Comparing Political Systems:

POWER AND POLICY IN THREE WORLDS

COMPARING POLITICAL SYSTEMS:

POWER AND POLICY

IN THREE WORLDS

Fourth Edition

GARY K. BERTSCH
University of Georgia

ROBERT P. CLARK
George Mason University

DAVID M. WOOD
University of Missouri-Columbia

Macmillan Publishing Company
NEW YORK

Editor: Bruce Nichols
Production Supervisors: Lisa G. M. Chuck and Charlotte Hyland
Production Manager: Richard C. Fischer
Text Designer: Patrice Fodero
Cover Designer: Brian Sheridan
Cover photographs: J. Langevin/SYGMA; Patrick Forestier/SYGMA; and Bigwood/Gamma-Liaison
Photo Researcher: Barbara Schultz, PAR/NYC
Illustrations: Academy Artworks, Inc.
This book was set in Palatino by C. L. Hutson, Inc., and was printed and bound by
Halliday Lithographers. The cover was printed by New England Book Components.

Copyright © 1991 by Macmillan Publishing Company,
a division of Macmillan, Inc.

Printed in the United States of America

Earlier editions copyright © 1978, 1982, and 1986 by John Wiley & Sons, Inc.;
copyright © 1986 by Macmillan Publishing Company.

Macmillan Publishing Company
866 Third Avenue, New York, New York 10022

Collier Macmillan Canada, Inc.
1200 Eglinton Avenue East
Suite 200
Don Mills, Ontario M3C 3N1

LIBRARY OF CONGRESS CATALOGING-IN-PUBLICATION DATA

Bertsch, Gary K.
    Comparing political systems: power and policy in three worlds /
Gary K. Bertsch, Robert P. Clark, David M. Wood.   —4th ed.
        p.   cm.
    Includes bibliographical references and index.
    ISBN 0-02-309020-0
    1. Comparative government. I. Clark, Robert P., 1940–
II. Wood, David Michael, 1934–   . III. Title.
JF51.B48 1991
320.3—dc20   90-13444
                                               CIP

Printing: 1 2 3 4 5 6 7   Year: 1 2 3 4 5 6 7

PREFACE

This preface is directed toward both old and new users of a text that originated a decade and a half ago. The fourth edition of *Comparing Political Systems: Power and Policy in Three Worlds* is appearing at a time of great structural change in the politics of many of the world's nations, including some nations that are among the most important international political actors and focal points of political attention, such as the Soviet Union, Germany, and South Africa. The recent trends in these and other countries mainly have been in the direction of *democratization* of previously authoritarian regimes. This has been particularly true in the case of Eastern Europe's Poland, Czechoslovakia, Hungary, Romania, Bulgaria, and Yugoslavia, as well as the Soviet Union and East Germany. Within the Soviet Union itself, there has been not only movement in the direction of democratization but also movements for autonomy and even independence of individual, ethnically distinct republics, such as Lithuania, Estonia, Azerbaijan, and Armenia. As for Germany, the collapse of the communist monopoly in the German Democratic Republic and the removal of restrictions on the movement of people between East and West Germany were preludes to a dizzying advance toward German reunification. The consequence has been that, at least on the continent of Europe, it is no longer possible to speak of the "communist bloc" of countries that once constituted the core of what we will call the "Second World."

Although changes in many Second World states have captured the headlines, there have been significant changes in the Third World as well. The dramatic economic growth of countries such as South Korea and Brazil has been matched by progress toward mass democracy, so that distinctions between these leading developing countries and the trailing First World states of Greece and Portugal are becoming fuzzier every day.

Most of the events just mentioned occurred in the late 1980s, and their ramifications continued to materialize almost daily as this edition went to press. The events bring back into focus the threefold division of the nations of the world that has oriented previous editions of this text. Former editions were written under the assumption that it is useful from the standpoint of *comparative* political analysis to divide the world's countries into three categories, which we, following popular usage, labeled the First, Second, and Third Worlds. This distinction was based on several criteria, the most important of which were both political and economic, involving the three distinct types of strategies for and experiences with modernization and industrial development in the three worlds. In relative terms, First World modernization was largely indigenous, its stages of industrialization generated with internal capital and resources. The pace was more gradual than in the Second World, where it was forced by the state and usually was externally generated or at least so assisted. External stimulus was featured in Third World modernization, but the resulting growth rates often have been sporadic, because relatively few Third World countries have been able to sustain growth. Weaknesses of Third World states and resistance by opponents of modernization have played a very important role in making Third World efforts to modernize and industrialize less impressive (until recently, at least) than those of Second World states.

Cultural and geographical factors played a secondary role in our classification of countries. When the first edition was published in 1978, the First and Third Worlds could be differentiated from one another on the basis of levels of economic development, with only a minor amount of overlap. Geographically, First World countries were found almost entirely in the Northern Hemisphere, with Australia and New Zealand as the exceptions, and most of them were in Western Europe, with the United States, Canada, and Japan as the exceptions in the Northern Hemisphere. Most of these countries shared a common Western cultural heritage. Third World countries were found mainly to the south of the First World countries, located on or near

the continents of Asia, Africa, and South America. Culturally, they exhibited a great deal of diversity. There was also a political feature distinguishing First World countries, all of which had operating democratic systems, or what we (after Robert Dahl) termed *polyarchies*, which emphasized the characteristic of pluralistic competition for power among political parties in free elections and open policy-making processes. A few Third World countries, such as Venezuela and Costa Rica, could be called polyarchies, but most Third World countries at that time were nondemocratic military regimes or single-party dictatorships.

Political criteria were much more prominent in defining the separate (and not necessarily intermediary) category of the Second World. These were countries run by Communist Parties adhering to the principles of Marxism-Leninism. Although there were important differences among them in the way Marxism-Leninism was interpreted (e.g., among the USSR, China, and Yugoslavia), they shared the common political distinction from First World countries of being one-party dictatorships rather than multiparty polyarchies. There was significant overlap with the First World in terms of economic development, with some Second World countries, notably East Germany and Czechoslovakia, being more industrially advanced than some First World countries, such as Portugal or Ireland. But the Second World as a whole fell well below the First World as a whole in terms of gross national product per capita, although it was—and still is—difficult to find reliable measures for Second World economic development. There was also overlap in economic terms between the Second World and the Third World. Again, political differences were more important than economic ones in distinguishing the two worlds. The Second World countries appeared to present a more stable political picture than did most of the Third World, because Communist Parties, in some cases backed by the presence of Soviet (or Vietnamese) troops, possessed a coherent set of purposes and an apparent organizational capacity to accomplish their social and economic objectives while keeping opposition neutralized and silent. There was also a geographical distinction to be made, as Second World countries, like most of the First World, were found in the Northern Hemisphere and to the north of most of the Third World countries. But like Third World countries, those of the Second World showed considerable cultural differentiation, especially when Second World countries in Eastern Europe and East Asia were compared.

The threefold division had the advantage of corresponding to the different courses in comparative politics offered by colleges and universities. However, changes in the world were making it more likely that curricula would have to be revamped. By the time the second and third editions of the text were published in 1982 and 1986, respectively, the economic basis for grouping a large number of countries in the single Third World category was beginning to erode. The Newly Industrialized Countries (NICs) were not only rapidly catching up with and passing the lower tier of the First World in economic terms, they were presenting a formidable challenge to First World countries with more advanced industrial sectors (textiles, steel, even automobiles), which had long exercised leadership. The "four dragons" of East Asia (South Korea, Taiwan, Singapore, and Hong Kong), following a path previously defined by Japan, were rapidly reproducing the economies and many of the social patterns of the First World, but, unlike Japan since the post–World War II era, they were not yet reproducing democratic political forms. Similar "economic miracles" of rapid growth were occurring in Latin America (e.g., Brazil) and in Southeast Asia (e.g., Thailand) with political change similarly lagging behind economic and social change.

Since 1986, there has been an acceleration of regime change from authoritarianism toward democracy or at least toward the reestablishment of multiparty systems in parts of the Third World. Among the more advanced industrial Third World countries, significant political changes in a democratic direction have occurred in South Korea, Brazil, Chile, Argentina, and Uruguay. What might be called *predemocratic* changes have occurred in South Africa, with a loosening of restrictions on the political participation of Black Africans, who nevertheless are still (at this writing) denied the right to vote for members of the South African parliament. Among poorer countries, very dramatic changes have been seen in Pakistan, the Philippines, and Nicaragua, but the process of democratization seems more reversible there than in the economically more advanced countries.

Democratization appears to have been reversible in one of the communist countries in which important changes were occurring in the late 1980s. In China, the Communist Party leaders under Deng Xiaoping decided in June 1989 not to let the student-led movement toward democracy go any further and they cracked down with armed force and considerable bloodshed at Beijing's Tiananmen Square and elsewhere in China, to the bitter disappointment of many who had seen China as likely to continue on its path of reform. At the time, there were signs that the Chinese reform movement would be contagious and spread to the rest of the communist world. In fact, indigenous developments were already well under way within most of the Eastern European communist regimes and were too strong to be set back by the Chinese crackdown. The difference was that the Soviet Union under Mikhail Gorbachev, which seemed to have had the military strength to turn back a democratic revolution in neighboring countries, allowed the revolutions to go forth, perhaps bowing to the inevitable in so doing. Even in those countries, where Soviet troops were stationed, principally in East Germany and Czechoslovakia, they were kept to their barracks, while the indigenous forces set aside their arms. In Romania, security forces loyal to the hard-line Ceausescu regime were defeated in a brief civil war by an insurrectionary movement that was, in essence, *led by* important elements of the regular Romanian army. In contrast, in China, Deng Xiaoping had replaced troops of questionable loyalty with more reliable troops from the provinces before the order was given to massacre young democracy demonstrators in Tiananmen Square.

How do we account for the above-mentioned changes and encouraging trends toward democracy, not only in the more industrially advanced Second World countries but also in those of the Third World? We will argue that rapid changes in technology and the global economy have made all industrial countries dependent on world markets. Consequently, the better educated and more sophisticated populations of these countries can no longer be isolated from the rest of the world culturally or politically than they can be economically. Closed regimes in the Second or Third World that attempt to stand between their people and the outside world have been unable to isolate them from the information explosion and from knowledge of the quantity and variety of goods and services that are now available to people in the open societies of wealthier nations. Increased access to information has given rise to demands for a greater share of material well-being as well as for political power. Such demands were met earlier in this century in the most industrialized

countries of what we have been calling the First World. In the poorest countries, the portion of the population that is urbanized and educated may still be too small to constitute the critical mass needed to force democratization. China provides a good example.

However, although it is possible to argue that a similar democratization process is accompanying a more advanced stage of economic development in the two categories of countries we are calling the Second and Third World, it is also true that once the process began in Eastern Europe in late 1989, it proceeded more swiftly—indeed, with dizzying speed—than tends to be the case in Third World countries where such a process can be identified. We believe this is due to two ways in which those communist countries differed from other countries of the world. First, power was highly concentrated in East European political systems and backed up with an awesome array of military might. This made the communist regimes appear invulnerable for a long time, but it also meant that they could fall like a house of cards as soon as it became known that their military underpinnings were no longer reliable. In Third World countries, unpopular regimes sustain themselves on the basis of ethnic, religious, regional, and ideological divisions among their potential opponents as much as on the efficiency of the armed forces at their disposal. Indeed, in many Third World states, there remains resistance to the very idea of modernization. This is related to the second way communist countries are different, which is that an educated and sophisticated populace in an industrially advanced communist country, particularly one whose population is relatively homogeneous in ethnic and religious terms (e.g., Poland), can more quickly become alert to the existence of a common hatred for the regime and a common desire to end it than can be true in a Third World country in which there is still substantial resistance to the communication and formulation of common political understanding between various parts of the country. The countries of Eastern Europe are geographically compact, and they are connected to one another, facilitating the flow of information between, as well as within, countries.

The present edition of this book will devote considerable attention to the political, economic, social, and cultural changes going on in all three worlds in the 1990s. This is particularly true of Part II, which deals with what we continue to term the Second World. Because events in the Second World recently have occurred with such rapidity and can be expected to continue to do so, we have found it preferable not to draw detailed "still photographs" of the present Second World political systems as if they have been in existence for a long time and are expected to continue to be so. Instead, we have concentrated on the process of change in communist systems. Our objective is more to *explain* these changes than to give a running account of what the changes have been. A new departure has been the inclusion of Japan among the First World countries systematically dealt with in Part I, which we continue to entitle "Power and Policy in Western European Democracies". The title is retained because the generalizations we draw are based on politics in four Western European countries: Britain, France, West Germany, and Italy. Japan is employed, along with the United States, to enhance the generality of common characteristics and to show the limits of those generalizations that are Western Europe specific. It should be added that the term *West* Germany (for the Federal German Republic) is used throughout Part I, and *East* Germany (for the German Democratic Republic) in Part II.

Discussion of the process of German reunification is in the Postscript to Chapter 7 of Part I.

Because the book is divided into three parts and is organized around common topics and chapters in each part, instructors have two basic alternatives in using the book. The instructor can take one part (e.g., the Third World) at a time and focus on cross-national comparisons within that particular world. The Introduction provides common terms and definitions that are used throughout all three sections, facilitating comparison within and across worlds. After the book has been finished, the Conclusion will assist in making comparisons among the three worlds. This approach may be desired by those who prefer to control the substantial variance found across the three worlds by concentrating on "one world at a time." The alternative approach considers all three worlds simultaneously by taking common chapters (e.g., Chapters 3, 10, and 17) from each of the three parts. The Introduction can aid in this approach as well, by providing a common theoretical perspective (i.e., the stress on modernization and its relationship to democratization) and common concepts. This strategy emphasizes simultaneous cross-national and cross-world comparison and may be desired by those who prefer a more global approach.

Each of the three parts is also available in paperback form from Macmillan. Together they form a series based on the same framework and containing essentially the same material as this volume. David M. Wood is the author of *Power and Policy in Western European Democracies*; Gary K. Bertsch, of *Reform and Revolution in Communist Systems*; and Robert P. Clark, of *Power and Policy in the Third World*.

We wish to acknowledge the invaluable contributions by the many individuals who assisted in this project and improved the content in innumerable ways. We would particularly like to acknowledge the constructive reviews and suggestions of many instructors who used the first three editions, and Sam Watson who coauthored Chapters 11, 12, and 13. We would also like to thank those who reviewed the fourth edition in manuscript form. All have aided us in making considerable improvements to the text. For whatever deficiencies the book contains, we assume the responsibility.

GARY K. BERTSCH
ROBERT P. CLARK
DAVID M. WOOD

CONTENTS

Contents

Contents

Contents

xiv

Comparing Political Systems:

POWER AND POLICY
IN THREE WORLDS

POLITICS AND HUMAN VALUES

Toward a Better Understanding of Politics: Why and How We Classify and Compare Nations

Comparison and analysis are the two central themes around which the field of comparative politics is organized. We believe we can better understand the political process and the political performance of countries if we can compare politics in one country, or set of countries, with politics in another. Comparison is an integral part of our intellectual activity and one in which we are constantly engaged. To compare means to look for similarities and differences, for good features and bad, for things that seem to work, and for those that do not. We compare political systems to examine the different ways they are organized, the differences in the way they carry out certain tasks, and the degree to which they succeed or fall short of their goals. Comparison is only the first half of our task, however, for we also want to analyze what we have found. Analysis here means to uncover the causes and consequences of the differences we have found

through comparison. If we are careful and thoughtful in our comparisons, we should be able to go one step further and explain why different political systems do things in different ways (the causes of variation) and what difference it makes to those who live in these countries (the consequences). In this book, we will call attention to and compare certain important characteristics of political systems, which, we believe, will help us explain political performance.

Before we examine and compare political systems, we first should classify them, that is, group them according to certain characteristics that we feel are important to understanding and explaining their similarities and differences. We have classified the world's political systems according to the way they are managing the processes of industrialization and modernization. Our classification scheme focuses on the strategies governments adopt to deal with modernization and industrialization, the success with which they implement these strategies, and the levels of performance they achieve in the process.

1

Modernization of a society implies two separate—but closely related—processes. At one level, people must modernize their way of thinking, rejecting notions of fatalism, mysticism, and historical rigidity and embracing the more modern concepts of science, historical causation, and the belief that a person can influence individual fate by exercising reason and skills. Modernization of the individual means increased educational opportunity and access to the network of mass communications. People come to value their own capacity to create a better world. They shed ancient taboos and inhibitions that had imprisoned thought. And they come to value this enhanced human capacity not only in themselves but also in others of their society. At another level, a society must be organized to enhance the physical and mental abilities of each person. Such organization requires the bureaucratization of task-performing institutions, the implementation of assembly-line and mass-production techniques, and the adoption of decision-making methods that emphasize rationality and systematic analysis. Thus, the improved knowledge, information, and skills of individuals can be mobilized to greatly increase human productive capacity.

Industrialization implies the increased application of technology to allow humans to manipulate the natural world to meet their demands and needs (and, not infrequently, to permit them to exercise power over others). Industrialization involves the discovery and application of techniques for transforming relatively inefficient energy sources into efficient ones. This brings about advances in materials processing, changes in transportation and communication technologies, developments in building and construction techniques, and many other related transformations. The result is a vast expansion of society's capacity to satisfy the human craving for greater material well-

being. As the size of the pie of goods and services grows, all groups within a society may potentially gain some share of the benefits.

The dual processes of modernization and industrialization have political implications that radiate in two directions from these revolutionary changes. On one hand, political institutions must be transformed into modern agencies of change that are capable of guiding and directing the industrialization process where it has already been established and of initiating it where it has not yet begun. This process may cause a further accretion of power by political elites. On the other hand, the political system is called on to resolve the numerous social, economic, and cultural conflicts that arise from the very process of industrialization. New groups emerge that must be appeased in this process. In the long run, industrialization frequently brings with it a broadening of the distribution of political power.

To cope with the problems of industrial growth and modernization, governing elites throughout the world have sought to increase their capabilities, their capacity for performing certain essential jobs that the unorganized and unaided citizens of the country cannot perform for themselves. This process of improving a government's capabilities is referred to here as *political development*. These tasks call for extractive capabilities, such as the ability to tax income and to conscript young men and women for military service. They require that governments regulate the behavior of citizens by passing laws and punishing those who violate them. Thus, a strengthening of the law enforcement arm of the state is necessary. Government must have the power to remove resources (such as land) from one group and distribute them to another group.

But government leaders also find that they must develop the ability to sense what their citizens want from the political system, so that their expanding needs and rising aspirations may be satisfied. Intermediary links between ordinary citizens and their political leaders must develop, whether these be legislative bodies, political parties, organized interest groups, electoral systems, or the press. And, finally, governments must generate and communicate symbolic messages to their people to satisfy the psychological needs of the citizens to trust the government and to have faith and confidence in its decisions.[1]

Three Political Worlds

Table I.1 illustrates how we have classified the 170 relatively self-governing states that are identified in the *Political Handbook of the World: 1987*.[2] The *First World* consists of twenty-four industrial democracies located principally in Western Europe and North America. These countries account for about 15.5 percent of the world's estimated 1987 population and take up about 23.5 percent of its surface area. The *Second World*, the sixteen Communist Party and post-communist states located principally in Eastern Europe and Asia, accounts for slightly less than one-third of the world's population (32.2 percent) and slightly more than one-quarter of its land area (26.8 percent). About half the world's population (52.1 percent) and land area (48.9 percent) are found in the *Third World*, a category that includes 102 states by our count. Finally, we identify twenty-eight states whose status is uncertain, such as tiny European principalities (Andorra) or isolated Pacific islands (Western Samoa). These unclassified states account for about one-tenth of a percent of the world's population and about seven-tenths of a percent of its surface area.

This classification rather closely reflects the predominant tensions between and among competing models and ideologies in international politics (e.g., East-West, North-South conflicts), and it is also explicitly tied to varying political approaches to the management of modernization and industrialization. Thus, the scheme primarily is political in nature rather than based on such criteria as economic status or geography—we classify states according to the way they have attempted to meet the challenges of industrial change and modernization.

The strategy chosen by political leaders to guide a country through these difficult changes frequently emerges from a political process in which questions like these are asked and answered.

Which government capacities or powers should be given priority? How should the overall mix of powers be blended together?

Which institutions must be created and which eliminated to speed up the process of change?

How rapidly and at what cost is development to take place?

What kinds of social, cultural, and economic changes must occur for political development to take place?

Which values should receive top priority? Which groups should receive these values first?

Which groups in society should pay the costs of development?

The countries of the world can be classified according to how they answer these questions.

In our framework, the First World countries in North America and Western Europe were on the whole successful at managing the tensions of modernization and industrialization

Table I.1 Classification of 170 States as of 1987

Name of State	Population (millions)	Area (thousands of square miles)
FIRST WORLD		
1. Australia	16.1	2,966.1
2. Austria	7.6	32.4
3. Belgium	10.0	11.8
4. Canada	25.9	3,851.8
5. Denmark	5.1	16.6
6. Finland	4.9	130.1
7. France	55.5	211.2
8. Germany, Federal Republic of[a]	60.9	95.9
9. Greece	10.1	50.9
10. Iceland	0.2	39.8
11. Ireland	3.6	27.1
12. Israel	4.5	8.3
13. Italy	57.4	116.3
14. Japan	122.8	143.7
15. Luxembourg	0.4	0.9
16. Netherlands	14.7	13.1
17. New Zealand	3.3	103.1
18. Norway	4.2	149.3
19. Portugal	10.2	35.5
20. Spain	39.4	194.9
21. Sweden	8.4	173.7
22. Switzerland	6.5	15.9
23. United Kingdom[b]	56.8	94.2
24. United States	242.7	3,615.1
Total	771.2	12,097.7
SECOND WORLD		
1. Albania	3.1	11.1
2. Bulgaria	9.1	42.8
3. China, People's Republic of	1,075.8	3,691.8
4. Cuba	10.4	44.2
5. Czechoslovakia	15.6	49.4
6. Germany, Democratic Republic of[c]	16.7	41.8
7. Hungary	10.6	35.9

4

Table I.1 (*Continued*)

Name of State	Population (millions)	Area (thousands of square miles)
SECOND WORLD (*Continued*)		
8. Kampuchea	7.2	69.9
9. Korea, Democratic People's Republic of[d]	21.0	46.5
10. Laos	4.4	91.4
11. Mongolia	2.0	604.2
12. Poland	38.1	120.7
13. Romania	23.0	91.7
14. Union of Soviet Socialist Republics	282.7	8,649.5
15. Vietnam	61.3	128.4
16. Yugoslavia	23.8	98.8
Total	1,604.8	13,818.1
THIRD WORLD		
1. Afghanistan*	18.4	249.9
2. Algeria	23.2	919.6
3. Angola	8.4	481.4
4. Argentina	31.6	1,072.2
5. Bahrain	0.4	0.2
6. Bangladesh*	106.8	55.6
7. Belize	0.2	8.9
8. Benin*	4.2	43.5
9. Bhutan*	1.5	18.2
10. Bolivia	6.8	424.2
11. Botswana*	1.2	231.8
12. Brazil	141.7	3,286.5
13. Brunei	0.2	2.2
14. Burkina Faso*	8.2	105.9
15. Burma	38.2	261.8
16. Burundi*	5.0	10.8
17. Cameroon*	10.1	183.6
18. Central African Republic*	2.8	240.5
19. Chad*	5.4	495.8
20. Chile	12.3	292.3
21. Colombia	32.0	439.7

(*Table continues on p. 6.*)

Table I.1 (*Continued*)

Name of State	Population (millions)	Area (thousands of square miles)
THIRD WORLD (*Continued*)		
22. Congo	2.1	132.0
23. Costa Rica	2.6	19.6
24. Dominican Republic	6.6	18.8
25. Ecuador	10.3	109.5
26. Egypt	50.6	386.7
27. El Salvador*	5.3	8.3
28. Equatorial Guinea	0.3	10.8
29. Ethiopia*	45.5	471.8
30. Gabon	1.5	103.4
31. Gambia[e]	0.8	4.4
32. Ghana*	14.4	92.1
33. Guatemala	8.9	42.0
34. Guinea*	5.9	94.9
35. Guinea-Bissau	0.9	13.9
36. Guyana*	1.1	83.0
37. Haiti*	5.5	10.7
38. Honduras*	4.7	43.3
39. India*	779.4	1,222.5
40. Indonesia	170.0	741.1
41. Iran	46.8	636.3
42. Iraq	17.0	167.9
43. Ivory Coast*	9.9	124.5
44. Jamaica	2.4	4.2
45. Jordan	3.8	37.7
46. Kenya*	22.0	224.9
47. Korea, Republic of[f]	42.9	38.0
48. Kuwait	1.8	6.9
49. Lebanon	3.4	4.0
50. Lesotho*	1.6	11.7
51. Liberia	2.5	43.0
52. Libya	4.1	679.4
53. Madagascar*	10.6	226.7
54. Malawi*	7.3	45.7
55. Malaysia	16.4	127.3

6

Table I.1 (*Continued*)

Name of State	Population (millions)	Area (thousands of square miles)
THIRD WORLD (*Continued*)		
56. Mali*	8.3	478.8
57. Mauritania*	1.9	397.9
58. Mauritius	1.1	0.8
59. Mexico	83.0	761.6
60. Morocco	24.6	269.8
61. Mozambique	15.0	309.5
62. Nepal*	17.2	54.4
63. Nicaragua	3.4	50.2
64. Niger*	6.7	489.2
65. Nigeria	97.4	356.7
66. Oman	1.4	120.0
67. Pakistan*	102.1	310.4
68. Panama	2.3	29.2
69. Papua New Guinea	3.6	178.3
70. Paraguay	3.5	157.0
71. Peru	20.7	496.2
72. Philippines	57.4	115.8
73. Qatar	0.3	4.2
74. Rwanda*	6.6	10.2
75. São Tomé and Principe	0.1	0.4
76. Saudi Arabia	7.0	829.9
77. Senegal*f	6.8	75.8
78. Sierra Leone*	4.0	27.7
79. Singapore	2.6	0.2
80. Somalia*	4.7	246.2
81. South Africa, Republic of	34.4	471.9
82. Sri Lanka*	16.5	25.3
83. Sudan*	23.5	967.5
84. Suriname	0.4	63.0
85. Swaziland	0.7	6.7
86. Syria	11.3	71.6
87. Taiwan	19.9	13.6
88. Tanzania*	23.4	364.9

(*Table continues on p. 8.*)

Table I.1 (*Continued*)

Name of State	Population (millions)	Area (thousands of square miles)
THIRD WORLD (*Continued*)		
89. Thailand	53.6	198.5
90. Togo	3.1	21.6
91. Trinidad and Tobago	1.2	1.9
92. Tunisia	7.3	63.2
93. Turkey	54.3	301.4
94. Uganda*	15.5	91.1
95. United Arab Emirates	1.8	32.3
96. Uruguay	2.9	68.0
97. Venezuela	17.1	352.1
98. Yemen Arab Republic*	8.5	75.3
99. Yeman, People's Democratic Republic of*	2.4	130.0
100. Zaire	31.8	905.6
101. Zambia	7.1	290.6
102. Zimbabwe	8.6	150.8
Total	2,594.5	25,248.6
MIXED SYSTEMS, STATUS UNCERTAIN OR OTHERWISE UNCLASSIFIED		
1. Andorra	0.05	0.175
2. Antigua and Barbuda	0.08	0.172
3. Bahamas	0.24	5.4
4. Barbados	0.26	0.166
5. Cape Verde Islands	0.33	1.6
6. Comoro Islands	0.43	0.7
7. Cyprus	0.68	3.6
8. Djibouti	0.43	8.8
9. Dominica	0.08	0.29
10. Fiji	0.73	7.1
11. Grenada	0.1	0.133
12. Kiribati	0.07	0.335
13. Liechtenstein	0.03	0.06
14. Maldives	0.19	0.1
15. Malta	0.39	0.122
16. Monaco	0.03	0.0007

Table I.1 (*Continued*)

Name of State	Population (millions)	Area (thousands of square miles)
MIXED SYSTEMS, STATUS UNCERTAIN OR OTHERWISE UNCLASSIFIED (*Continued*)		
17. Namibia	1.23	318.3
18. Nauru	0.009	0.008
19. St. Lucia	0.12	0.238
20. St. Vincent	0.13	0.15
21. San Marino	0.02	0.024
22. Seychelles	0.06	0.107
23. Solomon Islands	0.27	11.0
24. Tonga	0.1	0.27
25. Tuvalu	0.008	0.01
26. Vanuatu	0.14	4.6
27. Vatican	0.001	0.00017
28. Western Samoa	0.17	1.1
Total	6.378	364.6
Grand Total	4,976.9	51,529.0

[a] West Germany.
[b] Great Britain.
[c] East Germany.
[d] North Korea.
[e] Senegal and Gambia joined in Confederation of Senegambia, 1 February 1982.
[f] South Korea.
SOURCE: Arthur S. Banks, ed., *Political Handbook of the World: 1987* (Binghamton, New York: CSA Publications, 1987).
Note: Third World nations marked with an asterisk (*) are identified as extremely poor, or Fourth World, nations by Helen C. Low and James W. Howe, "Focus on the Fourth World," in James W. Howe, ed., *The U.S. and World Development: Agenda for Action 1975* (New York: Praeger, 1975), Table 1, pp. 48–49.

while at the same time encouraging the growth of pluralist democracy. In many of these countries, industrialization began rather early, as early as 1750 in England and by the end of the nineteenth century in most of the remaining countries. There was little outside pressure on these states as they industrialized because there were no comparable countries undergoing similar processes in other parts of the world, although competition between and among First World states grew sharper with the maturation of industrialization and eventually contributed to two world wars. Some of these countries also enjoyed the luxury of pursuing their goals at a relatively leisurely pace, frequently spreading the modernization process over several generations. In Great Britain, the consolidation of a modernizing elite took place over a span of about 180 years; in the United States, it took about ninety years, and in some of the countries on the European continent, the average was about seventy to seventy-five years.

It would be a mistake to see the processes of industrialization and modernization spreading evenly and peacefully across all of the countries of the First World. The states that industrialized and modernized later, including Germany and the southern European fringe (Portugal, Spain, Italy, and Greece), faced much greater difficulty in dealing with these challenges, perhaps *because* of their relatively later start in the transformation. Whatever the cause, all these countries endured some form of dictatorship or authoritarian regime before they could achieve a stable industrial economy and a modern society. In the 1990s, the place of Portugal and Spain in the First World of industrial democracies seems assured. Even mature industrial democracies are shaken occasionally by challenges from groups that feel they have been left out of the process of change, such as the Celtic fringe (Ireland, Scotland, and Wales) of the British Isles, the American South or its Indian tribes on reservations, or French-speaking Quebec in Canada.

Nevertheless, although it seems that industrial growth and modernization were not free of conflict in the First World, these processes did go forward rather peacefully when compared with the stormy passage to modernity that confronted other states where these processes came later. In the First World, the impetus for modernization came from important leading segments of the economic and political communities within the nation rather than from outside the country, with the consequence that the policies of industrialization and modernization did not become mixed with the equally contentious issues of national self-determination and anticolonialism, as was the case elsewhere. Where the principal drive for change came from native modernizing elites as opposed to foreigners—a phenomenon we call *modernization from within* (following John Kautsky[3])—antimodern groups were more easily won over or absorbed into the modernizing elite itself. In some countries, like Canada and the United States, industrialization and modernization came with the culture of the British colonizers and, meeting with only primitive native tribes, proceeded to spread almost unopposed across the land. In England, traditional segments of the population, including villagers, peasants, and aristocrats, were pushed from their rural pursuits into an urban capitalist economy over the span of several generations. Even the relatively more violent French experience did not result in the destruction of the traditional forces but rather eventually absorbed these forces into the modern society that emerged after the French Revolution.

Generally, then, traditional guilds merged into modern labor unions, aristocratic landowners became capitalist farmers, and peasants moved to the cities to become wage earners in factories. There were high human costs in the process; the literature of the period is full of accounts of slums, pollution, child labor, sweatshops, and other abuses. But in most cases the forces that naturally opposed modernization—peasants, aristocrats, and small shopkeepers and artisans of the villages and towns—could be dealt with by absorption or transformation. It was not necessary to destroy them outright to advance the cause of modernization. As a consequence, politics in the First World tended to be much more pluralistic, in the sense that autonomous and competing centers of power were not only tolerated but actually protected, and there was relatively less emphasis on the need to concentrate total power in the hands of a single individual, institution, or level of government.

Today the level of economic well-being that First World countries have attained helps to moderate the political conflicts that arise from the competition of economic interest groups. New issues are arising as the issues of the industrial era recede into the background. But First World political systems remain stable.

In Communist Party states, what we call the Second World, matters were and are quite different. In such countries as the Soviet Union and China, the processes of industrialization and modernization were delayed for decades before revolution brought communists to power. When they did begin the process of modernization, the new elites encountered severe obstacles in pursuing their goals; the entire process was much more shattering than it had been in the First World. For one thing, the impetus toward modernization in prerevolutionary times had tended to come from sources external to the country, what John Kautsky calls *modernization from without*.[4] Before the change in power, external capital funded what little industrialization there was in these countries. The Marxists who came to power with the revolution were themselves bearers of ideas and techniques imported from abroad.

Within the country, traditional antimodern forces resisted communist-directed change so strongly that the modernizing elites often had to engage them in violent struggle and destroy or expel them. In the countries that followed this path, landed aristocrats saw their land confiscated, peasants were regimented and often forced to collectivize their efforts, and urban laboring classes were mobilized into state-controlled unions. Thus, the process of industrialization followed a strategy that featured a Communist Party and centralized state apparatus

much more authoritarian than its counterpart in the First World. Power was concentrated so that it might be used to advance revolutionary objectives in the face of stiff resistance.

Finally, in Communist Party countries, because the process of industrialization occurred at a time when major world powers had already industrialized, there was great external pressure on Second World states in the form of threats, economic boycott, intervention, and war. Accordingly, communist governments frequently found themselves isolated, encircled, and under attack from those states of the First World that had industrialized earlier. All these characteristics taken together produced in the Second World a Communist Party state that gathered into its hands enormous power intended to change its society in a short time and to introduce radical shifts in both the country's political patterns and its economic order. Although most Second World governments emerged from violent beginnings, historically they fit into three different groups, depending on the exact circumstances surrounding their origins. The original Second World state, the Soviet Union, was born from internal revolution that came in the midst of large-scale suffering and destruction during World War I. A second group of socialist states, particularly those in Eastern Europe—including Czechoslovakia, Hungary, and Poland, was established after World War II out of the desire of the Soviet Union to foster a buffer of allied political systems on its western border. A third group grew out of a struggle for national liberation against foreign colonial domination—these states include China, Cuba, and Vietnam. In all three groups communism emerged in the wake of armed conflict.

Another set of characteristics typifies the Third World states of Latin America, Africa, the Middle East, and Asia. These states were also late starters in the industrialization process, most of them beginning even later than most Second World countries. The majority of Third World states were not independent before World War II; those that were (including most of Latin America) did not embark on their industrialization drive before 1914. Apart from their relatively late start, however, the distinguishing characteristic of the Third World states is the inability of modernizing elites to resolve their struggle with the anti-modern forces, either by absorbing and transforming them, as in the First World, or by destroying or expelling them, as in the Second World. In the Third World, the modernizing elites have tried to foster economic and political change without disturbing the complex power relationships that link together the wealthy and the poor in the traditional rural sectors of the country. This, in turn, has led in many instances to what A. F. K. Organski calls the syncratic state, a government based on a loose coalition of both modern and traditional elites who pursue modernization without changing the basically traditional nature of their society.[5]

The causes and effects of this phenomenon are many. With few exceptions, political change in Third World countries has been halting, erratic, violent, and marked by radical swings in public policy as first one group and then another captured the state policy-making apparatus. The process is complicated because this struggle takes place within an international economic, political, and military arena in which powerful forces are seeking to perpetuate the global inequities of wealth and power that have existed since 1945. These forces have varied over time and space, but the common result for the Third World countries has been economic dependence on the more affluent parts of the world. Although generalizations about such a large and disparate group of countries are hazardous, we argue that Third World states are having extreme

difficulty in managing the tensions of industrial and political change.

Some observers of politics in developing countries occasionally refer to still another category of state, the Fourth World, where poverty is especially striking. The relative prosperity of a few oil-rich Third World countries has obscured the fact that a significant number of very poor countries, including densely populated states like Bangladesh, India, and Pakistan, are simply not moving ahead in their progress toward industrial growth. According to some approaches, then, it makes sense to separate these states into a Fourth World; we have marked those countries with an asterisk in Table I.1. Despite this apparent split of the developing world into two camps, we choose to treat them as a single category. This book is about politics, political style, and public policy. Measured on that dimension, Brazil and Taiwan have much more in common with their poorer neighbors like Bolivia and the Philippines than they do with industrialized countries. A relatively good performance on the scale of per capita gross national product (GNP) should not be allowed to obscure what we think is an important political phenomenon.

There are today also a growing number of states that could be placed in more than one category. Some Third World states, like Venezuela and Mexico (as well as some others in Latin America), seem to have consolidated pluralist democracy and probably should be included with the First World before too much more time passes. Other Third World states, including Angola, Libya, and Mozambique, have adopted a political order based on Marxist principles. For the time being, however, we prefer to suspend judgment on these transitional cases and to treat them where many of their own leaders perceive their interests and identity to lie—with the Third World.

What Do People Want?

Agendas

We take up the three worlds separately in this text in part because their political institutions and the roles that ordinary people play in their political systems differ from one world to another, as the text will amply demonstrate. But it is also true that there are different *agendas* of issues that the political systems in the three worlds are processing. In the realm of economics, for example, many Third World countries are preoccupied with the basic problem of feeding their growing populations, portions of which may be not only below the poverty line but even on the verge of starvation. Furthermore, Third World economies are locked in a dependent relationship with a capitalist world economy that is dominated by the strongest First World economies of the United States, Japan, and the European Community. First World countries have elevated their populations above starvation and have upgraded the definition of poverty. The communist and post-communist countries of the Second World are struggling to reform and restructure their economies to boost their countries' economic output and the social well-being of their populations. This is proving to be a very difficult challenge. This challenge led to the collapse of communism in most East European governments in 1989 and could do the same to their successor regimes if they are not more successful in raising the living standards of their people.

Defense spending has become an issue on the agenda of First and Second World countries, not only as a question of the amount that is spent, but also in terms of the objects toward which defense spending is directed. But defense spending in general, and nuclear weapons in particular, are only two of many issues that have found their way onto the political agendas of the First World democracies. In relatively open, pluralist systems like those of Western Europe and North America, lobbies and interest groups clamor for attention to their problems. Usually their strategies are restricted to the small circles of political professionals who constitute the policy-making elites of the industrial democracies, but occasionally the issues burst onto the public scene through mass protest or some other traumatic event, such as terrorism, natural disaster, or dramatic social conflict.

In the 1980s we saw that there are groups and movements in the Soviet Union and Eastern Europe that are also forcing political leaders to pay attention to them. In Poland especially, the Solidarity movement, which began among workers in the shipyards, mines, and factories, reached revolutionary and mass proportions. What Solidarity sought was greater freedom of political expression, the right to dissent and to form a "loyal opposition." In Poland, a devout Catholic country ruled by an atheistic party, the issue of religious freedom was inevitably a part of the agenda as well.

The difference between political participation in the First and Second Worlds is that greater freedom of political expression is seen more as a means to other ends in the First World and as an end in itself in the Second. First World citizens seek ends such as reversal of the spread of nuclear weapons or of environmental pollution, of equal treatment of women and minority groups, of the "right to life" or the "right to choose" in the abortion issue. To reach their goals, which really involve major changes in public policy, they must capture the attention of the public through the mass media. It is not always the case that those in authority are not listening, but unless they fear the loss of votes in the next election, they won't necessarily respond. But the media are available if the groups can dramatize their demands. In the late 1980s, many anticommunist groups in the Second World pursued the goal of expanding political participation. The resulting protests reached revolutionary proportions by 1989 and many East European Communist governments were overthrown or simply collapsed. Political participation has become a more meaningful process in most countries of the Second World.

Third World political systems vary considerably in the degree to which they are open to citizen participation. For the majority of Third World peoples, participation is far beyond their range of preoccupation, because bare existence for themselves and their families is an everyday, pressing concern. Even awareness of the political system and what is on the country's agenda is confined to an educated urbanized minority. Human rights issues as framed by subgroups within this minority tend to emphasize the rights of ethnic and religious groups seeking greater recognition of their economic and political needs rather than on the rights of the average citizen to political expression, religious freedom, or even freedom from want. Human rights issues in the Third World tend to pit community against community, often to the advantage of political elites who can play divide-and-rule games, unless they are too closely identified with one tribe, one sect, or one language group of the population.

As we pass from the 1980s to the 1990s, however, there is ample reason to be optimistic as far as the cause of democracy in the Third World is concerned. In the last half of the 1980s, there were a number of promising developments that led to the retreat of dictatorships and the restoration of constitutional democracies, particularly in Asia (the Philippines, South Korea,

and Pakistan) and Latin America (Argentina, Brazil, and Chile). In addition to the strong defense of democracy in a number of traditionally open and democratic Third World regimes, such as India and Venezuela, this trend seems to suggest that much of the Third World has passed through its phase of military regimes and now is ready to extend the benefits of political participation to a growing number of its citizens. Problems still persist, however, particularly in the Middle East and in Africa below the Sahara.

Values

In the late 1980s and early 1990s, you could listen to news broadcasts on television or read news accounts in the print media that brought you information about any number of important, dramatic, even traumatic events around the world. By emphasizing the dramatic or even sensational in the news, these accounts probably hid from view the important differences in the ways people around the world react to such happenings, for what really matters in these instances is the way they reflect what people want most for themselves and others, their most important goals and objectives. We call these desired things and attitudes human *values*.

For many years, scholars from different fields of knowledge, including psychology, sociology, political science, and economics, have studied what humans value in different cultural and economic settings.[6] To date, no one has developed a list of universal human values that is acceptable to all scholars in all cultures and that at the same time is precise and capable of being investigated empirically. Thus, in this book, we must work with a set of human values derived from criteria other than what is provided by universal scholarly consensus. To organize our inquiry into comparative political performance, we have decided to work with four human values: *power, respect, well-being,* and *enlightenment.*

We do not claim that our four values are universal or sacred, only that they are useful as an organizing principle to guide our work. They tend to be among the most important human values dealt with in a political context around the world, and they span the entire range of important values, from the inner needs of individuals to the public requirements of social collectivities. In addition, these four values reflect our normative concerns. We favor democratic *power* distributions, universal *respect* for all peoples, equitable distribution of the ingredients of *well-being,* and universal access to *enlightenment.* Of course, others have different priorities. The task of a political scientist is to blend the empirical foundations of one's discipline with one's normative concerns as a human being.

Simply placing labels on concepts such as power and respect does not tell us much about what people want or about how governments help them achieve these values. Each of the four values must be defined in some detail if we are to know what to look for in our inquiry. Yet, as we will soon discover, each value may be interpreted differently in different countries or areas of the world. Where it is necessary to do so, we point out major differences between the value definitions we develop here and those that prevail in other countries.

Power. The first human value, *power,* means the ability to influence the behavior of others. In a political context, power can be conceived of as the capacity to change or influence policy outcomes. If a handful of elites have complete power to determine policy decisions, policy outcomes will reflect their particular scale of values. The extent to which power is distributed among the broader population determines the degree to which the values of ordinary people are reflected in policy outcomes. Although most governments in their official self-justifications consider democracy an overriding political goal, few have been successful in distributing power democratically within their societies. As we will see, political realities do not always correspond with political ideals.

Because power is not only a value in itself but also a determinant affecting the allocation of other values, it is the most important. The American, French, and Russian revolutions all were fought to wrest power from an entrenched elite and to place it in the hands of deprived sections of the population. Power itself—and the ways it is wielded and distributed within a political system—is at the heart of politics.

Two aspects of power stand out and call for further discussion. On one hand, all governments need to accumulate and consolidate sufficient power to be able to govern effectively. Without sufficient official power, governments cannot mobilize their armed forces to repel attack, spend money to meet the welfare needs of their people, or command the loyalty of a civilian bureaucracy. On the other hand, the distribution of power between citizens and government and among competing groups of citizens is also a pressing policy question in all nation-states. To varying degrees, rank-and-file citizens need to feel that they are able to influence the actions of their government, so power must be distributed effectively between the people and their government. Furthermore, many groups of citizens see the need to increase their power position with regard to other groups in society. As the principal institution for distributing power in society, the government is responsible for attending to the needs of these people.

The problem of power as a human value is, then, double-edged: (1) governments must acquire enough power to be able to govern; and (2) the people must obtain enough power to influence their government and competing groups in society. In the case of governments that are solidly entrenched, the acquisition of power has already been accomplished, and the distribution of power is the dominant issue. Our discussion principally focuses on power distribution. Nevertheless, there are many governments in the world, primarily in the less-developed regions, where the central problem is one of acquiring enough power to be able to meet the challenges of their society. Where necessary, then, our discussion shifts to an analysis of how governments in developing countries acquire enough power to become viable and to solve the problems that confront their people.

Respect.   The second human value, *respect*, refers to the desire of most people to enjoy secure and supportive relationships with others, including (in our usage) political authorities. In our dealings with other people, most of us prefer to associate with those who respect our feelings and our ways of thinking, who encourage us to feel self-confident in their presence, who do not try to punish or abuse us for what we think or do, and to whom we give our loyalty and affection. There is a counterpart process in the political world that matters a great deal to citizens and government alike. The different dimensions of respect—honor and prestige, respect for human rights, affection and loyalty—are all elements that contribute to the idea of community. *Political community* refers to a group of individuals who communicate with, work together with, and understand one another. Without a strong sense of political community, a political system will face excessive conflict and turmoil.

To enhance the development of community within a political system, respect must be accorded to all groups and individuals. If a particular race, ethnic group, or social class is not provided with respect through the laws of a country and if it is not allowed to vote or is not accorded equal opportunities in education and employment, it is not likely to feel like a part of a larger political community. Political systems characterized by discriminatory policies and actions tend to have societies divided by deep political cleavages—and these sometimes may express themselves in violent political conflict. The potential for violence is greatest in countries where respect is not widely distributed.

Well-being.   The third basic value at stake in politics, *well-being*, refers to the enjoyment by groups and individuals of income, goods, services, health, safety, and comfort. Although there seems to be a universal desire for increased well-being, ideologies and political systems hold different images of the proper distribution of wealth and other elements of well-being. *Capitalism* appears more individual oriented. Although attempting to provide equal opportunities, capitalist political systems allow individuals to achieve whatever levels of well-being are within their grasp. Thus, some individuals are able to accumulate great wealth and to enjoy an abundance of services, safety, and comfort. At the same time, certain individuals and groups live at the poverty level in these systems and suffer from crime, relatively poor health care, and social and physical deprivation. Capitalist belief systems remain ambivalent about these conditions and about inequality in general.

On the other hand, *Marxist* ideology and traditional *communist* political systems spoke in favor of more equitable distribution of well-being. They emphasized social equality and were willing to deprive the economically privileged of their wealth and shut off opportunities for material accumulation beyond a maximum standard. The traditional communist system stressed the collective good over that of the individual. Such systems purported to allocate values more equally than non-communist states. Although environmental and other constraints made it difficult for the leaders of communist countries (e.g., China), to raise dramatically the level of well-being for the whole population, redistributive policies made it possible for the poorer classes to be above the level of abject poverty.

One of the fascinating political developments of recent years involves the changing approaches to well-being in the communist and post-communist governments of the Second World. Most of these governments are privatizing their economies and allowing individuals greater opportunities to expand their incomes and improve their individual well-being. There is a clear trend away from a collectivist and statist approach to well-being and to an approach based on individual initiative and private enterprise.

Enlightenment. The term for our last value, *enlightenment*, is one with many different meanings, depending on whether one's focus is philosophical, historical, or educational. We define enlightenment as the process by which individuals learn about themselves and their world, whether by means of formal education, acquisition of information from the mass media, or transmission of informal social mores through family, peer group, or neighborhood.

Although educational opportunities in a given country are affected by economic factors, significant political choices still must be made. Education is an important means of overcoming economic deficiencies because human potential must be enhanced if economic development is to proceed. Still, the choices to be made are not always obvious. Should quality education be guaranteed to all, regardless of race, social class, or ethnic origin? Should the objective be mass enlightenment or the development of an intellectual elite capable of giving leadership in the process of modernization? Here, too, the question concerns allocation of resources. How can resources be allocated to gain the maximum benefit to society? In some countries undergoing modernization, the choice has been to raise the general level of all groups in the population although this may be costly in terms of a de-emphasis on quality, elite-oriented education. Two Western capitalist countries, the United States and Great Britain, made quite different choices in this respect during their periods of rapid industrialization in the nineteenth century. Today, many British observers feel that their choice of an elitist educational system was costly in view of the wide distribution of advanced technological skills now needed in modern industrial society. They compare their country unfavorably with the United States in this respect.

Enlightenment means much more than education. In many countries, the mass communication media are the subject of great controversy, as they disseminate information that may be threatening to an incumbent regime. Many government leaders have controlled their nation's press or have expelled foreign journalists because of the threat they pose to their survival. Even in countries where the press is relatively free politically, questions concerning censorship, pornography, and the role of the press in trials and at times of crisis have come to the surface. Information, especially that broadcast through public channels, is not a free good and is usually subject to some controls in the name of the public interest.

Even cultural and ethnic learning—once thought intensely private matters beyond the reach of the state—have come under public scrutiny in many countries. In some countries, such as Iran, regional separatism is kept alive by informal means, despite official measures to suppress distinct languages and cultural traditions. In other countries, such as Belgium, special regional sensitivities are protected by constitutional and other measures. In our highly politicized world, even one's innermost thoughts and modes of expression become the subject of public debate, if not of regulations.

Power, well-being, respect, and enlightenment represent four important human values. From time to time, we refer to them collectively by the term *human dignity*. Human dignity refers to a preferred state of being that many government leaders attempt to achieve through their allocation of our four values. Theoretically, the highest state of human dignity would be reached when a society received its preferred (ideal) mixture of values.

There are different conceptions of the term *human dignity* in today's world. In this book, the concept carries with it the notion that each human being is considered an end in himself or herself and is not a mere instrument to enhance the values of some higher entity, for example, a state, a party, or a dictator. We obviously cannot claim that all governments employ policies designed to maximize the Western concept of human dignity. A glance through a newspaper will uncover examples of governments that deny their people many, or even all, of the values listed. The approach of each government in meeting its society's problems will differ, depending on the relative weight it places on such competing factors as dissent and conformity or on the rights of the individual and the rights of the collectivity. We strive in the pages ahead to be sensitive to the different concepts of human dignity in the world today, yet we tend to emphasize personal standards as yardsticks against which to measure the performance of governments.

The Fundamentals of Politics

Politics *does* make a difference. We believe that there is no country in the world where decisions of political leaders could not bring about a more equal distribution of the four basic values outlined above. Yet we also are acutely conscious of the caveat, "There is no such thing as a free lunch." Redistributive decisions in one realm will inevitably be costly in another. Thus, the decision to confiscate private wealth, for example, through a heavily progressive tax on personal income or through a levy on corporate income, will have the effect of reducing the pool of private savings that can be devoted to capital investment and, thus, to economic growth. But failure to redistribute may mean that the rich will get richer faster than the poor—society may become less egalitarian rather than more so. These dilemmas face political decision makers in all parts of the world.

As we use the word, *politics* refers to the process by which certain values or things people want are distributed. We see politics as a process by which public goals are translated into governmental actions and value outcomes. Public *goals* are what people hope to accomplish, the expressed objectives of political leaders, groups, or ordinary citizens. *Actions* are decisions resulting in legislation, programs, or some other activity intended to achieve public goals. *Outcomes* are the consequences of political action.

What results from the actions, and what impact do they have on people? These results are the outcome of politics. Because the general result of this process is policy, we will occasionally use the term *policy-making process* to describe these events. The essence of the process is the distribution of values. However, there are many other social institutions, such as schools, churches, businesses, and labor unions, that also distribute the things people want. What makes the political process of distribution different is its public scope and authoritative character.

This means that politics is a public process in the sense that it affects all the members of a population whether or not they agree with the outcome, have participated in the process, or, in fact, are even aware that a public decision has been made. The all-encompassing coverage of the political process distinguishes it from other social institutions whose impact is, for the most part, restricted to their members. Occasionally, to emphasize the fact that politics deals with the values of the public as opposed to private interests, we will also use the terms *public policy* and *public policy-making process*.

Politics is an authoritative process because most citizens abide by the government's policy even though they may not agree with its content. The authority of a regime to make policy for an entire population stems not only—and maybe not even primarily—from the justice or wisdom of the policy but also from the willingness of the people to attribute such authority to the regime. Such attribution may come from the way a decision is made as much as from the content of the specific policy.

This book examines and compares the political process that shapes the distribution of values in countries from all parts of the globe. Although elites and masses influence the making of public policy, they do so within the framework of reg-

ular and predictable patterns of behavior or institutions. Thus, our focus on the policy process includes an examination of the political and governmental structures within which the power to make policy is located. Although we devote much discussion to explaining governments and their role in the policy-making process, we must broadly cast our net to include all actions relevant to the policy process. Thus, we often refer to political systems rather than to governments. Governments traditionally represent formal institutions (the executive, the legislature, etc.) and the political elites staffing them who are involved in the making of policy. Because of the nature of modern political life, only a minority of a society usually is directly involved in the determination of policy. These individuals are referred to as political elites; although they play crucial roles in the political process, they are not the sole participants.

The concept of a political system is more inclusive than government and incorporates all individuals and institutions involved in the political process. For example, in explaining Soviet policy toward the West, one must understand the role of its formal governmental organs and political leaders. But that alone will not produce a complete understanding. The student of politics must also examine the influence of other less formal factors, such as the military-industrial complex, political groups, and the flavor of international opinion. If this is true of the Soviet Union, it is likely to be even "more true" in the case of more open, democratic political systems in which there is a regular pattern of interaction among government decision makers and groups representing different sections of the general population. For all political systems, we are interested in the forces that help shape policy, whether they are near to, or remote from, the actual policy makers. We are also interested in the consequences of the policies made for different groups within a society. The political system includes the influences bearing on the policy makers, the impacts of their decisions on the public, and the resulting public reactions.

How the Book Is Organized

This book is divided into three main parts, each of which is devoted to countries that exhibit one of the major political styles: the Western European democracies of the First World (Part I), the communist and post-communist states of the Second World (Part II), and the developing countries of the Third World (Part III). Within each part, we compare countries with two questions in mind.

1. What similarities and differences exist among political systems regarding the *goals* that determine the allocation of values, the *actions* devised by political leaders to achieve these goals, and the degree of success attained in pursuing these goals, or the *outcomes*, of policy?

2. What important factors determine or shape the goals, actions, and outcomes of public policies produced by different political systems? Are *political structures* and *institutions* crucial, or is the social, economic, and cultural *environment* surrounding the political process more important?

By *political system* we mean a process of structured interaction among actors within a country. These actors are directing themselves toward particular goals that are designed to produce certain outcomes that will either promote or detract from human dignity as we have defined it. The decisions of government are the actions that will bring about such outcomes, but the decisions themselves are due to the interaction of goal-seeking actors, including the decision makers themselves. For example, the proponents of nuclear energy and the environmentalists both want to promote the value of well-being. The former believe that nuclear energy can well solve the energy shortages that threaten our present standard of living. On the other hand, the environmentalists fear the possible consequences of nuclear energy for the biological environment and even for the future of life itself. Each group calls on the government to exclusively adopt its own conception of well-being. Government decision makers must choose between the competing goals. The choices undoubtedly will reflect the values of those holding decision-making power as well as of those of the contending groups. The decisions will then be implemented, with consequences for both energy supply and environmental quality. These consequences are what we call the outcomes. The total impact of all actions taken in the political system will, then, lead us to reassess the extent to which human dignity is being promoted in that society.

However, events may occur outside the political system that also will have consequences for the level of human dignity. In fact, the political system itself does not exist in a vacuum. Political actors seek to realize their goals through government action because they find certain aspects of their lives unsatisfactory. In the beginning, at least, most of these aspects are not political in nature. Economic uncertainty, racial conflict, and external threats to the national security originate in various ways outside the political system itself owing to dislocations in other systems: the economy, the ecology, the social structure, the general culture, the international political arena. The sum total of these other systems constitutes what we call the *environment* of the political system.

In each part of the text, two chapters treat environmental characteristics of a social and economic nature that directly impinge on the political system. The first chapter shows the *historical* links among social, economic, and political factors that have been common to countries at similar stages of development and that also help to account for differences among countries that have many elements of similarity. The environment of the political system is dealt with in a different way in the second chapter. Here we describe the *contemporary economic and social structures* of the countries under examination. Regardless of the level of development, contemporary political systems face a wide variety of recurring and severe economic problems, such as unemployment; inflation; scarcity of raw materials, energy sources, and food; poverty; cyclical fluctuations; and structural underdevelopment. Similarly, social conflict stemming from ethnic or religious cleavage is not confined to the Third World, although it may be more of a problem in those countries.

The third chapter in each part links the political system to its environment through its treatment of *political culture* and *political socialization*. Political culture may be seen as the pattern of attitudes and beliefs that people hold toward their political system; political socialization refers to the process by which members of the system are taught these attitudes and beliefs. One aspect of political culture, for example, has to do with the ideas an ordinary citizen has about his or her own ability to influence the political process. In some countries, like Great Britain, many citizens feel competent to exert their influence on the political elites of the country; in many other countries, like Italy, the Soviet Union, and Mexico, the level of civic competence may be far less. These differences obviously have an impact on the willingness of citizens to participate actively in the politics of their nation.[7] In addition, within the study of political culture, we are able to consider the similarities and differences among political goals as they are articulated by the ideologies of various sets of political elites.

Political socialization is also dealt with in the third chapter. In many Third World countries, for instance, young people traditionally have been socialized into a localized system of beliefs and values through which they are taught that the community is the center of their life and strangers are to be regarded with suspicion. These socialization practices reinforce age-old communal strife as well as breed an attitude of hostility against efforts by the central government to develop nationalist sentiment. In countries seeking to develop rapidly, such as China, modernizing elites have found it necessary to disrupt conventional family structures to control the politically relevant lessons taught to the children of the country. In many Third World countries, however, the government's failure to achieve this sort of breakthrough has meant the growth of ethnic, linguistic, and religious associations that aggravate communal strife and weaken the nation's ability to develop rapidly.

Three chapters deal directly with the political system itself. In two of these, the fourth and fifth chapters, we describe *political structures* and *the roles played by individuals* within them; the sixth chapter evaluates *policy-making styles and processes*. What we have in mind is the distinction between an essentially descriptive account of the similarities and differences among the institutions in different political systems (the fourth and fifth chapters) and an analysis (the sixth chapter) of those structures and roles in terms of the allocation of values.

Each part concludes with a seventh chapter that evaluates *political performance*. We attempt to assess the extent to which a political system's goals, actions, and outcomes contribute to enhancing human dignity. We make this rather abstract concept operational by comparing a political system's espoused goals with actual performance in the area of the four basic values.

Our evaluation of political performance also involves an explanatory feature. After appraising performance in terms of goals, actions, and outcomes, we want to isolate the factors that determine different performance levels. Here, our analytical distinction between environment and political system comes into play. Can a relatively high level of human dignity be attributed to qualities of the political system of a given country, or must we emphasize its environmental advantages, such as its high level of economic development?

Finally, in the concluding chapter of the book, the summarized evaluations are brought together and the similarities and differences among the three worlds are analyzed.

Why Study Comparative Politics?

One is often jolted by students questioning, "What difference does all of this make to me personally? How can I use this information in my life?" Although different scholars and teachers of comparative politics would answer these questions differently, we believe the study of politics in other countries is important to a student for at least three reasons.

1. The United States contains 5 percent of the world's population but annually consumes more than 30 percent of the world's energy and output of goods. These data tell you two things. First, the United States is in a distinct minority in the world; second, the other 95 percent of the earth's population is becoming increasingly important to the United States. In the energy crises of the 1970s, it became obvious that oil-producing countries, like Saudi Arabia and Iraq, possessed a good deal of influence over our government and our standard of living. U.S. politics of the 1990s will require a better understanding of the various issues surrounding our relations with other nations. These issues should make us want to know more about the 95 percent of the world's population whose fate is each day more closely intertwined with our own.

2. We must learn more about foreign countries to make sense of our own government's efforts to influence those countries and to achieve U.S. objectives. Since World War II, the United States has been involved in two major wars (producing nearly 100,000 dead Americans) and literally dozens of minor conflicts—ranging all around the globe, from Grenada to Berlin to Iran. We have spent more than $100 billion in foreign assistance since the Marshall Plan days of the late 1940s to improve (and influence) foreign economies; each year we also spend approximately $300 billion on weapons and other military items to defend our nation. Finally, since the early 1950s, we have created an intelligence network in the Central Intelligence Agency (CIA) and the Federal Bureau of Investigation (FBI) that has angered and shocked some American observers for what they feel are unwarranted intrusions into our private lives. Why have these things come about? What is it about the countries beyond our borders that makes some of them threats to us, others allies, and still others a cause of great concern because of their very weakness? Could any of these expenditures be better made somewhere else? To know the answers to these questions, we must know more about the countries with which we share this planet.

3. Through our study of comparative politics, we can develop the skills of analysis and inquiry so necessary for knowledge of our own political world, locally, nationally, and internationally. How many of you have ever felt bewildered by political events that you could not understand? Most of us have had this experience. In this book, as you work toward a better understanding of foreign countries, you will also learn inquiry and analysis skills that later can be turned toward better understanding the government of your own country. For example, we will help you ask and answer questions such as: Where does power *really* reside? What roles do mass publics play in policy making? How do some political leaders use the symbols of democracy to mask the reality of authoritarianism? How can the individual citizen make his or her influence felt at the point where it will count most? Our inquiry into politics in France or the Soviet Union or India will, of course, yield one kind of answer, but the questions are the same for understanding politics in St. Louis, Atlanta, or Washington, D.C.

Notes

1. Gabriel A. Almond and G. Bingham Powell, *Comparative Politics: A Developmental Approach* (New York: Little, Brown, 1966), chap. 8.

2. Arthur S. Banks, ed., *Political Handbook of the World: 1987* (Binghamton, New York: CSA Publications, 1987).

3. John Kautsky, *The Political Consequences of Modernization* (New York: Wiley, 1972).

4. Ibid.

5. A. F. K. Organski, *The Stages of Political Development* (New York: Knopf, 1967).

6. The literature on human values is extensive. The interested reader can begin with Hadley Cantril, *The Pattern of Human Concerns* (New Brunswick, N.J.: Rutgers University Press, 1966); Harold Lasswell, *A Pre-View of Policy Sciences* (New York: Elsevier, 1971); Abraham Maslow, ed., *New Knowledge in Human Values* (Chicago: Regnery, 1970); Gunnar Myrdal, *Value in Social Theory* (Boston: Routledge & Kegan Paul, 1958); and Milton Rokeach, *The Nature of Human Values* (New York: Free Press, 1973).

7. Gabriel A. Almond and Sidney Verba, *The Civic Culture: Political Attitudes and Democracy in Five Nations* (Princeton, N.J.: Princeton University Press, 1963).

PART I

POWER AND POLICY IN WESTERN EUROPEAN DEMOCRACIES

East Berlin crowd listens to Helmut Kohl before the March 1990 elections in East Germany.

C H A P T E R 1

HISTORICAL BACKGROUND

Since World War II, most of the countries of Western Europe have consistently been classified by their own standards as democracies. The extent to which the reality has approached the Western ideal of democracy, considered as an equal distribution of power, has, however, varied. It is true that democracy is a goal toward which Western countries strive. Political scientists seldom claim that the ideal concept of democracy can be used as a descriptive term, that is, as a category to which Western political systems, in fact, belong.[1] American political scientist Robert A. Dahl has suggested that, instead of the word *democracy*, we use the term *polyarchy* to characterize the type of political system that predominates in the First World countries of Western Europe, in North America, and in parts of the western rim of the Pacific Ocean.[2] Polyarchies are political systems in which the many rule, not just in the formal sense of universal or near-universal suffrage but in the sense that there is a meaningful degree of competition among groups contending for power. The many who choose among these contenders have meaningful choices to make,

and in making them they determine who will be making the decisions of goverment. But when we look at the distribution of power within the polyarchy, we see that, as individuals, the few who make the decisions of government have considerably more power than have the many, again as individuals, even though the many choose the few. Hence, unlike the ideal of democracy, power is not distributed equally, although it has also been argued that power is more equally distributed in the polyarchies of the First World than it is, or ever has been, anywhere else. Peter L. Berger suggests that, not only does the polyarchy maximize the power of ordinary people in fact, if not in ideal terms, but it also attains a wider distribution of respect than can be found in other forms.[3] This is in part because the competition for power is sufficiently equal to ensure that power will remain fairly equally distributed, and in part because temporary majorities will not be strong enough to diminish the amount of respect enjoyed by individuals and groups that are temporarily, or even permanently, in the minority. In comparison with most other countries of the world, the polyarchies examined share these advantages, but, as we shall see, they differ from one another in the degrees and the ways in which the advantages are realized.

It will be noted that most polyarchies are rather advanced economically and socially. Indeed, they compete economically with one another and are also their own principal trading partners. It is characteristic of polyarchies that they rank high on the various indexes of socioeconomic strength. Actually, most of the more advanced industrial countries of the world are polyarchies, with the notable exceptions of the Soviet Union, East Germany, and Czechoslovakia, which are communist (Second World) countries. But recent changes have moved these countries toward the status of polyarchies as well.

Another characteristic of most polyarchies is that they have parliamentary systems of government. Indeed, almost all of the Western European polyarchies currently have parliamentary systems or, as in the case of France, parliamentary traditions. Furthermore, more polyarchies have multiparty systems (that is, more than two major political parties) than have two-party systems, as in the United States. Again, this is particularly true of Western Europe. Even Great Britain, traditionally regarded as a two-party country, has some of the characteristics of a multiparty system. (See Table 1.1.)

The five political systems we compare are the five most populous polyarchies in the world other than the United States, and they include the four most populous polyarchies in Western Europe. All are advanced industrially. Although the range is wide, the gap between the most and least prosperous of these five countries, West Germany and Italy, has been narrowing in the past decade. All except France have parliamentary systems of government; France has a difficult-to-classify mixture of parliamentary and presidential elements. All, including Great Britain, have multiparty systems by the definition employed here. (See Chapter 4.)

In this fourth edition of the textbook, we have decided to include Japan among the major First World polyarchies that are systematically compared. This is in part because Japan is, after all, a First World polyarchy and, although the principal geographical focus is on Western Europe, Japan can scarcely be ignored when we attempt to generalize from the Western European examples to the First World polyarchies as a type. Japan has enjoyed the highest rates of economic growth and has experienced rates of unemployment and inflation that are among the lowest in the First World. But Japan does not share a deep commitment to Western cultural values, having selectively borrowed elements of the values of power, well-being, enlightenment, and respect that the West has to offer. Particularly, in this volume we call attention to certain cultural and institutional elements relevant to Japanese politics that are distinct from those typically found in Western Europe. This raises the question of whether Japan's economic success has been because of or in spite of the ways in which she differs from the West. Should we look to the cultural and structural ways in which Japan differs from Great Britain, France, West Germany, and Italy for the reasons that Japan has had a better economic record than the four other countries in the past decade or so, or should we expect to find the reasons in the borrowings Japan has made from the West? The student may be moved, in fact, to ask whether the success that Japan has shown in adapting to the value requirements of capitalism as an economic system and of polyarchy as a political system points the way to future successes by other non-Western countries, particularly those of East Asia, which share certain cultural characteristics with Japan. The case of

Table 1.1 First World Polyarchies

Country	Type of Government	Area 1,000s of sq km	Area Population (in millions)	Urban Population (% of total population)	GNP* per capita (1987)
Australia	Parliamentary	7,687	16.2	86	$11,100
Austria	Parliamentary	84	7.6	57	11,980
Belgium	Parliamentary	31	9.9	97	11,480
Canada	Parliamentary	9,976	25.9	76	15,160
Denmark	Parliamentary	43	5.1	86	14,930
Finland	Mixed presidential/ parliamentary	337	4.9	60	14,470
France	Mixed presidential/ parliamentary	547	55.6	74	12,790
Germany, Fed. Republic of	Parliamentary	249	61.2	86	14,400
Greece	Parliamentary	132	10.0	61	4,020
Iceland	Parliamentary	103	0.2	—	16,600
Ireland	Parliamentary	70	3.6	58	6,120
Israel	Parliamentary	21	4.4	91	6,800
Italy	Parliamentary	301	57.4	68	10,350
Japan	Parliamentary	372	122.1	77	15,750
Luxembourg	Parliamentary	3	0.4	—	18,550
Netherlands	Parliamentary	41	14.7	88	11,860
New Zealand	Parliamentary	269	3.3	84	7,750
Norway	Parliamentary	324	4.2	74	17,190
Portugal	Mixed presidential/ parliamentary	92	10.2	32	2,830
Spain	Parliamentary	505	38.8	77	6,010
Sweden	Parliamentary	450	8.4	84	15,550
Switzerland	Parliamentary	41	6.5	61	21,330
United Kingdom	Parliamentary	245	56.9	92	10,420
United States	Presidential	9,363	243.8	74	18,530

(*Source*) The list of polyarchies is adapted and updated from Robert A. Dahl, *Polyarchy: Participation and Opposition* (New Haven: Yale University Press, 1971), pp. 84, 232. Data in the columns are taken from the World Bank, *World Development Report 1989* (Oxford: Oxford University Press, 1989), pp. 165, 225, 230. Population figures are from the latest census data available in 1987.

* GNP = gross national product.

France, West Germany, Italy, Japan, and the United Kingdom are in italics in all figures and tables to emphasize their use as comparative cases.

South Korea, which has registered even more spectacular economic success than Japan of late and has been moving by degrees toward polyarchy, may be particularly worth watching in the years immediately to come.

In this chapter, we discuss the history of the Western European polyarchies and Japan in an attempt to answer some of the questions just raised as well as such questions as these: How have the political systems of these countries (and those of other polyarchies) developed? What are the historical reasons for the similarities and differences between them? Why have they been able to develop economies that are generally more advanced than those of most other countries in the world? Are there historical reasons for these differences among them with respect to economic success? Although we cannot answer these questions fully in this introductory textbook, we can point to certain major developments in the history of advanced industrial societies generally and in particular of the four major Western European countries that are partially responsible. We also emphasize the development of Europe's social structure since the beginning of the Industrial Revolution in the eighteenth century. Our assumption is that the major political upheavals and economic changes during the past two centuries in Europe have been closely related to the conflicts among various social groups for larger shares of power, respect, well-being, and enlightenment.

The discussion is divided into four parts, each taking a stage in the path of Western Europe and Japan toward modernity: (1) the preindustrial social, economic, and political structures of Western Europe as found in the early eighteenth century just before the Industrial Revolution and in Japan before the middle of the nineteenth century; (2) the early industrialization period—an era of rapid change and great upheavals—that began about 1750 in Western Eu-

rope and a century later in Japan and lasted until around 1870 in northwestern Europe and perhaps until World War I in northern Italy and Japan; (3) the era of mature industrialization, beginning in the 1870s and 1880s and lasting until World War II; and (4) the post–World War II era in which Western Europe and Japan were developing the characteristics of *postindustrial society*.

Preindustrial Western Europe

At the outset, it should be noted that what we are describing is the process of *modernization* as it took place initially in Western Europe. Modernization in Western Europe followed a different path from what took, or is taking, place in most other countries of the world. For the most part, the industrialization of Western Europe was self-generated; whereas other countries have relied extensively on external stimuli for their industrialization, Western Europe already had certain factors that helped to facilitate self-generated industrialization.

Preindustrial Economies

Of prime importance in understanding the beginnings of industrialization is the fact that the economic system known as *capitalism* was already well established in Western Europe, and had been developing there for about three centuries before the advent of industrialization. During the period from around the middle of the fifteenth century until the middle of the eighteenth century, a transition took place from agrarian feudalism to industrial capitalism. It was a period in which the economic basis of social standing and political power was shifting from landed wealth to financial capital accumulated particularly in the growth of commerce among European cities, and between Europe and its expanding colonial empires. Capitalism is a dynamic economic system, in which a circular process occurs in the conversion of financial means that are at least in part in private hands, into the manufacture of goods and the provision of services. The realization of financial gain from these activities is then accumulated and put back into the cycle in the form of further investment. Wealth accumulates both in the form of liquid capital that can be reinvested and in the concrete material means of goods production and service provision, such as buildings, machines, and ships and wagons for conveying goods from place to place. The process can at any time be in a phase of expansion or of contraction, but over time, capitalism has produced an immense growth of both the financial and the material means for gains in human well-being. Capitalism is distinguished from *socialism*, the alternative method of accumulating wealth for a society, in that at least part of the financial resources provided and a large portion of the gain realized are by *private* entrepreneurs, who provide inspiration and take the risks for new industrial and commercial ventures. Under socialism, the state spreads the risk across society, and the inspiration is likely to come from state officials. During the three transitional centuries before the beginning of industrialization, capitalism moved from being a rather peripheral feature to becoming the central reality of economic life in Western Europe. In its earliest stages, as more recently elsewhere in the world, capitalism received considerable impetus from the state, which had first to accumulate power in its hands before it could use this power to assist in the development of capitalism and eventually industrialization.

Western Europe in this 300-year period was primarily agrarian, as are most of the Third World countries today. This means that the vast majority of the working population was engaged in agriculture. Many worked as agricultural laborers on large aristocratically owned estates; others divided their time between working for such landowners and working for themselves on their own small plots of land. Many people were independent small landowners able to subsist as such, but probably finding it impossible to accumulate wealth because of the heavy state taxes or manorial dues owed to a local lord. Other impediments were the seasonal uncertainties and the rather primitive state of agricultural technology.

In the smaller towns, the economy was dependent on the nearby countryside. These were market towns where farmers sold their produce and where goods that the farmer might buy were manufactured and sold. Itinerant merchants supplied farmers and townspeople with other goods that were not produced locally; this was about the extent of the economic intercourse between the town and the outside world. Only in the larger cities were goods produced for wider distribution. Because such manufacturing and its marketing often required substantial amounts of capital, the cities became financial centers. At that time (before industrialization), manufacturing existed only on a small scale. The factory system had not yet been introduced. The main source of energy was still the workers themselves.

Social Structure

The cities had grown sufficiently large by the seventeenth and eighteenth centuries that there was a distinctive urban social class structure. It was based essentially on the ownership of property, which had not yet come into much conflict with the traditional social hierarchy of feudal times. At the top of the social scale was the aristocracy, whose economic and social position was based on the ownership of land and the possession of political power. The leading families of England and France, as well as those of the smaller political units in Germany and Italy, owned land but were also firmly established socially in the leading cities, especially Paris, London, and the other political capitals. Thus, they were found at the pinnacles of both the rural and the urban social hierarchies.

The urban middle class constituted a mixture of elements that was not yet too complex. Ownership of property conferred status within the middle class, and those with the most substantial fortunes were at the top of the social hierarchy, just below the aristocracy. During the century or so before industrialization, upward mobility, at least within the middle class, was becoming increasingly possible. It was this class that was accumulating the wealth necessary to capitalize the coming industrialization. The conservative influence of the aristocracy and of established craftspersons in the towns was giving way to ambitious entrepreneurship. Markets were opening up in the New World and in the European cities for goods, such as clothing and housewares, that could be produced inexpensively on a large scale by using rural laborers. Although such workers were less skilled than urban artisans, they could produce qualitatively by specializing in particular operations—a foreshadowing of the soon-to-emerge factory system.

Rural society was more hierarchical and had fewer class distinctions than urban society. Below the landed gentry on the rural social scale came the various gradations of peasants. The relative number of independent farmers and agricultural laborers varied widely from one part of Europe to another and from region to region within a given country. There were proportionately more independent farmers in northwestern Europe, but more agricultural laborers toward the south and east.

Preindustrial Political Systems

The politics of the preindustrial period in Western Europe were dominated by the aristocracy or at least by those aristocrats who were concerned with national political matters. Attention focused on monarchs, whether their titles were emperor or empress, king or queen, grand duke, or elector. Aristocratic factions would vie with one another for the monarch's ear, and one measure of the monarch's personal power was the ability to keep factions divided and to maintain alternative sources of support, such as the church or the urban middle class.

Within the towns and cities, the middle class and artisans were rather formidable forces in their own right. In Western Europe, including parts of western Germany and northern Italy, they generally controlled their own local affairs and resisted monarchical intrusion. The development of parliamentary bodies in such countries as England and the Netherlands represented the determined effort of the urban middle class to resist arbitrary monarchical taxes. As the transitional 300-year period proceeded, in the larger and more powerful states of Western Europe—particularly in France, Prussia, and Sweden—monarchs were able to consolidate their own power territorially and to reduce the independent power bases of both the aristocracy and the towns. This was accomplished in part because of the skill employed by monarchs, or more accurately their chief ministers and advisers, in playing on the conflicts between the two principal estates of town and countryside, but also through a tacit alliance between the court and the leading financial and commercial interests.[4]

The system of mercantilism was developed in conjunction with the overseas expansion of European state power in the Americas and into areas bounded by the Indian Ocean. This was a method of accumulation of both wealth and power by the monarchical state through the achievement of surpluses in external trade, and through the plundering of conquered peoples. It enabled the powerful states to provide financial support for capitalist ventures, just as the enhanced power of the state to control internal affairs provided budding capitalists with the security to pursue risk-taking ventures. Part of the wealth accumulated in private hands returned to the state in the form of tax revenues, which funded the intra- and extra-European military endeavors of the state. As the wealth and power of the state expanded, that of a new class, the *bourgeoisie*, did as well. But its arrival to full political status in most countries had to await the explosion of privately held wealth that was the consequence of industrialization.

Early Industrialization

Industrialization Defined

The Industrial Revolution as a general European phenomenon began in the middle of the eighteenth century and ran its course in a little more than a century. As a localized phenomenon, however, it occurred at different times in different places and is still taking place today in many parts of the world. In Europe, it began in Great Britain and then spread to the northwestern part of the continent—to France, Belgium, and the Netherlands—by the late eighteenth century. Several decades later, it began to take hold in Germany and Sweden and still later in the Austro-Hungarian Empire; but it

did not spread to much of Italy or elsewhere in southern Europe, or to the Russian Empire until the end of the nineteenth century. By the early nineteenth century, industrialization was under way in North America, and it started in Japan toward the end of that century. In the earliest countries to industrialize, about 100 years were needed to complete what is often called the rapid industrialization stage. But early industrialization took longer in France because of factors that are discussed later in this chapter. By contrast, in some of the later industrialized countries—notably Germany, Sweden, and Japan—the early phase of industrialization was telescoped to about half the time, undoubtedly in part owing to the fact that the groundwork had been laid in other countries and, thus, the learning period could be greatly shortened.

We can define *industrialization* as the shift in the manufacturing industries from primary dependence on human energy to dependence on inanimate energy sources, thereby dramatically increasing productivity, or output rate per worker. This shift is accompanied by a reorganization of production so that larger numbers of workers are using machines driven by inanimate power to produce a substantially larger volume of goods for a much wider market than before industrialization. The factory system, an aspect of industrialization, means narrowing the tasks assigned each worker. Artisan production usually meant that each worker was responsible for the entire production process—from the raw material to the finished product. Now, each stage was assigned to a worker who specialized in only one or a few of the operations for producing the goods. The work hours were long and the work itself tended to be tedious and dehumanizing. The earliest decades of industrialization entailed the greatest human suffering. In every country when it occurred, at least one generation was sacrificed so that future generations could enjoy the fruits of its efforts.

The Origins of Industrialization

Scholars disagree as to why the Industrial Revolution started when and where it did.[5] Before the dawn of industrialization, there was a class of fledgling industrial capitalists in Western Europe who were already experimenting with more efficient forms of production, discovering far-flung markets, and accumulating wealth. The ability of this class to break away from traditional patterns of production and marketing, especially in Great Britain, enabled it to experiment with still newer forms. As for the development of the requisite technology, it meant a pragmatic fitting of means to specific ends. According to the great German social scientist Max Weber,[6] there emerged a certain "spirit of capitalism," a spirit that blossomed more easily in Protestant northwestern Europe than elsewhere. Protestant culture had freed itself from the inhibitions imposed on the individual by Roman Catholicism, thereby developing a greater faith in the human capacity to create and improve, and a belief in something like the modern concept of progress.

French economic historian Fernand Braudel acknowledges that there is a geographic correlation between Protestantism and the advancement of capitalism in Europe after about 1600. But he refuses to accept that Protestantism was the fundamental cause for that development. Capitalism had begun in southern Europe with the development of the Italian banking system over a century earlier, at a time when the countries of northern Europe were virtual colonial outposts of the South, according to Braudel.[7] The Protestant Reformation could thus be seen as providing the ideology supporting a "war of liberation" in which the poorer north-

ern countries established first their political, economic, and cultural independence from the South and later their economic supremacy. In strictly economic terms, an analogy can be drawn with mid-twentieth-century Japan and with today's newly industrial countries on the eastern fringe of Asia, which are successfully penetrating the markets of advanced industrial countries with products that can be manufactured more cheaply by societies that have less developed material needs. From this perspective, Protestantism in northern Europe, in its strictures against lavish consumption and its glorification of the work ethic, made a virtue out of harsh economic necessity and justified turning it to the advantage of societies adopting that ethic. A similar ethic seems to prevail in East Asia today.[8]

By the eighteenth century, certain factors characterized British society that made it unique, even in northwestern Europe. At that time, the population of Great Britain was growing about twice as fast as that of France and approximating the growth rate of Prussia. This helped create a domestic market for new industrial products. More important, the rigid social structure that prevailed in central Europe was less pronounced in Great Britain. Workers' wages were higher, they ate better, and they spent a smaller portion of their income on food than did their counterparts on the Continent. The percentage of small businessmen, artisans, and independent farmers in the active population was higher than in most other countries. Both in the cities and in rural areas, the gradations between the upper, middle, and lower classes were more gentle; upward mobility was easier; and social barriers were more relaxed. There was a strong tradition of entrepreneurial initiative that went back to the Middle Ages. Aggressive entrepreneurship could emerge from almost any social class or geographical area within the kingdom. Like the innovative Dutch, the British were experimenters, tinkerers; they were less afraid to take risks than most of their continental counterparts; and they were less bound to traditional ways of doing things.[9]

It is not coincidental that industrialization got its start in a country in which absolutism never quite took hold. The Tudor monarchs of the sixteenth century—Henry VII, Henry VIII, and Elizabeth I—had succeeded in bringing order out of the chaos that England had experienced during the fifteenth-century War of the Roses, but they had not attempted to overturn the powers and privileges of the medieval Houses of Parliament. By contrast, the Estates General, the French version of Parliament, lapsed into nonexistence during the long seventeenth-, and eighteenth-century Bourbon reigns of Louis XIII, Louis XIV, and Louis XV. The Tudors had been successful in accomplishing their political aims without confronting Parliament, preferring to wield influence through skillful coalition building. But their seventeenth-century successors, the Stuarts, sought to establish the principle that the monarch ruled by Divine Right, the claim to absolute power unfettered by countervailing bodies such as the Houses of Parliament or the courts. In other words, the Stuarts were asserting what the French monarchs were able to establish— absolute rule over a large territorial domain, or absolutism for short. But in England, Parliament rebelled and mounted sufficient military force to overturn two Stuart monarchs during the seventeenth century. In the eighteenth century the British[10] monarch was considered a coequal of the two Houses of Parliament, rather than an absolute ruler, in the enactment of legislation, largely because Parliament had demonstrated a healthy capacity to challenge the king's will—a possibility that was hardly conceivable in absolutist continental systems, even where some sort of representative body still existed.

It is arguable, along the lines of Adam Smith, the great Scottish political economist of the period, that, despite the accumulation of great wealth in France during the period of absolutism before the French Revolution of 1789, industrialization could not have begun there, because, unlike England, the monarch held the power to expropriate private wealth for noneconomic undertakings, creating an atmosphere of uncertainty as to whether even the most promising ventures into untested manufacturing realms could succeed. The earliest industrial experiments were more likely to be attempted in countries like Britain and Holland, where the power of the monarch was curtailed by the countervailing power of bodies representing the interests of private holders of wealth, secure in their belief that the capitalist flow of resources into risky undertakings would only fail to bring private gain if the undertakings themselves were ill conceived, not because of unpredictable diversions of potential gains into the state treasury. This is not to say that early industrial initiatives were not taken in France; indeed, the earliest centers of modern textile manufacturing developed there. But it was in Britain that the "critical mass" of venture capital and practical know-how was accumulated and deployed the most effectively.

By the early nineteenth century, Great Britain had established a half-century lead over her nearest rivals. France found she could not overcome this lead in the nineteenth century. French economic growth was sluggish and fitful throughout the century, even though the French Revolution of 1789 removed absolutism and many of the feudal restrictions and impositions that had previously hindered the budding capitalist class. For the most part, the French bourgeoisie preferred the safety of the small family firm with its assured but nonexpanding market and its handful of loyal workers, who could be protected from economic hazards by the patronizing policies of their employers. During the nineteenth century, the French people shifted from rural to urban life much more gradually than the British. Whereas 50 percent of the British population was urbanized by 1850, the same had not occurred in France even by 1900.

During the early nineteenth century, Germany and Italy were not yet unified nations. Both were still divided into a number of small and medium-sized political units that remained largely agrarian. By the 1840s, German entrepreneurs were beginning to exploit the vast mineral resources of the lower Rhineland. Encouraged by a change in state policy and able to take advantage of technological advances achieved elsewhere, German industry was soon expanding. By 1870, German technology had pulled alongside that of other leading countries in Europe. As for Italy, its unification in 1859–60 did not facilitate immediate industrial development. Like other southern and eastern European countries, Italy lacked indigenous capital and central state financial support, and would have to wait for an infusion from outside. Given Italy's poor resource potential, relatively little capital was invested throughout the nineteenth century. On the other hand, its population growth was rapid, especially in the cities, which were overcrowded in the nineteenth century, not unlike those of Third World countries today.

Early Industrial Societies

Observing British society in the mid–nineteenth century, Karl Marx came to the conclusion that industrialization was bringing about a simplification of the class structure, reducing the number of relevant social groups to essentially two: the capitalist class and the proletariat, that is, the owners of the dominant means of production and the workers whom they employed. Although the other classes were certainly not disappearing, it is true that these were the two most dynamic classes during early industrialization, in terms both of their growing numbers and of their growing importance to the smooth functioning of the economic order. Although these classes could be found before 1750, they really burst onto the scene during the next 100 years, growing rapidly in numbers and transforming the social structure of every industrial country. Each took a place alongside the older classes, thereby threatening their status, political power, and economic security. Politically as well as economically, these new classes were to be the instruments of change. More often than not, the older classes became the resisters of change, the reactionaries and conservatives.

The capitalist class is not as easy to distinguish from its neighbors in the upper echelons of society as is the proletariat in the lower reaches. Capitalists are distinguishable from other segments of the middle class in terms of their psychological makeup and style of action as much, perhaps, as in terms of their economic activities. During the period of early industrialization, the true capitalist was probably in a minority among business owners. Peter N. Stearns makes a useful distinction between the middle class and what he calls "the middling class."[11] The former was made up of adventuresome, risk-taking capitalists; those in the latter group were content simply to maintain their positions. There appear to have been proportionately more of the dynamic capitalists in Great Britain than in France (at least until the late nineteenth century) and more in Germany than in Italy. The French term for the middling class is *petite bourgeoisie*, meaning, perhaps, small-time middle class. It has often been used as a term of contempt in the twentieth century, but only because capitalism as a value system has taken firmer root. Typical nineteenth-century French business family heads could defend their conservatism in a way most of their contemporaries would understand.

At the lower levels of the social hierarchy, we see a common development everywhere with industrialization: the rapid increase in the size of the industrial proletariat—a class that scarcely existed before industrialization, indeed, whose very definition arises from industrialization. In part, the industrial working class was created through the *déclassement* of artisans in the manufacturing sectors that turned to the factory system. Small artisan shops could not compete with mass-production techniques, and many journeymen (and even some master artisans) found themselves with no alternative but to adapt to the machines and become what are termed skilled workers. But most of the new proletarian ranks were made up of uprooted peasants, those who had lost their means of making a living owing to the growing commercialization of agriculture. During early industrialization, a phenomenon began that later became increasingly common—people moving across political or ethnic borders from the less economically advanced countries to the industrial centers of Western Europe. One of the earliest migrations was of Irish workers to the new industrial cites of the English northwest.

Also during early industrialization, there began a commercialization of agriculture. Independent peasants were assuming the status of modern farm owners in parts of France and Germany. By controlling the political system, the landed aristocracy was able to secure protective tariffs to shore up their domestic markets, which were also expanding because of the growth of the railroad. In Great Britain, however, earlier tariff legislation was repealed in 1846, representing a victory for industrial capital over agricultural interests and reflecting the degree to which Great Britain had already become an industrial nation. It was an acknowledgment that the country could not be self-sufficient in food production. Other European countries, lacking Great Britain's industrial advantage, did not follow suit, and their farmers remained protected. Although it can be said that industrialization led eventually to the decline of agricultural employment, this was not yet a massive phenomenon in Europe during early industrialization.

Political Changes

Early industrialization was the stage in which the political power of the capitalist class made the most rapid gains. However, these were not as striking as the economic gains. The aristocracy was edged a little to one side, but it certainly had not lost its grip on political power. Although the House of Lords lost ground to the House of Commons after the Reform Act of 1832, individual members of the British aristocracy took note of the fact and managed to retain positions of power for the next few decades. British capitalism probably did not reach equal political stature with the aristocracy until about 1870. By then, Great Britain was a mature industrial nation.

The German aristocracy was even more successful in retaining its power; it continued to dominate politics after unification in 1871 as it had done before in the separate German states.[12] The position of the monarchs and their aristocratic supporters was shaken momentarily by the Revolution of 1848, but when the dust had settled, the monarchs were once again secure on their thrones and the newly introduced legislative bodies were firmly controlled by aristocrats. Some of the states of southwestern Germany had emerged from the period of constitution writing with relatively liberal regimes, giving the middle class an opportunity to share in political power; but with unification, these states became subordinate to the Imperial government, where power was concentrated in the hands of the emperor, his hand-picked chancellor, and a coterie of aristocratic advisers and officials. The legislative body, the Reichstag, was a forum in which middle-class spokesmen could vent their political frustrations, but it was little more than that—at least in the early years of the Empire. German capitalists remained content with their sizable economic rewards during the period of early industrialization; they usually went along with aristocratic initiatives in foreign and domestic policies.

Paradoxically, it was in France that the middle classes, which had been relatively sluggish economically, registered the most evident gains over the aristocracy in the nineteenth century. Formally, at least, the French political system had gone further in removing aristocratic privileges, beginning with the Revolution of 1789 and continuing with a series of political upheavals thereafter—in 1830, 1848, and the 1870s. The power of the Bourbon aristocracy was seriously undermined when the Revolution of 1789 abolished feudal privileges and when Napoleon Bonaparte created an administrative career service that was open to all, regardless of the accident of birth. After Napoleon's fall in 1815, there was an effort to restore the position of the old aristocracy, but this ended with the Revolution of 1830. Universal manhood suffrage was adopted with the Revolution of 1848, and the principle of executive subordination to the legislature became established under the Third Republic in the 1870s.

Although the political star of the middle class was on the rise in early industrial Europe, that of the working class was just beginning to appear on the horizon. By the end of the early industrial period, as artisans began to reconcile themselves to becoming skilled workers, they began to turn from unorganized, spontaneous expressions of anger and anxiety to better-organized, focused industrial action. It was the artisans who sparked much of the development of organized trade unionism around the middle of the nineteenth century. Artisans were coming to realize that industrial workers were their natural allies in the struggle against the common enemy, the capitalist. Even so, the road upward was steep. Universal manhood suffrage, first extended in some countries in 1848, was maintained in France but withdrawn in Germany, to be restored on a limited basis with the establishment of the unified German Empire in 1871. In Great Britain, it was extended gradually to different groups of people but was not fully established until 1918; however, skilled workers enjoyed the right to vote by the 1880s. Universal manhood suffrage was not established in Italy until 1913. But this was before the extension of the suffrage to women in any of our countries, in all of which women's suffrage was attained at least a generation after the early period of industrialization had run its course. In Britain it occurred on a limited basis (middle-class women over thirty) in 1918; and in Germany all women acquired the right to vote in 1919. But in France and Italy women did not gain the right to vote until the end of World War II. The two world wars (1914–18 and 1939–45) were both instrumental in removing opposition to suffrage expansion.

Whenever the right to vote was extended to a new social group, there was usually a time lapse before the results of the suffrage expansion would be manifested in new forms of political organization. In France, workers remained largely alienated from the political system until the socialist movement began to turn its attention to action within the political system late in the century. Less alienated politically, British workers divided their votes between the aristocratic Conservative Party and the capitalist Liberal Party. The powerful Labour Party of the twentieth century dates back only to 1900. In Germany, the response was swifter. The Marxist Social Democratic Party was already entrenching itself within the German working class before 1871. Thereafter, it quickly became the most powerful socialist party in Europe, although, owing to government repression and manipulation, it did not become a potent electoral force until after 1890. In general, one could say that during the later years of the early industrialization period, the groundwork was being laid for the members of the working class to enter the political systems of Europe. They were arriving economically in terms of their significance to the new forms of production and in terms of their growing ability to organize for industrial action, but they had not yet arrived politically.

Preindustrial and Early Industrial Japan

It is customary to begin the history of modern Japan with what is called the "Meiji Restoration," which began with a palace coup in 1868. The feudalistic Tokugawa Shogunate was overthrown by a group of provincial leaders, bureaucrats, and scholars who were bent on ending Japan's isolation from the rest of the world. The Japan of the mid–nineteenth century had for 250 years been ruled as a "centralized feudal regime," while the island country was forcefully closed to outside influences, including nearby China. Although Japan was formally an empire with a reigning emperor, the real rulers were the heads of the aristocratic Tokugawa family,

who had seized power in 1600, assuming the ancient title of shogun, and moving the effective seat of government from Kyoto, where the emperor resided, to the city of Edo, today known as Tokyo. Strong feudal lords (*daimyo*), resembling the dukes and barons of medieval Europe, held extensive land and ruled their areas of the country, but they were dependent on the shogun for military protection. By closing the country to foreign influence, the Tokugawa rulers prevented Japan from falling into the status of a colonial dependency of a stronger European state. This fierce determination of her rulers to retain independence did not die with the Tokugawa regime, but was continued by its successors after 1868.

Isolation also meant that Japan shared only very marginally in the economic growth associated in parts of Western Europe with the preindustrial and early industrial development of capitalism during the same period. However, although Japan retained many features that were similar to the earlier Western feudal system, the cities and towns were spawning a merchant class that was gaining in economic strength, accumulating wealth that would serve as an important source of indigenous capital once industrialization began. Isolation from the rest of East Asia also meant that, by and large, Japan was passed over by the military events of the region during the seventeenth to nineteenth centuries. The long era of peace and stability meant that a significant portion of the warrior class (*samurai*) could give up their weapons for scholarly pursuits, emerging by the late 1700s (the period of Enlightenment in Western Europe) as a sort of window to the West, acquiring what knowledge they could of Western scientific achievements and gradually constituting themselves as a critical intelligentsia preparing the way for the revolutionary transformation of Japan that took place after 1868.

The Meiji Restoration, named for the fifteen-year-old emperor who came to the Imperial throne at that time, reunited the emperor with the effective government of the state; but the real rulers were a coalition of lower-ranking *samurai* based mainly in two of the outlying provinces of Japan. These "oligarchs" wanted to modernize Japan so that the economic dependency that had been forced on her through the naval might of the Western powers could be overcome and Japan could take her place among the self-sufficient and militarily secure nations of the world. The leading figures of the government traveled to the West, visiting the United States, England, France, and Germany, borrowing technology and legal–political ideas. The latter then served as the basis for selection of elements of the Japanese Constitution of 1889. It was based on a new legal system patterned after the French and German code law systems, and it incorporated a set of governmental institutions borrowed selectively from wherever the leaders saw something of merit. For example, the bicameral Parliament was patterned in form after the British House of Commons and House of Lords. But the British system of ministerial responsibility to Parliament was not borrowed. Instead, the German system with a chancellor and cabinet responsible to the emperor, rather than to the Parliament (called the Diet in both Germany and Japan), served as the preferred model. Indeed, the Japanese constitution makers saw the situation of their country as very similar to that of Germany, whose leaders in the later nineteenth century similarly regarded democracy as a premature luxury during a time when priority was assigned to catching up industrially with the most advanced nations of the world. Accordingly, this first Japanese constitution gave only 1 percent of the adult population the right to vote. This was extended further by periodic relaxations of the property requirement until universal male suffrage was adopted in 1925. As in France and Italy, women were not given the right to vote until after World War II.

During the period of constitution building of the 1870s and 1880s, the groundwork was being laid for rapid industrialization of the following twenty-five years. At the time of the Meiji Restoration, the adult literacy rate of Japan stood at more than 40 percent, already as high as that in most contemporary Western countries. Thereafter, educational expansion in Japan kept pace with or even exceeded that in the more advanced European countries, which meant that the new skills for an industrial economy could be rapidly acquired by an educated, literate, intelligent population. This factor should be kept in mind when one asks how Japan could industrialize much sooner than could other Asian countries. Also important is the success of the Meiji leaders in centralizing government and creating an efficient bureaucracy, enabling the state finances to be brought into order and a single currency to be created.

In the 1870s Japan began the development of her railroad, telegraph, and postal systems. In the agricultural sector, tax reform and modernization of property holding brought about a new class of self-sufficient farmers, ending forever the system of serfdom and, for that matter, the feudal landowning class. Agricultural production grew rapidly in the late nineteenth century, so that, unlike that other island nation, Great Britain, emphasis on industrialization did not mean growing dependency on overseas agricultural production to feed the population.

The "take-off" period of early industrialization began around 1886 and lasted until the eve of World War I, or about a twenty-five-year period. Extensive government initiative characterized the early establishment of heavy industry, including steel and shipbuilding. Although Japan was dependent on imports of machinery from the more advanced West, she was able to achieve a cotton textile industry that substituted for imports from abroad, largely through rapid mechanization of production, bringing Japanese textile production up to world competitive standards. During this period, partly as a result of the development of a Japanese armaments industry, Japan became one of the primary military powers in East Asia, defeating China and Russia in brief wars in 1894–95 and 1904–05, respectively, and acquiring the beginnings of her colonial empire in the process. By World War I Japan was entering the mature stage of industrial development, approximately a half-century behind Britain, perhaps a quarter-century behind Germany and the United States, but arguably not much more than a decade behind France.

Industrial Maturity

Organized Capitalism

The next stage in industrialization—industrial maturity—differs from early industrialization not so much because of any overwhelming technological revolution, such as had occurred in England in the late eighteenth century, but because of a rapid acceleration of trends that had already started. During this period, Great Britain's industrial lead diminished and finally came to an end. Germany reached Great Britain's level and then fell back, although only momentarily, with its defeat in World War I. The United States emerged as the world's new industrial giant, and Japan moved into the second echelon of industrial countries through the rapid industrialization just discussed. France finally experienced an industrial upsurge at the end of the century; Italy began her industrialization around 1900, reaching industrial maturity after

World War II. But, despite great differences in levels of economic development, there were certain similarities among them that permit developmental comparisons *from the 1880s until just after World War II*, the period we are labeling "industrial maturity."

The most striking economic change during this period was the emergence of massive monopolistic or oligopolistic corporations in vital economic sectors, which replaced the smaller competitive firms of the preceding period. Anti-combination laws were sometimes relaxed to permit this development; large corporations could acquire a much greater amount of capital and thus could promote the technological advances of the era. Joint stock corporations in Britain and the United States accumulated large amounts of capital through the purchase of stock by a multitude of small investors. In other countries, notably Germany, large investment banks capitalized companies in different industrial sectors, assuming an important role in steering the direction of investment through occupation of strategic positions on company boards of directors. Businesses grew into giant bureaucracies, employing thousands of workers and generating an intermediate supervisory and clerical staff. The latter became the truly new social element of the period—the white-collar workers. Women entered the workforce in large numbers as part of this new social category. The lives of most people were becoming more highly organized. Mass-production and assembly line techniques accelerated, and the distance between employer and employee became much greater. In the larger corporations, the employer became virtually invisible, screened from blue-collar and white-collar personnel by layers of managerial staff.

The development of giant corporations stimulated trade unions to organize on a larger scale as independent craft unions joined together to form large federations. Late in the period, un-skilled and semiskilled workers in mass-production fields, such as the automotive industry, were becoming organized as well. In response, the capitalists attempted to organize the industrial sectors. Where laws prohibited the formation of trusts or the combination of competing firms for purposes of market control, trade associations formed to exchange information across a sector. Furthermore, huge industrial cartels began to emerge, representing vertical (rather than horizontal) integration, so that industrialists could better control the supply and cost of needed raw materials and capital goods as well as the markets for their products within industry itself. By the 1920s, industrial concentration and trade union organization had reached the point where serious industrial conflict was a significant concern. Capitalists in the European countries enjoyed varying degrees of success in dealing with the trade union challenge, but in all of our countries before World War I and until after World War II, the state curbed the power of the working class on behalf of employers' interests. Although socialist parties were achieving political power in Scandinavia, and although they secured a tantalizing share of power once or twice in Great Britain, Germany, and France, capitalism was able to retain its hold in most of Europe between the wars. This was even reinforced by fascism in Italy and Germany.

Karl Marx had predicted that class conflict in advanced capitalism would assume revolutionary dimensions. Nevertheless, despite the sharpness of class conflict during this period, it is clear that the conditions for life for the vast majority of people were improving dramatically and that the social structure was experiencing profound changes. Wages were rising during the entire period, whereas prices continued to

decline at least until about 1900 and to rise slowly enough most of the time thereafter to allow real wages to rise each decade, with the exception of the 1930s, the decade of the Great Depression. The resulting rise in purchasing power stimulated the perfection of mass-production techniques and the mass distribution of new commodities such as household appliances and bicycles, then automobiles. This certainly helps account for the increased willingness of socialist parties to work within the system toward the end of the century. The parties of the working class were beginning to compete with the middle-class parties for votes and seats in Parliament, hoping gradually to attain majority strength and to enact reforms rather than trying to replace capitalism with socialism through violent means.

Other trends were making it less likely that the transition to parliamentary socialism would be a smooth one. The four decades before World War I were marked by recurrent economic recessions that affected all countries more or less simultaneously. Each recession meant significant unemployment. Financial sources would dry up mysteriously for awhile and then just as mysteriously would begin to flow again. Whatever the state of the market, industrialists could not expand their operations without the needed capital. What was happening was that the pace of industrialization had increased so much that people were losing confidence in its ability to sustain itself. Despite the growth of the domestic market, increases in productivity were even greater, especially because new industrial nations had entered the field. Colonialism, which had once supplemented the domestic market as an outlet for goods, was no longer adequate because the most recently colonized areas, especially those in Africa, although valuable as sources of raw materials, were too primitive to be able to use the sophisticated products of Western Europe. Still, the imperialistic quest forged ahead.

By the time of the Great Depression, capitalists and their political allies were beginning to recognize the advantages of turning to the state to ameliorate industrial conflict. After World War II, a much more enlightened capitalism was to see the advantages of trying to eradicate the sources of social unrest, poverty, and economic insecurity. Such insights were relatively few and far between among the pre–World War I ruling classes. Some of the social reforms that had been undertaken had been instigated by aristocratic conservatives who sought to outflank their liberal rivals and win working-class votes as well as keeping workers from turning out of frustration in a more radical direction. Before World War I, it was often difficult to distinguish between liberals and conservatives on socio-economic matters. Actually, in each country there had emerged a ruling class made up of aristocrats and businessmen who controlled the powerful leverage points of the private sector, especially the banks. Political leaders, whether liberals or conservatives, radicals or moderates, were essentially extensions of the ruling class. The real political conflicts were between this combined ruling class on the inside and the socialist parties and trade unions on the outside.

The century beginning around 1870, which roughly corresponds to what is here called industrial maturity, is also the time in which there emerged what Scott Lash and John Urry have labeled "organized capitalism."[13] Industrial capital was sufficiently concentrated and the units in which it was concentrated sufficiently well organized that the rapid technological changes of the period could be managed through a combination of private- and public-sector guidance. Although the prevailing rhetoric empha-

sized the necessity that the state play only a minimal role in the economy, in fact that role was growing. Also growing was the power of organized groups in society, including the trade unions. Capitalism was becoming organized "both at the top and at the bottom."[14]

World War I and Its Aftermath

Much of the blame for the events leading up to World War I can be placed on political leaders whose perspective on the world focused too narrowly on such balance-of-power factors as the number of armed divisions, battleships, and square miles of territory held. The desire for peace as a value in itself seems to have been virtually beyond their range of vision, perhaps because no one could yet foresee the devastation that mature industrial powers were capable of inflicting on one another.

The loudest calls for peace were coming from those to whom the ruling circles had turned a deaf ear—the socialists. The generation in command of Europe's socialist parties at the turn of the century—leaders such as Jean Jaures in France and Karl Kautsky in Germany—were committed internationalists as well as socialists. They saw socialism, and, indeed, the working-class movement generally, as an international phenomenon. The class conflict knew no national boundaries; the struggle between nations was simply an in-house fight among different branches of the capitalist class. Thus, it certainly was not in the interest of the proletariat to participate in it. National conscription was a way in which the capitalists of one country recruited the workers of that country to fight the workers of other countries on behalf of capitalist objectives. Therefore, true socialists should fight war and militarism just as they should fight capitalism. To these socialists, it was quite logical that a socialist should be a pacifist.

As war became more and more likely, the European socialists found themselves forced to decide what approach they would adopt if it should come about. Many followed the example of the French Marxist Jules Guesde in supporting the war effort in their own countries, whereas others, like Vladimir Ilyich Lenin and Rosa Luxembourg, saw this as a sellout of the workers to capitalism. In short, the war had a devastating effect on European socialism. Because both the leaders and the followers were already uncertain where socialism stood in the era of mature industrialism, the commitment of many to its fundamentals turned out to be rather superficial in the face of the much stronger pull of nationalism.

World War I brought about a profound transformation in the distribution of power, both in Europe and worldwide. Temporarily, the defeat of Germany and the Revolution in Russia left France as the most powerful nation on the continent. On a worldwide scale, it appeared at first that the decline of Germany and Russia had removed the principal threats to the supremacy of the British Empire. But new rivals were coming forth, in the Pacific at least. Both the United States and Japan had emerged from the war considerably strengthened as naval powers. Moreover, Great Britain was finding that her far-flung empire constituted an enormous financial drain, leaving the mother country weakened in the face of postwar inflationary pressures and monetary crises.

It now is clear that World War I left the world divided into two types of powers—the relatively contented and the relatively discontented. In the former category were the principal victors—Great Britain, France, and the United States. In the latter category were Germany, the principal loser; Russia, seriously weakened by revolution and civil war but, as the new Soviet Union, the possessor of enormous potential for development into a stronger power than the old Russian Empire; Italy, technically a victor as a result of her switching sides during the war, but dissatisfied with her meager gains in the peace settlement; and Japan, gradually expanding her power base in the western Pacific, but acutely aware of her dependence for raw materials on islands and East Asian rimland areas to the south that were controlled by other powers. This division between the satisfied and the dissatisfied powers was to become the basis for a new alliance system, foreshadowing a second, even more devastating, worldwide conflagration.

Totalitarian Dictatorship

In the meantime, developments within the discontented nations were leading toward a new kind of division—between the democracies and the "totalitarian dictatorships."[15] One by one the discontented powers as well as some of the smaller countries of Europe were abandoning the form or the substance of democracy for various types of autocratic rule designed to achieve a unity of purpose in the quest for a stronger position in the world. The first major country to move in this direction was Russia. In late 1917, the Bolsheviks had already converted a budding constitutional democracy into a one-party dictatorship. During the ensuing civil war and even during the period of relaxation that followed in the early 1920s, the power of the Communist Party bureaucracy and the state police was steadily expanding. Following Lenin's death in 1924, the party secretary, Joseph Stalin, drew the various instruments of power together and, after a series of successful clashes with his principal rivals, became the unchallenged supreme ruler by the late 1920s.

By this time, another dictator, Benito Mussolini, had consolidated his preeminent position in Italy. Invited by King Victor Emmanuel III in 1922 to assume the premiership as a temporary solution to a political crisis, Mussolini manipulated the deputies in Parliament and gained emergency powers. Then, he systematically eliminated his opposition, beginning with the extreme left and moving to the right. Eventually, he and his Fascist Party ruled as a one-man, one-party dictatorship, much as Stalin and his Communist Party did in the Soviet Union.

While Stalin and Mussolini were establishing their leadership, in Japan military leaders and nationalistic politicians were in the process of undermining the unstable Japanese parliamentary regime. In 1931 they pushed the more liberal politicians aside and established a de facto military dictatorship. In the years that followed until Japan's defeat in World War II, the regime showed some similarity to those of Stalin and Mussolini, in that opposition found itself discredited and hemmed in by restrictions. But, as Edwin O. Reischauer has noted: "There was no dictator and the system was not the product of a well-defined, popular movement, but more a vague change of mood, a shift in the balance of power between the elite groups in Japanese society, and a consequent major shift in national policies, all occurring within the framework of the constitutional system established in 1889."[16] Totalitarianism came to Japan only with World War II itself, but the shift in leadership and policy focus in the 1930s started Japan along the road that led to war in the Pacific.

The extreme right in Germany, as elsewhere in industrially mature Western Europe, drew most heavily on those strata of society that had been the least dynamic during the stage of early industrialization and that had found themselves displaced during industrialization. Left behind by the dynamic sectors of organized capitalism, the petite bourgeoisie and small farmers were incapable of competing or coping with the industrial and commercial giants of the twentieth century. Right-wing attacks on trade unionism and communism probably focused more on the symptoms than on the causes of people's fears and frustrations, but the attacks appealed to the members of this class, especially where, as in Italy and Germany, they could be associated with frustrated national aspirations. Because a minority of Jews in certain countries such as Germany and France had achieved conspicuous success in business or politics, the Jews as a people became special targets for vitriolic attacks, again appealing to the frustrations of downwardly slipping social groups.

In Germany in the early 1920s anti-Semitism, combined with anti-communism, produced a number of right-wing threats to the new Weimar Republic during a time of postwar inflation and unemployment. In 1923 this unrest was further stimulated by the French occupation of the Ruhr and subsequent runaway inflation in Germany. In the fall of 1923, a rebellious segment of the army took control of the government of Bavaria and called on the central government in Berlin to yield power to the right wing. When Berlin refused, an obscure right-wing leader, Adolf Hitler, with the help of the former head of the General Staff, General Erich Ludendorff, staged an unsuccessful bid to gain power in Munich. Hitler was arrested and given a short jail sentence. Thereafter, the Weimar Republic found temporary solutions for its economic problems and began a five-year period of political stability. Nevertheless, Hitler had gained the public notoriety he needed to enable him to expand his organizational base, the National Socialist (Nazi) Party, to the national level.

By the early 1930s, the Great Depression, which had started earlier and hit with greater force in Germany than in most other advanced countries, had undermined the fragile stability of the Weimar Republic. Hitler's National Socialists as well as the Communists on the far left registered a series of spectacular gains in the Reichstag (parliament) elections of 1930 and 1932 and in the presidential election of 1932. By late 1932, the parties that were loyal to the Weimar Republic had virtually lost their majority in the Reichstag, and the country could be governed only by means of presidential emergency powers. Secret negotiations went on among conservative politicians and preeminent industrialists, leading to President Paul von Hindenburg's invitation to Hitler, in January 1933, to assume power as chancellor. This scenario resembled that of Mussolini's rise to power. Once again, a popular demagogue was invited to assume power because of his reputed ability to hold the left in check and, again, by a ruling elite who believed it could control his actions when in power. Even more rapidly than Mussolini, however, Hitler proceeded to eliminate all competing parties—those of the right, center, and left—and to construct a dictatorship in which the other power centers—the military, industrialists, and state bureaucracy—were subordinate to Hitler and his Nazi colleagues. The system of terror and domestic repression established by the Nazis was rivaled for its scope and ruthlessness only by that of Stalin at the height of the Great Purges in the late 1930s. By the eve of World War II, the Nazi and Soviet dictatorships stood as models of *totalitarianism*, a type of regime in which the individual is totally subordinate to the whims of the rulers of the state.

Totalitarianism is a system of rule that is fostered by political leaders seeking to engage an entire population in far-reaching projects for social, economic, and cultural change. Both Stalin and Hitler were preoccupied with strengthening their nations in preparation for the world war that each saw coming in the near future, the war that Hitler would, in fact, instigate. To accomplish this, each opted for a herculean program of mass mobilization. In Hitler's Third Reich, the individual was to be subordinated to the interests of the *Volk* ("nation"). Loyal German citizens would enthusiastically dedicate themselves to the tasks prescribed by the *Fuhrer* ("leader") and the Nazi Party, tasks designed to muster the maximum of human energy toward the goal of war preparedness. Even such previously private matters as the question of what career one might follow or whom one might marry were no longer left entirely up to individual choice but were required to fit within the regime's prescripts.

Totalitarianism attacks not only individual freedom of choice, but also (at least in theory) the individual psyche, aiming to mobilize the thoughts and feelings of individuals as well as their actions. Two means are employed toward this end: terror and propaganda. Terror is the instrument of a police state that creates diffuse uncertainty as to what is legal and what is illegal behavior. The individual must be constantly on guard lest a careless act or utterance lead to arrest, imprisonment, or death. The intense preoccupation that this uncertainty necessitates robs the individual of the freedom to express thoughts that do not fall within the bounds of what the regime officially permits. Simultaneously, the regime's propaganda bombards the citizen with its exclusive interpretation of situations and events inside and outside the country through a monopoly of the mass media and a forced screening out of contrary information emanating from whatever source.

The Nazi regime employed terror in essentially three domains: (1) as part of its racial purification program, designed to eradicate non-Aryan elements from the German population; (2) as part of Hitler's effort to eliminate political opposition, both inside and outside the Nazi movement; and (3) as a weapon against the German population at large, to enforce conformity to the regime's expectations and to weed out potential troublemakers. The instruments employed consisted of a confusing array of special police agencies, the most notorious of which were the Gestapo ("state police") and Hitler's elite corps of enforcers, the Schutzstaffel (SS; "Black Shirts"). It was the SS under Heinrich Himmler that maintained the concentration camps in Germany and eventually in German-ruled Eastern Europe. These were used systematically to snuff out the lives of millions of Jews.

Nazi propaganda was assisted by the perpetration of a myth, repeated and repeated until most Germans had internalized it—or so, at least, was the intention. The fundamental premise on which the myth rested was the superiority of the German people as the purest strain of the Aryan racial type. High points in the history of Germany were emphasized in the schools, whereas the lows were ignored or excused on the basis of the treachery of racial enemies. Especially stressed was the role allegedly played by Jewish business and political leaders in undermining the German war effort between 1914 and 1918. This, in turn, justified the Nazi demand for vengeance and the restoration of lost territory—if necessary, through military means. The myth of racial superiority was used to support Nazi claims to Eastern territory, the *Lebensraum* ("living space") rightfully owed to the German people although currently occupied by "inferior" Slavic and Jewish peoples. These peoples were marked for enslavement or, in the case of the Jews, extermination. The more extreme consequences of this doctrine may not have been spelled out to the German people, but the premises from which it might be inferred were systematically put forth in the schools, in the media, and in numerous speeches by Hitler and his propaganda chief, Joseph Goebbels. Pervading all of these messages was the glorification of Hitler as the infallible leader, with the implication that those anointed by Hitler as his principal collaborators—Himmler, Goebbels, Hermann Goering, and the *Gauleiters* (district party chiefs)—were to be obeyed without question as Hitler surrogates, chosen by the leader to implement his will and, in the event of his death, to carry on the work of "the 1,000-year Reich."

Although the word *Socialist* appeared in the party's title, in truth, the Nazi regime shored up German capitalism and enhanced the interests of employers, while doing away with independent trade unions and mobilizing the industrial workforce for war preparedness. This enhanced the profit-taking ability of German big business, although at a price—the reinstitution of central planning that even in the mid-1930s reached a scale rivaling that of World War I. In a sense, "organized capitalism" reached its pinnacle in Nazi Germany. Although it has also been argued that a social revolution took place in Hitler's Germany,[17] it took the form of the undermining of the aristocracy's superior social and political position inherited from pre–World War I Germany. The beneficiaries were those of the middle class who were to survive World War II. Any lowering of the social barriers between bourgeoisie and proletariat did not take place during the Nazi era.

World War II

After the consolidation of Nazi rule in Germany, the world witnessed a series of daring expansionist thrusts by the dissatisfied powers. Italy invaded Ethiopia in 1935; Germany reoccupied the demilitarized Rhineland in 1936; Germany and Italy intervened successfully in the Spanish

Civil War (1936–39) to ensure victory for the forces led by General Francisco Franco; Japan moved out from its base in Manchuria, which she had occupied in 1931, to invade China proper in 1937; Germany forced Austria to join in a single German state ruled from Berlin in early 1938; German troops moved in the fall of 1938 into the Sudetenland (a part of Czechoslovakia inhabited by ethnic Germans) and into the rest of Czechoslovakia a few months later. Great Britain and France protested these various moves but did nothing to stop them.

By early 1939, it had become clear that what were to become known as the Axis Powers— the coalition of Germany, Italy, and Japan— had informally divided the world into spheres of influence; they felt strong enough to impose their will on the French and the British, who were timidly shrinking from confrontation, and on the Americans, who were deeply ensconced in isolation. In fact, Hitler enjoyed a fair amount of sympathy in these countries, especially from right-of-center politicians who saw him as a bulwark against communism. This perspective received a severe jolt when, in August 1939, Hitler concluded a mutual nonaggression pact with Stalin, thus neutralizing the other have-not power in any potential world conflict. Shortly thereafter, Germany and Russia invaded Poland from different directions, tearing apart the buffer state. This was too much for Britain and France, which had guaranteed Poland's security from just such an onslaught, and World War II began in September 1939. When Hitler turned his attention to the west, he quickly defeated and occupied France; Great Britain barely managed to escape a similar fate as the Royal Air Force (RAF) fought the Luftwaffe (German air force) to a standstill in the skies over the English Channel during the summer of 1940.

The alliance of the have-nots was relatively short-lived. When Hitler invaded the Soviet Union in May 1941, he gave Great Britain an instant ally. The Allied coalition was completed when the Japanese attacked Pearl Harbor in December 1941. Although Japan had little interest in what was happening in Europe or North Africa, her rulers saw the United States as the main obstacle to consolidation of a "Greater East Asian Co-Prosperity Sphere," a Japanese sphere of influence in the South Pacific and in Southeast Asia that would relieve Japan of her dependence on the rest of the world for raw materials. Her rulers hoped that the destruction of the U.S. Pacific fleet at Pearl Harbor would cripple American capacity to frustrate Japanese aims, and at first they succeeded.

Meanwhile, what was left of the French forces outside Occupied France had gradually come together under General Charles de Gaulle, and they participated alongside the British and Americans beginning with the North African campaign. Gradually, after the reversal of the tide in early 1943 at the battle of Stalingrad, the Soviet forces began pushing the Germans and their allies westward, while the British and Americans were winning battles in North Africa and then in southern Italy. After the establishment of the Western Front in France in June 1944, the ring soon closed on Germany, which surrendered in May 1945. Three months later the war in the Pacific came to an end with the Japanese surrender. Victory was total. The damage visited by the war on civilian populations in most of the belligerent countries had been catastrophic, and the prognosis for the future of mature industrial capitalism in most of these countries was not good.

The Postwar Period (1945–60)

At the end of the war, Europe lay devastated. Germany was in ruins, her territory occupied by Allied troops. In all of the belligerent countries, economies needed rebuilding, with little or no capital available for the task. Great Britain and France still had commitments to their overseas empires, which promised to be more of a financial drain than an economic asset. The Soviet Union had extended its armed might far into Central Europe. Unless the United States was willing to retain its forces on the Continent, Western Europe would be vulnerable to any further Soviet expansionism. Germany was no longer a viable counterweight to Soviet power, and Soviet troops were occupying the smaller countries of Central and Eastern Europe, which had once been regarded as a buffer zone between Germany and Russia. At the end of the war, it was agreed that there would be four zones of occupation in Germany administered by the United States, Great Britain, France, and the Soviet Union. Berlin was also to be under four-power administration, although it was located well within the Soviet zone of occupation. The Soviet Union and Poland incorporated chunks of pre-Hitler Germany into their own territory (see map on page 56).

By 1947, it had become clear to the Western powers that the world was once again dividing itself into hostile blocs. In a series of initiatives taken between 1947 and 1949, the United States, Great Britain, and France moved to consolidate Western Europe politically and militarily. A bizonal Economic Council was established in the British and American zones of occupation to begin the process of restoring Germany's economy. Massive American economic assistance began flowing into Europe under the auspices of the Marshall Plan. Although West Germany was not a sovereign unit when the Marshall Plan began in 1947, it received a large share of the assistance. By this time, Italy, the other defeated Axis Power in Western Europe, had been restored to full membership in the international community. Its government partici-

pated fully in the economic and political steps leading to Western Europe's recovery.

Japan, too, lay devastated after World War II and was subjected to Allied Occupation. In this case, however, one of the victors, the United States, was the sole occupying power. Under General Douglas MacArthur the American occupiers sought to instill in Japan a basic commitment to political and social democracy. The political side "took" in the acceptance of a sweeping "amendment" to the Constitution of 1889 by the emperor, who was permitted to continue his reign as even more of a figurehead than he had been before the war. The new constitutional arrangements were wisely patterned after the British parliamentary system, a model toward which Japan had been moving in the 1920s before the reimposition of oligarchical rule in the 1930s. The occupying authorities also attempted to break up the monopolistic hold on Japanese heavy industry by a few powerful family combines, the "zaibatsu," but this exercise in economic democracy, which would have gone farther than what antitrust policy in the United States had ever successfully accomplished, did not prove to be as long-lasting as the strictly political reforms incorporated in the constitution. Although it took about a decade for the Japanese economy to get back on its feet, assisted in the early years by American economic aid, the Korean War provided a substantial boost, launching Japan on the remarkable economic growth of the 1950s and 1960s. The Korean War, as well as the coming to power of the Communists in China, also created an atmosphere of anti-communism in Japan that helped solidify the rule of center-right politicians in the 1950s, just as the Cold War was doing in most Western countries during that decade.

By the late 1940s in Western Europe, the Western powers were moving to establish an effective military posture against the Soviet threat. In 1949, the North Atlantic Treaty Organization (NATO) was created. Then, in 1950, a beginning was made to unify Western Europe economically and politically through the announcement by the French Foreign Minister, Robert Schuman, of his plan to integrate French and West German coal and steel production. The first unit of today's European Community (EC)—the Coal and Steel Community (ECSC)—came into being in 1952. By this time, Western Europe had successfully completed its rebuilding program, thanks to American assistance and to the lessons learned by the failures of prewar economic policy. How these lessons were interpreted in postwar economic policy is part of the discussion in Chapter 2 of the transition from mature industrial to "postindustrial" society.

In domestic politics, the left emerged from World War II considerably strengthened in most Western European countries. Socialists and communists shared power in the early postwar governments of France and Italy as well as in several smaller countries.[18] But with the onset of the Cold War in 1947, the communists voluntarily left or were forced out of governments. Power, then, shifted to the right, with Socialist parties losing power or having to share it with center and center-right parties. Exceptions to these trends were the Scandinavian countries, which continued to be governed by coalitions dominated by the Socialists through the 1950s and 1960s, and Great Britain, where the Labour Party emerged the victor in the election of 1945 and remained in power until 1951. During these early postwar years, the Labour government under Clement Attlee was able to put into effect an extraordinary program of economic and social reform, most of which the Conservatives were to leave intact during their long tenure in power from 1951 until 1964.

In West Germany and Italy, the threat of communism immediately to the east helped propel voters in the direction of right-of-center parties after 1947. By the time the German Federal Republic (West Germany) came into being in 1949, the division of Occupied Germany into two hardened semisovereign entities was an established, if not yet accepted, fact. Because the eastern part of Germany (German Democratic Republic) was dominated by the Soviet-backed Communists, communism in West Germany was shunned by the voters. Torn between revulsion to communism and the suspicion that a too-Western-oriented foreign policy might postpone German reunification indefinitely, the Social Democrats were likewise disadvantaged at the polls, although not to nearly the same degree as the Communists. This opened the field for the new Christian Democratic Union (CDU), a union of former Catholic and Protestant parties led by former Cologne Mayor Konrad Adenauer. By the early 1950s, Adenauer's party had established its predominance over smaller center and right-wing parties.

In somewhat similar fashion, the strictly Catholic Italian Christian Democrats established its predominance over all rivals in the early postwar years. Left-oriented voters divided their support in the early years between the Communists and the Socialists. In the center and right regions of the political spectrum, however, the Christian Democrats easily outdistanced five smaller parties. With nearly a majority of seats in Parliament, the Christian Democrats could reward and punish potential partners, maintaining a stranglehold on the principal instruments of power. Somewhat similar, but even less encumbered by the necessity to accommodate smaller coalition partners, was the position of the center-right party in Japan, the Liberal Democratic Party. Both the Italian Christian Democrats and the Japanese Liberal Democrats had such a lock on power in their respective countries, in fact, that they could afford the luxury of open factional infighting. Neither party could boast a leader able to maintain himself in power for very long before having to cede leadership to one of his rivals in another faction of the party, a condition that contrasted with the fourteen-year reign of Konrad Adenauer as West German chancellor.

The withdrawal of the French Communist Party from government in 1947 had a significant impact on French politics. However, no party of the center-right was able to establish its supremacy in the ensuing years as happened in West Germany, Italy, and Japan. Instead, loose and shifting coalitions of fairly evenly matched parties, ranging from the Socialists on the left to the Independent and Peasant Party on the right, shared power between 1947 and 1958. In the meantime, war hero General Charles de Gaulle, after resigning as head of the provisional government in early 1946, waged a protracted battle to discredit the new Fourth Republic. He attracted a loyal movement of Gaullist followers who formed a political party in 1946. The combined pressure of strong opposition from Communists on the left and Gaullists on the right helped destabilize the Fourth Republic, which staggered from one crisis to another until it finally collapsed in May 1958 in the wake of a civilian/military revolt in Algiers, staged to protest the way the government in Paris was running the Algerian War. The result was the return of de Gaulle to power and a radical shift of voter support to parties of the right, enabling de Gaulle to solidify the position of his new republic, the Fifth. By 1960, parties of the center and right were in power in all five of our countries. The pendulum had shifted away from the reformism of the first postwar years to the conservatism of the consolidation years. Postwar politics in all of the countries, except, perhaps, France, were measurably more stable than the politics of the years between the wars.

In presenting the history of these contemporary polyarchies, we have shown the development of the elements of the political system on the one hand, and the elements of the economic, social, and international environment on the other. In the past 250 years these countries have been transformed from preindustrial to highly sophisticated industrial systems. Elements of the agrarian and semifeudal societies of the early eighteenth century have largely disappeared. Today power is much more widely distributed among various societal groups. In studying the background of contemporary political systems, we are not considering simply the ways in which political systems and their environments emerged in the past; we are also concerned with the received tradition of the present. When we are learning about countries with such richly received traditions as those of Western Europe and Japan, we must be alert to those developments of the past that help us understand (1) how these countries differ today from newer nations elsewhere and (2) how these countries differ from one another.

Suggestions for Further Reading

Bracher, Karl Dietrich. *The German Dictatorship: The Origins, Structure and Effects of National Socialism*, trans. Jean Steinberg (New York: Praeger, 1970).

Gerschenkron, Alexander. *Economic Backwardness in Historical Perspective: A Book of Essays* (Cambridge, Mass.: Harvard University Press, 1966).

Jansen, Marius B. *Japan and Its World: Two Centuries of Change* (Princeton, N.J.: Princeton University Press, 1980).

Kindleberger, Charles P. *Economic Growth in France and Britain: 1851–1950* (Cambridge, Mass.: Harvard University Press, 1964).

Kunio, Yoshihara. *Japanese Economic Development: A Short Introduction* (Oxford: Oxford University Press, 1979).

Landes, David. *The Unbound Prometheus: Technological Change and Industrial Development in Western Europe from 1850 to the Present* (Cambridge: Cambridge University Press, 1969).

Maier, Charles S. *Recasting Bourgeois Europe: Stabilization in France, Germany, and Italy in the Decade after World War I* (Princeton, N.J.: Princeton University Press, 1979).

Milward, Alan S., and **S. B. Saul.** *The Development of the Economies of Continental Europe, 1850–1914* (Cambridge, Mass.: Harvard University Press, 1977).

Moore, Barrington, Jr. *Social Origins of Dictatorship and Democracy: Lord and Peasant in the Making of the Modern World* (Boston: Beacon, 1967).

Poggi, Gianfranco. *The Development of the Modern State: A Sociological Introduction* (Stanford, Calif.: Stanford University Press, 1978).

Rostow, W. W. *Politics and the Stages of Growth* (Cambridge: Cambridge University Press, 1971).

Stearns, Peter N. *European Society in Upheaval: Social History since 1750*, 2nd ed. (New York: Macmillan, 1975).

Thompson, E. P. *The Making of the English Working Class* (New York: Random House, 1963).

Tilly, Charles, ed. *The Formation of National States in Western Europe* (Princeton, N.J.: Princeton University Press, 1975).

Wallerstein, Immanuel. *The Modern World System: Capitalist Agriculture and the Origins of the European World-Economy in the Sixteenth Century*, Vol. 1 (New York: Academic Press, 1974).

_____. *The Modern World System: Mercantilism and the Consolidation of the European World Economy, 1600–1750*, Vol. 2 (New York: Academic Press, 1980).

Wray, Harry, and **Hilary Conroy,** eds. *Japan Examined: Perspectives on Modern Japanese History* (Honolulu: University of Hawaii Press, 1983).

Notes

1. Arend Lijphart, *Democracies: Patterns of Majoritarian and Consensus Government in Twenty-One Countries* (New Haven, Conn., and London: Yale University Press, 1984).

2. Robert A. Dahl, *Polyarchy: Participation and Opposition* (New Haven, Conn.: Yale University Press, 1971).

3. Peter L. Berger, *The Capitalist Revolution: Fifty Propositions about Prosperity, Equality and Liberty* (New York: Basic Books, 1986), p. 220.

4. Gianfranco Poggi, *The Development of the Modern State: A Sociological Introduction* (Stanford, Calif.: Stanford University Press, 1978), Chs. 3 and 4.

5. For an illuminating discussion of industrialization, see David Landes, *The Unbound Prometheus: Technological Change and Industrial Development in Western Europe from 1850 to the Present* (Cambridge: Cambridge University Press, 1969).

6. Max Weber, *The Protestant Ethnic and the Spirit of Capitalism*, trans. Talcott Parsons (New York: Scribner's, 1958).

7. Fernand Braudel, *Civilisation materielle, economie et capitalisme, XVe–XVIIIe siecle*, Vol. 2 (Paris: Armand Colin, 1979), pp. 505–509.

8. Berger, *The Capitalist Revolution*, pp. 140–171.

9. David Landes, "The Creation of Knowledge and Technique: Today's Task and Yesterday's Experience," *Daedalus* 109 (Winter 1980), 111–120.

10. In 1707 the Act of Union brought England, Wales, and Scotland together under a United Kingdom. Thus, the term *British*, referring to the whole island of Great Britain, became a more appropriate term than *English* for reference to the political system.

11. Peter N. Stearns, *European Society in Upheaval: Social History since 1750*, 2nd ed. (New York: Macmillan, 1975), pp. 119–120.

12. Germany and Italy did not achieve unification until the second half of the nineteenth century. Italy was unified in 1860 and Germany in 1871, following Prussia's victory in the Franco–Prussian War. Unification meant the end of separate identities for the various parts of the two countries. Compare the map on page 54 with that on page 55.

13. Scott Lash and John Urry, *The End of Organized Capitalism* (Cambridge: Polity Press, 1987), Chs. 1–3.

14. Ibid., p. 4.

15. For the most authoritative 1950s formulations of this concept, see Carl J. Friedrich and Zbigniew K. Brzezinski, *Totalitarian Dictatorship and Autocracy* (Cambridge, Mass.: Harvard University Press, 1956); and Hannah Arendt, *The Origins of Totalitarianism*, 2nd ed. (New York: Meridian, 1958).

16. Edwin O. Reischauer, *The Japanese* (Cambridge, Mass., and London: Harvard University Press, 1977), pp. 100–101.

17. See David Schoenbaum, *Hitler's Social Revolution: Class and Status in Nazi Germany, 1933–1939* (Garden City, N.Y.: Doubleday, 1966).

18. The distinction between *socialist* and *communist* goes back to the Bolshevik Revolution in Russia and the establishment by Lenin of the Third International. Parties that remained part of the Second International, or pre-1917 world organization of socialist parties, are called "Socialist." Those following Lenin's lead are called "Communist." See Chapter 4 for contemporary differences and for a clarification of the terms *left*, *center*, and *right* used in this section.

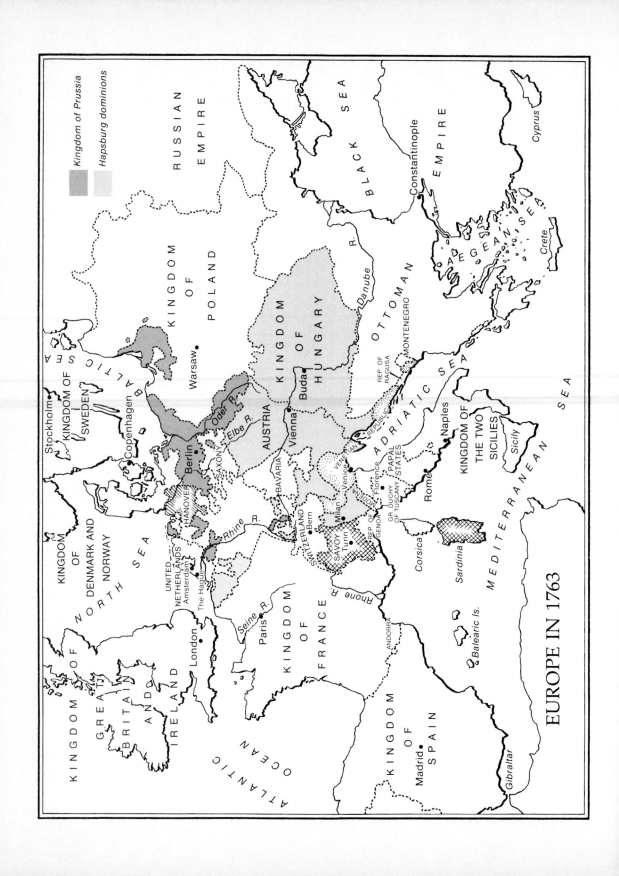

EUROPE IN 1763

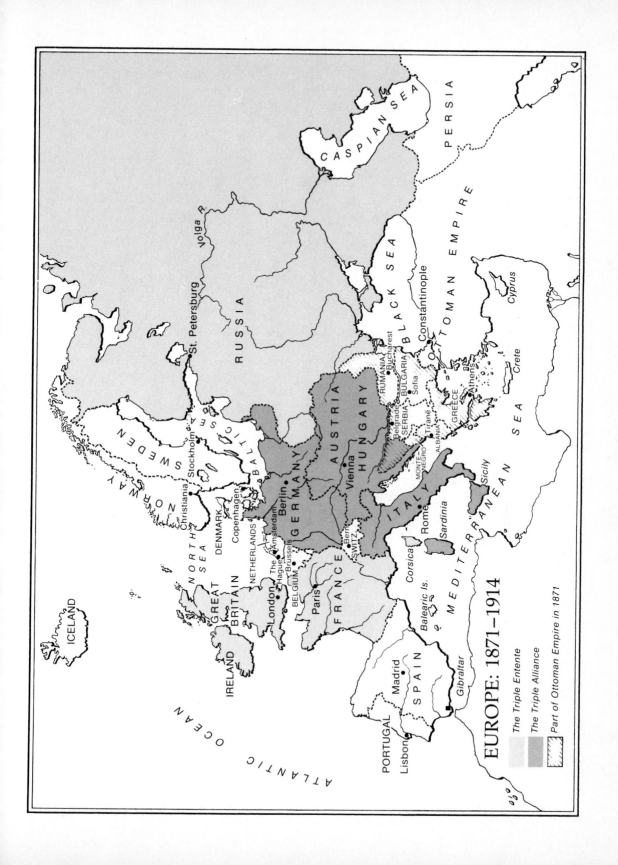

EUROPE: 1871–1914

ATLANTIC OCEAN

ICELAND

NORWAY
SWEDEN
Christiania
Stockholm
St. Petersburg
Volga R.
RUSSIA
CASPIAN SEA
PERSIA

NORTH SEA
DENMARK
Copenhagen
BALTIC SEA
OTTOMAN EMPIRE

GREAT BRITAIN
IRELAND
NETHERLANDS
The Hague
Amsterdam
London
Brussels
BELGIUM
GERMANY
Berlin
AUSTRIA
Vienna
HUNGARY
Bucharest
RUMANIA
BLACK SEA
Constantinople

Paris
FRANCE
Bern
SWITZ.
ITALY
Rome
Belgrade
SERBIA
BULGARIA
Sofia
Tiranë
MONTE-
NEGRO
ALBANIA
GREECE
Athens
Crete
Cyprus

PORTUGAL
Lisbon
SPAIN
Madrid
Gibraltar
Corsica
Sardinia
Sicily
Balearic Is.
MEDITERRANEAN SEA

The Triple Entente
The Triple Alliance
Part of Ottoman Empire in 1871

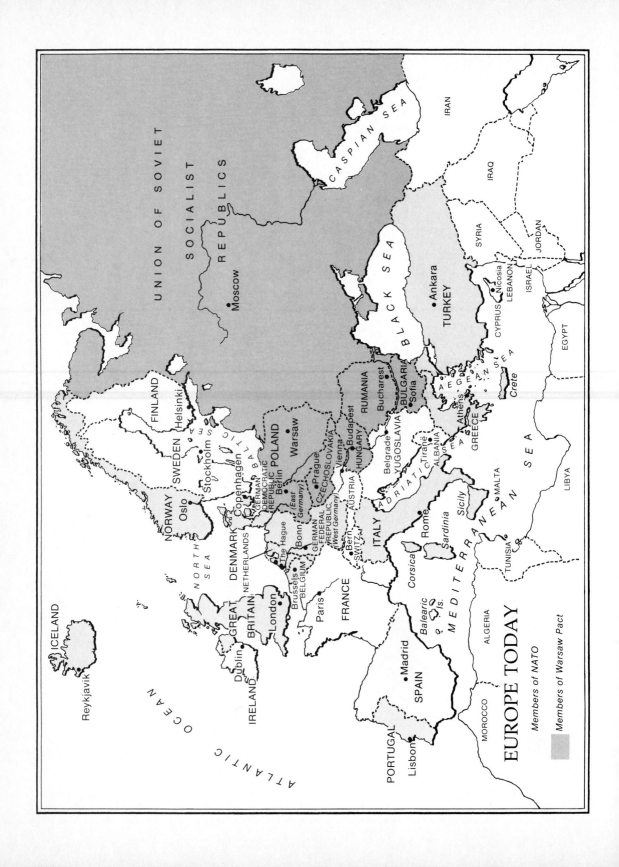

CHAPTER 2

POSTINDUSTRIAL ECONOMY AND SOCIETY

The economic and social environments of the Western European political systems have experienced substantial changes since World War II. Some scholars have gone so far as to suggest that, by the 1960s, quantitative changes, such as dramatic increases in the gross national product (GNP) and a marked alteration in the proportions of the various occupational groups in the workforce, resulted in a qualitative leap, that a corner has been turned, and that we are now experiencing what they call *postindustrial society*.[1] If so, the first two postwar decades were the "late industrial" years during which postwar economic and social policy adjustments were laying the groundwork that enabled the corner to be turned.

Late Industrial Social and Economic Policies

In all of our four Western European countries, the postwar period witnessed the expansion of the welfare state, featuring cradle-to-grave pro-

tection of those members of society unable, for whatever reasons, to cope with economic misfortunes. The upheavals of the 1920s and 1930s had left a lasting mark on Western Europe; leaders of both left and right in all countries converged on the Keynesian fiscal and monetary means of steering between the extremes of depression and runaway inflation. The result was a much improved level of personal security for individuals and families after World War II. Especially noteworthy were the provision of free medical care in Great Britain, through the National Health Service established in 1946, and the virtually equivalent result obtained in West Germany, through the extensive National Health Insurance Scheme. In Japan, as in the United States, more reliance was placed on private-sector provision of welfare, as in the worklife assurance of employment that Japanese corporations have provided their employees. However, there did not develop in the early postwar years in Japan a reliable pension or social security program caring for the needs of those beyond working age; nor was the security of employment enjoyed by workers in the large corporations an advantage enjoyed by the majority of the workforce, who were employed in smaller firms that were in a less secure position in the Japanese "dual economy."

But the more dynamic economic sectors in Japan and Western Europe pulled along the weaker sectors as all of our countries experienced a period of economic growth producing a remarkable transformation of their economies in the first two postwar decades. Although they were poor second cousins to the United States in the late 1940s, all of them experienced unprecedented economic growth in the 1950s and 1960s, to the extent that West Germany, France, and Japan, at least, became fully modern competitive equals by the 1970s. Even in Great Britain and Italy, countries whose economies suffered recurrent problems, the transformation in the lifestyles of ordinary citizens after World War II was dramatic.

One of the striking things about this record of economic success across five different countries is that there were considerable differences in approaches to economic policy, due to differences in past experiences and in the constellations of political forces and personalities in power. Participation by parties of the left in the earliest postwar governments resulted in important economic policy innovations in Great Britain, France, and Italy. Prominent among these were the extensive nationalizations of industrial sectors. In Great Britain and France, the postwar left-dominated parliaments converted the coal industry, railroads, major investment banks, and the electricity and gas supply utilities (among others) from private to public ownership. In Italy, nationalization was less of an innovation because the central government had already been buying into private industry during the Mussolini regime. Government financial participation through giant holding companies continued to spread in the postwar period, most notably in the energy sector.

In France, the governments of the latter 1940s began to make use of the leverage given them by government ownership to provide the leading wedge of a system of state economic planning, which was designed in the early years to modernize the war-damaged and seriously outdated French economy. Expansion of the public sector provided stimulus to the private sector by making energy, transportation, and raw materials more readily available at lower costs. The central planners assigned priorities to different industrial sectors and encouraged development of those with high priority through subsidies and tax incentives. As France emerged into the 1950s, this system of "indicative planning," which was to be given part of the credit for the subsequent economic boom, was developed further, providing French manufacturers and distributors greater certainty regarding the size of future markets and the availability of unfinished and semifinished goods needed in the productive process. France was one of two countries we are dealing with where the role of the state was probably decisive in fostering postwar economic growth. Japan was the other.

Once the Japanese government regained control over the pressure points that could influence the economic regeneration of the country, it followed a planning course that bore some resemblance to that of France, although the Japanese government was farther to the right and had closer links to industry than did the French government in the early postwar years. Because they were able to rely on an ample agricultural base, the French planners could hold the international economy relatively constant in their calculations and concentrate on building or rebuilding those industries that any relatively self-sufficient mature industrial economy would need. By contrast, Japan's dependence on the rest of the world for agricultural commodities and raw materials was, if anything, more acute than before the War, when she could rely on her colonial empire to supply a major portion of her needs. Therefore, her planners looked farther ahead than those in France, to the industries that would provide the greatest export mileage to earn Japan the U.S. dollars necessary to afford the commodities unavailable at home. Not only was massive government assistance, directed by the Ministry for International Trade and Industry (MITI), used to steer Japanese industry in the planned directions, as in France, but leading bankers and industrialists were at the very center of the priority assigning process, agreeing with their partners in MITI as to the appropriate uses to which both private- and public-sector investment would be put. Whereas mutual suspicions between the public and private sectors had to be broken down gradually in the evolution of French planning, a cooperative, information-sharing atmosphere prevailed from the outset in Japanese planning.

By contrast with the strong role played by the state in France and Japan, in West Germany the more conservative Christian Democrats, led by Chancellor Adenauer and Economics Minister Ludwig Erhard, evolved an economic system that relied much less on the state sector and placed its faith in the play of the free market. The market was expected to generate its own incentives, with the state intervening primarily in the interests of stabilizing the value of the deutsche mark and maintaining a steady money supply. Depending on the orientation of the economist, either Erhard's "social market economy," the French system of indicative planning, or the Japanese system of international trade-oriented industrial planning is cited as the model of effective economic policy for this period of late industrial recovery. The fact is that all three

economies established remarkable records for economic growth coupled with relative stability, especially in the late 1950s and early 1960s. On the other hand, Great Britain and Italy, both of which opted for more mixed, eclectic, economic policy strategies, were to experience less impressive economic records during the same time span—Great Britain with relatively low growth rates and chronic balance-of-payments problems, and Italy with a record of economic instability and geographically uneven growth, despite an overall growth rate that was very high.

Postindustrial Economy

Postindustrial society has been reached when a majority of a nation's workforce is employed in the *service sector* rather than, as in mature industrialism, in manufacturing. This is now true of all five of our countries. The term *post-industrial* has either positive or negative connotations depending on whether one is dependent on employment in the industry that is supposedly outdated (in which case the term may appear threatening) or whether one is optimistically looking forward to an economy in which computers and robots will perform the tasks that industrial workers once sweated over, and the "industry" remaining in the economy will be clean, safe, and healthy high-tech and service industry. In fact, all five of our countries, as has the United States, have moved a considerable distance from the era of smokestack industry and blue-collar labor. The changes that have taken place have accompanied the general process by which "organized capitalism" has become disorganized.[2]

Disorganized Capitalism

Scott Lash and John Urry have provided a comprehensive list of the economic and social features of "disorganized capitalism," a list that encompasses both the positive and negative features of postindustrialism. The first feature is at the heart of the matter:

(1) The growth of a world market combined with the increasing scale of industrial, banking and commercial enterprises means that national markets have become less regulated by nationally based corporations. From the point of view of national markets there has been an effective *de*concentration of capital.[3]

They are saying that capitalism has become disorganized at the national level, largely because it has become international in scope and organization. With the loss of national focus, the process of collective bargaining between management and labor becomes decentralized, and the economic policy that was previously made by national governments in close cooperation with private industry loses a good deal of its significance for industry. This is because the attention of private industry has become diverted beyond the national level. As for organized labor, because it is unable to come to grips with anonymous employers that may not even be headquartered in the same country, it finds it more rewarding to bargain with employers at the level of the individual manufacturing unit, whether these be branch plants of multinational corporations (MNCs) or local firms hiring local workers.

Three other features of economic change are central to disorganized capitalism, according to Lash and Urry:

(2) Increased importance of service industry for the structuring of social relations (smaller plants, a more flexible labour process, increased feminization, a higher "mental" component . . .).

(3) Decline in average plant size because of shifts in industrial structure, substantial labour-saving capital investment, the hiving off of various sub-contracted activities, the export of labour-intensive activities to "world market factories" in the Third World, and to "rural" sites in the First World. . . .
(4) Industrial cities begin to decline in size and in their domination of regions. This is reflected in the industrial and population collapse of so-called "inner cities," the increase in population of smaller towns and more generally of semi-rural areas, the movement away from older industrial areas. . . .[4]

Accompanying these changes in demography and economic geography are changes in the occupational structure, and thus the class structure, of society. (5) The size of the manual workforce in manufacturing industry declines, first in relative terms, and then absolutely. In turn, (6) there is an expansion "of the number of white-collar workers and particularly of a distinctive service class (of managers, professionals, educators, scientists, etc.)."[5] This last feature is at the heart of the earlier writing about postindustrial society at the time these phenomena were first being recognized in the early 1970s. It is discussed in the next section, after which we turn to the phenomenon of "deindustrialization" and the high levels of unemployment that have characterized postindustrial societies since the 1970s.

The Service Economy

Industrial society differed from preindustrial society because of the declining role of agriculture in the economy and the lower percentage of persons employed in the agricultural sector, especially when compared with the growing ranks of the industrial proletariat. By the same token, postindustrial society differs from industrial society because of the increasing importance of the service sector and the growing ranks of persons employed in the service sector as compared with both agriculture and industry. What is the service sector? According to Daniel Bell, it includes the following areas, where services rather than goods are produced: transportation, utilities, trade, finance, insurance, real estate, health, education, research, leisure, entertainment, and, finally—a catchall category—government. In the United States, the first country to achieve postindustrial status, employment in the goods-producing sectors of the economy increased from 25.6 million in 1940 to 29 million in 1968. In the service-producing sectors, employment increased from 24.3 million to 51.8 million during the same period.[6] Between 1968 and 1976, the number employed in the goods-producing sectors remained static, whereas the number in the service sector increased by another 7 million.[7] Among the service sectors, employment increased most rapidly in government, especially at the state and local levels.

Whether or not all First World countries have reached postindustrial status is a matter of definition. The most frequently used criteria are the percentage of employment of a country's workforce that is employed in service-sector occupations, and the country's gross domestic product (GDP) per capita. The combined rankings in the right-hand column of Table 2.1 give a very rough indication that the United States and Canada can be safely placed within the postindustrial society category, whereas Spain remains outside. The eight other countries are probably over the threshold into postindustrial society.

In Western Europe as in the United States, the service sector of the economy has become increasingly important in recent decades. This has meant that certain kinds of occupations

Table 2.1 Rankings of Eleven First World Countries on Postindustrial Indicators (1987)

	Percent of Employment in Service Sector	GDP per Capita	Combined Rankings
United States	1	3	2.0
Canada	2	5	3.5
Sweden	6	2	4.0
Japan	8	1	4.5
Netherlands	3	7	5.0
France	7	6	6.5
West Germany	10	4	7.0
Australia	5	9	7.0
United Kingdom	4	10	7.0
Italy	9	8	8.5
Spain	11	11	11.0

(*Source*) Organization for Economic Cooperation and Development, *OECD Economic Surveys 1988/1989: United Kingdom* (Paris: OECD, 1989), pp. 130–131.

have become more prominent than they were before. In general, nonmanual employment has increased more rapidly than manual employment. It was pointed out in Chapter 1 that, with the achievement of mature industrialization, a new social class—white-collar workers—appeared on the scene. This component of the workforce continues to grow in postindustrial society, but especially in the professional and technical category rather than in such white-collar occupations as secretaries and office clerks. Between 1958 and 1974, those in the professional and technical occupations increased by 77.5 percent in the United States, the largest increase in any single category.[8] This category includes those with the highest educational requirements, such as doctors, lawyers, engineers, teachers, scientists, and computer specialists.

As society becomes more complex, there is a growing demand for skills that involve the application of *knowledge* to large-scale problems. If Western Europe was slower than the United States to reach postindustrial society, it may not be simply because of inferior material resources and the disadvantages of working on a smaller national scale. European educational systems have been slow to change, whereas the American educational system has been decades ahead in the development of mass education and in the transition from the nineteenth-century classical curriculum to the more practical curricula of the twentieth century. The pool of talent available to meet the demanding standards of a postindustrial occupational structure is more restricted in Europe. On the other hand, if anything, the Japanese educational system has been freer than the American of traditional overhangs that impede the acquisition of the most up-to-date knowledge and skills. Indeed, Ezra N. Vogel attributes much of Japan's industrial surge of recent decades to the fact that, not only has she been able to borrow state-of-the-art technology from wherever in the world it can be found, but Japan can truly be called an "information society."[9] In Japan, according to Vogel, the quest for all relevant information bearing on a problem does not rely simply on its being retrievably stored in libraries or computer data banks, but on its being widely disseminated to all members of organizations, public or private, where it is needed to bear on decisions. Organizational members immerse themselves in available information and participate jointly in the decision to be made, rather than relying on the advice of a few experts, as would more likely be resorted to in the United States or Western Europe. Whether it would be correct to attribute Japan's economic success primarily to this characteristic, it is true that Japan was being labeled a "postindustrial society" not long after the term became fashionable, and sooner than it was applied to most Western European countries, precisely because of the high value placed on information, or what we are calling "enlightenment" in this text.[10]

Perhaps in part because of the higher earnings in real terms that workers in the skilled and professional categories realize today, there has been a growing demand for a wide variety of services, whose performances do not themselves require advanced education or refined skills. Thus, even in parts of northern England where unemployment among manual workers is high, there has been a striking growth of retailing and catering activities as those people who do have jobs have been spending significant portions of their incomes on consumption of goods and services that many could not afford ten years ago—for example, the sale of gourmet foods in grocery stores, of video recorders, of expensive suits, or of wine instead of beer in the pubs. The persons who sell these items are salesclerks and waiters or waitresses, normally classified as service-sector employees. Often they are employed on a part-time basis making earnings that are well below the average for manual workers, and for secretaries and other full-time white-collar workers. Such jobs have minimal educational or training requirements. In some ways the growth of the service economy has created a new postindustrial proletariat, one that is poorly organized in comparison with the factory workers of mature industrialism, and probably largely unorganizable, because of the high turnover in jobs of young people who perceive their location in this employment status to be temporary. In the meantime, the percentage of the workforce found in manual occupations is declining, and higher levels of unemployment have made it more difficult for trade unions to maintain the membership numbers of former days.

Deindustrialization and Unemployment

The growth of the service sector has been much sharper in relative than in absolute terms. Whereas service employment has replaced manufacturing employment in percentage terms, it has been slow to make up for the number of manufacturing jobs that have been lost. Some service-sector categories are "labor-intensive," as in the case of catering, retailing, and tourism; others are less so. In the meantime, manufacturing has been experiencing technological transformation that has made virtually all branches of manufacturing more capital-intensive and less labor-intensive than they once were. Moreover, some branches of manufacturing are in decline in terms of their shares of gross domestic product as well as in numbers of jobs. First World countries are giving over the production of lower-cost steel, textiles, clothing, automobiles, and electronic products to Third World countries, whose wage structures

are such that they can produce goods on a labor-intensive basis more cheaply. Some First World countries (Britain is the most startling example) have moved from the status of net exporters of manufactured products to net importers, compensating for the imports they buy with the proceeds of services or primary products (food, raw materials) that they have to sell to other countries. These are structural changes that are unlikely to be reversed. To the extent that other economic problems have been created by deindustrialization, especially unemployment and inflation, they are no longer likely to follow cyclical patterns as they did during industrial maturity. They are chronic problems that require long-term solutions rather than being susceptible to countercyclical manipulation. Yet the economic theories that we have used to cope with them have been developed at a time when economic problems were viewed as cyclical.

To the economist, unemployment is part of a larger phenomenon—underemployment of the nation's productive forces. As stocks of goods accumulate unsold in warehouses and retail outlets, factories shut down and employees lose their jobs. Some businesses weather the storm by cutting back production; others are swept away forever. Workers without jobs are forced to seek new employment. They often find that the only options are the unacceptable ones— moving to another part of the country (or to another country) to find work or going through the arduous process of retraining for a skill that is in greater demand. The impact of a recession on the individual and his or her family is often tragic, representing the loss of hope for a better future. To a country, recession means missed opportunity owing to unused productive capacity. Markets at home and abroad may be permanently lost to competition from companies in other countries because businesses have folded or have cut back production. Recession also means that national income falls short of its full potential; the standard of living of the nation fails to improve. Indeed, the standard of living for certain categories of the population actually declines as certain disadvantaged groups feel the brunt of unemployment.

The causes of recession and unemployment are varied. When economies of countries are compared with one another, it becomes clear that some countries suffer more severely than others during a worldwide recession. The relative losers lose to the relative winners because their producers cannot compete on an equal basis in the world market. If world demand is shrinking, it will be shrinking more rapidly for the less competitive and may not even be shrinking at all for those whose productivity and cost structures put them in a position to take over the markets of the losers. But why does a worldwide recession come about? The simple answer is that there is a worldwide shrinkage of consumer demand, a factor that itself may result from a variety of causes. Among these is government economic policy, especially the policies of the governments responsible for the largest economies, such as the governments in Washington, Tokyo, and Bonn. Government policies designed to curtail inflationary forces and trade deficits have an impact on the level of productive activity. If the measures (such as action to raise interest rates or fiscal policies designed to reduce consumer spending power) are too strong or are carried out for too long, the first consequence may be a downturn in economic activity, leading to a recession rather than to the desired result of bringing rates of inflation down to acceptable levels. Again, if we are talking about a major First World economy, declining demand in that country will mean a decline in world demand for the products of other countries. This may momentarily assist

the balance of payments of the first country by improving its trade balances, but if the result is worldwide recession, it will mean that all countries will suffer from rising unemployment and a decline in living standards.

The more profound causes of unemployment, however, are structural rather than cyclical. They are the causes touched on in the opening paragraph of this section. The "second industrial revolution," symbolized by the advent of the microchip, has meant that many industries in postindustrial countries have turned to automated means of production that require fewer workers to turn out the same volume of products. If, for example, the textile industry in one country fails to join the new wave of technological modernization, it will be overcome by the competition of its rivals in other countries where automated production has been adopted. Firms in the country that stands still will fold or cut back production, with loss of jobs. Thus, the size of the workforce will decline, no matter whether the industry opts for automation or allows itself to be left behind by its overseas competitors.

Related to this is a third reason that unemployment has risen in postindustrial countries: competition from newly industrializing countries (NICs), which are able to produce the same goods at lower cost, not because of automation, but because wages for workers in these countries remain at a much lower level than those of First World industrial workers. Continuing with the example, employment in the First World textile and clothing industries further declines as manufacturers attempt to compensate for their relatively high labor costs by making production more capital-intensive.[11] Situations such as this have led some economists to despair of the possibility that First World unemployment percentages can ever again be reduced to their pre-1970s levels. Other economists point to the

West German children riding their bicycles alongside a Ruhr factory near Duisburg.

growing service-sector fields such as "fast food" and retailing as the eventual answer to the present scarcity of jobs for unskilled and semi-skilled workers.[12]

Left-of-center politicians, whether American Democrats or European Socialists and Communists, often appear to be saying that one must choose between protecting the value of money (avoiding inflation) and maintaining full employment (avoiding recession), and that the choice to be made is clear. They hold that, when the values that make up human dignity are considered, one must protect the underprivileged and disadvantaged. This means taking whatever action is necessary to maintain workers in their jobs, even if this runs the risk of adding to inflationary pressures. Those on the left are all the more inclined to approach the economic dilemma in this fashion because there are equally strong voices on the right who agree with the premise that one must choose between monetary stability and full employment, in the short run at least, and who argue that human dignity is best advanced if we protect the purchasing power of the dollar, the pound, or the yen.

The debate between left and right continues to be centered around versions of two theories that have been carried over into postindustrial economies. The first, *Keynesianism*, has its origins in the era of industrial maturity; the other, *neoclassical economics*, has roots that go back to the earliest years of industrialism.[13] One of the prime assumptions of Keynesianism is that there is a "trade-off" between unemployment and inflation, such that governments, in trying to contain one, will exacerbate the other. If left to itself, the economy will move through cycles, oscillating from one extreme of high unemployment with low inflation to the other of high inflation with low unemployment. Government fiscal policies can smooth out these cycles, keeping them within a much narrower range and allowing entrepreneurs greater certainty and employees greater job security. This is based on the belief that consumer demand is the primary driving force for economic activity, and that it can be at any time at too low or too high a level relative to the existing supply of goods and services. These levels are subject to manipulation in either direction by government taxing and spending policies, which either take money out of the hands of consumers to curtail inflation or put it into their hands to stimulate the economy, thus creating more jobs.

The neoclassical school of economics that is often labeled *monetarism* argues that Keynesian countercyclical policies over time are counterproductive and that they worsen the problem that they are trying to keep under control. When government has sought to stimulate an economy that is experiencing only modest levels of resource underemployment, it has produced the expectation among both buyers and sellers of commodities and labor that higher levels of in-

flation will result. This creates a sort of "self-fulfilling prophecy" in which wages and prices are pushed up in anticipation of that very thing happening. This will result in a decline in demand for commodities and labor, which will in turn result in an increase in unemployment. Thus, government efforts to raise economic energies produce the opposite effect. Instead of a trade-off between unemployment and inflation, the two rise simultaneously, a phenomenon that has been labeled "stagflation," that is, economic stagnation along with inflation.

There has been enough evidence to support the neoclassical claim since the early 1970s to raise the stock of neoclassical economics in the press, in public opinion, and in the eyes of government policymakers. The monetarist talks about money supply as the central variable to be controlled, rather than consumer demand. The monetarist seeks to smooth out business cycles, just as does the Keynesian, although the method recommended is to bring the increase in money supply down to modest levels and to keep it there, because it is fluctuations in money supply caused by government policies that are responsible for business cycles. Neither monetarism nor Keynesianism places emphasis on the idea that longer-term structural changes in the productive forces of an economy may be reducing government's ability to control both unemployment and inflation simultaneously, while also rendering obsolete the phenomenon of business cycles encountered during industrial maturity.

Another sort of neoclassical economist puts emphasis on the "supply side" of the economy, arguing that orthodox economics, whether of the Keynesian or the monetarist variety, has been preoccupied with cyclical phenomena to the exclusion of structural problems that affect the quantity and quality of goods produced and services supplied. "Supply-siders" see the cause of both inflation and high unemployment to be insufficient investment in the modernization and equipment of home-based firms that produce goods, perform services, and supply jobs in the domestic economy. To supply-siders, the culprit is a tax structure that provides the wrong incentives to investors and feeds an over-expanded government that siphons off too many resources from the national economy in taxation without making compensating additions to the capital stock of the economy. Reduced taxation will provide the incentive for firms, individuals, and institutions to invest in increased productivity that will increase the supply of goods and services at lower cost, thus withstanding competition, creating jobs, and stimulating demand to meet the growing supply.

One problem with the supply-side prescriptions is that they assume that the extra capital available to investors as a result of tax cuts will be employed in the most productive directions. But Keynesians and socialists have argued that this gives no assurance that they will not be used for investment abroad, or in relatively unproductive exploits such as real estate. They argue that a genuine concern for the supply side would necessitate that government pay attention to the direction of investment, making sure that it is in sectors of the economy where future growth potential exists and where technological change and changing patterns of international competition have been taken into account. In part, investment could be influenced by the structure of tax incentives government offers to investors to judge investments in certain directions. Some supply-siders might go along with these suggestions. But the logical outcome of government guiding investment would be a "hands-on" government planning approach that goes well beyond Keynesian prescriptions and would be anathema to neoclassical economics of any stripe. Some *socialists* have argued that,

with proper state control of economic resources, the problems of both unemployment and inflation could be better addressed. Government could make full use of the labor-saving potential of the electronics revolution to reduce working hours and to use the surplus produced to improve the quality of life of the mass of citizens who now have an abundance of leisure time on their hands. This would be a radical solution, but capitalism has made radical adjustments to crises in the past and has maintained itself as a system. Nevertheless, socialist solutions that stress central government planning are not popular at the end of the twentieth century, especially in the wake of the collapse of socialist economies in Eastern Europe.

Postindustrial Social Structure

It was emphasized in Chapter 1 that a prominent feature of mature industrialism in Europe was intensified conflict between social classes. But in this chapter we have seen that the relatively simplified industrial class system has become complicated by the growth of the service sector, by the decline of manufacturing employment, and by the growth in importance of knowledge as a resource in economic affairs. A review of its more complex postindustrial class structure will enable us to assess the impact of social structure on the politics of postindustrial society. We focus on the hierarchy of social groupings that is based essentially on occupation and on the prestige assigned by society to each occupational category. In other words, we look at the varying shares that different social classes have of the four values of power, respect, well-being, and enlightenment. Do postindustrial societies distribute these values differently from those in earlier periods?

The Complexities of Contemporary Social Structure

One factor that complicates the analysis of class structure for all Western European countries is that, even if one focuses on occupation for assigning individuals or families to positions on the scale, there is no single, unambiguous scale. Instead, one must deal with the concurrent existence of old and new occupations that require different criteria for placing them somewhere in a hierarchical order. Italian sociologist Luciano Gallino has suggested that the social structure in Italy today can be understood only if one realizes that there exist simultaneously a "traditional," a "modern," and a "contemporary" class structure.[14] The continuation of an agrarian economy in southern Italy, with its dominant land-owning class and numerically large peasantry, is a carryover of traditional society into the late twentieth century. In our terms, southern Italian society is still largely preindustrial or early industrial, although important changes are taking place. In different parts of northern and central Italy, what Gallino calls modern and contemporary social structures can be found. Gallino's modern class system corresponds roughly to what we describe as mature industrial society, whereas his contemporary class system would be what is found in postindustrial society. The industrial working class is numerically the largest in modern society, whereas those in the service sector predominate in contemporary society.

In some ways, southern Italy resembles the semi-industrial nations of parts of the Third World that exist economically in a symbiotic, but essentially dependent, relationship with the core nations of the First World. Investment capital comes from the north, but return on investment returns to the north. Migrant workers move from south to north, learning skills in northern industry and sending money to families back home. But many remain where the higher-paid jobs are found, and never return with their skills to their home region. Much of the technically sophisticated, highly paid supervisory personnel in the new industries of the south are northerners sent by their firms or agencies for tours of duty in the south; but their career objectives lie northward. As for the manual workforce in the newer plants that have been built in southern Italy, as in the less developed regions of other First World countries, automation has made it possible for large corporations to employ semiskilled workers in the branch plants in "peripheral" regions, confining the skilled work to maintenance and repair shops in the original "core" regions where these firms began their lives.[15] This means that the industrial workforce in the core regions is more highly skilled, is better paid, and enjoys higher rates of unionization and greater job security than that of the periphery.

Whether one is working for a large corporation in a more prosperous region or for the same firm in a poorer area with lower wage rates, one is still part of the relatively advanced and stable sector of what is called the "dual economy." By this we mean that large corporations move on a "faster track" than many, if not all, smaller businesses. Large corporations are more apt to employ the most advanced technology, meaning that their streamlined workforces are highly efficient. Large corporations are, on the average, able to provide better pay, working conditions, and employment security for each of their workers than are smaller firms for his or her equivalent. That is, a woman employed as a technician in a large engineering firm in a medium-sized city will have a better job by these measures than will her counterpart in a smaller engineering firm in the same city. This is because (1) the large corporation produces

Constrasts in postindustrial societies: a pastoral scene in rural Scotland and an urban street scene in industrialized England.

more efficiently than the smaller one, and can afford to pay its workers more and provide better fringe benefits; (2) the large corporation is sufficiently diversified that it can carry unprofitable portions of its activities longer on the backs of its more profitable ones, or failing that, be able to transfer many of its employees to other parts of its operations—advantages the smaller firm that specializes in a single product line cannot offer its employees; and (3) there is a greater likelihood that the workforce in the larger firm is effectively unionized to promote better pay, better fringe benefits, and greater job security. These characteristics of the "dual economy" can be found in all First World countries to a greater or lesser degree, but it appears that the differences between advantaged and disadvantaged workers on either side of the divide are defined particularly sharply in Japan, where, in the absence of strong independent trade unions, the workers are dependent on the capacities of the firms they work for to define the positive and negative attributes of the jobs they hold. Larger firms organize their workforces themselves, guarantee their workers jobs for life, and solicit inputs into corporate decision making from the workers, who after all have a considerable stake in their companies' futures. Smaller firms in sectors where there is considerable competition and the struggle for survival is fierce are simply not in a position to accord such advantages to their workers, and the labor market in such a sector is more fluid that that in the more stable sectors.[16]

Nevertheless, the generalizations we make about the "dual economy" must be understood in light of certain postindustrial countertrends. As large corporations become multinational, they diversify and decentralize their operations so that the fact that parts of their operations are found in particular countries is of less significance to them than it once was. Security of

employment has declined even in the more stable sectors of Japan's dual economy in recent years.[17] On the other hand, the advent of the microchip and the rise of the service sector have made it possible for smaller firms in some fields to operate more efficiently than larger ones, or to find market niches that are profitable for firms operating on a smaller scale, whereas they are not worth bothering with from the larger firm's standpoint. The recent buoyancy of the Italian economy, which in 1986 surpassed Great Britain on the scale of GNP per capita, moving into fourth place among our five countries, has been attributed in part to the proliferation of small manufacturing firms.[18] Found in traditional manufacturing areas of northern and central Italy, these firms typically have a few employees headed by one or two skilled workers. Often these are craftspeople who have lost their jobs or taken early retirement from large firms, and used lump severance payments to capitalize ideas they had dreamed up while watching increasingly standardized products being produced by increasingly automated processes requiring ever less skill and ingenuity. This is another example of ways in which the occupational structure of postindustrial society has become too complex to be understood in simplified dualistic terms.

Postindustrial Social Classes

At the top of today's stratification system in Western Europe, the old aristocracy has been largely displaced by the executives of private corporations, as well as by professionals of various kinds (doctors, lawyers, government officials) who are in a favorable market position concerning the supply of, and demand for, their services. For example, a recent study of pay inequalities in Western European countries found that managers earn on the average 328.5

percent of the average earnings of full-time industrial workers in France, and 367.9 percent in Italy.[19]

In the middle range of the postindustrial stratification system, occupational categories are the most diverse. One finds both the declining ranks of small-business owners and independent farmers and the growing numbers of scientific and technical professionals, middle-management personnel, white-collar workers, and manual workers with marketable skills. The professional and managerial categories are the better paid, sharing with the upper-income earners a better education and a more favorable market position. Younger men and women in these categories may aspire to considerably higher incomes later in their careers as they move up the corporate ladder or shuttle back and forth between the public and private sectors. What distinguishes these various types of professionals from those below them in the middle-income ranks is their possession of knowledge that enables them to manipulate postindustrial technology and economic factors. They have invested time early in their careers to acquire this knowledge. The investment has more often than not been the result of early socialization in middle-class families, where acquisition of knowledge and investment for future gain are values on which high priority is placed. It is also likely to reflect a superior education at the primary and secondary levels, more readily available to middle-class than to working-class children in the relatively stratified Western European educational systems.

The distinction between manual and nonmanual workers has always been the basis of analysis of class structures under capitalism. Marxists believe that the class structure is based on exploitation of wage earners by their employers. Traditionally, Marxists either ignored

classes that fell in between these two or else lumped them together with one or the other. Thus, nonmanual workers might be seen as part of the bourgeoisie or as part of the proletariat, with the former tendency being by far the more prevalent. Today one can question whether the earlier classifications of industrial Europe are still relevant—whether, for example, the social, economic, and political distance between skilled workers and unskilled workers has not become greater than that between white-collar workers and skilled workers. Indeed, it might be argued that by function and training, skilled workers belong more to the category of engineers and technicians than do the white-collar workers such as store clerks, secretaries, and key punch operators. The latter may be more akin to the unskilled-worker category, especially in levels of pay and in vulnerability to unemployment. Again, we see the importance of levels of education in leading to differences in life chances. Although most skilled workers have not gone to universities, in most European countries, as well as in Japan, there are public and private training programs based in part on the old apprenticeship systems that bring skilled workers into the full-time workforce only after considerable time has been invested in bringing them up to marketable standards.

Further contributing to the breaking down of the class system of industrial society is an easing of the traditional rigidities of the typical Western European educational system. Most European countries have until fairly recently made a relatively inflexible distinction at the secondary level between schools that prepare the student for university education and the professions and schools that prepare the student for various manual and nonmanual occupations which can be entered on finishing school at age sixteen or seventeen. The grammar school in

Great Britain, the *lycée* in France, and the *Gymnasium* in Germany are traditional means by which the "cream of the crop" are separated at around the age of twelve from the majority of their age group and are prepared for their roles in life that will mean higher income and status. Despite the fact that these schools were maintained by the state and were free and open to anyone qualified, children from middle-class families had a much better chance of meeting the entrance requirements than did children from working-class families. With the establishment of *comprehensive schools* in Western European countries, the distinctions between upper and lower "streams" remain, but they are administered more flexibly than before. This has reduced the disparity between the classes in the likelihood of one's advancement to higher education. In the 1960s and 1970s there was a massive expansion of the state-supported university system, but the net result was to improve the chances of middle-class children for higher education much more than to improve those of working-class children. In Japan, as we will see in Chapter 7, the chances of working-class children for higher education are appreciably better than those in Western Europe. Nevertheless, the point to be emphasized in the present context is that the expansion of higher education in Western Europe has broadened the pool of talent from both strata that is entering the expanding middle ranks of the occupational structure. Therefore, changes in educational opportunities appear at one and the same time to be reducing the proportion of the population left to compete for the less remunerative and less secure jobs of both a manual and a nonmanual nature in postindustrial society, while reinforcing the gulf between the more and the less advantaged occupational positions, a gulf that runs through many families, dividing not only working-class parents from their better-educated offspring, but also dividing the better educated from their disadvantaged siblings and childhood friends.

Women and Immigrants in the Workforce

The above generalizations leave aside a crucial factor of increasing significance in Western Europe as well as in the United States and Japan: the fact that large percentages of white-collar workers are women and that overwhelmingly the largest percentages of women are found in the lowest-paid white-collar jobs. In Western Europe, as in the United States, efforts are being made by governments and by private employers to place more women in higher-paid positions of greater responsibility. Yet, the chief beneficiaries thus far have been women with advantageous social and educational backgrounds. Young women from middle-class families are entering universities in greater numbers and are coming out with qualifications that enable them to compete with men on a more equal basis in the liberal professions and for junior management positions. But young women from working-class families are even less likely than their male counterparts to go on to higher education; nor are they anywhere nearly as likely to go on to technical schools or the apprenticeships that will lead to their becoming skilled workers. Accordingly, on leaving school at around age sixteen, perhaps having learned to type and take shorthand, they seek jobs as store clerks, secretarial assistants, or members of typing pools.

Prospects for advancement are limited for women in the lowest-paid white-collar jobs. The expectation of their employers is that they will soon get married and raise families, thus becoming dependent on their husbands for their future economic and social positions. After the child-raising years, they may return to similar jobs at about the same rank as before, but with even less chance for future promotion to higher-paying jobs because they have less future ahead of them. What this adds up to is the fact that, when one says that the white-collar worker has better long-term job prospects than the manual worker, it is clearly the *male* white-collar worker that one has in mind. In terms of both the tangible and intangible rewards of their work, women in the lower-paid clerical jobs should probably be classified with the semiskilled and perhaps even the unskilled workers at the bottom of the occupational scale.

An industrial proletariat still exists in Western Europe. It consists of manual workers who now perform the tasks that technological advances have not yet rendered unnecessary—and perhaps never will. These include a wide variety of jobs, from watching over and occasionally adjusting the automated machines to serving as waiters in restaurants, from collecting trash to sweeping public buildings. If women occupy the lowest-paid levels of the nonmanual occupational categories, migrant workers, both men and women, are their counterparts in the manual categories. Like women white-collar workers, migrant workers occupy the jobs that are the worst paid and the least likely to enjoy union protection. As individuals, they are marginal to the employment structures of the countries where they work. As a class of workers, however, they are indispensable. They perform tasks that must be performed by someone if the factories are to be kept running and the streets are not to become blocked by mountains of garbage. Workers (especially men) indigenous to the more highly industrialized regions and

countries of Western Europe will no longer engage in such work. If necessary, they prefer unemployment compensation while waiting for more desirable jobs to reopen. To meet the need for unskilled labor at a time of near full employment, governments and employers in northern Europe (and recently in Italy as well) encouraged the immigration of hundreds of thousands of unskilled workers from countries along the shores of the Mediterranean and, in the case of Great Britain, Commonwealth citizens from West Indian, Asian, and African countries that were formerly part of the British Empire.

During the 1960s, large numbers of young men from Portugal, southern Italy, and Spain; from Greece, Turkey, and Yugoslavia; and from Algeria, Morocco, and Tunisia arrived in northern Europe and became important percentages of the working populations of Belgium, France, Great Britain, Switzerland, and West Germany, among others. In France, by 1968 their numbers had reached 6.3 percent of the labor force, including 8.7 percent of skilled workers, 10.6 percent of semiskilled workers, and 21.6 percent of unskilled workers. Moreover, they concentrated in the larger cities. Immigrants in the West German cities of Frankfurt, Munich, and Stuttgart constituted 17 percent of the population of those cities by the early 1970s. Approximately one-third of the immigrants in Great Britain and France lived in the London and Paris areas. This meant approximately 500,000 residents in each city. Paid the poorest wages and discriminated against by landlords, they occupied the lowest standard of housing, often crowded several to a room.[20]

When economic conditions took a turn for the worse in the 1970s, the governments of the host countries sought to restrict the flow of immigrants, and, indeed, the numbers of workers entering these countries declined. But, because indigenous workers could not be found to take over jobs that were still available in the recession, many of the immigrants who originally had entered on a temporary basis stayed. Much of the influx of the 1970s came in the persons of wives and children who had earlier been left behind. Second-generation southerners were now entering the schools and the job market in increasing numbers. What had been regarded as a temporary expedient, to assist the economy in a boom period, now was becoming a chronic social condition. Homogeneous societies like those of West Germany and France were becoming multiethnic, and neither governments nor private corporations nor trade unions were geared to deal with the resulting problems. There has been increasing militancy on the part of migrant workers. They have formed their own organizations and have engaged in wildcat strikes, sit-ins, and demonstrations, sometimes touching off backlash violence by native workers who feel economically and socially threatened. In France, a right-wing political party has capitalized on this unrest. Called the *Front National*, its candidate received 14 percent of the popular vote in the presidential election of April 1988. By 1989 a right-wing party in West Germany, the *Republikaner* (Republicans) was pursuing a similar anti-immigrant line. But its "anti-foreigner" message became confused with the influx into West Germany of several 100,000s of ethnic Germans from East Germany and elsewhere in Eastern Europe. Postindustrial society may have lessened the social distance among the relatively highly paid and skilled indigenous men workers (manual and nonmanual), but it seems to have created the roots of a new class struggle, which may be all the harder to resolve because occupational and economic bases of distinction are overlaid by racial, linguistic, and gender distinctions.

Postindustrial Inequality

Despite growing affluence, the shares of the expanding pie have been inequitably distributed in postindustrial society, and those with the smallest shares—in many cases the elderly, the handicapped and disabled, single mothers, orphans, and the unemployed—might be right to perceive the social order as unjust. A study sponsored by the Organization for Economic Cooperation and Development (OECD), published in 1976, lent some support to this possibility. The author of the study, Malcolm Sawyer, measured income distributions in twelve selected First World countries. He measured both pretax and post-tax income, employing a variety of standard measures that gave somewhat different, but not radically different, results. In measures of pretax income, France and the United States consistently showed the greatest inequality, and France consistently showed the most unequal distribution of income after taxes in Western Europe. Figure 2.1 shows the shares of post-tax income of the two lowest deciles of the population in each of the twelve countries. It can be seen that the poorest 20 percent in France had 4.3 percent of the post-tax income, whereas the comparable group in West Germany had 6.5 percent, in Italy 5.1 percent, and in Great Britain 6.3 percent. On the other hand, the richest 20 percent in France had 46.9 percent of the post-tax income. The comparable percentages were 46.1, 46.5, and 38.7 for West Germany, Italy, and Great Britain respectively.[21]

These intercountry differences probably mask differences in the trends of postindustrial societies toward or away from greater social

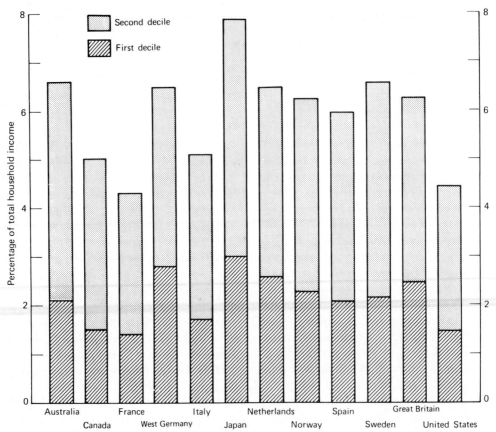

Figure 2.1 Shares of lowest two deciles in post-tax household income distribution. [Malcolm Sawyer, "Income Distribution in OECD Countries," in Organization for Economic Cooperation and Development, *Occasional Studies* (Paris: OECD, 1976), p. 15.]

equality. In 1979 the British Royal Commission on the Distribution of Income and Wealth reported its findings from a comparison of studies undertaken in several First World countries from the early 1950s to the mid-1970s. Very tentatively the Commission concluded that, insofar as the distribution of total personal income among households (family and single-person units) is concerned:

There was a trend toward greater inequality in the USA after 1967. A similar but more uneven trend was evident for the UK from the same date, having been preceded between 1959 and 1967 by a decline in the level of inequality. The Japanese estimates indicate a long run trend toward greater inequality, though this was not confirmed by . . . less complete . . . data. . . . In West Germany there has been little change since 1955 whereas in France an increase in inequality between 1956 and 1962 was reversed between 1962 and 1971. If the trend has persisted since 1971 then more up-to-date French data might show a level of inequality of roughly equal magnitude to other European countries in our study.[22]

It may be the case that France, less urbanized and industrialized in 1960 than the other countries in the study, assumed a social profile closer to that of the other First World countries during the next decade. But the finding that inequality appeared to be growing among some of the most advanced industrial countries during the

same period of time, and at a time of relatively high economic growth—relative to the most recent decade at any rate—leads one to suggest that, despite the "trickle-down" gains for all classes, those at the top of the scale were gaining the most. It should be stressed, however, that these are estimates of pretax inequality. Posttax figures for Britain and West Germany show little change in either direction over the late 1960s and early 1970s.[23] The same may likewise be true of France, whose tax structure was regressive by Western European standards.

According to economist Lester C. Thurow, the high levels of inflation and unemployment of the 1970s probably resulted in greater inequality in First World countries than was ac-

"Instant slums" outside Paris. These are called Bidonvilles (shanty-towns, or literally "tin-can towns"). Such slums in France and in other Western European countries house North African and other immigrant workers who perform low-paid service labor.

tually found in the mid-1970s.[24] Inflation produced an unwillingness on the part of middle-income earners to continue "to pay the transfer payments necessary to keep the income of the bottom quintile rising in pace with the rest of the nation."[25] Furthermore, inflation motivated middle-class wives, who have the education and skills to enable them to enter the postindustrial workforce at relatively high levels of remuneration, thus expanding the share of the pie held by upper-middle- and middle-income households, advantages that lower-income families usually do not possess. Thurow also sees rising unemployment as directly contributing to growing inequality, because market trends are distinctly unfavorable to the employment hopes of unskilled and semiskilled workers at the lower end of the income scale. Although his findings apply to the United States, the same phenomena have occurred in Western Europe, and thus the same reasoning applies. It seems reasonable to conclude that postindustrial society does not, of itself, generate forces that will lead to greater equality. If this is true, there will have to be some political impetus if First World societies are to become more equal or even to remain at approximately their present state.

Preindustrial Social Divisions and Politics[26]

During mature industrialism, political parties in Western Europe could be distinguished from one another as parties of the left or the right partly in terms of the social classes to which they directed their appeals. Parties of the left, particularly those calling themselves Socialists and Communists and seeing their intellectual inheritance in the writings of Karl Marx, primarily sought the voting support of the industrial working class, whereas parties of the right aimed their messages at the various por-

tions of the middle class. This was never a perfect correlation, particularly because of the tendency of a sizable minority of the working class to vote for the party or parties of the right. By the early post–World War II years, it was generally assumed that social class, or the division between manual and nonmanual workers, was the most important factor in determining whether voters voted for parties of the left or parties of the right.[27] Early in the century this assumption helped account for the long-range optimism of socialist parties in Western Europe, for they set the assumption of stable working-class support alongside the assumption that, with growing industrial maturity, the size of the working class would continue growing until socialist parties could be assured of majority voting support from the electorate as a whole.[28] Postindustrial society has confounded these expectations. Indeed, no party in any of our Western European multiparty systems has been able to gain a majority of the popular vote for any but fleeting moments during the entire post–World War II era.

There are two principal reasons for this failure on the part of socialist parties to reach majority status among Western European electorates. First, as previously noted in this chapter, social class structures have become more complex, with the portion of the working population properly labeled "manual worker" receding in size. Second, social class has declined in importance as a determinant of party voting.[29] In one First World country after another, the evidence mounts against the assumption that social class is any longer the primary basis of party politics. As social class has declined in electoral importance, other identifying features of electorates—some of which are older characteristics, some newer—have gained in significance. In the remainder of this chapter we concentrate on two of the longer standing social distinctions in Western Europe—religion and ethnicity. In

Chapter 3 we look at some post-industrial dividing lines of growing political significance.

Religion

Historically, religion has played a very important role in the politics of all Western European countries. The Protestant Reformation had an immense impact on the countries of northern Europe, as did the reaction to it of the Roman Catholic Church in southern Europe. Religious political parties have, at different times and in different places, been central to the politics of almost all continental Western European countries. Our four Western European countries can readily be characterized as follows: Great Britain is a Protestant country, France and Italy are Catholic countries, and West Germany is approximately half Protestant and half Catholic. But the situation is actually much more complex than that.

In the first place, in the late twentieth century, despite signs of a renascence here and there, organized religion has not been such an important factor in the average European's life as it was earlier in the century. Many people, especially in urban areas, are atheists, agnostics, or nominal church members who never attend services. Church membership figures in Western European countries usually far exceed that portion of the membership that could be regarded as "religious." This is particularly true in Great Britain, where 61 percent of the population identify themselves with the established Church of England, but where actual Church of England attendance is only a small fraction of the potential.[30] Generally, the same holds true for the Scottish Presbyterians (the established Church of Scotland). Although British Catholics and non-Anglican Protestants show higher attendance rates, those Britons who take religion seriously are decidedly a minority of the overall population.[31]

Religion is more important to more people in the three other countries, and it has greater political significance elsewhere than it has in Great Britain. The Anglicans tend to vote Conservative and the other religions lean to Labour, but social class is much more important in Great Britain in accounting for the two-party vote than is religion. Although class as a factor in British party voting has been declining since the early 1970s, it has not been replaced by religion or any other social factor as the principal determinant.[32] In West Germany, 50 percent of the population is Protestant and 46 percent Catholic. A majority of Catholics support the CDU, the successor to the old Catholic Center Party of the Weimar Republic. But the Christian Democrats have renounced a strictly confessional orientation. They have sought Protestant support and have obtained about one-third of the Protestant vote. Indeed, they have captured about 50 percent of the vote of self-employed, middle-class Protestants, which helps account for the inability of their rival, the Social Democrats, to gain much more than 50 percent of the Protestant vote.[33]

Although France and Italy are both Catholic countries, Roman Catholicism is much more solidly entrenched in the latter. In France, there has always been a very strong strain of anticlericalism. This is not the same as a personal philosophical position about the existence of God. The anticlerical French need not be atheists or agnostics, although many are. What distinguishes the anticlerics is their opposition to any church influence in political matters. What is sought is a complete separation of church and state, which means, for example, the abolition of state subsidies to religious schools.

Although anticlerics are difficult to distinguish from other French men and women, at least for purposes of census taking, voting studies show that there is a strong relationship between anticlericalism and left-wing voting. This can be seen from electoral maps of France that show what regions of the country have the strongest left-wing voting. Anticlericalism flourishes in the south and southwest, the regions that have consistently provided the greatest support for the left for more than a century. It has also been found that strong adherents to the Catholic faith in France tend to vote right of center. For example, in a 1981 survey, the Socialist Party was chosen by only 28 percent of weekly churchgoing Catholics, whereas it was chosen by 47 percent of the nonreligious and nonchurchgoing Catholics. By contrast, the Gaullists, the leading party of the right, were supported by 26 percent of the former group and only 9 percent of the latter.[34]

This distinction between church attendance and nonchurch attendance is also important in Italy and West Germany. Parallel studies in the two countries showed that, in both cases, church attendance was the most important variable explaining left-wing versus right-wing voting; it was more important than social class, trade union membership, or, in the case of West Germany, Catholicism versus Protestantism.[35] Thus, religion in its usual sense—that is, one religion versus another or religion versus nonreligion—as an environmental factor affecting politics in postindustrial societies, may no longer be so important as it once was. But, in some Western European countries, the intensity of religious participation still plays an important role in politics. This is particularly true in countries with substantial Catholic populations; other examples include Austria, Belgium, the Netherlands, Spain, and Portugal.

Ethnicity

In two of the smaller Western European countries, Belgium and Switzerland, there is another important factor—the concentration of people who speak different languages in separate regions of the country. In Belgium, the division is between French-speaking Belgians (Walloons) in the south and Dutch-speaking Belgians (Flemish) in the north. In Switzerland, there are four separate regionally based linguistic groups, of which the most important are the French-speaking Swiss in the west and the German-speaking Swiss in the north and east. Political party support in both countries has been profoundly affected by these linguistic divisions, but in Switzerland they have not disrupted the overall political harmony in this century. The opposite has been true in Belgium. There, the numerically superior Flemish have claimed that the Walloons enjoy a privileged political and economic status, and the Walloons resent the economic decline of their region relative to prosperous Flanders. Disruptions of the Belgian political system have sometimes approached the scale of those in Canada, where a similar division can be found between French-speaking and English-speaking Canadians.

In each of our four Western European countries, the principal language group far exceeds the minorities in terms of its share of the population. West Germany has no significant geographically based minority. In Italy and France, linguistic minorities are found in border areas that adjoin other countries: the Alsatians on the French side of the Franco–German border speak a dialect that is similar to German; the Basques and Catalans in southern parts of France that adjoin the corresponding regions of Spain have their own languages; the French-speaking Italians are found in the Alpine region adjacent to France; and the people of the South Tyrolean Alps speak German but live on the Italian side of the Austro–Italian border. In all these areas, except Alsace, there are movements seeking attachment to the appropriate ethnographic entity. The most serious conflict has been in the French Basque region. Basques on the French side of the Franco–Spanish border have harbored fugitive Basque separatists from the Spanish side. This has been a source of strain in relations between Paris and Madrid, although both governments have taken steps in recent years to seal off the border to the refugees.

There is a different kind of problem for certain minorities in regions of France and Great Britain where there are no international boundary lines dividing linguistic groups who speak the same language. In these cases, a combined cultural and economic deprivation is felt by the minorities in relation to the dominant populations. In France, this is the case of the Bretons in Brittany, the westernmost region of the country, and of the Corsicans on the Mediterranean island of Corsica, which is legally and administratively an integral part of France. In Great Britain, it is true of the Welsh and the Scots. In all of these cases, the political system has been affected—by outbursts of violence in Brittany and Corsica and by the electoral success of Welsh and Scottish nationalist parties. The responses in these cases have been halting attempts by the central government to provide greater material resources to the aggrieved regions and to experiment with means of giving more power to regional levels of government to stave off the demand for full-scale independence. Regionally based ethnicity bears watching as an old source of a new strain in postindustrial societies, especially if social class and religious divisions become less important politically than they once were and if economic disparities between regions within a country continue.

The Anomaly of Northern Ireland

In a class by itself is the division between peoples in Northern Ireland, an area that is physically part of the island of Ireland but is politically a part of the "United Kingdom of Great Britain and Northern Ireland," which we have been referring to as "Britain" or "Great Britain" (i.e., the larger of the two main islands of the British Isles). At the time Catholic Ireland gained its independence from the United Kingdom after World War I, heavily Protestant Ulster (the northern six counties of Ireland) remained part of the United Kingdom and remains so today. Its population is divided along what are both religious and ethnic lines. Between 35 and 40 percent of the population are historically indigenous Irish Catholics; the remaining 60 to 65 percent are Protestants, mainly Presbyterians whose ancestors migrated to Ulster from lowland Scotland two or three centuries ago. Religion is a more salient dividing line than ethnicity today, as church attendance is much higher for both Catholics and Protestants in Northern Ireland than it is for either religion in Great Britain. But sociologists argue that the dividing line is as much a social class division as a religious one. All of the indicators of well-being, employment indicators, levels of pay, and standard of living favor the Protestants, who, until 1969, dominated the government of Northern Ireland, which was allowed a great deal of autonomy from control by the British Parliament.[36]

In 1969 the Catholics staged civil rights demonstrations that produced intergroup violence and eventuated, in 1971, in the British government's dismissing the local parliament and establishing direct rule from London. The arrival of the British army stimulated resistance from more militant Catholics organized in the Irish Republican Army (IRA). Militant Protestants are also organized in paramilitary fashion, and their political parties have defended the social, economic, and political advantages of Protestants with single-minded determination. Most Catholics today support the independence of

Northern Ireland from Great Britain and its unification with the Irish Republic in the south. But militant Protestants have made it clear they will turn to violent means themselves if the governments in London and Dublin were to move overtly in that direction. Talks have gone on between the two governments, both of which believe some form of joint Protestant–Catholic rule must form the basis of an ultimate solution for Northern Ireland itself, but there is not a clear-cut agreement on the question of who should have ultimate sovereignty, the United Kingdom or the Republic of Ireland. In Northern Ireland itself, too much of the present political leadership of both communities appears too far removed from willingness to seek a compromise solution for it to be a realistic hope before the arrival of the twenty-first century. However we view the social basis of the conflict in Northern Ireland, the violence it has produced far exceeds that in any other part of the First World. In Great Britain itself, religious conflict has not produced such violence since the early 1700s.[37]

In summary, it would seem clear that socioeconomic environmental factors are important in influencing politics. The level of a country's economic development and the degree of equality in the distribution of well-being among its social groups will help determine the shape of its political system. But these economic factors will undoubtably be affected by the country's predominant social cleavages, some of which have existed since before the Industrial Revolution.

Suggestions for Further Reading

Acquaviva, S. S., and M. Santuccio. *Social Structure in Italy: Crisis of a System*, trans. Colin Hamer (London: Robertson, 1976).

Atkinson, A. B., ed. *Wealth, Income and Inequality* (Oxford: Oxford University Press, 1980).

Bell, Daniel. *The Coming of Post-Industrial Society* (New York: Basic Books, 1973).

Coates, David. *The Context of British Politics* (London: Hutchinson, 1984).

Gallie, Duncan. *Social Inequality and Class Radicalism in France and Britain* (Cambridge: Cambridge University Press, 1983).

Goldthorpe, John H. *Social Mobility and Class Structure in Modern Britain* (Oxford: Clarendon Press, 1980).

Hirsch, Fred, and John H. Goldthorpe, eds. *The Political Economy of Inflation* (Cambridge, Mass.: Harvard University Press, 1978).

Jacobs, Jane. *Cities and the Wealth of Nations: Principles of Economic Life* (New York: Random House, 1984).

Krejci, Jaroslav. *Social Structure in Divided Germany* (New York: St. Martin's, 1976).

Lash, Scott, and John Urry. *The End of Organized Capitalism* (Cambridge: Polity Press, 1987).

Marceau, Jane. *Class and Status in France: Economic Change and Social Immobility, 1945–1975* (Oxford: Clarendon Press, 1977).

Offe, Claus. *Disorganized Capitalism: Contemporary Transformations of Work and Politics* (Cambridge, Mass.: MIT Press, 1985).

Okimoto, Daniel L., and Thomas P. Rohlen, eds. *Inside the Japanese System: Readings on Contemporary Society and Political Economy*

(Stanford, Calif.: Stanford University Press, 1988).

Parkin, Frank. *Class Inequality and Political Order: Social Stratification in Capitalist and Communist Societies* (New York: Praeger, 1971).

Sabel, Charles F. *Work and Politics: The Division of Labor in Industry* (Cambridge: Cambridge

University Press, 1982).

Taylor, Robert. *Workers and the New Depression* (London: Macmillan, 1982).

Vogel, Ezra N. *Japan as Number One: Lessons for America* (Cambridge, Mass., and London: Harvard University Press, 1979).

Notes

1. Among many works that discuss postindustrial society, see Daniel Bell, *The Coming of Post-Industrial Society* (New York: Basic Books, 1973); Leon N. Lindberg, ed., *Politics and the Future of Industrial Society* (New York: McKay, 1976); and Alain Touraine, *The Post-Industrial Society*, trans. Leonard F. X. Mayhew (New York: Random House, 1971).

2. Among the earlier uses of this term is that by the German Socialist Claus Offe. See his *Disorganized Capitalism: Contemporary Transformations of Work and Politics* (Cambridge, Mass.: MIT Press, 1985).

3. Scott Lash and John Urry, *The End of Organized Capitalism* (Cambridge: Polity Press, 1987), p. 5.

4. Ibid., p. 6.

5. Ibid., p. 5.

6. Bell, *The Coming of Post-Industrial Society*, pp. 129–142.

7. Statistical Office of the European Communities, *Basic Statistics of the Community*, 16th ed. (Luxembourg: The European Communities, 1978), p. 18.

8. Bell, *The Coming of Post-Industrial Society*, p. 135.

9. Ezra N. Vogel, *Japan as Number One: Lessons for America* (Cambridge, Mass., and London: Harvard University Press, 1979), Ch. 3

10. Taketsugu Tsurutani, *Political Change in Japan: Response to Postindustrial Challenge* (New York: McKay, 1977); Ardath W. Burks, *Japan: A Postindustrial Power* (Boulder, Colo., and London: Westview, 1981).

11. Donald B. Keesing and Martin Wolf, *Textile Quotas against Developing Countries*, Thames Essay no. 23 (London: Trade Policy Research Centre, 1980).

12. Angus Maddison, "Economic Growth and Structural Change: Issues and Prospects," in Irving Leveson and Jimmy W. Wheeler, eds., *Western Economies in Transition: Structural Change and Adjustment Policies in Industrial Countries* (Boulder, Colo.: Westview Press, 1980), pp. 41–60.

13. Jane Jacobs, *Cities and the Wealth of Nations: Principles of Economic Life* (New York: Random House, 1984), Ch. 1.

14. Luciano Gallino, "Italy," in Margaret Scotford Archer and Salvador Giner, eds., *Contemporary Europe: Class, Status and Power* (London: Weidenfeld and Nicolson, 1973), pp. 110–115.

15. Charles F. Sabel, *Work and Politics: The Division of Labor in Industry* (Cambridge: Cambridge University Press, 1982), pp. 71–77.

16. Tadashi Hanami, *Labor Relations in Japan Today*, 1st paperback ed. (Tokyo: Kodansha Interna-

tional, 1981), pp. 89–90.

17. Edward J. Lincoln, *Japan: Facing Economic Maturity* (Washington, D.C.: Brookings, 1988), p. 4.

18. Sabel, *Work and Politics*, pp. 220–231; "The Flawed Renaissance: A Survey of the Italian Economy," *The Economist* (February 27, 1988), special section, pp. 4–9.

19. Duncan Gallie, *Social Inequality and Class Radicalism in France and Britain* (Cambridge: Cambridge University Press, 1983), Ch. 1, fn. 33.

20. Thierry Baudouin et al., "Women and Immigrants: Marginal Workers?" in Colin Crouch and Alessandro Pizzorno, eds., *The Resurgence of Class Conflict in Western Europe since 1968*, Vol. 2 (New York: Holmes & Meier, 1978), p. 74.

21. Malcolm Sawyer, "Income Distribution in OECD Countries," in Organization for Economic Cooperation and Development, *Occasional Studies* (Paris: OECD, 1976), pp. 3–36. Estimates in the study are carefully made from a variety of sources, including government statistics and surveys of households. Narrow differences among countries should be interpreted cautiously; wider differences should be quite reliable.

22. Report no. 7 of the Royal Commission on the Distribution of Income and Wealth, reprinted in part in A. B. Atkinson, ed., *Wealth, Income and Inequality* (Oxford: Oxford University Press, 1980), pp. 93–95.

23. Ibid., p. 94.

24. Lester C. Thurow, "Equity, Efficiency, Social Justice and Redistribution," in Organization for Economic Cooperation and Development, *The Welfare State in Crisis* (Paris: OECD, 1981), pp. 140–145.

25. Ibid., p. 142.

26. Because of the absence of politically relevant *pre*industrial cleavages in Japan, we confine our discussion in this section to our four Western European countries. *Post*industrial cleavages in Japan are considered, along with those in Western Europe, in the next chapter.

27. Robert R. Alford, "Class Voting in the Anglo-American Political Systems," in Seymour M. Lipset and Stein Rokkan, eds., *Party Systems and Voter Alignments: Cross-National Perspectives* (New York: The Free Press, 1967), p. 68.

28. Adam Przeworksi, *Capitalism and Social Democracy* (Cambridge: Cambridge University Press, 1985), pp. 16–19.

29. Russell J. Dalton, *Citizen Politics in Western Democracies: Public Opinion and Political Parties in the United States, Great Britain, West Germany and France* (Chatham, N.J.: Chatham House, 1988), Ch. 8.

30. Richard Rose, "Britain: Simple Abstractions and Complex Realities," in Rose, ed., *Electoral Behavior: A Comparative Handbook* (New York: The Free Press, 1974), p. 517.

31. Ibid., pp. 517–518; Dalton, *Citizen Politics*, p. 162.

32. Regional differences in Great Britain, where unemployment levels and other economic indicators show substantial differences between the more prosperous south of England and the poorer northern English regions and Scotland and Wales, are becoming of greater political importance. In 1987 the Conservative Party won 51.8 percent of the vote in the south, against 36.6 percent of that in northern England, 29.5 percent of the Welsh, and 24 percent of the Scottish vote. For Labour, the percentage of the southern vote was only 20.9, against 42.1 percent in northern England, 45.1 percent in Wales, and 42.4 percent in Scotland. David Butler and Dennis Kavanagh, *The British General Election of 1987* (London: Macmillan, 1988), p. 284.

33. Derek W. Urwin, "Germany: Continuity and Change in Electoral Politics," in Rose, ed., *Electoral Behavior*, pp. 133, 148; Dalton, *Citizen Politics*, p. 164.

34. Dalton, ibid.

35. Urwin, "Germany," and Samuel H. Barnes, "Italy: Religion and Class in Electoral Behavior," in Rose, ed., *Electoral Behavior*, pp. 109–170, and 171–225, respectively.

36. Although he accepts this statistical evidence, Richard Rose contends that it is still religion, rather than social class, that is the predominant politically relevant social cleavage in Northern Ireland. *Governing without Consensus: An Irish Perspective* (Boston: Beacon Press, 1971), pp. 286–387.

37. David Coates, *The Context of British Politics* (London: Hutchinson, 1984), p. 184.

CHAPTER 3

POLITICAL CULTURE

It should be clear from the preceding chapter that First World economies have been struggling in the past two decades and that the accompanying social strains have been growing in severity. In subsequent chapters, we will see how the political systems of these countries have adjusted to these strains. In some cases, as in Great Britain and France, important changes have taken place in voting patterns, partisan alignments, and public policy goals. The West German and Japanese political systems, which earlier underwent the greatest transformations from pre–World War II patterns, had been the most resistant to the winds of change, probably because, as we have seen, the economy and social order in the two countries have been the least subject to strain during the past decade. But, even in West Germany, if not in Japan, the 1980s brought some political surprises. Thus, we can see a relationship between the stability of the socioeconomic order and political stability. Disequilibrium in one realm is likely to produce discontinuity in the other.

Social and economic strains do not simply translate into political events without first having some impact on the people who make the political events. In First World polyarchies, the political stage is a relatively crowded one. Political actors include not only the elites who make the principal policy decisions that affect society, but also ordinary citizens—citizens acting as voters and in other ways participating in the political process. The importance of voters for political outcomes should be obvious to anyone who has witnessed the changes at the top that have occurred as a result of elections in Great Britain, the United States, France, West Germany, and Italy since 1979. But political participation of other kinds—participation in strikes, public meetings, and demonstrations and even acts of violence—have an impact on the political system, although often a less calculable impact than that of dramatic changes in voting behavior.

How do ordinary citizens respond politically to the traumas of daily life? The answer depends on how citizens view politics. Do they see it as a very distant realm inhabited by a few knowledgeable persons, or as an arena affording opportunities for personal involvement and potential relief from social, economic, and even psychological ailments? In other words, what are the political beliefs of ordinary citizens? How do they perceive the values of power, well-being, enlightenment, and respect to be distributed within their society, and what responsibility do they assign to government for these distributions? What role do they see for themselves in reinforcing or bringing about changes in these distributions? Do the citizens of different countries have different political beliefs? In what ways do different segments of the population of the same country differ in their political beliefs? The study of political culture is the study of such belief systems. It enables us better to explain and make predictions about the ways traumatic events affect the political behavior of citizens in different societies.

Definitions

The term *political culture* was coined in the 1950s by the political scientist Gabriel A. Almond.[1] Its meaning has changed somewhat since then as perspectives borrowed from social psychology have come to have greater influence in the fashioning of the concept. According to Almond and G. Bingham Powell:

Political culture is the pattern of individual attitudes and orientations toward politics among the members of a political system. It is the subjective realm which underlies and gives meaning to political actions. Such individual orientations involve several components, including: (a) cognitive orientations, knowledge, accurate or otherwise, of political objects and beliefs; (b) affective orientations,

feelings of attachment, involvement, rejections, and the like, about political objects; and (c) evaluative orientations, judgments, and opinions about political objects, which usually involve applying value standards to political objects and events.[2]

Essentially, Almond and Powell are saying that political culture is a pattern of individual attitudes and orientations toward political objects. The key words are (1) *pattern*, (2) *individual attitudes and orientations*, and (3) *political objects*.

Let us begin with the second of these elements. "Attitudes and orientations" should lead us into the realm of individual psychology. How do people think and feel about themselves and about the world around them? How they think or feel, of course, is not necessarily an indication of how they will act. At best, it simply gives us some insight into their *potential* for action. One must also take into account the situational opportunities and constraints that surround any such potential action. I might have a very strong feeling that the mayor of my city is corrupt and has been robbing the city blind for years. Yet I might hesitate to take action unless I know others feel the same way and unless I believe something could be done to get the mayor out of office. Still, if many people feel the same way I do (impotent), that is one significant reason why the mayor has been able to get away with it for so long. If such people could know who shared their view and realize that the discontent was widespread, perhaps the mayor could be ousted from office. The potential is there; the problem is to convert the potential into action.

This brings us back to the first element—the pattern of attitudes and orientations. Suppose that only a tiny minority of relatively well-educated citizens opposed the mayor, whereas the vast majority of people were either apathetic or believed he was doing a good job. The mayor would have less to be concerned about in this situation than if the city were polarized, that is, fairly evenly divided between strong supporters and strong opponents. Here we see the difference between two attitudinal patterns: a consensual and a polarized pattern; these patterns can be depicted graphically as distribution curves. (See Figure 3.1.) The J-shaped and normal curves represent consensual patterns, whereas the U-shaped curve indicates polarization. In the case of the J-shaped pattern, there is what one might call a one-sided consensus because there is a minority that is far removed from the majority in this case. The normal curve reflects something of a middle-of-the-road consensus. Here, it would be easier to work out a compromise between the competing opinions than in the first situation.

The final element of our definition is the political object toward which the attitudes and orientations are directed. In the case at hand, the incumbent mayor is the political object. But political culture encompasses a much wider array of political objects; these may include a number of questions of public policy, how government should allocate scarce resources among competing needs. Also included are attitudes and orientations toward the structures of politics and government and how power is distributed between citizens and their government and between government offices. In other words, the political culture of a country is the pattern of attitudes and orientations of its citizens toward power, well-being, respect, and enlightenment, and how they are distributed.

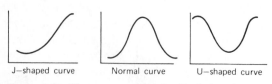

J—shaped curve Normal curve U—shaped curve

Figure 3.1 Three types of attitudinal distribution.

In studying political culture, we may want to know whether certain political attitudes and orientations are distributed among the entire population of a country or only among a portion of its citizenry. We have already used the political culture of a single city as an example. Any national political culture can be subdivided into a variety of political *subcultures* if certain groups that can clearly be differentiated on the basis of certain attributes also have distinct political orientations. For example, the youth of a country, who are distinguishable on the basis of age, may also share distinct political beliefs and feelings. Perhaps women or the elderly or Catholics share sufficiently distinctive political orientations to warrant being treated as subcultures in certain countries. In Chapter 4, we consider the political elites of our five countries—those public officials and influential private citizens with the greatest share of political power—and ask whether there are distinct subcultures among political elites, that is, the different ideologies that divide political parties, such as Socialists and Conservatives, from one another. In some countries, such as the United States, the ideological differences between political parties are probably not fundamental enough to warrant the judgment that all but their most active members belong to different subcultures. In other countries, however, the ideological walls are steeper and thicker, and such subcultures can be found.

We should not be surprised to learn that French communist ideology constitutes a separate political subculture. But the active Communists, after all, constitute only a small minority of the population, almost professionally separate from the rest—like doctors, lawyers, or engineers. What about the masses of people? In postindustrial society, do typical French people differ enough from typical Britons or Germans to make it worthwhile to examine differences in political culture? If you have ever traveled in these countries, perhaps you can answer this question. People *do* differ in how they feel about things, and their reactions may seem unpredictable to anyone who is unfamiliar with their culture. By and large, Britons were able to empathize with the trauma that Watergate represented to Americans, but they could also better sympathize with the plight of a disgraced president, whose stature as a world leader they respected, than could most Americans. Germans, on the other hand, could understand neither. They could not relate to the agony most Americans were experiencing. Obviously, Richard M. Nixon had done wrong; obviously, he should be removed from office. What was all the fuss about? The French displayed a third reaction—cynicism. To them, all politicians are corrupt and what Nixon did was no better or worse than what most politicians do. But if Americans wanted to clean up their political system, they should have started much earlier; in any event, it probably would not have done much good.[3]

How can people living in such close proximity to one another have such different responses? Part of the answer lies in the fact that people are brought up differently in these countries. Here we come to the subject of *political socialization*. Each country has typical ways in which children are brought up and typical ways in which adults are politically influenced that continue to reshape the orientations they learned in childhood and adolescence. In these social learning experiences, one acquires a set of "correct" attitudes that enables one to get along with one's fellow human beings with a minimum of friction. This training and conditioning process is only partly at the conscious level. Parents have certain ideas about how to bring up their children, but most of them are not trained child psychologists. Children growing up in France during the presidency of Charles de Gaulle may

have gotten a clear impression from their parents that the general was greatly admired and respected, even though their parents may never have said anything explicitly to this effect. Later on, this same respect and admiration may have transferred to the office of the president itself, with de Gaulle's successors benefiting from the "halo effect." Whatever orientations children gain from parents will not easily be changed later in life.

Certain kinds of political orientations are also learned in school. In Western European polyarchies, children are not as likely to learn partisan affiliations as they are to learn of their position in the larger world. No longer screened from this world by the warmth of the family circle, children begin to experience the various authority patterns with which they will have to live later on, and they begin to get an idea of their position in the hierarchy of respect within the general society. The relatively elitist educational systems of Western Europe help transmit a stronger sense of class difference than is true of the schools in the United States and Japan. European children going through the privileged upper stream are likely to have greater confidence in their ability to influence political events than are children in the lower stream, who are learning that they will have lesser shares of well-being, respect, and enlightenment. But as larger numbers of young persons in Western Europe have gone on to higher levels of education, so the level of confidence of the younger generation as potential wielders of political influence exceeds that of older people.

Political socialization takes place elsewhere as well. Peer influences can be quite important in shaping attitudes both in school and later on in various occupations and organizations. Such influences may reinforce or conflict with those learned in the family and the school. In postindustrial society, many individuals are exposed to influences that lead them to become quite different from their fathers and mothers. The acceleration of change has been so great in recent decades that could a time machine transport average Italian adults from the 1940s to the 1990s, their efforts to adjust to the new Italy might bring about a severe trauma requiring confinement in a mental institution. Older Italians have gone through precisely this process, but at a slower pace, which has enabled them to build up their psychological defenses. But how well can an Italian of twenty communicate with an Italian of seventy? Change the word *Italian* to *American* and see what your answer is.

Television and the other media have also helped break down the attitudes acquired early in life. The process of challenge probably begins in late childhood, accelerates in adolescence, and comes to full bloom in adulthood. The degree to which the media are deliberately purveying certain messages varies from country to country. The matter of government control over French broadcasting is one of the most important issues in France, and has been ever since the Gaullist leadership began shaping media messages more than thirty years ago. Opponents of the Gaullists argued that they used radio and television to condition attitudes in ways that helped them remain in power. Today the Gaullists are making similar complaints about their Socialist successors. But the potential influence of the media goes far beyond partisan advantage and disadvantage. The crises of inner cities, the tragic struggle of Northern Ireland, terrorist attacks, the killing of fish by chemical pollution of the Rhine River, the grim economic statistics of the last decade—all reach the livingrooms of people in Western polyarchies. So does emotionally charged good news, such as the steps taken toward democratic regimes nearby in Eastern Europe. No matter how ob-

jectively these traumatic events are portrayed by media news staffs, they are bound to affect people's confidence in the efficacy of political systems and in the dependability of their own future.

Political Allegiance

Allegiant and Alienated Political Cultures

When political scientists compare the political cultures of different countries, much of their attention is focused on what we have called the value of *power*. Political scientists have asked two very general sorts of questions about attitudes toward the distribution of power. The first relates to the way people view the structure of political elite roles within the political system; the second concerns people's view of themselves and of people like themselves as nonelite political actors. The political elite is a body larger than that set of individuals who hold important public offices at any given time. In Western Europe and Japan (as we will see in Chapters 4 and 5) the political elite includes the leaders of the opposition party or parties who hold seats in the legislative body (parliament) and who stand ready to replace the leaders of the majority party or parties who presently hold power.

The first aspect of political culture is the study of how nonelites perceive the political elites of their country. When we ask how people view political elites, we are not asking simply how well they like the incumbents. Such questions are frequently found in public opinion polls: People are asked how well they think President George Bush or Prime Minister Margaret Thatcher is doing, for example. In studying political culture, we ask a more fundamental question: how well people believe the country is being run by *whoever* is in power. This question has a longer-term quality to it. It is a question about what political scientists call the *regime*. We are interested in how well the ordinary citizen feels his or her country has been run in recent experience, including periods of time during which more than one president or prime minister or, for that matter, political party has been in power. In essence, we are asking both (1) how well the system of political institutions is structured to ensure that the most appropriate team of political elites will be in a position to make public policy and (2) how reliable the *entire pool* of political elites is.

Individual citizens who have positive attitudes toward their political institutions and political elites can be termed *allegiant*. They are so in more than the sense that they have a strong national identification, meaning a sense of patriotism. They also believe that their system of government is one that works, at least most of the time, and that the people who specialize in the work of government are capable of making it work. *Alienated* citizens, on the other hand, are those who lack confidence in their governmental system and in their political elites. They may not trust those in power, they may be disenchanted with all politicians, and they may very well be searching for substantial changes in the structures of the system that will make it work better. It is possible to go from the level of the individual to the citizenry as an aggregate and say that the political culture of a country is allegiant or alienated if a strong majority of the citizenry shares attitudes of one type or the other. These two types of political culture are depicted in Figure 3.2.

It is easier to define aspects of political culture, such as political allegiance, than it is to measure them. Ideally, one would like to be able to determine how every citizen of a particular country

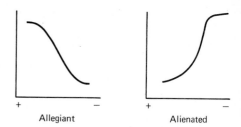

Figure 3.2   Two types of political culture.

felt at a given time about the political elites. Although this is impossible, the next best thing—the public opinion poll or attitude survey—is in principle available and reliable. Prohibitive costs, however, have limited its use on a cross-national basis so that, although we have many good surveys of the political attitudes of people in individual countries, they can seldom be combined with similar studies of other countries to enable comparative analyses. One of the pioneering cross-national studies in this field—a five-nation survey conducted by Gabriel A. Almond and Sidney Verba in 1959–60[4]—is still a landmark, but its findings are now quite out of date. Therefore, we supplement some of those findings with more recent studies made either cross-nationally or within single countries.

Almond and Verba asked their respondents in the United States, Great Britain, West Germany, Italy, and Mexico the following question: "Speaking generally, what are the things about this country you are most proud of?"[5] The respondents came up with their own answers rather than being compelled to answer in categories supplied by the interviewer. The responses were then coded into a discrete number of categories. (See Table 3.1.)

The Americans and British most often cited aspects of their governmental or political institutions, including social legislation. Nearly twice as many Americans as British said they felt most proud about aspects of their political

Table 3.1   Aspects of a Nation in Which Respondents Report Pride (by Nation)

Percentage Who Said They Were Proud of:	U.S.	U.K.*	West Germany	Italy
Governmental, political institutions	85%	46%	7%	3%
Social legislation	13	18	6	1
Position in international affairs	5	11	5	2
Economic system	23	10	33	3
Characteristics of people	7	18	36	11
Spiritual virtues and religion	3	1	3	6
Contributions to the arts	1	6	11	16
Contributions to science	3	7	12	3
Physical attributes of country	5	10	17	25
Nothing or don't know	4	10	15	27
Other	9	11	3	21
Total percent of responses[†]	158	148	148	118
Total percent of respondents	100	100	100	100
Total number of cases	970	963	955	995

(*Source*) Gabriel A. Almond and Sidney Verba, *The Civic Culture: Political Attitudes and Democracy in Five Nations* (Princeton, N.J.: Princeton University Press, 1963), p. 102. Reprinted with permission of Princeton University Press.
* Great Britain.
[†] Percentages exceed 100 because of multiple responses.

system, but more British cited this category than any other aspect of their country or its people. Only negligible percentages of the Germans and Italians mentioned this category at all. The largest percentage of German respondents mentioned characteristics of the people, such as industriousness and efficiency, and the success of the West German economy. As for the Italians, the largest single category was "nothing, or don't know." The physical attributes of the country came ahead of any category dealing with the qualities or achievements of the Italian people. Clearly, allegiance to the political system was higher at that time in the United States and Great Britain than in West Germany or Italy.

Recent Developments

In the past twenty years, changes have taken place in mass attitudes in the countries Almond and Verba studied.[6] In a recent study of attitudes toward democracy in our four Western European countries and the United States, Ulrich Widmaier found that there had been a general tendency for support for democracy to decline during the troubled economic times of the late 1970s and early 1980s.[7] This expressed itself differently in the five countries. In the United States, support for democracy declined gradually from a very high level before the economic decline began, and even by the early 1980s it rested at a higher level than was true in the four other countries.

The next highest level was found in Widmaier's own country, West Germany, where, he noted, support for democracy had risen dramatically in the 1960s and early 1970s but had declined somewhat since then. France and Britain showed fluctuations during the period studied, but they seemed to be related to different factors that might explain them. In the case of France, Widmaier noted that support for democracy rose around the times elections were held and declined thereafter. He interpreted this to mean that the French voters' hopes for democracy were raised each time the evenly balanced parties went into combat against each other, but typical French cynicism set in again once the outcome had been declared and the new incumbents had settled into office. As for Britain, support for democracy closely followed support for the incumbents. Thus, for example, when public opinion polls were registering an upsurge in support for Prime Minister Margaret Thatcher at the time of the Falklands (Malvinas) War, the attitude surveys on which Widmaier relied were showing a similar improvement in British views of democracy. In Italy, support for democracy was lower than in the other countries and showed less movement over time. However, in all five countries, levels of support for democracy were lowest in the mid-1970s and the early 1980s, when economic fortunes were likewise at a low ebb. They rose again in the mid–1980s with the return of good economic times.[8]

The substantial differences in patterns of support for democracy among these five countries suggests more caution in interpreting the findings than Widmaier displays. For one thing, the term *democracy* itself may have different meanings in different political cultures. It has always enjoyed a sort of "halo effect" in the United States, whose people see themselves as the pathbreakers who have led the rest of the world in making the abstract concept of democracy work in reality. The American view of democracy probably had a substantial impact on the generations of West Germans who have grown up since World War II, experiencing an educational system that features civics courses that are, if anything, more sophisticated than those found in American schools. Such explicit socialization in democratic norms and values is not found in British, French, or Italian schools, where greater continuity prevailed between prewar and postwar educational patterns. The tendency of the British to subordinate their view of democracy to their view of the way the government is performing at the moment suggests that democracy is not a concept that is grasped early and retains strong emotional attachment in Britain, as it does in the United States and seems to do in West Germany. It also suggests that questions about attitudes toward democracy do not really reach the deepest levels of political allegiance in European countries. Older symbols, relating to the nation-state, may reach further.

There have been other recent studies of political allegiance that have gone deeper into the subject for each of these countries. The increased allegiance among citizens of West Germany has been a consistent finding. In 1978, a sample of West Germans was asked to specify what things about their country made them proudest, and the results were noticeably different from what Almond and Verba found in 1959–60. The percentages who volunteered some aspect of governmental or political institutions had risen from 7 percent to 31 percent, the second highest category after the economic system, which had risen to the 40 percent level.[9] Although West Germans were still proud—indeed, even prouder—of their economic record in 1978, they were now registering allegiance to the political system in much higher frequencies than twenty years before. It can be imagined that the sustained superiority in economic performance of West Germany had built up a stock of *specific support* among its citizenry. This is allegiance to the existing regime that is based on a positive evaluation of its performance but that is not necessarily indicative of a deeper sense of allegiance to the political institutions. The latter has been termed *diffuse support* by political scientists.[10] It may be developing in West Germany, but one wonders whether the high levels of allegiance shown in recent surveys would be sustained in the face of a sustained reversal in the performance of the West German economy. However, it seems safer today than twenty years ago to predict that democracy as a general system of government will continue to receive support. This has been shown in survey after survey taken over the past two decades in which West Germans in overwhelming percentages consistently expressed positive feelings toward democracy and rejected authoritarian forms of government.

The positive movement of West Germans along the allegiance/alienation dimension is all the more striking because, if anything, the movement of American and British citizens has been in the opposite direction in the past twenty years. The evidence for Americans is quite clear. Periodically, Americans have been asked about their levels of confidence in various political and social institutions. Comparisons of results for 1966 and 1972 show a remarkable decline in confidence for all institutions, including the medical profession, major companies, organized labor, and the various branches of national government. Among the latter, the Supreme Court declined from a 51 percent expression of public confidence to 28 percent in the six-year period. The Senate and House of Representatives were supported by only half as many respondents in 1972: 21 percent for both houses of Congress versus 42 percent in 1966. Support

for the executive branch declined from 41 percent to 27 percent. This declining confidence appears to have been accompanied by a growing cynicism among Americans. The percentage of those who agreed with the statement that government is "run by a few big interests" increased from 29 percent in 1964 to 65 percent in 1974.[11] The latter figure can be compared with that of only 27 percent in West Germany who agreed with the statement the same year. Also in 1974, 47 percent of British respondents agreed with the same cynical proposition, a figure approximately midway between those for West Germany and the United States.[12]

Although West Germans are gaining in allegiance and Americans seem to be moving in the direction of disaffection, if not alienation, the evidence for Great Britain is less clear. Cynicism appears to have reached only a moderate level in the evidence just cited, but it is noteworthy that the strong support for the British two-party system, registered in election after election in the 1950s and 1960s, dropped off significantly in the 1970s, both in terms of the votes for the two major parties in elections and in terms of the levels of party identification. As in the United States, increasing numbers of voters, especially young voters, are showing a lack of attachment to the two political parties that have dominated British politics since World War II. However, it should be pointed out that the identification of Britons with the social classes of the industrial era has also declined in postindustrial Great Britain. Loss of party identification can be partially explained by the fact that the two political parties, Labour and Conservative, are strongly associated in the public mind with the manual and nonmanual classes of the industrial social order.[13]

It is possible that the British have recently withdrawn specific support from their political elites, at least to an extent; it is not so certain that the same can be said of the diffuse support that had accumulated in Great Britain over centuries of gradual political development.[14] Surveys have shown that the British still support the institution of the monarchy in overwhelming numbers, something that cannot be said of any of the American political institutions, including the presidency and the Supreme Court. However, British respondents also acknowledge that the monarch has little power, so that the appropriate American analogue might be a purely symbolic feature of the American political system, such as the flag or the Washington Monument.

More to the point, perhaps, is the continued support in Great Britain for the system of law and for the obligation of the citizen to obey the law. Higher percentages of British respondents, in a 1979 survey, were willing to give approval to police using force against illegal demonstrations than was true of American or West German respondents.[15] One comparative study of teenagers in London and Boston found satisfaction with the political system to be higher among British young people, but expectations of democratic performance to be lower. Perhaps Britons are less alienated because they have not demanded as much responsiveness from their political system as have Americans.[16] To repeat, it appears that specific support has declined in recent years but that the stock of diffuse support, built up over a long period of time, has scarcely been depleted, despite the waning of British power in the world and the country's dismal economic record of recent decades.

Almond and Verba found a substantial degree of alienation and cynicism among their Italian respondents in 1959. This fit the stereotypes that most observers shared in viewing the Italian political culture of the time. During the 1960s, with the Italian economy booming, attitude surveys revealed more positive assessments, especially in policy-related areas, such as jobs, housing, and income. The political system

seemed to be gaining its share of popular credit for improving well-being in Italy. But the 1970s brought a reversal in this trend. In 1971, only 17.5 percent of an Italian national sample agreed with the statement that "there is something basically wrong with the social and political system." By 1974, the percentage had risen to 34.6. In 1975, more than 77 percent of respondents assigned to government great responsibility for solving problems in the fields of jobs, crime prevention, and inflation. Less than 18 percent evaluated government performance positively in any of these areas. It is unlikely that evaluations have improved in the years since 1975. Still, as Joseph LaPalombara has emphasized, political cynicism is worn as a sort of badge of honor by Italians. One wonders how seriously it should be taken.[17]

In light of the evidence from the United States, Great Britain, and Italy, the West German case seems all the more striking. It is difficult to escape the impression that economic success can engender and help sustain political support, whereas poor or mediocre economic performance can have the opposite effect. Especially when one considers the disastrous earlier German experiment with democracy, the Weimar Republic, does the West German case seem significant. Generalizations about the German national character have long stressed the tendency of the German people to accept authority unquestioningly as a civic obligation. The early attitude surveys taken after the establishment of the Federal Republic of Germany indicated that the acceptance of the authority of the state, its laws, and the actions of its official state agents—bureaucrats and the police—did not necessarily mean a strong attachment to the existing political leadership found in the governing and opposition parties. More recent studies have found that not only are the governmental institutions of the Federal Republic accepted today, but the phenomenon of competing political parties, always viewed with ambiguity at best, has now become an accepted feature of the institutional framework.[18]

France: Allegiance or Alienation?

In the case of France, the fact that Almond and Verba did not include that country in their study deprives us of a similar baseline for comparing today's political culture with that of thirty years ago. Nor have French scholars been preoccupied with asking the same kinds of questions about political culture as have students of American, British, and West German political cultures. There is some evidence regarding attitudes toward the two most recent political regimes that have prevailed in France—the Fourth and Fifth Republics. As in West Germany and, briefly during the 1960s, in Italy, evaluations of the new French regime improved swiftly during the economic boom years of the 1960s.[19] French citizens assess the Fifth Republic instituted by General Charles de Gaulle more positively than they do its predecessor, but the disparity is in no way as striking as that between West German evaluations of the Weimar and Bonn republics.[20]

Students of French political culture have focused a great deal of their attention on French attitudes toward authority, viewed in the abstract and studied in a variety of settings, such as offices of large bureaucratic organizations and classrooms at various educational levels.[21] The prevailing view is that most of the French are ambivalent toward authority, whether it be found in their more immediate small-group experiences or as they view the authority of their political leaders and the state. There is a strong distaste for manifestations of authority that are experienced at too close range. The French reputedly have an abhorrence of face-to-face contact with those who hold authority over them. They prefer that authority remain impersonal and distant and that they be expected to adhere

to formal rules that apply equally to all in the same situation as well as that allow them a maximum of freedom to assert their own individuality within the framework established by these rules. If authority becomes too immediate and oppressive, the French may well rebel against rules that they consider arbitrary or unjust. The rebellion may be covert, taking the form of surreptitious noncompliance with the rules—as in the case of tax fraud or of students ridiculing teachers behind their backs—or it may take a more overt and collective form—as in 1968, when tens of thousands of French men and women discovered, almost spontaneously, a common resentment against the authority of the French state and went on a collective strike that eventually evaporated as suddenly as it had formed, once the pent-up resentment had been sufficiently vented.

The other side of this ambivalence is a need for order and a fear of chaos that will be reasserted when rebellion against authority threatens to get out of hand. General de Gaulle is said to have fit the French expectation of authority especially well, in that he was an aloof, aristocratic figure, preferring Delphic generalities to specific commands. It was reassuring that de Gaulle was *there*, as living proof that the capacity of the state to maintain law and order was intact; and it was especially comforting in that de Gaulle did not appear to be making excessive demands on his people to achieve goals of *his* choosing, goals that they as individuals had not chosen for themselves. His grand designs tended to be directed outward toward the leaders of other countries, especially the superpowers and his European neighbors. His people could watch his maneuvers, as they would watch a spectator sport or the performance of a great actor, without feeling any obligation being thrust on them, other than the obligation to admire. Contrast this style of leadership with that of John F. Kennedy, which was better attuned to the

American culture. Kennedy said, "Ask not what your country can do for you; ask what you can do for your country." At the same time in history, de Gaulle was saying, in effect: Ask not what you can do for France; observe and be proud of what de Gaulle does for France.

French ambivalence toward authority is also related to a tendency, as in Germany, to disassociate the state from the current political regime.[22] In the French case, the concepts of state and nation are intermingled. Throughout the many successive political regimes that France has experienced since the French Revolution of 1789, the state has remained relatively intact, meaning that the bureaucracy, the courts, the army, and the diplomatic corps have not experienced great upheaval, whatever has happened at the political level. The state, with its permanent bureaucratized institutions housed in their elegant old buildings, is the living proof of the nation's permanence. By contrast, state and nation for West Germans cannot be so readily equated. Whatever its historic meaning as a geographic and cultural expression, Germany did not exist until 1871; its boundaries were subject to radical fluctuation between 1918 and 1945. Thereafter, what was left of its former territory was divided into two separate states fashioned on rival political and social philosophies. With the removal of physical barriers between the two Germanies in November 1989, we again see the territorial question attaining a predominant place on the political agenda on both sides of Germany. Although the West Germans continue to feel a strong sense of civic obligation to obey the commands of the state and do not feel the same sense of ambivalence toward the state's authority as do the French, there is not the same confidence in the state's permanence. Had support been withdrawn from the Bonn Republic (the political regime), one could not have predicted with confidence that there would not be a convulsion affecting the

structure and authority of the West German state and threatening the viability of West Germany as a political entity. Should support for the French Fifth Republic be withdrawn, on the other hand, the institutions of the state would likely survive without difficulty even if a Sixth Republic came into being.

In fact, the question of regime support is at the heart of the issue of how German reunification should take place. Those who, like West German chancellor Helmut Kohl, believe that East Germany should simply "join" the existing Federal Republic (FRG), are asserting that the FRG is an established, legitimate regime, whereas the East German regime (the German Democratic Republic) is not. Those who, like West German opposition leader Oskar Lafontaine, would prefer the creation of a new all-German regime with a new constitution, agree that the East German regime lacks popular support; but they believe that, for a reunited Germany to be established on a secure basis, the existing FRG must be replaced with a constitutionally based regime that will be designed from the outset to be permanent, which the FRG was not. Only then can the new regime begin to accumulate the support of both East and West Germans that will eventually evolve into support of the diffuse kind. (See the Postscript at the end of Chapter 7 for a more extended discussion of German reunification).

Attitudes toward Political Participation

Earlier Findings

The second aspect of political culture that concerns us is the question: How do people feel about themselves—ordinary citizens—as political actors? Much of the Almond and Verba study was directed toward answering the question: Do people believe that they—as ordinary citizens—can influence the decisions made by those in power? This question taps people's perceptions of the way political power is, in fact, distributed. Such perceptions may not actually be correct. People may naively feel that they have a greater share of power than they in fact have, or they may be overly cynical, believing that power is concentrated in fewer hands than it really is. But whether their perceptions are correct or not, they are of interest because they can help predict the way people will act. It is likely that citizens who believe they have access to the political system would be more apt to try to do something about a political situation they regard as unfavorable. On the other hand, citizens who cynically detach themselves from a political system they believe is rigged against them would be more likely to ignore opportunities that may actually be available to them.

To answer this, Almond and Verba asked their respondents questions designed to discover levels of what they called *civic competence*. The citizen who feels competent is one who believes he or she actually has the capacity to influence government decisions. Almond and Verba asked whether the individual, if confronted with an unjust national regulation, felt

he or she could do something about it.[23] Table 3.2 presents the percentages who responded affirmatively to this question about both a nationally and a locally imposed regulation. Intercountry differences are not particularly great on the question of local decisions, but the differences are striking at the national level. Clearly, more Americans and Britons felt they were competent to influence national decisions than did West Germans or Italians.

Almond and Verba made certain judgments on the basis of the response patterns to their whole array of questions.[24] They found that the Italians were highly distrustful of one another, were preoccupied with self-protection, and were dubious that the government can be enlisted to help them.[25] They believe that government is run by the few in the interest of the few; democracy is an illusion. Therefore, why not accept the fact and live with it? Italians find they can get along most comfortably in life if they let the politicans worry about politics while they worry about the welfare of their family. In this way, Italians avoid disappointment; therefore, their cynicism may be of positive value for them psychologically.

Almond and Verba made a more complex judgment of West German political culture. They observed what they called political detachment

Table 3.2 Percentage of Respondents Who Said They Could Do Something about an Unjust Local or National Regulation (by Nation)

Country	Can Do Something about Local Regulation	Can Do Something about National Regulation
United States	77%	75%
Great Britain	78	62
West Germany	62	38
Italy	51	28
Mexico	52	38

(*Source*) Gabriel A. Almond and Sidney Verba, *The Civic Culture: Political Attitudes and Democracy in Five Nations* (Princeton, N.J.: Princeton University Press, 1963), p. 185. Reprinted with permission of Princeton University Press.

and subject competence among the West Germans.[26] Voter turnout is high in West Germany, and Almond and Verba found that the West Germans were more knowledgeable about politics than were their respondents in the other countries. But they also found that the Germans were more preoccupied with economic than with political matters. Voting is seen as a civic obligation, and keeping informed about political matters is only prudent for people in a country that has undergone such drastic political upheavals in this century. But Almond and Verba's study shows that a majority of West Germans in 1960 did not feel particularly competent to influence political events, and there was no majority who even felt one ought to try. The conclusion is that, although the West Germans were not necessarily antidemocratic, they had not yet internalized truly democratic norms and values. On the other hand, it appeared that they felt themselves competent as *subjects*, that is, as consumers of the goods and services provided by government. Relatively large percentages of West Germans trusted government administrators and the police to treat them fairly. Apparently, the professional traditions of these officials could be relied on as a protective device against arbitrary official behavior, despite the inclination of the German people not to exercise effective popular control.

To characterize Great Britain and the United States, Almond and Verba coined the term *civic culture*.[27] A civic culture is a political culture in which citizens value popular participation in political affairs and an equal distribution of political power, but where they are sufficiently content with the political system that they have no motivation to participate very actively in politics. Most of the time they prefer to leave politics to their leaders, the specialists. Almond and Verba found that the British were more passive than the Americans, but the differences were not great; therefore, they labeled the former

a *deferential* civic culture and the latter a *participant* civic culture. In both cases, the commitment to democracy was strong enough to ensure that the political system would operate essentially as a democracy; but the commitment was not so strong that large numbers of people would be constantly intervening in the decision-making process, overloading the normal channels and threatening to destabilize the system. Almond and Verba felt that the civic culture is a solid underpinning for stable democracy. The future of democracy seemed more certain in Great Britain and the United States than it did in West Germany and Italy.

What about France, which was not included in the five-nation study? Students of French political culture are generally agreed that the French tend to be cynical (like the Italians) about the extent to which France is indeed a democracy.[28] In 1969, a survey was taken in France that asked a number of questions similar to those in the Almond–Verba study. Among these, the respondents were asked if they agreed with the following statement: "The people decide how the country shall be run through the vote." The percentage of the French who responded positively (58 percent) was lower than that for any of the five Almond–Verba countries, in which the percentages ranged from 83 percent (Great Britain) to 62 percent (Italy).[29]

More Recent Findings

Once again, we must ask whether attitudes in the various countries have changed in the years since the Almond–Verba study. If we take the idea that these countries have since entered or are now entering the postindustrial era, we might expect certain changes to have occurred. Russell J. Dalton has called attention to certain socioeconomic changes associated with postindustrialism that might suggest a growth of participant orientations: (1) The growth of gov-

99

ernment involvement in society since the middle of the twentieth century has increased citizens' awareness of the importance of government's decisions for their lives. (2) The growth of the service sector and the expansion of educational opportunities has meant that more persons rely on their intellectual skills in their occupational lives, which may mean that more have developed the capacity to analyze public affairs and make their own judgments. (3) The last point has been reinforced by improvements in the flow of information between citizens, through the growth of voluntary associations and the availability of electronic means of storing, retrieving, and communicating information. (4) New issues have arisen involving ordinary citizens more directly, a point that is developed later in this chapter. Dalton has reviewed the findings of various recent studies of political participation and has concluded that the amount of change that has occurred since 1959–60 depends on the country examined and the type of political participation one has in mind.[30]

Three of the countries Almond and Verba examined—the United States, Great Britain, and West Germany—were included in a more recent five-nation study in which the focus of attention was on popular attitudes toward political participation. The international team of researchers who conducted the study in the mid-1970s was headed by an American, Samuel Barnes, and a West German, Max Kaase.[31] The Barnes–Kaase team conducted surveys in the Netherlands and Austria as well as the United States, Great Britain, and West Germany. An important feature of this study was to answer those critics of Almond and Verba who stated that they had paid insufficient attention to modes of political participation often considered *unconventional*. Activities such as demonstrations, unofficial strikes, boycotts, and sit-ins had not been prevalent in the late 1950s, and, in neglecting to inquire into popular attitudes toward these less

common modes of behavior, Almond and Verba's study rapidly became outdated as the instances of unconventional participation multiplied during the 1960s and 1970s.

Many of the questions Barnes and Kaase asked differed from those that Almond and Verba had posed, but, in some cases, comparison of the two time periods is possible. Regarding conventional modes of participation, Barnes and Kaase asked what types of activities respondents actually had engaged in, such as attending public meetings, contacting public officials, or trying to convince friends to vote in particular ways. Leaving aside those respondents who had done no more than read about politics in newspapers or discuss politics with friends in a neutral fashion, we find the percentages for the more active respondents listed in Table 3.3.

In 1974, when the Barnes–Kaase survey was administered, Americans still rated at the top of the scale in political participation, at least of the conventional type. But the British no longer ranked higher than the West Germans—quite the contrary. As in the case of the allegiance/alienation dimension, democratically relevant attitudes have increased in West Germany. Table 3.3 also suggests that today the West Germans rank high among Western Europeans in their propensity to employ conventional modes of

Table 3.3 Conventional Political Participants

Country	Percent
United States	42%
West Germany	28
Austria	21
Netherlands	20
Great Britain	16

(*Source*) Samuel H. Barnes et al., *Political Action: Mass Participation in Five Western Democracies* (Beverly Hills: Sage, 1979), p. 85. Copyright © 1979 by Sage Publications, Inc.

participation. At least in northwestern Europe, the British political culture now appears to rank among the least participant.

A similar impression is gained if we look at the Barnes–Kaase findings on civic competence. The Almond–Verba study found the United States, Great Britain, and West Germany to rank first, second, and third, respectively, in both local and national civic competence. Table 3.4 displays percentages for both 1959–60 and 1974 for these three countries as well as percentages for 1974 for the Netherlands and Austria. The rankings for local competence have changed, with West Germany replacing Great Britain in second place. The rankings for national competence remain the same. But it is noteworthy that the gap between West Germany and the Anglo-Saxon countries has narrowed markedly. Civic competence has increased among West Germans at the local level, whereas it has declined among the British at both levels and among Americans at the local level, but not at the national level.[32]

When Barnes and Kaase asked their respondents about unconventional modes of political participation, they shifted the focus from activities in which respondents *had* engaged to those in which they *would* engage given proper stimulus. The principal dividing line was between legal activities considered unconventional, such as legal demonstrations and boycotts, and activities that were illegal as well as unorthodox, such as rent strikes. In terms of the percentages of those who said they would engage in the illegal type of activity, the ranking of the United States, West Germany, and Great Britain remained the same (in that order); the only change was the rise of the Netherlands from fourth to first place (tied with the United States), with 46 percent of the respondents willing to engage in at least one of the illegal activities (compared with 31 percent in West Germany and 30 percent in Britain.[33]

Reviewing these and similar findings, Russell Dalton poses two competing explanations for the rise of unconventional participation in these industrialized polyarchies. The first is that there has been a rise of dissatisfaction with the performance of these political systems on the part of disadvantaged and alienated persons, that is, a decline in allegiance and a rise in alienation. As we have seen, the evidence for this on a cross-national basis is mixed, appearing stronger, or at least more consistent, in the United States than in Western Europe up to the beginning of the 1980s. But, when the corre-

Table 3.4   Percentage of Respondents Who Said They Could Do Something about an Unjust or Harmful Local Regulation or National Law, 1959–60 and 1974

Country	Local Regulation		National Law	
	1959–60	1974	1959–60	1974
Netherlands	—%	62%	—%	43%
Great Britain	78	64	62	57
United States	77	71	75	78
West Germany	62	67	38	56
Austria	—	43	—	33

(*Source*) Samuel H. Barnes et al., *Political Action: Mass Participation in Five Western Democracies* (Beverly Hills: Sage, 1979), p. 141. Copyright © 1979 by Sage Publications, Inc.

lates of unconventional participation are examined on an individual level, it is seen that unconventional participants tend to be more highly educated and younger than conventional participants. This suggests the validity of a second thesis, according to Dalton. It may be that the boundary lines between conventional and unconventional participation are shifting, and at least some of what was considered unconventional for an older (and less well educated) generation is considered conventional by those who have reached adulthood since the Almond–Verba study, given their own experiences.[34] We examine further evidence to support this interpretation at the end of this chapter.

Italy and France

In the past (as noted earlier), the Italian and French political cultures have not seemed to have as heavy an incidence of participant orientation as has been the case with the other countries we are examining. Earlier studies focused primarily on conventional modes of participation. It is clear that France and Italy have been among those European countries in which the rise of unconventional, including illegal and even violent, political activity has been most striking since the late 1960s. However, speculation that the Italians rate high in propensity for unconventional activity is belied by a survey taken in 1975 in which Italians were asked whether they would engage in various forms of activity. Violent forms were overwhelmingly repudiated, and, at most, only about 20 to 25 percent of respondents indicated a willingness, in theory, to engage in any illegal activities.[35] This can be compared with the figure of 30 percent that Barnes and Kaase found for Great Britain and West Germany. It must be remembered that Italy is a Catholic country. Despite strong support for the Italian Communist Party (PCI), a great many Italians are taught by the

church and at home to respect the authority of the established government and the police who enforce its laws. This is especially true because the established government is primarily in the hands of the Christian Democratic Party and, therefore, enjoys the church's blessing. It is even likely that many communist voters would disdain illegal activity. The PCI has become an established part of the structure of political institutions in Italy, and communist leaders have little desire to see those institutions rocked by widespread acts of defiance of the state's authority, as they have demonstrated in condemning terrorist acts and in seeking to discourage unauthorized strikes in industrial disputes.

What we might call the theory of French political culture suggests that the typical Frenchman or -woman, ambivalent about established authority, will avoid conventional modes of participation approved by those in authority and potentially involving face-to-face contact. They will avoid such contact with the authorities themselves and with other like-minded citizens in any organized context in which the legitimacy of the authorities is mutually acknowledged.

Although France is officially a Catholic country, nonbelievers and lukewarm Catholics are found with greater frequency there than in Italy. Thus, the restraining hand of the church and Catholic family are less likely to inhibit attitudes toward unconventional participation in France. The other side of the coin is that the French would not be expected to engage in sustained, organized protest. Their ambivalence toward authority would mean oscillation between periods of intense antagonism and periods in which the desire for order and predictability would return. The tendency of French leftist groups toward endless internal bickering and splintering into innumerable offshoots would be an expression of the reputed French disdain for long-term stability in relations with peers as well as with those in authority. However, the success of the French Socialist Party (PS) in channeling youthful energies into the successful campaigns of the 1981 presidential and legislative elections challenges these speculations. More of the French may today be gaining respect for, and confidence in, conventional modes of political action.

Japanese Political Culture

Until now we have deliberately left the Japanese political culture out of consideration. This is because the Japanese have a system of social values and norms that differs markedly from that typically found in Western countries. Whereas Western value systems are predominantly individualistic in nature, that of Japan, like other Asian countries, is essentially collectivistic. This means that the very question of whether the Japanese are allegiant or alienated toward their political system lacks cognitive meaning, if, as we have done so far, it is thought of in an individualistic sense (i.e., in the sense of the relationship between the individual and the state). To the Japanese, individuals are a part of a social order that is hierarchical and all-encompassing. Given centuries of isolation from the rest of the world, this society is viewed by its members much as is an extended family in agrarian societies[36]—and, remember, Japan was an agrarian society until early in this century. Holders of authority in the state are seen as the natural leaders of this extended family, and challenges to their authority are unthinkable, not because authority holders are considered to be always right, but because the individual is not an autonomous actor who can counterpose his or her judgment against them.

In smaller social settings, as in the immediate family, the neighborhood, or the workplace, conflicts do occur, but they tend to be resolved in favor of the views held by those in positions of power and authority within the group. Appeals to the seniority or higher social status of the stronger person will suffice to remove the substance of the weaker person's disagreement.[37] Yet traditionally, or during the centuries of isolation and feudalism, conflict among different groups within Japan were frequent and often cataclysmic. As Japan became more vulnerable to the rest of the world from the sixteenth century onward, her leaders made great efforts to draw society together into a tightly knit defensive posture. Individuals, families, towns, and other groups within society were expected to defer to the common interest as defined by society's rulers. But the potential for explosive group conflict existed just below the surface, making it imperative for individuals, when dealing with other persons from other parts of society, to subordinate individual needs to social needs and thus to stifle potential conflict voluntarily.[38] In our terms, the Japanese concept of respect involves the desire for respect for one's group rather than for one's self as an individual. Or, perhaps better put, Japanese self-respect is dependent on how well one believes one has conformed to group expectations—that is, how well one has earned the respect of the group.

The Japanese, therefore, are group-oriented rather than self-oriented[39] to such an extent that questions about their own sense of political efficacy can have little meaning to them unless there is a group reference. The company for which they work might be such a reference, and the individual may rely on the company-as-group, and of course the executives of that company, to promote his or her interests as an employee in the political arena. Individual Japanese with strong objections about aspects of Japanese life, such as conservationists concerned about the threat of population pressure on the natural habitats of migratory birds, will feel politically efficacious only as members of organizations committed to their goals. But if the organization takes on the character of a community of persons with strong dedication to the cause, its members may be capable of employing unconventional means of participation at great potential risk to themselves as individuals, subordinating what we might consider to be their own personal interests to the needs of the group as defined by the group's leaders. If asked an abstract survey question such as "Could you do something about an unjust law?" the individual Japanese would be less likely than the Westerner to give a positive answer yet be more willing than the Westerner to engage in self-sacrifice on behalf of a collective objective. Had Japan been included in the original Almond–Verba study or, for that matter, the more recent study by Barnes and Kaase, it is difficult to say what the results would have been, because the questions asked and the categories employed grow out of Western political science preoccupations.

Nevertheless, Japan has experienced the same social and economic trends that were discussed as postindustrial phenomena in the preceding chapter and that Dalton argues are bringing about changes in Western political cultures. We consider certain accompanying features of postindustrial political culture that have been hypothesized by political scientists such as Dalton and Ronald Inglehart in the final section of this chapter and return to the question of whether Japanese political culture has any traits that liken it to the political cultures of other advanced industrial countries.

Factors Underlying Political Participation

The differences among our Western European countries with respect to the dimensions of conventional and unconventional participation do not stand out as clearly as do those on the allegiance/alienation dimension. A possible explanation may be that there are underlying factors that account for attitudes toward participation essentially in the same ways in all of our countries. For example, Almond and Verba found that civic competence increased in all countries with level of education. Citizens with university-level educations, for example, would be more likely than those who had not completed secondary education to display civic competence, regardless of whether they were American, German, or Italian.

Demographic Factors

In point of fact, the relationship between level of education and political participation is one of the most consistent findings in the research on political culture.[40] Studies have also found that it is a stronger predictor of political participation than are indicators of social class, such as occupation and family income. The consistent finding that level of education is the strongest predictor of political participation can be explained in terms of the heightened awareness and understanding of politics that the student gains at the higher levels of education. Alternatively, it may reflect a higher personal investment and stake in a system that can be influenced by political participation.

Other possible predictors of political participation are gender, age, and religion. Of the three, Barnes and Kaase found that gender was the most strongly related to conventional political participation. Age and religion bore little or no relationship to conventional participation, although there was a tendency for participation to increase with age, only to level off in the oldest age brackets. In all five countries, men were more likely to participate through normal channels than were women, but the difference was greatest in West Germany, least in the United States. This suggests that one aspect of the greater liberation of women in the United States is their greater involvement in politics, whereas the gap between West German men and women remains relatively wide.

With respect to unconventional participation, age assumes an importance at least equal to that of education. In fact, in the United States, Great Britain, and West Germany, age was a somewhat better predictor of attitudes toward unconventional participation than was education. The relationship is a negative one in the case of age; that is, the older the individual, the less likely he or she is to favor unconventional participation. The relationship between education and unconventional participation is a positive one; that is, the higher the educational level, the greater the inclination toward unconventional participation. Gender and religion showed some relationship to unconventional participation, but the correlations are weaker than in the cases of age and education. Men are slightly more likely than women to favor protest activity. Those who have no religious belief or little intensity of belief (whatever their religion) are somewhat more likely than the more intensely religious to favor unconventional participation.

Political Socialization

The strong relationship between level of education and conventional political participation is a standard finding that we should expect on the basis of common sense. But that the social category most likely to engage in unconventional activities is that of younger people with higher levels of education would not have been so self-evident before the era of the campus protests of the 1960s and 1970s. Those with higher levels of education would have been expected to display a greater appreciation for the beneficial qualities of the democratic political system because they were the very people who had benefited most from the educational opportunities provided by that system and could also command the other values that education can bring. Because young people were typically less likely than their elders to participate in conventional ways, it might also have been expected that they would not show a penchant for unconventional participation. Nor did many students in either the United States or Western Europe spend much time protesting perceived political injustices before the mid-1960s.

When the student rebellions began, the older generation was hard pressed to understand the new phenomenon. These young people certainly were not behaving in ways taught them by their parents. Young people participating in demonstrations and university sit-ins, on the other hand, could not comprehend the lack of comprehension on the part of their parents. Observers of this new dimension of political conflict in the First World—parents versus children—began to speak of a generation gap.

Concern about a generation gap came at about the same time that political scientists were exploring an area of research that was new to them and that they conceived to be closely related to the study of political culture. The study of *political socialization* is the study of the ways in which political orientations are transmitted from generation to generation through the mediation of institutions in which older people communicate with younger people. Especially noteworthy among these institutions are the family, the school, and the media of communication. Something seemed to be happening in Western society that was interfering with traditional lines of communication between the generations. The same sort of break in continuity was being observed in studies of political socialization in Third World countries, but it was to be expected there, given the fact that such countries were undergoing rapid modernization. What students of political socialization in the First World in the 1950s and early 1960s failed to recognize was that rapid change was occurring in the First World as well, and that it was affecting the perceptions the younger generation held of their elders and of the institutions in which the authority of the older generation had always prevailed. The family, the school, and the political system were becoming arenas of conflict that centered around the question of the right of the older generation to command the obedience of the younger generation. It was a conflict between the power asserted by the older people as their right and the respect demanded by younger people as their right. What has been happening to the process of political socialization in Western Europe during this era of institutional change?

If we begin with the traditional role played by the primary socializer—the family—we are struck immediately with the more authoritarian nature of the family in our three continental European countries than in Great Britain or the United States. Almond and Verba found a higher percentage of Britons and Americans than of West Germans or Italians who (1) remembered having had an influence in family decisions as children, (2) remembered being free to protest family decisions, and (3) remembered that they had actually protested family decisions on occasion.[41] In the past, the typical European (non-British) family was dominated by the father, whereas the father and mother played (and continue to play) more equal roles in family decision making in the United States. The latter is also true among British middle-class families. However, in the British working class, the father was an authoritarian figure, although he was traditionally absent when it came to bringing up the children. Thus, the mother played a greater role by default. The resulting authority pattern was probably more ambiguous than that found in a working-class family on the Continent.

Traditionally, authority patterns learned in the family served as models as the child grew up. If he or she had experienced the father having the final decision-making responsibility and had been used to obeying these decisions without question, the child would assume this pattern to be normal and, thus, expect to find it in later-life situations. In this connection, European (including British) school systems were more authoritarian than the American, as the Almond–Verba study documented.[42] The authority of the teacher was absolute. In French schools, the child learned certain principles by rote and was then expected to reproduce them to the teacher's satisfaction. If the child failed, the teacher might call on the ridicule of the other children as a means of reinforcing the expectation.[43] In Italy and in parts of France and West Germany, religious instruction in the public schools or instruction in church schools added the absolute authority structure of the Catholic Church to an already authoritarian pedagogical system.

Once again, it should be pointed out that the Almond–Verba surveys were conducted thirty years ago. In the meantime, important changes have taken place in Western Europe, some of which were discussed in Chapter 2. A decrease in family size has made it more likely that the wife will work at least part of the time to supplement the family income. This increases her status within the family and gives her a stronger voice in the family decision-making process. With a more pluralistic family power structure, the children are not so overwhelmed that they cannot exert influence, especially as they grow older. The schools have been doing a certain amount of experimentation in curriculum development and teaching methods, often along American lines. West Germany has gone especially far in this direction. Ever since the Allied

Occupation, a concerted effort has been made to democratize the educational system with respect to both the authority patterns within the schools and the explicit content of the teaching.[44] German children are given a much more extensive civics education than are British, French, or Italian children, and the content is often of a superior quality to what can typically be found in American schools. A recent study has shown a marked increase in the past two decades in the tendency of West Germans to discuss politics with one another. It is true of all generations, but the tendency of West Germans born after World War II to discuss politics is substantially greater than is that of their elders. The advent of television as well as quantitative and qualitative educational improvements have helped bring about this change.[45]

As in the case of West Germany, the American occupiers of Japan after World War II paid considerable attention to the structure and content of the educational system, with the explicit objective of changing what had been an authoritarian structure and a traditional content. From the time of the Meiji Restoration, Japanese educational authorities had wrestled with the problem of how to control the process of psychological modernization of the Japanese so that modern technology could be learned while traditional Japanese values would not be swept aside in favor of subversive Western value systems. What steps were taken in the late nineteenth and early twentieth centuries to liberalize education were reversed during the decade preceding World War II, as nationalism and emperor worship were reinforced in the school curricula. Any teacher who believed that children should gain the capacity to think through public issues on their own and participate in the political process was stifled.[46]

The American occupation of Japan from 1945 to 1951 failed in several of its objectives to democratize Japanese education. Control over the West German educational system became decentralized in the hands of the state (*Länder*) governments, thus permitting a certain amount of educational pluralism to develop. Despite the wishes of the Occupation authorities to decentralize Japanese education, it reemerged with control over curriculum concentrated in the hands of the central Ministry of Education. This has meant that the conservative politicians who have ruled at the center have made sure that the traditional values retained their place. Although General MacArthur had hoped, probably unrealistically, that the school system would adhere to the Western liberal principle of separation of church and state, traditional religious values still form part of what the students learn today. Perhaps most important, the Japanese teenager lives under what could almost be called a totalitarian regime of preparation for state examinations that will determine his or her future, with much more time spent on studies both inside and outside school than is true of students in Western countries. Much of the time spent involves rote learning; it does not involve much consideration and discussion of controversial ideas.[47] These conditions have persisted in postindustrial Japan, such that one wonders whether the impact of education on participant orientations in Western countries is reproduced there.

There is evidence in political socialization studies to suggest that postindustrial society, with its higher levels of education and increased media exposure of young people, is witnessing the declining political influence of traditional political socializing agencies, especially the family and the political party.[48] As was noted in Chapter 2, the industrial maturity link between family, social class, and party identification has been breaking down in the past decade or so in Western Europe. It is possible that these long-standing agents of political attitude shaping have become weaker as well. British political scientist Dennis Kavanagh argues that people in Western societies have become more adept at "determining their own political attitudes" based on the wide array of conflicting messages about politics that reach them from many directions, and that attitudes are less likely than once was the case to fit neatly into predictable patterns along class and party lines. Thus, the likelihood that two individuals, one of whom is allegiant and the other alienated politically, will be from predictable social backgrounds—the one from a middle-class family and pursuing a professional career, the other growing up in a working-class family and holding down a blue-collar job—is less today than it was a generation ago, just as it is less likely that the one will vote to the right and the other to the left.[49]

Kavanagh sides with the "recency" side of the "primacy versus recency" argument among students of political socialization. That is to say, he feels that political attitudes are more likely to be shaped by influences experienced in one's adult life than by those in childhood and adolescence. Earlier influences may still show up in today's attitudes, but the individual is not foreordained as a political thinker by the beliefs that prevailed in the family and neighborhood where he or she was raised. More people are exposed to information and ideas about politics today in a way that does not reinforce attitudes learned early in life. Or perhaps the attitudes learned earlier in life are not as clear and consistent as they tended to be before the arrival of the mass media, such that the recent adult is freer than were his or her parents to choose among a variety of ways of thinking about and reacting to political stimuli.[50]

The Value Gap

What has brought about the generation gap? Why has it manifested itself in an expanded

repertory of political participation modes? An answer to these questions was implied in the preceding section. In making it more explicit, we draw on the work of American political scientist Ronald Inglehart, who has examined the changing structure of values in First World countries.[51]

Inglehart has been interested in whether the affluence and relative security of postindustrial society has shifted people's value preferences from a preoccupation with getting on in daily life to more abstract, less mundane values. In our terms, this would mean a shift from the values of well-being and power to those of enlightenment and respect. He hypothesized that older citizens, having experienced the Great Depression and World War II, would be more concerned with maintaining a healthy economy, as well as domestic and international order. Younger citizens would see less value in such things because they had experienced them all their lives. Instead, they would be concerned with expanding the scope of individual expression, both politically and in their personal lives. Table 3.5 indicates that Inglehart's expectations were essentially borne out by the findings. In all five of the countries included in the table, the percentage of respondents exhibiting what he called *materialistic* values increases as one moves to successively older age categories (cohorts), whereas the percentage of his respondents exhibiting *postmaterialist* values declines.[52] The same was true of the five smaller countries included in his study—Belgium, the Netherlands, Luxembourg, Denmark, and Ireland.

Table 3.5 also reveals several differences among the larger countries. For one thing, the range of percentages from younger to older respondents is greater for three of the countries—West Germany, France, and Italy—than it is for the other two—the United States and Great Britain. Inglehart explained this by citing events that caused a greater generation

Table 3.5 Value Type by Age Cohort in Five Countries, 1972–73 (Percentage of Each Country's Respondents in Each Age Cohort)

Ages	West Germany		France		Italy		U.S.		Great Britain	
	Mat.*	P-M†	Mat.	P-M	Mat.	P-M	Mat.	P-M	Mat.	P-M
19–28	24%‡	19%	22%	20%	26%	16%	24%	17%	27%	11%
29–38	39	8	28	17	41	8	27	13	33	7
39–48	46	5	39	9	42	7	34	13	29	6
49–58	50	5	39	8	48	6	32	10	30	7
59–68	52	7	50	3	49	4	37	6	36	5
69+	62	1	55	2	57	5	40	7	37	4
Total point spread across cohorts	38 + 18 = 56		33 + 18 = 51		31 + 11 = 42		16 + 10 = 26		10 + 7 = 17	

(*Source*) Ronald Inglehart, "The Nature of Value Change in Postindustrial Society," in Leon N. Lindberg, ed., *Politics and the Future of Industrial Society* (New York: McKay, 1976), pp. 70–71. Reprinted with permission of Longman Inc.
* Mat. = Materialistic value system.
† P-M = Postmaterialistic value system.
‡ Percentages do not total 100 for each country because of respondents in intermediate categories.

gap in continental Europe than in the Anglo-Saxon countries. World War II was experienced more directly and probably left a greater and more lasting impression on the generations who experienced it in Germany, France, and Italy than on generations in the United States and Great Britain; in addition, postwar economic growth has been more rapid in the former countries than in the latter, suggesting that younger people in the former countries have become as accustomed as younger people in the latter countries to expecting progressive improvement of material conditions.

In addition to his independent research, Inglehart participated in the Barnes–Kaase five-nation study and measured the relationship between his materialism/postmaterialism dimension and the Barnes–Kaase measures of conventional and unconventional political participation. He found a strong association between materialism/postmaterialism and con-ventional/unconventional participation, postmaterialists being more favorably disposed than materialists to protest activity.[53] Extending Inglehart's theory, therefore, we can suggest that the reason younger people are more inclined to protest what they perceive to be wrong in their societies is not that they have a greater sense of material deprivation than do their elders; rather, they are likely to have a different ordering of value priorities. Among those values that they are likely to rank in high position are (1) the value of power, which they believe should be distributed more widely in their societies instead of being concentrated in the hands of the few, especially when the few are apt to be older persons; and (2) the value of respect, which they feel is denied to them to the extent that there are limits placed on their ability to communicate their political beliefs. Material values (well-being) are of lesser concern to them, but this does not mean that they are, for that reason, politically quiescent; quite the contrary. In the case of their parents, the experience of enhanced material well-being had occurred in their formative years. The solidification of these gains remained a principal preoccupation for them as they grew older, and has not completely left them even today. Moreover, in Western Europe, at least, few of them were afforded the opportunity for higher education, something their sons and daughters have had available in much greater numbers. These young persons do not experience material deprivation, but it is possible that the value deprivation they *do* feel is of a greater magnitude than that of their parents.

Although Japan was not included in the earlier Inglehart studies of value change in industrialized countries, there have been surveys undertaken over the years in which similar values were tested with different age groups in the Japanese population, and some of the same questions have been asked in periodically repeated surveys over a number of years. If these have turned up findings similar to those of Inglehart, then we may have reason to wonder whether the group-oriented emphasis that the Japanese political culture puts on the values of power and respect (see the treatment of Japanese political participation, discussed earlier) still holds among the younger generation, which, like the younger generation in Western Europe, is better educated than its elders. Japanese political scientist Nobutaka Ike[54] summarized one series of surveys of Japanese values in which respondents were asked to choose which among several alternatives were their "goals in life." It was found that over a fifteen-year period from 1953 to 1968, the percentage who answered that "work hard and get rich" was one of their major goals had held fairly constant, but that the goal "just lead a life that suits your tastes" had risen in frequency of choice from 21 percent of the respondents in 1953 to 32 percent in 1968. The latter was particularly true of the youngest

cohort of respondents, ages twenty to twenty-four, 34 percent of whom chose this highly "individualistic" value in 1953, while 51 percent did so in 1968.

On the other hand, a very traditional goal— "resist all evils in the world, and live a pure and just life"—had lost favor over time, supported by only 17 percent in 1968, against 29 percent fifteen years earlier. There was some evidence that materialism was receding as in Western Europe. The percentage of respondents who agreed with the proposition that schoolchildren should be taught "that money is the most important thing" had fallen from 65 percent in 1953 to 57 percent in 1968.[55] But what was replacing both traditional values and materialistic values among the youngest generation was individualistic pursuit of self-determined goals, something even the older generation of Western Europeans had taken for granted when they were young. According to Ike, "in Western culture, which has long stressed individualism, youth may seek a sense of belonging, whereas in Japanese culture, which has emphasized the group, youth may yearn for individuation and privatization."[56] Unlike Ike, Scott C. Flanagan believes that what Western youth seek is more complex than this. There is a commitment both to ideal goals and to fulfillment of self.[57] For some Western youth these would be in contradiction with one another; for others the two would be compatible, as in the case of young people who find *self*-fulfillment in the pursuit of "*other*-directed" causes such as the ecology movement espouses.

Among the elements that Inglehart expected to find within a postmaterial value system was an ecological concern, the value of preserving our natural environment for future generations.[58] This might be considered a long-term perspective on the value of well-being, that is, well-being not for the here and now but for the future. Or it might be seen as the assertion of the right of future generations to the same respect generations currently alive are given. For a growing number of First World citizens, ecology is of the utmost importance. The Green Party of West Germany (see Chapter 4) has attained considerable political prominence in the 1980s with a program that features four "pillars": ecology, social responsibility, grassroots democracy, and nonviolence.[59] Of the four, ecology has the widest support among Green Party members, who came together behind this program in 1979–80 from a wide variety of earlier political and ideological loyalties.

The ecological perspective is holistic, in the sense that all things related to life are seen as interconnected and interdependent. This accords with a desire to see the power concentrations of modern states broken down into smaller entities that are closer to the problems of human beings living within their everyday environments. The Greens raise the value of environmental well-being to a higher priority than the values of economic well-being and national security, which, materialists would argue, can only be adequately promoted by the nation-state with power instruments concentrated in the hands of its government. The Greens see a radical divergence between their agenda—which includes nuclear disarmament, governmental decentralization, the ending of sexist exploitation, the controlling of automobile emissions, and elimination of acid rain, nuclear waste, and other forms of pollution—and the agendas of the other political parties that accord such items low priority. Inglehart's terminology has not been part of the Green lexicon, but their arrival on the scene in the 1980s accords generally with his predictions of a decade earlier.

Inglehart's principal study was undertaken in the early 1970s, before the economic difficulties associated with the 1970s had been perceived as a chronic condition of postindustrial society. It has often been observed in more recent years that young people have turned their backs on the idealism of the previous two decades and are showing greater tendencies toward conformity with their elders' expectations because they are concerned with their futures in terms of economic security. In fact, follow-up studies that Inglehart undertook later contained some evidence that postmaterialism had receded among the very youngest age cohort, making them more materialistic than their immediate elders, the Sixties generation.[60] But the differences are slight, and, at any rate, the youngest cohort is less materialistic than are the cohorts of the parents and grandparents of today's teenagers. As we have seen, younger people appear to be less allegiant and more inclined (in all countries) toward protest activity than are their elders.[61]

As we move to the study of political parties and party systems in the next chapter, it is worth noting that Inglehart's theory of value change points to the growth of parties of what are called sometimes "the New Left" or "the New Politics," parties that burst on the scene in the later 1960s and have undergone a series of subgenerational shifts every half-dozen years or so, including the Green phenomenon. Inglehart appears to relegate to his materialist category another new, or perhaps resurgent, political phenomenon—the New Right—which is particularly strong in France, but which has come close to or actually succeeded in capturing control of conservative parties in other countries, notably the United States and Great Britain since the mid-1970s. Yet, as Flanagan has argued, the New Right is not necessarily materialist in the strictly economic sense of the word. Its economic philosophy stresses national self-restraint from material overindulgence in order to achieve longer-term material benefits, in a sense similar, though not identical, to the longer-term view of the Greens.[62] Its stress on moral issues, such as "the right to life" and "law and order" are materialist only in the concept-stretching sense in which Inglehart defines the term. To Flanagan, both the New Left and the New Right are "nonmaterialist" (and, we could add, equally postindustrial) manifestations of the breakdown of early socialization patterns just discussed. This still raises the question of whether different groups in society support the New Left and the New Right or whether adherence to one or the other is essentially a random matter. And it leaves open the further question of why the New Left has taken different forms and achieved different measures of success in different countries, and likewise the New Right. The converse of these questions is: What has been happening to the "Old Left," the "Old Right," and, for that matter, the "Old Center"?

As for Japan, the survey findings that Ike and Flanagan have reviewed leave considerable room for doubt as to whether "New Right" and "New Left" have the same meaning that they do in the West, and even whether such terms have any relevance to Japanese politics. As we shall see, there are still "Old Right" and "Old Left" political parties in Japan, but if younger people are seeking meaning in themselves instead of in large causes—turning away, as Ike suggests, from the traditional loyalty to larger bodies of persons, including especially the family and the nation—then they are becoming apolitical and less available for mobilization on behalf of causes that can be related to these primordial loyalties.

Suggestions for Further Reading

Almond, Gabriel A., and Sidney Verba. *The Civic Culture: Political Attitudes and Democracy in Five Nations* (Princeton, N.J.: Princeton University Press, 1963).

———, eds. *The Civil Culture Revisited* (Boston· Little, Brown, 1980).

Baker, Kendall, et al. *Germany Transformed: Political Culture and the New Politics* (Cambridge, Mass.: Harvard University Press, 1981).

Barnes, Samuel H., et al. *Political Action: Mass Participation in Five Western Democracies* (Beverly Hills: Sage, 1979).

Barzini, Luigi. *The Italians* (New York: Bantam, 1965).

Christopher, Robert C. *The Japanese Mind: The Goliath Explained* (London and Sydney: Pan Books, 1984).

Dalton, Russell J. *Citizen Politics in Western Democracies: Public Opinion and Political Parties in the United States, Great Britain, West Germany, and France* (Chatham, N.J.: Chatham House, 1988).

Dogan, Mattei, ed. *Comparing Pluralist Democracies: Strains on Legitimacy* (Boulder, Colo., and London: Westview, 1988).

Hart, Vivien. *Distrust and Democracy: Political Distrust in Britain and America* (Cambridge: Cambridge University Press, 1978).

Inglehart, Ronald. *The Silent Revolution: Changing Values and Political Styles among Western Publics* (Princeton, N.J.: Princeton University Press, 1977).

Kavanagh, Dennis. *Political Science and Political Behaviour* (London: George Allen & Unwin, 1983).

LaPalombara, Joseph. *Democracy, Italian Style* (New Haven, Conn., and London: Yale University Press, 1987).

Nakane, Chie. *Japanese Society* (Berkeley and Los Angeles: University of California Press, 1972).

Schonfeld, William R. *Obedience and Revolt:* *French Behavior toward Authority* (Beverly Hills: Sage, 1976).

Wylie, Laurence. *Village in the Vaucluse*, 3rd ed. (Cambridge, Mass.: Harvard University Press, 1974).

Zeldin, Theodore. *The French* (London: Fontana, 1984).

Notes

1. Gabriel A. Almond, "Comparative Political Systems," *Journal of Politics* 18 (1956), 391–409.

2. Gabriel A. Almond and G. Bingham Powell, *Comparative Politics: A Developmental Approach* (Boston: Little, Brown, 1966), p. 50.

3. These generalizations are based on direct observations by the author in Western Europe during 1974.

4. Gabriel A. Almond and Sidney Verba, *The Civic Culture: Political Attitudes and Democracy in Five Nations* (Princeton, N.J.: Princeton University Press, 1963).

5. Ibid., p. 102.

6. See the collection of essays in Gabriel A. Almond and Sidney Verba, eds., *The Civic Culture Revisited* (Boston: Little, Brown, 1980). These essays evaluate the Almond–Verba study in light of findings of more recent studies.

7. Ulrich Widmaier, "Tendencies toward an Erosion of Legitimacy," in Mattei Dogan, ed., *Comparing Pluralist Democracies: Strains on Legitimacy* (Boulder, Colo., and London: Westview, 1988), pp. 143–167.

8. Ronald Inglehart shows differences between Western European countries in life satisfaction, relative levels of which remain fairly constant between countries, but political satisfaction levels fluctuate more unpredictably. Ronald Inglehart, *Culture Shift in Advanced Industrial Societies* (Princeton, N.J.: Princeton University Press, 1990), p. 33.

9. David P. Conradt, "Changing German Political Culture," in Almond and Verba, eds., *The Civic Culture Revisited*, p. 230.

10. David Easton, *A Framework for Political Analysis* (Englewood Cliffs, N.J.: Prentice-Hall, 1965), pp. 124–126.

11. Alan I. Abramowitz, "The United States: Political Culture under Stress," in Almond and Verba, eds., *The Civic Culture Revisited*, pp. 189–190.

12. Conradt, "Changing German Political Culture," p. 235.

13. Samuel H. Beer, *Britain against Itself: The Political Contradictions of Collectivism* (New York and London: Norton, 1982), pp. 110–120.

14. Philip Norton, *The British Polity* (New York and London: Longman, 1984), pp. 32–34.

15. Samuel H. Barnes et al., *Political Action: Mass Participation in Five Western Democracies* (Beverly Hills: Sage, 1979), p. 88.

16. Vivien Hart, *Distrust and Democracy: Political Distrust in Britain and America* (Cambridge: Cambridge University Press, 1978), p. 42.

17. Findings reviewed by Giacomo Sani, "The Political Culture of Italy: Continuity and Change," in Almond and Verba, eds., *The Civic Culture Revisited*, pp. 308–310. But see the argument

by Joseph LaPalombara that Italians are critical of their politicians in the same way they are of their football stars and opera singers. They demand perfection in performance and when, rarely in the case of politicians, it is attained, they applaud wildly. This may not be true political alienation. LaPalombara, *Democracy, Italian Style* (New Haven, Conn., and London: Yale University Press, 1987), pp. 88–91.

18. David P. Conradt, *The German Polity*, 3rd ed. (New York and London: Longman, 1986), pp. 55–58.

19. Henry W. Ehrmann, *Politics in France*, 3rd ed. (Boston: Little, Brown, 1976), p. 131.

20. Support for the Fifth Republic no longer is confined to voters on the right, as power passed to the left in the 1980s, and the regime rather easily survived the experience of "cohabitation," or the sharing of power by left and right in the 1986–88 period.

21. See the discussions in Ehrmann, *Politics in France*, Ch. 3; and John S. Ambler, *The Government and Politics of France* (Boston: Houghton Mifflin, 1971), Ch. 3.

22. That is, the political regime may change but the state, as a set of permanent bureaucratic institutions, is seen to carry on unchanged. Americans and Britons do not tend mentally to separate the concepts of state and regime, in part because the two have not been disjoined historically.

23. Almond and Verba, *The Civic Culture*, p. 184.

24. Ibid., pp. 402–414.

25. Ibid., pp. 135–136, 267. See also Edward C. Banfield, *The Moral Basis of a Backward Society* (New York: The Free Press, 1958).

26. Almond and Verba, *The Civic Culture*, pp. 428–439.

27. Ibid., pp. 440–469.

28. A classic analysis is Laurence Wylie, *Village in the Vaucluse*, 3rd ed. (Cambridge, Mass.: Harvard University Press, 1974), pp. 206–239.

29. Ambler, *The Government and Politics of France*, p. 54.

30. Russell J. Dalton, *Citizen Politics in Western Democracies: Public Opinion and Political Parties in the United States, Great Britain, West Germany, and France* (Chatham, N.J.: Chatham House, 1988), Ch. 8.

31. Barnes et al., *Political Action*, pp. 57–94.

32. Some British scholars are highly critical of the concept of civic competence. They argue that negative responses to questions such as those the cross-national studies have posed may reflect negative evaluations about the political system (especially its economic performance), not a weak sense of personal efficacy. This would make the findings of declining allegiance and lower civic competence in Britain consistent with one another. Evidence to support such a contention is at best mixed. See Alan Marsh, *Protest and Political Consciousness* (Beverly Hills: Sage, 1977), Ch. 6; and Hart, op. cit.

33. Barnes et al., *Political Action*, p. 81.

34. Dalton, *Citizen Politics*, pp. 66–70.

35. Sani, "The Political Culture of Italy, p. 306.

36. Robert C. Christopher, *The Japanese Mind: The Goliath Explained* (London and Sydney: Pan Books, 1984), Ch. 2.

37. Mitsuyuki Masatsugu, *The Modern Samurai Society: Duty and Dependency in Contemporary Japan* (New York: American Management Associations, 1982), pp. 77–92.

38. Ibid., pp. 1–9.

39. Chie Nakane, *Japanese Society* (Berkeley and Los Angeles: University of California Press, 1972), Ch. 1.

40. The discussion in this section is drawn from material in Barnes et al., *Political Action*, pp. 97–135.

41. Almond and Verba, *The Civic Culture*, p. 331.

42. Ibid., pp. 332–333.

43. Wylie, *Village in the Vaucluse*, pp. 84–87.

44. See Sidney Verba, "Germany: The Remarking of Political Culture," in Lucien W. Pye and Sidney Verba, eds., *Political Culture and Political Development* (Princeton, N.J.: Princeton University Press, 1981), pp. 130–170.

45. Kendall L. Baker et al., *Germany Transformed: Political Culture and the New Politics* (Cambridge, Mass.: Harvard University Press, 1981), Chs. 2 and 3.

46. J. E. Thomas, *Learning Democracy in Japan: The Social Education of Japanese Adults* (London: Sage, 1985), Ch. 3.

47. Ibid., pp. 53–54.

48. Dalton, *Citizen Politics*, Ch. 8.

49. Dennis Kavanagh, *Political Science and Political Behaviour* (London: George Allen & Unwin, 1983), Ch. 3.

50. Ibid., pp. 44–46.

51. Ronald Inglehart, "The Nature of Value Change in Postindustrial Society," in Leon N. Lindberg, ed., *Politics and the Future of Industrial Society* (New York: McKay, 1976), pp. 57–99.

52. Materialists, in our terms, express a preference for stability of economic well-being and political power. Postmaterialists seek a redistribution of all values to those in society who are relatively deprived of them; but they are most concerned with the values of power and respect.

53. Ronald Inglehart, "Political Action: The Impact of Values, Cognitive Level, and Social Background," in Barnes et al., pp. 343–380.

54. Nobutaka Ike, "Economic Growth and Intergenerational Change in Japan," *American Political Science Review* 67 (December 1973), 1194–1203.

55. Ibid., p. 1198.

56. Ibid., p. 1203.

57. Scott C. Flanagan, "Value Change and Partisan Change in Japan: The Silent Revolution Revisited," *Comparative Politics* 11 (April 1979), 260–261.

58. Ronald Inglehart, *The Silent Revolution: Changing Values and Political Styles among Western Publics* (Princeton, N.J.: Princeton University Press, 1977), p. 45. Inglehart's findings did not support the expectation that ecological goals fit within his postmaterial value cluster. However, this only means that ecology has a broad appeal to people in many walks of life in Western Europe, as in the United States.

59. Fritzof Capra and Charlene Soretnak, *Green Politics* (New York: Dutton, 1984), Ch. 2.

60. Ronald Inglehart, "Political Dissatisfaction and Mass Support for Social Change in Advanced Industrial Society," *Comparative Political Studies* 10 (1977), 452–472; and "Postmaterialism in an Environment of Insecurity," *American Political Science Review* 75 (December 1981), 880–900.

61. This is not to suggest that a majority of young people are clearly postmaterialistic. Inglehart has consistently found that those from lower-income families exhibit the materialism of their elders. This may be especially true of those who are upwardly mobile, for whom the term *Yuppies* has traveled across the North Atlantic from the United States.

62. Ronald Inglehart and Scott C. Flanagan, "Value Change in Industrial Societies," *American Political Science Review* 81 (December 1987), 1303–1318.

C H A P T E R 4

POLITICAL PARTIES

Parties, Participation, and Pluralism

In First World political systems, political parties serve as a medium through which ordinary citizens are able to express their political preferences in a way that reaches the attention of the makers of public policy. This is because, as voters, citizens may choose to support one of the parties presently in power with their votes or to shift their support to an opposition party. If enough voters do likewise, the party or parties in power could find themselves outside government looking in after the election. So those who make policy must be alert to voter preferences, both directly in terms of their policy preferences and indirectly in terms of their preferences between competing political parties and candidates.

Parties serve as a medium for political participation both as mobilizers of popular support at election time and as organizations in which ordinary citizens participate as more or less active members. In Western Europe and Japan,

parties play a more distinct role in structuring political participation than is true of parties in the United States. This is partly due to the nature of political party organization in these countries. In the United States, those who vote regularly for the Republican Party's candidates are likely to think of themselves as members of that party. In Western Europe and Japan, the larger parties have an official definition of what a party member is; there is usually a dues-paying requirement and perhaps a certain minimal expectation of participation in party activities. The membership will therefore be easily identifiable and stable; it will not fluctuate wildly from year to year, and the party itself will function on a continuous basis. Party meetings will be held—locally as well as nationally—with regularity, whether it is an election year or not. Party activity will naturally increase at election time, just as it does in the United States; but the point is that the ground troops are already in place, ready for action. They do not have to be recruited on the eve of the campaign.

What this suggests is that the political party in the countries we are studying offers opportunities as a channel for popular participation, but one must first establish his or her credentials as a party regular before having any hope of playing a weighty role either in the electoral or in the public policymaking process. The rules of the game of popular participation are thus more firmly established in Western Europe and Japan. Because the two major parties are looser and more fluid in the United States, the participant may be in a position to help redefine the rules as well as to influence the outcome. Nevertheless, the existence of a larger number of political parties in most First World countries means that the individual has a variety of choices. This may be a reason why voter turnout rates are higher in most other First World countries than in the United States.

On both sides of the Atlantic (and of the Pacific), the electoral process is the principal means by which most people participate in politics. The political parties are the instruments through which the electorate expresses its preferences at election time as follows: (1) Those citizens who are active in the political parties may have a role in selecting candidates for elective office, and (2) the choices that are offered on the ballot are usually distinguishable to the average voter according to the differences between the parties they represent. The first point is more true of the United States than of other First World countries, which do not have primary elections for choosing the parties' candidates. The second point is more true of Western Europe and Japan, where the voters may not be clearly aware of who the candidates for legislative office are, but they feel competent to choose anyway because of the candidates' party (or factional) affiliations.

In each of the political systems we are studying, two or more political parties interact with one another in what we call a *party system*. The central focus of this interaction is the contest among political parties for the power to govern the country—a contest that takes place at two levels: (1) in elections, where the voters determine the respective share each party will have of the seats in parliament, and (2) within parliament, where the distribution of seats among the parties and the coalitions worked out among them will ultimately determine what party or parties will constitute the government. These are *pluralistic* party systems, because there are two or more parties among which competition is meaningful. It makes a difference how people choose among these parties. If the choice goes in one direction, one party or coalition of parties will govern the country, with one set of policy consequences; if it goes in another direction, there will be a different set of governors and policy consequences.

Italian political scientist Giovanni Sartori has made two important observations concerning pluralistic party systems: First, they operate very differently with quite different consequences for human dignity than do political systems in which there is only one political party of consequence. Second, there is, however, the danger that pluralistic party systems may become *too* pluralistic, with adverse consequences for the capacity of those governing the country to make headway in the pursuit of human dignity. In other words, *viable* pluralistic party systems are found in a range that is terminated by the one-party system at one end and what Sartori calls "extreme pluralism" at the other.[1] Although there may be more than one party, it may be the case that a single party so dominates the other parties that the party system is pluralistic in form only. Critics of the Japanese party system have sometimes characterized it in this fashion.[2] Or it may be the case that there are many parties of roughly equal strength and of sufficiently divergent policy views, so that it becomes impossible for coalitions of parties to solidify around common programs that will enable effective government to persist. Sartori sees the Italian party system as belonging to the extreme pluralism category.[3]

In Sartori's view, there are three important variables that differentiate party systems which should be taken into account in deciding whether a given party system is close to the one-party or the extreme pluralistic end of the continuum, or somewhere safely in between them. These are (1) the nature of the *ideological spectrum* the parties occupy, (2) the number of parties of significance in the system, and (3) their relative strengths.[4] Let us begin with the fascinating and complicated subject of party ideologies.

The Ideological Spectrum

In Chapter 3 our focus was on the political beliefs of ordinary citizens. Political culture is a diffuse set of attitudes that are generally shared by large numbers of citizens. The individual citizen may or may not be able to relate his or her political attitudes to an integrated set of political beliefs that we would dignify with the label *ideology*. Only a minority of citizens have this capability. Usually, they are those who are more highly educated, who follow politics regularly, and who at least discuss politics on a regular basis with friends and associates. Political ideologies are more highly developed than is political culture. They can usually be traced to the writings of influential political philosophers who fit into established philosophical traditions, and they can be assigned recognizable labels, such as *liberalism*, *conservatism*, or *socialism*. This chapter considers the political parties in Western Europe and Japan that are readily identifiable in terms of political ideologies and that compete with one another for power—contesting elec-

tions and seeking government office on the basis of their stated, ideologically based programs.

Ideology plays a more important role for European political parties than for their American counterparts. Americans, who are used to thinking of themselves as Democrats or Republicans as long as they more or less consistently vote for the candidates of one or the other party, have difficulty understanding that political parties in Western Europe have corporate identities that separate them clearly and distinctly from the body of voters to whom they appeal for votes. The parties, in effect, are groups of men and women who fill party offices and actively participate in party functions. They constitute a small minority of the population. Thus, if French political parties are sharply at odds with one another on ideological grounds, that does not necessarily mean that the average French man or woman cares much about these battles between activists.[5] If French voters divide their votes among a relatively large number of parties, it could be because the French political elites give them a relatively large number of choices. The separate ideological families in France are subsets of political activists—the minority of the French who devote their time and energy to such matters. Thus, to speak of ideologies that divide political parties from one another in Europe is to speak of several different political subcultures—essentially elite subcultures.

Let us briefly survey the range of these subcultures as they are typically found in Western Europe. We use the traditional left–right spectrum because most subcultures can be fairly easily placed along it. (See Figure 4.1.). Two of the eight subcultures, *liberalism* and *conservatism*, have their origins in the nineteenth century; one, *democratic socialism*, was a turn-of-the-century creation; the remainder are distinctly twentieth-century phenomena.

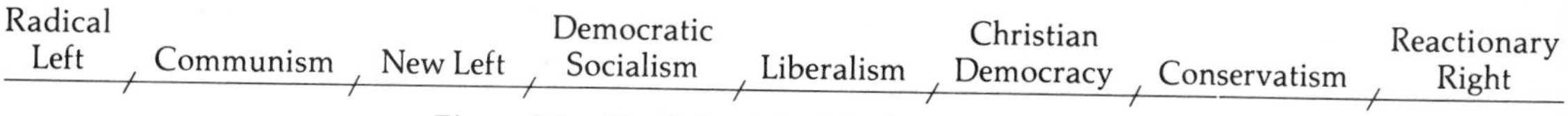

Radical Left	Communism	New Left	Democratic Socialism	Liberalism	Christian Democracy	Conservatism	Reactionary Right

Figure 4.1 The left–right ideological spectrum.

Nineteenth-century liberalism and conservatism differed from one another primarily in terms of the struggle to democratize European political systems. Liberals favored a measured, steady reform that would expand the electorate and reduce the power of the entrenched aristocracy, whose privileges and prerogatives conservatives sought to protect. In Europe today, there is little to distinguish liberalism from conservatism; both accept political, economic, and social institutions essentially as they are. Although conservatives resist efforts to redistribute well-being, respect, and enlightenment through government action, liberals are amenable to moderate reform but are not likely to be in the vanguard advocating it. Liberalism and conservatism have both adapted to modern capitalism. Indeed, it is not clear to what extent they can any longer be regarded as separate subcultures, although most Western European countries have separate liberal and conservative political parties.

Socialism as an ideology and as a subculture goes back nearly as far as liberalism and conservatism. In the nineteenth century, there were both utopian and scientific versions of socialism existing side by side; the former was more prevalent in France, whereas the latter was more prevalent in Germany, the home of Karl Marx. By the end of the century, Marxist socialism was the predominant variety, but there was emerging within Marxism a doctrinal conflict over the appropriate means for achieving the agreed-on ends. The revisionist wing of the movement became stronger after the turn of the century as its prescription to work within the parliamentary democratic system began to

pay dividends. What we now call *democratic socialism* is the product of early twentieth-century revisionism. The democratic socialists advocate a substantial redistribution of the values of well-being, respect, and enlightenment in favor of those social classes that have relatively small shares of them. However, they do not believe a major redistribution of power is also necessary because parliamentary democracy enables classes that are weak in other resources to use their superior numbers to gain the necessary power to make redistributive decisions.

Western European *communism*, on the other hand, is a direct descendant of that branch of socialism that remained faithful to the Marxist revolutionary blueprint. Until recently, at least, these Communists denied that a fundamental redistribution of well-being, respect, and enlightenment could take place unless the political system were radically changed. Thus, if the Communists had come to power in Western European parliamentary democracies, they would have used their newly acquired political resources to destroy the power base of the capitalist class, thus removing resistance to socialist redistribution and achieving "dictatorship of the proletariat." Recently, however, communism has become more ambivalent about how to achieve socialist goals. Leading Communists in Italy, the country in Western Europe where communism is strongest, have argued (much as the democratic socialists have argued all along) that it would not be necessary to change the rules of parliamentary democracy. Although this would mean living with capitalism longer than the Communists in the Soviet Union, Poland, or East Germany were willing to do, contemporary Western European communism seems content to let the existing distribution of power remain intact while working on the redistribution of other values. Thus, differences between communism and democratic socialism have been considerably lessened.

In the mid-1970s, the term *Eurocommunist* was applied to most of the Western European Communist parties, implying that they had evolved in a direction different from that of the Soviet Communist Party (CPSU) and its fraternal parties in Eastern Europe. The term was first assumed by the Spanish Communist Party (PCE), which even went so far as to deny that it was any longer a Marxist–Leninist party, preferring to be regarded as simply a Marxist party, thus implicitly denying any necessity to follow the guidance of the CPSU, the party of Lenin. Both the Italian and the French parties permitted themselves to be labeled Eurocommunist, but there have been important differences between the two parties, including differences of an ideological nature. The Italian Communist Party (PCI) went a considerable distance in pragmatically adapting its program to the expectations of the ruling Christian Democrats with whom it sought a partnership. This search for a *historic compromise* led the PCI into close working relationships with private capitalists in those cities where the PCI held power, as well as with the Christian Democrats in the Parliament, where the PCI has frequently played a cooperative role in the fashioning of legislative compromises. More recently, the PCI has sought the establishment of a "popular front" coalition with the Socialist Party (PSI). PCI leader Achille Ochetto intends to bring about a change in the party name, removing the word "Communist." The French Communist Party (PCF) persisted in a determined opposition to the parties in power until the victory of the Socialist Party in the 1981 legislative election. Their participation in the Socialist-led government formed in that year ended only three years later. Many observers who take at face value the claim of the PCI that they have abandoned the objective of a dictatorship of the proletariat are more skeptical of the same claim when it is made by the PCF. One indicator of the difference between the two parties is the fact that the Soviet invasion of Afghanistan was denounced by the PCI, whereas the PCF defended it. However, the upheavals in 1989–90 affecting Communist parties in Eastern Europe may have removed some of the causes of disagreement among Western European Communists, as the Leninist model of one-party rule appears to be on its way to becoming a museum piece of modern history, at least in the nearest Eastern European neighbors.

Younger Socialists have moved into the vacuum left by the communist drift away from the extreme left since the mid-1960s. Calling themselves Marxists, Leninists, Trotskyites, Maoists, or anarchists, they have rejected Moscow-oriented communism as defensive of the status quo. But their position on the distribution of basic values in Western capitalist systems is essentially the same as that of the revolutionary Socialists at the turn of the century or of the Communists of the 1950s. They feel that only a thorough destruction of the capitalist base of power will make it possible to achieve a radical redistribution of other values. This *radical left* differs from the earlier brand of communism by dividing its criticism equally between Western capitalism and the socialist regimes of Eastern Europe. Because inequalities persist in the latter regimes, the radical left in Western Europe argues that this is a form of state capitalism that does not differ in principle from the private capitalism of the West. But their wholesale rejection of the Western institutional structure places them on the far left of the ideological spectrum. Political parties of the radical left, such as the Democratic Proletarians in Italy, have seldom received more than 1 or 2 percent of the popular vote in recent national elections.

Another primarily twentieth-century development in some Western European countries was the emergence of Christian democracy, which came about as an effort to reconcile Europe's Catholics with parliamentary democracy and with economic and social reform. Before World War II, there had been strong Catholic elements who rejected democracy and sought to preserve the existing distribution of values in society. These groups were especially strong in the Mediterranean Catholic countries—Italy, Portugal, and Spain—but they constituted at least a minority among the politically active Catholics in France and Germany. In all of these countries, some leading Catholics embraced fascism. Yet, Catholics also played an important role in resisting Mussolini's fascist rule in Italy and the German occupation of France during World War II. In France and Italy, Christian democracy, which stemmed from smaller parties of earlier decades, earned its democratic credentials during the resistance and emerged from the war with a large mass following. In Germany, Christian democracy was made up of the leaders of the old Catholic Center Party of the Weimar Republic, who had gone into deep retirement during the Nazi years and emerged after the war untainted. But Christian democracy in West Germany has taken a somewhat different turn from that in Italy and France because half of the West German population is Protestant. In West Germany, Christian democracy has been able to appeal to liberal and conservative middle-class Protestants as well as to Catholics of all social classes.

What is Christian democracy today? It remains the ideological basis of two strong political parties—in Italy and West Germany—whereas its political expression in France became weaker and weaker, until today there is no longer a Christian Democratic Party, properly speaking. The party's survival in Italy and West Germany has depended on the capacity of Christian democratic leaders to broaden their appeal, adopting in their party platforms elements of conservatism, liberalism, and even democratic socialism. In the early years after World War II, Christian democracy in all three countries had a strong reformist strain, a commitment to a truly democratic political system and to moderate redistribution of well-being, respect, and enlightenment. After the onset of the Cold War in the late 1940s, these reformist aspects became increasingly muted in favor of a strong anti-communism. In the 1950s, it was customary to classify Christian democracy with conservatism. But since the early 1960s, the willingness of Christian democratic political leaders to cooperate with the Democratic Socialists in programs of moderate reform has made it much harder to place them very far to the right on the ideological spectrum. Christian democracy today is a mixture of many ideological elements with considerable pragmatism and even opportunism. It is probably safest to locate Christian democracy in the center-right of our ideological spectrum.

As for the *far right*, it is not as easy to find bona fide right-wing extremists in Western Europe as it was a few decades ago. With respect to political movements, there is nothing even faintly resembling the virulent Nazis in Germany or Mussolini's Fascists in Italy. Short-lived right-wing movements have appeared from time to time, such as the Poujadists in France in the mid-1950s, which was a movement of small-business owners who were protesting the dislocations that affected them as France moved toward a postindustrial society. Today's longest-lived right-wing party, the Neo-Fascists in Italy, is a somewhat similar phenomenon, likewise appealing to threatened social groups and gaining its principal strength in the less advanced southern portion of Italy, just as the Poujadists were strongest in the rural areas of central and southwestern France. It is not easy to characterize what today's reactionary right represents ideologically. In some ways, it resembles the radical left in its aversion to big capitalism and big government. But prewar Nazism and fascism showed that bringing the reactionary right to power will only lead to bigger capitalism and bigger government without effecting any real redistribution of well-being, respect, and enlightenment, whatever the upheavals in the structure of power. The racism of the Nazis finds some faint echoes today, as in campaigns against immigrant workers carried on in France by the National Front, a party that rose very rapidly in electoral strength through the 1980s, peaking at 14% for its leader, Jean-Marie Le Pen in the 1988 presidential election. A similar phenomenon in West Germany, the *Republikaner*, rapidly captured attention in West Germany in 1989. However, the strong nationalism of the Republikaner was made redundant by the rising voices from left, center, and right calling for German reunification.

As Western European countries have entered postindustrial society, *new left* parties have emerged of late, attracting the support especially of the educated "postmaterial" youth, whose preoccupation is with the expansion of political rights, including the right to engage in forms of political action labeled in Chapter 3 as "unconventional." One such party has been the Radical Party in Italy, which came from almost nowhere in the 1979 national election to capture 3.4 percent of the popular vote and eighteen seats in the Chamber of Deputies. Sometimes encompassed within new left parties and sometimes constituting separate parties on their own are the Environmentalists (or Greens). The Green Party in West Germany was strong enough in the 1983 parliamentary election to take crucial segments of votes away from the larger parties. It captured 5.6 percent of the popular vote and twenty-seven seats, becoming the fourth party in the Bundestag, or lower house of Parliament. In 1987 it increased its share of the popular vote to 8.3 percent, and of seats to forty-two.

Another type of fringe party found in many Western European countries is the regional or ethnic separatist party—exemplified by the Scottish Nationalist Party in Great Britain and the South Tyrolean People's Party in Italy—

Jean-Marie Le Pen, leader of the French right-wing party, National Front.

which, at a minimum, seeks greater autonomy for the region in which its ethnic minority is concentrated. In some cases, as for some Scottish Nationalists, actual independence from the larger nation is sought. It is difficult to fit many of these new or resurgent parties into the traditional left–right spectrum that reflects the "materialist" agenda of issues of advanced industrialism. As we saw in Chapter 3, postindustrial society is bringing forth a new agenda to which the older parties are trying to adjust.

Table 4.1 matches ideologies with the more important political parties in our five countries. Some parties defy classification, such as the Union for French Democracy (UDF), which is a mixture of Liberals, Christian Democrats, and Conservatives. For want of a better solution we categorize them as liberals, in order to distinguish them from the French Gaullists (RPR), whom we have placed in the conservative category. However, both the UDF and the RPR are broad coalitions of elements much like the Christian Democrats in Italy and West Germany. Some Gaullists are liberals, others are clearly conservatives, and still others, in their strong nationalism at least, resemble adherents of the reactionary right. Indeed, it was customary to classify the forerunner of the contemporary

Table 4.1 Location of Political Parties on the Ideological Spectrum

Country	Radical and New Left	Communism	Democratic Socialism	Liberalism	Christian Democracy	Conservatism	Reactionary Right
Great Britain			Labour Party	Democrats (SLD) Social Democrats (SDP)		Conservative Party	
France	Ecologists	French Communist Party (PCF)	Socialist Party (PS)	Union for French Democracy (UDF)		Gaullists (RPR)	National Front (FN)
West Germany	Greens	German Communist Party (DKP)	Social Democratic Party (SPD)	Free Democratic Party (FDP)	Christian Democratic Union (CDU)	Christian Social Union (CSU)	Republikaner
Italy	Proletarian Democracy (DP) Radicals (PR) Greens	Italian Communist Party (PCI)	Italian Socialist Party (PSI)	Republican Party (PRI) Social Democratic Party (PSDI)	Christian Democratic Party (DC)	Liberal Party (PLI)	Italian Social Movement (MSI)
Japan		Japan Communist Party (JCP)	Japan Socialist Party (JSP)	Democratic Socialist Party (DSP) Komeito		Liberal Democratic Party (LDP)	

Gaullist Party, the Rally of the French People (RPF) of the late 1940s and early 1950s, as a party of the far right. Still, in terms of the behavior of the Gaullist leadership since the party came to power in 1958, it seems appropriate to classify the party as conservative, but it is a very practical, flexible kind of conservatism—like that of the British Conservative Party.

A similar judgment can be made about the ruling party in Japan, the Liberal Democratic Party. Two parties in the center of the Japanese party spectrum, the Democratic Socialist Party (DSP) and the Komeito, or "Clean Government Party," are very difficult to classify in Western terms. They are placed in the liberal category here, mainly because of their center position between Japanese socialism and conservatism. Both call themselves "socialist," but the DSP gets substantial financial support from private business, and the Komeito, a Buddhist party dedicated to peace and a clean environment, combines elements of liberal reformism with what in the West would be associated with Christian democracy on the one hand, and the new left on the other.

Ideology and Organization

Traditionally, the parties of the left and right in Western Europe were distinguished from one another not only in terms of their beliefs and programs, but also in terms of the ways in which they were organized. Socialist parties, being parties of the working class, sought large mass memberships, particularly of industrial workers, who could be readily organized in advanced industrial society because of their concentrations in large factories and in homogeneous residential areas. Liberal and conservative parties of the center and right sought to mobilize the financial contributions of wealthy supporters, while confining party membership to a relatively small circle of middle-class activists. Thus, according to French political scientist Maurice Duverger, democratic socialist parties were *mass parties*, while liberal and conservative parties were *cadre*, or "framework," parties.[6]

In postindustrial societies, parties of the left, center, and right are not as easily characterized in organizational terms as they were nearly four decades ago when Duverger made the mass/cadre distinction. On the left, parties that previously relied heavily on working-class support have had to come to grips with the fact that the industrial working class is diminishing in size and is losing what cohesion it once had. Democratic socialist and even communist parties have had to redouble their efforts to capture middle-class support if they wish to hold the shares of the popular vote they once enjoyed. This has meant a dilution of the working-class bases of socialist parties and a decline in membership, as middle-class supporters have been harder to recruit to dues-paying membership status and the pool of available working-class members has been evaporating. On the other hand, those parties of the center and right that have broadened their party programs in order to appeal to working-class as well as to middle-class voters (e.g., the British Conservative Party and the French Gaullists) or to Protestants as well as to Catholics (the Christian Democrats of West Germany) have found their memberships growing as they reach into new social categories that are amenable to organizational efforts. Thus, as parties of the advanced industrial era have become "catch-all" parties,[7] trying to reach as many voters as possible with the broadest possible appeals, the old organizational differences have disappeared. At least the larger parties of Western Europe are no longer strictly mass parties or strictly cadre parties, although some smaller parties are found in the latter category. They are parties with respectable dues-paying memberships, but their focus is electoral. They rely on the financial support of both the dues paid by their formal membership and the substantial contributions made by wealthier adherents; and they make use of both the army of doorbell-ringing ordinary members and the media skills of paid professionals. Although there are slight differences in organizational form as one moves from one party to another, such differences assume less importance in light of the trends discussed in Chapter 2 under the heading "Disorganized Capitalism." It is not that political parties have become less organized than they once were; it is that party organization has become a standardized, professionalized feature of all parties that are successful in attracting significant shares of the popular vote. It would be relatively easy to substitute the organizational characteristics of one party for those of its most serious rival with relatively little adjustment trauma for the personnel involved.

A more telling question to ask about the ways in which today's political parties in First World countries are structured is to ask abut the nature of intraparty conflict. Some political parties have easily identifiable ideological left and right *wings*. Within-party conflict in such parties is nearly as serious as the ideological warfare that goes on between parties. Political scientist Richard Rose has distinguished between the British Labour and Conservative parties in these terms. The Labour Party, he says, is a party of *factions*, whereas the Conservative Party is a party of *tendencies*.[8] In the Labour Party there are readily identifiable left and right wings that take different positions on a wide variety of issues and that have stable memberships, almost as if there were two separate political parties within one Labour Party. The Conservatives, on the other hand, divide in different ways on different issues. Thus, there are certain party members who are opposed to capital punishment and others who favor it, but some of those who are at odds with one another on this issue will join forces against still other members on the issue of whether Britain should be a member of the European Common Market. Each of these pro and con positions is a tendency, but a set of tendencies will not add up to stable factions that could be disruptive of Conservative Party unity, as the constant battle between left and right has done in the Labour Party.

There is another meaning of the word *faction* that has been applied in particular to two of the parties we are considering here: the Italian Christian Democratic Party (DC) and the Japanese Liberal Democratic Party (LDP). Both parties are the largest vote getters in their countries, and both have monopolized or held the lion's share of power since normal politics resumed after World War II. Both have publicly identifiable factions, but they are factions defined more in terms of the *persons* who belong to them than of the ideological beliefs their members share. It is possible to give rough "left" or "right" labels to some of the factions that vie for leadership of the DC and the LDP, but many others occupy shifting ground somewhere between the center-left and center-right of the within-party spectrum. More appropriately, the factions are named for their present or past leaders. Their inner cores are sets of parliamentary members of the respective parties, led by one or more nationally prominent figures, who ordinarily will be found occupying ministerial positions in government, or party organizational posts, or both. Younger members of a given faction count on the support of their seniors for promotion up the political ladders so that they will in turn become faction, party, and governmental leaders later in their careers.

Most observers feel that the Italian and Japanese type of factionalism just described is less damaging to internal political unity than is the ideologically defined factionalism often found in parties of the left in Western Europe. However, the other side of the coin is that a great deal of energy is expended in the DC and LDP in interfactional maneuvering and bargaining. On the face of it, both parties have been strong enough to have provided effective policy leadership during the many years they have dominated their political systems; yet, especially in Italy, the infighting that has gone on between factions has assumed greater significance for the contestants than just the policy issues that an outsider would think are at stake. Still, it could be argued that both countries have been governed more effectively than the critics would lead us to expect, especially when we look at indicators of economic growth and international trade balances.[9] The ideological factionalism found in the British Labour Party has been one of the prime targets for criticism of the poor economic record of Britain during the years of Labour government in the 1960s and 1970s.[10] At any rate, the amount of pluralistic competition within party systems is a function not only of the number of parties in the system, but also in the degree to which the parties are factionalized in either of the senses discussed here.

Party System Pluralism

In the two preceding chapters we have examined the structure of social cleavages and the pattern of psychological orientations (political culture) as they relate to politics in Western Europe and Japan. It has typically been the function of political parties in these parts of the world to translate social cleavages and mass political orientations into political action, through the medium of the contests between parties for power. These contests take place within the framework of what we call *party systems*. They involve competition between political parties for the support of members and electors and a system of cooperation and conflict between parties in the process of forming governing coalitions and making public policy. The party system will reflect the principal lines of cleavage within a society (Chapter 2) and the principal political subcultures (Chapter 3) by appealing to different sets of voters with competing party leaders, competing slogans, and competing ideologies. Those parties that succeed in gaining power or a share of it in governing coalitions will put their leaders in office and see that the leaders adhere more or less closely to the promises the parties have made to their adherents in the electorate.

However, we must not suppose that there are one-to-one translations of voter wishes into party intentions and of party intentions into the actions of their leaders when in government office. Intervening factors can distort the one translation or the other. Some of these factors are indigenous to the party system itself; others are external to it, operating elsewhere in the political system or in its environment. Factors internal to the party system, such as fragmentation, polarization, and coalition formation, are discussed in this chapter, as is an influential external factor, the way the system of elections is organized. Additional external factors are discussed in other chapters: The changes occurring in the economy were discussed in Chapter 2, the rules of parliamentary practice are discussed in Chapter 5, and the ways in which conflicts of interest between major interest groups in society, such as trade unions and employers groups, are resolved are discussed in Chapter 6. Such constant or uncontrollable factors can influence the electoral fortunes of political parties as well as their capacity to make good on their promises once in office.

There are many ways of characterizing political party systems, depending on the purpose of the analysis. Since we are concerned with the problem of where party systems fall in the range between too little pluralism and too much pluralism,[11] we focus on three criteria for differentiating party systems that are related to this problem. These are (1) the degree of fragmentation, (2) the distribution of strength across the ideological spectrum, and (3) coalition patterns. The first of these, *fragmentation*, combines two measurable characteristics, the number of parties in a system and the strengths of those parties. The fewer the number, the less the fragmentation; and the more even the strengths of the parties, the greater the fragmentation. A four-party system ordinarily would be more fragmented than a three-party system. But if the strength of the three parties in the latter system is evenly distributed, each party having one-third of the voters' support, it would be more fragmented than would a four-party system in which two parties each had 45 percent of the voters' support and the remaining two parties each had 5 percent. That is, voter support is more concentrated in the four-party system than in the three-party system. Presumably, it would be easier to draw together a majority coalition when you start with a 45 percent party as one of the building blocks than it would be when you have to find ways of reconciling two proud 30–35 percent parties in the same coalition government. Fragmentation, then, makes the cohesion of government more tenuous, thus adversely affecting the productivity and ultimately the stability of government. This, at least, is what theorists of party systems have argued for a long time.[12]

There are a number of indexes that political scientists have devised for party fragmentation, some of the best known of which are rather complex. One of the simplest, the *index of aggregation*, measures the converse of fragmentation.[13] It divides the percentage of the largest party by the number of parties in the system. We follow the practice of regarding a party as being "in the system" if it obtains at least 2 percent of the popular vote in legislative elections. By this measure, aggregation has been greater in the United Kingdom in the last four elections (aggregation index = 14) than in France (aggregation index = 7). Party system aggregation has an average index of 14 in West Germany, substantially higher than that of Italy, which is 8. Japan, with an average index of 9, is closer to the more fragmented systems.

The *distribution of strength across the ideological spectrum* refers to the left–right spectrum outlined in the previous section and the distribution of party strengths across that spectrum. Even if all of the ideological types are represented in a particular party system, if the strongest parties are concentrated near one point on the spectrum, the system could be labeled left-leaning, centrist, or right-leaning, depending on the location of that point. Another party system might have more of a bimodal distribution with twin peaks on the left and right, such that it could be labeled *polarized*, although the degree of polarization would depend on whether the large parties of left and right are of the extremes or of the more moderate left and right. The party systems could be differently characterized depending on whether we are talking about the distribution of electoral strength or the distribution of strength in Parliament. Thus, the British party system appears to have a rather centrist appearance if electoral strengths of the parties are considered, as the center Liberal and Social Democratic Alliance captured more than 20 percent of the popular vote in 1987, but, because the number of seats it obtained in the House of Commons constituted only about 3 percent, it nearly disappears from a diagram of parliamentary party strength, and the British system appears moderately polarized between the Labour Party on the near left and the Conservative Party on the near right. At this stage we concentrate on the distribution of party strength as reflected in the popular vote, and then later we look at the parliamentary distribution when we consider the effects of electoral systems on party systems.

Figure 4.2 shows how our five party systems appear when the distribution of party electoral strengths across the ideological spectrum[14] is diagrammed. From the figure we can see that the mild polarization of the British party system finds echoes in the West German and Japanese party systems, in each of which a Democratic Socialist Party and a party of the moderate right are the two strongest. In France and Italy, there are Communist parties with sufficient strength to extend the left bloc in Parliament farther to the left, creating greater polarization, especially

as there is some strength on the far right in each country as well. Both the French and the Italian party systems exhibit both polarization and the highest levels of fragmentation among the five countries.

Coalition formation occurs in party systems in cases where no party is strong enough to command a majority in the legislative body, called the House, the Assembly, the Chamber, or the Diet, depending on the country in question. (See Chapter 5.) In three of our five countries—France, West Germany, and Italy—coalitions are usually necessary because of the fact that seldom, if ever, can one party gain a majority in its own right. In Britain and Japan, on the other hand, coalitions have not been found in recent decades, because one party has, with rare exceptions, always had a majority of seats in parliament. Whether coalitions are found or not, the same question can be asked: Does power remain anchored at one point on the left–right spectrum, or does it alternate between left and right over the course of, say, a twenty-five-year generation? In Britain, alternation is fairly frequent, with power having changed hands between left and right four times in the past twenty-five years. In France, changes have occurred three times during that span and in West Germany, twice. But power has remained anchored on the right in Japan and in a broad area of the Italian spectrum stretching from center-left to center-right. In the Italian case, the width of the coalition has expanded and contracted from time to time, but it has remained anchored around the center of the spectrum. Italy is the only one of the five countries to exhibit coalitions of the center, a characteristic Sartori associates with extreme pluralism, because the parties on the extreme left and right of the spectrum are not seen as suitable partners by those closer to the center. So the center parties remain one another's coalition partners by de-

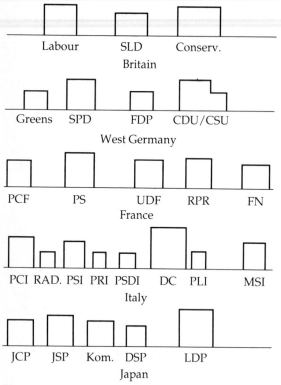

Figure 4.2 Party left–right spectrums for five countries.

British Labour party supporters demonstrating their opposition to Conservative Prime Minister Margaret Thatcher during the June 1987 general election campaign.

fault. In the four other countries, the coalitions have been clearly either to the left or to the right of center, although France edged slightly toward a center coalition in mid-1988. The coalition patterns and locations of government and opposition in the five party systems as of mid-1988 is depicted in Figure 4.3.

Electoral Systems

It is a long-accepted generalization among political scientists that the number of political par-

ties a country has is, in part at least, dependent on the type of electoral system it has. Two-party systems tend to be found in countries with *single-member district plurality* electoral systems, and party systems with more than two parties, especially party systems with five or more parties, are associated with *proportional representation*. The United States and Great Britain are said to have two-party systems, and Italy, always with more than five parties, is said to have a multiparty system that features extreme pluralism.

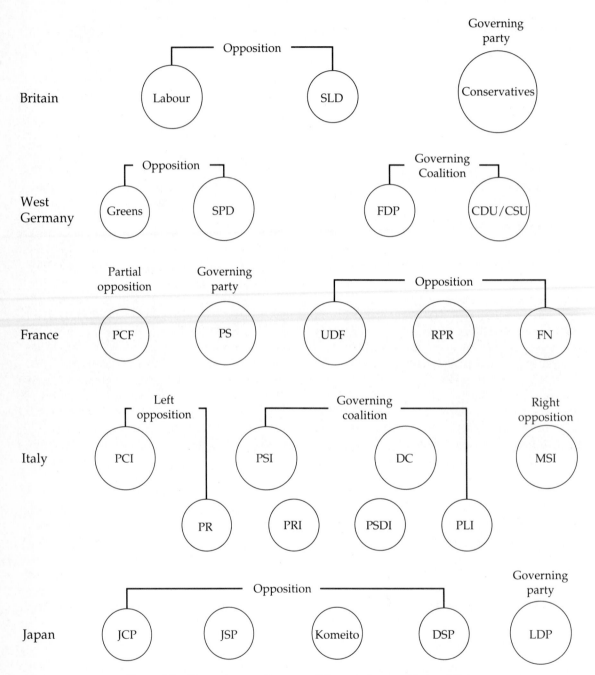

Figure 4.3 Governing parties or coalition, and opposition parties.

But do the United States and Great Britain really have two-party systems? And does it matter whether they do or they do not? Are there not important differences between three-party systems and, say, eight-party systems? In other words, the dividing line between two and three parties is a rather arbitrary one and may not capture a significant distinction. Look at the British party system today. In the general election held in June 1987, the two leading parties, Labour and the Conservatives, together gained 73 percent of the popular vote. The third largest contending unit, the Alliance of Liberals and Social Democrats, captured 23 percent, whereas other parties, including Scottish Nationalists, Welsh Nationalists, Ulster Unionists, Communists, the right-wing National Front, and various independents, totaled nearly 5 percent. Clearly the two largest parties far outdistanced the others, but can we really omit the Liberals and Social Democrats from consideration? Is the British party system not really at least a four-party system?

One reason political scientists have clung to the two-party label for Great Britain is that, at least until very recently, the British electoral system has seriously discriminated against all but the two largest parties. As in the case of the U.S. House of Representatives, Great Britain is divided into geographical units, each returning 1 member to the 650-member House of Commons. When a general election is held, all 650 seats are contested. Some of these are safe Labour seats, returning the Labour candidate in election after election; some are safe Conservative seats. Few can be taken for granted by the Alliance. In fact, Liberal and Social Democratic strength is quite evenly distributed around the country, unlike that of the Scottish, Welsh, and Ulster parties, which, of course, is concentrated in their respective geographic regions. Because only one candidate can win the

seat in a given constituency and because the winner is whoever gains a plurality—not necessarily a majority (more than 50 percent) of the votes—the Alliance often runs a strong second to one or the other of the two major parties, but seldom takes the first spot. Thus, in June 1987, although the Alliance won 23 percent of the popular vote, it captured only 22 of the 650 seats. With 73 percent of the popular vote, the two largest parties obtained 93 percent of the seats. So, is the British party system a two-party system or a four-party system, or even an eight-party system?

Now let us look at the situation in West Germany, whose party system bore some resemblance to that of the British until recently. There, too, the three leading parties have been a large party on the left, the Social Democrats (SPD); a large party on the right, the Christian Democrats (CDU/CSU); and a smaller party in the center, the Free Democrats (FDP). In January 1987, the two larger parties (the Christian Democrats are federated with the Bavarian CSU) gained 81 percent of the popular vote, and the FDP obtained 9.1 percent. If this result has occurred in Great Britain in June 1987, the Alliance would have been fortunate to have gotten its twenty-two seats. Yet, the FDP captured 46 seats out of 497. This enabled them to hold the balance of power between the two major parties, neither of which had secured a majority of seats in the Bundestag.

It is the electoral system that accounts for the more advantageous position of the FDP. West Germany has a complex combination of proportional representation and the single-member plurality system; however, the proportional representation principle predominates. This means that seats are distributed among parties in proportion to their percentages of the popular vote. Half of the 497 Bundestag seats are based on single-member constituencies, as in Great

Britain. The other half are distributed on a proportional basis among party lists drawn up at the state (*Land*) level. The distribution among Land lists corrects for any disproportion that arises in the single-member district results so that the total distribution of seats among the parties will be proportional to their percentages of the national popular vote.

Proponents of the proportional representation system argue that it is only simple justice to allow a party the parliamentary representation it has earned. Otherwise, the votes of those who support a party such as the British Liberals are often discounted. The counterargument stresses the fact that proportional representation tends to encourage the proliferation of parties. The horrible example often cited is the Weimar Republic of Germany (1919–33), where a pure system of proportional representation encouraged literally dozens of parties to vie for Reichstag seats and actually rewarded many of them. Building and maintaining governing coalitions under such circumstances is extremely difficult. The framers of the Bonn electoral law had the Weimar experience in mind when they sought to modify the extreme proliferating effect of proportional representation. They accomplished this by denying representation in the Bundestag to any party that could not gain at least 5 percent of the national list vote. This rule has kept the Communist Party out of the Bundestag since the earliest years of the Federal Republic, and it has worked to the disadvantage of right-wing parties and various regional splinter parties. Among the smaller parties, only the FDP was able to remain above this minimum level before March 1983. The advantage that the FDP gains by means of proportional representation is somewhat offset by its uncertain future. In March 1983, the FDP fell to 6.9 percent of the popular vote, thus coming close to elimination from the Bundestag. In the meantime, the Green

Party, which had gained only 1.5 percent of the vote in 1980, climbed to 5.6 percent in 1983, thus increasing to four the number of parties with seats in the Bundestag. In 1987 the two parties both increased their shares of both votes and seats. (See Table 4.2.)

Italy, on the other hand, retains a multiplicity of parties. There are nine listed in Table 4.2, which excludes parties of a strictly ethnic-regional character. This is because Italy is the only one of our five countries to have essentially unrestricted proportional representation. However, five of the Italian parties are of a distinctly minor nature, typically polling 5 percent or less of the popular vote. It seems likely that only the proportional representation system is keeping them alive at the national level.

The capacity of proportional representation to encourage the proliferation of political parties has also been seen in the case of France since World War II. During the Fourth Republic, France had a proportional representation system that discriminated in favor of parties of the center that were able to form electoral alliances with one another, but which nevertheless permitted six or seven parties to play important roles in the National Assembly at any given time. When the Fifth Republic came into being in 1958, the electoral system was changed to a single-member district basis, the system that is found there today. But is is not a plurality system like that in Britain. Rather, a majority of votes in a district are required for a candidate to be elected on the first ballot. Failing that, a second ballot is held a week later, at which time a plurality of votes, or more than any other candidate obtains, is all that is required to win the seat. This system encourages alliances of parties of the left to form against alliances of parties of the right. The candidates of the left who do not receive the largest number of votes for left candidates on the first ballot will step aside and urge their

Table 4.2 Distributions of Seats and Votes in Three Recent Legislative Elections

United Kingdom

Party	1979 Votes	1979 Seats	1983 Votes	1983 Seats	1987 Votes	1987 Seats
Labour	36.9%	268	27.6%	209	30.8%	229
Liberal (Alliance)	13.8	11	25.4	23	22.6	22
Conservative	43.9	339	42.4	397	42.3	376
Others	5.4	16	4.6	21	4.3	23

France

Party	1981 Votes	1981 Seats	1986 Votes	1986 Seats	1988 Votes	1988 Seats
Communists	16.2%	44	9.8%	35	11.3%	27
Socialists and Left Radicals	37.5	285	32.7	214	37.5	276
Giscardists (UDF)		64		131		130
Gaullists (RPR)	40.0	85	44.7	158	40.5	128
National Front	0.4	—	9.7	33	9.6	1
Others	5.9	13	3.1	—	1.1	13

West Germany

Party	1980 Votes	1980 Seats	1983 Votes	1983 Seats	1987 Votes	1987 Seats
Greens	1.5%	—	5.6%	27	8.3%	42
SPD	42.9	218	38.2	193	37.0	186
FDP	10.6	53	6.9	34	9.1	46
CDU/CSU	44.5	226	48.8	244	44.3	223
Others	0.5	—	0.5	—	1.3	—

Italy

Party	1979 Votes	1979 Seats	1983 Votes	1983 Seats	1987 Votes	1987 Seats
Communists	30.4%	201	29.9%	198	26.6%	177
Greens	—	—	—	—	2.5	13
Radicals	3.4	18	2.2	11	2.6	13
Socialists	9.8	62	11.4	73	14.3	94

(Table continues on p. 114.)

Table 4.2 *(Continued)*

	Italy					
	1979		*1983*		*1987*	
Party	*Votes*	*Seats*	*Votes*	*Seats*	*Votes*	*Seats*
Social Democrats	3.8	20	4.1	23	3.0	17
Republicans	3.0	16	5.1	29	3.7	21
Christian Democrats	38.3	262	32.9	225	34.3	234
Liberals	1.9	9	2.9	16	2.1	11
Italian Social Movement	5.3	30	6.8	42	5.9	35
Others	5.9	12	4.7	1.3	5.0	15

	Japan					
	1980		*1983*		*1986*	
Party	*Votes*	*Seats*	*Votes*	*Seats*	*Votes*	*Seats*
Communists	9.8%	29	9.3%	26	8.6%	27
Socialists	19.3	107	19.5	112	17.2	86
Komeito	9.0	33	10.1	58	9.4	57
Democratic Socialists	6.6	32	7.2	38	6.4	26
Liberal Democrats	47.9	284	45.7	250	49.5	304
Others	7.4	26	7.8	27	8.4	12

(Source). Great Britain: David Butler and Dennis Kavanagh, *The British General Election of 1987* (New York: St. Martin's, 1988), p. 283. France: J. E. S. Hayward, *Governing France: The One and Indivisible Republic,* 2nd ed. (London: Weidenfeld and Nicolson, 1983), p. 76; *The Economist,* June 11, 1988, p. 49, and June 18, 1988, p. 48. West Germany: Stephen Padgett and Tony Burkett, *Political Parties and Elections in West Germany: The Search for a New Stability* (New York: St. Martin's, 1986), p. 200; Christian Soe, ed., *Comparative Politics 88/89* (Guilford, Conn.: Annual Editions, 1988), p. 40. Italy: Frederic Spotts and Theodor Wieser, *Italy: A Difficult Democracy* (Cambridge: Cambridge University Press, 1986), p. 295; Mark Donovan, "The 1987 Election in Italy: Prelude to Reform," *West European Politics* 10 (1987), 127; Japan: Ronald J. Hrebenar, *The Japanese Party System: From One-Party Rule to Coalition Government* (Boulder, Colo., and London: Westview, 1986); *Keesing's Contemporary Archives* 32 (August 1986), 34555; *The Economist,* July 12, 1986, p. 29.

supporters to vote for the leading candidate of the left. Something similar will happen on the right, so that ordinarily on the second ballot the two strongest candidates are left facing one another. The first ballot has been likened to the primary elections in the United States, by which party candidates are nominated to appear on the ballot in the general election, which corresponds to the French second ballot. The system encourages weaker parties to remain in existence in the hope they will be able to win a few seats with the support of their partners on the same side of the political spectrum. It does not ruthlessly weed out the weaker parties, as does the single-member plurality system.

In the Fifth Republic, the two-ballot system for legislative elections has had the effect of reducing the number of effective contending parties to four, two on the left (the Communists and Socialists) and two on the right (the RPR and UDF). However, before the 1986 legislative elections, the then Socialist majority in Parliament succeeded in enacting a new electoral law that returned France briefly to proportional representation. The Socialists wished to distance themselves from the Communists, who had been losing electoral support and no longer appeared to be a very useful electoral alliance partner, while at the same time neutralizing the more effective alliance on the right. The strategy failed to produce a majority that would enable the Socialists to retain control of the government, but it did have the predicted effect of increasing the number of parties in the National Assembly from four to five, with the success of the right-wing National Front in attaining 10 percent of the popular vote, thus entitling them to the same percentage of seats in the Assembly under the proportional rule. Upon regaining a majority in the assembly despite the socialist maneuver, the RPR and UDF gave their support to a reversal of the electoral law change, restoring the single-member district, two-ballot system. The result of the subsequent 1988 legislative election was the virtual elimination of the National Front from the Assembly and therefore a return to the four-party system at the legislative level.

The different effects of the single-member district and proportional representation systems can be seen if we compare indexes of aggregation for our party systems in terms of the extent to which the index changes when we move from measuring the aggregation of electoral support among parties to an index of the aggregation of seats in parliament. Table 4.3 presents indexes of aggregation for both votes and seats for our four Western European countries and Japan in the early 1980s.

The table shows, first of all, that, in terms of the distribution of the popular vote among parties, Britain and West Germany have relatively aggregated party systems, whereas France and Italy have relatively fragmented ones, and the Japanese system falls in between. But, in terms of the seat distribution, the British and French systems appear the most aggregated, the Italian and Japanese the least, and the West German in between. The index of aggregation increases markedly for the British and the French systems, but only very modestly for the Italian and the Japanese, and not at all for the West German. Proportional representation clearly lives up to expectations in accurately translating votes into seats in West Germany, whereas the single-member district plurality system has the expected distortive effect in Britain. Distortion

Table 4.3 Indexes of Party Aggregation in Elections and in Parliament

Country	Year	Index (Votes)	Index (Seats)
United Kingdom	1983	14.1	30.5
France	1981	8.4	14.5
West Germany	1983	12.2	12.2
Italy	1983	6.6	8.9
Japan	1983	9.1	9.8

in France occurs in the aggregative direction as well, in this case because the Socialist Party in the 1981 legislative elections was able to outdistance not only its opposition on the right, but also its communist allies on the left. This put it in the position to win more seats than it would be entitled to on the grounds of strict proportionality. The French electoral system, unlike the British, allows more than two parties realistically to contend for voter support, but, like the British—indeed even more so—it piles up seats in the column of any party that is able to put appreciable daylight between it and its nearest rival. Some distortion also occurs in the Italian case, despite the fact Italy has a proportional representation system, because many of the electoral districts are small and do not have enough seats to distribute to the fourth, fifth, or sixth largest parties. This favors the two or three largest parties, especially the Christian Democrats, which obtained 34.3 percent of the popular vote in 1983, but 37.1 percent of the Chamber of Deputies seats.

In the case of Japan, the electoral system combines features of the plurality system and the proportional representation system in ways that favor the largest party, the Liberal Democrats, but that do not tend greatly to distort the translation of its share of the votes into its share of seats. Districts for the House of Representatives are of medium size—three to five seats. The seats are not distributed proportionately among party lists as in West Germany and Italy, but among individual candidates. In a constituency with three seats, the three candidates receiving the highest number of votes are elected, so that candidates of one party are competing against other candidates of the same party, as well as against candidates of other parties. Parties must calculate what share of the vote they can reasonably hope to attain and then put the optimum number of candidates

up for election. Too few candidates in a district would mean some other party would gain a seat that might otherwise go to one's own party; but too many candidates would risk losing the extra seat as well, because the vote might be too evenly divided between them, and another party with the optimum number of candidates would win the seat instead. This feature of the Japanese electoral system has tended to freeze the relative proportions of party strength that existed in earlier postwar years, making it very difficult for smaller parties to make up ground on the dominant LDP. Although it does mean a fairly accurate translation of the vote distribution into the seat distribution, the lack of surprises such as are possible in Britain and France is of dubious value, because it is purchased at the cost of interparty competitiveness.

Coalition Patterns

It should be clear by now that none of the five political party systems can be labeled two-party without serious qualification. On the other hand, two of them—the British and the West German—have at least the potential of behaving very much like two-party systems because each system has two strong parties that can serve as poles of attraction for the coalescence of the smaller parties. In fact, this is clearly what does happen in West Germany, and it potentially could happen in Britain. If one of the characteristics of a viable two-party system is that the two major parties alternate with one another in power, such has been the case in both of countries. In the 13 elections for the House of Commons since World War II, power has changed hands between the Conservatives and Labour six times, most recently in May 1979. Since the Bundestag was first established in 1949, there have been eleven elections in West Germany. Power really has changed hands there only twice. This occurred in 1969, when the Social Democrats came to power in a coalition with the Free Democrats; and in October 1982, when the FDP switched coalition partners a second time, abandoning the center-left coalition headed by Chancellor Helmut Schmidt and joining a new coalition government under CDU leader Helmut Kohl. If the West German electoral system was as sensitive to shifts in support for the two major parties as is the British, the most recent change in power holders probably would have occurred six years earlier, in October 1976, when the Christian Democrats recaptured the lead in popular votes but were outdistanced by the coalition of the Social Democrats and Free Democrats, a result that was reproduced four years later.

Because of its strategic position, the FDP is the key to whether or not power will change hands frequently in West Germany. Most of the time from 1949 to 1966, the FDP was in coalition with the CDU; then, in 1969, it joined a coalition government with the SPD. Between 1980 and 1982, some CDU leaders sought to woo the FDP away from the left-center alliance and into a right-center alliance; and some FDP leaders became increasingly attracted by the prospect. After the formation of the CDU/CSU–FDP government in October 1982, the issue was put to the voters, who approved the change in the March 1983 Bundestag election. Thus, in West Germany there is a two-*tendency* rather than a two-*party* system. Clearly, the strategic moves of the FDP have been taken cautiously at times when FDP leaders calculated the electorate would approve. There are two alternative coalitions; this means that the potential exists for a fairly frequent alternation in power, but that the process is complicated by rigidities in the coalition pattern. But the fact that the FDP has the potential at any time to switch partners means that its current partner

must be attentive to its policy preferences. Although the relatively small size of the FDP means that it is always the junior partner, it is a partner with considerable influence. Because of its central position on the left–right ideological spectrum, this influence is usually exercised in the direction of moderation. The FDP is often at odds with the Bavarian CSU, which occupies the far-right position in the governing coalition. Before it switched sides, the FDP was frequently in conflict with the left wing of the SPD, for similar reasons. Chancellors Schmidt and Kohl frequently have had to mediate these disputes.

The arrival of the Green Party on the national scene in West Germany complicates the coalition pattern. Although the percentage of the popular vote gained by the Greens in the 1983 and 1987 elections only barely enabled them to gain seats in the Bundestag (Table 4.2), it had been thought each time that they might take enough votes away from the FDP to close the doors of the lower house to the latter party. If this had occurred, assuming that the CDU/CSU had remained short of a majority of seats, it would have made the discovery of a majority coalition extremely difficult. The Greens have been publicly disdainful of the "parliamentary game" as it is normally played in West Germany as well as in other Western European polyarchies. They presumably would have resisted a coalition with the Social Democrats, something that the right wing of the latter party would not have wanted anyway. A return to the Grand Coalition government of the SPD and the CDU/CSU (1966–69) might then have become necessary, although it would not have been to the taste of many in both parties. As it happened in both elections, the FDP surmounted the 5 percent barrier, and the center-right government was maintained in office. But the Greens have served notice that the future of three-cornered coalition politics in the Federal Republic is very much in doubt.

This uncertainty has increased with the rise of the right-wing Republikaner, foreshadowing a possible five-party system.

Recent developments in Britain have likewise raised doubts as to the continued alternating pattern of the near two-party system there. After the May 1979 election victory of the Conservative Party led by Margaret Thatcher, internal strife in the Labour Party led to a schism in 1981, with four prominent ex-Cabinet ministers on the right of the party resigning their party membership and calling for the formation of a new Social Democratic Party. Later in the year, the new SDP joined the centrist Liberal Party in an electoral arrangement called the Alliance, designed to strengthen both against the two major parties in election contests. The Alliance succeeded in winning several by-election battles to fill vacant seats in Parliament during the next year and appeared to be poised to take enough parliamentary seats in the next general election to deprive the Conservatives of their majority. However, the success of the Thatcher government in bringing down inflation and the British victory in the Falklands (Malvinas) War of the spring of 1982 elevated Mrs. Thatcher's popularity just when the Alliance appeared on the verge of a breakthrough. Perceiving the occasion to be advantageous, the prime minister called an early election in June 1983 and the Conservatives scored an easy victory, raising the number of their seats in the House of Commons from 339 to 397 (Table 4.2).

The Conservatives were actually helped along to their victory by the success of the Alliance in taking votes away from the Labour Party, whose percentage of the popular vote dropped from 36.9 in 1979 to 27.6 in 1983. The Alliance took nearly the same percentage (25.4) as Labour and increased the share the Liberals alone had held in 1979 by 11.6 percent. Had the Alliance been able to gain an appreciably larger share of the vote (30–35 percent), it undoubtedly would have been at the expense of the Conservatives; so, although the Conservatives were helped by the Alliance to a smashing victory in 1983, the government was served notice that further gains by the Alliance could deprive Conservatives of their majority in the next election, given the effect of the electoral system in exaggerating swings in popular support. Meanwhile, the Labour Party under the youthful leadership of Neil Kinnock, elected leader in October 1983, attempted to repair the damage of the internal party divisions that were so devastating to the party in the period up to June 1983.

But the 1987 general election and its aftermath revealed that the long-term viability of a third force between Labour and Conservatives could not be taken for granted. As the election approached, differences between the Liberals and Social Democrats over policy issues began to surface. The Social Democratic leader, Dr. David Owen, showed considerably greater sympathy for the domestic and foreign policies of the Thatcher government than did the Liberal Party and its leader, David Steel, who were closer to the Labour Party on a number of issues, especially the question of nuclear disarmament. During the election campaign Owen even hinted that, in the absence of a single party majority, the Alliance should consider offering itself to the Conservatives as a coalition partner, whereas Steel insisted that the Alliance parties should keep their options open. Aware of the divisions in the Alliance ranks, many voters who might have voted Alliance a few months earlier turned to the Labour and Conservative parties or stayed away from the polls. As a result, although the Labour Party made modest gains, the Conservatives did not lose electoral ground, and they retained a considerable majority in Parliament (Table 4.2).

Neil Kinnock, leader of the British Labour Party, shown at the October 1983 Labour Conference, where he was elected to the leadership at the age of 41.

Following the 1987 election, the conflict between the Alliance leaders expanded into a conflict over the future of the Alliance itself. The Liberals remained fairly cohesive, but the Social Democrats split into two factions—the supporters and the opponents of David Owen and the positions he had taken during the election. Owen's opponents called for a fusion of the two parties into one, thus ending the confusion that had reduced voter support in the recent election. In this they had the support of most Liberals. Owen and his supporters preferred to hold onto a separate Social Democratic party. As a result, the SDP split, with the anti-Owenites joining the Liberals in a new party called the Social and Liberal Democrats (SLD), or "Democrats" for short. Owen remains the leader of what is left of the Social Democrats, which was reduced by the election and by defections to only three members of Parliament. If we drop this minority of a minority from consideration, Britain still appears to have a three-party system, but the "third party" in the center is considerably weaker than it was not too long ago.

In Italy and Japan, it is not clear whether there is even the potential for alternation between the two leading parties. The Christian Democrats in Italy have governed either alone or in coalition since 1946. The Communists have not had a share of power since 1947 and, until the mid-1970s, there was little likelihood that they would regain it. Until 1962, the Christian Democrats relied on the support of smaller parties in the center and on the right to maintain their majority. Then, the coalition pattern shifted to the left, with the Socialists replacing the Liberals as the principal coalition partner. Unable to gain a majority in their own right and unwilling to turn either to the Communists on the far left or to the neo-fascist MSI on the far right, the Christian Democrats and Socialists became virtual prisoners of one another, although the former were clearly the senior partner. Both parties were divided internally over whether to keep the coalition alive.

Finally, in 1974, the Socialists abandoned their partners and joined the Communists in opposition. This left the Christian Democrats without a majority. They continued on for several months as a minority government but were finally forced to call new elections for June 1976. Both of the major parties gained or maintained strength, whereas some of the smaller parties lost ground. But the parliamentary situation remained basically unchanged. A new Christian Democratic government was formed with the tacit willingness of the Communists to allow it some breathing space in exchange for a more progressive program. Following the June 1979 election in which the PCI lost twenty-seven Chamber of Deputies seats, a Christian Democratic–Socialist coalition again became possible. This is what was governing Italy in the 1980s, the Communists having returned to the role of constructive opposition. The principal innovation in the 1980s was the selection of non-DC leaders as prime minister. Before the 1983 election, the office was held briefly by Republican Giovanni Spadolini. From that election (in which the Socialists gained nine seats) until 1987, PSI leader Bettino Craxi was prime minister. In these cases the Christian Democrats supported the government in Parliament and held the largest number of ministerial posts. Since June 1987, the DC has again held the prime ministership, while governments have succeeded one another as coalitions of the same so-called pentarchy of five centrist parties— the Socialists, the Republicans, the Social Democrats, and the Liberals, as well as the DC. Although the present system works, the Italian party system remains fraught with uncertainty for the future. It is not really a two-tendency system of the type found in Great Britain and West Germany. There may be two political parties that are numerically superior, but no mechanism has yet been worked out by which there can be an orderly transfer of power as there was in West Germany in the late 1960s and early 1980s. Nevertheless, the Socialists have been gaining ground on the Communists over recent elections, and one might foresee the time, perhaps in the 1990s, when they will replace the PCI as the second largest party. As they have a greater potential for forming coalitions with smaller parties other than the Communists and the Christian Democrats, an alternative coalition headed by the Socialists may someday come to power, finally relegating the DC to unaccustomed opposition status.

There are a number of similarities between the Japanese and the Italian party systems, not the least of which is the predominant role of one party of the center-right. Like the Christian Democrats in Italy, the Liberal Democratic Party (LDP) in Japan has not been out of power for more than three decades. In Italy, in fact, the DC has been in power for more than four dec-

ades, but the Liberal Democrats in Japan did not merge into their present identity until 1955. However, since doing so, they have been able to govern most of the time by themselves, without the need for coalition partners. In the early years, as in Italy, the two strongest Japanese opposition parties were the Communists (JCP) and the Socialists (JSP). Unlike the Italian left, the Socialists have been stronger electorally than the Communists and are the second largest party in Japan in terms of both voting support and seats in Parliament. But partly because of the rigidities imposed by the electoral system discussed in the last section, the JSP has remained frozen at a level of support far below that of the LDP. For this reason, writers in the 1950s and 1960s referred to the Japanese system as a "one-and-one-half-party system."

There are two reasons why the term "one-and-one-half parties" is misleading. It is especially so today, but has always been so in a sense, because of the factionalized nature of the leading Japanese parties, and especially the LDP. As noted earlier in the chapter, another way in which the Japanese party system resembles the Italian is in the personalized factionalism of the parties. The LDP is said to consist of some four or five factions, each identified with one of the principal leaders of the party.[15] These leaders vie with one another for positions in the government, especially for the top prize of prime minister. In turn, their supporters among the LDP members of Parliament (Dietmembers) and supporters among regional and local-level politicians compete with one another on an interfactional basis for lower-level elected offices. The system for electing Dietmembers, described in the preceding section, contributes to the interfactional competition, because, as noted, voters choose not only between parties, but between competing candidates of the same party. Given the relatively fixed ratio of seats between the parties from one Diet to the next, it can be seen that, for Japanese who follow politics closely, the contest among LDP factions for Diet seats is more fascinating than the interparty contest. It is only a mild exaggeration to say that, far from having a highly aggregated party system with one dominating party, Japan really has an extremely pluralistic multiparty system, if we imagine each of the within-party factions as a party in itself. Nevertheless, when it comes to governing the country, the factions of the LDP are sufficiently cohesive that the party's monopoly of power is not threatened by such intraparty pluralism.

Also militating against the "one-and-one-half-party" label is the fact that the number of political parties with significant shares of votes and seats has grown over the years since the label seemed most applicable. After the merger of the Liberal Party and the Democratic Party into the LDP in 1955, Japan had only three national parties of significance—the LDP, the JSP, and the JCP—and of these, the Communists held only two Diet seats. In the 1960 election a fourth party emerged with seventeen seats, the Democratic Socialist Party, a right-wing offshoot of the JSP. This four-party system persisted in the Diet until the arrival with the 1967 election of the Clean Government Party, or Komeito. All five of these parties remain in the Diet today, all of them capable of capturing at least 10 percent of the popular vote and at least twenty-five seats in Parliament. In addition, a breakaway party from the LDP, the New Liberal Club (NLC), obtained representation in the Diet beginning in 1976. With that breakaway, enough seats were taken away from the LDP to threaten its ability to retain a majority in Parliament. In the latter 1970s and in the early 1980s, for the first time the LDP was forced to govern as a minority government and, for a time, even as a coalition government, with at least the token

incorporation of a few NLC ministers. Although the LDP majority was regained in 1986, the loss of the long-standing certainty that there will always be a majority makes the "one-and-one-half-party" label a dubious one when applied to Japan today.

Curiously, although France does not have two dominant parties (as West Germany and Great Britain do), something like a two-tendency system has emerged, with a fairly stable alliance on the right facing a fairly stable alliance on the left. Part of the reason for the two-tendency system lies in the two-ballot-type election for both president and legislative representatives that encourages electoral alliances. As is discussed at some length in Chapter 5, France's system of government differs from the parliamentary regimes of the four other countries. There are both an elected president and an elected legislative body. Because they share power, both elections are important. The balance of power established at the last legislative election can be upset by the next presidential election, and vice versa. To reiterate, France is divided into single-member constituencies, as is Great Britain. But a candidate must win a majority of the vote on the first ballot to be elected. Otherwise, there will be a second ballot the following week, during which any candidate who obtained at least 12.5 percent of the registered voters on the first ballot can remain in the race or withdraw. The second ballot operates the same way the single ballot does in Great Britain: Whoever receives a plurality of the vote will be elected for that constituency. The arrangement for the presidential election is similar, except that (1) France is one entire constituency, and (2) the second ballot is automatically a runoff between the two candidates who receive the most votes on the first ballot.

Because no French party is strong enough to win a majority in its own right in the majority of constituencies in legislative elections, the parties need to have allies who will agree with them in advance that there will be only one candidate mutually representing the parties against a common enemy on the second ballot. Traditionally, the left has been better able than the right to work out such arrangements. During the Third Republic (1870–1940), the Socialists and Radicals were quite successful in maintaining discipline between the two ballots. The expectation was that, in any given constituency, whichever candidate, Socialist or Radical, did better on the first ballot, the other would step aside and urge his supporters to vote for the first candidate on the second ballot. In the Fifth Republic, the Socialists and Communists have had a similar agreement. In response, the right has had to work out its own arrangement. From 1967 to 1988, with only one exception (1978) there has been only one candidate of the majority coalition (primarily the Gaullists and the Giscardist liberals) in each constituency on the first ballot.

For the presidential election, such prior agreements are not necessary because all except the two top candidates are automatically eliminated after the first ballot. But there is a special need for unity on both the left and the right. If the parties on one side cannot agree on a common candidate before the first ballot but those on the other side can, the common candidate will far outdistance his rivals on the first ballot so that the parties on the divided side will really have to scramble to try to secure support for the surviving candidate during the two weeks between the first and second ballots. An excellent example is the 1969 presidential election. Georges Pompidou, the only candidate of the right, was facing three rivals of the left and center. Pompidou won nearly twice as many votes as his nearest rival on the first ballot and then went on to win the runoff easily, partly

because one of the losing parties on the first ballot, the Communists, refused to support his second-ballot opponent. In 1981, neither the left nor the right presented a single candidate on the first ballot. The failure to do so was more costly to the surviving right-of-center candidate on the second ballot, incumbent President Valery Giscard d'Estaing. His defeated rival, Jacques Chirac, refused to give him a clear endorsement whereas the Communists endorsed François Mitterrand, the eventual victor. Thus, the presidential election as well as the legislative puts a premium on solidarity between the parties on either side.

One must not put too much stress on the importance of the electoral systems in France. The country has had electoral alliances of a fairly stable nature in the past. However, what was truly remarkable in the first twenty-three years of the French Fifth Republic was a stable governing coalition, consisting of Gaullists, Giscardists, and minor partners on the center right. At least three factors were responsible for this: (1) the strong leadership exercised by General de Gaulle in the early years of the Fifth Republic; (2) the superior electoral position of the Gaullists, which enabled them to play the role of senior partner, rewarding their allies for loyalty; and (3) the fact that the office of president of the Republic is the preeminent prize to be won and that, because important decision-making powers are concentrated in the president's hands, the coalition partners must mute their dissent.

With the capture in 1981 of the presidency and a majority in the National Assembly, the Socialists under François Mitterrand found themselves in a position similar to that enjoyed by the Gaullists between 1968 and 1974. Strictly speaking, it would not have been necessary for the Socialists to offer their Communist electoral allies a share of power, because the Socialists claimed a parliamentary majority in their own right. However, concern for maintaining Communist cooperation in the trade union movement was a potent reason for Mitterrand to offer the Communists four seats in his first cabinet (headed by his fellow Socialist Pierre Mauroy as prime minister). The positions were filled by relatively junior members of the PCF leadership, and they were not the most prominent or strategically significant ministerial offices. However, inclusion in the Socialist-dominated government meant that the Communists had to support that government's domestic and foreign policy initiatives. This they did with little public dissent for the first year of the Mitterrand presidency. But as his domestic policy began to move away from an initial reflationary and redistributive strategy and his pro-Western, anti-Soviet inclinations came into sharper focus, criticism from PCF leaders outside the government and communist trade union leaders began to mount. By mid-1984, the Communists were leading an outcry against the industrial restructuring carried on by the government (see Chapter 6) that was acknowledged to be increasing the already high level of unemployment. When, in July 1984, Mitterrand dismissed Mauroy as prime minister and appointed in his place Laurent Fabius, a young technocrat who had been the minister in charge of the disputed industrial policy, the Communists read the signal correctly and declined to be included in the new government. Thus, the one-sided coalition of the left was dissolved.

By the time the next legislative election was held, in March 1986, both parties of the left had shown losses in electoral strength in the various local elections held in between national elections, as well as in the election to the European Parliament of June 1984. But the decline in Communist Party strength had more than doubled the Socialist decline. On the right, the gains of the mainstream RPR and UDF were less impressive than that of the extreme right party, the National Front. These changes were solidified in the 1986 legislative election, which gave the RPR and UDF a majority in the National Assembly and necessitated a change in government.

Although there was speculation that President Mitterrand would resign with the loss of a Socialist majority in the Assembly, his seven-year term had two years to run, and he preferred *cohabitation* with Gaullist leader Chirac as prime minister rather than to return to the wilderness of opposition. For the next two years Mitterrand and Chirac shared power in an uneasy division of responsibilities in which, like Charles de Gaulle before him, the president shouldered primary responsibility for foreign affairs and the prime minister was mainly responsible for domestic policy. In some ways, this was like the Grand Coalition of the CDU/CSU and the SPD in West Germany in the 1960s. Only the parties of the extreme left and the extreme right were left outside. Although the Communists only managed to slow down their decline in support as registered in the public opinion polls, the National Front continued its gain, and its leader, Jean-Marie Le Pen, looked like he might be in a position to affect the outcome of the next presidential election. He did not fail to highlight the fact that the parties of the center-left and center-right were, in effect, governing together, applying the term "Gang of Four" to all four of the other parties: not only to Mitterrand's Socialists and to the RPR and UDF, in the coalition government under Chirac, but also to the Communists, which, many of its working-class voters believed, had sold out while its members had been ministers in a government that pursued an economic policy course seen as contributing to the rise in unemployment.

History came close to repeating itself in May 1988, when François Mitterrand won a second term as president, with an enhanced majority over his 1981 margin. Once again, he relied on Communist votes, although they were less numerous than they had been seven years earlier. The RPR and UDF showed greater solidarity behind Chirac as their second-ballot candidate than they had behind Giscard, who was not a candidate in this election. But Le Pen succeeded in capturing 14 percent of the first-ballot vote, and many of his supporters may have abstained on the second ballot or even shifted their votes to Mitterrand. Mitterrand appointed moderate socialist Michel Rocard as his prime minister, and it became his role to form a government that contained enough politically neutral or centrist ministers to ensure that the additional votes could be found either to the left (PCF) or to the right in order to get legislative measures through Parliament. Once again, Mitterrand dissolved the National Assembly and legislative elections were held in the month following the presidential elections. However, this time his Socialists failed to obtain an absolute majority in the National Assembly, falling thirteen seats short. Thus, the Rocard government is technically a minority government, rather than a coalition government, because only one party as such—the PS—is included within it.

Conclusion

Despite the various dissimilarities among our five political party systems, they do appear to fall into three separate categories, based on the distinctions by Giovanni Sartori discussed earlier in this chapter. In three of the cases, there is sharp, clear-cut competition between left and right, whether it is a case of a party on the left facing a party on the right or of a coalition of parties facing one party or another coalition. Sartori would call the West German and British cases "moderate pluralism," because they enable one party to control all or most government offices at a given time, but do not prevent the occasional changing of the guard, as there are two parties with this sort of governing potential. It will be recalled that these are the two-party systems with the consistently highest indexes of aggregation. One might ask how Sartori would judge the French system, where, since 1986 at least, there have been three parties of fairly even strength, preventing any single one of them from gaining exclusive control of government. Here there would not seem to be sufficient aggregation, or in Sartori's terms, too much pluralism, especially considering that there are also parties of the far left and far right that limit the options of the larger parties still further. Nevertheless, once formed, coalitions have held together reasonably well in France, including the "coalition" of cohabitation between President Mitterrand and Prime Minister Chirac. And, on the other hand, there have been three changes in power between left and right in the 1980s, which has not occurred in Britain and has happened only once in West Germany during the decade. Therefore, Sartori's term *moderate pluralism* seems applicable.

Actually, the existence of such left–right competition is remarkable when we consider the history of two of these three-party systems—the French and the German. If we go back to the 1920s in Germany, and as recently as the 1950s in France, we see a different sort of party system, one in which power is anchored in the center of the spectrum and opposition comes from the left and right extremes. In the Weimar Republic of Germany, the center parties were committed to the existing democratic regime. But during much of the Republic's life, these parties were scarcely able to maintain majorities in the Reichstag because of the anti-democratic parties on the left and right. A similar situation prevailed in France in the 1950s. For this reason, one has to view the present prospects for a return to center coalitions in France with some misgivings.

Anchoring power in the center of the political spectrum in a coalition of beleaguered parties that are committed to the preservation of the existing regime means there is no possibility of alternating power from left to right. Power remains where it is, or the regime falls. From the voters' standpoint, either they support the coalition in power or they face unknown upheavals. This is really not a choice for many voters who may feel disenchanted with the performance of the governing coalition. Some will abstain; others will vote for one of the parties opposing the governing regime under the assumption that it could not come to power anyway; still others will resign themselves to the continuation of the present regime and will vote accordingly, although not out of any great conviction. Under the circumstances, the disgruntled voter will feel disenfranchised.

This description is not far from the case today in Italy, whose party system comes closest to what Sartori called *extreme pluralism*. The characteristics of this system that keep it out of the moderate pluralism category have not changed appreciably since the early 1960s, when the Socialists were invited into what had theretofore been government anchored on the center-right. Since then it has been government anchored more symmetrically at the center. However, it does not exemplify extreme pluralism to quite the degree the Weimar Republic and the French Fourth Republic did so, because the Christian Democrats have remained easily the strongest party in the system, both in electoral terms and in terms of the position of indispensability they occupy for coalition formation. No party oc-

cupied such a position with any consistency in Germany of the 1920s or France of the 1950s. The Italian Christian Democrats have done so for more than forty years.

But the Italian Christian Democrats do not enjoy the same sort of hegemony as that of the Liberal Democratic Party in Japan. In the mid-1970s Sartori employed the term *dominant party system* to characterize Japan. Clearly it falls into a third category. There is pluralism, but not of the kind that allows power to be shared with other parties of any size and strength, let alone to be transferred to another party or coalition of parties entirely. Although our measure of aggregation does not quite capture the fact, because there are five parties that are able to surmount our rather arbitrary 2 percent barrier in Japan, it seems appropriate to consider the Japanese party system to be one of "minimum pluralism." But the loss of the earlier assurance on the part of the LDP that they will always have a working majority in the Diet suggests that the potential for Japan to move to moderate or even extreme pluralism is greater than it was before the late 1970s.

Finally, if the politics of postindustrial society is becoming the politics of "disorganized capitalism," as was broached in Chapters 2 and 3, is it possible that political party systems in postindustrial capitalist societies are becoming "disaggregated" party systems? One way in which this has been happening has been in the tendency of larger parties of the left and right to shed their close ties to segments of society that are themselves no longer as cohesive as they were during the height of industrial maturity. The nexus between working-class voters and democratic socialist parties has been weakened because of (1) the numerical decline of the working class, (2) the decline of working-class support for parties of the left, and (3) the resulting effort of democratic socialist parties to reach out to other classes in society for electoral support. On the right, the most reliable supportive groups for conservative and Christian democratic parties—farmers and the self-employed middle class—have also experienced numerical decline. Although the middle class as a whole has grown, it has been largely a new urbanized middle class, which has shown great volatility in shifting support among parties of the left, center, and right. With minor modifications, these trends are discernible in all five of our countries. Added to this volatility is the appearance of new issues in First World politics, of particular interest to young, well-educated voters. (See Chapter 3.) The cultivation of these trends has had two effects on party systems: It has reduced the percentage of support for the largest political parties in each system, an effect that has been particularly noteworthy in Britain, Italy and Japan; and it has increased the number of viable competitors, as in the case of the rise of the Greens in West Germany and the National Front in France.

Suggestions for Further Reading

Baerwald, Hans H. *Party Politics in Japan* (Winchester, Mass.: Allen & Unwin, 1986).

Bell, D. S., and Byron Criddle. *The French Socialist Party: Resurgence and Victory* (Oxford: Clarendon Press, 1984).

Butler, David, and Dennis Kavanagh. *The British General Election of 1987* (New York: St. Martin's, 1988).

Daalder, Hans, and Peter Mair, eds. *Western European Party Systems: Continuity and Change* (London: Sage, 1983).

Doring, Herbert, and Gordon Smith, eds. *Party Government and Political Culture in Western Germany* (New York: St. Martin's, 1982).

Duverger, Maurice. *Political Parties: Their Organization and Activity in the Modern State,* 2nd English ed., trans. Barbara and Robert North (New York: Wiley, 1959).

Hrebenar, Ronald J. *The Japanese Party System: From One-Party Rule to Coalition Government* (Boulder, Colo., and London: Westview, 1986).

Kavanagh, Dennis. *Thatcherism and British Politics: The End of Consensus?* (Oxford: Oxford University Press, 1987).

Lane, Jan-Erik, and Svante O. Ersson. *Politics and Society in Western Europe* (London: Sage, 1987).

Merkl, Peter H., ed. *Western European Party Systems: Trends and Prospects* (New York: The Free Press, 1980).

Padgett, Stephen, and Tony Burkett. *Political Parties and Elections in West Germany: The Search for a New Stability* (New York: St. Martin's, 1986).

Penniman, Howard H., ed. *Italy at the Polls, 1983: A Study of the National Elections* (Washington, D.C.: American Enterprise Institute, 1987).

Rose, Richard. *Do Parties Make a Difference?* 2nd ed. (Chatham, N.J.: Chatham House, 1984).

———, ed. *Electoral Behavior: A Comparative Handbook* (New York: The Free Press, 1974).

Ross, George. *Workers and Communists in France: From Popular Front to Eurocommunism* (Berkeley: University of California Press, 1982).

Sartori, Giovanni. *Parties and Party Systems: A Framework for Analysis* (Cambridge: Cambridge University Press, 1976).

Wilson, Frank L. *French Political Parties under the Fifth Republic* (New York: Praeger, 1982).

Notes

1. Giovanni Sartori, *Parties and Party Systems: A Framework for Analysis* (Cambridge: Cambridge University Press, 1976), Ch. 5.

2. Ibid., p. 299.

3. Ibid., p. 128.

4. Ibid., pp. 121–128.

5. For supporting evidence, see Philip E. Converse and Georges Dupeux, "Politicization of the Electorate in France and the United States," in Angus Campbell et al., eds., *Elections and the Political Order* (New York: Wiley, 1966), pp. 269–291.

6. Maurice Duverger, *Political Parties: Their Organization and Activity in the Modern State*, trans. Barbara and Robert North, 2nd English ed. (London: Methuen, 1959), pp. 63–71.

7. Otto Kirchheimer, "The Transformation of the Western European Party Systems," in Joseph LaPalombara and Myron Weiner, eds., *Political Parties and Political Development* (Princeton, N.J.: Princeton University Press, 1966), pp. 177–200.

8. Richard Rose, "Parties, Factions and Tendencies in Britain," in Rose, ed., *Studies in British Politics: A Reader in Political Sociology* (New York: St. Martin's Press, 1966), pp. 314–329.

9. Regarding Italy, see the argument by Joseph LaPalombara in *Democracy, Italian Style* (New Haven, Conn., and London: Yale University Press, 1987).

10. S. A. Walkland, "Economic Planning and Dysfunctional Politics in Britain 1945–1983," in A. M. Gamble and S. A. Walkland, *The British Party System and Economic Policy 1945–1983* (Oxford: Clarendon, 1984), pp. 92–151.

11. Sartori, *Parties and Party Systems*, Ch. 6.

12. Ibid., pp. 131–145.

13. Lawrence Mayer, "A Note on the Aggregation of Party Systems," in Peter H. Merkl, ed., *Western European Party Systems: Trends and Prospects* (New York: The Free Press, 1980), p. 517.

14. The height of each party's column in Figure 4.2 is based on its share of the vote in the three most recent legislative elections.

15. Ronald J. Hrebenar, *The Japanese Party System: From One-Party Rule to Coalition Government* (Boulder, Colo., and London: Westview, 1986), p. 248.

C H A P T E R   5

THE DISTRIBUTION OF GOVERNMENT POWER

In this chapter we consider most directly the question of how power is distributed in First World polyarchies. Chapter 6 discusses how power is used to affect the distribution of well-being; Chapter 7 assesses the outcomes of these uses of power. In this chapter, for the most part, we examine the formal power relationships among units of government. Wherever informal forces, especially the system of political parties, come into play and affect the working of the formal mechanisms, this is taken into account. Our focus is on those institutions and roles that, legally speaking, are *supposed* to have the power to make decisions for society as a whole. In First World polyarchies, the distinction between formal and informal power structures is somewhat easier to make than in the case of political systems in the Second and Third Worlds. Western polyarchies are characterized by an adherence to the form of their constitution and organic laws to a greater extent than is true elsewhere. A description of the forms does provide some understanding of the way a political system works in the First World, although it is certainly not the entire story.

In analyzing both the formal and the informal distributions of power in a country, it is convenient to make a distinction between what might be called the *vertical* and the *horizontal* distributions. Vertically, power is distributed among the various levels of government—national, regional, and local. We are concerned with the vertical distribution of power in the United States whenever we talk about the system of federalism—the distribution of power between the federal government and the states—or when we discuss the problem of the cities attempting to gain financial assistance from the federal or the state governments. The horizontal distribution of power, on the other hand, exists among units of government that are all located at the same level. Power, as we know, is distributed at the federal level in the United States among the three branches of government—legislative, executive, and judicial. Further, each of these branches has subunits so that power of the branch itself is further distributed. For example, the federal executive is divided into a multitude of agencies that vary widely in the amount of power they exercise and in their relationship to the White House. Let us begin our discussion of the formal distribution of power by seeing how our four European political systems and Japan divide power horizontally at the national level of government.

Horizontal Power Distribution

Parliamentary Systems

Britain, Italy, and Japan. In the first place, it is important to understand that most Western European political systems differ from the American political system in that power is distributed horizontally according to the principle of *parliamentarism*. Parliamentarism exists in a relatively uncomplicated form in Great Britain, Italy, and Japan. It is qualified in certain respects in West Germany, and it has been partially displaced in favor of the alternative system of presidentialism in France. Figure 5.1 depicts basic formal differences among British parliamentarism, American presidentialism, and the mixed French system.

In a parliamentary system of government, unlike the presidential type of system, the voters do not directly elect the executive head of government. They elect only the members of the legislative body, called Parliament. The head of government, usually called the prime minister (chancellor in West Germany), is then chosen on the basis of the distribution of political party strength in the newly elected Parliament. The prime minister must be someone who is able to hold together a majority of members of the Parliament. He or she will be the leader of the party with the most seats in Parliament, or perhaps the leader of a smaller party capable of forming a coalition with other parties large enough to ensure majority support for the prime minister. The prime minister will then form a

cabinet, consisting of heads of government departments (ministries) and drawn usually from among leading members of the party or the coalition of parties that the prime minister leads in Parliament. The prime minister and the cabinet may continue in office as long as they retain the voting support (confidence) of a majority of the Parliament. If they do not lose majority support, they may stay in office until the end of the Parliament's term (four or five years). Should the majority be lost on a vote of confidence or a vote of nonconfidence, the prime minister will resign or ask the head of state to dissolve Parliament, meaning that new elections will be held before the end of the Parliament's term.[1] Resignation may also come as a result of shifts in parliamentary support that are not formally registered in votes of confidence or nonconfidence.

The characteristics of parliamentarism as seen in Great Britain, Italy, and Japan are such that, in a formal sense, these three systems operate in an essentially similar fashion, but there are certain informal differences that make their actual functioning different in important respects. In all three, there is an organic relationship between the composition of the legislative body and the composition of the leading executive body, the cabinet. In each country, if a single political party wins a majority of the seats in Parliament at the general election, it has the right to form a cabinet on its own without seeking coalition partners. In fact, this happens regularly in Great Britain and Japan. It has happened only once since World War II in Italy—in 1948—when the Christian Democratic Party won a slim majority in both houses of Parliament, the Chamber of Deputies (the lower house) and the Senate (the upper house). Since that high point, the Christian Democrats have declined in strength. Although still the largest party in Parliament, they must find coalition partners to have the

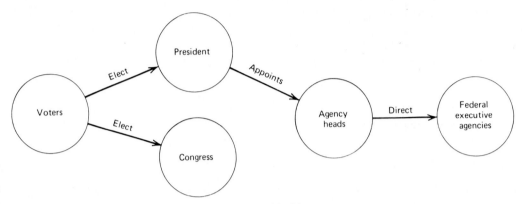

The American presidential system

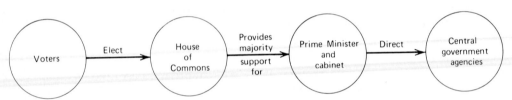

The British parliamentary system

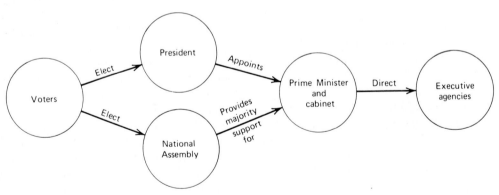

The mixed French system

Figure 5.1 Essential elements of three systems of government.

majority necessary to form and sustain a government.

In parliamentary countries generally, if a single party has won a majority, there will probably be a single-party cabinet. If a coalition of parties wins the majority, either the cabinet will be a coalition cabinet, made up of leaders of the parties in the coalition, or it will be a minority cabinet, like the Labour government in Great Britain from 1976 to 1979. The Labour Party held office by itself but required the support of other parties to remain in power. A similar situation has existed in both Japan and Italy at various times in recent years.

In comparison with the American presidential system of government, leadership of government in parliamentary systems is exercised by cabinets as bodies that *collectively* make decisions and are *collectively* responsible to Parliament. The prime minister may be, and often is, the strongest figure in the cabinet. In Great Britain (but usually not in Italy or Japan) some prime ministers have even been dominant figures. But political preeminence is not inherent in the office to the degree it is in the American presidency. Such generalizations, of course, are subject to considerable modification when specific personalities are compared. Compared with Helmut Kohl, Konrad Adenauer was a dominant chancellor. Compared with Margaret Thatcher, her predecessor James Callaghan was simply "one among equals," in his cabinet. But an indicator of the greater importance of the American chief executive is that there is an entire subfield of American political science that makes such comparative judgments about, say, Lyndon B. Johnson versus Jimmy Carter. A similar preoccupation is not found among West German or British political scientists, let alone Japanese or Italian.

The British and Italian lower houses of parliaments have five-year terms, at the end of

Westminster Palace, London, which houses the mother of parliaments, the famous Big Ben clock and tower.

which elections must be held. In Japan, the Diet has a maximum four-year term. If, however, a cabinet loses its majority in Parliament, it has the option of calling new elections, as Harold Wilson, then Great Britain's prime minister, did in September 1974; or it may resign and allow a new cabinet to be formed, as has happened frequently in Italy.[2] Thus, elections may be held before the end of the term, depending on the political situation and the judgment of the leaders of the existing cabinet.

Suppose that the result of an election is not a clear-cut one. Neither the February 1974 British election, the 1980 Japanese election, nor the 1987 Italian election produced an automatic majority. What then? Who decides what cabinet should be chosen? The place to look is the internal deliberating processes of the leading political parties: the Labour and Conservative parties in Great Britain; the Christian Democrats, the Socialists, and several smaller parties in Italy; and the Liberal Democratic Party in Japan. Formally, there is a sort of referee, although it would be misleading to emphasize the importance of this role. In all three countries, there is a head of state who performs essentially ceremonial and nondiscretionary functions. In Great Britain and Japan, it is the hereditary head of state, the queen in the United Kingdom and the emperor in Japan. In Italy, the head of state role is played by the president of the Republic. Parliamentary heads of state are to be distinguished from the political leader of the country—the head of government, called the prime minister in all three countries. Two of these rulers, of course, gained their positions through the accident of birth. Because the monarchical principle is so far removed from late twentieth-century democratic norms, it is unthinkable for the sovereign to exercise real political discretion. The Conservative and Labor parties in Britain elect their leaders, as does the Liberal Democratic Party in Japan. Thus, there is no scope for the hereditary sovereign to exercise a personal choice in naming the prime minister.

The president of the Italian Republic, on the other hand, is usually a politician of some prominence who has been elected to that office by members of the two houses of Parliament voting jointly. It is expected that the president will defer judgment to the leaders of the party (or parties) in power. During the life of the Italian Republic this principle has been followed, although with some notable exceptions. However, the extreme polarization of the Italian party system, as outlined in the previous chapter, means that the president can play a useful role in bringing the parties together behind a choice of one of their leaders for prime minister. One can even imagine a potential role for the president as a safety valve, a national asset held in reserve in case of total stalemate. Should the

party leaders be incapable of steering Italy out of one of her recurrent political crises, it might become necessary for the president of the Republic to take a more active part. The precedent, however, is ominous. It was the head of state in an earlier era, King Victor Emmanuel III, who handed power to Mussolini. This memory undoubtedly has played a part in convincing the leaders of the coalition parties to keep the reins of power in their hands.

One additional formal difference between the systems should be noted. Although the British, the Italian, and the Japanese parliaments are bicameral—that is, divided into two houses— the upper houses differ considerably in power. The House of Lords in Great Britain is a body of residual importance whose principal function may be to enable leading politicians, government servants, businesspersons, and trade union leaders to be honored for service to their country. Such an honor is likely to be given rather late in life, at a time when the individual is handing over responsibilities to younger colleagues. Elevation from the House of Commons to the House of Lords is actually a sort of political demotion when viewed in these terms. The Lords debate and amend bills coming from Commons, but they seldom refuse them passage, and the amendments stay in effect only if Commons (which usually means the cabinet) accepts them graciously. The Lords usually avoid direct confrontations with the majority in Commons. The upper chamber suffered two reductions in its power in this century (1911 and 1949) because the cabinet of the left felt it was necessary to overcome the real or potential opposition by the Conservative-dominated Lords to its legislative program. The clue to the weakness of the Lords is that, because of the hereditary principle, it has a permanent Conservative majority.[3] This has been tempered somewhat since the 1950s by the creation of life peers, new members of the House of Lords whose titles will not pass on to their heirs. Although many of these are Labour and Alliance peers or political independents, the Conservative majority remains. Thus, the composition of the House of Lords does not reflect changes in popular support for the parties. Its wishes are not taken into account when a new cabinet is being formed or when it is being decided whether the present one should stay in power.

By contrast, the Italian Senate is nearly a coequal of the lower chamber, the Chamber of Deputies. Legislation must pass both houses; the Senate can just as easily be a stumbling block as the Chamber. The cabinet must retain the support of the Senate as well as the Chamber to stay in power. Nevertheless, having two chambers in Italy is actually rather arbitrary and of limited significance for two reasons. First, the electoral systems for the two chambers are similar; they are both based essentially on proportional representation. (See Chapter 4.) Whenever one house is dissolved, the other is as well; therefore, elections are held at the same time, and the results are usually quite close. Thus, it is possible to form a cabinet on the basis of the distribution in either chamber without doing injustice to the distribution in the other. Second, major decisions about the disposition of legislative matters are made at party headquarters among leaders representing factions of the party in both chambers. A decision made for the party, whether Christian Democrats, Communists, or Socialists, will generally be binding on members of the party in both chambers, and the voting on legislation cannot be expected to differ significantly in either house.[4] This is not to suggest that there is never disagreement between the two; it is still important to recognize the formal coequal status of the Italian Senate in comparing its power with that of the House of Lords.

As for the Japanese upper house, the House of Councillors, it is an elective body, like the House of Representatives, the lower Diet chamber. But its composition differs from that of the House of Representatives, as there is a different type of electoral system—one that favors the ruling LDP even more than does the electoral system for the lower house. Like the House of Lords, the House of Councillors has only a delaying power, which is used sparingly, because the government is able to ensure through LDP party discipline that both houses will comply with its wishes.

When one turns fully to the informal aspects of the horizontal distribution of power, especially when one asks about the role of party systems, there is a sharp contrast between Great Britain's near two-party system and the Italian multiparty system, with Japanese legislative behavior resembling the British more than the Italian. The similarity between Britain and Japan is especially apparent in the high level of party discipline in Parliament. Members of parliamentary parties in both countries vote as blocs most of the time. If the control exercised by party leaders over these legislators shocks American students, they should remember that party discipline in legislative bodies is generally greater in Western Europe than it is in the United States. Great Britain is certainly no exception. As in Japan, the many in the major parties are directed by the few who are party leaders, although the proper term for Japan is *faction leaders*. The chief difference lies in the greater role the British members of Parliament (MPs) actually play in choosing their leaders and in their capacity to withhold their approval, forcing the leaders to bend to their will. But this rank-and-file control is not exercised very often. On a day-to-day basis, the leadership formulates policy, communicates it to the rank and file, and expects to see them filing into the appropriate division lobbies when a vote is called.

Mention should be made of the method of voting on important questions in the House of

Commons. Figure 5.2 shows the physical layout of the House. In contrast to the houses of Congress in the United States as well in most other parliamentary bodies, MPs do not sit in rows facing a common podium. Instead, they sit in rows of benches facing each other. On one side are the governing party's benches; on the other are the opposition's. Third- and fourth-party MPs sit on the opposition's side. Debate flows back and forth between the two sides. Much of it is informal and impromptu, a characteristic that is facilitated by the small size of the chamber because there are fewer seats than there are MPs.

On either side of the chamber are rooms known as division lobbies. MPs vote by filing into the appropriate lobbies whenever the division bell rings. The bell can be heard throughout Westminster Palace, in nearby MPs' offices, and out on the street as well, so that any MP in the vicinity is alerted. Actually, the party whips will have informed MPs when to expect the division. It is their job to see that the troops are marshaled whenever a vote is important. If the balance between the two parties is very close, MPs on both sides remain away only at the risk of their leaders' severe dipleasure. But

even if there is a comfortable majority, both sides will want to make a good showing. Too many absentees will indicate weakness in the current leadership's support on the back benches. The convenient aspect of the division lobbies from the leadership's point of view is that the whips can station themselves at the heads of the lobbies and make sure that their back-benchers are whipped in. To file into the opposite lobby takes an act of overt defiance, which most MPs would rather avoid most of the time.

However, too much should not be made of these physical aspects. Most observers find two other explanations for party cohesion in the House of Commons more persuasive.[5] In the first place, Labour and Conservative MPs are team players. The results of the divisions are like cricket scores. It looks better for the party in power to win a division by, say, 330 to 261, than by 305 to 286. The latter score would be at least a moral victory for the other side if the normal spread between the two parties is wider. Of course, if the party balance in Commons is very close, a poor result could actually mean the government's defeat. (This happened to the James Callaghan government in the spring of 1979.) Such a result on a motion of confidence would force the government either to resign or to call a new election. Although the latter is the more likely choice in Great Britain, it could still mean the loss of power if the electorate so decides (as also happened in 1979). Taking all these factors into consideration, the team player usually goes along with his or her mates.

A second consideration is the practical consequence for the MP of violating party discipline. If an MP should lose the backing of his or her political party, he or she would be in the political wilderness. Candidates without the backing of one of the major parties stand little chance in a general election in Great Britain. Although it

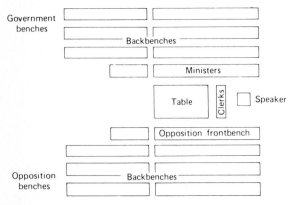

Figure 5.2 Floor plan of the House of Commons.

does not happen very often that a party in Parliament expels an MP from its ranks, it is possible that an MP who votes with the opposition on a crucial division will be dropped by the local party constituency association in favor of another candidate.[6] Moreover, within the parliamentary party, potential dissidents who are ambitious for higher office may find their path blocked by the leadership whom they have defied and who controls access to government office. However, despite all of that, party cohesion in the House of Commons declined in the 1970s. Back-bench dissent, or voting in the opposite lobby, occurred within the majority party on a number of important issues, causing difficulties for both Labour and Conservative governments. Party cohesion has generally held on motions of confidence and nonconfidence, but the dissent registered on important policy questions probably reflects a greater spirit of independence among back-bench MPs and, in the case of the Labour Party, serious within-party conflict over domestic and foreign policy.[7]

Japanese Dietmembers are likewise known for the high level of party cohesion they display in Parliament. However, in both the Japanese and Italian legislative bodies, votes are taken only after elaborate negotiations among factional leaders have been undertaken and common party positions worked out.[8] The result is a much more cumbersome process of *intra*party deliberations that must go on before a majority can be built behind a single position. The individual Italian or Japanese legislator may be able to influence this process, as can the MP in Great Britain with respect to particular policy areas where the interests he or she represents are at stake. But, for the most part, the legislator is dependent on his or her factional and party leaders to get results. Whether or not the leaders can get results depends on the stands of other leaders and on the overall distribution of party

strength in Parliament. However, once the decisions are made, in Japan cohesion will hold, whereas this has not been a certainty in Italy. This is because, until the practice was abolished in 1988, important votes in the Italian Parliament were taken by secret ballot, giving individual members of parties the opportunity to vote in unexpected ways. So-called sharpshooters were free to vote against a government in which their party participated—indeed, voting counter to the way the party leaders had pledged that the party would vote.[9] This is a principal reason that cabinets in the Italian Republic have had an average life of only ten months.[10]

When a British or Japanese party leadership comes to power after gaining a solid electoral victory, it can proceed to put its program into effect. However, this certainty is not possible in a party system like Italy's where no single party can hope to gain a majority. Even in a country like the Netherlands, where the differences between the parties on substantive issues are not as great as in Italy, it usually takes several weeks or even months of negotiation before a governing coalition can be formed with an agreed-on program. But in Italy, the members of a new coalition cabinet have come to power with only the vaguest idea of a common program. Policy tends to emerge on an ad hoc basis in response to urgent necessities when decisions can no longer be postponed. Under similar circumstances in France in the 1950s, the political system was characterized as *immobile*; and this term accurately describes the situation in Italy today.

West German Parliamentarism. Immobility of the above type had plagued the earlier German attempt to construct a polyarchy—the Weimar Republic (1919–1933). Just as in the Italian Republic today, a multiplicity of political parties had hampered policymaking. As was shown in Chapter 4, the West German party system has come a long way from the extreme multipartism of the Weimar period. As of 1949, however, when the Basic Law (constitution) of the new Federal Republic was being formulated, it was not at all clear whether or not there would be the same multiplicity of parties as in the past. Accordingly, the framers of the Basic Law added certain complications to the model of a parliamentary system to prevent the potential destabilizing effects of a multiparty system. Because of the subsequent consolidation in the party system, these complications have not been as significant in the Bonn Republic as they might otherwise have been.

The two most important additions to the normal rules of a parliamentary system are the so-called constructive vote of nonconfidence and the important role played by the upper chamber of Parliament, the *Bundesrat* (Federal Council). In most parliamentary systems, when the cabinet decides that a vote in Parliament will be a motion of confidence, it must resign or call for new elections if defeated. Under the West German Basic Law, resignation is forced on the federal chancellor (the West German counterpart of a prime minister) only if the vote of no confidence has been on an opposition motion that names a new chancellor and passes by a majority vote. If this does not occur, the chancellor may remain in office even if his or her majority has been lost on the vote of confidence, or he or she may call for new elections. This was the situation facing Chancellor Willy Brandt in 1972. He had lost his majority in the lower house, the *Bundestag* (the Federal Diet), but no alternative chancellor could secure a majority. Therefore, Brandt called for new elections, which his coalition (SPD-FDP) won comfortably; this changed the balance in the Bundestag in his favor and gave him a reliable majority. In October 1982, a constructive vote of no confidence

Helmut Kohl, the West German chancellor, addressing the lower house of the Parliament, the Bundestag. Former Chancellor Helmut Schmidt is in the background.

was adopted by the Bundestag for the first time in the history of the Bonn Republic. SPD Chancellor Helmut Schmidt was defeated and a new chancellor, Helmut Kohl, leader of the CDU, was elected in his place.[11]

Both the 1972 and 1982 cases show the importance of having few political parties in West Germany. The calculations necessary to avoid a loss of confidence in the first place or, once it is lost, to find a new majority are much easier to make when there are only four political parties operating at the national level. The number of potential defectors from a governing coalition are far fewer than in the Weimar Republic, and there are fewer alternatives to any given coalition. As noted in Chapter 4, the appearance of the Greens as a fourth party in the Bundestag complicates matters. However, had the extreme multiparty system prevailed after 1949, it is conceivable that the provisions of the Basic Law on motions of confidence would have been used more often. This might have increased the importance of the president of the Republic, who plays a neutral role in the political process, as does the Italian president, unless a stalemate arises between the chancellor and the Bundestag.

The role of the upper chamber, the Bundesrat, is a unique feature of the Basic Law. Its composition is based neither on the hereditary principle that prevails in the House of Lords nor on direct popular election found in the Italian Senate and the Japanese House of Councillors. It reflects the fact, as is outlined later, that West Germany is a federal republic and, therefore, gives an important place in its system to its regional units of government, the *Länder*. Members of the Bundesrat are actually members of the Land cabinets who are sent to Bonn to represent the interests of their governments in the upper house of Parliament. The Bundesrat enjoys an absolute veto over the acts of the Bundestag whenever they directly affect Land interests. This is true for more than half the bills adopted by the lower house because much federal legislative policy is actually administered by the Länder. On other legislative measures, the Bundesrat has a suspensory veto, meaning that bills must be repassed by the Bundestag by a majority (in certain cases by a two-thirds majority) if they are to become law without the Bundesrat's consent.

These powers actually put the Bundesrat in a strong position, not only with respect to the Bundestag itself, but also with respect to the federal chancellor and the cabinet, who reflect the wishes of a majority in the Bundestag. When the party balance in the Bundesrat differs from that in the Bundestag, as it did before 1982, the opposition party or coalition is in a position to stymie the actions desired by the party or coalition in power. Until 1982, the situation was one in which the SPD-FDP coalition with a majority in the lower house faced a majority of CDU/CSU votes in the upper house. This is all the more likely to occur because, unlike the case of Italy, members of the upper house are not chosen at the same time as those of the lower house. Land elections, which determine the composition of Land governments, are staggered at different times during the period between federal elections. This partial veto power held by the upper chamber in West Germany (potentially, at least) interferes with the responsibility of a cabinet to its majority in the lower one. A cabinet could bend to the wishes of the majority in the upper house and find itself losing the confidence of the majority in the lower house. When this danger exists, the party or coalition in power has no choice but to give the opposition a role in its policy-making deliberations.

Thus, the Basic Law has some built-in features that could, under certain circumstances, produce instability or immobility. On the other hand, a cabinet can keep going despite the loss of its Bundestag majority as long as it has the support of the federal president and the Bundesrat. But what the framers of the Basic Law may have gained in flexibility, they seem to have lost in terms of the parliamentary theory of democracy. Neither the president nor the Bundesrat is directly elected by the people. Still, because the party system has permitted stable government, power has been concentrated in the chancellor and the cabinet at least as much as in the case of the British prime minister and cabinet.[12] Once again, a high degree of party discipline works to the advantage of party leaders. Because they have the support of a majority in the popular house of Parliament and because this majority has been chosen from essentially only two alternatives by the voters, the democratic link is there.

The Mixed French System

From the establishment of the Third Republic in the 1870s until the fall of the Fourth Republic in 1958 (except for the brief interlude of German occupation, 1940–1944), France, too, had a parliamentary system of government. However, because of the fragmented party system, cabinet coalitions were unstable and government was weak throughout the Third and Fourth Republics. The Fifth Republic, instituted under the leadership of Charles de Gaulle in 1958, represents a departure from French parliamentary traditions in a number of important respects. As the Fifth Republic has matured, it has developed features that are more typical of a presidential system—as in the United States. The result has been a combination of constitutional elements.

As Figure 5.1 indicates, French voters elect both the lower house of Parliament (the National Assembly) and the head of state (the president of the Republic). This feature of the Fifth Republic constitution resembles the American presidential system, as does the fact that the terms of the president and the National Assembly do not coincide, the former being elected for a seven-year term and the latter for five years. On the other hand, like the monarch in the British parliamentary system, the French president appoints a prime minister, whose role is to preside over the cabinet. In the French case this is not a mere formality: The French president exercises discretion in this choice. However, the choice must be one that can be supported by the National Assembly, because the prime minister can be forced to resign if a motion of censure is adopted by the Assembly. This could potentially neutralize the president's control over the prime minister, although the president has the power in such cases to dissolve the National Assembly, forcing a new legislative election that might return a majority favorable to a prime minister of the president's choosing. Circumstances such as these have occurred three times in the history of the Fifth Republic—in 1962, when Prime Minister Georges Pompidou, appointed by President de Gaulle, was defeated on a motion of censure; and in 1981 and 1988,

French President François Mitterrand. With his Socialist Party, he won the presidential and legislative elections of May–June 1981, and was reelected seven years later.

when the election of François Mitterrand as president on both occasions produced the situation in which a president of the left faced a National Assembly majority of the right. In all three cases the assembly was dissolved and the subsequent elections produced an assembly that was more compatible with the president's wishes. However, in 1986, new legislative elections produced a National Assembly with a majority of the right facing a president of the left—Mitterrand. For two years the president had to "cohabit" power with a prime minister—Gaullist leader Jacques Chirac—he would have preferred not to appoint.

Several features of the constitution of the Fifth Republic were designed to reduce the hold of Parliament over the process of policymaking and turn power decisively over to the executive. In the Third and Fourth Republics, Parliament's ability to withdraw majority support from cabinets on short notice deprived the latter of the capacity to make strong, coherent policy—at least in areas where Parliament was sharply divided (for example, on colonial policy during the Fourth Republic). Among the new procedural means, several enable the prime minister and the cabinet virtually to ignore or circumvent the legislative process. For example, the National Assembly has been deprived of the power to lay down more than the basic principles of legislation in many areas; in other areas that are relegated to the administrative sphere, it cannot legislate at all. Furthermore, in those areas where the Assembly can still legislate, the prime minister is authorized to deny it an actual vote! Whenever the prime minister declares that a bill is a matter of confidence, the bill will pass without a vote, unless the opposition puts down a motion of censure. In that case, the motion must pass by an *absolute majority* (that is, 50 percent plus one of all members of the Assembly—not just a majority of those voting). During the life of the Fifth Republic, some prime ministers have been more heavy handed than others in using these and other provisions in short-circuiting Parliament. But the stability of governing majorities has consistently made sure that the power of Parliament in the Fifth Republic to assert its will against the prime minister and cabinet has not been as great as that of its predecessors.

Although it was not necessarily the intention of its framers, the Constitution of 1958 departed further from the parliamentary principle by creating a potentially powerful president of the Republic without incorporating a system of checks and balances, such as that found in the American Constitution. Since 1965 the president has been elected for a seven-year term. The more important powers of the office include (1) the power to decide when to dissolve the Assembly, something the president could do before only on the advice of the prime minister; (2) the power to put a question to the voters in the form of a popular referendum (on the advice of the prime minister); (3) the power to choose the prime minister without having to secure approval for this choice by a parliamentary vote; (4) the power to conduct the nation's foreign policy; and (5) the power to declare a state of emergency, thus suspending Parliament's power to legislate. The last of these was a cause of grave concern to many French observers, but it was deemed a necessary evil because of the Algerian War, which was raging at the time the constitution came into effect and because of the near-military coup that had brought down the Fourth Republic.

Charles de Gaulle was elected the first president of the Fifth Republic in December 1958 and served until his resignation in 1969. Of the various powers available to him, the emergency power—potentially the most extensive—was exercised with moderation and essentially within constitutional limits. He declared a state of emergency only once, in April 1961, in the face of an imminent coup d'état by army generals in Algeria. The powers he assumed at that time were phased out gradually with what experts regarded as only minor breaches of legality. There was no doubt in anyone's mind that a real emergency existed and that strong measures were needed to save the Republic. By contrast, in another civil crisis seven years later, the May–June revolt of 1968, de Gaulle refrained from invoking the emergency clause, Article 16. Nor has it been used by any of his successors.

In other areas, de Gaulle seemed to be fashioning the role of the president into something beyond that of a mere referee among competing political forces. He appointed his own prime minister, Michel Debré, who had been a loyal follower of the general from the beginning; he also decided who the members of Debré's cabinet should be—a practice he continued with subsequent cabinets. Furthermore, he intervened on a daily basis in policy decisions, essentially devising his own national security strategy and often interjecting his views among those of his ministers in the area of domestic policy.

In short, de Gaulle acted much more like the very partisan and powerful president of the United States than like the neutral and largely powerless heads of state of Great Britain, Italy, Japan, and West Germany. His prime minister was not expected to be a political leader in his own right, but rather a policy coordinator and manager of the majority in the National Assembly; however, the long tenure of Georges Pompidou as prime minister (1962–1968) enabled him to transcend the limits of the role and ultimately to rival de Gaulle himself. Yet Pompidou as president (1969–1974) and his successor, Valery Giscard d'Estaing (1974–1981), largely continued to exercise the function of the presidential office along the lines established by de Gaulle. The president of the republic is by far the most powerful figure in the French political system.

That having been said, it must be acknowledged that the unique circumstance of *cohabitation* between a president of the left (Mitterrand) and a prime minister (Jacques Chirac) and parliamentary majority of the right, which was the case between 1986 and 1988, restricted the normal presidential powers. In order to have a relatively free rein in the sphere of foreign affairs, Mitterrand found it necessary during this time to allow Chirac wide scope to formulate and implement domestic policy. In fact, this worked to the president's advantage, because it was a period of improving relations with the Soviet Union and other Eastern block nations, whereas the domestic ventures of the prime minister lurched from one disappointment to another. Accordingly, Mitterrand won reelection to the presidency in 1988, rather easily outdistancing Chirac on the second ballot. In the following legislative elections, however, his Socialists failed to gain an absolute majority in the National Assembly. This means that his prime minister, moderate Socialist Michel Rocard, has had the spotlight focused on his efforts to sustain coalitions behind his domestic policy. Mitterrand plays a more passive role similar to the one he played during cohabitation. It appears that France has moved beyond the period of recurrent crises that marked the de Gaulle presidency and that forced him to play a more active role than perhaps he himself had regarded as ideal, even though necessary in the circumstances. Indeed, whenever possible, de Gaulle preferred to remain publicly aloof from domestic political infighting, exposing his prime minister and other members of his government to the risk of public opprobrium when things went wrong. Mitterrand has by both choice and necessity played a similar role.[13] But, again, at no time in the Fifth Republic has the presidency reverted to the figurehead status of the Third and Fourth Republic presidents or of the heads of state of our four other countries.

Probably the most controversial use President de Gaulle made of the presidency was his attempt on two occasions to use the popular referendum to amend the constitution. Although Article 89 of the Constitution of 1958 provides several methods of constitutional amendment, all of them require the participation of both parliamentary chambers—the National Assembly and the Senate. Yet in October 1962 and April 1969, de Gaulle submitted constitutional amendments to the voters without first consulting the two chambers. The first, which changed the method for selecting the president to direct popular vote, was adopted by the voters with a wide margin.[14] The second, designed to change the composition and powers of the Senate and to give certain powers of the central government to new regional units of government, was rejected—which brought about de Gaulle's retirement from politics. Both referendums were heavily criticized by non-Gaullists. Part of the criticism was directed at the unconstitutional method of amendment, a criticism that probably carried more weight with political elites than with the general public.

In fact, the referendum of October 1962 profoundly changed the spirit of the Constitution of 1958. It introduced something foreign to French political traditions. The idea of a popularly elected president had been anathema to dyed-in-the-wool republicans ever since the middle of the nineteenth century, when the only previous popular presidential election had resulted in the victory of Napoleon Bonaparte's nephew and the consequent transformation of the Second Republic into the Second Empire. By making the president of the republic a popularly elected official, the 1962 amendment went a long way toward changing the French system of government from a modified parliamentary system to a near-presidential system. Because the longest standing and most copied presidential model is the American one, it may be worthwhile to compare the present Fifth Republic with the American political system (Figure 5.1). In both systems, whatever the original intentions, the president is the central figure in the structure of power. Both presidents name whomever they choose to their cabinets. Both are in charge of foreign and defense policies. Both are popularly elected, with major attention in the election being given to the personalities of the competing candidates. Both carry a great deal of authority with the public, the press, the legislature, and their subordinates in the executive branch of government.

Nevertheless, the president of the French Fifth Republic has a greater share of horizontal power than does the president of the United States. The French president is elected for a seven-year, rather than a four-year, term and unlike the case of the American president, there are no constitutional limits on the number of times a French president can be reelected. The American president cannot do three things that are permitted to the French president under the Constitution of 1958:

1. The U.S. president cannot dissolve Congress and call new elections. The terms of members of Congress are fixed, and the dates of the elections are determined by the U.S. Constitution. However, the French president cannot dissolve the National Assembly twice during a one-year period.

2. The American president cannot submit a proposition to the voters in the form of a referendum. De Gaulle made effective use of this device in mobilizing support for his objectives in the Algerian War. Presidents Lyndon B. Johnson and Richard M. Nixon might have found a similar device useful in handling the war in Vietnam.

3. The American president cannot declare a state of emergency, thus suspending the legislative powers of Congress. American presidents sometimes assume extraordinary powers during a crisis, but their actions can be revoked by Congress or declared invalid by the Supreme Court. The French Parliament is powerless to act if Article 16 is invoked, and no judicial body in France is as powerful as the U.S. Supreme Court.

On the other hand, there is a counterweight in the French system that is not found in the American system—the capacity of the National Assembly to censure the president's hand-picked prime minister, forcing either the prime minister to resign or the president to dissolve the Assembly. It is this provision that made it inadvisable for Mitterrand to choose a Socialist colleague as his prime minister after his party had lost the legislative education of 1986. If the U.S. Congress had this power, it could remove members of the president's cabinet from office by a majority vote. But this is not a means for removing the French president. There is a procedure in the French Constitution that resembles impeachment and removal from office of the American president. The French president can be indicted by an absolute majority of both chambers in an open ballot and then be tried by a High Court of Justice made up of members of Parliament elected by their colleagues in the two chambers. However, according to Article 68, "The President of the Republic shall not be held accountable for action performed in the exercise of his office except in the case of high treason." This would seem to constitute a greater limitation on the capacity of the French Parliament to remove a president from office than is true in the case of Congress, which has twice instituted impeachment proceedings against a president thought to be guilty of "high crimes and misdemeanors." Thus, rather paradoxically, the French president seems to be more immune from removal by the legislature than is the American president, but the latter's cabinet cannot be brought down on a motion of censure.

In fact, what the French Constitution seems to guarantee is that, in normal times, the president will have enough power to fashion policy, to gain its acceptance by Parliament, and to coordinate its implementation, relatively free of the kind of roadblocks and detours that often confront American presidents. The French president enjoys the position normally held by British and West German cabinets that are assured of stable majorities in their respective parliaments. Even an American president whose party has majorities in both houses of Congress faces cross-party coalitions that can block passage of certain bills. The threat of dissolution might make quite a difference here, but it would also disrupt the balance in the American system that has developed during two centuries of trial and error. On the other hand, the French president enjoys at least as much immunity against removal from office as does the American president, in a position superior to that of the British prime minister and the West German chancellor, who serve only as long as they can retain the support of majorities in Parliament. What this means is that the French president has the best of both the parliamentary and the presidential worlds. If we are speaking of the normal situation (i.e., leaving cohabitation aside), it seems that this is the single most powerful government office in the countries we have been examining.

But the "normal" situation is not always the case. The constitution, because it mixes together elements of the presidential and the parliamentary systems of government, has the potential for deadlock between executive and the legislature even more severe than what often beset the Third and Fourth Republics. Thus far, either the French voters or their elected officials have managed to avoid absolute deadlock, although the period of cohabitation is unlikely to be remembered as one of inspired, dynamic government. There are some very delicate balances in the French system. Perhaps it is not possible to combine the two constitutional principles into one system without running the risk of deadlock. The flexibility may be there to enable the political elites to work out their difficulties, but the heat of partisan battle may dictate otherwise. Still, we have seen problems in the other countries. In Great Britain and West Germany in the early 1980s, the former certainty that stable majorities could be found in Parliament was lessened by the appearance of new actors on the scene, the Alliance in Great Britain and the Green Party in West Germany. In Italy, there is the great difficulty of finding a stable majority as long as the Communists are not invited to share power. Even in Japan, there has been uncertainty about the ability of the LDP to maintain a clear-cut majority in the Diet. In all five countries, the least workable situation seems most likely to materialize whenever the balance between left and right is closest, because the ability of executive leaders to command the support of legislative majorities is most uncertain at such times. Under such conditions, the usual executive initiative-taking role and more passive role of the Parliament can be undermined by the potential veto capacity held by the latter.

Administrative Elites

On the right-hand side of Figure 5.1 are the administrative agencies that implement the policies formulated by presidents, prime ministers, and cabinets and enacted into law by legislative bodies. In Western Europe and Japan, administrative authority is largely in the hands of permanent civil servants, especially those in the higher ranks—the *administrative elites*.

For our purposes, the term *administrative elite* is reserved for higher echelon civilian administrative officials. In Western Europe, the line between the political heads of government agencies and neutral civil servants who are their subordinates is drawn at a higher level of the administrative hierarchy than it is in the United States. At the top levels of executive branch agencies in the United States, the patronage system remains, to the extent that at least the top two or three layers are staffed with fellow partisans of the president who have been rewarded for their service to the party and to the president. In most Western European countries, on the other hand, only the top-line position in each department is held by a leader of the party or parties in power. Below that level are high-ranking civil servants, who are chosen, in

large part, for their demonstrated merit according to criteria established for the civil service of that country. These civil servants are highly educated experts in the art of governing. They are expected to maintain neutrality between the contending political parties, and, unlike American higher officials, they are insulated from the political infighting of the legislative body. When compared with the United States, the principle of political neutrality of high-ranking government officers in at least three of our countries holds up, but, when compared with each other, it appears that the British higher civil service maintains a higher level of political neutrality than do the others, although the reasons this is so differ from country to country.

The leading study of administrative elites in First World countries is *Bureaucrats and Politicians in Western Democracies*, by Joel D. Aberbach, Robert D. Putnam, and Bert A. Rockman.[15] During the early 1970s the authors interviewed more than 1,400 politicians and civil servants in seven countries, including the four Western European countries covered in this text. A similar study was undertaken in Japan in the middle 1970s by Michio Muramatsu and Ellis S. Krauss.[16] Both studies examined the different role perceptions of administrators and politicians in the countries studied. Aberbach et al. set forth four models of role relationships between political leaders and administrative elites and classified their respondents according to which of the models they carried in their heads while they performed the duties of their respective offices.

The first model (Type I) is close to the one set forth at the outset of this section. It is a very formal relationship in which politicians make policy decisions, which administrators implement faithfully. Although this may be a sort of constitutional ideal of Western democracies, as the politicians are elected by the voters and the administrators are appointed by the politicians, in fact this image did not recommend itself to many politicians or bureaucrats in any of the countries as an approximation either of the way things should operate or of the way they do in fact operate.

Both politicians and bureaucrats recognize that the civil servant is invaluable to the policy-maker as a supplier of information the policy-maker needs to make competent decisions. The civil servant is the real expert on the substance of the issue at hand, but the politician recognizes the *value* implications behind the issues. The way the decision goes will have important consequences for the values of power, well-being, enlightenment, and respect. The second model of political and administrative roles (Type II) draws a dichotomy between *fact* and *value*. It is the political leader's job to decide between values and the administrator's job to supply the politician with the relevant facts, including the facts bearing on what the value consequences of each decision will be. The administrator in this model plays a crucial role in policymaking. It is not a passive role, simply waiting for a decision to be made so that it can be implemented; rather, it is an active role of providing the information the policymaker needs to make an informed decision. In the studies in question, administrators were much more inclined than policymakers in each country to define their roles vis-à-vis policymaking in something like these terms. This was particularly true of civil servants in West Germany and Italy. For example, more than 80 percent of the civil servants in these countries saw the role of the administrator as that of technician, whereas the percentages fall to 66 percent and 59 percent in the cases of British and French administrators.[17] On the other hand, Italian administrators were much less likely than those in any of the other Western European countries studied to express

a tolerance for political interference in what they considered to be their sphere of activity.[18] In Japan, it was found that administrators had an aversion to politics similar to that of the Italians, and that the Japanese were as likely to say that "technical considerations should outweigh politics" (49 percent of the Japanese administrators) as were the West Germans (50 percent), although not as much as the Italians (77 percent). On this question, only 21 percent of the British administrators agreed.[19] In general, it appears that the Type II model is popular with the West German, Japanese, and especially the Italian higher civil servants, but less so with the British and the French.

The third model suggested by Aberbach et al. (Type III) is one in which the politician supplies the energy and will to accomplish policy objectives, whereas the administrators react to the politician's initiatives, trying to be helpful when possible, but seeking to strike an equilibrium between the wishes of their political "masters" and the network of interest groups and other bureaucratic agencies with which they work on a continuing basis. The politicians are there for brief periods; the civil servants stay on in their jobs. The latter must make certain that the former do not so upset things that the environment in which they work will become a hostile one. This means that they will often attempt to dissuade the politicians from courses of action that appear too rash and will attempt to steer them into safer waters. Viewers of the television series "Yes, Minister" and "Yes, Prime Minister" will recognize this tendency in the relationship between the British political leader and the top-ranking permanent civil servant. Much of the recent literature critical of the British civil service has suggested that this third model is, indeed, eminently applicable to Britain.[20] In fact, Aberbach et al. conclude their study by arguing that their findings identify Type III as uppermost in the minds of higher civil servants in all of the countries they studied. Although the second model is one those interviewed frequently cited as a formal statement of the role relationship, when pressed for a more realistic picture, they brought in elements of the third model. We might say that in Italy, Japan, and West Germany, the formal model serves as a stronger inhibition against subtle bureaucratic undermining of political will than it does in Britain. There are reasons for this, as we can see in the next section.

Finally, the fourth model tested in these studies (Type IV) removes any distinctions between politicians and administrators at the top levels, blending them together into a hybrid type. This may take the form of the political leader with administrative experience or of the politician taking over the functions of the bureaucrat. In either event, gone are any inhibitions against bureaucratic involvement in politics, including interest brokering, the making of choices between competing values, and the exercise of political will. In essence, the administrative elite becomes part of the political elite. Aberbach et al. find this to be most true of the United States, where persons playing roles similar to those of higher civil servants in Western Europe and Japan are, in fact, political appointees. Significantly, they found that the role image most prevalent among American civil servants is that of *trustee* (74 percent), which they define as a "focus on one's role as representative of the state."[21] This suggests that the permanent civil servants in the United States see themselves as providing the continuity that is otherwise lacking in a system where so many of the leading personnel change when new leadership comes to the executive branch. France is another case in which the trustee role is chosen by many administrators (77 percent). An even larger number in France (82 percent) saw elements of the *pol-icymaker* in their role, which suggests that French administrators find little to inhibit them from playing a strong administrative role, while at the same time they regard this as necessary from the standpoint of protecting the interests of the French state. Of our five countries, France seems to be the one whose higher civil servants, even those who are not political appointees, most closely approximate the Type IV hybrid image.

The Socialization of the Administrative Elite.[22] Part of the explanation for these differences can be found in the administrative traditions of the five countries, traditions that have been handed down from generation to generation through the process of socialization. In part, this process takes place in the family. A fair percentage of recruits to the administrative elite in all five countries come from families headed by civil servants. But, in general in these countries, a very high percentage of the administrative elite is recruited from the upper strata of society, is educated in the most prestigious schools and universities, and enters the ranks of the civil service at a level commensurate with its education and high enough to guarantee that these individuals will end their service careers in positions of considerable responsibility.[23] Family and school socialization patterns for Europe's and Japan's upper classes do not vary greatly from country to country. What is different is the type of professional training recruits to the upper administrative ranks have received, both in their formal education and in the years of their apprenticeship as higher civil servants. Three essential patterns may be distinguished for our five countries: the classical *generalist* (Great Britain), the *legalist* (West Germany, Italy, and Japan), and the *technocrat* (France).

In Great Britain, the administrative elite is a well-defined minority within the civil service, known until recently as the administrative class. It consists of only a few hundred officials in the top nonpolitical ranks of agencies headed by ministers. Below this elite is a much larger body of subordinate officials who follow the orders of their administrative class superiors. However, they may in turn be responsible for supervising the activities of large numbers of employees. Elite civil servants have university degrees, whereas those below them may or may not, and if they do, they will probably not be as distinguished as the degrees held by those in the elite category. The examination for the elite-level civil servants is partly an academic-style written examination and partly a test of the candidate's capacity to respond to situations designed to simulate actual administrative experiences. Because the curriculum in the elite university–preparatory secondary schools is classical in its orientation—emphasizing history, literature, languages, and philosophy—and because the civil service examination allows university graduates with a humanistic education to specialize in their subjects, well-rounded generalists are not at a disadvantage and may even have an advantage over their more technically specialized peers.

The British education system produces liberally educated generalists at the baccalaureate level. Therefore, the administrative class of the British civil service is filled with generalists, whose forte is the ability to master the general terms of a particular problem and to offer a solution that takes a maximum number of considerations into account. The solution may not, however, be a clean, economical way of optimizing any given objective. To achieve that end, the technical specialist—the economist, the natural scientist, the accountant, the engineer— may be better equipped. But the British way has been to keep the expert "on tap, not on top." Administrative agencies consign the highly trained specialists to staff positions, which are subordinate in the hierarchy to generalists, who occupy the principal decision-making posts. This practice has been heavily criticized since the 1960s by academic specialists in public administration and, most significantly, by the Fulton Commission, which made a number of sweeping recommendations for changing the civil service. Although the Fulton Report appeared in the late 1960s, its most important recommendations—to phase out the administrative class and to place specialists on an equal footing with generalists—have been implemented very slowly, if at all. Although the administrative class has now ceased to exist as such, its spirit is likely to continue to pervade the British administrative elite.[24]

The counterpart of the British generalist in the West German, Japanese, and Italian administrative services is the higher civil servant with a generalized legal education. In these countries, officials trained in law are more likely than those with other academic specialties to be found at the topmost levels of the administrative hierarchy, although, in West Germany, economics has been gaining in favor in recent years as a preferred academic background second only to law. Civil servants in these countries are expected to pay strict attention to the procedural and substantive legalities of their work. This helps to ensure a relatively impartial bureaucracy, in West Germany at least, but it may also lead to overly cautious and even obstructive implementation of the state's business—a characteristic that numerous critics of the Italian bureaucracy have noticed. In both Italy and Japan, impartiality between political parties may not appear particularly important to civil servants, as power has not shifted to the Opposition since the present regimes came into being following the post–World War II occupations.

The route for legally trained candidates to administrative elite positions in West Germany leads from the Gymnasium (upper-stream secondary school) through the university to a first state examination in law. The requisite qualifications are determined by the state, and the universities are expected to gear their curriculum in law to fit these expectations. This is unlike the situation in Great Britain, where university standards have been used since the late nineteenth century to determine the content of the examinations. Success in the first state examination will enable the German aspirant to begin a training period of about two-and-one-half years in one of the administrative agencies at the federal, Land, or local level or in the administrative service of a court at one of these levels. Here, the prospective civil servant will build on this background in the study of law and prepare to take a second state examination, which will determine whether he or she is qualified to become a higher level civil servant (*Beamter*). The criteria for admission to this elite are precise and objective, unlike those in Great Britain where a fair amount of emphasis continues to be given to the intangibles of style.

If anything, training in the law is even more exclusively the academic mode of entry into the Italian and Japanese administrative elites than it is in West Germany. However, the recruitment process is not as carefully regulated in Italy as it is in West Germany. In the Federal Republic of Germany, one seeks to enter the civil service of the federal government or of one of the Länder just as, in Great Britain, one is recruited into the civil service of the central government. In both countries, generalized criteria apply, regardless of the government agency or level in which the recruit ultimately will be employed. In Italy, on the other hand, one seeks employment in a given ministry, not (in general) in the service of the Italian central government. And, to be assured of employment in that ministry, one ought to have family or political connections in addition to a law degree. Without such connections, the waiting period may last

several years, no matter how well the recruit does in the entrance examination. Here, the power of the Christian Democratic Party (DC) can be clearly perceived. Certain ministries have been headed by leaders of the DC for years. Different factions of the party regard particular ministries as their exclusive fiefdoms. This is especially true of those factions whose power base is located in the area south of Rome. Ambitious young people from southern Italy are more likely to be attracted to a relatively secure position in the central government than to a riskier, if potentially more rewarding, job in the private sector.

As in other aspects we have examined, the fact that one party is dominant and that that party is factionalized means there are similarities between the recruitment of Italian and Japanese civil servants. Besides the fact that legal training is paramount for both, it is also the case that connections with one or another of the ruling party's factions is a means in both countries of attaining a post in the appropriate ministry. But the academic standards are higher for admission to the higher civil service in Japan than they are in Italy. Typically, those recruits who attain the most attractive initial posts and who are most likely to be "high flyers," rising rapidly in their early years, have received their degrees from either the University of Tokyo or the University of Kyoto, the two most prestigious Japanese universities. In this respect they resemble their British counterparts from "Oxbridge."[25]

In the four countries thus far considered in this section, civil servants who have been trained in such academic disciplines as economics, mathematics, engineering, and the natural sciences—disciplines that are most apt to put them in touch with the most decisive changes taking place in postindustrial society—are more likely to have positions that are subordinate and advisory to the more traditionally educated civil servants, who hold the real decision-making power in the administrative elite. This is not the case in France, which has a long-standing tradition of relying on the state to take a dynamic part in driving and shaping the economy. The elite corps of highway and mining engineers were already playing a major role in laying the basis for French industrialization early in the nineteenth century. After World War II, France established a model for training an administrative elite by creating the École Nationale d'Administration (ENA), where recruits to the higher civil service undergo a three-year training program containing a heavy dose of economics—not the classical laissez-faire economics that prevailed in France and elsewhere in Western Europe before the War, but rather the Keynesian, growth-oriented economics that rapidly caught on in government circles in France after World War II. Graduates of ENA have come to occupy top-ranking positions in the central agencies that direct and regulate the French economy, including the Ministry of Finance and the important Planning Commissariat. Aside from ENA, there is the École Polytechnique, which provides the finishing academic touches for future state engineers, some of whom will spend their entire careers in the Ministry of Industrial Production or the Ministry of Transport. These various kinds of technocrats can anticipate careers in which they will eventually reach high-level positions with important decision-making responsibilities. The expert, whether economist, legal specialist, or engineer, can eventually hope to get to the top rather than to remain on tap in the French bureaucracy.

The Role of the Administrative Elite in Policymaking.   What are the consequences of these differing socialization patterns for the positions that administrative elites occupy in the horizontal power structures of our four countries? As noted earlier, these elites differ with respect to the self-perceptions they carry with them in fulfilling their role specifications; these self-perceptions, in turn, affect their actual performances. Generally speaking, it can be said that the British administrative elites are relatively self-restrained in their approach to the exercise of administrative discretion, whereas the French are relatively free of self-restraint. The West German, Italian, and Japanese administrative elites fall somewhere in between these two other types.

Administrative neutrality is a well-established tradition in both Great Britain and Germany. However, it has been severely strained in the latter country at certain times in the past and recently has been challenged by the appearance of politically oriented administrators occupying positions that are held by neutral civil servants in Britain. In Great Britain, the role of the neutral civil servant prepared to serve whichever party comes to power goes back to the middle of the past century. If it were ever in doubt, it met the supreme test after World War II, when the Labour Party came to power and put into effect its sweeping program of economic and social reform. Although the program contained many items that must have been fundamentally at odds with the personal views of many senior civil servants, the Labour ministers later said that the administrative elite carried out the directives of the Labour government as loyally as they had those of earlier Conservative governments. The higher civil servant is a career officer whose professional standards require a high degree of intelligence employed in the mastery of detail and in the assessment of the implications of alternative courses of action. It is the duty of civil servants to advise their political superiors about these implications; however, even if civil servants privately disagree with the latter's judgment, they will implement the chosen action with skill and dispatch. That, at least, is the formal role image of the British administrative elite.

There is, however, the other side of the coin. Although the senior civil servant has been trained as a generalist, he or she has spent a career in government service. If successful, the civil servant has gained the reputation of being a quick study, which means that one can master the essential details of whatever problem might arise. The civil servant is very likely, therefore, to be more of an expert and less of a generalist than his or her political superior, the minister. As a result, it would be foolish to suggest that such civil servants do not have a great deal of influence on the policymaking process, especially where complicated adjustments to the needs of particular interest groups are concerned. They have information, something their minister, who may be new to the job, desperately needs. In this respect, British civil servants may even have an edge over their counterparts in Italy, where turnover in particular ministerial positions occurs less often than it does in Great Britain. Of the civil servants examined here, the British seem to come closest to the Aberbach et al. Type III of politician–bureaucrat relations. They try to see that their ministry maintains an *equilibrium* in its relationship with powerful groups in its environment. If this means translating the intentions of the occasional headstrong minister into less threatening policy implementation, so be it.

The lawyers who occupy important positions in the West German administrative structure are probably not as deferential to their political superiors as are their British counterparts. After all, they regard themselves as experts. They view the politicians as generalists against whose intervention they (the specialists) must safeguard their professional standards. In the past, this insistence has escaped the boundaries of administrative neutrality. For example, the So-cialist ministers in the early Weimar Republic (about 1920) did not benefit from the civil servants' willingness to carry out their wishes as did the Labour Party ministers in Great Britain during the late 1940s. When Adolph Hitler came to power, he made certain that he would not encounter the same obstructiveness, so he abolished the security of tenure that the German administrative elite traditionally had enjoyed. This was restored after World War II for the reconstituted West German administrative elite; and, since that time, the civil service has rediscovered the principle of political neutrality. This time, when the Social Democrats replaced the Christian Democrats in power, they could count on the loyal implementation of their programs.

Nevertheless, the advent in 1969 of the Social Democratic–Free Democratic coalition was accompanied by the implantation of persons loyal to the coalition parties in some top positions and important auxiliary positions normally occupied by career civil servants. Besides the desire to be able to rely on the loyalty of the top administrators, this was done to ensure a greater sensitivity to political considerations on the part of higher civil servants than could be expected from the traditional, legally minded German administrator. This is perhaps the major reason that West German respondents to the Aberbach et al. study could not so readily be classed in the Type II category, which confines the role of the civil servant to that of supplying information while ministers make the decisions. The more politically oriented administrative elites of the post-1969 West German government see themselves in Type III or even Type IV roles, with any meaningful distinction between politics and administration removed.

This suggests that the higher West German and French civil servants are coming to resemble each other. High-ranking French civil servants expect to have an important voice in the policy-making process, and they do. Their demanding, relatively highly specialized academic training, capped with a final period of socialization at one of the grands écoles, gives them a sense of their own self-importance. The self-assurance exhibited by the French diplomatic corps in international negotiations, often to France's advantage, can be observed among the higher civil servants who are responsible for administering domestic policy as well.

The high degree of formal concentration of power in the hands of the executive of the French central government enhances the position of the administrative elite in the horizontal power structure. Deputies in the National Assembly cannot hope to influence the course of policy-making through their own legislation. Often, what they want to accomplish can be achieved only through administrative action or, if legislation is necessary, only if the government will draft it and present it to Parliament. Either way, it will be necessary to work with civil servants who will be sure to incorporate their own views into whatever decision is made by the appropriate ministry. The political heads of these executive units frequently are former civil servants who have moved to the political level either directly or indirectly from the permanent civil service.[26] Even when ministers have not had administrative experience, they will include in their inner cabinets rising young members of the Conseil d'État or the Finance Inspectorate—men and women on loan from their respective agencies. Their role will be frankly a political one, to aid the minister in making decisions that will enhance his or her career. Such rising young stars are likely to move back and forth between administrative and political positions in their careers. The newer breed of French administrators who have come out of

ENA since World War II are pragmatic men and women of action.

Whatever advantages there may be when the state is expected to play a dynamic, innovating role—stimulating other social institutions to change in keeping with the changing times—this aggressive type of role presents a problem from the standpoint of political theory. Administrative self-restraint is a guarantee that the ultimate rulers will be representatives of the people. Professional civil servants who have the security of tenure are responsible, first and foremost, to their own professional standards. If those standards permit a forceful, imaginative policymaking role, then considerations of what the public really wants are likely to take second place to the civil servants' beliefs as to what is best for the public.

An additional reason there may be cause for concern in the French case is the tendency of higher civil servants to leave their government jobs in mid-career and take executive positions in industry, or else to enter politics in the hope of being elected to Parliament and then assuming ministerial positions when and if their parties come to power. These prospects can hardly be conducive to the most public-spirited application of their responsibilities as public servants. A very similar situation is found in Japan, where civil servants, particularly in the ministries concerned with economic policy, can look forward to occupying high-ranking positions in industrial or banking firms whose interests have been in their hands while they have occupied important government positions. In both France and Japan, observers of this phenomenon have noted a certain arrogance in public posturing of the administrative elites. This is suggested also by the high number of French administrators who saw their roles as *trustees*, removed from effective public control.[27] This description of the Japanese administrator by Muramatsu and Krauss is similar:

> Almost all of the Japanese civil servants believe that political parties often needlessly intensify political conflicts, and a large majority of them also believe that the clash of interest groups seriously endangers the national welfare. Further, they believe that it is they, not the parties or legislature, who ensure reasonable public policy and that technical factors should have precedence over political ones.[28]

Muramatsu and Krauss claim that Japanese civil servants are "more like the classical bureaucrats of Italy"[29] than like the civil servants of the other countries we are studying. By this they mean that the formal legal training of civil servants in both Japan and Italy make them particularly defensive against the intrusion of politics into their domain. This may well be true of the Japanese, as it was of the traditional German, civil servant. But it is not an element of Italian culture to hold fast to legalities to the exclusion of all other considerations, and we have seen that the Japanese political culture stresses that such modern concerns are in constant conflict with more traditional values and loyalties, to family, village, and friends. (See Chapter 3.) But one wonders if "modern concerns" of administrative neutrality and adherence to legal norms have the meaning in Italy they do for the elegantly educated Japanese administrative elite. In Italy, if it is a question of adhering to a legal principle as opposed to the interests of one's political friends, there may not be much conflict for the administrator. If these friends have been responsible for one's getting a job in the bureaucracy in the first place, for example, as a favor to a member of one's family, the civil servant will find an excuse to ignore the legal principle. In the eyes of an Italian, this is not necessarily corruption. It may even be regarded as highly moral behavior—loyalty to one's family and friends, displaying reliability (in their eyes), and even demonstrating a sense of one's responsibilities. Such personal responsibilities come before the abstract responsibilities associated with the role of public servant. A jealous guarding of one's status also leads to a conservative stance regarding ideas for reform. Italian civil servants are not the dynamic force for innovation their French counterparts are reputed to be.[30] They also lack the firm commitment to political neutrality found in Great Britain. Accordingly, the Italian civil service is a force to be contended with in the policymaking process. But it is not likely to be a force for change.

The Vertical Distribution of Government Power

When we speak of the vertical distribution of power in a political system, we mean the relationship among various levels of government rather than among different units at the same level. In any system of government, there will be at least a national (or central) level of government and a local unit that corresponds to the city, town, or village in which people reside and interact with one another. Usually, there are also one or more intermediate levels between the center and the localities. There may be some sort of district that is larger than the locality, which includes several nearby localities and the adjoining countryside—a district that resembles the county in the United States. In some countries, there will be a larger intermediate level, which can be called a regional level—an area that comprises more than one city and a significant proportion of the country's population or territory. The states in the United States would fit this definition, as would various kinds of regional units in the countries we are studying. Western polyarchies differ substantially from one another with respect to their intermediate and local units and the distribution of power among national, intermediate, and local units.

The first, and most basic, distinguishing question is: What, if any, regional level of government is there? There are two types of answer to this question among Western polyarchies. Either there is a regional level with powers that are clearly defined by a constitution and protected from encroachment by the central government, or there is not. If there is such a regional level, then the system can be called *federalism*; if there is no regional level or it is weak and dependent on the center, the system should be termed a *unitary* one. The United States is generally regarded as having a federal system of government because the regional units—the states—have powers reserved to them by a constitution, and these powers are protected by a court system that is pledged to uphold the constitutional balance. Great Britain, on the other hand, has a unitary system in that the regional level of government is very weak, to the extent that it exists at all, and the local level of government is dependent on Parliament for whatever powers it has. The courts in Great Britain defer to acts of Parliament. There is no constitutional distribution of powers to which Parliament must defer when it defines what local government units may and may not do. Of our five political systems, only West Germany can properly be called a federal system; the four others are unitary systems.

Unitary Systems

In our four unitary systems, cities, towns, and villages generally constitute what is often called the first tier of local government. In France and Italy, this first tier is made up of *communes*, irrespective of their size; in Great Britain and Japan, the terms for the units vary depending on their size. In all four countries, there is a second tier comparable to the American county: It is called the *county* in Great Britain, the *département* in France, the *province* in Italy, and the *prefecture* in Japan. Both tiers of government in all four countries exercise powers that have been granted to them by laws enacted through the normal lawmaking processes of the central government. They are not, however, simply administrative arms of the central government any more than, say, the city of Detroit is just an administrative arm of the state of Michigan. They have their own elected councils, which make policy for the local area subject to certain restrictions imposed from above.

As in the United States, local units of government do not monopolize the administration of government policies within their boundaries. In Detroit, there are offices of both the federal and the Michigan governments, with administrative responsibilities and jurisdiction within the city of Detroit. Similarly, there are central government field offices in Newcastle, England; Nancy, France; Naples, Italy; and Nagoya, Japan—the post offices in these cities, for example. But, to varying degrees, the city governments are responsible for such things as maintaining law and order, fighting fires, and collecting refuse.

Among unitary systems there is a wide variety of ways in which the relationship between central and local levels of government is organized. This variation is between countries and between different functional areas of government as well. In general, the legislative body of the central government is free in a unitary system to change the boundaries and powers of local governments at will; but powerful political forces may make such change impossible or may make only certain kinds of change possible. For example, a political party that holds power nationally may be restrained by local leaders of that party from making certain changes in the powers of local governments they control, even though to do so might make fulfillment of the national party's program easier. Within a given country, implementation of policy may vary in the enthusiasm with which local governments carry it out, and even in the direction that it takes from one area of the country to another, because different political parties or coalitions of interest groups are powerful in different localities.

In Italy today—and until recently in France and until the "MacArthur constitution" in Japan—there is a single official of the central government, called the *prefect*, with power to bring local governments into line within the intermediate level of government under his or her control. The prefect has the powers to veto acts of local councils and to withhold funds otherwise provided by the central government. In Japan today, executive power at both the local and the intermediate levels is held by locally elected, rather than centrally appointed, officers. The same has been true of France since the office of prefect was eliminated by legislation during the period of the Socialist government in the early 1980s. It was replaced by the office of councillor of the republic, who is weaker than the prefect was, but still retains the power to nullify acts of the local governments after the fact, rather than to stop them from being taken in the first place, as was in the prefect's power. Some observers are skeptical as to how much difference the reform has actually made, especially in less populous areas that are heavily dependent on government financial support. The reform seems to have strengthened the hand of elected officers in larger cities and in some départements, but elected officials had

been gaining on the prefects in an informal process of decentralization before the socialist reform. The exact significance of the decentralization continues to be debated by students of French sub-national government.[31]

In these unitary systems, central government agents have always acted in a very crowded political–administrative environment in which their authority frequently is challenged not only by local units of government, but by other agents of other divisions of the central government. Each of these actors views policy from a different perspective, and conflicts are inevitable.[32] Centralization has never been as monolithic as stereotypes of these systems suggest; but the very complexity of the process defeats efforts to make it less technocratic and more democratic.

In First World polyarchies generally, power is sufficiently divided on the vertical dimension as well as on the horizontal, that whoever holds the upper hand at the central level faces an extremely difficult task trying to get local authorities, even if they are of the same political persuasion, to conform to central policy objectives. And in the case of local authorities with markedly different policy objectives, the frustration of central power holders can be acute. This has been the case especially of governments that have been trying since the high-inflation years of the 1970s to bring the spending of local government under control. During the 1960s and 1970s, in most First World countries local governments took on added responsibilities for providing social services such as public housing, transportation, higher education, and welfare. Many of these functions were added at the behest of central governments trying to keep their own administrative burden from becoming unmanageable; others were assumed at the initiative of the local governments themselves. Whatever the case, by the late 1970s local government spending had increased to the point of becoming the largest component of public spending in many Western countries. By the late 1970s, central governments were seeking to contain government spending generally as part of macroeconomic policies strongly influenced by monetarist economic thinking. (See Chapter 2.) However, they were not always able to convince local governments to rein in their spending and often lacked the political strength to force them to do so. Some governments were able to reduce the amount of central grants used to fund local programs, but this could be countered by local governments' raising the taxes imposed on their residents.

In 1979 the new Conservative government led by Margaret Thatcher came to power in Britain and pledged to bring the high levels of local-authority spending under control. During the early and middle 1980s, it was able to steer legislation through Parliament designed to set upper limits not only on local-authority spending, but also on the rates, or property taxes, that can be levied on local businesses and private residences. In 1988 legislation was enacted to replace residential property taxes with a poll tax, or a tax on each local resident that would be the same regardless of income or wealth. This is designed to make the less affluent voters more aware of the costs as well as the benefits of local-government spending programs, but it has been heavily criticized as regressive (i.e., as extracting a higher percentage of the assets of lower-income than of higher-income persons). Businesses will no longer be taxed by the local governments, but will be taxed at rates determined by the central government, the proceeds to be remitted to the local governments by the central government. This very substantial withdrawal of traditional local revenue-gathering power has been matched by withdrawal of other powers in the areas of law enforcement, education, housing, and economic regeneration of depressed local economies.[33]

In some ways, this recentralization of government in Britain runs counter to the trend toward disaggregation of social, economic, and political institutions discussed in earlier chapters. The trends in Italy and France appear to be toward greater decentralization, with the creation of elected regional bodies in Italy in the 1970s and in France in the 1980s. A 1974 movement in that direction in Britain, with the creation of elected county councils in large metropolitan areas, was canceled in 1986, with some of the functions of these bodies, instead of being devolved back to the smaller governmental units, being concentrated in nonelected bodies under central government control. It remains to be seen whether the centralization going on in Britain at present can be sustained in the face of strong centrifugal forces represented by local business, labor, and community groups organized both locally and regionally, especially if the resurgence of the economy registered in the period from 1985 to 1989 can be sustained. Local resistance to central control can take a variety of forms. The fact that the central state acts in the various parts of its territory through a multiplicity of agencies, and that the various localities have representation in the legislative body on which government is dependent, makes it likely that the current centralizing thrust of the Conservative government will lose its momentum. It does not have close parallels in other First World countries.[34]

West German Federalism

Federalism in the United States is of a type that political scientist Gordon Smith calls a *dual* system of vertical power distribution.[35] The federal government and the states each have their own spheres of power. Under the U.S. Constitution, the federal executive implements policy that has been enacted in the form of legislation by Congress. Spheres of power that have not been explicitly granted to the federal government in the constitution are, according to the Tenth Amendment, reserved to the states. We know, of course, that the meaning of the constitution has been stretched considerably as the powers of the federal government have expanded. But the states continue to exercise primary responsibility in many areas that are of direct importance to people's lives—providing for public education, maintaining public order, and caring for the indigent, the elderly, and the mentally infirm. The federal government plays an important auxiliary role in these areas, but the discrepancies in the quality of the service and in the amount of money per capita spent by individual states attests to the fact that state prerogatives are jealously guarded against extensive federal encroachment.

In West Germany, there are fewer obvious regional disparities in the quality of public services than in the case of the United States. Part of the reason for this is that the Basic Law of the Federal Republic encourages greater per capita revenue and expenditure standardization among the Länder, as part of what Smith calls a *fused* system of vertical power distribution.[36] It must also be acknowledged, however, that West Germany is a much smaller country than the United States and one would, therefore, expect less diversity. Moreover, except for Bavaria and the two city-states of Hamburg and Bremen, the Länder are new entities emerging from boundary rearrangements by the Allied Occupation after World War II and, thus, do not maintain such local particularisms as do, say, a Mississippi or a New Hampshire. Still, regional differences have always been important in German life, and it must be remembered that Germany as a national political unit has existed for only about 120 years. Parts of what is now West Germany, such as Bavaria, Baden, and Wurttemberg, were sovereign states before 1871.

Under the Basic Law, both the federal government and the Länder possess explicitly delineated spheres of power. The most important powers held exclusively by the federal government are, as for any sovereign state, those pertaining to national security. For the Länder, education, religion, and cultural affairs are among the more important areas that are exclusively within their jurisdiction. There is a further area of concurrent powers—for example, transport, nuclear energy, and criminal law—where both may legislate but with the stipulation that federal law supercedes Land law. In still other areas, the federal government may enact broad framework laws, but implementation is left up to the governments of the Länder. The federal government plays more of a supervisory role than a direct administrative one. This means that, in relation to the other countries with which we are dealing, the Federal Republic of Germany maintains a relatively small central bureaucracy. Public employment is, relatively speaking, dispersed in West Germany.

On the other hand, the federal government holds the upper hand with respect to taxation. The taxes with the highest total yield, including the income tax, go into the federal treasury. These are then distributed to the Länder so that they can implement federal policy. This has much more of a redistributive effect than have revenue distributing systems tried in the United States. Taxes collected in the richer Länder, like Hamburg and Baden–Wurttemberg, are used to help bring public services in the poorer Länder, such as Lower Saxony or the Saarland, up to a common national standard. This financial power gives the federal government considerable leverage to make sure the states are carrying out federal policy as intended by those in power in Bonn, but the primary purpose of the arrangement is to equalize resources to implement policies determined at both central and regional levels.

Divided Germany before the 1990s. West German states (Länder) are separated by broken lines.

Two counterweights protect the Länder against excessive federal control. The Federal Constitutional Court plays a role resembling that of the U.S. Supreme Court in refereeing the system. Even by American standards, this is an activist court that seeks to accommodate the Basic Law to existing social realities. Important constitutional decisions have sometimes gone against the Länder and sometimes against the federal government. The second counterweight is an organ discussed earlier—the Bundesrat. Through this body, the state governments are able to play a direct role in the federal legislative process. Although the federal government has powerful means for guiding and controlling the management of Land affairs, the Länder can help shape the ways in which this guidance and control will be exercised.

As for the local level of government in the Federal Republic, there has been an increasing tendency of the federal government, as in the United States, to bypass the states and deal directly with local units of government—the counties (*Kreise*) and the municipalities. Both federal government and Länder have shown a tendency, with the intensification of economic problems in the late 1970s and early 1980s, to increase their shares of revenue at the expense of the localities, while at the same time shifting responsibility for implementing policies downward to the local level. This has helped stimulate a citizens' movement in defense of local autonomy, which has stressed the problems of urban decline and ecological peril. Part of the same "citizens' initiative" phenomenon that has given rise to the Green Party, this movement has been particularly threatening to entrenched Social Democratic city governments and has had the local support of Christian Democrats and Free Democrats reflecting middle-class urban concerns—yet another example of political disaggregation in postindustrial society.[37]

Although central–local relations do not seem to be at the forefront of the Japanese policy agenda in the same way they are in the Western European countries considered here, the problems of the cities have been a focus of the citizens' action movement there as in West Germany. They also have arisen within the British Labour Party to challenge its traditional centralist focus and suggest that the vertical dimension of power is becoming a battleground in the face of the centralizing tendencies of the Thatcher government. The "politics of disaggregation" can be expected increasingly to feature such conflicts between "center" and "periphery" in the years to come.

Conclusion

In summary, it seems clear that the greatest concentration of power in the countries we have examined is found in France. This is true on both the horizontal and vertical dimensions. If we take as the standard for horizontal concentration the amount of executive predominance over Parliament, the French president has more power than the cabinets of the strictly parliamentary countries. This power is reinforced by the strong role played by French civil servants. On the vertical scale, France has had a high concentration of power in the central government, and long-standing habits at both the central and local levels will not readily be erased by recent efforts to decentralize the system. Closely following France in these respects is Japan, with the long reign of the Liberal Democratic Party having meant an accumulation of power in the executive, facing a relatively docile legislature. Japan's elite civil servants do not escape the control of the LDP politicians as readily as their French counterparts have habitually been able to do in what has, except for the 1960s and early 1970s, always been a more evenly balanced system politically, which no set of politicians is quite able to dominate. On the vertical plane, the recent French reforms may have brought the French and Japanese systems closer together. Formally, they are unitary systems; informally, networks of local politicians are able to steer courses that escape tight central control.

In the West German and British parliamentary systems, there is a more collective form of leadership than is found in France, although perhaps with more scope for the head of government to lead than is the case in Japan and certainly more than is found in Italy. As in Japan, power is held securely in West Germany and Britain by the cabinet as a collective body, with little scope for Parliament to play more than a marginal role collectively in policy-making. In Italy, on the other hand, the existence of a minority or weak coalition government and the inefficiency of the bureaucracy makes it difficult for the cabinet to assert its will over Parliament. Secret voting and instantaneous coalitions of opposition parties with "sharpshooters" in the majority parties have made it necessary for governments to spend much of their time minding their legislative fences, a problem that is hardly unknown to U.S. presidents. Thus, power is more dispersed in the horizontal sense in Italy than in any of the other countries. West Germany, on the other hand, with its federal system, goes farthest toward decentralization on the vertical scale, although the country has a higher degree of actual centralization than is found in the United States. Like the cities and states in West Germany, the local units of government in Britain and Italy have a longer tradition of autonomy and of corporate identity than do those in France and Japan, so when the various reorganizations of the unitary systems are sorted out, it is still safe to say that Britain and Italy fall somewhere in the middle of our scale of vertical power distribution.

Suggestion for Further Reading

Aberbach, Joel D., et al. *Bureaucrats and Politicians in Western Democracies* (Cambridge, Mass., and London: Harvard University Press, 1981).

Armstrong, John A. *The European Administrative Elite* (Princeton, N.J.: Princeton University Press, 1973).

Ashford, Douglass E. *British Dogmatism and French Pragmatism* (London: George Allen & Unwin, 1982).

Conradt, David P. *The German Polity,* 4th ed. (New York and London: Longman, 1986).

Drucker, Henry, et al., eds. *Developments in British Politics 2* (rev.) (New York: St. Martin's, 1988).

Gurr, Ted Robert, and Desmond King. *The State and the City* (Basingstoke and London: Macmillan, 1987).

Hayward, Jack. *The State and the Market Economy: Industrial Patriotism and Economic Intervention in France* (New York: New York University Press, 1986).

Loewenberg, Gerhard, and Samuel C. Patterson. *Comparing Legislatures* (Boston: Little, Brown, 1979).

Nordlinger, Eric A. *On the Autonomy of the Dem-*

ocratic State (Cambridge, Mass., and London: Harvard University Press, 1981).

Norton, Phillip. *The British Polity* (New York and London: Longman, 1984).

——— . *The Commons in Perspective* (New York: Longman, 1981).

Reischauer, Edwin O. *The Japanese* (Cambridge, Mass., and London: Harvard University Press, 1977).

Richards, Peter G. *The Local Government System* (London: George Allen & Unwin, 1983).

Rose, Richard, and Ezra Suleiman, eds. *Presidents and Prime Ministers* (Washington, D.C.: American Enterprise Institute, 1980).

Smith, Gordon. *Politics in Western Europe: A Comparative Analysis*, 4th ed. (London: Heinemann, 1983).

Spotts, Frederic, and Theodor Wieser. *Italy: A Difficult Democracy* (Cambridge: Cambridge University Press, 1986).

Suleiman, Ezra N. *Elites in French Society: The Politics of Survival* (Princeton, N.J.: Princeton University Press, 1978).

Notes

1. A vote of confidence is a vote in Parliament on a motion introduced by supporters of the prime minister; a vote of nonconfidence is a vote on a motion introduced by the opposition. Dissolution of Parliament is an act that prematurely terminates the life of the present Parliament and means that new parliamentary elections will be held.

2. This presents the alternatives a bit too sharply. It is possible for a government to soldier on for a few months without a majority if a negative majority cannot (or will not) vote it out of power on a confidence or nonconfidence motion.

3. Paradoxically, the House of Lords has been quite active in amending legislation passed by the Conservative-dominated House of Commons elected in 1983 and in 1987. This appears to be partly because dissent within the ranks of Conservative MPs is lost in the large majority the Thatcher government holds in Commons. Conservative peers have thus joined non-Conservative peers in forcing the government to take a second look at the more controversial provisions of its bills, a function that the House of Commons is not performing as adequately as it might with a slimmer majority.

4. This was less than a certainty as long as important votes in the Chamber were taken by secret ballot. Individuals or factions within parties could break ranks and defeat, even bring down, the government on such votes. The practice of secret voting was abolished in 1988.

5. Robert J. Jackson, *Rebels and Whips* (London: Macmillan, 1968).

6. As a result of recent changes in party rules, the "deselection" of sitting MPs has occurred more frequently than in the past in the Labour Party, but it is an extremely rare occurrence in the Conservative Party.

7. Philip Norton, *Dissension in the House of Commons 1974–1979* (Oxford: Oxford University Press, 1980).

8. It should be noted, however, that the enactment of many bills in the Italian Parliament is done by smaller committees where party control may not be as strong as it is in the entire Chamber

or Senate, thus providing the individual legislator somewhat wider scope.

9. Joseph LaPalombara, *Democracy, Italian Style* (New Haven, Conn., and London: Yale University Press, 1987), p. 114.

10. Frederic Spotts and Theodor Wieser, *Italy: A Difficult Democracy* (Cambridge: Cambridge University Press, 1986), p. 115.

11. Stephen Padgett and Tony Burkett, *Political Parties and Elections in West Germany: The Search for a New Stability* (New York: St. Martin's, 1986), pp. 236–248.

12. Until recently it was customary to remark on the greater role played by the West German chancellor vis-à-vis his cabinet than of the British prime minister. This undoubtedly reflected the strong personal authority of long-standing chancellors Konrad Adenauer and Helmut Schmidt. However, recent commentary suggests that Margaret Thatcher has come to enjoy a similar preeminence, especially since the Falklands (Malvinas) War. Gillian Peele, "Government at the Center," in Henry Drucker et al., eds., *Developments in British Politics* (London: Macmillan, 1983), pp. 100–105; Dennis Kavanagh, *Thatcherism and British Politics: The End of Consensus?* (Oxford: Oxford University Press, 1987), p. 264.

13. President Mitterrand has at least wanted to be *seen* to be detached from day-to-day policymaking. It is likely that his real role is stronger than what outward appearances would suggest. Olivier Duhamel, "The Fifth Republic under François Mitterrand: Evolution and Perspectives," in George Ross et al., eds., *The Mitterrand Experiment: Continuity and Change in Modern France* (Cambridge: Polity Press, 1987), pp. 153–154.

14. Under the Constitution of 1958, the president was to be elected by a sort of electoral college that was made up of more than 80,000 members, consisting mainly of small-town mayors and councillors. This was the mode by which de Gaulle was first elected in December 1958.

15. Joel D. Aberbach, Robert D. Putnam, and Bert A. Rockman, *Bureaucrats and Politicians in Western Democracies* (Cambridge, Mass., and London: Harvard University Press, 1981).

16. Michio Muramatsu and Ellis S. Krauss, "Bureaucrats and Politicians in Policymaking: The Case of Japan," *American Political Science Review* 78 (March 1984), 126–146.

17. Aberbach et al., *Bureaucrats and Politicians*, p. 97.

18. Ibid., p. 220.

19. Muramatsu and Krauss, "Bureaucrats and Politicians," p. 134.

20. Peter Kellner and Lord Crowther-Hunt, *The Civil Servants: An Inquiry into Britain's Ruling Class* (London: Macdonald, 1980). More balanced is James B. Christoph, "High Civil Servants and the Politics of Consensualism in Great Britain," in Mattei Dogan, ed., *The Mandarins of Western Europe: The Political Role of Top Civil Servants* (New York: Wiley, 1975), pp. 25–62.

21. Aberbach et al., *Bureaucrats and Politicians*, pp. 87, 97.

22. In the preparation of this section, John A. Armstrong's *The European Administrative Elite* (Princeton, N.J.: Princeton University Press, 1973) was very useful.

23. Aberbach et al., *Bureaucrats and Politicians*, Ch. 3; Muramatsu and Krauss, "Bureaucrats and Politicians," pp. 130–131.

24. Kellner and Crowther-Hunt, *The Civil Servants*.

25. Muramatsu and Krauss, "Bureaucrats and Politicians," p. 130.

26. According to the constitution of the Fifth Republic, ministers may not simultaneously be members of Parliament. Such a prohibition is not found in our four other countries.

27. Aberbach et al., *Bureaucrats and Politicians*, p. 97.

28. Muramatsu and Krauss, "Bureaucrats and Politicians," p. 132.

29. Ibid.

30. Spotts and Wieser, *Italy*, pp. 128–136.

31. Yves Meny, "France: The Construction and Reconstruction of the Centre, 1945–86," *West European Politics* 10 (October 1987), 52–69; Steven C. Lewis and Serenella Sferza, "French Socialists between State and Society: From Party-Building to Power," in Ross et al., eds., *The Mitterrand Experiment*, pp. 109–110.

32. Jack Hayward, *The State and the Market Economy: Industrial Patriotism and Economic Intervention in France* (New York: New York University Press, 1986), Ch. 2.

33. Ted Robert Gurr and Desmond King, *The State and the City* (Basingstoke and London: Macmillan, 1987), Ch. 5.

34. Ken Newton, "The Local Financial Crisis in Britain: A Non-Crisis Which Is Neither Local Nor Financial," in L. J. Sharpe, ed., *The Local Fiscal Crisis in Western Europe: Myths and Realities* (London and Beverly Hills: Sage, 1981), pp. 222–225.

35. Gordon Smith, *Politics in Western Europe: A Comparative Analysis*, 4th ed. (New York: Holmes & Meier, 1983), p. 225.

36. Ibid.

37. Joachim Jens Hess, "The Federal Republic of Germany: From Cooperative Federalism to Joint Policy-Making," *West European Politics* 10 (October 1987), 70–87.

C H A P T E R 6

ECONOMIC POLICY-MAKING: CASES IN INDUSTRIAL RELATIONS

Introduction

The formal institutions and roles of government are an important indicator of where power is located in Western polyarchies. Presidents, prime ministers, cabinets, civil servants, and parliaments make decisions that have a major impact on the ways in which well-being, respect, and enlightenment are distributed among the populations of polyarchies. The power to make significant decisions is not confined to leaders and agents of government, however. Private citizens and institutions also hold power in countries where a private sector exists together with the public one and where the state does not attempt to control all facets of social life. Two important institutions that hold potential power are private business enterprises, especially the giant corporations; and trade unions, representing workers' interests. The former, through their capacity to determine levels of prices, wages, and investment for an economy, can collectively have a greater impact than can the economic policy decisions of government. The power of private corporations can, of course,

be effectively checked by organized trade unions, but only in certain areas, such as the determination of wages. Big business and big labor may even combine their forces to nullify any government efforts to counter inflation through successive wage and price increases.

Economic-Sector Interest Groups

Farmers' and Business Groups

In the private economic sphere, as distinct from the state administrative and political circles, three types of interest groups play an important part in influencing economic policy in all Western European countries: farmers' associations, business associations, and workers' organizations. All three are regularly consulted by their governments in the making of economic policy and in the determination of each country's position on economic matters within the European Community (EC), of which all four of our Western European countries are members. (See Chapter 7.) In postindustrial societies, economic policy-making has become a central preoccupation of political elites in general. The leaders of the major economic interest groups are therefore an essential element in the power structure of each country. Their advice is solicited when major economic decisions are to be made, and they can often precipitate events that will compel government decision makers to come to grips with unpleasant situations.

Farmers' associations carry considerable weight in the economic policy-making process of all First World countries, despite the decreasing size of the farm population. In all five of our countries, independent farmers tend to support the parties in the center and on the right. In France and Italy, the parties on the left have a share of votes of sharecroppers and agricultural workers in the regions where they are numerous, but the leading farm associations in these countries represent independent farmers who produce for the larger market. Thus, the farm associations are not in the best position to bargain between parties on the left and the right. In Great Britain, they are tied closely to the Conservative Party; in Italy and West Germany to the Christian Democrats; and in Japan to the Liberal Democrats. Only in France, where they can shift their votes back and forth between parties of the center and the right, can they exert some leverage through the ballot.

Nevertheless, in all five countries the economic role of the farmers is crucial. Whether the country is relatively self-sufficient in farm products, as France is, or partly dependent on imports, as Great Britain and West Germany are, the agricultural sector has an important impact on the balance of payments. France and Italy earn a substantial part of their foreign currencies through agricultural exports, especially to their Common Market partners. The EC's Common Agricultural Policy (CAP) has been worked out and is continually being adjusted with the interests of the key farm produce sectors of each member country in mind. Farmers' interest groups do a lot of lobbying both in their own national capitals and in Brussels, the headquarters of the EC.

There are three types of *organized business* interests in Western Europe and Japan, as in the United States: large private corporations, trade associations (of firms in the various productive and distributive sectors), and peak employers' confederations. The employers' confederations are the principal spokespersons for employers in national-level conflicts with organized labor, such as wage disputes, disagreement over working conditions, government policy issues (e.g., wage and price controls), and questions of the participation of workers in the management of the firm. In each of our five countries, there is a leading peak confederation: the Confederation of British Industries (CBI), the National Confederation of French Employers (CNPF), the Federation of German Employers (BDA), the General Confederation of Italian Industry (Confindustria), and the Japan Federation of Employers' Associations (Nikkeiren). With the exception of Confindustria, these tend to be dominated by the larger firms, which maintain specialists in employer–employee relations and related matters. Contacts among employers' spokespersons, leading politicians, and high-ranking civil servants tend to be very close, especially in France and Japan, where parties of the center-right have held onto power for a long time and where traditions of administrative neutrality are weaker than in Great Britain and West Germany.

Sector-specific trade associations play an important part in the overall economic planning for growth and modernization and in the development of trade policy nationally and internationally. Trade associations work closely with government experts and officials of the

EC in developing these policies. Their ability to commit an entire industrial or commercial sector makes their cooperation indispensable. The major opponent of a given trade association (for example, that for the West German chemical industry) is the corresponding trade association in a competing country (for example, the British chemical industry's). But in negotiations at the EC level, cooperation may be more important than competition, since promotion and protection of the industry in Western Europe against outside competitors will be emphasized. The interlocking relationships among trade association officials, national political leaders, high-ranking civil servants, and the "Eurocrats" based in Brussels are making it increasingly impossible to view national economic policymaking in isolation.

To further complicate the picture, the major industrial giants—private corporations such as British Petroleum, Fiat, or Siemens—have an impact on both national and European-level economic policy-making, over and beyond that of the trade and employers' associations to which they belong. Political contributions by corporation and their leading officers, private friendships between the latter and leading political figures, and the movement of corporate managers back and forth between employment in the private and public sectors all lead to the conclusion that the corporate directorate in postindustrial countries constitutes an important, if unmeasurable, part of the power elite.

Furthermore, many of the leading private firms in Western Europe are subsidiaries of the gigantic multinational corporations, many of which have headquarters elsewhere, especially in the United States and Japan. This has led to a substantial body of critical literature in Europe, asserting that the multinationals are Trojan horses that enable American interests to sub-

stantially influence not only the economics but also the political systems in Western Europe.[1] Much of the discussion in Western Europe has emotional overtones, reflecting resentment over the preeminent economic, political, and military position of the United States since World War II. However, the discussion may be losing some of its urgency as European-based multinationals have reversed the process in the past two decades. It is difficult to assess to what extent parent corporations are able to control the actions of their affiliates abroad. But it cannot be denied that the multinationals make it difficult for Western European governments to regulate these businesses because too harsh a regulatory policy could drive a certain firm out of a country, resulting in considerable hardship for the local economy.

Trade Unions

Can *organized labor* rival organized business as a political force in Western polyarchies? That business interests have a secure position within the power structure of each country (although varying in degree from country to country) would be difficult to refute. Like the United States and despite a generally larger public sector, Western European countries are, in the final analysis, capitalistic. Although governments as well as the EC can regulate and induce certain behavior on the part of the private sector, their economies are still at the mercy of decisions made by a relatively small number of corporation heads. On the employees' side, there is a potentially similar power in that trade unions can bring economic activity to a standstill through use of the strike weapon. Nevertheless, there is considerable variation among our five countries with respect to how well trade unions are

Striking French medical students lie on a bridge over the River Seine in Paris, blocking traffic. This action in early 1990 was part of an effort to call attention to their working conditions in French hospitals and clinics.

actually equipped to use this weapon to their advantage.

Industrial relations in Western Europe have been in a state of flux since the 1960s.[2] Collective bargaining has not been as well established as it is in the United States. Efforts to institutionalize it more firmly have led to more-or-less formal arrangements at the national level between employers' and employees' organizations. For example, minimum wages may be agreed on by representatives of the two sides of industry at meetings presided over by members of the government and high-ranking civil servants. But the actual level of wages above these minimums will vary from industry to industry and from plant to plant within an industry, depending on the relative bargaining power of the workers and employers at these levels. Often the unions are left out of this process altogether because agreements are worked out in committees that represent management and employees; for this purpose, the employees elect their representatives directly with or without union participation in the election. In France, bargains reached locally with one union will apply to all workers, even though in some cases a majority belong to unions that were not a bargaining party.

However, wildcat strikes may break out, which the national employees' federations cannot control. Local workers, whether members of unions or not, can present their national leadership with *faits accomplis*. Although the latter may oppose such strikes at the outset, they often are obliged to support them to maintain some semblance of union solidarity. Because the national leadership of the unions often has little control over local activity, employers and government may both be at the mercy of worker demands for higher wages. When concessions are made in one industry or even by one firm, it becomes harder to resist parallel demands

elsewhere, and so the inflationary spiral continues. In fact, governments may find themselves having to combat not only the trade unions but also the employers whenever they attempt to pass a higher-wage bill on to the consumer in the form of higher prices.

Nevertheless, there is fairly wide variation in the strength of organized labor as it faces both the employers and the state in our five countries. Relatively speaking, until recently at any rate, workers have been in the weaker position in France and Japan, and in the stronger in Great Britain, Italy, and West Germany— for different reasons. Three factors account for these judgments: (1) the unity of the trade union movement nationally, (2) the strength of the unions at the plant level, and (3) the strength of the central government as a potential adversary seeking to frustrate union objectives.

In France, all three factors have worked against the emergence of a strong trade union movement. There are three major national confederations of trade unions in France, each with a different ideological orientation. The Communist-dominated *Confédération Générale du Travail* (CGT) is the oldest and largest, but the long-standing exclusion of the Communist Party from government kept the CGT in an isolated position, not only in its relations with the government but also in its relations with other workers' confederations. Of the two major noncommunist confederations, the largest is the *Confédération Française Démocratique du Travail* (CFDT), an offshoot from a Christian Democratic confederation. The smaller one, *Force Ouvrière* (FO), is centrist in its leanings and is also more anti-Communist than the CFDT, which has sometimes found that cooperation with the CGT is advantageous. The division of French organized labor extends from the national level to the various industrial sectors and even to the plant level, where the unions put up com-

A demonstration in Paris by car workers. The two left-wing French trade unions, CGT and CFDT, are both identified by banners as sponsors of the demonstration.

peting candidates for election to local workers' committees. Wherever more than one union confronts the employer, the latter will be in a position to divide and conquer.

At the national level, the French trade unions face not only a united employers' movement, but also a highly centralized and technically expert government. Trade unions send representatives to the various committees that participate in formulating the five-year plans, but they are usually outclassed by the highly proficient representatives of the trade associations and the appropriate ministries. Moreover, because the right was in power continuously from

1958 until 1981, trade unionists felt that they were dealing with a monolith when it came to national-level decisions on wages, prices, and other issues that are vital to workers' well-being. Business interests were well represented politically in the economic ministries in the persons of Gaullist and Giscardist ministers. The higher civil servants have often had a tour of political duty in the service of the leaders of these political parties, and they may have aspirations of ending their careers in management positions in private corporations. With the left in power in the 1980s, the trade unions were no longer on the outside looking in with respect to economic policy-making. However, their ability to influence government decisions has declined since the first year of the Socialist government, as economic policy has come to accord more with employers' interests. Much the same judgments regarding the second and third source of trade union weakness can be made about the Japanese trade union movement, which, aligned with the left opposition and representing only a modest proportion of the workers, plays a minor role in economic decision making, except when it bears on the few industries where it is strong.[3]

The Italian labor movement is also divided between Communist-leaning and non- or anti-Communist confederations. The largest, the *General Confederation of Italian Labor* (CGIL), is made up of workers who are members of, or tend to support, either the Communist or the Socialist Party. However, the Communists are in the principal leadership positions; and, unlike the case of the CGT in France, they are less isolated politically and can have a greater voice in industrial disputes both nationally and locally. The Christian Democratic trade union confederation, moreover, is allied with the left wing of the DC, which favors closer cooperation with the Communists in policy-making. Thus, the trade unions in Italy speak with a more united voice both nationally and locally than those in France. Trade union strength is further enhanced by the weakness and internal division of the Italian government. Lacking a majority in Parliament, the Christian Democratic governments have had to include the Socialists and to woo the Communists for support. Such support has been gained only by making concessions that benefit the Italian labor movement. Still, employers' interests are well represented in the DC's leadership, which means that the concessions are often passed on to the consumer, as

can be attested by the high rate of inflation in Italy.

A mixed image likewise emerges from examining the West German labor movement. Here the movement is not divided. The *German Trade Union Federation* (DGB) has the overwhelming majority of organized industrial workers affiliated with it. But the greatest strength of the West German trade union movement is in the large national federations, organized on an industry basis, such as the metalworkers and chemical workers, both affiliated with the DGB. Until the 1970s, union members were not effectively organized at the plant level because the national federations preferred to negotiate nationally with employers and the government. Although the DGB leadership is heavily Social Democratic, Catholic trade unionists are also affiliated with it, and an effort has been made to maintain harmonious relations with both CDU- and SPD-led governments. A great deal of give-and-take has occurred in negotiations at these levels, and the unions have shown a greater tendency than their counterparts in France, Italy, and Britain to forgo resorting to strikes in return for assurances by the government that the standard of living of the German working class will continue to rise. Since the late 1970s, as recession has deepened, the West German trade unions' national organizations have become more militant, especially since the arrival of the center-right government in 1982.

As in West Germany, organized labor in Great Britain is united under one confederation—the *Trades Union Congress* (TUC). The political links of British trade unions are tighter than is the case in the four other countries. National federations are affiliated directly with the Labour Party, and a portion of the dues that trade union members pay to their federations is automatically turned over to the party, unless members contract out by signing a statement of refusal to have their union dues so used. Because only a small percentage of trade unionists contract out, the majority of British trade union members are indirect members of the Labour Party. Or, to put it another way, approximately five-sixths of the membership of the Labour Party is indirect membership. The same ratio of votes is cast by the trade unions at the annual Labour Party conference as a result of this arrangement, which means that, whenever the unions speak with a united voice, they dominate the party. When this voice is at odds with that of the party's parliamentary leadership, the latter finds itself isolated from its rank and file—a vulnerable position. But such direct conflict between the parliamentary leaders and the trade unions seldom arises. Indeed, since 1981 the trade unions have had a 40 percent share in the election of the party's parliamentary leader. In recent years, the trade union movement and the Labour Party have both been divided internally, with the leadership of the TUC and of the party serving as mediators on divisive issues.

Such close ties between the trade unions and one political party can be disadvantageous whenever that party is out of power and economic policy is being made by the opposite party. Moreover, the unions cannot expect even a Labour government simply to translate their wishes into public policy without significant alterations. Since the period of acute industrial unrest in the late 1960s and early 1970s, the Labour Party has been at pains to convince the voters that trade union self-restraint is more likely to be exercised at the urging of a Labour than of a Conservative government. The claim was sufficiently credible that, after narrowly gaining power in February 1974, Labour was able to strengthen its hold in a second election

eight months later. But the claim was no longer credible to British voters five years later. After a series of strikes in the winter of 1978–79, which the Labour government had been unable to prevent, Labour was voted out of power. In the 1980s, the Conservative government was able to claim that, not the Labour party, but rather the Conservatives, are best able to hold the trade unions in check.

What makes British trade unions more powerful than those in France or Japan, if not those in West Germany or Italy? It is certainly not because they speak with a single voice when addressing the government or the employers. In fact, the TUC can only exhort powerful unions, such as the Transport and General Workers' Union or the Amalgamated Engineering Union—both of which have hundreds of thousands of members and both of which sometimes have militant leftists among their leaders. Such giants are free to steer their own courses even if these conflict directly with the policy of the Labour Party and the TUC. Paradoxically, the power of the trade unions since the 1960s has stemmed in considerable part from their disunity or, more specifically, from the inability of national union leaders to control the actions of their rank and file at the local level. A moderate national leadership, attempting to cooperate with the government in a policy of wage restraint, may find that the local branches are electing militant leftists, even Communists, to the key positions of representation at the plant level.[4] Some of these same conditions have developed in continental European countries, but the fact that their unions are weaker at the local level means that the grass roots of organized labor cannot impose awkward situations on national policymakers as well as they can in Great Britain. Still, as we shall see, disunity has become less impressive as a source of strength for the British trade unions in the era of Conservative government under Margaret Thatcher in the 1980s.

Declining Trade Union Strength

There are reasons to believe that developments in the postindustrial era are working against comprehensive and cohesive working-class organization in Western democracies. In Chapter 2 emphasis was placed on the higher levels of unemployment that have come about in part because of long-range trends rather than, as before, because there are troughs in the business cycle. These trends—technological change and the rise of newly industrialized countries providing competition for the manufactured products traditionally produced by advanced industrial economies—have brought on a decline in demand for the skills of certain kinds of workers who prevailed in an earlier era when they formed the backbone of the trade union movement. The skilled worker (or craftsman) and the assembly line unskilled or semiskilled worker are in numerical decline. Union organization in the large factories of the mid–twentieth century reached peak levels because of the large number of workers performing routine tasks on the assembly line or, as in the case of the trained craftsmen, doing repair work on the machines or precision work on various components that were not amenable to assembly line processing.[5]

Earlier in the century, the growth of the unskilled categories of workers faced the existing trade unions—largely comprising the older crafts and skills—with the dilemma of whether to assimilate the new workers or to protect the distinctions in terms of pay and status between skilled and unskilled workers, thus forcing the unskilled to form their own unions. In some cases the former route was taken, resulting in the formation of large and usually powerful industry-wide comprehensive unions; in other cases the union movement remained highly fragmented, with different unions organizing different segments of the workforce within the same industry and even within the same plant.

Today, the trade union movement, already weakened by (1) the decline in the number of manual workers, (2) disadvantages in trying to organize the growing service sector, and (3) the declining bargaining strength of workers' organizations when unemployment is chronically high, must overcome not only the divisions between skilled, semiskilled, and unskilled workers, but also the tendency of workers of whatever skill level to doubt the relevancy of trade unions to their needs. Such workers see their own interests as tied closely to those of their employers; they view the real threat to their livelihoods as not the capriciousness of the employer, but the threat posed by competition from other workers whose skills may be substituted for their own.

Still another contribution to declining trade union strength is the parallel phenomenon of the growth of small satellite firms making components or providing services for the larger corporations that were once performed within the corporation itself, but are now "farmed out" to save labor costs in a competitive market. The satellite firms are able to survive when the economy is buoyant, but many of them fall by the wayside in harder times. For the most part, they employ unskilled workers, who will return to the status of the unemployed when the firm discontinues operations, and whose earning power when at work is below that of workers in more stable factory employment. These conditions are similar to those found in service-sector jobs that rise and fall on the basis of the ups and downs of the economy: jobs in retailing, fast food, and the tourism sector.

The growth of both satellite manufacturing and marginal parts of the service sector has led to the identification of the "dual economy" phenomenon, or the division between the stable sector and the unstable sector of the economy.[6] In the stable sector many types of jobs are more secure, workers are unionized, and pay is higher. In the unstable sector the opposite conditions prevail. To varying degrees these elements of postindustrial "disorganized capitalism" can be found in all five of our countries. The ways in which it affects the policy-making process depend in part on the traditional relationship between the state, the employers, and the unions in each country.

Economic Policymaking

Pluralism

The policy-making process in all First World polyarchies features the interaction of major economic interest groups with one another and with the state in a continuous process involving both conflict and cooperation. When contrasted with the policy-making processes of Second and Third World countries, policymaking in the First World roughly corresponds to the *pluralist* model, according to which the conflict between major actors takes place within an agreed-on set of rules of the game. Over the long run, gains by one side are balanced by those of the other, with the government playing a mediating role. Public policies can be understood as the outcomes of contests between the competing groups in which both sides have agreed in advance to comply with these outcomes or to seek to change them through normalized processes. Whether public policy sides with one of the contenders or another, it will be a reflection of the momentary balance of power between the contenders, a balance that the temporarily weaker is free to seek to rectify.

Pluralism is the image of the policy-making process that most interest groups and political parties in First World countries present in seeking to justify their actions. They will say that they have acted according to established procedures and within normal channels or that they have acted to keep such channels open— or, in extreme cases, to reopen them—when others have closed them. They will insist that they respect the rights of their opponents and are merely acting to ensure that their own rights will be respected. On the other hand, they may accuse their opponents of seeking to circumvent legality and to deny legitimate rights. Trade unions may accuse employers of constituting a privileged class interested only in preserving their unjustly large share of the wealth; employers' groups may accuse the unions of trying to divide society into warring classes, thus weakening the nation in the face of economic and international dangers. In all such efforts, the pluralist image is put forth as both normal and desirable. Others are accused of seeking to subvert a system that would work to the advantage of everyone if all would approach it with goodwill.

Corporatism

Some political scientists have challenged the pluralist image of Western economic policymaking, arguing that it treats the *state*[7] as a neutral reflector of group pressures, when in fact the state has interests of its own that it is all too ready to interject into the policymaking process. Some of these writers have incorporated the state into a Marxist framework, but most are adherents to the corporatist school, that sees *corporatism* as a more viable alternative to pluralism, both as a description of how economic policy actually *is* made and as a prescription of how it *ought to be* made.[8]

Corporatists share the belief that the adverse economic conditions of recent years are attributable to the selfish actions of groups in society that have placed their own particular interests ahead of the interests of all. This can be seen in the inflationary spirals, wherein producer groups sought to pass the burden of price increases on to the consumer, that is, to the economically weak who were not in a favorable position to protect their purchasing power. To combat this tendency, government must intervene to curb the power of the acquisitive. But government is often in too weak a position to do so because its leaders are dependent on the same groups for their power. Elections are seen as a bidding process in which promises of tax cuts, wage indexing, increases in social security benefits, and job-creating spending programs vie with one another for available votes.

The largest share of blame for these problems is usually reserved for the working classes, who are said to undermine economic stability through their excessive demands. The central aim of corporatism has always been to bring wage demands and class conflict under control, subordinating them to what is perceived to be in the general interest. What this means, first and foremost, is the interest of the employer in maintaining profit levels and of the government in maintaining economic stability. Instruments that are used to bring about wage restraint range from coercive strikebreaking actions by government to incentive schemes designed to induce voluntary compliance on the part of wage earners and their organizations. In practice, these can be grouped into two sets, the instruments of what we might call *negative* and *positive* corporatism.[9]

Negative corporatism would take the form employed by Fascist Italy and Nazi Germany

before World War II, a form in which independent trade unions were dissolved and state-dominated workers' organizations were created in their place. This resulted from a bargain between employers and government, in which state controls over production were accepted by employers in return for the state's guarantee of a compliant labor force. Forced to live on lower wages than a free labor market would otherwise have brought them, the workers could take some consolation, in Germany at least, from the fact that jobs were once again relatively plentiful after the early dark days of the Great Depression. The justification for this exploitative system was the assumption that society was a corporate entity whose functioning parts were intimately interdependent. Action taken on behalf of the employers' interests would be to the benefit of all groups, and action on behalf of the selfish interests of one group would be detrimental to the interests of all. Thus, cooperation in the common effort was both normal and desirable. Conflict was seen as abnormal and counterproductive.

The more *positive* version of corporatism, and the version that is more widely advocated in Western Europe today, has been promoted most consistently by left-of-center Christian Democrats and by right-of-center Democratic Socialists, in other words by occupants of the broad center of the left–right spectrum. (See Chapter 4.) This maintains some of the same assumptions as negative corporatism—that society is an interdependent corporate entity and that cooperation is a more normal mode of behavior than conflict. But it also harbors a more optimistic view of the likelihood that workers and their organizations will voluntarily moderate their claims on society so that all in society will enjoy the benefits of cooperative effort. In this version, workers should be induced to cooperate with employers and with the state through efforts to maintain stable prices. In countries where positive corporatism has been implemented, trade unions and employers' organizations are given representation on consultative bodies with the right to be heard before major economic policy decisions are made by government. Democratic Socialists would go farther and grant workers a legitimate share in the profits and even the management of the firms in which they work as a means of sensitizing them to the large stake they have in the health of the economy and of each of its functioning units.

Advocates of positive corporatism contend that the problems of British economic policy-making stem from failure to carry corporatism farther than it was carried in the 1970s. Citing relatively successful examples of state–industry cooperation in West Germany, Austria, and Sweden, they argue that successes registered in keeping both unemployment and inflation from approaching double figures were due to systems of consultation and mutual restraint in income demands by economic actors that made it possible for goods to be priced at internationally competitive levels. This in turn enabled employment to be maintained at home in sectors that were during the same period in decline in inflation-prone Britain. Countries in which positive corporatism allegedly worked best were those in which cooperative mechanisms had been established shortly after World War II and had thus become ingrained. Cooperation and mutual self-restraint had become habitual by the time the crisis of the 1970s arrived.[10] In Britain, experiments with corporatism had come only after the economic situation had begun to deteriorate, and, when introduced, they were not far-reaching and were ultimately unsuccessful The problems of the British economy were due to uncontrolled pluralism, not excessive corporatism, according to this view.[11]

In broad terms, positive corporatism is found in countries where there exists a combination of two defining characteristics: (1) a *strong state tradition* and (2) a *cohesive trade union movement*. These defining characteristics are especially important when it comes to applying the concepts of pluralism and corporatism to economic policy-making. In countries with strong state traditions, the issue (so prevalent in American debates on economic policy) of whether the state should play a role in the economy is rarely raised. Because the state has historically played an important role in shaping and guiding the private sector, the question tends to be *what* the state should do, not *whether* it should do anything to cope with challenges to economic well-being. In positive corporatism, the state plays a role as partner with the private sector and the trade unions, unlike negative corporatism, where the state helps employers control their workers. The role of the state is more secure in positive corporatism than it is in countries characterized by pluralism, where active, as opposed to passive (reactive), state involvement in the economy has not been universally accepted as legitimate. The state in the pluralist policy-making model is a mediator between interests but is not itself actively engaged until the conflict has matured through a complicated process of sifting of issues that are sufficiently salient to receive public attention.

As already noted, the cohesion of trade unions is also a crucial defining feature of corporatism when it comes to economic policymaking. In positive corporatism, the trade unions play a positive role in helping shape economic policy alongside the state and private business interests. If cohesive trade unions prevail, corporatism is facilitated because bargaining partners can make commitments on behalf of their memberships with the certainty that they will be able to honor them. Corporatist bargaining requires mutual trust between the bargaining partners, trust that no one will attempt to take undue advantage of the willingness of others to make concessions. But in some countries with strong state traditions, notably France and Japan among our countries, what might appear to be corporatist relations between the public and the private sector fall short of positive corporatism in that the unions are too weak, and their role in policymaking is too poorly established, for a balanced triangular relationship between state, employers, and unions to exist. In Japan there are elements of what we have called negative corporatism, where a strong state

Pickets in front of the London headquarters of the British Broadcasting Corporation, 1989. These members of the National Union of Journalists are striking over a pay dispute with BBC management.

acts on behalf of the interests of employers to keep the workers' movement weak. In France it seems more the case that a strong state acts autonomously of both employers and trade unions to make economic policy, in what some have called a *statist* policy-making pattern. It is probably most accurate to say that both Japan and France display a mixture of statist and corporatist (both positive and negative) elements, with the mix varying with the type of economic policy and the sector of the economy concerned. But, in general, where trade unions are incohesive, as they are in Britain as well, trade union bargainers will be uncertain of the support of those they represent and will be unable to make firm commitments or to convince those with whom they are bargaining that their commitments are reliable. In the absence of this certainty, pluralist contests of strength or else statist impositions of unbargained, unmediated solutions are what is likely to result.

In our five countries we can observe four kinds of combinations of state traditions and trade union cohesiveness. Japan, West Germany, and France have active state traditions, whereas Italy and Britain do not, although in the Italian case the Fascist experience provides a twenty-year exception. But, whereas trade unions in West Germany are strong, those in France and Japan are weak, providing two cases in which the state and the employers have successfully coalesced to keep workers' organizations at bay. In the case of the passive-state-tradition countries, unions are relatively cohesive in Italy and relatively incohesive in Britain, although this has not always meant union weakness in the latter case or union strength in the former. Our two-way classification of the five countries is shown in Figure 6.1.

The West Germany combination has strong elements of corporatism; those of Italy and Britain are essentially pluralistic; the French and

Trade Unions

		Cohesive	Incohesive
State Tradition	*Active*	Positive corporatism (West Germany)	Statism (Japan, France)
	Passive	Labor-driven pluralism (Italy and Britain, 1970s)	Capital-driven pluralism (Italy and Britain, 1980s)

Figure 6.1   Models of industrial relations.

Japanese cases are primarily statist. However, trade union cohesion in Italy is a fragile phenomenon that may not hold up against the factors that are weakening trade unions in post-industrial society. Also, it would appear that the term *statist* as applied to industrial relations fits the French case better than it does the Japanese.

Case Studies in the Politics of Industrial Relations[12]

These competing models of economic policy-making have been applied in numerous analyses of the way policy is made in advanced industrial countries.[13] A great deal of disagreement exists over how comprehensively a given model applies to any particular country. If positive corporatism seems to fit the way industrial relations disputes are settled in West Germany, for example, is it as applicable when we turn to an examination of the making of West German monetary and fiscal policy? Does any single model extend in any country to such diverse socioeconomic policy realms as housing policy, transport policy, and international trade policy? Obviously, the answer will be different from one country to another and from one policy area to another. However, in certain policy areas it is clearer which of the models best applies to a given country; five case studies follow involving industrial relations policies and the related problem of the unemployment produced by industrial restructuring. The cases involve, first, the setting of wages and prices prior to the advent of deeper recession and higher unemployment in the 1980s, illustrating the tension between the competing approaches to the problem of stagflation. Second, the phenomenon of deindustrialization, which was more apparent in the early to mid-1980s, changed the agenda of industrial relations policymaking, which is also reflected in the cases. The case of West Germany illustrates the fact that the positive corporatist approach, successful in coping with stagflation, has been less successful in dealing with the problems of deindustrialization. The Italian case illustrates that efforts in the 1970s to impose elements of positive corporatism on a pluralist base have given way to a resurgence of what can almost be considered negative corporatism in the 1980s. In both countries deindustrialization has changed some of the environmental conditions affecting policymaking. These more recent developments are touched on briefly in the West German and

195

Italian cases, then dealt with more fully in the French, Japanese, and British cases, discussed in the sections that follow.

West Germany and Italy: Industrial Relations When Unions Are Strong

The intervention of the German state in the economy goes back to the German Empire in the nineteenth century, and it continued in each successive regime until the early years of the Bonn Republic. During the first fifteen years of the new regime, the official economic policy stance of the West German government accorded with its overall commitment to what it called the "social market" strategy. This set of economic policies was most closely identified with Christian Democratic Economics Minister Ludwig Erhard, who eventually succeeded Konrad Adenauer as chancellor. The strategy was to permit economic forces as much autonomy as possible to pursue their own interests, a policy guided by the laissez-faire assumption that state interference in the economy would impede natural productive forces, stifling the incentives to innovate and take risks. It also expressed the strong German aversion to inflation, stemming back to the disastrous experiences of the early 1920s. The most intervention the Erhard policy would permit was orthodox monetarist control over the supply of money. Erhard placed his faith in a stable growth in money supply to moderate demand and limit price increases during full-scale economic expansion. Given the seemingly voluntary moderation on the part of employer and employees, the policy attained substantial success, to the mutual satisfaction of the government, the employers' organizations and private corporations, and the trade union leadership.

So long as the Erhard strategy and tactics were working, there was no reason to call into question its basic assumptions that minimized the role of the state in the economy. Yet when West German industrial relations are compared with those of its neighbors, one central fact stands out: the existence of rather elaborate and stringent legal constraints in the employer–employee bargaining process. Unlike the situation in Great Britain, for example, unofficial strikes are illegal in West Germany, meaning that national union leaders, challenged by insurrection on the shop floor, can cloak themselves in a wrap of legality and refuse to support unofficial strikes and their objectives. This serves to reinforce the determination of national union leaders to cooperate with employers in following a policy of wage restraint. It also suggests a somewhat stronger role for the state in practice than the Erhard philosophy allowed in theory. In fact, West German law and the enforcement structure maintained to ensure compliance with the law had a corporatist flavor to it, and, compared with some Western European countries, it gave an advantage to the employers.

That corporatism was the underlying economic outlook of a large share of the West German elite became evident as the recession of 1966–67 took hold. Its almost immediate political impact was to discredit Chancellor Erhard and force him out of office. In December 1966, a new government was formed—the Grand Coalition of Christian Democrats and Social Democrats, led by Kurt Georg Kiesinger, the CDU chancellor, and SPD leader Willy Brandt, as vice-chancellor and foreign minister. Seeking a way out of the recession, the leaders of both partners of the coalition were willing to renounce those aspects of the Erhard policies that restrained the state from intervening in the economy. The new economics minister, Keynesian economist Kurt Schiller of the SPD, developed a new West German economic policy: the policy of "concerted action." It meant that the state would take a more active role in controlling economic fluctuations through fiscal as well as monetary policy, a commitment that had been reached in Great Britain and France more than a decade earlier. But the Grand Coalition went a step farther and announced an income policy that would involve the state in putting forth wage and price guidelines for acceptance by both employers and employees.

The Schiller experiment indicated that there was substantial support among West German elites for some version of positive corporatism involving government leadership. The Brandt government (1969–74) continued to seek employer and trade union cooperation in limiting wage and price increases and in containing industrial unrest. The effort was assisted by the success gained by the national trade unions in establishing their presence at the plant level. Whereas localized disputes previously had been negotiated with the firm by works councils elected by employees, in the early 1970s trade union representatives began to actively seek election to the councils and came to control them in numerous instances.

The Brandt and subsequent Helmut Schmidt coalition governments had the majority of workers supporting their political and economic objectives. National trade union leadership was supportive most of the time, having to withdraw some distance from the government whenever plant-level militancy was at its height. This tended to vary with the fortunes of the West German economy, which was subject to greater fluctuation in the 1970s than in earlier periods, but not, it should be emphasized, when compared with other postindustrial economies in the 1970s.

During the 1970s, the SPD under Brandt and Schmidt sought to secure greater worker support for its policies by advancing the objective of worker participation in management—*Mitbestimmung*, or codetermination. The idea was to elevate the institution of the works council from the plant level to the level of the business firm's corporate headquarters and to give workers representation on the governing boards. To achieve this objective, the SPD leadership was forced to negotiate with the coalition partner, the Free Democrats, a party with considerable financial dependence on business interests. The compromise meant the limitation of codetermination to larger firms and to those corporate policies that directly concern the interests of the workforce, not to decisions of major economic importance, such as pricing policy or industrial mergers. The failure to extend codetermination farther undoubtedly limited its effect as a means of gaining worker acceptance of the corporatist framework.

What distinguished the West German pattern from that in our three other countries in Western Europe was a pair of important characteristics: (1) Industrial conflict was consistently lowest in West Germany, even in periods where it was intense by West German standards; and (2) agreement among West German elites (including trade union leaders) on the efficacy of positive corporatism is not found in Great Britain, Italy, and France, where elites typically diverge in their outlooks on industrial relations. The West German pattern was especially characteristic of the period of coalition government when the SPD was the senior partner, a condition reinforced by electoral victories for the coalition in 1972, 1976, and 1980. With the return to power of the CDU/CSU in 1982 in a new center-right coalition with the FDP, the pattern has changed in a more conflictive, and thus less corporatist, direction. The return of the right to power has taxed the ability and willingness of trade union leaders to withstand the pressures of the militant left within their ranks.

Rising levels of unemployment in the early 1980s, accompanied by declining real wages, brought the value of positive corporatism into question for some West German trade unionists. The pursuit of "positive sum politics" had been accompanied by the greater centralization of national trade unions and a growing distance between the professional union officials at the national level and the membership on the shop floor.[14] Members' jobs were threatened by the twin nemeses of recession and automation, especially in the face of a center-right government that was adding to recessionary trends with its deflationary policies. Neo-Marxists on the Social Democratic and trade union left renewed their demand that the forty-hour workweek in West Germany be reduced to thirty-five hours without reduction in workers' income, so that capitalist employers would be unable to continue to profit through laying off workers. Instead, existing workers' incomes could be maintained, while younger unemployed workers could be added to the workforce to fill the hours opened up by shortened workweeks. Two of the most militant industrial unions, the gigantic metalworkers' union and the printers' union, put forth this proposal in early 1984, but it was rejected by employers and the Kohl government on the grounds that it would raise the cost of producing West German steel and automobiles, making them less competitive internationally, with an adverse effect on the entire West German economy. It would create jobs for Japanese workers, not those at home, it was argued.

In May 1984, the metalworkers and printers began selective strikes, especially affecting production in the automotive and related engineering industries. Employers in those industries retaliated by "lockouts," or temporary closings of the plants not yet hit by the strike.

This meant that many thousand more workers were off work than were actually on strike. By late June, 450,000 workers were out of work. Those locked out or laid off were ruled ineligible to receive unemployment benefits, which meant a heavy burden on strike funds used by the unions to support members' families during the strike. But the combined strike and lockout was costly to employers as well. In late June, metal industry management and unions agreed to submit the dispute to mediation. Agreement was reached rather quickly on the general principle of a 38½-hour week, to be interpreted flexibly from firm to firm. The center-right government, which had sided with the employers, was not a party to the agreement. Thus, the framework for resolution of the conflict was pluralist rather than corporatist. Still, the speed with which agreement was reached once mediation began in this, the longest West German strike since 1957, suggests that positive corporatist reflexes were still operant in West Germany.

In contrast to the case of West Germany, where elements of National Socialist negative corporatism were systematically weeded out, the early postwar Italian system of industrial relations was strongly influenced by the two decades of Fascist rule the country had experienced. Benito Mussolini's state had explicitly opted for a system of negative corporatism in which state-controlled trade unions assisted the government and the employers in enforcing labor discipline. Although the constitution and statutory law of the new Italian Republic repudiated the fascist system and removed legal restrictions on both employers and employees, Italian employers did not easily give up the corporatist model to which they had grown accustomed during the Fascist years. The weakness of the trade unions during the 1950s allowed employers to impose a negative corporatist reality on a pluralist legal framework, despite, or perhaps in part because of, the fact that workers' organizations and political parties espoused an intransigent Marxism.

Economic circumstances worked against the success of trade union militancy. Rapid modernization and economic growth occurred in the 1950s in Italy as they did elsewhere in Western Europe, but the early period of underemployment lasted somewhat longer because industrialization was less far advanced and there was an overabundance of semiskilled and unskilled workers, especially in southern Italy. Organizationally, the trade unions in Italy were very nearly the weakest in Western Europe. Their memberships tended to be confined to the minority of skilled workers, and they were notably weak in the semi-industrialized southern regions.

At the national level, the unions did not speak with one voice. The largest, the *General Confederation of Italian Labor* (CGIL), had strong links with the opposition Communist and Socialist parties. The Catholic union, the *Italian Confederation of Workers' Syndicates* (CISL), was linked with the left wing of the ruling Christian Democratic Party. The tactic of divide and conquer worked well for employers throughout most of the 1950s. Finally, at the plant level, what presence the unions had was rendered ineffectual by management's practice of ignoring plant works councils, created immediately after World War II and often containing union members. Although the employers' refusal to negotiate wage agreements with the works councils was illegal, the Christian Democratic governments of the 1950s looked the other way. *Confindustria,* the employers' organization, enjoyed easy access to the Christian Democratic governments and especially to the ministries that administered industrial relations policy. Such access was totally lacking to the CGIL. Thus, Confindustria was able to gain tacit state approval for its negative corporatism.

By the late 1950s, Italian industrialization was in full expansion. The demand for both semiskilled and unskilled labor was growing not only in Italy but also in northern Europe, where industries were attracting immigrant workers from the south. These twin pulls reduced Italian unemployment and improved the bargaining position of the trade unions. The incidence of strikes began to increase. The employers who felt the impact most severely were often the most modern and competitive, those whose market was global. The strikes put them in a disadvantageous position relative to firms in countries where industrial unrest was minimal. In many such cases, the employer was the state. The Italian state sector had been expanding substantially during the growth period in areas where the expansion had been greatest—petrochemicals, for example. But those firms most affected by the strikes included American-based multinational corporations as well as large private Italian corporations, notably Fiat and Olivetti. An additional reason that these public, semipublic, and private giants were the most affected was that the unions were best organized in precisely these same firms.

The influx of southern Italian workers into northern cities provided the Communist Party with an opportunity to increase its base of support. During the 1960s, the Italian Communist Party and the Communist-linked trade unions made a concerted effort to reach the growing number of semiskilled and unskilled workers occupying the lowest-paid jobs, often in smaller firms where union organization was the weakest. The disoriented and estranged workers from the south were a uniquely available target. For them, the Communist Party and the trade union offered a sort of home away from home. The Communists provided assistance in finding housing and recreational facilities. In return, the newly recruited were socialized to accept the communist world view. At the same time, however, that world view was changing. The growing prosperity, the more positive attitude of the government and of many of the northern employers, and the rising electoral support for the PCI were factors that mitigated the communist tendency to see the world exclusively in terms of class conflict. Cooperative arrangements of a semicorporatist nature were being developed between unions and management at the local level during this period, encouraged by local governments under Communist leadership. For the moment, however, in the late 1960s, the consequence of the growing strength of the PCI and the CGIL was an increase in industrial militancy that coincided, as in other countries, with an upturn of the economy.[15] Industrial unrest in Italy between 1968 and 1973 resulted in a number of gains for workers and for the trade union movement. Most important was the achievement of legislation in 1970 that established the right of trade unions to organize workers at the shop level, a right that many employers had successfully denied the unions in the past. From this point, the unions succeeded in gaining control of works councils with which management would have to negotiate concerning wages and conditions of work. The strikes also secured substantial increases in real income for the workers, bolstered by revamped indexing arrangements that promised automatic increases in the future to keep workers' incomes ahead of price inflation, thus serving to exacerbate inflationary tendencies. The PCI played an active role in supporting these demands and in neutralizing the government as a recourse for beleaguered employers. The rising strength

of the PCI was verified by substantial gains in the municipal elections of 1975 and the parliamentary elections of 1976. Finally, the 1970s saw the tentative beginnings of a move to merge the CGIL and the CSIL into a single trade union confederation. However, greater progress was made in this direction at the local level than nationally.

In the early 1980s, the position of employers hardened as they perceived the center of political gravity to have shifted back toward the right, away from a conciliatory policy toward the unions. By 1984 the northern industrial triangle of Turin, Milan, and Genoa had fallen on severe times. Rationalization of automobile production methods (Turin) and steel production (Milan) as well as the worldwide decline of shipbuilding (Genoa) had resulted in massive unemployment. The government, led by Socialist Bettino Craxi, reflected the mood of employers, which was to keep real wages in check by reducing the power of trade unions to bargain for increases. Early in the year Craxi proposed that the automatic wage increases for the year, indexed to rise with inflation, be cut by one-third, in order to bring Italian inflation down from its chronic double figures. Employers' groups and the two non-Communist trade unions gave their agreement to the proposal, although the employers argued that it did not go far enough. But the Communist-led CGIL refused its accord. To their surprise, Craxi proceeded to implement the policy by decree.

The Communists and the CGIL, who had staged two massive one-day strikes in response to Craxi's action, complained that the prime minister had broken with the long-standing practice of gaining the approval of all interested parties in wage-level decisions. Actually, this positive corporatist view of the process had been valid only for the previous fifteen years since the unions had gained coequal status with employers' groups at the end of the 1960s. Craxi's ability to defy the unions and the Communist Party suggests at least a temporary return to the negative corporatist pattern of the 1950s and 1960s. When high levels of unemployment have occurred in Italy, it generally has been the case that union solidarity diminishes and government's tendency to support the employers' interests is reestablished. In West Germany, a lack of support from government in 1984 was not enough to prevent union militancy from forcing concessions from employers.

The shift in government policy toward the trade unions in Italy reflects the fact that, at bottom, the Italian policy process is a pluralistic one in which government policies reflect the relative strengths of competing interest groups at any given time. In West Germany, both trade unions and employers are able to successfully insist on their established rights in the bargaining process, secure in the belief that, no matter what economic changes may do to their respective cohesiveness and firmness of purpose, the state will honor their claims to be heard and to maintain their rights. This difference is partly a result of the more established position of the West German than of the Italian state. In West Germany, the state is assured of the acceptance by both trade unions and employers of its decisions as legitimate. Unions may strike against employers and employers may lock out workers, but neither will act in such a militant fashion toward the state. Both may be seeking to influence state policy in their direction, but the role of the state is usually to facilitate negotiation between the industrial parties and to register the agreements they have reached, without playing a decisive role as an actor in its own right. The role that the Italian state will play is less predictable, not because the state itself is in a strong position, but because its temporary leaders are in a weak one. They are

able to act in ways that appear decisive, as Craxi did in 1984, only at a time when the prevailing economic situation clearly favors one side over the other—the workers in the late 1960s and early 1970s, and the employers in the 1980s. In pluralistic fashion, they are bending to the prevailing wind. The stronger West German state has an interest in preserving a relative balance between trade unions and employers; if the state intervenes, it will be to preserve that positive corporatist balance rather than to add its weight to further unbalance an already unbalanced situation.

France and Japan: Strong States and Weak Trade Unions

The French pattern of industrial relations has traditionally exhibited characteristics similar to the situation that prevailed in Italy prior to the 1960s. A divided and restricted trade union movement faced employers (the *patronat*), who believed in maintaining their authority over their employees even at the expense of peaceful industrial relations. They relied, when possible, on economic conditions to give them a superior bargaining position. The French Communist Party (PCF) has always played a role similar to that of the PCI in the 1950s. It has maintained strong links with the largest trade union (the CGT) and has avoided cooperation with the employers and with the state except when able to operate from a position of strength—which was seldom the case in France before the late 1960s. Employers frequently were able to deal with non-Communist trade unions, arriving at settlements to which the state gave its accord.

During the Fourth Republic, the policies of the divided governments tended to be ad hoc and inconsistent. With the return to power of General Charles de Gaulle, certain changes took place that brought the picture into sharp focus.

Through strengthening the executive constitutionally and through his own personal authority, de Gaulle was able to strengthen the hand of the government relative to the competing interest groups. Greater administrative coordination was achieved through the lessened role of the National Assembly as a conduit for group influences toward the bureaucracy and by reason of the fact that loyal Gaullists commanded the ministries relevant to economic policy. These ministries hitherto had been divided among leaders of different political parties. In the Fifth Republic, until 1981, the party in power was a party of the right, more favorably disposed to the propertied classes, whereas the political left, including the non-Communist left, was relegated to protracted opposition. Thus, the trade unions were at a disadvantage with respect to the state, whatever their position with respect to employers might have been at any given time.

In the Gaullist perception of economics, the interest of the state in maintaining a productive and stable economy came first. This proceeded from the commitment of de Gaulle to a strong French posture in international affairs, including his insistence that France be equipped with an effective, credible nuclear deterrent. Considerable state resources were channeled into scientific research and technological development. At the same time, his government sought to cope with growing needs and demands in society for such services as education and health delivery systems.

As the Gaullists saw the situation, the combined demands being put on the state were fraught with inflationary potential, a potential that could threaten the willingness of investors to gamble on the French economic future. Investment capital came second only to the state in the Gaullist system of priorities. Therefore,

the government economic policy turned from emphasis on economic growth for its own sake to emphasis on improving productivity through technological development and through joining employers in pressing for greater worker productivity as a prerequisite to satisfaction of wage demands. Deflationary policies in the mid-1960s further weakened the workers' position by building a certain "tolerable" level of unemployment into the economy. Despite a number of days lost to strikes that was high for the time in Western Europe, the lack of unity in the French trade union movement meant that long-term strikes could not be sustained. Thus, bolstered by the moral support of the Gaullist state, employers usually could hold out against wage demands.

The strong showing of the ad hoc coalition of Communists and Socialists in the 1967 legislative elections was a sign that working-class disenchantment was beginning to improve the chances of a solid opposition to Gaullist policy. The explosion of May 1968, in which students protested against the overcrowded and alienating conditions in the system of higher education, led to confrontations with the police and, ultimately, to work stoppages in factories. The latter began as sympathy strikes directed against government antistudent actions, but they soon developed into a general strike of workers all over France who demanded higher wages and changes in industrial organization. The demands and the tactics of the French workers were little different from those arising at about the same time in other countries. What distinguished the French explosion were its dimensions. The general strike was of sufficient scope and intensity to threaten the existence of the Fifth Republic. In retrospect, it is clear that it forced de Gaulle to reorder his domestic and foreign policy priorities and, ultimately, to leave office after unsuccessfully testing his popularity in a referendum he easily could have won a few years earlier.

The governments of the right and center-right headed by Presidents Georges Pompidou and Valery Giscard d'Estaing sought to defuse French industrial relations such that it could not again pose a threat to the regime as it had in 1968. Legislation passed in 1968 had legitimized the presence of trade unions in individual firms and plants for purposes of collective bargaining. Governments in the 1970s encouraged employers to establish dialogues with local trade union branches and to negotiate local agreements on wages and conditions of work. Progress was registered in this direction, especially in the early 1970s before the onset of economic decline following the 1973–74 oil shocks, but recognition of local unions was often confined to the moderate unions rather than to the more militant CGT and CFDT. As the economic situation worsened later in the 1970s, the moderate FO became a particularly favored union for employers to negotiate with, trading off benefits for the unions and their members for union acquiescence in the rationalization of manufacturing, involving the shedding of jobs. Under the law, efforts by the CGT and CFDT to fight such developments were largely futile, whereas membership in FO expanded or held its own while the larger confederations were losing members. In difficult times the workers were interested in the relative security FO could promise, rather than the distant panaceas promised by the more militant unions.

The government of the left that came to power under President François Mitterrand in May 1981 portended a radical reversal in the relative positions of employers' and workers' organizations. The government took office with a list of seven major private corporations to be brought under state ownership along with investment banks and the steel and armaments industries. This was designed to give the state greater control over investment decisions in key sectors of the economy and to enable it to substitute itself for the employers in relations with the trade unions representing the employees in the sectors affected. The government also was pledged to reverse the deflationary policies of the previous right of center government under President Giscard d'Estaing, which, they alleged, had created large-scale unemployment and depressed real wages. The reversal would take the form of a reflationary policy, deliberately countering the deflationary trend in other First World countries, which would bring unemployment down through stimulating demand and investment in import-substituting industries. There was also a strong redistributive thrust to the government's program, designed to end the relatively high French levels of income inequality that cross-national studies had revealed during the 1970s. (See Chapter 2.) This would be effected through increased taxation of the higher-income and -wealth brackets, accompanied by improved social security benefits for lower-income earners. Finally, new industrial relations legislation was introduced and enacted, further extending the rights of unions at the firm and plant levels and making it still more difficult for employers to nullify the unions that were, or were seeking to become, the most representative defenders of their workers' interests.

During most of the first year of the new government, all of those aspects of the program were partially or fully implemented, including most of the promised nationalizations, reflation through deficit financing, imposition of a wealth tax, expansion of social security, shortening of the workweek from forty to thirty-nine hours without loss of income for the workers, and enactment of the industrial relations legislation, the Auroux Laws of 1982. The trade unions, usually left out of the economic policy-making process in the past, now enjoyed access to the governmental decision makers and to the management of state-sector firms. The national coal board, *Charbonnages de France*, was headed by a Communist director, and the newly nationalized firms came under the management of persons sympathetic to the government's aims. However, in the private sector, hostility to the new measures mounted in the months after the left came to power. Private investment declined and representatives of business groups refused to cooperate with the government in bargaining over wages and working hours. As the year wore on, indicators of inflation, the balance of trade, and the value of the French franc vis-à-vis the dollar began to show considerable deterioration, and unemployment refused to come down in response to the reflationary policy. To be sure, the government was unfortunate in coming to power in the midst of worldwide recession, but the combined impact of worsening indicators and employers' refusal of cooperation began strengthening the centrist voices within the government.

During the second year of the Mitterrand government, from spring 1982 to spring 1983, a tortuous process of reassessment of economic policy took place. Faced with continued stagflation at a time when other countries were choosing to attack inflation while letting unemployment rise, the government reluctantly came to the conclusion that it must follow suit. The turn to deflation was designed in part to restore business confidence in the government, so that a tripartite relationship involving government, employers, and trade unions could be established. This would make it possible to effectuate an incomes policy in which both wages

and prices could be brought under control. The government counted on the continued support of the trade unions, assuming that, for the unions to undermine a Socialist government, even when it was pursuing policies favorable to the class enemy, the only result could be the loss of that government's capacity to mitigate the adverse effect of the policies on the workers. Although the Communist-led CGT, ironically, gave the government greater support than the Socialist-leaning CFDT, in general trade union support was sufficient to usher in a period of positive corporatism, as employers and employees cooperated in holding the inflationary line. By the summer of 1983, with real wages down and profits up from the year before, inflation was coming back down into single-digit proportions, while unemployment continued at levels only slightly higher than those of the year before Mitterrand came to power.

The policy reversal was beginning to take its toll by mid-1983 in closings in the private sector and in the necessity to subsidize firms in the public sector in order to cover losses. The private-sector development was adding to the unemployment totals, whereas public-sector subsidization was designed to keep unemployment within bounds. Massive subsidies in the coal and steel sectors ran counter to the general austerity thrust of government policies, and, in the fall of 1983, Finance Minister Jacques Delors proposed to cut them substantially in the following year's budget. This brought about the resignation of the Communist director of the coal board and signaled the beginning of a more militant opposition to the new direction of economic policy on the part of the trade unions. The cut in public-sector subsidies coincided with the development of a new approach to industrial policy generally, in which the government would encourage the modernization of declining industries, recognizing that this would bring with it considerable loss of jobs—a projected 200,000 for 1984—through the effect of automation and acceptance of the fact that the industries in question were overmanned. To obtain the support of the trade unions once again, the pill was sweetened by the promise of substantial financial support for the workers concerned, enabling them to find new, subsidized employment, in many cases with government-assisted retraining.

Although the CGT tentatively accepted the new direction, the CFDT, with a larger proportion of lower-paid (especially immigrant) workers, who would experience the heaviest incidence of the job losses, opposed the policy and tested it out in one of the first places of application, the state-owned Talbot (formerly, Peugeot) car plant in Poissy, in the outskirts of Paris. Among the CFDT complaints was the fact that the government had not consulted the unions at Poissy before announcing its policy, which would mean the loss of jobs of 1,900 workers, most of them immigrants. The government had planned to pay the immigrants to return to North Africa, but, in the face of the strike, it promised to make provisions for finding new jobs in France for those who wanted to remain. As the strike ended, it also was announced that the government would provide redundant workers with payment for two years to enable them to train for new jobs or, alternatively, to help them find employment in their own regions (especially the industrial north and Lorraine) where they could employ their own skills. This was in response to pressure from the CGT, whose continued support for government economic policy was becoming increasingly problematic.

Trade union unrest came to a head in March 1984, when a two-day strike of public-sector employees was called by the CGT and other unions in response to a government decision to hold public-sector pay increases to 5 percent at the same time inflation was running at 9 percent. Seemingly in support of the Socialist government, the CFDT did not call its members out on strike, although many of them struck anyway. The CFDT leader, Edmund Maire, claimed that his confederation was dissociating itself from the strike because it was over the false issue of wages, ignoring the real issue of jobs. More concerned than the CGT with those most threatened with job loss in the face of the government's industrial modernization policy, the CFDT was clearly distancing itself from the better-paid and more job-secure workers who were better defended by the other unions. The strike demonstrated once more that, when French worker militancy rises, it can seldom express itself in more than short-term strikes designed to put a point across symbolically, whether the government be of the right or the left. But the increased militancy represented a defeat for the government's efforts to build a positive corporatist consensus behind its economic policies. Thus, the Socialist government found itself in the uncomfortable position of having greater support for the main lines of its economic and industrial policies from employers and the parties of the right than from its own base in the trade unions. At the same time, its popular support generally was declining, a trend that culminated in the Socialists' defeat in the legislative elections of March 1986. It is not too far-fetched to suggest that the temptation of the Socialists to utilize the economic policy tools of a strong state in order to overcome the resistance of their erstwhile trade union allies turned out to be as irresistible as the original urge to use the same state weapons as means of righting the balance between employers and unions that was implemented in Mitterrand's first year.

According to the criteria outlined earlier in this chapter, Japan shares with France the twin qualities of having a strong state and divided trade unions when it comes to industrial relations policy and to economic policy in general. But when we look more closely at the two cases, we find the Japanese state playing a more passive role in industrial relations policy than does the French state, and a more passive role in industrial relations policy than in other economic policy realms, especially that of industrial *development* policy, where the Japanese governments have met with considerable success in avoiding the pitfalls of deindustrialization that the other advanced industrial countries have faced, a record that is looked at in the next chapter. In any event, the fact that the state is regarded as strong by the trade unions in both countries adds to the weakness of both the French and Japanese trade unions when they face employers, not only because the unions are divided among themselves, but also because the state appears in both countries most of the time to be in league with the unions' opposite number in industrial relations: the employers.

The lines of division within the trade union movement are different in Japan from the ideological–partisan divisions in France, although there is a sort of left–right division among Japanese unions as well.[16] Whereas less than 20 percent of French workers belong to unions, the Japanese unions organize about 30 percent of the workers, a figure that itself falls short of the Italian, British, and West German levels, all of which are found between 40 and 50 percent.[17] But a feature of the unionized Japanese workers that distinguishes them from those in these Western European countries is that more than 90 percent of them belong to what are, in the first instance, *company* unions. In both the public and the private sectors, in large firms as well as small, the typical Japanese

union member belongs to a union whose membership is confined to the economic unit (private company or government agency) where he or she works. In France and other Western European countries, the worker joins a national union federation which may or may not have a presence in the place of work. In West Germany the federation the worker joins is likely to enjoy a "closed shop" status in the plant or office (i.e., it is the only federation to which the worker may belong), but it is a federation that enjoys similar status in many other plants or offices, and in a given company it may exist alongside another union or other unions whose members fall into different categories of workers (e.g., office workers rather than factory workers, or supervisory personnel rather than machine operators). But in Japan the typical worker does not join a national federation; instead, he or she becomes a member of the local company union along with other workers, of whatever category of job, within the same company. The company union in turn may belong to one of the two largest union confederations, *Sohyo*, a fairly militant union of the left, or *Domei*, a moderate union that is often in sympathy with the policies of Japan's Liberal Democratic government. As in France, the peak confederations are distinguished from one another along ideological lines, but the ideology of the confederation is more remote from the concerns of the Japanese worker who joins a company union than it is for the French worker who consciously joins one union rather than another because it is, say, a CGT rather than a CFDT union.

According to Tadashi Hanami,[18] Japanese workers, after signing on to work for a new firm, will be drawn to the company union in order to become more socially solid with a new "family." The only choice to be made is whether to belong to a union or not; it is not, as in the typical French case, which of two or more possible unions to join. The distant ideological affiliation of the company union is therefore not likely to be an important consideration for the new employee. However, indirect affiliation with Sohyo or with Domei can have consequences in the case of industrial disputes. The more militant Sohyo has been known to get its members into impossible positions in bargaining with the companies in which they work, such that their employers may be able to entice them away from the Sohyo-affiliated union into a breakaway union that may later affiliate with Domei or remain independent. If a majority of workers can be drawn into the new union, it then becomes the official union for the company. Both the workers who made the change and those left behind will be motivated to come back together again, putting behind them all previous antagonisms toward one another and toward the employer.

In a famous study of Japanese society, Chie Nakane argues that in Japan, unlike in many other societies, individuals identify with the social organization, or "frame," to which they belong, rather than the social type, or "attribute," to which an outsider might assign them.[19] Thus, a daughter-in-law becomes an integral part of her husband's family, although born a member of another family, if the couple live in the household of the husband's parents. The same is true of servants living in the household. Both the daughter-in-law and the servant are considered part of the household and consider themselves so, whereas a daughter who has married and goes elsewhere to live with her husband thereby becomes an outsider. Similarly, when a young person becomes an employee of a business firm, he or she becomes a "family member" of the firm. The firm virtually becomes the individual's entire world. Indeed, if a new male employee is single, he may look for a female employee of the same firm to marry, so that the marriage will not be strained by the fact that husband and wife belong to different "families" in their places of employment.

Thus, the Japanese worker identifies with the firm as the frame and not with his or her particular skill category or attribute, and certainly not with other Japanese workers elsewhere who might happen to share certain political beliefs. This is why there will not be more than one union per firm and why, if there is a conflict within that union, loyalty to the firm will force the workers to resolve the conflict so that a one-union firm can be reestablished, or else a *no-union* company will be the result of the conflict.

Paradoxically, when conflicts do occur in the relations between Japanese management and labor, they often assume very emotionally explosive and sometimes even violent proportions. This is because, according to Hanami,[20] within the family the rule of the head of the household may not be challenged. To do so is to risk becoming an outcast. One must, in fact, have taken leave of one's senses to challenge such absolute authority overtly. In the company, employees who challenge the authority of the head of the firm do so in ways that demonstrate a temporarily altered personality state. They change their appearance, discarding the usual dark business suits and behave in bizarre ways far removed from the daily routine. When the conflict is over they return to their former selves, as if to say, "That was not me; it was someone else. I am not to be held accountable." And both employers and employees proceed ahead as if there had not, in fact, been such a confrontation.

Accordingly, Japanese industrial disputes are usually short-lived. They will end either by the employer's giving up just enough of what the employees demand so that "face" is saved on both sides, or by the employer's succeeding in splitting the union, a technique alluded to earlier.

Failing either of those solutions, a state agency will be called on to mediate the dispute. In certain ways this outline is similar to what occurs in France. Strikes break out frequently in France and are usually both angry and short-lived. Management tries to divide the workers and, as in Japan, frequently can succeed. Or the dispute may end fairly amicably by each side making concessions, failing which the state may enter into the action. But there are important differences. Although a Sohyo-led strike in Japan may involve certain ideologically motivated nonnegotiable demands, not unlike those conducted in France under CGT or CDFT auspices, French strikes are often called at the national level; Sohyo, on the other hand, lends its support to strikes that arise within a particular firm. The French strikes are often scheduled to last for only a day or for a specified and brief period of time, the object being more to demonstrate the strength of the union within the workforce than to gain specific benefits for the union's members. Such strikes really do not have measurable outcomes, in the same sense as do industrial disputes in other countries, including Japan. Finally, although the state may become involved in both countries, it is a more active involvement in France than in Japan, and it may be initiated at the highest levels of government. The French state is likely to impose a solution that one or both of the parties to the dispute may be too weak to refuse. The semi-autonomous Labour Relations Commission that mediates industrial relations disputes in Japan seldom arbitrates, a process that obliges the parties to the dispute to accept the solution imposed by the arbitrator. Rather, it mediates or conciliates, trying to persuade both parties of their own interest in reaching a decision that only they, as members of the same "family," can achieve. Despite these differences, it still should be noted that the Japanese state retains

considerable strength in reserve that it could use in case industrial militancy came to threaten Japanese economic viability. The sympathies of the Liberal Democratic government, like those of the right-of-center governments during most of the Fifth Republic, are, in the final analysis, with the employers. The fact that neither government has had to exercise its latent authority over industrial relations in heavy-handed fashion is perhaps due more to the fact that private-sector employers in both countries have the best of it in arguments with their workers most of the time.[21] In this sense, the more balanced industrial relations of West Germany and Italy find the state acting in ways that either reflect (Italy) or restore (West Germany) the balance when it is threatened; the unbalanced industrial relations of France and Japan are not in balance because of the strong position of the state to make sure, if necessary, that the imbalance remains as it is.

Great Britain: Unions and the State at the Mercy of Economic Forces

The economic problems that other countries have faced in the past decade were encountered much earlier in Great Britain. The British were early pioneers in the virgin territory of postindustrial stagflation. Throughout the 1950s, the consequences for the working class of Great Britain's worsening economic picture were obscured by rising real incomes. The Conservative government's commitment was to Keynesian economics minus the heavy array of controls the Labour government of 1945–51 had carried over from World War II. Great Britain had evolved too far in the direction of state intervention for a complete return to free-market economics, something many Conservatives had never been enthusiastic about anyway. But the basic underlying philosophy applied to industrial relations was essentially that government intervention in the economy should not extend to employer–employee relations. Rather, the outcome of such contests, it was held, should reflect the relative strengths of the contestants.

Rising purchasing power and living standards reduced the perception of interclass hostility among British workers. In the later 1950s, impressed by the Conservatives' repeated electoral victories, the Labour Party abandoned its commitment to a more socialist Great Britain. On the one hand, the existing mixed economy and welfare state could be improved; on the other hand, perpetuation of a private industrial sector could now be tolerated.

The interventionist pluralism of the Labour Party contained a corporatist potential, which could be stimulated by adverse economic conditions. When the party returned to power in 1964 under Harold Wilson's leadership, it chose an incomes policy of wage and price restraint, banking on the support of the trade unions for a Labour government. But given the perception on the part of union leadership that their bargaining position with the employers was a strong one, union compliance with wage restraint was halfhearted at best, especially as grassroots pressure was intensifying and the incidence of wildcat strikes sharply increasing. In 1968–69, the volume of strike activity reached new postwar highs for periods with the Labour Party in power.

Unlike the West German legal system, British law contained no means by which unofficial strikes could legally be contained. Nor were there regulations allowing for periods of cooling off or for compulsory resort to state-appointed mediators or arbitrators. By the time the Wilson government had concluded that wage restraint was not going to work, a considerable amount of pressure had built up from the Conservatives and from employers' associations for legislation restricting strike activity and (implicitly) restraining employees' bargaining position relative to that of employers. The Wilson government introduced legislation to the House of Commons designed to limit the right to strike by imposing fines on workers engaging in unofficial strikes and on trade unions resorting to strikes before exploring government-induced opportunities to negotiate. Although the legislation also provided for expansion of union rights in gray areas not previously covered by legislation, the unions mounted a campaign against it and, with support from Labour back benchers in the House of Commons, forced the Wilson government to withdraw it and abandon its experiments with corporatist policy instruments.

After the reversal of the Labour policy initiative, it was the Conservatives' turn. Following the Conservative victory in the June 1970 elections, the government of Edward Heath introduced legislation similar to that of the Wilson government, although providing a wider array of countermeasures and antistrike penalties. It was enacted into law as the Industrial Relations Act of 1971. By 1972 it had been rendered ineffective due to noncompliance on the part of trade unions and/or employers.

The Heath government also turned to another instrument designed to curb the power of organized labor to push successfully for inflationary wage claims. In 1972, Heath reversed his government's opposition to wage and price controls and, after failing to gain union support for voluntary wage restraint, instituted a statutory incomes policy. This imposed rigidly enforced limits on wage and price increases, thus abruptly reducing the power of labor in its bargaining relations with management. Although the policy met with relative success in its first year, it fell apart in the wake of the Arab oil embargo that followed the October 1973 Arab–Israeli war. With their bargaining power sud-

The British coal miners' strike of 1984–85 was nowhere more intense than in South Yorkshire. The confrontation between rock throwing miners and police guarding a pit entrance at Barnsley took place in October 1984. Below are Yorkshire miners, still defiant, returning to work at the end of the strike in March 1985.

denly enhanced by the nations' energy shortage, the National Union of Mineworkers called a strike in the coal mines. Heath countered by declaring a state of emergency, which a number of other unions defied by striking in sympathy with the miners. The winter of 1973–74 was made particularly severe through reduction of industrial activity to a three-day week and through numerous work stoppages and shortages of supplies. Finally, Heath called an election for February 1974, stressing the issue of whether the government or the unions were running the country. Although no party won a majority in the election, Labour returned to power as a minority government, having a plurality of seats in the House of Commons. Harold Wilson then proceeded to negotiate a settlement of the miners' strike that was favorable to the miners' demands touched off an inflationary wave of wage settlements.

Thereafter, the Labour governments of Harold Wilson and his successor, James Callaghan, followed an incomes policy that sought voluntary cooperation from the unions as part of a "social contract," with a counterpart element of legislation that strengthened the legal position of the unions, especially restricting employers' ability to interfere with the unions' right to organize and represent employees. Through the mid-1970s, the unions were able to gain rank-and-file acceptance of these policies as the British economy struggled through a period of recession coupled with an inflation rate that at times reached higher than 20 percent. But, as unemployment and inflation figures began to descend to more normal ranges, the disincentive against unofficial strikes lessened and industrial unrest resumed. A series of interconnected strikes in the state sector in early 1979 further undermined a weak Callaghan government, and the Labour Party, after an adverse vote of confidence in the House of Commons, suffered

defeat at the hands of Margaret Thatcher and the Conservatives in the general election of May 1979.

Margaret Thatcher had captured the leadership of the Conservative Party when Edward Heath had failed to gain a vote of confidence as Leader of the Opposition from Conservative members of Parliament in early 1975. In addition to two consecutive electoral defeats, Heath had been blamed for the inconsistency of his economic policies during his 1970–74 government. The market-oriented right wing of the Conservative Party, which had felt abandoned by Heath when he turned to a more interventionist policy in 1972, now reasserted itself and elected a leader with whom they felt an ideological affinity. When Mrs. Thatcher came to power, she appointed a monetarist, Sir Geoffrey Howe, as chancellor of the exchequer; and her government committed itself to a policy of allowing market forces a maximum of independence to pursue their own interests free of government controls.

As part of its determination to rid the British economy of inflationary pressures, the Thatcher government committed itself to legislation that would considerably reduce trade union strength. This time the Conservatives preferred to enact their reform legislation in piecemeal fashion, avoiding a single massive assault on the workers' organizations. Unlike the Heath legislation, the Thatcher bills, enacted in 1980, 1982, and 1984, were directed toward the national trade union federations acting in their official capacities, rather than to unauthorized work stoppages arising on the shop floor. Although this appeared at first to be a more cautious approach, cumulatively the measures represented a more formidable assault on union power than that mounted by Heath. They were aided considerably by the rising levels of unemployment in Britain in the early 1980s, partly engendered by the government's deflationary policies. The trade union legislation complemented the government's general economic strategy and was assured of smoother passage through Parliament and acceptance by the electorate as a result of popular sentiment at the time that was highly unfavorable to the union movement.

The new laws had two central purposes regarding industrial relations. The first was to curtail the unions' capacity to engage in "secondary picketing," or attempting to halt work at firms other than the ones employing the picketers. This form of picketing was outlawed unless it could be demonstrated that it directly related to a dispute going on with the picketers' employers involving wages or conditions of work. Suits could be brought against unions authorizing such picketing by the employers affected or other workers prevented from working by the illegal action. Potentially crippling damages could be awarded by courts out of union funds. The second aspect of the legislation involved the phenomenon of the closed shop, whereby the employer agreed not to hire nonunion workers and could legally refuse employment to or could fire workers not belonging to the authorized union. Court action could be brought against employers taking such actions if the closed-shop agreements had not been voted on by at least 80 percent of the employees in the firm. Both of these measures struck at the heart of union power. The first sharply curtailed the unions' ability to magnify the impact of one another's strikes by engaging in supportive strikes in other industries or other firms. The second jeopardized the unions' organizational capacities. During the 1970s, British union membership had been growing to the point where by 1979, it exceeded 50 percent of its potential membership, making it one of the "densest" union movements in Western Europe

and, in the eyes of the Conservatives, excessively increasing its bargaining advantage. Whereas Conservatives argued that the measures added up to a restoration of the balance in industrial relations that had tilted in the trade unions' favor before 1979, the Labour Party and its trade union supporters feared that the laws had tilted the balance very much in the opposite direction. Indeed, trade union membership dropped off sharply in the early 1980s, with a loss of about two million members from 1980 to 1986.[22]

Today the Conservatives claim that the purpose of their industrial relations policies is to rid Britain of the creeping corporatism that has been developing at least since the Wilson government of the 1960s, and that was restimulated by the policies of the Heath government and its Labour successors in the 1970s. To the "neoliberals" around Mrs. Thatcher, the "corporate state" is only one step removed from the socialist state. Corporatist consultation of government with economic interest groups in the making of economic policy means that an overwhelmingly large concentration of economic power is arrayed behind the decisions of the state. In order to free the economy of state controls, it is necessary to break the hold of the interest groups—especially the trade unions, but the employers' groups and other special interests as well—on the process by which economic policy decisions are made. Paradoxically, the influence of these groups must be removed so "government will be free to govern," which for the Conservatives means so "the government will be free to remove itself from the economy." The paradox is that, in order to reduce the influence of the unions and even to reduce the size of the state sector, the government must take a number of decisive actions, actions of political will that promise to increase the intensity of confrontation between the state and other forces in society. An illustration of this occurred in the coal strike that began in March 1984.

Throughout the life of the Thatcher government, British industrial decline had been as severe as that occurring in any First World country. Plant closures and sizable layoffs were at least monthly occurrences during the early 1980s. Occasionally the government would engage in a rescue operation, as in the case of the automobile manufacturer British Leylands. But in most cases, the government encouraged industrial rationalization with its inevitable reductions in the size of workforces. This was particularly true in the case of the state-owned British Steel Corporation, which scaled down to a more competitive size while offering steelworkers substantial assistance in the form of handsome "redundancy" (severance) payments and pensions, as well as investment in new industry in areas where steel mills closed down, so that workers losing their jobs could find new employment locally. Where possible, younger workers were relocated to more modern steel plants elsewhere in Great Britain. In late 1983 the man who had presided over the steel rationalization program, Ian MacGregor, took over as head of the National Coal Board (NCB) with the intention of implementing a similar program in the coal industry.

What the Thatcher government and the new coal chairman faced in the coal industry was a trade union federation, the National Union of Miners (NUM), whose leadership under its president Arthur Scargill was much more militantly hostile to the Thatcher-led state than were the leaders of the steelworkers' federation, who had agreed to MacGregor's terms after a brief strike. Shortly after MacGregor took command of the NCB, Scargill announced an overtime ban, whereby miners would confine their workweek to a minimum in order to cut down production of coal, which was already in oversupply with worldwide demand at a low ebb. As later became apparent, this was for the purpose of keeping British coal stocks as low as possible against the time when the full-scale strike that Scargill anticipated should occur. The moment came in March 1984, after MacGregor announced the imminent closing of some twenty coal pits in various parts of Great Britain, entailing the loss of 20,000 miners' jobs. Earlier guarantees of both Labour and Conservative governments that miners not eligible for retirement would be reemployed in nearby pits were not included in MacGregor's package, which resembled what he had offered to steelworkers when he headed the BSC. With the support of Scargill and the Communist head of the Scottish branch of the NUM, Mick McGahey, miners in Scotland, Wales, and parts of northern England voted to strike rather than accept MacGregor's package. But elsewhere, in newer mines not scheduled for closing, where miners earned substantially more through bonus schemes than in the less productive mines, miners refused to vote for a strike, and the mines continued to operate. This was particularly true of Nottinghamshire and several other mining areas in the Midlands. In order to try to force the Nottinghamshire miners to cease working, hundreds of "flying pickets" traveled the short distance from South Yorkshire, where the miners had voted to strike, to persuade them, by threat of violence if necessary, not to deplete the overall national strike effort by continuing to produce coal. This example of secondary picketing, illegal under the Conservative legislation of 1980 and 1982, was met by quickly mobilized police drawn from Nottinghamshire and elsewhere in Britain. Clashes between the pickets and police were very bloody in the early stages of the strike, with one death and hundreds of injuries occurring in the first weeks. Although the police effort was clearly coordinated from the cabinet level, the government attempted to remove itself as much as possible from any appearance of involvement in the conflict. Although this would have seemed the obvious occasion on which to test the legislation against secondary picketing, MacGregor's superior, the energy secretary, restrained him from seeking a court order that could have led to massive fines and perhaps the jailing of NUM leaders, but that would also have escalated the violence.

The strike continued until March 1985. Since the strikers were ineligible for unemployment benefits while on strike, there was a steady movement of returnees to the mines. Scargill and the government (acting by proxy through MacGregor) were engaged in a test of wills, with each apparently bent on destroying the other. But both were flawed by a fundamental weakness that prevented either from delivering the knockout blow. In Scargill's case, it was the absence of either a united NUM or a united British trade union movement behind him. Although about three-quarters of the miners were on strike at the height of the conflict, Scargill was reluctant to ask for a national NUM vote authorizing the strike, since this would have required a 55 percent majority for adoption and he could not be sure that such a large percentage would support in secret the strike that they were supporting by their public action of refusing to work. As for the rest of the trade union movement, although the miners received sporadic support in the transport sector from railway workers and dock workers, who could interfere with the movement of imported coal, Scargill failed to convince the moderate steelworkers' union to boycott imported coal in steel mills that were barely surviving in the face of depressed demand for steel. These factors eventually wore down the miners' enthusiasm for the strike, and the NUM capitulated.

In the case of the Thatcher government, memories of Edward Heath's unsuccessful confrontation with the miners in 1974 and of the downfall of the Callaghan government due to the wave of strikes in 1978–79 provided strong inhibition against taking more direct action to end the coal strike. The official rhetoric was that the state should have no place in the midst of an industrial dispute. But its legislation to curtail strike activity had been little used by firms in the private sector, which preferred to settle conflicts through bargaining rather than to confront unions directly through legal action. In any event, most of the coal mines were in the public sector, and the NCB was headed by a Thatcher appointee. The government was restraining him from taking stronger action while it was simultaneously coordinating the massive police effort to keep the industrial conflict below the threshold of violence and to allow miners wishing to keep working to do so. In the meantime, the Labour Party, embarrassed by the strike, sought to evoke positive corporatist images of reconciliation and mutual interest, which fell on deaf ears among the leaders of the NUM. The British economy felt the effects of the strike in the form of reduced output in the steel and other industries, as well as in a somewhat increased dependence on imports of foreign coal. But the principal losers were the striking miners and their families, for many of whom the benefits offered by the National Coal Board in compensation for loss of jobs began to look more appealing than the continued loss of income and dependence on community and family support.

This British case departs in some ways from the image of pluralism associated with a weak state. During the 1960s and 1970s, governments of both the Labour and the Conservative parties were stymied in their dealings with unions, not because they were facing a unified labor movement, such as that found in West Germany or, until recently at least in Italy, but precisely because the autonomy of individual unions and local branches of unions frustrated efforts of the state and, under Labour governments, of the state and the national trade union leadership to maintain a cooperative system of industrial relations. But by the time Margaret Thatcher assumed the prime ministership, the combined scourges of stagflation and de-industrialization that Britain experienced in the 1970s had weakened the bargaining position even of local union branches and had exhausted the patience of the British public with trade union militancy. Mrs. Thatcher came to power at a time when many voters, including many who had voted for the Labour Party, wanted the state to take a strong hand in industrial relations.

Conclusion

A feature common to the foregoing cases is that there is a certain *rhythm* to industrial relations policy in First World countries, a rhythm that may extend to economic policy in general. The rhythm is associated with the phenomenon of business cycles, which have not been eliminated by the advent of postindustrial society, only elevated in intensity in the phenomenon of stagflation. When the economy is at the productive end of its pendulum swing, workers are in an advantageous position relative to their employers because labor is then a scarce commodity, much in demand. But at times when the pendulum has swung to the opposite extreme and unemployment is high, the advantage shifts to the employer. When workers perceive conditions to be favorable to their demands,

they can afford to take risks, and the rank and file become more amenable to the militancy of their left wing. When employers feel the labor market to be in their favor, their negative corporatist instincts come to the fore.

In the 1980s, whether official government rhetoric has been neoliberal (Britain), positive corporatist (West Germany and Japan), socialist (France), or mixed but essentially pluralist (Italy), the tendency of government industrial relations policy has been increasingly to favor the interests of employers over the interests of labor. The reasons for this are by no means to be found exclusively in electoral politics, since the elected Socialist government of France has been moving in the same direction as has the elected Conservative government of Great Britain, although it has not covered as much ground. More to the point have been the interconnected phenomena of slow growth, unemployment, and industrial restructuring that have both weakened trade unions and convinced governments that unions pose a potential obstacle to the changes that must take place if the nation's industry is to regain international competitiveness. Thus, the politics of industrial relations has featured much less tripartite consultation in which the unions enjoy a co-equal status, and more unilateral government policy-making seen by unionists as damaging—as well as more unilateral actions by employers, such as closures, layoffs, and even lockouts that are tolerated and even encouraged by governments. Adding to the weakened position of the unions in advanced industrial countries is the fact that a "postindustrial fault line" has developed within the workers' movement, between those workers on the safe side of postindustrial structural change and those who find their jobs crumbling away. This line of cleavage can cut right through a union, as in the case of the British miners; it can isolate workers from others in the movement, as in the case of automobile workers in West Germany and Italy; it can reinforce already existing divergences between skilled and un-skilled (especially immigrant) workers, as in France; and it can enable employers to divide workers from their union, as can occur in Japan. The result has been fertile ground for divide-and-conquer tactics on the part of governments as diverse in basic philosophy as those of Margaret Thatcher and François Mitterrand. In short, it can bring together many of the elements of what we have called negative corporatism.

However, these converging tendencies would seem valid only as long as the underlying economic hard times continue. If governments are successful in strengthening economic structures in time to join in whatever growth the worldwide economic future holds, then slimmed-down union movements may be able to recapture a position of rough equality with slimmed-down industry. This should be true in countries where governments perceive the model of positive corporatism to be the one that works best in most circumstances, an attitude that appears to be true of the governments currently holding power in West Germany, Italy, and probably France and Japan. But the neoliberal model of the Thatcher government in Great Britain appears to have imbedded within it a long-range goal of curtailing union power that may not be within the best British pluralistic traditions, not to mention the aspirations of the positive corporatists in the moderate wings of all of the British political parties, including the Conservative Party itself. In trying to face down the British trade union movement, it is taking on a powerful force in a pluralistic society and risking a confrontation not only with the unions, but also with the long-established consensual instincts and preference for fair play of the British political culture.

Suggestions for Further Reading

Beer, Samuel H. *Britain against Itself: The Political Contradictions of Collectivism* (New York and London: Norton, 1982).

Beyme, Klaus von. *Challenge to Power: Trade Unions and Industrial Relations in Capitalist Countries*, trans. Eileen Martin (Beverly Hills: Sage, 1980).

Cerny, Phillip G., and Martin A. Schain, eds. *French Politics and Public Policy* (New York: Methuen, 1980).

Crouch, Colin, and Alessandro Pizzorno, eds. *The Resurgence of Class Conflict in Western Europe since 1968*, 2 vols. (New York: Holmes & Meier, 1978).

Flanagan, Robert J., et al. *Unionism, Economic Stabilization, and Incomes Policies: European Experience* (Washington, D.C.: Brookings, 1983).

Goldthorpe, John H., ed. *Order and Conflict in Contemporary Capitalism: Studies in the Political Economy of Western European Nations* (Oxford: Clarendon Press, 1984).

Grant, Wyn, ed. *The Political Economy of Corporatism* (Basingstoke and London: Macmillan, 1985).

Hanami, Tadashi. *Labor Relations in Japan Today*, 1st paperback ed. (Tokyo: Kodansha International, 1981).

Johnson, Chalmers. *MITI and the Japanese Miracle* (Stanford, Calif.: Stanford University Press, 1982).

Lehmbruch, Gerhard, and Philippe C. Schmitter, eds. *Patterns of Corporatist Policy-making* (Beverly Hills: Sage, 1982).

Offe, Claus. *Disorganized Capitalism: Contemporary Transformations of Work and Politics* (Cambridge, Mass.: MIT Press, 1985).

Olson, Mancur. *The Rise and Decline of Nations: Economic Growth, Stagflation and Social Rigidities* (New Haven, Conn.: Yale University Press, 1982).

Rose, Richard, ed. *Challenge to Governance: Studies in Overloaded Polities* (Beverly Hills: Sage, 1980).

Sabel, Charles F. *Work and Politics: The Division of Labor in Industry* (Cambridge: Cambridge University Press, 1982).

Shonfield, Andrew. *Modern Capitalism: The Changing Balance of Public and Private Power* (New York and London: Oxford University Press, 1965).

Smith, W. Rand. *Crisis in the French Labour Movement: A Grassroots' Perspective* (New York: St. Martin's, 1987).

Notes

1. For example, Jean-Jacques Servan-Schreiber, *The American Challenge*, trans. Ronald Steel (New York: Atheneum, 1968); Christopher Tugendhat, *The Multinationals* (New York: Random House, 1972).

2. For a useful overview of industrial relations in the First World, see Klaus von Beyme, *Challenge to Power: Trade Unions and Industrial Relations in Capitalist Countries*, trans. Eileen Martin (Beverly Hills: Sage, 1980).

3. The role of trade unions in Japan is discussed at greater length later in this chapter.

4. For a treatment of these various factors, see Leo Panitch, *Social Democracy and Industrial Militancy: The Labour Party, the Trade Unions and Incomes Policy, 1945–1974* (Cambridge: Cambridge University Press, 1976).

5. This section draws on Charles F. Sabel, *Work and Politics: The Division of Labor in Industry* (Cambridge: Cambridge University Press, 1982).

6. Ibid., Ch. 2.

7. We have left the term *state* rather vague until now, perhaps reflecting a pluralist bias of our own. Pluralism conceives of First World *governments* as being divided into many branches, departments, and subunits that are susceptible to penetration by interest groups that will influence them to take sides in their own conflicts. The corporatist perspective tends to take the state as a unit that pursues its own interests. These interests may be concurrent with certain interests of autonomous groups and in conflict with other interests. For a "state autonomy" argument that runs counter to the pluralist tradition, see Eric A. Nordlinger, *On the Autonomy of the Democratic State* (Cambridge, Mass., and London: Harvard University Press, 1981).

8. See Wyn Grant, "Introduction," in Grant, ed., *The Political Economy of Corporatism* (Basingstoke and London: Macmillan, 1985), pp. 1–31.

9. We prefer these terms to *state* and *societal* corporatism broached by Philippe Schmitter, which imply too much state domination of the private sector in the first form and too small a role for the state in the second to accommodate the principal historical examples, which are probably Fascist Italy under Mussolini for state corpo-

ratism and today's Austria for societal corporatism. As we are concerned here with contemporary relations between the state and economic interest groups, the range of examples to which the term *corporatism* ought to apply is much narrower than Schmitter's terms suggest; hence our terms *negative* and *positive* corporatism. Both imply a role for the state as well as for employers' and workers' organizations, but the state acts in such a way as to give employers the advantage over workers in negative corporatism, whereas more of a balance is struck in the positive variety. The former implies a belief by the various actors in a "fixed- or negative-sum game," the latter a belief in the existence of a "positive-sum game" from which everyone benefits.

10. See the various essays in Gerhard Lehmbruch and Philippe C. Schmitter, eds., *Patterns of Corporatist Policy-making* (Beverly Hills: Sage, 1982), especially Manfred G. Schmidt, "Does Corporatism Matter? Economic Crisis, Politics and Rates of Unemployment in Capitalist Democracies in the 1970s," pp. 273–258.

11. From a somewhat different starting point, this conclusion has likewise been reached by Samuel H. Beer, *Britain against Itself: The Political Contradictions of Collectivism* (New York: Norton, 1982), Part 1: "Pluralistic Stagnation."

12. These case studies draw on, among others, Colin Crouch and Alessandro Pizzorno, eds., *The Resurgence of Class Conflict in Western Europe since 1968*, vol. 1 (New York: Holmes & Meier, 1978); Anthony Carew, *Democracy and Government in European Trade Unions* (London: Allen & Unwin, 1976); Geoffrey K. Ingham, *Strikes and Industrial Conflict: Britain and Scandinavia* (London: Macmillan, 1974); E.C.M. Cullingford, *Trade Unions in West Germany* (Boulder, Colo.: Westview, 1977); Robert J. Flanagan et al., *Unionism, Economic Stabilization, and Incomes Policies: European Experience* (Washington, D.C.: Brookings, 1983); W. Rand Smith, *Crisis in the French Labour Movement: A Grassroots' Perspective* (New York: St.

Martin's, 1987); Sabel, *Work and Politics*; and two London newspapers, the *Guardian* and the *Observer*, 1983–84.

13. For example, David Coombes, *Representative Government and Economic Power* (London: Heinemann, 1982); John Zysman, *Governments, Markets, and Growth: Financial Systems and the Politics of Industrial Change* (Ithaca, N.Y.: Cornell University Press, 1983).

14. Wolfgang Streeck, "Organizational Consequences of Neo-Corporatist Cooperation in West German Labour Unions," in Lehmbruch and Schmitter, eds., *Patterns of Corporatist Policymaking*, pp. 74–75.

15. Flanagan et al., *Unionism*, pp. 518–522.

16. Tadashi Hanami, *Labor Relations in Japan Today*, 1st paperback ed. (Tokyo: Kodansha International, 1981), p. 92.

17. Smith, *Crisis in the French Labour Movement*, p. 13; Japan Institute of Labour, *Labour Unions and Labor–Management Relations*, Japanese Industrial Relations Series, no. 2 (Tokyo, Japan Institute of Labour, 1985), p. 9. The French figure for union membership declined during the 1980s and may now be closer to 10 percent than to 20 percent.

18. Hanami, *Labor Relations*, Ch. 1.

19. *Ibid.*

20. *Ibid.*

21. In both France and Japan, trade union strength and militancy are greater in the public than in the private sector. In the public sector the state cannot remain a passive observer of conflict between the two other parties; it is a direct party to the conflict and it may, for political reasons, be less resistant to union demands than are private employers.

22. Dennis Kavanagh, *Thatcherism and British Politics: The End of Consensus?* (Oxford: Oxford University Press, 1987), p. 239.

THE PERFORMANCE
OF POLITICAL
SYSTEMS

We come now to an overall evaluation of our five polyarchies as promoters of human dignity. How should we assess the performances of these political systems with respect to our four dimensions—power, well-being, enlightenment, and respect? In the preceding chapters, we have made a number of evaluative statements, but an overall assessment remains for this concluding chapter. We devote principal attention to the value of *well-being*. Although this means an imbalance in our treatment of the four values, we consider that the overwhelming predominance of material issues on the agendas of First World political systems in the late twentieth century justifies giving them predominant consideration. First, we undertake brief assessments of the performances of the five political systems regarding the three other values.

Power

In analyzing First World polyarchies, we have been concerned mainly with how power is dis-tributed within the political system rather than with how much power the political system has been able to mobilize as it faces the outside world. Historically, the larger countries have found it necessary to have a relatively high concentration of power internally in order to be prepared for whatever threat might arise externally. The frequent wars on the continent of Europe have testified to this necessity. Today, the Western European polyarchies no longer threaten one another militarily. Whatever threat exists, whether of Soviet military power or of economic and political domination by the United States, has come from outside the region. Such dangers have seemed real enough (in the recent past, at least) so that certain Western Europeans have wanted a closer association with one another through a regional political organization. Later in the chapter, we take note of the progress that has been made in that direction.

First World political systems have retained enough power in the central organs of government so that each country has been able to speak with one voice in international affairs. This has not meant such a high degree of concentration that ordinary citizens have no access channels to the policymaking process or that the pluralistic nature of highly industrialized and urbanized societies has not been able to express itself through representative political institutions. The Second World countries, even those that are now relatively advanced industrially, have found it necessary until very recently to concentrate power. The Third World countries have often sought to limit free access to policymaking circles although their leaders sometimes find that their resources for implementing policies are limited.

In comparison with the United States, it appears that power is more highly concentrated both horizontally and vertically in Western Europe and Japan. Among the First World countries, power is more dispersed in the United States than elsewhere, both because of the constitutional dispersion on the vertical and horizontal scales and because of the strong political culture bias against allowing power to be too highly concentrated in a few hands. The reaction against an imperial presidency, aroused by the sometimes high-handed tactics of the Lyndon B. Johnson and Richard M. Nixon administrations, was, from a European perspective, a reassertion of intrinsic American values and a renewal of American determination to have these values prevail. In Western Europe and Japan, more reliance is placed on the political leaders' commitment to relatively explicit value systems and on senior government officials' commitment to their professional standards. These political and administrative professionals can be held to their standards by their equally professional colleagues. There may be considerable cynicism in France and Italy as to how much those in power are really acting on behalf of the best interests of the citizenry at large, but people also believe that the system will operate in such a way as to prevent the worst

excesses. In Great Britain and West Germany, there is a strong belief that political leaders and public officials will adhere to well-established legal norms and that the opposition will see that they do so in fact. The latter belief is thoroughly entrenched in Great Britain; the relatively orderly course of political events in the Bonn Republic has gradually implanted it in the West German political culture as well. As for Japan, trust in government officials approaches British and West German standards, even though the capacity of opposition parties to keep government incumbents in check is weaker than in any of our Western European countries.

This suggests that political culture acts to restrain the concentration of power less in the polyarchies we are examining than in the United States. In actual performance, it can be said that elites have exercised a considerable amount of self-restraint in ensuring that power will not be concentrated beyond certain well-recognized limits. The notable exception is France. Power has always been rather highly concentrated on the vertical scale in France. Steps toward regional decentralization have been taken haltingly and with obvious reluctance on the part of central power holders until quite recently. Horizontally, the concentration of power has varied considerably from regime to regime. In devising the political institutions of the Fifth Republic, General Charles de Gaulle and his advisers were acutely aware of the debilitative effect that power dispersion at the center had had on the capacity of the Fourth Republic to respond to external challenges. Today, one might suggest that they had overcompensated.

The Fifth Republic established an imperial presidency that was the envy of Richard M. Nixon. Without de Gaulle's imperious personality, the authority of the French president has diminished somewhat, but the president remains the supreme policymaker in the French political system, with no need to answer to Parliament. However, whether French presidents have used their powers to full potential has varied among incumbents, according to personal styles and political circumstances. Since 1986, President François Mitterrand has interpreted it more passively than he did previously or than his predecessors. Even though power is, in principle, more highly concentrated in a parliamentary than in a presidential system, the combination of the presidential and parliamentary features in the Fifth Republic gives the French president the best of both worlds, as explained in Chapter 5. To be sure, power is concentrated in the cabinet in Great Britain, West Germany, Italy, and Japan, and the British prime minister and West German chancellor are in superior positions vis-à-vis their respective colleagues. But prime ministers and chancellors must retain the support of their fellow partisans in parliaments. The political demise of such figures as Anthony Eden and Harold Wilson in Great Britain, of Konrad Adenauer and Helmut Schmidt in West Germany, and of numerous short-term prime ministers in Italy and Japan attests to the uncertain base of personal political support that these parliamentary leaders need. By contrast, the French president is assured of holding office for seven years.

It should be recalled that we are talking about political systems in which, whatever may be the concentration of formal (or government) power, informal (nongovernment) power is generally dispersed. There are a number of political parties that are not quasi-government organs, as they are in Second World and some Third World systems; and each country has strong parties in the opposition. There are also a number of interest groups that contend with one another for scarce resources and counteract the power of one another and of the government itself. Where parties alternate in power, as in

Great Britain and West Germany, the advantage one group (such as organized labor) might have is offset by the disadvantage of being too closely tied to the fortunes of one party or coalition. Where one party or coalition has enjoyed power for many years, as in Italy, the advantage that one group (such as an organized business) might have is threatened by the danger that the opposition might come to power and turn that advantage into a disadvantage. What this suggests is that there are built-in adjustive mechanisms in First World polyarchies (although Japan may be an exception) that assure a kind of rough balance between contending political forces over the long run, at least, if not in the short run.

Enlightenment

The goal of providing an adequate education for everyone through the secondary level and of making a college education widely available has long been backed by the U.S. government. In the early 1980s, 6.7 percent of the American gross national product (GNP) was being spent by all levels of government on education, as compared with 5.3 percent for Great Britain, 5.8 percent for France, 4.5 percent for West Germany, and 5.7 percent for Italy and Japan.[1] However, some other First World countries—Sweden, Norway, the Netherlands, and Canada—were exceeding the U.S. commitment in these terms, spending for education between 7 and 8 percent of GNP. The United States leads the First World in expenditure on *higher* education and in percentage of the relevant age group enrolled in higher education, but student–faculty ratios exceed 30 to 1 in American colleges and universities. In Italy and Great Britain they are between 20 and 25 to 1; in France, West Germany, and Japan they are 10 to 1 or even below. In the primary grades the American pupil to teacher ratio looks better than the ratio at the higher education level, standing at 19 to 1, midway between the Japanese rate of 24 to 1 and the Italian rate of 14 to 1.[2]

It is tempting to suggest that, at the higher levels of education, if not at the primary level, the United States has sacrificed educational quality for quantity as compared with most other First World countries. In Chapter 2 we emphasized the role of the secondary schools in Western Europe in sorting out children destined to go on to the university from those who will finish school at the secondary level and go into blue-collar and nonprofessional white-collar occupations. This goes a long way to explain the much larger proportion of American young people who attend colleges and universities because, for the most part, American secondary education is not similarly segregated. The possibility of being able to go on to institutions of higher education is not decided once and for all at age eleven or twelve for the majority of American students as it has been for European students. On the other hand, the quality of secondary education available to the favored European minority is undoubtedly higher than it is for the average American high school student who plans to go on to college. The first two years of college often serve the same function as the last years of secondary school do in Europe in giving the American student the intellectual tools necessary to specialize at higher levels, something the European student begins to do immediately on entering the university. Thus, it can still be said that the American outcome is better quantitatively, but that qualitatively it is somewhat inferior.

Still another perspective is offered by Japan, where the effort of the state to maintain an educational system of high quality is matched by the determination of Japanese parents and their offspring to take fullest opportunity of the possibilities offered. Getting ahead in Japanese society through education has long been a culturally sanctioned commitment, which makes it possible for us to rate the opportunities for upward mobility in that society as higher than in most First World countries. Students work very hard, pursuing goals that have been instilled in them early in life, to pass the rigorous entry examinations for university entry. This desire to achieve is not confined to children from middle-class families as it has been in Europe. Approximately 20 percent of students in Japanese public (not private) universities and colleges come from the 20 percent of families with the lowest incomes. In other words, who enters Japanese public institutions of higher education is "virtually unaffected by parental income"; thus "social factors are probably less important for educational attainment in Japan than in almost any other OECD country."[3] The reasons would seem to be found more in Japanese culture than in the way the system of education is structured. There is evidence that failure can be severely damaging psychologically, but success in entering a university is almost an assurance of a good position in government or in a private corporation, whatever one's social origins. The technical capacity of Japan's industry owes something to its educational system as well. Although the number of degree holders in mathematics and in scientific and technical subjects is not unusually high,[4] the test scores of Japanese elementary and secondary schoolchildren in mathematics are among the highest in the world,[5] which is another indicator not only of the quality of the educational system, but of the built-in drive of the students themselves.

Despite the potential qualitative disadvantages of the American educational system, European countries have been demonstrating their belief in the superiority of something like the American approach by pushing for reform of secondary-level education in the direction of the *comprehensive school*, which brings together students of all intellectual levels and does not prematurely foreclose the possibility of certain youngsters' ever going on to the university. Steps have been taken under the impetus of democratic socialist parties in most Western European countries to reform their educational systems, but progress has been faster in some countries, such as Great Britain, where more than 80 percent of students in secondary education are in comprehensive schools, as a result of the rapid advance of comprehensivization in the later 1970s, and especially Sweden, where the comprehensive principle had been firmly established by 1970.

France and Great Britain are two countries for which educational reform has been high on the policy agenda in the past decade.[6] In the eyes of the Conservative government of Margaret Thatcher, comprehensivization of secondary education had proceeded too fast and too far in the decade before they came to office. For the French Socialists under François Mitterrand, educational reform efforts under their predecessors had not proceeded far enough. Mrs. Thatcher's education secretary, Sir Keith Joseph, sought to put more emphasis on the quality of education and less on the quantity, by concentrating state financial resources on a core curriculum that would ensure that British schoolchildren would learn the basics of English, mathematics, and science. The aspects of concentrating financial resources has probably been more successful than that of improving educational quality. Nor has the Thatcher government been very successful in its effort to rejuvenate private education in the country, thus giving families (most probably middle-class families) an alternative to the comprehensive school for their children.

In France, the Socialist government, favoring state-supported comprehensive education, moved in the opposite direction from the Conservatives in Britain concerning the balance between public and private schools. There has been a centuries'-old conflict in Catholic France regarding the relationship between church and state in the educational sphere. Most private schools in France are what are called parochial church schools in the United States, and since 1959 they have been maintained partially through state subsidization in return for their adhering to certain minimum state-determined standards. Socialists traditionally have opposed state financial involvement in the private schools, and when the new government took office in 1981 it sought to make continued state aid contingent on a much fuller private school conformity to Ministry of Education's standards for the state school curriculum. The Catholic Church, Catholic lay organizations, and conservative political parties mounted a vociferous campaign against the proposed legislation, culminating in a day-long march of more than 1 million demonstrators. The opposition succeeded in forcing the government to revise the legislation, making it less threatening to the autonomy of the Catholic schools. Whereas the French Socialist government, like its Conservative opposite number in Britain, failed in its primary objective in the area of educational reform, it did succeed in diverting substantial public resources in the direction of education and in increasing the size of the state school teaching force at the same time Margaret Thatcher's government was whittling down the size of British teaching staffs. The high budgetary priority the French Socialists assign to education is in no small way connected with the fact that a large proportion of party members and even Socialist deputies in the National Assembly are professional educators.[7]

Enlightenment is available to citizens in all Western European countries in the form of a free press, which is not subject to government censorship or constrained to serve as government's mouthpiece, as is frequently the case in Second and Third World countries. In some Western European countries—Great Britain, for example—government secrecy frustrates efforts by the press to engage in the sort of investigative journalism common in the United States and in the scandal-oriented French, Italian, and West German presses. But the practice of government leakage of information has been developing in Britain of late, especially in defiance of the security-conscious Thatcher government. Journalists in Britain must be careful, however, not to run afoul of the Official Secrets Act of 1911, which provides penalties for writers and publishers who publish classified material. In all four countries a pluralistic press can be found, with readers able to choose among numerous daily and weekly newspapers, many of national circulation (in contrast to the more localized press in the United States) of varying political viewpoints. Like the American press, the bias in Western Europe of most major papers tends to be to the right, but virtually every major political party (left, center, and right) has one or more newspapers with relatively high circulation faithfully supporting its leaders and their policy positions. In each country there are distinguished newspapers that cover government and politics with critical objectivity and provide a forum for a wide range of political viewpoints. Examples are the *Times* and the *Independent* in Great Britain and *Frankfurter Allgemeine Zeitung* in West Germany. But there are also numerous offerings of a less serious nature that cater to appetites for a more sensational rendering of the news, inviting comparison with what one finds at grocery store checkout counters in the United States. More so than in the case of the educational system, what is regarded as the ordinary press in Western Europe may reach both qualitative extremes with greater

frequency than in the United States. In Japan, the press tends to be more uniform, politically neutral though critical of the government, and probably of higher average quality than is found in the Western countries we are discussing.

Television and radio broadcasting are subject to a wise variety of structural arrangements throughout Western Europe. Our four European countries differ sharply from the United States, however, in that television is state owned and state controlled. To the extent that private broadcasting exists, as it does in Great Britain alongside of the state-owned but autonomous networks of the British Broadcasting Corporation (BBC), it is in the form of concessions granted by the state and subject to the supervision of a state agency (the Independent Television Authority in Britain). Such limited pluralism can also be found in West German television, where the separate states are responsible for mass media policy and different states operate their different channels, and in Japan, whose public–private mix is similar to the British. Whether pluralism exists as now in France or there is a near-national state monopoly, as in Italy, an effort is made to provide viewers (and listeners) with a choice between serious public affairs programs and lighter fare. It is safe to say that the quality of broadcasting is superior to what it is in the United States, where the privately owned networks are predominant. However, there are frequently heard complaints, especially in France and Italy, of bias in public affairs broadcasting, including straight news programs, in favor of government parties to the detriment of the opposition. But in both countries television broadcasting has been opened to private initiative in recent years. The most frequent complaint in Great Britain and West Germany is that controversy has been contained within limits that are not threatening to the cross-party establishments. Whether or not this claim is true, the intellectual content of what controversy there is appears to be on a higher level than that usually found on the major networks in the United States, not to mention the sports and entertainment networks, which have no counterpart as yet in Western Europe. The arrival of cable television there, still on a relatively modest scale, may change this picture. At best, it will result in a greater variety of offerings to a diversified public without detracting from the level of quality programming.

Respect

Almost by definition, the First World comprises countries in which (at least most of the time) governments are bound by legal norms that restrain them from acting in ways that would violate local concepts of human rights. In a survey of political systems in all parts of the world, it was found that thirty-two countries had high scores for maintaining civil liberties and political rights relatively free of government interference. Of these, sixteen were in Western Europe. Great Britain, France, West Germany, and Italy were all among the sixteen. Japan was one of the countries outside Western Europe to be found in the highest category. Of the countries normally considered to be in Western Europe, only one, Greece, fell into the "second freest" category on a scale from 1 to 7.[8] It should be noted that the study distinguishes between "political" and "individual" freedoms. Whereas all five of our countries were in the highest category regarding political freedoms, only three of them (the United Kingdom, Italy, and Japan) were in the highest category regarding individual freedoms. West Germany and France are placed in the second-highest category, apparently for different reasons. In the case of West Germany, it was because of the 1979 anti-

terrorist legislation that restricted the rights of certain groups to organize and carry out their activities, whereas, in the case of France, it was because "the political composition of government affects the nature of what is broadcast [by the media] to the advantage of incumbents."[9] Still, despite these exceptions, all five countries are placed in the overall category of "free" countries where basic human freedoms are respected. At least five general reasons can be cited for this favorable record:

1. Most First World countries have long-standing legal traditions in which the rights of individuals are clearly defined. In the case of the United States and Great Britain, the common-law traditions handed down from medieval England consist of a body of precedents found in earlier court decisions with a number of legal norms applying to the relationship between the individual and the state. These have been supplemented by acts of the national legislatures in both countries as well as by state legislatures in the United States; such acts are then subject to court interpretation. In a very real sense, judges make law in common-law countries, because they are continually reinterpreting old precedents in the light of modern circumstances. However, British judges use considerably greater self-restraint in preferring to be guided by precedent, whereas American judges are more willing to alter law to fit new situations.

In continental European countries, including France, West Germany, and Italy, systems of code law prevail. These derive from the Roman law tradition. In such legal systems, laws originally enacted by Parliament or promulgated by the sovereign have been codified into complex bodies of categories and subcategories that contain the legal norms that apply in various kinds of cases. The role of the courts is more limited in such countries than it is in Great

Britain and the United States because the codes are specific and thus the courts have limited discretion in handling particular cases. It is up to the legislative bodies in these countries to determine what new laws will apply to new situations not envisaged in the codes. Still, in both kinds of system, bodies of law exist that clearly define rights and obligations, at least in settled areas of the law; institutions exist to ensure that these laws are observed—by itself, this is a greater safeguard for the individual than where the law is uncertain and at the mercy of the whims of those in power. This is also certainly true in the case of the Japanese legal and judicial systems, which represent a twin borrowing—of continental European code law at the time of the Meiji Restoration, and of the American system of legal safeguards for persons accused of crime, incorporated during the MacArthur period.

2. In addition to their ordinary role of interpreting and applying the law, courts in First World countries perform the function of restraining the executive (or law enforcement) arm of government. Government actions that go beyond delegated powers or that violate established norms may be revoked by court actions. In common-law countries, the courts may declare executive actions ultra vires, that is, beyond the scope of power granted by the legislature and, therefore, unenforceable. In code law countries, there is a network of administrative tribunals that hear cases brought by individuals against state officials. Although technically part of the bureaucracy, they are noted for standards of impartiality and consistent adherence to precedent. Moreover, in both types of legal system, there are appellate courts at the top of the ordinary court system that can reverse the decisions of the lower courts on the ground that norms protecting individual rights

have been violated in the administration of justice.

Finally, there is the power of judicial review, that is, the power to declare legislative actions unconstitutional—in some cases on the ground that they violate rights listed in a country's constitution. In the United States, the U.S. Supreme Court possesses such power, which is emulated by constitutional courts in West Germany and Italy, both of which have been active in insisting that constitutional provisions for human rights be respected. The supreme court of Japan also possesses the power of judicial review, but except in certain cases involving the interpretation of provisions of the constitution relating to human rights, the supreme court has been reluctant to make use of its powers against the more political branches of the government. No such body exists in Great Britain, where, indeed, there is no written constitution and where courts are bound to enforce the Acts of Parliament without applying separate standards to judge their constitutionality. But Parliament itself is expected to exercise self-restraint in its capacity to determine the content of the constitution through its ordinary acts, and by and large it does exercise such restraint.

In France, the Constitutional Council established by the constitution of the French Fifth Republic seemed originally to have quite limited powers to judge the constitutionality of legislation. Until the mid-1970s it could decide on the constitutionality of laws enacted by Parliament only when cases were brought to it by the president of the republic, the prime minister, or the president of one of the two chambers of Parliament. In fact, few laws were referred to it until, after his election as president of the republic in 1974, Valery Giscard d'Estaing sponsored a constitutional amendment that enabled challenges by the opposition parties to parliamentary acts to be brought to the Constitutional Council on the petition of sixty members of either parliamentary chamber. This opened the door for many more challenges, whose number rose modestly during the Giscard presidency but then precipitously between 1981 and 1986 when a Socialist government faced a conservative court appointed largely by its predecessor, much as Franklin Roosevelt faced a conservative Supreme Court in the United States in 1933 when he first took office with his New Deal program of legislation. Changes in the council's composition more recently have brought it more in line with the renewed Socialist government under François Mitterrand and Michel Rocard, but during the 1981–86 period there were thirty-four pieces of Socialist legislation that were revoked either in whole or in part.[10] This puts the French Constitutional Council now in the same class as the constitutional courts of West Germany, Italy, and Japan which, within certain limits, have the power of judicial review enjoyed by the American Supreme Court.

There is also a potential for a sort of *European* judicial review to be exercised by the European Court of Justice (ECJ), an organ of the European Community (EC), which is discussed later in this chapter. The treaties on which the powers of EC governing bodies are based largely deal with economic issues, but they relate in certain ways to what are usually considered human rights matters. In attempting to bring about equal conditions of employment among member countries, for example, they put acts of national parliaments that discriminate on the basis of sex, race, or national origin (if from another EC country) in violation of European Community law. The ECJ can declare acts of national legislative bodies (e.g., the British Parliament) to be in violation of treaty obligations, in effect, unconstitutional in EC terms. It is then up to the courts in the country concerned to refuse to honor a law of its own parliament unless it is changed to conform to treaty obligations. This "split-level" exercise of judicial review is emerging slowly in practice, but it is coming into practice even in countries like Britain, where the courts traditionally have not exercised judicial review of national legislation.

3.   In the continental countries and Japan, judges have a status similar to that of higher civil servants. They have security of tenure within their professional ranks, but their promotion from lower to higher courts is politically controlled, at least in part. Therefore, independence of political superiors is not assured, a matter that provoked considerable criticism in France early in the Fifth Republic. American and British judges are politically appointed (unless elected, as is true of the majority of American state and local judges), but also enjoy lifetime tenure. British judges are drawn from the exclusive ranks of the *barristers*, which in effect means they are drawn from a pool of, at most, a few hundred senior, highly educated, well-paid lawyers. Recruitment of American judges is from the legal profession in general, which is not professionally divided in the elite/nonelite way the British profession is. Who will be appointed to the higher benches is much less predictable than it is in Britain or the continental countries, where the range of possibilities is narrower and the leeway of the appointive authority therefore more restricted.

Students of the subject are not in agreement regarding the question of whether the narrow basis of judicial selection in Western Europe makes judges more independent of or more dependent on the political executive than are those in the United States. Security of tenure of U.S. federal judges means that most of them outlast the presidents who appointed them. Thus a court at any given time is unlikely to be peopled only by the appointees of the incumbent president. Western European judges may be independent of executive control while remaining tied to professional norms that restrict their range of judgment. Perhaps these mixtures of discretion and constraint are better than too much of either, at least from the standpoint of respect for human rights. Too much discretion might allow a judiciary to interpret the law in ways that are either too out-of-date or too far in advance of the cultural definitions of human rights and obligations that prevail at a given time. Too little discretion would leave the judges without the flexibility needed to right wrongs whenever they are committed against human dignity by other agents of the state or by their own judicial colleagues.

4. Because of the pluralistic nature of the First World's political systems, the role played by the political opposition, and the ready availability of channels of public communication, it is unlikely that gross violations of human rights will go unprotested. These phenomena interact with and reinforce one another. Thus, the greater the level of individual freedom, the more confidence individuals will have in group action, including political opposition and the collective public voicing of dissent. Many political systems in the world attest to the fact that the opposite characteristics form a syndrome as well: repression of voluntary groups, of political opposition, and of public dissent, as well as disdain for the many safeguards for the individual that are taken for granted in Western polyarchies.

5. Postindustrial societies are witnessing the emergence of a new agenda of public policy problems. Here, we should include a heightened concern for human rights. Critics of the violations of human rights in the Soviet Union and other Second World countries, many Third World countries, and in the Republic of South Africa have shown an increased unwillingness to allow long-standing abuses to continue simply at the discretion of those countries' leaders. Many of the same critics have also directed attention to the continuing denials of respect in their own countries. Progress has been made in areas such as equal rights for minority groups and for women. The former has especially been a problem in the United States and Great Britain, with their significant populations of racial minorities, as well as in Northern Ireland, with its large Catholic minority. Progress probably has been swifter in the United States (although only after many decades of neglect), where there has been a greater willingness on the part of the dominant racial group to look at the problem and attempt to find solutions to it—a willingness, no doubt, stimulated by the militancy of the minority groups themselves. This was not the case in Northern Ireland, where British troops had to take civil power away from the Ulster Parliament because of blatant discrimination by Protestants against Catholics. Although France, West Germany, Italy, and Japan do not have similar minority groups whose rights are so seriously in jeopardy, these countries have been slower than the United States and Great Britain to promote equal rights for women in areas such as employment opportunities and divorce law. But, in all the cases mentioned, there seems to be a growing awareness of the problem as one of human respect.

Although we can say confidently that First World countries as a group display better human rights records than do the other two groups of countries, it is also the case that the First World is on the cutting edge of technological advance in an era in which changes in technology and the foreseeable (let alone the unforeseeable) consequences of those changes have been truly astounding. Threats to the environment from industrial pollution and efforts by government to protect the environment through regulation can be seen as issues involving the rights of private firms to conduct their businesses free of government regulation, or they can be seen as cases of human rights (i.e., as involving respect for the individuals in society who might be physically harmed by toxic effluents or atmospheric waste).[11]

We are dazzled by the anticipated benefits in the realms of the prolongation of human life, the explosions of knowledge, and the immense increases in productivity. But some of the technological breakthroughs hold forth the danger of depriving individuals of accustomed rights to privacy and to control over their own persons while threatening to concentrate enormous power in the hands of scientists, physicians, and information technology specialists and, through them, to the governments and multinational corporations that employ them. First World legal systems, moving with their traditional professional deliberateness and political caution, cannot keep up with changes that are affecting our daily lives. The extent to which electronic devices have taken over the center of our working and leisure time in the past decade is perhaps the most visible manifestation of these changes for most persons. Information technology can cut both ways: It can not only expand our horizons as thinking and learning humans, but it can also limit and condition that thinking and learning in a variety of subtle ways. What is more sinister, it can be a means of simplifying the process by which information about us is gathered, stored, systematized, and transferred between organizations that are interested in us for reasons with which we may not be in sympathy.

Advances in biotechnology promise to revolutionize the processes of human reproduction and genetic inheritance. At the same time that they are in the process of expanding the options available to parents, they are also bringing about a nightmare of conflicting perceptions of the respective rights of parents and children, fathers and mothers, natural and surrogate parents, pregnant women and embryos, religious and secular authorities, all of which involve the clash of conceptions of human dignity and the rights of various categories of persons to have respect as individuals. Such conflicts ultimately may be sorted out by political processes. It is to be hoped that pluralistic systems of conflict resolution and policy-making will be equal to the task and that superior state power will not force issues to premature closure. Weighted in favor of pluralism are the ever-increasing capacity of the electronic media to expand horizons and the fact that technological know-how is widely dispersed throughout the world at large and not confined to a small conspiratorial elite, which means that the process can be kept open and legal systems constantly adjusted to new realities while older values are not lost from sight.

When compared with their own traditions and established standards, First World countries have not gotten universally high marks in recent years. Thus, student and working-class unrest has been met in some Western European countries, including the four largest, with violent police action or repressive legislation removing legal safeguards for certain groups of citizens. Such actions have been defended as required because of the threat of terrorist attacks, such as assaults on embassies, airliner hijackings, or the kidnapping and assassination of prominent public figures. The dilemma is quite clear, especially for countries with uncertain traditions of political stability. Is it worse to deprive acknowledged enemies of the public order of their individual rights, or to allow them relative freedom they may use to deprive innocent citizens of their freedom and sometimes their lives? This is not an easy question for anyone, but especially not for people with memories of political warfare between strong-armed groups of the left and the right.

Even in the United Kingdom, where the instinct to protect the individual from arbitrary action is probably as strong as it is anywhere in the world and where leadership has been taken in certain human rights areas (such as the rights of homosexuals), traditional rights, such as habeas corpus and the right to a speedy trial, have been suspended—in Northern Ireland, because of the civil strife going on there. As noted in the previous section, tightened interpretations of the Official Secrets Act lately have produced some notable violations of press freedom. Significant lapses in all five countries in the matter of human rights make it difficult to give highest marks to them for the value of respect, especially if we recognize that the basic concern for the value of the individual has grown out of the Western tradition.

Well-Being

The Record

The economic difficulties experienced by First World countries in the 1970s and early 1980s raised considerable speculation as to the future of postindustrial society. The problem of stagflation was treated in Chapter 2 as a general phenomenon affecting all postindustrial countries. However, when we look at the economic record on a country-by-country basis, we are more impressed by the differences in this record among countries than by the similar fates of postindustrial countries. Let us look at the recent record. In so doing, we compare our five countries with the largest economy in the First World, the United States.

Table 7.1 provides us with an overview of the productive capacities of the six economies

and of their growth patterns from 1981 through 1986. Although the American economy is by far the most productive in terms of total output, it is not far ahead of Japan on a per capita basis. West Germany had surpassed the United States in gross domestic product (GDP) per capita briefly in the 1970s, although the United States regained its lead by 1981. France, Great Britain, and Italy are ranged behind these leaders. But an examination of growth rates in the 1980s shows that Japan's economy has grown at a more rapid pace than have the others. West Germany, Italy, and France, all of which in earlier decades had grown at more rapid rates than the United States and Great Britain, had fallen behind those two countries in growth rates by the mid-1980s.

Inspection of Table 7.1 also shows that the American and British growth rates are the only ones that were not at lower levels in 1981–86 than in the preceding five-year period. Reasons for the higher growth rates of Japan, Great Britain, and the United States can be found in the data in the bottom row, where the annual percentage of fixed capital formation is also presented. It can be seen that investment in France was actually negative in the 1980s, whereas that in West Germany and Italy has not been sufficient to assure superior economic growth.

The British investment figures are particularly impressive when it is considered that, for the preceding five-year period, 1976–81, Britain actually disinvested, which helps account for the fact that Britain fell below Italy for the first time in the mid-1980s in GDP per capita. Table 7.1 suggests that Italy's lead may be short-lived. However, it should also be recognized that these official figures do not include the so-called informal economy, or unreported economic activity that eludes the gaze of tax collectors. This is said to be particularly buoyant in Italy, although it undoubtedly plays a not-negligible, if unmeasurable, role in every country. If we

Table 7.1   Economic Growth in Six Countries

	France	West Germany	Italy	Japan	United Kingdom	United States
GDP per capita (1986)	$13,077	$14,611	$10,484	$16,109	$9,651	$17,324
Percentage annual growth (1981–86)	1.7	1.7	1.9	3.6	2.6	2.9
Percentage annual growth (1976–81)	2.3	2.5	2.6	4.6	0.5	2.8
Capital formation, annual growth (1981–86)	−0.7	0.3	0.3	3.5	4.4	4.4

(*Source*) Organization for Economic Cooperation and Development, *OECD Economic Surveys: United Kingdom* (Paris: OECD, 1988). For percentage of annual growth (1976–81) figures, OECD, *OECD Economic Surveys: Germany* (Paris: OECD, 1984), p. 28.

were in a position to accurately measure the totality of economic activity in each of these countries, it might be that Italy's lead over Britain has existed for considerably longer and that the chances of Britain's recapturing a lead over Italy are slim.

The data in Table 7.2 suggest that the average American enjoys greater material well-being than the average European or Japanese. The greatest gap is found in energy consumption, which includes both domestic use and use by manufacturing, commercial, and administrative units. But the American lead is considerably greater in energy use than in GDP per capita, which suggests a much greater use by consumers than in the other countries. This is further reflected in the long lead of the United States in the number of passenger cars and television sets per capita. When we move from private consumer items to *collective* (or publicly provided) goods, the United States no longer leads the league. The United States is in the middle in the number of doctors per 1,000 population, and, in a measure of the adequacy of national health care delivery systems (infant mortality), the United States has a higher rate at 10.6 infant deaths per 1,000 live births than

does Japan (5.9), France (6.9), West Germany (9.1), or Britain (9.4). Only Italy, at 10.9, exceeds the high American rate, of the countries dealt with here. On the other hand, as noted earlier in this chapter, the United States, and to a lesser extent Japan, leads the Western European countries in quantitative measures of education.

The Western European countries are more dependent on world trade than is either the United States or Japan, at least if total trade figures are examined. In Table 7.3, combined 1986 exports and imports are listed as percentages of total GDP. Of the four major Western European countries, Italy and France are relatively self-sufficient, being able to meet most of their food consumption needs with domestic production. This is not the case of West Germany or Great Britain, although food production has been growing in these, as in all First World countries. But some of the smaller Western European countries are even more dependent on foreign trade. Imports and exports approach 60 percent of GDP for Belgium; Irish exports reached 51 percent of GDP in 1986. But, large or small, most Western European countries usually show a negative balance of trade in goods, importing a higher percentage of GDP

Table 7.2   Indicators of Living Standards in Six Countries

	France	West Germany	Italy	Japan	United Kingdom	United States
Private consumption per capita (1986)	$7,389	$7,116	$6,963	$7,132	$7,156	$11,500
Energy consumption per capita (kg of oil equivalent, 1986)	3640	4464	2539	3186	3802	7193
Passenger cars per 1,000 population (c. 1984)	360	441	355	221	312	473
TV sets per 1,000 population (early 1980s)	297	377	244	250	336	621
Doctors per 1,000 population (c. 1983)	2.1	2.5	3.6	1.3	0.5	2.3

(*Source*) Organization for Economic Cooperation and Development, *OECD Economic Surveys: United Kingdom* (Paris: OECD, 1988), pp. 106–107. For energy consumption, World Bank, *World Development Report 1988* (New York: Oxford University Press, 1988), p. 241.

than they export. The major exception is West Germany, which consistently has shown a healthy positive balance in the 1970s and 1980s. Japan, though not as heavily trade dependent, has also shown positive balances, but not as substantial as those of West Germany. The favorable West German trade record has been a source of complaint for its partners in the European Community (EC) because their own negative balances are in part attributable to West Germany's success—often as their principal trade partner. It should be noted that when trade in services and financial transactions are added, some countries such as Britain and the United States are more likely to show positive balances.

The positive German and Japanese trade balances are both a consequence and a cause of the fact that both have enjoyed relative economic stability in a period when most countries have

Table 7.3   Foreign Trade in Goods in Six Countries

	France	West Germany	Italy	Japan	United Kingdom	United States
Exports of goods as percentage of GDP (1986)	16.5	27.2	16.2	10.8	19.5	5.2
Imports of goods as percentage of GDP (1986)	17.8	21.3	16.7	6.5	23.0	8.8
Balance (row 1 minus row 2)	−1.3	+5.9	−0.5	+4.3	−3.5	−3.6

(*Source*) Organization for Economic Cooperation and Development, *OECD Economic Surveys: United Kingdom* (Paris: OECD, 1988), pp. 106–107.

experienced high levels of unemployment and inflation. The West German record has been more consistent than the Japanese. West Germany has been less successful than Japan in holding down unemployment; but, with respect to price increases, Table 7.4 shows that West Germany has held inflation to modest levels, whereas prices in other economies soared in the 1970s. The Japanese experience in the 1970s was erratic regarding inflation. Japan had double-digit inflation rates similar to those in France during most of the crisis period of the mid- and late 1970s; but it was able to bring price increases under control at the end of the decade, and they have been among the lowest in the First World in the 1980s. As noted in Chapter 2, all six countries have seen unemployment rise in the 1980s. Only in Japan has the rise in unemployment been modest. On the other hand, all but Italy had brought inflation down substantially by the mid-1980s, and Italy was able to do so by 1988.[12]

When one considers unemployment and inflation on a comparative basis, as we are doing here, the relatively good and relatively bad rates stand out and become virtual absolutes. West Germany appears to get very high marks for maintaining economic stability, but in the mid-1970s (at least), the West Germans were not so impressed with their own performance, and the coalition government led by Helmut Schmidt had a lot of explaining to do in the election campaign of 1976. The coalition lost ground to the Christian Democratic opposition that year.

Table 7.4 Indicators of Economic Instability in Six Countries

	France	West Germany	Italy	Japan	United Kingdom	United States
Unemployment						
Average unemployment rate,						
1964–73	2.2	0.7	5.5	1.2	3.1	4.4
1974–79	4.5	3.2	6.6	1.9	5.1	6.6
1983	8.4	8.2	9.7	2.6	11.6	9.6
Unemployment rate, late 1988	10.2	8.5	16.5	2.5	7.7	5.4
Inflation						
Average annual percentage change in consumer prices,						
1961–70	4.0	2.7	3.9	5.8	4.1	2.8
1971–80	9.0	5.9	12.2	11.1	13.6	6.6
1980–86	8.8	3.0	13.2	1.6	6.0	4.4
1988	3.0	1.6	5.3	1.1	6.4	4.2

(*Source*) For unemployment: Organization for Economic Cooperation and Development, *Economic Outlook* 35 (Paris: OECD, 1984), 43; *The Economist*, December 17, 1988, p. 109. For inflation: Organization for Economic Cooperation and Development, *Economic Outlook* 35 (Paris: OECD, 1984), 51; World Bank, *World Development Report 1988* (New York: Oxford University Press, 1988), p. 271; *The Economist*, December 17, 1988, p. 109.

By the 1980 elections, however, with West German unemployment and inflation figures remaining approximately where they had been four years before, the coalition regained most of its lost ground. Then, in 1983, with the higher levels of unemployment a more salient matter than the lower inflation, Schmidt's Social Democrats lost substantial electoral support to the new center-right coalition and to the emergent Green Party on its left. In the meantime, a British government had been voted out of office and Italian governments had struggled through a period in which there had been a real possibility that the Communists would gain a share of power. During the same election years in which the West German coalition twice survived challenges, two incumbent American presidents were defeated at the polls. Seven months after the second Schmidt victory, the French president was repudiated by the majority of French voters amid rising unemployment figures and continued double-digit inflation. In Japan, on the other hand, the turning around of the inflation rate preceded a surprising recovery in the 1980 election for the governing party, which had experienced several years marked by scandals, internal dissidence, and seeming voter disaffection. More recently, governing parties in Britain and the United States have twice been reelected amid signs of economic recovery, preceded by a substantial reduction in the inflation rate. It would be difficult to refute the proposition that electoral success for incumbents in postindustrial political systems is closely tied to the recent economic record and especially to the indicators of economic stability.

Structural Adjustment Policies

The foregoing indicators of comparative levels of well-being among our countries relate to what are usually called *macroeconomic policy* objectives.

Governments attempt to attain objectives concerning economic growth, consumption levels, energy conservation, trade balances, and levels of unemployment and inflation through the manipulation of broad economic policy levers, particularly fiscal policies involving budget balances between revenue and expenditure and monetary policies involving control of the money supply. (See Chapter 2). But governments have found that these instruments of macroeconomic manipulation are inadequate to solve the problems of sectors of their economies that are becoming less competitive in the face of technological change and competition from countries able to produce the same goods or supply the same services at lower cost. Economists have come increasingly to argue that macroeconomic policy should be systematically supplemented by what is called *microeconomic policy*. This involves gaining greater control over the factors that go into the *supply* of goods and services for a country's domestic markets and for international markets. Countries that are successful in maintaining positive trade balances, it is said, are those that are most successful in finding the appropriate mix of microeconomic policies; in other words, their governments have been the most astute in dealing with the problems of *structural adjustment*.

An example of the difference of emphasis that is involved when we look at structural adjustment as a microeconomic, rather than a macroeconomic, problem is the shift in our focus from overall levels of *unemployment* besetting a country's economy to the levels of *employment* found in different sectors of the economy and how these are changing over time. Table 7.5 provides a breakdown of some representative sectors of the six economies examined in the previous section. Percentages in the table are of gains or losses in employment for the period 1973–83. The sectors are placed roughly into

Table 7.5 Employment Adjustments in Selected Economic Sectors for Six Countries, 1973–83

	France	West Germany	Italy	Japan	United Kingdom	United States
Traditional sectors						
Agriculture	−3.0	−3.2	−2.6	−2.4	−1.4	−0.6
Basic metals	−2.1	−2.4	+0.5	−1.9	−5.0	−4.2
Textiles	−4.0	−5.4	−0.7	−3.6	−5.8	−2.5
Modern industrial sectors						
Chemicals	−1.2	−0.8	−1.0	−1.9	−2.7	+0.3
Motor vehicles	−1.5	−1.4	+0.3	+0.2	−3.2	−1.2
Electricity, gas, water	+0.4	+0.6	+1.2	+1.3	−0.4	+1.7
Food	−0.4	−1.2	+0.0	−0.1	−2.1	−0.7
Service sectors						
Transportation	+1.1	−0.6	+1.4	+0.3	−0.9	+0.8
Retailing	+0.8	−0.2	+2.0	+1.5	n.a.	+2.2
Financial services	+2.2	+1.2	+3.8	+3.2	+2.6	+3.4

(*Source*) Organization for Economic Cooperation and Development, *Structural Adjustment and Economic Performance* (Paris: OECD, 1987), p. 163.

three categories: traditional economic sectors (agriculture, basic metals, textiles), modern industrial sectors (chemicals, motor vehicles, food, and electricity/gas/water), and service sectors (transportation, retailing, and financial services). It is clear that the service sectors have shown gains in employment in all countries, and the traditional industries have shown universal losses. Financial services have shown the largest job gains in all six countries; textiles have shown the greatest losses in all but Italy (exceeded by agriculture and chemicals) and the United States (exceeded by basic metals). Differences between countries are striking. Thus, we see that Italy, Japan, the United States, and France have shown employment losses only in manufacturing industries, whereas West Germany and Britain have experienced losses of jobs in some of the service sectors as well. Indeed, financial services

is the only sector in which Britain has shown job gains.

In postindustrial society, we expect employment to decline in manufacturing and to increase in the service sector. Within manufacturing, the traditional heavy industries that once were labor-intensive have become more capital-intensive, and the same has been true in the chemical and automobile industries. Thus, the fact that Italy and Japan actually showed employment gains in motor vehicles, and the fact that Britain and West Germany showed job losses in transportation, and West Germany in retailing, appear counterintuitive from the standpoint of the concept of postindustrial society. Of course, this could be because Italy and Japan are not taking advantage of labor-saving opportunities in the production of cars, or that Britain and West Germany have been auto-

Table 7.6 Value Added in Selected Economic Sectors for Six Countries, 1973–83

	France	West Germany	Italy	Japan	United Kingdom	United States
Traditional sectors						
Agriculture	+0.5	+1.0	+2.0	−1.3	+1.9	+0.3
Basic metals	−0.2	−0.8	+0.9	+0.1	−3.9	−4.8
Textiles	−1.5	−1.7	+1.1	+2.9	−3.5	+1.0
Modern industrial sectors						
Chemicals	+2.8	+1.2	+2.8	+5.1	+0.1	+1.4
Motor vehicles	+0.8	−1.5	+1.6	+3.3	−3.7	+0.5
Electricity, gas, water	+2.8	+2.9	+0.0	+4.7	+1.5	+1.8
Food	+2.6	+1.4	+2.6	+1.6	+0.4	+0.4
Service sectors						
Transportation	+2.6	+3.3	+3.1	+2.4	+0.9	+2.7
Retailing	+2.1	+1.3	+2.3	+5.9	−0.3	+2.3
Financial services	+2.9	+3.7	+2.8	+4.4	+3.9	+2.3

(*Source*) Organization for Economic Cooperation and Development, *Structural Adjustment and Economic Performance* (Paris: OECD, 1987), p. 163.

mating their transportation sectors. Table 7.6 shows the annual growth rates of *value added* in the production of these categories of goods and services. When we compare individual countries across the manufacturing/service sector divide, we see that West Germany and Britain have shown increases in value per unit in the transportation sector, but that they have shown losses in the vulnerable industrial sectors of basic metals, textiles, and motor vehicles, compared to gains in all three of these fields by Italy and Japan, in two of them (textiles and motor vehicles) by the United States, and in one of them (motor vehicles) by France. In other words, some countries have been able to continue increasing their output of goods. This has meant shedding the labor needed to produce these goods in some cases. In other cases the expansion in production has been great enough that there have been employment gains as well.

These countries clearly have found the technology and work organization necessary to produce more efficiently in order to meet international competition successfully. Others have not been able to make up for job losses with productivity gains that enable them at least to retain their market shares.

The reasons for these differences are many. They relate to the factors that go into the production of goods and the provision of services: labor, capital, and technology.

Labor. We have earlier noted that the Japanese and American educational systems produce higher percentages of academically oriented students prepared to go on to college or university than do those of our European countries. One measure of this is the percentage of seventeen-year-olds in general education, as opposed to the percentage in vocational training or already in the workforce. In 1984 it was 81 percent in the United States and 63 percent in Japan; the other countries ranged from 32 percent in West Germany to 18 percent in Britain. However, when those seventeen-year-olds who are in some form of school-delivered vocational training are added to those in general education, the Japanese percentage rises above the American, to 90 percent. The French, West German, and Italian also rise fairly steeply, to 63 percent, 50 percent, and 47 percent, respectively, whereas the British rises only to 30 percent.[13] This was before the introduction in Britain of the Youth Training Scheme, which today takes many of the remaining 70 percent of seventeen-year-olds out of the job market and seeks to prepare them more adequately for jobs than the regular educational system did. Still, we may here see one reason why Britain between 1973 and 1983 experienced declines in both jobs and output in many industrial sectors: The educated or otherwise trained labor force was not available on the scale it was in other advanced industrial countries.

In Chapter 6 we saw that the relationships between organized labor, employers, and the state vary substantially among our countries. In general terms, in those countries where labor is most accommodative to the claims of both management and the state for greater productivity and lower per-unit wage costs, we would expect industry to have the greatest competitive advantage. We saw that the institutional arrangements for industrial relations in Japan and France give employers a distinct advantage over labor, particularly in Japan, whereas the opposite has been the case in Britain and Italy, at least until lately. In West Germany the two appear roughly even in strength, but the relationship is cooperative, rather than conflictual. Table 7.7 gives some indication of how the six countries rank with respect to the accommodation of industrial relations to economic realities.

The percentages, all less than 1.0, represent the extent to which wages respond to increases in unemployment. The relatively low percentages for the United Kingdom and West Germany represent relatively sluggish responses, sug-

Table 7.7   Decrease in Nominal Wage Growth Resulting from a One-Percentage-Point Increase in the Unemployment Rate (sample period in the 1980s)

Country	Percentage
Japan	0.88
United States	0.60
Italy	0.60
France	0.33
United Kingdom	0.15
West Germany	0.14

(*Source*) Organization for Economic Cooperation and Development, *Structural Adjustment and Economic Performance* (Paris: OECD, 1987), p. 133.

Table 7.8 Measures of Labor Market Flexibility

Country	1979 Industry Wage Differentials	Regional Movers—1980 Percentage of Total Population
Japan	34.0	2.6
United States	26.8	3.3
France	23.9	1.3
West Germany	—	1.3
United Kingdom	20.4	1.1 (England and Wales)

(*Source*) Organization for Economic Cooperation and Development, *Structural Adjustment and Economic Performance* (Paris: OECD, 1987), pp. 135–136.

gesting that organized labor is better able in those two countries than in the others to resist the pressure against nominal wage increases that unfavorable labor market conditions (as reflected in unemployment increases) are likely to entail. The order of countries is not what we might expect from the review of industrial relations in the preceding chapter. Italian unions appear less able to deliver wage-level stability to their members than we might have expected, whereas West German unions appear better able to do so. But it should be noted that the ordering of the countries is close to what we might expect when we look at the employment and output losses to de-industrialization shown in Tables 7.5 and 7.6. Greater wage flexibility in Japan, the United States, and Italy may help account for the greater buoyancy of industrial sectors in those countries that are in deeper trouble in the three other countries.

Two other measures of labor market flexibility produce approximately the same orderings of countries as the one in Table 7.7 (Italian figures unavailable). In Table 7.8 we see coefficients for four of the countries concerning variation in wage levels within manufacturing industries. This gives some idea of the extent to which firms anticipating growth can attract skilled workers with substantially higher pay, whereas firms in trouble can keep their labor costs within bounds by paying lower wages. In 1979 Japan showed the greatest variation in this respect, followed by the United States, France, and the United Kingdom, in that order.

The second measure in Table 7.8 involves geographical mobility within a national labor market for five of the six countries. Here the United States shows a population with a greater capacity than elsewhere to "move to the jobs" wherever they are available, thus reducing market "friction," or the lag that occurs between the creation and filling of job vacancies. Japan is second on this scale, well ahead of the other three—France, West Germany, and England/Wales. The ordering in Table 7.8 is again quite close to the ordering for structural adaptability of economies as displayed in Table 7.5 and 7.6.

Capital and Technology. Aside from the education indicators, the above measures pertaining to the quality of the *labor* input into the supply of goods and services in a country reflect only very indirectly the efforts its government makes to influence the competitive standing of national industry. Governments have policies designed to affect wage levels and geographical mobility, but they can be thwarted by institutional and cultural factors beyond government's control. Government can also influence the allocation of *capital* to industry by programs designed to steer industrial activity in more promising directions in the light of technological and world market trends. Government aid to industry includes subsidies that may or may not have the effect of stimulating investment into new products or new technology for more efficient production. In general terms, the United States, Japan, and West Germany are countries that avoid heavy subsidization of industry, whereas France, Britain, and Italy have engaged in subsidies ranging from 3.5 to 4 percent of industrial value added in recent years.[14] This ordering provides little reason to judge subsidization as being conducive, in general terms at least, to successful industrial restructuring, as the more successful countries have, for the most part, been those low on the subsidization scale.

When we take a more qualitative look at industrial investment expenditures to see whether resources are being devoted toward research in and development of new technologies (R&D), we find much the same ordering of countries as we do for government subsidization (i.e., the countries whose governments subsidize industry most heavily are also the countries in which the overall commitment to R&D is the weakest). This can be seen in Table 7.9, which also indicates that the countries with the greatest overall commitment to R&D are the countries in which the government's share of R&D funding is the smallest. Finally, the table also shows that the countries with the greatest R&D commitment are those with the greatest per capita output of the information technology sector, which might be considered a measure of the extent to which the Second Industrial Revolution has taken hold. It would appear that the governments of Japan and, to a lesser extent, the United States and West Germany, instead of intervening financially in their industries for whatever purpose, have sought to maintain the proper climate for private-sector adaptation to the technological and market changes that have been occurring. It should also be noted that the state sectors in the three other countries are

Table 7.9   Indicators of National Commitment to Research and Development

	R&D per Capita in $ (1983)	Share of Public Funding in National R&D (1983)	Output of Information Technology Industries as Percentage of GNP (1984)
United States	$379	49.2%	1.4%
Japan	257	24.0	2.3
West Germany	272	39.4	1.3
France	223	54.0	1.1
United Kingdom	218	50.2	0.9
Italy	94	52.4	0.9

(*Source*) Organization for Economic Cooperation and Development, *Structural Adjustment and Economic Performance* (Paris: OECD, 1987), pp. 95, 104, 254.

larger than they are in Japan, the United States, or West Germany. This has tended to mean government assistance to state-owned industries, keeping them operating at a greater capacity for a longer period than otherwise might have occurred had they been in private hands. Governments have found it harder to escape political responsibility for job losses in state-owned than in privately owned industry and have acted to keep them in existence for a longer period of time, postponing the inevitable day of reckoning.[15]

It is possible that one should look more to the micro- than to the macroeconomic level for an understanding of the recent reversals of economic fortunes by macroeconomic measures experienced by the United States and Great Britain. Conservative governments under Ronald Reagan and Margaret Thatcher have taken credit for, first, the reduction of inflation and, then, the reduction of unemployment (which has gone farther in the United States than in Britain), arguing that their macroeconomic strategies known as "Reaganomics" and Thatcherism" have been responsible for these records of relative success. However, Reagan's "supply-side" economics with its emphasis on tax reductions and Mrs. Thatcher's monetarism with its commitment to a stable money supply produced undesirable macroeconomic side effects; budgetary deficits in the United States and, initially at least, higher unemployment in Great Britain. It is possible that what has begun to turn manufacturing and productivity levels around in the two economies has been a renewed confidence placed by government leaders in the capacity of private industry to regenerate itself and the withdrawal of assurance that the state will step in to rescue firms that cannot keep up with the times. It took a while for the message to sink in, especially in Britain where the habits of reliance on the state were stronger,

and it is still too early to know if in the long run, these experiments will prove to have been successful.

As for Japan, one could argue that this is a case of both macro- and microeconomic success accompanying a more interventionist approach, thus casting the above "North Atlantic" examples into doubt as generalizable to the rest of the world. Two answers might be given to this argument. In the first place, the Japanese state has gradually withdrawn from the process of detailed planning of national economic development, leaving this more and more in the hands of the leaders of large multinational corporations. Second, when, in the postwar period, the Ministry for International Trade and Industry (MITI) played a stronger role, it was in a period that included postwar reconstruction designed to help the Japanese economy catch up rapidly with the advanced Western industrial countries and, later, to enable Japanese industries not to persist without change in the face of international competition, but to adapt to new technologies and market conditions. Once the adaptive habit had been thoroughly learned by private industry, the state could retire to a less-obtrusive position, ready to step in to help in dire emergencies, but relatively confident that industry would exhibit the astuteness necessary to make such emergencies rare occurrences.

Human Dignity and the European Community

We cannot conclude our discussion of the performance of the leading First World polyarchies without mentioning an effort that some of them have made *collectively* to enhance human dignity on at least certain dimensions. The European Community, as it has developed over the years, has probably performed best on the dimension of well-being, because the principal steps taken toward European integration have been economic ones. The members of the European twelve are currently France, West Germany, Italy, Belgium, the Netherlands, and Luxembourg (the original six), as well as Great Britain, Denmark, Greece, Ireland, Spain, and Portugal (the six that have entered the EC since 1973). Clearly, the outstanding accomplishment of the EC has been the establishment of a common market among the twelve countries for industrial and agricultural products, which has meant the removal of tariff barriers among them and the establishment of joint restrictions on the importation of products from nonmember countries.

For the six original countries, at any rate, the Common Market served as an additional stimulus to economic growth during the 1960s. For the later entrants, this has not been so obvious. The 1973 entry of Great Britain, Denmark, and Ireland coincided with the energy crisis and with the concomitant reversal in the general economic fortunes of the Western polyarchies. The EC could not prevent the member countries from responding separately to the energy crisis. The addition of Greece, Spain, and Portugal in the 1980s has intensified the division between affluent northern European countries on the one hand, and poorer Mediterranean countries that have more serious economic problems that now must be shared in certain respects with the others. Nevertheless, it should be noted that achievements of the EC in the economic sphere have been remarkable if measured against original expectations. Given the history of protectionism and economic warfare before World War II (and even stretching back into the nineteenth century), such developments as the pooling of coal and steel production in the 1950s and agreement on a Common Agricultural Policy (CAP) in the 1960s are truly remarkable.

It is possible to view the EC from a standpoint that is not idealistic, but eminently practical. For the countries that first formed the Common Market, at least, the new organization became an *instrument* of their economic policies—an extension of other instruments employed at the domestic level. Each member government, from this standpoint, saw the EC as meeting a particular need in its own efforts to deal with economic problems. For the French, the CAP has been, among other things, a means by which a large, inefficient agricultural sector could be assured of sheltered markets in the partner countries while time was bought for a policy of encouraging consolidation and mechanization of French farms. This has been accomplished (to a considerable extent) through the EC policy of imposing levies on farm commodities imported into the EC from non-EC countries. The levies are collected by member governments and the proceeds distributed to farmers in the member countries. This involves the payment of large sums by the governments of food-importing countries, especially Great Britain and West Germany, through the medium of the European Commission, to the governments of food-exporting countries, which, in turn, disburse the funds to their farmers. Because the French farm sector is the largest of the twelve countries, it has been the main beneficiary of the policy along with the French state, whose burden of farm subsidization has greatly been eased.

There have been considerable advantages for the other original member countries as well. West Germany and the Benelux countries are heavily dependent on foreign trade, and the Common Market represents an assurance of a high volume of such trade. In fact, trade among the member countries increased rapidly after 1958, adding substantially to the factors promoting rapid economic growth in these countries. More specifically, it meant for West German manufacturers the opening up of the large French market that previously had been guarded behind relatively high tariff barriers. For Italy, the advantages have included the availability of additional sources of development funds for the southern region and sympathetic partners when credits are needed to keep the weak lira viable, features that later attracted Ireland, Greece, Spain, and Portugal to membership. Industry in the modern north of Italy has also benefited from the expanded market, just as has industry in the other original member countries. In addition, the more efficient of the Italian farmers share in the benefits of the CAP.

The CAP has also been an attraction for Danish, Irish, Greek, and Iberian farmers as well as for their governments. In the case of Great Britain, whose farm sector is a very small portion of its economy but whose farmers generally are highly efficient, the CAP is viewed (not by the farmers themselves) as a negative feature of the EC, involving high British contributions to the EC budget through the levy system, most of which goes to farmers across the Channel. Nor do many Britons perceive great advantages to the industrial and commercial sectors of their economy resulting from EC membership. By the time Great Britain entered the EC in 1973, her economy was lagging far behind those of her new partners, who had enjoyed the full benefits of the earlier boom period. But the boom was over, and membership in the EC no longer could provide the stimulus to British manufacturers to modernize and become more competitive, as it had done for French and Italian manufacturers fifteen years earlier. Although Prime Minister Thatcher and her Conservative government wish Great Britain to remain within the fold, they are determined to bring about a reform of the CAP that will make the EC less burdensome to British consumers and taxpayers.

In 1985 the twelve heads of governments of the EC agreed on an elaborate set of measures, labeled "Project 1992," designed (1) to finally remove all restrictions to trade between member countries that previously had existed in the form of regulations and mutually agreed quotas that had the same effect as tariff barriers, and (2) to complete steps that had been begun toward creating a common market for transportation and other services (e.g., banking and professional certification). These have been prime objectives of the British government under Margaret Thatcher, which is committed to the principle of freedom of trade and has especially pushed for a common market for financial services, with respect to which Britain should have a comparative advantage. However, in other ways the agreements are less the object of British enthusiasm. The completion of a barrier-free market within Europe is likely to be accompanied by the erection of common EC barriers against goods and services of non-EC countries, a prospect that Western European countries such as Sweden and Switzerland as well as the United States and Japan are viewing with some apprehension. Also, the trade measures have been accompanied by a loss of the British veto power and a modest boost in the powers of the European Parliament (discussed later), which represented concessions on the part of a British government jealous of its sovereignty.

On the other hand, the EC has accomplished very little in getting the member countries to coordinate their policies in other sectors. Thus, it has had relatively little effect on redistributive policies, on educational policies, or on upholding human rights. These are areas in which the performance of the member countries is uneven and often falls short of their own aspirations. However, it should be added that the *prospect* of membership in the EC may have played a role in hastening the democratization of Greece,

The European Summit in Madrid, in June 1989. In the front row are the Presidents and Heads of Government of the twelve European Community memberstates. Behind them are their twelve foreign ministers.

Spain, and Portugal, which were governed autocratically before the mid-1970s. Democratization of countries in Eastern Europe may well qualify Poland, Hungary, and Czechoslovakia (and perhaps others) for associate status, a sort of half-way house to membership. As for East Germany, when reunification with West Germany takes place, the eastern part of the enlarged Germany will simply become a region of an existing EC member-state.

It might be expected that experience in dealing with common problems within a common decision-making framework would encourage national political elites to transfer certain elements of national sovereignty to EC executive and legislative bodies and that some sort of European parliamentary system would emerge, gradually taking on a shape somewhat like what prevails in most of the member countries. In fact, the institutions that could assume such roles already exist. There is a community executive in the form of the European Commission, which consists of seventeen commissioners who are appointed by the member governments. If this body were to become truly responsible to the rudimentary legislative body—the European Parliament—the dominant role of the national governments, as currently exercised in another body—the Council of Ministers—might diminish over time.

The European Parliament consists of members directly elected by the voters in their countries. The first direct elections to the Parliament took place in June 1979 and since then have occurred at five-year intervals. It is the hope of committed Europeans that a popular base will enable the European Parliament to be more assertive in EC affairs, even to the extent of encouraging the European Commission to form an alliance with it and promote policies that may be unacceptable to some of the member governments, thus defying the Council of Ministers. The European Commission had adopted a very cautious stance toward the Council ever since its knuckles were rapped by General de Gaulle in the mid-1960s, but the decisions of 1985 have signaled a resurgence of Commission confidence and assertiveness. If carried too far, such an alliance of European organs would be contrary to long-standing government policies of the three most powerful member states—West Germany, France, and Great Britain—which seem to view the EC as a useful vehicle for intergovernmental cooperation and the occasional coordination of their foreign policies toward the rest of the world, especially the United States and the Soviet Union.[16] These governments are themselves responsible to their own parliaments or, as in the case of the French president, directly to the electorate. Opponents of greater European integration can argue that abandoning national sovereignty would actually be giving up well-established national systems of democratic control for a yet-to-be-tested system at the EC level.

Clearly, arguments can be made on either side from the standpoint of our set of value commitments. In principle, the EC could be an admirable vehicle for the integration of national policies that would enhance well-being, enlightenment, and respect for the peoples of Western Europe. Democratization of the EC would mean effective popular control over what is potentially a formidable concentration of power to produce good or evil. But a very real question is whether such democratization could actually be made to work and whether officials of the EC with the power to make decisions affecting human lives would not be so remote from those people as to render the latter powerless. As we have seen, many valid questions can be raised along these lines when we look at the way contemporary postindustrial societies are governed within existing national units.

Postscript (Germany 1990) and Conclusion

In the spring of 1990, the near certainty that East and West Germany will soon be reunited into a new German state is riveting the attention of observers of the Western European as well as the Eastern European scenes. Elsewhere in the First World, events such as the survival of Liberal Democratic party rule in Japan following the February 1990 Diet elections, and the eruption of violence in Britain in the wake of the poll tax introduced by the Margaret Thatcher government in April 1990, have had to fight for media attention alongside East German and Hungarian elections and the struggle of Lithuania for independence from the Soviet Union. In fact, the events in Central and Eastern Europe are bound to have a profound impact on all five of the political systems that have been the concern of the past seven chapters. The most profound impact, of course is that upon West Germany, which will cease to be *West* Germany upon reunification, although it may still bear the name Federal German Republic.

The swift succession of dramatic events that are leading to the outcome of reunification began in the early fall of 1989, when, one after the other, the Communist governments of Hungary and Czechoslovakia decided to permit East Germans who had crossed into their countries to emigrate to Austria and West Germany. The East German government attempted to stop the flow of emigrants, many of whom were young, educated people, with good prospects of jobs in West Germany at considerably higher pay than those available in East Germany. This resulted in a spontaneous outburst of protest demonstrations in Leipzig, East Berlin and other cities that forced the removal from power of President Erich Honecker. On November 9, a hastily formed replacement government of lesser known Communists attempted to quell the uprising by removing the ban against emigration, or, in symbolic terms, by opening the Berlin Wall that had for nearly thirty years prevented free movement between East and West Berlin. This opened up the floodgates for a massive migration of East Germans into West Germany that averaged over 2,000 persons per day by the first months of 1990. In the wake of what was, in effect, a popular vote of non-confidence, the harderline Communists gave way to a reform-minded government, which made it clear that its principal objective was to achieve a true democracy in East Germany and to move toward reunification with West Germany.

Very quickly, the West German government echoed the call for reunification, and in early December 1989, Chancellor Helmut Kohl alarmed his NATO allies/European Community partners, as well as the Soviet government, by outlining a plan for a confederation of the two German states that would be a step toward an eventual federation. The four powers that had occupied Germany after World War II then moved to gain some control over the fast-moving process and, in a conference at Ottawa, Canada, attended by foreign ministers of both German governments (the "two"), and of the United States, the Soviet Union, Britain and France (the "four"), the so-called "two plus four" plan was agreed upon, whereby these six governments would work out the agreements that would lead to a unified Germany under conditions acceptable to all six. Eventually the agreements would be submitted to a larger body of all European states, East and West, for their accord. The acceptance of this plan by the Soviet Union removed any serious doubt that reunification would occur. From that point it became a question of how soon it would happen.

In the early months of 1990, a new political process came into being in East Germany, as elections for a new parliament were scheduled for mid-March, and West German political leaders, including Kohl for the Christian Democrats (CDU), Foreign Minister Hans-Dietrich Genscher for the Free Democrats (FDP), and former Chancellor Willy Brandt for the Social Democrats (SPD), crisscrossed the DDR (German Democratic Republic) in search of votes for their counterpart parties in the East. Most observers expected the SPD to win fairly handily, given their historic strength in the Berlin area and the industrial region of Silesia, and there were suggestions that Brandt would become the first President of the newly united Germany. But this was to reckon without the strategic advantage held by Kohl, who was able to focus East Germans' attention upon his call for economic concessions to East Germany and for the speediest possible reunification. Social Democratic leaders were more circumspect, believing that East Germany should not be railroaded into joining the Federal Republic, but that the new German regime should be the result of negotiation between more nearly equal partners. Election of a Social Democratic government in East Germany would ensure that Kohl's views could not easily prevail. Meanwhile, the existing communist government, headed by reform-

CDU Kohl- fast reunification
SPD Brandt- gradual "

East German citizens are applauded by West Berliners as they drive through Checkpoint Charlie after the historic opening of the Berlin Wall by the East German government, November 1989.

minded Communist Hans Modrow, although resigned to the fact that it would not remain in power beyond the election, was campaigning on the demand that a future East German government should put the needs of East Germans first. Trailing far behind all of the above in the polls were various New Left, indeed post-materialist, parties resembling the West German Greens, that could justifiably claim credit for starting the stunningly successful protests of the previous fall, but which were unable to

mobilize the support of most voters, who had themselves stayed on the sidelines in the fall events until it was clear which way things were going. In the March 18, 1990, East German elections most voters were to prove themselves decidedly materialistic. As an electoral force, the Green movement proved itself to be essentially a Western phenomenon.

The big winner in the March 18 elections was the East German version of the Christian Democratic Union of Helmut Kohl. The coalition of the Christian Democrats and two smaller conservative parties gained 48 percent of the popular vote and the same percentage of seats in the parliament. Although it was the second largest single party to emerge from the elections, the Social Democrats gained a very disappointing 22 percent of both votes and seats. The Communist party of Hans Modrow obtained 16 percent of both and the Liberals 5 percent. However, the Liberals were once again, as almost always in the Bonn Republic, in a position to hold the balance of power between left and right, as their 21 seats were enough to put the Christian Democratic-led coalition over the 50 percent mark.

But, for a variety of reasons, Christian Democratic leader Lothar de Maizière preferred to negotiate the formation of a Grand Coalition of his own three-party alliance with the Liberals and the Social Democrats. He reasoned that, in view of the momentous nature of the decisions to be reached, it would be best to associate all of the parties with West German counterparts in the responsibility for making them. Moreover, the constitution of the DDR specifies that amendments to it may pass only with a two-thirds majority, which would be assured only if the Social Democrats were added to the coalition. The formation of a Grand Coalition government in early April meant that the Bonn coalition of CDU/CSU and FDP would not face its exact mirror image in East Berlin and raised the possibility that reunification negotiations between the two German governments would have important issues to resolve.

Probably the issue gaining the most public attention at the time the new government was formed was the question of the conversion rate between West German and East German currencies—the Deutschemark (DM) and the Ostmark (OM). Although Kohl and Genscher had campaigned on the promise of a one-to-one conversion rate, voices within the Bonn government argued that this would put too severe a strain on the West German economy, with inflationary implications that might necessitate an unpopular tax increase before the December 1990 Bundestag elections. The suggestion of a one-to-two conversion rate (i.e., one DM would cost East Germans two OM) gave rise to howls of protest and renewed demonstrations in East Berlin at the opening of the newly elected Parliament. The conversion rate issue is part of a larger complex of issues involving the question of how much of their superior living standards West Germans can be expected to sacrifice, at least in the short run, in order to upgrade the material conditions of their Eastern brethren. The more equal the currency exchange rate, the more purchasing power East Germans would gain, which would mean upward pressure on West German prices. But to impose a conversion rate closer to the true market rate, which, depending on the definition, might be somewhere between one-to-five and one-to-ten, would be to condemn East Germans, at least in the short run, to a continuation of their much lower standard of living at a time when West German technological efficiency is taking over sectors of the East German economy and producing unemployment.

Although a compromise on the monetary issues was worked out over time, it has become clear from the sudden media spotlighting of East German economic conditions that the vaunted German capacity for hard work and efficient production has been much truer of West Germans than of East Germans. The massive influx of less educated and less skilled East Germans into West Germany in early 1990 brought attention to the lack of effective incentives toward hard work and career self-propulsion in the East than are found in the West. Integration of the two economies in *sociocultural* terms may prove to be a long-term process, indeed. Added to the problems of economic performance, and likewise attributable to the wrong kind of incentive system, are the dismaying disparities in pollution control between East and West that are so great as to have momentarily silenced Green protests against the *relatively* innocuous sins of West German industry. In industrial regions such as those around Halle and Leipzig in southern East Germany, industrial pollution has reduced the life expectancy average prevailing elsewhere in the country by as much as five years. To modernize East German industry in order to bring it up to Western technological standards of productivity, safety, and cleanliness will require a massive private and public investment at a time when the West German taxpayer will be asked to shoulder some of the burden of a welfare system designed to go much further than that in the West to make material conditions within society more equal. In West Germany the social market economy means that the ability to survive in competition determines one's place in society with the state smoothing out the rough edges. In East Germany individuals have been sheltered to a much greater extent from economic competition and assured of a modest, but safe, niche in society. Somehow these two opposed value commitments must be reconciled.

We can visualize the problem of amalgamating East and West Germany as involving the confrontation of two separate political cultures that have evolved from what was once a single, although certainly variegated one. Recalling our definition of political culture from Chapter 3, it is a statistical distribution within a given population of orientations toward politically relevant objects. When a population is split apart, the processes of political socialization and generational change can produce over time two separate distributions of political orientations. If an attempt is made, two generations later, to put those two subpopulations back together again, the best that one can hope for over the first decade or so, would be two very distinct political *sub*cultures with an overlay of agreement on basic objectives among political elites. The two subcultures can be expected to harbor quite different distributions of orientations regarding some, and maybe all, of our four basic values reviewed in the present chapter, adding up to quite different concepts of human dignity.

Clearly, the West German concept of human dignity is much more *individualistic* in tendency than is the East German concept. In East Germany, the underlying Marxist-Leninist philosophy of the long-ruling Communist party puts the collectivity ahead of the individual. Individuals advance along the four value dimensions that make up human dignity in so far as the society as a whole advances. Values are seen in class-collective terms: that is, the *power* of the working class collectively to advance its objectives against class enemies; the *respect* that workers and other formally undervalued groups should be accorded by those in society who have been more privileged; the advances in *well-being* to be gained by society as a whole as a result of the solidarity shown by workers engaged in building a more abundant economy; and the gains in mass *enlightenment* through the equalization of educational opportunities for the masses. Ordinary citizens in Eastern European countries appear to have become alienated from the regimes that have promoted those values and cynical toward the values themselves. It can even be said that the mass egress in 1989–90 of more than a million ethnic Germans from East to West represents a reassertion of the individual through an unwillingness any longer to share in collective misery and to seek improvement in well-being for oneself and one's family by an act that diminishes the human resources available to the collectivity to which one formerly belonged.

But this is a very negative sort of individualism, to the extent that it is not accompanied by a commitment to the relevant features of the competing value system represented by the part of Germany into which the hundreds of thousands are immigrating. There, individualism, even in a strictly materialistic sense, is accompanied by an acceptance of the competitive system of capitalism, where material advancement is, to a greater extent, dependent upon one's acquiring skills that are in demand, the rewards for which will depend upon supply and demand conditions in the open market. Many East Germans interviewed by Western media as the prospect of reunification looms have expressed reservations about such an economic system, seeing it as a potentially dehumanizing system where materialistic values supercede all others. What attracts them to the West is apparently the style of life enjoyed by Westerners when they are at their leisure, or else when they are working in the headier atmosphere of the young professionals depicted in Western films and televised dramas. The West represents variety and excitement in place of the drabness and boredom of life in the East. But one wonders how it will appear to those for whom it will also come to represent longer hours of boring work.

There is another aspect of human dignity, which we have touched on in Chapter 2, that is also getting a good deal of attention in connection with the prospective reunification of Germany. This involves the question of the *respect* Germans hold for other peoples. This is usually phrased in terms of respect of Germans for non-Germans, but, it is worth noting as well that the greater the cultural disparities between West Germans and East Germans, the greater the possibility that each subculture will deny the "other Germans" the respect that Germans on each side ordinarily give one another. But, setting that possibility aside, it remains the case that Germans as a people do not have a lustrous historical record when it comes to according respect to people inside or outside their country

who are not themselves Germans. Instances from pre-1945 German history when some Germans did reveal a sense of identification with humankind at large, have been seriously obscured by the record of Germany during the Nazi regime, and especially during World War II.

Much of the discussion of a potential resurgence of German ethnocentrism that might be unleashed by reunification has centered on the experience of the Holocaust, when 6 million Jews were exterminated by the Nazis while the "Aryan" German population looked away. Incidents of West German intolerance toward Turkish *Gastarbeiter* today provide evidence to support the argument that even the more outward looking West Germans have not changed fundamentally, and that, once the details of reunification have been worked out, the government of a new Germany will feel strong enough to ignore the displeasure of the rest of the world and seek to remove non-German minorities from the country. The questions raised by the Kohl government about the postwar territorial settlement, and whether the border between East Germany and Poland should be regarded as legally fixed, added fuel to speculation about a renewed German nationalism. Further misgivings have been stimulated by the rise in 1989 of a right-wing, nationalist and anti-immigrant party, the *Republikaner*, which has demanded the restoration of Germany's pre-1937 boundaries as well as the expulsion of Turks and other non-German minorities. Although it is recognized that such manifestations attract overt support from only a small percentage of the West German population, the fear is that they express only the tip of the iceberg. And it is further believed that the iceberg is greater in East Germany than in West Germany, especially the anti-Semitic iceberg, for the schools and the media in Communist East Germany had systematically denied what their counterparts in West Germany had come in recent years to acknowledge: the responsibility of their own part of Germany for the Holocaust. In East Germany the regime had taken the stance that Nazi crimes against humanity were an artifact of the capitalist system, which still prevailed in the West, not the East. Hence, later generations in the West should feel guilt over what their forebearers had done, but not those in the East. Lacking a feeling of guilt regarding the consequences of anti-Semitism, East Germans were free to indulge themselves in the old-style feelings of ethnic hatred without any sense of *déjà vu*.

In fact, the framework we have employed in this text precludes an analysis which suggests that certain value commitments, however pleasant or unpleasant they may appear to us, are *inherited* traits of people of one nation more than of another. Our framework suggests that differences in value systems, while historically conditioned, are primarily a consequence of differences in the life experiences of present generations. If there is reason to think that East Germans may be less tolerant of non-Germans than are West Germans, we would suggest it is not because the former have not had their "Germanness" knocked out of them, but because their life experiences, particularly those of a socioeconomic nature, have been quite different. In terms of the value of respect, as well as that of well-being discussed above, East Germans appear to be more materialistic than West Germans. Tolerance of others is not likely to be a well-developed quality for people whose lives have given them little occasion to elevate their self-images and aspirations. Just as Ronald Inglehart's studies show that postmaterialism is found in higher amounts among educated persons from middle-class families than among working-class offspring of working-class parents, similar studies would undoubtedly find that a greater incidence of the latter type of

person in East Germany would yield a more materialistic value system than that found in West Germany. Intolerance manifests itself among East Germans vis-à-vis Jews, Poles, and Vietnamese immigrants among others; but perhaps no more so than it does among Russians toward Lithuanians, or among Serbs toward Croats, or, for that matter, among Israelis toward Palestinians (and vice versa in all three examples).

If it is true that the cultural patterns of East and West Germany are dissimilar in certain politically relevant respects, then it may also turn out over time that the political party system of West Germany will not be exactly reproduced in East Germany. In March 1990, Chancellor Kohl may have succeeded in reaching a materialistic core of the East German political culture by appealing to German nationalism and the desire for economic betterment. His West German Social Democratic Opposition had incorporated too much of the postmaterialist value system into their public image to convince a large portion of East Germans that the Social Democrats were in tune with their basic preoccupations. But in time, the commitment of Kohl and other West German conservatives to a capitalistic, individualistic version of materialism may leave many East Germans longing for the socioeconomic safety net the old regime provided. At that point a Communist party with a reformed public image might reemerge as an indigenous regional party supported by many East Germans.

Whatever the mistakes and sins committed in its application, Marxism, as a pure value system, remains attractive to many of the world's underprivileged. It can not readily be classified in materialist versus postmaterialist terms, because, while it sees economics as the underlying driving force of all human activity, it profoundly condemns a social and political order that rewards and reinforces successful acts of human acquisitiveness. In this sense, Marxism is altruistic, or *other*-oriented, whereas capitalism is self-oriented, regarding selfishness as a good thing, at least in the abstract. Although they are rejecting a system that has failed to deliver on its more materialistic promises, many East Germans may not be prepared to embrace the underlying premises of the alternatives the West German political parties are offering.

In conclusion, it seems appropriate to remind ourselves that the Western value system that lies at the heart of the concepts employed in this text, like any value system, contains a set of ideals that are nowhere realized, or even approximated, in practice. One clash of systems and ideals that has been going on since the Bolshevik Revolution, indeed, since Karl Marx wrote, appears to have been resolved in favor of the *current* manifestations of Western values, at the expense of its *current* leading challenger, Marxism–Leninism. But the clash of values, and, happily, the reconciliation of values, will go on into the next century.

In the present century, democracy provided, after World War II, the context that facilitated a reconciliation between some of the promises and programs offered as alternatives by capitalist and socialist value systems. But inequality and poverty continue to be found even in the economically most advanced countries of the world, as well as ignorance and impatience with unpopular ideas. These consequences of the imperfect realization of our ideals will have to be met by a rededication to those ideals. The problem of preserving the natural environment against the onslaught of modern science and industry will be brought under control only when modern science and industry are more intensively directed toward environmental protection and recovery. If one system of ideas has proven itself unworkable in practice, it does not follow that an alternative system, that to which First World states formally adhere, has proven itself eminently workable. The exploration of alternatives requires a pragmatic application of the comparative method of analysis, akin to the scientific method of experimentation. By this method we can reject certain propositions that experience shows us to be false; but, likewise, we can not take as proven propositions that only a handful of cases tell us have not been falsified. If capitalist democracies appear to have worked better at an advanced stage of industrialization than have single-party socialist regimes, we can not say it has been proven that capitalist democracy is superior to any other conceivable form of regime. Such a conclusion would be based on too narrow a set of observations, nor would it give us an answer to the question: Which, if either, is responsible for those successes First World societies *have* registered, capitalism or democracy?

Suggestions for Further Reading

Alt, James E., and K. Alec Chrystal. *Political Economics* (Brighton, England: Wheatsheaf Books, 1983).

Andrain, Charles F. *Politics and Economic Policy in Western Democracies* (North Scituate, Mass.: Duxbury, 1980).

Ardagh, John. *Germany and the Germans: An Anatomy of Society Today* (New York: Harper & Row, 1987).

Ehrmann, Henry L. *Comparative Legal Cultures* (Englewood Cliffs, N.J.: Prentice-Hall, 1976).

Eulau, Heinz, and Michael Lewis-Beck, eds. *Economic Conditions and Electoral Outcomes: The United States and Western Europe* (New York: Agathon, 1985).

Gamble, Andrew. *Britain in Decline: Economic Policy, Political Strategy and the British State,* 2nd ed. (Basingstoke: Macmillan, 1985).

Gastil, Raymond D. *Freedom in the World: 1986–1987* (Westport, Conn.: Greenwood Press, 1987).

George, Stephen. *Politics and Policy in the European Community* (Oxford: Clarendon Press, 1985).

Heidenheimer, Arnold J., et al. *Comparative Public Policy: The Politics of Social Choice in Europe and America,* 2nd ed. (New York: St. Martin's Press, 1983).

Hibbs, Douglas, Jr. *The Political Economy of Industrial Democracies* (Cambridge, Mass., and London: Harvard University Press, 1987).

Lincoln, Edward J. *Japan: Facing Economic Maturity* (Washington, D.C.: Brookings, 1988).

Lindberg, Leon N., and Charles S. Maier, eds. *The Politics of Inflation and Economic Stagnation: Theoretical Approaches and International Case Studies* (Washington, D.C.: Brookings, 1985).

Riddell, Peter. *The Thatcher Government* (Oxford: Martin Robertson, 1983).

Ross, George, et al., eds. *The Mitterrand Experiment: Continuity and Change in Modern France* (Cambridge: Polity Press, 1987).

Sassoon, Donald. *Contemporary Italy: Politics, Economics and Society since 1945* (London and New York: Longman, 1986).

Tufte, Edward D. *Political Control of the Economy* (Princeton, N.J.: Princeton University Press, 1978).

Wallace, Helen, et al., eds. *Policy-Making in the European Community,* 2nd ed. (New York: Wiley, 1983).

Notes

1. United Nations Educational, Scientific and Cultural Organization, *UNESCO Statistical Digest, 1986* (Paris: UNESCO, 1986), passim.

2. Ibid.

3. Organization for Economic Cooperation and Development, *Structural Adjustment and Economic Performance* (Paris: OECD, 1987), p. 76.

4. *UNESCO Statistical Digest,* p. 207.

5. R. A. Garden, "The Second IEA Mathematics Study," *Comparative Education Review* 30 (February 1987), 47–68.

6. The following comparison is based on a study by John S. Ambler, "Constraints on Policy Innovation in Education: Thatcher's Britain and Mitterrand's France," *Comparative Politics* 20 (October 1987), 85–105.

7. Ibid., p. 99.

8. Raymond D. Gastil, *Freedom in the World: 1986–1987* (Westport, Conn.: Greenwood Press, 1987), pp. 40–41.

9. Ibid., p. 18.

10. John T. S. Keeler and Alec Stone, "Judicial–Political Confrontation in Mitterrand's France: The Emergence of the Constitutional Council as a Major Actor in the Policy-Making Process," in George Ross et al., eds., *The Mitterrand Experiment: Continuity and Change in Modern France* (Cambridge: Polity Press, 1987), p. 167.

11. This is an area in which the Japanese Supreme Court has taken leadership away from the Japanese government in protecting a new category of human rights. Edwin O. Reischauer, *The Japanese* (Cambridge, Mass., and London: Harvard University Press, 1977), p. 264.

12. "The Flawed Renaissance: A Survey of the Italian Economy," *The Economist* (February 27, 1988), special section, p. 4.

13. OECD, *Structural Adjustment*, p. 72.

14. Ibid., p. 229.

15. Although it is true that West German industry does not appear by the measures displayed in Tables 7.4 and 7.5 to be making structural adjustments as effectively as those of Japan, the United States, and Italy, it will be recalled that West German trade figures are the most favorable of our six countries. Perhaps there is a *qualitative* element to West German manufacturing that stems from effective capital investment and R&D targeting as well as accumulated skills and know-how that maintain an exporting edge even for industries that exhibit relative decline by other indicators.

16. It should be noted, however, that in 1990 the governments of West Germany and France promoted a review of options for an Economic and Monetary Union and even a Political Union. The former might lead to a single currency for EC countries and to a central banking system; the latter might involve a democratization of EC institutions. The British government is resisting these steps, which the German and French governments see as essential if Project 1992 is to be successful in stimulating economic integration and regeneration in Western Europe.

PART II

REFORM AND REVOLUTION IN COMMUNIST SYSTEMS

A statue of Lenin being removed from downtown Bucharest, Romania.

C H A P T E R 8

HISTORICAL SETTING

Karl Marx and the Nineteenth Century

Communist history cannot be understood without studying the man one American journalist called the least funny of the Marx brothers.[1] The philosophy of Karl Marx has had a greater impact on twentieth-century life than any other political philosophy or creed. The son of a Jewish lawyer who later became a Christian, Karl Marx was born in Germany in 1818. During his education at the universities of Bonn and Berlin, he became attracted to the philosophies of Georg Hegel and Ludwig Feuerbach. On graduation, Marx became a political writer and joined the staff of the liberal newspaper *Rheinische Zeitung*. After he was named editor, he became involved in various revolutionary causes and, in protest against the Prussian government, moved to Paris in 1843. In France, Marx undertook the serious study of what he called scientific socialism and met many prominent socialist thinkers. One not so prominent at that particular time but who later

became one of the era's great radical philosophers was another German, Friedrich Engels.

Engels, the son of a wealthy German manufacturer, had been sent abroad by his father to oversee the family's business interests. While earning his livelihood from the system he so vigorously condemned, Engels came to France where he became involved in socialist thinking and writing. When he met Marx, they formed a deep bond that lasted through Marx's lifetime.

In 1848 Marx and Engels wrote one of the most important political documents of modern history. This document was a short but stirring call to arms for the working class and became the creed of the Communist Party. Known as the *Communist Manifesto,* it contains the immortal words: *"Workers of the world unite! The proletarians have nothing to lose but their chains."* In concise, ringing language, the *Communist Manifesto* sets forth the basic tenets of Marxist philosophy. Telling of the bourgeoisie's (the owners') exploitation of the proletariat (the workers), Marx predicted a proletarian uprising and an end to capitalism and exploitation.

Marx returned to Germany for a short time following publication of the *Manifesto* but was tried for sedition and expelled from the country in 1849. He then went to England, where he remained for the rest of his life. During his years in Great Britain, Marx worked long hours in the reading room of the British Museum on his chief endeavor, *Das Kapital*. Although the first volume appeared in 1867, the second and third volumes did not appear until after his death in 1883. In contrast to the *Communist Manifesto*, which is a rousing declaration, *Das Kapital* is a mammoth, plodding, scientific study of capitalism that describes its origins and its predicted demise. Because his writings and theories were based on observed facts, Marx wanted to distinguish himself from the utopian socialists. He believed he had developed a scientific theory of socialism. The utopians hoped for socialism; his theory predicted that it was inevitable.[2]

Marx's lifelong endeavor was to discover the laws of human and social development and to provide evidence of their scientific validity. Believing that the world was governed by predictable forces, he spent most of his life trying to understand them. He had a voracious appetite for reading and his typical day in the British Museum began early and ended late. During this exhaustive research he reached several important conclusions.

According to Marx, all traditional societies—for example, feudal or capitalist—were divided into two main classes. Because the interests of these two classes were constantly at odds, they were involved in class struggle. The *Manifesto* notes:

The history of all hitherto existing society is the history of class struggles. Freeman and slave, patrician and plebeian, lord and serf, guildmaster and journeyman, in a word, op-
pressor and oppressed, stood in constant competition to one another.[3]

In nineteenth-century Europe, the class struggle between the bourgeoisie (those in control of the means of production) and proletariat (the working class) was generated by the Industrial Revolution. Capitalism had developed in Europe and although economic development soared, great human costs were incurred. Those in control of the means of production were exploiting the working class in the production process. According to Marx, the proletariat had no means of production and were forced to sell their labor to live. Marx predicted that the exploited working class would develop a political consciousness and throw off the ruling bourgeoisie. This revolution would result in a new form of society—a form called socialist—in which the working class would rule. Because classes would be dissolved, exploitation and class struggle would disappear. This societal form would finally evolve into communism, a perfect state free of classes, exploitation, material scarcity, and government coercion.

Marx was a man of his times. He lived in nineteenth-century Europe and observed some of the worst features of industrialization. Attracted from the countryside to the cities, the new working class was subjected to treatment incomprehensible by today's standards. Because labor unions and collective bargaining had not developed, the proletarian class had no voice against the powerful bourgeoisie, was paid subsistence wages, and lived in deprivation and poverty.

As a humanitarian and social scientist, Marx was forced to rebel against the injustices he saw. Not a man of the sword, although he believed in violence, he utilized the written word to call attention to the degraded state of mankind. Marx wanted the quality of life to be im-

Karl Marx (1818–83), seen here with his eldest daughter, Jenny, was described by some as a warmly affectionate family man. Because of his radical political views, Marx was forced to leave his native Germany. After meeting his collaborator Friedrich Engels (1820–95), Marx settled in England, where he prepared his major works.

and suffered from poor housing, lack of nutrition, and inadequate medical care. His two sons and a daughter may have died as a result of these conditions. He was often without any means of subsistence and had to rely on the financial support of his friend and collaborator, Engels.[4]

But to Marx, the physical suffering was minor compared with his broken dream of proletarian revolution. Marx hoped and predicted that workers' uprisings would occur in nineteenth-century Europe. By his death, however, there had been no major proletarian revolution and no founding of a Marxist state. Although we must acknowledge Marx's contribution to the beginning of modern social science analysis, we must also recognize that he was a product of the period in which he lived and was limited by it. It is obvious that he did not predict many of the developmental nuances of the twentieth century.

By the end of the nineteenth century, socialism and revolution were discussed by students, workers, revolutionaries, and other interested observers across the continent. Throughout the coffeehouses of Europe, revolutionaries of different viewpoints and motives plotted to end the injustices they perceived around them. Many were without direction, lacking either political theory or power; others found inspiration and guidance in the writings of Marx and had firm ideas on how power could be obtained. One such individual was the Russian, Vladimir Ilyich Ulyanov, later to become known by the pseudonym Lenin.[5] Born in Simbirsk (renamed Ulyanovsk), Russia, in 1870, Lenin was the son of a school inspector and a teacher. Although the Ulyanov family was of an apparently conservative and religious background, the children were radical and became involved in a plot to overthrow the tsarist autocracy. Lenin's sister, Anna, and brother, Alexander, were arrested

proved for the impoverished masses and he wished to develop a theory that demonstrated improvement was not only possible but inevitable and scientifically predictable.

Before his death in London in 1883, Marx experienced constant hardship and frustration. He and his family lived near the poverty level on charges of belonging to a revolutionary organization conspiring to kill the tsar. Alexander was hanged in 1887 along with four fellow conspirators for his complicity in the abortive plot.

One year later, in 1888, Lenin was introduced to Marxism and before long began writing revolutionary materials that plotted the overthrow of the tsarist government. Traveling between St. Petersburg, the capital of tsarist Russia, and the nations of Europe, Lenin established his credentials as a Marxist and a revolutionary. On his return to Russia in 1897, he was arrested and sent to Siberia, where he was incarcerated until 1900.

By the spring of 1900, Lenin was a free man in the city of St. Petersburg (renamed Leningrad

Vladimir Ilyich Lenin (seated, third from left) with fellow revolutionaries prior to 1917.

in 1924). Dedicated to the overthrow of the autocracy that had imprisoned him and had executed his brother, Lenin plotted with other Russian Marxists. When he returned to exile in Switzerland and Germany, he published the article "What Is to Be Done?" in the party journal, *Iskra* (The Spark). In that article, he argued for a small, centralized, revolutionary organization to lead the uprising, as opposed to a broad-based, mass movement. The plan was accepted by a faction of the Russian Marxists, who adopted the name Bolsheviks, and Marxism was soon put to the test.

The Bolshevik Insurrection

At the beginning of the twentieth century, the autocracy of Russia under Tsar Nicholas II was in serious trouble. Europe was industrializing and generally prospering, but Russia, always comparatively backward, was falling further and further behind. Economic difficulties, including a scarcity of food and consumer goods, declining services, and poor wages, were worsened by ill-advised military ventures. The Russo-Japanese War of 1904–05 proved an embarrassing defeat to Imperialist Russia and a great drain on her available resources. Then, Russia became involved in World War I at enormous cost, and the human and physical resources of the state were further depleted.[6]

During the 1907–17 period, Russian Marxists were a disorganized, faction-ridden organization, unprepared to assume political power or even to apply pressure to the failing tsarist regime. Many were in exile (Lenin) or imprisoned (Stalin); most of the remainder were involved in ideological disputes and intraparty fighting. One major conflict among the Marxists was between the Bolsheviks and the Mensheviks. Whereas the Mensheviks favored a broad-based

movement and a more evolutionary path to power, the Bolsheviks were inclined toward a small, conspiratorial movement that could assume power quickly and decisively. Led by Lenin, the Bolsheviks prevailed over all other revolutionary and opposition movements and brought about the communist takeover.

The stage was set for a Bolshevik victory with the abdication of Tsar Nicholas II in February 1917 and the political vacuum that followed. Power was assumed by the noncommunist but democratic-liberal and socialist Provisional Government under Alexander Kerensky's leadership. By November 1917, however, it too had proved incapable of quickly resolving Russia's difficulties. Returning from Switzerland to St. Petersburg in April 1917, Lenin organized the insurrection. Under his leadership, the Bolsheviks prepared for their takeover by appealing to the masses with such slogans as "Bread, Peace, Land" and by organizing a conspiratorial military organization. Careful planning, utilization of a new organizational weapon (the Communist Party), the use of armed force and propaganda, and the revolutionary leadership all aided in the successful seizure of the Winter Palace on the night of November 7, 1917. The initial Bolshevik victory in St. Petersburg was incredibly easy: The provisional government had few answers and little support; the Russian army had been so consumed by World War I that it had no energy or inclination to try to keep power from the revolutionaries; and other opposition and revolutionary groups were largely ineffective. Suddenly in power, Lenin was confronted with almost insurmountable economic and social problems as he began the construction of the first Marxist state.

It may appear surprising that the tsarist regime and the traditional political structure could be toppled by such a small band of untested revolutionaries. But the victory was neither as difficult nor as easy as it may seem. Imperial Russia was a sick and dying state; even if it had been able to cope with the challenges of modernization, its entanglement in World War I proved costly. This situation left the Bolsheviks with a vulnerable opponent, and when the political vacuum developed in 1917, the organized, determined, and politically astute communists grasped power. The revolution was not easy in the sense that major difficulties for the Bolsheviks came after they had seized power, not from the defeated tsarist autocracy, but rather from other groups (Mensheviks, Socialist Revolutionaries, many anticommunist groups) that challenged the Marxist leaders. Although the Bolsheviks had grasped power, a struggle for the rule of Russia would continue for many years.

To the Bolsheviks' dismay, the writings of Marx were of little help in the ensuing years. Although Marx went to great lengths to explain the impending fall of capitalism and the victory of socialism, he wrote little *about the nature and construction of socialism* and, therefore, was of minimal help to the new Russian leaders as they began their difficult task. As a result, Lenin and the communist leaders had to set out largely on their own. Their problem was worsened because Russia was not "prepared" for the socialist victory, in the sense that it had not gone through, although it definitely had begun, the capitalist stage of industrialization and development. According to Marx, socialism would triumph after capitalism had outlived its usefulness. But the Bolsheviks' seizure of power came before Russia had completed that important stage of development. As a result, Lenin and his fellow leaders had to complete Russia's industrialization before they could devote their attention to the construction of communism.

Other pressing problems also confronted the Bolsheviks in the immediate postrevolutionary period. World War I continued to drain Russian resources. In addition, Bolshevik rule was not readily accepted throughout the Russian state, and a bloody civil war broke out (1918–21) that saw Western intervention (including the United States) on the side of the anticommunist forces. Subsequently, Western hostility and suspicion of the Bolsheviks and communism precluded the possibility of assistance from abroad. So, although the Bolshevik victory of 1917 placed the Marxists in power, it in no way guaranteed the future success of communism.

Lenin's first objective was to get Russia out of World War I. On March 3, 1918, Russia signed the Treaty of Brest-Litovsk, obtaining peace with the Central Powers in return for yielding valuable land and resources. The communist leaders then began consolidating the homeland. During the Civil War, opposition movements were eliminated as the Communist Party moved to assert dictatorial control. Then, to facilitate economic recovery, the leaders adopted the New Economic Policy (NEP) (1921–28) that permitted a partial return to private enterprise and eventually got the economy back on its feet.

During the postrevolutionary construction years, the communist leaders were concerned with survival, both of the state and of their regime. The Communist Party became a leading organizational tool for consolidating power and organizing political rule. In these building years, the ideals of proletarian rule and democracy were lost among the pressing needs for survival. According to most Western observers, the ideal of a dictatorship of the proletariat in which the workers were supposed to rule became in reality a dictatorship of the Party.[7]

After the death of Lenin in 1924, this dictatorship invested increasing power in the hands of one man, Joseph Stalin. Although a dying Lenin warned the Party against Stalin's ascendancy to power, a struggle ensued and Stalin

Joseph Stalin (1879–1953) delivers an order to his foreign minister, Vyacheslav M. Molotov, at Yalta in 1945. Stalin placed the USSR on the road to becoming an industrial and military power, but his oppressive rule cost greatly in terms of social welfare, democracy, and human rights and took Soviet ideology far afield from classic Marxism.

soon achieved dominance. During his rule (1926–53), Stalin revised Marxism in many ways. Differences in degree grew into differences of kind. The combination of environmental forces (for example, the need to industrialize) and Stalin's pathological character resulted in a highly centralized, totalitarian state. Most observers agree that Stalin's imprint on Marxism during these formative years of development took communism far afield of the more humanitarian theories of Marx, and this Stalinist brand of communism was exported to Eastern Europe and China at the end of World War II.[8]

At the time of the Bolshevik victory, the Russian leaders expected victorious revolutions elsewhere in Europe.[9] During the early 1920s, optimism about this possibility began to fade. The recognition that these victories would not occur quickly or easily was made official by Stalin in 1924 when he formulated his famous "socialism in one country" doctrine. According to this doctrine, attempts to promote world revolution would be abandoned.[10] Because capitalism had temporarily stabilized itself, it was better to turn inward and concentrate efforts on building Russia into a bastion of socialism.

Closely tied to the Bolshevik victory was the establishment in 1921 of the second Communist Party state, Mongolia. Dominated through history by both Imperial Russia and Imperial China because of its unfortunate location between the two more powerful countries, Mongolia finally gained statehood in 1911. Shortly thereafter, the Russian Civil War brought Red Army troops to Mongolian soil. Using Mongolia as a base of operations, renegade White Russian bands were tracked down and destroyed by the Red Army and the partisan Mongols. In 1921, the victors established the Provisional Revolutionary Mongol People's Republic. Since that time, the Soviet and Mongolian states have had close ties and relations.

Although Marxist states were established in Russia and Mongolia early in the century, no other revolutions were successfully carried out until after World War II. But the absence of new Marxist states did not mean the absence of communist revolutionary activity. The most violent, intense, and significant activity occurred behind the Great Wall of China.

Revolution in China

A powerful determinant of present-day diversity in communist states is the past. Examining this point, one scholar argues that the remarkable differences between Chinese and Russian revolutionary outcomes can be attributed in large part to the influence of distinct prerevolutionary sociopolitical structures and patterns of economic development. According to Theda Skocpol, old regime structures helped to shape specific variations in the revolutionary outcomes not merely by surviving but also by influencing the communists' consolidation and use of state power.[11] China's prerevolutionary experience was certainly of great importance.

China's ruling tradition was one of upper-class government, the city ruled over the countryside through a network of local gentry and warlords, and the few ruled over the many. To the peasant, the central government seemed remote and unconcerned with the problems of the masses. A Chinese folk poem expresses what must have been the feelings of the masses.

We work when the sun rises,
We rest when the sun sets.
We dig wells for drink,
We plow the land for food.
What has the Emperor to do with us?

The institutions of family, gentry, and government perpetuated ancient Confucian traditions and provided the mortar that gave China its long, stable history.[12] But the events of the nineteenth century drastically changed the course of Chinese history. Conceived of by its leaders and the masses as the Central Kingdom, China was now battered by Western imperialism, resulting in intense national humiliation. This was intensified in the latter part of the century by unequal treaties imposed on China by the European powers and by her defeat to Japan in the Sino-Japanese War (1894–95). During this period, parts of China, such as Hong Kong and Shanghai, became Western colonies, where the local populace was subject to foreign law. Evidence of this is the now-famous photograph of a sign in a city park of Shanghai: NO CHINESE OR DOGS ALLOWED!

The twentieth century presented not only the dawn of a new Chinese culture but, more importantly, the birth of Chinese nationalism. One of the leaders of this movement was Dr. Sun Yat-sen, a radical but compassionate politician, educated in the Chinese classics and Western medicine. In 1911, the Manchu dynasty was toppled. Sun assumed leadership and established a Chinese republic based on democracy, socialism, and nationalism. The revolutionary's accomplishment brought about the end of more than 2,000 years of dynastic rule in China, but even he was unable to cope with the political, social, and economic problems that contributed to the fall of the Manchus. One major problem was posed by the warlords. From 1916 to 1926, China was torn by strife among provincial dictators, who pitted Chinese against Chinese in their greed for increased power and wealth. Combined with the humiliation at the hands of the imperialist European powers, this internal conflict made it difficult for Sun and his supporters to unite the Chinese and promote social and political development.

By the second decade of the twentieth century, China found a more interested and active sector of the Chinese population committed to speak out against foreign and domestic exploitation. In the spring of 1919, large groups took to the streets to protest foreign domination and imperialism. Known as the May Fourth Movement, a wave of patriotism touched off street demonstrations and political harangues that motivated the Chinese delegation to refuse to sign the Treaty of Versailles at the 1919 Paris Peace Conference, an agreement that would have legitimated and prolonged foreign imperialism in China.

In the early part of the century, several Chinese scholars became acquainted with Marxism and other varieties of socialism, and interest grew when the antiquated Russian autocracy was overthrown in 1917. Many Chinese intellectuals followed the events in Russia closely and began to study the Russian experiment with Marxism; one was Li Dazhao[13] (1888–1927), a history professor and chief librarian at Beijing University. While studying Marxism, Li met with students in his office, which became known as the Red Chamber. One of the young intellectuals attending these meetings was Mao Zedong, a man soon to take a leading role in the growing Chinese drama.

A major reason for the growing appeal of Marxism-Leninism in China resulted from the Soviet position in imperialism. To many Chinese intellectuals, Marxism-Leninism represented the key to Chinese development. It told them how to be scientific and "modern" in dealing with the problems of development and how to be uncompromisingly anti-imperialist and nationalist in being Chinese. Soon Russian agents from the Communist International (Comintern) arrived in China to aid Chinese Marxist-Leninists in promoting communism. In July 1921, the Chinese Communist Party (CCP) was established and a new actor joined the revolutionary cast.

The Russian Comintern agents advised the Chinese communists to form a united front with the Nationalists [Kuomintang (KMT)], which was under the leadership of Dr. Sun Yat-sen.

Mao Zedong (1893–1976) on the reviewing stand at a mass political rally in Beijing. After establishing communism in China in 1949 by ousting Chiang Kai-shek and the Nationalists, Mao developed a more radical brand of communism, and split with the Soviets in the early 1960s.

Although the native communists found this a bitter pill to swallow because they preferred to organize for revolution on their own, it was sweetened somewhat by the fact that the Nationalists were also committed anti-imperialists. The alliance, although often shaky, lasted through Sun's death in 1925 and the rise of his successor, Chiang Kai-shek. However, in April 1927, Chiang turned on the communists in Shanghai, slaughtered them by the thousands, and established himself as the head of the new Chinese government. Stalin then ordered the Chinese communists to seize power, but this only resulted in the killing of more communists. After Stalin's disastrous plans led to the eviction of all Soviet advisers and a new annihilation of the Chinese communists, the CCP grew more estranged from the Russian communists.

It was during this period that Mao advanced to power. Through a trial-and-error process, Mao groomed the CCP into a political force that would redirect the course of Chinese history. In 1934, Nationalist military pressure forced the CCP troops to take an epic trek—the Long March—across 6,000 miles of difficult terrain. One-hundred-thousand Chinese began the march; only 20,000 survived. The conclusion of the Long March, in the northern city of Yanan in the province of Shaanxi, began an important stage of CCP development, commonly called the Yanan period. During these years, Mao consolidated his power within the Party and formulated the ideological and military plans that would carry the communists to victory. Building on the power of human will, Mao engaged the CCP in a "proletarian revolution" in a peasant society which lacked any semblance of capitalist infrastructure. Mao and the CCP called on the power of the Chinese peasantry to accomplish what was theoretically impossible: the founding of a Marxist state in China.

Chinese involvement in World War II aided the communists' ascendancy to power. When Japan brutally invaded China beginning in 1937, Chiang Kai-shek was faced with an important decision—whether to concentrate his forces and efforts against the Japanese, which he referred to as a disease of the skin and body, or against Mao and the communists, which he considered a disease of the heart and spirit. Considering the latter the more pressing evil, Chiang set out once again to destroy the CCP forces. While the Nationalist and communist forces were engaged in a civil war, Japan launched a relentless attack on the Chinese mainland that destroyed Chinese industrial capabilities and caused widespread suffering. Under such conditions, the Nationalist government had limited capabilities, few answers, and even less success at resolving the pressing social and economic difficulties facing the Chinese people. The government and KMT Party under Chiang were marked by corruption and were out of touch with the Chinese masses. At the same time, the war gave Mao and the CCP time to consolidate their forces, to appeal to the Chinese intellectuals and masses, to fight the Japanese, and, ultimately, to build up their strength to challenge and defeat the Nationalists. Just as World War I encouraged the downfall of tsarist Russia, World War II did the same to Nationalist China.

With the Japanese surrender in 1945, the communists and the Nationalists tried to negotiate an agreement to end their conflict. Although the United States attempted to mediate the dispute, the negotiations failed and the two factions reverted to a state of civil war. Although the Nationalists had superior equipment and support, the communists were able to draw on the vast Chinese populace to defeat Chiang's forces. The Nationalists retreated to the Chinese island of Taiwan (Formosa) and in 1949 the communists controlled the entire Chinese mainland. It was at this time that the People's Republic of China (PRC) was formed.

The Russian and Chinese revolutionary experiences were quite different. Whereas the Bolshevik takeover occurred quickly and the real test of the new leaders came after the revolution, the Chinese takeover took several decades.[14] This meant that when Mao and his comrades finally took office in 1949, they had been tested under fire. They were a united, cohesive, militarized group. Because they had won power on their own, they were loath to have someone else dictate to them concerning their postrevolutionary development. As we will see, who wins power is of considerable importance in determining who gives orders after power is won.

Following World War II, China's neighbor, Korea, also became communist. Similar to the division and occupation of Germany after World War II, Korea was divided at the 38th parallel into northern and southern zones with the USSR and the United States serving as occupational powers. During the three-year Soviet occupation of the North (1945–48), the Red Army installed communist-oriented leaders to manage the affairs of the occupied zone. The head of the communist government was Kim Il Sung, a military figure who had fought along with the USSR in World War II. The Soviets initially set up a coalition government—the North Korean Provisional People's Committee—before establishing a more monolithic communist regime. Although the Korean communists were not initially in a particularly strong position, Soviet assistance and the fusion of the socialists and communists into the Workers' Party provided the necessary power base to ensure a communist government in North Korea. In 1950, the communist regime of North Korea attempted to take over South Korea; this brought about U.S.

and U.N. military involvement on the side of South Korea and Chinese involvement on the side of North Korea. When the Korean armistice was signed on July 27, 1953, the division of Korea into a communist North and noncommunist South was perpetuated.

Communists Come to Power in Eastern Europe

Perhaps more so than in Asia, World War II markedly altered the political setting of Eastern Europe. Before the war, none of the Eastern states were communist; within a few years of the war's conclusion, all eight countries were governed by communist regimes.[15] What had happened in this short span to prepare the way for communism? We can identify two distinct patterns: (1) Communist Parties winning power during World War II, principally through their own internal efforts (Yugoslavia and Albania); and (2) Parties obtaining power through the occupation, pressure, and assistance of the Soviet Union (Czechoslovakia, Poland, Romania, East Germany, Bulgaria, and Hungary).

Communist Victory from Within

Yugoslavia is a state of recent political origin. Prior to World War I, the South Slavic peoples—who comprise contemporary Yugoslavia—were subjects of larger European empires or lived in independent states. Most of the southern part of the land area was under the administration of the Ottoman Empire, whereas the north was part of the Austro-Hungarian Empire. From the ashes of World War I came a new state, the Kingdom of Serbs, Croats, and Slovenes, later—in 1929—to be called Yugoslavia.

The South Slavic ethnic groups of this new state represented different cultures, languages, religions, and traditions. The northern part of the country used the Latin alphabet, was Catholic, and was mostly Western in culture and tradition; the southern part was inhabited by nationalities who used the Cyrillic alphabet, were Orthodox or Moslem in religious faith, and held more to Eastern cultures and traditions. This complex mix of nationalities and ethnic groups generated intense conflict in Yugoslavia between the two world wars. To quell such conflict, unite the country, and move the state toward its goals, autocratic King Alexander established a dictatorship in 1929. This centralized form of government only exacerbated the existing problems and undermined still further the regime's fading support.

Through the 1920s and 1930s, a small group of Yugoslavs were attracted to Marxist philosophy and what it might do for Yugoslavia. One such individual was Josip Broz, later known as Tito, a young man who had been wounded fighting for the Austrians in World War I and had been taken to Russia as a prisoner of war. On his release in Russia, he became interested in the Bolshevik cause and later returned to Yugoslavia to promote the ideals of socialism and communism. Although King Alexander outlawed the Communist Party, Tito and the Yugoslav communists were able to organize a secret Party that relied on Moscow for guidance and direction.

On March 25, 1941, the government under Prince Paul, who replaced the King after his assassination in Marseilles, signed the Tripartite Pact guaranteeing collaboration with the Nazis. In the national uproar that followed, the army revolted, deposed the government, and repudiated the pact. Yugoslavia virtually was without a government until the end of the war. In its place, various movements organized, including the Chetnik movement representing the Serbs and the Ustashi, which was pro-Nazi and primarily Croatian. But the most successful was the communist movement led by Josip Broz Tito.[16]

Tito and the communist partisans, gaining considerable support from all the South Slavic groups of Yugoslavia, waged a courageous battle against the Nazis as well as against such other anticommunist Yugoslav forces as the Chetniks. Because Tito and the communists were perceived by the West as the most effective force against the Nazis, they ultimately won the backing of the Allied Powers. After years of guerrilla warfare in the mountains of central Yugoslavia, the victorious partisans recaptured the land from the Nazis and quickly established a Communist Party state. This was all accomplished with little aid or advice from the hard-pressed Soviets, a fact significantly affecting the Yugoslav experience as a socialist state.

The communists' advent to power in Albania was closely tied to the Yugoslav movement. During World War II, Albania was occupied by Italy and later Germany. As in Yugoslavia, various resistance groups arose, one communist-inspired. This movement received both aid and advice from Yugoslav emissaries and, under the leadership of Enver Hoxha, seized power in 1941 and has held it to the present day. The fraternal ties that originally characterized Albanian and Yugoslavian relations, however, soon deteriorated into fear and suspicion. Today, Albania is a small, undeveloped enclave on the southern boundary of Yugoslavia.

Communist Victory from Without

During and following World War II, the Soviet Union was instrumental in uniting antifascist groups and, subsequently, for eliminating noncommunist alternatives and placing Communist

Party regimes in power in the remaining six East European states. In view of Soviet military predominance in the area at the end of the war, the USSR was in a strong position to determine the character of the postwar governments in these liberated states. The Teheran Conference of 1943 and the Yalta and Potsdam conferences of 1945 gave the Soviet Union great freedom in determining the political character of postwar Eastern Europe. Some contend that it could have gone so far as to incorporate the liberated areas into the USSR.[17]

The Soviets chose not to adopt the more radical policy of incorporating these European states into the Soviet Union; instead, they opted for the more gradual policy of national fronts. This meant that the governments in the liberated states were to be reconstituted into coalition governments with the communists sharing power; at the proper moment, the communists were to seize complete control. Although there are certain similarities in all cases, there are sufficient differences to warrant brief discussion of each.

The communists' advent to power in Czechoslovakia occurred under unique circumstances. In the prewar Czechoslovak state, the communists were an influential and respected political party. Liquidated by Adolph Hitler in 1939, the Czechoslovak government under the noncommunist President, Eduard Beneš, went into exile in London for the duration of the war. But back at home, the Czech and particularly the Slovak communists formed underground resistance movements to fight against the Nazis. While in London, the Czechoslovak government maintained good relations with both the Soviet and the home communists and, with the liberation of the country, President Beneš returned to preside over a coalition government with strong communist representation. Although the coalition appeared to be working well, the com-

munists staged a coup in 1948 (strong Soviet involvement was suspected) and occupied broadcasting stations, government buildings, and other key power organs. Quickly and decisively the coalition was transformed into a solid Communist Party regime under the leadership of Klement Gottwald.

Like Czechoslovakia, the prewar Polish government went into exile in London during World War II. Resisting the Nazis at home under terrible odds were the Home Army and underground government. These resistance forces recognized, and were recognized by, the Polish government in exile. Although this noncommunist government initially maintained reasonably good relations with the Soviet Union, a series of disputes ensued, resulting in full Soviet support of the Polish communists. In 1942, a group of Polish communists traveled from Moscow to occupied Poland to join the native communists who had stayed at home. One of these who came from Moscow was Wladyslaw Gomulka, who was to become the head of the postwar Soviet-oriented regime. As the Nazis were driven from the country, a predominantly communist Committee of National Liberation was formed to administer the liberated areas. Following the full liberation of the country, the Committee acted as a provisional government and assumed control of the Polish state. Although the Western powers intervened at the 1945 Yalta Conference and succeeded in having representatives of the London government included, the communists retained predominant influence. With the help of the Soviet Union, local communists were eventually successful in eliminating political opposition and in placing Gomulka and his associates in full control.

As in the Polish case, the takeover in Romania was a relatively protracted process occurring at the end of World War II. The takeover began with the Soviet Red Army's "liberation" of the country from Nazi occupation and Soviet diplomatic pressures based on the national-front policy. This included disarming the Romanian army, prohibiting noncommunist political parties, and severely restricting political suffrage. Western pressure in 1945 again added noncommunists to the coalition government but dominant power remained in the hands of the communists under the leadership of Peter Groza. Elections held in an atmosphere of communist intimidation, the arrest of opposition leaders, and the abdication of King Michael placed communists in a position of power under the Secretary-General of their Party, Gheorghe Gheorghiu-Dej.

In East Germany, the Soviet Red Army was the sole occupying power following the war and automatically was placed in a position of exclusive control. Walter Ulbricht, a German who had returned from Moscow to Berlin with the Red Army, assumed the key ruling position in the new government. Although political parties continued to exist and performed certain political and administrative functions, the occupying Soviet officials and German communists assumed total control. In October 1949, the German Democratic Republic (East Germany) was formed and the dedicated communist, Ulbricht, and his monolithic Socialist Unity Party were firmly in command.

The Soviet Red Army entered Bulgaria on September 8, 1944, and departed late in 1947. During that three-year period, domestic anticommunist opposition was crushed and dominant political control of the Bulgarian Communist Party was assured. The day after the Red Army's intervention in 1944, a Soviet-backed coup brought power to a socialist movement called the Fatherland Front. Under the leadership of General Kimon Georgiev, a government was formed that placed communists in key leadership positions. After a series of political purges and pressure tactics, the communist-dominated Fatherland Front won 78 percent of the vote in the 1946 elections. This new Bulgarian government was headed by a former General-Secretary of the Comintern, a longtime communist and friend of the Soviets, Georgi Dimitrov.

As in Bulgaria, Soviet intervention in Hungary placed native communists on the inside track to power. Because Hungary had taken an active part in military operations against the Soviet Union, the Red Army took an aggressive position concerning postwar political developments. The occupying Soviet Army purged noncommunist leaders, accused many of collaboration with the Nazis, and, by 1947, had moved Hungarian Marxists into power, including the leader of the Hungarian communists, Mátyás Rákosi. Having spent 16 years in Hungarian prisons for being a communist, Rákosi was now intent on achieving absolute power in the postwar Hungarian state. Although noncommunist parties initially had considerable influence (in the open election of 1945 the Smallholders Party's victory led to the formation of a noncommunist coalition), Rákosi and the Soviets soon achieved a dominant position through the controlled 1947 elections.

Suddenly and somewhat unexpectedly, the political character of Eastern Europe was radically transformed. The proud young states of pre–World War II Europe were now cast behind what became known as the Iron Curtain. The Soviet Union's strategy had succeeded remarkably well in establishing communist regimes in its neighboring states of Europe. It had established a buffer zone, which helped calm Soviet fears of German invasion and of American aid to a resurgent Europe. Caught up in their own concerns of postwar reconstruction, the Western powers were slow to react. Soviet involvement in and control of

Eastern Europe was so complete and so successful that by the time the West fully recognized what had been done, diplomatic action was hopeless. A military response from the Western powers would have undoubtedly brought another violent military conflict. In its place, the Cold War developed—a period of extreme ideological hostility and enmity between the West and the Communist Party states of Europe.

The Special Cases of Cuba and Southeast Asia

Given its proximity to the United States and the continuing acrimony in United States–Cuban relations, the establishment of a communist government in Cuba takes on special interest and meaning. Closely tied to and highly dependent on the United States, pre-Castro Cuba was run by an unpopular and corrupt dictator named Fulgencio Batista. Fidel Castro, a gifted revolutionary who had apparently not yet become a Marxist or communist in the 1950s, plotted and then fought against the dictatorship in an effort to promote representative democracy. As a result of growing Cuban sympathy and the support of other groups and sectors in Latin America and even in the United States, Castro was able to stage a successful revolution against Batista's corrupt and inefficient army.

Castro and his minuscule force of less than 100 persons (subsequently reduced to around a tenth of that) began their takeover with an invasion from Mexico in 1956. Basing their guerrilla warfare in the Cuban mountainous region of the Sierra Maestra, Castro and his forces attacked depots, cities, bases, and other key targets throughout the country. With growing popular support and revolutionary power, Castro forced the Batista regime to surrender in January 1959 and took over the reins of government. Unlike so many of the other countries discussed, the Cuban countryside was not in a state of total revolution and disorder. Rather, Castro was able to take over a country with a flourishing economy and a relatively healthy populace.

Contrary to considerable opinion, available evidence suggests that the Cuban revolution was not initially directed by a Communist Party or by any political or ideological organization other than Castro's nationalistic, revolutionary band. Apparently, at that time, Castro did not consider himself a Marxist-Leninist.[18] Although there was a Cuban communist group, known as the Popular Socialist Party, the first contact between it and Castro's forces did not take place until 1958. The communists were extremely skeptical of Castro's movement and placed their faith in a popular-front strategy that would unite all anti-Batista forces.

At what point Castro, or Castro's Cuba, became communist is still debatable. Castro was and is a radical with a deep desire for the social transformation of Cuba, but he is not a disciplined communist in the sense of being a strict adherent to Marxism-Leninism or the Soviet Union. Although communist ideology played a minor role in the revolution and the initial period of Cuban transformation, that soon changed. It seems clear in retrospect that Castro felt Cuban socialism was threatened by the United States in such challenges as the U.S.-supported invasion in 1961, known as the Bay of Pigs, which prompted him to turn to Soviet patronage and, thus, eventually to Soviet-style communism.

The territory today known as Vietnam had been under French control since the late nineteenth century. During World War II, the rather larger area of Indochina was the scene of warfare between national troops under Ho Chi Minh and the Japanese occupational forces. With the defeat of the Japanese and the withdrawal of the Chinese Nationalist troops from the northern part of the Indochinese peninsula, Ho established the Democratic Republic of Vietnam (North Vietnam). At first, the French accorded it provisional recognition; then, negotiations broke down and the Ho regime initiated military action against French forces and the South Vietnamese (September 2, 1945). Carrying on a people's war, Ho and the Vietnamese communists were involved in almost constant struggle for the next quarter of a century, first against France (1946–54) and later against the United States. The United States had come to the aid of the South Vietnamese in the 1960s. On April 30, 1975, the American forces were withdrawn from Vietnam. Under the party leadership of First Secretary Le Duan (Ho Chi Minh had died in 1969), the North Vietnamese entered Saigon and brought an end to the partition of Vietnam.

Generally refused an enclave on Cambodian soil by the royalist government under Prince Norodom Sihanouk, Ho Chi Minh's Cambodian communist allies spent most of their time exiled in North Vietnam. With Lon Nol's successful right-wing coup against Sihanouk in 1970, about 1,000 Cambodian communists returned home to wage war against the new republic under Nol. The bloody war that had been raging in Vietnam during the 1960s and had spread to Laos now engulfed Cambodia as well. Old and new revolutionaries, known as the Khmer Rouge resistance movement, waged a relentless guerrilla war against the new and weak Cambodian Republic supported by the United States. The revolutionaries, under Pol Pot, won the conflict and ousted Lon Nol in 1975 and adopted a new constitution the next year that established an independent state called Democratic Kampuchea. The Pol Pot regime used extreme bru-

tality, killing millions, to impose terror and a rigid ideology in this once peaceful land. Finally, in December 1978, the Vietnamese communists invaded and occupied Kampuchea and installed a puppet regime headed by President Heng Samrin. Talks took place and agreements were signed in 1989, intended to end Vietnam's occupation of Cambodia.

During the Vietnamese conflict, the Laotian communist movement, known as the Pathet Lao, controlled the northeastern section of Laos bordering on North Vietnam. Advised and supplied by the North Vietnamese, the Pathet Lao exploited the ineptitude and weakness of the royalist government and spread its control over an expanding portion of the country. Finally, in December 1975, the Lao People's Revolutionary Party emerged from the coalition government to abolish the monarchy and establish the Lao People's Democratic Republic.

It should be apparent by now that the establishment of communist regimes in Vietnam, Cambodia (Kampuchea), and Laos did not bring immediate peace and prosperity to the area of Southeast Asia. Conflict continues to rage at staggering costs to the people of that troubled region.

A Comparative Overview

It is clear that communism came to many different countries under a variety of circumstances and for many different reasons. We will now try to identify the most significant similarities and differences by considering the following questions. Generally speaking, *how* did communist movements come to power? *When* and *where* did they come to power? *Who* led these successful movements? And, perhaps the most interesting and important question, *why* did they come to power? As students of comparative politics, our guiding purpose is to establish some general patterns that explain the advent of communism throughout the world.[19]

How Did Communist Movements Come to Power?

Most observers of Communist Party states agree that the way in which a Party comes to power is important in determining how it uses power and makes policy in subsequent years. Communist Parties that come to power through independent revolutionary movements—for example, the USSR, China, Yugoslavia, Cuba—have had more freedom in planning and carrying out policy than states—for example, Mongolia, Bulgaria, East Germany—in which the Party came to power through the outside influence of the Soviet Union.

Communist Parties have come to power as a result of independent internal movements, through the imposition of a Communist Party regime by an outside force, or as a result of some combination of the two. The first column in Table 8.1 summarizes the experiences of each country. The two major powers within the communist world, the Soviet Union and China, came to power primarily as a result of internal movements. In addition, two countries in Eastern Europe, Albania and Yugoslavia, as well as Cuba and Vietnam had independent movements and became communist largely as a result of their own actions.

In the remaining countries of Eastern Europe, the Soviet Occupation at the end of World War II led to the imposition of communist-dominated regimes. Although the conditions, timing, and exact strategies varied somewhat from case to case, the idea of a national front served as the guiding policy. Coalition-type governments were initially installed but were soon transformed into communist-controlled governments. Although it occurred in a different part of the world, the communist ascendancy to power in North Korea was initially similar to the East European experience, particularly to that of East Germany and Poland. North Korea escaped Soviet domination after 1950, however, when China's influence increased and growing Sino-Soviet competition in North Korea allowed the Koreans to follow a more independent road.

The Vietnamese and Cuban revolutions were quite different from the East European examples where the Soviet Union played a dominant role. Ho Chi Minh and Fidel Castro were both nationalists and revolutionaries intent on ending exploitation and imperialism and bringing democratic socialism to their governments. Unlike the East European cases, they were successful in doing so without major assistance from or the occupation of an outside power. With few exceptions, those regimes that established communism on their own exhibited greater independence and autonomy in the international arena. On the other hand, with the notable exceptions of Romania and North Korea, those coming to power as the result of an outside occupation showed less independence of action, particularly in relation to the USSR. In addition, those leaders coming to power by means of the independent route (e.g., Mao, Tito, Castro) enjoyed relatively cohesive, stable reigns. Although there are exceptions, such as North Korea, those placed in power by outsiders tended to be less popular among their own people and more susceptible to Soviet interference, power struggles, or other developments resulting in abbreviated tenure.

In summary, communist movements can be and have been generated by internal and external forces. Thus, we can conclude that both domestic and international factors determine the manner in which communism develops in various nations.[20]

Table 8.1 Chronological Listing of Successful Communist Movements

	Attributes for Comparison			
State	*How*	*When*	*Where*	*Who*
Soviet Union	Independent movement	1917	Europe	Vladimir Ilyich Lenin
Mongolia	Armed occupation (USSR)	1921	Asia	Sukhe-Bator and Khorloin Choibalsan
Albania	Independent and outside (Yugoslavia)	1944	Europe	Enver Hoxha
Yugoslavia	Independent movement	1945	Europe	Josip Broz Tito
Vietnam	Independent movement (unification)	1945 (1975)	Asia	Ho Chi Minh (Le Duan)
North Korea	Armed occupation	1945	Asia	Kim Il Sung
Romania	Armed occupation (USSR)	1945	Europe	Gheorghiu-Dej
Bulgaria	Independent and outside (USSR)	1946	Europe	Georgi Dimitrov
Hungary	Armed occupation (USSR)	1947	Europe	Mátyás Rákosi
Poland	Armed occupation (USSR)	1947	Europe	Wladyslaw Gomulka
Czechoslovakia	Independent and outside (USSR)	1948	Europe	Klement Gottwald
East Germany	Armed occupation (USSR)	1949	Europe	Walter Ulbricht
China	Independent movement	1949	Asia	Mao Zedong
Cuba	Independent movement	1959	Latin America	Fidel Castro
Laos	Independent and outside (Vietnam)	1975	Asia	Kaysone Phomvihan
Cambodia	Independent (Outside—Vietnam)*	1975 (1978)	Asia	Pol Pot (Heng Samrin)

* Vietnam invaded Cambodia in 1978 and installed the puppet regime headed by Heng Samrin.

When and Where Did Communist Movements Occur?

The chronological listing in Table 8.1 shows that most successful movements occurred at the end of World War II. With the exceptions of the Russian (1917) and Mongolian (1921) takeovers at the end of World War I and the relatively recent Cuban and Southeast Asian experiences, most successful movements followed the serious disorders of World War II. Wars and other major destabilizing forces establish the conditions for revolutionary change. In one way or another, communist victories tended to come in the wake of international or civil war.

Geographically speaking, communist movements have been victorious in both East and West. Although most occurred in Eastern Europe, movements in Asia and Latin America illustrate that communism was not bound to any one part of the world.

Past communist movements and takeovers also show no particular bounds in terms of culture. When communism first took hold in Russia, some experts attributed its success to the nature of Russian culture. Their Slavic culture, "soul," and general spiritual characteristics (according to these theorists) made them well suited to an ideology emphasizing collectivism and socialism. Because of these spiritual and cultural requisites, scholars noted, communism was unlikely to go to other parts of the world. Subsequent movements and the spread of communism to the different cultures in Asia and Latin America seemed to invalidate this idea of cultural requirements.

Communism also came to power in countries at different levels of economic development. Most had been agricultural societies at the early stages of economic growth. Some, such as Czechoslovakia and East Germany, had rather advanced economic systems; others had been at intermediate stages of development; still others, in Asia, had very primitive economic systems. Overall, it is fair to say that communist movements and takeovers have occurred under many different geographical, cultural, and socioeconomic conditions.

Who Led These Victorious Movements?

Were Lenin, Mao, Tito, Ho Chi Minh, Castro, and others indispensable elements in the revolutionary process or could victory have been achieved without them? Perhaps more important: Which came first—the revolution or the revolutionary? To evaluate an individual's impact on a process as complex as revolution is difficult and risky. What can be said is that most had extremely capable leaders, men who well understood their countries and the military and organizational dynamics of the revolutionary process. Leaders like Mao and Tito were able to seize on international forces (e.g., World War II) and to combine them with domestic needs to build successful resistance and revolutionary forces. Although they were "great" leaders in many respects, we can probably observe that the social and economic forces were larger than the men. If a Tito, Mao, Lenin, or Castro had not existed, it is likely that some other individual would have come to the fore and directed the revolutionary movement. "Great" men cannot necessarily make history, but they can influence it by recognizing and exploiting emergent social forces. At the very least, the individuals listed in Table 8.1 were the right men in the right place with the foresight and ideas to bring revolutionary visions to fruition.

Why Were the Communist Movements Successful?

Table 8.1 contains no entry with the heading *Why?*. Although the why of successful movements is far too complex to summarize in a brief word or two, we can make some broad generalizations about the trends leading to the demise of the old state systems and to the establishment of communism.

All the regimes that preceded the establishment of communism suffered from a number of severe shortcomings. Most had lost the confidence of the broader society, and their leaders were unable to inspire and gain the support of the mass populace. Often there was government corruption and inefficiency that resulted in disillusionment and disappointment with the old autocracy. The difficulties of the times were further exacerbated by forces of international and civil war, conflicts in which the armies were either unable or unwilling to protect incumbent regimes. In every case, either internal or international wars (and often both) contributed to the final collapse of the old regime. What followed was disorder, economic stagnation, and a political vacuum.

But why were the successor states communist rather than some other political doctrine or creed? One reason for the success of communist movements concerns the use of a new organizational weapon, the Communist Party. Centralized, conspiratorial, and militant, the Party became the organizational agent for effecting revolutionary change. Operating in a period of political disorganization and general social disorder, the organized Communist Parties of the revolutionaries capitalized on the unstable setting to grasp the reins of power. It is in this respect that the leaders often showed the attributes of the great-men syndrome. Understanding the use of organizations and the domestic and international contexts in which they were operating, the leaders assumed and consolidated political power.

The revolutionary leaders and the Parties they represented also understood the meaning and role of military power. "Power grows out of the barrel of a gun," proclaimed Mao Zedong. Use of the Communist Party as a military as well as a political organization was a major factor in most takeovers. In some states, armed force meant the intervention of the Soviet Army and a period of military occupation. This factor represented a key element in the communists' ability to assume and retain political power, especially in those states often referred to as being in the Soviet bloc.

Although comparison is difficult because of the many differences among the communist movements, we can identify some general patterns concerning the advent to power. Authoritarianism, misrule, mass discontent, and alienation, when combined with international warfare and foreign imperialism, are the factors that have led to a toppling of old state systems. Then, organized resistance and revolutionary movements, led by astute leaders operating within centralized Communist Party organizations, often with the armed assistance of the USSR, helped establish new communist systems. Because there are obviously other states that have experienced such conditions and have not gone communist, we should not consider these patterns universal laws. At the same time, there are enough similar conditions and forces to point up general patterns that involve the establishment of communist rule.

A Review of the Communist Experience

Before we move into our examination of contemporary issues, it will be useful to put the historical experience of communism in broader perspective. First, we should note the significance of the application of Marxism-Leninism in Russia and the deep impact that the Soviet experience has had on subsequent communist

276

development. It was in the authoritarian Russian setting that communist rule took on its oppressive, centralized features. Power was consolidated under the heavy hand of dictatorial Soviet rulers, not the least of which was Joseph Stalin.

Stalin did much to pervert the original, Marxist goals of communism. Stalin had a pathological personality and mistrusted the people he ruled and those he ruled with. He imposed great human costs on Soviet society as he ruthlessly and coercively pursued his conception of building a Soviet, communist state. Terror, repression, and the centralization and arbitrary uses of power became key elements of Marxism-Leninism-Stalinism, or what has often been referred to as the Stalinist model of communism.

It was this Stalinist model of communist rule that was subsequently exported to and imposed on China and Eastern Europe. Although it may not be entirely accurate to call Mao a Stalinist, it is fair to say that he was willing to use terror, coercion, and centralization of political power in his quest to build communism in China. Stalin himself, the Communist Party of the Soviet Union, and the Soviet Red Army did much to impose the Stalinist model of communism in the East European countries after World War II. Although there were indigenous communist movements in most of these states, it was Soviet power that determined the postwar character of communist rule in Eastern Europe.

This was a scenario for disaster. The proud nationalities of Eastern Europe stagnated under Soviet dominance. The imposition of the centralized political system generated frustration, discontent, cynicism, dissidence, and apathy among the people. The centralized, command-type economic system impeded the development of these states' economies. There were numerous uprisings in Eastern Europe over the postwar period—in East Berlin in 1953, Poland and Hungary in 1956, Czechoslovakia in 1968—which suggested that there were problems and cleavages in what we generally referred to as the Soviet bloc. The national aspirations of these countries were in conflict with Soviet goals of a Soviet-led, international communist movement.

The first major crack in the facade of communist internationalism came with the dispute between Stalin and Tito and Yugoslavia's expulsion from the Soviet bloc in 1948. When Stalin sensed that Tito was failing to toe the Soviet line, he excommunicated the Yugoslavs from the communist camp. Yugoslavia moved to develop what it called its own "road to socialism" outside of the Soviet bloc.

Other East European countries would have liked to have done the same but were not permitted to do so until Gorbachev brought about his changes in the late 1980s. In Hungary in 1956 the Hungarian leadership and people sought to gain sovereignty over the building of socialism in their country. After the Yugoslav experience, the Soviet leadership was unwilling to see their hopes of Soviet-directed internationalism suffer another setback. When Hungary declared its neutrality and attempted to withdraw from the Warsaw Pact in 1956, the Soviet Army suppressed the national uprising. Before Soviet control was forcibly reasserted, some 7,000 Soviet soldiers and 20,000 Hungarians were killed.

The next great setback to a united movement of socialist states came with the growing disaffection between the Chinese and the Soviets in the late 1950s. Resulting in an open split in 1960, the Sino-Soviet dispute buried all illusions concerning the possibility of socialist harmony.[21] Chinese and Soviet animosities reached unprecedented heights in the late 1960s as both sides prepared for war. The Sino-Soviet border became the site of encampments of huge armies

Gorbachev and other communist leaders at the 1989 celebration of forty years of communism in East Germany, just prior to the collapse of communist rule throughout Eastern Europe.

and occasional military skirmishes. The Soviet communists' ideal of a united communist movement under their leadership dissolved as ideological and national differences came to divide the Second World.

There were other significant problems in the communist movement as well. A critical one involved economics. As the years passed, it became increasingly clear that the centralized system of state socialism could not compete with capitalism and the various hybrid forms of socialism and capitalism that existed in Western Europe, the Far East, and North America.

It is believed by many that the stagnation of the socialist economies was one of the most powerful forces leading to the demise of the Stalinist form of communism as the world had come to know it.

There are other factors that contributed to the demise of Stalinism. The repression of the people, lack of human rights, growing human costs, and other such forces led to tremendous disaffection with the Stalinist model in Second World societies. This in turn led to a significant decline in the legitimacy of the communist rulers, particularly those of a Stalinist bent. By the

1980s, it had become increasingly clear that traditional communist leaders had not provided the values that they long promised their people.

With the passing of the ideological Mao and conservative Brezhnev regimes, China and the Soviet Union had an opportunity to engage in new thinking and reform. Deng Xiaoping engineered an opening and reforming of China in the 1980s, and Mikhail Gorbachev began the process in the Soviet Union after his assumption of power in 1985. Although both developments were significant, it was the glasnost, perestroika, and reform movements under Gorbachev that had the greatest impact on what happened elsewhere in the Second World. When Gorbachev began to emphasize the themes of openness, democracy, and sovereignty within the communist movement, he unleashed a powerful dynamic of great significance. Where it will lead is difficult to tell, but by 1990 it had ushered in a tumultuous period of reform and revolution in the Second World.

Suggestions for Further Reading

Billington, James H., *Fire in the Minds of Men: Origins of the Revolutionary Faith* (New York: Basic Books, 1980).

Brzezinski, Zbigniew K., *The Soviet Bloc: Unity and Conflict*, rev. ed. (New York: Praeger, 1961).

Burks, R. V., *The Dynamics of Communism in Eastern Europe* (Princeton, N.J.: Princeton University Press, 1961).

Carr, Edward H., *The Bolshevik Revolution, 1917–1923*, 3 Vols. (New York: Norton, 1985).

Dallin, Alexander, *Diversity in International Communism: A Documentary Record, 1961–1963* (New York: Columbia University Press, 1963).

Drachkovitch, Milorad M., ed., *Marxism in the Modern World* (Stanford, Calif.: Stanford University Press, 1965).

Drachkovitch, Milorad M., and **Branko M. Lazic,** *The Comintern: Historical Highlights, Essays, Recollections, Documents* (New York: Praeger, 1966).

Fairbank, John K., *The Great Chinese Revolution, 1800–1985* (New York: Harper & Row, 1986).

Fejto, Francois, *A History of the People's Democracies* (New York: Praeger, 1971).

Gasster, Michael, *China's Struggle to Modernize* (New York: Knopf, 1972).

Goodrich, L. Carrington, *A Short History of the Chinese People*, 3rd ed. (New York: Harper & Row, 1959).

Hammond, Thomas T., ed., *The Anatomy of Communist Takeovers* (New Haven, Conn.: Yale University Press, 1975).

Hunt, R. N. Carew, *The Theory and Practice of Communism*, 5th ed. (Baltimore: Penguin, 1963).

Johnson, Chalmers, *Peasant Nationalism and Communist Power* (Stanford, Calif.: Stanford University Press, 1962).

Kennan, George F., *Russia and the West Under Lenin and Stalin* (New York: New American Library, 1961).

Laqueur, Walter, and **Leopold Labedz,** *Polycentrism: The New Factor in International Communism* (New York: Praeger, 1962).

Lichtheim, George, *Marxism: An Historical and Critical Study*, 2nd ed. (New York: Praeger, 1965).

McCrea, Barbara P., et al., *The Soviet and East European Political Dictionary* (Santa Barbara, Calif.: ABC-Clio, 1984).

Meisner, Maurice, *Mao's China: A History of the People's Republic* (New York: Free Press, 1977).

Pares, Bernard, *A History of Russia*, 5th ed. (New York: Knopf, 1949).

Schapiro, Leonard, *The Origins of Communist Autocracy* (Cambridge: Harvard University Press, 1955).

Seton-Watson, Hugh, *From Lenin to Khrushchev: The History of World Communism* (New York: Praeger, 1960).

_____, *The East European Revolution*, 3rd ed. (New York: Praeger, 1956).

Selden, Mark, ed., *The People's Republic of China: A Documentary History of Revolutionary Change* (New York: Monthly Review Press, 1979).

Snow, Edgar, *Red Star over China* (New York: Random House, 1938).

Trotsky, Leon, *A History of the Russian Revolution*, trans. Max Eastman (3 vols.) (New York: Simon & Schuster, 1932).

Ulam, Adam B., *Expansion and Coexistence: Soviet Foreign Policy, 1917–1973* (New York: Praeger, 1974).

_____, *Titoism and the Cominform* (New York: Praeger, 1971).

Volgyes, Ivan, *Politics in Eastern Europe* (Chicago: Dorsey Press, 1986).

Zagoria, Donald S., *The Sino-Soviet Conflict, 1956–1961* (Princeton, N.J.: Princeton University Press, 1962).

Zinner, Paul E., *Revolution in Hungary* (New York: Columbia University Press, 1962).

Notes

1. The adjectives *communist, Marxist-Leninist*, and *Second World* are used interchangeably to refer to the states we will be addressing in the chapters that follow. Because some of these states are moving away from communism and Marxism-Leninism as we enter the 1990s, these first two terms will not always be useful and accurate descriptions in the future.

2. For a useful collection of the basic writings of Marx and Engels, see Robert C. Tucker, *The Marx-Engels Reader*, 2nd ed. (New York: Norton, 1978).

3. Ibid., pp. 335–336.

4. Isaiah Berlin has written a splendid book about Marx's life: *Karl Marx: His Life and Environment*, 3rd ed. (London: Oxford University Press, 1963); also see David McLellan, *Karl Marx: His Life and Thought* (New York: Harper & Row, 1974).

5. David Shub, *Lenin, a Biography* (New York: Penguin, 1976); Rolf Theen, *Lenin: Genesis and Development of a Revolutionary* (Princeton, N.J.: Princeton University Press, 1980).

6. Several books analyze the decline of tsarist Russia. Among the best are Hugh Seton-Watson, *The Decline of Imperial Russia, 1855–1914* (New York: Praeger, 1952); and M. T. Florinsky, *The End of the Russian Empire* (New Haven: Yale University Press, 1931).

7. Solzhenitsyn argues that the roots of the dictatorship of the Party are to be found in the nature of the ideology itself.

8. Two excellent accounts of Stalin and his rule are Robert C. Tucker, *Stalin as a Revolutionary*, 1879–1929 (New York: Norton, 1973); and Adam B. Ulam, *Stalin: The Man and His Era* (New York: Viking, 1973).

9. At the Third International Party Congress (First Congress of the Comintern) held in 1919, Lenin told the delegates that conflict between the capitalist and socialist worlds was inevitable and that socialism would soon result from proletarian uprisings throughout Europe.

10. Stalin's policy conflicted with Leon Trotsky's theory of permanent revolution (formulated in 1905). The fiery Trotsky was expelled from the country in 1929 for his views and was assassinated by a Stalinist agent in Mexico in 1940. Trotsky's book, *The Revolution Betrayed* (New York: Pathfinder Press, 1972), provides an interesting personal account of this and related issues.

11. Theda Skocpol, "Old Regime Legacies and Communist Revolutions in Russia and China," *Social Forces* 55 (2) (1976), 284–315.

12. The ancient traditions are deeply embedded in China and represent conservative forces even today. For an excellent analysis of the past, see Mark Elvin, *The Pattern of the Chinese Past* (London: Eyre Methuen, 1973); for a contrast of the past with the present, see Lucian W. Pye, *China* (Boston: Little, Brown, 1972); also see John K. Fairbank, *The United States and China*, 4th ed. (Cambridge: Harvard University Press, 1979).

13. Chinese names are transliterated in the Pinyin system now standard in China. Familiar names, like Confucius, Kuomintang, Chiang Kai-shek, and Sun Yat-sen are not rendered in Pinyin but follow the Wade-Giles system used in the past.

14. For an analysis of the Chinese approach, see Chalmers Johnson, *Peasant Nationalism and Communist Power* (Stanford, Calif.: Stanford University Press, 1962).

15. For an excellent account, see Hugh Seton-Watson, *The East European Revolution*, 3rd ed. (New York: Praeger, 1956).

16. For an interesting account of the life of Josip Broz Tito, see Milovan Djilas, *Tito: The Story from the Inside*, trans. Vasilije Kojbic and Richard Hayes (London: Weidenfeld: Nicholson, 1981).

17. In fact, it did so in the case of Latvia, Lithuania, Estonia, and the eastern sections of Czechoslovakia, Romania, Poland, and Germany.

18. For an account of Castro's ideological philosophy prior to and during the Cuban revolution, see Hugh Thomas's monumental work, *Cuba: The Pursuit of Freedom* (New York: Harper & Row, 1971).

19. The advent of communism in Communist Party states is analyzed in Thomas T. Hammond, ed., *The Anatomy of Communist Takeovers* (New Haven: Yale University Press, 1975). Also see Hugh Seton-Watson, *From Lenin to Khrushchev: The History of World Communism* (New York: Praeger, 1960).

20. It should be noted that Marxist rule was brought to Chile in 1970 through the ballot box. Although elected, the communist-oriented government of Salvador Allende Gossens was subsequently overthrown by military leaders in 1973.

21. See Donald Zagoria, *The Sino-Soviet Conflict, 1956–61* (New York: Atheneum, 1964).

CHAPTER 9

THE SOCIAL AND ECONOMIC SETTINGS

By the end of the 1980s, everyone knew that the Marxist-Leninist experiments were in trouble. Communist systems had neither achieved the progress their leaders promised nor had they established conditions conducive to achieving their goals in the future. No less a figure than Mikhail Gorbachev admitted that the Soviet Union and other communist states had failed to create the conditions necessary for the building of communism. Because such conditions tell us much about the communist experiments of the past and prospects for the future, it is worthwhile to examine the environmental settings characterizing the Second World states.

This chapter will focus on economic and social conditions. When addressing the economic settings, we will note that the centralized, Stalinist-type economic systems failed in the Second World countries and required their leaders to search for better models and methods for promoting economic development. When examining the social settings, we will find that the Second World systems have provided neither the living standards (what we refer to as the level of well-being) nor the equality that was promised under socialism. We will also see that ethnic and national differences remain in these countries and, in many cases, have intensified and resulted in deep cleavages that do not allow relations based on the "brotherhood and unity" promised by the Marxist-Leninist leaders.

These economic, social, and ethnic (or nationality) problems represent important elements of the setting in which politics takes place. These conditions were not in correspondence with or conducive to promoting the ideals of communism. Therefore, the challenges confronting communist leaders and their peoples in the 1990s are formidable. Although we will consider in the pages ahead many of the sixteen Second World states discussed in the previous chapter, we will concentrate our attention on the Soviet, Chinese, and some selected East European cases.

The Economic Setting

Economics is at the heart of Marxist ideology and the current Second World predicament. Marx predicted that the socialist revolution would occur in capitalist countries that had undergone the Industrial Revolution. In point of fact, communism arose in agriculture-based societies where the industrial sector was a very small percentage of the working population. In East European societies, the industrial sector of the societies ranged between 5 and 40 percent (see Table 9.1). The societies of Asia—China, Cambodia (Kampuchea), Laos, and Vietnam— were less industrially and more agriculturally oriented than their European counterparts. The United Nations estimates that nearly 80 percent of China's present-day labor force still works in agriculture. Therefore, although Marx predicted that industrial development would precede and economic abundance and equality would come with the victory of socialism, the social and economic conditions of most aspiring Marxist states did not correspond with these ideals.

In the Soviet Union, the initial challenge facing Lenin and the communist leaders after the Bolshevik victory was Russia's reconstruction. After removing the country from World War I, the Bolsheviks went about the task of consolidating power and building socialism within their country. In 1918, Lenin's decree nationalized

heavy industries, land, and the means of production; private ownership of land and industry was strictly forbidden. During the ensuing period of civil war and foreign intervention (1918–21), however, little could be done to set up a rational system of economic administration. It was during this period of "war communism" that Soviet economic output fell to 20 percent of what it had been before the outbreak of World War I.

To get the economy going again, the Soviet leaders adopted the New Economic Policy (NEP) in 1921. Although large industries remained nationalized, this new policy called for a mixed economic strategy that denationalized small industries and agriculture. Representing a temporary return to capitalism, the NEP saved the Bolshevik government from bankruptcy and got the Soviet economy back on its feet again. By 1926, economic output had reached its prewar levels.

With Lenin's death in 1924 and Stalin's assumption of power, Russia's leadership embraced the monumental task of rapid industrialization. With the first Five-Year Plan of 1928–33 (a centralized plan coordinating economic goals and policies for the entire country),

Table 9.1 Working Population (%) before Socialism, by Sector of Economy

	Czechoslovakia (1934)	Hungary (1930)	Poland (1931)	Romania (1930)	Bulgaria (1935)	Yugoslavia (1936)
Industry	38.3	24.1	19.4	7.7	8.0	9.9
Agriculture	25.6	53.0	60.6	76.9	80.0	76.3
Trade	9.2	5.9	6.1	3.3	2.4	4.2
Other	26.9	17.0	13.9	12.1	9.6	9.3
Total	100.0	100.0	100.0	100.0	100.0	99.7

(*Source*) Walter D. Connor, *Socialism, Politics, and Equality: Hierarchy and Change in Eastern Europe and the USSR* (New York: Columbia University Press, 1979), p. 31.

the Stalinist strategy of economic development began to materialize. Because there was no real possibility of bringing foreign capital into the country (the socialist leaders did not want to become dependent on the capitalist West and the West was suspicious of, and unwilling to support, Russian development) Soviet economic policy had to devise a method of generating capital internally. By adopting a policy that exacted high costs from the peasantry and that funneled nearly all economic surpluses back into the industrial sector, the Soviets attempted to accumulate funds on their own. To achieve the Communist Party's economic goals, Stalin established a centralized administrative structure and readopted the policies of nationalization of industry and collectivization of agriculture. Designed to mobilize the population to attain unreasonably high economic goals, this developmental policy incurred great human costs. Individuals or groups who disagreed with nationalization or the collectivization of agriculture were sent off to Siberia or annihilated.[1] The human costs surrounding Stalin's programs were high—millions were killed or died—but the economic benefits were substantial. Even in view of the devastation and economic setbacks caused by World War II, the Soviet economic strategy propelled the USSR to the stature of a world power by the end of the Stalinist era in 1953. Utilizing a command-type economic system based on government control of the means of production, central planning, and a high rate of capital investment, production in the Soviet Union drew close to and even surpassed that of some of the Western powers.

The Soviet Union's economy continued to grow in the post-Stalin era. In 1950, the Soviet GNP was estimated at less than one third that of the United States. By 1965, Soviet GNP had grown to approximately half that of the United

States and three times that of Great Britain. The general economic goal through the first 70 years of Soviet development was that of basic capital investment. Stated simply, the Soviets opted for the development of heavy industry—hydroelectric plants, steel mills, and so forth—at the expense of the consumer sector. As we will see later, however, the Soviet strategy was not nearly as successful as it might earlier have appeared. With the benefit of hindsight, most observers in the Soviet Union and abroad now consider the strategy a tragic mistake.

Assuming power in 1949, Mao Zedong and the Chinese communists faced a far less developed economy, more devastated country, and a more chaotic economic system than the Bolsheviks confronted. The economy was in such a deteriorated state that it did not even have the capacity to manufacture the primary vehicle for Chinese transportation, the bicycle. Unlike the Bolsheviks, Mao and his compatriots did not rush to nationalize industry and collectivize agriculture. To stimulate economic recovery, they attempted to use capitalist industry and redistribute agricultural land among the peasants; nationalization and collectivization would occur gradually over the span of several years. This policy of gradual transformation was carefully followed during the 1949–52 period and resulted in political consolidation, economic growth, and improved internal and international prestige. Slowly, the leadership began to transform privately owned enterprises into a cooperative form of state/private management. At the outset of the first Five-Year Plan in 1953, these joint enterprises accounted for approximately half of China's economic output; by 1956, practically all private enterprises had been changed to the cooperative operation. The first Five-Year Plan (1953–57), based on a general conception of Stalin's model but benefiting from the hindsight of Soviet mistakes, resulted in substantial material growth and economic progress. Utilizing aid and advice from the USSR and East European states, China appeared well on the way to economic recovery.

Soon after the second Five-Year Plan was proclaimed (1958–62), however, the recovery encountered a number of serious setbacks, the first of which was the Great Leap Forward campaign beginning in 1958. Based on the Maoist line of "going all out and aiming high to achieve greater, quicker, better, and more economical results in building socialism," this radical program was intended to make China a world economic power in a matter of decades. With expectations of surpassing Great Britain in industrial output in fifteen years, the strategy called on both modern and traditional methods of development (what the Chinese refer to as "walking on two legs"). Among other naive strategies and policies, Chinese citizens were encouraged to build smelter furnaces in their backyards to increase the output of steel. Sacrificing quality for quantity and suffering from poor planning and execution, the Great Leap Forward resulted in a large step backward. Planning became difficult, product quality declined, economic imbalances were experienced, and the idealistic but misguided campaign ended in disgrace.

The period of 1959–61 also brought a series of problems, including natural calamities such as droughts and floods, that further reduced Chinese economic capabilities, diminished agricultural production, and hindered development. In their midst came the Soviet Union's withdrawal of material aid and technical assistance in the summer of 1960. Precipitated by a growing ideological dispute, the Soviet Union's withdrawal interrupted many developmental programs that relied on foreign assistance.[2] At this point in Chinese reconstruction, the economic future looked bleak indeed.

In the early 1960s, the Chinese brought an end to the Great Leap Forward program and began to reevaluate their economic policies. This period ushered in an emphasis on greater self-reliance and a search for policies uniquely suited to Chinese needs and capabilities. The reappraisal changed the general strategy from one emphasizing heavy industry (the Soviet Union's approach) to one emphasizing agriculture. The new order of priorities became agriculture first, light industry second, and heavy industry third. As recovery proceeded and the third Five-Year Plan entered its second year in 1967, however, the economic system encountered another destabilizing campaign. Intended to "take firm hold of the revolution and stimulate production," the Great Proletarian Cultural Revolution (GPCR) of 1966–69 once again set the economic system into a state of disarray. Young revolutionaries, the Red Guards, were dispatched to the factories and other social and economic organizations to stimulate production through revolutionary and ideological means; their political intrusion incurred great economic costs. Such policies that were intended to rejuvenate the revolutionary spirit of the populace continued to disrupt the Chinese economy until Mao's death in 1976.

The East European economic settings were also contrary to the building of communism. Always economically behind their West European counterparts, the East European economies were further damaged by the devastations wrought by World War II. For example, during their evacuation of Yugoslavia at the end of World War II, the Nazis destroyed much of the country's transportation system and industrial facilities. The Yugoslavs began the task of reconstruction by nationalizing and collectivizing private holdings according to the Stalinist mode of development. However, growing friction between Joseph Stalin and the Yugoslav leaders culminated in a decision that shocked the communist world. Unexpectedly, in 1948, Stalin expelled the Yugoslavs from the international communist organization, Cominform, and initiated a sudden freeze in Soviet-Yugoslav relations.[3]

A few years after the expulsion, the Yugoslavs began considering alternatives to the Soviet command-type economic system. Slowly experimenting with and implementing a number of reforms, the Yugoslavs moved to a decentralized form of market socialism that based production more on the laws of supply and demand and less on the commands of a central economic plan. Movement to a market-based economy was in part motivated and certainly hastened by the Soviet's economic blockade of Yugoslavia that followed the expulsion from the Cominform. Weathering this blockade and several natural catastrophes with economic assistance from the United States, the Yugoslavs began a steady period of economic growth. Through the 1950s and 1960s, the Yugoslav economic growth rates were among the highest in the world. The good news resulting from economic experimentation was not to last, however. In the 1970s and 1980s there was clear evidence that the Yugoslav economy was in serious decline.

Although some countries fared worse than others, World War II also unleashed destructive forces on the economies of the other East European states. The extent of these damages and the amount of reparation required by the region's victor, the Soviet Union, largely determined the initial pace and extent of postwar recovery.[4] In many cases, the Soviets stripped factories of machinery or dismantled entire plants for shipment to the USSR to help pay for war damages. By the early 1950s, however, all the states were back to their prewar levels of production. East Germany was the last to reach this level because of its unusually high reparations to the USSR.

Following Stalinist policies of Soviet economic development, the economies of the East European states were virtually all nationalized by 1950. Forced to emulate the Soviet economic model and working within the supranational Council for Mutual Economic Assistance (CMEA or COMECON) established in 1949, the different states adopted rather similar economic policies and procedures.[5] Attempting to expand the industrial base (particularly mining, machine building, ironworks, and steelworks) while simultaneously retarding personal consumption, the states hoped to increase the margin for capital investment. The resultant economic systems were inefficient and unable to promote the well-being of their societies. Economic recovery from the ravages of war was achieved at high costs, including poor working conditions, low salaries, and a scarcity of basic consumer goods.

Economic Forms and Reforms

The ideal of communism described by Karl Marx envisioned an economic system based on the principle "from each according to his abilities, to each according to his needs." This principle presupposed an economic system in which there were no shortages and where the members of society did not have to pay for food, goods, or services. Individuals were to work and produce according to their abilities and consume only what they needed.

To move toward the ideals of communism, the Second World states all established some sort of socialist economic system. Under socialism, workers produce according to their ability and are paid according to their contribution. In this economic system, theoretically speaking, the factors of production are owned collectively and controlled by the public. Marx believed that this system was a lower stage than communism, unjust because more important work would be more highly rewarded than less important work; however, it would accomplish certain necessary benefits. Basically, socialism would produce a system of material abundance in which the state would "wither away," and the "oppressive government of men" would be replaced by the "administration of things." For Marx, socialism would provide the necessary socioeconomic prerequisites for the emergence of true or pure communism.

The Second World states have displayed a variety of socialist institutional arrangements and policy preferences, each officially designed to facilitate the evolution from socialism to communism. Because the state rather than the public owned the factors of production, the Soviet Union's traditional economic system was often referred to, especially by its various detractors, as one of state socialism. In such a system, state ministries and government bodies at different levels invest in, own, and manage the factors of production. Because industries and enterprises receive their directives from central planning agencies, the term command-type system also has been used to describe this type of economic system. Although the market and the idea of supply and demand have some effect on production, the planning agencies assume primary power and responsibility for determining the type and level of economic output. Under such a system, profits and losses accrue to the state, not to the enterprise or to the workers.

Although a basic purpose and desired benefit of the centralized, administered system of state socialism were economic efficiency, many economists have called attention to considerable waste and inefficiency in the Soviet and East European systems. The administered system was expected to be useful in tackling high-priority tasks, such as the development of heavy industry or the decision to promote intensive capital investment. However, vesting ownership in the state and control in the government ministries ruled out important economic dynamics that promote efficiency and development. A key example involves the attitude and commitment of the average worker. Marx contended that under capitalism, workers had become alienated from their work, but under socialism they were to regain control of their work because the work enterprise was to be publicly owned. But under a centralized system of state socialism, workers once again were exploited and given little control over or incentives in their work.

There were a number of reactions to this development in the form of experimentation with alternative forms of socialism. The first was the Yugoslav experiment, with their self-managing form of socialism. Referred to by a variety of terms, including decentralized socialism, laissez-faire socialism, or a mixed free enterprise/public ownership system, the Yugoslav experiment represented an attempt to resolve some of the problems of state socialism. Hoping to eliminate excessive bureaucracy, low productivity and efficiency, and a relative absence of motivation and initiative, the Yugoslavs developed a hybrid economic system that combined elements of both socialism and capitalism.

Beginning in the 1950s, Yugoslavia began to abandon many features of the Stalinist command-type system. In a series of reforms, Yugoslav leaders deemphasized centralized planning, provided economic enterprises with more decision-making autonomy, and made competition and profit a central motivating feature of the economy. All these and additional policies came under the movement toward self-managing, market-oriented socialism.

Although accounts of the motivating forces behind self-management vary, some say it included Yugoslavia's desire to put power in the hands of the worker, where, according to Marx, it rightly belongs. This involved the establishment of workers' councils in economic enterprises. These councils of elected workers were to assume major responsibility for running the affairs of the firm. Under this system, central government planning was deemphasized while the autonomy of the enterprise was increased. Considerable authority was transferred from central planning ministries to the enterprises themselves, and the enterprises began to base their decisions more on the market and less on the government's commands. However, as we will see later when we examine the economic crisis of contemporary Yugoslavia, these attempts at reform were no panacea. They did not bring about Yugoslav prosperity.

Early Yugoslav reform efforts came under hostile attack from both the Chinese and Soviet leaders. A pamphlet published in Beijing in 1964 noted:

> Although the Tito clique still displays the banner of "socialism," a bureaucrat bourgeoisie opposed to the Yugoslav people has gradually come into being since the Tito clique took the road of revisionism, transforming the Yugoslav state from a dictatorship of the proletariat into a dictatorship of the bureaucrat bourgeoisie and its socialist public economy into state capitalism.[6]

During the 1960s and 1970s the Soviet leaders also looked critically on the economic revisionism being followed in Yugoslavia and warned leaders in the other European socialist states to stay clear of the Yugoslav heresy.

Taking the advice of the Soviet leaders, the East European states adopted more orthodox (i.e., Soviet-styled) economic strategies and systems. In these states, an initial mixed-economy (i.e., capitalist and socialist) period after World War II was followed by the adoption of a command-type system emulating the Soviet model. Launching Five-Year Plans that emphasized industrial development, nationalizing trade and industry, and subordinating labor unions to the Communist Party, the economic models of the other East European states looked much like that of the Soviet system.

Increasingly, however, many of the East European states began to experiment with reforms. Some observed with keen interest the economic experimentation and reform in Yugoslavia. Many felt that the planned economies established in their countries at Soviet insistence after World War II were impeding optimal development. Having experienced prewar histories of rather successful economic growth and possessing definite economic potential, some economic planners in these states blamed their difficulties on the Soviet-style administered system. Although the responses in the 1960s and 1970s differed from country to country, many were eager to experiment with new economic forms. As a result, policy changes intended to bring about economic liberalization and reform were initiated at different times in a number of the countries, particularly Czechoslovakia, Hungary, and Poland. However, because the USSR perceived these policies as endangering the preservation of the command system, the Soviets intervened and forced these countries back into more orthodox positions. One such example was the Czechoslovak experiment in the late 1960s when they attempted to undertake far-reaching social and economic reforms. One dimension of this experiment was economic liberalization designed to take some of the planning and policy-making functions away from the Party and central ministries. Although significant economic progress was being made and other social and political reforms were gathering momentum during the spring of 1968 (the so-called Prague Spring), Soviet reservations about these reforms resulted in military intervention that brought an end to Czechoslovak economic and political liberalization.[7] Organizing a joint intervention by the Warsaw Treaty Organization (WTO) states, troops and tanks from Bulgaria, East Germany, Poland, Hungary, and the Soviet Union marched onto Czechoslovakian soil on August 20, 1968, and brought an end to Czechoslovakia's attempt to develop socialism with a "human face."[8] Many Czechoslovak leaders, including the Communist Party leader, Alexander Dubcek, were ousted as the country returned to the more orthodox position that characterized the economic systems of the other WTO and COMECON states.

In January 1968, the Hungarian communists began implementation of their own program of economic liberalization, the New Economic Mechanism (NEM).[9] By carefully depoliticizing the program and by proceeding cautiously, the Hungarians gradually decentralized and strengthened the Hungarian economy without provoking the sort of Soviet intervention that occurred in Czechoslovakia. Under the NEM, centrally determined quotas and prices were slowly replaced by general national guidelines, the introduction of profit incentives, and the privatization of many sectors of the Hungarian economy. Hungarian economic reforms really picked up steam in the late 1980s. For example, revolutionary laws were introduced in 1989 that included a number of provisions intended to promote private enterprise. For example, one law allowed the transformation of state enterprises into joint stock companies giving Hungarian citizens full involvement in these enterprises. It permitted Hungarians to buy and sell shares in such companies and even

allowed foreign investors to buy Hungarian companies.

The appointment of the reform-minded Mikhail Gorbachev as the Soviet Party leader in 1985 finally brought significant economic experimentation and change to the Soviet Union. Under the general concept of *perestroika* (restructuring), the Soviet leaders hoped to reform the overly centralized, stagnant economy by introducing what officials then referred to as more "intensive development policies." These policies emphasized greater entrepreneurship, initiative, efficiency, decentralization, and accountability. The early Gorbachev years stressed *uskoreniye*, or acceleration, which involved greater discipline, improved effort, and increased conservation. Later, in 1987, Gorbachev and his associates began to talk about more radical reforms.

Gorbachev emphasized repeatedly in the late 1980s that economic restructuring and domestic development were the highest priorities of his rule. His economic reforms were in response to the fact that the Soviet economy had stagnated and had generated little hope for economic progress in the future. The 1981–85 average annual growth rates of 2 percent in the USSR were simply too low to fulfill Soviet hopes and expectations. Using terms like "radical reform" and "profound transformation," Gorbachev began to encourage fundamental change in the economic management of the Soviet economy.

Although many of the specifics were lacking, the broad outlines of radical change, intensive development, and accelerated economic growth were made clear early in Gorbachev's tenure. The 1986–89 Five Year Plan and the economic guidelines to the year 2000 proposed that the economy grow at 4.5 percent a year, considerably above the 1981–85 levels. How was this to be brought about? Perestroika was Gorbachev's plan. Soviet workers were to become more efficient and productive. There were to be organizational changes intended to decrease the central government's micromanagement of the economy and to increase the roles of enterprises and the territorial units of the Soviet state. There was to be technological progress and new machinery, better managers, and improved methods. These and other proposals were part of the Soviet strategy of perestroika.

The strategy was outlined in 1987 in an official document entitled "Basic Provisions for Radical Restructuring of Economic Management." Gorbachev referred to this document in his book *Perestroika* in the following way: "Perhaps this is the most important and the most radical program for economic reform our country has had since Lenin introduced his New Economic Policy in 1921."[10] The proposals in the 1987 Basic Provisions were intended to change the highly centralized, command-type Soviet system to one where local units were given greater power and central government authorities were relegated to a planning role.

Among other things, the 1987 Basic Provisions established the Soviet enterprises (i.e., the firms)—rather than the central government and its planning bodies—as the primary actors in the Soviet economy. This principle was embodied in considerable detail in the 1987 Law of the USSR on State Enterprises. The 1987 law promised enterprises more independence and required them to be economically self-sustaining. They had to be self-financing and self-accounting, that is, responsible for their own profits and losses. The provisions also acknowledged that worker-incentive systems (meaning significant wage differentials) were important and made worker organizations (enterprise work collectives) responsible for electing the enterprise leaders.

The 1987 provisions were intended to reduce the role of the central government so that enterprises could operate more efficiently. In the past, GOSPLAN (the State Planning Committee) and other high level bodies attempted to control all economic activity, that is, to micromanage the Soviet economy. The new provisions called for central-planning organs to be relieved of the day-to-day management of the economy and to refocus their efforts on broader guidance and implementation of the country's economic activity. By removing themselves from micromanagement of the economy, they were to allow enterprises and local territorial units within the Soviet Union to assume more decision-making authority and accountability.

The 1987 Basic Provisions also dealt with other important issues, such as wages and social well-being. The provisions rejected the idea of wage leveling (i.e., equality) and argued that wage differentials can act as important incentives to workers. The provisions also called attention to the human factors of development and for an increase in the level of the nation's prosperity and the standard of living.

By the end of the 1980s, it was apparent to all that perestroika and the Gorbachev reforms would not quickly and easily revive the failing Soviet economy. In 1989, Leonid Abalkin, a leading Soviet economist and deputy prime minister of the government, drew attention to a colossal budget deficit of $165 billion and called it the most important economic problem facing the country. The $165 billion would put the USSR's deficit at approximately 11 percent of the Soviet GNP, much higher than the worrisome U.S. deficit, which during the same period stayed at about 4 percent of the American GNP. To deal with the deficit, Abalkin said the Soviet government would have to slash military and civilian spending and shift many government projects to private financing.

Other official reports were calling attention to Soviet economic problems. A bleak report published in the government newspaper *Izvestia* in January 1989 concluded that the country's economic situation was precarious. According to the report, agricultural output grew only 0.7 percent in 1988, far short of the 6.3 percent target in the government's economic plan. National income grew 4.4 percent in 1988 instead of the targeted 6.6 percent goal. Gorbachev attempted to buoy the spirits of the Soviet people, indicating that there were a number of reasons for the continuing Soviet economic difficulties in the late 1980s. He cited such causes as the investments required by the war in Afghanistan, the tragic 1988 earthquake in Armenia, the nuclear accident in Chernobyl, and the drop in oil export prices. Although these and other reasons no doubt helped explain the continuing economic difficulties in the Soviet Union, it was also apparent that the changes Gorbachev referred to as perestroika were not working well and were unable to bring quick relief to the Soviet economy.

Following the Soviet lead and in response to serious economic decline in their own country, Polish leaders introduced an important economic reform program of their own in the late 1980s. Among other things new Polish laws removed all limits on the size of a private business, which meant that Polish capitalists were to be allowed to own factories with thousands of employees. The new laws also said that any business activity not legally prohibited may be freely undertaken. This reversed the previous principle of state control, under which no private business activity could be undertaken without official authorization. A new Polish law on foreign investment allowed foreign companies to set up operations with an unlimited number of employees. That meant that Americans could go to Poland (and increasingly to the Soviet Union and other communist countries as well) and establish private businesses that were under the total ownership of American capitalists.

In early 1990, the Polish leaders adopted a series of radical economic reforms designed to greatly accelerate the transformation of their economy from one based on socialist principles to one based on principles of the free market. Some of the economic shock measures undertaken in Poland included decontrol of almost all prices; the abolition of most consumer subsidies; widespread privatization of state enterprises; and the devaluation of the Polish currency, the zloty, in an effort to make it convertible on international exchanges.

After Mao's death in 1976, the Chinese also realized their economic stagnation and began to consider reform. In 1984, the leaders announced sweeping economic reforms, what Deng Xiaoping referred to as a "revolution." The reforms called for greater decentralization of industrial management and more competition among factories. At the core of the reforms was an attempt to invigorate the state enterprises by granting them more autonomy. The reforms were intended to introduce more market forces in industry and make businesses compete so that, in the Chinese communists' words, "only the best survive." Another key component of the reforms was the drastic modification of centralized planning. The reforms reduced the scope of mandatory planning to include only items that were vital to the national interest and people's livelihood, such as the production of energy and raw materials. Service industries and the production of small commodities, on the other hand, were to be left to market forces.

There was further evidence of dramatic change in China in the 1980s. In 1984, the Chinese Communist Party newspaper, *People's Daily*, said that although the works of Marx and Lenin should be studied, they were not necessarily applicable to the contemporary problems and challenges confronting China. In a front-page commentary, *People's Daily* noted that "Marx died one hundred and one years ago. . . . We cannot depend on the works of Marx and Lenin to solve our modern day questions." This dramatic statement was qualified somewhat the next day when the newspaper ran an inconspicuous three-line "supplementary correction" that said the last part of the commentary should have read: "We cannot depend on Marx and Lenin to solve *all* our modern day questions." (Italics added.) A few days later, a senior Chinese Communist Party ideologist told foreign journalists that although Marx was a great revolutionary whose ideas still underpinned Chinese theory, he did not provide practical answers and advice on how to build a socialist economy. The ideologist noted that some of Marx's theories were far from enough to resolve the contemporary problems of socialist economic construction. These and related developments underscored the fact that the 1980s were a time of economic challenge and change in much of the Second World.

The Social Setting: Well-Being and Equality

The Marxist-Leninist experiments brought neither well-being nor equality to their societies. This is not to say that people are living in these states in utter poverty or that the gap between the "haves" and "haves nots" has not been reduced under socialism. Rather it is to say that observers both within Second World systems (including the highest level leaders) and from abroad agree that socioeconomic progress has not been impressive and certainly not as great as was promised by past communist leaders.

Let us begin by observing, first, general indicators of economic and social standing, and second, how equally these economic and social resources have been shared within the societies.

Economic and Social Well-Being

We can begin by looking at the Gross National Product (GNP) figures for each of the countries; GNP tells us something about the size of the national economies (see Table 9.2). Although the Second World countries vary considerably in economic size and strength, the GNPs tend to be considerably smaller (with the exception of the USSR) than those of the more developed economies of the First World. When examining GNP per capita figures, which tell us how this overall, national economic strength looks when spread among the entire population, we see that the Second World societies are far behind the United States and much of the highly industrialized countries of the First World. The 1986 GNP per capita figure for Americans ($17,478) was about double that of the Soviet Union ($8,442) and most of the East European states. However, the real standard of living for Americans is even more than double, as we will see later, because of the high level of Soviet spending for defense and investment. That is to say that although there have been considerable economic resources in many Second World states, an extraordinarily large portion of them has been invested in capital and military development and an unusually small portion in the consumer realm. Therefore, the GNP per capita figures for these states are inflated, overstating the amount of economic resources that have been available for social and consumer investment.

There are also important differences within the Second World. Although the Soviet GNP

Table 9.2   Socioeconomic Indicators, 1986

Country	GNP (billion US $)	GNP per capita (US $)	Global Economic-Social Standing*
Albania	4.2	1,391	55
Bulgaria	44.4	4,955	33
Cambodia	1.1	147	130
China	314.9	299	94
Cuba	20.0	1,999	40
Czechoslovakia	103.8	6,688	29
East Germany	146.5	8,808	16
Hungary	66.0	6,212	28
Laos	0.8	227	120
Mongolia	1.7	880	67
North Korea	25.7	1,231	55
Poland	188.6	5,034	37
Romania	91.8	4,024	46
Soviet Union	2,357.0	8,442	25
Vietnam	14.0	229	101
Yugoslavia	85.1	3,659	43
USA†	4,219.2	17,478	4

* Represents average rankings of 142 countries, based on GNP per capita and education and health indicators.
† The USA is included for comparative purposes.
(*Source*) Adapted from Ruth Leger Sivard, *World Military and Social Expenditures, 1989* (Washington, D.C.: World Priorities, 1989), pp. 47–55.

per capita of $8,442 is far below that of the United States, Yugoslavia ($3,659) is far below that of the USSR, and China ($299) far below that of Yugoslavia. Perhaps the two most important observations we should make when examining the figures in Table 9.2 are, first, that the economies of the Second World lag far behind those of the United States and other industrialized countries of the First World, and second, there is a great range of socioeconomic resources within the Second World.

The differences in the GNP, GNP per capita, and Economic-Social Standing figures among the states listed in Table 9.2 have a direct impact on the standards of living found in the various countries. Economic development is of course a major factor determining the physical or material quality of life. Because the economic indicators describing the U.S. economy are much stronger than those for the Soviet Union, we can infer that much more money is available for investing in the American people. And because the indicators of economic development are much higher in the Soviet Union and East European countries than in their Asian counterparts, so too is the standard of living. That means that the amount and quality of housing, the availability of food and social services, and so forth are much better in the Soviet Union—no matter how bad they may be—than in places like Vietnam, Cambodia, and China.

Most Second World countries have done fairly well in providing the basic necessities of life such as food, housing, and health care; very few people are starving in these states and few are without some form of housing and health care. The caloric intake and protein consumption of Soviet citizens, as a matter of fact, compare well with the highly industrialized countries of the West. And social services such as pension systems, worker benefits, health care, and urban transportation are not bad and, in fact, sometimes better than those found in the West.

These and some other indicators of the quality of life in communist systems look good on paper. For example, the number of Soviet physicians and hospital beds per capita is far higher than that found in the United States. However, the quality of health care, food, and social services tends to be very poor in communist systems. Medical doctors are poorly trained and often inattentive. Hospital beds are available but often cramped in overcrowded and unsanitary facilities. The difficulties encountered by the Soviet government when responding to the great tragedy of the 1988 earthquake in Armenia called attention to some of the Soviet shortcomings in the provision of medical and emergency social services.

Additionally, although the caloric and protein intake in the Soviet Union and East European countries is high, the quality of the diet is very poor. Meat and fresh produce are often unavailable, and long lines in front of meat markets and produce and department stores continue to be seen throughout much of the Second World. Their dietary and consumption standards are far below those of their neighbors in Western Europe.

Although housing is cheap in Second World states, it is often of poor quality and space is very cramped. The average living space for families in the Soviet Union is estimated to be less than half of what it is in the United States. Twenty percent of Soviet urban families in the mid-1980s lived in communal apartments, where they shared kitchens and bathroom facilities. During the same period, 25 percent of the state-controlled urban residences contained no running water, and 10 percent had no sewerage or central heat.

The availability of housing has also been a major problem in most of these states. Because there is a severe shortage of housing units, many who desperately need living quarters have to wait long periods of time before receiving any housing. This shortage has many social consequences; for example, it deters many people from marrying at a young age. Moreover, because marriage often means living with one's in-laws for years waiting for cramped apartment space to become available, the housing shortage also contributes to divorce. Clearly, the Soviet and other Second World systems are still struggling with the challenge of improving the availability and quality of housing for their people.

There is also a shortage of consumer items throughout much of the Second World. People generally have plenty of money but very little to buy. In the 1980s, the number of televisions per capita in the Soviet Union was one half that in the United States, the number of radios one fourth, and the number of automobiles less than one tenth. Before recent changes, East Germans had to wait fifteen years for a little Trabant, the underpowered, smoke-belching car of the GDR.

Consumers in Second World systems have lived in environments of general deprivation when compared with the standards of the West. Although well-being is much more than food, housing, and the ability to buy consumer goods,

These empty shelves in a Warsaw meat market in 1989 were representative of the food shortages throughout Eastern Europe and the Soviet Union in recent years.

these conditions do tell us about what communist systems have been able to do to promote the physical quality of life. The material deprivation existing in these states had a great deal to do with the growing expression of discontent and resulting political changes that swept over Eastern Europe in the late 1980s. The East European standard of living was considerably below what was found in counterpart states in the West. When the East Germans streamed through the Berlin Wall in 1989, their expressions of amazement with the West's material abundance were a clear indication of the different standards between East and West. Other Eastern societies, like Romania, lived in even more deprived environments than the East Germans. Due to the malaise in the Romanian economy and the dictator Ceausescu's austerity programs, the average Romanian citizen lived a life of extreme material deprivation in the 1980s. Many homes were allowed to burn only one light bulb and to turn on the heat for only a few hours a day in the dead of winter.

The material deprivation so prevalent in the Second World is likely to grow in the short term as many Second World states undertake economic reform programs. Many in the Second World are learning that the transformation from a command to a market economy can be painful; that there is no quick fix. The economic shock treatment applied to Poland in early 1990 initially resulted in even greater shortages of goods and longer lines than what had existed under the traditional Polish command economic system.

The inflationary pressures, unemployment, currency devaluations, disruptions of supply, and shortages that accompany the tearing down of a communist economic system are making life very frustrating for many in the Second World today. Their standard of living is being destabilized and threatened by the reform processes that many expected to be a cure-all. They are being told by political leaders and economists at home and in the West that in the long run they will be better off under a market system. They are asked to be patient and accept uncertainty. For people who for years have lived in a highly stable and predictable, if not prosperous, economic environment, the present uprooting and change in their lives must be very unsettling. Just how long their patience and tolerance for economic reform will last remains an unanswered question.

If communist systems have not done so well in providing a reasonable level of physical well-being, how have they done in promoting equality, that is, an equal distribution of available resources among their people? Before trying to answer this question, let us see what Marxist-Leninists think about equality.

Equality

In the *Communist Manifesto*, Karl Marx and Friedrich Engels wrote, "The history of all hitherto existing society is the history of class struggles." According to Marxist theory, modern industrial society had given birth to the proletariat and bourgeoisie, the two antagonistic classes of the capitalist stage of development. With the establishment of communism, a new historical epoch was to occur. This socioeconomic system was to be free of classes and exploitation and based on the principles of social and material equality.

The avenue leading to communism, said Marx and Engels, leads through the socioeconomic stage of socialism, in which property is made public and private ownership abolished. According to Marxist theory, private property is the force that divides people during the capitalist stage of development. If you forbid private property, you dissolve the basis for class antagonism.

During the early period of their rule, the Communist Parties moved to nationalize—sometimes quickly, at other times more gradually—private property and place power, at least theoretically, in the hands of a proletarian dictatorship. Although the dissolution of private property was gradual in some states, such as in China where Mao wanted to use the capitalists and avoid class warfare, or incomplete, as in some East European societies where small private farms and businesses continued to exist, large holdings of private property were outlawed and transferred to collective social or state ownership. Under socialism, the proletarian dictatorship was to be a temporary arrangement preceding communism, the idealized classless society. The basic question concerning this theory and the hypothesized developments involves their validity. Would socialism necessarily lead to equality? Would class boundaries and distinctions dissolve under Communist Party rule? Would this lead to the development of the classless community of peoples envisioned under communism?

The experience of the Second World states suggests that, although some inequalities were radically reduced, development of a classless society under socialism was not, at least in the short run, an easy task. There were a number of forces making the transition difficult if not impossible, and these involve some central features of an industrializing society. Most social theorists maintain that a division of labor is a necessary prerequisite to or at least a component of industrialization. Division of labor refers to the structure of jobs and the specialization of occupational skills needed to achieve industrial development. For example, an industrializing society requires engineers, planners, and workers; these occupations vary in terms of training and skills. As we have noted, the guiding principle of socialism is "from each according to his abilities, to each according to his contribution"; therefore, those occupations that contribute more important skills receive greater rewards. All the countries we are studying adopted this philosophy of a differentiated reward system during their socialist phases of development. The communist ideal of "from each according to his abilities, to each according to his *needs*" remains an unachieved ideal today.

Although Vladimir Ilyich Lenin and the Bolsheviks initially instituted a policy of wage leveling, they soon opted for a system providing incentives in the form of sizable wage differentials. Through the 1930s and 1940s, Stalin was willing to rationalize inequality in wages as a necessary incentive to attract workers into desired occupations. Soviet industrialization during this phase of development required skilled workers, planners, and engineers as well as clerical and administrative personnel. These and other occupations provided crucial functions required of an industrializing society, and they represented the division of labor that characterizes all modernizing societies. Although Nikita Khrushchev launched a campaign in the 1950s to reduce these wage differentials, they were never eliminated. Table 9.3 indicates the differentials among some selected occupations in the USSR and four East European countries after the Khrushchev period. Using worker salaries as a base unit (100), the data indicate that although pay generally became more egalitarian between 1960 and 1973, particularly in the USSR, significant differences according to occupation remained. Such differences remain through the present.[11]

It is easy to see why a growing specialization and division of labor had made the establishment of a classless society difficult. When you have considerable differences between the highest- and lowest-paid workers, you encounter strong forces encouraging the formation of classes. Some communists would attempt to refute this argument by noting that although Second World societies do exhibit occupational wage differences among individuals and groups, they do not represent the traditional classes of earlier forms of society. In a capitalist society, they would argue, the *bourgeoisie* control and exploit the working class. In earlier societies (primitive, slave, feudal, and capitalist), the nature of class differences led to an inevitable class struggle—"the history of all hitherto existing society." Therefore, Marxists contend that although wage and status differences may exist in socialist societies and may lead to a system of social stratification, they will not result in the social classes and resultant conflict of old. Although the issue is debatable, we can at least conclude that social divisions are present in Second World societies and that they do have some of the characteristics of social classes under capitalism.

Occupational and income differences are among the primary elements associated with social stratification in contemporary Second World societies. A top-ranking engineer or a dean in a university is much more likely to have a disproportionate share of respect, well-being, enlightenment, and power than a blue-collar worker. The official ideology maintains that all occupational roles contribute equally to the building of socialism, but some are considerably more valued than others. A nuclear physicist at Moscow State University, an engineer in Beijing, and a director of an economic enterprise in Yugoslavia command a higher income and status than rank-and-file workers. In addition, their opportunities for attaining the values associated with enlightenment are greater, as are their opportunities for achieving a preferred state of well-being and political power.

The gap between the highest- and lowest-paid occupations tends to be smaller in Second World than in First World states. In many First World states such as the United States, salary differences can be more than 300 to 1, meaning that the highest-paid people earn more than 300 times what the lowest-paid people earn. A considerable body of research supports these points. The distinguished American sociologist Gerhard Lenski has noted that the range of salaries and incomes generally seems to have been reduced in Marxist societies to a level well below that in most comparable non-Marxist societies.[12] His research indicated a ratio of 50 to 1 between top salaries and the minimum wage in the USSR in the 1970s, 40 to 1 in China before Mao's death, and 7.3 to 1 in Cuba. (Again, the corresponding ratio in the United States in recent years has been approximately 300 to 1.) As Lenski cautioned, these figures should not be taken at face value, and they do not provide a direct

Table 9.3 Average Pay by Occupational Category*

	1960	1973
Bulgaria		
Intelligentsia	142.1	132.1
Routine nonmanual	93.8	95.5
Worker	100.0	100.0
Peasant	92.1	91.5
Czechoslovakia		
Intelligentsia	116.8	120.4
Routine nonmanual	77.0	81.3
Worker	100.0	100.0
Peasant	79.2	98.1
Hungary		
Intelligentsia	157.2	142.4
Routine nonmanual	94.8	92.4
Worker	100.0	100.0
Peasant	na[†]	94.1
Poland		
Intelligentsia	156.7	144.3
Routine nonmanual	105.1	100.1
Worker	100.0	100.0
Peasant	na[†]	77.5
USSR		
Intelligentsia	150.9	134.1
Routine nonmanual	82.1	84.5
Worker	100.0	100.0
Peasant	57.7	76.5

* Intelligentsia, routine nonmanuals, workers (all in state industry), and peasants (workers in state/socialist agriculture).
† Not available.
(*Source*) Adapted from Walter D. Connor, *Socialism, Politics, and Equality: Hierarchy and Change in Eastern Europe and the USSR* (New York: Columbia University Press, 1979), p. 231.

measure of differentials in living standards. However, Lenski concluded that the Marxist experiments have, in fact, resulted in a reduction of inequality in income and living standards in Second World societies. At the same time, he called attention to a number of Marxist failures, including: (1) the persistence of very high levels of political inequality, (2) the persistence of worker alienation, (3) the persistence of gender inequality, (4) the persistence of urban-rural inequality, and (5) the failure of Marxist societies to give birth to the new socialist man.[13]

Urban and rural distinctions also contribute to a stratified society. The differences between life in Moscow, Warsaw, or Belgrade and the backward peasant life of the villages is extreme. Urbanization has been a major agent of social change and, in some respects, has had a leveling effect on a host of social differences. The common experiences of city life have softened some occupational and cultural differences, whereas life in the agricultural areas often remains parochial and provincial. The social differences between a typical college student in New York City and one in Moscow are considerable but tend to be less significant than those between a Russian student in Moscow and his counterpart in a remote Siberian village.

Communists stood and fought for the emancipation of sexes as well as of workers. In some respects, however, gender tends to stratify societies within the Second World because women predominate in many of the unskilled, "physical" professions (e.g., construction workers, machine operators, bus drivers). Unlike the situation in some First and Third World societies, in socialist states women represent an extremely large and important sector of the total work force. In addition to their predomination in many of the unskilled occupations, women also represent an important sector of the work force in many professional occupations. For example,

Soviet women outnumber men in such occupations as economic planner, doctor, and dentist.

The greatest gender discrimination in the Soviet Union, and traditionally in other Second World states as well, has been in the area of politics. Although there is a relatively high proportion of women in ceremonial political roles, there is a very small percentage in positions of real power in either the Party or the government. Underrepresentation of women is also evident in some nonpolitical directing posts, such as those in hospitals, factories, and in the field of higher education. Another interesting and more subtle form of discrimination seems to take place in the home. After putting in a full day as a machine builder, bus driver, or economic planner, a woman typically returns home to assume the major household responsibilities. Perhaps to a greater extent than in the West, Soviet and East European men do little to share in the burdens of housework. Social discrimination against women, deeply embedded in the traditional value structures of Second World cultures, will have to be eradicated before a genuine equality of sexes can be achieved in these societies.

We should now be aware that standards of living and their associated systems of social stratification vary considerably among the socialist states comprising the Second World. Although some of these differences can be attributed to political choices, environmental factors such as socioeconomic development help determine who gets what in the socialist states. Nobody gets very much in China simply because there is not very much to go around. The average citizen gets a little more in the Soviet Union, primarily because the state is at a somewhat more advanced economic level. Furthermore, the average citizen in Leningrad or Moscow enjoys a higher standard of living than his or her counterpart in the less developed republic of Kazakhstan, largely owing to the fact that the socioeconomic capabilities of the Russian region are higher than those of Kazakhstan.

However, there are political choices that account for some of the differences in the values people enjoy. For example, Communist Party officials have traditionally enjoyed a better standard of living than the average citizen in Second World states. Until recently at least, these officials have been given top priority in the distribution of state goods and property. They have allowed themselves to bypass the numerous lines and waiting lists the average citizen has had to endure to acquire everything from cars to shoes. They have had the nicest homes and eaten the best food. They have shopped in special stores, open only to them, where they have bought imported consumer goods unavailable anywhere else in their country. Their children have gone to the best schools and been given the most attractive jobs the state has had to offer. Some communist leaders have used their position in the Communist Party to amass huge personal wealth. The Swiss bank accounts, elaborate homes, and luxurious lifestyle of the late Romanian communist dictator Nicolae Ceausescu, for example, have proved to be the equal of any personal fortune built by a monarch or successful capitalist.

In addition to the benefits that have been granted to Communist Party officials in the past, other social groups within Second World states have also received economic and social advantages that run contrary to Marxist principles of social equality. One of these groups has been the star athletes of most Second World states. Communist leaders have long viewed international sports competitions like the Olympic Games as opportunities to enhance the reputation of their states and a means to add legitimacy to their own rule. Their rationale was

that if communist athletes were judged to be best in the world, the system they lived in and were governed by could more easily be promoted as also being the best in the world. To guarantee that their athletes would be the best in the world, communist leaders had to make sure that their sports stars were catered to in all aspects of their personal and professional lives. East Germany was perhaps the best example of this. By offering many of the material advantages to star athletes that they themselves enjoyed, communist leaders provided the necessary incentives to ensure that their athletes worked hard and strove to do their best in international competitions. Judging by the resounding success communist athletes have typically enjoyed in these competitions over the last two decades, it is safe to say that the athletes did what was expected of them by their leaders—they brought medals home to their motherland. It will be interesting to see how well the athletes of Eastern Europe compete in the future in their changing environments.

Ethnicity and Socialism

The Second World settings are also very much affected by the sociocultural features of nationality and ethnicity. In the *Communist Manifesto*, Marx and Engels predicted that nationality was a dying force in the contemporary world. They believed that with the increasing freedom of commerce in the international market and with the growing uniformity of production and conditions of life, national differences would dissolve. Furthermore, as exploitation and antagonism between classes began to cease under socialism, so too would hostility among nations and nationalities. As national differences began to disappear (again, according to Marx and Engels), we would witness the development of internationalism within the socialist world. In this phase of historical development, workers of the world would be united by the bonds of socialist or proletarian internationalism and the forces of nationalism and ethnocentrism would cease to exist.

As we witness events in the contemporary world, we can see that Marx and Engels underestimated the power of nationalism. Nationality, or nationhood, is a strong and enduring sociocultural force that grows out of the history, geography, language, and culture of groups of people. As we approach the twenty-first century, we seem to be witnessing a growth rather than a decline in nationalism in the Second World.

Although we usually refer to the "nations" of the communist world, strictly speaking, this is misleading. Some of the Second World "nations" are composed of many distinct nations or nationalities, each with its own language, customs, and sense of the past. For example, the Soviet Union is a multinational state and includes such nationalities as Russians, Ukrainians, Armenians, Georgians, Lithuanians, Tatars, a variety of Asian nationalities, and many, many others. There are more than 100 national and ethnic groups in the Soviet Union. And although Russian, the official language of the state, tends to be spoken by most members of all groups, the Soviet Union still displays a rich mix of languages that represents many distant points in Europe and Asia.

The largest Soviet nationality by far is the Russians, who comprise just over half of the total population (see Table 9.4). The bulk of these Russians resides in the Russian Republic (RSFSR), which stretches from Moscow and Leningrad eastward to the Pacific (see the map of the USSR), although many Russians live in other republics as well. The Russian Republic in the Soviet Union is huge, almost twice the size of the United States. The Russian Republic contains sixteen autonomous republics, five autonomous regions, and ten national areas, representing a heterogeneous multinational mosaic of groups. The next largest Soviet nationalities are the Ukrainians, who reside primarily in the Ukrainian Soviet Socialist Republic, and the Uzbeks, who inhabit the Uzbek Soviet Socialist Republic. The fourth largest is the Byelorussians, or White Russians, and they too have a republic within which they predominate.

Administratively and constitutionally, the early Soviet leaders designed a federal political arrangement to reflect the extreme diversity in the society. This federal structure divided the Soviet state into the fifteen union republics and the autonomous republics indicated on the map. The units coincide with the complex array of national and ethnic groups in the state and vary in status according to the size and strength of the groups. Although the constitution guaranteed these federal units important rights and privileges, past Soviet leaders did not honor them. This all began to change, however, during the Gorbachev period.

Growing nationalism is one of today's pressing challenges, if not the most critical challenge, that will affect the future of the Soviet Union. After decades of repression, national differences began rising to the surface, often violently, with the appearance of glasnost in the late 1980s. A brief review of a few important cases will help convey how critical an issue today's ethnic and national relations is to the Soviet future.

One case involves the growing unrest in Central Asia, the area in the Soviet Union that is populated by most of the USSR's 45 million Moslems. Because the Soviet Union has the fifth largest Islamic population of any country in the world, and because of the growth of Islamic nationalism and the fear of Islamic fundamentalism in the USSR, the Soviet authorities

Table 9.4   Major Nationalities of the USSR, 1979 (with populations >1 million)

Nationality	Population	Percent of Total	Linguistic Group	Traditional Religion
Russian	137,397,089	52.4	Slavic	Orthodox
Ukrainian	42,347,387	16.2	Slavic	Orthodox
Uzbek	12,455,978	3.6	Turkic	Islam
Belorussian	9,462,715	3.6	Slavic	Orthodox
Kazakh	6,556,442	2.5	Turkic	Islam
Tatar	6,317,468	2.4	Turkic	Islam
Azeri	5,477,330	2.1	Turkic	Islam
Armenian	4,151,241	1.6	Indo-European	National Christian
Georgian	3,570,504	1.4	Iberian	Orthodox
Moldavian	2,968,224	1.1	Romance	Orthodox
Tadjik	2,897,697	1.1	Iranian	Islam
Lithuanian	2,850,905	1.1	Baltic	Roman Catholic
Turkmen	2,027,913	0.8	Turkic	Islam
German	1,936,214	0.7	Germanic	Lutheran
Kirgiz	1,906,271	0.7	Turkic	Islam
Jewish	1,810,875	0.7	Yiddish	Judaism
Chuvash	1,751,366	0.7	Turkic	Orthodox
Latvian	1,439,037	0.5	Baltic	Lutheran
Bashkir	1,371,452	0.5	Turkic	Islam
Mordvinian	1,191,765	0.5	Finnic	Orthodox
Polish	1,150,991	0.4	Slavic	Roman Catholic
Estonian	1,019,851	0.4	Finnic	Lutheran

(*Source*) Tsentral'noe statisticheskoe upravlenie, *Chislennost' i sostav naseleniia SSSR po dannym vsesoiuznoi perepisi naseleniia 1979 goda* (Moscow: Finansy i Statistika, 1985), 71–73; Barbara A. Anderson and Brian D. Silver, "Estimating Russification of Ethnic Identity Among Non-Russians in the USSR," *Demography* 20 (November 1983), 466; Philip G. Roeder, *Soviet Political Dynamics* (New York: Harper & Row, 1988), p. 372.

are deeply concerned about the increasing discontent in that part of the country. Our case begins in 1986 with the removal of First Secretary Dinmukhammed Kunaev, the powerful leader of the Kazakh Republic since 1964, and the appointment of a nonresident Russian as his successor. The leaders in Moscow considered Kunaev, the Kazakh leadership, and many of their supporters as corrupt and felt that they had to bring in an outsider to manage a far-reaching purge. However, the appointment of an ethnic Russian with no experience in Kazakhstan showed extraordinary insensitivity to Kazakh national sentiments and set off violent rioting in Alma-Ata, the capital of the Kazakh Republic. Thousands stormed through the capital city, looted stores, burned cars, waved Kazakh-language banners, and attacked Russians and their

The proclamation of Lithuanian independence shown here is a clear indication of the continuing presence and power of national identity in the Soviet Union.

property. Although early reports referred to these disturbances as being the result of "hooligans," subsequent dispatches suggested that Kazakh officials also were involved and bore some responsibility for the rampage. A resolution of the central Community Party authorities in Moscow charged that the former Kazakh leadership had committed serious mistakes in implementing the country's nationalities policies. Although the Kazakh movement was largely repressed, the 1986 uprising and ensuing events were among the many signals that the

Soviet Islamic minorities would no longer tolerate in the age of glasnost what they perceived to be Russian domination of their political and economic affairs. Ethnic tensions and disturbances in Islamic areas such as Uzbekistan and Tadzhikistan in the late 1980s indicated that other Central Asian nationalities also had strong feelings about their situations. As we will see later in this book, nationality in the Soviet Union raises complex questions and concerns about proper allocation of the values of power, respect, well-being, and enlightenment. The Islamic minorities, along with many others, do not think they are receiving their fair share.

Another case took place in the late 1980s in the southern area of the USSR, but west across the Caspian Sea in the region known as the Caucasus. This case involves a virulent dispute between the Christian Armenians and the Moslem Azerbaijanis and the relationship of both to the Soviet state and centralized Communist Party rule. Both nationalities have long been concerned with what they consider Russian discrimination and their less-than-ideal situations in the Soviet Union. But it was Armenian concern over an enclave of Armenians who reside in Nagorno-Karabakh, an autonomous region close to the Armenian republic but officially under the jurisdiction of the Azerbaijan republic that precipitated violence and bloodshed in 1988. Armenian concerns were extensive and elaborate, but basically they felt the Azerbaijanis were repressing the social and cultural development of their fellow Armenians who were living on Azerbaijan soil in Nagorno-Karabakh. Accordingly, they demanded that the Armenian enclave in Azerbaijan be united with Armenia. Simultaneously, they raised broader Armenian concerns, including expanded Armenian autonomy vis-à-vis the central government in Moscow; increased teaching of the Armenian language; the creation of Armenian military units where Armenians could serve on their own soil rather than in the far reaches of the Soviet state; and the elimination of hazardous industrial sites on Armenian soil. This final demand took on further significance in the aftermath of the tragic earthquake that destroyed whole cities and killed approximately 50,000 Armenians in December 1988.

Although Gorbachev and Communist Party leaders in Moscow considered and acceded to some of the Armenian demands in the late 1980s, they were unwilling to put Nagorno-Karabakh under Armenian control. This brought about a further deterioration in relations among the concerned parties and an outbreak in violence in which many were killed. Demonstrators defied government bans on public rallies, and hundreds of thousands flocked to air their grievances in Yerevan and Baku, the respective capitals of the republics of Armenia and Azerbaijan. By the close of 1988, more than 100,000 people had fled their homes, and military forces were brought in to preserve the peace. In an attempt to defuse the violent ethnic dispute that had brought virtual martial law to the two republics, the Soviet government decided in 1989 to put the disputed territory of Nagorno-Karabakh under the direct rule of the central government in Moscow, thereby ending sixty-five years of Azerbaijani control over the contested region.

The tragic earthquake that struck Armenia made the situation even more serious. This natural disaster provided further evidence to Armenians of their disadvantaged situation and Soviet discrimination. Armenians criticized the Soviet government for their inadequate rescue and reconstruction efforts. When Armenian nationalists tied these criticisms to the larger issue of what they perceived to be a cavalier and callous Soviet disposition toward Armenian concerns, they were arrested, which further heightened Armenian nationalist sentiments. The Azerbaijan-Armenian conflict subsequently exploded on numerous occasions and resulted in the imposition of Soviet troops and martial law on Azerbaijan soil in early 1990. Although much is uncertain as this book goes to press, we can expect the Armenians and Azerbaijanis to continue to press their demands for power, respect, well-being, and other values to which they feel entitled.

Another proud nation in the Caucasus, the southwestern part of the Soviet Union, is the

Georgians, who also are deeply concerned about the values to which they feel entitled. The Georgians are a fiercely nationalistic nation, and many are pressing for independence from the Soviet Union. In April 1989, twenty independence demonstrators were killed in the Georgian capital of Tbilisi as they pressed their demands in a clash with Soviet authorities. Georgian concerns continue to fester in this nationalistic region of the Caucasus.

Our final Soviet case involves the Baltic nationalities—the Estonians, Latvians, and Lithuanians—and their efforts to expand their power, well-being, and respect vis-à-vis the central Soviet government in Moscow. Like the Armenians, the small Baltic nationalities have suffered much throughout history. Their cherished independence between WWI and WWII was ended as a result of Soviet annexation of their territories in 1940. The Stalinist government accused and arrested many Baltic nationals as class enemies, moved Russian authorities into key positions, unleashed a frontal assault on private farming and enterprise, and did great damage to the thriving economies in this proud region. The experience of the Baltic nationalities under Soviet rule has not been a pleasant one. The Estonian, Latvian, and Lithuanian nationalities do not feel they have received the values they deserve.

In the context of increasing openness and growing discussion about the relationships between the central and republic governments in the late 1980s, Baltic nationalism underwent a powerful resurgence. A significant event that triggered the reactions of the Baltic peoples involved discussions in Moscow about Gorbachev's reform program and the future of republic-federal government relations. Whereas the Baltic groups desired more political and economic freedom, some in the central government in Moscow wanted to maintain the central government's traditional domination of the republics and local governments.

The reactions of the Estonians convey the concerns of the Baltic nationalities, so let us focus for a moment on the Estonians. Feeling spiritually closer to the West (and particularly to Finland) than to the Soviet Union, the Estonians were keen to take advantage of glasnost and perestroika to bring about changes promoting their national interests. Accordingly, as a first step in reaction to the discussion in Moscow, the Estonian parliament adopted by unanimous vote in 1988 a resolution giving Estonian authorities the right to refuse to apply Soviet laws. This declaration of Estonian sovereignty was a clear and dramatic statement intended to increase the republic's power in relation to the central Soviet authorities. It proclaimed Estonian sovereignty and power in all matters except defense and foreign policy. An estimated 900,000 of the 1.5 million Estonian populace signed petitions protesting Soviet policy and favoring the Estonian declaration. The other Baltic nationalities—the Latvians and Lithuanians—shared the Estonian point of view. An estimated 1.5 million of 3.6 million Lithuanians and 300,000 of 2.6 million Latvians signed similar petitions.

The Lithuanians took even more serious actions in the late 1980s to push for their interests. The Lithuanian parliament passed proposals to create a commission to rewrite the Lithuanian constitution and to make Lithuanian rather than Russian the official language and the traditional, independent Lithuanian flag the official flag of the republic. In 1990 the Lithuanian government declared its independence from the Soviet Union, provoking a dramatic showdown with Secretary Gorbachev and the Soviet authorities. As this book goes to press, resurgent Baltic nationalism continues to challenge Soviet authorities as Estonian, Latvian, and Lithuanian leaders attempt to promote the interests and values of their proud peoples. If Soviet authorities cannot convince these and the other constituent nationalities that their best interests are served by belonging to the Soviet Union, they will be confronted with growing secessionist movements. Because of this, most observers believe that the Soviet Union will lose substantial territory by the end of this decade.

Yugoslavia is also a multinational state that continues to be confronted with nationalist movements that challenge the unity and future of Yugoslav communism. Comprised of five South Slavic nationalities—the Croats, Macedonians, Montenegrins, Serbs, and Slovenes— as well as sizable non-Slavic nationalities like the Albanians, the federal Yugoslav system has traditionally given these constituent nationalities a higher level of independence and autonomy than counterpart groups have received in the Soviet Union. This has not brought an end to nationalist tensions, however, as many groups continue to be unhappy with their situations and roles in the Yugoslav union. The largest nationality, the Serbs (comprising 40 percent of the total population of the country), feel that they should have more power in view of their size and importance within the country. Smaller nationalities from more developed regions like Slovenia feel they should have more autonomy to allow them to pursue a more independent course of economic development. The major minority from the most deprived part of the country, the Albanians, feel they should have more aid and autonomy. These and other conflicting demands, along with increasing economic problems, brought Yugoslavia to the brink of ethnonationalistic conflict in the late 1980s. In 1990 the Slovenian communists walked out and aborted the National Party Congress, leading Yugoslav newspapers to write about the end of the Communist Party (or League of Communists) as it is known in Yugoslavia. Ethnonationalism continues to be a troublesome impediment to the idealistic Yugoslav visions of brotherhood and unity that were held in earlier days.

China is another example of a heterogeneous multiethnic state in the Second World. Although 93 percent of the population is of the basic Chinese nationality (the Han), it is divided into groups characterized by many social, cultural, and linguistic differences. Among the Hans, the spoken language in one region, such as in Canton, may be unintelligible to people from other regions. The Chinese do, however, share a unified written language. In addition to the Han people, China has over 50 million members of minority groups, more than double the total population of Yugoslavia. Of these, more than fifty groups have been designated as minorities and have been given ninety-eight autonomous areas at the provincial, intermediate, and county levels. These autonomous areas, usually named after the group or groups who predominate, provide the minorities greater freedom and government rights—although all these rights are subordinate to national programs, laws, regulations, and organizations. The map of China outlines the twenty-one provinces and five autonomous regions. Autonomous regions are areas heavily populated by non-Chinese minorities. Some of these minorities, like the Tibetans, continue to challenge the authority of the central leaders. Poor relations between the central authorities and Tibet resulted in a major Tibetan rebellion in 1959 and difficulties that continue to the present time.

The economic, social, and ethnic conditions surveyed in this chapter are important when considering the context in which politics takes place. When conditions are bad—when economic resources are limited, when social needs are going unmet, when national unity is strained by ethnic conflict—the challenges of governing are much greater. And that is where many of the Second World states find themselves as we enter the 1990s. Before moving on to our analysis of government and politics, we will consider in the next chapter political cultures, another part of the setting in which politics takes place.

Suggestions for Further Reading

Banac, Ivo, *The National Question in Yugoslavia: Origins, History and Politics* (Ithaca, N.Y.: Cornell University Press, 1984).

Barnett, A. Doak, *China Economy in Global Perspective* (Washington, D.C.: Brookings Institution, 1981).

Bennigsen, Alexandre, and Marie Broxup, *The Islamic Threat to the Soviet State* (New York: St. Martin's Press, 1983).

Bergson, Abram, *Soviet Post-War Economic Development* (Stockholm: Almqvist & Wiksell, 1975).

Bialer, Seweryn, *Politics, Society, and Nationality Inside Gorbachev's Russia* (Boulder: Westview Press, 1989).

Conner, Walker, *The National Question in Marxist-Leninist Theory and Strategy* (Princeton, N.J.: Princeton University Press, 1984).

Conner, Walker D., *Socialism, Politics, and Equality: Hierarchy and Change in Eastern Europe and the USSR* (New York: Columbia University Press, 1979).

Eckstein, Alexander, *China's Economic Revolution* (Cambridge: Cambridge University Press, 1977).

Fischer-Galati, Stephen A., *Twentieth Century Rumania* (New York: Columbia University Press, 1970).

Griffith, William E., *Albania and the Sino-Soviet Rift* (Cambridge, Mass.: MIT Press, 1963).

Hewett, Edward A., *Reforming the Soviet Economy* (Washington, D.C.: Brookings Institution, 1988).

Jancar, Barbara Wolfe, *Women under Communism* (Baltimore: Johns Hopkins University Press, 1978).

Matthews, Mervyn, *Poverty in the Soviet Union: Lifestyles of the Underprivileged in Recent Years* (New York: Cambridge University Press, 1986).

Moore, Barrington, Jr., *Authority and Inequality under Capitalism and Socialism* (Oxford: Clarendon Press, 1987).

Nelson, Daniel N., ed., *Communism and the Politics of Inequalities* (Lexington, Mass.: Lexington Books, 1983).

Sirc, Ljubo, *The Yugoslav Economy under Self-Management* (New York: St. Martin's Press, 1979).

Tyson, Laura D'andrea, *The Yugoslav Economic System and Its Performance in the 1970s* (Berkeley: University of California, Institute of International Studies, 1980).

U.S. Congress, Joint Economic Committee. *China's Economy Looks Toward the Year 2000,* Vols. 1 and 2 (Washington, D.C.: U.S. Government Printing Office, 1986).

U.S. Congress, Joint Economic Committee. *Gorbachev's Economic Plans,* Vols. 1 and 2 (Washington, D.C.: U.S. Government Printing Office, 1987).

Notes

1. Stalin's collectivization drive of 1929–36 was a radical program to transfer the private ownership of land to collective farms under state administration. The drive ended with the abolition of 90 percent of private farming and the deportation of over 1 million peasant households. For a detailed history of Stalin's collectivization drive, see Robert Conquest, *Harvest of Sorrow: Soviet Collectivization and the Terror Famine* (Oxford, Oxford University Press, 1986).

2. These and other events resulted in the so-called Sino-Soviet conflict, a dispute characterized by hostile interstate relations between the two communist powers. See Donald Zagoria, *The Sino-Soviet Conflict, 1955–1961* (Princeton, N.J.: Princeton University Press, 1962).

3. The Communist Information Bureau (Cominform) was established in 1947 to bind the East European socialist states more closely to the USSR. In a letter of March 27, 1948, addressed to the Yugoslav communists, Stalin and the Soviet Central Committee castigated the Yugoslav leaders and excommunicated them from the socialist camp. Because they considered themselves loyal to the Soviet Union, this was initially a bitter blow to the Yugoslav communists. For a firsthand account of their reactions and subsequent search for alternative economic and social policies, see Vladimir Dedijer, *The Battle Stalin Lost* (New York: Universal Library, 1972).

4. For a discussion of Soviet demands for reparation payments from the new Communist Party regimes to cover war damages inflicted by the Axis Powers, as well as other forms of Soviet involvement in the postwar economic setting

of Eastern Europe, see Nicholas Spulber, *The Economies of Communist Eastern Europe* (Cambridge: MIT Press, 1957).

5. COMECON was established as a response to the Western Marshall Plan and was intended to coordinate reconstruction, planning, production, and foreign trade within Eastern Europe. It originally included Bulgaria, Czechoslovakia, Hungary, Poland, Romania, and the USSR. Subsequently, it was broadened to include Albania, Cuba, East Germany, and Mongolia.

6. *On Khrushchev's Phoney Communism and Its Historical Lessons to the World* (Beijing: Foreign Languages Press, 1964), p. 47.

7. The Soviet leaders were worried by factors other than economic liberalization. There were fears, for example, concerning Western influence and involvement in Czechoslovakia and the possibility that the reforms would result in a Czechoslovak withdrawal from the Warsaw Treaty Organization (WTO) and COMECON pacts.

8. The Warsaw Treaty was signed in 1955 by Albania, Bulgaria, the German Democratic Republic (GDR [East Germany]), Hungary, Poland, Romania, and the USSR as a response to the establishment of the North Atlantic Treaty Organization (NATO). Like NATO, the treaty pledged mutual military assistance in the event of an attack on one of the signatories. The so-called Brezhnev Doctrine that grew out of the 1968 intervention in Czechoslovakia broadened the assistance to include perceived domestic threats to socialism.

9. For details on the Hungarian NEM, see Ivan Volgyes, *Hungary: A Nation of Contradictions* (Boulder, Colo.: Westview, 1982).

10. Mikhail Gorbachev, *Perestroika: New Thinking for Our Country and the World* (New York: Harper & Row, 1987), p. 33.

11. Wage differentials remain a characteristic of all socialist societies, even the most egalitarian, the Chinese.

12. Gerhard Lenski, "Marxist Experiments in Destratification: An Appraisal," *Social Forces* 57(2) (1978): 370–371.

13. Ibid.: 371–376.

Boundaries of Soviet Socialist Republics (S.S.R.)

Boundaries of Autonomous Soviet
Socialist Republics (A.S.S.R.)

O C E A N

Wrangel I.

B E R I N G

S E A

SEVERNAYA
ZEMLYA

NEW SIBERIAN
ISLANDS

L A P T E V

S E A

S O C I A L I S T   R E P U B L I C S

YAKUT A.S.S.R.

S E A

O F

O K H O T S K

R E P U B L I C

S O C I A L I S T

Sakhalin I.

Kuril Islands

BURYAT-MONGOL
A.S.S.R.

TUVA
A.S.S.R.

MONGOLIAN

REPUBLIC

CHINA

S E A

O F

J A P A N

NORTH
KOREA

SOUTH
KOREA

JAPAN

EASTERN EUROPE

The Eight Communist States

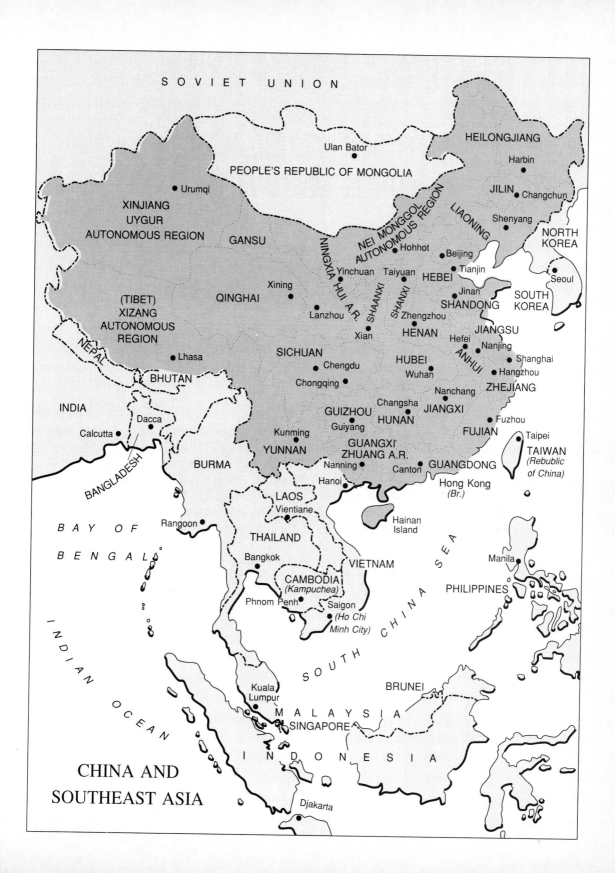

CHINA AND
SOUTHEAST ASIA

C H A P T E R   10

POLITICAL CULTURE AND POLITICAL SOCIALIZATION

What do we know about the political attitudes and ideas of the millions upon millions of people who live in Second World societies? What do they want? Do they support their leaders? Are there signs of psychological and attitudinal change in these societies? How are they responding to the experiences of reform and revolution? These important questions take us to the topics of political culture and political socialization.

Because of the past leaders' commitments to build communism, and because of the importance of the human dimension in the process of political change, the concepts of political culture and political socialization are of special significance in our study. Gabriel Almond, the distinguished American political scientist, has noted, "Every political system is embedded in a particular pattern of orientations of political action."[1] This pattern of attitudes and beliefs that people hold toward their system is referred to as political culture; it represents the orientations that define the setting in which politics takes place. The political culture of the Soviet Union is the total composite of that society's ideas about political life. Orientations about

glasnost and perestroika, justice and democracy, welfare and equality, and reform and revolution represent dimensions of the larger Soviet political culture. As in all other states, these orientations have an influence on power, politics, and policy in Second World political systems.

Although we may refer to a Chinese political culture, a Soviet political culture, and so forth, we should realize that it is a simplification to speak of the total set of attitudes and values of the populace and to consider it a homogeneous whole. Obviously, like other societies, those of the Second World are heterogeneous in their beliefs and values, just as they are in social and economic characteristics. However, when we discuss and compare societies, it is useful to have a concept to refer to the general attitudinal and psychological setting within political systems. Political culture is the term for such a concept.

How can one study something as abstract as political culture? What does one try to observe? Some researchers have conducted massive opinion surveys of large samples of national populations. For example, in their book *The Civic Culture*, Almond and Verba surveyed at-

314

titudes and values of over 5,000 citizens from the United States, Great Britain, West Germany, Italy, and Mexico to better understand the political cultures of these states.[2] Although some Second World states are beginning to allow such studies, this quantitative approach to the study of political culture was generally not possible in Communist Party states in the past because their governments were unwilling to allow Western scholars to study issues that they considered so sensitive. In this book, we take an inductive approach and base our study on a growing body of research conducted by native and foreign scholars. Although this research is not always based on scientific surveys, it draws on the personal contacts and research of scholars who know these countries well.

Political culture has certain things in common with—but is quite distinct from—a state's ideology. Although the term has been conceptualized in many ways, ideology commonly refers to the set of arguments and beliefs used to justify an existing or desired social order. Although there is bound to be considerable overlap, the ideologies of the Second World states deviate in certain important respects from their political cultures. Whereas in the past, Marxist-Leninist ideology traditionally represented the official arguments and beliefs put forth by Communist Parties to explain and justify their social order, the political cultures of Second World countries have always represented many personal values opposed to Marxism-Leninism. Ideology and political culture differ. There is much ideological and cultural change taking place in Second World states, which makes it even more challenging for authorities who hope to mold attitudes among their citizens that correspond with the changing ideology.

This issue and attempts to mold political culture introduce us to the concept of political socialization. Most political scientists conceive of political socialization as the process by which official or prevailing attitudes and beliefs are transmitted to a society, particularly to newcomers, such as children or immigrants. When the Communist Party states suddenly adopted the ideology of Marxism-Leninism in their political past, in a sense all of their citizens were newcomers and great efforts had to be made to inculcate political orientations conducive to the building of socialism. Because the prerevolutionary societies in these countries had distinctive, noncommunist traditions and political cultures of their own, the transmission of new political orientations to the populace was exceedingly difficult. The leaders of the new Marxist-Leninist states realized that if their political and economic policies were to be carried out successfully, traditional political beliefs had to be replaced. In their place, the leaders hoped to develop a new set of attitudes and values, ones that corresponded with and supported their interpretations of Marxist-Leninist doctrine and their drives for modernization and rapid industrialization. As we will see in the pages that follow, this task was more challenging than anyone imagined.

Changing the Traditional Political Cultures

When Vladimir Ilyich Lenin, Mao Zedong, Fidel Castro, and others assumed power in their states, the traditional political cultures were not conducive to, and in many respects were even hostile toward, changes the leaders felt were necessary for building socialism. The political orientations of the people in these countries had been molded over hundreds, even thousands, of years. Centuries of tsarist rule in Russia and imperial rule in China resulted in undemocratic, elitist political cultures. We must remember that most of the Second World societies that became communist were primarily composed of peasants, with the bulk of the population working the land. These people generally accepted the prevailing social hierarchy: the strong ruled, the weak were ruled. In most Second World countries, the traditional belief was that those who governed had been chosen by divine mandate. The coronations and the ritualistic ceremonies such as those accorded the Russian tsars, Chinese emperors, and East European kings and ruling families made the rulers and masses acutely aware of the divine significance of the rulers' power. The masses were expected to remain passively in the background sowing the crops, working in factories, or laboring in whatever jobs they could find. The thought of political participation and the ideas of democracy were as remote as distant America. When the peasants heard news of democratic rule in the West, they neither understood its meaning nor comprehended its significance to their traditional ways of living. As the age of democracy grew in other parts of the globe, the masses of Second World countries remained largely isolated and, for the time being, unaffected by the winds of change.

When the Yugoslav Communist Party seized power in 1945, for example, the existing political culture was based on authoritarian, elitist, and nonparticipant norms. Centuries of foreign domination by the Ottoman and Austro-Hungarian empires as well as the more recent periods of nineteenth- and twentieth-century rule under indigenous authoritarian regimes served to mold a resigned, apathetic, and conformist society. The authoritarian Stalinist approach to political life, initially followed by Tito and the Yugoslav communists at the end of World War II, corresponded with the nonparticipant political culture of the past. The masses had never been widely consulted and involved in the affairs of politics before the war and did not really expect to be included afterward.

In Confucian China, the traditional political culture was steeped in the ideal of harmony with nature and a strict, hierarchical set of social and political relations. Power was entrusted to the emperor or empress, his or her supporting officials, and those who had worked their way up the hierarchy through intellectual attainment. To the masses, political power was the right of the emperor; the hierarchy was viewed as natural and the government tended to be remote. On those few occasions when the common peasant or laborer had contact with the government, the authorities appeared unjust and harsh. Because of this experience, the large bulk of the society was resigned to a life of political passivity and acquiescence. In a large peasant society, the common man and woman had little interest in, and few orientations about, politics. An early Chinese communist leader commented on this fact in 1922:

The peasants take no interest in politics. This is common throughout the whole world, but is particularly true in China. . . . All they care about is having a true Son of Heaven [emperor] to rule them, and a peaceful bumper year.[3]

Mass values about democracy and power in China, Russia, and much of the Second World were shaped by centuries of authoritarian rule. Although the leaders of these countries—the rulers, ministers, counselors, representatives, magistrates, and others who served the empires—possessed a set of political orientations that represented an authoritarian political culture, the masses were characterized by a general absence of political sentiment.[4] They held few political feelings and were uninvolved in politics because of their traditional isolation from political affairs. To transform this massive parochial, nonparticipant sector of society into one that would support and advance the ideas of communist rule was a major task facing the new leaders in the postrevolutionary periods.

Because the leaders of the communist political systems recognized that the building of communism would be difficult, if not impossible, with the political culture (and subcultures) inherited from the presocialist states, they adopted heavy-handed strategies of political socialization to mold the orientations required for their new societies.

Perhaps it should be pointed out that all countries, including the United States, attempt to foster attitudes and beliefs in their people that are supportive of their systems of government. For example, in the United States, children at an early age are taught the Pledge of Allegiance, "The Star Spangled Banner," and the stories of our founding fathers. We may call it civics or citizenship training, but it is political socialization aimed at instructing the newest generation about the values of our political system. The key question in regard to this topic is not whether political socialization exists, for it exists in all societies; we must instead examine who determines what ought to be taught, how it is accomplished, and how far governments go in attempting to change the belief structures of their people.

A variety of different tactics were used over the decades in the Second World countries to reform the minds of the citizenry. After the revolution in China, emphasis was placed on thought reform, self-criticism, and rectification programs; those with "bourgeois mentalities" were given the opportunity to reform themselves and become productive members of Chinese society.[5] In some countries, more coercive methods, such as deportation, imprisonment,

terror, and even death and genocide, were used to mold political cultures. Stalin was notorious for brutal tactics as he ruthlessly sought to transform Soviet society to suit his purposes. Still others used less violent and sometimes more subtle methods. One of Castro's strategies in dealing with Cubans of hostile or nonconforming political orientations was to deport them or simply let them leave. Thousands of Cubans came to the United States during the 1960s and again in 1980 because, among other reasons, they were unable or unwilling to change their beliefs and opinions concerning socialism in Cuba.[6]

There are numerous agents of political socialization (i.e., institutions or instruments by which political values and orientations are transformed) that were at work during the Marxist-Leninist experiments. Among the most important was the family. Although there were some families that were committed to the building of communism in Second World states through the years, there were as many, and perhaps more, who were not. Most families in Second World states historically did more to promote the preservation of traditional (e.g., religious) or familial values than the official, communist values.

One agent of socialization that plagued the socialization intentions of communist leaders was the church. Particularly in the East European states where the Catholic and Orthodox religions are deeply embedded in the cultures of the people, the church proved to be a troublesome institution with which communists had to contend. At some points in communist history, officials undertook aggressive and oppressive campaigns to eradicate religion from their countries. At other points, when they needed to mobilize support for the government and promote unity within the country, they eased their politics of persecution.[7]

After many years of rejecting religion, recent leaders in Second World states have come to accommodate the church. Mikhail Gorbachev was the first Soviet communist leader to meet a Roman Catholic pontiff.

The agent of political socialization that traditional communists took the most interest in and (unlike family life and religion) over which they found it easiest to exert considerable influence was the school. The educational systems in Second World states historically were controlled by the Communist Party. Through the coordinating arm of a central ministry for education, the Communist Parties had great influence in designing curricula, selecting texts, and setting instructional policies within the schools. Although the Party leaders did not typically become directly involved in these activities, they did recommend certain policies, which were implemented through the ministries and by the local organs. The content of courses, textbooks, and the general educational philosophy, however, varied markedly among the different Second World states.

Perhaps the most politicized and ideologically infused education system in communist history was that of the Chinese during the Maoist period (1949–76). During the Great Proletarian Cultural Revolution (GPCR) (1966–69), Maoist doctrine accompanied almost every lesson. In elementary school mathematics, for example, the exploiting capitalist and the downtrodden peasants were typically found in the daily exercises:

PROBLEM: If a peasant works 4 plots of land and the capitalist takes the products of 3, what does that leave the peasant?

The writings of Chairman Mao played a major role in the educational process during the Cultural Revolution. Pictures from China showed the ever-present *Little Red Book* held proudly by the Chinese grade-schooler. Bulletin boards and texts were adorned with pictures of the communist leaders and the slogans they extolled to mobilize the masses. Even at the more advanced levels of Chinese education, including the universities, ideology represented a significant element in the curriculum and course content. One did not even approach the topics of

In Chinese classrooms during the Maoist period, revolutionary posters and slogans accompanied daily lessons. Although the post Mao leaders decreased the emphasis on ideological education, it remains a part of the socialization system.

medicine or physics without recognizing the relevance of Maoist ideology. Western observers witnessed college seminars dedicated solely to the reading of Chairman Mao's revolutionary thought.

Another influential agent of socialization carried out in the past through the schools involved youth organizations. These youth groups ranged from the elementary-grade Young Pioneers to the high-school and college-age youth leagues. Although all Second World states had similar groups, they varied widely in functions and behavior. The Chinese Communist Youth League in the 1970s, for example, constituted the primary training ground for what the leaders called revolutionary successors. It had a militant philosophy and was infused with the Chinese revolutionary spirit. During this period, Young Pioneers in China were even instructed in the arts of making revolution. Whether marching in parades, chanting Maoist slogans, or operating rifles with live ammunition on the firing range, these elementary schoolers were taught the finer points of Maoist strategy for revolutionary warfare.

Social service and political education were, historically speaking, important functions of the organization for teenage youth in the Soviet Union, the Communist Youth League (Komsomol).[8] Former Soviet leader Leonid I. Brezhnev referred to their mission as that of "bringing up youth in the spirit of communist commitment" and of carrying on the "cause of their fathers, the cause of the great Lenin." However, many teenagers in the Soviet Union today seem bored by the group activities; they often complain that they are ineffective organizations for social work and that the activities do not interest them.

The mass media—television, radio, newspapers, books, and the like—historically were also controlled by the Communist Parties and represented important agents of political socialization. In the past, television networks scheduled heavy doses of ideological and political programming. These propaganda programs assumed a variety of formats but always presented the Communist Party, government, and the country's leaders in a complimentary light. Propaganda, historically, has not had the pejorative meaning in Second World states that it typically had held in the West. Lenin felt that all Party members should act as theoreticians, propagandists, agitators, and organizers. Propaganda meant advertising the Communist Party's work in an attempt to win new adherents to the cause. In the past, even those television programs that were expressly intended for entertainment would typically have a political message; the vast majority of novels, short stories, and magazine articles included the same. This concern with ideology had a sobering effect on the written word in all socialist countries. The loading of ideology into almost everything, from newspaper reports to romance novels, severely reduced the quality of writing. Writers unwilling to yield to ideological themes—often some of the very best writers such as Vaclav Havel in Czechoslovakia—were forced to pick other professions to survive.

Although the emphasis was definitely on youth in the socialization process, adults were certainly not ignored. The Communist Parties and trade unions had vast networks concerned with ideological training and propaganda. Often the training was tied to one's job; classes and programs were offered to heighten workers' political consciousness and to call attention to the continuing class struggle. Although many adults ignored such activities, the social pressures were great enough to generate a significant level of participation.

Historically, the primary agent of political socialization in Second World states was the Communist Party itself. As will be noted in more detail in Chapter 11, the Communist Party traditionally controlled public information in the Second World states and, in so doing, played a powerful role in determining what people saw, heard, and learned. Because of their organization and socializing strategy, the Communist Parties attempted to oppose the agents of socialization that ran counter to the desired political culture (e.g., the church, the family) and used those agents that were under their direction (mass media, schools, youth organizations). For example, Communist Party organizations were present in factories, collective farms, and other places of work. Members of these organizations were expected to be exemplary citizens and to set good examples for their peers. In addition, the mere presence of Party members and Party organizations in the work place and throughout the society had a powerful socializing impact of its own. Party propaganda was the responsibility of special departments of the Central Committee in most Communist Parties. "Agitprop" activities (a shortened version of agitation plus propaganda) were controlled by the Communist Parties and furthered by such organizational vehicles as the ZNANIYA (Society for the Dissemination of Political and Scientific Knowledge) Society in the Soviet Union and equivalent organizations in other states.

Finally, in the past when these less coercive agents of socialization failed, the Communist Parties were quite willing to utilize a number of more coercive agencies to deal with citizens who threatened regime goals and political culture. Included in these agencies were local militias, intelligence agencies, and the armed forces. In the Soviet Union, for example, the KGB (Committee for State Security) has been charged with guaranteeing the security of the Soviet state. In exercising this responsibility, the KGB

Science and ideology have coexisted in Soviet education, as shown by the artifacts in this classroom in Moscow. Soviet advances in science attest to the success of its educational system. Success in the area of ideological indoctrination has been far less clear.

(and its counterparts in other Second World states) in the past had wide-ranging authority to combat "counter-revolutionary activities" and "crimes against the state." The frequent presence of unidentified KGB operatives in Communist Party, governmental, military, and other organizations has had a powerful impact on attitudes and behavior in Second World societies.

Now that we have reviewed the traditional political cultures and the historical agents used to change them, we will look at the type of political cultures the communist leaders have desired.

Desired Political Cultures

Although the question of desired political cultures today is in a state of considerable uncertainty and flux, we can examine the type of political cultures those responsible for the building of communism desired in the past. We can get some idea of what the Soviet leaders wanted by reviewing what they have traditionally referred to as the "Moral Code of the Builder of Communism":

Devotion to the pursuit of Communism; love for the socialist homeland and for the countries of socialism;

Conscientious labor for the good of society; whoever does not work does not eat;

The concern of everyone for the conservation and increase of social property;

A high consciousness of social obligation and intolerance toward infringements of social interests;

Collectivism and comradely mutual aid; one for all and all for one;

A humane relationship and mutual respect among people; one person to another person—friend, comrade, and brother;

Integrity and truthfulness, moral purity, simplicity, and humility in social and personal life;

Mutual respect in family life; concern for the upbringing of children;

Implacable opposition to injustice, parasitism, dishonesty, careerism, greed;

The friendship and brotherhood of all the peoples of the USSR; intolerance toward nationalist and racist hostility;

Implacable opposition toward the enemies of communism; the pursuit of peace and the freedom of nations.

Mao also recognized the importance of political socialization and the desirability of a new political culture. More than forty years ago, he noted:

It is necessary to train a great many people as vanguards of the revolution. People who are politically far-sighted. People imbued with the spirit of struggle and self-sacrifice. People with largeness of mind who are loyal, active, and upright. People who never pursue selfish interests, but are whole-heartedly for liberation of the nation and society. People who fear no difficulties, but remain steadfast and advance courageously in the face of difficulties. People who are neither high or mighty nor seekers after the limelight, but are conscientious and full of practical sense. If China has a host of such vanguard elements, the tasks of the Chinese revolution will be successfully fulfilled.[9]

Like the Soviet leaders, Mao also wanted an ideologically committed and politically active society. Mao placed great emphasis on political participation and, during certain periods of his rule, mobilized what might have been the highest level of mass political activity in modern history. Yet Mao and the Chinese leaders also placed severe limits on the nature of participation. The people were expected to work within the system, and this meant parroting Maoist slogans and supporting the official Party doctrine. There was to be no dissent but rather a united, mobilized populace led by the so-called Great Helmsman, Mao Zedong.

Mao's successors also recognized the importance of political culture to Chinese development and attempted to outline its ideal features. A 1980 statement emphasized the following points:

1. loving the socialist motherland;
2. utilizing Western things useful to the four modernizations and rejecting things unhealthy and against the national spirit;
3. making the ideal of communism a guide to action; and
4. cultivating and strengthening communist ethics.[10]

The political culture desired by the post-Mao leaders has been what we might call both "Red" and "expert." Red means that the culture is to be communist; it should recognize the importance and validity of communism and abide by a code of communist morality. Expert means that the culture also should be based on knowledge, skills, and scientific know-how. The political culture desired in contemporary China is based on many of the ideological principles of the Maoist period but it adds a new dimension—knowledge—which is required by an emphasis on modernization. Although the post-Mao leaders have experimented with the development of a more modern political culture (i.e., less ideology, more skills and knowledge), they have been explicit in setting certain boundaries and reminding the people that the Chinese Communist Party (CCP) is still in charge.

Although the revolutionary changes that came to Eastern Europe at the end of the 1980s have put the issues of political socialization and culture in a state of uncertainty and flux, the desired political cultures of the past show considerable similarity to what was desired in the Soviet Union. Like their Soviet counterparts, through the first few decades of communist rule the East European leaders were intent on molding the dedicated and loyal citizens needed for the building of communism. This would require a "new communist person," one who would support socialism and the Communist Party leadership and contribute unselfishly to the common good.

In the early 1970s Ivan Volgyes conducted a study of these East European socialization efforts.[11] Volgyes' content analysis of East European newspapers identified eight themes that captured what was desired by the Communist Party leaders. Rank-ordered for their importance, from the most frequently found to least found, the themes were:

1. the building of socialism
2. anti-imperialism
3. socialist morality
4. patriotism
5. anti-individualism
6. socialist commonwealth
7. antinationalism
8. anti-Stalinism

This ranking indicates that the leaders' socialization efforts as reflected in East European newspapers in the early 1970s were most concerned with the people's commitment to the building of socialism (or communism). They also desired a commitment to anti-imperialism, socialist morality, patriotism, and other important themes. As we will note later, their efforts did not succeed.

Political Cultures Today

Political cultures in Second World states today are extremely complex and in a state of considerable flux. They are complex because they are a consequence of the traditional and diverse political cultures that preceded the establishment of communism; the revolutionary cultures that Lenin, Mao, and other communist leaders attempted to establish after the advent of communism; and the dramatically changing environments in which individuals and groups find themselves in these states today. Contemporary political cultures are not homogeneous in the sense that everyone holds the values and orientations that were once desired by the ruling elites. Rather, the diverse and heterogeneous political cultures today show all of the complexities, paradoxes, and uncertainties of societies undergoing rapid social, political, and economic change.

Because we want to examine those orientations that most significantly affect politics, we will address those related to the four values outlined in the introduction of this book: power, respect, well-being, and enlightenment. For a political system to allocate these values in an authoritative and peaceful manner, the citizens of a particular state ideally should have reasonably uniform expectations concerning their proper distribution. If 50 percent of the population feels that political power ought to be totally confined to a small number of leaders within the Communist Party, and the other 50 percent strongly feel it should be broadly shared among the entire society or by various opposition groups, it will be difficult for policy makers to satisfy all the people with their decisions. On the other hand, if the society widely shares one distribution or the other, or if its members are largely apathetic, the policy makers will have an easier time governing the society. A useful way of viewing the political cultures, then, will be to examine mass orientations and behavior relating to the four values defined earlier.

Power

The first value and dimension of political culture involves the role of the individual citizen in the political system. Should Soviet, Chinese, or East European citizens be involved, or should they leave political affairs in the hands of a small number of political elites? Should their society be a multiparty system where various individuals and groups can compete democratically for political power? Based on the Marxist goal of worker control and mass participation, traditional communist leaders purportedly wanted to destroy what they perceived to be dictatorial precommunist power relations that prohibited mass involvement in political affairs. These elitist power relations were to be replaced with what they argued would become a more democratic set of social and political relationships. Accordingly, such institutions as legislatures, public courts, and mass organizations were established in all Second World states to facilitate, according to the communists, the goals of worker and mass participation. Although some involved in the early communist experiments may have been committed to developing democratic political cultures and political systems, the totalitarianism brought about by Stalinist rule quashed most hopes surrounding these idealistic goals. What developed were authoritarian political cultures where Party leaders ruled and the rest of society was expected to follow.

Two leading scholars of Soviet political culture used the term *subject-participatory* to describe this aspect of the political culture of the 1960s and 1970s in the USSR.[12] Barghoorn noted "subject participatory denotes the relationship among Soviet citizens of subordination to superiors in one or more bureaucratic chains of command and the obligation of all citizens to do their best to assure the performance of the collective."[13] Barghoorn contended that although some political participation occurred in the Soviet communist past, it did so "within a framework of values, directives, and controls emanating from a ramified national bureaucracy subject to the commands of the Moscow Politburo."[14] Some observers of the Soviet Union feel that participation today is much less controlled than Barghoorn described it in the 1960s and 1970s.

However, it is clear that over the many years of pre- and postcommunist Soviet development, political orientations reflecting the subject-participatory culture have been deeply ingrained in the society. The typical Soviet citizen, whether inhabiting the far eastern reaches of the Russian Republic or the political center in Moscow, possesses a set of beliefs and attitudes defining his or her subject role in the political system.

Gorbachev attempted to change some of this and supported more democratic power relations after coming to power in March 1985. Speaking directly to the question of democratization and perestroika, Gorbachev argued that the Soviet Union could not succeed in restructuring and reforming Soviet society unless the people became more directly involved in political life.

And although Gorbachev and the Communist Party leaders still held the preponderance of power in the late 1980s, important changes were taking place in their and in most other Second World states. Although the Communist Parties wanted to remain the central source of power in the political systems, the leaders recognized the importance of expanding more meaningful mass participation in the affairs of state. This meant giving lower-level socioeconomic and political organizations—and the people themselves—greater opportunities to become involved. It meant making meaningful participation a reality. In this regard, one of Gorbachev's goals was to make the people feel that they had a stake in saving and rebuilding socialism.

What had developed over the years in the Soviet Union and most other Second World societies were feelings of helplessness, passivity, and cynicism among the people. Because the authorities were in charge and the risks of trying to influence policy and bring about change were considerable, most people became politically passive and alienated. Being rational human beings, they concluded that the high costs of trying to participate outweighed any benefits. They blamed, at least privately, their societies' ills on the leaders and were cynical about the leaders' promises and exhortations. This was one of the major obstacles that Gorbachev and reformers like him had to overcome. To build a healthier political culture conducive to Soviet development, they had to convince the people that they were serious about and valued their participation in political life. They had to instill a new sense of pride, involvement, and commitment among the people, and the people had to come to feel that they could contribute to and benefit from the reform process. Some of this began to happen with the reform movement of the late 1980s, but such changes will not come easily or be cost free to the Soviet Union. Political scientists have established that political cultures are slow to change. Yet, although much remains uncertain about how the Soviet people will view participation and power relations in their future, it is clear that change is possible.

Gorbachev's reform program of the late 1980s reminds us that it may be easier to change a leader's ideas about politics than the people's ideas. No one could deny the new ideas coming out of the Soviet Party hierarchy in the late 1980s, but much of the populace remained highly conservative and cautious abut change. Many were afraid of glasnost and democracy. Al-though the Party wanted people to get involved, to do so meant they had to make choices, to take a position, to "stick their neck out." Given past experiences in the Soviet Union, many people were reluctant to do this. However, Gorbachev and the other leaders tried to convince the people that they were serious about democratization and that the people would benefit by becoming more involved in the political process.

Even more significant developments took place in Eastern Europe during the late 1980s. The leaders and the people were viewing Gorbachev's reform efforts and wondering about their relevance in and implications for their societies. Throughout most of the decade, the Polish communist authorities fought to deny the independent labor movement Solidarity an official role in the political process. In the early 1980s, they temporarily imprisoned Solidarity's leader, Lech Walesa, declared martial law, and stood firmly opposed to most efforts to democratize the political process. In this repressive context, Polish political culture grew more and more cynical. The people lost faith in their leaders and political system. They identified more with Solidarity, the Catholic church, and various opposition movements than with the communist leaders. There was an extraordinarily high level of negativism and cynicism throughout the society, and the country was in a crisis and headed in a destructive direction during most of the 1980s. However, toward the end of the decade, the leaders showed greater flexibility toward the possibility of political reform, the role of Solidarity, and the opening of the political system. To bring about progress in Poland, the leaders began to appreciate the need to democratize the political process and convince the people that it was in their interest to participate, and by the late 1980s, the Polish political system was undergoing significant reform.

Soviet May Day parades in the era of glasnost are not the carefully staged displays of Marxist-Leninist and patriotic fervor they once were. At the 1990 parade, an environmentally conscious demonstrator holds a placard that reads "other countries do not know where man breathes so freely," while wearing a gas mask. After years of promoting the Soviet environment as being cleaner than those found in the capitalist West, Soviet officials have more recently admitted that environmental conditions in their country are deplorable and will take years to remedy.

Discussions among the communists, Solidarity, the Catholic church, and others—the so-called roundtable talks of 1989—resulted in democratic reforms, including free elections. These elections brought about a democratic expression of the will of the Polish people and resulted in the rejection of the communist slate of candidates and the first noncommunist government in contemporary Eastern Europe. These and other developments suggest important changes in the values surrounding political power in contemporary Poland.

The people's values about power were changing elsewhere in Eastern Europe in the late 1980s. Gorbachev's glasnost, perestroika, and democratization programs were spreading across the borders into all of the states of the region. The Soviets encouraged East European reform and said that they would not intervene and scuttle the democratization movements as they had been prone to do in the past. These and other factors encouraged a major democratization movement that swept across Eastern Europe and resulted in the dramatic decline of communist rule in 1989. Communist leaders were forced to step down. Citizens took to the streets chanting, "We are the people." Groups of citizens organized opposition parties. Legislatures became meaningful institutions of democratic discussion and policy making. Political cultures were being transformed. The people had become a powerful force in East European politics.

Unlike Lenin and Stalin, who had a deep-seated distrust of the untutored and politically unsophisticated rank-and-file people, Mao was convinced of the need for mass involvement. The adventurous Great Leap Forward and the turbulent Cultural Revolution exemplified the Maoist concept of mass participation. At the height of the Cultural Revolution, Mao orchestrated the induction of a large number of mass elements into the Communist Party hierarchy and gave them positions of Party and government responsibility at all levels. For a time, even the Central Committee of the Communist Party included representatives drawn from model workers among the Chinese masses.

It is, however, inappropriate to equate Mao's emphasis on mass participation with pluralist, participatory democracy. In the final analysis, Maoist participation primarily served as an instrument of legitimation and mobilization. The populace had little or no influence over the decision-making process and had to operate within the parameters of political behavior as defined by the Maoist leaders. Cooperation or recruitment of mass elements was totally at the leaders' discretion. The people's representatives were only a cog in the Maoist political machine

and wielded little real power. They were not even allowed to work in the interest of their constituents. They generally occupied a supernumerary position, and when they had outlived their usefulness or when there was a major political reversal, they would be quickly dismissed.

Although it is still difficult to accurately judge to what extent the traditional elitist culture was replaced by the Maoist brand of populism in the 1950s and 1960s, there is reason to believe that some of the young people came to assume somewhat more participatory values and a more active, yet constrained, political role. There was always an undercurrent of opposition in China, but political dissidents were seldom in the national spotlight until the 1980s when they, too, emerged from anonymity and obscurity to be a formidable force. Astrophysicist Fang Lizhi, outspokenly critical of the communist system and ardently supportive of the democratic movement, has been viewed by some as the nation's conscience. Maverick writers like Liu Binyan, Wang Ruowang, and Wu Zhuguang have castigated the radical excesses and perversities of the past and openly deplored the Chinese leadership's procrastination in implementing political reforms. Even prominent Marxist theoreticians, such as Wang Luoshui and Su Shaozhi, challenged some fundamental premises of the official ideology and advocated profound reform of the obsolescent Marxist and Maoist orthodoxy that had put a constraint on Chinese modernization and democratization.

The 1980s were a period of growing openness in China (i.e., until the fateful crackdown that became know as the Tiananmen Square massacre of 1989). During this period, intellectuals and students were demanding more power for the people and a less dictatorial role for the Chinese Communist Party. They wanted to see the value of power more democratically shared, rather than monopolized by the communist elites. Although it was difficult to discern the aspirations of the rank-and-file Chinese, most observers foresaw a trend toward more democratic values in the 1980s, something akin to what seemed to be taking place in the Soviet Union and Eastern Europe.

These hopes and aspirations were brutally crushed in June 1989 when the student occupation of Tiananmen Square in the capital of Beijing was violently put down by the Chinese Army. The students had been demonstrating for democratic reforms and challenged the leadership to make the kinds of changes that were being made in the Soviet Union and Eastern Europe. Although it is too early to assess the full consequences of the Chinese crackdown, it is apparent that the democratic aspirations in Chinese political culture suffered a major setback.

Some have argued that there have always been participatory values in the Chinese communist experience that related to political culture and the political process. Some observers saw Mao's China (1949–76) as a system of mass involvement and referred to it as a mobilization system in which all individuals—leaders and peasants alike—were expected to become actively involved in the struggle for socialist construction.[15] From the early years of Chinese communism until Chairman Mao's death in 1976, Mao was the primary mobilizer and undertook a variety of campaigns and programs to encourage political participation. Following the ideal of populism, the leaders expected all citizens to participate in communal affairs and to serve the people.

Although communist leaders and middle-level political, social, and economic officials tend to support the principles of self-managing socialism, they are still uncertain about sharing policymaking power with the people and relinquishing

their positions of control. They may theoretically share and support the ideals of a more democratic society, but they remain skeptical of the efficiency, effectiveness, and overall feasibility of industrial or multiparty democracy. And although the mass populace tends to distrust the sincerity of its leaders, it also has certain doubts about the desirability of mass democracy. Is it the most efficient and productive system? Do the masses have the knowledge and training to assume such integral responsibilities in political and economic life?

Despite the exceptions in China just discussed, values surrounding power in many of the Second World countries today have an opportunity to change. With the democratic developments in Eastern Europe, for example, people are finding new opportunities to speak out, to become involved in political campaigns, and to vote. These developments are all very new and we are not certain how all of the people will react. We do know, however, that the traditional norms about power relations are changing in these societies and that important elements of the traditional political cultures are undergoing change.

Respect

In his opening remarks at the 24th Congress of the Communist Party of the Soviet Union in 1971, General Secretary Brezhnev spoke of the need for action, "whereby trust in and respect for people is combined with principled exactingness toward them" to create a "businesslike comradely atmosphere." What have trust and respect meant in the Soviet context and why are they important in the building of communism? The qualities of which Brezhnev spoke are a vital element in the political process because they pertain to the subjective feelings governing interpersonal and intergroup relations. Traditionally, citizens in Communist Party states were told to be comrades, which meant that they were to have a common outlook and common interests. To promote comradeliness meant to encourage a common class perspective. Communist citizens were expected to possess similar attitudes and to relate to one another in a respectful, trusting way.

As we observed the ethnic strife that pervaded certain Second World states at the beginning of this decade, we can appreciate the importance of a cohesive community of people who can work together and relate to one another on the basis of trust and respect. Clearly, the diverse peoples of the Soviet Union are still unable to do this. Until Gorbachev came to power, Soviet authorities did everything possible to convince the rest of the world that they had solved their nationality problem. Before the coming of glasnost, Soviet authorities were able to suppress and cover up many of the national cleavages and animosities that existed in Soviet society. However, as Soviet society opened up in the 1980s, it became increasingly apparent that an ideal political culture based on values of comradeliness and goodwill had not been established. Violent displays of ethnonationalism—for example, between the Armenians and Azerbaijanis in the late 1980s—showed that these historical animosities continued to boil. The Estonian, Latvian, and Lithuanian distrust and, in some cases, hatred toward the Russians showed that ethnicity and nationalism still divided people in what is supposed to be a Soviet *union*.

Gorbachev spoke frequently at the turn of the decade about the need of the diverse Soviet people to respect one another. We are one family, he said, and in order for families to survive and flourish, individuals must tolerate and support one another. Given the historical an-

imosities and cleavages in Soviet society, this is no easy undertaking.

Are the Chinese doing any better in developing respectful and comradely relations among their people? In this regard, years ago, Ezra F. Vogel outlined the original Maoist objectives as well as the important changes he thought were taking place during the early period of Chinese communist rule.[16] Vogel described a movement away from what we know as friendship (a personal, private relationship among close companions) to the concept of comradeship. Comradeship in the Maoist context was to be based on a universal ethic in which individuals were to treat all other individuals as equal members of a political community. With the emphasis on collective rather than private relationships, comrades were obligated to mutually reinforcing roles within their society. The emphasis on the collective and helping was reflected in the Maoist slogan and required reading, "Serve the People."[17] In attempting to establish comradely relations of this sort in China, the Western concept of private trust was suppressed. Under the system of comradeship, one would not tell a comrade a secret, something one wanted withheld from others. If a comrade knew, for instance, that you cheated on your income tax or that you took more than your allotment of rice from the storehouse, he or she would be expected to report you to the people's court. If you were found guilty of these transgressions, you would engage in self-criticism and admit to your crime against the people. In attempting to establish a public surveillance system where no indiscretions avoided the public eye, Maoist China tried to build a society free of corruption, crime, and graft. The personal costs reminded some of the coldhearted efficiency of Orwell's "Big Brother," and the long-term benefits were of questionable significance.

Most observers agree that the intensive Maoist political indoctrination failed to dethrone the Chinese traditional culture. Ultimately, it was unable to expunge the faith in interpersonal relationships from the minds of the leaders, not to mention the common people. In the twilight of the Mao era, patronage networks played a pivotal role in political elite recruitment and circulations. After Mao's demise, nepotism and favoritism again gained ascendancy. In many cases, Communist Party leaders seemed to accept ascriptive attributes such as family background and blood lineage in lieu of achievements and meritocratic standards as criteria for political promotion.

In the post-Mao era, the emphasis on comradeship and other more ideological themes decreased. Groupism, altruism, and other desired Maoist values were deemphasized, and materialism and consumerism set in. The post-Mao leadership lifted the taboo against material incentives and encouraged private enterprise, at least on a small scale. "To get rich is glorious" became a leading slogan of the 1980s. The post-Mao ideology posited a stereotype of an exemplary citizen who could reconcile political rectitude with business acumen. In this context, the nation approached a money-making frenzy. The principle of service to the people went into abeyance, and the life of most people, be they student, teacher, worker, or soldier, revolved around his or her performance with respect to finances. At various times, some leaders, obviously overwhelmed by twinges of nostalgia, tried to revive the cult of Lei Feng and Wang Jie, the puritanical heroes whom Mao put forward as paragons of virtue, but these leaders generally ended up as objects of ridicule. Their plan went awry because people dismissed the Maoist values as anachronisms. Some suggest that the Chinese Communist Party's Tiananmen Square massacre of June 1989 proves that the Party's austere socialist values can be imposed only by force.

In Eastern Europe, respect among people, and between the people and communist authorities, declined precipitously in the postwar period. Much of this resulted from the Soviet Union's imposition of a Stalinist model of government on societies that were largely opposed to communist rule. Because the people were forced to accept political and economic systems they despised, they engaged in fraudulence and subterfuge to get around the system. This involved blackmarket financial affairs, bribes, political and economic favoritism, corruption, and the like.

Another feature of the Stalinist model involved the coercive elements of the secret police and political informants. Because many members of the society were on the payrolls of the Communist Parties to keep an eye on everyone from acknowledged dissidents to rank-and-file citizens, there was a continual element of suspicion in many of the interpersonal relationships within the society. Although the official ideology preached comradely relations among the people, this suspicion and other consequences of the Stalinist system did much to impede those relations. There tended to be more fear, distrust, and suspicion than trust, respect, and comradeship in the East European states under communist rule.

There was also little respect between the people and their communist rulers. The people did not respect the communists because they considered them, for the most part, corrupt instruments of Soviet imperialism. As time passed and the communist authorities were unable to provide the socialist paradise they had promised, the people's respect for the leaders declined further. The leaders, in turn, showed little respect for the people. The communist authorities considered themselves the "vanguard of the

330

people" and showed little sensitivity to the needs and concerns of the common people. They became isolated, often living in opulent and privileged settings, and showed little respect for the rank-and-file worker.

Well-Being

What are Second World attitudes and aspirations concerning the value of well-being? What do the people expect in the way of health care, social services, and consumer goods? What are their attitudes concerning a fair and proper distribution of these values? At the 24th Soviet Communist Party Congress in 1971, General Secretary Brezhnev announced, "The growth of the people's well-being is the supreme goal of the Party's economic policy." At the 25th Party Congress five years later, he noted that the most important goal remained "a further increase in the people's well-being." That was to involve improvements in working and living conditions; progress in public health, culture, and education; and everything that facilitates "improvement of the socialist way of life." Similar pledges were given by Gorbachev at more recent Party Congresses. But what do the people think of these pledges and the state of well-being in their society?

First, we should note that the Soviet Union is a welfare state that was founded upon a commitment to meet the needs of its people. It spends the equivalent of billions of dollars on education, health care, social security, and, at tremendous cost, on the massive bureaucracy that coordinates these programs. However, in contrast to the leaders' promises of upgrading the material and social well-being of the Soviet populace, the contemporary scene shows considerable shortcomings. There are critical shortages in housing and basic foodstuffs as well as poor service in many of those programs (e.g., medical and dental care) the regime has prided itself on the most.

The dominant orientations of the Soviet populace reflect the contradiction between the communist ideal, where goods and services are to be in abundance and allocated on the basis of need, and the Soviet reality of reward on the basis of work. For the most part, the more poorly paid seem reconciled to their less privileged position in the income hierarchy, whereas the better paid tend to believe that a differential system of rewards is the only fair and reasonable way to handle income.

The American visitor views the Soviet living standard as one of general deprivation. To us, the most striking feature of this aspect of Soviet political culture is the general passivity of the population in accepting the status quo. Although there were some strikes and signs of discontent in the late 1980s, most people accepted their circumstances with little hope for change. Most Soviets neither work very hard nor expect very much. A commonly heard saying in the USSR captures the average citizen's values: "We pretend to work and they pretend to pay us." Soviet values are not conducive to fulfilling the productive potential of a country with considerable human and natural resources. These are the values that have contributed to the stagnation of Soviet development.

But how do Soviet citizens view their living standards and their personal well-being? One effort to find out in the 1980s was the Soviet Interview Project (SIP), a major study by Western social scientists to discover from Soviet emigrants how they saw their lives and the Soviet system. The data were gathered from interviews with 2,793 Soviet emigrants who arrived in the United States between 1979 and 1983. There are, of course, biases in a survey of this sort; the respondents were emigrants, which might suggest that they would have attitudes more critical of the Soviet system and quality of life than those of Soviet citizens who did not emigrate. Although these and other possible sources of bias no doubt affected the interview project results, the data do reveal some interesting and useful insights about Soviet political culture.

The Soviet interviewees were positive toward some aspects of their systems and negative about others. For example, the interviewees were asked for evaluations of their standard of living, housing, and other aspects related to the quality of their physical well-being. Although these people had chosen to leave the Soviet Union, they were surprisingly satisfied with their former standard of living, housing, jobs, and health care systems (see Table 10.1). When combining the "very satisfied" and "somewhat satisfied" responses, we see that about 60 percent were satisfied with their standard of living and health

care, 70 percent with their housing, and 80 percent with their jobs.

If these Soviet citizens were reasonably satisfied with their physical quality of life, why did they choose to leave the Soviet Union? The interviewers asked this question and found that whereas only 27 percent considered an economic motive as an important reason, more than 40 percent cited ethnic, religious, and political reasons. Interestingly, the Soviet interviewees did not show as much dissatisfaction as we might expect with what we in the West see as an inferior quality of life. There were, however, aspects of the Soviet system that they would have liked to change. When responding to the question posed in Table 10.2, the political system was clearly the leading candidate for change. The other aspects of the Soviet system they would have liked to alter represented a variety of political and economic issues that Gorbachev and the other Soviet leaders are now addressing.

Table 10.1 Self-Assessed Satisfaction SIP General Survey

		How satisfied were you with:				
		Standard of Living	Housing	Goods	Job	Health Care
Very satisfied	% =	11.3	23.3	5.1	31.8	19.3
Somewhat satisfied	% =	48.8	43.8	17.8	47.1	42.6
Somewhat dissatisfied	% =	25.2	13.7	23.2	13.5	21.3
Very dissatisfied	% =	14.7	19.2	53.9	7.6	16.8
TOTAL	N =	2,750	2,770	2,738	2,238	2,680
Missing values	N =	43	23	55	555	113

(*Source*) SIP General Survey Codebook. Adapted from Daniel N. Nelson and Roger B. Anderson, eds., *Soviet-American Relations* (Wilmington, Del.: Scholarly Resources Inc., 1988), p. 4.

Table 10.2   What Things in the Soviet System Would You Be Sure to Change?

	1st Answer (%)	2nd Answer (%)	3rd Answer (%)	Total (%)
Political system	27.0	6.6	6.5	40.1
Allow private enterprise	9.3	10.5	9.8	29.6
Control of speech	3.5	8.8	13.6	25.9
Collective-farm system	9.4	9.3	7.1	25.8
Enforce rights	3.5	11.1	10.2	24.8
One-party system	6.3	6.0	4.4	16.7
Economic planning	2.4	3.3	3.8	9.5
Internal passports	1.3	3.6	3.1	8.0
Everything	6.5	0.5	—	7.0

(*Source*) SIP General Survey Codebook. Adapted from Daniel N. Nelson and Roger B. Anderson, eds., *Soviet-American Relations* (Wilmington, Del.: Scholarly Resources Inc., 1988), p. 19.

An important component of this dimension of political culture concerns a society's expectations for the future. Past Soviet policy regarding material well-being has been very sensitive, almost paranoid, on the question of rising expectations. One of the reasons for the Communist Party leadership's traditional reluctance to loosen foreign travel has no doubt been tied to their fear of increased mass expectations, which the government would be unable to meet. Rising and unmet expectations have been more prevalent and, as a result, more of a problem among East European populations, where contact with the West has been greater. In addition, the populations of these countries have been less passive than the Soviet populace and frequently have made their feelings known.

The Polish people have vented their frustrations on numerous occasions. Just before Christmas in 1970, for example, the Polish leaders instituted a major price increase in a variety of foodstuffs. Perceiving a substantial reduction in their level of material well-being, the Polish populace protested the government's policy, rioted in some coastal cities, stopped working, and burned down the Communist Party headquarters in one major city. This action led to the removal of the Party leader, Wladyslaw Gomulka, and abolition of the price increases. The next Party leader, Edward Gierek, attempted a new set of price increases in 1976 and also encountered mass dissatisfaction. The government was forced once again to rescind the increases. Gierek was ousted in 1980 during the workers' strikes, when he, too, proved incapable of meeting the aspirations and demands of the Polish people. The explosions of mass discontent throughout Eastern Europe in 1989 had a distinct economic base and represented the people's rising expectations. The resulting political changes in Eastern Europe call attention to the power of a society's expectations and the impact that orientations concerning the fair and proper allocation of well-being can have on political life.

These developments also have implications for the Soviet Union. As the awareness and sophistication of the Soviet populace have increased with the policy of glasnost, we have seen them develop more critical attitudes and become more involved in important questions of social and political affairs. By 1990, many Soviet officials believed that they were running short on time; if significant improvements were not made in the standard of living, mass unrest would develop in Soviet society.

With the Maoist emphasis on equality and the collectivity, the Chinese people were to deemphasize private material interests and to work for the interests of society as a whole. To solve the problems of mass starvation and the general deprivation that characterized much of Chinese society at the time of the communist assumption of power in 1949, a massive program of economic redistribution was adopted. Because egalitarianism was not previously a dominant part of Chinese political culture, redistribution emphasizing material equality did not meet with universal approval. This became a focal point of Chinese socialization efforts, and during the radical 1966–76 period, the Chinese moved decisively to promote equality of well-being. Subsequently, these values were revised as the leaders moved to establish a link between individual effort and individual reward.

For example, in the 1980s, "from each according to his abilities, to each according to his contribution" was construed as an endorsement and justification of inequality in distribution. People were exhorted to improve their standards of living through hard work and private initiative. They were dissuaded from envying others' affluent lives and told that wealthy people and societies worked hard to earn what they enjoyed. As a result, a new generation of wealthy people began to emerge in China. Although some economic effects of the policy trickled down to the broader population and the regime legislated for some safeguards against the income and social polarization that began to result, relative

deprivation had become a major social problem and irritant in China by the end of the 1980s. A large segment of the population who considered themselves to be the losers in the post-Mao era resented their failure and the beneficiaries of the economic reforms. It was hard for those who became accustomed to more equal distribution in China to acquiesce to the widening gap between themselves and others. In the late 1980s, there were numerous reports of sporadic strikes and demonstrations in protest against the new economic policy.

In Eastern Europe during this same period, societal values concerning well-being were marked by anger, frustration, and hostility toward the communist governments. With stagnant economies and spiraling inflation, standards of living were dropping precipitously. The people were angry and outspokenly critical of their leaders. When East Europeans remembered the better times of the past and looked across their borders at the relative affluence in West European countries, they felt a deep sense of deprivation. The presence of relative deprivation reached revolutionary levels in the late 1980s and contributed to the changes in political leadership and orientation that are described elsewhere in this book.

Today the East European systems appear to be moving in a direction that will take them further away from social equality in well-being. This move in the direction of privatization and away from state socialism inevitably will result in the state having even less control over the growing economic inequalities that are likely to develop. It will be interesting to see how the East European people react to these new developments.

Overall, one gets the impression that self-interest is the dominant value defining well-being in most societies, including the Second World societies. Although there are differences among people and countries, most individuals tend to place their personal interests before those of the collectivity. If the leaders of these states were suddenly to adopt the principle, "from each according to his abilities, *to each according to his needs*," people would probably react according to how this new policy would affect them. If they expected to raise their level of well-being, they would tend to support the new policy. If they were engineers, successful writers, or athletes and already making and enjoying more than they really needed, they would be likely to oppose it. In other words, attitudes and values concerning well-being in most Second World societies may not be all that different from those in the West.

Enlightenment

The final dimension of political culture to be examined concerns the value of enlightenment. After seizing power, communist leaders set out to develop a new set of values, ideas, skills, and behaviors—in other words, a new socialist being—to begin the building of communism. Thus, one way of examining the enlightenment dimension of political culture is to examine the people in terms of a set of standards outlined by T.H. Chen to describe this new being.[18]

1. *Absolute selflessness*. The model Maoist citizen, according to Chen, was to hold no ambitions beyond serving the cause of the revolution and China. In traditional communist ideological parlance, selflessness was an expansive and comprehensive concept signifying unreserved and steadfast commitment to communism, patriotism, and collectivism and unconditional subordination of personal interests to those of the revolution, motherland, and one's peers. Paul Kochakin, a legendary hero in Nikolai Ostrovsky's autobiographical novel

The Making of Steel, became a household name during the Stalinist era in the USSR. The Soviet propagandists conferred an aura of sainthood on him because he personified selfless and wholehearted dedication to the Bolshevik Revolution, for which he sacrificed his youth, his love, his family, and his health.

The Maoist conception of selflessness was capsulized and embodied in Mao's "Three Much Read Articles," which moralized about the desirability of selflessness as a revolutionary virtue. The trio idolized and idealized by Mao—a contemporary soldier, a foreign volunteer doctor, and a fictitious ancient character—were designated as role models for the whole population.

Although the Chinese and other communist leaders sought to instill the quality of selflessness among their citizens, they were largely unsuccessful. Most people living in Second World states are patriotic and may at times be willing to sacrifice their individual interests for what they perceive to be in the best interests of their country. But in everyday life, one gets the impression that they think first of themselves, then of their families and friends, and then perhaps remotely of their fellow citizens and country.

The grandiose Great Leap Forward movement in China, premised on mass spontaneity, voluntarism, and selflessness, ended up a fiasco largely because people placed personal concerns above those of the collective. Major components of the movement, such as communalization, egalitarianism, and abolition of material incentives, did not correspond with people's personal value preferences. No matter how inspiring and uplifting the Maoist exhortations were, the populace was soon disenchanted and demoralized, and the Maoist attempt to ignore technological and physical constraints and build progress on human willpower collapsed.

The call for selfless devotion in China rose to a crescendo during the Cultural Revolution. Because the Maoists drew an analogy between self-centeredness and villainy, there was a stigma about showing any concern for oneself. Posters bearing Mao's dictum, "Serve the people," were ubiquitous and people vied with one another in reproaching themselves for their alleged failures to comply with Mao's instruction in a daily liturgy of pledging allegiance to the principle of "combating selfishness." Anyone who had the audacity to openly work in his own self-interests would incur severe criticism and become an object of ridicule. However, this does not mean that Maoist China became a virtuocracy and every citizen a paragon of selflessness. The irony was that as the Maoist moralizing reached its greatest height, the social moral code disintegrated.

During the post-Mao era, the Chinese leadership downplayed the significance of selflessness. Generally speaking, four factors contributed to its decline. First, the value seems to be in conflict with human nature in China. On the one hand, Chinese take pride in helping others. On the other hand, when it comes to a question between personal and public interests, they generally feel that the former should prevail over the latter. Second, a disproportionately large segment of the population lived through the ordeal of persecution and other trials and tribulations during the Cultural Revolution. When their positions were precarious, human instinct for survival would override other considerations, and altruism was considered a luxury they could not afford. Third, the Maoist leaders themselves did not always set a good example. Their addiction to power belied their hypocrisy and selfishness in the eyes of many Chinese citizens. Fourth, continuous emphasis on selflessness would be in conflict with the resurrection of material incentives and private

initiative and stifle efforts to rehabilitate and revitalize the economy.

The political cultures characterizing Soviet and East European societies also fail to show the selflessness desired under communism. In environments of economic hardship and shortage, people have a tendency to put their personal interests before those of others. Self-interests appear to transcend selflessness in most Second World societies today.

2. *Obedience to the Communist Party*. Like selflessness, commitment to the leaders and to the Party was once intended to be a dominant feature of communist political culture. Chen quotes the words of the song "East is Red," which the Chinese children were taught to express their worship of Chairman Mao:

The East is Red,
The sun rises.
China has brought forth a Mao Zedong.
He works for the People's happiness.
He is the people's great savior.

Chairman Mao loves the people,
He is our guide.
He leads us onward
To build the new China.

The Communist Party is like the sun,
Whenever it shines, there is light.
Where there's the Communist Party,
There the people will win liberation.

To instill in the citizenry a deep sense of reverence for and submission to the Communist Party and its leadership, the Maoists portrayed a pantheon of communist heroes. The most prominent among them was Lei Feng, an army squad leader posthumously lionized for his martyrdom, heroism, and selflessness.

Although support and respect for the Communist Parties and leadership have been desired features of all Second World political cultures, they clearly have been absent in most. In many of these countries, the Communist Parties have been totally discredited in the eyes of the people. Why should the people obey a Party that today is generally viewed as having ruined the country? The recent rejection of Communist Party candidates in East European elections has displayed the peoples' values on this issue.

In China, the Maoist regime's political excesses and poor performance over the years, especially during the Cultural Revolution, alienated much of the populace and compromised the Party's reputation. By the eve of Mao's death, both his and the Party's prestige plummeted to a nadir. Popular resentment of endless power struggles and economic shortcomings translated into a skepticism of the political system and its guiding principles of Marxism and Maoism. This was evident from the pervasiveness of what was referred to as the three crises in China—the crises in trust, confidence, and credibility—that jeopardized the legitimacy of the regime.

After Mao's death, the pragmatic and reform-minded leadership mounted strenuous efforts to redeem the Communist Party's damaged reputation. It repealed many unpopular Maoist policies as an antidote to political radicalism. The new regime's initial success in economic reconstruction, development, and depoliticization at first won support. However, as the economic reform ran into difficulty and caused dislocation and inflation, more and more people began to voice their grievances against the post-Mao regime as well. The Chinese Communist Party's image was further damaged as a result of its brutal suppression of the democratization movement in 1989. Although it is too early to determine the full implications of the Party's crackdown on Chinese political culture, most analysts feel it has turned more of the Chinese people against the Party.

3. *Class consciousness.* The model communist citizen was also to be on guard against remnants of the class struggle, such as bourgeois ideas at home and abroad, and the global threat of capitalist imperialism. Because of intense indoctrination by the schools, the arts, and the media during the Maoist period, the Chinese were immersed in class-struggle thinking and were expected to assume a political consciousness as part of their belief systems.[19]

There is little evidence to suggest that class consciousness is of any real significance in the belief system of the majority of people living today in Second World societies. Although most Soviet students have been taught to explain in class terms the Great Patriotic War or race relations in Africa, it is not something they think of frequently or feel strongly about; the same holds true for the Chinese. In contrast to Mao's China, where the people were continually warned of class enemies and where class warfare was said to rage endlessly, there is today a much more relaxed atmosphere surrounding the idea of class struggle in the Second World states.

4. *Ideological study.* Ideological study in Mao's China meant the study of Mao Zedong's political writings; the works of Karl Marx, Friedrich Engels, and Joseph Stalin; and contributions by certain other Chinese Party officials. At the height of the Cultural Revolution (1966–69), the Maoist cult surrounding ideological study achieved unprecedented heights; there was saturation of Maoist ideology in every aspect of an individual's life. Mao's teachings became the ultimate ethical code for the whole nation. Everybody had to make a daily ritual of reading his *Little Red Book*, a collection of revolutionary aphorisms and moral precepts. Academic work in all fields became an exegesis of the Maoist scriptures, and the quality of scholarship was evaluated

During Mao's reign, art and culture in China were expected to communicate the goals and values of the revolution. "The Red Detachment of Women," a folktale made into a revolutionary ballet, exemplifies the adoration of Mao and his *Little Red Book*.

on the basis of the ability to recite Maoist tenets. Whereas almost all books were labeled as remnants of feudalism, capitalism, and revisionism and withheld from publication and circulation, Mao's works came out in stunning profusion and inundated the nation.

After the post-Maoist leadership embarked on the reform and modernization policies, ideology no longer dominated the national agenda. Although the Chinese communist leaders claimed to have inherited Mao's ideological mantle and paid lip service to it, they renounced the primacy of the Maoist dogma. Few Chinese people bothered any longer with

ideological study and redirected their efforts at staying clear of the political authorities and making money. Mao's books were largely ignored and could no longer be found in the average Chinese household.

After the mass demonstrations and political protests of spring 1989 had been brutally suppressed by the Chinese army, the Chinese Party leadership turned back to ideological training and indoctrination in an effort to prevent future dissent and unrest among Chinese students and workers. The old ideological works that had largely been in storage throughout most of the post-Mao period reemerged in classrooms and factories across China. Courses in communist ideology once again became a required part of university curricula; workers once again had to partake in ideological sessions at their place of employ. While commitment to ideological training on the part of the Party may not have been as strong or as fervent in the post-Tiananmen period as it was in Mao's heyday, ideology had once again become an integral part of the Party's plan for political control and socialization of the Chinese people.

Ideological study today has become passé in the Soviet Union and is rejected in Eastern Europe. Although the Soviet school curricula contain Marxist-Leninist requirements, students and teachers generally oppose it and want to see ideological study reduced. Ideological study has been more strenuously opposed in Eastern Europe. Noting that about one-fifth of their college classroom hours were devoted to the study of Marxism and that most other classes were taught from a Marxist perspective, Hungarian students demonstrated in 1988, resisting this form of governmental control of their curriculum. Likewise, during the height of the Solidarity movement in the 1980s, the independent union of Polish university students pressured the government into removing classes on dialectical materialism from the required curriculum. As a result of the revolutionary changes that swept across Eastern Europe in 1989, there is now very little communist ideological study in any of these Second World systems.

5. *Labor and production.* The new communist citizen in Mao's China was expected to thrive on, and enjoy, manual labor. During the Maoist period, for example, all students were required to engage in productive labor for the state in addition to their normal academic study. Schools and universities were to become centers of production as well as centers for learning. Mao's China was a picture of men and women at work: peasants marching in the fields, students and laborers working side by side in farms and factories.

The drive to indoctrinate the higher-educated stratum of society in the importance of manual labor culminated in the massive "sending-down" campaigns before and during the Cultural Revolution. Compulsory participation in productive labor was consonant with the advocacy of Maoist anti-intellectualism and populism. It was designed to humiliate the presumably arrogant intellectuals, eliminate a divorce of theory from reality, and bridge the gap between the urban and rural areas. Mao's insistence on political reeducation through productive labor demoralized and antagonized those in the scientific and technological professions whose contributions were subsequently solicited for the modernization efforts. The Maoist strategy interfered with routine scientific and technical work. Later, the post-Mao leadership revoked the Maoist prescriptions and exempted students and professionals from the bulk of their duties involving manual work. Recently, however, Communist Party officials have raised alarm about a new tendency among young students to despise manual labor. To remedy the situation, in the late 1980s, some educational systems began to alternate classroom instruction with field experiences on farms and in factories. This trend gained added support in the repressive environment following the Tiananmen Square crackdown.

6. *The Red/expert blend.* The enlightened socialist citizen was also to be both committed to communist ideology (i.e., Red) and an expert, with specific skills and talents that would contribute to the construction of communism. The different blends of Redness and expertness seen throughout communist history, however, have illustrated some significant contrasts among the various Second World states. Mao's China in-

variably placed greater emphasis on the ideological side (Red) and less on the technical, scientific aspects (expert) of socialist construction. During this period in China, the "Red and expert" formula served as a theoretical justification for the denigration of technocrats and intellectuals and the domination of workers over professionals. In practice, political virtuocracy invariably took precedence over meritocracy. Lack of professional competence seldom disqualified a politically reliable candidate from recruitment or promotion.

For most of its history, the Soviet Union took a more middle-of-the-road position. Although the Soviet leadership did not emphasize the value of extreme Redness, neither did it allow the more unfettered development of the technocratic experts; what it did was emphasize both. The enlightened citizen was to be not only ideologically committed but also trained and educated to bring the most advanced skills and training available to his or her work setting. The new emphasis on glasnost in the Soviet Union suggests that this and other dimensions of Soviet political culture are changing. The East European states began making decisions in the 1980s that placed greater emphasis in their political cultures on technical merit and productivity and less emphasis on ideological considerations. This trend was given a big boost with the political revolutions of 1989. Red was out, and professional merit was in. Most of the East European leaders and people came to the conclusion that the heavy emphasis on Redness in their postwar societies was one of the significant factors that led to economic stagnation and social malaise. If you do not have well-trained and competent people involved in development programs, they concluded, it is difficult to compete in the increasingly competitive global economy.

In concluding our discussion of enlightenment, we should call attention to the recent developments in Eastern Europe that are likely to have significant implications for the enlightenment element of political cultures in that part of the Second World. As this book was being written, the Berlin Wall was coming down and formerly repressive states like Romania were opening their borders to allow free passage of their citizens in and out of the country. Although it is difficult to predict where these and related changes will lead East European countries, and what impact this will have on the political cultures of their societies, we can be assured that in the 1990s the attitudes and values surrounding enlightenment likely will be changing. The heavy emphasis on communist ideology appears to be a thing of the past, as these societies are beginning to experiment with elements of pluralist democracy including multiple parties, free elections, and noncommunist governments. Although difficult challenges face these societies as they attempt to rebuild their political cultures and systems, exciting opportunities clearly exist.

Subcultures, Countercultures, and Dissidence

Although the postwar Second World leaders were dedicated to building unified, communist political cultures in their societies, they came to realize that it was an impossible task. Most of these societies are complex and heterogeneous and contain a variety of subcultures, countercultures, and dissidents within their broader populations. Although these individuals and groups may share certain values with the dominant political culture, they also hold many distinct values of their own.

Subcultures can be based on a diverse set of characteristics. We can divide populations geographically and find distinct subcultures; we can also divide societies by age, social or occupational attributes, ethnic differences, and so forth. Another meaningful and useful way to explore subcultures is by dividing societies into political elites and masses. The masses, for example, hold values that are often quite different from those held by the political elites. The presence of subcultures, countercultures, and dissidence in China is particularly interesting in view of Maoist efforts to wipe out the old and create a new communist political culture. Even during the most repressive days of the Maoist period, individuals and groups challenged the ideology and values that the regime tried to impose. In 1955, Hu Feng, a celebrated literary figure who had won recognition as the Chinese Communist Party's poet laureate, dissented from the Maoist policy on literature and art issues, articulated the embittered literary workers' resentment of the authoritarian Communist Party controls, and stated their demands for the stoppage of unwarranted Party surveillance. The fact that the Communist Party had to respond not only by putting Hu behind bars but also by launching a nationwide political campaign to round up his followers was clear proof of the existence of an anti-Party subculture within cultural and educational circles during the Maoist period.

Then, during the liberalization drive in 1957 (generally referred to as the Hundred Flowers Movement) many Chinese began to speak out during this fleeting Maoist period of glasnost. Inspired and emboldened by the Maoist leaders' conciliatory gestures approving of a new openness, a significant number of China's political, economic, cultural, educational and scientific elites came out to voice their disillusionment with the communist regime's shortcomings and their skepticism about the feasibility of communism. The vehemence and scale of criticism provided considerable evidence of the intensity and significance of the anticommunist subcultures. In panic and with great exasperation, the Maoist leaders decided to strike back. As a result, the so-called Anti-Rightist crackdown ended the short-lived Hundred Flowers Movement and was used as an instrument for retribution for political dissent and heresy. Mao found the dissidents guilty of maligning socialism, opposing the Communist Party's development strategy, and advocating anticommunist ideology. In the face of repression in subsequent years, the Chinese counterculture replaced their frontal attack with subtle, circuitous criticism in articulating their political and ideological preferences.

In the post-Mao period, the criticism became more open. Some writers and scientists, like Liu Binyan, Wu Zhuguang, Wang Ruowang, and Fang Lizhi, delved into the Chinese communist experience to identify and expose the problems inherent in the Chinese communist system. Their views and opinions were echoed by thousands of young students and intellectuals. They won considerable support for their courage and became national celebrities among their subcultural supporters. The conservatives among the communist elites resented their "pernicious" influence and had many of them purged in early 1987 on a charge of agitating for student demonstrations in support of liberalization and democratization. Student demands for democracy and reform grew, however, resulting in the violent confrontation between students and communist authorities in June 1989 in Tiananmen Square. The authorities used military force—the Peoples' Liberation Army (PLA)—to quash the democracy movement, pushing it underground and to foreign lands. Some of the students came to the United States, where they set about organizing change for China from abroad.

In the late 1980s, other subcultures, some of which were diametrically opposed to communist values, gained ascendancy in China. Some were motivated by materialistic and consumer concerns. Materialism seemed to be triumphing over revolutionary asceticism. Many of the younger generation, who did not live through the ordeal of precommunist chaos and famine, were no longer inspired by revolutionary ideals; rather, they were obsessed by desires for modern comforts and consumer goods such as color TVs, refrigerators, stereos, and bigger apartments. Patriotism and ethnocentrism seemed to give way to worship of the West. Many Chinese young people had a fixation with Western culture and art and made a fetish of imported goods. Dazzled and mesmerized by the affluence of the West, many young Chinese were ready to desert their motherland mired in poverty and backwardness in search of their fortunes in foreign lands.

The late 1980s saw a mass exodus of Chinese students and people from all walks of life to the United States, Japan, and Europe. Still more were biding their time, anxiously awaiting their exit visas. Many government-sponsored students chose to be expatriates after completion of their studies abroad. The number of international marriages skyrocketed because they were an avenue for emigration to and resettlement in the West.

Other Chinese were motivated out of concerns for democracy and human rights. Many thoughtful young men and women were exposed to Western ideology and dismissed Marxism and Maoism as irrelevant anachronisms. Adoption of Western philosophy and democratic concepts was very much in vogue in China in the late 1980s. It would not be an overstatement to say that the existentialist Paul Sartre, psychoanalyst Sigmund Freud, and the Soviet leader Mikhail Gorbachev had a far larger following than did any Chinese among the educated young people of China.

Finally, in China, many of the ethnic minorities have remained tied to their subculture value systems. During the first few years of communist rule, the regime gave preferential treatment to the minority nationalities and showed remarkable tolerance for their indigenous values, habits, and customs. Later, however, as minority leaders demanded more administrative autonomy and cultural tolerance, the Communist Party rescinded its original conciliatory and concessionary policy and decided to clamp down on ethnic opposition. It orchestrated a crusade against local nationalism and purged many officials who were of ethnic extraction. Ethnic insurgency erupted in many areas during the period of economic depression in the late 1950s and early 1960s, in protest against communist interference in religious, social, and cultural life and the majority Han's colonization of their homelands. The government resorted to brutal force in suppressing a variety of rebellions—for example, in the theocracy Tibet.

In the Soviet context, political subcultures, countercultures, and dissidence also can be viewed in a variety of different ways. There are differences based on age (e.g., youth culture), religion (e.g., Jews, Moslems, Christians), and political persuasion (e.g., democratic pluralists versus totalitarian communists). Frederick C. Barghoorn has distinguished different political subcultures on the basis of social structure.[20] Classifying Soviet society in terms of intelligentsia, workers, and collective farmers, Barghoorn identified attitudes and behaviors that distinguish each group from one another and from the dominant political culture. According to this approach, different orientations toward politics are largely defined by one's position in the social structure. Because the intelligentsia are a somewhat privileged stratum in Soviet society, they have higher levels of education and sometimes expect higher levels of power, respect, and well-being than do the less privileged and less educated sectors.

Subcultures can also be distinguished in different age groups in the Soviet Union. Interviews conducted in 1988 by the Soviet Institute of Sociological Research revealed that different age groups held rather different values about important aspects of the Soviet system (see Table 10.3). Younger people were far more skeptical than the older generations about the ability of the one-party system to promote democracy. The younger were more supportive of multicandidate elections and more tolerant of street demonstrations to air grievances. Surprisingly, perhaps, the old were more supportive of Gorbachev and his policy of perestroika. As the

Table 10.3   Voices from Moscow: What They Say about Their System

	Age				
	18–29	*30–44*	*45–64*	*65+*	*Total*
One-party system in U.S.S.R. promotes development of democracy					
Agree	46%	50%	53%	60%	51%
Disagree	34	32	25	13	28
Elections to regional Soviet should be conducted under a multicandidate system					
Yes	80	83	76	65	77
No	2	3	5	4	4
Interests of minority groups in U.S.S.R. are infringed on					
Not at all	61	65	65	84	66
Partially	27	22	20	6	20
Severely	4	2	1	1	2
It is acceptable for people with grievances to hold street demonstrations					
Yes	44	40	34	13	35
No	49	48	56	75	54
Support Gorbachev's domestic policies					
Completely	65	74	85	94	78
Less than completely	32	23	14	4	19
Support perestroika					
Strongly	65	66	83	83	73
With reservations	31	33	13	11	23

Based on a poll of Moscow residents conducted by The Institute of Sociological Research of the Soviet Academy of Sciences for The New York Times and CBS News. A total of 939 Moscow residents were interviewed by telephone on May 7, 8, 14, and 15, 1988.

(*Source*) The *New York Times*, May 27, 1988.

data in Table 10.3 indicate, different generations can hold rather different attitudes about politics in Second World states.

Subcultures can also be distinguished on the basis of nationality. Because there are so many nationalities and ethnic minorities in the Soviet Union, there are many national subcultures. These nationalities produce beliefs, values, and opinions that can have a powerful impact on politics. The Baltic nationalities had such an impact in the late 1980s. Representing formerly independent states, nationalities like the Estonians, Latvians, and Lithuanians hold values that place great emphasis on national autonomy. They want the Soviet state to provide them with more political, economic, and cultural freedom to promote their national interests. Such values have motivated the Baltic nationalities to make a number of demands on Moscow, including requests for independence.

National subcultures, then, can hold rather different preferences about the allocation of such values as power, respect, well-being, and enlightenment. On the issue of power, for example, many national groups—such as the Baltic nationalities, the Georgians, the Armenians, and others—feel that their power ought to be expanded. They feel that the Soviet state has concentrated far too much power in the central government in Moscow. They also feel that they have not received the respect that is due them. In their opinion, the central authorities have suppressed their national cultures and contributed to the Russification of their territories. They also believe that their well-being has been stunted through the economic system imposed on them by Moscow. And, finally, through the communist controlled information and socialization policies of Moscow, they have not been allowed to mold the enlightened citizenry that will serve their national interests and cultural development. As a result of such values, a number of Soviet nationalities

are making demands of great significance to the political process and to the future of the Soviet state. In fact, such values are of an intensity and character to threaten the very existence of the Soviet Union.

Similar national subcultures exist in other Second World states. Yugoslavia, for example, has a number of nationalities that are finding it very difficult to coexist and cooperate in the Yugoslav federation. Because of cultural, religious, and economic differences, these groups hold political orientations that contrast, and often conflict, with one another. Some of the groups (e.g., the Albanians) who inhabit less developed areas of Yugoslavia feel that the government should do more to equalize the level of well-being among different national regions.[21] Because their levels of well-being are considerably below those in the more developed regions, they feel funds should be taken from the developed regions and invested in their areas to aid social and economic development.

These and other differences of opinion associated with nationality in Yugoslavia are reflected in both elite and mass political cultures, and on many occasions they have resulted in political conflict pitting one republic or group of republics against another. Many Albanians in the province of Kosovo demonstrated and rebelled on numerous occasions in the 1980s to indicate Albanian dissatisfaction with their situation in the Yugoslav union. Other festering inter-national disputes and animosities were rekindled. By the end of the decade, the historical Croatian-Serbian feud was boiling. Croatians were increasingly outspoken about their fears of Serbian dominance in the Yugoslav union. With the country on the verge of economic collapse, ethnonationalism was ripping the delicate fabric of the Yugoslav state.

There were many other cleavages expressed in East European political cultures in the 1980s. Most of them were repressed and kept out of the press and public eye by the communist authorities. However, with the opening of these societies in the late 1980s, the full meaning and significance of the cultural differences came into public view. There were differences between generations, national and religious groups, and social classes. Perhaps the most significant differences had to do with the precise political values that were to guide East Europe's experiments with political democracy and economic reform in the 1990s. Although there was considerable sentiment to move in the direction of multiparty democracy and market-oriented economies, there were significant differences when it came to specifics. Many of these societies were rejecting communism but had much to do to create new democratic political cultures.

We thus can conclude this chapter by noting that the communists did not succeed in creating a new communist person and new political cultures. Although one could observe a certain level of conformity and even some level of acceptance and support of the ideals and values of the regime among the people throughout most of the Second World states in the past, there was little real progress in the development of unified and genuine communist political cultures.

In their book written more than ten years ago on political culture and political change in Communist Party states, Archie Brown, Jack Gray, and others summarized the results of considerable research on this question.[22] In all of the countries examined, there was little evidence to suggest that communism had been able to change human nature and political culture in a fundamental way. We should acknowledge that the amount of time devoted to communist change has been relatively brief when viewed in the course of human history and that more fundamental changes may still come about in the countries that remain communist; however, their and our conclusions still raise some important questions about the creation of communist political cultures. Because Second World leaders have been unsuccessful in creating their desired political cultures, they must make decisions in environments marked by considerable differences of opinion on the proper distribution of such values as power, respect, well-being, and enlightenment. This means that policies will be made in a politicized environment where different groups and individuals will prefer different decision and policy outcomes. Like the historical and socioeconomic forces reviewed in Chapters 8 and 9, the attitudinal and behavioral forces reviewed here are contextual determinants of considerable importance to politics and policy making in Second World states.

Suggestions for Further Reading

Avis, George, ed., *The Making of the Soviet Citizen: Character Formation and Civic Training of Soviet Education* (London: Croon Helm, 1987).

Black, Cyril E. and **Thomas P. Thornton,** *Communism and Revolution: The Strategic Uses of Political Violence* (Princeton, N.J.: Princeton University Press, 1964).

Brown, Archie, *Political Culture and Communist Studies* (London: Macmillan, 1984).

Brown, Archie, and **Jack Gray,** eds., *Political Culture and Political Change in Communist States,* 2nd rev. ed. (New York: Holmes & Meier, 1979).

Chen, Theodore Hsi-en, *The Maoist Educational*

Revolution (New York: Praeger, 1974).

Curry, Jane Leftwick, *Dissent in Eastern Europe* (New York: Praeger Publishers, 1983).

Dallin, Alexander and **George W. Breslauer,** *Political Terror in Communist Systems* (Stanford, Calif.: Stanford University Press, 1970).

Gorbachev, Mikhail, *Perestroika: New Thinking for Our Country and the World* (New York: Harper & Row, 1987).

Lenin, Vladimir I., *Imperialism: The Highest Stage of Capitalism* (New York: International Publishers, 1939).

Matthews, Mervyn, *Education in the Soviet Union: Policies and Institutions since Stalin* (London: Allen & Unwin, 1982).

Metzger, Thomas A., *Escape from Predicament: Neo-Confucianism and China's Evolving Political Culture* (New York: Columbia University Press, 1977).

Mickiewicz, Ellen P., *Split Signals: Television and Politics in the Soviet Union* (New York: Oxford University Press, 1988).

Millar, James R., ed., *Politics, Work, and Daily Life in the USSR: A Survey of Former Soviet Citizens* (Cambridge, Mass.: Cambridge University Press, 1987).

Nelson, Daniel N., *Elite-Mass Relations in Communist Societies* (London: Macmillan Press, 1988).

Nove, Alec, *Glasnost in Action* (Winchester, Mass.: Unwin Hyman, 1989).

Ramet, Pedro, *Religion and Nationalism in East European Politics* (Durham, N.C.: Duke University Press, 1985).

Remington, Thomas F., *The Truth of Authority: Ideology and Communication in the Soviet Union* (Pittsburgh: University of Pittsburgh Press, 1989).

Solomon, Richard H., *Mao's Revolution and the Chinese Political Culture* (Berkeley: University of California Press, 1971).

Tucker, Robert C., *Political Culture and Leadership in Soviet Russia: From Lenin to Gorbachev* (New York: Norton, 1987).

Volgyes, Ivan, ed., *Political Socialization in Eastern Europe* (New York: Praeger, 1975).

Welsh, William A., ed., *Survey Research and Public Attitudes in Eastern Europe and the Soviet Union* (Elmsford, N.Y.: Pergamon, 1980).

White, Stephen, *Political Culture and Soviet Politics* (New York: St. Martin's Press, 1979).

Notes

1. Gabriel A. Almond, "Comparative Political Systems," *The Journal of Politics*, 19(3)(1956): 395.

2. Gabriel A. Almond and Sidney Verba, *The Civic Culture: Political Attitudes and Democracy in Five Nations* (Princeton, N.J.: Princeton University Press, 1963).

3. Chang Kuo-tao, cited in Jerome Chen, *Mao and the Chinese Revolution* (London: Oxford University Press, 1965), p. 193.

4. An authoritarian political culture represents a set of beliefs and attitudes supporting or at least tolerating nondemocratic political rule.

5. Robert J. Lifton, *Thought Reform and the Psychology of Totalism: A Study of "Brainwashing" in China* (New York: Norton, 1961).

6. See Richard R. Fagen, *The Transformation of Po-*

litical Culture in Cuba (Stanford, Calif.: Stanford University Press, 1969).

7. Stalin's persecution of religion was abandoned in 1941 in an effort to foster greater support and national unity to address the Nazi threat. Nikita S. Khrushchev resumed the more oppressive policies and initiated a campaign (1960–64) to eliminate religious life completely from the Soviet Union. Gorbachev relaxed the oppressive policies again in the late 1980s.

8. In the Soviet Union, the Komsomol accepts people of ages fourteen to twenty-eight; the Pioneers, nine to fourteen; and the Octobrists, seven to nine.

9. Cited in "Transform Schools in to Instruments of Proletarian Dictatorship." *Peking Review* 19(11)(1976): 7.

10. Wang Renzhong, "Striving for the Future of Socialist China," *Beijing Review* 23(24)(1980): 16–19.

11. Ivan Volgyes, "Political Socialization in Eastern Europe," *Problems of Communism*, 23(1): 51.

12. The term *subject-participatory* comes from Almond and Powell's three basic varieties of political culture: a "parochial" political culture where individuals manifest little or no awareness of the national political system; a "subject" culture where individuals are oriented to the political system and the impact it has on their lives but are not oriented to participation; and a "participant" political culture of individuals oriented to engage actively in the political process. (Gabriel A. Almond and G. Bingham Powell, Jr., *Comparative Politics: A Developmental Approach* [Boston: Little, Brown, 1966].)

13. Frederick C. Barghoorn, *Politics in the USSR*, 2nd ed. (Boston: Little, Brown, 1972), p. 23.

14. Ibid., p. 25; the Politburo is the highest decision-making authority within the Communist Party.

15. Mobilization systems utilize government control to activate the people in the quest for high-priority goals. See Franz Schurmann, *Ideology and Organization in Communist China* (Berkeley: University of California Press, 1966).

16. Ezra F. Vogel, "From Friendship to Comradeship: The Change in Personal Relations in Communist China," *The China Quarterly* 21 (1965): 46–60.

17. "Serve the People" was one of the three political writings that was required by the Chinese government for all citizens.

18. These six standards are drawn from Theodore Hsi-en Chen, "The New Socialist Man," in C. T. Hu, ed., *Aspects of Chinese Education* (New York: Columbia University Press, 1969), pp. 88–95.

19. The arts in China were viewed as a forum for heightening the class consciousness of the masses during Mao's time. Revolutionary operas and ballets were written to convey the themes of class struggle and consciousness.

20. Barghoorn, op. cit., pp. 48–86.

21. The autonomous province of Kosovo, inhabited primarily by Albanians, was rocked by rioting and demonstrations in the 1980s as Albanians sought a greater share of resources in the Yugoslav federation.

22. Archie Brown and Jack Gray, eds., *Political Culture and Political Change in Communist States*, 2nd rev. ed. (New York: Holmes & Meier, 1979).

COMMUNIST PARTIES AND THEIR POWER: PAST AND PRESENT

The late 1980s were a period of incredible change for the Communist Parties of the Second World. Most of the Second World societies in Eastern Europe, for example, saw their top Party leaders overthrown. Thousands of Party officials in Eastern Europe were voted out of office in competitive elections. All of the East European Communist Parties were either seriously weakened or destroyed, and a proliferation of noncommunist parties emerged in the region. By 1990 in most Second World states, Communist Parties were no longer the sole and uncontested holders of power they had been throughout the postwar era.

Because it is difficult to anticipate what will happen in the 1990s, much of this chapter will be devoted to the past. We need to examine the characteristics of one-party rule and why it has recently failed in so many Second World states. We will also look at membership in the Communist Parties and other issues such as organizational structure, personnel, and past Party rules and practices. Then we will examine the revolutionary changes of the late 1980s and what they have meant to Communist Party rule in the Soviet Union, China, and the countries of Eastern Europe.

Historical Setting

Karl Marx and Friedrich Engels provided the practioners of communism precious little guidance concerning the proper organization of the postrevolutionary Marxist state. "Now that we've won, what do we do?," Vladimir Ilyich Lenin and Leon Trotsky asked themselves after the Bolshevik victory in 1917. How should they organize political power and activity to solve the pressing social and economic problems facing the Russian state?

Lenin understood the importance of political organization. As one leading scholar put it:

One trait that made [Lenin] a pioneer of twentieth-century politics was his insight into the crucial role of organization. Lenin realized that . . . all human activities . . . are carried out in and through organizations and associations.[1]

In what is perhaps his most important work, *What Is to Be Done?*, Lenin recognized the need for a particular type of organization that could be used to facilitate the revolutionary goal of socialist construction. Years before the Russian Revolution, Lenin's political organization, the Communist Party, was created and molded into a highly centralized, authoritarian, and militant "party of a new type"[2] and one that became the sole guardian of communist political rule.

Under Lenin's leadership, the Communist Party represented the key institution for consolidating power and forging the messianic construction of communism. Using great organizational and leadership skills and adhering to the ruthless principle that the ends justify the means, Lenin concentrated political power within the organizational structure of the Party. What was initially viewed by the Bolsheviks as the dictatorship of the proletariat became, for all intents, a dictatorship of the Communist Party. During the Leninist and Stalinist stages of development, the Party grew into a dictatorial, bureaucratic organization that controlled the goals, actions, and policy outcomes of the Soviet political process.

Lenin attempted, however, to include some semblance of democratic values within the Party dictatorship by adopting the principle of democratic centralism. This formula represented an intended merging of both democratic and centralistic (or dictatorial) powers, in which members of the Party were encouraged to debate policy matters freely until the point of decision. Once a vote had been taken and a decision was made, however, centralism was required and further discussion and debate, outside normal Party channels, was forbidden. Although this principle did allow some level of democratic debate within the Party, it did not alter the underlying primacy of dictatorial Communist Party rule, in which a small minority of the

state's population monopolizes the primary institution of political power. One-party rule administered according to the principle of democratic centralism was the single most distinguishing characteristic of traditional Second World communist political systems.

The traditional supremacy of the Communist Party as an omnipresent and omnipotent decision-making body manifested itself in several important ways. First, the Party ensured its domination and control over the political system through a fusion of the Party and government. Second, the Party controlled the national economy through state ownership and central planning. Third, the Party had the nation's armed forces at its disposal; and fourth, the Party imposed its official ideology on the population through political indoctrination and enforcement of stringent rules outlawing ideological heresy.

Communist Party Membership in the 1980s

Who belonged to Communist Parties before the major changes of the late 1980s? As Table 11.1 indicates, only a small minority of Second World societies were members of ruling Communist Parties. In the mid 1980s, membership ranged from a high of about 16 percent in Romania to a low of 0.1 percent in Cambodia. Why did so few people belong to the Parties? There were a variety of reasons for the minority status of the traditional Communist Parties. First, the leaders wanted it that way. They preferred minority Parties that supposedly included only the most dedicated, ideologically committed citizens. This made it easier to maintain Party discipline and purity and to ensure the Party's role as the so-called revolutionary vanguard of the society. Second, Party membership was often

Table 11.1 Communist Party Membership in the 1980s

Country	Communist Party Name	Party Membership	Communist Party Membership as Total Percent of Population
China	Chinese Communist Party	46,001,951	4.3
USSR	Communist Party of the Soviet Union	19,037,946	6.7
Romania	Communist Party of Romania	3,640,000	15.9
North Korea	Korean Workers' Party	2,500,000	11.7
East Germany	Socialist Unity Party	2,324,386	14.0
Yugoslavia	League of Communists of Yugoslavia	2,168,000	9.3
Poland	Polish United Workers' Party	2,130,000	5.6
Vietnam	Vietnamese Communist Party	1,900,000	3.0
Czechoslovakia	Communist Party of Czechoslovakia	1,705,490	10.9
Bulgaria	Bulgarian Communist Party	932,055	10.4
Hungary	Hungarian Socialist Workers' Party	870,992	8.2
Cuba	Communist Party of Cuba	523,639	5.1
Albania	Albanian Party of Labor	147,000	4.8
Mongolia	Mongolian People's Revolutionary Party	88,150	4.4
Laos	Lao People's Revolutionary Party	40,000	1.1
Cambodia	Khmer Communist Party	7,500	0.1

(*Source*) Richard F. Staar, ed., *Yearbook on International Communist Affairs* (Stanford, Calif.: Hoover Institution Press, 1988).

demanding and not many people wanted to do it. Members were expected to serve as model citizens and often found their lives scrutinized by other Party members. Finally, many people were reluctant to join Parties that were viewed as bankrupt or discredited political organizations by large sectors of society.

There were a number of factors, however, that still led some people to join the Party, and at least three should be mentioned. First, some individuals were achievement oriented and had high aspirations for success. Joining the Party could open doors that might otherwise be closed. Second, some joined the Party because of the political influence it provided them. If in the past one wanted to pursue a career in politics or in some line of government service, membership in the Party was practically mandatory. In many cases, it gave a person leverage in competing for positions in traditionally non-governmental sectors. Finally, there were always some who joined because of a spirit of communist conviction. Committed to the Marxist-Leninist doctrine, they felt that the best way to promote communism and the betterment of society was within the organizational structure of the Party.

The Communist Parties attempted to attract members from all sectors of their societies, although most had difficulties keeping the peasant and workers' ranks sufficiently high to justify their proletarian basis and heritage. At one time or another, most of the Parties had to undertake campaigns to increase the number of peasants, workers, and minority nationalities among their memberships. The substantial increase (over 8 percent) in worker representation in the Community Party of the Soviet Union (CPSU) between 1957 and 1980 was the result of a recruitment campaign begun by Party leaders Nikita Khrushchev and Leonid Brezhnev to increase working class involvement.

Procedures governing entrance into the Parties varied somewhat from country to country and over time. The procedures followed in the Soviet Union in the 1960s and 1970s, however, are fairly representative and illustrate the general standards that were maintained. When an individual wanted to join the CPSU, he or she had to be recommended by three persons, each of whom must have been a Party member for five years and known the candidate for at least one year. Once the application was prepared and brought before the local primary Party organization, a two-thirds majority vote was required for admission as a candidate member. After serving for one year in this provisional status—a period when the candidate's work was closely monitored by superiors—the application was again voted on by members of the local primary organization. If the individual received a two-thirds vote, his or her file was sent to the next Party level (usually city or district), where it was normally approved.

It was not always easy to join a Communist Party. In Maoist China only a small fraction of candidates whose applications were forwarded with grassroot endorsements were considered and accepted for membership. An exhaustive, thorough scrutiny of background and commitment preceded a final decision on the candidate's fate. Many aspirants and hopefuls were screened out for trivial defects in character. In the 1980s, the eroding prestige of the Chinese Communist Party (CCP) greatly dampened the popular enthusiasm for Party membership. Although the post-Mao leadership lifted many restrictions on induction and actively solicited applications from intellectuals, the number of newly filed applications steadily declined. Most people balked at the prospect of joining the Party because they felt that only those who wanted to ingratiate themselves into the Party's favor and advance their careers at their friends' and co-workers' expense would still be interested in Party membership. By the end of the 1980s, the question of Party membership generated increasing cynicism and skepticism throughout the Second World. What was once hailed to be an honorable and responsible act of service to one's country had, in the eyes of most, become an act of self-aggrandizement and delusion. As we will see, there are several reasons for this and most of them represent a serious indictment of the quality of Communist Party rule.

Organizational Structure

Primary Organizations

Figure 11.1 illustrates the typical organization of the traditional Communist Party, from the lowest-level primary organization (what formerly were called the local Party cells) to the highest-level Party leader. The organizational structure of the Party approximated a pyramid, at the bottom of which were thousands of primary organizations based in factories, schools, collective farms, and the like. When an individual joined the Party, it was this local organization that received and processed the application. Recruitment of new members and ideological work (spreading official propaganda, political education, and so on) were major responsibilities of the primary organizations. These organizations also served as ideological caretakers within factories, schools, and other institutions as they tried to propagate attitudes and behavior corresponding to the Party's expectations. By linking every social, economic, and territorial unit within the state, the primary organizations were intended to provide the central Communist Party with a communication network that reached to the grassroots of their

society. There were over 400,000 primary organizations in the Soviet Union in the late 1980s.

One distinctive feature of the Chinese Communist Party (CCP) organizational policy during the Maoist era was the fusion of the Party, local government, and economic management at grassroot levels. For a long time, local Party leaders (called Party secretaries) served in important supervisory and management capacities in addition to concurrently acting as ideological watchdogs for their superiors. There was a positional overlap and the Party leadership always exercised authority in local administration and management. Non-Party managers, directors and superintendents were generally figureheads and performed largely ceremonial duties. The rationale for totally integrating the Party organization into government and administration was the perceived need for unified leadership under the control of the Communist Party.

The usurpation of administrative powers by Communist Party leaders and committees represented costly and unwarranted intervention into purely technical and professional affairs. These Party officials ended up making decisions in areas that were often beyond their true responsibilities and capabilities. Significantly, the reform movements of the 1980s in China, Eastern Europe, and the Soviet Union featured a bifurcation of Party and government administration. Deng Xiaoping and Mikhail Gorbachev both were ardent proponents of the separation of Party and government. Deng was explicit about his endorsement of reduced Party control over economic enterprises in comments he made in 1986:

> The substance of reform should primarily be separating the Party from government administration, finding a solution to how the Party should exercise leadership, and how to improve leadership.[3]

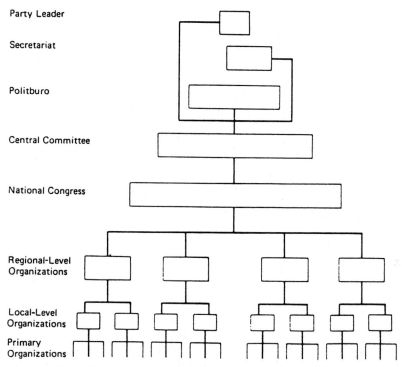

Party Leader

Secretariat

Politburo

Central Committee

National Congress

Regional-Level
Organizations

Local-Level
Organizations

Primary
Organizations

Figure 11.1 Communist Party organizational structure.

Although the 1989 crackdown and reversal of the reform programs in China raised certain questions about the Chinese communist commitment to this principle, most observers expect the trend to continue. Of course, more than a few former Party functionaries appeared unreconciled to the erosion of their powers, and there has been evidence suggesting that the policy favoring a separation has been opposed, circumvented, and boycotted in China.

Regional- and Local-Level Organizations

Traditionally, the vast majority of Party members worked in part- and full-time capacities within the regional- and local-level networks. The central Communist Party organization provided the regions—the republics and provinces—with a certain degree of autonomy in the administration of Party affairs. These regional organizations typically coordinated their own Party conferences and had organizational structures that closely corresponded with those of the national Party organizations.

The regional-level Party organizations in the Soviet Union had always been based on a federal structure. At the regional level, the Parties of the fifteen Soviet republics—for example, Russia, Armenia, Estonia, and so forth—had the highest status. A major issue for the Soviet Union as it entered the 1990s was the relationship between the central and republic Party organizations. Some regional Communist Party organizations, such as that of the Lithuanians, declared their independence from the Communist Party of the Soviet Union (CPSU).

Next in order of importance were the regions and areas within the Soviet republics, followed by the towns, rural and urban districts, and so on down the list. Each of these units had its own Party organizations and networks, including full-time committees, officials, and elected delegates to represent the unit at the next highest level.

The Communist Party in China (CCP) was also divided into regional and local Party networks. The degree of regional Party autonomy had been hotly debated in China and had been subject to the shifting desires of the central Party leaders. During the initial stage of the Great Proletarian Cultural Revolution (1966–69), for example, the provincial Party structures were assaulted and dominated by both the national leaders and such grassroots groups as the Red Guards. In the 1980s, the provinces regained some semblance of regional autonomy and became a stronger force in making policy within their respective regions. Many of the leaders who emerged in the post-Mao era gained their experience in the regional organizations.

The Yugoslavs traditionally had the most formalized and autonomous regional Party organizations. Each of the six republics (Bosnia-Hercegovina, Croatia, Macedonia, Montenegro, Serbia, and Slovenia) and two autonomous provinces (Kosovo and Voyvodina) had regional congresses, central committees, and the usual executive Party organs. Meeting regularly, these organs and their members had considerable power in determining regional Party policy. In fact, the central Party organization lost power in the political arena over the last few decades and that of the regional Party organizations

grew. The republics' vigorous pursuit of regional interests resulted in a high level of interregional conflict, leading many to remark that Yugoslavia long had, in reality, a de facto multiparty system—that is, the Croatian Communist Party, the Serbian Party, and so forth.

National Party Congress

In all traditional Communist Party states, delegates from the regions and lower-level organizations gathered every four or five years to attend the national Party congresses. Called the All-Union Party Congress in the USSR and the National Party Congress in China, these large and highly ceremonial meetings were filled with considerable Party fanfare.

In theory, the delegates came to the national congresses to elect the new Central Committee that would serve until the next congress. In fact, however, the slate of candidates was typically prepared in advance by the leaders themselves, which resulted in the unanimous election of the official slate. Traditionally, rank-and-file delegates had little, if any, effect on the selection of their highest leaders. The content of the speeches, the selection of the Central Committee, and the congress in general was carefully orchestrated by the top Party leadership.

Some of this began to change in the 1980s. By the end of the decade, Party congresses in the Soviet Union and China were meetings of considerable importance and called attention to the dramatic changes taking place in the politics and policies of communist states. The 1986 27th Party Congress of the CPSU in Moscow marked the end of the Brezhnev and the beginning of the Gorbachev era. In power as Party leader for about one year, Gorbachev used the 27th Congress as an opportunity to outline his vision for Soviet reform. To do so took considerable time. Gorbachev's opening speech ran five and one half hours and addressed all major aspects of Soviet foreign and domestic policy.

The 27th Congress also approved a new set of Party rules outlining the rights and duties of the Party member and adopted a Party program that outlined the need for perestroika and radical reform of the economy. The 27th Congress endorsed the 12th Five Year Plan for the 1986–90 period and a document charting Soviet social and economic plans to the year 2000.

Gorbachev and the Party leaders convened another important meeting called a Party conference (rather than congress) in June 1988. By convening the 19th Party Conference, the first such meeting in forty-seven years, they reintroduced the convention of holding Party conferences at intervals between the Party congresses. Among other important developments, the 1988 Conference offered valuable insights into the politics surrounding Gorbachev's reform program. For example, whereas most of the Party leadership seemed to support perestroika and economic reform, some Party conservatives, such as Yegor Ligachev, were highly skeptical

Gorbachev confers with Yakovlev and Ligachev at the historic Communist Party Conference in June 1988.

about Gorbachev's goals surrounding glasnost and democratization. The debates were critical, spontaneous, and often electrifying. For the first time in history, Communist Party policies were being debated in more open and democratic ways, in full view of the world and an astonished Soviet television audience.

By the time the 28th Party Congress convened in Moscow during July 1990, the divisions apparent within the CPSU at the 19th Party Conference had grown deeper and become more clearly defined. Again before the people of the Soviet Union and the world, Party leaders argued vehemently with one another over the future course and pace of reform the Party should undertake. Conservative delegates castigated Gorbachev and his reform program for abandoning Marxism-Leninism. Radical delegates demanded that the Party embrace social democracy and relinquish its control over state resources. Near the end of the Congress, Boris Yeltsin, an outspoken member of the radical faction of the Party, announced his decision to quit the Party from the rostrum of the Congress. Following his announcement, instead of returning to his seat, Yeltsin dramatically walked out of the hall where the delegates had convened. Several other members of the radical reform faction of the Party later joined Yeltsin in renouncing their Party membership. The 1990 Soviet Party Congress demonstrated the extent to which the traditional communist principles of democratic centralism and Party solidarity before the public had been abandoned by members of the CPSU in the Gorbachev era.

An important Party congress was held in China in the late 1980s. Meeting in Beijing from October 25 to November 1, 1987, the 13th Party Congress of the CCP addressed the major question of Chinese reform. To open the congress, then General Secretary Zhao Ziyang presented a report to the approximately 2,000 assembled delegates entitled "Advance Along the Road of Socialism with Chinese Characteristics." Zhao emphasized that China was in the primary stage of socialism and would continue to be so for at least another 100 years. He noted that the primary stage of socialism was a long-term and necessary transitional stage, which China had to go through to build communism from a backward, underdeveloped economic base. Zhao outlined the Party's goal to turn China "into a prosperous, strong, democratic, culturally advanced, and modern socialist country" of the future. Zhao was ousted in the aftermath of the Tiananmen Square massacre in 1989 and had little time to see his vision realized.

Central Committee

Because of their large size, the infrequency of their meetings, and the fact that the highest-level leaders were making the decisions, the national Party congresses traditionally had little meaningful power as policy-making bodies. Although affected by some of the same factors, the Central Committees were far more influential bodies. The Central Committees were large, generally ranging from 100 to 300 members within the different states, but not nearly so enormous as the Party congresses that supposedly elected them. Meeting periodically, usually every few months or so, the Central Committees theoretically were considered the most important Party organization within their states. The traditional Central Committee of the CPSU historically had been the organ that directed the considerable activities of the Party and of the local organs. This involved selection and appointment of leading personnel; direction of the work of central governmental and public organizations; creation and direction of various Party organs, agencies, and enterprises of the Party; appointment of the editors of the central newspapers and magazines operating under Party control; and allocation of funds from the Party budget.

Historically, the Central Committees in all Second World countries were vested with a number of important functions. First, the Central Committees were required to ratify Politburo decisions to give them legitimacy. Second, with their memberships recruited from all parts of the country, the Central Committees served as an effective and important link between the apex of the political pyramid and its base. Third, Central Committee membership was one of the highest accolades for Party veterans. The Party honored its outstanding members with Central Committee membership in recognition of their meritorious service. Fourth, tenures as Central Committee members were also part of the apprenticeship to top Party and governmental positions.

The Central Committees historically were the conclave of the country's most influential and powerful people. Among its members were the leading personnel of the central and regional Party apparatuses and government agencies. The Committees also embraced national dignitaries and prominent figures from the military, industrial, and intellectual sectors; in short, they assembled in their midst the highest bureaucrats and functional elites who ran the country.

The memberships and meetings of the Central Committees in the 1980s reflected the important changes taking place within Second World systems. In April 1989, Mikhail Gorbachev and his associates engineered a sweeping purge of 110 of the 301 members of the CPSU Central Committee. The removal of the Brezhnevites, or what were called the dead souls—from the title of the novel by Nikolai Gogol—included such Party stalwarts as Andrei Gromyko, long-time Foreign Minister of the Soviet Union, and Nikolai Tikhonov, former Prime Minister of the Soviet state. This 1989 meeting was also noteworthy for the startling outpouring of opinion, which was published in great detail in the Communist Party newspaper *Pravda*. Although many of the speeches and discussions were in support of the Gorbachev reform policies, many regional Party officials used the occasion to criticize the central Party organization—and implicitly Mr. Gorbachev himself—for mismanaging the economy, undermining the authority of the Party and the military, and allowing for a dangerous rise in nationalist sentiments. Like other aspects of Soviet politics, Central Committee meetings became more open and democratic.

At the 28th Soviet Party Congress in July 1990, delegates to the Congress directly elected the Party leader and the Politburo for the first time. Previously the delegates to the Congress had elected the Central Committee which in turn chose the Party leader and members of the politburo. The change in voting procedures made it increasingly unlikely that the Central Committee could again oust a Party leader, as it had done Nikita Khrushchev in 1964, in the future. By mid 1990, the Soviet Central Committee had lost many of its traditional powers.

Politburo, Secretariat, and Party Leader

Although in theory the Central Committees held considerable power throughout communist history, they did delegate the bulk of it to the bodies and individuals they elected—the Politburos, the Secretariats, and the Party leaders (see Figure 11.1). The Politburo was an exceedingly important decision-making institution with a great deal to say concerning who got what in Second World states. Generally meeting at least weekly, this group of Party members traditionally was responsible for transacting the highest level and most important business on the nation's agenda. The Politburos were considered the most significant and powerful policy-making bodies in Second World states.

Formal power to make policy was given to the Politburo, but the Secretariats had considerable power and important responsibilities of their own. The Soviet Party statutes in the 1980s noted that the CPSU Secretariat was to direct the Party's work and organize the fulfillment of Party decisions. As the organizational arm of the Politburo, the Secretariats supervised the implementation and execution of Party policies. Meeting almost daily, these bodies occasionally overshadowed the Politburos, particularly in times of crisis, by making policy proposals, issuing decrees, and ensuring administrative execution.

These high-level Party bodies were subject to considerable change in the past and are likely to be subject to even more in the future. The Chinese Communist Party (CCP) Central Committee Secretariat was abolished in 1967 and reestablished in February 1980. During that period, the Politburo Standing Committee, often thought of as the Secretariat but, in fact, a different body and more powerful than the CCP Politburo, indeed was the most important decision-making body in China. During the unstable period following Mao's death in 1976, for example, the Politburo Standing Committee convened an enlarged Politburo session and undertook a number of important actions of great consequence to the future course of Chinese politics. Perhaps the most important was the purging of Mao's wife, Jiang Qing, and three additional members of the CCP Politburo, the so-called Gang of Four. In the 1980s the CCP Central Committee Secretariat once again became a major locus of power. Because of the absence of formal rules outlining the sharing and use of power in the upper Party echelons as well as a general disregard for statutes and

rules during times of crisis, the power relationships between these highest organs were always rather fluid.

As a result of their heavy supervisory, implementation, and execution functions, the Party Secretariats controlled and relied on large bureaucracies to assist them in these tasks. The bureaucracies were divided into departments organized according to broad policy areas. In the CPSU Secretariat in 1989, for example, Viktor Chebrikov was in charge of legal policy; Yegor Ligachev, agricultural policy; Vadim Medvedev, ideology; and Aleksander Yakolev, international policy. Generally, each member of the Secretariat was in charge of a certain department and specialized in that department's designated policy areas. In overseeing policy implementation and execution in these different departments, the secretaries had a major impact on the policy process.

Also elected by the Central Committees, the Party leaders—at the beginning of 1990, Mikhail Gorbachev in the Soviet Union and Jiang Zemin in China—traditionally have been the highest ranking officials in their states, outranking the top government officers, such as the President or the Premier. The first among equals in their states and in their Parties, the Party leaders presided over the work of the Politburos, controlled the central Party apparatus, and acted as the primary spokespersons for the Party and for the state.

Because political power was heavily concentrated in the hands of the top Party leaders during the decades of traditional Communist Party rule, these leaders had a deep impact on the governing of Second World systems. Lenin was the supreme leader of Russia from 1917 to 1924.[4] After Joseph Stalin's assumption of power (he became General Secretary of the Party in 1922), the position of Party General Secretary soon overpowered all other political offices, including the leading government positions. In his so-called last testament, Lenin warned his associates against the appointment of Stalin as General Secretary, noting that Stalin already had become too powerful and did not use his power with sufficient caution. Shortly before his death, Lenin added a postscript to his testament, suggesting that Stalin be removed from his post. As history shows, Stalin was not dislodged; rather, he decisively moved to increase his power within his role as General Secretary of the CPSU.[5] Under his administration, the role of Party leader became the dominant position in Soviet politics, a pattern that held until 1990, when the Soviet Union continued to consider political reforms that would lead to a different constellation of power.

After Stalin's death in the spring of 1953, a power struggle between Nikita S. Khrushchev and a number of high CPSU officials ensued. Having a solid political base by virtue of being a member of both the Secretariat and the Politburo, Khrushchev soon became the dominant figure and had his title upgraded to First Secretary.[6] Unlike Stalin's leadership as General Secretary, however, Khrushchev's was never as totalitarian and autocratic. Not only was he less powerful, but his reign of power was shorter. In the fall of 1964, while on vacation in the Crimea, Khrushchev was summoned back to Party headquarters in the Kremlin and ousted from his job. Because of shortcomings in his agricultural policy, the embarrassment and failure of the Cuban missile episode, the bifurcation of the Party, and other alleged shortcomings, the career of the impulsive Khrushchev was abruptly brought to an end.[7] Replacing Khrushchev as head of the CPSU was Leonid I. Brezhnev, who headed the Party for two decades, longer than both Lenin and Khrushchev. Beginning his leadership of the CPSU under Khrushchev's former title of First Secretary,

Brezhnev assumed Stalin's upgraded title of General Secretary in 1966 and the state presidency in 1977.[8]

In November 1982, General Secretary Brezhnev died at the age of 75. Considerable attention focused on the Kremlin as the Soviet leaders prepared to choose a successor. American Kremlinologist Myron Rush noted that the most striking feature of the Brezhnev succession was the absence of clearly qualified candidates who possessed not only good health but also broad political experience.[9] Many of the candidates were older than Brezhnev; others had careers that were highly specialized. Brezhnev's apparent choice for a successor was Konstantin Chernenko, who had the unfortunate image of being Brezhnev's aide and an undistinguished staff man who had never been the responsible head of a high-level Party or government organization. Despite Brezhnev's apparent desire to make Chernenko his heir, Yuri Andropov, former head of the Soviet Committee for State Security (the KGB), decisively moved to assume the top Party spot. Having capitalized on Brezhnev's physical frailties and political vulnerabilities during the final years of the former Party leader's life, Andropov brought some strong qualifications to the job. Described by Kremlinologist Rush as highly intelligent, dispassionate, and cool under fire, the 68-year-old Andropov quickly took over the top Party and government positions, something that had taken Brezhnev thirteen years to accomplish. Once in office, Andropov sought to wipe out corruption and turn around the Soviet Union's decline.

However, Andropov's reign was short-lived. By August 1983, nine months after assuming Brezhnev's mantle, Andropov had disappeared from public view. According to official medical reports, Andropov had developed serious kidney problems; his condition sharply deteriorated in January 1984, and he died the next month.

Many predicted that the Soviet Union would then turn to a younger successor, perhaps the 53-year-old Mikhail Gorbachev or the 61-year-old Grigori Romanov. However, the CPSU Politburo stuck with the most experienced generation and chose Brezhnev's original heir, 73-year-old Konstantin Chernenko. However, Chernenko also proved to be a short-term leader and thirteen months later succumbed to ill health. Having long suffered from emphysema, Chernenko died in March 1985.

Soviet leadership then underwent a swift, and what proved to be a far-reaching, transformation in the course of a single day. Chernenko's death was announced in the afternoon of March 11, 1985, and by evening, Mikhail Gorbachev was installed as the new CPSU General Secretary. A native Russian, Gorbachev was born in 1931 in the Stavropol region, an agrarian area in the Russian heartland. According to his official biography, his parents were peasants and he worked on local collective farms as a youth. Bright, talented, and ambitious, Gorbachev went to study law at Moscow University in 1955. Unlike previous high CPSU officials, most of whom had little advanced education, Gorbachev earned a degree from Moscow University and another degree, in agricultural economics, from a correspondence school. Representing a new kind of Soviet leader, Gorbachev was the first leader to come from a generation that did not take part in World War II and the first who had received a full education in the postwar era.

After graduating from Moscow University, Gorbachev went back to Stavropol and began his rapid climb up the political ladder. He first became head of the Komsomol, later took charge of the collective farms in the region, and then, in 1970, became First Secretary of the Communist Party in Stavropol. In 1978, he was brought to Moscow to fill the vacant post of the CPSU Central Committee Secretary for Agriculture. The next year, in a remarkable and meteoric rise, Gorbachev was catapulted into the CPSU Politburo, first as a candidate member and, in 1980, as a full member. Although passed over for the top job when Brezhnev died in 1982 and again in 1984 when Andropov died, he used the time to acquire more experience and to expand his power base. During this period, Gorbachev acquired considerable responsibility for matters concerning the economy, culture, ideology, personnel, and various aspects of international affairs.

When Chernenko's health began to fail in 1984 and 1985, forcing him to drop more and more of his official activities, Gorbachev assumed a leading role in the work of the CPSU Secretariat and Politburo. Although a power struggle was being waged behind the scenes at the highest levels of Soviet politics, the political momentum was very much on Gorbachev's side. Working to his advantage were personnel changes made during Andropov's brief tenure. Andropov brought a number of younger people into the top Party leadership who were natural allies to Gorbachev. By the time Chernenko's health failed, and with KGB support and the acquiescence of the Soviet army, Gorbachev had assumed an almost unassailable position.

Although the Politburo vote making Gorbachev the Party leader was not unanimous, Gorbachev quickly became a powerful leader. Two weeks after taking power, he began a campaign to sweep out incompetent, corrupt, and aging Party officials and replace them with younger, better educated, and more technocratic-minded successors. Gorbachev was now in charge, and Soviet communism was in for a period of substantial change.

Along with Gorbachev came new ideas and thinking. The new thinking involved *glasnost,* increased information and honesty in public life, *perestroika,* a restructuring of the economy, and *demokratizatsia,* a democratization of political life. Gorbachev proved to be a remarkable tactician in furthering these revolutionary objectives in the early days of his rule. He demoted or ousted his opposition and in rapid succession introduced a panoply of new reforms. By the end of the 1980s, he had set off a chain of events that would transform the Second World and the nature of Communist Party rule.

In a deft play of power in 1988, Gorbachev took over the governmental position of President with the forced retirement of 79-year-old President and Politburo member Andrei Gromyko. (This will be discussed in more detail in the next chapter.) Gorbachev also engineered other changes in the Politburo, including the retirement of the 74-year-old Mikhail Solomenstev and 68-year-old Anatoly Dobrynin, foreign policy specialist and former ambassador to the United States who apparently lost his position due to the rapid rise of a close Gorbachev associate, 64-year-old Aleksandr Yakovlev. A strong ally of Gorbachev's, Yakovlev took over the top foreign policy job in the Secretariat and assumed the powerful number-two position behind Gorbachev in the Politburo. To bring additional new blood and support for his reform program into the Politburo, Gorbachev elevated the 59-year-old Vadim Medvedev to full Politburo membership, allowing him to bypass his normally expected service as a nonvoting candidate member. Promoted to candidate membership was the 59-year-old Aleksandra Biryukova, who became the first woman to serve on the CPSU Politburo in twenty-seven years.

Until September 1976, the People's Republic of China had known only a single leader of the Chinese Communist Party (CCP). As one of the founders of the CCP in 1921, this leader, Mao Zedong, held a variety of positions in the Party before becoming its head during the period of the Long March (1934–35). When the People's Republic was proclaimed in October 1949, Mao concurrently became Chairman of the Republic and Chairman of the CCP. The Chairman of the People's Republic was considered the head of state in China, putting Mao in charge of a number of executive and ceremonial responsibilities. Giving up the head-of-state role in 1959, Mao remained the reigning head of the CCP until his death in 1976.

Although choosing Mao's successor was a favorite pastime of many Sinologists, most were surprised when Hua Guofeng, a relatively unknown Party official from the province of Hunan, assumed the dual roles of Chairman of the CCP and Premier of the State Council in 1976. Hua's meteoric rise was generally believed to be the result of an effort to break a stalemate in an intra-Party factional fight over succession. From the outset, both Hua's heir apparency and the authenticity of what was purported to be Mao's message, "With you [Hua] in charge, I am at ease," which Hua used to legitimize his leadership, were challenged. Lacking a power base of his own and experience at the helm, Hua was predestined to be a transitional leader. Deng Xiaoping, the resilient and pragmatic leader, and the so-called moderates in the CCP—those who opposed the ideological excesses of Maoism and favored more pragmatic reforms to modernize China—skillfully challenged and successfully dislodged Hua from his leadership posts.

In September 1980, Hua resigned as Premier in favor of Zhao Ziyang, then a member of Deng's moderate coalition. Although Hua cited the Party principle of collective leadership (to be discussed later in this chapter) as the reason for his resignation, it was apparent that he was

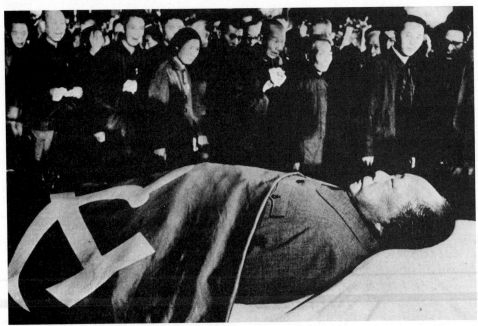

Chinese mourners file by Mao's body at his funeral in September 1976. At that very moment, an intense struggle for succession was underway. It resulted in the elevation of Hua Guofeng to take on Mao's mantle and the purging of the "Gang of Four," which included Mao's wife, Jiang Qing.

losing a struggle for power with the moderates. Two months later, Hua also resigned the Chairmanship of the CCP's Military Commission and, most importantly, the overall Chairmanship of the Party, which went to another member of the moderate coalition, Hu Yaobang. These demotions were officially announced in June 1981, when a lengthy Party resolution critically assessed both Mao and Hua. Hua was charged with fostering a cult of personality, propagating erroneous policies and opposing correct ones, and committing other transgressions.[10] The changes in the CCP leadership put the moderates Deng, Zhao, and Hu in a position of dominance in the Chinese political structure.

After Hua was deposed, the moderate coalition split into two factions, the reformists and the conservatives, with the top leader, Deng Xiaoping, as the ultimate arbiter. The reform-oriented Party leader, Hu Yaobang, was soon on a collision course with the more conservative senior leaders. Hu favored a quickened tempo of reform and rejuvenation of China's political system; the conservatives wanted to go slow. In late 1986 and early 1987, student demonstrations provided ammunition for the conservatives opposing Hu's political and economic reforms. They capitalized on Hu's reluctance to crack down on the dissident students and accused him of favoring "bourgeois liberalization." In a cacophony of malicious attacks, the Politburo stripped Hu of his Party leadership and designated Zhao Ziyang as his successor at the Party's 13th Congress in 1987.

Zhao was also a reformer, and his Party leadership was also short-lived. Once again, student demonstrations brought down the CCP's Party leader. What started out as student demonstrations praising Hu Yaobang, who had died on April 15, 1989, became a major democratization movement involving millions of Chinese, primarily students, in the hearts of major Chinese cities most notably in Tiananmen Square in the center of Beijing. Party leader Zhao Ziyang was tolerant of the demonstrations and wanted to avoid the use of force in bringing them to an end. Others, including longtime leader Deng Xiaoping and the conservative Premier Li Peng, were more concerned with stability and called in troops to quash the student demonstrations. Behind the bloody violence in Tiananmen Square was an intense power struggle, which led to the ouster of Party leader Zhao Ziyang and the appointment of his successor, the 62-year-old Jiang Zemin, the Party leader from Shanghai.

Deng Xiaoping, Zhao Ziyang, and Li Xiannian stand side by side at an anniversary celebration of the Chinese Revolution. As a consequence of the political protests and conservative backlash of spring 1989, Zhao was removed from his position as General Secretary of the Chinese Communist Party.

The power struggles and leadership changes taking place in the Soviet Union and China in the 1980s provided an important lesson about Communist Party rule in Second World states. We sometimes had the impression that communist leaders, once in power, were firmly in command. Although they did have considerable power at one time, once Second World states began to reform, that power became increasingly fragile.

Past Party Rules and Practices

Unlike Western political parties, the traditional Communist Parties required more from their members than occasional financial contributions, verbal support, and turnout at key elections. What was expected of Soviet Party members in the 1980s was outlined in the CPSU Party Rules. Parts I and II of the rules set down the rights and responsibilities of members and described the procedures for admission and expulsion. Parts III to VI of the rules described the structure and powers of Party organs and the principles guiding Party elections, leadership, and decision making. Parts VII to IX explained the CPSU's relationship to government, to the Komsomol, and to the military.

Party members in China were also guided by certain rules and obligations in the 1980s. These included:

1. To adhere to the Party's political and ideological line of Marxism-Leninism–Mao Zedong thought.
2. To uphold collective leadership and oppose the making of arbitrary decisions by individuals.
3. To safeguard the Party's centralized leadership and strictly observe Party discipline.

4. To uphold Party spirit and eradicate factionalism that undermines the Party's unity.
5. To speak the truth, match words with deeds, and show loyalty to the cause of the Party and to the people.
6. To promote inner-Party democracy and to take a correct attitude toward dissenting views.
7. To guarantee that the Party members' rights of criticism, policy formulation, and implementation are not encroached upon.
8. To provide genuine democratic elections within the Party and give full expression to the voters' wishes.
9. To criticize and fight against such erroneous tendencies as factionalism, anarchism, and extreme individualism and evildoers such as counterrevolutionaries, grafters, embezzlers, and criminals.
10. To adopt a correct and positive attitude toward comrades who have made mistakes.
11. To accept supervision from the Party and the masses and to see that privilege seeking is not allowed.
12. To study hard and become both Red and expert in order to contribute to the four modernizations.[11]

A variety of procedures and practices also were important to traditional Communist Party life and politics. Collective leadership was one practice and was intended to avoid a return to the highly dictatorial, "one-man" rule of Joseph Stalin. Therefore, decision making in Party organs at all organizational levels was to be a collective exercise. Although Party leaders and secretaries were the first among equals, they still had to gain the support of their peers. Although the so-called one-man rule under Stalin truly never was a reality, it led all states, in the post-Stalin era, to more fully embrace the principle of collective rule.

Democratic centralism was supposed to be another important practice at work in the Communist Parties of Second World states. Developed by Lenin to reconcile both freedom and discipline, democratic centralism was based on the following principles: (1) election of all Party bodies, (2) accountability of Party bodies to their organizations and higher bodies, (3) strict discipline of the minority to the majority on all decisions, and (4) the binding of decisions of higher bodies on lower bodies. Theoretically, there were to be both democratic and centralistic elements in these principles. In actuality, centralism and control usually prevailed.

Another past practice or set of practices is noteworthy, partly because of the general absence of Party rules and partly because of the changes taking place today in Communist Parties. This concerns the problems of circulation and rotation of Party leaders and the issue of succession once leaders die or are removed. The Yugoslavs did the most in the past to formalize both rotation and succession of Party leaders.[12] Until the changes of the late 1980s, efforts in most of the other states to formalize turnover within Party organs were largely ineffective. For example, at the 23rd Congress of the CPSU in 1966, Brezhnev and his colleagues abolished the requirement (adopted at the previous Congress in 1961) that there would be a regular, specified turnover in Party leadership bodies. The requirement was intended to avoid the election of the same leaders time after time and to bring some new blood into decision-making circles. Little came of the 1961 proposal, but in the late 1980s Gorbachev proposed secret balloting and a choice of candidates in Party elections within the context of his democratization and political reform program. Gorbachev's belief that the average citizen and Party member must be given a greater sense of participation began to affect the traditional principles regarding the selection of Party leadership. In this regard, Gorbachev is quoted as saying, "A house can be put in order only by a person who feels he is the owner."

In May 1988, the CPSU Central Committee approved proposals that limited service of all Party officials to two consecutive five-year terms. Election for a third consecutive term required approval by no less than 75 percent of the membership of the relevant Party organization. The proposed limitation covered membership in the CPSU Secretariat, the Politburo, and even the office of General Secretary, the post occupied by Mikhail Gorbachev. Much remains to be done to make genuine elections and term-of-office limitations a reality, but in the late 1980s there was evidence that the Soviet Party leaders were serious about these proposals.

Another traditional Party practice was called nomenklatura. Nomenklatura referred to a list of positions, both in the Party and in society at large, that the Party maintained and for which Party approval was necessary before personnel changes, removals, or replacements could be made. The nomenklatura list in the USSR included an extensive list of high positions in the military, scientific organizations, the mass media, and other important sectors of Soviet life. This practice allowed traditional Communist Parties to control appointments to key positions throughout their societies. Party officials actively used the nomenklatura practice in the past to remove undesirables, select officials who met Party standards, and control appointments to the most important positions in society.

The importance of the nomenklatura practice, and certainly the number of positions on the list, began to decline in the 1980s throughout most of the Second World states. At the 13th Party Congress in 1987, China endorsed plans to reduce the number of jobs whose hiring was controlled by the CCP.[13] As the East European

Communist Parties began to crumble in the late 1980s, one of the first practices to be discarded was the nomenklatura system. Changes also are being contemplated in the Second World states where Communist Parties remain in control.

Recent Developments

Soviet Union

Mikhail Gorbachev has faced opposition from within the Communist Party of the Soviet Union since he was chosen as the Party General Secretary in March 1985. Originally, Gorbachev's opposition within the Party consisted of holdovers from the Brezhnev era: Party careerists who profited from the corruption allowed under Brezhnev and refused to acknowledge the need to reform once Brezhnev left the political scene.

By the time the 27th Party Congress of the CPSU concluded in February 1986, Gorbachev and his Party supporters had been able to remove most of the old Brezhnev guard from power and put in their place younger officials who recognized that if the Soviet Union was to maintain its stature as a superpower into the twenty-first century, both the Soviet state and the Soviet Communist Party would have to undergo a lengthy period of reform and renewal.

The replacement of the Brezhnevites by Gorbachev did not signal an end to opposition to his reform policies within the Party, however. Where reformers had been united in their common pursuit of removing the old Brezhnev guard from power, once that goal had largely been accomplished, the unity of the reform movement collapsed within the Party. Some Party officials began to assert that Gorbachev was proceeding too quickly and too broadly with his perestroika and glasnost reforms. Party leaders like Yegor Ligachev, a reformer himself in comparison with many of the ousted Brezhnevites, began to criticize Gorbachev for trampling upon the memory of those who had worked so hard to achieve the ideal state of communism in the Soviet Union before he came to power.

Gorbachev faced opposition from Party conservatives who resisted reform, but he also came under attack from other factions within the Communist Party, who believed that his reforms were not radical enough to solve the pressing problems that the Soviet Union was facing in the late 1980s and continues to face in the 1990s. Party leaders like Boris Yeltsin and economists and academicians like Abel Aganbegyan and Oleg Bogomolov grew increasingly frustrated with the slow pace of the reform process under Gorbachev.

Since the ouster of most of the old-guard Brezhnevites from the CPSU in the first year and a half of his rule, Gorbachev has strived to keep himself in a moderate, middle-of-the-road position relative to his critics from both the radical and conservative reformist factions within the Party. He has become a master at playing one faction off the other, always reserving for himself and his supporters the role of final arbiter between competing factions.

Gorbachev has made sure that he has kept the middle ground for himself by lashing out against conservatives and radicals alike when he has felt his role as Party leader being challenged. For example, in 1987, Boris Yeltsin, a radical reform member of the ruling Politburo and Party leader in the city of Moscow, was removed from his positions of authority by a temporary coalition formed between conservative reformers and Gorbachev and his supporters. In this instance, Gorbachev saw Yeltsin as too radical a proponent of change and aligned himself with conservatives like Ligachev to remove Yeltsin from power. By so doing, Gorbachev appeared as a moderate relative to Yeltsin and could not be targeted by conservatives as being too far out on a limb in pursuing his visions of glasnost and perestroika.

Unfortunately for Gorbachev, Boris Yeltsin did not fade into anonymity after he was stripped of his power base within the Party in 1987. In subsequent years, Yeltsin ironically became a primary benefactor of Gorbachev's efforts to transfer the locus of Soviet power from the Party to revamped and more powerful governmental institutions. In 1989, Yeltsin was elected to the Congress of People's Deputies and became a leader of a radical bloc of deputies within the new legislature. His political comeback and outspoken criticism of both the Party and Gorbachev's reform program proved immensely popular with the Soviet people. In 1990, he was elected as the new President of the Russian Republic and renounced his Party membership, proclaiming that he no longer intended to serve the interests of the Party, but rather the people. While Gorbachev had effectively removed Yeltsin as a threat to his role as leader of the Party, via his reforms he had created a new power base, the Soviet government, from which Yeltsin could once again challenge his role as supreme leader of the Soviet Union.

In 1988, following a series of attacks by conservatives on his policies of perestroika and glasnost in newspapers around the Soviet Union, particularly in Leningrad, Gorbachev, in coalition with radical reformers, took action against the recognized head of the conservative opposition within the Party, Yegor Ligachev. Ligachev had been serving as head of the ideology department within the Secretariat of the CPSU. The head of the ideology department had long been recognized by Western Kremlinologists and Sovietologists as the second most powerful position within the Soviet Communist Party, behind only the position of General Secretary. The powerful and respected Mikhail Suslov served as ideology chief under Brezhnev for many years, and Gorbachev himself served in this coveted position under Chernenko.

From his position as the number-two Party man, Ligachev could wield considerable power to subvert and even challenge Gorbachev's reform policies. During a Central Committee plenum in 1988, Ligachev was demoted from his position as ideology chief to that of agricultural secretary, the same position Gorbachev had held when he first arrived on the national political scene in 1980.

At the 28th Party Congress, Ligachev with the support of his conservative allies set out to recapture his number two position within the Party. The title and nature of the number two Party position had changed since Ligachev lost it in 1988. Since Gorbachev had assumed the new, more powerful presidency of the Soviet Union, he had found it increasingly difficult to manage the day-to-day affairs of both the Soviet state and Party. He decided to concentrate his time and energy in his role as head of state and turn day-to-day management of the Party over to a deputy Party leader. This new deputy Party leader position became the second most important in the Party, replacing that of ideology chief. At the 28th Party Congress, unable to unseat Gorbachev as Party leader, Ligachev sought election as deputy Party chief in the hopes that he could control day-to-day management of the Party and move the Party in a more conservative direction. Gorbachev opposed Ligachev's candidacy and supported Vladimir Ivashko, an ally and fellow reformer from the Ukraine. Ivashko defeated Ligachev by a vote of 3,109 to 776. Following his defeat and exclusion from the Politburo by the 28th Congress, Ligachev returned to his home in Siberia to pen a book.

The actions taken by Gorbachev against Yeltsin and Ligachev can be seen as two very bold and shrewd political moves. By playing the radical and conservative factions of the Party against each other, Gorbachev was able to secure his position as Party leader by holding onto the political middle ground. Gorbachev's strategy was very similar to that employed by Stalin in his battles against both Trotsky and Bukharin following Lenin's death in the mid-1920s.

Until February 1990, Gorbachev's political balancing act between radical and conservative critics had worked marvelously. By that time, however, the middle ground in which Gorbachev had anchored his policies had eroded. The Soviet Communist Party had become polarized. The radical reformers increasingly had become more radical in their policies, whereas the conservatives had become more and more conservative. One group of reformers had gone so far as to organize their own caucus, the Democratic Platform, within the Party, which called for "radical reform of the Soviet Communist Party in the direction of a completely democratic parliamentary party, acting in a multiparty system."[14] In such conditions, it becomes almost impossible for a middle-of-the-road, moderate position to win the day because the constituencies to which the moderate leader must make his case hold too-extreme views. In the words of the British Sovietologist Peter Frank, "The center ground became depopulated, leaving Gorbachev satisfying neither the reformist radicals nor the traditional conservatives."[15]

Therefore, by February 1990, Gorbachev had to make a choice as to which camp he wanted to join, the radical reformers or the conservatives. At the Central Committee plenum held from February 5 to 7, Gorbachev did so; he chose to count himself as a radical reformer. He primarily did this by endorsing and seeking the removal of Article 6 from the Soviet Constitution. Article 6 of the Soviet Constitution read:

The leading and guiding force of Soviet society and the nucleus of its political system, of all state organizations and public organizations, is the Communist Party of the Soviet Union. The CPSU exists for the people and serves the people.

The Communist Party, armed with Marxism-Leninism, determines the general perspectives of the development of society and the course of the domestic and foreign policy of the USSR, directs the great constructive work of the Soviet people, and imparts a planned, systematic and theoretically substantiated character to their struggle for the victory of communism.

All party organizations shall function within the framework of the Constitution of the USSR.

Article 6 of the Soviet Constitution guaranteed the Communist Party of the Soviet Union a monopoly of political power within the country. Opposition parties were not allowed, and only the Communist Party could control the government. The willingness of Gorbachev and the CPSU to have Article 6 withdrawn from the Soviet Constitution had tremendous significance. It meant that after more than seventy years of one-party dictatorship, political pluralism and a multiparty state in the Soviet Union now were possible. Suddenly, the Soviet people had a number of political parties from which to choose. This led Aleksandr Yakovlev, a key supporter of Gorbachev, to note that Soviet society itself "will now decide whether it wishes to adopt our [the CPSU] policies."[16]

In addition to advocating the removal of Article 6 from the Soviet Constitution, Gorbachev also took radical measures related to the powers of the CPSU Politburo, the traditional base of Soviet communist power. Following Gorbachev's lead, the delegates to the 28th Party Congress elected a new 24-member Politburo in July 1990, which by design included him as the national Party leader and the Party leaders of the fifteen Soviet republics. The new Politburo was quite different from a traditional Soviet Politburo in that it had twice as many members; was elected by delegates to the Party congress, rather than the Central Committee; was not dominated by Great Russians; did not include many Party leaders who held high positions in the Soviet government; and met monthly instead of weekly. Before and during the Congress, Gorbachev argued that the Soviet government, and not the Party's Politburo, should decide state policy. He insisted that the Politburo be relegated to a role of setting long-term goals for the Party and for the state. By electing more disparate, and less influential individuals to the Politburo, delegates to the 28th Party Congress apparently obliged their Party leader.

In the late 1980s, another challenge to Gorbachev's role as Communist Party leader and to the integrity of the Party itself emerged in the Soviet Union. Rather than being concerned with the pace and comprehensiveness of perestroika and glasnost, reforms largely targeted at Soviet society and the Soviet state, as the radical and conservative reformist factions within the Party had been, this new challenge was directed more toward internal Party policy, came from nationalist forces at the regional Party level, and pitted the local Communist Parties in the Soviet republics against the Russian-dominated central Party hierarchy in Moscow.

In late 1989 and early 1990, the Soviet Republic of Lithuania in a series of startling moves abolished the local Communist Party's monopoly of power; created a multiparty system with a legislature composed of freely elected representatives; held the first freely contested, multiparty elections in Soviet history; and, on March

11, 1990, declared itself independent from the Soviet Union.

To be competitive in the February 1990 elections for the newly created Lithuanian legislature, the Lithuanian Communist Party on December 20, 1989, declared itself independent from the Communist Party of the Soviet Union. Agirdas Brazauskas, the leader of the Lithuanian Communist Party, justified his Party's move by underscoring the power of Lithuanian nationalism and the belief that any political party viewed by Lithuanians as being under the control of Moscow and Great Russians stood little chance of ever hoping to accumulate power within an independent, pluralist Lithuania. Lithuanians despised Great Russian control over their land. They believed that they had been an occupied country since Stalin forcefully annexed the independent Republic of Lithuania into the Soviet Union in 1940.

In respect to the violent turmoil that engulfed the Soviet Republics of Armenia and Azerbaijan in the late 1980s, the local Communist Parties in those two republics largely lost their ability to rule autonomously. Regional Party leaders frequently were caught between taking orders from Moscow and appealing to popular pressure to fan the fire of ethnic unrest throughout the Caucasus. In most cases, they chose the latter course and even instigated some of the ethnic violence in the region. Although the CPSU claimed to retain dejure rule over Armenia and Azerbaijan, defacto local rule was in the hands of the Armenian National Movement and the Azerbaijani People's Front, aggressive popular-front organizations that had more than a few local Communist Party members included in their membership.

Gorbachev's response to the challenge posed by rebellious regional Communist Parties was, not surprisingly, one of moderation. He neither approved of regional fragmentation of the CPSU, as local leaders like Brazauskas and the Estonian Communist Party leader Vaino Valjas would have liked him to, nor forced submission of the regional Parties to Moscow's control, as many CPSU leaders in Moscow, particularly of Great Russian heritage, wanted. He adopted a wait-and-see, middle-of-the-road position.

As with his position concerning the pace of his economic and political reforms at the state and societal level, however, it is most probable that in the future Gorbachev will have to make a choice between two polarized alternatives to reconcile national differences in the CPSU. He will have to either allow regional Communist Parties to go their separate ways from CPSU control in Moscow altogether or crack down on the regional Parties, purge the nationalist leaders of those Parties, and impose Party discipline through leaders imposed by Moscow.

Eastern Europe

As the year of 1989 commenced, it was fair to say that the Soviet Union led all of the Second World states of Eastern Europe in terms of its commitment to democratic reform, openness, and economic restructuring. By the end of March 1990, however, Hungary, Poland, Czechoslovakia, and East Germany had passed the Soviet Union on the road to political pluralism and a market-oriented economy; Bulgaria, Yugoslavia, and Romania had at least caught up to the USSR, and only Albania remained lagging behind, a position to which the small Balkan country had by now grown quite accustomed.

In discussing the impact of recent developments in Eastern Europe on the Communist Parties in the region, perhaps the best way to proceed is chronologically, touching upon key events affecting the Parties in the various countries as they happened in time. Before beginning the discussion, however, one should keep in mind that as this book goes to press, the different states and Communist Parties in these societies are at different points along the road to institutionalized political pluralism and market economies. To date, most of the paths that Eastern European countries have been taking to reach their destination have been similar in nature. None, however, has yet reached the end of the road, and pitfalls and curves may befall these countries before they finally do reach their sought-after destination of a democratic, market-centered political and economic system.

As mentioned earlier, as 1989 opened, all of the Eastern European states were more or less ruled by traditional Communist Party regimes. Conditions of a one-party dictatorship and of a centrally planned economy predominated; opposition parties to communist rule were banned, and the government and legislatures of these countries were under the control of the Communist Party.

Hungary's Communist Party took the initial bold step in 1989 by agreeing in February to allow the creation of independent, opposition political parties within the country. The Polish Communists followed the Hungarian lead in April by signing an agreement with Solidarity, the historically persecuted Polish opposition trade union movement. The Polish government legalized Solidarity and called for the holding of elections in which Solidarity could run for 35 percent of the seats in the lower house (the Sejm) and all 100 seats in a newly created upper house (the Senate) of the Polish legislature. In May, the Hungarians dismantled the barbed wire fence along their border with Austria, becoming the first Soviet Bloc country to open its border with Western Europe.

At this point in the discussion, perhaps an important question needs to be raised. Why would a traditional Communist Party willingly agree to legalize opposition parties that might

Thousands of demonstrators pack Wenceslas Square in Prague resulting in the resignations of Czechoslovak Communist Party leaders in November 1989.

In late November 1989, Nicolae Ceausescu, by this time the last Communist Party dictator remaining in the Warsaw Pact states, categorically rejected the democratic reforms being adopted elsewhere in Eastern Europe. By Christmas night, Ceausescu along with his wife Elena had been convicted of treason by a revolutionary tribunal and been shot to death. The fall of Ceausescu, unlike the fall of every other traditional Communist Party regime in Eastern Europe during 1989, was not peaceful. Scores were killed as Ceausescu's dreaded Securitate, the secret police, tried to halt their dictator's demise by shooting down protestors in Bucharest and Timisoara and later waging open warfare with the Romanian Army as it heroically abandoned Ceausescu in favor of the Romanian people.

Following Ceausescu's demise, state power in Romania fell into the hands of the eleven-member executive board of the Ruling Council of National Salvation. The National Salvation Front outlawed the Romanian Communist Party in January 1990 and promised to hold free elections in Romania. The primary leaders of the Front, including its President Ion Iliescu, its Prime Minister Petre Roman, Silviu Brucan, and Cazimir Ionescu, all were former communists who worked for Ceausescu at one point but were discredited and removed from office before his fall.

There was some question as this book went to press as to whether the Council of National Salvation in Romania was truly representative of the democratic interests of the Romanian people or whether it was just a new group of communists attempting to seize power and reestablish a one-party dictatorship in Romania. The Front's decision to hold a monopoly of state power until elections could be held and its harassment and intimidation of fledgling or reborn opposition parties like the Peasants'

On December 11, Mladenov proposed that Bulgaria hold free elections and remove the Party's monopoly on power from the constitution as soon as possible. Mladenov later became the President of Bulgaria. He had to resign his position, however, after the political opposition in Bulgaria obtained a videotape of Mladenov asking his Party colleagues the question "Shouldn't we bring the tanks in?" during a 1989 antigovernment demonstration. The exposition of scandal for political gain and public accountability, two characteristics of Western politics, had come to Bulgaria.

Party, Liberal Party, and Social Democratic Party raised doubt as to whether the revolutionary violence in Romania was yet over and whether a few more steps had to be taken by the people of Romania before they could achieve their goal of a pluralist democracy.

On January 22, 1990, the Yugoslav Communist Party voted to give up its forty-five-year monopoly on power and to permit a new political system in which other parties could compete. The League of Communists of Yugoslavia, the official name of the Yugoslav Communist Party, was, like most other Communist Parties in Eastern Europe, in a state of crisis. The Yugoslav Party crisis, like the crisis within the Communist Party of the Soviet Union, was a product of many factors, including strong nationalist divisions within Yugoslavia and the desire of regional Communist Parties representing different national groups to separate themselves from the national Party. The Slovenian Communist Party declared itself independent from the League of Communists of Yugoslavia as the 1990s opened, and other regional Parties are likely to do so in the future, further amplifying the disintegration of the Yugoslav Communist Party into independent factions divided along both Communist/Social Democratic lines as well as ethnic/national lines.

Finally, as this book goes to press, the small Balkan country of Albania remains the odd man out in Eastern Europe. Albania is unique in the Second World in that after Stalin's death no moderation of the repressive Stalinist communist model took place as it did in all other Second World states around the world. Albania chastised its communist brethren for their heresy and withdrew from the international communist community to pursue an austere isolationist course. That course remained remarkably steady for over forty years, although under Party leader,

Ramiz Alia, some moderation took place in the late 1980s and early 1990.

Under Alia, who in 1985 replaced Enver Hoxha, the longtime Albanian Communist Party leader, Albania abandoned its strict isolationism and opened diplomatic relations with some countries, most notably the Federal Republic of Germany; relaxed travel and emigration restrictions for its people; and increased Albanian society's access to Western consumer goods, including televisions. The Albanian people, largely by watching Italian, Greek, and Yugoslav television, became aware of their relative backwardness compared to the rest of Europe. Viewing Alia's moderation of orthodox Stalinism as an opportunity to pursue their freedom, the Albanian people by the start of the 1990s were seeking to bring political change to their country. Mass protests and strikes erupted throughout the country in 1990 and many Albanians sought refuge in Western embassies, hoping to gain safe passage out of their country. With the world watching, a reluctant Albanian leadership allowed many of its citizens to emigrate.

China and Other Second World States

Following the June 1989 crackdown by the People's Liberation Army on the massive student demonstrations in Tiananmen Square in Beijing and in other major cities around China, the Chinese Communist Party entered a period of retrenchment, relative to the reforms made in political and economic policies in the country throughout most of the 1980s. With Deng Xiaoping ailing from both the frailties of his advanced age and the loss of his role of final arbiter between radicals and conservatives in the Party, with the purging of Zhao Ziyang and most of his supporters from the upper echelons of power following the Tiananmen massacre, the conservative Premier Li Peng has ascended to new heights of power since June 1989.

Under the direction of Li Peng, the Chinese state and the Chinese Communist Party have implemented policies to rejuvenate ideological steadfastness of cadres in the face of perceived threats from "bourgeois liberalism" both at home and abroad. Ideological training has been stepped up at universities throughout China in an attempt to subdue the source of pressure for democratic change that erupted in the spring and summer of 1989. Student leaders of the democracy movements have fled China; gone into hiding in China; or been arrested, sentenced, and, in some cases, put to death for their revolutionary fervor. Similar to these leaders of the democracy movement, the spirit among the Chinese people for change once again has become latent and gone underground. It would be a mistake to conclude that it has disappeared, however. When the time is right, perhaps at the time of Deng's passing or during the next power struggle behind the doors of the Great Hall of the People, the democracy movement in China will once again come into the open and press even harder for change. Until such a time for opportunity presents itself, Tiananmen Square likely will remain quiet.

Traditional Party leaders at the helm of Communist China, North Korea, and Vietnam currently are keeping a watchful eye on the events transpiring in Outer Mongolia. The Mongolian People's Republic is a relatively obscure Second World state sandwiched between the Soviet Union and China, with a human population of about 2 million and a sheep population of close to 13 million. By the end of March 1990, the Mongolian People's Revolutionary Party (the Communist Party of Mongolia) had brought to East Asia political and economic reform comparable to that taking place in Eastern Europe and the Soviet Union. The ruling Politburo under the direction of Party leader Jambyn Batmonh had agreed to give up its monopoly on power and proposed that Party officials and dissidents work together on a new constitution. This constitution would allow for rival political parties to compete in democratic elections to the Great People's Hural, the national legislature. Batmonh also called for an Extraordinary Party Congress to convene in April 1990 to choose a new Central Committee and agree on a new Party policy, including an official name change of the Party to the Mongolian People's Party. As if Outer Mongolia were an infected neighbor, China looked cautiously on the changes taking place in that country in early 1990. China seemed preoccupied with the possibility that unrest in Mongolia could spill over and cause unrest first among the 3 million ethnic Mongolians living in China and then, more significantly, among the Chinese population at large.

Besides the maintenance to date of traditional Communist Party regimes in China, North Korea, and Vietnam, momentum for reform also has been lacking in Cuba. Fidel Castro remains the communist dictator in Cuba. One would think, however, that Castro's anxiety over a potential coup against him has been increasing, in light of the defeat of Daniel Ortega in the February 1990 elections in Nicaragua, the violent overthrow of fellow dictator Nicolae Ceausescu in Romania, the increased efforts by the United States to broadcast news into Cuba via both Radio and Television Marti, and the reluctance of the Soviet Union to continue their massive funneling of aid to the Caribbean island nation. Castro and his regime have been increasingly dependent on this aid in recent years, as the Cuban economy continues to stagnate and world commodity prices for sugar, Cuba's chief export, continue to flounder.

Conclusion

If Lenin, Trotsky, and other founders of the original Communist Party in Russia were to come back today and see the present condition of the Communist Party of the Soviet Union—not to mention the international communist movement as a whole—they most likely would shake their heads in disbelief and disgust. They would no longer consider the Party they founded and the Parties they directed through the Communist International, or Comintern, as being communist anymore.

The nineteenth-century ideas and philosophies of Marx and Engels always have had and continue to attract their followers. In the late nineteenth and early twentieth centuries, the original proponents of Marxism and their descendents split into different factions. Each faction represented a different interpretation of Marxist philosophy. The two predominant factions both within Russia itself and internationally were the social democratic and communist traditions.

Too often today, people identify Marxism only with communists and Communist Parties. In point of fact, such democratically and pluralist-inclined organizations as the Labour Party in Great Britain and the Social Democratic Party in the Federal Republic of Germany can trace their political roots back to Marx just as easily as can any Communist Party. The split that generated the development of independent, social democratic and communist traditions of Marxist thought occurred both over the speed with which the "dictatorship of the proletariat" was to be established in a country and the degree to which nationalism and national institutions

were to be respected by proponents of Marxist philosophy.

The original position of most Marxists was that Marxist political parties should engage in social democratic practices, that is, come to power legitimately in countries through national electoral processes. They would do so by respecting the existing political institutions of the state and by working with political parties in coalition to create conditions in the society that would eventually lead to the establishment of the "dictatorship of the proletariat" and advancement toward the communist ideal as originally defined by Marx.

The social democratic parties that exist today in Western Europe to an extent have perverted the original Marxist social democratic tradition, in that they do not seek or see in the future the establishment in their respective countries of Marx's dictatorship of the proletariat. Although they in essence have abandoned the Marxist dialectic claiming that history will end with the establishment of communism, they have not abandoned the emphasis that Marx put on the importance of the physical and economic well-being of the society as a whole, and on the welfare of the working class in particular. Social democratic parties in Western Europe have been largely responsible for the creation and protection of the welfare state in their societies in the post–World War II era.

In the early 1900s, a small minority of Marxists became dissatisfied with the social democratic Marxist tradition of their movement and developed an independent effort. This new movement called for the rapid and revolutionary accumulation of state power and the creation of a dictatorship of the proletariat in a country, irrespective of national laws, institutions, and customs. These more radical Marxist followers were led by Lenin and Trotsky. Lenin and Trotsky despised both social democracy and nationalism. Social democracy was too passive and weak for the communists; they believed that Marx's ideal state could be achieved forcefully and quickly in societies if a true dictatorship of the proletariat or "party of a new type" existed.

Lenin and Trotsky did not think of people as being divided into different nations and ethnic groups. They believed that people were primarily divided by different social classes. To them, workers in Germany had more in common with workers in Great Britain than with Germans of the bourgeois class. Lenin and Trotsky believed that the upper classes used patriotism and nationalism to keep workers from identifying with each other on a universal class basis. As a result, they felt that nationalism had to be eradicated so that workers could properly develop their class consciousness and unite in opposition to the bourgeoisie.

As we have seen in this chapter, a number of Communist Parties in Second World societies today have willingly abandoned their position as "dictatorships of the proletariat" in their countries in favor of participating in a multiparty system. Some have abandoned the communist tradition of Marxism and adopted the social democratic tradition. By definition, then, they are no longer Communist Parties as the founders of the communist movement conceived of Communist Parties. In addition to turning toward social democracy, many present-day Communist Parties have embraced nationalism. In societies that blame traditional communism and communists for their sorry standard of living, some of these parties see nationalism as the one potential platform that might help attract voters in future competitive elections. As one can see, Lenin and Trotsky would not be pleased with what happened to their tradition of Marxism in 1989 and with what likely will continue to happen to it throughout the 1990s.

Suggestions for Further Reading

Beck, Carl, et al., *Comparative Communist Political Leadership* (New York: McKay, 1973).

Bialer, Seweryn, *Stalin's Successors: Leadership, Stability, and Change in the Soviet Union* (Cambridge: Cambridge University Press, 1980).

Borkenau, Franz, *European Communism* (London: Faber and Faber, 1953).

Breslauer, George W., *Khrushchev and Brezhnev as Leaders: Building Authority in Soviet Politics* (Winchester, Mass.: Allen & Unwin, 1982).

Brown, Archie, ed., *Political Leadership in the Soviet Union* (Bloomington, In.: Indiana University Press, 1990).

Bunce, Valarie, *Do Leaders Make a Difference? Executive Succession and Public Policy under Capitalism and Socialism* (Princeton, N.J.: Princeton University Press, 1981).

Carter, April, *Democratic Reform in Yugoslavia* (Princeton, N.J.: Princeton University Press, 1982).

Conquest, Robert, *Power and Policy in the USSR: The Struggle for Stalin's Succession, 1945–1960* (New York: Harper & Row, 1967).

Djilas, Milovan, *The New Class* (New York: Praeger, 1957).

Hahn, Werner G., *Democracy in a Communist*

Party: Poland's Experience since 1980 (New York: Columbia University Press, 1987).

Hill, Ronald and **Peter Frank,** *The Soviet Communist Party,* 3rd ed. (Winchester, Mass.: Allen & Unwin, 1986).

McCauley, Martin and **Stephen Carter,** *Leadership and Succession in the Soviet Union, Eastern Europe, and China* (New York, M.E. Sharp, 1986).

Miller, R. F., J. H. Miller, and **T. H. Rigby,** *Gorbachev at the Helm: A New Era in Soviet Politics* (London: Croon Helm, 1987).

Rush, Myron, *How Communist States Change Their Rulers* (Ithaca, N.Y.: Cornell University Press, 1974).

Rusinow, Dennison, *Yugoslavia: A Fractured Federalism* (Washington, D.C.: Wilson Center Press, 1988).

Schapiro, Leonard B., *The Communist Party of the Soviet Union* (New York: Random House, 1970).

Schulz, Donald E., and **Jan S. Adams,** eds., *Political Participation in Communist Systems* (New York: Pergamon, 1981).

Terrill, Ross, *Mao: A Biography* (New York: Harper & Row, 1980).

Voslensky, Michael, *Nomenklatura: The Soviet Ruling Class* (New York: Doubleday, 1984).

Notes

1. Alfred G. Meyer, *Communism*, 4th ed. (New York: Random House, 1984), p. 46.

2. For a discussion of Lenin's "party of a new type," see Bertram D. Wolfe, "Leninism," in Milorad M. Drachkovitch, ed., *Marxism in the Modern World* (Stanford, Calif.: Stanford University Press, 1965), pp. 76–84.

3. *Beijing Review* (20), May 18, 1987: 16.

4. Lenin was referred to as Premier, because he was chairman of the Council of People's Commissars and also a member of the Politburo, which at that time had no formal head.

5. Stalin ruled in the dual position of head of both Party and state. Although the tendency in most Second World states during the post-Stalin era was to divide these posts, General Secretary Leonid I. Brezhnev combined them once again in 1977 by assuming the ousted Nikolai V. Podgorny's role as President. Brezhnev's successors, Yuri Andropov, Konstantin Chernenko, and Mikhail Gorbachev, also assumed both positions.

6. Georgi M. Malenkov initially replaced Stalin as head of both Party and state. His leadership evolved into a triumvirate in which he shared power with Vyacheslav M. Molotov and Lavrenti P. Beria. Beria's arrest and Khrushchev's rapid ascent to increased power in 1953 led to Khrushchev's election as First Secretary in September of that year.

7. Khrushchev lived out the remaining years of his life in retirement on the outskirts of Moscow, in a dacha (country home) supplied by the state.

8. For an excellent review of the Brezhnev era, see Jerry F. Hough, "The Man and the System," *Problems of Communism* 25 (2) (1976): 1–17.

9. Myron Rush, "Succeeding Brezhnev," *Problems of Communism* 32 (1) (1983): 2.

10. See "The Resolution on Certain Questions of Our Party since the Founding of the People's Republic of China," *Beijing Review* 24 (27) (1981): 10–39.

11. "Guiding Principles for Inner-Party Life," *Beijing Review* 23 (14) (1980): 11–20.

12. In 1978, Tito suggested that yearly rotation should be applied to almost all LCY organs, from the commune to the federation. In 1979, the Central Committee endorsed the practice. See Stephen L. Burg, "Decision-Making in Yugoslavia," *Problems of Communism* 29 (2) (1980): 1–20.

13. See John P. Burns, "China's Nomenklatura System," *Problems of Communism* 36 (5) (1987): 36–51.

14. *Time*, February 19, 1990: 35.

15. *The Observer*, January 28, 1990.

16. *The New York Times*, August 2, 1990: 1.

GOVERNMENT IN THE SECOND WORLD: PAST AND PRESENT

If Second World states historically were ruled by Communist Parties, what was the function of their governments? Were the Party and government distinguishable in any important ways? Which was more important in shaping overall state policy and influencing policy outcomes?

In many of the Second World countries we are studying, the revolutions of 1989 and the elections of 1990 brought fundamental changes to the governmental process. What exactly did these changes entail? Have actors and institutions outside the Party become more powerful than they once were in these states? If so, how and why?

We will address the questions posed above in this chapter. We will do so by first examining how institutional and power relationships traditionally were structured in Second World states. We will describe the traditional methods of government that were utilized in the majority of Second World states before the events of the late 1980s and early 1990s. And we will analyze how one particular state, the Peoples Republic of China, still practiced such methods as the 1990s commenced.

Next, we will take an in-depth look at the impact the various reform programs of Mikhail Gorbachev have had on conventional methods of government in the Soviet Union. Finally, we will take a close look at the major changes that in the late 1980s and early 1990s altered the processes of government in the states of Eastern Europe. We will analyze the reforms that have been undertaken and the means by which they have begun to be formalized and institutionalized in states such as Poland, Hungary, and Czechoslovakia.

Traditional Processes of Government in the Second World

The Relationship between the Party and Government

In traditional communist political systems, the Communist Party led and set policy while the government followed and implemented policy. Traditional communist governments were designed to take policy directives of the Party and translate them into the rules and regulations that organized socialist life. Darrell Hammer, an American Sovietologist, once described this relationship by quoting an authoritative Soviet text: "No important decision is ever taken by an organ of government, or by an administrative organ, without corresponding instructions from the Party."[1]

Constitutions in traditional communist political systems outlined a set of government institutions of significance to the policy process. Conventional communist constitutions called for representative assemblies with legislative authority. Many included provisions for a collegial or collective head of state, usually called a presidium, that possessed legislative authority in addition to administrative responsibilities. Most established executive or ministerial bodies, typically called councils of ministers, which were entrusted with the functions of policy implementation and execution.[2]

Because the idea of separation of powers was rejected as a bourgeois theory, the government assemblies, presidiums, and councils set up by the constitutions of traditional communist states were dominated by the Communist Parties. Communist Party centralism and terrorism— not democracy or constitutional liberalism— were the underlying features of the processes of government in the most orthodox Second World states.

Party leaders believed that if they created constitutions and institutions patterned along Western lines, they could disguise the Party dictatorship that really existed in their states. They saw in the promulgation of constitutions and the establishment of parliaments opportunities to insulate the Party from criticism at home and abroad.

The creation of a subservient government gave the Party many advantages. When Party planning or policy resulted in popular discontent at home, the Party could blame the government for poor implementation of Party policy, rather than having to accept the responsibility. If a Party leader did not want to agree to an internationally popular proposal put forth by the West or an international organization, he or she could use the government at his or her disposal to scuttle it, instead of doing so directly.

Conventional Communist Party leaders viewed governmental institutions as necessary administrative tools, but when those institutions obstructed revolutionary politics or became outmoded, they were simply ignored, altered, or dismantled. The reasons are manifold as to how political leaders vested with overarching powers could ignore or restructure the government. In addition to the fact the Communist Party controlled the government, the populace had little if any influence on key political processes. Party leaders could with impunity overstep their authority or arrogate to themselves executive powers that were not constitutionally established.

There largely were no prescriptive rules and norms in traditional communist political systems that specified and defined the scope of the respective functions, powers, and responsibilities of the Party and government organizations. This allowed the Party leaders much latitude in making decisions. The subordination or subservience of the state bureaucracy to the Party also helped to assure the Party a ruling monopoly and hegemony over the policy-making process.

Past observers of traditional communist political systems called attention to the close relationship between the Party and the state bureaucracy and described it as inseparable or as an interlocking directorate: "The central Party organs give guiding instructions to the ministries . . . while not restricting their operational independence."[3] This overlapping and interlocking relationship between Party and bureaucracy in the past applied to all levels of conventional communist government. From the federal level down through the local villages, Communist Party members staffed all the organs of the Party and the state administration.

Traditional Government Structures in the Second World

To develop a better understanding of the setting in which governmental processes took place in traditional (i.e., pre 1990) communist political systems, we need to describe in more detail the government structures and institutional actors that were part of such systems. Therefore, in this section of the chapter, we will take a closer look at such orthodox communist state actors as the legislature, the council of ministers, the state bureaucracy, and the defense council to see the role and function these institutions played in the government of traditional Second World states.

Legislature. The legislative body of the traditional communist government may have been designed to mirror a Western parliament, but unlike a Western parliament, the conventional communist legislature was not a significant policy-making body that could initiate and independently decide on legislation. Rather, the traditional legislature was a ceremonial organ, whose primary functions were to ratify policy proposals of the more powerful Party organizations, such as the Politburo, and to legitimate the actions of the Communist Party.

The political impotence of the legislatures in traditional Second World states was indicated by the unusually short time they were in session; typically, they met once or twice a year, usually for less than a week each time. Representatives in these ceremonial bodies never debated or disagreed on the passage of legislation; all of their votes were unanimous.

Deputies were elected to traditional communist legislatures for a set term, on the basis of universal suffrage and secret printed ballots. Although only one name usually appeared on the ballot for each official position, election returns made public by communist state governments often showed that 99.9 percent of the population consistently voted in national elections. They did so for the simple reason that traditional Communist Party doctrine considered voting an obligation. Communist Party pressures were great, and citizens felt obligated to vote.

A more important stage in selecting deputies to a traditional communist legislature occurred before the election itself. Selection of the official slate appearing on the ballot was very much engineered and controlled by the Communist Party. Names forwarded to electoral commissions to be placed on the ballot were almost always determined from nomenklatura lists maintained by the Party.

More so than the legislature as a whole, the smaller presidium of the traditional communist legislature, which was usually elected by the larger legislature, was a relatively influential body within most conventional communist political systems. Much more professional and less diverse in membership than the legislature, the presidium usually had the right to conduct legislative affairs and make decisions while the legislature itself was not in session. As a result of the short and infrequent meetings of traditional communist legislatures, this provided presidiums with enhanced responsibility and power.

Western observers often gave the title of president to the chairman of the presidium of the national legislature of a communist state,

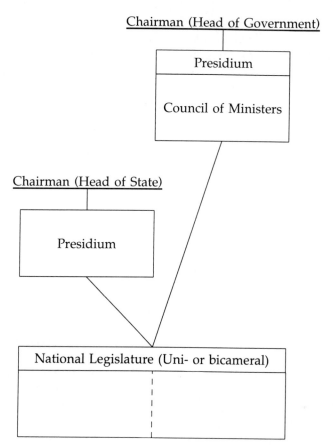

Figure 12.1 The structure of a traditional Second World government.

although the power of the office was nowhere near that of the president of the United States or the president of France. Historically, in most communist states, whoever held the chairmanship of the presidium of the national legislature was considered to be the head of state.

Council of Ministers. The executive arm in traditional communist political systems, the council of ministers, was generally composed of the heads of all ministries, chairpersons of regional councils of ministers, and chairpersons

of important state committees. The chairman of the council of ministers, the prime minister, was legally head of government in most traditional Second World states. Because the traditional council of ministers had a large number of members, a smaller body, the presidium of the council of ministers (not to be confused with the presidium of the national legislature) often acted in the council's name.

The council of ministers and the ministries were important government institutions in conventional communist political systems, both in theory and in reality. Typically, the presidium of the council was constitutionally prescribed the powers and responsibilities for issuing decrees, in a fashion similar to the presidium of the national legislature; it directed and coordinated the work of the national ministries and carried out the plans of the Party.

State Bureaucracy. Conventional communist state bureaucracies were enormous. Adhering to the leading role of the Communist Party in social and economic development, Party leaders established massive bureaucracies to carry out their messianic visions of building communism. For example, there were many commissions, councils, ministries, and committees under the umbrella of the council of ministers. All of these bodies had their own bureaucracies, with hundreds and often thousands of additional offices, committees, and assorted bodies. Many employed hundreds of thousands of civil servants and had administrative structures that stretched throughout the country.

The state bureaucracy included many ministries with their own areas of responsibility and specialization, e.g., Foreign Affairs, Defense, Agriculture, and Health. Each was headed by a minister and thousands of officials. There was little mobility from ministry to ministry within the traditional communist bureaucracy, as there historically has been among departments and agencies of the United States government. Traditional government officials usually were knowledgeable specialists who worked their way up the bureaucratic ladder within a particular ministry. The primary function of these ministries was to implement and coordinate Party policy in their specialized areas and supervise activities at the regional and local levels. The large industrial and agricultural bureaucracies within conventional communist systems often became highly specialized, compartmentalized, and parochial.

A ministry common to all traditional communist states was the ministry of planning. The ministry of planning's responsibilities were much heavier and larger than those of the Office of Management and Budget in the United States. A large ministry with numerous deputy ministers, the ministry of planning primarily was charged with the planning and coordination of the complex and cumbersome centrally controlled economic system common among conventional communist states. Every year, the ministry of planning in each traditional communist state had to set, review, and confirm production and prices for hundreds of thousands of goods.

In addition to ministries, the state bureaucracy in conventional Second World states consisted of a number of important commissions, such as the military-industrial commission. The military-industrial commission usually cut across ministry or departmental lines. This commission was in charge of the defense industry, a very high-priority sector of most traditional communist states. The military-industrial commission worked closely with other state ministries and bodies to ensure preparedness in the defense sector.

Defense Council. One key position of power familiar to Americans that we have not identified yet as existing within conventional communist political systems is that of commander-in-chief. Party leaders in traditional communist states historically did not want outsiders to know either who or what policy-making body would be at the helm of state in times of crises or national emergencies. The office that held the responsibilities of commander-in-chief was never identified in any conventional communist constitution.

Through careful analysis of historical communist political behavior, however, Western observers were able to learn of a very secret organ of power within traditional communist political systems: the state defense council. They also discovered that the chairman of this council held the powers historically reserved for a commander-in-chief. The exact composition and functions of the state defense council in traditional Second World governments were never very clear. Most observers believed that the council was chaired by the leader of the Communist Party, the General Secretary, and included such key positions as the minister of defense, the head of the secret police, the foreign minister, and the chief of the military's general staff. It has long been thought that the council primarily was created and designed to assume supreme authority in the event of war, extreme international tension, or national emergency. It was never as clear, however, as to what the role of the state defense council played in peacetime. Some believed it was the key policy-making body in traditional communist states, more powerful than even the Politburo or the Secretariat. Others were equally convinced that the defense council remained dormant in times of peace and was only activated and convened in a crisis situation.[4]

The Party, the Military, and the Secret Police: A Fragile Truce

Owing to communist sensitivity, internal security, and regime stability, the state security apparatus had a special role in traditional communist politics, far greater than that of the Federal Bureau of Investigation or the Central Intelligence Agency in the United States.

Most traditional communist states had two types of secret police forces. One typically was a security organization designed to spy both at home and abroad. The other was more of a national guard, designed to quash dissent and restore order when popular discontent got out of hand. Traditionally, the security organization was an independent state committee within the government, whereas the militia-styled force was part of the interior ministry. The security organization was the more powerful of the two.

Because traditional Second World states had closed societies, Party dictatorships, and lacked institutionalized means for leadership succession, the importance of the security apparatus in the process of government cannot be downplayed. The security apparatus kept tabs on everyone—ordinary citizens, dissidents, military and bureaucratic personnel, and even top Party leaders.

When a power struggle arose within the Party, as it inevitably would, the faction that had the security apparatus on its side had a powerful ally in its bid for power. If it was successful in its struggle, it had clear knowledge that it had better keep the security apparatus happy or it might lose its next bid.

Because of the information it had in its files, the security apparatus had considerable ability to influence Party power struggles. The Party, however, was not so foolish as to open itself up to potential overthrow or dominance by the security apparatus. The security apparatus in traditional Second World states was kept in line by the Party in a number of ways. First, the security forces were controlled by both a department within the Central Committee Secretariat and the council of ministers. In addition, there usually were two other departments within the Central Committee Secretariat whose sole purpose was to keep tabs on the activities of the security apparatus—one department to track domestic agents, the other to track agents abroad. Finally, the Party would try to prevent any potential coup by the security apparatus by placing its leaders into choice Party positions, so they also would have a stake in the future of the Party.

The security apparatus was not the only state actor in pursuit of state power that the Party had to worry about staging a coup against it. The military also was a potential threat. The military was a very significant actor in conventional communist political systems, if for no other reason than it was the only institution that, if not held in check or pacified, had the power to overthrow the Communist Party, government, and secret police.

Because the military had the potential to be such a powerful force on the political stage, the Communist Parties in nearly all conventional communist political systems took calculated steps to insure that the military establishment remained, like the security organization, under its watchful eye. The Party primarily did this in two ways. First, it established watchdog departments within the Central Committee Secretariat to monitor the activities of the military, and second, it played the military off the security apparatus, by allowing the apparatus to infiltrate both the armed services themselves and the military intelligence.

To conclude, there were three institutions capable of exercising state control in traditional communist political systems: the Party, the military, and the security apparatus. The Party maintained control over policy making, the military had the guns, and the security apparatus had knowledge of who had done what when. These three pillars of power constantly vied against each other for power. If one looked like it was accumulating too much power, the other two would gang up against it and restore a balance of power among all three institutions.

Historically, in most Second World states, the Party was first among equals primarily because the military and the security apparatus hated each other more than they hated the Party. The one common interest the three actors had was keeping the population suppressed, for if the population was aroused, it could shift the balance of power among the three state actors in favor of one or in favor of the people or oppositional groups outside the ranks of power. The overthrow of Nicolae Ceausescu by the Romanian army, and the popular revolutions in Poland, Hungary, and Czechoslovakia in late 1989 all are classic examples of what can happen to the fragile balance of power among the Party, the military, and the security apparatus when the people force themselves into the power equation of a traditional communist state.

China 1990: A Case Study of Traditional Communist Government

Despite the fact that the preceding outline of traditional methods of communist rule was placed in the past tense, those methods have not been abandoned by all Second World states and they could make a return appearance in some of the states that in recent years have undertaken reform processes. One case in particular that demonstrates that traditional communist methods of government have not yet departed the Second World is that of China. Let us now look at China to see how the generalized methods of communist rule that were developed in the first part of this chapter apply to her specific story.

Communist Party control over the Chinese government takes two important forms. First, Party officials concurrently serve as government officials. For example, the People's Republic President in 1989, Yang Shangkun, also held Communist Party posts in the Politburo and the Chinese Communist Party Central Military Commission. Occupancy of dual positions in the Central Committee of the Communist Party by vice-premiers, councilors, and ministers of the State Council within the government is taken for granted in China. Second, Party committees and their secretaries supervise and monitor routine government operations and report to the central Party authorities.

Although the post-Mao moderates have made the separation of Party and government functions a top priority in their efforts to reform the Chinese political process, they have brought relatively little change to traditional power relationships. Many Party functionaries have been ambivalent toward the moderates' plans for political reform. Little progress has been made in this direction, especially at the top and medium levels of the Chinese government. If in the future China were to resume a reformist

political strategy that was comparable to the one it had appeared to assume in the late 1980s until the Tiananmen Square massacre, the role and significance of government institutions in the Chinese political process might increase.

In constitutional terms, the National People's Congress is the Chinese legislature. The NPC is a unicameral legislature because Chinese Party leaders want to promote the point that their state operates on the basis of a unitary system. The constitutionally prescribed functions of the NPC are discussing and ratifying Party and government reports, state plans and legislative drafts, and electing and approving government officials.

The 1982 constitution refers to the NPC as the highest organ of state power in China. In reality, however, it is far less significant. Although it is supposed to convene yearly, the constitution provides the nation's leaders with

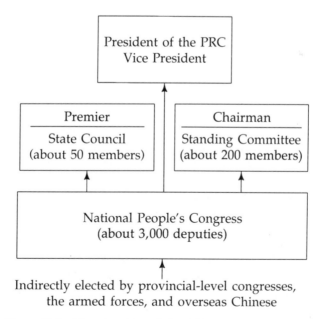

Figure 12.2 The structure of the Chinese government.

considerable flexibility for canceling or postponing meetings of the NPC.

Representatives to the NPC are elected for five-year terms by the provincial-level congresses, the armed forces, and overseas Chinese. The NPC elections are indirect in the sense that rank-and file citizens do not cast ballots for specific candidates. The nomination, selection, and election of delegates in China are handled through organizations in a way that is heavily dominated by the Chinese Communist Party.

The real function of the NPC has been to symbolize the regime's legitimacy and popular base. It is intended to provide the political system with a democratic facade and serve as an instrument for ratifying (some might say rubberstamping) Party resolutions into law. Virtually all Party and state apparatuses traditionally have been immune to NPC oversight and surveillance.

The presence of a large number of Party and government officials in the NPC detracts from its utility as a mechanism for checks and balances. The typical NPC session shows submissive deputies vying with each other in paying homage to the Party and its leaders. The unanimity with which Party decisions are passed is suggestive of the NPC's unquestioning obedience and subservience to the Party.

However, for a time during the reformist period in the 1980s, NPC deputies no longer were content with this submissive position and tried to seek autonomy and assert their authority. For example, in 1986, the NPC withheld ratification for a controversial bankruptcy law because many deputies had misgivings about its efficacy and social implications. Some proponents of an overhaul of the Chinese political system during this period even envisioned a reincarnation of China's legislature as an effective and independent locus of power, accountable to its constituencies and capable of effecting substantial results. However, few optimists remained, at least in the short term, after the Tiananmen Square massacre and the 1989 reassertion of traditional Communist Party authority.

The Standing Committee exercises most of the important functions of the NPC. A smaller body of high officials who frequently meet in Beijing, the Standing Committee has a compact, cohesive, and permanent structure with a membership of approximately 200, enabling it to exercise more effectively the NPC's formal powers of legislation and oversight. It also enjoys a certain degree of autonomy because a stipulation in the Chinese Constitution precludes other state officials from becoming eligible for its membership. Because it has potential as a genuine parliamentary body, some reformers in the late 1980s were contemplating amendments to the existing Chinese Constitution to transform the Standing Committee into a regular parliament that would hear and examine government reports and inspect and inquire about the performance of state organs. Once again, however, the bloody crushing of the student demonstrations in Tiananmen Square in June 1989 put an end to such talk of reform.

The head executive body, and the most important one in the Chinese government, is the State Council. From its inception in 1954 until early 1976, the State Council was headed by Premier Zhou Enlai. Upon Premier Zhou's death in 1976, Hua Guofeng became the new premier and leader of the State Council. In 1980, Hua was ousted, and the premiership was passed to Zhao Ziyang, an energetic reformer. After his election as Party Secretary General in early 1988 and in compliance with injunctions in force at that time against simultaneously holding both dominant Party and governmental positions, Zhao resigned his premiership in favor of Li Peng, a Soviet-trained engineer-turned-bureaucrat and the adopted son of the deceased Premier Zhou Enlai. Interestingly, Li Peng, in concert with Deng Xiaoping, was a primary player in bringing about the backlash against Zhao and his reformers in the spring of 1989.

The State Council consists of the premier, four vice premiers, half a dozen state councilors, and numerous heads of ministries and commissions. Many of the high Party leaders simultaneously hold positions on the State Council. Unlike the NPC, the State Council always has been and continues to be an important organ in Chinese politics. Although hardly an independent decision-making body, the State Council plays a significant role in the governing process because the Party cannot dispense with the expertise of its professionalized and specialized staff.

The State Council is particularly important in the implementation of Chinese Communist Party policy. As the highest executive body, the State Council directs and supervises the Chinese administrative structure. Assuming the responsibility for implementing the Party's policy proposals and for coordinating the economy and foreign and domestic affairs, the State Council shares political power with the CCP Politburo and Standing Committee. Under Zhao's stewardship in the late 1980s, the State Council distinguished itself as a bulwark of modernization and reform.

Above the State Council is the president of the Republic (head of state), a post that is different than that of chairman of the Standing Committee of the National People's Congress. In 1988, the president of the Republic post was assumed by Yang Shangkun, a member of the Politburo. Mao held this post from 1954–59 and passed it on to Liu Shaoqi, who held it from 1959–66, when he was purged. The post was abolished but restored in 1982, when Yang's

predecessor, Li Xiannian, assumed the head-of-state role.

In the 1980s, although moderate and reformist Chinese leaders presided over the elimination and merger of many ministries, the Chinese bureaucracy today still remains large and highly entrenched. The State Council directs numerous ministries. For example, one of them, the State Planning Commission, was established in 1952 as the Chinese ministry responsible for the planning of the state-run economy. The Chinese bureaucratic system is characterized by higher levels of provincial power than is seen in most traditional communist systems. Both the national ministries and the provincial organs can serve as powerful actors in the Chinese governmental process.

The Chinese military, the People's Liberation Army (PLA), has historically played a more important role in Chinese politics than militaries in other traditional communist states. During the civil-war years in China, the CCP and the PLA were indistinguishable; during Mao's reign, the PLA clearly was the most powerful bureaucracy in politics. Deng Xiaoping, the supreme leader in China in the 1980s, primarily owed his status and power to the ranks loyal to him within the PLA. Because of its willingness to implement a Deng-ordered crackdown on demonstrations and dissent in 1989, the PLA's power once again appeared to be on the rise.

Because of the closeness between the military and the Party in China, the security apparatus, which includes the People's Armed Police, historically has been weaker than the average security apparatus in a traditional Second World state. The relative weakness of the Chinese security apparatus vis-à-vis the PLA can be seen in the Party's response to both actors failing to promptly carry out orders relative to the crushing of the student demonstrations in Tiananmen Square. Both actors hesitated, and there was insubordination in the ranks of each, yet, only the security apparatus was significantly purged by the Party after order had been restored.

Governmental Reform in the Soviet Union

"The most perilous moment for a bad government is when it seeks to mend its ways. Only consummate statecraft can enable a king to save his throne when, after a long spell of oppressive rule, he sets to improving the lot of his subjects."[5]

—Alexis de Tocqueville

Since Mikhail Gorbachev first came to power in 1985, he has proposed a number of reforms targeted at the traditional method of government dominant in the Soviet Union since Joseph Stalin. Each of the reforms Gorbachev has proposed to date may be placed into one or more of four broad classifications: democratization, economic and political restructuring (perestroika), openness (glasnost), or "new thinking." Gorbachev has referred to the implementation of the four types of reform as being absolutely essential, if the Soviet Union ever is to break the shackles of its traditional methods of government and become a "rule of law state," characterized by the "direct involvement of the Soviet people in politics."

This section of Chapter 12 will be devoted both to outlining the goals of the various reform programs identified and to analyzing how much progress Gorbachev and his reform-minded allies have made in implementing them. What successes and what failures have Soviet reform communists experienced in attempting to implement their reform programs? Have the ac-

tions of Soviet reform communists matched their stated goals? Have they been practicing what they preach? How strong are the challenges to continued reform communist rule in the Soviet Union from both traditional communist and anticommunist forces? Let's take a look.

Outline of Reforms

The stated purpose of Gorbachev's democratization and restructuring reforms has been to break down in an orderly and evolutionary (as opposed to revolutionary) manner the monopoly of power that the Communist Party of the Soviet Union has enjoyed for more than 70 years in all aspects of social, political, and economic life, and to transfer that power to a reformed, restructured, and revitalized Soviet government. This reformed government would be held accountable to the Soviet people at large—and not to the Party—so that the Soviet Union finally might escape the spiritual and economic stagnation that has plagued it and achieve its true potential as a Great Power, not just a superpower, in the twenty-first century.

Policies of openness and toleration toward an independent press, political opposition groups, and free debate over the Soviet Union's past and future have been looked upon by reform communists in the Soviet Union both as a means to win popular support for their programs in the face of traditional communist opposition and as a means of generating new and fresh ideas that may cure the Soviet Union of its spiritual and economic malaise.

In an attempt to create a calm international environment conducive to the long-term growth of their domestic reform programs, as well as from a desire to transfer scarce economic resources to those programs so that they may have a fighting chance for success, Gorbachev and his allies in the Party and government have advocated a conciliatory, benign Soviet approach to international affairs. Disarmament proposals and announcements of Soviet intentions to de-mobilize forces, cut defense spending, and alter traditional military doctrine have emanated from the Kremlin on a fairly consistent basis since Gorbachev came to power in 1985.

Taken together, all of the offers, proposals and concessions the Soviet Union has made related to defense and foreign policy make up a package of substantial reforms in their own right. These are a different breed of reform than the programs described above, however, for they generally are believed to be sought after by Soviet leaders not for their own sake, but rather as a means to help support other, more domestically focused reforms. The term usually attached to this outwardly focused reform package of defense cuts and benign Soviet be-havior around the world is "new thinking."

Not surprisingly, reaction in the West to the "new thinking" line promulgated by the Kremlin has been mixed. Some have viewed Soviet offers and moves such as its withdrawal from Af-ghanistan, its abandonment of the Brezhnev Doctrine in Eastern Europe, and its signing of the INF Treaty with the United States as proof positive that the Soviet Union is sincere in its attempt to alter its aggressive international tendencies of the past.

Others are not so sure that overall Soviet strategy has changed as much as the tactics used to implement that strategy. They view "new thinking" as a Soviet strategy designed to gain a breathing spell, a *peredyshka*. During this "breather," they will seek a "realignment of the correlation of forces" (i.e., strengthening of Soviet military power) in a manner that will make them even stronger in the future, when they will decide to return to their more tradi-tional foreign and defense policies of expansion and coexistence.

Implementation of Reforms

Culminating, on December 1, 1988, a hotly con-tested two-year process of discussion and de-bates, the Supreme Soviet (the name of both the traditional and the reformed legislative body in the Soviet Union) adopted institutional changes which were envisioned by Gorbachev and his fellow reformers as the first phase of a concerted and serious attempt to reform and reorganize the Soviet government and the broader political system. Gorbachev described the changes as a major step leading to the de-mocratization of Soviet society.

Among other things, the political reforms created a new national parliament with broad legislative authority; competitive elections and limited terms of office; a powerful, expanded post of President; and enhanced responsibilities for executive bodies of the central government.

The reforms called for by Gorbachev in 1988 began to be implemented in 1989. First, a new 2,250-member unicameral legislature called the Congress of People's Deputies was created and seated by means of competitive elections. De-puties were selected for membership in the Congress on the basis of secret balloting in mul-tiple candidate elections held throughout the country in the spring of 1989.

By arrangement, 750 deputies were selected from all-union public organizations. One hundred of these seats were reserved by law for candidates from the Communist Party, whereas the other 650 were allotted to orga-nizations such as trade unions, cooperatives, youth leagues, and scientific groups. Another 750 seats were assigned to territorial districts, each with 257,300 voters. The residents in a given territorial district then voted in competitive elections to see who would be their district's representative to the Congress. Finally, the last 750 seats were allotted to regional units of the

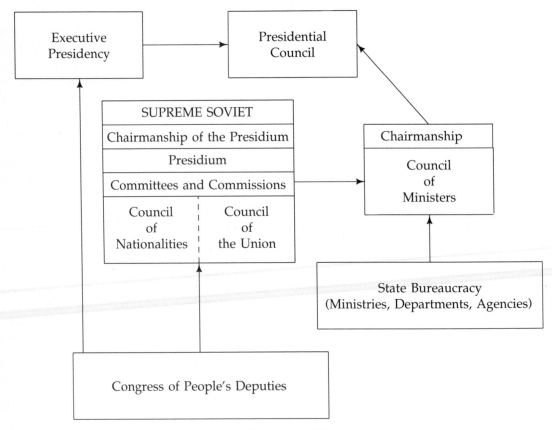

Figure 12.3 Structure of the reformed Soviet government.

Soviet federal structure. For example, each union republic received 32 seats. The union republic then held 32 elections within its borders to determine who its representatives would be.

The first Congress of People's Deputies convened in Moscow on May 25, 1989. The Congress is considered to be the highest state body in the Soviet Union and meets once or twice a year to establish state priorities in economic, social, political, and defense spheres.

In January 1989, the Communist Party selected its deputies to the Congress of People's De-

puties. First, nominees were submitted to the CPSU Politburo by the CPSU Central Committee and the Central Committees in the constituent republics. In a four-hour meeting on January 10, 1989, the Politburo alone chose the deputies who would represent the Party in the Congress, leaving the Central Committees and others with no say in the final selection process. Although all Party members had a chance to be nominated, and 31,500 were purportedly nominated from across the country, Gorbachev and the central Party leaders, particularly those in the Politburo, kept the authority for themselves to decide who the Party's representatives would be.

Some aspects of the 1989 election of the 1,500 deputies from territorial and regional jurisdictions to the Congress of People's Deputies suggested more democratic developments. The late Andrei Sakharov, a nominee for the citywide Moscow seat along with Boris Yeltsin, the former Politburo member, and Vitaly Vorotnikov, a member of the Politburo at the time, drew enthusiastic pre-election support. Sakharov's support motivated Yeltsin and Vorotnikov to take their chances in other electoral districts. Subsequently, however, Sakharov withdrew from the territorial election on the principle that he should have been a nominee of the Soviet Academy of Sciences, which had been assigned a number of seats on the basis of its status as an all-union organization.

Sakharov ultimately was elected by the Academy of Sciences, and Yeltsin won by an overwhelming margin in his electoral district. Many higher Party leaders were soundly rejected by the voters, indicating that new democratic trends had been set in motion in Soviet society.

Once the new Congress of People's Deputies had been seated, it elected a reconstituted, streamlined 542-member Supreme Soviet. Unlike the traditional Supreme Soviet that it replaced, the reconstituted Soviet meets twice a year for two or three months' duration, rather than its typical one- or two-day, twice-a-year sessions of the past. The new Supreme Soviet did keep the bicameral structure of its predecessor. One house of the new Supreme Soviet is called the Council of the Union, and the other is called the Council of Nationalities. Both houses of the new Supreme Soviet have 271 members.

Delegates to the Supreme Soviet come from the ranks of the Congress of People's Deputies. The Congress puts forth its own nominees and then votes. Those chosen move on to become

President Gorbachev presides over a meeting of the Congress of People's Deputies, an institution of increasing importance in the USSR. The late dissident and People's Deputy Andrei Sakharov stands at the podium, addressing the Congress.

members of the Supreme Soviet while simultaneously maintaining their seats in the Congress.

Twenty-three permanent committees and commissions are attached to the Supreme Soviet. Their responsibilities include not only preparation of legislation for consideration by the Supreme Soviet but also oversight of key executive actors who are responsible for implementation of the legislation once it has become law. For example, the Supreme Soviet Committee on Defense and State Security oversees the Soviet armed forces, internal police, and security apparatus.

The Supreme Soviet has a Presidium. The Presidium of the Supreme Soviet is a collegial body whose membership includes the Chairman of the Council of the Union and the Chairman of the Council of Nationalities, the two houses in the Supreme Soviet, the chairmen of the Union-republic supreme soviets, and the chairmen of the permanent commissions and committees of the Supreme Soviet. The Presidium of the Supreme Soviet is headed by a Chairman, who is elected by the Congress of People's Deputies from within its own ranks. The Chairman of the Supreme Soviet acts as the parliamentary speaker for the Supreme Soviet. In spring 1990, the Chairman of the Presidium of the Supreme Soviet was Anatolii Lukyanov.

The initial reforms of the Soviet constitution adopted in 1988 established the Chairman of the Presidium of the Supreme Soviet as President of the Soviet Union. The 1988 amendments to the Soviet constitution conferred important levers of state power on the Presidium of the Supreme Soviet as a whole and its Chairman in particular. For example, the right to declare war or to proclaim a state of emergency was granted to the Presidium. Its Chairman had the right to negotiate and sign international treaties, and from the General Secretary of the Party, he took control over the State Defense Council.

In March 1990, however, the Congress of People's Deputies approved new amendments to the Soviet constitution. These new amendments created a new executive Presidency within the Soviet government. This new Presidency was designed to stand alone, independent of the Presidium of the Supreme Soviet. Shortly after its creation, Mikhail Gorbachev assumed the mantle of the new Presidency, giving him the top leadership positions in both the Communist Party and the government in the Soviet Union.

The executive Presidency of the Soviet Union is an extremely powerful office as designed by the 1990 amendments to the Soviet constitution. The President of the Soviet Union has the power to propose legislation, negotiate treaties, overrule decisions of state bodies if they violate the constitution and endanger people's rights and freedoms, veto laws passed by the Supreme Soviet (the veto may be overridden by a two-thirds vote by each house), declare war, and to declare a state of emergency or martial law (but only after a warning to the republic concerned and the consent of that republic's presidium, or approval by a two-thirds vote in each house of the Supreme Soviet). In addition, the Soviet President is considered to be the Commander-in-Chief of the Soviet armed forces and the head of state.

The President of the Soviet Union can be removed from office by a two-thirds majority vote of the Congress of the People's Deputies, but it must be proved that he has violated the Soviet constitution. There is no provision for removing the President for immoral or irrational behavior. Although Gorbachev was elected President by the Congress of People's Deputies, plans have been drawn for the next election to the post to be held on a direct, popular-vote basis. The anticipated date of that election is late 1994, with the new popularly elected President entering office in early 1995 to serve the first of two possible five-year terms.

Along with the new office of the President, the constitutional amendments of 1990 provided for the creation of a new consultative body, the Presidential Council, to advise the President. This body appeared to be designed to take over the tasks reserved in the past for the Politburo of the Party and the State Defense Council. In other words, it is very powerful. Its membership is at the discretion of the President, except for the Chairman of the Council of Ministers (the prime minister), who must be included by design.

The Supreme Soviet elects the Council of Ministers, a body that does not appear that different from its traditional predecessor. Headed by the Prime Minister (Nikolai Ryzhkov in March 1990), the Council includes about a dozen first deputy prime ministers and deputy prime ministers, as well as various ministers and heads of other government bodies. What is different about this body is the process by which it is appointed. In the past, members of the Council of Ministers were handpicked by the top Party leaders. In 1989, the Supreme Soviet began playing a key role in determining the elections and confirmation of the new Council of Ministers, going so far as to reject 12 nominees from the Communist Party itself.

A final institution important in the new Soviet government is the Council of the Federation. The Council of the Federation includes the President of the Soviet Union and the presidents of the fifteen Soviet republics. Because the reformed and new governments of the individual republics of the Soviet Union were demanding greater autonomy from Moscow and indigenous political and economic control in the late 1980s and 1990, the Council of the Federation is likely to take on increased importance as the 1990s progress. Having the power to formulate treaties between the Soviet national government and the republics, the Council of the Federation will play a major role in any attempt on the part of Soviet leaders to create a loose confederation of sovereign states out of the union of socialist republics that has existed in the country since 1922. In such a confederated political order, the foreign and defense policies of the individual republics would likely be controlled by the national Soviet government, while the individual republics would maintain autonomy in other policy areas.

The inaugural sessions of the new Congress of People's Deputies and the reconstituted Supreme Soviet were televised across the entire USSR, and what the people witnessed was amazing. Heated debates about the most important and sensitive political issues, pointed criticism of higher Party officials, including Mikhail Gorbachev himself, and dramatic statements both for and against further reform. The stark contrast between the former, traditional Supreme Soviet and its vibrant, more democratic successor was apparent to all who witnessed the historic sessions of 1989.

Although significant democratization of the Soviet government has been undertaken, it would be inaccurate to say that the separation of powers and the checks and balances that have been built into the reformed Soviet political system have come anywhere close to approximating the pervasiveness of such principles in the political systems of the United States and other First World countries. The Communist Party of the Soviet Union remains very powerful in the Soviet Union, and the reforms that have been implemented in the Soviet government have had its blessing. What will happen when the government defiantly challenges the will of the Party is yet to be determined.

The will of the government has yet to deviate from the will of the Party largely because there are still so many Party members occupying key positions in the reformed Soviet government. The Party holds a vast majority of the seats in both the Congress of People's Deputies and the Supreme Soviet. The President, Prime Minister, and Chairman of the Presidium of the Supreme Soviet all are leaders of the Communist Party. Many departmental secretaries of the CPSU

Central Committee Secretariat serve as Chairmen of Supreme Soviet committees.

It should be duly noted, however, that the Communist Party that dominates the reformed Soviet government is far different from the Party that controlled the more traditional one. The CPSU is not the monolithic force it once was. The principles of democratic centralism and unity through terror are no longer applicable to the Party. The CPSU is highly factionalized. Party members are divided over the pace of social, economic, and political reform and over the resurgence of nationalism that has occurred throughout the Soviet Union during the reform era. The Party is so factionalized that it is no longer possible to talk, as was done traditionally, about "the will of the Party."

Threats to Reform

The reform communist leaders in the CPSU have had to deal with significant opposition to their programs of democratization, restructuring, openness, and "new thinking" from traditional conservatives, radical liberals, and ardent nationalists, both from within their Party and outside of it.

The reform communists' frustration and anxiety with their more doctrinaire brethren stem from the difficulty they have had in getting their reform proposals implemented through traditional channels and methods of communist rule. In many instances, lower-level Party and traditional state officials have not had the same enthusiasm for change and reform of the traditional Soviet economic, political, and social system that the leaders on high have. Party and state bureaucrats have enjoyed the perks granted to them by the old system. Why would someone want to implement reforms that might cost them their jobs and positions of power?

As Mikhail Gorbachev began in the late 1980s to scale back military spending and the role of the military in Soviet affairs, he encountered a certain amount of resistance within the military. So far, Gorbachev and the Communist Party have been firmly in control. However, the Soviet military remains a powerful actor, and we can expect them to continue to compete for what they consider their fair share of Soviet resources.

Gorbachev has long tried to eliminate the retrenchment and inertia toward his reforms from within the ranks of the Party and traditional state bureaucracies. During the first several years of his regime, he attempted to do so through a purging of personnel from within the traditional political system. When that didn't work, it is argued, he decided to create a new system, which would move the locus of power out of the bureaucracy and into the hands of a reformist government.

In fact, many Western analysts believe that Gorbachev's primary motivations in restructuring the Soviet government have been to eliminate the threat to his reforms posed by traditional conservatives within his Party. By proposing and then occupying the powerful Presidency, Gorbachev, they believe, has created an alternative power base for himself, independent from the Party, that might enable him to maintain his power even if he should be removed from his position as Party General Secretary by a conservative coup within the CPSU Central Committee.

Unfortunately for the reform communists, radical reform factions have developed within the Communist Party and in the new institutions of the reformed Soviet government that want to go much further and much faster than they do in reforming the political and economic system away from traditional methods of communist rule. One example is the Interregional Deputies Group in the Supreme Soviet. The

Group backs a political platform that advocates a free-market system and 100 percent popular-vote elections for the Soviet Union.

Many members of the Interregional Deputies Group were dissatisfied with the powers granted to the executive Presidency by the constitutional amendments of 1990. During debate over the amendments in the Supreme Soviet, they argued that expanded presidential power was not consistent with the reform communists' stated goal of democratization. Some warned that the expanded presidential powers set dangerous precedents for the future.

Another force that has threatened the programs of the reform communists is the intense mass appeal of newly emerging noncommunist national fronts, informal groups, and political parties within Soviet society. Taking advantage of the relaxation of repression in the age of glasnost and the repeal of constitutional provisions prohibiting political parties other than the CPSU, new political movements and organizations sprang up throughout the Soviet Union in the late 1980s and early 1990. Many of these new rivals to Party rule seek not the reform of the traditional communist Soviet political system but its overthrow (see Figure 12.4).

In an era of increasing national consciousness in the Soviet Union, the new political parties and mass movements of the Baltic republics have been particularly critical and outspoken of centralized communist rule. During the reformed Soviet government's consideration of constitutional changes in early 1990, for example, legislators from the new political parties in the Baltic republics made dramatic appeals and proposed reforms that would give their republics greater say. Initially, the non-communist leaders of the Baltic republics just asked the Supreme Soviet to pass reforms that would give the republics more power vis-à-vis the central government. By the spring of 1990, however, they

had moved toward outright seccession and independence from the Soviet Union.

Reformed Government in Eastern Europe

The revolutions of 1989 and the elections of 1990 have brought fundamental change to traditional methods of government in the Second World states of Eastern Europe. Communist Parties in these states mostly have collapsed, and the levers of state power have been passed to reformed and reconstituted governments. These governments have been freely elected and largely are composed of multiparty coalitions that span the spectrum of political thought.

Although the path to reform government in the states of Eastern Europe has been unique to each of the countries in the region, there have been some similarities among the countries in what has taken place. There has also been an underlying set of factors at the international-system level that has impacted Eastern Europe as a whole.

For these reasons, the first part of this section of the chapter will focus on the Second World states of Eastern Europe as a whole. Drawing on the individual reform stories of the various states, as well as regional factors produced by the international system, we will try to develop a general model that lays out the different stages through which the Second World states have had to pass on the road to reform.

Our model will serve as a comparative guide for us when we examine in the second part of this section the reform route that one specific Eastern European state—Hungary—has taken. We will take a closer look at Hungary and describe how its processes of reform have been both similar to and different from any general post-communist norm.

Confederation of Anarcho-Syndicalists

Founded: May 1989

Membership: 1,000

Leaders: None

Wants total abolition of the state. In favour of co-operatives, but anti-capitalist

Democratic party

Founded: January 1989

Membership: 2,000

Leaders: Lev Ubozhko,
Rastislav Semenov

Centre-left breakaway from Democratic Union (see below). Mr Ubozhko modestly describes himself as "the only leader who, standing at the head of the state, can pull it out of catastrophe"

Orthodox Constitutional Monarchy party

Founded: May 19 1990 (birthday of Nicholas II)

Membership: unknown

Leaders: S. Yurkov-Engelgardt,
Neliya Milovanova

Wants to unite the Russian Orthodox church, the army and KGB under a restored constitutional monarchy. Members swear allegiance to the grand duke Vladimir Kirilovich Romanov. Other monarchist groups want the tsar to be elected by a nationwide assembly

Constitutional Democratic party

Founded: May 1990

Membership: 500

Leader: Leonid Podolski

Centre-left. Based on an organization called the Union of Constitutional Democrats, which is in turn a revival of the pre-revolutionary anti-tsarist Cadets party

Liberal Democrats

Founded: March 1990

Membership: 3,000-4,000

Leader: Vladimir Zhirinovsky

"No ideology, our theory is common sense." Pro free market. Split away from the Democratic Union. Described by former allies as "trash" and "an arm of the KGB"

Party of Free Labour

Founded: February 1990
(but not yet a formal party)

Membership: unknown

Leader: Igor Korovikov

Pro-business. The party of the co-operatives, it has money but limited popularity. Will not admit Communists

Christian Democratic Union

Founded: April 1989

Membership: 2,500

Leader: Alexander Ogorodnikov

Centre-right. Implacably anti-Communist, it has close links with western Christian Democrats. Wins respect because its founder is a long-time religious dissident. Plans to set up an umbrella group called the Russian Democratic Forum

Russian Communist party in the CPSU

Founded: January 1990

Membership: 2,000

Leaders: Boris Gidaspov,
Nina Andreeva

Neo-Stalinist, in favour of strict central planning and Russian imperialism. The fundamentalists of the Communist party hostile to President Gorbachev and *perestroika*. The faction is not recognized by the national Communist party but has won the acceptance of the local Leningrad party

Socialist party

Founding congress planned in June

Membership: 1,000

Leaders: Boris Kagarlitsky,
Vladimir Makhonov,
Lev Volovik

Socialist. Connected with the strike committees of the unofficial trade-union movement. Wants to give state property and economic control to local governments

Democratic Union

Founded: May 1988

Membership: 2,000

Leaders: None (very democratic)

Uncompromisingly anti-Communist. The earliest and bravest of the informal political parties, determined from the beginning to behave as if the Soviet Union were a proper democracy. Its pioneer demonstrations were broken up by the KGB. It continues to boycott elections as insufficiently free, but its influence is falling as the country becomes more democratic and members leave to set up other parties

Russian Popular Front

Founded: December 1988

Membership: Up to 40,000

Leaders: Vladimir Ivanov
M. Skurlatov

Favours the free market, democracy and the spiritual rebirth of Russia. One of the largest of the new parties, it attempts to do in Russia what the Popular Fronts are doing in the Baltic and TransCaucasian republics. Oddly mixes western democratic and Russian Orthodox values. It is split between the liberal Ivanov faction and the social democratic Skurlatov wing

Social Democratic Party of Russia

Founded: May 1990

Membership: 5,000

Leaders: Oleg Rumyantsev,
Nikolai Tutov

Centre-left. Well-organized, with good links to West European social democratic parties. Linked also with the reformist wing of the Communist party, but rules out a coalition with Communists. It is part of the Social Democratic Association, founded in Estonia in January. It failed to attract better-known social democratic deputies, who are drifting towards the Russian Peoples' party. Split between Muscovites (who want a centralized party) and Lengingraders (for a decentralized one)

Marxist Platform of the Communist party

Founded: April 1990

Membership: unknown

Leaders: Yegor Ligachev,
Vadim Bakatin

Conservative Communists, the mirror image of the Democratic Platform (see below). Likes some elements of *perestroika*, but dislikes the party's loss of monopoly power

United Workers' Front

Founded: October 1989

Membership: more than 5,000

Leader: Veniamin Yarin

Marxist-Leninist. Stands for central planning, guaranteed full employment and a minimum wage. Closely allied with, and often indistinguishable from, the Marxist Platform of the Communist party. It has strong support in the large but polarized industrial cities of Leningrad, Moscow and Sverdlovsk. Its leader is a populist working-class hero in the Peronist mould

Democratic Platform of the Communist party

Founded: January 1990

Membership: 500,000

Leaders: Vyacheslav Shostakovsky,
Gavriil Popov,
Boris Yeltsin

Social Democratic. The "left-radicals" (ie, reformers) of the Communist party. They want to turn the party in to a Socialist one, encouraging free enterprise and ending Communist control of factories, the army and KGB. Target of attack by party conservatives. Embraces many of Russia's most respected reformers, but they seem unlikely to take over the party, so many (but how many? and how coherently?) will split away

Russian People's party

Organizing committee exists, but party not yet formally founded

Membership: –

Leaders: Nikolai Travkin,
Yuri Afanasyev

Centre-left. Intended to be the home for disaffected Communist reformers if or when they leave the Communist party. Mr Travkin urged the new unofficial trade-union organization, the Confederation of Labour, to affiliate but it turned him down. The army trade union, Shield, and April, an influential reform group of the Soviet Writers' union, may, however, join

Figure 12.4 Communist Party factions and independent parties in the Russian republic, ranked on a scale of importance from one to ten. [From *The Economist* (May 26, 1990), p. 52.]

The Rejection of Traditional Methods of Communist Rule

Traditional Eastern European Communist Party leaders witnessed the emergence of increased opposition to their rule throughout the 1980s. This opposition was represented in such diverse forms as independent trade union movements; underground religious and human rights organizations; national, cultural, and environmental conscious groups; secret student and literary clubs; demonstrations; strikes; the dissemination of non–Party-sanctioned publications (samizdat); and the ever-growing sense of frustration among society at large, reflected in declining worker productivity and mass apathy. The pursuit of communism via a single-Party socialist system became an exercise in futility.

With the rise to power of Mikhail Gorbachev and the advent of his reform programs in the Soviet Union, the traditional communist leaders in Eastern Europe began to face opposition to their methods of rule not only from their societies at large but also from reform factions within their own Communist Party.

Historically in Eastern Europe, if a Party member toed Moscow's line, his chances for enhanced power within the Party were far greater than if he did not. With the advent of Gorbachev's reformist line and the refusal of old-line communist leaders in Eastern Europe to accept it, a good number of Gorbachev's newly converted Eastern European protegés in the mid-1980s probably did not truly believe in his reforms, but rather saw in them an opportunity to enhance their own power once any decision came down from Moscow that the hard-line, traditional Communist leadership must go.

Those who sought Moscow's intervention to remove traditional Communist Party leaders in Eastern Europe gradually learned, however, that the Kremlin of Gorbachev did not operate in the same manner as the Kremlin of his predecessors, relative to the domestic affairs of Eastern European states. The Gorbachev regime had publicly hinted on numerous occasions early on in its rule that it simply had too many other problems to worry about than the internal politics of Eastern European states. On the basis of 1956 Hungary and 1968 Czechoslovakia, however, few in Eastern Europe were willing to give Gorbachev's pronouncements the benefit of the doubt. Because of a belief that a sudden policy reversal in Moscow was possible, reform communists in Eastern European Parties and opposition groups at large within these Second World societies initially remained cautious in their calls for change in their country's traditional communist political system.

Unlike the past, however, the liberalized line in Moscow was not reversed when the call for change in Eastern Europe reached the point of the dissolution of traditional Party rule. This time, Party officials in Moscow had told the truth. They really were not going to intervene militarily, economically, or politically to prevent the dissolution of Party dictatorships in Eastern Europe.

By early 1989, the communist reformers and opposition groups in various Eastern European states had become convinced that what Gorbachev had been saying for years was indeed true, and with the promise of economic rewards being offered by the United States and countries of Western Europe for accelerated movement toward a pluralist, democratic political system, they began to make their respective assaults on state power. Without the support of Moscow to which they had grown so accustomed throughout the Cold War period, the traditional Communist Party dictators and their loyalists stood little chance of survival once they were exposed to an angry populace.

Alexander Dubcek and Vaclav Havel confer during a 1989 demonstration that led to the end of Communist Party rule in Czechoslovakia.

Initially, the reform communist faction of the Party and the opposition at large within Eastern European societies worked together to remove traditional Communist Party leaders from their positions of power. This was done by a reform communist bid for power from within the Party, which was reinforced by expressions of support from influential opposition forces outside the Party. These two factors, coupled with Moscow's ambivalence, resulted in a swing in the balance of power within the Party in favor of the reform communists, who, once they held a majority in the Central Committee of the Party, proceeded to purge the traditional communists from their positions of power.

For the most part, the purging of the traditional communist leaderships was done peacefully, without much loss of life. The exception to the rule, however, was in Romania. In Romania, the traditional communist dictator, Nicolae Ceausescu, refused to gracefully step down in the face of popular and intra-Party opposition. Rather, he ordered his secret police force, the Securitate, and the Romanian Army to engage in a slaughter of his opponents. The Romanian Army balked at such orders and instead sided with the opposition. After a series of bloody battles between the Securitate and the Romanian Army, which was aided by bands of civilian militants, the Army and the opposition prevailed, and the Ceausescu regime was overthrown.

The Implementation of New Governments in Eastern Europe

Once the Eastern European reform communists had gained control of their Parties, they soon realized that the opposition that had once supported them now increasingly wanted them to share their Party's reins of power. The opposition did not want just a reformed communist system; they wanted an entirely new system, based on the pluralist democratic systems of the West.

Confronted with this challenge to their newfound rule, the reform communists agreed to

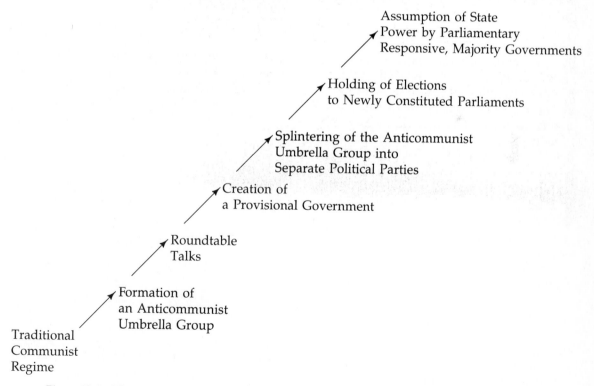

Assumption of State
Power by Parliamentary
Responsive, Majority Governments

Holding of Elections
to Newly Constituted Parliaments

Splintering of the Anticommunist
Umbrella Group into
Separate Political Parties

Creation of
a Provisional Government

Roundtable
Talks

Formation of
an Anticommunist
Umbrella Group

Traditional
Communist
Regime

Figure 12.5 The process of transition from communist to pluralist regimes in Eastern Europe.

enter into roundtable negotiations with the opposition to hammer out reform methods of government that would be acceptable to both sides. The reform communists had little if any choice but to propose and enter the roundtable process. For example, the reform communist leaders in Poland found that the popular support commanded by Solidarity made it impossible to govern without recognizing and working with the free trade union movement.

A reform communist refusal to negotiate or to release the reins of dictatorial control would have been an adoption of the the same line that had supposedly been done away with by the purging of the traditional communists. The reform communists were too attuned to the increasing importance of popular support in governing within the region since the exit of dominant Soviet influence to make such a mistake. They recognized the need to command mass support and were, therefore, willing to allow the growth of independent political movements, more powerful assemblies, and more competitive elections. By so doing, reform communist leaders hoped to win enough acclaim from their populace to enable them to hold onto some of their power once their state's traditional political system had been reformed.

During the roundtable negotiations, the opposition parties won major concessions from the Party: The Party agreed to rescind state constitutional provisions granting it a monopoly of power; legalize opposition parties; have competitive, multiparty, free elections to a reformed national parliament based on Western European lines, which would assume state power from the Party once elected; and include noncommunists in a provisional government that would rule the country until parliamentary elections could be held.

The institutions of the provisional government were those of the traditional communist gov-

ernment with two major differences. First, the provisional government no longer took orders from the Party Politburo and Secretariat. Second, many of the seats and ministerial positions in the government were occupied no longer by subservient communists, but rather by leading figures of the umbrella opposition group.

During the provisional government phase of reform, most leaders of both the Party and the umbrella opposition were more concerned with positioning themselves for the upcoming parliamentary elections than with governing the country via the provisional government. In preparation for the elections, both the Party and the umbrella opposition split into various new parties representing all points of the spectrum of political thought. In Czechoslovakia, for example, almost forty new political parties were formed after the creation of the provisional government in that country. There now are parties throughout Eastern Europe in competition with each other, standing on such diverse platforms as traditional communism, reform communism, socialism, social democracy, lib-

This March 18, 1990 voting in East Berlin represented the first free election in East Germany since the 1930s.

eralism, religious conservatism, environmentalism, nationalism, populism, and even fascism.

The elections to the new national parliaments that have taken place in Eastern Europe have been conducted on the basis of secret ballots with universal adult suffrage. They have to a large extent been patterned after parliamentary elections in Western Europe. Elections in Western Europe differ from those in the United States in that there is more emphasis on the vote a party gets rather than the vote a particular individual gets. For example, in the United States, if an individual wins a majority of the votes in a Senate race, that individual occupies the Senate seat for which he has competed. In most European countries, however, that individual may or may not occupy the seat for which he has contested, depending on the desire of his party and the rank of his name on a party list.

In Europe, the number of seats a party is assigned in the parliament is based on the percentage of the total vote it receives in an election. In most cases, parties draw up lists of candidates that they consider once the number of seats allotted to them has been determined. The number-one candidate on the list fills the first available party seat, the second on the list the second seat, and so on down the line. Because the parties make out their lists under assumption that a clean sweep of all the seats in parliament is possible, inevitably, some candidates on the party list are not awarded seats because the party does not, in fact, win all of the seats available. Because of this fact, the ranking of the names on the party lists becomes very important.

Once the elections have taken place in Eastern European states and the seats in parliament have been allotted to the various deserving parties, the next step in reform has been for the majority party in parliament to form a government under the direction of one of its leaders, who assumes the title of prime minister. If no party has been awarded a majority in parliament by the electoral process, a coalition government consisting of a major party and one or two minor parties in alliance with one another has had to be formed. This coalition government controls the majority of seats within the parliament but is less stable than a single-party majority government because it is made up of different parties that often have very different platforms. They have aligned out of mutual self-interest to share power.

The prime minister of the coalition government typically comes from the party with the most seats in the parliament within the government coalition. The minor parties generally are rewarded by the prime minister for their participation in the coalition by the appointment of leaders of their party to ministerial positions within the government.

In addition to a prime minister who heads the legislative body of the government, most Eastern European states have made provisions for the election of a chief executive, or president. The office of president in most Eastern European countries appears to most closely resemble the office of president in France, in that the presidents in Eastern Europe will have strong state powers to handle national emergencies and state crises, to choose the prime minister, to veto legislation, and to dissolve parliament.

The Hungarian Reform Experience

Unlike the situations in some other Second World states of Eastern Europe, organized opposition to traditional communist rule in Hungary was not that strong before the cataclysmic events of 1989 and 1990. The Hungarian people, after all, had already been burned once by attempting to reform their traditional communist political system. The Soviet invasion of their

Election results are for the lower house of parliament, and percentages of the vote are for the first round of voting in 1990.

Bulgaria

Elections on June 10th and 17th, 1990, for a 400-seat, single-chamber two-year parliament.

	% of vote	seats
Bulgarian Socialist party (formerly communists)	47	211
Union of Democratic Forces (anticommunist alliance)	36	144
Agrarian Union (farmers)	8	16
Movement for Rights and Freedom (ethnic Turks)	6	23
Other	3	6

East Germany

Election on March 18th, 1990, for a single-chamber, 400-seat parliament.

	% of vote	seats
Alliance for Germany (Christian Democratic coalition)	48	193
Social Democrats	22	87
Democratic Socialists (formerly communists)	16	65
Liberals	5	21
Others	9	34

Hungary

Election on March 25th and April 8th, 1990, for a single-house, 386-seat, four-year parliament.

	% of vote	seats
Democratic Forum (center-right)	25	165
Free Democrats (center-liberal)	21	92
Independent Smallholders (farmers)	12	43
Socialists (reform communists)	11	33
Young Democrats (center-liberal)	9	21
Christian Democrats	7	21
Hungarian Socialist Workers (unreformed communists)	4	0
Social Democrats	4	0
Other	7	11

Czechoslovakia

Elections on June 8th and 9th, 1990, for a two-year federal parliament with 150-seat House of the People (101 from Czech republic, 49 from Slovakia) and 150-seat House of the Nations (75 from each).

	% of vote	seats
Civic Forum/Public Against Violence (Czech/Slovak anticommunist alliance)	47	87
Communists	14	23
Christian Democrats	12	20
Moravian and Silesian Autonomists	5	9
Slovak National party	4	6
Coalition of other minorities	3	5

Figure 12.6 Elections in Eastern Europe 1990. [Adapted from The Economist (June 23, 1990), p. 46; and *Report on Eastern Europe* (July 13, 1990), p. 41.]

Poland

This is a special case. The last general election was in June 1989 for a parliament with 460-seat lower house and 100-seat upper house, the Senate. In the free election for the Senate, the anticommunist movement, Solidarity, won 99 seats. Elections for the lower house were semi-free. There, Solidarity could compete for only 35% of the lower house seats.

	% of vote	seats
Solidarity....................	35	161
PUWP (Communists)......	37	173
Polish Peasant Party	16	76
Democratic Party...........	5	27
Former procommunist Christian Groups	5	23

Romania

Election on May 20th, 1990, for a two-year parliament with 396-seat lower house and 190-seat upper house.

	% of vote	seats
National Salvation Front (ex- and not-so-ex-communists, military officers, former dissidents)	66	233
Democratic Hungarian Union.....................	7	29
Liberals (center-right)	6	29
Greens.....................	3	12
National Peasants (farmers)	3	12
Others	15	81

Figure 12.6 (Continued)

country in the fall of 1956 and the subsequent crushing of the revolutionary Nagy regime had killed thousands of Hungarians.

In the years after the 1956 revolution, the Hungarian people reached a sort of tacit agreement with their communist overlords. The people agreed to tolerate traditional communist rule if the regime provided them with a better standard of living than their communist brethren in the rest of the Soviet bloc.

The traditional Hungarian communist regime in the post-1956 era was headed by Janos Kadar. Kadar ruled Hungary with an iron hand. He was intolerant of dissent, yet he was willing to experiment with reform of the traditional Stalinist economic model to attempt to pacify his people with an above-average socialist standard of living.

In the late 1960s, Kadar and his Party designed the New Economic Mechanism for the Hungarian economy. The New Economic Mechanism reduced the burden placed on workers by the central planning bureaucracy by transferring some management decisions to managers at the local-enterprise level. The workers initially responded to this plan by producing more and better-quality goods. The NEM also allowed Hungarians access to Western consumer goods not available anywhere else in the Soviet bloc.

When Mikhail Gorbachev and his reform programs came along in 1985, the imagination of the Hungarian people did not run wild, but the imagination of many mid-level, technocratic, young Communist Party members did. Reform communism was attractive to them because they recognized that the aging policies of the New Economic Mechanism no longer were able to generate the standard of living to which the Hungarian people had grown accustomed. In an effort to preempt political unrest, these reformers recognized that the Hungarian economy needed an infusion of new thinking. They turned to Gorbachev-styled reforms in both the economic and the political arena to solve their problems. They also saw in the Gorbachev line an opportunity to launch a challenge to Kadar's age-old grip on state power.

The enthusiasm the reform faction of the Hungarian Communist Party developed toward perestroika and glasnost soon outdistanced the Soviet Party itself in terms of its daring and boldness. Before long, the Hungarian people began to take notice of what was going on in their suddenly not-so-monolithic Party. The Party was splitting along reform and traditional lines. The traditional faction was being led by Party leader Janos Kadar. The reformist wing was being led by men such as Imre Pozsgay, Gyula Horn, Miklos Nemeth, and Rezso Nyers.

In May 1988, Kadar, via an intra-Party coup, was removed from his position as Party leader after thirty-two years in power. His replacement, Karoly Grosz, was a compromise choice between the reformist and traditional factions of the Party. Over the next year, a tug of war took place within the Party over its future direction. The reformists radicalized their programs in an effort to win increasing popular support. The traditional communists used their positions within the apparat to scuttle the implementation of new reforms.

By January 1989, the reformist faction of the Hungarian Party had succeeded in gaining a majority within the Party's Central Committee and traditional Hungarian legislature. It had successfully purged many old-line communists from the Party rank and file.

During January 1989, the traditional Hungarian legislature approved bills legalizing freedom of assembly and freedom of association for the Hungarian people. In February 1989, the Hungarian Communist Party Central Committee approved the creation of independent political parties in the country. In May 1989,

the Central Committee forced the former Party leader Janos Kadar into retirement from his ceremonial position as President of Hungary. In June, the reformists in the Central Committee replaced Karoly Grosz as Party leader with one of their own, Rezsos Nyers. Miklos Nemeth, another reformer, became Prime Minister.

Throughout the summer of 1989, the political scene in Hungary was in a state of flux. The Communist Party was disintegrating over factional battles between reformers and traditionalists, and between different leading personalities within the reformist faction itself. Opposition to communist rule, long dormant because of severe repression, had been reborn and rejuvenated. More than sixty parties (including one called the Winnie the Pooh Party!) had been formed in rapid succession since the approval of the February 1989 Party decree that allowed for opposition parties.

On September 19, 1989, roundtable negotiations between the Party and an umbrella opposition group concluded. The two groups reached an agreement allowing for the creation of a multiparty political system within Hungary. In exchange for the promise of free elections to parliament, the reform communists supposedly were reserved the right to provide the country's head of state. The new president was expected to be directly elected by the people before the new parliament was chosen, thereby giving the Party's likely candidate, Imre Poszgay, a good chance of winning.

Also at the roundtable talks, it was agreed that the Party's militia, the 60,000-strong Workers' Guard, would be turned over to a provisional government, which would hold sway over the country until the parliamentary and presidential elections could be held. The provisional government was to be led by the standing Prime Minister, Miklos Nemeth, and was to include representatives from both the

Party and the opposition. Seats were to be opened in the traditional legislature and were to be competed for by both members of the Party and the opposition in special elections.

In October 1989, the Hungarian Communist Party, officially the Hungarian Socialist Workers' Party, renounced Marxism and renamed itself the Hungarian Socialist Party. The leaders of the new Socialist Party, largely the same people that controlled the reformist wing of the traditional Communist Party, committed themselves to the creation of a market economy and a multiparty, democratic political system in Hungary. Shortly after the conclusion of the October Party Congress that had ratified the name change of the Party, the traditional communist faction within the new Socialist Party broke away and re-formed the Hungarian Socialist Workers' Party.

On October 23, 1989, on the thirty-third anniversary of the 1956 uprising, Hungary was proclaimed a free republic and the provisional government approved at the roundtable talks in September, under the leadership of Miklos Nemeth, took control of the state. The special elections to the open seats in the traditional legislature resulted in a string of defeats for the Socialist Party and inclusion of opposition leaders in the provisional government.

On November 26, Hungarians decided by referendum not to choose a president until they had chosen their new parliament. This was a real blow to the leaders of the Socialist Party because they thought an agreement had been struck at the roundtable talks that would allow the presidential elections to take place before the parliamentary elections.

The Socialists believed that their candidate for president, Imre Poszgay, would win in a presidential election held before the parliamentary elections because of his popularity as the Party man who peacefully negotiated away the Party's monopoly of power in Hungary. They thought he could not win in a presidential election held after the parliamentary elections. The Socialist Party was not expected to fair well in the elections for parliament (because they were the former Communist Party), and it would be difficult for a candidate from a minority party in parliament to win a national office such as the presidency.

Once the provisional government set March 25, 1990, as the date for parliamentary elections in Hungary, a flurry of Western-style campaign activity took place. A bitter campaign evolved between two leading parties once loosely linked to the anticommunist opposition. One of the parties, the Democratic Forum, emphasized traditional Christian values and conservative social policy in a manner similar to the center-right Christian Democratic Parties of Western Europe. The Democratic Forum also advocated a careful transition from socialism to a free-market economy and a convertible Hungarian currency; favored integration with Western Europe and a continued American role in Europe; and took up a nationalistic stance concerning the protection of Hungarian minorities living abroad, particularly those living in the Transylvania section of neighboring Romania.

The other leading party, the Alliance of Free Democrats, accused the Democratic Forum of being both overtly nationalistic and chauvinistic on the basis of its stance on the Hungarian minority issues. In addition to the two parties' differences on the minority issue, there were differences between the two relative to the pace at which Hungary should be integrated into the rest of Europe. The Free Democrats advocated a much more rapid shift away from the traditional methods of communist rule than the Democratic Forum. The Free Democrats called for radical moves toward a free market, laying out plans to privatize 35 to 40 percent of Hungary's business assets within two to three years after the elections, and 70 to 80 percent before ten years passed.

The Hungarian multiparty parliamentary elections held on March 25, 1990, were conducted on the basis of a two-tiered voting system. The two-tiered system allowed voters to vote on two ballots, one giving party preference and the other selecting individual local candidates. Any candidate receiving 15 percent of the vote qualified for a runoff, which was held on April 8, 1990.

The two big winners in the March 25 elections were the Democratic Forum and the Alliance of Free Democrats. The Democratic Forum won 24 percent of the total vote, and the Alliance of Free Democrats 21 percent. Of the other sixty parties that desired seats in the new Hungarian parliament, only six achieved the necessary 4 percent of the total vote to be granted representation. (No, the Winnie the Pooh Party was not one of these six!) Sixty-four percent of eligible Hungarian voters voted in the March 25 elections.

Following the runoff elections of April 8, seats in the first freely elected parliament in Hungary since the imposition of communist rule were distributed. No single party held a majority of seats in the new parliament; therefore, a coalition government had to be formed. The Democratic Forum, the party that won the most seats in the elections, was able to form a majority government by entering into an alliance with two smaller parties, the Smallholders and the Christian Democrats. Together, the three parties in the governing coalition in Hungary controlled 229 of the 386 seats in parliament.

The Socialist Party, primarily consisting of the reform communists responsible for the abolition of the Party's monopoly of power in Hungary, received only 11 percent of the total vote in the parliamentary elections. The traditional Communist Party, the Hungarian Socialist Workers Party, failed to earn 4 percent of the total vote in the election and was denied representation in the new parliament. By the spring of 1990, one could safely assume that communist rule had effectively come to an end in Hungary.

In May of 1990, Arpad Goncz, a founder of the Free Democrats and writer jailed for six years during the 1956 uprising, was selected by the Hungarian parliament to serve as the interim President of Hungary until national popular elections could be held. The Democratic Forum, the dominant party of the majority coalition within the new Hungarian parliament voted for Goncz, a member of the opposition Free Democrats, as interim President after securing promises from the Free Democrats that Goncz would call on the Democratic Forum to form a government and that they would supply the needed votes when legislation required a two-thirds majority. Shortly thereafter, Jozsef Antall, the leader of the Democratic Forum, was named Prime Minister of Hungary and called upon by Goncz to form a government. Peaceful bargaining and compromise between rival political parties had come to Hungary.

Suggestions for Further Reading

Barnett, A. Doak, *Cadres, Bureaucracy, and Political Power in Communist China* (New York: Columbia University Press, 1967).

Bialer, Seweryn, *The Soviet Paradox: External Expansion, Internal Decline* (New York: Knopf, 1986).

Bialer, Seweryn, and Thane Gustafson, eds., *Russia at the Crossroads: The 26th Congress of the CPSU* (Winchester, Mass.: Allen & Unwin, 1982).

Brown, J.F., *Eastern Europe and Communist Rule* (Durham, N.C.: Duke University Press, 1988).

Carter, April, *Democratic Reform in Yugoslavia: The Changing Role of the Party* (Princeton, N.J.: Princeton University Press, 1982).

Cocks, Paul, *Controlling Communist Bureaucracy* (Cambridge, Mass.: Harvard University Press, 1977).

Colton, Timothy J., *Commissars, Commanders, and Civilian Authority: The Structure of Soviet Military Politics* (Cambridge, Mass.: Harvard University Press, 1979).

Harding, Harry, *Organizing China: The Problem of Bureaucracy, 1949–76* (Stanford, Calif.: Stanford University Press, 1981).

Hough, Jerry F., and Merle Fainsod, *How the Soviet Union Is Governed* (Cambridge, Mass.: Harvard University Press, 1979).

Knight, Amy W., *The KGB: Police and Politics in the Soviet Union* (Winchester, Mass.: Allen & Unwin, 1988).

Lane, David, *Elites and Political Power in the USSR* (Brookfield, Vt.: Edward Elgar, 1988).

Little, D. Richard, *Governing the Soviet Union* (New York: Longman, 1989).

Lovenduski, Jean and Jean Woodall, *Politics and Society in Eastern Europe* (Bloomington, In.: Indiana University Press, 1987).

Nelson, Daniel and Stephen White, eds., *Communist Legislatures in Comparative Perspective* (London: MacMillan and Albany: State University of New York Press, 1982).

Pye, Lucien, *The Dynamics of Chinese Politics* (Cambridge: Oelgeschlager, Gunn & Hain, 1981).

Pravda, Alex and Blair Ruble, *Trade Unions in Communist States* (Winchester, Mass.: Allen & Unwin, 1988).

Ra'anan, Uri and Igor Lukes, eds., *Inside the Apparat: Perspectives on the Soviet System from Former Functionaries* (Lexington, Mass.: Lexington Books, 1990).

Sharlet, Robert, *The New Soviet Constitution of 1977: Analysis and Text* (Brunswick, Ohio: King's Court Communications, 1978).

Starr, Richard F., *Communist Regimes in Eastern Europe*, 5th ed. (Stanford, Calif.: Hoover Institution Press, 1988).

Vanneman, Peter, *The Supreme Soviet: Politics and Legislative Process in the Soviet Political System* (Durham, N.C.: Duke University Press, 1977).

Notes

1. V.A. Vlasov, *Sovetskii gosudartvennyi apparat* (Moscow: Gos. idz-vo i urid. lit-ry, 1959) p. 361, cited in Darrell P. Hammer, *USSR: The Politics of Oligarchy* (Hinsdale, Ill.: Dyrden, 1974), p. 278.

2. For an analysis and the text of the 1977 Soviet constitution, see Robert Sharlet, *The New Soviet Constitution of 1977* (Brunswick, Ohio: Kings Court, 1978).

3. I.N. Ananov, *Ministerstva USSR* (Moscow: Gos. idz-vo i urid. lit-ry, 1960) p. 22, Ibid., p. 277.

4. For a description of the duties of the traditional state defense council, as told by former Party insiders, see Uri Ra'anan and Igor Lukes, eds., *Inside the Apparat* (Lexington, Mass.: Lexington Books, 1990), pp. 84–95.

5. Alexis de Tocqueville, *The Old Regime and the French Revolution*, trans. Stuart Gilbert (New York: Doubleday Anchor Books, 1955), p. 277.

THE POLICY PROCESS AND ECONOMIC REFORM IN SECOND WORLD STATES

For decades, Second World states were described as Communist Party dictatorships. Political scientists generally referred to the policy process as totalitarian, meaning that the Communist Party and the elites who sat at the top of the Party hierarchy had almost total control over the making and implementation of policy. Was this an accurate description of the policy process in Second World states? And what about the present and future?

This chapter will examine and discuss different models and concepts that can be used to better understand the creation and implementation of policy in the Soviet Union, China, and selected East European states.

An Overview of the Policy Process

To simplify and aid in the understanding of something as complicated as politics and the policy process, political scientists use models, that is, simplified representations, to help capture important elements of reality.

Until the 1960s, the totalitarian model guided most studies of communist systems. This model drew attention to a highly organized, dictatorial process where individuals and groups outside of the top Party leadership had no significant political power. Two early proponents of this model, Carl Friedrich and Zbigniew K. Brzezinski, noted that the totalitarian system involved an unavoidable compulsion on the part of the rulers to absorb or destroy all social groups obstructing its complete control.[1]

Certainly, there was a considerable amount of totalitarian rule in the Second World during the Stalinist period. The Soviet political system was a dictatorial state in which the Communist Party dominated social, political and economic life. Stalinist totalitarianism was exported to communist China and the East European states after World War II and remained dominant in most Second World states throughout the 1950s and 1960s.

Although the widely used totalitarian model drew attention to some very important features of communist political systems, an increasing number of scholars in the post-Stalin era began to feel that it also obscured some equally important aspects of the policy process. H. Gordon Skilling, for example, contended that the totalitarian model focused too much attention on outputs (the decisions made by the Party leadership) and too little on inputs.[2] Skilling argued that groups and actors outside the formal Party leadership could make inputs (e.g., demands) that affected the political process in traditional communist systems.

This viewpoint resulted in new concern with the input side of the policy process and brought increasing attention to the competing interests and bargaining that went on prior to the formal making of decisions in the post-Stalin era. Scholars with these interests began to use group, or pluralist, models to study power and policy in communist systems—that is, by the 1970s, many Western analysts felt that increasing numbers of groups and political actors both inside and outside the Communist Party hierarchy were becoming influential in the policy process. With the decline of terror tactics following Stalin's death, the increasing complexity of social, political, and economic decisions, and the growing expertise of different sectors of society, the conditions were set for a more open, sometimes pluralistic process. Jerry F. Hough contended, for example, that these tendencies had become so prevalent that a new pluralist model of communist politics was needed.[3] Although some were critical of the group and pluralist models,[4] these newer approaches brought attention to the presence of interest group competition and to some measure, at least, of political pluralism in communist-run societies.

The introduction of this text called attention to different phases in the policy process—the setting of goals, taking action, and producing outcomes. The models of totalitarianism and pluralism help us to better understand these phases. We want to know, for example, who sets the goals and formulates policy objectives and proposals. Who makes the decisions and takes the actions? Who implements the policy and produces policy outcomes? To help answer these questions, we will now examine the policy process and the issue of economic reform in the Soviet Union, China, and Eastern Europe.

Politics, Policy-Making, and Economic Reform in the USSR

When Lenin and his associates took over after the Bolshevik revolution in 1917, they were ill prepared to create and manage a socialist economy. When setting goals for the new socialist state, Lenin was guided by both Marxist ideals and the political exigencies of the moment. Believing that private ownership and capitalism were the roots of much evil, Lenin nationalized heavy industries, land, and the means of production. He and his associates hoped to rationally and comprehensively make economic policy and were willing to resort to totalitarian means to do so. Private ownership of land and industry was strictly forbidden.

However, during the 1918–21 period of civil war (the so-called war communism period), economic output fell to 20 percent of what it had been before the outbreak of World War I. The Soviet economy was in shambles. This forced the Bolshevik leaders to back away from their idealistic goals for building communism. Although large-scale industries and the banking systems remained nationalized, decisions were made to allow agriculture and small businesses to be run by private entrepreneurs. This phase of Soviet economic policy, the so-called New Economic Policy (NEP) of 1921–28, illustrated the presence of both totalitarian and pluralist incremental modes of decision making. Lenin and the Communist Party would have liked to have moved decisively in putting together a new socialist economic system. Social, economic, and political realities, however, forced them to pay attention to other groups and centers of political power in the system and move incrementally toward their goals of socialism and communism.

With Lenin's death and Stalin's assumption of power, the USSR moved far in the direction of totalitarianism. Stalin and the Communist Party leaders dominated the economic planning and policy-making processes. Agriculture was collectivized, businesses and industry were nationalized, and private labor and ownership were strictly outlawed. Communist Party planning and control were carried out through Five-Year Plans. Stalin and other Party leaders set the goals; the Party-dominated governmental organizations such as GOSPLAN, the Council of Ministers, and Supreme Soviet took action; and the various ministers and ministries were expected to produce the outcomes that would fulfill the Five-Year Plans. Although the Stalinist policy model and political system brought about the industrialization of the Soviet state, it did not do so without problems. In fact, the Stalinist system was repressive, wasteful, and inefficient.

In the post-Stalin years, leaders such as Khrushchev, Kosygin, and Brezhnev sometimes tried to address the problems of waste and inefficiency in the Stalinist command-administrative system. However, unwilling to consider all of the information, alternatives, and cost-and-benefit analyses available to them, they largely proceeded on the basis of totalitarianism to pursue the Stalinist economic model. They were unwilling to consider reform that would give workers, firms, and regions more economic autonomy, and they were loathe to reduce the role of the Communist Party and the central government in the economic policy process. Although they attempted to control economic policy making and rationally and comprehensively proceeded on the basis of Five-Year Plans, they increasingly were bogged down in what many have called bureaucratic pluralism and its consequent incrementalism.[5]

By the 1970s, the Soviet political process was marked by a diversity of interests, which resulted in clashes and compromises among the different leaders and agencies. Under these conditions, in the words of Jerry F. Hough, incrementalism became the "hallmark of the system."[6] As a result, the Soviet system entered a period of stagnation.

What happened? How did the highly centralized, totalitarian leadership of the Soviet Union under Stalin evolve under Brezhnev into a group of political brokers who mediated the competing demands of different government and bureaucratic sectors? With the death of Joseph Stalin and the deconcentration of power that Khrushchev's rule ushered in, some political power devolved from the highest Party bodies to different bureaucratic and state organs. Although Khrushchev was an impulsive policy maker who would often take adventurous action to attain high-priority goals, his policies of liberalization and decentralization dispersed considerable autonomy and policy-relevant authority throughout the Soviet system.

Khrushchev's successors, Leonid I. Brezhnev and Aleksei N. Kosygin, moved the USSR even further in the direction of pluralism and incrementalism. Basing their leadership on a system of collective rule, these leaders provided the specialized state, Party, and scientific complexes with considerable policy-making autonomy in their fields. To avoid the loss of support that had led to Khrushchev's ouster, Brezhnev and Kosygin tried to keep their subordinates happy by giving the various departments an incremental budgetary increase each year.[7]

When Gorbachev came to power, some facets of the policy-making process began to change. Gorbachev proved to be a bold and decisive leader and wanted the system to break with the past and adopt the radical reforms embodied in glasnost and perestroika. Although he attempted to move radically, rationally, and comprehensively, many remnants of the old incrementalism remained.

It was clear by the time Gorbachev came to power in 1985 that the period of rapidly accelerating economic growth had ended and the command-type, Stalinist economic model had outlived its usefulness. The Soviet economy was now characterized by decelerating growth; although the economy was still growing, it was growing at a slower rate than before and much more slowly than the Soviet leaders desired. Under such economic conditions, it would be difficult for the Soviets to achieve their high-priority goals. Most observers believed that although the Soviet economy would not collapse, it would deteriorate even further in the future, in view of labor shortages, low productivity, and increasing energy prices. These economic pressures confronted Gorbachev with some very difficult challenges. What could be done to improve the Soviet economy?

A leading American economist outlined four alternatives that confronted the Soviet leaders in the 1980s.[8] The "conservative" alternative represented preserving and carrying on into the future the existing economic system with minor incremental changes. The "reactionary" approach represented a return to the highly disciplined economic system of the Stalinist period. This alternative would place a high priority on discipline and order and mean an even greater assertion of centralized CPSU control of the economy. The "liberal" alternative would

maintain traditional planning methods while liberalizing restrictions on private initiative and competition. Finally, the "radical" approach would represent the most significant change and emphasize decentralization of planning and management and utilize elements of private enterprise and competition.

Although considerable evidence suggested that fundamental changes—that is, the liberal or radical approaches—were required to right the Soviet economy, Brezhnev and Kosygin opted for the conservative alternative. The choices made and changes pursued in the Soviet Union under their leadership tended to be incremental and ad hoc rather than comprehensive and rational. Why was this so? Berliner argued that it was because they let short-term politics rather than long-term economics dictate their choices.[9] The pre-Gorbachev leaders opted for the conservative strategy because it would not rock the boat and was in line with their short-term political interests. Scientific, rational analysis might have suggested radical solutions, but short-run political considerations in the USSR ruled them out.

When Gorbachev entered office in 1985, some of this began to change. The Soviet economy required innovative and fundamental reform. Gorbachev and his associates began to move in the direction of liberal and even radical reform. Although most agreed that such reforms were necessary, they faced a fundamental dilemma in how to proceed. They could use totalitarian methods and try to force through radical reform. If they did so, however, they could be seen as dictators, a fact that would be in conflict with their goals of glasnost and democratization. Furthermore, they would risk losing both the ideas and the involvement of the people, on which economic reform ultimately depended.

On the other hand, Gorbachev and his associates could move more democratically and cautiously, step by step, in line with the principles of pluralism. This alternative also had costs. Allowing full debate and democratic pluralism could result in deadlock and delay. This would provide time for the opposition to organize. The reforms could become mired in bureaucratic pluralism. The "muddling through" and stagnation so prevalent during the Brezhnev years could have continued under Gorbachev as well.

The Gorbachev approach has turned out to be a complex blend of totalitarianism and pluralism. When Gorbachev took office, he realized that to reform the economy and move the Soviet Union forward, he would need the support of the people, including those at the top of the Party hierarchy who made the decisions, those in the bureaucracy who implemented the reforms, and those in the factories and on the farms who carried them out.

Gorbachev began by giving attention to all of these groups. He brought reformers into the highest Party and governmental bodies and got rid of the "deadwood" that was standing in the way of restructuring and reform. He promoted economists and advisers who shared his visions of glasnost, perestroika, and democratization and got rid of those who resisted. He was willing to use totalitarian tactics to form his new team and shape up the stagnant Soviet society.

Gorbachev also took his reform program and ideas for change to the people. Adroitly using the power of his personality and the Soviet media, he sought to convince the Soviet people that change was in their interests. He tried to persuade them to support perestroika rather than to become cynical and take to the streets when progress seemed remote or when prices had to be raised. He told them to work hard and be patient. He had to convince students and pensioners, intellectuals and workers, that perestroika and economic reform would be in

their interests and that their patience, sacrifice, hard work, and cooperation was vital. He appealed to tradition, patriotism, and pride.

While Gorbachev was assembling his team and launching the ideas of perestroika and change in 1985–86, relatively little reform was actually taking place. This was the goal-setting stage and an opportunity for Gorbachev to think through and illuminate his policy objectives. Skillfully using Party meetings and organized media campaigns, Gorbachev sought to mold support for the inevitable challenges that radical change would encounter.

In the winter of 1986–87, the Gorbachev reformers began to move ahead, to translate their goals into action. After having decided on a series of radical reforms introducing private labor and enterprise, independent cooperatives, greater autonomy for enterprises, and joint ventures and expanded economic relations with the West, Gorbachev went to the critical Party and governmental organizations to garner their support. The Central Committee of the CPSU ratified much of what Gorbachev and the reformers in the Politburo wanted in the way of economic reform. As you will recall from the chapter on the Communist Party, the Central Committee traditionally has had the power to elect and dismiss the Party leader, in this case, Secretary Gorbachev. Nikita Khrushchev and Party leaders in other communist states had been ousted when they lost the support of the Central Committee. In the mid- and late 1980s, many wondered if this would also be the fate of Gorbachev and his reform program.

Gorbachev used the power of his leadership to bring reformers into the Central Committee, demoting those who were ambivalent or opposed. He also used his strength in the Central Committee to bring his supporters into the Politburo and Secretariat. He promoted his close adviser, Aleksander Yakolev, to the Secretariat in 1986 and to full Politburo membership in 1987. He made his close friend Eduard Shevardnadze a full member of the Politburo and Foreign Minister in July 1985. Without the support of these and other high Party leaders, Gorbachev's radical reform program would have had little chance for success.

During the 1985–90 period, Gorbachev proved to be highly skilled and successful in consolidating his power and building his team in the key Party and governmental bodies. Without such support, he would have become increasingly vulnerable to all of the pluralistic forces that had a stake in the reform process. If the Party leadership did not move decisively to push the reform program forward, there was always the danger of becoming mired in the excessive bureaucratic pluralism and incrementalism of the Brezhnev period.

It should be noted here that although Gorbachev was adept, he was unable to win the unqualified support of all who were at the top of the Party and government organizations. Many observers saw Yegor Ligachev as a conservative reformer and opposed to some of Gorbachev's radical initiatives. Others called attention to the opposition of Vladimir Shcherbitsky, longtime Politburo member and Party chief of the Ukrainian Communist Party, and to Andrei Gromyko, longtime Foreign Minister and fellow Politburo member. Gorbachev adroitly dealt with these challenges. Gromyko retired quietly from the Politburo and active political life in 1988; Ligachev was reassigned the portfolio for Soviet agriculture which, in view of its great problems, was a no-win situation and would surely keep him too busy, Gorbachev hoped, to interfere with his reform program. Shcherbitsky was forced to resign.

However, a program as bold and far reaching as perestroika cannot be introduced without generating opposition within a conservative, traditional society like the USSR. In January 1988, Gorbachev himself called attention to the presence of this opposition by noting criticism from the left and right. He went on to note that voices from the right were saying that he was undermining the foundations of socialism. One of those voices came from the editor and pages of *Sovetskaia Rossia*. At a January 1988 meeting between Gorbachev and Soviet media representatives, the editor V. Chikin warned Gorbachev that the radical reforms could lead to the resumption of capitalism and "ideological homelessness."[10] Then in March 1988, a dramatic page-long article appeared in *Sovetskaia Rossia*. Supposedly written by a Leningrad chemistry teacher, Nina Andreeva, the article defended the honor of Stalin and went on to criticize much of the Gorbachev reform program, including glasnost, perestroika and democratization. Various theories abounded about the motivations behind the article, including one that linked it to Politburo conservative Ligachev.

The editorial signified the presence of a troublesome conservative coalition whose highest-ranking member in the late 1980s was Ligachev. This coalition included Party functionaries, some military and bureaucratic officials, writers, journalists, and intellectuals who remained wedded to more traditional Soviet policies. Some opposed perestroika and the reform program for philosophical reasons, and many feared it because of its implications for their personal self-interests. Having risen to comfortable positions and salaries under the old system, many saw a diminution of their power and, in some cases, the loss of their jobs with the advent of the Gorbachev reform program.

This conservative coalition also commanded powerful support from large sectors of the working class. Preferring the predictability and stability of the stagnant past, many resented the new freedoms of expression, the outbreak

Gorbachev faced opposition from both the political right and left in the late 1980s. Here he calms a group of deputies from the Soviet Congress during the winter session of 1989.

of ethnic nationalism, and the growing entrepreneurship in Soviet society. Seeing important self-interests in jeopardy, members of the conservative coalition worked in various ways to obstruct the radical reform programs.

Although some individuals and groups thought Gorbachev and the reformers were going too far and too fast, others felt they were not going fast enough. Politburo member Boris Yeltsin criticized Gorbachev and his colleagues for these reasons and was dropped from the Politburo. This did not silence Yeltsin, as he successfully ran for the Soviet parliament and continued to criticize the timidity and slow pace of Gorbachev's reforms. Later, he was voted into an even higher office, becoming President of the Russian republic in 1990. Others, for example, in the Baltic republics of Estonia, Latvia, and Lithuania, demanded greater reform and wanted the central government to provide them far more power over their own affairs.

Both from within and outside of the Party, those who criticized Gorbachev's economic reforms as not going far enough to stimulate Soviet economic recovery increased their calls for the Soviet leader to radicalize his program in early 1990. The increased pressure on Gorbachev came as a result of both the persistent evidence that perestroika was not working fast enough to improve the Soviet standard of living, and the successful adoption of shock economic programs by several of the reformed noncommunist governments of Eastern Europe. Shock treatment advocates argued that only a rapid transformation toward the free market could cure the popular discontent within the Soviet Union and keep the country together in the face of growing centrifugal nationalist forces.

Responding to the demands for adoption of economic shock measures by the Soviet Union, in early 1990, Gorbachev dispatched Leonid I. Abalkin, Deputy Prime Minister, and a team of economic specialists to draft an economic program that might stimulate accelerated Soviet economic growth through free market measures. At a meeting of the Presidential Council in April 1990, the shock program was presented by Abalkin to Gorbachev. Gorbachev flatly rejected it, later stating:

> Let market conditions be put in place everywhere. Let's have free enterprise and give the green light to all forms of ownership, private ownership. Let everything be private. Let us sell the land, everything. I cannot support such ideas, no matter how decisive and revolutionary they might appear. These are irresponsible ideas, irresponsible.[11]

The reasons for Gorbachev's rejection of a shock economic program for the Soviet Union appear to have been more related to politics than a conviction by the Soviet leader that such measures would not work. Gorbachev felt that by adopting a shock program he would lose the middle ground between left and right in Soviet politics that he so cherished. Any further destabilization and deterioration of the Soviet standard of living caused by radicalized reform efforts might provide ammunition for Party conservatives in an effort to dislodge Gorbachev from power. The conservatives might possibly point to the economic upheaval of a shock program as a harebrained scheme. Having recognized these factors, Gorbachev apparently saw any further radicalization of perestroika as simply too great a risk to take at the time.

In addition to those in the Party, many in the bureaucracy felt that Gorbachev was going too far in some areas and not far enough in others. Many were uneasy about the impact of perestroika on their jobs. In the fall of 1988, Gorbachev announced that 700,000 ministry jobs would be cut and that at some industrial enterprises and collective farms, half of the managerial positions would be abolished. Gorbachev also announced that 40 percent of Party secretaries at the primary level had been voted out of office and 60 percent of Party leaders on the shopfloor were being replaced. It was clear that Gorbachev and the reformers were taking actions that would affect people's careers and lives. Resistance was inevitable.

As Gorbachev's reform programs were promulgated, it became increasingly clear to Soviet workers that perestroika was going to raise the expectations and standards placed on them by the Party and state. At the same time, perestroika did not seem to be allowing them to buy more or to be raising their standard of living. Many workers wondered what good perestroika was if it meant they had to work harder and receive fewer benefits. As a result of worker concern, organizations like trade unions took a great deal of interest in Gorbachev's initiatives. Although

free and independent trade unions like those we know in the West, or like Solidarity in Poland, did not exist in the Soviet Union, "official" state unions became more outspoken during the late 1980s and less obedient to the powers that be in the Soviet Union. In the era of glasnost, official unions became genuinely concerned with the Soviet workers they represented and less afraid to speak out and protect their interests.

During the summer and fall of 1989, thousands of Soviet coalminers expressed their displeasure with perestroika by bypassing official unions altogether and organizing a series of wildcat strikes. For several months, informal groups of miners walked off their jobs in various regions of the country, from the Ural Mountains and Siberia to the Ukraine and the Donetsk Basin. The miners' actions triggered a national economic crisis, which had to be addressed by Gorbachev and other key Soviet leaders. Workers striking in a supposed workers' state was something new for Soviet leaders. Gorbachev, his associates, and the miners reached a compromise, which resulted in the striking miners returning to work in exchange for concessions by the Soviet state. Violence and severe economic hardship largely were averted in the 1989 labor unrest. Both Party and state leaders throughout the Soviet Union learned, however, that future labor crises loomed on the horizon if perestroika did not start improving the economic situation and raising the living standard. The power of organized labor and strikes was rediscovered by Soviet workers in 1989 after years of repression and subserviency.

Gorbachev and the reformers also had to contend with powerful institutional groups like the Soviet military. Although the military leaders recognized that a strong economy was vital to maintaining a strong defense and were therefore inclined to support reforms that would strengthen the military, they were loathe to accept reformist policies that were likely to weaken or take resources away from the military sector. When Secretary Gorbachev announced military cuts late in the 1980s, including a unilateral cutback in Soviet military spending, he created considerable unease and resistance in the military. Groups like these lobbied hard to protect their share of the allocation of Soviet resources.

A Soviet economist described the complex planning and decision-making process surrounding Gorbachev's reforms as "bargaining between enterprises and ministries over . . . the allocation of resources" and noted that "the bureaucratization of the economy has taken on dangerous proportions."[12] Enterprises, ministries, and other pressure groups forcefully articulated their interests in a variety of ways to see their policy preferences served. Although Gorbachev and the reformers wanted to proceed decisively to do what they considered best for the country, various centers of power like the conservative political and bureaucratic opposition groups, the trade unions, the military, and so forth worked hard to see their interests served. In the age of glasnost and democratization, it was difficult for Gorbachev and his associates to avoid the pluralistic pressures and the sort of incrementalism that could stymie the reform program.

Perhaps the most powerful force driving the Soviet reformers in the direction of incrementalism was the sheer complexity of economic reform itself. With no master plan, Gorbachev and the reformers were experimenting without knowing what would ensure successful economic reform. Reality meant that they never had the time or information to consider all of the alternatives, costs and benefits, and likely outcomes. Gorbachev often expressed his frustrations about this reality. On the one hand, he wanted to move quickly and decisively and

introduce comprehensive reforms. On the other hand, he recognized the importance of what he called a "socialist pluralism of opinions," where people would speak out for what they thought was best.

When examining the setting of goals and the taking of actions surrounding economic reform in the Soviet Union, the political leadership in the form of Mikhail Gorbachev was a critical factor. Gorbachev and his associates led the reform movement. They wanted to pursue rational, decisive, and comprehensive reform. However, because of the complexity of the reform process and the plurality of opinions about what should be done, the Soviet reformers were often driven in the direction of incrementalism. This was not their preference, of course, because they wanted to reform the Soviet economy according to rational and comprehensive principles.

When Gorbachev proposed reform of the Soviet political system in the late 1980s, one had the impression that he was reacting to this fundamental dilemma, that is, how to promote rational, comprehensive decision making and yet allow the socialist pluralism of opinion and democratization that every modern society needs. The political reform proposals set forth during the period suggested that Gorbachev and his associates favored movement toward a bifurcated, two-tiered political system. On the top tier were Gorbachev and the ruling elite, who were to maintain strategic control of overall policy. On the second tier was the plurality of opinions—from groups, ministries, provincial and local governments, and informal groups—involved in a more democratic, competitive struggle over the allocation of Soviet resources. Such a political system was intended to help reconcile the forces of totalitarianism and pluralism very much present in contemporary Soviet politics and policy making.

Politics, Policy-Making, and Economic Reform in China

The Chinese politics surrounding economic policy-making and reform show both similarities to and differences from the Soviet case. Mao adopted important features of the Stalinist political and economic system. Like Stalin, Mao was the critical actor in Chinese economic policy-making for decades. He played a major role in setting goals, initiating action, and producing outcomes. Mao fit the mold of the totalitarian leader. Michel Oksenberg describes Mao in the following terms:

> Mao was, to the end of his life, a revolutionary and a totalitarian ruler. He believed the only way to transform China was rapidly, violently, comprehensively; its elites and institutions would have to undergo continual transformation. China's problems were so vast that efforts to attain peaceful, gradual change would be lost in the morass of bureaucracy. In his view, to transform China required vision and extraordinary confidence that a politically involved Chinese populace—given no respite to cultivate individually-determined pursuits—could overcome their common plight of poverty and weakness. To unleash the masses in all their fury required leaders capable of interacting directly with the social forces in society unmediated by intervening bureaucracies. Mao saw institutions such as the Party, government, or army as having little intrinsic value. They were to be used instrumentally, as divisions in war, their credibility and authority expended in his larger efforts to make China a strong, prosperous, socialist China.[13]

In reality, however, Mao neither held total control nor was able to be completely rational and comprehensive in the making of economic policy for China. Oksenberg goes on in his article to tell us that although Mao structured the Chinese political system to allow himself to intervene according to his idiosyncratic impulses, competing factional groupings had considerable influence on him. Oksenberg also suggests that the evolution of domestic policy choices was not based on careful analysis of the alternatives but more frequently on personal preferences and political exigencies.

Using case studies of various policy issues, we can see various blends of totalitarianism and pluralism at work in Maoist China. Examining five policy issues in China during Mao's reign—the Twelve-Year Agricultural Program, administrative decentralization, the commune movement, the Socialist Education Campaign, and the ideological rectification campaign—Parris H. Chang examined how policy was made and who was making it in the 1950s and 1960s.[14] Chang found a variety of important actors in the decision-making process in addition to Mao. Other actors included the Chinese Communist Party (CCP) Politburo; the CCP Standing Committee; the Party's Central Committee; Party officials at the provincial and local levels; the People's Liberation Army (PLA); the bureaucracy; and extraparty forces, such as the Red Guard and revolutionary rebels. The actors involved varied according to the policy area. For example, Chang noted that those institutions involved in setting goals, taking action, and producing outcomes in the area of rural policies included at the national level the Ministry of Agriculture; the Agricultural and Forestry Staff Office; the CCP Central Committee Rural Work Department; and the CCP Secretariat, Politburo, and Central Committee.[15]

How, then, was policy made in Mao's China? Chang answers this question by contending that:

Policy in Communist China was not made by a few leaders alone; actors possessing different political resources participated, directly or indirectly in each stage of the policymaking process and affected in a variety of ways, the decision-output of the regime.[16]

At the same time, Chang cautions, it is necessary to recognize the enormous power wielded by Mao. When Mao was most active—for example, during the second half of the 1950s—the policy-making process was more personalized and totalitarian. Mao used other institutions and actors to initiate, accept, and carry out the policies he preferred. For example, when other Party leaders favored a "go-slow" approach toward collectivization of agriculture in 1955, Mao vehemently argued for stepping up the tempo in a secret speech to provincial Party secretaries. By skillfully using others, Mao was able to overcome the go-slow opposition and launch an intense nationwide campaign to accelerate agricultural collectivization.[17]

The policy-making process became more open and less totalitarian in the post-Mao period. In the early 1980s, Oksenberg and Bush described China as having moved from "revolutionary totalitarianism" to "reformist authoritarianism."[18] They saw the Maoist "totalitarian revolutionaries" as having attempted a rapid, violent, and comprehensive transformation of China. In contrast, the "authoritarian reformers" of the 1980s were committed to more gradual and peaceful change within a more stable political framework. Although Deng, Zhao, and other reformers remained authoritarian and tolerated no organized opposition to their rule, they adhered to a more open, institutionalized form of collective rule. Decision making was more likely to involve the relevant Party and governmental bodies and to be based upon compromise and consensus. The authoritarian

reformers shifted the policy-making process away from Maoist totalitarianism to a more institutionalized process of governing through the Party and governmental bureaucracies.

Oksenberg argues that whereas Mao was committed to revolutionary change, Deng was committed to reform. Whereas Mao was a totalitarian committed to a dialectic path of development, Deng was an authoritarian who sought to pursue a steady, persistent course. Whereas Mao sought to bypass the bureaucracy, Deng sought to restore it.[19] Overall, Deng's major objective was to improve the standard of living of the populace. This required the setting of new goals and policies to achieve the desired outcomes.

Not everyone supported Deng's reformist ideas in the post-Mao period. With the death of Mao in 1976 and the ouster of the Maoist faction known as the Gang of Four, the new leaders soon polarized into two camps and held quite different goals to guide future Chinese policy. The traditional faction led by Mao's heir apparent, CCP Chairman Hua Guofeng, was composed of those who gained ascendancy under Mao's patronage. This faction favored continuity and opposed the comprehensive and radical reforms desired by Deng Xiaoping. The reformist faction, led by Deng and his more pragmatic associates, wanted to discard the Maoist model and implement a fundamental economic restructuring.

To build political support for their new goals, Deng and his cohorts initiated a "de-Maoification" campaign to rid Chinese society of its ideological inhibitions and lay the foundation for their new economic plans. The prelude to the campaign was a nationwide debate orchestrated by Deng and his faction on the theme "practice is the sole criterion of truth." Through such debates, this reformist faction wanted to convince the Chinese people that what works in practice, rather than Maoist ideology, ought to be the criterion guiding Chinese economic policy. The Deng faction won the struggle, and Hua and the traditionalists lost their positions of power in the early 1980s. Once in a dominant position, the reform faction of Deng Xiaoping, Zhao Ziyang, and the new Party leader Hu Yaobang announced the end of Maoism, with its emphasis on collectivism and self-reliance, and spelled out their new goals for building the Chinese economy. These goals were to reduce centralized control, emphasize the market mechanism, and open the Chinese economy to the world.

Although the reformers were now in power, there was continuing controversy within the leadership over such issues as the possible dismantling of central planning and state ownership and whether China should strive to become a full-fledged market economy. The more radical wing of the reformers argued for fundamental and far-reaching reforms, including significant constraints on centralized control and an expansion of market forces. The most zealous champions of radical reform were Deng's two protegés, Hu Yaobang and Zhao Ziyang. Hu had taken over the Party leadership and Zhao the governmental premiership from the defeated Hua Guofeng. This duo established their credentials as the primary goal setters and policy actors in the post-Mao reform period. These radical reformers spent the early 1980s outlining their plans for fundamental reform, a process referred to as "the destruction of the old and the establishment of the new."

Soon pitted against this more radical wing of reformers were a group of more conservative reformers in the Politburo and Central Committee. The leader of this faction was Chen Yun, a veteran leader and former Party vice-chairman whose forte was economic management and policy. In the 1950s, Chen figured prominently as China's premier economist. He was demoted during the Great Leap Forward because he was at variance with Mao and skeptical of his economic fanaticism. During the Cultural Revolution, he was for a time on the verge of being exiled by the Red Guards for his dissent from Maoist economics. Ironically, he emerged in the 1980s as the standard-bearer of economic conservatism.

Chen, other ranking leaders, and Party dignitaries were averse to the far-reaching economic changes proposed by the more radical reformers and wanted to safeguard the primacy of central planning and state ownership. Market mechanisms, they argued, should only serve as a supplement to the socialist economy. These more conservative and radical protagonists of post-Mao politics would be locked in a fierce fight throughout the 1980s over the orientation of economic reform.

Similar to Gorbachev in the Soviet Union, Deng Xiaoping played a critical role in the reform process by maintaining the middle ground and arbitrating disputes between the two competing reform factions. By staying above the fray, Deng was able to protect the power he had achieved in his victory over the Maoist traditionalists. He was the supreme leader during the reform period in China. Sometimes playing the role of dictator, sometimes calling for greater democracy, Deng frequently utilized his considerable political skills and power to manage political change and the policy process in China.

During the early 1980s, top priority was given to rural reform, the centerpiece of which was the introduction of the production responsibility system. The new policy stipulated that farmland and other means of production be allocated to households on a contractual basis, and that households supercede production teams and communes as the key economic unit in the countryside. This reform was tantamount to the decollectivization and privatization of Chinese agriculture.[20] Concurrent with rural reform in the early 1980s was experimentation with reforms in other sectors. The regime authorized some pilot schemes of enterprise autonomy in preparation for the more radical reforms to follow. However, even such a limited first step upset some hardliners. The emerging trends of social stratification and even polarization provided an impetus for expanding a campaign against "spiritual pollution." The campaign was launched to combat the Western ideology which was perceived by some Communist Party officials as getting a foothold in China and diluting Marxism and the Chinese cultural heritage. Disgruntled Communist Party cadres took advantage of this opportunity to vent their wrath and to obstruct the reform.

In spite of all this, rural reform turned out to be a success. Zhao Ziyang and Hu Yaobang were able to override the more conservative opposition. In their euphoria over success in the rural reform, the radical reformers announced in 1984 at the Third Plenum of the Twelfth Party Central Committee a broader industrial reform package encompassing enterprise autonomy, a tax-for-profit system, price reforms, expanded wage incentives, and a variety of other reform measures. It was evident from the blueprint that the radical coalition envisioned a more thorough reform in lieu of the previous piecemeal experimentation in the agricultural sector. If implemented in its entirety, this reform package would have meant the virtual decimation of the socialist economic system. Although the radical reformers still paid lip service to socialism, they could not allay the fear and opposition of conservatives headed by Chen Yun and Peng Zhen. Initially, Chen and the conservatives acquiesced primarily because success in rural reform had given the more radical reformers much leverage in influencing and

determining the orientation of the broader economic reform. They bided their time, and when the ill-designed and ill-fated broader reform program ran into trouble, they pounced on the radicals' mistakes and tried to scuttle the reform program.

From the outset, the more conservative reformers had serious reservations about radical economic reforms and were reluctant to give them their full support. Their opposition to and obstruction of extensive, rapid economic reform were not only ideologically and politically motivated but also associated with concerns for its social, economic, and cultural implications. Most of the conservatives were avowed communists who had strived all their lives to build a communist society. The economic reforms challenged many of the fundamental premises of Marxism that they had espoused. In addition, the institutional change called for in the economic reforms entailed the delegation of power to their subordinates and the recruitment and cooptation of new elements, which they considered an erosion of Party organization and authority.

Furthermore, to the conservatives, the idea of a market economy was akin to restoring capitalism. They saw the relaxation of state controls and price deregulation as engendering rife corruption, runaway inflation, and social stratification and polarization, which, in turn, fueled popular alienation and cynicism. They also saw the influx of "decadent" Western culture as a consequence of the radical reformers' open-door policy. Western culture, they argued, was polluting the minds of the people and causing a drastic increase in the incidence of crimes and other social evils. In the conservatives' opinion, economic reform was opening Pandora's box.

Criticism of the radical reformers also came from middle- and lower-level cadres and ordinary citizens. Economic reform threatened the role of the Chinese cadre corps. It threatened their ability to maintain their privileged positions because of the new emphasis on merit and the abolition of life tenure in Party positions. When local and regional leaders found the reform policies unpalatable, they criticized or tried to boycott or circumvent them. They argued laxity in discipline and growing regionalism had reached alarming proportions and raised the specter of the reemergence of fiefdoms prevalent during the turbulent precommunist period of warlordism.

The radical reform program of the 1980s also generated the opposition of many who were not materially benefiting from the reforms. In the course of the economic reforms, there were some who were well connected or blessed with business acumen who took advantage of the newly available opportunities for entrepreneurship and made a considerable amount of money. However, growing disparities in incomes and standards of living made many ordinary people feel deprived and therefore resentful of the reforms. Economic reform in the 1980s also brought an end to guaranteed employment, a system sarcastically referred to as the "iron rice bowl." It brought to an end the practice of equal wage remuneration irrespective of the significance of one's work contributions. As a result, less diligent and competitive personnel found their former positions and security threatened. The danger of unemployment, which never existed under Maoist communism, now loomed large. It goes without saying that many Chinese people had misgivings about the new reforms. Some of them preferred the Maoist period, when a secure livelihood was guaranteed despite the fact that many things were in short supply.

Economic policy-making and the reform process were affected by a variety of political forces. For example, to justify and legitimize their goals and preferred policy actions, both the competing factions invoked the powers of ideology. Each side had at its disposal a brain trust composed of writers, researchers, and scholars steeped in Marxist and non-Marxist theories. Establishment theoreticians subscribing to orthodox economic doctrine congregated under the banner of conservatism, whereas the newly emergent, more Western oriented economic thinkers gravitated toward the radical reformers' camp. Writers in both camps couched their articles in the Marxist political jargon so as to give weight to their arguments, but some reform-minded researchers even incorporated non-Marxist theories and ideas into their writings.

The promotion, demotion, and recruitment of Party and government officials were utilized to influence the reform process. Expansion of factional representation and its reduction of the adversary in the various decision-making bodies was highly contested and served the purpose of increasing leverage in the competition for power. Appointment or dismissal of key figures like Hu Yaobang, Li Peng, and Deng Liqun had far-reaching repercussions. The proponents and opponents of reform also used demonstrations, protests, work stoppages and slowdowns to influence the policy process. Although we are unable to say that leaders in the competing camps instigated or abetted these activities, their policies often benefited and suffered from such events.

The reform process was also affected by nonpolitical forces. Soon after the inception of the urban reform, the Chinese economy encountered a number of difficulties. Starting in 1984, problems like uncontrolled economic growth; excessive increase in capital goods investment, credit, and consumption; price hikes; inflation; and depletion of foreign exchange reserves began to gain saliency. This development provided ammunition for the conservatives, who called attention to the potential costs of full-scale reform and pressed for modifications to the existing reform program. Due to opposition and economic difficulties, the radical reformers were forced to begin pulling back a bit in the mid-1980s.

A significant sign of conservative resistance and backlash was the removal of the reformer Hu Yaobang from the Party leadership in January 1987. Hu continually criticized and demeaned Mao's theoretical contributions to socialism while praising Western democratic theorists and freedoms. Hu's reformist inclinations had gone too far for the conservatives to accept. Finally, the Party conservatives gained enough strength to oust him, although they were forced to appoint another reformer, Zhao Ziyang, to replace him.

Another sign of conservative backlash and the struggle for control over Chinese economic policy during this period was the changing political slogans. For example, contrary to the radical reformers' exhortation in the early 1980s that "to get rich is glorious," the so-called No. 1 Directive of the 1987 Central Committee preached the "superiority of socialism" over capitalism and deemphasized material incentives to promote production. Attempting to redefine the goals of Chinese economic policy, the conservative faction attacked the threat of "bourgeois liberalization" and reemphasized more orthodox economic principles.

Although Zhao and the radicals had to consent to Hu's ouster as a way of placating the conservatives, they refused to compromise on the larger issues of economic reform. However, the reform program had brought unintended consequences and more ammunition for the conservative faction. Prices were soaring, and budgetary and trade deficits were on the rise. Government mints were operating at full capacity, and for the first time since the early

period of Chinese hyperinflation in the late 1940s, new large-denomination bank notes went into circulation. Zhao Ziyang and the radical reformers diagnosed the problem as the inadequacy of reform. They remained committed to further reform and advocated stopping the practice of putting ceilings on the prices of thousands of commodities so that market mechanisms could play a larger role in the distribution of goods and services.

The freeing of prices from centralized control exacerbated the already very serious problems of inflation and corruption. China's financial system fell into disarray in the late 1980s. The inflation rate grew by leaps and bounds, jumping to 50 percent in 1988. The supply of goods faltered, and staple foods like meat, eggs, sugar, cooking oil, and even salt had to be rationed.

But Party leader Zhao and the radical reformers wanted to stay the course. They insisted that the decontrol of the pricing system would produce the desired effect in due course. At a succession of Politburo conferences held from June to September 1988, Zhao tried to enlist support for his ambitious price reform. Concerned by the magnitude of the crisis, even his followers became noncommittal, whereas his critics in the Politburo castigated him for his rashness in pushing for radical price reforms. There were heated debates at these meetings, but the conservatives overruled all of Zhao's proposals. Finally, Deng himself began to waver and indicated his readiness to scale back the bold restructuring. At the Third Plenum of the Thirteenth Central Committee held in late September 1988, the Party leadership decided to put a two-year moratorium on the radical reform program. In the late 1980s, much of Zhao's economic decision-making power devolved on Li Peng and Yao Yilin, who called for a slowdown of the reform. Though Zhao retained his General Secretaryship for the time being, his authority on economic issues had significantly declined.

In 1988–89, Li and Yao presided over a retrenchment and austerity program, with emphasis on controlling consumer demand, curbing inflation, doing away with economic overheating, and slowing down overly rapid industrial growth. The reversal was a heavy blow to Zhao and his radical reform program. Although Zhao and the radical group had not yet conceded defeat and were still trying to pursue their bold economic reforms, there was considerable uncertainty as China approached the end of the decade.

The events in Tiananmen Square of May and June 1989 brought about the defeat of the radical

Students put up a poster at Beijing University in April 1989 announcing support for a class boycott showing opposition to Chinese government policies.

reform faction. Zhao Ziyang was closely associated with the students' protest movement, and when Deng Xiaoping decided to crush the democratization movement, Zhao was ousted. The conservative hardliner Li Peng assumed control, and the course of radical reform and the possibility of growing pluralism in China suffered a major setback.

In summary, the Chinese policy process was the arena of intense competition between the conservative and radical reformers in the 1980s. The conservative faction approached the reform process cautiously and set limits on the extent and speed of the reform. The radical reformers, on the other hand, wanted to advance the reform and strove to do so rapidly and on all possible fronts. The continuing factional competition in the 1980s pushed China through periods of reform and retrenchment, or what some have referred to as a cyclical, experimental pattern of Chinese reform.[21] China had no comprehensive plan and therefore was forced to experiment. Harding quotes Deng Xiaoping as saying, "We are engaged in an experiment. For us, [reform] is something new, and we have to grope to find our way."[22]

Harding argued that the 1980s brought a reduction in the scope and role of the Chinese state and an increase in popular participation.[23] He also observed, however, that all of the opportunities for political participation were limited. When it came to reform, restrictions remained on what could be said and who could say it. Accordingly, the debate over Chinese economic reform primarily took place among elites and within Party and state organs. Although the process was not one of complete totalitarianism, neither was it one of democratic pluralism.

However, the Tiananmen Square massacre in 1989 signaled a return to more totalitarian rule in China. The Party leaders, including Deng

Xiaoping, were frightened by both the student movement in China and the revolutionary changes in Eastern Europe. Their response was to protect communism through repression and a return to more dictatorial rule. By 1990, China was clearly out of step with the political change that had come to Eastern Europe and the Soviet Union.

Politics and Economic Reform in Eastern Europe

As a result of the export by the Red Army of the traditional Soviet communist political system to many of the Second World states of Eastern Europe, and the indigenous rise of such traditional systems in Yugoslavia and Albania, Stalin's totalitarian command-administrative economic model was largely copied and implemented in the East European states after World War II. At that time, the East European leaders took strides to nationalize industry; collectivize agriculture; develop and implement five-year production and distribution plans; set and subsidize fixed prices; achieve complete employment of the work force through the assignment of individual citizens to specific jobs; and insulate their domestic economies from the free markets of the West via inconvertible currencies and inconsequential, bartered foreign trade.

The original Eastern European version of the totalitarian command-administrative model was virtually identical to the Soviet prototype, in that the economy was controlled almost exclusively from the center. The central planning ministries, under directions from the Party hierarchy, controlled all aspects of the economy. Enterprises and the individual workers were merely supposed to carry out the orders coming from the center; they were not to make their own economic decisions.

Many of the problems associated with the command-administrative economic model that arose in the Soviet Union in the post-war period also became evident in Eastern Europe. Irrational pricing, supply bottlenecks, overemphasis on heavy industrial production, quota-induced production of inferior and useless goods, excessive autarchy, and worker apathy all took their toll on the economies of the communist states of Eastern Europe.

The orthodox command-administrative economic model did not remain intact in Eastern Europe for very long after its introduction. For a variety of factors, both economic and political, Eastern European leaders attempted to modify and reform the traditional Stalinist model. Yugoslavia was the first communist state to do so. In 1948, Stalin expelled Yugoslavia from the Cominform. This action isolated Yugoslavia from the rest of the Eastern European communist states and their economic resources. Without economic assistance from the Soviet Union, in particular, the Yugoslav economy faced a grave crisis in the late 1940s. To receive economic help from the West, the Yugoslav leadership had to moderate their totalitarian decision making. Part of this moderation involved reform of the Stalinist economic model that Tito and the other Yugoslav communists had advocated before their dismissal from the Cominform.

The Yugoslav leadership reformed their economic system by introducing principles of self-management. Under self-management, instead of the workers and managers of individual enterprises being solely directed by central planners, they were allowed a larger say in what and how much they had to produce. The workers and managers were to some extent given control over the operation of their enterprises.

By introducing self-management reforms and including new actors in the process, the Yugoslav communists served to pluralize state economic decision making. They did so in hopes of jump-starting worker incentives by giving them a measure of control over their own destiny and in hopes of appeasing free-market advocates in the West who refused to sponsor assistance to the isolated communist state unless they backed away from economic totalitarianism. It was believed in Belgrade that adoption of self-management reforms would lead to economic recovery and would prevent civil unrest.

Although the other communist states of Eastern Europe ignored the process of reform in Yugoslavia while Stalin was alive, once the dictator was dead and his policies had been criticized by Khrushchev, other Eastern European communist leaders took a closer look at the advantages economic reform could offer them and their states.

After Gomulka had achieved power in Poland in 1956, he initiated decentralizing economic reforms in that country. Gomulka was a Polish nationalist, and by pluralizing decision making and distancing his economic policies from Moscow, he sought increased legitimation for his regime in the eyes of the Polish people. He thought by developing a Polish brand of socialism he could escape the puppet label attached to so many of the communist leaders in Eastern Europe and win support and assistance from the West. A similar rationale served as the basis for economic reforms in Czechoslovakia in the late 1960s under Alexander Dubcek.

In Janos Kadar's Hungary, the New Economic Mechanism, a decentralizing and liberalizing economic reform program, was introduced in the late 1960s to pacify a populace that had suffered through the brutal suppression in 1956 of the Hungarian Revolution by Soviet armed forces. For a brief moment in Hungary in 1956, the traditional communist political system had been overthrown. When Kadar was put in power by the Soviets, he had little if any le-gitimacy in the eyes of the Hungarian people. When the Prague Spring in Czechoslovakia got out of hand in 1968, Kadar recognized that such unrest and antagonism of Moscow could erupt in Hungary as well. The New Economic Mechanism was designed to prevent such an occurrence by creating a better standard of living for the Hungarians than was enjoyed by their communist brethren.

The reforms undertaken by Second World states in Eastern Europe to traditional Stalinist economic systems during the Cold War can best be described as attempts to develop hybrid economic systems combining elements of both capitalism and socialism, pluralism and total-itarianism, market and command-type economic systems.

The resulting "market socialism" economic systems of communist Eastern Europe allowed for some private ownership of property, some decentralization of economic decision making to the firm and managerial level, some increased emphasis on the production of consumer goods and services, and some wage differentiation among workers. At the same time, however, price setting, state firm monopolies, centrally planned distribution, inconvertible currencies, and bureaucratic oversight and intrusion continued unchanged. State firms did not have to face competition or bankruptcy; central planners still set overall, if not micro-, policy; and workers and farmers still had little incentive for hard work because personal rewards from the system were miniscule.

By the late 1980s, the economic stagnation and malaise that the people of Eastern Europe had suffered through under both orthodox and market socialism contributed to the overthrow of traditional communist regimes throughout the region. With the rise of noncommunist regimes to state power in Eastern Europe by the start of the 1990s, new institutions, policies, and decision-making processes were being created to replace those of the former communist regimes.

As this book went to press, the economic institutions, policies, and decision-making processes of the various Second World states of Eastern Europe were in a considerable state of transition. Their final nature, composition, and structure were uncertain. The apparent trends, however, were that the new governments in Eastern Europe were moving away from centrally planned or even hybrid market-socialism economic models and decision-making processes, and toward First World models based more on pluralism and the free market.

Competing factions, spanning the spectrum of economic and political philosophy, were being allowed to participate in the policy-formulation processes in many of the new Eastern European regimes. Although advocates of orthodox communism no longer held a monopoly of power over economic policy and decision making, within the new noncommunist, pluralist regimes, even their opinions were allowed to be heard in policy debates. This was in stark contrast to the anticommunists' predicament when traditional communist economic models and decision-making processes were dominant throughout Eastern Europe; under those models, opponents of the Communist Party were not allowed to participate in policy debates or decision-making processes. In most of the new regimes in Eastern Europe, every group or party is afforded the opportunity to put forth policy alternatives and to engage in pluralistic politics to determine what state policy will be.

There is a popular adage in the West that trying to move gradually from a planned economy to a market economy is like trying to ask a nation to shift gradually from driving on the right hand side of the road to driving on the left hand side of the road. Based on the steps

An early meeting of the Hungarian Stock Market in February 1989, a clear example of the economic reform that has come to Eastern Europe.

its noncommunist government took as the 1990s commenced, Poland seemed determined not to let its economy crash! The reformed Polish government, on January 1, 1990, commenced a rapid economic conversion program designed to make the difficult transition from a command economy to a market economy in a little more than a year's time.

In Poland, numerous plans were drawn up, bills proposed, and laws passed, calling for privatization of industry, agriculture, banking, equity and bond markets, and property. The noncommunist Polish government moved to rapidly dismantle state-planning bureaucracies, end state subsidies, free up prices, and make their currency, the zloty, convertible on Western markets. They sought investment, information, and advice—but not necessarily outright loans or grants—from the First World. They hoped for integration into the European Common Market but, at the same time, did not desire to end their historical trading ties with the Soviet Union.

Polish leader General Woyciech Jarulzelski and Solidarity leader Lech Walesa, sit together at the first meeting of the newly created Polish Senate on July 3, 1989. The Senate is an important institution in determining Polish economic plans for the future.

The relatively high level of consensus for rapid economic conversion to free-market systems in Poland was not as clear-cut in other Eastern European states at the start of the decade. In Hungary, for example, the two dominant political parties in the new noncommunist government, the Democratic Forum and the Alliance of Free Democrats, were split over the pace and scope of reform of the Hungarian market socialist economy. The Free Democrats advocated a rapid push toward a free-market economy, with privatization programs and conservative social policies that would make Margaret Thatcher or Milton Friedman proud. The Democratic Forum, on the other hand, was not so eager to cast aside social welfare programs and state intervention in the economy. The Forum increasingly looked toward the social democracies of Western Europe, particularly the Swedish model, for ideas as to how they would like Hungary's

economy and economic policy processes to take shape in the future.

In some Eastern European states, the long shadow cast by traditional Communist Party supporters in the bureaucracy, the military, the government, and even society at large continued to interfere in movement toward pluralist economic decision-making processes and in adoption and implementation of free-market reforms. In Czechoslovakia, for instance, many members of the provisional, noncommunist government were hesitant in early 1990 to push forward plans for rapid economic conversion to a market economy before national elections could be held. They feared potential voter backlash at the polls over any economic crises that rapid conversion policies might produce, and they were afraid of the communists' ability to pounce on and manipulate such social dissatisfaction in attempts to subvert the new government.

By the start of the 1990s, Bulgaria and Romania had not moved as far away from traditional communist economic models and decision-making processes as some of the other Eastern European states. Opposition parties, groups, and factions were finding it difficult to gain access to the economic policy process in these two states. The communists in Romania and Bulgaria, while paying lip service to economic and political reform, largely retained control over the state economy and really sought more to reform the existing economic system along incremental, hybrid market socialist lines than to pursue adoption of a true free-market economic system and pluralist economic decision-making processes.

Conclusion

This chapter has attempted to apply totalitarian and pluralist models to the processes of economic decision making in Second World states. We have focused on the Soviet Union, China, and several Eastern European countries. Through our study, we have discovered that as the decade of the 1990s began, there was considerable variance among Second World states in the way they set their economic policy. No one particular model of decision making applied across the board.

China, for example, experimented throughout the 1980s with liberalization of their traditional command-administrative economic system. The policy-making process seemed to become a bit more pluralistic. Actors outside of the Party hierarchy and central bureaucracy increasingly were allowed to participate in economic decision making. Following the events in Tiananmen Square in the spring of 1989, however, China put its economic reform program on hold and reverted to its more traditional, totalitarian methods of making economic policy.

Economic policy making in the Soviet Union in early 1990 was caught up in the reforms of Mikhail Gorbachev. Gorbachev and his associates in the Communist Party of the Soviet Union were engaged in a balancing act, attempting to placate Party traditionalists while trying to please radical free-market reformers.

Gorbachev was calling for a complicated hybrid economic system—somewhere between socialism and capitalism. He recognized the need for privatization and market competition in the Soviet Union but had yet to free the economy from the guise of intrusive planners and bureaucrats. Gorbachev was holding the middle ground, and by 1990, the Soviet approach to economic reform appeared to be mired in pluralist incrementalism.

Various states in Eastern Europe, particularly Poland, Hungary, and Czechoslovakia, had moved beyond acceptance of a hybrid command economy by the start of the 1990s. Most parties in the new noncommunist leaderships desired free-market economic systems based on Western models; however, there were significant differences of opinion over the nature and pace of the transition process. Some wanted to make the move rapidly, as evidenced in the "shock treatment" pursued in Poland. Others preferred to make a slower, less abrupt transition. Still others appeared reluctant to make the transition at all. The differences and resulting debates in the reformed governments of Eastern Europe were a clear indication that totalitarianism had declined and pluralism was growing in the former Soviet satellite countries.

Suggestions for Further Reading

Aslund, Anders, *Gorbachev's Struggle for Economic Reform* (Ithaca, N.Y.: Cornell University Press, 1989).

Barghoorn, Fredrick C. and **Thomas F. Remington,** *Politics in the USSR* (Boston: Little, Brown, and Co., 1986).

Chang, Parris H., *Power and Policy in China,* 2nd

enlarged ed. (University Park, Pa.: Pennsylvania State University Press, 1978).

Chung, Han-ku., *Interest Representation in Soviet Policy-Making: A Case Study of the West Siberian Energy Coalition* (Boulder, Colo.: Westview, 1987).

Colton, Timothy J., *The Dilemma of Reform in*

the Soviet Union (New York: Council on Foreign Relations, 1986).

Dawisha, Karen, *Eastern Europe, Gorbachev, and Reform: The Great Challenge* (Cambridge: Cambridge University Press, 1988).

Falkenheim, Victor C., ed., *Chinese Politics: From Mao to Deng* (New York: Paragon House Publishers, 1989).

Friedberg, Maurice and **Heyward Isham,** eds., *Soviet Society under Gorbachev: Current Trends and Prospects for Reform* (New York: St. Martin's Press, 1987).

Gross, Susan, *Pluralism in the Soviet Union* (New York: St. Martin's Press, 1983).

Harding, Harry, *China's Second Revolution: Reform After Mao* (Washington, D.C.: Brookings Institution, 1987).

Hewett, Ed A., *Reforming the Soviet Economy: Equality Versus Efficiency* (Washington, D.C.: Brookings Institution, 1988).

Hoffman, Erik P., and **Robbin Laird,** *The Politics of Economic Modernization in the Soviet Union* (Ithaca, N.Y.: Cornell University Press, 1982).

Hough, Jerry F., and **Merle Fainsod,** *How the Soviet Union Is Governed* (Cambridge, Mass.: Harvard University Press, 1979).

Lampton, Michael D., ed., *Policy-Implementation in Post-Mao China* (Berkeley: University of California Press, 1987).

Lieberthal, Kenneth and **Michel Oksenberg,** *Policy Making in China: Leaders, Structures, Processes* (Princeton, N.J.: Princeton University Press, 1988).

Reynolds, Bruce L., *Chinese Economic Policy: Economic Reform at Midstream* (New York: Paragon House Publishers, 1989).

Rusinow, Dennison, *The Yugoslav Experiment, 1948–1974* (Berkeley: University of California Press, 1977).

Skilling, H. Gordon, and **Franklyn Griffiths,** eds., *Interest Groups in Soviet Politics* (Princeton, N.J.: Princeton University Press, 1971).

White, Stephen and **Daniel Nelson,** eds., *Communist Politics: A Reader* (New York: New York University Press, 1986).

Notes

1. Carl Friedrich and Zbigniew K. Brzezinski, *Totalitarian Dictatorship and Autocracy* (Cambridge, Mass.: Harvard University Press, 1956). The authors outlined the five essential features of a totalitarian system as: an official ideology, a single mass party, a monopoly of control of all means of armed combat, a monopoly of control of mass communication, and terroristic police control.

2. H. Gordon Skilling, "Interest Groups and Communist Politics," *World Politics* 18 (3) (1966): 435–451.

3. Jerry F. Hough, "The Bureaucratic Model and the Nature of the Soviet System," *Journal of Comparative Administration,* 5(2) (1973): 134–167; and "The Soviet System: Petrification or Pluralism?," *Problems of Communism* 21 (2) (1972): 25–45.

4. William E. Odom, "A Dissenting View on the Group Approach to Soviet Politics," *World Politics* 28 (4) (1976): 542–568; and Andrew C. Janos, "Interest Groups and the Structure of Power. Critique and Comparisons," *Studies in Comparative Communism* 12 (1) (1979): 6–20.

5. Incremental policy making, often called the process of muddling through, deals with policy matters, as they arise, on a more or less ad hoc basis and results in decisions that deviate from present policy only marginally. This form of policy making essentially is short term, or remedial, and does not place much emphasis on long-range planning and analysis or on the foresight necessary to promote future social and ideological goals.

6. Jerry F. Hough, "The Brezhnev Era: the Man and the System," *Problems of Communism* 25 (2) (1976): 1–17.

7. Hough, "The Soviet System": 29.

8. See Joseph S. Berliner, "Managing the USSR Economy: Alternative Models," *Problems of Communism* 22 (1) (1983): 40–56.

9. Ibid.: 54.

10. *Pravda*, January 13, 1988: 38.

11. May 14, 1990, *The New York Times*, p. A1.

12. *Kommunist* (3) (February 1988): 75–76.

13. Michel Oksenberg, "Economic Policy-Making in China," *China Quarterly* (90) (1982): 165–194.

14. Parris H. Chang, *Power and Policy in China*, 2nd enlarged ed. (State College, Pa.: Pennsylvania State University Press, 1978).

15. Ibid., pp. 186–187.

16. Ibid., p. 181.

17. Ibid., p. 189.

18. Michel Oksenberg and Richard Bush, "China's Political Evolution: 1972–82" *Problems of Communism* 31 (5) (1982): 1–19.

19. Oksenberg, "Economic Policy-Making in China": 170.

20. Not surprisingly, some resistance to the imposition of household farming occurred. Rural Communist Party cadres greatly resented the weakening of their privileged positions resulting from the decollectivization of agriculture and disbandment of the commune system. The replacement of the egalitarian distribution system by the one favoring competition and differential rewards offended many farmers accustomed to the life of collectivism and equality.

21. See, for example, Harry Harding, *China's Second Revolution: Reform After Mao* (Washington, D.C.: The Brookings Institution, 1987), p. 93.

22. Ibid., p. 87.

23. Ibid., pp. 174–183.

CHAPTER 14

POLITICAL PERFORMANCE IN SECOND WORLD SYSTEMS

One year after Karl Marx's death in 1883, Friedrich Engels, using Marx's research notes and materials, wrote:

> Democracy in government, brotherhood in society, equality in rights and privileges, and universal education, foreshadow the next higher plane of society to which experience, intelligence and knowledge are steadily tending. It will be a revival, in a higher form, of the liberty, equality and fraternity of the ancient gentes.[1]

After many difficult decades of trying to build this higher form of society, it is clear that the ideals represented within it are more remote than ever. On May Day 1990 in Red Square, Moscow, a placard borne aloft during the unofficial parade read "Seventy Years on the Way to Nowhere!" What went wrong? Why didn't the Marxist-Leninist experiments result in democracy, respect, well-being, and enlightenment? This chapter will focus on these four values to summarize and assess the records of political performance in the Second World states.

Power: Democracy or Dictatorship?

Power relationships are of central importance in our examination of Second World rule. Mikhail Gorbachev began his address on political reform at the November 29, 1988 meeting of the Supreme Soviet by noting, "The question of power is the most important question in any society." He went on to say that the question "acquires a special significance in revolutionary periods when the old political system is being broken down and a new one established, when the orders and rules by which society will have to live and develop for a whole historical epoch are being instituted."[2] This is the sort of period in which the Soviet Union and many other Second World systems find themselves today. We will begin our examination by focusing on *goals*, *actions*, and *outcomes* in the Soviet case and will divide the Soviet experience into the pre-Gorbachev (1917–85) age and the more recent period.

A number of goals motivated the Soviet leaders concerning the distribution of power in the pre-Gorbachev period. Although Lenin once went so far as to say communism would not be achieved until full democracy was implemented, he and subsequent Soviet leaders were obviously not guided, at least first and foremost, by democratic goals. Rather, the primary goal was to see that the Communist Party of the Soviet Union (CPSU) maintained a monopoly of power. This was such an important goal that it was written into the Soviet constitution.

The Soviet leaders undertook many actions over the years to achieve this primary goal. They prohibited any organized opposition to their power and structured the political system to facilitate their authoritarian style of centralized one-party rule. On occasion, they encouraged mass involvement in the political process and requested the advice of experts outside of the formal Party and governmental hierarchy. But although there was some mass and expert involvement in the Soviet system prior to the Gorbachev period, it was strictly within the bounds prescribed by the CPSU.

In the Gorbachev period, the Party leadership finally confronted the costs of centralized Communist Party rule and began to recognize the need to reform the political system and to broaden the distribution of power. On the first point, Gorbachev rhetorically asked the delegates to the historic 19th Party Conference in June 1988 why the Soviet Union required a radical reform of its political system. He answered his question by noting:

First and foremost, comrades, it is a fact—and we have to admit this today—that . . . the political system established as a result of the [1917] revolution underwent serious deformations. This made possible the omnipotence of Stalin and his entourage, and the wave of repressive measures and lawlessness.[3]

Gorbachev went on in his speech to outline a new set of goals regarding political reform and the distribution of power in Soviet society:

First, everything must be done to include millions upon millions of people in administering the country in deed, not in word.

Second, maximum scope must be given to the processes of the self-regulation and self-government of society, and conditions must be created for the full development of the initiative of citizens, representative bodies of government, party and civic organizations, and work collectives.

Third, it is necessary to adjust the mechanism of the unhindered formation and expression of the interests and will of all classes and social groups, their coordination and realization in the domestic and foreign policies of the Soviet state.

Fourth, the conditions must be created for the further free development of every nation and nationality, for the strengthening of their friendship and equitable cooperation on the principles of internationalism.

Fifth, socialist legality, law and order, must be radically strengthened so as to rule out any possibility of power being usurped or abused, so as effectively to counter bureaucracy and formalism, and reliably guarantee the protection of citizens' constitutional rights and freedoms, and also the execution of their duties with respect to society and the state.

Sixth, there must be a strict demarcation of the functions of party and state bodies, in conformity with Lenin's conception of the Communist Party as a political vanguard of society and the role of the Soviet state as an instrument of government by the people.

Finally, seventh, an effective mechanism must be established to assure the timely self-rejuvenation of the political system with due consideration for changing international and external conditions, a system capable of increasingly vigorous development and of introducing the principles of socialist democracy and self-government into all spheres of life.[4]

On this and numerous other occasions, Gorbachev outlined his goals for what he called "the democratization of our society."

By the end of the decade significant actions were taken and efforts made to reform the Soviet political system. Gorbachev pushed through measures to give more power to the Soviets; to separate Party and government responsibilities, to place more emphasis on secret ballot, multicandidate, competitive elections; to give more power and responsibilities to the regions and national minorities. In 1990, the Soviet leaders went so far as to repudiate Article 6 of the Soviet Constitution, which formally guaranteed the Communist Party's monopoly of power.

No one can deny that historic changes were being made in the Soviet political system and in the distribution of power in the late 1980s and at the turn of the decade. Although it is too early to evaluate all of these changes and their consequences, the following observation should be made. Gorbachev and the Soviet Party leaders were willing to experiment with reforms that were beginning to bring about significant power redistributions within the broader society. This period was clearly an opportunity for the expansion of democratic processes in what had traditionally been one of the world's least democratic states. As we will note later, however, this democratization has begun to undermine the very existence of the Soviet state.

Even more revolutionary redistributions of power came to the states of Eastern Europe during the same period. After initially resisting the democratization that was taking place in

the Soviet Union, the pace of political reform began to pick up in Eastern Europe in the late 1980s and finally exploded with the historic transformations of 1989. Poland started first, when the communist authorities entered in direct talks (the so called roundtable talks of 1989) with Solidarity, the Catholic church, and other noncommunist forces. These talks brought about the elections that resulted in a mandate for the noncommunist forces and the first clear use of the ballot box to vote communist governments out of power.

The redistribution of power away from the traditional ruling Communist Parties and into the hands of opposition groups and parties then unfolded in stunning and rapid succession. Within months, the prevailing power relationships within the East European states had been radically transformed. Traditional Communist Party rule was out and multiparty democracy was in. The goal of a Communist Party monopoly of power was being replaced by a serious but perilous movement toward democracy.

The Chinese Communists also considered political reforms in the 1980s but turned out to be much more reluctant about democratization than their Soviet and East European counterparts. From Mao's time to the present, the Chinese leaders have remained wedded to the primacy of Communist Party rule. During Mao's reign, the Party dominated in an intrusive and arbitrary way all aspects of Chinese society. The Party, and its top leaders, clearly were the power elite within the Chinese system. Of course, there were some efforts to build democratic participation—for example, through such concepts as the mass-line and activities like mass demonstrations during the Cultural Revolution. However, these activities were controlled by Mao and/or the Communist Party and had little to do with democratic rule. The mass-line idea, one of Mao's so-called democratic inventions, was supposed to provide a two-way flow of communication between Party members and the masses. In reality, however, the Party reserved almost complete decision-making autonomy and the masses had very little impact on the policy-making process. Overall, the Maoist period was one of arbitrary Communist Party and personalized (i.e., Mao and his associates) rule.

Although the primacy of Communist Party rule remained in China in the 1980s, some important changes began. Convinced that the overcentralization of power impeded economic development, engendered corruption, and contributed to the malaise among the people, Deng Xiaoping and his fellow reformers made some moves toward a limited diffusion of power. For example, many veteran Party officials were urged to retire and open up jobs for younger, better-educated people. There also was a rejuvenation of the government and bureaucracy, providing opportunities for better-trained, more technically competent people to play a role in decision-making processes. Greater separation of Party and government was also seen, which allowed people who were not Party members to play increasing roles in social and economic activities, particularly at the lower levels. The Chinese even began to experiment with direct and multicandidate elections, allowed greater decentralization of power to the regions, and implemented economic reforms that took some power, however limited, away from the central Party leaders. In 1987, Harry Harding observed that:

The Party no longer interferes in the detail of the daily lives of most citizens. A system of law, which guarantees the Chinese people certain substantive and procedural rights, increasingly constrains the exercise of political power. Greater opportunities have been opened for Chinese outside government, particularly intellectuals, to express their views on national policy. Discussion of political issues, both in private occasions and in public forums, is more lively, frank, and detailed. And the tone of political discourse is less charismatic, more secular, less ideological, and more rational. On balance, the political system is more open and relaxed than at any time since 1949.[5]

Harding went on to caution, however, that China was still not characterized by political pluralism and had not fundamentally transformed the basic features of a one-party Leninist political system. He emphasized that although the Communist Party leaders consulted with a larger number of people in the making of policy, it still allowed "no independent political parties, no autonomous mass media, no independent social or professional associations, and no true contest for political power."[6] The Communist Party's crackdown on the reform and democratization movements in the late 1980s and in 1990 confirmed that the Chinese authorities would try to resist the revolutionary changes that had come to the Soviet Union and Eastern Europe.

Yugoslavia's experience with the question of political power has been particularly interesting and is deserving of special consideration. The Yugoslavs began their experiment with communist rule in the dictatorial Stalinist tradition. When Tito and the Yugoslav communists took over power after World War II, they imposed a one-party dictatorship similar to the ones found in the Soviet Union and other East European states. In 1947, however, the Yugoslavs broke with the Soviet bloc and began to develop their own model of communism. Compared with its Soviet, East European, and Chinese counterparts in the 1960s and 1970s, it featured a number of democratic innovations that suggested movement toward a broader distribution of power.

The earliest and perhaps most significant reform involved the Yugoslav experiment with industrial democracy and what has often been referred to as self-managing socialism. The Yugoslavs began this experiment in the 1950s when they set up workers' councils to encourage workers to participate, along with management and Communist Party officials, in the process of industrial decision making. Subsequently, workers' councils and other participatory decision-making bodies were established in all social, economic, and political organizations within the society. The Yugoslav constitution was rewritten to require that schools, factories, and all other organizations manage their own affairs. The Yugoslav leaders boldly spoke about their desires to make Yugoslavia a more democratic, self-managing society.

Other democratic trends seemed to be developing in Yugoslavia in the 1960s and 1970s under the broad rubric of self-managing socialism. Considerable power was decentralized from the federal government in Belgrade to the regional governments in the constituent republics. The republics—Croatia, Slovenia, Serbia and so on—took on considerable power and could challenge and sometimes defeat the federal government on important matters of policy. The federal government hoped that the decentralization of power in a truly federal system could ensure "unity through diversity" and have a better chance of commanding the support of the multinational Yugoslav people than a highly centralized system as existed in the Soviet Union at that time.

The Yugoslavs also experimented with the fundamental principle of Communist Party rule. They undertook both symbolic changes—for example, renaming the Communist Party the "League of Communists of Yugoslavia" (LCY)—and significant reforms. They decentralized considerable LCY power to the regional Party organizations, leading some observers to speak decades ago of a Yugoslav multiparty system—that is, a country with regional Communist Parties that were often at odds with one another. In the 1960s, Yugoslav communist leaders talked about "divorcing" the Party (LCY) from power, by establishing a greater separation of Party and government. What they had in mind was a Party that would still be very much involved in guiding and, in reality, controlling the country but would turn over increasing power to the government and self-managing institutions. The Party also experimented with rules requiring greater circulation and rotation of Party officials. This was intended to allow more people opportunities to assume leadership roles and avoid the personalized and centralized rule of the traditional, Stalinist Communist Party state.

Yugoslav leaders were guided by two primary and conflicting goals concerning the distribution of power in their political system. Although attempting to pursue, on the one hand, the democratic ideals of self-governing socialism, they were unwilling until recently to relinquish the Party's leading role. Yugoslav leaders wanted both self-government and Party rule and undertook actions to pursue both of these principles. The outcomes in Yugoslavia reflected these competing and conflicting goals. Self-management made some inroads into the traditional power relationships within the society. Some of the authoritarian arrangements of the past were replaced with more democratic processes, involving large and varied groups of people. But the process of democratization was still incomplete and was likely to remain that way as long as the LCY maintained its dominant role. Divided deeply along republic (i.e., national) lines, the LCY could develop neither the democratic consensus nor the totalitarian power to move the country forward. Although Yugoslavia also moved toward greater democratization and away from Communist Party rule in recent years, the challenges of stable democracy in this divided Balkan state are exceedingly great.

Respect: Community or Conflict?

To what extent did Second World systems create political communities of love and friendship? And to what extent were they divided by class and conflict? An examination of the value of respect will give us a clearer idea.

Soviet leaders long ago realized that the class divisions and ethnocentrism that plagued and contributed to the collapse of tsarist Russia would have to be resolved if they were to be successful in developing a unified Soviet commonwealth. Social and national cleavages were deeply cast in the old Russian state; radical goals and policies were required to overcome them. The initial goal that guided the post-revolutionary leaders was state survival, which Lenin, Stalin, and others pursued through the repressive policies of centralized rule in hopes of promoting societal cohesion and political integration. The Soviet leaders also sought to establish respect and a spirit of comradeliness among the diverse Soviet peoples. These traits, the leaders hoped, would contribute to the goal of a unified Soviet state.

To encourage the development of these traits, the leaders emphasized the common struggles of the Soviet peoples, the bonds that united them, and the importance of cooperation and friendship among the different ethnic and national groups. At certain times in the past, some might have thought that these efforts had reduced ethnocentrism and discriminatory relations among the Soviet peoples. However, recent research and experience suggests that interethnic differences persist, and the Soviet leaders have been unable to create what Soviet leaders traditionally referred to in the past as a "fundamentally new social and international community" of Soviet people. What social harmony existed in Soviet society was imposed by suppression. It did not emanate naturally from social and ethnic relations in the society. Anti-Semitism among large sectors of the Soviet people continues, and strong ethnonational tensions have exploded into full view. There appears to be little community of shared interest among the diverse Soviet peoples. The destructive disputes between the Armenians and Azerbaijans and the assertion of national pride and demands for independence among the Baltic nationalities are among the numerous examples indicating that the Soviets have not solved their nationality problems. Gorbachev has pleaded with the Soviet people, telling them that "we are one family." As we enter the 1990s, destructive feuds continue, indicating serious differences within the Soviet "family."

Another traditional shortcoming in the USSR concerned the system's disrespect for human rights and the personal freedoms taken so seriously in the Western democracies. Past Soviet constitutions elaborated in great detail the citizens' economic guarantees that formed the centerpiece of the Soviet's traditional definition of human rights: the right to housing, education, work, leisure, medical care, and maintenance in old age. Less prominent and heavily qualified were the political rights, including freedom of speech, press, assembly, demonstration in the streets, religion, and privacy. The constitution diluted these rights by declaring that they were granted only "in conformity with the interests of the working people and for the purposes of strengthening the socialist system." An explicit limitation aimed at dissidents noted, "The exercise of rights and freedoms shall be inseparable from the performance by citizens of their duties."

We should note, however, that Soviet human rights policy has considerably improved during the Gorbachev period. Many political prisoners have been set free; many minorities and former "refuseniks" have been allowed to emigrate. Dissidents, such as the late Andrei Sakharov, were returned from exile and allowed to speak out and even run for political office. Magazines and journals are addressing sensitive issues and themes that were strictly forbidden in the past.

But along with the opening of Soviet society and improvements in human rights problems come new challenges and difficulties for the Soviet people. During the present period of change and transition in the Soviet Union, the social contract on which order, respect, and trust are based is changing. In this environment of change and uncertainty, some Soviets have called attention to a disintegrating social and moral order. Some make references to a dead, sick, or corrupt society. There has been a rise in organized crime in the USSR. Many reports call attention to bands of disciplined, organized criminals who bribe officials to achieve desired ends such as protection from the law, prized apartments or property, raw materials for business projects, and so on. They also use their organization to exploit prostitutes, black-marketeers, and law-abiding citizens who are trying to start cooperatives and private enterprise. It has never been easy to promote love and respect, brotherhood and unity, among the Soviet peoples, and it has become no easier under glasnost, reform, and perestroika.

Other Second World states have encountered similar problems when trying to achieve a secure and supportive community from their diverse nationalities and ethnic groups; the Yugoslav policy makers also wanted brotherhood and unity but pursued rather different policies than the Soviets. Traditionally, Yugoslav policy actions showed greater respect for human rights and local autonomy. Yugoslav socialization policies were less coercive, more respectful of the people, and more patient concerning the considerable time required to bring about the desired changes. Government actions in the area of federalism and self-management granted high levels of political and economic autonomy to the various ethnic groups and local organizations, reflecting more respect for the interests and concerns of the diverse Yugoslav peoples.

Although Tito and the Yugoslav policy makers may have tried to do more to allocate respect to all groups and regions on the basis of universalistic norms and principles, the regional groups, such as the Albanians, Serbs, and Croats, often have been unwilling to accord respect and trust to one another. When faced with difficult political choices that critically affect the national republics and provinces—such as whether to take the profits of the richer republics to subsidize the development of the poorer—Tito tried to decide in the collective, or Yugoslav, interest. Many contemporary regional leaders, however, are unwilling to place Yugoslav interests before the interests of their own national or ethnic group. As a result, political decisions often degenerate into nationalistic squabbles pitting one nationality against another.

The value of respect in Yugoslavia dropped to a postwar low in the late 1980s along with the declining economy and deteriorating interethnic relations. The people of Yugoslavia were angry. Their standard of living was plummeting and they vented their frustrations on any convenient target. Often it was the government, and at other times, neighboring ethnic groups. No matter who was the target, antagonistic ethnic and social relations in Yugoslavia

440

had reached a critical and dangerous stage. There is more conflict than community in contemporary Yugoslavia.

As a result of the deep social and regional cleavages of traditional China, the value of respect and the goal of societal integration also commanded high attention from its postrevolutionary leaders. To unify the society, Mao and the communist leaders hoped to transform the Chinese populace by developing a new socialist person. Emphasizing the themes of respect, equality, and comradeship, the Mao leadership once was thought to have achieved considerable success. But with the benefit of hindsight and more information, we now know that Maoist China was far from the paradise of harmony, love, and mutual respect that the leaders sought to convey. Large segments of the population discriminated against others on the basis of class background, family connections, social status, and geographic origin. People of the privileged classes, such as the political, economic, and cultural establishment, were often unwilling to associate with those considered to be inferior. Overall, the Maoist regime did little to promote the values of comradeship it so deeply desired to instill.

Perhaps the most significant outcome of Mao's policies was the level of equality—at least *income* equality—evident in the Chinese system during the 1960s and 1970s. In a society with a long and strong tradition of elitist, hierarchical relations, Mao's actions altered a social characteristic that many observers had thought impossible to change. However, along with this trend toward increased income equality came reductions in economic efficiency and development.

In the post-Mao period, egalitarianism was deemphasized to promote higher productivity and economic efficiency. The post-Mao reforms emphasized initiative, competition, and "getting rich" as being more important to China than equality. Increased corruption, however, followed. In the 1980s, corruption among Party officials, new entrepreneurs, and government bureaucrats became a problem of unprecedented dimensions. Some observers have said the country was turned into a "kleptocracy," where the values of greed and materialism replaced the former superficial commitment to comradeship. The economic reforms expanding entrepreneurship provided opportunities for profiteering, which generated resentment among sizable sectors of the Chinese people. Social relations declined, and gambling, prostitution, and crime were on the rise.

What about human rights in China? Interestingly, considerably little has been said and written in the West over the years about Chinese human rights policy, compared with the considerable attention given this problem in the Soviet Union. In fact, Mao's record on human rights was at times as dreadful as that of Stalin's. For example, shortly after the communist takeover in 1949 and during the Cultural Revolution in the late 1960s, the Maoist regime put due process in abeyance and utilized what we would refer to as kangaroo courts to mete out capital punishment for millions of people. There were also thousands of political prisoners who suffered under the harsh and arbitrary strictures of Maoist rule. Friendship was to give way to "comradeship," a euphemism for interpersonal relations based on mutual suspicion. People were reluctant to confide with their former friends. Respect and trust had disappeared.

The 1980s witnessed considerable improvement in the regime's performance with respect to human rights and civil liberties. Although the new regime continued to incarcerate some political dissidents, such as Wei Jingsheng, there no longer were reports of mass imprisonment and mass execution for political reasons. Another significant change in the 1980s was that ordinary people were emboldened to voice their grievances against the regime's policies in public, a felonious offense punishable by death or stiff prison terms in the Maoist past. Although there were conservative backlashes and the movement toward human rights liberalization was slow and limited, the Chinese people in the 1980s enjoyed much more freedom of speech and press than in the past. During this period, the mass media began to carry out vigorous investigative reporting and exposed corruption and incompetence.

The democratization movement and confrontation in Tiananmen Square in 1989 and the convulsive events that have brought dramatic change to much of the Second World place new challenges on the Chinese authorities in the 1990s. The leaders' initial response has been conservative and repressive. They have dug in their heels and denied the changes taking place around them. They lied to the Chinese people and to the world about the massacre in Tiananmen Square. They lied about the yearning for democracy and human rights in their society. Such an approach shows little promise for promoting trust and respect in Chinese society.

Traditional social and elite-mass relations in Eastern Europe showed some of the same negative consequences of repressive, dictatorial rule. The leaders lied to the people, and the people lost respect for the leaders. In the repressive and economically deprived environments, people worried first and foremost about themselves. Values of love, respect, and true comradeship were lost in the struggle for survival. The social contract was no longer viable. The societies became morally ill. No one spoke more eloquently about this problem than the new Czechoslovak President Vaclav Havel in his 1990 New Year's Day address to the Czechoslovak people (see excerpts from address).

'The Great Moral Stake of the Moment'

Perhaps not since Abraham Lincoln's Second Inaugural has a head of state delivered a speech as searching as Vaclav Havel's New Year's Day address to Czechoslovakia. The new president challenged his compatriots to face their past collusion with communist rule and their future responsibility for their own freedom. Excerpts:

For the past 40 years on this day you have heard my predecessors utter variations on the same theme, about how our country is prospering, how many more billion tons of steel we have produced, how happy we all are, how much we trust our government and what beautiful prospects lie ahead. I do not think you put me into this office so that I, too, should lie to you.

Our country is not prospering. The great creative and spiritual potential of our nation is not being used to its fullest. Whole sectors of industry are producing things in which no one is interested, while things we need are in short supply.

The state, which calls itself a state of the working people, is humiliating and exploiting the workers. Our outdated economy is squandering energy . . . A country which could once be proud of the standard of education of its people spends so little on education that today it ranks 72nd in the world. We have laid waste to our soil and the rivers and the forests our forefathers bequeathed us, and we have the worst environment in all of Europe today. . . .

The worst thing is that we are living in a decayed moral environment. We have become morally ill, because we have become accustomed to saying one thing and thinking another. We have learned not to believe in anything, not to care about one another and only to look after ourselves. Notions such as love, friendship, compassion, humility and forgiveness have lost their depth and dimension, and for many of us they represent merely some kind of psychological idiosyncrasy, or appear as some kind of stray relic from times past, something rather comical in the era of computers and space rockets. . . .

The previous regime, armed with its arrogant and intolerant ideology, denigrated man into a production force and nature into a production tool. In this way it attacked their very essence and the relationship between them. It made talented people who were capable of managing their own affairs . . . into cogs in some kind of monstrous, ramshackle, smelly machine whose purpose no one can understand. It can do nothing more than slowly but surely wear itself down, along with all the cogs in it.

When I talk about a decayed moral environment . . . I mean all of us, because all of us have become accustomed to the totalitarian system, accepted it as an inalterable fact and thereby kept it running. In other words, all of us are responsible, each to a different degree, for keeping the totalitarian machine running. None of us is merely a victim of it, because all of us helped to create it together.

Why do I mention this? It would be very unwise to see the sad legacy of the past 40 years as something alien, handed down to us by some distant relatives. On the contrary, we must accept this legacy as something which we have brought upon ourselves. If we can accept this, then we will understand that it is up to all of us to do something about it. We cannot lay all the blame on those who ruled us before, not only because this would not be true but also because it could detract from the responsibility each of us now faces—the responsibility to act on our own initiative, freely, sensibly and quickly. . . .

Throughout the world, people are surprised that the acquiescent, humiliated, skeptical Czechoslovak people who apparently no longer believed in anything suddenly managed to find the enormous strength in the space of a few weeks to shake off the totalitarian system in a completely decent and peaceful way. We ourselves are also surprised at this, and we ask where the young people, in particular, who have never known any other system, find the source of their aspirations for truth, freedom of thought, political imagination, civic courage and civic foresight. How is it that their parents, the generation which was considered lost, also joined in with them? How is it possible that so many immediately grasped what had to be done?. . .

Of course, for our freedom today we also had to pay a price. Many of our people died in prison in the '50s, many were executed, thousands of human lives were destroyed, hundreds of thousands of talented people were driven abroad. . . . Those who resisted totalitarian government were persecuted, [as were] those who simply managed to remain true to their own principles and think freely. None of those who paid the price in one way or another for our freedom today should be forgotten. . . .

Neither should we forget that other nations paid an even higher price for their freedom today, and thus also paid indirectly for us, too. The rivers of blood which flowed in Hungary,

Poland, Germany and recently in such a horrific way in Romania, as well as the sea of blood shed by the nations of the Soviet Union, should not be forgotten . . . it was these great sacrifices which wove the tragic backdrop for today's freedom or gradual liberation of the Soviet-bloc nations, and the backdrop of our newly charged freedom, too. . . .

This, it seems to me, is the great moral stake of the present moment. It contains the hope that in the future we will no longer have to suffer the complex of those who are permanently indebted to someone else. Now it is up to us alone whether this hope comes to fruition, and whether our civic, national and political self-confidence reawakens in a historically new way.[7]

The new East European leaders and their societies are now facing tremendous challenges. Among other things, they must establish a new social contract that brings out the best in their people. In their efforts to transform their economic and political systems, they must build civic cultures that will promote private initiative and public cooperation, personal integrity and social respect. They are swimming in uncharted waters and will find this a challenging task.

Well-Being: Welfare or Poverty?

The value of well-being represents an area of social policy of considerable importance to Second World states. In his speech to the 24th CPSU Congress in 1971, General Secretary Leonid I. Brezhnev claimed that the country's principal goal was raising the standard of living. At the 25th Congress in 1976, he reemphasized that goal by pledging:

> "a further increase in the Soviet people's well-being, the improvement of their living and working conditions, and significant progress in public health, education, and culture."

At subsequent Party congresses, similar pledges were made.

When examining the actions and outcomes, we encounter a mixed picture. It is apparent that some things were done in the area of social services. The Soviet Union is a welfare state. Housing is exceedingly cheap although always in short supply; medical care, health services, and education are free; employment is guaranteed. Yet, when comparing the average Soviet citizen with his or her West European counterpart, he or she clearly is deprived of many goods and services associated with a higher standard of living. For example, housing is exceedingly scarce, forcing many families to share apartments or to wait for years to be provided an apartment suited to their needs. Second, medical care generally is of poor quality. Third, consumer goods are in critically short supply. Soviet department stores show a limited variety of modern appliances, clothing, and other consumer goods that we take for granted in the West. True, the Soviet leaders continue to speak of altering this situation, but the extent to which change is possible, at least in the short term, is a matter of some contention.[8]

The Soviet economy is having severe problems, and there is not nearly enough money in the Soviet budget to bring about necessary improvements in the social and consumer sectors. Like the United States in the late 1980s, the Soviet Union during that period also was running a huge budgetary deficit. Although figuring the USSR's size and comparing the Soviet deficit with the American one are difficult, one leading Soviet economist and deputy prime minister, Leonid Abalkin, estimated the Soviet deficit at $165 billion in 1989 and called it the most important economic problem facing the country.[9] A $165 billion deficit would be about 11 percent of Soviet GNP, which would suggest that the Soviet deficit was considerably larger than the American deficit, which was about 4 percent of the American GNP in the late 1980s.

Because perestroika was unable to bring about a rapid turnaround in the economy—Abalkin predicted it would be at least six years before perestroika produced a significant improvement in the standard of living—the Soviet leaders faced hard choices as they approached the 1990s. What would it be: guns or butter? Social programs or military spending? There was not enough money to bring about necessary improvements in health care, old-age pensions, child care, food and housing, and all of the other services of a welfare state. Gorbachev and the Soviet people knew that they would have to do better. Perestroika was the plan, but even in the most optimistic scenario, the relief would be neither immediate nor guaranteed. Albalkin said cuts would have to be made in both military and civilian spending; in addition, the government would be forced to shift many government projects to private financing, something previously heretical in the Soviet state. By the end of the decade, the Soviets had

Antiaircraft missiles on display in Moscow's Red Square at the anniversary celebration of the Great October Revolution. Although heavy spending in the military sector moved the USSR into "superpower" status, it meant considerable deprivation for the consumer.

announced a 14 percent cut in the military budget, a 20 percent cut in capital investment related to civilian construction, and an expansion in the role of private and cooperative financing and building of housing.

In an April 1990 report to the U.S. Congress, the Central Intelligence Agency (CIA) and the Defense Intelligence Agency (DIA) confirmed the bleak assessments on the state of the Soviet economy.[10] Among other things, the report noted that the:

1. Production of energy and industrial materials had fallen and that industrial production had registered its worst performance since World War II.

2. The combination of inflation and shortages had made daily life extremely difficult for all but the most privileged segment of the population; according to Soviet sources, 15 percent of the population was living below the poverty line.

3. Shortages in consumer goods and inequalities in their distribution had contributed to a growing number of strikes and ethnic clashes.

Heavy Soviet spending on the military left little money for environmental protection, as indicated by the pollution from this Estonian phosphate plant.

To deal with these and related economic stringencies, the CIA and DIA reported that the Soviet leaders had reduced defense spending by 4 to 5 percent; military procurement was cut by 6 to 7 percent; the production of tanks was halved; uniformed military manpower was reduced by 200,000; military deliveries to Third World countries were reduced by nearly $2 billion; and substantial military withdrawals were made from Eastern Europe. Although these were important steps designed to redress the traditional "guns and butter" imbalance, few believed that they would have a significant impact on improving the social well-being of the Soviet people in the short run.

Because of the lower level of economic development and the much greater number of people, the problem of providing all citizens with a reasonable level of well-being has been even more severe in China. Accordingly, the primary goal guiding the Chinese policy makers in the postrevolutionary period was the provision of a minimal level of economic security.

These provisions in a historically underdeveloped area like China require high rates of economic modernization and industrial production. Although there have been notable achievements, China remains a colossus mired in poverty and economic backwardness. In terms of GNP per capita, it still trails behind more than a hundred countries in the world. Although the mass of Chinese people are better fed, better clothed, and enjoy a longer life span than ever before, they are not keeping up with the advances of other parts of the Far East.

To encourage economic growth, the post-Mao Chinese leaders undertook dramatic economic reforms in the 1980s. In the agricultural sector, they broadened the rights of peasants to farm on their own and to engage in profitable activities. In the industrial sector, they reduced governmental control and placed greater emphasis

Chinese factory workers' flats usually consist of one room inhabited by parents and child. Kitchens and bathrooms are generally shared with other families. Although this space seems inadequate by Western standards, it is an improvement over the prerevolutionary period in China.

on competitive market forces. The overriding goal in both agriculture and industry was to promote initiative, competition, and efficiency. By so doing, the leaders hoped to promote modernization and social well-being in China.

Like the Soviet Union, China's economy has been unable to support all of the social needs of a welfare state. And with the post-Mao deemphasis on equality, the gap between the haves and have nots began to rise. Successful entrepreneurs were able to provide for their needs, while those dependent on the state often suffered from the provision of minimal services. While the standard of living for a minority rose, the masses were struck by rising prices and a decline in the quality of life.

Former Party leader Zhao Ziyang recognized the problems confronting China in the 1980s and outlined three basic goals for improvements in an address to the 13th Party Congress in 1987. He claimed that the first goal involved a doubling of the 1980 GNP and the solution of food and clothing problems. The second step involved another doubling of the GNP by the end of the century, and the third was to reach the per capita GNP level of an average developed country by the middle of the next century. These long-term goals did little to assuage the concerns and improve the living standards of the Chinese people. Expectations and feelings of deprivation among the masses were rising in China. To avoid the dangerous consequences of excessive deprivation, frustration, and cynicism in the future, the Chinese leaders must be able to demonstrate progress toward their goals.

Contemporary China is a blend of the new and old.

447

The former Communist Party states of Eastern Europe were overthrown for a variety of reasons, but one of the most important was their inability to provide the levels of social well-being so long promised their societies. The people of East Germany had been told that they were building a workers' paradise, yet when the Berlin Wall came down, they found the paradise (at least in terms of standard of living and social well-being) on the other side. The people of Romania had been forced to live in extreme deprivation under the dictator Nicolae Ceausescu and had one of the lowest standards of living in Europe.

The peoples' well-being in Eastern Europe also was affected by the deteriorating physical environment. Because the governments could not afford the high cost of environmental protection, many people were forced to live in environs of sticky soot, carbon monoxide, nitrogen oxide, sulphur, heavy metals, and other unhealthy materials spewed from industrial plants. Much of Eastern Europe had become an ecological disaster, and the governments could not afford to address the growing problem. Overall, the highly centralized command economies had not produced sufficient resources, and much of the meager resources produced was invested in programs (e.g., military) that did little to improve the living conditions of the people (see Table 14.1 for indicators of some of these conditions in the 1980s). Such conditions generated considerable resentment in these societies, fueling the explosions of discontent that characterized the 1989 revolutions.

Well-being is one of the values that is more amenable to quantitative evaluation and comparison. A useful way of examining and comparing government actions, for example, is to see where they spend their money. Table 14.2 gives us some idea of how much money each Second World government spent per capita in the mid-1980s on the military, education, and health. Before examining the data, we should remember that because of their weak economies, Second World states did not have very much to spend. Second, of what they did have, far too much was spent on the military. Examining military spending as reflected in Table 14.2, we see that the USSR spent far more per person (and overall) than any other Second World state. Although it spent somewhat less per person than the United States, it spent far more as a percentage of its gross national product (GNP). The USSR was clearly the big spender in the defense sector in the 1980s. Observing the domestic consequences of military spending, Soviet leader Gorbachev announced cuts in Soviet military expenditures by the end of the decade. China had comparatively little to expend and invested less per capita in the military sector than any of the East European states.

Turning to education expenditures listed in Table 14.2, the USSR and East Germany were the clear leaders, although both spent substantially less than the United States. The education and health expenditures of the Laotians, Vietnamese, and North Koreans were extremely low and explain the low quality of health care and schooling found in these countries. When combining health and education expenditures and comparing them with military expenditures, some interesting facts appear. Whereas the United States, for example, spent $1,002 per person a year on defense and $1,445 on health and education, the Soviet Union spent $816 and $559, respectively.

Actions in terms of government expenditures are, of course, related to policy outcomes. Table 14.1 provides a number of indicators of such outcomes, describing levels of health care, nutrition, and so forth in the Second World states in the 1980s. Examining in the first column the number of people per physician, we find that the Soviet Union purportedly had the best ratio

Table 14.1 Health and Nutrition Indicators, 1986

Country	Population per Physician	Population per Hospital Bed	Infant Mortality* Rate per 1,000	Life Expectancy	Calorie Supply† per Capita	Protein Supply† per Capita	Percent of Population with Safe Water
Albania	671	170	39	72	na‡	na	92
Bulgaria	339	110	16	72	3,634	106.3	96
Cambodia	14,404	410	130	48	na	na	3
China	1,673	460	32	69	2,628	62.0	na
Cuba	455	190	15	73	3,107	78.9	82
Czechoslovakia	327	80	15	71	3,673	103.3	74
East Germany	424	100	9	73	3,800	112.7	90
Hungary	304	100	20	70	3,561	101.7	84
Laos	6,353	370	110	47	na	na	21
Mongolia	401	90	45	64	2,829	92.5	100
North Korea	na	740	24	69	3,199	93.6	100
Poland	497	180	18	71	3,298	101.8	67
Romania	475	110	22	70	3,396	101.8	77
Soviet Union	235	80	24	69	3,396	105.6	100
Vietnam	3,233	430	64	61	na	na	41
Yugoslavia	549	160	25	72	3,542	101.5	68
USA	462	190	10	75	3,692	106.5	100

* Deaths of infants under one year old per 1,000 live births.
† Per capita supply of food, in calories, and of grams of protein per day; the figures of caloric supply relate to 1984–1986 average.
‡ Not available.
(*Source*) Adapted from Ruth Leger Sivard, *World Military and Social Expenditures, 1989* (Washington, D.C.: World Priorities, 1989), pp. 50–55; and *Production Yearbook; 1988* (Rome: Food and Agricultural Organization of the United Nations, 1989), pp. 293–294.

in the world (235 people for every physician). However, we must be cautious about the use of such statistics. Although the Soviet Union may have an impressive quantity of doctors, it also has many glaring deficiencies in the quality of its health care system.

With the exception of the Albanians, the East European states also do very well on the people-per-physican indicator. The Asians, on the other hand, do very poorly. The second column, de-

scribing the population per hospital bed, reflects the same trend. When examining the three indicators of nutrition in Table 14.1, the Soviets and Europeans do quite well once again, whereas the Asians lag far behind. Cambodia (Kampuchea) and Laos are among the few states in the world with calorie-supply-per-capita levels below 2,000 per day. Cambodia (Kampuchea) suffered tragic losses in the 1970s through starvation and war. In 1975, the country had a

**Table 14.2 Public Expenditures per Capita:
Military, Education, Health in 1984**

Country	Military (US $)	Education (US $)	Health (US $)
Albania	56	na*	32
Bulgaria	179	219	160
Cambodia	na	na	na
China	18	8	4
Cuba	148	124	64
Czechoslovakia	272	241	278
East Germany	432	335	228
Hungary	146	234	196
Laos	na	3	na
Mongolia	93	na	11
North Korea	123	na	12
Poland	167	228	201
Romania	62	73	75
Soviet Union	971	442	270
Vietnam	na	na	na
Yugoslavia	146	140	157
USA	1,164	928	783

* Not available.
(*Source*) Adapted from Ruth Leger Sivard, *World Military and Social Expenditures, 1989* (Washington, D.C.; World Priorities, 1989), pp. 50–55.

population of approximately 8 million; by 1980, as many as 4 million had died. No nation on earth suffered more during the last two decades than this once tranquil and fertile land.

Enlightenment: Erudition or Ignorance?

Policy choices concerning the nature and distribution of enlightenment—what one should know about oneself, one's work, and one's world—have been the focus of considerable controversy and debate in political systems throughout the world. Should the goal be the development of a citizen broadly trained in the humanist, liberal tradition, or the development of a more narrow, ideologically trained zealot? Should enlightenment be determined by the people, or controlled by the state? These and other choices confronted policy makers in Second World states as they attempted to mold populations that contributed to the construction of communism.

Past Soviet policy emphasized the molding of a new socialist person through a social and educational system tightly controlled by the

Communist Party. Enlightenment was what the authoritarian and ideologically motivated Party leaders wanted it to be. Education, the mass media, the arts, and all opportunities for access to information were carefully monitored and controlled by Communist Party authorities. What largely resulted was a passive, bored, and stagnant society that was conducive to neither the building of communism nor the general development of Soviet society.

Soviet policies and performance concerning enlightenment changed significantly during the Gorbachev period under the theme of glasnost. In his book *Perestroika*, Gorbachev spoke about glasnost in the following terms:

We want more openness about public affairs in every sphere of life. People should know what is good, and what is bad, too, in order to multiply the good and to combat the bad. . . . Glasnost, criticism and self-criticism are not just a new campaign. They have been proclaimed and must become a norm in the Soviet way of life. No radical change is possible without it. There is no democracy, nor can there be, without glasnost. And there is no present-day socialism, nor can there be, without democracy.[11]

The content of newspapers changed considerably under glasnost and served as a good indicator of the opening of Soviet society. By the end of the 1980s, Soviet citizens were reading daily about shortcomings in their society, including the problems of perestroika, bureaucratic inefficiency, and the Stalinist heritage. In a break with tradition, the media were allowed to report on Soviet disasters, and newspapers began to give fuller accounts of such events as the nuclear power accident in Chernobyl, the tragic earthquake in Armenia, and the independence movements in the Baltic republics.

Letters to newspaper editors, long a safety valve in the Soviet Union allowing citizens to let off steam, began in the 1980s to print letters that addressed much more sensitive issues. Letter writers complained about all sorts of things, including glasnost and the Communist Party itself. Typical letters read, "All we have is glasnost—but you can't eat glasnost, you can't clothe yourself in it." The KGB and other formerly taboo topics came under scrutiny. Some letters raised questions about the KGB and its role in a modern society. Some letters denounced Stalin as a murderer and tyrant, whereas others praised him as a great leader and the architect of the Soviet state. Soviet editors came to brag about the number of letters received, considering them a barometer of public trust. The government newspaper, *Izvestia*, boasted that it had received more than 450,000 letters in 1988. The outspoken weekly magazine *Ogonyok* announced that it had received 600,000, a tenfold increase since 1985. And *Literaturnaya Gazeta*, a weekly newspaper read primarily by intellectuals, was pleased to announce its receipt of 110,000. Although still a tiny minority in Soviet society, people expressing opinions can be found more and more.

The Soviet press also began to publish articles and statistics showing some of the darker sides of Soviet life. In February 1989, Soviet authorities released detailed crime statistics for the first time in more than fifty years, calling attention to a sharp increase in Soviet crime. "Perhaps this will shock many people," *Izvestia* commented, "but it is better to know the reality of things. . . ." General Anotoly Smirnov, chief of the Interior Ministry's information center responsible for releasing the statistics, reported specific numbers in specific categories. For example, he reported that there had been 16,710 murders and attempted murders in 1988, 37,191 cases of aggravated assault, 17,658 rapes and attempted rapes, 67,114 holdups and burglaries, and 165,283 thefts of state and public property. Overall, these and other crimes showed a 17.8-percent increase over the previous year. Smirnov went on to say that his ministry would regularly publish such statistics in the future, to give the society a clearer picture of Soviet crime, a topic that had been classified as a state secret since 1933.

The Soviet people also began in the 1980s to learn more about their leaders. A Soviet youth paper revealed that members of the ruling Politburo were paid 1,200 to 1,500 rubles a month and that Mikhail Gorbachev got a bit more, or about $30,000 a year. The highest salaries, however, went to leading Soviet military figures, who received as much as $2,000 rubles a month. The article also revealed that Gorbachev had given his $600,000 in royalties from his book *Perestroika* to the Soviet Communist Party Central Committee. In the pre-Gorbachev period, such personal information about Soviet leaders was tightly controlled.

Included in the printed media's new openness were direct attacks on the Communist Party's policies and Gorbachev himself. As noted in an earlier chapter, the Soviet periodical *Sovetskaia Rossia* published an article in 1988 defending Stalin and questioning Gorbachev's reform policy. In 1989, the Leningrad literary and political monthly *Neva* published a scathing attack of the Soviet Communist Party and of Gorbachev. The article asserted that the Party had become an interest of the "new class" and was ignoring the needs and interests of the people. The article argued that "we have to admit that it was the Party leadership that brought the country to economic crisis and moral decline." Publications like these represented a significant broadening of the boundaries of Soviet debate and fundamental changes in Soviet society. As fear diminished, and education and glasnost

increased, people were prepared to criticize their leaders and the communist values they represented.

Another change related to the jamming of foreign radio broadcasts into the Soviet Union. Since the early 1950s, Soviet authorities had gone to considerable expense to interfere with foreign broadcasts of the British Broadcasting Corporation (BBC), the U.S. government's Voice of America, and Radio Liberty, an American-financed station. The Soviets stopped jamming these stations in 1987 and 1988. Not only were the Soviet leaders broadening the boundaries of their domestic debate, but they were allowing Western broadcasters to contribute to it.

Glasnost also had significant consequences for the arts. Soviet films and books addressed topics that were strictly forbidden in the past. The authorities allowed the publication of formerly banned books like *The Foundation Pit*, a brutally irreverent fable by Andrei Platonov about the building of Soviet communism. They also allowed films and theater that addressed controversial themes. "Repentance" was a film made for television in the republic of Georgia but which was shown throughout the Soviet Union and worldwide in the late 1980s. Although Stalin is not mentioned by name, the film portrays the brutality of the Stalinist dictatorship and suggests that Soviet society still has not adequately dealt with the terrors of Stalinism.

Perhaps the most important development relating to enlightenment in the USSR concerns what began to happen in Soviet schools in the 1980s. Glasnost was carried into classrooms at all levels, and there was a refreshing openness in the study of history, politics, and economics. Students began to discuss the Stalinist heritage, the problems of perestroika, and the differences between communism and capitalism in ways that were unheard of in the past. The conservative American president, Ronald Reagan, was allowed to go before students at Moscow State University and lecture them on human rights and Western democracy. People were exposed to a broader range of opinions than had ever existed in the Soviet past.

Although we should not ignore these and other developments related to glasnost and enlightenment in the Soviet Union, we also should not overstate them or underestimate their fragility. Communist Party leaders remain in control of the instruments of political socialization in 1990, and they could close the opening of Soviet society even faster than they opened it. However, significant changes have taken place in the Soviet Union that will make it difficult to return to the closed society of the past.

Chinese policy and performance in the area of enlightenment has also changed considerably from what it was during the Maoist past. As indicated earlier, Mao thought all Chinese citizens should be selfless, imbued with a collective spirit, and willing to endure personal hardships in service to the public good and the building of communism. Mao and the CCP leaders undertook a variety of actions to develop these new minds, new outlooks, and new behaviors. They adopted a strategy of political socialization that utilized fanatic and heavy-handed indoctrination in the schools, the mass media, and the arts. The printed and spoken word was to serve the revolution, and a politically conscious populace was thought to be necessary for victory.

Although all of the consequences of Maoist fanaticism, such as the Cultural Revolution, are not yet clear, the apparent reverence to Mao's word has all but disappeared in contemporary China. The 1980 reformers under Deng Xiaoping deemphasized Mao's teachings and political conformity and emphasized pragmatism and productivity. There also was a broadening of

As illustrated by these three students at the Technical University of Jiaotang, Chinese education is trying to stay abreast of the computer age.

the boundaries of political debate and opinion. The Chinese Communist Party in the 1980s was no longer above criticism, and dissidents were allowed to enter the public debate. China went through a period of great change in the 1980s and so did the values of its people.

Illustrative of the changes were the value orientations of some sectors of the younger generation. In the late 1980s, more and more people had lost interest in both politics and education. Many were more interested in money and pleasure. A highly materialistic and even hedonistic generation had emerged. College degrees were devalued and considered not worth the time and energy invested because they could not make people rich. At the same time, an increasing number of Chinese made a cult of Western-style consumerism. Some of them would go to any length to go to the West, in their opinion the paradise of opportunity and affluence. It is clear that enlightenment in contemporary China was coming to mean something quite different than it had during the Maoist period.

Beginning with the crackdown in Tiananmen Square in 1989, the Chinese Communist Party attempted to reverse the tide. Whereas they engineered a liberalization of the conservative Maoist policies in the 1980s, in 1989 and 1990 they began a return to a more conservative line. "Redness" was again emphasized over expertise; ideology was stressed in the schools and workplace; revolutionary heroes and models were brought back into the lessons and textbooks. Chinese policy was undergoing a reversal that put it very much at odds with what was going on in the Soviet Union and Eastern Europe.

Without doubt, the most dramatic changes in the area of enlightenment at the turn of the decade took place in Eastern Europe. Still under conservative leadership in the mid- and even into the late 1980s, some of the states, such as Czechoslovakia, East Germany, and Romania, were slow to change. However, with the revolutionary transformations of 1989, East European enlightenment practices were radically altered. The teaching of Marxism-Leninism was taken out of the schools; ideology and the Communist Parties were taken out of the workplace. There was freedom of speech, press, travel, and religion. For the first time in forty years, East Europeans were free to inform themselves about their country and the world. It was a time of incredible change. Dissident writers and playwrights became presidents (e.g., Vaclav Havel in Czechoslovakia and Arpad Goncz in

Hungary); noncommunists took over the ministries of education and culture; the press and mass media were suddenly free. It was indeed an historic change, a period of enlightenment.

When considering the changes that swept across Eastern Europe in 1989 and the already high state of education and communication in these societies, one realizes the great potential in these societies. One of the tragedies of the communist experiments was the repression of this human potential. Because of the heavy hand of the Communist Party and state, the proud and able people of Eastern Europe were unable to contribute fully to their societies. Although much remains uncertain about the East European futures, the recent expansions in enlightenment should help to contribute to positive political and economic change.

Conclusion

Our four-value framework has been useful in helping us review some of the important consequences of the Marxist-Leninist experiments and Communist Party rule. We found that the traditional communist states of the Second World did not allocate power in a manner that led to socialist democracies; they did not build unified societies where people respected and supported one another in pursuit of common goals; they did not generate economic abundance, a high standard of living, and equality; and they did not create a new, enlightened citizenry conducive to the building of communism.

Because of their inability to perform—whether measured by their own or Western standards—they were forced to reconsider what they were doing and to begin to do something about it. What was done, is being done, and will be done in the 1990s is of historic significance. Mikhail Gorbachev and Deng Xiaoping started the process in the 1980s by moving their societies in the direction of reform. While the Chinese backed away from the reform process in 1989 and moved toward a policy of retrenchment, the Soviets accelerated their reforms. Many of the East European states took an even bolder approach in 1989 and 1990 by attempting, through revolution, to move from Communist Party dictatorships to pluralist democracies in one radical stroke. But what is the future of reform, revolution, and retrenchment in the Second World? What are the factors that will influence these states' success in dealing with the tremendous challenges ahead? What will affect the allocation of values in the 1990s and into the next century? Although we should be modest about our ability to predict the future, the following factors will no doubt affect it. The first is the difficult challenge of actual reform and revolution. There are no precedents or blueprints for moving from communist dictatorships and state socialism to pluralist democracies and market economies. The leaders are forced to experiment, to try to reform through trial and error. This is exceedingly difficult and risky business.

The experiences of the Soviet Union and China in the late 1980s are indicators of the nature of the challenge. By 1990, most observers agreed that the Soviet reforms were in trouble. Perestroika and glasnost had not put food on the table, and the Soviet people's support for reform was wearing thin. One had an uneasy feeling that the Soviet experiment was in peril. One was reminded of Tocqueville's famous passage on the beginnings of the French revolution. Suffering is endured patiently but becomes intolerable the moment it appears there might be an escape. In China, the process of reform had also encountered problems and underwent a serious reversal in 1989. Reforming the two

giants of communism was not proving to be an easy task.

The possibilities for positive change in some of the other Second World states are more promising. The smaller, less heterogeneous, more governable East European states stand a better chance of meeting the challenges of revolution and reform in the 1990s. The people of East Germany will find their transition to be eased considerably by their fellow Germans in the West. The other East European states hope to have their economic situations eased by expanding economic relations with their neighbors in Western Europe. As we look to the 1990s, we should recognize that the challenge of reform, the allocation of values, and human dignity will be quite different among the Second World states. There no doubt will be both successes and failures.

Another factor that will affect the chances for success will be the quality of political leadership. Mikhail Gorbachev did a remarkable job bringing about change in the 1980s. It was a clear indication that a great leader could make a difference. Yet, as we have seen, there were challenges to his leadership from the right and from the left. Some thought he was going too far too fast and that he was being excessively critical of the Soviet past. Others thought that he was not going far and fast enough and that the reform process was becoming bogged down in incremental rather than radical reform. Overall, however, we should note that Mikhail Gorbachev provided strong leadership for the Soviet reform process and deserved much of the credit for what had been accomplished by the beginning of the decade.

Some thought that Deng Xiaoping would play a similar role in China. During the 1980s, Deng and other moderate leaders were able to push the Chinese reforms forward. However, Deng was frightened by the 1989 democratization movements in both China and Eastern Europe and brought a halt to what he had earlier referred to proudly as China's "second revolution." By 1990, the powerful leadership of Mikhail Gorbachev and Deng Xiaoping was affecting the reform movements in the two Second World giants in very different ways. The quality of leadership provided the East European states will also make a difference and have much to do with the allocation of values and the state of human dignity in these societies in the 1990s. If leaders can outline their visions, win the confidence of the people, and effectively govern these changing societies, their chances for success will be reasonably bright. On the other hand, the absence of leadership may be disastrous, as demonstrated in Yugoslavia in the late 1980s. Having adopted a highly decentralized, multinational system of collective and rotating leadership in the post-Tito period, the Yugoslavs in effect created a vacuum of leadership in their society. Because the collective presidency and Party bodies called for a sharing of leadership functions among representatives of the republics and provinces, and because the regional organizations were deeply divided on many important political choices along national-regional lines, the Yugoslav leaders were locked in a stalemate. Although most recognized that reform was important and necessary to save the Yugoslav union, and although radical reform programs were put forward, the Yugoslav leaders were unable to agree on and implement the most critical reform measures. Yugoslavia was in a state of crisis, and its leadership largely was paralyzed by the end of the decade.

A third factor involves the quality of government itself. We will be seeing increasingly different forms of governments in the Second World in the 1990s. Some of them will remain the traditional Second World governments controlled by the Communist Party. Others will enter into complicated new forms of coalition government that will include communists and noncommunists. Still others will completely break with communism and constitutionally elect new leaders to put together policies and programs emulating those of the West European democracies. In all the scenarios, the governments will be under tremendous pressure to enact and carry out policies that can bring progress to these societies.

Not only must policies be made, they must be implemented in ways that bring about necessary changes. This raises the issue of the incredible challenge of implementation facing Second World governments and their bureaucracies. Responsible for the implementation of reform policies, the bureaucracies have considerable influence in facilitating or impeding reform. The giant bureaucracies in the Soviet Union and China did more of the latter than the former in the 1980s. Finding much in the reforms that was threatening to their self-interests, important sectors of the bureaucracies tried to sabotage the reform process. Created to implement the policies, the Soviet and Chinese bureaucracies often acted as constraints to the leadership's reform initiatives. In other countries, such as Yugoslavia, the federal bureaucracy was unable to act and eventually lost the support of the people. The political leadership was excessively decentralized, the federal bureaucracy was divided and without sufficient power, and Yugoslavia was "muddling along" near the brink of disaster.

The fourth factor of considerable importance to the reform process concerns the people themselves. Ultimately, the reform process and the allocation of values depends on the people of the Soviet Union, China, and the other Second World states. If the people support the reforms, if they agree with the goals and actions of the leaders, if they contribute fully in their daily work settings to promote economic output within their societies, the prognosis for reform is much brighter. However, the situation is extremely complicated and less than ideal in all of the countries we are considering.

There is no national consensus behind the reform programs in many of the countries we are considering. In the Soviet Union, for example, Gorbachev and the reformers have gone to great lengths to get the people to support perestroika and glasnost. Although many people do, many more seem to be passive and reluctant, and some very much opposed. There is no common interest or vision in Soviet society today. Surprising as it may seem to us in the West, some sectors of Soviet society long for the Stalinist past and consider the reform policies of Gorbachev a threat to the more authoritarian and stable society they prefer. The Soviet people also are divided along national-regional lines. The non-Russian nationalities want to increase their power and promote their values in the Soviet state, whereas many of Russian origin are fearful of a crumbling of the Russian empire and of losing all of the values their dominance implies.

The people of the Second World societies will also have a considerable impact on the reform process, by the way they go about their work and daily lives. In many of these societies, people have grown accustomed to lax and unproductive work environments. Soviet people often say, "They [the government] pretend to pay us and we pretend to work." For perestroika and economic reforms in these societies to succeed, people will have to work harder and produce more. Soviet economic reform and competitiveness in the global economy will not succeed if the Soviet people continue to cling to the work ethic of the past. If the reformers can reorganize their economic systems to bring out the best in their workers, they will have tapped

a great reservoir of human resources that can contribute much to the reform process. On the other hand, if the people go about their work and lives as usual, they will prove to be a formidable constraint to the reform and development process.

All of the factors addressed above involve politics, what some have called the "art of the possible." If the leadership, the governments, and the people can coalesce around a viable reform process, they can bring about significant changes in their society. On the other hand, if the leadership and the governments are divided, if the bureaucracies are resistant, and the people opposed to or reluctant about the reforms, the likelihood for progress is low.

Economic forces will also be very much involved with what happens in the Second World states. If the leaders can adopt economic policies that stimulate economic growth and improve the level of well-being, they will win support from the people and buy the time needed to move forward with their reforms. The East Europeans' moves toward privatization and market economies are both dangerous and promising. Although the new pricing systems, austerity programs, and related changes will no doubt bring about increased economic hardship in the short run, they may establish the foundations for more competitive economies in the long term.

The last factor to be mentioned concerns the influence of external forces. Although the most powerful determinants of the reform process and the future of Second World societies are those domestic factors mentioned above, there are some powerful forces in the international system that will have some bearing on reform and the allocation of values in the 1990s. For example, the improvement in East-West relations begun in the 1980s may result in a significant dampening of the arms race, which will lead to considerably lower levels of military expenditures in Second World societies. This in turn would allow these systems to invest more of their resources in the civilian sectors and make more available for allocation to education, social services, and consumerism.

Finally, global and regional economic relations will have much to do with the outcome of the economic and political experiments in the Second World. The Marshall Plan had a tremendous impact on the postwar economic reconstruction and development of Western Europe. The European Community and East-West economic relations can have a similar impact on the East European countries in the 1990s. Significant economic forces involving trade, technological,

and monetary cooperation already have been set in motion and no doubt will influence the processes of change and development.

As we can see, there are many factors that can and no doubt will affect the reform processes and the allocations of values of the Second World states. Many important developments are taking place in these countries as this book goes to press. Because it is difficult to predict just what will happen in the years ahead, it will be important for you, the student, to follow these affairs carefully and to make observations and judgments of your own. With the opening of these societies, you have more information at your disposal and much more to study than ever before.

Suggestions for Further Reading

Bergson, Abram, *Planning and Performance in Socialist Economies. The USSR and Eastern Europe* (Winchester, Mass.: Allen & Unwin, 1989).

Brezezinski, Zbigniew, *The Grand Failure: The Birth and Death of Communism in the Twentieth Century* (New York: Charles Scribner's Sons, 1989).

Butterfield, Fox, *China: Alive in a Bitter Sea* (New York: Times Books, 1982).

Connor, Walter D., *Socialism's Dilemma: State and Society in the Soviet Bloc* (New York: Columbia University Press, 1988).

Curry, Jane Leftwich, *Dissent in Eastern Europe* (New York: Praeger, 1983).

Dawisha, Karen, *Eastern Europe, Gorbachev, and Reform* (New York: Cambridge University Press, 1988).

Garton Ash, Timothy, *The Polish Revolution* (New York: Schribner, 1984).

Harding, Harry, *China's Second Revolution: Reform after Mao* (Washington, D.C.: Brookings Institution: 1987).

Herlemann, Horst G., ed., *Quality of Life in the Soviet Union* (Boulder, Colo.: Westview Press, 1987).

Hewett, Ed A., *Reforming the Soviet Economy: Equality versus Efficiency* (Washington, D.C.: The Brookings Institution: 1988).

Karlins, Rasma, *Ethnic Relations in the USSR: The Perspective from Below* (Winchester, Mass.: Allen & Unwin, 1988).

Kaser, Michael, *Health Care in the Soviet Union and Eastern Europe* (Boulder, Colo.: Westview Press, 1976).

Lasswell, Harold, Daniel Lerner, and **John D. Montgomery,** *Values and Development: Ap-*

praising the Asian Experience (Cambridge, Mass.: MIT Press, 1976).

McFarlane, Bruce, *Yugoslavia: Politics, Economics, and Society* (London: Pinter Publishers, 1988).

Matthews, Mervyn, *Patterns of Deprivation in the Soviet Union under Brezhnev and Gorbachev* (Stanford, Calif.: Hoover Institution Press, 1989).

Miller, R. F., J. H. Miller, and **T. H. Rigby,** *Gorbachev at the Helm: A New Era in Soviet Politics?* (London: Croon Helm, 1987).

Moore, Barrington, Jr., *Authority and Inequality under Capitalism and Socialism: USA, USSR, and China* (Oxford: Oxford University Press, 1987).

Nathan, Andrew J., *Chinese Democracy* (New York: Alfred A. Knopf, 1985).

Roeder, Philip G., *Soviet Political Dynamics* (New York: Harper and Row, 1988).

Sacks, Michael Paul, and **Jerry G. Pankhurst,** eds., *Understanding Soviet Society* (Winchester, Mass.: Unwin Hyman, 1988).

Scalapino, Robert A., *Communism in Korea, Part I: The Movement* (Berkeley: University of California Press, 1972).

———, *Communism in Korea, Part II: The Society* (Berkeley: University of California Press, 1972).

Skilling, H. Gordon, *Czechoslovakia's Interrupted Revolution* (Princeton: Princeton University Press, 1976).

Notes

1. Friedrich Engels, "The Origin of the Family, Private Property and the State," reprinted in Robert C. Tucker, ed., *The Marx-Engels Reader* (New York: Norton, 1972), p. 659.

2. *Pravda*, November 30, 1988.

3. As excerpted in *The New York Times*, June 29, 1988.

4. Ibid.

5. Harry Harding, *China's Second Revolution: Reform After Mao* (Washington, D.C.: The Brookings Institution, 1987), pp. 199–200.

6. Ibid., p. 200.

7. *Newsweek*, January 15, 1990; 42.

8. For details, see Mervyn Matthews, *Patterns of Deprivation in the Soviet Union under Brezhnev and Gorbachev* (Stanford, Calif.: Hoover Institution Press, 1989).

9. As reported in *The New York Times*, January 26, 1989.

10. "The Soviet Economy Stumbles Badly in 1989." Presented by the Central Intelligence Agency and the Defense Intelligence Agency to the Technology and National Security Subcommittee of the Joint Economic Committee, Congress of the United States, April 20, 1990.

11. Mikhail Gorbachev, *Perestroika: New Thinking for Our Country and the World* (New York: Harper and Row, 1987), pp. 75, 79.

PART III

POWER AND POLICY IN THE THIRD WORLD

Violetta Chamorro celebrating her victory in the 1990 Nicaraguan elections.

CHAPTER 15

THE IMPACT OF COLONIALISM ON THIRD WORLD POLITICS

In all probability, historians of the next century will look back on the period from 1500 to 2000 as the time of one of the most remarkable and significant events in world history: the expansion of Europeans beyond their continent to explore, populate, and dominate most of the rest of the world and to bring with them the ideologies, technologies, and institutions of modernity. In historical terms, the period of European domination of the globe was relatively brief. By 1776, less than 300 years after it had begun, the tide of European expansion began to ebb in the Western Hemisphere, first in the north, with the American Revolution, and then, thirty to forty years later, in the south, with the breakup of the Spanish and Portuguese Empires. The reversal of colonialism is lasting about as long as its launching, but the rapid dissolution of empire around the world since 1945 seems to establish the trend quite firmly. By 2000, it seems, most legal colonial relationships will be eliminated, and national self-determination will be worldwide.

European colonial domination of non-European peoples must be the point of departure in our journey to the Third World because it was the European contact that initiated the spread of industrialization and modernization around the world. As historian L. S. Stavrianos wrote, "The Third World emerged in early modern times as the result of a fateful social mutation in northwestern Europe. This was the rise of a dynamic capitalist society that expanded overseas in successive stages, gaining control over widening segments of the globe, until by the nineteenth century it had established a worldwide hegemony. . . . [T]he phrase 'Third World' connotes those countries or regions that participated on unequal terms in what eventually became the global market economy."[1]

Without the colonial experience, most of the states of the Third World would not even exist, at least in the form that we know them today; indeed, entire regions, such as Latin America and Indochina, would carry different labels when we located them on a map. The European colonial influence brought to the peoples of the Southern and Western hemispheres the social, intellectual, and material inventions that had allowed Europe to break out of its own Dark

Ages; the introduction of these cultural innovations would prove to have much the same effect on the so-called backward peoples of the globe. That the introduction of these inventions has not brought to the Third World similar levels of material prosperity and political progress is due partly to the colonial experience itself; partly to its remnants, which still characterize Third World relationships with the industrialized West; and partly to the inability of Third World political elites to exploit the value of European ideas and technologies.

The Colonial Period

By some accounts, premodern life was brutal, savage, unpredictable, and ignoble. The population was divided into two groups: the landed gentry who controlled the only real source of wealth—the land—and the peasants who tilled the land for their masters. Traditional populations were rural, agrarian, ill educated or illiterate, cut off from all external influences, and subject to the ravages of famine, pestilence, war, plagues, and natural disasters. Life spans were short, personal civility was lacking, the social order was shot through with suspicion and distrust, and there seemed to be little opportunity for members of the society to realize any of their higher ambitions beyond obtaining enough food to get through the day.

I. R. Sinai has painted for us a dramatic picture of the life of Asian peasants in *The Challenge of Modernization*:

> Enveloping all these communities [of peasants] there is a sense of life robbed of all significance. Man is both degraded and mocked. The peasantries are all haunted by the fear that the earth will lose its fertility. . . . They are obsessed by an almost panic concern

to maintain the size of their populations. Surrounded by malignant demons and spirits, threatened by the unruly forces of nature and society, they were led to seek the intervention of occult powers whom they must try to propitiate or coerce by means of offerings, spells, worship, to protect their precarious though unchanging position in the natural and social order . . . war, famine and disease desolated them, conquerors swept over them, tax collectors . . . robbed them, but these villages remained unchanged and unaffected, always ready to resume the old burdens and to submit tamely to the same degrading routine.[2]

According to other versions, life in premodern societies, although certainly hard physically, was stable and secure and provided people with what they needed most—a sense of belonging, a feeling of one's place in the universe. Society was divided into two classes, a poor majority and a wealthy elite. But the aristocracy cared for and looked after the peasants or serfs and managed their lives in a remarkably efficient manner, given the overall scarcity of goods for society generally. Furthermore, the fact that traditional society lived in extended families spread out into clans made it possible for individuals who suffered from some particular problem to be supported by the resources of the entire community. From this perspective, premodern societies were internally consistent and logical and, above all, their system worked. Because their village political system was closely linked to their village social system, the two functioned in harmony. If food and shelter were not abundant, at least they were adequate to meet the needs of the villagers. Land was usually owned and cultivated in communal style. The actual land was the property of the village, and the fruits of the harvest belonged more or less

A small boy carries water to his home in a remote village in Ecuador. The boy's clothing and the materials used in building the dwellings identify the village as traditional. Millions of citizens of Third World countries continue to live in similar villages despite the modernization of their country's major cities.

equitably to all members of the community. Perhaps most important, there was stability and consistency in the lives of traditional people. The continuity of their traditions sustained them in times of trouble and taught them in times of plenty not to expect much improvement in the future.

Political scientist John H. Kautsky has analyzed traditional societies in terms of their social and economic class structure as well as their fragmented and isolated physical setting. For Kautsky, traditional societies are those that are entirely unaffected by the impact of modernization and that are composed minimally of an aristocracy and several primitive agrarian societies under its rule.[3]

Kaustky notes that the societies of traditional countries were highly decentralized. That is, they consisted of numerous small villages spread throughout remote valleys or along winding rivers, with little central control or direction of their lives. Because communications were restricted to face-to-face conversation and transportation was limited to that powered by humans and animals, remote villages enjoyed the luxury (or suffered the disadvantages) of being fairly free from control by central government authorities, despite what the theoretical powers of those political authorities might have been.

The economic basis of traditional society was overwhelmingly agricultural. As much as 80 to 90 percent of a traditional society's labor force was employed in tilling the land and in related activities. (The comparable statistic for a modern industrial society, such as the United States, is 5 percent or less). Because land was the basis for the society's economic structure, ownership of the land was the basis of power. Power, in turn, was very unequally distributed between a landed aristocracy, who owned the land and who received most of the benefits from its use, and a massive, poor peasant class. Government for the aristocrats was little more than a device to manage the subordinate classes, to extract what surplus there was from agricultural pursuits, and to spend that surplus in the time-honored aims of the aristocratic classes: making war, amusing themselves, and fighting with other aristocrats for the privilege of maintaining their position. They did not envision any societal change, but they surely would have opposed such change if they could have imagined it.

They opposed the spread of capitalism to their jurisdictions, and they sought to keep the lower rural classes bound to them in every way.

The peasant classes generally accepted this arrangement, because they, too, benefited from the system. They did not benefit in a material sense as we in the modern world would understand it. Their lives were impoverished, and they lacked even a semblance of the advantages of a wealthier society: health care, housing, and entertainment, for instance. But, in their complex relationships with the upper classes, the peasants enjoyed a security that emerged from a stable place in the constellation of social units within which they lived. To change this would have implied movement, from a village to a larger town, as well as social movement to another kind of unit. Societal modernization would have meant submitting oneself to the impersonal control of the economic work unit. All these changes would have been not only unfavorable and unlikely to the peasant, but also threatening and frightening. As long as the society remained traditional, neither peasants nor aristocracy had anything to fear because the fatalism and apathy of rural premodern life prevented the lower classes from even imagining improvement in their lives.

Like traditional societies, traditional people differed markedly in their makeup from those with more modern perspectives. As we discuss in greater detail in Chapter 17, the set of attitudes and values that defines the traditional way of life emphasizes fatalism, apathy, suspicion of strangers, and the choice of low-risk alternatives to the solving of life's problems. We have more to say later about how these attitudes and values affect, and are affected by, the modernization process.

Around the world, traditional societies have been under the influence of modernization for at least several generations. It would be an error, however, to conclude that traditional ways of life have crumbled and eroded, leaving only modern societies in their place. In every instance in which a traditional society has been affected by modernization, the result has been an amalgamation of the two forces, a social order that is more or less modernized but with significant traces of traditionalism still intact and still important. Despite the apparent disparity between the physical and economic power of traditional and modern societies, the former have shown the resilience and absorptive capacity to withstand the influence of the latter.

Europeans first encountered the traditional world in a sustained way in the Western Hemisphere, or, to be more specific, in the island chains that cross the Caribbean Sea and in the littoral washed by its waters. Spreading inland through Mexico, Central America, and south through Peru and Chile, the Spanish conquistadores carried the power of Spain abroad in the name of the king and of the Roman Catholic Church. On the eastern side of the South American continent, separated from the Spanish colonies by a line confirmed by the pope in 1506, Portuguese explorers established their hold over what would become Brazil. (In addition, during the sixteenth century, the Portuguese established their rule over Angola and Mozambique in Africa as well as over the Spice Islands and the East Indies.)

Spanish rule in Latin America (and, to a great extent, in the Philippine Islands) was characterized by its legalist basis, its centralist allocation of powers, and its authoritarian treatment of dissent. Despite the distances separating Madrid from its colonial holdings and the time required to traverse them, Spain insisted on maintaining tight control over its various colonies. At the same time, Spain's insistence on the rigid fulfillment of the law to its exact letter encouraged local de facto autonomy accompanied by a good deal of cynicism about the need to obey the laws issued from Madrid. Finally, there were no opportunities for dissent to be voiced from the colonies, despite the early growth of local settler colonies in several major cities, including Buenos Aires, Caracas, Lima, and Mexico City. Local political participation was regarded by the Spanish monarchy as radical and upsetting. Thus, in 1810, when the Spanish colonies began to cut away from Spain in the aftermath of the Napoleonic wars, there was little heritage of local self-government and practically no indigenous business or political elite interested in pursuing the objective of enhancing human dignity. Instead, there were the still-rigid cultural artifacts of traditional society.[4]

After the decolonization process was completed in Latin America in the early 1820s (with the exception of the Caribbean countries of Cuba, Haiti, and Santo Domingo [now the Dominican Republic], which would come to independence later), the former Spanish-Portuguese colonial domination was replaced by a neocolonial (or quasi-colonial) relationship between Latin America and Great Britain and, later, between Latin America and the United States. In these relationships, the important currency of power was not law or constitutional prerogative, but money and its material products: trade, commerce, raw-material extraction, manufacturing, and the attendant social changes. As a consequence of differential rates of industrialization, Latin American countries became the suppliers to Great Britain and the United States of industrial raw materials and exotic consumer goods while serving as a market for the manufactured products exported from the two industrializing countries.

Other European countries began their process of expansion somewhat later, and other parts of the world were exposed to European influence only at the beginning of the eighteenth century or later. During the seventeenth and eighteenth centuries, the principal expansionist countries were Great Britain, France, Belgium, and the Netherlands. Their efforts at expansion were turned first toward South and Southeast Asia and later toward sub-Saharan Africa.

The entry of Great Britain and the Netherlands into the colonial arena differed greatly from that of Spain and Portugal. The Iberian influence had been spread first by soldiers and subsequently by agents of the church; in the case of the British and Dutch, trade and political and strategic advantages were the foremost concerns. Accordingly, the two governments formed joint public–private companies to trade with newly discovered areas. In 1600, the British East Indies Company was founded, followed two years later by the Dutch East Indies Company. Other European powers followed suit and, throughout Asia in the eighteenth century and throughout Africa later, trading posts and economic enclaves sprang up, injecting Western currencies, influence, and thought into traditional societies.[5]

Through the first three-quarters of the nineteenth century, colonial influences spread primarily by informal means and in accord with economic, political, and strategic impulses. The colonial powers sought to penetrate the traditional regions of Asia and Africa by means of trade, and they negotiated commercial agreements or treaties with tribal chieftains or village heads. Western control was strong but still informal. The system of informal trade penetration had an inherent bias toward expansion of control and toward more formal dominance of the remote areas. As each trading area was secured, the local commercial official in charge became responsible for maintaining order in the region, including the frontier regions that marked the area off from neighboring, still-uncivilized zones, where traditional societies lay untouched by the colonial system. At the first sign of disturbance on the border, the colonial power seized the opportunity to expand its influence and to establish new boundaries around its zone of influence. In this act, however, the authorities unwittingly lengthened the boundary to be secured and magnified the possibilities for additional disturbances in the future, which would necessitate even further encroachment into previously unsettled lands. The expansionist imperative of colonial trading arrangements was unmistakable.

By 1870, pressures for formal political control over colonial preserves had mounted to such a degree that the European powers launched a series of expansionist moves that effectively divided up almost all of the remaining unclaimed land area of the globe. From 1870 to 1900, the European colonial states added to their direct political control abroad more than 10 million square miles of territory and about 150 million people (about 20 percent of the earth's land area and about 10 percent of the world's population). Great Britain was the largest beneficiary of this expansion. Nearly half the land area and nearly 60 percent of the people brought under colonial rule became subjects of the British government. The British Empire stretched from the Indian subcontinent westward to Egypt, the Sudan, Uganda, Kenya, and other areas of Africa; to British Guiana in South America; and to Malaya and Burma in Southeast Asia. The French were second in the scramble for colonies, claiming 3.5 million square miles and about 26 million persons, mostly inhabitants of Africa and Southeast Asia. Germany, Italy, and Belgium also acquired significant colonies in Africa; in the Pacific, Japan and the United States joined in the expansion. The hardest hit region was Africa. In 1870, only about 10 percent of the continent was under alien control; by 1900, only 10 percent remained independent.

Traditional societies in the Middle East remained isolated from European colonization efforts until after World War I. The war brought about the destruction of the Ottoman Empire, and the Versailles Peace Conference of 1919 was the scene of unscrupulous bargaining and division of the spoils of war in the area. Under the League of Nations mandate system, Great Britain and France established control over most of the Middle East, excluding Turkey, Iran, and Saudi Arabia. Syria, Iraq, and Lebanon were designated as mandates, and Palestine was established as the special responsibility of Great Britain, despite the protests of the Palestinians.

One of the ironies of the entire colonial experience involves the role of the great wars in extending the system and in bringing it to a close. World War I was fought by the United States as a struggle for the right of self-determination of all peoples, but it resulted in the expansion of colonial empires into areas previously saved from colonialism. In contrast, World War II had little to do with self-determination as a cause, yet it left in its wake conditions that led directly to the dissolution of nearly all the formal colonial possessions around the world. In 1945, the Japanese had been driven out of all of their colonial holdings, as had Italy. Germany had been denied expansion once again. In addition, Great Britain, France, Belgium, and the Netherlands had all been so weakened by the war that they were unable to maintain control over their possessions for more than a decade or two. The year 1945 would mark the beginning of the end of Europe's 500-year-long domination of the world. As European power receded, it left behind the emerging political systems of the Third World as well as, many would say, a lingering system of informal, neocolonial influence and control.

An Assessment of Colonial Rule

The world *colonial* describes a relationship between two groups of people who are culturally alien and geographically distant from one another. The essence of this relationship is its asymmetrical, unbalanced, or unequal nature. The power relationship between the two peoples is asymmetrical because one group is strong and dominant, the other weak and dependent. And the distribution of the costs and benefits of the relationship is asymmetrical as well, since the dominant group receives most of the benefits of the relationship, and the dependent group bears most of the costs. Finally, the relationship is not amenable to change since the weak have little or no access to the political institutions of the distant, dominant state, and few instruments of power by which to influence its policies.

The exact nature of the colonial relationship derives from the various ways in which each side may perceive its links with, and its privileges and obligations toward, the other. The powerful, dominant state may wish to absorb the dependent people and make them citizens in its own society with full privileges and responsibilities; or, conversely, the strong state may wish to keep the weak group at arm's length, extracting the benefits from the relationship without incurring any of the costs. The former case is exemplified by the United States in regard to American Indians, former slaves, Mexicans living in California, and Hawaiians. The French also tried to assimiliate colonial peoples into their society, as in the case of the Algerians and the Vietnamese; they even granted them seats in the national legislature and positions in the national cabinets. The Portuguese did likewise in their colonies in Africa, Angola, and Mozambique. On the other hand, the Dutch in Indonesia allowed native rulers to continue in power more or less undisturbed and made no effort to transform Indonesians into citizens of the Dutch state. The British fell somewhere in between. They were interested primarily in the maintenance of order; where native rulers could accomplish this task, they were left alone; where native rule faltered, the British substituted their own bureaucracy. In each case, the British objective was to implant the rule of law and government by representative institutions without necessarily intending for all colonial peoples to become Britons or even loyal British subjects.

From the point of view of the weaker side, however, the colonial bond was inherently an unstable one. If the weak found the relationship to their liking, they moved closer to the dominant country and eventually were absorbed into it; this happened with Alaska and Hawaii. At times, this took place even if the weak peoples were not particularly fond of the colonial regime, if they thought they had no choice, or if they perceived long-run benefits to be derived from closer association with their powerful ruler. For many years, the quasi-colonial relationship between Panama and the United States was of this type. In most cases, however, the weaker peoples were unhappy with their subordinate relationship, and they became more so as the waves of modernization and nationalism swept through the Third World. The outcome in these cases was guerrilla insurgency, terrorism, and wars of national liberation. Such violence marked the passage to national independence of virtually all of Latin America, Algeria, Israel, Angola, Bangladesh, Indonesia, Vietnam, Malaya, Kenya, and other states. The success of these independence movements can be explained partially by the declining economic and political value of the colony to the mother country. To a large degree, however, the struggles were successful because of the distance between the insurgent colony and Paris, London, or Madrid. In cases such as Algeria, where the

European country had established overseas settlements, separation was much more difficult and violent because the central authority fought much harder to retain control over the colony.

An accurate assessment of the colonial experience should weigh all of the things the Europeans brought to their colonies, both the good things and the bad, both the benefits of colonialism and the costs.[6]

The most immediate effect of European colonization was on the population, both in size and distribution. The arrival of Europeans in Asia, Africa, and Latin America had a devastating impact on the health of the peoples of those lands. The introduction of European diseases unknown in distant lands, such as measles and smallpox, exposed native peoples to savage epidemics that swept unchecked through village after village, decimating entire local populations. The arrival of Europeans also caused major changes in the use of agricultural land, which led, in turn, to changes in diet that were harmful to Third World populations. Forced native labor and the relocation of populations to areas more in accord with European commercial needs also took their toll. According to one estimate, the Amerindian population of New Spain (Mexico and parts of Central America) numbered between 20 and 28 million in 1519, but had declined to only slightly more than 1 million by 1605. These effects were only part of the story in Africa, where the traffic in human beings through the Western Hemisphere slave trade resulted in the forced removal of about 10 million blacks between 1451 and 1870. Some 80 percent of these slaves ended up in what are now parts of the Third World: Spanish America, Brazil, and the French Caribbean.[7]

Another contribution of the Europeans to traditional countries has been modern technology, which for the Third World has been a mixed blessing. Some specific examples of technology introduced into traditional countries will help to clarify the costs and benefits of such a contribution.

Transportation technology, including railroads, highways, and small airports, has obviously contributed greatly to the opening up of remote interior portions of many Third World countries. An analysis of the spatial spread of modernization within a newly independent country would reveal that the impact of modernization was heavily influenced by the transportation infrastructure built by the colonial power and left behind after its departure.[8] The control of the new government over its jurisdiction is shaped strongly by the existing rail, air, and road facilities constructed by the mother country. Frequently, however, the metropolitan country constructed the transportation network to serve some economic necessity that had little to do with the development of the colony. Because Third World areas usually served the industrialized world as sources of raw materials and exotic tropical food products, the transportation facilities were built primarily to facilitate the exportation of these commodities. The remaining needs of the colony for internal lines of communication and transportation, for instance, were ignored. In some Central American countries today, for example, the only railroads in existence are those constructed by the banana companies to move their produce to the seaports and, from there, to markets in North America and Europe. Any relationship to the internal needs of the host country was purely coincidental. The same thing was true of communication facilities, including telephone, telegraph, radio, television, and print media (newspapers, magazines, and postal services).

A second important technological contribution made by European colonizers to the Third World lies in the area of hygiene and health care. We have just seen how the early impact of European colonialism had such a negative effect on Third World populations. In more recent times, however, through the introduction of mass inoculations, public health clinics, prenatal and postnatal care, food shipments under programs such as "Food for Peace," and other advances, the Western world has helped lower the death rates of many Third World countries. No doubt this is to be applauded. Yet, as we will learn in Chapter 16, the combination of falling death rates, as a consequence of Western health care techniques, and of stable birthrates, as a consequence of rigid social structures, attitudes, and mores, has produced a population explosion in the Third World.

Manufacturing and farming technologies have also had mixed blessings for Third World countries. With little thought for their total impact, Western business representatives pressed backward areas to adopt Western techniques in manufacturing (mass production, assembly line techniques) and in farming (heavy use of equipment, pesticides, and fertilizers). These technologies have improved the individual worker productivity in many traditional countries and, thereby, have made more products available on the market, perhaps even at a reduced price. But there have been costs to these innovations. Modern manufacturing techniques have reduced the need for labor and have displaced many workers, thereby reducing the aggregate purchasing power of the society. The same thing has happened on the farm. Fewer workers are needed to produce more food, so that aggregate demand falls and more and more heads of families are out of work. Furthermore, Third World countries are discovering that the adoption of Western manufacturing technologies makes them more vulnerable to external pressures. The use of modern industrial facilities makes the economy more dependent on foreign sources of raw materials and energy, especially petroleum. In agriculture, the use of petroleum-based fertilizers has cost many Third World countries a great deal as the cost of crude oil has risen since 1973.

A fourth kind of technology introduced by the European states was in the form of weapons and other military equipment. Western domination over traditional societies was greatly facilitated, if not actually made possible, by their use of firearms and other lethal technologies to force the more backward peoples to submit to their rule.[9] Later, as the natives learned to turn this new technology against their masters and as the number of weapons available in the developing world increased enormously, modern weapons technology helped accelerate the destruction of the European colonial empires. Yet, after helping emerging countries gain their independence, modern weapons technology is certainly making political life in the Third World more difficult. These weapons of radically increased lethality make local disputes much more costly in terms of human life and property, as the evidence from the Lebanese civil war of 1975–76 or the Iran–Iraq War in the 1980s will attest. As the Western powers freed their colonies, they left behind not only the military equipment of a modern army but also the military organization needed to use it. After a while, the new military leaders frequently came to power in these states, determined to impose on them the order and discipline of the barracks. As we note in Chapter 19, military intervention in politics has been one of the most serious problems Third World states have had to deal with since 1945. In addition, the adoption of military technology from the Great Powers or from other industralized states tends to make the recipient countries dependent on the countries of origin for training, ammunition, and replacement parts, even after the dominant–dependent relationship has formally ended.

Perhaps the most significant aspect of the introduction of Western technology through the colonial system has been the change in the attitudes of Third World citizens with regard to nature. We discuss more extensively in Chapter 17 the question of the prevalent personality structures and attitudes in both traditional and modern countries. Many traditional people possess what behavioral scientists call a fatalistic view of life, which means that usually they believe that human beings cannot change nature but, instead, must adjust to nature's force. Modern persons, however, feel that they can change nature through technology. Generally, the technology brought to traditional societies by colonists may have wrought its most important change in the minds of traditional peoples.

Another important European contribution to the traditional lands of the Third World has been education.[10] By education we mean a formal, school-based transmission of knowledge as well as the more informal socialization techniques based on family, kin groups, and, in many instances, the mass media. All of these educational media are considered at length in Chapter 17.

In most instances, when Europeans arrived in the traditional societies of Latin America, Africa, or Asia, they found no native educational systems. Traditional communities utilized the family and other village-based organs of communication to transmit certain essential lessons to their young; beyond that, these cultures were simply not organized to make education a formal, institutionalized endeavor.

It was not until after World War II that most colonial administrations began to take measures to improve public-supported education in their territories. Prior to the 1940s, the support of the colonial government for public education had been very scanty and had depended more on local funds than on any allocations from the wealthy mother country. For example, in 1942, Indonesia, with a population of more than 70 million, could count fewer than 1,000 natives who had completed a college education. During British control of Egyptian education, which nominally came to an end in 1922, the rate of illiteracy remained more than 90 percent of the total population. In Tunisia in 1945, under the French protectorate, fewer than 10 percent of the eligible children were attending primary schools. Even in countries that had shaken off colonial rule earlier, such as Latin America, the remnants of an underfinanced and mismanaged educational system left 80 percent of the population illiterate at the close of World War II.

If the overall quantity of European-supported education can be severely criticized, it is still true that in certain very specific qualitative terms, the impact of European education has been significant throughout the Third World. Western education, especially higher education in Paris or London, eventually created the articulate, activist, nationalist leaders of the native middle class—the intelligentsia of the local societies—and these people provided the leadership and the ideas for the dissolution of colonial ties.

Beyond the leadership elites of Third World nationalist movements, Western education had an equally important impact on the masses of Africa and Asia, primarily by heightening their awareness of their own ethnic and national identities. Citizens of Western countries often forget just how modern are the notions of nationalism, national identity, and ethnic self-determination. Only since the end of the eighteenth century have people started to think of themselves as citizens of a nation-state whose boundaries were larger than, and transcended, those more narrow enclosures of language, ethnic heritage, village grouping, clan, or religion. Western-introduced education, with civics training directed from the mother country, aided by textbooks with Western-style national maps and other symbols, helped divert young attentions away from traditional identifications and toward the broader self-image. Many traditional areas acquired their present national, territorial label only as a result of the decisions of their colonial rulers. In the Western Hemisphere, ancient kingdoms were destroyed and replaced by colonial administrative structures, which, in turn, gave way to independent nation-states. The Incan Empire fell to the Spanish conquerors who established the viceroyalty of Lima, which eventually became the nation-state Peru. In West Africa, the British grouped together tribes that had literally nothing in common, and they called their creation Nigeria. The same process was repeated in the Indian subcontinent. After termination of British rule, the state of Pakistan was created to shelter the religious freedoms of millions of Muslims who felt that if they were included in a larger unit with predominantly Hindu India, their rights to worship would be suppressed. The label *Indochina* is itself of European origin, as were the various subregional identities forced on the Vietnamese people by the French. Despite the artificial character of these national identities, nationalist leaders in the Third World have discovered that the symbols of nationhood are powerful weapons to wield against their former European masters. The typical citizen of, say, Nigeria, might not have known what Nigeria stood for in the late 1950s, but he or she at least knew that it stood against continued British rule and therefore merited support and allegiance. Once independence is achieved, the uniting force of nationalism becomes thin and fragile and separatist movements have frequently aggravated what is, at best, a very difficult process of nation building. But, with all its weaknesses, the idea of the nation-state as

the core of one's identity has proven to be one of the most powerful motivating forces in modern world politics.[11]

Another major European colonial impact on the Third World is the result of the modern system of commerce and trade, including the ways in which this system disrupted traditional methods of relating individuals to one another and to some broader social unit.[12]

Whatever else might be said about traditional societies as they were on the eve of European intrusion, they at least fed themselves relatively satisfactorily. As noted, traditional society was agricultural in character; the overwhelming majority of its workers were employed in growing food for the community. The land was generally owned by some sort of communal arrangement, although the exact nature of the land-tenure system obviously varied widely across the Southern Hemisphere. Private ownership constituted the exception and not the rule. Land was dedicated to the cultivation of one of the three kinds of crops from which traditional peoples could maintain a more than subsistence diet: cereal grains (wheat, maize, and rice), tubers (sweet potatoes, potatoes, and yams), and legumes (beans, lentils, and peas). These were the only foods that satisfied the nutritional and commercial requirements of traditional peoples before colonialization; the evidence shows that they were all grown and cultivated extensively throughout the area now known as the Third World. Virtually all of a community's food needs were self-met; there was little need for, or interest in, trading and little surplus available to be traded.

With the arrival of the Europeans and their ideas of trade and commerce, the traditional techniques of farming, the traditional forms of land tenure, and the traditional crops were all cast aside in favor of more modern ways to employ the great agricultural riches of the Third

World. First, the intruding colonial powers altered traditional forms of land ownership and allowed private citizens to purchase large plots of land, to enclose this land, and to plant on it whatever they wished. In Latin America, the Spanish government went one step further and rewarded the adventurers and conquistadores with huge grants of land; the grants included ownership of the native Indians who happened to reside in the villages on this land. In Asia and Africa, the colonial countries first confiscated the land from village or communal ownership, then sold it to private companies or individual citizens who were supposed to use the land productively. This usually meant that the land was to be used not to grow crops for local consumption, but for trade to the colonial countries. Because Europe was already rich in cereal grains, tubers, and legumes, the lands of the Third World were turned to the production of crops that had little nutritional value but that commanded high prices in the developed markets of Europe and North America. Thus was born the agricultural system of the colonial world, the dedication of rich farmland to the cultivation of coffee, cocoa, sugar cane, pepper, hemp, bananas, rubber, peanuts, and tobacco. In other instances, if land contained rich mineral deposits, it was exploited not for what it could grow but for what lay under it; the flow of minerals also began to mark trade patterns between the industrializing countries and their colonies to the south. During the nineteenth century, copper, tin, iron, nitrates, and coal were all shipped from the colonial empires to the industrial center. In the twentieth century, these flows have been joined by perhaps the most important raw material for an industrial society, petroleum.

Most of these linkages have mattered little economically to the industrialized countries, but they have been catastrophic to the Third World.

Instead of land being used to grow food to feed the communities that till the soil, we see land used to grow exotic, tropical crops for shipment abroad to grace the tables of Europeans or Americans. Instead of communal ownership of the land, with an equitable distribution of its fruits, we see the concentration of the land in the hands of a few favored entrepreneurs and the resultant impoverishment of the remainder of the people. Instead of the steady and secure working of the soil for what it gives to the community, we see the extension of the cash nexus to the workers, linking them precariously to the whims of a market system not only beyond their control but also literally beyond their comprehension.[13]

Clearly, modernization of the techniques for owning and exploiting the soil is not, in itself, destructive of the ways in which people live. Every modern state of Europe experienced the same transformations in its drive to modernity. The rural agrarian classes had to be pushed in the direction of capitalist exploitation of the soil; property had to be enclosed and private ownership adopted for the incentives of the market to compel full and efficient use of the land; and the rural working class had to be forced off the land and into the cities for an urban industrial class to come into existence to support modernization. The way in which these transformations took place in a country like Great Britain was beneficial and helpful for the overall development of the society.

In the colonized areas, however, the intrusion of modern trade and commerce has destroyed traditional lifestyles without substituting, or aiding in the development of, alternatives. Agricultural and mining products did not remain in the community or even in the country but, instead, were sent abroad. The modern commercial sectors of the traditional countries constituted economic enclaves, separate and isolated communities; they were cut off from the colony and had their own set of laws and social services. The benefits of these enclaves rarely were extended to the larger community. The proceeds from the sale of these products were usually kept in the financial system of the mother country or, at best, were returned to the enclave to improve its standard of living but without touching the lives of the great majority of natives. Rural workers were forced from their communal lands and made to labor for European owners and managers at highly unstable wages. They worked at jobs that depended not on natural forces, like the weather—which could be seen and felt—but on distant forces, like the international market economy—which were neither experienced firsthand nor understood. Bert N. Adams wrote that in Africa, colonists used both political coercion—conscription or slavery—and economic coercion—the head or hut tax—to force natives to leave the land and provide the human raw material for Western economic ventures in mines and factories.[14] Local industry did not grow, because the enclaves imported what they needed for their own use. Worker productivity did not rise, because the enclaves were not faced with local competition and, therefore, did not need to lower production costs. Social services were not provided and wages were not stabilized or improved, because native workers had not mastered the skills of labor organization and collective bargaining. The colonial system created many economic inequities by needlessly disrupting traditional modes of economic cooperation without replacing them with more stable, more productive arrangements that would spread the benefits of modernization evenly throughout the world.

The introduction of European forms of agriculture, trade, commerce, and manufacturing had the additional important effect of altering the already-existing traditional class structure, which, as we have seen, was limited primarily to a small land-owning aristocracy and a large rural agrarian lower class. The arrival of the colonial economic system caused the emergence of a new socioeconomic class, a small but growing commercial and industrial middle class whose principal advantage was its ability to deal effectively with the representatives of the foreign power. The members of this growing middle class achieved their special status by virtue of their ability and willingness to leave behind their distinctive traditional languages and culture and to embrace the new European languages and customs. As a consequence, those in this new class rose rapidly in the economic and social structure of the new state, leaving behind those less willing or able to adapt. It is for this reason that contemporary struggles for national liberation from colonial rule quite often had a class origin as well as an ethnic and linguistic stimulus. As Third World nationalists struggled to throw off foreign domination, they were also fighting to unseat from power those ruling groups who had succeeded in adapting to the colonial or neocolonial system. This additional class dimension of these struggles helps us understand more fully why the conflicts over national liberation in the Third World were as violent as many of them were and why they pitted native against native during the early phases of the struggle.

The final result of the European domination of the Southern Hemisphere was a cultural inferiority complex—a belief inculcated in the colonial peoples that Europeans were superior to them in economic and political relationships and, therefore, deserved to rule them. When the Europeans began their conquest and colonization of the traditional peoples of the Third World, they regarded their new charges as little children, too primitive to be trusted with their own fate. Because, the conquerors reasoned, it was obvious which group was the more powerful, it was obvious which group should rule and which should submit. The dominant colonial administration managed to justify its own arrogance by reference either to religious superiority (as in U.S. President William McKinley's agonizing decision to assume responsibility to bring Christianity to the Philippines), to race (as in Rudyard Kipling's reference to "the white man's burden"), or to a general cultural superiority (as in the French insistence on their civilizing mission). The British held only the utmost contempt and disregard for the abilities of the Indians. Lord Cornwallis is quoted as saying, "Every native of Hindustan is corrupt," and Lord Wellesly described Indians as "vulgar, ignorant, rude, familiar, and stupid." As late as 1934, Indians were considered genetically inferior and therefore not qualified to hold jobs on a par with the British.[15] Whatever the origin, this feeling of religious, racial, or cultural superiority naturally conveyed itself to the natives, both in the formal sense (through the colonial education system) and in the countless informal tensions that characterized the prevailing master–servant relationship.

Ironically, it was also the European introduction of the psychological attributes of modernity, particularly their emphasis on self-rule and self-determination, that eventually led to the creation of a class of nationalist intellectuals who rejected the idea of European superiority and who were determined to expel the light-skinned invaders from their country. Psychologists have learned that a culturally modern person accepts ultimate responsibility for the success and failures of life and that external powers or forces cannot be blamed instead. Consequently, the more modern people become in attitudinal terms, the more they are inclined to reject external attempts to rule them and to

assert their own responsibility for self-governance. Apparently, within the group of Western-educated nationalists who have led the struggle against European domination in the Third World, this assertion of personal responsibility has assumed great importance. This has resulted in the demand of colonial states that they be permitted to rule themselves, even if the outcome is not necessarily comfortable or fruitful. As they often state, "We would rather be governed like hell by ourselves than well by someone else."

After centuries of seeing their country governed from abroad, aided many times by members of their own society who were willing to cooperate with the foreigners, ardent nationalists like Juan Bosch of the Dominican Republic can only agonize over the desire for independence and self-control of their nation's destiny. Bosch's cry of anguish stands for similar expressions heard throughout the Third World since World War II:

[For the American Ambassador], dealing with me was no easy matter. . . . I was sensitive to anything that might affect Dominican sovereignty. My poor country had had, from the first breath of its life as a republic, a string of political leaders who had dedicated all their skills and resources to looking for any foreign power on which to unload our independence. . . .

I felt wounded, as if it were a personal affront, at the spectacle of so many men without faith in the destiny of their own country. In my childhood, I had seen the Dominican flag coming down from the public buildings to give way to the U.S. banner. No one will ever know what my seven-year-old soul suffered at the sight. . . .

Perhaps I love my little Antilles country so passionately because when I became aware of it as a nation, I realized that it was not that at all, but a dominion. This caused me indescribable pain, and often kept me awake a long time after I had been sent to bed. . . . By the time I was ten, I was ashamed that Santana, who annexed the country to Spain in 1863, and Baez, who wanted to turn Samana [Bay] over to the United States, were Dominicans. As the years passed, that pain and that shame became transformed into passionate patriotism.[16]

As a consequence of these dramatic attitudinal changes in developing countries, the leaders of the nationalist movements in the Third World look toward modern industrial society with a complex mixture of love and hate, fear and admiration. On the one hand, they ardently desire to liberate their countries and their people from the suppression of foreign domination, but they realize that to accomplish this feat, they must modernize their societies and industrialize their economic structures. In short, they must turn their backs on the traditional ways of doing things and embrace modernity with all of its pitfalls and shortcomings. The symbols of industrial society, such as steel mills and modern capital cities, become more than that—they are transformed into the very expression of national independence. On the other hand, these nationalist intellectuals try desperately to retain the essence of their traditional ways and to avoid the flaws of modern industrial society. They laud the "golden age" of their peoples before the arrival of the Europeans, and they seek ways to preserve the fragile and intricate social structures of the traditional village-based communal life, which is under constant assault from modernization. Not surprisingly, these attempts to blend modern and premodern ways of life generate substantial tensions in political ideology and everyday life

among many Third World peoples.[17] We consider the psychological and cultural implications of this phenomenon in Chapter 17.

The Decolonization Process since 1945

As observed earlier, 1945 and the end of World War II signaled the end of Europe's formal domination of its far-flung empires. The devastation of the war left the major colonial powers battered and exhausted; they had little interest in renewed struggle over their fringe territories. The early victories of Japan, on the other hand, had shown the world's nonwhite races that a non-European power could defeat a predominantly white nation in combat; this restored a great deal of self-confidence in the Third World's peoples. Finally, the principles of self-determination, as taught in the Western schools and as enunciated in the United Nations Charter, began to have an effect on the nationalist elites of Africa and Asia. The result was a swelling surge of anti-imperialist sentiment that rocked the European colonial powers and forced them to reconsider their imperial pretensions.

In 1945, the largest empire in the world was that of Great Britain. More than one-fourth of the world's population, about 600 million people, were governed from London. By 1948, about two-thirds of this total were living in independence. In these years, the states of South Asia—India, Pakistan, and Ceylon (now Sri Lanka)—were created. Burma, Egypt, Iraq, and Jordan also successfully asserted their independence. Following the partition of Palestine, Israel claimed its independence, and, by the early 1950s, informed British opinion recognized the inevitability of the disintegration of its empire. In 1956 and 1957, the granting of independence

477

PERIOD	Number of Countries Gaining Independence	Eight Selected Countries
Never Under Direct Foreign Rule in Modern Times	6	Iran
Before 1820	7	Mexico (1810)
1821–30	8	Brazil (1822)
1831–40	2	
1841–50	2	
1851–60		
1861–70		
1871–80		
1881–90		
1891–1900		
1901–10	1	
1911–20	2	
1921–30	2	Egypt (1922)
1931–40	3	
1941–50	11	India (1947) Indonesia (1945)
1951–60	7	Nigeria (1960)
1961–70	39	Tanganyika (1961), Zanzibar (1963) united to form Tanzania (1964)
1971–80	11	
1981–90	2	

Figure 15.1 Distribution by decades of achievement of independence by 102 Third World countries, with specific years for eight selected countries. [From: *Encyclopedia of the Third World*, by George Thomas Kurian. Copyright © 1978 by George Thomas Kurian. Reprinted with the permission of Facts on File, Inc., New York; and Arthur S. Banks, ed., *Political Handbook of the World: 1987* (Binghamton, New York: CSA Publications, 1987).]

to the Sudan, Malaya (Malaysia), and Ghana initiated the process of emancipation on a large scale. Today, the British Empire consists of a few scattered islands in the Western Hemisphere (such as Bermuda) and a handful of strategic points that Great Britain refuses to yield, including Gibraltar and the Falkland Islands. In 1983, Britain fought a short but extremely violent war with Argentina to retain control over the Falklands, strategically located in the South Atlantic.

The second largest empire in 1945 was that of France, and, although France fought much harder than Great Britain to retain its colonial holdings, the outcome was the same. In the mid-1940s, Syria and Lebanon were given their independence, and in 1954, after the disastrous French–Indochina War, Cambodia (now Kampuchea), Laos, and the two halves of Vietnam left the French sphere. In 1956, Tunisia and Morocco were freed after agitation and guerrilla war. In 1958, after Charles de Gaulle's return to power, France's African holdings were reduced—first (1958) Guinea and later (1960) the remainder of French Equatorial and West African possessions as well as Madagascar were liberated. Algeria was the possession that France was most reluctant to release, probably because of its proximity to the mother country and because of the many French citizens living in Algeria. But by 1962, the violence and destruction of the Algerian war had so weakened French resolve that the colonial relationship there was terminated as well. As of the middle of the 1980s, French possessions included some scattered holdings in the Western Hemisphere (French Guiana, Guadeloupe, and Martinique) and some islands in the Pacific. Nevertheless, colonial relationships die away only very slowly. As late as 1989, the French government still maintained troops in six African countries that were former French colonies: Central African

Republic, Chad, Djibouti, Gabon, Ivory Coast, and Senegal. To be sure, the troops were stationed in these countries at the request of the host government; but that fact simply highlights the continued dependency relationship that characterizes neocolonialism.[18]

The same story applies to the smaller colonial systems still in existence in 1945. The Japanese Empire was divided among the victors of the war: the United States, the Soviet Union, and China. Korea was partitioned and granted its dual independence. Italy's overseas possessions—Ethiopia, Libya, and Somalia—were quickly freed. In 1946, the United States granted independence to the Philippines and statehood was granted in 1959 to two other possessions—Alaska and Hawaii. Okinawa was returned to Japan in 1972. The Dutch lost Indonesia almost immediately after the war; and Belgium gradually loosened its hold on its African possessions—the Belgian Congo (now Zaire), Burundi, and Rwanda.

The Third World empires that lasted the longest were those that belonged to countries that lived under dictatorial rule at home, Spain and Portugal. However, even in these cases, inevitable changes in the mother country (the deaths of Francisco Franco and Antonio Salazar) have brought new governments to power; the result has been a rapid decolonization of the Spanish Sahara (now under control of Morocco) and of Portugal's possessions—Angola, Guinea, and Mozambique.

What may prove to be the last significant instance of decolonization and state building took place during 1989 and early 1990. Since 1915, South Africa had ruled the region known as South West Africa, which it had captured from Germany. The natives of the region, known to them as Namibia, had begun to agitate for independence after World War II; and in the early 1960s, the South West Africa People's Organization (SWAPO) began a guerrilla insurgency to force South Africa to free the region. The issue was complicated greatly by the presence of both South African and Cuban troops in the civil war being waged in neighboring Angola. As long as Cuban forces remained in Angola, South Africa was determined to retain its hold on the important buffer area in South West Africa. Finally, after years of negotiation, an arrangement was brokered by the United States and the Soviet Union that provided for the withdrawal of all foreign troops from Angola, followed by the gradual transition to independence of Namibia. The transition began on April 1, 1989; and despite some early misunderstandings about troop movements and relocations, the United Nations-monitored transition went ahead more or less on schedule. Elections were held in November 1989, for a constituent assembly that was to write a new Namibian constitution. The SWAPO won forty-one of the seventy-two seats in the assembly, and the remainder were divided among six opposition parties. The new constitution, which provides for a multi-party democracy and limits a president to two five-year terms, was finally approved in February 1990. The country formally became independent in March.

Conclusions: Ethnonationalism and Human Dignity

Formal, legal control of the Third World from Europe and North America seems to be definitely coming to a close. However, this does not indicate a lessening of the tensions of ethnonationalism, the belief that people should be governed only by others of their same ethnic group.[19] When we consider that dozens if not hundreds of self-aware ethnic groups are com-

Guerrilla fighters of the Eritrean Liberation Front (ELF) raise their weapons in celebration of a victory in the struggle against the government of Ethiopia. The ELF is one of the many ethnic and regional separatist movements given impetus by the spread of decolonization around the world since World War II. The fighters are holding both AK-47 rifles, manufactured in the Soviet Union, and American-made M-14s, indicating their ability to receive aid from many different sources.

pressed into the boundaries of only about 150 distinct nation-states, we see immediately the revolutionary potential of ethnic pride and self-defense.

In the Third World, the phenomenon of decolonization, with all its ramifications, has yet to run its course. Two special problems emerge. First, the trend toward ethnic self-consciousness in newly created states has a momentum of its own that has led to the fragmentation of several of the countries left behind by the former European colonial powers and to unsuccessful threats to the stability of several others. At the beginning of the decolonization period in Africa, secession attempts such as those of Katanga (in the Congo) and Biafra (in Nigeria) failed; many other African states may feel that they have successfully weathered the storm. In South Asia, on the other hand, Bangladesh (formerly

East Pakistan) has successfully separated itself from Pakistan (itself a separation from India), and the potential in Southeast Asia for fragmentation continues to be severe. We should expect more such upheavals in the future as previously submerged peoples attempt to build a political order that is more rational and more responsive to ethnic feeling than that imposed by foreign rulers. We return to this theme in Chapter 16.

The second residual problem is the continued struggle against economic and other forms of domination still exercised by the industrialized nations over Third World peoples. As we discuss in greater detail in Chapter 16, the poor countries can be expected to take more forceful steps to redress the balance of resources and wealth distribution around the world. The abortive efforts of Chile's late President Salvador Allende to bring his country's resources under Chilean control and the oil embargo of 1973 were only the opening shots in this new phase of the decolonization struggle.

Indeed, many of the policy decisions made by the governments of Third World countries can best be understood as part of the very long process of undoing what was done to them by the colonial experience. You may find it easier to understand politics in the Third World in 1990s by remembering that these events and policies owe their origins to hundreds of years of foreign rule with all its benefits and imperfections.

Suggestions for Further Reading

Apter, David, *Rethinking Development* (Beverly Hills: Sage, 1987).

Bagchi, Amiya Kumar, *The Political Economy of Underdevelopment* (Cambridge: Cambridge University Press, 1982).

Betts, Raymond F., *Europe Overseas: Phases of Imperialism* (New York: Basic Books, 1968).

Black, Cyril E., *The Dynamics of Modernization* (New York: Harper & Row, 1966).

Cohen, Benjamin J., *The Question of Imperialism: The Political Economy of Dominance and Dependence* (New York: Basic Books, 1973).

Danmole, Mashood B., *The Heritage of Imperialism* (New York: Asia Publishing House, 1974).

Deutsch, Karl W., and **William J. Foltz,** eds., *Nation-Building* (New York: Atherton, 1963).

Easton, Stewart C., *The Rise and Fall of Western Colonialism* (New York: Praeger, 1964).

Emerson, Rupert, *From Empire to Nation: The Rise to Self-Assertion of Asian and African Peoples* (Cambridge, Mass.: Harvard University Press, 1960).

Fieldhouse, D. K., *Economics and Empire, 1830–1914* (Ithaca, N.Y.: Cornell University Press, 1973).

Foster, George M., *Traditional Cultures and the Impact of Technological Change* (New York: Harper & Bros., 1962).

Furnivall, J. S., *Colonial Policy and Practice* (Cambridge: Cambridge University Press, 1948).

Furtado, Celso, *Economic Development of Latin America: A Survey from Colonial Times to the Cuban Revolution* (Cambridge: Cambridge University Press, 1970).

Hodgkin, Thomas, *Nationalism in Colonial Africa* (London: Muller, 1956).

Hunter, Guy, *Modernizing Peasant Societies: A Comparative Study in Asia and Africa* (New York: Oxford University Press, 1969).

Hyam, Ronald, *Britain's Imperial Century, 1815–1914* (New York: Barnes & Noble, 1976).

Kautsky, John H., *The Political Consequences of Modernization* (New York: Wiley, 1972).

Kitching, Gavin, *Development and Underdevelopment in Historical Perspective* (London: Methuen, 1982).

Lichtheim, George, *Imperialism* (New York: Praeger, 1971).

Magdoff, Harry, *Imperialism: From the Colonial Age to the Present* (New York: Monthly Review Press, 1977).

Mannoni, Dominique O., *Prospero and Caliban: The Psychology of Colonization,* trans. Pamela Powerland (New York: Praeger, 1956).

Rangel, Carlos, *Third World Ideology and Western Reality* (New Brunswick, N.J.: Transaction, 1986).

Seton-Watson, Hugh, *Nations and States: An Enquiry into the Origins of Nations and the Politics of Nationalism* (Boulder, Colo.: Westview Press, 1977).

Stavrianos, L. S., *Global Rift: The Third World Comes of Age* (New York: William Morrow & Company, 1981).

Thornton, Archibald P., *Imperialism in the Twentieth Century* (Minneapolis: University of Minnesota Press, 1977).

Wallerstein, Immanuel, ed., *Social Change: The Colonial Situation* (New York: Wiley, 1966).

Wolf, Eric R., *Peasants* (Englewood Cliffs, N.J.: Prentice-Hall, 1966).

Notes

1. L. S. Stavrianos, *Global Rift: The Third World Comes of Age* (New York: William Morrow & Company, 1981), pp. 31–32.

2. I. R. Sinai, *The Challenge of Modernization* (New York: Norton, 1964), pp. 34–35.

3. John H. Kautsky, *The Political Consequences of Modernization* (New York: Wiley, 1972), Ch. 1. See also Robert E. Gamer, *The Developing Nations: A Comparative Perspective* (Boston: Allyn & Bacon, 1976), Ch. 2.

4. Claudio Veliz, "Centralism and Nationalism in Latin America," *Foreign Affairs* 47 (1) (1968), 69–83.

5. Benjamin J. Cohen, *The Question of Imperialism: The Political Economy of Dominance and Dependence* (New York: Basic Books, 1973), Ch. 2.

6. For a detailed discussion of the same theme, see Rupert Emerson, *From Empire to Nation: The Rise to Self-Assertion of Asian and African Peoples* (Cambridge, Mass.: Harvard University Press, 1960).

7. Amiya Kumar Bagchi, *The Political Economy of Underdevelopment* (Cambridge: Cambridge University Press, 1982), Ch. 3.

8. Peter R. Gould, "Tanzania 1920–63: The Spatial Impress of the Modernization Process," *World Politics* 22 (2) (1970), 149–170. Also Bagchi, ibid., Ch. 4.

9. John Ellis, *The Social History of the Machine Gun* (New York: Random House, 1975).

10. A useful compendium of articles on this subject is James S. Coleman, ed., *Education and Political Development* (Princeton, N.J.: Princeton University Press, 1965).

11. Donald Horowitz, *Ethnic Groups in Conflict* (Berkeley: University of California Press, 1985).

12. Celso Furtado, *Economic Development of Latin America: A Survey from Colonial Times to the Cuban Revolution* (Cambridge: Cambridge University Press, 1970). See also Frances Moore Lappe and Joseph Collins, *Food First: Beyond the Myth of Scarcity* (New York: Ballantine, 1977).

13. This idea is explored extensively in Jeffrey M. Paige, "Inequality and Insurgency in Vietnam: A Reanalysis," *World Politics* 23 (1) (1970), 24–37.

14. Bert N. Adams, "Kinship Systems and Adaptation to Modernization," *Studies in Comparative International Development* 4 (3) (1968–69), 50.

15. Saleem Qureshi, "Political Violence in the South Asian Subcontinent," in Yonah Alexander, ed., *International Terrorism: National, Regional and Global Perspectives* (New York: Praeger, 1976), p. 160.

16. Juan Bosch, *The Unfinished Experiment* (New York: Praeger, 1965), pp. 162–163.

17. Mary Matossian, "Ideologies of Delayed Industrialization: Some Tensions and Ambiguities," *Economic Development and Cultural Change* 6 (3) (1958), 217–228.

18. *The Economist*, April 22, 1989.

19. Walker Connor, "The Politics of Ethnonationalism," *Journal of International Affairs* 27 (1) (1973), 1–21.

C H A P T E R 16

SOCIAL AND ECONOMIC PROBLEMS IN THE THIRD WORLD

Introducing the Third World

French demographer and economic historian Alfred Sauvy is credited by many with having coined the term *Third World* in 1952 to describe those newly emerging countries trying to find a "third way" or "middle way" to development that would avoid the excesses of both Stalinist communism and Western capitalism. During the mid-1950s, the term passed into general usage to describe or label those states in Africa and Asia that tried to remain neutral in the ideological battle then raging between the United States and the Soviet Union. Gradually, however, as the national liberation and revolutionary struggles of the early 1960s drew attention to the poverty and political dependency of the developing world, "Third Worldism" came to embody a wide-ranging critique of the industrial states and the international economic system that, according to many Third World leaders, was responsible for the relative disadvantage suffered by poor people in poor countries.[1]

In 1986, British author Nigel Harris pronounced "the end of the Third World."[2] What

is rapidly disappearing, according to Harris, is not, of course, the poor of the world, but rather the *ideology* of global economic exploitation of poor countries by rich. The old dichotomy, wrote Harris, of rich industrial First World states plundering poor, raw materials–exporting Third World countries has given way to "an interdependent, interacting global manufacturing system [that] cuts across the old view of a world . . . marked by the exchange of raw materials for manufactured goods. But the new world . . . is far more complex and does not lend itself to the simple identification of First and Third, haves and have-nots, rich and poor, industrialized and non-industrialized" (p. 200).

Perhaps the globally integrated manufacturing system *has* blurred the lines between the rich and the poor of the world, but we believe the concept of the Third World still has *political* validity in the 1980s and 1990s. As we use the term, the Third World consists of the independent countries of Central and South America and the Caribbean, the Middle East and North Africa, sub-Saharan Africa, and Asia and the Pacific. We exclude from our definition all the states in these regions that have adopted clearly and unequivocally the development pattern of either the industrial Western democracies or the centrally directed authoritarian regimes inspired by Marxist-Leninist philosophy. Thus, we eliminate not only the Communist Party states of the regions listed, such as North Korea, Vietnam, Cambodia (Kampuchea), Laos, and Cuba, but those that are clearly in the camp of the Western democracies, such as Israel and Japan. Some states are inclined strongly in one direction or another; a similar list made a decade from now might not even include them in the Third World at all. These states might include Marxist-oriented countries such as Ethiopia, Angola, and Libya, as well as those firmly established as Western democracies such as Mexico and Venezuela. It is still too early to locate these countries without question outside the Third World boundaries, so we continue the customary practice of including them in the Third World until the outlines of their political style become somewhat clearer. Organized and defined in this way, the Third World consists of 102 states: 24 in Latin America, 18 in Asia and the Pacific, 19 in the Middle East and North Africa, and 41 in Africa south of the Sahara. (These figures are as of 1989, and do not include the newly created state of Namibia.)

Third World countries are neither Western industrialized democracies nor authoritarian Marxist regimes, but what exactly are they? The Third World category contains a very wide variety of social, historical, economic, political, and ethnic dimensions.[3] We find huge states, such as Brazil (more than 3 million square miles—larger than the United States, excluding Alaska) and Argentina and India (more than 1 million square miles each). We also find some very tiny countries that are small islands, like São Tomé, or cities that have separated from their surrounding country, like Singapore. Third

World states differ widely in population, too—from mammoth India, whose more than 800 million people make it the second most populous country in the world, to the tiny oil-rich states in the Arabian peninsula, such as Qatar with a population of only about 400,000. The Third World has landlocked countries, like Bolivia, and long island chains, like Indonesia. There are countries that are rich agricultural areas, like the rice areas of Southeast Asia, and there are regions where the wealth is derived from the minerals drawn from beneath the ground, such as the oil areas of the Middle East. The Third World has states that have been independent and active members of the international system for more than 150 years, like Argentina, and it has countries that have existed for barely a few years, like Papua New Guinea, formerly a member of the British Commonwealth administered by Australia. And, as we will note shortly, the states of the Third World do not even share their condition of poverty; several, such as South Korea and Brazil, have become rising industrial countries, and a few enjoy some of the highest per capita incomes in the world.

The Third World accounts for about 49 percent of the earth's land area and slightly more than 53 percent of its total population. Africa contains more than one-third of the land area of the Third World, but it is relatively sparsely populated, with only about 18 to 19 percent of the Third World's population. The same is generally true of Latin America, with about 31 percent of the area and 15 percent of the population. Densely populated Asia, in contrast, accounts for only about 14 percent of the area but more than 55 percent of the Third World's population. The Middle East is relatively low on both dimensions: about 19 percent of the land area and about 11 percent of the population. (See Figure 16.1.)

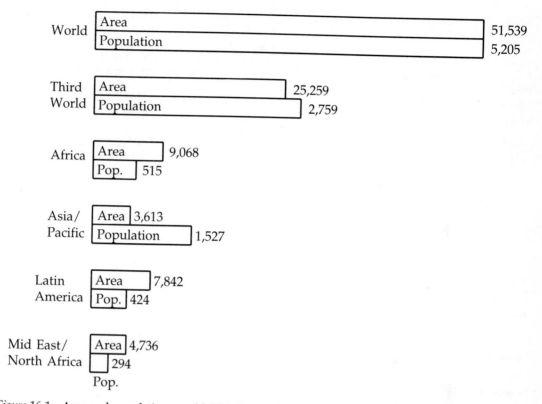

Figure 16.1 Area and population, world, Third World and regions, 1989. [Banks, ed., *Political Handbook* (1989). Note: Area in thousands of square miles, population in millions, both as of 1989.]

Table 16.1 summarizes these same data for eight selected Third World countries. Throughout this book, in the presentation of tabular data as well as in other kinds of illustrative examples, we use these eight countries (Brazil, Egypt, India, Indonesia, Iran, Mexico, Nigeria, and Tanzania) to highlight certain key points about Third World politics. These eight countries, all significant members of the international community in their own right, were selected to represent the Third World only in a most general sense. It would be arbitrary to try to reduce the diversity of the Third World to only eight examples. The countries are offered as "typical" developing states although, no doubt, others could have been chosen that would have portrayed somewhat different characteristics of the Third World.

Global Inequality: An Overview

From the vantage point of the political leaders of the Third World, the question of how to enhance human dignity through public policies quickly focuses on one central issue: inequality.

Table 16.1 Area and Population of Eight Selected Third World Countries, 1989

Country	Area (1,000s sq. mi.)	Percentage of Regional Total	Population (millions)	Percentage of Regional Total
Africa				
Nigeria	356.7	3.9	104.1	20.2
Tanzania	364.9	4.0	24.8	4.8
Asia/Pacific				
India	1,222.5	33.8	828.9	54.3
Indonesia	741.1	20.5	178.0	11.7
Latin America				
Brazil	3,286.5	41.9	149.4	35.2
Mexico	761.6	9.7	84.5	19.9
Mid East/N. Africa				
Egypt	386.7	8.2	53.6	18.2
Iran	636.3	13.4	56.1	19.1

Third World leaders who desire to raise the level of human dignity of their citizens must face the fact that the desirable goods, services, and values of life are distributed in a grossly unequal way among the earth's inhabitants. Public policies aimed at enhancing human dignity must deal with this inequality and find ways to redistribute the world's wealth and power more equitably, both across national boundaries and within their countries. If this could be accomplished, they believe, other indicators of human dignity would be improved accordingly.

The dimensions of global economic inequality are stark. The World Bank's *World Development Report* for 1987 divides the bank's 128 member states (with more than 1 million population) according to level of income. (See Table 16.2.) Of the earth's approximately 5 billion people, nearly half (about 2.4 billion) live in countries with "low-income economies" and an average

per capita Gross National Product (GNP) of $270. Of this number, more than half (nearly 1.4 billion) live in the Third World; most of the remainder live in China, a Second World state in our classification system. Another 674 million Third World people live in what the Bank calls "lower-middle-income economies," with an average per capita GNP of about $820, while a few Third World countries, with a population of slightly less than 450 million, have reached the level of "upper-middle-income economies," with a per capita GNP of $1850. Only a scant handful, four countries with only 18 million people, have reached prosperity, and these are the "high-income oil exporters" of the Middle East. In contrast to most Third World states, however, the "industrial market economies" of Western Europe and North America enjoy a per capita GNP of $11,810.

Moreover, the gap between rich and poor countries has been steadily growing. (See Figure

16.2.) From 1960 to 1987, the per capita GNP of the developed countries rose from $5,519 to $11,392, whereas that of the developing countries (including China) grew from $372 to $731. (all amounts expressed in 1986 dollars). After two and a half decades of concerted development effort, the developing world had not

reached the point in the late 1980s where the developed countries had been in 1960, and indeed the gap between the two groups of countries had widened from about $5,147 to about $10,661.

This, then, is the economic dilemma confronting the Third World today. The industrial-

Table 16.2 The World Bank Economic Classifications, 1985

Category	GNP per capita ($)	World	No. of Countries	Pop. (millions)
Low-income economies	270	First	0	0
		Second	4	1105.6
		Third	33	1333.8
Lower-middle-income economies	820	First	0	0
		Second	0	0
		Third	36	674.6
Upper-middle-income economies	1,850	First	3	24.3
		Second	4	93.6
		Third	16	449.5
High-income oil exporters	9,800	First	0	0
		Second	0	0
		Third	4	18.4
Industrial market economies	11,810	First	19	737.3
		Second	0	0
		Third	0	0
Nonreporting nonmember economies	na*	First	0	0
		Second	8	353.8
		Third	1	8.8
All categories		First	22	761.6
		Second	16	1553.0
		Third	90	2485.1
Total			128	4799.7

* na = not available.

(*Source*) World Bank, *World Development Report: 1987* (New York: Oxford University Press, 1987), Table 1, pp. 202–203.

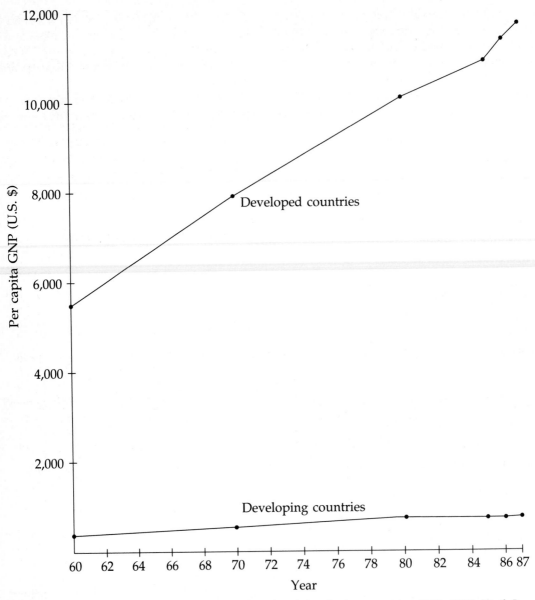

Figure 16.2 Growth of per capita GNP in developed and developing countries, 1960–1987. [Ruth Leger Sivard, *World Military and Social Expenditures: 1989* (Washington, D.C.: World Priorities, 1989), Table 1, p. 46.]

ized West, beginning from a much higher economic base, continues to register large gains, while the still-poor Third World can look forward to only modest improvement for the remainder of this century. For all but a few oil-rich states and a comparative handful of newly industrializing countries like Brazil and South Korea, it certainly seems to be the case that "the rich get richer and the poor get poorer."

Comparisons of economic growth of developed and less developed countries by means of GNP per capita figures are apt to be somewhat superficial for several reasons. First, a considerable portion of the population of the Third World lives and works outside the money economy so that its economic transactions will be less likely to appear on the balance sheets of national accounts statistics prepared in the capital city.[4] Second, we should not lose sight of the importance of inflation, a force that accounted for so much of the change in GNP figures during the last half of the 1970s and that probably caused the income figures of the industrialized countries to rise faster than those of the less developed world. Finally, the Third World could actually be registering faster growth of GNP per capita in percentage terms than the industrialized countries and still be dropping behind in absolute terms because of the relatively larger initial base of the developed economies.

Behind these dry statistics, however, are real human beings, most of whom live in constant anxiety about the stability of their jobs and incomes. In the mid-1970s, a worldwide Gallup Poll found that two-thirds of all respondents in Latin America, Africa, and Asia said that they worried "all" or "most of the time" about meeting family expenses. Half of them reported insufficient money to provide their families with food, and an even higher percentage said there were times when they could not afford to buy their families clothes. About half were unable to pay for the simplest medical care. As a consequence of such material poverty, only 28 percent of Latin Americans, 8 percent of Africans, and 6 percent of Indians interviewed considered themselves fully satisfied with their lives.[5]

Economic inequality is the easiest kind of document, but the unequal distribution of wealth around the world is felt by human beings in ways that directly affect their health and wellbeing. In developed countries, life expectancy is about seventy-three years, whereas it is only about fifty-nine years in the developing world, forty-nine years in Africa, and fifty-two years in southern Asia. More than 90 percent of the population of the developed countries has access to safe drinking water, whereas in the less developed world, the figure is only slightly more than fifty percent. The countries of the developed world spend more than $469 annually per capita on health services; in the developing world, the figure is only $11. In fifty-two Third World countries, more than 15 percent of the population was undernourished, by the standards of the United Nations Food and Agricultural Organization, a standard that specifies only 1,600 calories per day, whereas the typical diet of the developed world averages about 3,100 calories per day. In 1985 in the United States, each citizen consumed about 7,000 kg of oil-equivalent of energy; in the low-income countries, the average was slightly higher than 300.[6]

Any textbook discussion of the quality of life in the Third World must somehow attempt to communicate to American univeristy students what it means to live, work, and die in the grinding poverty and dismal surroundings of poor countries. In huge cities from Asia to Latin America, what makes life in the Third World distinct for most of its poor is the sense of absolute despair and dreariness that is cast over their lives.

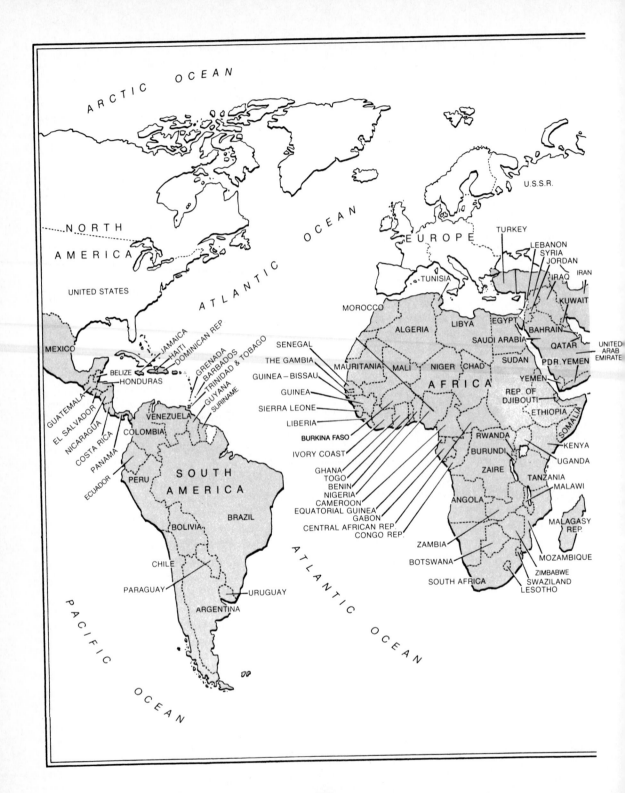

ARCTIC OCEAN

NORTH AMERICA

UNITED STATES

ATLANTIC OCEAN

MEXICO

JAMAICA
HAITI
DOMINICAN REP
GRENADA
BARBADOS
TRINIDAD & TOBAGO
GUYANA
SURINAME

BELIZE
HONDURAS

GUATEMALA
EL SALVADOR
NICARAGUA
COSTA RICA
PANAMA
ECUADOR

VENEZUELA
COLOMBIA

PERU

SOUTH AMERICA

BRAZIL

BOLIVIA

CHILE

PARAGUAY

URUGUAY

ARGENTINA

EUROPE

U.S.S.R.

TURKEY
LEBANON
SYRIA
JORDAN
IRAQ
IRAN
KUWAIT

TUNISIA

MOROCCO

ALGERIA
LIBYA
EGYPT
BAHRAIN
QATAR
SAUDI ARABIA
UNITED ARAB EMIRATE
SUDAN
PDR. YEMEN
YEMEN
REP. OF DJIBOUTI

AFRICA

SENEGAL
THE GAMBIA
GUINEA – BISSAU
GUINEA
SIERRA LEONE
LIBERIA
BURKINA FASO
IVORY COAST
GHANA
TOGO
BENIN
NIGERIA
CAMEROON
EQUATORIAL GUINEA
GABON
CENTRAL AFRICAN REP.
CONGO REP.

MAURITANIA
MALI
NIGER
CHAD

ETHIOPIA
SOMALIA

RWANDA
BURUNDI
KENYA
UGANDA

ZAIRE
TANZANIA
MALAWI

ANGOLA

MALAGASY REP.

ZAMBIA
MOZAMBIQUE
BOTSWANA
ZIMBABWE
SWAZILAND
SOUTH AFRICA
LESOTHO

PACIFIC OCEAN

ATLANTIC OCEAN

492

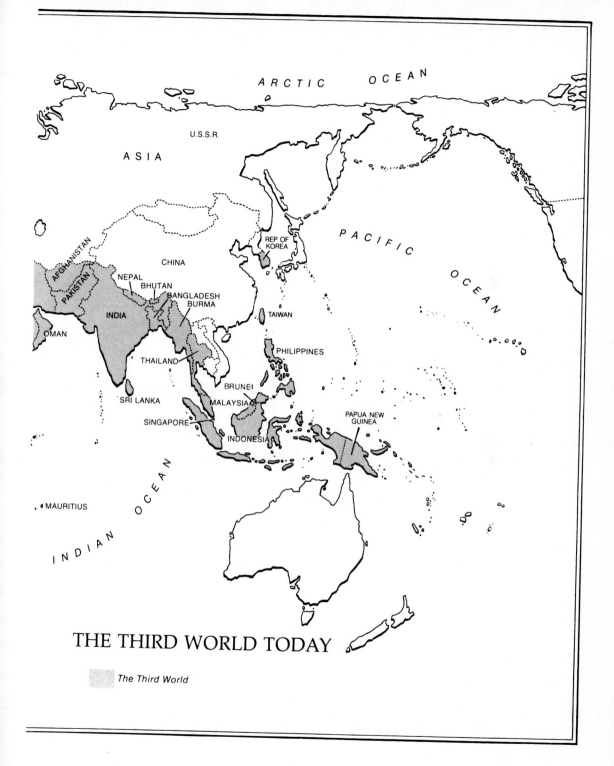

ARCTIC OCEAN

U.S.S.R.

ASIA

AFGHANISTAN

CHINA

PAKISTAN

NEPAL

BHUTAN

BANGLADESH

BURMA

INDIA

REP OF KOREA

PACIFIC OCEAN

TAIWAN

OMAN

THAILAND

PHILIPPINES

SRI LANKA

BRUNEI

MALAYSIA

SINGAPORE

INDONESIA

PAPUA NEW GUINEA

MAURITIUS

INDIAN OCEAN

THE THIRD WORLD TODAY

The Third World

Consider the life of a twenty-nine-year-old pedicab driver in one of Indonesia's larger cities, Jogjakarta. His name is Sarjono, and he pedals his cab more than twenty miles a day for daily earnings of about $3.20. One quarter of his earnings must go to rent his pedicab; the remainder is spent on food for the day (rice, less than a pound of fish, a few vegetables). Milk, eggs, fruit, meat—even clothes for his two children—are luxuries. He pays $45 a year to rent a dark, dirt-floored room on one side of a bamboo-walled hut owned by a second family that occupies the main part of the house. All four members of his family sleep in the same room, which also serves as the kitchen, living room, and dining area. For a toilet, Sarjono's family and neighbors all share a hole in the ground shielded by a partition from the rest of the shacks in the neighborhood. Sarjono is typical of literally tens of thousands of young Indonesian men and women whose desperation has driven them to this kind of minimal existence, and frequently to a life of crime, prostitution, and drugs.[7]

In Brazil's beautiful city of Rio de Janeiro, the poor try to escape the slums by selling their corneas or their kidneys through ads placed in newspapers, or their blood to slum-based commercial blood banks. Even though the practice is illegal, corneas can be sold for as much as $40,000 and kidneys for as much as $30,000. In 1980, a Brazilian documentary film on the blood business sparked a nationwide debate by telling the true story of an unemployed Rio man who supported his family by regularly selling blood, only to drop dead of anemia at the door of a supermarket.[8]

India's once-great cities of Bombay and New Delhi have similarly become the scene of urban frustration and desperation that frequently boil over into random crime and violence. In New Delhi, where street begging has been illegal since 1961, anti-begging squads of police roam the streets to arrest hundreds of beggars each day and deport them to poorhouses outside the city. By the next day, most of those arrested have returned to the streets, where they make as much as $4 or $5 daily. India has an estimated 6 million beggars. In Bombay, a city of 9 million, more than 1 million people live on the streets and sidewalks; their homes are torn pieces of burlap sacking stretched over bamboo poles.[9]

Manila, capital city of the Philippines, is another huge Asian city where the quality of life nears disaster for hundreds of thousands of the urban poor. According to the United Nations, the city's urban poor now number nearly 35 percent of its 8 million inhabitants, and the squatter population—people who live on unclaimed land or even on garbage dumps—is growing by 5 to 6 percent each year. The thousands of people who have migrated to Manila from the country's rural areas in search of jobs, houses, and a better way of life have found little but a life sustained by begging, scavenging for refuse, and crime. They have fostered a second generation of slum dwellers who have little future except begging, drugs, and prostitution.[10]

If life in big cities is bad, rural villages in the Third World can seem even worse. In small, remote Third World villages, the combined pressures of rural poverty and isolation lead to sporadic outbreaks of violence and even interfamily blood feuds. One such town, tiny Exu in the remote interior of Brazil's desperately poor northeast, has no paved roads and only one telephone for its 5,000 inhabitants, but its two cemeteries are silent reminders of a family feud that has claimed thirty lives since it began over a tragic love affair in 1949.[11] Not much has changed in rural Latin America since the following description was written of Los Toldos, Argentina, the birthplace of María Eva Duarte, the famous wife of Argentine dictator Juan Pe-rón:

> No one who has not seen such a pueblo can imagine the dreariness of it. It lies like a worm cast on the platter of the plains, its squalid little buildings crumbling back into the dust from which they have been built. Dust lies everywhere, a foot thick on the unpaved road where a passing troop of cattle raises a white cloud that for a while stagnates in the hot air and then settles slowly on the earth again. Dust seeps into the small houses whose pink and yellow plastering has faded to the dun of dust; the grit of it settles on the food and on the clothes and on the skin and teeth and in the very heart of man. Dust and silence everywhere, a deathly stillness broken only by the mongrel dog crossing the road to scratch itself or an iron windmill that clanks as it turns which way to the wind. Flies buzz above offal cast out in a yard and men's voices are raised in momentary anger, or a woman scolds at a whining child.[12]

Such descriptions help us understand the true meaning, the human meaning, of inequality in the Third World.

The Causes of Inequality: Some Popular Theories

Because global economic inequality is such an obstacle to human dignity in the Third World, it has received a great deal of attention from political leaders and scholars who have attempted to find the causes of the problem and, thereby, to discover a solution to it as well.

Many different theories have been proposed to explain the causes of poverty in the Third World. Some place the causes outside the Third World, for example, in the nature of the international system. Other theories locate the cause of poverty within the national political systems of Third World countries. If the theory focuses primarily on the world outside the Third World, it may emphasize either the intentional thwarting of legitimate Third World desires by profit-hungry capitalists in league with imperialistic Great Powers or it may concentrate on the impersonal, relatively automatic workings of an international system composed of industrial and raw material–exporting countries. If the theory deals with conditions inside the countries of the Third World, it may deal with some of these themes: resource deficiencies; rigidities in social structures (with special emphasis on the population explosion, education, or urbanization); ethnic, linguistic, or racial characteristics; psychological factors; or political structures and processes. Because this textbook is about politics, Chapters 18, 19, and 20 examine these latter factors and take up in detail assertions that Third World states generally lack the kind of political order necessary to bring about badly needed social and economic reforms. In Chapter 17, we discuss the political culture and socialization processes of Third World countries, and we examine the psychological factors included in the preceding list. In this chapter, we summarize the remaining theories concerning the causes of poverty in the Third World.

International Sources of Third World Poverty

One of the most prominent theories used to explain the poverty of backward peoples has been the idea that the rich countries exploit and suppress the poor. The motivation of the wealthy countries varies. In some theories, the villains are huge corporations that manipulate politics behind the scenes in the wealthy countries. These corporations employ the great power of their home countries not only to secure markets for their products, but also to exploit the poor countries as sources for needed raw materials. In other theories, the true mischief makers are not business leaders, but the government elites who establish Great Power influence throughout the poorer countries so that they can play the game of international power politics on the territory of states that cannot defend themselves from being used in this manner.

The best known of the economic theories are those associated with Karl Marx and Vladimir Ilyich Lenin. Their work has been interpreted and updated in our times by three prominent American economists, Paul Baran, Paul Sweezy, and Harry Magdoff.[13]

The imperialistic imperative of modern capitalist society, say these writers, derives from the inevitable tendency of monopoly capitalism to generate insufficient demand at home to absorb its surplus production. Lenin wrote of this as a problem of underconsumption that stemmed from the growing discrepancy between what workers produce (increasing worker productivity) and what they are allowed to consume (decreasing share of output to workers in the form of wages). Critics of traditional Leninist theorizing respond to this assertion by pointing to the vigor of the trade union movement in the industrialized countries and the consequent capacity of the workers to gain an increasing share of what they produce. In an effort to modernize Lenin's theory and bring it into line with twentieth-century politicoeconomic realities in the capitalist states, Baran and Sweezy have altered conventional Marxist-Leninist theory to stress the tendency toward excess surplus that derives from the expansion or growth imperative of monopoly capitalism. That is, modern business philosophy in capitalist society condemns

to extinction any firm or corporation that does not try to maximize its share of the market and, thereby, grow in the process. Hence, there develops the trend toward mergers and oligopolies within the industrialized states and the counterpart trend toward the spread of multinational firms abroad. Despite the growing proportion of industrial output diverted into the hands of labor, profits (the equivalent of surplus in the Baran–Sweezy formulation) rise even faster and the investing class (the capitalist enterpreneurs) is at a loss to find ways to dispose of, or to absorb, these profits. The answer, say the Marxists, lies in the poorly developed markets of the Third World.

According to this reasoning, the capitalist monopolies and multinational firms of the industrial economies have spread abroad in an effort to use the purchasing power of the Third World consumers to drain off, or absorb, the excess production of the industrialized West. To do this, the multinational firms must maintain significant control over the economic and political fortunes and directions of the weak states of the Third World. The overseas outlets of the Western firms must be permitted to bring their products into the developing countries free of import restrictions, such as duties and licenses. Local Third World firms that might compete with Western products are to be discouraged from operating and should be denied the working capital they need to become established. The consumption tastes of Third World consumers must be manipulated through Western-dominated mass media—particularly motion pictures, radio, and television—to induce them to purchase exotic items from the United States and Western Europe, even if they cost more. Labor unions in Third World states are discouraged from putting undue pressure on the local factories and manufacturing installations of the Western firms so that the multinationals can take advantage of cheap labor costs abroad. Finally, the governments of the host countries in the Third World must not regulate the Western-based firms, tax their local profits, or otherwise interfere in their operations. To achieve such a docile operating environment abroad, it is argued, large Western corporations have cooperated with, and used, the governments of the Western powers, particularly that of the United States, to suppress local reform movements in Third World states that have appeared to stand a chance of altering the privileged status of the foreign corporations. Proponents of the Marxist-Leninist theory of imperialism would use this argument to explain Western intervention against a number of radical Third World leaders, including Salvador Allende in Chile (1973), Jacobo Arbenz in Guatemala (1954), Mohammad Mossadegh in Iran (1953), Fidel Castro in Cuba (1961), Gamal Abdel Nasser in Egypt (1958), and the Sandinista government in Nicaragua in the 1980s.

Although the Marxist-Leninist theory of imperialism has received a great deal of attention and support from Western intellectuals and Third World political leaders, its principal drawback is its assertion that all of the above things will inevitably happen, regardless of what Western leaders desire, simply because of the inherent flaws in the capitalist system. Benjamin J. Cohen, in *The Question of Imperialism*, has called into question not the possibility of such outcomes, but the inevitability of them.[14] Is it not possible, asks Cohen, to find other ways of accounting for the dominant–dependent relationship between the powerful and the weak states in international relations? First, Cohen argues, monopoly capitalism does not necessarily lead to the production of an unabsorbable excess surplus (profit). Even in pluralist democracies in the larger Western states, labor unions have represented the working class suf-

ficiently well so that profits as a percentage of GNP have actually been gradually declining since the 1930s. Even if we admit the tendency toward the generation of excess profits, Cohen says, there are other ways in which these profits can be absorbed besides exploiting the Third World consumers. For one thing, businesses in the capitalist system may be induced to lower prices to increase consumption, especially if their sector of the economy is reasonably competitive, as many are. Second, the government can intervene in the economy to drain off these profits through transfer payments to the poor and middle-income citizens, thereby redistributing income and increasing consumption at home. Finally, the government may come to the rescue of the capitalists by absorbing these profits itself, primarily through expenditures on military equipment. Thus, says Cohen, imperial exploitation of the Third World markets is only one possible outcome of monopoly capitalism; there are others, depending on the shape of domestic politics in the First World.

This variation on the Marxist-Leninist theme leads us to another explanation of Third World poverty and weakness, derived not from the economic imperatives of monopoly capitalism, but from the military imperatives of the game of Great Power politics.[15] According to this version of imperialism, the Third World is kept in a state of weakness, poverty, and dependence by the Western powers because of the way in which Great Power struggles are carried out. As a result of nearly 100 years of bloody struggle in Europe, the major world powers have learned an important lesson: When possible, Great Power confrontation should be carried out on the soil of a third country that cannot prevent its territory from being used as a battleground for foreign struggles. If anything, the shift to nuclear weapons and the exponential growth in the lethality of Great Power arsenals have reinforced this belief. In the late nineteenth and early twentieth centuries, Great Powers confronted one another directly and worked out the prevailing rules of the game of international politics through a direct testing process. Today, the rules of the game emerge from a testing process carried out between proxies of the Great Powers on the soil of poor, weak states that have no stake in the larger struggle but whose leaders cannot defend their territory from these external interventions.

A brief review of the major confrontations of the Cold War reveals a recurring pattern. Korea, Vietnam, the Philippines, Malaya, the Middle East, Lebanon, the Suez Canal, the Congo, Nigeria, Angola, Rhodesia, Chile, Cuba, Guatemala, Nicaragua, and the Dominican Republic have three things in common. They are (or were) Third World countries or regions with little if any stake in the global struggle between the capitalist and Marxist versions of historical destiny. Next, they are usually in the "seams" between the shifting monolithic worlds dominated by Washington and Moscow. Finally, they constitute what geopoliticians call shatter zones, regions that are unable to govern their own political directions and to control their own internal political processes. These shatter zones are usually prone to internal disturbances and violence as first one force and then another struggles for, and gains, power. This disorder frequently offers the excuse for the Great Powers to intervene to restore order if only to forestall counterintervention by the adversary. The tendency of expanding economies to produce economic surplus, which is siphoned off into military expenditures, completes the theoretical circle by leading to the creation of large standing military establishments, which, then, look for ways to be used.

Still another way of looking at the problem of global inequalities to wealth and power—the structural approach—states that the poverty and dependence of the Third World stem not from any intentional policy decisions made in Washington, London, or Moscow but, instead, simply from the structure of an international system that is so constructed that raw material–exporting economies are condemned to lose their share of the benefits of production. One of the best-known structural theories is called the Prebisch thesis after its first exponent, Argentine economist Raúl Prebisch. As Secretary General of the United Nations Economic Commission for Latin America (UNECLA), Prebisch wrote the seminal essay in this field in 1949, *The Economic Development of Latin America and Its Principal Problems*.[16] Although originally intended as an explanation of the causes of underdevelopment in Latin America, the Prebisch thesis has now been adopted by many radical but non-Marxist regimes throughout the Third World as the best way to explain their economic relations with the industrialized world.

For many years (centuries, in fact), classical economists have followed the laissez faire position first articulated by Adam Smith in 1776, that the economic interests of all nations were best served under a system of free trade and economic specialization wherein each trading party performed the economic functions for which it enjoyed a relative (not an absolute) advantage. Smith and others of the free trade school were able to demonstrate that each trading partner benefited most from such specialization because the sum total of the economic pie grew most rapidly under such a system. Even though some states obviously benefited more than others, economic specialization and free trade made all partners better off than they would be under any other kind of arrangement because they provided for the most rational allocation of resources throughout the system. In other words, states that manufactured things best exported manufactured items; states that possessed rich deposits of raw materials should export those. Governments should refrain from intervening in the process through such devices as tariffs, subsidies, and taxes; intervention would distort the natural workings of the system. This system has been called the doctrine of *harmony of interests* by the British historian Edward H. Carr, because it asserts that all economic interests, worldwide, are in natural harmony, and that government interference can only make things worse.[17] Adam Smith referred to the system as the "invisible hand," meaning that the sum total of all individual private economic decisions was equivalent to raising the general welfare for all the parties to the system.

Prebisch's theory departs significantly from the classical laissez faire approach. According to Prebisch, the free trade system works against the interests of the countries that export raw materials (the periphery countries) and in favor of the interests of the industrialized, wealthy economies that export manufactured goods (the center countries). The reason for this stems not necessarily from any evil intent on the part of the center countries, but from the very structure of the international economic system.

The prevailing distribution of economic functions around the globe allocates the benefits of economic interchange in an unequal fashion, with the industrialized countries retaining more than their fair share of the benefits of trade. The center is able to retain a greater than fair share because of the impact of technology and social structure on economic productivity. In the center countries, their relatively greater access to manufacturing technology means that worker productivity can be linked to labor-saving devices instead of to increased employment. In addition, the organization of the workers into powerful unions means that the fruits of this increase in productivity are passed back to the

workers in the form of increased wages, leading, in turn, to increased savings, investment, and government revenues. Increases in productivity in the periphery, on the other hand, are lost through unnecessary consumption or through remittances back to the industrialized countries. We have already seen in other contexts some of the reasons for the inability of Third World countries to retain the benefits of increased productivity: The low state of development of labor unions means that the workers have little leverage to apply against the foreign companies; Third World business firms are unable or unwilling to accumulate large amounts of capital for reinvestment; the few manufacturing installations that do exist are not tightly linked to the host economy (the *enclave theory*) so that there is little technological spillover into the host country; and, finally, the host government is too weak to extract from the enclave industry any resources to devote to domestic development.

In addition to the problem of retention of the fruits of improved productivity, the raw material–exporting countries also are hurt by the prevailing price structure in the international economy. Prices for manufactured goods are relatively rigid, both at home and abroad, because of the strength of labor unions in the industrialized countries and because of the powerful position of multinational corporations and their ability to administer price levels or to control overall price structures for their products. The prices of raw materials and agricultural products, on the other hand, are very elastic and fluctuate wildly, creating alternate years of bonanza and depression. Thus, raw material–exporting countries cannot plan adequately for the future without knowing more definitely the levels of financial resources on which they will be able to draw. Finally, the link between income levels and demand also works against the prices of raw materials. In general, as one's income rises, the percentage of income devoted to manufactured products rises at a faster rate than does the percentage of income devoted to the purchase of raw materials and food. Because incomes are rising in both the center and the periphery countries, the demand for manufactured goods must rise more than the demand for unprocessed raw materials. In both instances, the outcome works against the countries that export raw materials.

There are other important aspects of Prebisch's theory that help explain the causes of Third World poverty. Investment capital, for example, helps perpetuate industrial control over the factors of production in the periphery by ensuring that all local production installations are geared to the export trade. Local savings and, therefore, local investment remain small because of the workers' inability to raise their share of the surplus and because of the government's inability to tax the sectors where the excess is located: foreign businesses and local traditional economic groups, such as landowners and traders. Inflation is a persistent structural problem, not because of an excess of demand, but because of the rigidities of supply: rigidities in agricultural production and transportation infrastructure; inadequacies in labor; and persistent pressure on the balance of payments because of the unpredictable changes in raw material prices on the world market. Rising interest rates in the major capital markets in New York and in Western Europe aggravate the already severe problem of Third World indebtedness and condemn many developing countries to increasing hardship and austerity just to pay the interest on their international loans.

Prebisch, unlike the Marxists, finds the solution to the problem of Third World poverty not only in the international system, but also at home. Internationally, Prebisch has recom-

mended that the center countries give special treatment to the raw material exports of the Third World and devote increased financial resources to aid Third World governments that are trying to reform their domestic economies but lack the funds to do so. But, asserts Prebisch, Third World governments must assume a major burden in reforming their internal economic structures to make them more responsive to demand pressures, to retain a greater share of the earnings of production within the country, to increase the taxation of possible sources of revenue to increase government income, and, perhaps most important, to build up domestic industry to the point where the nation consumes its own locally produced manufactured products no matter what the cost. Only through such import substitution, claims Prebisch, can the Third World emerge from its peripheral status in the foreseeable future.

In the 1960s and 1970s, a number of Latin American and European writers began to pull together the various strands of Marxist thought and center-periphery analyses developed by Third World nationalists to produce what became known as *dependency theory*.[18] There emerged quite a variety of interpretations of dependency theory, which quickly became one of the most widely held explanations of Third World underdevelopment, but they share most of the following ideas. The theory's central theme was articulated this way by Brazilian economist Theotonio dos Santos:

By dependence we mean a situation in which the economy of certain countries is conditioned by the development and expansion of another economy to which the former is subjected. The relation of interdependence between two or more economies . . . assumes the form of dependence when some countries (the dominant ones) can expand and be self-sustaining, while other countries (the dependent ones) can do this only as a reflection of that expansion. . . .[19]

Dependency theory goes beyond Prebisch to assert that the way the system works against poor countries on the international periphery is both global—in the sense that it affects all Third World countries wherever and however they launch their development effort—and intentional—in the sense that certain economic classes deliberately keep developing countries poor to advance their own fortunes. Based on many of the same ideas we have already discussed in connection with Marxist-Leninist theory and the ideas of Raul Prebisch, dependency theory holds that underdevelopment is the result of a dominant international capitalist system (embodied in multinational corporations) in league with local Third World elites who use their special advantages to maintain their privileged positions. Although the Third World cannot industrialize and develop economically as long as it is caught in the grip of a discriminatory international system, local elites cannot disengage from this system, because to do so would imperil their own standing in their countries. Indeed, the role of national elites in the Third World quickly became the focal point of the theory, especially in view of the proposed solutions to Third World poverty. If the disadvantages suffered by the Third World could be traced to the willingness of Third World elites to cooperate with the industrial countries and with multinational corporations, then the only way to break the dependency deadlock was through national revolutions that would replace these elites with leaders who would not sell out their people for their own class or individual interests.

In the late 1970s and early 1980s, however, several important changes in Third World economic and political fortunes began to emerge that caused economists to doubt the conclusions of Marxists, the center-periphery analysts, and the dependency theorists. First, nationalist revolutions failed in many countries, either because of their own internal weakness or because of external pressures from Western powers and multinational corporations. Nevertheless, the dire predictions of Third World analysts about their continued dependence on Western industry, capital, and technology seemed to be refuted by the experiences of a small number of countries that were becoming rising industrial economies in their own right. In 1986, for the first time developing countries earned more from the export of manufactures than from agriculture and mining. Between 1980 and 1986, the dollar value of their exports of manufactures rose by an average of 8 percent per year, doubling the share of manufactures in their total exports to 40 percent. In Chapter 21 we examine the recent record more closely as we assess the performance of Third World economies in the 1980s; here we only need to note that the successful industrialization of several Third World countries, led by the export of manufactured items to Europe and the United States, caused analysts of development to put forward yet another explanation of the Third World—*postimperialism*.[20]

According to the postimperialist writers, the global spread of monopoly capitalism need not necessarily doom the Third World to be perpetually the suppliers of raw materials to the industrialized West, and the impoverished customers of the finished products made from those raw materials. A number of case studies showed that, first, multinational firms could be induced to cooperate with Third World national economic policies as long as they (the firms) were allowed to earn a decent return on their investments and were not threatened with expropriation. Second, nationalist, Third World elites could come to power without revolutionary violence, and they could fashion and implement industrial development policies that would bring prosperity to their countries. Admittedly, in many instances these elites did not come to power through democratic means; but they frequently yielded power to constitutional regimes elected by democratic processes once the industrialization effort had become self-sustaining. The Third World success stories, such as South Korea, Singapore, Taiwan, and Brazil, showed that a global manufacturing system was emerging in the last two decades of the twentieth century, and that the Third World could play a vital role in helping that system function properly.

National Sources of Third World Poverty

Population. Before 1700, world population grew very slowly, probably at an average rate of about 0.2 percent per year. As far as demographers can tell, the population of the world in 1750 was about 0.5 billion. World population began to grow more rapidly at about the time of the Industrial Revolution and, although it has declined in certain areas and during certain historical periods, the overall pattern has been one of exponential growth rates. By 1850, world population stood at about 1.3 billion; by 1900, it was 1.6 billion; by 1970, it was 3.6 billion; and in the middle of the 1970s, world population exceeded 4 billion. Demographers now estimate that the world's population will continue to grow, although at a declining rate of increase, until sometime between 2050 and 2150, when a stable population will be achieved at somewhere between 8 and 15 billion persons.[21] The World Bank, for example, in its *World Development Report* for 1984, projected that world population will stabilize around the year 2150, having risen to more than 11 billion.[22] In the near term, between 1990 and 2025, according to World Bank estimates, world population will grow from 5.3 billion to 8.4 billion.[23]

The social phenomenon that we call the population explosion is caused by the demographic transition that occurs in countries that are experiencing modernization. During the first stage of the demographic transition—characteristic of traditional countries with a low standard of living—population levels are kept low and stable through a combination of high birth and high death rates. In traditional countries, the birth rate tends to be about 40 to 50 per 1,000 and the death rate is about 30 to 40 per 1,000; the resultant population growth rate is about 1 percent annually, meaning that the population will double in about seventy years. As a country begins to make the transition from traditional to modern status, however, it reaches stage 2, in which advanced technology and rising standards of living have a differential impact on birth and death rates. The introduction of advanced medical and hygiene technologies from abroad as well as an improved diet combine to reduce the death rate (particularly among infants) to perhaps 20 to 30 per 1,000, but birth rates remain at their traditional level or decline very slowly because of the resistance of customs and mores concerning desired family size. Therefore, population grows at the rate of 2 to 3 percent per year. Under these conditions, population will double every twenty-five to thirty-five years. The third stage of the demographic transition appears in countries that are more or less completely modernized and industrialized. Whereas death rates remain at about 20 to 30 per 1,000, birth rates also drop to about the same level. Eventually, if this happens for enough years in succession (about two generations are required), population levels off.

Most Third World countries are in the second stage of demographic transition. (See Table 16.3.)

This traffic jam in central Bombay, India, illustrates the effect of the uneven spread of industrialization to the large cities of the Third World. Rapid population growth and the increasing availability of automobiles even in poor countries have combined to overwhelm the road network of major cities such as Bombay.

Developed countries experienced population growth rates of less than 1 percent during the 1970s and 1980s, but the underdeveloped countries showed rates ranging much higher, usually between 2 and 3 percent annually. In 1980, the highest growth rates were those of sub-Saharan Africa, which, as a region, was growing 3.1 percent annually. Next highest were the Middle East and North Africa at 2.7 percent, followed by Latin America and the Caribbean at 2.5 percent, South Asia at 2.2 percent, and East Asia (excluding China) at 2.3 percent. Between 1970 and 1982, thirty-three Third World countries registered population growth rates of 3 percent or higher. For the period 1980–85, thirty-one countries were still growing at this rapid pace.

One of the effects of the high growth rates in the Third World will be to alter the current balance between industrialized and developing countries. (One important effect of Third World population growth has been to spur waves of migration from developing countries to Western Europe and North America. This trend is examined in Chapter 21.) At the beginning of the 1970s, the world's population was divided roughly 30:70 between the developed and less-developed countries (both Communist and Third World). By 2000, if current rates of population growth hold steady, the ratio will change to 20:80. Asia will contain 40 percent of the world's population and Latin America and Africa 10 to 12 percent. Europe, on the other hand, will decline to 6 percent of the total, the Soviet

Table 16.3 Population Data from Eight Selected Third World Countries

Country	Estimated Population 1985 (millions)	Annual Population Growth Rate (1965–80)	Estimated Population in Year 2000 (millions)	Year of Reaching Net Reproduction Rate of 1	Estimated Size of Stationary Population (millions)
Nigeria	100	2.5	163	2035	529
Tanzania	22	3.3	37	2035	123
India	765	2.3	996	2010	1,678
Indonesia	162	2.3	212	2010	363
Mexico	79	3.2	110	2010	197
Brazil	136	2.5	178	2010	292
Egypt	48	2.4	67	2020	132
Iran	45	3.2	69	2020	157

(*Source*) World Bank, *World Development Report: 1987*, Table 1, pp. 202–203; Table 27, pp. 254–255.

Union to 4 percent, and North America to 4.5 percent.

High rates of population growth affect Third World poverty levels in several important ways. The addition of so many new people to the population absorbs much of the new productivity that the developing states manage to squeeze out of an inadequate industrial base, an inadequate agricultural sector, and an inadequate social infrastructure (schools, hospitals, housing, etc.). Although the rates of population growth seem small, the bulk totals of new population every year are staggering. At present rates of growth, more than 80 million new persons are added to the world's population every year. To feed the yearly increment requires nearly 20 million tons of additional grain each year, about the size of the entire Canadian wheat crop. The resources of Sri Lanka are presently inadequate to support its 15 million people, yet in eighty years, by a conservative estimate, its population will exceed 30 million. To cope with its population increase, Egypt must build and

equip a city the size of Washington, D.C., each year. India must build ten such cities per year.

Population growth in developing countries occurs in a way that burdens economically productive sectors with new persons who are not immediately productive. Age distribution in a rapidly growing population shifts downward because the young segments of the population grow more rapidly than do the older ones. Thus, the proportion of the working-age population steadily declines. In the developing countries in 1980, the working-age population (ages fifteen to sixty-four) amounted to only 57 percent of the total population, whereas more than 40 percent are aged fifteen or younger. Whereas in industrialized countries there are approximately two working-age people to support each person who is either too young or too old to work, in the developing world the ratio is closer to one to one.

Another way in which rapid population growth increases the burden on the economically productive sectors is through the phenomenon of rapid urbanization. In every region of the Third World, cities are growing twice as fast as the general population. In Africa as a whole, from 1950 to 1980, the urban population grew at an annual rate of more than 7 percent. At that rate, urban areas in Africa will double in population in ten years. Latin America is even more densely urbanized. From 1960 to 1970, Rio de Janeiro, Brazil, grew at the annual rate of 4.1 percent; Santiago, Chile, 4.1 percent; Mexico City, 4.5 percent; Lima, Peru, 5.8 percent; and Caracas, Venezuela, 4.7 percent.

By the year 2000, if present trends continue, eighteen of the world's twenty-five largest cities will be located in the Third World. The list will be headed by Mexico City, with an incredible 31 million people, followed by São Paulo, Brazil, with nearly 26 million. The sudden and dramatic rise in urban populations is presenting the Third World's countries with insurmountable problems in housing, food, medical care, sanitation, transportation, and public security.[24]

A third impact comes from the relationship between lowered birth rates and per capita income and between these two factors and resource consumption. Although demographers are not certain about this, it appears that out of all the possible factors that could cause birth rates to decline, the only factor that is predictable consistently is per capita income. That is, as a country's per capita income rises, desired family size declines. (See Figure 16.3.) There are several reasons for this relationship. For one thing, the cost–benefit balance of each additional child tends to discourage having large families. For another, as per capita income rises, people become better educated and more aware of the need for population controls, as well as of the availability of contraceptive devices and information. Finally, as income rises, the status and role of women in society change, more women leave the home to enter the labor force, and

they tend to marry later and have fewer children, spaced further apart. Therefore, although government programs encouraging birth control (as in Sri Lanka) or encouraging male sterilization (as in India) may have some local impact, in the long run and in general, the world's population will stabilize only when and if per capita wealth increases beyond subsistence levels.

The principal drawback to this solution lies in the third variable, resource consumption. As an individual's income increases, his or her burden on the earth's resources and its pollution-absorption capacity also increases. Of the total increase in energy consumption in the United States from 1947 to 1973, nearly 60 percent was due to increased affluence; only 40 percent was due to increased population. Each wealthy person places a burden on the earth's resources about five times as great as his or her poor counterpart. (See Figure 16.4.)

From the vantage point of the Third World, the implications of these findings should be sobering. If birth rates can be reduced only by means of increasing per capita wealth, but if increased affluence spells a greater burden on already scarce resources, the prospects for economic progress by the world's poor nations appear dim indeed.[25]

Recent press reports suggest that population growth continues to present major policy problems for Third World countries, although there are signs that in a few nations the skyrocketing rates of the 1970s are beginning to abate somewhat. India's census figures released in March 1981 shocked government planners with the news that the country's population had climbed to 684 million, some 12 million more than projected. Despite nearly $1 billion spent on population-control programs during the 1970s, India's growth rate has remained about the same as it was in the 1960s, nearly 2.5 percent. In

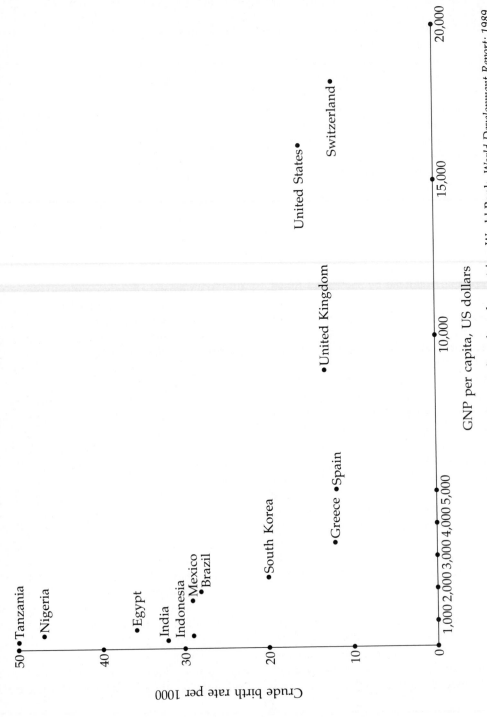

Figure 16.3 Crude birth rates versus GNP per capita, 1987, for selected countries. World Bank, *World Development Report: 1989* (New York: Oxford University Press, 1989. Table 1, pp. 164–5; Table 27, pp. 216–7.

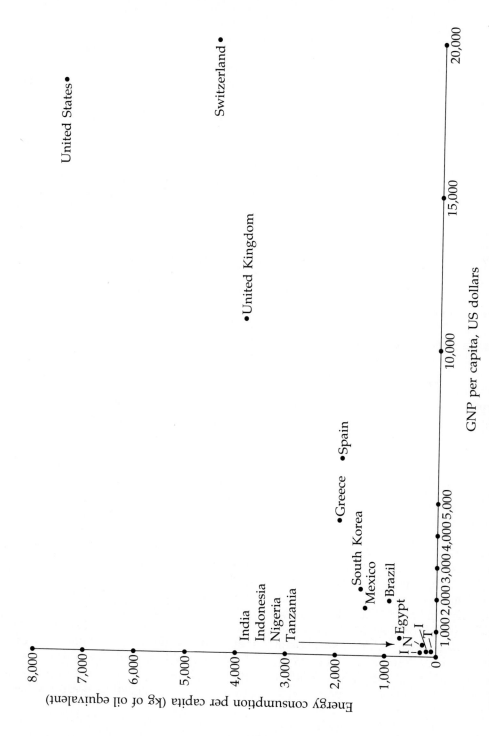

Figure 16.4 Energy consumption and GNP per capita, 1987, for selected countries. World Bank, *World Development Report: 1989* (New York: Oxford University Press, 1989), Table 1, pp. 164–5; Table 5, pp. 172–3.

Kenya, a population growth rate of 4 percent means that its 16 million population will double in eighteen years. In 1981, there were almost 650,000 more mouths to feed than in 1980. The average Kenyan woman has slightly more than eight children. On the other hand, in Brazil, the growth rate has declined from the predicted 2.7 percent to about 2.4 percent, principally because of increased literacy, more women working outside the home, and an increased exposure to modern urban lifestyles. Nevertheless, Brazil still adds about 3 million people (about the population of Israel) to its ranks each year and its urban corridor from Rio de Janeiro to São Paulo now holds more than 21 million people, which is projected to rise to 45 million by the year 2000.[26] In Indonesia, the problem is not only a high growth rate (2.3 percent between 1970 and 1982), but an intense concentration of its population in a comparatively small area. (Sixty percent of the people live on 7 percent of the land area.) To reduce this concentration, the Indonesian government planned in the early 1980s to move 65 million people to other parts of the country over twenty years. The World Bank estimated that this program would cost about $9,000 per five-person family, or about $5 billion per year for twenty years. After ten years, in 1987, only 4 million people had been moved and the whole project had been trimmed back to only $3 billion total costs.[27]

Agricultural Production and Food. A rapidly growing population would not be an undue cause for alarm if the society in question could somehow mobilize the resources to feed, house, and clothe its new members. This requirement places heavy demands on the agricultural sector to grow the needed food, fibers, and lumber to meet this demand. Unfortunately, the record shows that agriculture in the Third World is barely holding even with population growth;

in some instances, it is actually falling behind. From 1970 to 1980, food production per person rose in the developing countries as a whole by a mere 0.4 percent annually. In the middle-income countries of the Third World, food output rose 0.9 percent per year, but in the more populous low-income countries, per capita production actually declined 0.3 percent each year. The regions showing the best gains were Southeast Asia (1.4 percent) and Latin America (0.6 percent), whereas South Asia (0.0) and the Middle East (0.2) barely stayed abreast of population increases. Africa, in contrast, continued on the edge of agricultural disaster, with food output per person dropping 1.1 percent per year through the decade of the 1970s.

One of the key indicators of a country's level of development is the percentage of its workforce dedicated to agriculture. As a country industrializes, its agrarian workforce must become much more efficient, so that increasing numbers of rural workers can be freed to move to the cities to take on manufacturing jobs. In addition, these workers must be supported with increased food and fiber production. Consequently, a developing country's agricultural sector must produce more with fewer workers if the industrial sector is to flourish. Data from the World Bank's 1987 *World Development Report* show that Third World countries remain by and large overwhelmingly agrarian. (See Table 16.4.) The low-income economies, such as India and Tanzania, still have about 70 percent of their workforce employed in agriculture (a level registered by the United States in the 1820s) to produce only about one-third of their gross domestic product (GDP). Lower-middle-income countries, like Indonesia or Egypt, have managed to reduce their rural workforce to about one-half (the United States' level in 1860) to produce about one-fifth of their GDP. And the upper-middle-income countries, including Brazil and Mexico,

Table 16.4   Agricultural Data from the Third World in the 1980s

	Percentage of GDP in Agriculture, 1985	Percentage of Workforce in Agriculture, 1980	Food Production per Capita, 1983–85 (1979–81 = 100)
Low-income economies	32	72	120
India	31	70	120
Tanzania	58	86	108
Lower-middle-income economies	22	55	111
Indonesia	24	57	117
Egypt	20	46	115
Nigeria	36	68	109
Upper-middle-income economies	10	29	108
Brazil	13	31	115
Mexico	11	37	110
Iran	na[a]	36	109

[a] na = not available.

(*Source*) World Bank, *World Development Report: 1987*, Table 3, pp. 206–207; Table 6, pp. 212–213; and Table 32, pp. 264–265.

have cut their agrarian workforce to about one-third (the United States' in 1910) to produce one-tenth of their GDP. Thus, over half of all Third World inhabitants live in economies where the agricultural sector is still about 150 years behind that of the advanced industrial countries. The Third World must look to the agricultural sector for major gains in worker productivity; their failure to register these gains is a major cause of poverty in the developing countries.

The causes of underproduction in agriculture in the Third World are not only ecological, but technological and socioeconomic.[28] On the one hand, per acre crop yields remain low because of the poor nations' inability to devote high levels of agricultural technology to their farming effort. Such technologies as improved seeds, pesticides, herbicides, fertilizer, irrigation, animal husbandry, marketing, transportation, and storage of crops remain substantially beyond the reach of the average small farmer in virtually all of the Third World. The ability of the industrialized world to apply modern technology to farming means that the gap between rich and poor nations has been widening in agriculture, just as it has been in manufacturing. For example, in the period 1979–81, the Netherlands achieved a yield of more than five and a half tons of cereal gains per hectare of harvested area by applying more than 1,120 kilograms of fertilizer per hectare (1 hectare = 2.47 acres). In developing countries, with the exceptions of Egypt and South Korea, yields averaged about 1.67 tons per hectare, and fertilizer use averaged only about fifty-three kilograms per hectare.[29] This achievement by the industrialized countries explains how we in the West can consume more than 3,000 calories per day

Jamaica is just one of many Third World countries where government leaders are much concerned about rising population pressures. Billboards like this one are part of a major government effort to persuade Jamaican couples to use birth control devices. As a result of these efforts and other forces, Jamaica's population grew by only 1.5 percent per year in the 1970s, low by Third World standards.

and still dedicate only about 5 to 7 percent of our workforce to agriculture, whereas people in the developing world, with ten times as great a proportion of their workforce in agriculture, still consume only slightly more than 2,000 calories per day (the minimum to maintain reasonably good health according to many nutritionists).

The second major reason behind the low agricultural productivity of the Third World lies in the land-tenure system, or the way in which land is owned and exploited. In most Third World countries, the rural sector remains that part of society most strongly wedded to traditional, antimodern ways of living, and this is reflected particularly sharply in the way in

which land ownership is determined. The exact system differs across the Third World, but the effects are usually the same: little incentive to maximize production, unstable land title, uneconomic size and distribution of parcels, and a highly unequal distribution of social power in rural areas based on land ownership.

In Latin America, one of the areas with the greatest agricultural problems, the land-tenure problem is one of highly unequal distribution of land combined with uneconomical size of parcels.[30] This is the familiar phenomenon of the *minifundia*, the many extremely small parcels, existing alongside the *latifundia*, the few extremely large holdings. In Peru in 1961, for example, 88 percent of the parcels accounted for

about 7 percent of the land, whereas 1 percent of the holdings accounted for more than 80 percent of the land. In Chile, 37 percent of the farms contained only 0.2 percent of the land, whereas 6.9 percent of the parcels contained 81.3 percent of the land. Other countries outside Latin America also suffer from this problem. Even in Egypt, in 1961, after nearly ten years of vigorous land-reform activity by a progressive regime, 5.6 percent of the farm owners held 45.2 percent of the land, 59 percent of the owners held 8 percent of the land, and more than three-quarters of a million families (about 23 percent of the total) possessed no land at all.

In sub-Saharan Africa and in much of Asia, the problems of land tenure follow a somewhat different pattern. In Africa, much rural land is still owned communally, which means that individuals do not own the land, but work it for the benefit of the entire village. Each villager is assigned a parcel to work, and the proceeds are shared by the general population. There is little emphasis on production for commercial purposes, and most of the food and fiber are consumed within the village. Much of this land is now being encroached on by commercial plantations, which grow cash crops such as cocoa and peanuts for export. Young men leave their villages to join the flood of migrant farm laborers who move from plantation to plantation, trying to save money before returning to the villages. But their savings are quickly dissipated in uneconomic consumption, and, when they do return to their villages, they form a part of the growing rural *lumpenproletariat*—underemployed, landless, and mired in poverty.[31] The few who manage to obtain a small parcel of private property find themselves at the mercy of the swarms of intermediaries who control the farmers' access to the far-off markets: the brokers, the owners of the means of transport, the moneychangers, the mill and silo

Primitive farming techniques are still used in many parts of the Third World. This particular scene is from the Nile Delta region of Egypt. Since the construction of the Aswan Dam, the Nile doesn't flood this region, and irrigation is difficult without tools and technical assistance. Again, the uneven spread of industrialization creates imbalances that make life more difficult for poor inhabitants of the Third World.

managers, and so forth. The undue control of the farmers by intermediaries has also aggravated rural poverty in South and Southeast Asia. In Thailand, for example, government plans to establish new groups of prosperous small farmers in the rich rice lands upcountry from Bangkok failed to break the hold of the absentee landlords in the north and of the parasitic intermediaries in the other rice-growing areas.[32] As a consequence, although nonfarm GNP per capita rose nearly 60 percent from 1960 to 1970, from $739 to $1,156, the farm share of the same economic pie grew only slightly, from $103 to $139 in the same period.

Finally, let us not overlook the constraints imposed on Third World agriculture by the environment. Although there is little evidence of a global land shortage (only about 40 percent

of the world's arable land is presently being cultivated), relatively little new land is brought into cultivation each year in the Third World. In sub-Saharan Africa, vast areas remain unused because of virulent plant and animal diseases such as river blindness and sleeping sickness. In India, Brazil, and the Nile Basin, the major limitations are scant rainfall and the high costs of irrigation. In the Sahel region of Africa, northwestern Asia, and the Middle East, years of drought and unwise land-use practices are turning usable farm land into desert at the rate of 200,000 square kilometers each year.

What does all this mean in human terms?— 800 million people in the Third World with a diet so limited they do not have enough energy for routine physical activities, another 300 million children retarded in growth and mental development, 40,000 young children dead every day from malnutrition and infection, and 150 million Africans facing starvation daily.[33] A 1985 World Bank study shows dramatically the extent of low food consumption in the poor countries of the world. The Food and Agriculture Organization (FAO) and the World Health Organization (WHO) have calculated the amount of food a person needs to function at full capacity in all daily activities, and they have established two reference points for measuring dietary adequacy. The first benchmark is 80 percent of the FAO/WHO standard, a level below which stunted growth and serious health risks are common. The World Bank study reported that in 1980, 340 million people fell short of this consumption level, half of them in the Indian subcontinent and one-fourth in sub-Saharan Africa. The second benchmark is 90 percent of the FAO/WHO standard, a level at which growth is not severely stunted but where people do not obtain enough calories to lead a fully productive working life. In 1980, about 730 million people—one-third of the developing world outside China—fell below this standard. About 470 million of these people lived in the seven countries that make up the Indian subcontinent. About 150 million were in sub-Saharan Africa, and the remaining 110 million were in Latin America, North Africa, and the Middle East.[34]

Social Class Structure and Income Distribution. Another severe social problem affecting levels of human dignity in the Third World is that of highly unequal social class structures and the way in which these structures affect political power, wealth, and economic development.[35] At the bottom of the social scale are what French scholar R. Gendarme calls the urban subproletariat, or urban dwellers who are only occasionally employed; rural folk only recently arrived in the city and not yet accustomed to city life; illicit street vendors; and people with minor service trades, such as shoeshine boys, porters, and rickshaw drivers. In addition, the urban lower class includes servants of the rich, who may account for as much as 10 percent of the urban population, according to Gendarme. Rounding out the bottom of the social ladder are the masses of rural poor, landless farmers who work on an erratic basis and who live at a subsistence level. In Egypt, the landless rural population may amount to as many as 3.8 million persons, about 20 percent of the country's total rural population. In Iran, under the Shah (according to Gendarme), 60 percent of the country's rural families owned no land; in Ecuador, out of a total (rural and urban) population of about 3 million, 500,000 people receive no money income at all and about 1 million receive only between $30 and $40 per year.

At the next level up the social ladder, we find the urban artisan and working-class groups. The artisans, still a powerful force in traditional societies, work as tailors, shoemakers, potters, blacksmiths, and weavers. The urban wage

earners, on the other hand, work in factories, are accustomed to assembly line discipline and regular employment, and are settled into an urban routine that means they are more or less modernized. Factory employees account for about 15 to 20 percent of the total economically active population of an underdeveloped country, as opposed to 30 to 40 percent in an industrialized one.

The closest resemblance to a typical Western middle class one finds in the Third World consists primarily of civil servants, government bureaucrats, and army officers. Because the state frequently is the most progressive employer in a developing economy, large percentages of high school and college graduates can find work no other place and become absorbed into a very large bureaucracy. In Ghana, Peter Lloyd reports, 40 percent of the workers are employed by the government; in other West African states, the figure is likely to be as high as half of all workers.[36] The armies of developing states, although very small by Western standards, have come to play an extremely important role in the development of their societies, partly because of their more modern outlook, partly because of their superior social discipline, and partly because of their monopoloy of the armed forces in the country. We examine the military's role in Third World politics in greater detail in Chapter 19.

At the top of the social scale come the bourgeois and aristocratic classes. Despite their high social standing and their high income levels, this is actually a very heterogeneous social grouping; some of the upper classes are decidedly modern in their attitudes, whereas others are staunchly committed to retaining the country's traditional way of life. Within the upper class, we are likely to find landlords (a tiny fraction of the total rural population), who enjoy ownership of the vast majority of rural property;

the old aristocracy, who can trace their origins back to precolonial days and frequently assert some sort of royal lineage; the educated, nationalist elite found mostly in professions such as law, medicine, engineering, and architecture; and traders, business leaders, bankers, and other economic elites.

Income is distributed in a highly unequal fashion in virtually every Third World country for which we have reliable data. (See Table 16.5.) The top 20 percent of the population in each country earns as much as half of the country's income each year. The percentages decline sharply thereafter so that the bottom 20 percent in a typical Third World country earns from 3 to 5 percent of the total national income.

Moral considerations aside, in purely economic terms unequal income distribution does not necessarily mean that the country is not progressive or developing. Income is distributed unequally in all of the industrialized democracies, including the United States, where the top 20 percent of the population earns about 40 percent of the national income. Moreover, it appears that inequities in income distribution become sharper and gaps between rich and poor are greater in rapidly developing nations. (See Figure 16.5.) Income inequalities in developing countries appear to be much more of a social and political problem for at least three reasons: The low-income sectors of the population are so poverty-stricken that the gap between rich and poor is greater than in the industrialized countries, the affluence of the upper-income groups becomes much more visible, and the issue becomes politically much more volatile. Furthermore, because of the close links among income, education, and social power, the great disparities in income levels in the Third World also mean great disparities in power. One often hears radical regimes assert the need for land-tenure reform, not for eco-

Table 16.5 Income Distribution in Eight Selected Third World Countries in the Mid-1970s

Country	Percentage of Income to Richest 5 Percent	Percentage of Income to Poorest 20 Percent	Percentage of Population Living in Absolute Poverty	Ratio between Percentage of Income to Richest, Poorest Quintiles (year)
Nigeria	na*	na	30	na
Tanzania	34.0	5.0	54	8.7:1 (1969)
India	25.0	5.0	36	7.0:1 (1975–6)
Indonesia	na	na	51	7.5:1 (1976)
Mexico	36.0	4.0	10	19.9:1 (1977)
Brazil	27.0	5.0	8	33.3:1 (1972)
Egypt	20.0	4.0	na	8.3:1 (1974)
Iran	25.0	5.0	5	na

* na = not available

(*Source*) *The Book of World Rankings*, by George Thomas Kurian. Copyright © 1979 by George Thomas Kurian. Reprinted with the permission of Facts on File, Inc., New York. (Tables 60, 61, pp. 85–86); World Bank, *World Development Report: 1984*, Table 28, pp. 272–273; *World Development Report: 1987*, Table 26, pp. 252–253.

nomic purposes, but to break the political power of the landed gentry. Also, much of the income, wealth, and social power in Third World countries are concentrated in the hands of traditional groups whose members, as we saw earlier, are not only not interested in modernization and industrialization, but are determined to fight their introduction through public policies whenever and wherever they can.

Cultural Schisms in the Mosaic Societies. Third World countries have been characterized aptly as *mosaic societies* because they are made up of many separate pieces, each of which adds to the whole picture without being absorbed or assimilated into any other segment.[37] This is not a problem unique to the Third World. One survey of the question of *ethnonationalism*— the belief that people should be governed only by others of their same ethnic group—found that there are only fourteen countries in the

world substantially free of at least one significant minority, that Japan is the only one of these that has a large population, and that only 4 percent of the world's population lives in a nation-state that corresponds closely to a single ethnic group. This same survey went on to assert that, as of 1973, fifty-eight countries were "currently or recently troubled by internal discord predicted upon ethnic diversity."[38]

It obviously is difficult to generalize about such a problem, but it still seems that ethnic discord is a much more serious obstacle to national development in the Third World than it is in most of the industrial countries.[39] There are several reasons for this. Many Third World countries, particularly in Africa and Asia, are enclosed by artifical boundaries that were imposed on the country by the departing colonial power and do not reflect long-standing tribal or ethnic divisions. In addition, the struggle against the colonial power led many of the nationalist leaders to emphasize each person's inherent right to self-determination, an ideology that turns out to be a two-edged sword, that can be wielded by an ethnic minority against a newly created regime just as that regime used it against the colonial country. Also, modernization seems to exacerbate tribal, ethnic, or linguistic feelings. Sharp increases in mass media expose people to new cultural symbols, awakening in them a cultural consciousness that leads to new ideas about the "them" and "us" of their world. Rapid social change frequently drives bewildered traditional peoples back into the comparative safety of mystical religions and tribal cults, which tend to emphasize the dividing lines in human society. Rapid economic change can produce sharp inequalities in the distribution of the gains of industrialization; not infrequently, these economic inequities correspond to some kind of ethnic division. Finally, we must note the comparative fragility of many of the Third World's states, whose people have not yet become committed to the nation as a symbol of a going concern that deserves their loyalty and dedication. In such instances, ethnic divisions loom large as the cause of conflict, violence, and even the breakup of the country.

Third World countries are divided by the customary social faultlines seen elsewhere. (See Table 16.6.) Language is one such source of division. Ghana, with a population of 10 million, has five major languages; India has fifteen major languages and more than 1,600 dialects. In the Philippines, no one language can be understood by as many as one-third of the people. Nigerians speak three major languages; in Zaire, four languages are used for communication between European and natives, four others are used in primary education, and three more are used only in certain localities.[40] Even in Latin America, where the countries have had much time

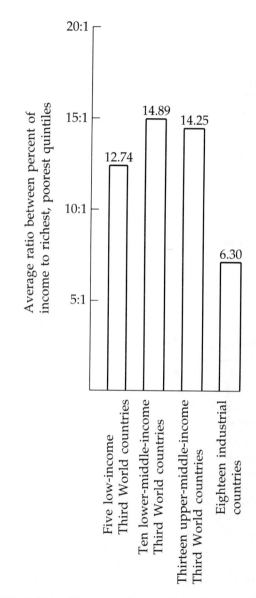

Figure 16.5 Changes in income distribution patterns by levels of income. [World Bank, *World Development Report: 1987* (New York: Oxford University Press, 1987), Table 26, pp. 252–3.]

Table 16.6 Ethnic/Linguistic Data from Eight Selected Third World Countries in the Mid-1970s

Country	Number of Separate Languages Spoken (Principal/Secondary)	Number of Significant Discrete Ethnic Groups (Principal/Secondary)	Homogeneity Index*
Nigeria	3/250	4/250	13
Tanzania	1/100	1/130	7
India	15/1600+	2-3/numerous	11
Indonesia	1/250+	2-3/300+	24
Mexico	1/5-10	1/3	70
Brazil	1/3-5	1/3-5	93
Egypt	1/2	1/5	96
Iran	1/5-8	1/40-50	24

* Ranges from 0 to 100; 100 represents complete homogeneity of ethnicity.
(*Source*) The data on ethnic homogeneity are from *The Book of World Rankings*, by George Thomas Kurian. Copyright © 1979 by George Thomas Kurian. Reprinted with the permission of Facts on File, Inc., New York. (Table 32, pp. 44–46); the data on languages and ethnic groups are from Kurian, *Encyclopedia of the Third World* (New York: Facts on File, 1978), 2 vols.

to resolve these problems, Indian languages such as Quechua and Guarani, present obstacles to communication in the Andean countries.

Religious beliefs are also sources of conflict in the Third World. Much of the conflict in Lebanon stems from the division of the population into six principal socioreligious groupings: the Christian Maronites (about 23 percent of the total population), the Greek Orthodox (7 percent), the Armenians (5 percent), the Sunni Moslems (26 percent), the Shiite Moslems (27 percent), and the Druze (7 percent). The chief division in Sri Lanka is between the 2.5 million people of the Tamil Hindu minority and the 9 million Sinhalese Buddhist majority. In the former South Vietnam, conflict among the Cao Dai (a syncretic Christian faith), the Catholics, and the Hoa Hao (a Buddhist sect) further weakened the already shaky political order and contributed to the downfall of the U.S.-supported regime.

Racial differences and tribal allegiances compound the problem of national unity, especially in Africa and Asia. Nigeria and Zaire (at the time called the Congo) experienced severe challenges from separatist movements soon after gaining their independence. In both cases the source of conflict was tribal loyalties and feelings of persecution (often aggravated by outside intervention). The presence of many racially different overseas minorities has sparked conflicts, for example, the Indians in several East African countries and the Chinese in Malaysia and Singapore. Even though many Latin Americans may proclaim that their countries are more tolerant of racial differences, persons of European origins seem to enjoy greater advantages economically, socially, and politically than do persons of mixed racial ancestry.

Nigeria is a Third World country that has experienced great strain from its ethnic diversity. Since independence from Great Britain in 1960,

Nigeria has suffered four military coups, one bloody attempted coup, and a civil war that lasted two and a half years (ending in 1970) and cost an estimated 1 million lives. For thirteen years, from 1966 to 1979, the country lived under military rule, and the armed forces seized power again in 1984. The principal cause of all this discord is the tribal animosities contained within the fragile and artificial state. There are 250 distinct tribal groups in the country; 47 percent of the people are Muslim and 34 percent are Christian. The civil war centered on the country's three major tribal groupings—the Yoruba of the west, the Hausa-Fulani of the north, and the Ibo of the east. After the breakdown of the shaky tribal coalition that had governed since independence, there followed a series of riots, charges of rigged elections, and two military coups that involved ethnic hostilities. Thousands of Ibos living in the north were killed and thousands more fled to their home region, which then seceded as the independent state of Biafra in 1967. Although the defeat of the Ibos resulted in the consolidation of Nigerian national identity, the Ibos have felt resentful ever since because of their treatment at the hands of the victors. Ibo property confiscated during the war still had not been returned as of 1980. Biafra's war wounded are not helped by the central government. Public works, such as roads and drinking-water supplies, have been left to deteriorate, and many badly needed projects remain uncompleted. It was not until late 1980 that Ibo civil servants from the days before the civil war had their federal government pensions restored. Much remains to be done to weld Nigeria's 250 ethnic groups into a single proud country.[41]

India is another major Third World country where ethnic and linguistic discord led to considerable violence in the early 1980s and now threatens the very fabric of the country itself.

Language is one major dividing line, as we have already noted. Hindi (spoken by only about 40 percent of the people) and English are jointly used as official languages at the national level, but fifteen other languages are used officially at the state level. Religious and ethnic ties are also strong centrifugal forces. In the remote northeast province of Sikkim, ethnic and tribal strife led to vicious communal fighting and separatist insurgency that forced the late Prime Minister Indira Gandhi to send in regular army forces in 1983 to restore order. At the other end of the country, along the Pakistan border, militant Sikh fundamentalists mounted a challenge to New Delhi rule that provoked an Indian army invasion of a Sikh holy site, the Amritsar Golden Temple, in 1984, at a cost of more than 300 lives.[42] The assassination of Mrs. Gandhi in late 1984 by her Sikh bodyguards was apparently in retaliation for the Amritsar attack. In 1987, Sikh terrorists killed more than 1,000 people; and the death toll from their attacks reached nearly 200 in the first month of 1988.[43]

Conclusions: Economics and Social Barriers to Human Dignity

As this brief discussion makes clear, Third World governments desirous of raising the levels of human dignity in their societies must first come to grips with a number of severe social and economic problems. The international economic system within which the Third World must live is one obvious source of difficulty. Multinational corporations and Great Powers use developing countries to further their own goals and ambitions; seldom does this treatment help the poor nations themselves.

Each Third World country, however, suffers from social and economic problems that will be just as intractable as those of the international arena. Explosive population growth absorbs increased industrial and agricultural production, meaning that even the most prosperous Third World economies must run harder and harder just to stay in place. Social class structure and inequalities in income distribution create political conflict, economic waste, and the misallocation of scarce resources. Ethnic, tribal, linguistic, and racial differences complete the list of the noneconomic obstacles to human progress.

The list is a formidable one. Even the most stable and creative of political systems would have difficulty in managing any of these problems in isolation, much less the entire set together. In the following chapters, we examine governments in the Third World as they attempt to cope with problems that seem at times to be overwhelming in scope and intensity.

Suggestions for Further Reading

Agarwal, Amar Narayan, and **S. P. Singh,** eds., *The Economics of Underdevelopment* (New York: Oxford University Press, 1963).

Angelopoulos, Angelos, *The Third World and the Rich Countries: Prospects for the Year 2000* (New York: Praeger, 1972).

Baran, Paul, and **Paul Sweezy,** *Monopoly Capital* (New York: Monthly Review Press, 1966).

Bauer, P. T., *Equality, the Third World and Economic Delusion* (Cambridge, Mass.: Harvard University Press, 1981).

Becker, David, and **Jeff Frieden, Sayre Schatz** and **Richard Sklar,** *Postimperialism: International Capitalism and Development in the Late Twentieth Century* (Boulder, Colo.: Lynne Reinner Publishers, 1987).

Bhagwati, Jagdish N., ed., *Economics and World Order: From the 1970s to the 1990s* (New York: The Free Press, 1972).

Chilcote, Ronald, *Theories of Development and Underdevelopment* (Boulder, Colo.: Westview Press, 1984).

Chilcote, Ronald H., and **Dale L. Johnson,** eds., *Theories of Development: Mode of Production or Dependency?* (Beverly Hills: Sage, 1983).

Connor, Walker, "The Politics of Ethnonationalism," *Journal of International Affairs* 27 (1) (1973), 1–21.

Elliott, Charles, *Patterns of Poverty in the Third World* (New York: Praeger, 1975).

Enloe, Cynthia, *Ethnic Conflict and Political Development* (Boston: Little, Brown, 1973).

Erb, Guy F., and **Valeriana Kallab,** eds. *Beyond Dependency: The Developing World Speaks Out* (Washington, D.C.: Overseas Development Council, 1975).

Harris, Nigel, *The End of the Third World* (New York: Penguin, 1986).

Holt, R. J., and **J. E. Turner,** *The Political Basis of Economic Development* (New York: Van Nostrand, 1966).

Horowitz, Donald, *Ethnic Groups in Conflict* (Berkeley: University of California Press, 1985).

Hoselitz, Bert F., *Sociological Aspects of Economic Growth* (New York: The Free Press, 1960).

Johnson, Harry G., eds., *Economic Nationalism in Old and New States* (Chicago: University of Chicago Press, 1967).

Kerr, Clark, et al., *Industrialism and Industrial Man* (Cambridge, Mass.: Harvard University Press, 1960).

Lloyd, Peter C., *Africa in Social Change,* rev. ed. (Baltimore: Penguin, 1975).

Mountjoy, Alan B., ed., *The Third World: Problems and Perspectives* (New York: St. Martin's Press, 1978).

Myrdal, Gunnar, *Asian Drama: An Inquiry into the Poverty of Nations* (New York: Pantheon, 1968).

————, *The Challenge of World Poverty* (New York: Random House, 1970).

Petras, James, *Critical Perspectives on Imperialism* and *Social Class in the Third World* (New York: Monthly Review Press, 1978).

Seligson, Mitchell A., ed., *The Gap between Rich and Poor: Contending Perspectives on the Political Economy of Development* (Boulder, Colo.: Westview, 1984).

Singer, Hans, and **Javed Ansari,** *Rich and Poor Countries,* 3rd ed. (London: George Allen & Unwin, 1982).

Thompson, Dennis, and **Dov Ronen,** eds., *Ethnicity, Politics, and Development* (Boulder, Colo.: Lynne Reinner Publishers, 1986).

Vogeler, Ingolf, and **Anthony de Souza,** eds., *Dialectics of Third World Development* (Montclair, N.J.: Allanheld, Osmun, 1980).

World Bank, *World Development Report: 1987* (New York: Oxford University Press, 1987).

Notes

1. Ronald Chilcote, *Theories of Development and Underdevelopment* (Boulder, Colo.: Westview Press, 1984).

2. Nigel Harris, *The End of the Third World* (New York: Penguin, 1986).

3. A good source of factual information about all the world's political systems is Arthur S. Banks, ed., *Political Handbook of the World: 1989* (Binghamton, N.Y.: CSA Publications, 1989). See also George Thomas Kurian, *Encyclopedia of the Third World* (New York: Facts on File, 1978), 2 vols.

4. "Grossly Deceptive Product," *The Economist,* September 19, 1987.

5. George H. Gallup, "What Mankind Thinks about Itself," *Reader's Digest* (October 1976), pp. 132–136. For a good discussion of poverty in the Third World from the vantage point of specific country case studies, see Charles Elliott, *Patterns of Poverty in the Third World* (New York: Praeger, 1975).

6. Sivard, *World Military and Social Expenditures, 1987–88,* Table III, pp. 46–51; World Bank, *World Development Report: 1987,* (New York: Oxford University Press, 1987), Table 9.

7. Paul Zach, "'Low Quality' Job Earns Indonesian Pedicab Driver $3.20 a Day," *Washington Post,* October 10, 1980.

8. Jim Brooke, "Kidney, Cornea Sale Flourishes in Brazil," *Washington Post,* October 19, 1981.

9. William Claiborne, "New Delhi's Beggars Are Banished to Poorhouses in the Suburbs," *Washington Post,* November 7, 1982; Stuart Auerbach, "Bombay Wallows in Poverty, Slums as Glitter Fades," *Washington Post,* August 19, 1982.

10. Keith Richburg, "Manila's Unseen Poor: No

Land, No Future," *Washington Post*, November 22, 1987.

11. Jim Brooke, "Northeast's Blood Feud Spills into Rio for 30th Death," *Washington Post*, November 9, 1981.

12. Maria Flores, *The Woman with the Whip: Eva Perón* (New York: Doubleday, 1952), p. 15.

13. Paul Baran and Paul Sweezy, *Monopoly Capital* (New York: Monthly Review Press, 1966); Harry Magdoff, *The Age of Imperialism* (New York: Monthly Review Press, 1969); Magdoff, *Imperialism: From the Colonial Age to the Present* (New York: Monthly Review Press, 1977).

14. Benjamin J. Cohen, *The Question of Imperialism: The Political Economy of Dominance and Dependence* (New York: Basic Books, 1973).

15. Melvin Gurtov, *The United States against the Third World* (New York: Praeger, 1974).

16. UNECLA, *The Economic Development of Latin America and Its Principal Problems* (Lake Success, N.Y.: U.N. Department of Economic Affairs, 1950).

17. Edward H. Carr, *The Twenty Years' Crisis, 1919–1939*, 2nd ed. (New York: St. Martin's Press, 1958).

18. Many of the key writings in dependency theory have been collected in Michael Smith, Richard Little, and Michael Shackleton, eds., *Perspectives on World Politics* (London: Open University, 1981), pp. 273–386. For additional readings, see Guy F. Erb and Valeriana Kallab, eds., *Beyond Dependency: The Developing World Speaks Out* (Washington, D.C.: Overseas Development Council, 1975). For an excellent critique of dependency theory, see Tony Smith, "The Underdevelopment of Development Literature: The Case of Dependency Theory," *World Politics* 31 (2) (1979), 247–288. See also James D. Cockcroft et al., eds., *Dependence and Underdevelopment: Latin America's Political Economy* (Garden City, N.Y.: Doubleday, 1972); Daniel A. Offiong, *Imperialism and Dependency: Obstacles to African De-*

19. Theotonio dos Santos, "The Structure of Dependence," *American Economic Review* 60 (May 1970), 231. Quoted in Chilcote, *Theories of Development*, p. 60.

20. David Becker, Jeff Frieden, Sayre Schatz, and Richard Sklar, *Postimperialism: International Capitalism and Development in the Late Twentieth Century* (Boulder, Colo.: Lynne Reinner Publishers, 1987).

21. Tomas Freijka, "The Prospects for a Stationary World Population," *Scientific American* 228 (3) (1973), 15–23.

22. World Bank, *World Development Report: 1984* (New York: Oxford University Press, 1984), p. 7.

23. *The Economist*, January 13 and 20, 1990.

24. Robert W. Fox, *Urban Population Growth Trends in Latin America* (Washington, D.C.: Interamerican Development Bank, 1975). See also *The Economist*, May 31, 1986.

25. Nathan Keyfitz, "World Resources and the World Middle Class," *Scientific American* 235 (1) (1976), 28–35.

26. Stuart Auerbach, "Indian Census Spurs Call for Birth Control Plan," *Washington Post*, May 12, 1981; Jay Ross, "Kenya's 4% Birthrate Said to Create 'Mind-Boggling' Problems," *Washington Post*, June 20, 1981; Jim Brooke, "Brazil's Population Growth Rate Decreases," *Washington Post*, February 2, 1981.

27. *The Economist* (London), August 4, 1984 and December 19, 1987.

28. Gunnar Myrdal, *The Challenge of World Poverty* (New York: Random House, 1970), Ch. 4.

29. World Bank, *World Development Report: 1984* (New York: Oxford University Press, 1984), Table 5.7, p. 94.

30. Celso Furtado, *Economic Development of Latin America: A Survey from Colonial Times to the Cuban*

velopment (Washington, D.C.: Howard University Press, 1982).

Revolution (Cambridge: Cambridge University Press, 1970).

31. Peter C. Lloyd, *Africa in Social Change*, rev. ed. (Baltimore: Penguin, 1975).

32. Brewster Grace, "Population Growth in Thailand, Part I: Population and Social Structure," *Reports* [American Universities Field Staff (Asia)] 22 (1) (1974), 7.

33. Nevin S. Scrimshaw, "The Politics of Starvation," *Technology Review* (August/September 1984), 18–27.

34. Lester Brown, "Sustaining World Agriculture," in Lester Brown et al., *State of the World: 1987* (New York: Norton, 1987), pp. 134–135.

35. R. Gendarme, "Reflections on the Approaches to the Problems of Distribution in Underdeveloped Countries," in Jean Marchal and Bernard Ducros, eds., *The Distribution of National Income* (London: Macmillan, 1968), pp. 361–388.

36. Lloyd, *Africa in Social Change*, p. 120.

37. W. Howard Wriggins, *The Ruler's Imperative: Stategies for Political Survival in Asia and Africa*

(New York: Columbia University Press, 1969), p. 22.

38. Walker Connor, "The Politics of Ethnonationalism," *Journal of International Affairs* 27 (1) (1973), 1–21.

39. Donald Horowitz, *Ethnic Groups in Conflict* (Berkeley: University of California Press, 1985); Dennis Thompson and Dov Ronen, eds., *Ethnicity, Politics, and Development* (Boulder, Colo.: Lynne Reinner Publishers, 1986).

40. Rupert Emerson, *From Empire to Nation: The Rise to Self-Assertion of Asian and African Peoples* (Cambridge, Mass.: Harvard University Press, 1960).

41. See the series of articles by Leon Dash in the *Washington Post*: "10 Years Later Ibos Still Feel Impact of Nigeria's Civil War," May 27, 1980; "Nigeria Acts to Conciliate Ex-Biafrans," October 2, 1980; "Nigeria Election Recriminations Revive Sensitivities of Civil War," December 28, 1980. Also see Michael Battye, "Nigerian Military Seizes Control; President Arrested," *Washington Post*, January 1, 1984.

42. *The Economist*, June 9, 1984.

43. *The Economist*, February 6, 1988.

C H A P T E R   17

CULTURE AND CHANGE IN THE THIRD WORLD

In Chapter 16, we outlined a number of major economic and social obstacles to raising the level of human dignity in the Third World. Much of what goes on in politics in developing countries is aimed at removing these obstacles by reforming the social, economic, and political structures. Despite the determined and, at times, heroic efforts of political leaders, only a few countries in the Third World seem to be making significant progress toward this goal. One reason for this difficulty may lie in the cultural features of the societies in question. If the attitudes, modes of thinking, and forms of interpersonal relationships do not support political and economic reform, the changes will not endure no matter how well designed or financed they may be.

For this reason, many Third World regimes now spend significant resources on policies intended to alter or influence the traditional cultures of their people. They do this out of a conviction that traditional cultures impede the implementation of policies to raise the level of human dignity. In this chapter, we examine some of the principal features of traditional and modern ways of thinking and discuss the links between these different modes of thought and the enactment of public policy. All policies have their costs, however, and we must also consider the costs of government programs aimed at changing the way people think.

Some people in every society wish to preserve the old, the tried, and the tested ways of thinking and doing. They perceive, with justification, that modern ways of thinking have disadvantages as well as advantages. Perhaps after reading this chapter, you will also decide that traditional values and habits should be conserved and that cultural modernization is too costly. Nevertheless, most Third World leaders who are trying to reform their societies believe that such reform must include some cultural changes. Whether or not this is wise, or even feasible, are questions you should be better prepared to answer at the end of this chapter.

From Tradition to Modernity: The Dimensions of Change

There seem to be almost as many definitions of the term *culture* as there are scholars and others who study the subject. One definition that seems useful in the study of Third World societies is that given us by Henri Aujac: "The totality of the intellectual character of a population, and the body of social, religious, ethical, scientific and technical features which constitute the culture."[1] Culture, according to Aujac, both sustains and is sustained by the general social order, evident in customs and informal systems of rules as well as in more formal laws, organizations, and institutions. In the view of British writer Peter Worsley, culture has three components.[2] The cognitive, or thinking, component of culture tells us who we are, and how and why we differ from others; the evaluative, or judging, component enables us to make value judgments about our world; and the conative, or doing, component shapes for us the answer to the question "What do I *do* given my current situation?" Culture, then, is that aspect of life that mediates between the individual and his or her surroundings, making it possible for a person to know (or know about) those surroundings, evaluate them, and act on them to produce a desired outcome.

As we use the terms, *traditional* and *modern* are ideal types or models that social scientists have developed to describe certain complex features of social change. These terms do not exist in the real world, but they are still helpful to us as we attempt to make sense out of the process of social and psychological transformation. All of us, and all societies with which we are likely to come into contact, are complex mixtures of traditional and modern ways of thinking and acting. All cultures, once they have been exposed to the forces of modernization, form a continuum from traditional to modern. None can be regarded as entirely of one type or the other.

Until fairly recently, many social scientists accepted the *convergence theory* of social change. They believed that as societies industrialized, they would become more alike culturally, or *converge*. This trend toward cultural sameness would be driven by the demands of industrialization. In preindustrial cultures, the principal criterion for selecting the appropriate behavior or (in simpler terms) "doing the right thing" in any given situation was *tradition*; people selected one behavior or one value over others because it was sanctioned by tradition; that is, things had "always" been done that way. In industrial countries, on the other hand, such choices are usually based on a different criterion: fact, logic, or direct (empirical) observation. When a society transforms itself from preindustrial to industrial, and its chief cultural criterion is changed from tradition to empirical fact or logic, we say that the society is becoming more *rational* and its values and institutions are becoming *rationalized*. The process of such a change is called, then, *rationalization*.

Whereas at one time it was thought that societies that were being made more rational would become more alike, or converge, we now understand that exactly the opposite is just as likely to happen. That is, as societies become more industrial, although they may undergo some (or even a great deal of) rationalization, many preindustrial and nonrational attitudes and values will persist and survive well into the industrial period. Thus, new, industrial, rational attitudes, institutions, and practices will be laid alongside traditional values and habits of thought to form surprisingly complex and varied cultures. As industrialization spreads around the world, then, diversity seems to flourish rather than to be threatened by the homogenizing influences of industrial life.[3]

Modernization is a multidimensional phenomenon, meaning that it is a process that affects most of the mental structures of an individual as well as most of the social institutions of which he or she is a part. People do not become modern only in certain parts of their personality but, apparently, must make the transition along a wide range of mental activities. In fact, if the changes do not take place across this wide range, the chances are greater that modernity will not become established within the individual's personality and a return to traditional modes of thinking, feeling, and acting will occur. More frequently what happens is that an attempt to reconcile traditional and modern values within a single individual produces psychological strain or tension, leading to forms of behavior that are unstable or unhealthy for society.

The changes involved in modernization affect four areas: personality, attitudes, cognition (or the handling of information), and behavior.[4]

Changes in Personality

At the very core of our mental structures lie the devices that people use to guide and direct the personality in its encounters with the environment as well as the protective techniques (defense mechanisms) that shield the personality from threat and attack. These structures are deeply embedded in the personality and are the outcome of very early childhood experiences, especially those arising within the family setting. Until recently, many psychologists regarded these structures as being virtually unchangeable after adolescence, except under traumatic conditions. Thanks to the work of Erik Erikson, ideas about this are beginning to change.[5] The dimensions of the personality that appear most relevant to modernity are those that have to do with one's openness to change, feelings of efficacy and optimism, an ability to empathize with others, and an inclination toward moderate risk taking.

A traditional person is inclined to be skeptical about the value of change. In fact, the very definition of *traditional* would probably include reverence for the old and the tested and suspicion of the new and the untried. A modern person, on the other hand, is not only open and receptive to change but looks about for it, even at the cost of uprooting self and family and moving to a different location. A modern person's readiness for change extends to more than just job, home, or customs; he or she also is inclined to be receptive to new modes of production or of cultivation and to new political forms. Change, even when it comes rapidly, is usually not threatening or unmanageable for the modern person.

A traditional person relates to the natural environment with a feeling of resignation and with a belief that he or she must accept what nature imposes without trying to alter the inevitable. This characteristic of the traditional person, which we call *fatalism*, is indicative of the degree to which the tradition-bound individual feels that life is controlled by external forces, beyond one's control. Typical of this sort of mentality would be the farmer who refuses to take resolute action to rid a crop of pests out of the belief that the pests are an act of God, against which the farmer cannot struggle. Modern people, on the other hand, act decisively to overcome nature and its obstacles. They believe that destiny is in their control and that they can influence events that have a bearing on their lives. A modern person feels efficacious and capable of resolving many of the problems that confront daily life without resorting to spiritual or external assistance.

A third dimension of personality affected by modernization involves a person's dealings with others. A traditional person does not trust others, especially if they come from beyond the immediate circle of friends or kin groups; strangers are to be suspected, not dealt with openly. Relations going in the opposite direction are also difficult because a traditional person lacks the ability to empathize with others, to put himself or herself in their position and to imagine how the world looks from their vantage point. A modern person, however, possesses the opposite of both of these characteristics. Modernity helps a person trust in others, especially if he or she has some sort of rule or legal document to ensure that the impersonal other can be expected to behave in a certain prescribed manner. Bureaucracy, that great social invention of the modern world, could not work if it were not for the tendency of modern people to trust others to conform to a written set of rules. A modern person also has the ability to empathize with others, to imagine the sorts of problems from which they may be suffering, and to adjust personal behavior to the feelings of others. Some social psychologists even assert that a modern person has greater respect for the dignity and worth of weak and poor people, of women and the aged, and of other groups that have been discriminated against until recent times.

Finally, a traditional person has a tendency to avoid taking risks in daily life. Fatalism, low sense of efficacy, and unwillingness to accept change combine to make a traditional person a low-risk person who tries to reduce all life choices to those guaranteed to come out successfully. New agricultural techniques, for example, are avoided unless they offer complete certainty of yielding a larger crop. Movement to the city, likewise, is avoided because to do so creates uncertainty and risk. A traditional person is not so much interested in achieving success as in avoiding failure; the best way to avoid failure is to attempt nothing unless success is guaranteed. In the real world, this is usually the equivalent of doing nothing. A modern person accepts a moderate amount of risk in life. He or she understands that certain tasks offer only a medium chance for success, but he or she feels that the outcome of the task can be influenced by throwing skill and intelligence into the balance. A modern person wishes to achieve positive things; merely avoiding failure is not sufficient. Modern psychology leads to the creation of an entrepreneurial class as well as to highly motivated and well-trained workers. In many ways, this dimension is the key to the economic development of a society.

Let us not conclude that traditional people avoid risk and eschew innovation solely because of their personality characteristics. In many instances, resistance to innovations may stem from flaws and rigidities in the surrounding economic and social institutions, from a very narrow margin of resources with which people can experiment, and from a very realistic appraisal of the prospects for change. As William Ogionwo discovered in his study of Nigerian farmers, traditional rural folk frequently have high aspirations, especially for their children, but they also have an accurate understanding of their fragile hold on economic survival, and of the social and economic practices that limit their ability to risk new and unproven techniques. Personality, then, is only one of several factors that lead to traditional behavior patterns.[6]

Changes in Attitudes

Moving away from the core of a person's mental activities, we come to a wide variety of social, economic, and political attitudes that mark an individual's day-to-day relationships with the world. As these attitudes and opinions are acquired somewhat later in life than the personality structures mentioned earlier, they are, in theory, more easily changed or discarded as new information about the real world becomes available. This is particularly true for individuals who are more modern and, therefore, relatively more open to change and new experiences.

There appear to be six major sets of attitudes that undergo change as a person makes the transition from tradition to modernity. First, the propensity to form and hold opinions begins to grow, thereby making it easier for a modernizing person to develop a wide and rich set of beliefs and feelings about new and unusual phenomena. A traditional person would be less likely to have numerous opinions about things far removed from daily life and more likely to answer "I don't know" to an interviewer's questions about such issues. A modern person, in contrast, forms, changes, and discards opinions at a rapid pace that reflects the rapidly changing world.

Second, modern and traditional people differ in their attitudes about time. Traditional persons, reared in primarily agricultural settings, gear their lives to much broader and vaguer notions of time requirements. Time for a rural dweller in a traditional country is linked to the seasons instead of to clocks or watches. Modern persons, however, are much more attuned to the formal requirements of clocks and watches. Schools, factories, businesses, and other complex institutions depend on their members arriving and departing more or less together or at specific times. The modern institution teaches its participants the importance of time, that is, if they have not already learned it.

Closely related to the attitudes they have about time are the feelings modern people have about planning. Modernity implies an ability to bring order out of chaos, to impose a rigorous framework of analytical thought over the otherwise unorganized data of our surroundings. A traditional person resists planning because what is going to happen will happen anyway without human intervention. A modern person, on the other hand, intervenes in the flow of events to plan, to develop preferred sequences of events, and to impose his or her own sense of order on the environment.

A modern person believes in the efficacy of science and the scientific method as a means for people to get nature under control. Some tradition-bound persons hold that the world is completely random with no structure and, thus, no predictability. Others hold that whatever structure may exist is unknowable to ordinary people and can only be reached through spiritual appeals to some divine power—efforts to apply rationality and science to real problems are doomed to failure. A modern person, in contrast, believes in the inherent rationality of the universe and, therefore, holds that science can be used to rid humanity of some of its worst problems. One interesting illustration of this dimension is in the area of birth control. A traditional person argues against artificial attempts to control or alter the conception of children; a modern person accepts not only the possibility of achieving this goal but also the desirability, if not the necessity, of doing so.

Modern and traditional people differ in their attitudes about how society should reward its members. Modern persons, who are more achievement-oriented, assert that society should distribute its rewards according to only one criterion: how well individuals perform their societally assigned task. Traditional people are more ascriptive, which means that they believe that society should reward its members according to some criterion (or criteria) other than role performance. Such criteria might include one's religion, race, language, ethnic group, gender, or age. Obviously, as society generally moves toward a more achievement-oriented means of rewarding its members, individual persons must abandon ascriptive modes of interacting with their fellow citizens.

Finally, we should mention the shift from particularism to universalism as an example of attitudinal change in a modernizing society. *Particularism* is the belief that a particular group has the right to promote its own specific interests without reference to the interests of any larger or more inclusive entity. *Universalism* implies a belief that one's ultimate loyalty should be directed toward a social or political entity larger than one's own narrow parochial grouping. When applied at the concrete level in a traditional society, particularism means the supremacy of one's clan, kin group, family, tribe, language group, religious order, or ethnic grouping. The explicit political application of universalism in a modern context means the granting of ultimate supremacy to the nation-state. Although some citizens in the industrialized West may have begun to shift their loyalty to transnational entities or even to some global entity (such as all of humanity), those residents of the Third World who are emerging into psychological modernity focus primarily on the nation-state as the political unit to which they attach their commitments.

Changes in Information and Behavior

From attitudes, let us move to the outer mental structures where we find the cognitive dimension of the personality, which deal with what we know about the outside world as opposed to how we feel about it. In a political context, the cognitive dimension is closely related to the conative aspect of personality, or the behavioral side of mental functioning. For this reason, we consider knowledge and behavior simultaneously with special emphasis on their political implications.

The single most important cognitive-behavioral aspect of modernization involves information and how a person gets it. A traditional person lives in a world largely lacking in information. Furthermore, he or she has few resources that would permit seeking out needed information. Literacy rates are apt to be quite low in poor and developing countries, which indicates that many people are effectively cut off from a flow of information through the printed media that most of us in the industrialized countries take for granted. In addition, electronic forms of the mass media—telephones, motion pictures, radio, and television—are hardly developed in most emerging countries, with the likely exception of the country's capital city. Table 17.1 indicates the relative poverty of information within which Third World citizens live. Modern people, in contrast, not only possess large amounts of information, but also devote significant resources to the search for more data that they can use to order their lives.

We see this transformation from traditional to modern most clearly when we consider the political behavior of the two types of individuals. Traditional persons typically do not have many political opinions, and they lack the necessary information that would enable them to form opinions about an issue. Modern individuals, on the other hand, possess ample attitudes and opinions about political issues; they know where and how to go about getting the information they need to form an opinion on any new issues that might arise in their surroundings. The same generalization applies to the exchange of political opinions. Traditional people do not share opinions with others because conversation about things they cannot change (the regime in the far-off capital, for instance) is a waste of time.

Table 17.1 Communications and Media Data from Eight Selected Third World Countries, Mid-1980s or Most Recent Estimate

Country	Literacy Rate (%)	Radios per 1,000 Population	TV Sets per 1,000 Population	Daily Newspaper Circulation per 1,000 Population
Nigeria	42	68	5.0	5.3
Tanzania	85	27	0.4	9.7
India	44	29	2.0	15.1
Indonesia	74	41	9.0	14.3
Mexico	90	290	103.0	132.9
Brazil	78	129	112.0	39.3
Egypt	44	152	83.0	75.9
Iran	51	79	51.0	22.1

(*Source*) Literacy rate (as of 1984): Ruth L. Sivard, *World Military and Social Indicators: 1987–88* (Washington, D.C.: World Priorities, 1987), Table III, pp. 46–51. Radios, TV sets (as of 1983): Arthur S. Banks and William Overstreet, eds., *Political Handbook of the World: 1982–1983* (New York: McGraw-Hill, 1983). Newspaper circulation: World Bank, *Social Indicators of Development 1987* (Washington, D.C.: World Bank, 1987).

Modern persons, however, appear quite ready to exchange opinions about political issues with each other, especially if the environment is supportive. There are, of course, many social settings within which it would be inappropriate or inadvisable for the holder of a minority opinion to engage the dominant majority in debate over some political issue; but, these exceptions aside, the exchange of political ideas in a modern society is much more frequent than in traditional surroundings.

As we move on to consider what modern and traditional persons actually do in politics, the contrast stands out even more starkly.[7] On the input side of politics, where citizens are supposed to bring their demands, grievances, and support to the attention of policymakers, traditional people are almost totally inactive. Their fatalism, their lack of faith in their own efficacy, and their reluctance to join with others in common enterprise frequently make them unable to mount an effective campaign to influence the political system. Their lack of information about politics makes them ignorant of how, where, and by what means to exert pressure, even if they were so inclined. Modern persons, on the other hand, not only possess the motivation, the activist spirit, and the interpersonal and organizational skills to advance their interests through the political input process, but also know how best to make their influence felt to achieve their goals. The gap between traditional and modern is somewhat less on the output side of the policy process, where people (and groups) are less concerned with influencing policy before it is made and more concerned with protecting themselves from its adverse effects during the implementation stages. People in traditional societies are apt to have a fairly well developed set of skills to protect themselves from the impact of a given policy. In addition, there are always the ever-present intermediaries whose main job it is to obtain special treatment from the state bureaucracy for their clients. We meet these intermediaries again as we move on in subsequent chapters to consider the government structures of Third World countries. In modern societies, however, the task of protecting a citizen or a group from the adverse impact of public policy falls more into the realm of legitimate interest-group activities and less into the jurisdiction of informal or corrupt intermediaries. All of this helps explain why, in modern political settings, we are more apt to find formal associations, interest groups, and political parties operating on both ends of the political process—to influence policy before it is made and to protect their members or clients afterward, when it is being implemented. Although such an arrangement appears to be largely institutional, it could not survive for long if the basic personality and political culture of modernity did not strongly support it.

Consequences of Rapid Cultural Change

If you consider the value changes we have discussed as a complete set, or package, of transformations that a person must experience as he or she makes the change from traditional to modern, it is obvious that we are talking about massive personality alterations. These alterations do not ordinarily come about easily or painlessly; in fact, there is usually considerable turmoil involved in cultural modernization. This problem begins to take on a political dimension whenever the personal turmoil suffered by modernizing men and women erupts into societal disturbances that cannot be contained within the existing social and political institu-

tions. Nevertheless, governments and modernizing elites in Third World countries cannot afford to ignore the problem of psychological change or to treat it as a given in their human resources environment; if the basic personality[8] of a developing nation is not brought along in tune with the demands of a modern society, the process of political change may founder and slip backward.

The psychological effects of rapid modernization are a particular version of what Alvin Toffler calls future shock, or change at such a rapid pace that one's mental and physical resources are overwhelmed.[9] Toffler was writing about the impact of high-speed change in modern, industrial society, but his observations also apply to persons caught in the dizzying whirl of psychocultural modernization.

Making the change from tradition to modernity requires unlearning or discarding inappropriate values, behavioral tendencies, information, attitudes, and personality structures and replacing them with their modern counterparts. Traditional people must reassess their repertoire of mental structures, determine which of these are inappropriate for a modern society, and cast them off in favor of others more attuned to the needs of modernity.

People learn in one of four ways. First, our environment conditions our behavior in certain directions by the granting or withholding of rewards or by the application and withdrawal of punishments. Through repeated encounters with sets of such rewards and punishments, we learn by the process of adding rewarded behavioral choices and discarding nonrewarded or punished ones. For more complex social activities, we rely on modeling (social learning), a process that enables us to learn entire packages of behaviors at once by observing others engaged in a particular action and then emulating them. In addition, we may transfer lessons learned in one sphere of activity to another area of our lives through the learning process known as generalization. And, finally, the process of exemplification allows us to internalize a rule or guideline of an institution and make it our own as a lesson for personal behavior. An example of this latter process would be seen in an individual who, after working in a factory that is run according to a set schedule of events, learned the value of scheduling personal events. We can assume, then, that the process of psychocultural modernization within an individual will be less disruptive and will endure longer if (1) the person is rewarded substantially for having made the shift; (2) the environment provides ample models in the form of other modern persons who can be emulated; (3) the person has an opportunity to transfer the lessons of modernity from one sphere of life (school, for instance) to another (business); and (4) the person is placed in institutions or organizations that are run along modern lines and that provide ample opportunity to copy their behavioral principles.

Under the best of circumstances, psychocultural changes of this magnitude involve what some psychologists call *object loss*, a condition marked by a person's perception that he or she has been deprived of, or must do without, some object (another person, an aspect of one's own self-concept, a tangible resource, or a cultural abstraction) that is invested with emotion and that is culturally defined as valuable.[10] In this particular case, the object that is lost is the set of values that were appropriate in a traditional setting but that are out of step in a modern surrounding. Some degree of object loss is inescapable. We all lose loved ones and valued objects as part of the normal process of living. Many such losses are well within the normal range of predictability, however, and society generally provides us with institutions, rituals,

and compensation to cushion us against the shock. Occasionally, however, entire social aggregates such as ethnic groups or social classes may experience object loss together as the result of the sudden change of some important group characteristic such as land ownership or income level. When this happens, social buffer institutions are less effective because society itself had a stake in maintaining the status quo ante. Rapid cultural modernization of a developing country is one such instance.

As a very general term, object loss embraces two more specific kinds of psychological disturbances that can affect the stability of developing countries. One of these is *relative deprivation*. This is a person's perception that there is a significant gap between the objects (goods, conditions of life, opportunities, symbols, etc.) to which he or she feels legitimately entitled (expectations) and the objects that he or she can reasonably hope to attain and keep (capabilities). The awareness of this gap is often called frustration, and the frequent outcome of a frustrating condition is the direction of aggression against a convenient and symbolic target.[11] A second kind of object-loss disturbance is called *cognitive dissonance*. Psychologist Leon Festinger asserts that one of the most important human drives is that which impels us to desire internal consistency of opinions, perceptions, expectations, and the whole general range of mental structures. A person holding contradictory values feels uncomfortable, and this discomfort energizes the person to seek to correct the condition. The awareness of internal inconsistencies or contradictions in one's values or attitudes is called cognitive dissonance, and actions taken to soften or eliminate these contradictions are called dissonance reduction.[12]

Up to now, we have dealt with object loss at a fairly abstract level. Let us now consider some concrete examples of relative deprivation and cognitive dissonance at work. India in the 1980s is a country severely challenged by the competition between tradition and modernity. Despite the country's status as a parliamentary democracy, most local problems are still solved by local bosses and intermediaries who are in a position to intercede in behalf of their clients or constituents with the prime minister in the capital city, New Delhi. Although the country was for many years governed by a woman, the status of women has barely progressed beyond feudalism. In 1985 in New Delhi, 460 women were burned to death under suspicious circumstances. Police allege that these bride burnings were carried out by the husbands of the victims usually because of insufficient dowry. Despite the country's emphasis on modern technology in its space and nuclear energy programs, the traditional Indian medical practice, *ayurveda*, which is based on herbs, vegetables, and the curative power of sunlight, is thriving; and ayurvedic doctors practice side by side with modern doctors in well-equipped big city hospitals.[13] As I. R. Sinai writes in describing Indian intellectuals caught between the traditional demands of family and kin group, on the one hand, and the modern requirements of adult experiences, education, and profession, on the other:

> People like me are heirs to two sets of customs, are shaped in our daily lives by dual codes of behavior. For example: my generation on the one hand declared its agnosticism and on the other tamely succumbed to the old rituals; we yearned for romantic love but were reconciled to marriage by the well-established method of matching horoscopes to a girl selected for us by our parents; outside our homes we smoked, consumed alcohol, and ate meat, when available, but at home we were rigidly puritan and vegetarian; we glibly talked about individual salvation although we belonged to a very closely knit joint-family system.[14]

Sinai is writing of cognitive dissonance, yet relative deprivation can also produce disturbances in rapidly modernizing societies. In some cases, stable, tradition-bound groups try to hold fast to unchanging expectations but find their resources eroding away under the pressure of modernization. In the East African countries of Kenya and Tanzania, for example, small farming villages are caught between the unrelenting increase in population and the finite amount of land available for cultivation. Because the traditional methods of passing land from one generation to another are not adequate to resolve this problem, the inhabitants of these small villages see the average size of the agricultural parcel dwindle away to the point of not being economically viable. In other instances, more modernized groups, such as urban, middle-class political leaders, see a gap develop between their high (and rising) expectations of what can be accomplished under an independent, democratic, national reform government and their perceptions of what actually does happen: not reform, but corruption; not economic progress, but decay; not self-denying leadership, but self-indulgent abuse of power. The result in numerous instances has been for the most powerful modernizing elite, the armed forces, to intervene to restore order and begin anew the drive to development. We return to this phenomenon again in detail in Chapter 19, when we consider government structures.

For the person in Latin America, Asia, Africa, or the Middle East who is caught in the midst of the turmoil of modernization, several broad kinds of mechanisms are available to help cope with the tensions of rapid change. Withdrawal, either partially through drugs or totally through suicide, offers one escape from modern life.

Indeed, we often find that developing countries are experiencing increases in drug use, alcoholism, and suicide rates as they try to transform their cultures. For many individuals who look to the supernatural for aid, mysticism, witchcraft, and magic play an important role. In many countries of the Third World—Mexico, other areas of the Caribbean, West Africa, and Southeast Asia—the transformation of society from traditional to modern has been accompanied by an increase in popular belief in sorcery, voodoo, witches, spirits, and other agents of supernatural power. Sometimes the mass devotion to these practices can be transformed into hatred and fear as happened in Haiti, where in the first three months of 1986 about 100 voodoo priests and followers were attacked and brutally murdered because they were thought to be poisoning people with secret potions.[15] Some of the frustration of psychocultural change is expressed in social pathology. Homicides, divorces, crimes of passion, theft, burglary, and other forms of socially disruptive aggression are on the increase as a frustrated and discontented individual, caught in the grip of forces he or she cannot understand, strikes out against symbolic targets, usually in the family and the immediate circle of friends and kin groups. And, finally, mental illness may rise along with levels of modernization as many people succumb to the stress and tension of rapid change.

What we have described are the negative effects of cultural change, the consequences that disrupt society and one's personal life and divert a reform government's attention away from larger, more institutional problems. That these individual-level responses to modernization can mean the undoing of the national development efforts seems obvious. Governments in the Third World have found that they cannot simply leave the traditional political culture alone and expect it to change as the nation's institutions change.

Neither can a modernizing regime ignore the danger signals in the rising rate of social pathology in its country: suicides, homicides, drug addiction, alcoholism, and the rest. Thus, whether they want to or not, modernizing governments must intervene in the very subtle and elusive process of psychocultural change to smooth its adverse effects and to speed it up if they can.

Iran, Islam, Revolution: A Case Study in Religion and Politics

People caught up in the turmoil of rapid political, economic, and social change are frequently left bewildered and confused by the destruction of traditional standards of thought and behavior with which they are apt to be most comfortable. In their search for a belief system to which they can anchor themselves in the midst of change, they will, at times, support the revival of religious fundamentalism, a return to the old values that served them so well in the past. Such a development has been taking place in the Islamic world since the early 1970s, and it has been one of the most significant events in the Third World since the start of that turbulent decade.[16]

The Islamic revival has affected the peoples living in a broad band of the Third World, running all the way from Mauritania and Morocco on the northwest shoulder of Africa to Indonesia and the Philippines in the Western Pacific.[17] The revival has taken on many different forms. In ethnically strife-torn Mauritania, the universal adherence of the country to Islam is used by the government to override social schisms.[18] In Turkey, Islamic fundamentalism appears in revolutionary terrorist organizations and neo-Fascist political parties that challenge the secularism of Turkey's national development elite.[19] Turkey's Islamic resurgence was cited as one of the principal factors that drove a young Turk named Mehmet Ali Agca to attempt to assassinate Pope John Paul II in Rome in 1981.[20] In Libya and Saudi Arabia, the revival accompanies efforts by these two regional powers to support allies and friends throughout the Middle East, and, indeed, the world. Libya uses Islamic fundamentalism to advocate revolutionary insurgency; Saudi Arabia, much more conservative, uses its immense wealth to support less prosperous Islamic countries, primarily through heavy donations to the Islamic Development Bank. In the Philippines, the Moro National Liberation Front, representing the Muslims of the southern island of Mindanao, has revived a centuries-old struggle against the central government, fighting both for autonomy for Muslims and against the settlement of Christians in their territories. In Malaysia, the country's first privately owned television channel, which began broadcasting in 1984, has angered Moslem traditionalists with its Western-style programming of soap operas, variety shows, and Hong Kong–made motion pictures, and has led to a national debate about government censorship of the television station. And in Egypt in 1981, following government attempts to suppress both Moslem and Coptic Christian religious extremists, President Anwar Sadat was assassinated during a military parade by a group of Moslem revolutionary conspirators within the Egyptian army.

In the late 1980s and early 1990s, as journalist Charles Krauthammer points out, the most turbulent region of the world was what he termed "the new crescent of crisis," that broad swath of territory running from Kashmir province in northern India west to the Central Asian republics of the Soviet Union (Azerbaijan, Tadzhikistan) and to Kosovo province in Yugoslavia, and then south to Lebanon, the West Bank, and the Gaza Strip. "All of these conflicts," writes Krauthammer, "are rooted in the same grievance: A Moslem population is demanding sovereign control over a piece of territory in which it constitutes a local majority. The Moslems are fighting for (1) dominion over their province and (2) domination over the local non-Moslem minorities. In all but Lebanon (which long ago achieved sovereignty), they demand (3) separation from the non-Moslem country to which they are now joined and (4) independence or unification with the Moslem heartland." This "global intifada" (to use Krauthammer's term) is not centrally directed, but it does have a geographical unity: The conflicts are all taking place at the edges of the Moslem world, where Moslems meet the surrounding non-Moslems.[21]

Of all the instances of the political impact of Islamic fundamentalism, however, the most dramatic and the best known to Americans has been the Iranian revolution and its aftermath. At the beginning of 1978, the Shah of Iran had seemed at the height of his power. He was undisputed ruler of his country, a position he had held formally since 1941 when his father abdicated in his favor and one that he had exercised vigorously since the failure of a nationalist revolution in 1953. At that time, and with increasing fervor from the early 1960s on, the Shah had attempted to lead his country through the turbulence of a massive social, economic, and political revolution without adequately preparing for the disturbances that such a development would inevitably unleash. Especially after the increase in oil prices in 1973 produced a bonanza in foreign exchange, the Shah combined vigorous developments with the buildup of a major military force to make Iran the dominant power in the Persian Gulf. Nevertheless, although development proceeded at a rapid pace, the Shah became intolerant of competing ideas and suppressed dissent with an increasingly heavy hand. Political repression and corruption spread rampantly, and crass Western materialism sickened the once-devout Muslims of the country.

The opposition to the Shah emerged from many different sources. The deterioration of the country's agriculture coupled with the failure of land reform fifteen years earlier produced a peasantry displaced to the city, where they swelled the ranks of the unemployed and discontented. Real growth declined after 1976, but the conspicuous gap between the wealthy few and the numerous poor grew ever wider. The urban proletariat, denied the right to protest and strike, soon joined the peasants as the mass of desperate lower-class Iranians looked for an institution to which they could turn for help. That institution was the only familiar one remaining intact and vital: the mosque. The Iranian revolution took an Islamic form for several reasons. Islam stands for tradition and contrasts most sharply with the Western features of the Shah's rule. The clergy, called mullahs, provided solace and a haven for the distressed of the big cities. Their dislike and distrust of foreigners (especially Americans) made them a likely core around which to mount anti-Shah propaganda. And the mosques and the mullahs offered the one institution capable of organizing a network of people who could be forged into a base for national political action.

For Iran, Islam and the anti-Shah movement were embodied in the Ayatollah Ruhollah Khomeini. He was not the only religious critic of the Shah, but he became the most powerful. He emphasized traditional Islamic and Persian virtues. He was incorruptible in a land where corruption abounded. He refused to compromise with the Shah in contrast to many more moderate leaders. All of these characteristics caused the people to rally to him in large numbers after his move to exile in Paris (from Iraq) in October 1978.

The movement against the Shah grew to a violent crescendo during 1978. Rioting spread through most major cities during the first half of the year. Martial law was imposed in August, but to little effect. The final blow was the strike of oil-field workers late in the year, causing panic in the nation's economy. On January 6, 1979, the Shah appointed a moderate leader to head a new government and ten days later, on January 16, left Iran on what was termed a vacation. In February, Khomeini returned from exile, the Iranian army buckled under the pressure, and the Shah's last government resigned. The Ayatollah's choice for prime minister was installed shortly thereafter and was recognized by most governments of the world.

The Iranian revolution was bloody but still far from being consolidated through the early 1980s. During 1979, until a new constitution could be adopted, the country functioned under the control of Khomeini and a clergy-dominated Revolutionary Council. Shortly after the adoption of the constitution, in December 1979, the country began to function under a quasi-parliamentary system heavily dominated by Islamic leaders. The new constitution established Shi'ite Islam as the official state religion, placed supreme power in the hands of the Muslim clergy, and named the Ayatollah as the nation's religious and political leader for life. Both an elected president and a unicameral legislature were provided for in the constitution, but they were subordinate to the Ayatollah. A Council of Guardians of the Constitution (destined to replace the Revolutionary Council) was empowered to nullify laws they consider contrary to the Islamic faith.

Shortly after the new government began to function, Abolhassan Bani-Sadr, a moderate Western-trained economist, was elected president of Iran with more than 70 percent of the vote in a field of six other official candidates. His government lasted seventeen months. He was dismissed by the Ayatollah in June 1981, allegedly for counterrevolutionary acts and for having been a puppet of Western interests. Even before his dismissal, Bani-Sadr had been in hiding to avoid capture and execution. His dismissal removed the last obstacle to a complete takeover of the country by Islamic fundamentalists and clergy who are determined to reverse the trend of modernization begun under the Shah. There were more acts of violence in 1981. The country's second-ranked political figure, Ayatollah Sayed Mohammed Hosein Beheshti, was killed along with twenty-three others in a bombing in June. In July, gunmen assassinated a provincial governor, and twenty-seven opponents of the government were executed in retaliation. In August, the country's president and prime minister were killed in a bomb blast. During the first several months of 1982, there were an estimated five to ten terrorist incidents each day in Iran's capital city, Tehran.[22]

The costs of the Iranian revolution, like the costs of the Shah's development program, have been heavy in terms of human dignity. Religious fundamentalism in Iran proved to be as violent as its predecessor, and just as autocratic. As British journalist John Simpson reported, "No one is sure how many men and women were executed in the first years of the revolution; Amnesty International has learned of 2,444 executions in the second half of 1981 alone.[23] Whether it will prove to be a more effective force for mobilizing the talent and energy of the Iranian people is still an open question. In the late 1980s, Iran was a study in contradictions. While vigilante squads roamed the streets of Tehran enforcing the strict Islamic moral codes, such as requiring the veil for women and prohibiting the consumption of alcohol, the cor-

Iranian women wearing the traditional veil, the "chador," demonstrate their support for Iran's ruler, the Ayatollah Khomeini, and for Iran's return to Islamic fundamentalist values. In 1979, under pressure from three days of mass demonstrations against compulsory wearing of the veil, Iran's premier announced that just a veil for the head would be sufficient. Nevertheless, vigilante squads continued to roam the streets to enforce the strict Islamic dress codes for women.

ruption and black market trade connected with the war against Iraq had created a new class of wealthy in the capital. In all, however, as one foreign correspondent put it, "Iran's torrid affair with revolutionary Islam has settled down to a more or less sedate marriage. Much of the passion has gone, there is plenty of bickering, and some disillusion; but the regime is secure, and the country seems pretty stable."[24]

On June 3, 1989, the Ayatollah Khomeini died, leading to foreign speculation that Iran would deteriorate into internal assassination and terrorism. Instead, the struggle for power between extremist, hard-line factions favoring a continuation of the Islamic fundamentalist revolution and those groups advocating a more moderate and pragmatic path took place almost entirely within the confines of a relatively peaceful campaign to elect a new national president as the Ayatollah's successor. Although some ninety-one persons registered to be considered as candidates for the newly strengthened office of president, most were screened out as unsuitable by the Council of Guardians. In the end, only one candidate thought to have a serious chance of being elected survived the screening: Ali Akbar Hashemi Rafsanjani, the current speaker of the Iranian parliament and acting commander-in-chief of the armed forces. On election day, July 28, Rafsanjani received 95 percent of the more than 14 million votes cast. His election sent yet another message to the outside world that the Iranian Islamic fundamentalist revolution would continue to moderate in the face of the economic, social, and political damages done by a decade of unremitting revolutionary fervor and the country's devastating war with Iraq.

Psychocultural Modernization: Social Agents and Public Policies

The various agents of psychological modernization can be arranged across a wide spectrum according to the type of mental activity they are designed to alter. (See Figure 17.1.) At the far left of the spectrum are the mental activities located at the core of an individual's personality.

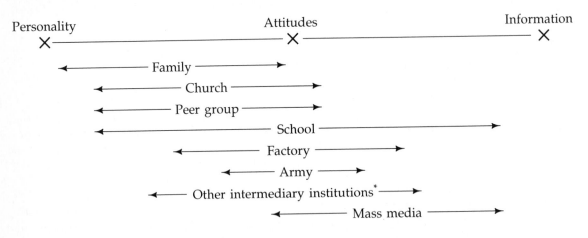

*Labor union, agricultural cooperative, neighborhood association.

Figure 17.1 Impact of various modernizing agents on three levels of mental activity (length of arrow indicates approximate range of impact of each agent).

In the center of the line fall the mental activities midway between the personality's core and its periphery, which we refer to as *attitudes*. At the far right of the scale are the mental activities that are most superficial, which we refer to as *cognitive*, that is, having to do with information.

Arrayed in similar fashion below the spectrum are the social institutions or agents of modernization that have special impact on certain specified areas of one's psychological functioning. The family, for example, being the first socializing agent encountered by the young child, has most of its impact on the core of mental activity, the personality. However, many family-taught lessons also pertain to attitudes, values, and preferences. Churches and peer groups, such as youth gangs or Scout troops, primarily affect attitudes, but they also have considerable impact on personality structures. The school probably affects a wider range of mental activities because it conveys information, influences attitudes and value choices, and also has some ability to transform personality structures. Several intermediary institutions, such as the factory, military service, labor unions, or agricultural cooperatives, are of obvious importance to the modernization process. Most of the work of these institutions is performed in the changing of attitudes, whereas relatively less of their activity has to do with the transmission of information. Finally, the mass communications media, such as radio, television, motion pictures, and newspapers, have a great deal of influence in the transmission of raw and distilled information, and they may alter individual attitudes although their ability to change deep-seated personality structures is relatively small unless they are supported by other institutional arrangements.

Public policies designed to shape and direct the modernization process must take into account the nature of the political culture in most Third World countries, the interplay between levels of mental activity, and the character of the social change agents.

Let us begin at the core of mental functioning. Traditional family practices, child-rearing practices, and peer-group pressures in Third World countries have been investigated in great detail by Western social scientists. The results of these investigations generally point to major problems for any government seeking to modernize its country's basic personality. In brief, the evidence is that traditional child-rearing practices and other early childhood socialization techniques found in the Third World do not prepare the youth to take an active and constructive role in modern politics. Although we cannot survey all of the many details of such widely varying techniques, let us focus on just a few typical characteristics to illustrate these conclusions. We divide our survey into three periods of early socialization: child rearing, social pressures of the extended family, and sex-role performance.

In many traditional cultures, such as those of Southeast Asia, child rearing typically begins with much permissiveness, indulgence, and affection. Young children are allowed virtual autonomy within their tiny universe; their every demand is granted; and all of their siblings and older relatives (aunts, uncles) take great pains to respond to the crying infant or toddler. Suddenly, however, without warning or preparation, the young child or adolescent is plunged into the world of the adult, both socially and sexually. There is much pressure placed on the child at this point to perform at very high standards, and there is severe punishment for failure. Child-rearing practices that have been indulgent and affectionate to this point now turn sullen and teasing; the child begins to lose the confidence that was his or hers as a two- or three-year old. This pattern of child rearing has been called the *betrayal syndrome* because of its

This rural elementary school in El Salvador must hold classes outside because of a lack of available building space. Literacy rates in Third World countries generally range between 50 and 75 percent. One important reason is the scarcity of school facilities in rural areas.

tendency to teach the small child that he or she cannot trust anyone in a position of authority, not even mother, and that the world is an unpredictable and malevolent place to be endured but not to be changed.[25]

Antimodern lessons continue to be learned through peer-group pressures in many Third World areas, as exemplified by the social forces of the Arab world. The Arab child is not a free agent in society, but is bound and constrained by numerous social commitments, duties, and obligations. Social groups take deep interest in the behavior of their members and judge this behavior. Many areas of social contacts must be consulted before acting, and many different individuals must be placated in the act. Social punishment is turned against nonconformist members of the group and takes the form of scolding, ridicule, face-to-face insults, shaming, and other forms of intimidation. The consequence of this form of social pressure is a basic personality that takes its cues for behavior from external sources instead of measuring its behavior against inner standards of excellence. Persons who grow up in this sort of environment frequently exhibit tradition-bound behavior patterns as adults, such as scapegoating, distrust of foreigners, belief in conspiracies, and the blaming of unseen forces for failure. Clearly these do not contribute to cultural modernization any more than did the more deeply rooted family child-rearing practices examined earlier.[26]

We conclude this brief inquiry into traditional early socialization practices by mentioning the pressure on sex-role performance under which young men grow to maturity in many Latin American countries. The drive to dominate others by proving one's masculinity is seen in many Latin American societies, including Mexico, Venezuela, and Argentina. This cultural phenomenon is labeled *machismo*, after the Spanish word *macho*, or male. From an early age, a young boy's father emphasizes his rapid sexual maturation, at times before the boy is physiologically or psychologically ready. This pressure leads many Latin American men to be aggressive in other social spheres, as well as to need to dominate others. A social order built on this kind of "lesson" will be one in which compromise and adjustment of interests will be seen not as moderation, but as weakness, and even as homosexuality.[27]

Although we have detailed several major ways in which traditional socialization practices leave antimodern residues in personality structures across the Third World, the fact is that most modernizing regimes in Latin America, Africa, and Asia simply cannot intervene directly into these intimate and very personal practices. Only in a few countries have governments sought to change the ways in which families shape the personality of their young; however, in most instances, these policies consist of removing children from the family environment before traditional lessons have been learned and placing them in state-run institutions, such as day-care facilities, nurseries, or kindergartens. In this way, radical governments, such as those in Cuba or China, have succeeded in breaking the grip of the family on future generations. But only the most revolutionary governments (those of the Second World) have been able to bring to bear enough political power and public will to throw off the influences of tradition as it is exemplified in antimodern child-rearing techniques. This is not to say that changes in child rearing will not occur through the natural workings of economic, educational, and social modernization. Peter C. Lloyd reports that elite families in West African countries, such as Nigeria, are already applying modern child-rearing techniques to bring their offspring into the modern world as positive, activist, change-oriented, achieving adults.[28] In several countries

of East Africa, including Kenya and Uganda, the large-scale migration of the family head from rural areas to cities in search of jobs is having a marked impact on youth socialization and child-training practices. By removing the head of the household for long stretches of time, the massive urbanization of Africa may have a lasting impact on the next generation by making the family less authoritarian and, thus, less tradition-bound.[29] But, significantly, these changes are occurring apart from government policy, not because of it. As far as public policy is concerned, family and peer-group socialization practices are beyond the reach of most Third World governments.

There are, nevertheless, many ways in which Third World governments can influence and shape the cultures of their people in hopes of making them more in tune with the demands of industrial life. Policies undertaken to "manipulate cultural factors for purposes of deflecting human habit in the direction of new and perhaps constructive endeavors" form the basis of what African political scientist Ali Mazrui calls "cultural engineering."[30] According to Mazrui, cultural engineering policies in Africa have been based on four fundamental principles: first, indigenizing what is foreign, or transforming European ideas and ways to make them conform to local customs and habits of thought; second, idealizing what is indigenous, or lauding the local ways of doing things; third, nationalizing what is sectional, or emphasizing the nation-state over the local tribe, village, or kinship group; and fourth, emphasizing what is African as a distinctive cultural tradition that transcends the new nation-states. Mazrui goes on to discuss a wide variety of policies aimed at reshaping the cultural traditions of Ugandans, Kenyans, and Tanzanians: emphasizing a single nationwide language; changing place names to recall pre-European heroes and events; revising history to stress the pre-European accomplishments of the people; encouraging artistic expression in pre-European art forms; controlling the behavior of the press to protect national unity; issuing "great documents" (proclamations, laws, etc.) that portray the proposed new society; designing political party systems and electoral mechanisms to transcend narrow ethnic or particularistic ties; encouraging the emergence of an entrepreneurial class through tax laws, stock ownership, and so forth; establishing a "national service" where all young adults can offer their services to their country on graduation from the university; encouraging the acquisition of material goods (and, thereby, increasing productivity) without encouraging luxury consumption; and many others.

One aspect of family life where Third World governments have attempted to make changes is in the role of women in society. Not all these changes have been enlightened, to be sure. In countries influenced by Islamic fundamentalism, public policies are directed at reducing the rights of women in the home, in social life, and in politics. In Pakistan, a 1984 law stipulates that in a trial two female witnesses are required to counter the evidence of one Moslem man. The law also provides that relatives of a murder victim will be compensated twice as much if the victim is a man than if it is a woman. The country's Islamic Ideology Council began in 1984 to discuss depriving women of the right to vote.[31] Other Third World governments have realized that they can gain control over their countries' high birthrates only by educating women and giving them more access to social and economic opportunities. For example, countries like Jamaica or Sri Lanka, which have succeeded in bringing their population growth rates down to less than 2 percent per year, also have well over half of the country's females enrolled in secondary school. In contrast, countries with growth rates of 4 percent or more will typically enroll only 10 to 15 percent of their females in secondary schools.[32]

We turn now to the intermediate socialization institutions: the school, the army, the factory, and other linkages, such as labor unions and agricultural cooperatives. In later chapters, we examine the role these intermediate institutions play in channeling population participation into the political arena and in providing much-needed information for policymakers concerning the effects of their decisions. In this section, however, we are most interested in the ways these institutions can be used to alter the basic personality of traditional groups.

Generally, modern institutions help modernize the people in them by means of the learning principle we discussed earlier, *exemplication*. Modern institutions of the sort we have just listed are organized, maintained, and operated according to a set of principles that are based, in turn, on a modern outlook on life. They are bureaucratic in nature, emphasizing the impersonal and predictable meeting of responsibilities. They are regular and routinized, again stressing the ability of people to predict the behavior of their superiors, subordinates, and peers. The emphasis on rules and on the fair application of these rules leads people to become more trustful of their environment and of impersonal, unknown others. Modern institutions are achievement-oriented, rewarding the people in them more for their performance of societally assigned roles than for some ascriptive characteristic, such as race or religion. In addition, many of these institutions, such as the armed forces, the factory, and the agricultural cooperative, offer to their members clear examples of people dominating nature. Members of these groups are taught to operate and maintain heavy equipment and machinery, to manipulate the natural world and to bend it to human needs, and to work productively with large amounts of energy and raw materials.

Completely traditional societies have few of these institutional arrangements within which people can learn to apply the rules of modernity to their daily lives. Thus, in many developing Third World countries, the first decisions regarding social change are frequently aimed at establishing or encouraging such institutions. Schools are usually first on the list, not only because of their impact on traditional modes of thought, but also because of their teaching of literacy to an illiterate populace.[33] In Turkey, after the modernizing revolution of Mustafa Kemal (Ataturk) in 1919, not only were local schools and universities made the recipients of rapidly increased investments, but certain important philosophical changes in education also were introduced. Village institutes were established to receive a select cadre of children who were removed from their family and village environment at the age of fourteen and sent to special boarding schools for future teachers. Religious instruction in schools was terminated, as was the teaching of Arabic and Persian, so the contacts that had linked the traditional Islamic groups with the nation's youth were severed. From 1923 to 1941, the number of students in Turkish elementary schools grew from about one-third of a million to nearly 1 million and college-level enrollment increased nearly fourfold.

The army is another intermediary institution that reform governments in the Third World have depended on, not only to educate large numbers of young recruits drawn from rural, traditional villages and low-income slums in big cities, but also to provide the officer corps its training in modernity, which frequently leads to the creation of new, forward-looking officers. In Ghana, under the late Kwame Nkrumah, the government sponsored the creation of the paramilitary Workers' Brigade, a uniformed organization that absorbed unemployed and ill-educated youths who had been cut loose from family and tribal ties and turned them into a loosely disciplined construction unit, used particularly in public-works building. In addition to serving its country and supplying symbolic evidence of the government's existence and activity, the Workers' Brigade also provided its members with rudimentary education, health care, social coordination, discipline, and a sense of responsibility.

A third kind of intermediary institution designed to aid in the psychological modernization of traditional peoples is the government-sponsored agricultural cooperative, as exemplified by the Comilla experiment in Bangladesh (formerly East Pakistan). In 1959 and 1960, the Pakistan Academy for Rural Development was launched in the Comilla District as an effort to eliminate rural backwardness in the region by means of a coordinated, comprehensive attack on many aspects of rural traditional agrarian society. Through the academy, villages and small farmers were first collected into cooperatives, which were linked together with each other and with the academy as the central coordinating force. The cooperatives were shown the benefits of mutual agreement in the joint solving of problems. The academy provided the cooperatives with substantial assistance in water development, operation and maintenance of tractors, marketing, and a number of important social services, such as midwife training and local elementary schools. But the key to the success of the Comilla experiment was the academy's insistence on mass participation in the project. Each cooperative decided jointly on the communal need for resources and jointly guaranteed each individual loan made to its members. Instead of simply being the recipient of technical help by a group of elite bureaucrats from the capital city, the Comilla cooperatives were genuine schools of modernity for their members.

If the agricultural cooperative has proven useful as a modernizing institution to help rural poor in the Third World, the housing cooperative has been shown to be equally effective in organizing and mobilizing the talent of the urban poor. In El Salvador in 1968, a small group of people organized by a local priest and a Peace Corps volunteer helped relocate about thirty families who were victims of flooding in the capital city, San Salvador. Only two years later, they had formed a low-cost housing cooperative as a nonprofit foundation with local business support, and by 1980 they had become a major producer of low-income, institutionally financed dwellings. The foundation emphasized low cost (each dwelling cost an average of $2,800 in 1982, including land), self-help (home buyers were taught how to do most of the construction work themselves), appropriate technology, close contact with the participating communities, community mutual help on new construction, and self-management of the projects by the people living in the community. Despite the upheavals suffered by El Salvador in the 1980s, the foundation continued its work, probably because its leaders saw it not just as a way to build houses, but also as a means of organizing and increasing the self-reliance of the urban poor.

The examples discussed are important reflections of public policy in Third World countries, where governments have tried to construct the intermediate institutions so badly needed to bring the mental structures of modernity to their still-traditional peoples. Although these examples are impressive, they are characteristic of only a minority of reform regimes. Governments throughout the Third World are discovering tremendous obstacles to the building of

institutional linkages between the modern and traditional sectors of their countries. Because this is a problem affecting mass popular participation in politics, we postpone until Chapter 18 any further discussion of the institutional aspects of political change.

The inability of nearly all governments to influence the formation of personality structures through family and peer socialization, and of most governments to shape attitudes through intermediary institutions, has led many regimes in the Third World to concentrate their efforts on the informational end of the spectrum: the creation and transmission of symbols, usually through the mass communications media.[34] The fact that the mass communication of patriotic and modern mobilizing symbols has little impact on the more deeply rooted mental structures of traditional people apparently matters only slightly, if at all, to Third World leaders. What these leaders seek is, first, to dominate the media of communication with the symbols of their regime and, frequently, of their person and, second, to prevent the mass media in their country from being used to criticize or dissent from government policies.

Many observers of politics in the Third World have commented on the tendency of leadership in these countries to be based on the personal appeal of a particularly charismatic figure, such as Juan Perón of Argentina, Gamal Abdel Nasser of Egypt, Sukarno of Indonesia, or Kwame Nkrumah of Ghana. In a country where the institutional forms of modern government are lacking or in disrepair, leaders such as these can offer to their people the symbol of action, of power, of the solutions to the many problems that assault them in their daily lives. No government in the world is fortunate enough to have tangible resources sufficient to distribute to each citizen to meet his or her needs; so, each government is thrown back onto its symbolic resources. That is, each government must distribute psychic benefits to those people who do not receive material benefits from a given policy decision. Where tangible or material resources are in especially short supply (as is the case in any poor country) and where loyalty to the national government is fading or non-existent, symbolic resources must fill the gap to buy time while the government tries to solve the countless material problems confronting it. This is the real meaning of symbolic or personalistic politics in the Third World.

Far more serious for anyone concerned about the state of civil liberties in the Third World today is the increasing use of press censorship by governments in developing countries to prevent criticism of their policies and decisions. (See Figure 17.2 and Table 17.2.) Reports reaching the West from various countries throughout the Third World indicate that the free press of these countries is under such an assault that it may not survive intact. A review of the state of freedom of reporting and of operations of the mass communications media in the Third World suggests that private news media enjoy substantial freedom to investigate and report the news in slightly more than two dozen countries.[35] And even in most of these countries, there is an official news agency and government control of at least one medium of communication to ensure that the government's position is reported to the people.

In another group of more than thirty-five countries, private news media do exist alongside the official, government-sponsored media. But the controls—both official and unofficial—placed on the private media are so strong that they constitute censorship. The style and degree of press censorship vary greatly within this group. In India, for example, news magazines and newspapers are required to submit all copy to government censors prior to publication. In

One of the most charismatic of contemporary Third World leaders. Libya's Colonel Muammar el-Qaddafi is shown acknowledging the enthusiastic response of a crowd of thousands in Lahore, Pakistan. Qaddafi was in Pakistan for the second Islamic summit, held in February 1974.

Mexico and Peru, government control over the source of scarce newsprint is sufficient to quiet potential criticism of government policies. In Tanzania, a 1968 law allows the president to ban any newspaper if he considers such action to be in the national interest. The constitution of Libya guarantees press freedom as long as it does not interfere with the principles of the Libyan revolution. In Turkey, a nominally free press censors itself through a press council court of honor, aided by official favoritism in the placement of advertising. At the extreme, in Uganda, under now-deposed President Idi Amin there was jailing and torture of journalists who insisted on reporting their criticism of the Ugandan government.

In more than thirty countries, all media are controlled by the state. In at least nineteen of these countries, there are no private communications sectors. All media of communication belong to the government.

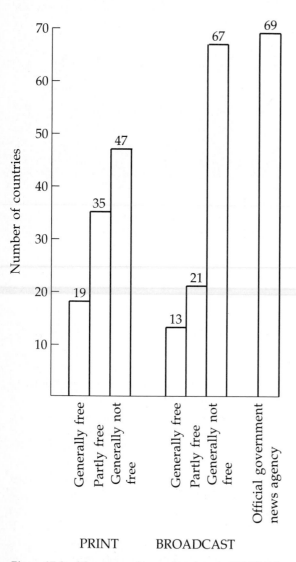

Number of countries

70 —
60 —
50 —
47
40 —
35
30 —
21
20 —
19
13
10 —

Generally free
Partly free
Generally not free

Generally free
Partly free
Generally not free

Official government news agency

67
69

PRINT   BROADCAST

Figure 17.2   Measures of press freedom in 101 Third World countries, 1985. [Leonard R. Sussman, "No Detente in International Communications," in Raymond D. Gastil, ed., *Freedom in the World: Political Rights and Civil Liberties*, 1985–1986 (Westport, Conn.: Greenwood Press, 1986), Table 9, pp. 100–103.]

In addition to controlling the news media in their own countries, many Third World governments are now seeking to restrict the news-reporting agencies in their countries to purely indigenous organizations and to exclude the Western-based international news agencies such as Reuters, United Press International, and the BBC. These Western agencies, say Third World leaders, are an embarrassment to developing countries because they print only the bad news about local conditions, never bringing out the good aspects of Third World politics. Furthermore, and probably a much more serious problem, some international news agencies have been reported to be fronts for the Central Intelligence Agency (CIA) and other organizations run by Western governments. For example, prior to the fall of the government of Marxist Salvador Allende, the CIA sent a number of foreign reporters to Chile to bring back unfavorable material on the Allende regime to affect the opinion of influential political and business leaders in the United States regarding the Allende government. Whether or not these plans to control foreign news agencies will come to fruition will depend greatly on the ability of Third World governments to develop their own international news agency to replace the Western-biased journalists. In view of their inability to develop such news agencies on a purely national basis, one is inclined to doubt the capacity of the Third World countries to mount a more sophisticated transnational effort in the foreseeable future.

Beyond policies designed to control the private news media, a few Third World governments are trying to stimulate the spread of mass communications into the traditional regions of their countries. In contrast with Communist regimes, such as that of Cuba, where television and radio are relied on heavily to exhort the public to be

Table 17.2   Indicators of Degree of Press Freedom in Eight Selected Third World Countries, 1987

Country	*Indicators of Degree of Press Freedom*
Nigeria	Newspapers publish relatively freely; however, in 1987 an outspoken weekly newspaper was banned for several months. The government maintains an official news agency and, since 1975, has controlled all radio and television broadcasting facilities.
Tanzania	The Newspaper Ordinance of 1968 empowers the president to ban any newspaper if he considers such action to be in the "national interest." The government has its own official news agency and owns and operates the two radio stations and the single television station in the country. Although there is no formal censorship, news contrary to government policy is not published.
India	Although Indian news media had been among the freest in Asia, they were subjected to rigid government censorship following the declaration of emergency in June 1975. Most emergency legislation was rescinded in April 1977, and press freedom guarantees were written into a constitutional amendment in 1978. The government supervises both radio and television broadcasting, but commercial television was introduced in 1976.
Indonesia	Newspapers have been tightly controlled by the government since 1974, and several were banned in 1978. In the spring of 1982, several major publications were suspended for failing to provide "responsible coverage" of the election campaign then under way. Several newspapers were banned in 1986 and 1987. All broadcasting is government controlled, and the government also operates the principal domestic news agency.
Mexico	The print media are privately owned but are operated under government regulation. The government does not censor newspapers but effectively controls what they write through its newsprint monopoly as well as through direct and indirect financial subsidies. Radio and television are privately owned and operate under government supervision.

(Table continues on p. 546.)

Table 17.2 (*Continued*)

Country	Indicators of Degree of Press Freedom
Brazil	Censorship of newspapers fluctuates according to the political climate, but the potential for government curbs on press freedom is very real. In 1977, for example, the government banned all political party statements on radio and television. Since 1978, censorship has been somewhat relaxed, although the country's leading opposition weekly was forced to cease publication in November 1981. Despite the government controls, Brazil's press has traditionally been vigorous and widely read. The government's National Telecommunications Department supervises and regulates television and radio broadcasting. The government announced the end of political control in March 1985. The 1988 constitution prohibits nearly all forms of media control.
Egypt	State supervision of the press was ended in 1978. Although the government still owns 51 percent of all newspapers and all television broadcasting stations, some criticism of government policy is allowed. There is some commercial radio service.
Iran	Twenty opposition newspapers were closed by government order in August 1979, and most of the remaining opposition publications were banned in 1981. In August 1981, the Iranian parliament approved a law making it a criminal offense to use "pen and speech" against the government. The government maintains its own news agency and has expelled a number of foreign journalists. Television and radio are all government owned.

(*Source*) Arthur S. Banks, ed., *Political Handbook of the World: 1987* (Binghamton, N.Y.: CSA Publications, 1987).

supportive of the government and of the revolution, Third World governments have in the past seemed little inclined to exploit the great symbolic potential of broadcasting and telecasting. In a handful of developing countries, however, this attitude is changing.

Mexico is one country where the government is doing something to reach rural areas through the mass media. High in the Sierra Madre mountains near Mexico's southern border with Guatemala, *Radio Indígena* (Indigenous Radio) broadcasts daily in five separate Indian languages, all offshoots of Maya, because virtually no one in the region speaks Spanish. The content of the broadcasts is decidedly practical, positive, and nationalistic. The bulk of the station's programming consists of helpful hints for the Indians, such as how to cure snake and tarantula bites and how to practice birth control. Bad news, especially about political affairs, is never mentioned, and the emphasis is always on the bright side of the government's accomplishments. Finally, the station's messages are always aimed at integrating the Indians more firmly into the Mexican nation; the folk tales and songs are usually geared to this objective. One technician at the station was quoted as saying, "We don't do sensitive or sensational news. We have government propaganda, good news, and useful information." No one knows how many people listen to *Radio Indígena*, but one indicator was seen in 1981 when the station reported that in a distant state capital a meeting would be held for people interested in regularizing the titles to their land. More than 20,000 men showed up at the meeting. Many had walked and traveled on buses for two days to get there.[36]

India is another Third World country where government leaders are waking up to the potential of television for getting their message out to the people. In 1980, only about 15 percent of India's people lived within viewing distance of a television transmitter. By dramatically increasing its expenditures on communications satellites and transmitting and relay stations, the government raised this figure to 30 percent by 1984, with a projection of 70 percent by 1985. Moreover, the government has purchased and installed community TV receivers for some 9,000 remote Indian villages, so even though the purchase of a personal TV set remains unthinkable for the vast majority of Indian families, they still can be reached by the Indian national network. If this ambitious program succeeds, India will constitute the largest potential television audience in the world.[37]

Conclusions: Cultural Modernization and Human Dignity

Human dignity begins in the minds of human beings. If a person is at peace with his or her surroundings and social order, outside observers should respect this peace. If a person believes that he or she enjoys a dignified existence, then we must accord that view our respect even though the person's outward appearance may contradict it.

It is important to avoid equating tradition with bad and modern with good. Many aspects of traditional life, such as the conservation of natural resources or the solidity of the family circle, are of great value and should be preserved. Likewise, there are some features of modern value structures that degrade human dignity, such as the social disintegration of big-city slums and the widespread destruction and waste of natural resources.

But this is a textbook about politics, and specifically about politics in the Third World. Regardless of what we may think of their decision, most reform-minded Third World political leaders believe that traditional modes of thought and behavior stand in their way, and they are determined to correct this problem. As far as we know, no society has ever set out on the journey to modernity and then subsequently decided to return to its traditional origins voluntarily; it is unlikely that any large group of individuals has ever done so either. In recognition of that fact, this textbook has adopted a working definition of human dignity that owes much to Western, modern ways of thinking.

In making this choice, we seek not to pass judgment on the wisdom of Third World leaders who have directed their societies toward modernity but, instead, to evaluate their methods of reaching that goal and to measure their success or failure. Given the nature of the goal (*i.e.*, modernity), certain aspects of traditional thought can certainly be regarded as obstacles or barriers. However, the costs of removing them will inevitably be high, and, because thinking is the most personal of all acts, each of us must decide whether the price is too high for the benefits to be derived.

Suggestions for Further Reading

Almond, Gabriel, and **Sidney Verba,** *The Civic Culture* (Princeton, N.J.: Princeton University Press, 1963).

Bryant, Coralie, and **Louise G. White,** *Managing Rural Development: Peasant Participation in Rural Development* (West Hartford, Conn.: Kumarian Press, 1980).

Coleman, James S., ed., *Education and Political Development* (Princeton, N.J.: Princeton University Press, 1965).

Doob, Leonard W., *Becoming More Civilized: A Psychological Explanation* (New Haven, Conn.: Yale University Press, 1960).

Enayat, Hamid, *Modern Islamic Political Thought* (Austin: University of Texas Press, 1982).

Esposito, John L., ed., *Islam and Development: Religion and Sociopolitical Change* (Syracuse: Syracuse University Press, 1980).

_____, ed., *Voices of Resurgent Islam* (New York: Oxford University Press, 1983).

Gurr, Ted Robert, *Why Men Rebel* (Princeton, N.J.: Princeton University Press, 1970).

Hagen, Everett E., *On the Theory of Social Change* (Homewood, Ill.: Dorsey Press, 1962).

Harrison, Lawrence, *Underdevelopment Is a State of Mind* (Lanham, Md.: University Press of America, 1985).

Hedebro, Göran, *Communication and Social Change in Developing Nations* (Ames: Iowa State University Press, 1982).

Inkeles, Alex, and **David H. Smith,** *Becoming Modern: Individual Change in Six Developing Countries* (Cambridge, Mass.: Harvard University Press, 1974).

Kahl, Joseph A., *The Measurement of Modernism: A Study of Values in Brazil and Mexico* (Austin: University of Texas Press, 1968).

Klass, Morton, *From Field to Factory: Community Structure and Industrialization in West Bengal* (Philadelphia: Institute for the Study of Human Issues, 1978).

Korten, David C., *Planned Change in a Traditional Society: Psychological Problems of Modernization in Ethiopia* (New York: Praeger, 1972).

Lauterbach, Albert T., *Psychological Challenges to Modernization* (Amsterdam, N.Y.: Elsevier, 1974).

Lerner, Daniel, *The Passing of Traditional Society* (Glencoe, Ill.: Free Press, 1958).

Lloyd, Peter C., *Classes, Crises and Coups: Themes in the Sociology of Developing Countries* (New York: Praeger, 1972).

McClelland, David, *The Achieving Society* (New York: The Free Press, 1967).

Mazrui, Ali A., *Cultural Engineering and Nation-Building in East Africa* (Evanston, Ill.: Northwestern University Press, 1972).

Moore, Wilbert E., *World Modernization: The Limits of Convergence* (New York: Elsevier, 1979).

Mortimer, Edward, *Faith and Power: The Politics of Islam* (New York: Random House, 1982).

Nash, Manning, *The Golden Road to Modernity: Village Life in Contemporary Burma* (Chicago: University of Chicago Press, 1965).

Ogionwo, William, *Innovative Behavior and Personal Attitudes: A Case Study of Social Change in Nigeria* (Cambridge, Mass.: Schenkman Publishing Company, 1978).

Pye, Lucian W., ed., *Asian Power and Politics: The Cultural Dimensions of Authority* (Cambridge, Mass.: Harvard University Press, 1985).

————, *Communications and Political Development* (Princeton, N.J.: Princeton University Press, 1963).

————, *Politics, Personality and Nation Building: Burma's Search for Identity* (New Haven, Conn.: Yale University Press, 1962).

————, and **Sidney Verba,** eds., *Political Culture and Political Development* (Princeton, N.J.: Princeton University Press, 1963).

Redfield, Robert, *A Village That Chose Progress: Cham Kom Revisited* (Chicago: University of Chicago Press, 1950).

Varma, Baidya Nath, *The Sociology and Politics of Development: A Theoretical Study* (London: Routledge & Kegan Paul, 1980).

Worsley, Peter, *The Three Worlds: Culture and World Development* (Chicago: University of Chicago Press, 1984).

Notes

1. Henri Aujac, "Cultures and Growth," in Mitchell A. Seligson, ed., *The Gap Between Rich and Poor: Contending Perspectives on the Political Economy of Development* (Boulder, Colo.: Westview, 1984), pp. 38–52.

2. Peter Worsley, *The Three Worlds: Culture and World Development* (Chicago: University of Chicago Press, 1984), esp. pp. 41–44.

3. This theme is the subject of Wilbert E. Moore's *World Modernization: The Limits of Convergence* (New York: Elsevier, 1979). See also Clark Kerr, *The Future of Industrial Societies: Convergence or Continuing Diversity?* (Cambridge, Mass.: Harvard University Press, 1983).

4. This analysis is based on the following works: Alex Inkeles and David H. Smith, *Becoming Modern: Individual Change in Six Developing Countries* (Cambridge, Mass.: Harvard University Press, 1974); Joseph A. Kahl, *The Measurement of Modernism: A Study of Values in Brazil and Mexico* (Austin: University of Texas Press, 1968); Daniel Lerner, *The Passing of Traditional Society* (Glencoe, Ill.: The Free Press, 1958); David McClelland, *The Achieving Society* (New York: The Free Press, 1967); Kenneth S. Sherrill, "The Attitudes of Modernity," *Comparative Politics* 1 (2) (1969), 184–210.

5. Erik Erikson, *Childhood and Society*, 2nd ed. (New York: Norton, 1963).

6. William Ogionwo, *Innovative Behavior and Personal Attitudes: A Case Study of Social Change in Nigeria* (Cambridge, Mass.: Schenkman Publishing Company, 1978).

7. Gabriel Almond and Sidney Verba, *The Civic Culture* (Princeton, N.J.: Princeton University Press, 1963).

8. The term *basic personality* means "that personality configuration which is shared by the bulk of the society's members as a result of the early experiences which they have in common," according to Ralph Linton in the introduction to Abram Kardiner et al., *The Psychological Frontiers of Society* (New York: Columbia University Press, 1945), p. viii.

9. Alvin Toffler, *Future Shock* (New York: Bantam, 1971).

10. Fred Weinstein and Gerald M. Platt, *Psychoanalytic Sociology* (Baltimore: Johns Hopkins University Press, 1973).

11. Ted Robert Gurr, *Why Men Rebel* (Princeton, N.J.: Princeton University Press, 1970).

12. Leon Festinger, *A Theory of Cognitive Dissonance* (Evanston, Ill.: Row, Peterson, 1957).

13. Stuart Auerbach, "Feudalistic Ways Persist in India, World's Largest Democracy," *Washington Post*, April 2, 1982; Nilova Roy, "Tradition Wars with Modernity in India," *Washington Post*, April 7, 1982; Jonathan Power, "Indian Villagers Slowly Accepting Women's Rights," *Washington Post*, February 13, 1984; William Claiborne, "Dowry Killings Show Social Stress in India," *Washington Post*, September 22, 1984, Elisabeth Bumiller, "The Wife and the Flame of Mystery," *Washington Post*, April 1, 1986.

14. I. R. Sinai, *The Challenge of Modernization* (New York: Norton, 1964), p. 64.

15. Julia Preston, "Voodoo Adherents Attacked in Haiti," *Washington Post*, May 17, 1986.

16. John L. Esposito, ed., *Voices of Resurgent Islam* (New York: Oxford University Press, 1983); Edward Mortimer, *Faith and Power: The Politics of Islam* (New York: Random House, 1982).

17. Daniel Pipes, " 'This World Is Political!' The Islamic Revival of the Seventies," in Steven L. Spiegel, ed., *At Issue: Politics in the World Arena*, 3rd ed. (New York: St. Martin's Press, 1981),

pp. 80–111.

18. See two articles by Leon Dash in the *Washington Post*: "Torn between Past, Present, Mauritania Lurches from Crisis to Crisis," May 24, 1981; "Tensions Mount in Mauritania's Delicately Balanced Caste System," May 31, 1981.

19. Kevin Klose, "Turkey, Searching for Modernity, Offers Fertile Field for Terrorism," *Washington Post*, May 25, 1981.

20. David Barchard, "Brother of Accused Turk Cites Islam, Fame as Motives in Shooting," *Washington Post*, May 16, 1981.

21. Charles Krauthammer, "The New Crescent of Crisis: Global Intifada," *Washington Post*, February 16, 1990.

22. Jonathan C. Randal, "Daily Ration of Violence Mars Life of Tehran Populace," *Washington Post*, April 19, 1982.

23. John Simpson, "Along the Streets of Tehran," *Harper's* 276, no. 1652 (January 1988), pp. 36–45.

24. *The Economist*, August 25, 1984; See also Adeed Dawisha, "The Iranian Revolution: The Thrill Is Gone," *Washington Post*, November 23, 1986.

25. Lucian W. Pye, *Politics, Personality and Nation Building: Burma's Search for Identity* (New Haven, Conn.: Yale University Press, 1968).

26. Sania Hamady, *Temperament and Character of the Arabs* (New York: Twayne, 1960).

27. Carl E. Batt, "Mexican Character: An Adlerian Interpretation," *Journal of Individual Psychology* 25 (2) (1969); 183–201.

28. Peter C. Lloyd, *Africa in Social Change*, rev. ed. (Baltimore: Penguin, 1975), pp. 181–190.

29. Ali A. Mazrui, *Cultural Engineering and Nation-Building in East Africa* (Evanston, Ill.: Northwestern University Press, 1972), especially Ch. 13.

30. Mazrui, ibid., p. xv.

31. *The Economist*, August 4, 1984.

32. World Bank, *World Development Report: 1984* (New

York: Oxford University Press, 1984), Ch. 6, and pp. 198–199, 254–255.

33. James S. Coleman, ed., *Education and Political Development* (Princeton, N.J.: Princeton University Press, 1965).

34. Lucian W. Pye, ed., *Communications and Political Development* (Princeton, N.J.: Princeton University Press, 1963).

35. Arthur S. Banks, ed., *Political Handbook of the World: 1987*. Binghamton, N.Y.: CSA Publications, 1987).

36. Marlise Simons, "Radio Brings the World to Mexican Indians," *Washington Post*, June 20, 1981.

37. William Claiborne, "Television, Controversy Flicker into India's Remote Villages," *Washington Post*, July 3, 1984.

POLITICAL PARTICIPATION IN THE THIRD WORLD

Proponents of liberal democracy customarily assume that there is a direct and causal relationship between mass participation in politics and levels of human dignity. In other words, public policies designed to raise the level of human dignity in a society are the product of an increase in mass participation in the political process, primarily through voting in elections and exposure to mass communications.

In this chapter, we examine this idea as it is applied to politics in the Third World. We are interested specifically in uncovering the connections between mass participation in politics and public policies in Third World countries. If an increase in mass political participation has not brought about an increase in the level of human dignity in many developing countries, the fundamental theoretical cornerstone of liberal democracy would certainly be of dubious validity in typical Third World settings. Furthermore, if we discover this to be the case, we must ask why the link between mass participation and human dignity seems to have been broken, at least in the case of many Third World polities. Let us consider, then, how in the Third

World individual citizens who are not political professionals relate to the government and how those relationships affect public policies.

Dimensions of Political Participation

The words *political participation* mean many different things to different people, depending on the political culture in which they live. We use the meaning developed by political scientists Samuel P. Huntington and Joan M. Nelson: "activity by private citizens designed to influence governmental decision-making."[1] Political participation has to do specifically with overt, observable behavior or activity. In Chapter 17, we considered the more elusive inner states of political actors—the attitudes of tradition and modernity. In this chapter, we move one step closer to the actual performance of political systems by examining the actions taken by citizens to influence their government's decisions. We are concerned with the behavior of private citizens, the individuals who do not make politics a profession but who engage in political behavior as an avocation or only intermittently. We examine only the activities intended to influence or alter some action or decision forthcoming from a government agency. Many events have political ramifications, even if they are unintended. These may range from a natural disaster, such as an earthquake, to an act designed to influence some other area of human society (a strike or boycott, for example) but that spills over into the political sphere unintentionally. We limit our inquiry to the activities expressly intended by the actor to influence government policy. The definition includes all forms of activity intended to alter public policy, including violent and nonviolent behavior and legal and illegal action.

Finally, we discuss both autonomous and mobilized behavior in the political arena. This distinction may have relatively little significance for Americans, but it is of major importance for citizens of the Third World. In brief, the distinction is this: Political participation is *autonomous* when the actor intends his or her behavior to influence government decisions; it is *mobilized* when the action is intended by someone other than the actor to influence policy. In many traditional settings in the Third World, individual citizens engage in politically relevant behavior (such as voting or attending rallies) not because they believe their actions will influence government policy, but because some influential or powerful figure in their community (such as a village chief or a union boss) has instructed or encouraged them to undertake such activities. When we reach our discussion of the patron–client system in Third World politics, we refer extensively to the idea of mobilized political participation.

Many observers of traditional politics believe that we should not include mobilized partici-

pation in our study because it is not really participation inspired by an individual citizen's belief in his or her own efficacy. We believe, however, that a complete understanding of politics in the Third World cannot be gained without including this kind of participation. Mobilized participation may become or lead to autonomous action, either because the participants learn to incorporate it into their repertoire of political behavior, or because what starts out as mobilized participation from the vantage point of the actor ends up being regarded as autonomous by the policymakers who are on the receiving end of the participants' messages. Many Third World governments actively reach out to mobilize their own citizens through mass mobilization parties or other institutional linkages. These official mobilization efforts arise from a government's desire to show to potential opponents the popular support it enjoys, either generally or for a particular policy or decision. Because this aspect of politics is so profoundly important in the transitional societies of the Third World, we cannot ignore such behavior or its implications.

We have so far been using the term *political participation* as if it were a phrase that stood for or represented only one kind of behavior. Actually, the concept of political participation covers a variety of behavioral patterns that encompass (1) electoral activity, including voting, working in campaigns, seeking to persuade others to vote for a given candidate or party, or otherwise trying to alter the outcome of an election; (2) lobbying, which means contacting government officials to influence their attitudes and behavior on issues that affect significant numbers of people; (3) organizational activity other than lobbying that is designed to influence the general climate within which policymaking takes place (such as efforts to influence public opinion on a given issue); (4) individual contacting of public officials to express grievances on a matter relating to a single inidividual; and (5) violence, meaning efforts to influence government decisions by doing physical damage to persons or property.

Even though most studies of political participation focus on voting behavior and other forms of electoral activity, we must understand that the other categories are widely used throughout all political systems. However, in any given political system, the precise mixture of forms of participation may vary considerably. A government that has outlawed elections and parties obviously is not encouraging much electoral activity. That simply means that we must look deeper to discover the ways its citizens are expressing their demands, their needs, and their opinions to the government.

Elections in Third World Politics

We begin our survey of political participation in the Third World with a look at electoral behavior. At least at the level of rhetoric, most Third World governments have committed themselves to the principle of popular sovereignty as expressed through universal suffrage, mass voting, regular elections, free competition, and honest counting of the ballots. In many Third World countries, mass voting is not only encouraged but coerced. Nevertheless, levels of voting vary quite widely. (See Table 18.1.) Although voting levels tend to be quite high in the Second World states and somewhat less so in the Western democracies, these levels fluctuate greatly in the Third World. As a general rule, however, about one-third to one-half of all citizens register to vote in the Third World and about 75 to 90 percent of those registered

actually turn out. However, in a number of countries (including Tanzania and Egypt), where the president is elected by indirect ballot or plebiscite, the number of persons who actually vote is apt to be misleading.

It is difficult to assess voting turnout in the Third World because of a scarcity of precise and comparable data. Nevertheless, we can offer some tentative and cautious comparisons based on available figures. For the 1960s, we have data on voting in twenty-one Third World countries, where the average turnout was 64.5 percent. By the 1970s, the number of countries holding elections for which results are available had more than doubled, to fifty; but the average turnout had declined to 61.9 percent, despite the fact that five Third World states claimed that 100 percent of their countries' adults had voted. (In the United States, 56.8 percent voted in 1964; 54 percent in 1976.)[2] Finally, in the 1981–1982 period, thirty-two Third World states held elections. In the eighteen cases for which data are available, an average of 70.4 percent turned out.[3]

Elections in many Third World countries have been notorious for the way in which the dominant political forces have suppressed opposition parties, coerced illiterate peasants and city workers into voting for the approved candidates, used "goon squads" to harrass political rallies and to disrupt campaign headquarters, and miscounted ballots or conveniently lost entire ballot boxes in hostile precincts. The list of violations of honest election principles could continue at length. Although few outside observers are in a position to attest to this, national elections in many Third World countries fall far short of offering the voter an honest choice between two or more candidates who have an unfettered opportunity to campaign freely, to see that the ballots are counted, and to take power if victorious. On more than one occasion,

Table 18.1   The Role of Elections in Eight Selected Third World Countries

Country	Indicators of Voting Turnout
Nigeria	In 1964, 28 percent of eligible voters voted; in 1974, 34 percent; in 1983, 39 percent. Elections frequently marred by charges of fraud, violence. The 1983 election nullified by military coup four months later. First elections since 1983 coup were held in December 1987 to choose members of local councils. There were 13,000 candidates for 301 councils, and the government issued 72 million voting cards for a population estimated between 97 and 105 million. (There has been no census since 1963.) Parties are still prohibited. National elections scheduled for 1992.
Tanzania	In 1975, there were 5 million registered voters out of a population of 16 million. Presidential elections take the form of a plebiscite held every five years, where voters vote "yes" or "no" for another term for the incumbent (Julius Nyerere since 1962). In 1975, 67.5 percent of eligible voters took part in plebiscite. Parliamentary and local elections offer voters choices among candidates drawn from the CCM party. Most recent elections were held in October 1985 for both the presidency and parliamentary seats.
India	Registered voters rose from 48 percent of the population in 1971 (271 million out of 560 million) to nearly 55 percent in 1977. Voter turnout as percentage of adults rose from 56 percent in 1967 to 67 percent in 1977. In December 1984, Indians elected Rajiv Gandhi to succeed his assassinated mother, Indira, as prime minister in the largest democratic election ever held in the world up to that time. Some 230 million Indian voters went to the polls; Gandhi's party, the Congress (I), won more than 50 percent of the vote and 394 out of 509 parliamentary seats being contested. A number of important state elections were held in 1985 and 1987. In November 1989, more than 275 million Indians voted for Parliament; the Congress (I) Party won only 191 seats, and Gandhi was turned out of office.
Indonesia	In 1971, 48 percent of the population registered (58 million out of 120 million), and 94 percent of the registered voted. In 1977, the government claimed 100 percent of the population aged twenty years or older turned out. In 1982, estimated 74.3 million voted out of total population of 152.6 million (about 49 percent). In April 1987, the ruling Golkar Party won 73 percent of the vote, with 91 percent of the adult population voting. The party won 299 of the 400 parliamentary seats being contested; the army appoints 100 additional seats in the Parliament.
Mexico	Voting turnout was 49.8 percent in 1967, 62.6 percent in 1977, and about 70 percent in 1982. State elections in 1985 were marred by charges of vote fraud, violence, and intimidation. National elections held in 1988 again resulted in a victory for the PRI, but by the narrowest margin in the party's fifty-nine-year history. Turnout exceeded 70 percent.

(Table continues on p. 556.)

Table 18.1 (*Continued*)

Country	Indicators of Voting Turnout
Brazil	Registered voters estimated 30 to 35 percent of the population in 1978, about 46 percent in 1982. President not elected by direct popular vote between 1962 and 1985. Turnout in state, local elections estimated at 44 percent in 1966, 56 percent in 1974, and 43 percent in 1982. In 1985, first civilian president in twenty-one years elected by special electoral college; Congress approves direct elections of president. In 1987, constitutional assembly votes to limit presidential term to four years. Direct presidential elections were held in November 1989, with more than 80 million persons casting ballots.
Egypt	In 1984 parliamentary elections, 12.3 million voters registered (about one-fourth of the total population), and 43 percent of the registered (5.1 million) cast valid ballots. Voting for president is indirect. Parliamentary elections held in 1987 with very low turnout, in some districts below 20 percent. Later in year, Parliament nominates President Mubarak for a second six-year term; he is reelected without opposition.
Iran	In 1981, about 70 percent of adults participated in presidential elections. Presidential elections held in 1985; incumbent wins easily over four other opponents; twenty-four other opposition candidates denied right to compete for the office. Presidential elections held in 1989 after Ayatollah Khomeini's death; 14 million voters participated.

(*Source*) For Nigeria: "Nigerian Election Recriminations Revive Sensitivities of Civil War," *Washington Post*, December 28, 1980; John de St. Jorre, "Nigerian President Sees Vote as 'Encouragement' to Other African States," *Washington Post*, August 12, 1983; *The Economist*, December 19, 1987. For Tanzania: George Thomas Kurian, *Encyclopedia of the Third World* (New York: Facts on File, 1978), vol. 2, pp. 1379, 1383; Louis A. Picard, personal correspondence; Charles Taylor and David Jodice, eds., *World Handbook of Political and Social Indicators*, vol. 1: *Cross-National Attributes and Rates of Change* (New Haven, Conn.: Yale University Press, 1983), Table 2.6, p. 77. Raymond D. Gastil, ed., *Freedom in the World: Political Rights and Civil Liberties, 1985–1986* (Westport, Conn.: Greenwood Press, 1986), Table 7, p. 76. For India: Kurian, *Encyclopedia*, vol. 1, p. 635; Kurian, *The Book of World Rankings* (New York: Facts on File, 1979), Table 37, p. 52; Taylor and Jodice, eds., *World Handbook*, vol. 1, Table 2.6, p. 77; William Claiborne, "Indians Vote a Landslide for Gandhi," *Washington Post*, December 29, 1984. For Indonesia: Kurian, *Encyclopedia*, vol. 1, p. 662; Taylor and Jodice, eds., *World Handbook*, vol. 1, Table 2.6, p. 76; "Suharto's Party Wins Mandate in Indonesia," *Washington Post*, May 7, 1982; *The Economist*, May 2, 1987. For Mexico: Taylor and Jodice, eds., *World Handbook*, vol. 1, Table, 2.6, p. 77; Gastil, ed., *Freedom* (Westport, Conn.: Greenwood Press, 1982), Table 6, p. 28; *The Economist*, September 5, 1987. For Brazil: Kurian, *World Rankings*, Table 37, p. 52; Kurian, *Encyclopedia*, vol. 1, p. 188; Taylor and Jodice, eds., *World Handbook*, vol. 1, Table 2.6, p. 77; Jackson Diehl, "Brazil Vote Gives Military Limited Backing," *Washington Post*, November 21, 1982; *The Economist*, April 25, 1987. For Egypt: David Ottaway, "Ruling Party Crushes Opposition in Egyptian Election," *Washington Post*, May 30, 1984; *The Economist*, April 11, 1987; Jane Friedman, "Egypt Votes on New Term for Mubarak," *Washington Post*, October 5, 1987. For Iran: Gastil, ed., *Freedom* (1982), Table 6, p. 27; Arthur S. Banks, ed., *Political Handbook of the World: 1987* (Binghamton, N.Y.: CSA Publications, 1987).

in fact, the army has stepped in to nullify elections after the vote showed an unacceptable candidate on the verge of winning (as in Peru in 1962) or to declare certain political groups or parties to be illegal and therefore not entitled to present candidates (as in Argentina several times during the 1970s).

Electoral competitiveness and honesty are distributed unevenly across the Third World. According to the *World Handbook of Political and Social Indicators*, during the mid-1960s, 26 percent of Third World states held competitive and reasonably free elections; about 35 percent had elections that deviated significantly from the competitive and free norm; nearly 17 percent held elections that were markedly uncompetitive and in which there was widespread fraud; 5 percent held no elections at all; and 15 percent could not be judged for lack of data.[4]

According to the *Freedom in the World* report for 1982, voters went to the polls in thirty-two Third World countries in 1981–1982. The elections met the conventional tests of democracy (open campaign, general adult suffrage, honest vote counting, no intimidation or violence) in only five countries (Colombia, Costa Rica, Dominican Republic, Honduras, and Trinidad and Tobago). In seven cases, only a single candidate, party, or slate of electors was permitted. In three countries, the results of the election were annulled by a military overthrow of the government. In three cases, elections were more or less open, but accompanied by severe violence. In twelve countries, the competition was severely restricted in some way, such as by jailing opposition candidates, counting votes dishonestly, excluding certain parties, or limiting the right to vote to certain groups. In one case, the balloting consisted of open (not secret) voting in a referendum, and in one case the openness of the election was not clear. In other words, in the early 1980s only about one election in

six in the Third World was held under democratic conditions.[5]

During the middle years of the decade of the 1980s, however, democracy began to be restored in a number of important Third World countries, and elections openly conducted and scrupulously respected increasingly were the route to national power. According to the *Political Handbook of the World* for 1987, elections of one sort or another were held in 58 of 102 Third World states between 1983 and 1987.[6] (The forty-four countries that did not celebrate elections during this four-year period included military dictatorships such as Chile and monarchies such as Saudi Arabia, as well as democracies such as Venezuela, whose political calendar simply did not call for elections during the period considered.) Of the fifty-eight elections recorded, thirty-one would be considered as not competitive, primarily because of the absence of opposition candidates or because the chief executive was named by some secondary body, such as a council of electors or a national assembly, whose members had been chosen in a nondemocratic manner. Twelve of the fifty-eight contests could be defined as partially competitive. Some opposition was permitted, but the field was not open to all who wished to compete; there was some press coverage, but it was subjected to censorship; and so forth. In fifteen countries, then, or barely one-fourth of those holding elections, the contests were open and fully competitive.

Latin America was the Third World region where fully competitive elections reappeared in greatest numbers. Of the fifteen contests described above as fully competitive, twelve took place in Latin America. In December 1983, Raúl Alfonsin began a six-year term as Argentina's president, ending seven years of military rule. In May 1984, José Napoleon Duarte became El Salvador's first constitutionally elected president in more than fifty years. In November 1984, Uruguay held national elections to end eleven years of military rule. In January 1985, Tancredo Neves was elected by a special electoral college as Brazil's first civilian president after twenty-one years of of military rule. Neves died before he could assume office, and his place was taken by Vice President José Sarney. In 1986 Brazilians elected a constituent assembly to write a new constitution to replace the one imposed after the 1964 military coup, and in 1987 that assembly voted to include direct presidential elections in the constitution. In July 1985, Alan García became Peru's first elected president to take power from another elected president in forty years. In August 1985, Victor Paz Estenssoro was sworn in as Bolivia's president, the first time in more than twenty years that power had been passed from one constitutionally elected government to another. And in January 1986, in Guatemala Vinicio Cerezo was inaugurated as the country's first civilian president in eighteen years, and in Honduras José Azcona was sworn in, marking the first time in more than fifty years that one elected civilian succeeded another as chief executive of that country. In 1989, elections were held in ten Latin American or Caribbean countries. In eight of these, the voting was carried out in a relatively calm, free, and open atmosphere with more or less free competition among multiple candidates and honest tabulation of the results. In several instances (Argentina, Bolivia, Honduras, and Uruguay) power was passed from one democratically elected leader to another under conditions of economic and political instability; in several others (Brazil, Chile, and Paraguay) the election marked the end of a military dictatorship and the beginning of constitutional government. Unfortunately in two cases (El Salvador and Panama) the elections were marred, in the first case by insurgent and counterinsurgent vio-

lence, in the second by voting irregularities that led eventually to the nullification of the outcome by military strongman Manuel Noriega. In 1990, six more Latin American or Caribbean countries were scheduled to hold national elections: Colombia, Costa Rica, the Dominican Republic, Guatemala, Nicaragua, and Peru.

There were other promising signs of the restoration of democracy in important Third World countries in the 1980s. India, the world's most populous democracy, survived the assassination of its president, terrorist sectarian violence, and grinding poverty to hold national elections in 1984 and 1989 and critical state elections in 1985 and 1987. In Turkey, elections in November 1987 returned Prime Minister Turgut Ozal to office for a five-year term in the first civilian-run contest since the 1980 military coup. In December 1987, in South Korea Roh Tae Woo was elected president with 36 percent of the popular vote and became the first directly elected president in the history of the country. In addition to India, other significant elections were held in the Third World in 1989, including Sri Lanka (where voting went on in the midst of a bloody ethnic insurgency), Namibia (where the elections paved the way for the drafting of the country's first constitution), South Africa (where elections brought to power the white government that eventually freed Nelson Mandela and launched the country's transition to racial tolerance and political democracy), and Taiwan (where the ruling Koumintang Party allowed organized opposition for the first time since establishing its rule on Formosa in the aftermath of the Chinese Civil War).But perhaps the most dramatic sign of the return of electoral competition to the Third World was the coming to power of Corazon Aquino in the Philippines in 1986.

Even if elections were conducted in a spotlessly clean and scrupulous manner, however, we would still be concerned about the way in which the average citizen of the Third World views his or her role in elections or the electoral process. No matter how meaningful the elections might be, if they do not convey to the typical villager, peasant, or worker of the developing world a sense of efficacy, elections do not effectively serve the purpose of mobilizing traditional folk into a modern political process.

In his book on village life in Burma, Manning Nash describes the meaning of the electoral process for one set of Burmese villagers.[7] The process began, Nash observed, with a visit by the village headman and the local patron, the village's richest man, to the national capital for a talk with the organizers of the Union Party. Upon their return to the village, the word was passed around the village that the patron, U Sein Ko, had decided to join the Union Party, and others from the village were expected to do likewise. The book to enroll new members was kept in U Sein Ko's house. Aspiring members passed by the house for a ceremonial visit and cup of tea; this was followed by enrollment in the party. There were no campaign activities, no mass-enrollment effort, and only one mass meeting (attended by about forty men of the village) at which U Sein Ko's son was chosen to head the local party organization. On election day, U Sein Ko's prestige and power as the local patron were sufficiently strong to mobilize 90 percent of the villagers to vote for the Union Party candidate. They voted not out of a conviction that they were influencing policy, but out of a complex set of traditional Burmese cultural mores: that society was organized around a local man of power, that followers joined this powerful figure to enjoy his protection from outside forces, and that voting for the Union Party candidate entitled the villagers to receive U Sein Ko's protection from government policies. Thus, we can see that voting plays a very special role in the lives of Burmese villagers, a role that may have little or nothing to do with the policy process or with politics generally.

The Philippines: A Case Study in Third World Elections

Recent Philippines presidential elections offer us an important example of the role of elections in Third World politics. In 1972, President Ferdinand Marcos—serving the third year of his second four-year term—imposed martial law on his country in a move some said was intended to keep himself in office. (The constitution of the Philippines, at that time, limited the president to two four-year terms, as is the case in the United States.) On January 17, 1981, eight years later, Marcos lifted the martial-law edict and initiated the process of changing the country's constitution to permit his reelection. The changed constitution was approved by the electorate in a referendum on April 7, which opponents labeled as a fraud. The amended constitution allowed a president a succession of six-year terms for as many times as he wanted and the people approved. Unsurprisingly, Marcos presented himself as a candidate for another term under the new constitution. Against him were presented two token candidates, one of whom ran on a platform favoring American statehood for the Philippines. Opposition groups again charged Marcos with fraud and attempted to organize a boycott of the elections. Election day, June 16, 1981, was marked with some violence (thirteen persons were reported killed in clashes with government troops), and arrests of forty-five boycott leaders. The government asserted that 85 percent of Philippine voters had cast ballots; opposition groups argued that the number was less than

60 percent. Marcos won overwhelmingly, with 86 percent of the vote.[8]

After 1981, despite Marcos's efforts to consolidate both his own status and the growing power of his wife, Imelda, opposition to his rule continued to grow. In August 1983, the assassination of popular opposition leader Benigno Aquino at the Manila airport upon his return from exile led to massive unrest throughout the country. In December, the country's leading business executives offered to pay to have the official voting registration lists brought up to date and purged of so-called ghost voters in an attempt to restore confidence in the electoral process. In May 1984, despite widespread vote fraud and violence (an estimated 122 killed in election-related attacks), the anti-Marcos opposition coalition and independent candidates combined to win more than 70 of the contested 183 seats in the Philippines legislature, the National Assembly. Even the president was prompted to note what he termed "an undercurrent of dissent" that a highly manipulated electoral process could not conceal.[9]

In 1985, despite growing unrest and opposition to his rule, Marcos seemed determined to carry on in power. In January, Armed Forces Chief General Fabian Ver was named by an inquiry commission as one of two dozen conspirators in the plot to assassinate Aquino. Although General Ver was subsequently acquitted of the charges, public opinion ran high against the implied role of President Marcos in the killing. In November, Marcos bowed to pressure from the United States and agreed to hold new elections. Aquino's widow, Corazon, promptly declared herself in the race.

The elections were held in February 1986 under close scrutiny of the world's press corps as well as representatives of the U.S. Congress. Although the Philippines National Assembly declared Marcos the winner, Aquino appeared to be the winner in an independent count of the votes, and she called for a campaign of strikes and boycotts to protest the outcome. President Ronald Reagan publicly blamed Marcos for the fraud and violence connected with the election and sent envoy Philip Habib to meet with both Marcos and Aquino. After the U.S. Senate voted overwhelmingly to condemn Marcos' election as a fraud and a House of Representatives subcommittee voted to cut off aid to the Philippines, elements of the Filipino armed forces, led by the country's defense minister and acting chief of staff, seized the nation's military headquarters and demanded Marcos's resignation. On February 26, Marcos and an entourage of family and followers flew into exile aboard a U.S. Air Force hospital aircraft to Guam and then to Hawaii.

Elections were to continue to play a major role in the restoration of democracy in the Philippines. In February 1987, nine out of ten eligible Filipino voters turned out to approve (by about an 80 percent margin) a new constitution that, among other things, confirmed Mrs. Aquino as president until 1992. In May 1987, a 90 percent turnout again reflected mass support for the election of a new National Assembly, the first freely elected since 1971. About two-thirds of the 200 members of the House of Representatives were supporters of Mrs. Aquino. When this new Assembly met for the first time in July, Mrs. Aquino formally gave up her right to rule by decree. Finally, in January 1988, about 80 percent of the registered voters turned out to elect more than 16,000 local government officials, the first such open local elections in nearly two decades. Although Mrs. Aquino continued to face formidable problems in her country, the remarkable transformation of the Philippines from an autocratic dictatorship to a reasonably open and competitive democracy would provide her with a base of power from which to begin

In November 1984 following the assassination of Indian Prime Minister Indira Gandhi by her Sikh body guards, furious Hindus rioted in their rage against India's Sikh population. In most of the country's largest cities, Hindu mobs burned Sikh homes and businesses and lynched Sikh bystanders. An estimated 200 Sikhs died in the riots.

autonomy. As of 1990, these conflicts are still unresolved.

The war in Angola, which began in 1975, was complicated enormously by foreign intervention of both global powers and regional neighbors. Fighting against the Angolan government was a guerrilla army known as UNITA, with the support of the South African army and government. The South Africans intervened because Angola harbored an insurgent organization, known as SWAPO, which operated across the border in Namibia, which SWAPO claimed it wanted to free from South African rule. To counter the South African and UNITA attacks, the Angolan government relied on aid from the Soviet Union and the presence of a reported 20,000 Cuban troops. As of the end of 1987, an estimated 213,000 persons had died as a result of this war, some 200,000 of them civilian. In 1989, all foreign troops were withdrawn as part of the deal that led to the independence of Namibia.

In Central America, Great Power intervention has also aggravated what began as a series of internal insurgencies. In 1978, a long guerrilla war against the Nicaraguan dictator, General Anastasio Somoza, exploded into a major civil war and the general's flight into exile. He was replaced by the radical Sandinista government, which attracted the attention and the support of Cuba and the Soviet Union. At about the same time, rural insurrections erupted in neighboring El Salvador and Guatemala, and the United States responded with aid to these regimes as well as to the key noncombatant, Honduras, and to the guerrilla force fighting against the Sandinistas, the so-called contras. As of late 1987, these four countries, with a combined population of about 22 million, hosted official armies of nearly 200,000 troops (not counting foreign advisers), as well as guerrilla insurgent forces of more than 25,000, and had experienced 150,000 political killings since 1979. The United States sent about $1 billion in military aid and about $4 billion in economic aid to its friends in the region, and the Soviet Union contributed about $500 million in military aid to Nicaragua, helping that country build up an army equal in size to the armed forces of all the other Central American countries combined. Elections in Nicaragua in 1990 offered the promise of ending that country's violence; but El Salvador continued to suffer the effects of its insurgency as the 1990s began.

Of all the conflicts in progress around the Third World at the end of 1987, the Iran–Iraq war was by far the most bloody and costly. This war, which began in September 1980, had by the end of 1987 already lasted longer than the Korean War or either World War. The war had multiple and complex beginnings, including personal hatred between the countries' two leaders (Iraq's President Hussein and Iran's Ayatollah Khomeini), and religious (Sunni ver-

sus Shi'ite Muslims) and ethnic (Arab versus Persian) conflicts that date back for centuries. The war was probably sparked by Iraq's fears that the Islamic fundamentalist resurgence in Iran would threaten to spill over into its neighbor and weaken Hussein's hold on his country. Exact casualty figures are unknown, but reliable estimates are that the war cost more than 350,000 killed and some 650,000 wounded. The casualty figures were so high because of Iran's use of human wave attacks against the superior fire power and military technology of the Iraqis. Finally, the mutual exhaustion of both sides facilitated a United Nations–mediated cease-fire in July 1988. Despite an inability of the warring parties to negotiate a final settlement of the conflict, the cease-fire held into 1990.[15]

In Chapter 17, we discussed the psychological disturbances arising from object loss in rapidly changing societies, such as those we typically find in the Third World. Rapidly changing ideas about political participation also result in heightened levels of disorder and strife, primarily as a consequence of the uneven penetration of modern institutions into a society. Education, government propaganda, and the mass media are the first elements of modernity to impinge on the consciousness of traditional folk; their aspirations and expectations are raised thereby, and they begin to hope that they can achieve some improvement to their lot through government action. However, the other institutions of modernity that we have described— the political party, the associational interest group, the agricultural cooperative, the neighborhood association—all appear much later in the modernization process, and they often fail to appear at all. We have here the classic revolution of rising expectations. Ideas about what people think they should be achieving in politics begin to outreach the institutions available to help them achieve these objectives. The results are frustration, anger, aggression, and a generally increased level of political instability.

One should not conclude, however, that high levels of instability necessarily are associated with political reform. One of the most important features of a developing society is the gap between the rural, traditional segment and the modern segment. This absence of an articulating link between traditional and modern is paralleled by a similar gap between those who have power and those who do not. This means that there seldom are linkages between political violence and the actual making of public policy. The high level of political violence witnessed in many Third World countries does not actually affect the prevailing political structures, because the violence takes place in a distant arena that is sealed off from the centers of power. As long as the forces of law and order (the police and the army) remain loyal to the government, isolated outbreaks of rioting, terrorism, or guerrilla war can be contained remarkably easily without having much impact on public policymaking. Of course, when the army *does* lose confidence in the regime in power, it is a relatively simple matter for it to intervene to overthrow the government and to install a military dictatorship. We consider this problem in detail in Chapter 19.

Increased Participation: The Institutional Dimension

Political participation is something that individual persons engage in; political institutions exist merely as the psychological and cultural context within which individuals interact, in politics as well as in any other area of society. When we say, for example, that a certain political party supports a specific candidate or demands a certain kind of policy, we are actually engaging in a sort of shorthand to describe these events. The party as an institution can support or demand nothing; these activities are undertaken by specific individuals who act and speak in the name of the party, a privilege given to them by other members of the party and conferred on them symbolically by granting to them a certain role (party chairperson, for example). Thus, although only individuals act, the institutional context within which they act is all-important because it strongly influences how others will react to their behavior.

The experience of the industrialized countries of Western Europe and North America suggests that successful industrialization both stimulates and requires the growth of mass-based institutions, including political parties, labor unions and other interest groups, and communications media. However, political leaders of the Third World are confronted with a major problem in their efforts to mobilize previously traditional groups and to weld them tightly into the modernizing political system. In Chapter 17, we saw some of the difficulties they encountered in designing institutions that would convert traditional personalities into modern ones with a minimum of disruption. In this chapter, we see the same kind of difficulties experienced in a somewhat different context—that is, how to mobilize previously inert citizens and make them active citizens, without disruption or political decay.[16]

Many Third World countries are characterized by what anthropologist Manning Nash has called multiple societies.[17] The *multiple society* is a divided social order consisting of two separate social systems that are bound together by a single set of economic, political, and legal bonds. One social system of this divided society is national in scope, is urbanized (usually living in the capital city), identifies with the states as an abstract concept, maintains relations with

An Iraqi army artillery unit lays down fire against Iranian troops in the third year of the war between the two Persian Gulf countries. At the time the photo was taken in February 1983, the war had already taken more than 250,000 lives. As of the end of 1987, the death toll had risen to more than 350,000.

other countries, and is in touch with the trends of modernity around the world. The national segment supplies the country with its political, economic, and intellectual elites. It has access to resources of economic and political power and is the arena within which the contests over the use of these resources is focused. The other social system (or systems) of the multiple society is region-based or village-based. It lives in the countryside, small towns or villages, or in big-city slums and rarely identifies itself as a part of the nation. It is traditional in attitude but may be undergoing certain aspects of the transition to modernity, particularly in the economic sphere. Its only resources are regional in nature, and even these are tiny when compared with the resources of the national elite.

The tension of political modernization arises from the difficulties encountered in attempting to link together these two halves of the multiple society. The two halves are poorly connected. The national segment is the planner, the organizer, the decision maker for the nation; the rural, village segment is rarely more than the raw material for political purposes. Communications rarely pass freely between the two segments.

Three devices, or social forms, have been used to link together the two segments of the multiple society. These are (1) the mass communications media; (2) modernizing political institutions, such as the political party and the interest group; and (3) the patron–client system.

We have already discussed in another context government use of the mass communications media (Chapter 17).[18] We found, as you may recall, that the mass media had little lasting effect on the more profound dimensions of attitudinal change. In the same way, we find that the mass media are of little value in providing the linkages needed to mobilize the village-based segment of the multiple society and to give it a vigorous role in policy-making at the national level. There are several reasons why the mass media are inefficient instruments for mobilizing mass participation. Use of the mass media requires an investment of something of value, such as money, time, energy, or attention span. In the rural and low-income areas of the Third World, all of these things are in extremely short supply, and there is rarely little surplus left to expend on an activity for which there is so little demonstrable reward. The mass media are of value only in communicating information and in providing people with an intellectual framework that they can use to make sense of their surroundings. We have been stressing here the institutional context of participation because, among other reasons, the institutions of participation act as a school of modernization by making traditional peoples aware of the importance of interpersonal exchanges and dealings. In providing traditional peoples with only information, the mass media offer only one dimension (and by far the least important one) of political participation. Without the institutional surroundings of the political group or party, the new participants will not learn the valuable lessons of how to get things accomplished by working with others in politics.

Perhaps the most significant reason why the mass media cannot mobilize rural folk is that they tend to be channeled through the single source of power and authority in each village or neighborhood. In a moment, we will encounter the patron–client system so prevalent in Third World local politics, and we will begin to get some idea of how politics is carried on in the day-to-day life of traditional peoples. For now, let us just observe that the political boss, or patron, of each village, tribe, or neighborhood effectively controls the mass media, just as he or she controls everything else of value. What the people know of the mass media is usually what the patron wants them to know. In the remote Mexican village of Cham Kom, for example, anthropologist Robert Redfield found that only two or three men regularly read a newspaper, among them the village patron, Don Eus: "The knowledge that other people in Cham Kom have of the matters reported or urged in these papers comes to them largely as Don Eus, having read the paper, explains the contents as the men sit together in the plaza in the evening.[19]"

Manning Nash found much the same sort of situation in small villages in Burma where, at least in one case, the village patron received a copy of the city newspaper and left it in a special place outside his home for others in the village to peruse at their convenience. No one else in the village received the publication, leaving the village chief in virtually complete control over the mass media exposure of the people of the village.[20] Because traditional culture holds that the validity of information is determined by its source and not by the degree to which it conforms to some abstract standard of scientific correctness, traditional society cannot use the mass communications media as a tool to transform its people into active, mobilized citizens.

This brings us to the set of modernizing institutions considered so important by Western scholars: the political party and the associational interest group, the agricultural cooperative and the labor union, the neighborhood civic association, and the ethnic interest group. (See Table 18.3 for description of status of political parties and interest groups in eight selected countries.)

Political Parties

Historically, political parties have appeared in political systems under one or more of three conditions.[21] First, in the older parliamentary systems of Western Europe and North America, parties were preceded by the emergence within parliament of factions that organized themselves internally and then turned their attention to the winning of electoral support from within the broader populace. Clearly, the development of parties under these circumstances had to be accompanied by the growth of the electorate, which, in turn, was linked to reforms in the electoral law. In the Third World, the only area where this development had a chance to occur was in the more advanced regions of Latin America, particularly Argentina and Chile. There, liberal and conservative parties came into being during the mid-nineteenth century. However, where these groupings did emerge, they failed to enlist popular support and became stunted in their growth, either because they were unable to relate to the needs of the masses or because their unprincipled exploitation and manipulation of the electoral laws caused a wholesale degeneration of public morality,

which led eventually to military rule, as in Argentina.

Parties can also emerge during a specific developmental crisis that has to do either with the legitimacy of the regime, with the establishment of an integrated national society, or with the channeling of large numbers of newly mobilized persons into political activity. In the new states of Africa and Asia, the struggle against the colonial rulers provided the setting for the creation of nationalist parties. Their main function was to mobilize popular support for the battle against the colonial country and to convince everyone concerned (including themselves) that their country had the right to exist as a separate social and political entity. Where large unassimilated ethnic groups declined to pay homage to the new national entity, it was expected that the nationalist mobilization party would provide them with the new identification they needed. There are several classic examples of such a party: the Congress Party of India, the Convention People's Party in Ghana, and the Tanganyika African National Union (TANU) of Tanganyika (now Tanzania). In other cases, parties like Malaysia's Alliance Party or the Democratic Party of the Ivory Coast (PDCI) have been particularly effective in overriding ethnic and regional loyalties and in mobilizing disparate peoples into a single, embracing national system.[22] In those instances where a single nationalist party was not formed prior to independence, such as in Nigeria, much greater latitude was given to the unassimilated ethnic and tribal minorities; consequences for national unity in Nigeria have been quite negative.

Another condition accompanying the formation of political parties has to do with the social modernization of the country and the need to harness the unleashed social forces and turn them to some political benefit. In this case, political parties emerge from a society that is

Table 18.3 Data on Political Parties and Labor Unions in Eight Selected Third World Countries in the 1980s

Country	Status of Parties, Labor Unions
Nigeria	1966 ban on parties lifted in 1978. Parliamentary democracy restored in 1979 but destroyed once again in late 1983 by a military takeover of the government. Even though local government elections held in December 1987, parties still prohibited. Democracy to be restored gradually by 1992. All unions belong to a single labor federation which represents about 2 percent of the workforce. Most strikes are illegal, but in practice government intervention in work stoppages has varied widely. There has been a marked reduction in work stoppages. Only sixty-nine occurred between May 1984 and May 1985. In previous years, hundreds per year were normal.
Tanzania	The sole legal political party is the Chama Cha Mapinduzi (CCM), the Revolutionary Party of Tanzania, formed in 1977. About 15 percent of labor force represented by the sole official union, the National Union of Tanzania Workers, which is an arm of the Ministry of Labor. All other unions are banned. Strikes are illegal.
India	Multiparty system with most ideological viewpoints represented by legal parties, including Marxist. Since independence, Indian politics dominated by the Indian National Congress, one of the oldest political parties in the Third World (founded in 1885). In 1969, the Congress separated into two factions, the leading one of which, led by Prime Minister Rajiv Gandhi, was the country's governing party until 1989. In December 1984, the Congress (I) Party won more than 50 percent of votes cast and about 80 percent of the seats in India's 509-seat Parliament. However, in subsequent elections in 1985 and 1987 at the state and local levels, the party lost ground with the voters. In November 1989, the Congress (I) Party won only 191 seats, and Gandhi was defeated as prime minister. About 5 percent of the labor force is unionized. Union control over workers is weak, membership is unstable, and wildcat strikes are common. However, unions represent one of the largest organized groups in politics and serve as mass base for many of the political parties.

(Table continues on p. 570.)

Table 18.3 (Continued)

Country	Status of Parties, Labor Unions
Indonesia	There are three official parties, all created and sponsored by official agencies of the government, including the armed forces. In 1987 elections, the ruling Golkar Party won 71 percent of the vote against two minor opposition parties, and 299 of the 400 parliamentary seats being contested. Legal parties must endorse the five pillars of "Pancasila": belief in one god, nationalism, humanitarianism, representative government, and social justice. About 10 percent of the labor force is unionized. Only one trade union is allowed. Political activity by unions is forbidden. Although the right to strike is guaranteed by law, in practice it is greatly circumscribed.
Mexico	Officially a multiparty system, but the ruling party, the PRI (Institutional Revolutionary Party), customarily wins more than 90 percent of the vote. Since 1985, the PRI has faced growing challenges from the conservative National Action Party (PAN), which is strongest in the northern states along the U.S. border. After state elections in 1986, the PAN charged the PRI with vote fraud to retain its dominance over the country. Internally, the party leadership effectively silenced dissenters in 1987 to retain its relatively closed method of nominating the party's candidate for president, which is tantamount to winning the election. In 1988, the PRI candidate was again elected president, but by the narrowest margin in the party's history. About 20 percent of the labor force is unionized. Unions are relatively free, but industrial disputes are submitted to compulsory arbitration by the government.
Brazil	In 1979, the officially sanctioned two-party system was abolished and replaced with an apparently more open multiparty system. All parties were legalized as of May 1985. Of the more than fifty registered parties, eight won legislative seats in 1986 elections. In 1989, free and competitive presidential election was held, for the first time since 1960. About half the labor force is unionized, but industrial disputes are controlled by Ministry of Labor. The country's four major labor

organizations are administered by the government. The constitution guarantees the right to strike.

Egypt
Egypt has a de facto one-party system. The leading party, the National Democratic Party, is descended from the old Arab Socialist Union, which was the country's sole legal party until 1978. The formation of opposition parties is subject to government regulation. In 1983, the Parliament passed law making the National Democratic Party effectively the only party able to win seats. The system uses proportional representation, with a minimum of 8 percent of the vote required for representation. The NDP controls more than 90 percent of the Parliament's seats. A few tiny opposition parties are allowed to exist, but the principal opposition party, the Wafd, has been outlawed and dissolved. About 20 percent of the workforce is unionized. The Egyptian Trade Union Federation is the sole authorized labor union. Strikes are not prohibited, but government regulations make legal strikes extremely difficult.

Iran
Parliamentary system established following overthrow of Shah, but parties must conform to concept of Islamic Republic to be approved. Multiple parties contested presidential elections in January 1980 and again in 1985 and 1989. The ruling party since 1979 has been the Islamic Republic Party, led by a group of Moslem clergy loyal to the Ayatollah Khomeini. Unions not organized on independent basis, but oil workers have demonstrated considerable power to hurt economy through strikes. The syndicate is the basic unit of labor organization. There are sixty-seven approved syndicates. Several short-lived strikes in 1984 were dealt with severely. Labor organizations are instruments of government control.

(Source) George Thomas Kurian, Encyclopedia of the Third World, 3rd ed. (New York: Facts on File, 1987), 3 vols.; Banks, ed. Political Handbook (1987); U.S. Department of State, Country Reports on Human Rights Practices for 1979 (Washington, D.C.: U.S. Government Printing Office, 1980); Charles Taylor and David Jodice, eds., World Handbook of Political and Social Indicators (New Haven, Conn.: Yale University Press, 1983), vol. 1, Table 2.9, pp. 85–87; The Economist, December 19, 1987, September 12, 1987, May 2, 1987; Washington Post, December 30, 1984, July 21, 1983.

being assaulted by the forces of modernization—communications, economic development, mass education, the disruption of traditional social forms and attitudes—and that lacks the organizational framework to discipline itself. The alternative appears to be chaos; men and women are uprooted psychologically and lack social and political reference points. The modernizing nationalist reform party is created, then, not to lead the nation to independence (that has already been accomplished) but to help establish order in a disorderly world. There are a few clear-cut examples of such a party, particularly in Latin America: Acción Democratica in Venezuela, the Institutional Revolutionary Party ("*Partido Revolucionaro Institucional*" [PRI]) in Mexico, and the National Liberation Party of Costa Rica. In other areas of the Third World, modernizing parties would include the Republican People's Party of Turkey and the Destourian Socialist Party of Tunisia.

Regardless of the social or political origins of parties in the Third World, they seldom perform exactly the same kind of functions that are carried out by their counterpart organizations in Western democracies. In the United States, we are accustomed to thinking of political parties as possessing four characteristics (at least in theory): (1) organizational continuity, a life span that outlasts the life of the current leadership; (2) an organizational structure that is permanent and that extends down to the local level; (3) a leadership determined to capture and hold decision-making power, not simply to influence the exercise of such power; and (4) an effort to persuade voters to vote for their candidates.

Political parties in the Third World are, at the same time, both more and less than this formulation. The more successful parties are well organized down to the local block level. Tunisia's Destourian Socialist Party has more than 1,000 cells with an average of 100 to 400 members

each and operates effectively at the lowest precinct sphere of local politics. In addition, the party has formed close working alliances with the country's only labor union and has formed within itself an artisans' and shopkeepers' section, a farmers' union, a student group, a youth section, a scout organization for young boys, and a women's organization. Effective modernization parties, such as Acción Democratica of Venezuela, provide social services for their members that go far beyond the mere mobilization of voters. A typical local office of one of these parties could be expected to provide information on jobs to an unemployed member, housing for a newly arrived person, or recreation for the member who wishes to spend his or her idle hours with friends. Peru's leading leftist party, the American Popular Revolutionary Alliance (APRA), provides its members with a free dental clinic and a low-cost dining hall in Lima, and distributes free cornmeal and other foodstuffs.[23]

But if some political parties do more than their Western counterparts, many (perhaps most) do considerably less. Most organizations that call themselves parties in fact only faintly resemble what we would recognize by that name. Many are only the personal creations of a specific individual or family, and they fade away after that person's death or loss of interest in politics. Many others have some ideological base but lack the organizational basis to carry through the periods out of power. Most parties are underfinanced and understaffed, and they suffer from a lack of experienced personnel who can manage complex bureaucracies.

Perhaps the most significant difference between political parties in the Third World and their counterparts in the First World is that in most Third World countries parties are not organized to provide electoral competition, mobilize voters, win elections, and hold power for some recognizable political purpose. Out of 102 Third World countries, in 1987 only 24 had a multiparty system in which parties competed more or less freely with one another for power. Most of these multiparty systems were found in Latin America, the region that has the most openly competitive democracies (including Costa Rica and Venezuela), but the list also included the world's most populous democracy, India. In twenty-seven cases, including Algeria, Burma, and Zaire, only one party was permitted to exist; all electoral competition was prohibited, either by constitution or by legislation. In twenty-four other instances, parties were allowed to exist, but since a single party had come to dominate the rest, we refer to these as de facto one-party states. Mexico was the best known of these states; other examples were Indonesia and Taiwan. In these systems, the dominant party or single party existed not to mobilize voters or win elections but, instead, to act as a communications and education channel that tied together the rural, traditional segment of society with the modern, urban segment. Finally, in twenty-five cases parties were banned altogether. In some of these instances, the party prohibition arose out of an illegal seizure of power, as in Libya; in others it was the product of a still-traditional dynastic regime, such as Jordan or Saudi Arabia. (In two cases, the status of the party system was uncertain as of late 1987.)[24]

In the latter half of the 1980s, however, there were clear signs that the foundation of some of these de facto one-party systems was beginning to crumble under the pressure of the forces of industrialization and modernization. In Mexico, the PRI entered the 1988 campaign for president confident of victory, since every PRI candidate had won the country's highest office since the party's founding nearly sixty years earlier. By emphasizing the redistribution of farmland to Mexico's landless peasantry, the PRI had managed to cement its hold on power by reliance on a rural–labor coalition. In the 1980s, however, two powerful challenges to the party's dominance appeared, both fueled by rural unrest. In the still-traditional south of Mexico, small leftist parties began to gain ground in local elections on the platform of greater redistribution of farmlands as well as increased government investment in improving these lands. In the north, the more conservative National Action Party (PAN) was attracting thousands of disaffected peasants with their call for more privately held land and less farmed by the age-old communal ejido system. The party's 1988 presidential candidate, Carlos Salinas de Gortari, was assured of victory; but his margin was narrower than that of any of his predecessors.[25]

Interest Groups

Going beyond the political party, we find a wide variety of interest groups. For ease of discussion, let us categorize these interest groups according to whether or not the rationale for their existence is economic.

Generally, countries that are still relatively traditional in economic and social makeup are also countries where the most active interest groups are those that cut across economic lines and are based on noneconomic criteria for membership. In many emerging African countries, urban neighborhoods frequently are organized by tribal or ethnic associations that exist to serve the social needs of their kinfolk recently arrived in the city from the countryside. According to Peter C. Lloyd, these ethnic associations assist recent arrivals to find housing and employment, incorporate them into a group that shares their culture and their language, and act as an informal conflict-resolution device for disputes between members of the association.[26] Local-government ties with these associations are usually limited to some sort of informal advisory status, but occasionally the associations assist the local municipal administration by acting as a law enforcement authority in the local neighborhood. Other traditional noneconomic interest groups might revolve around such criteria as religion, language, or kinship patterns. One would expect that, as a society modernizes, the bases for such grouping would erode considerably; but the activity of distinct ethnic groups in American politics, such

as the activity of people of Italian or Polish origin, should make us aware that noneconomic criteria for human association persist in even advanced industrial states.

As a country's economic system modernizes, it also becomes more differentiated. This means that its members begin to take on tasks and role assignments that are more and more specialized and that require specialized knowledge and working conditions. This is the basis for the growth of interest groups based on economic self-interest. Of these, the most important politically is the trade or labor union.[27] Trade

The city of Caracas, Venezuela, must house a population of over two million, about one-fifth of the nation's total. Slum dwellings, called "ranchos," cover the mountains surrounding the city and contrast sharply with the city's modern skyscrapers. The government would like to destroy the shantytowns and move the slum dwellers into the nearby high-rise apartments, but the modern buildings cannot be erected fast enough to accommodate the city's exploding population.

unions in Third World countries differ substantially from their Western counterparts. Although Western (particularly American) unions concentrate on their economic needs first, in the Third World, trade union activity has been distinctly political, with less interest shown in pursuing a specifically economic approach. Because trade unions in the Third World are especially weak compared with Western trade unions, they rely much more on official or political party support and nurturance; such support frequently leads to control and political dominance.

There are several major sources of trade union weakness in developing countries. The still-traditional state of the country's economy means that many, if not most, of the workers are employed in jobs that are hard to unionize: subsistence agriculture, service tasks in urban areas (domestic servants, street vendors), and so forth. Rural farm workers are difficult to organize because of their geographical isolation. Consequently, trade unions rarely represent more than a small fraction of the workers in any given country. The 1987 edition of the *Encyclopedia of the Third World* reports trade union membership data for forty-two countries, not including those where union activity is legally prohibited.[28] Of these forty-two cases, in twenty-eight, one-quarter or less of the workforce was organized; in seventeen countries, the figure is 10 percent or less. In only four countries does union membership represent half the workforce or more. The average proportion of the unionized workforce for the forty-two cases was 22.2 percent. In addition, most Third World unions lack regular and independent financial support. Most of the workers in low-income areas lack the means to contribute regularly to union treasuries. Strike funds and other financial resources of modern union activity must be obtained either from official sources or from sources outside

the country (the competing American and Soviet-sponsored international trade union movements). In many countries, such as Zambia and Malaysia, ethnic or tribal allegiances cut across the working class and split the labor movement into quarreling factions. Add to these problems the lack of administrative personnel and the rampant graft and corruption within Third World unions, and one can see why the working class is only weakly represented, if at all, in these countries.

A second reason for the increased politicization of Third World unions has to do with the level of economic development of the country. During a country's early stages of development, there is a great need for investment capital, which can come from only two places. Either foreign sources must supply the financial aid through government loans or through private investment (both of which are distasteful to Third World governments), or an economic surplus must be created within the country itself. If the latter strategy is adopted, the citizens of the country must be forced or persuaded to produce more than they consume, at least for the first decade or two of the development plan. This objective runs exactly counter to the rationale for trade unions, that is, to obtain increasing financial returns from the economic system for their members. This conflict is often referred to as the struggle between the consumption and savings imperatives of economic development. Although some economists assert that there is no necessary conflict between the two, most governments believe that there is such a conflict and that the only way to resolve the struggle is by persuading the working classes to accept a certain sacrifice for the initial period of the development effort. Peasants are not usually affected by this call for sacrifice because they produce and consume so little already that they could have little impact on development no matter what they did. Most upper- and middle-income groups are likewise little affected, because their political power makes them immune to such government confiscatory taxation policies. Obviously, few free and independent trade unions would accept such a bargain and most union members would overthrow any leadership that tried to impose such an arrangement of the members. Thus, governments in developing countries must bring unions under their official jurisdiction to make them compliant members of the national development effort.

As a consequence of these factors, trade unions in the Third World are much more tightly controlled by political organizations than in the West. They are rarely free and independent in the sense that American unions are free. Data available in the late 1980s indicate that, of 102 countries, in 34 the trade unions were completely free or mostly free to organize and bargain collectively, whereas in 52 they were completely controlled by the government, either directly by the government's ministry of labor or indirectly by being integrated into the country's single or dominant political party. In seven countries, no union activity was permitted at all, and in nine cases sufficient data were not available for classification. The ultimate power of trade unions—the right to strike—was also sharply restricted throughout the Third World. In only 26 of 102 countries did unions enjoy the right to strike in theory (as guaranteed by law or by the constitution) as well as in practice. In twenty-five cases, although the right to strike existed in law, it was denied in practice. In twenty-two instances, the right was both illegal and denied in practice. In a few states (four), strikes took place even though they were prohibited by law. Data were not available in twenty-five cases, but presumably in most of these the right to strike was denied either in theory or in practice, if not both.[29]

Until now, governments in the Third World have been fairly successful in preserving peace in the industrial labor movement. There are some early warning signs, however, that labor unions in key developing countries are becoming restive and impatient. In Mexico, despite the prestige and power attributed to the Mexican Workers' Federation (CTM), younger leaders are beginning to challenge the older leadership, and charges of corruption and selling out to Mexican industry are having the effect of weakening the strength of the labor bureaucrats. In Brazil, Latin America's most dynamic and popular labor leader, Luis Ignacio da Silva, offered such a strong challenge to the military regime that they succeeded in convicting him of leading an illegal strike and sentenced him to three and one-half years in prison. After democracy was restored to Brazil in 1985, the country's powerful industrial trade unions refused to cooperate with the government's attempts to dampen inflation by restricting wage increases. Between March and May 1985, there were more than thirty-eight significant strikes, involving workers in airlines, the postal service, teachers, and subway and bus drivers. In early 1987, when the government tried to persuade the workers to accept wage restraints while prices were allowed to rise by 30 percent, strikes broke out across the country and troops had to be sent in to the country's paralyzed oil refineries. In Argentina, as the military relinquished control to a democratically elected regime in 1983, the formerly suppressed industrial unions began to reassert their powerful influence in both electoral politics and the country's social welfare system. In 1984 and again in 1985, the Argentine General Confederation of Labor called massive general strikes involving as many as 100,000 workes to protest President Raul Alfonsin's economic policies that would have curbed inflation by holding down wages and creating severe unemployment. In the Philippines in 1987, President Corazon Aquino's policies were sharply challenged by an increasingly restive labor movement as well as by rising numbers of illegal wildcat strikes. In August, after the government announced a fuel price increase, a massive general strike and street demonstrations crippled transportation and slowed work in factories and offices all over the country. Police were forced to suppress the strikers with live ammunition, seriously wounding four. In South Korea in 1987, the restoration of political democracy was accompanied by an upsurge of economic unrest, where workers' rights to protest long hours and low wages had previously been kept in check by an authoritarian regime. In August, a two-week-long wave of strikes, stoppages, and sit-ins affected nearly 300 companies, idled 200 factories (including all five of the country's automobile manufacturers), and sent some 35,000 workers out onto the streets. These are clear signals that the economic cramp of the 1970s may have led to major explosions in the 1980s in the major industrial countries of the Third World.[30]

Roughly the same degree of underdevelopment in trade union organization is seen in Third World organizations that represent middle-class professional and business interests. Perhaps as many as half the countries in the Third World report having something like a chamber of commerce but, in most instances, these business organizations are just small clubs that operate in the capital city. Only a few countries possess highly differentiated business-sector interest groups that cover the entire range of a modernizing economy. Even in a relatively advanced country like Chile, where the private business sector is well represented by interest groups of long standing, only a minority of business leaders actually bother with the work of such groups, out of indifference, the press of business, or a feeling that political action is not likely to produce tangible benefits for business interests.[31] Because of their relatively high level of development and because of the high degree of American business influence, Venezuela and Mexico have developed very large, well-financed, and well-organized business- and manufacturing-interest associations that have a great deal of influence with their respective governments. But these two countries are a minority among Third World states.

The wealthy members of a nation's economy have ways of making their influence felt without the assistance of formal organizations or interest groups. Wealthy landowners, industrialists, and the representatives of foreign corporations are usually able to get the attention of the president or other top officials of a country merely by virtue of their strategic location in the system, apart from any special organization representation they may enjoy. The wielding of influence by Western multinational corporations, such as Lockheed Aircraft or International Telephone and Telegraph, to gain special favors in the developing world is already well known. Other examples of such foreign business intervention in Third World politics are Gulf Oil Company's payment of $460,000 to Bolivian President René Barrientos from 1966 to 1969 to obtain special favors for its operations in Bolivia, and United Brands' payment of $1.25 million to Honduran military dictator Oswaldo Lopez Arellano in return for exemptions from Honduran export taxes. Such tactics for gaining influence are equally well employed by the wealthy within the nation. Even governments that profess a radical and uncompromising hostility to the traditional business and agrarian elites of their countries are usually found to be doing business with them behind closed doors, reformist rhetoric to the contrary notwithstanding.

In addition to the groups already mentioned, there are at least three other kinds of interest groups that span both economic and noneconomic criteria for membership: students, peasants, and neighborhoods. Students groups in all parts of the world came into prominence during the 1960s as the source of unrest and disorder as well as the voice for radical changes in many societies. In a few countries, such as South Korea and Venezuela, students came close to disrupting society sufficiently to bring about the downfall of the government. In Latin America, particularly, where the principle of the inviolability of a university campus has been used for generations to protect student protestors, the role of students in politics has been especially important. Many prominent Latin American political leaders, such as Fidel Castro of Cuba and Romulo Betancourt of Venezuela, got their start as leaders of student political groups.

In several countries, in addition, peasant groups or leagues have been formed to represent the needs and demands of the low-income, landless workers of the soil. Sometimes peasant leagues are created by government agricultural ministries or by political parties as mobilization devices to gain political support (as in Venezuela) or as administrative devices to assist in the implementation of land reform programs (as in Egypt). At other times, as in Brazil, peasant leagues have been formed essentially free of official control, in which case they usually are suppressed by government action. In either case, they seldom are the channel for the mass mobilization hoped for by Western observers.

Finally, in many cities neighborhood associations are formed to force government attention to persistent urban problems that they cannot solve by themselves—garbage collection, crime control, water, housing, paved streets, and so forth. In most Third World countries, but especially in Latin America and South Asia, a prime urban problem is that of the squatters,

the illegal residents of urban slums or shanty-towns. In cities like Lima or Caracas, the squatters have formed associations to establish some primitive organization framework to administer their neighborhoods and to pressure the national government into granting them legal title to their lands. In many cases, where these associations have been careful to limit their demands to very narrowly stated aims and where they have been willing to resort to disruptive action to achieve their objectives, they have been reasonably successful.

Patron–Client Politics: The Failure of Institution Building

Institutions are the key to absorbing increased political participation in rapidly modernizing societies. Yet the record shows relatively few effective modernizing (and modern) institutional linkages between traditional, low-income peasants and urban workers, on the one hand, and the modern, nationalistic city elites, on the other—a mass mobilization political party in Mexico or Venezuela, the village institutes in Turkey, an agricultural cooperative in Pakistan, ethnic or tribal associations in Nigeria or Ghana. The scarcity of such examples shows how thinly modernization is penetrating into the Third World in an institutional sense.

Why are so many Third World political leaders unable to build the institutional bridges out to the traditional folk of their countries? For one thing, many members of the modern, well-educated elites in developing countries cannot understand the ways in which traditional, lower-status people calculate the costs and benefits of their daily lives. The Westernized education received by the modernizing elites has often blinded them to the essential rationality of the traditional style of life. They have forgotten, if they ever knew, the ways in which the elemental forces that play on the lives of traditional people impel them toward personal calculations that appear irrational to Western-trained observers. Often, the city elites in Third World countries cannot even speak the language spoken by rural villagers; if they do share the same language, they do not speak similar dialects. In any case, communication of the simplest sort is difficult, if not impossible. The urban, modern elites—the visiting bureaucrat, planner, or agricultural extension agent—cannot empathize with, or even communicate with, the intended client.

Even where the bureaucrats of the national government are committed to a style of reform in the countryside that is intended to benefit the peasants, they frequently expect the peasants to respond to their plans as if some sort of modern class consciousness existed among the rural workers. When the peasants refuse to respond favorably to these plans and institutions, the bureaucrats become exasperated with their backward or childlike clients and impatiently decide to coerce the peasants into actions and decisions that the bureaucrats believe are manifestly in their own interest. In Chile, during the reformist regime of Salvador Allende, bureaucrats from the capital swarmed over the countryside intent on building a more modern and just social order. Land was to be expropriated from the large landowners and placed in collectives to be worked communally by the peasants. The proceeds would be pooled and then redistributed equally, with a percentage going to the state to pay for the whole enterprise. To the surprise of the modernizing bureaucrats, the peasants would silently nod their assent to the project and then quietly go about the business of sabotaging the collectives. The bureaucrats were astounded at the lack of consciousness of their clients; frequently, they were provoked

into using coercion to motivate the peasants to act more according to their own rational interests (as those interests were defined by the bureaucrats).[32]

As a consequence, elites cannot construct institutional arrangements that can induce, support, and reinforce modern behavior and attitudes. The characteristics of such arrangements, such as new farming techniques or novel methods for selecting a village chief, depend to a large extent on shared standards of rationality; these, in turn, derive in essence from the ideas of modernity. Remove these ideas, and the shared standards of rationality and the institutional arrangements will collapse because of the unwillingness of the people to internalize their lessons and to assimilate them into their daily lives. The problem is aggravated when the agents of social and technological change are merely temporary visitors in a rural area. A few months after bringing some innovation to the village, they may return to the comfort of the city, abandoning the villagers to their fate with the new equipment, seeds, medicines, or books. Small wonder that the villagers are reluctant to commit themselves to an unknown factor in their struggle to eke out a bare subsistence from the soil. Experience with the new miracle grains in Asia showed that the only farmers who were willing to adopt the new methods and seeds were those who were already wealthy and could afford to risk a bad crop. Those who lived perpetually on the edge of starvation were unwilling to risk any departure from the prevailing norms.

The nineteenth-century French social observer Alexis de Tocqueville called our attention to the "art of associating together," by which he meant the ability of people to join together in common enterprises. In traditional cultures we frequently find many people unwilling to join with others, especially if the others are not of their kin group or ethnic circle. After all, where everyone lives so close to the margin of survival, there is little reason to trust one another, especially in the context of a formal institution such as a political party. In modern institutions, trust is derived from formal, impersonal features, like laws, rights, obligations, and constitutional provisions. In traditional institutions, trust derives from personal familiarity, thereby sharply limiting the number of people who will meet the requirements of mutual trust in any consensus-based political organization.

Finally, and perhaps most important, reform governments in the Third World frequently fail to construct modernizing institutions in traditional areas because powerful traditional political forces resist such institutionalization. These traditional forces may be religious (priests, witch doctors, shamans), political (village chiefs), or economic (large landowners, peasants). Whatever the source of their power, these individuals resist modernizing institutions because they understand clearly that the introduction of these institutions into their community will undermine their power, their privileges (where they have them), and their accustomed way of life. Not surprisingly, they fight back with the tools and weapons at their disposal, such as money, graft, bribes, rural insurgencies, refusal to implement the law, and voodoo and other ritualistic devices. And, in most places in the Third World where this confrontation is taking place, the forces of tradition are winning or, at least, holding their own.

As a result, mass local politics in many parts of the Third World has fallen under the control of numerous patron–client systems, or what John Duncan Powell calls "clientelist politics."[33] These patron–client relationships stand midway between the tribal chieftaincies of the traditional, precolonial era and the modern, bureaucratic, rule-oriented authority relationships of urban,

industrial politics. The patrons in question may be people of immense power, such as large landowners and priests, or they may be persons of modest influence, such as moneylenders, ward bosses, and other kinds of intermediaries. Their clients may be poor, illiterate peasants, small shopkeepers, or even urban workers. But, however they are constructed and wherever they are, patron–client political systems are extremely important to Third World politics for several reasons: (1) they constitute the primary (and, often, the sole) channel for rural and urban poor to be involved in political activity; (2) they have great influence over the ways in which public policies are implemented at the local level; and (3) they are (or can be) valuable sources of information for modernizing elites who are attempting to formulate a policy to solve some recurrent problem. In the terms of this chapter, however, patron–client politics is most significant because of what it says about the failure of Third World elites to construct modernizing institutions to guide the newly mobilized citizen into productive and constructive political participation.

Conclusions: Political Participation and Human Dignity

Mass populations in the Third World are not inert and helpless lumps of clay as they are often depicted in Western literature. In some ways, citizens participate in politics to as great a degree as they do in modern, industrialized nations; in a few instances, they may even participate more than their Western counterparts. Yet this increased political participation does not translate evenly into public policies that are aimed at enhancing human dignity. It is almost as if there were a short circuit in the connection between mass participation and public policy in many developing countries.

In this chapter, we have identified the causes of this break in the link between participation and policy. The mass media are seen as an insufficient mobilizing agent because they fail to involve the citizen in an active role in the political process. The various institutions of political participation—parties, interest groups, and the like—exist only in fragmentary form and are often coopted by the very government that they exist to influence. Even well-meaning reformist bureaucrats have difficulty in constructing the institutions of mass participation because of cultural and economic reasons we presented earlier.

In the absence of these other channels for involvement, Third World citizens are mobilized (if that is the correct word in this case) by patron–client systems or are provoked by their frustration into unstructured violence. The aggressive features of political life in developing countries have been fully documented and seem to stem from the unsettling experiences of change unrelieved by any opportunity for the citizen to intervene in the process of modernization. The patron–client system exists not to influence policy but, instead, to confer on a selected powerful few the privileges of an elitist society while maintaining the rhetoric of liberal democracy.

In sum, mass participation in Third World politics frequently fails to elicit progressive public policies because there are few institutions to transmit popular needs and demands and to link together the mass of the village and the slum with the national elites in the capital city.

Suggestions for Further Reading

Alba, Victor, *Politics and the Labor Movement in Latin America* (Stanford, Calif.: Stanford University Press, 1968).

Davies, Ioan, *African Trade Unions* (London: Penguin, 1966).

Day, Alan J., and **Henry W. Degenhardt,** eds., *Political Parties of the World,* 2nd ed. (Detroit: Gale Research, 1984).

Delury, George E., ed., *World Encyclopedia of Political Systems and Parties* (New York: Facts on File, 1983).

Feierabend, Ivo K., Rosalind L. Feierabend, and **Ted Robert Gurr,** eds., *Anger, Violence and Politics: Theories and Research* (Englewood Cliffs, N.J.: Prentice-Hall, 1972).

Galenson, Walter, ed., *Labor in Developing Countries* (Berkeley: University of California Press, 1962).

Hodgkin, Thomas, *African Political Parties* (London: Penguin, 1961).

Huizer, Gerrit, *The Revolutionary Potential of Peasants in Latin America* (Lexington, Mass.: Heath, 1972).

Humphrey, John, *Capitalist Control and Workers' Struggle in the Brazilian Auto Industry* (Princeton, N.J.: Princeton University Press, 1982).

Huntington, Samuel P., *Political Order in Changing Societies* (New Haven, Conn.: Yale University Press, 1968).

Huntington, Samuel P., and **Joan M. Nelson,** *No Easy Choice: Political Participation in Devel-*

oping Countries (Cambridge, Mass.: Harvard University Press, 1976).

LaPalombara, Joseph, and **Myron Weiner,** eds., *Political Parties and Political Development* (Princeton, N.J.: Princeton University Press, 1966).

Leiden, Carl, and **Karl M. Schmitt,** *The Politics of Violence: Revolution in the Modern World* (Englewood Cliffs, N.J: Prentice-Hall, 1968).

McKenzie, William J. M., and **Kenneth Robinson,** eds. *Five Elections in Africa* (Oxford: Clarendon, 1960).

Miles, William F. S., *Elections in Nigeria: A Grass Roots Perspective* (Boulder, Colo.: Lynne Reiner Publishers, 1987).

Millen, Bruce H., *The Political Role of Labor in Developing Countries* (Washington, D.C.: Brookings Institute, 1963).

Randall, Vicky, ed., *Political Parties in the Third World* (Newbury Park, Calif.: Sage, 1988).

Smith, T. E., *Elections in Developing Countries* (London: Macmillan, 1960).

Spalding, Hobart, *Organized Labor in Latin America: Historical Case Studies of Workers in Dependent Societies* (New York: Harper & Row, 1977).

Stockholm International Peace Research Institute, *SIPRI Yearbook 1987: World Armaments and Disarmaments* (Oxford: Oxford University Press, 1987).

Vega, Luis Mercier, *Guerrillas in Latin America: The Technique of the Counter-State* (New York: Praeger, 1969).

Weiner, Myron, *Party Politics in India: The Development of a Multi-Party System* (Princeton, N.J.: Princeton University Press, 1957).

Notes

1. Samuel P. Huntington and Joan M. Nelson, *No Easy Choice: Political Participation in Developing Countries* (Cambridge, Mass.: Harvard University Press, 1976).

2. Charles Taylor and David Jodice, eds., *World Handbook of Political and Social Indicators*, vol. 1: *Cross-National Attributes and Rates of Change* (New Haven, Conn.: Yale University Press, 1983), Table 2.6, pp. 76–78.

3. Raymond D. Gastil, ed., *Freedom in the World: Political Rights and Civil Liberties* (Westport, Conn.: Greenwood Press, 1982), Table 5, pp. 25–29.

4. Charles Taylor and Michael Hudson, eds., *World Handbook of Political and Social Indicators*, 2nd ed. (New Haven, Conn.: Yale University Press, 1972), Table 2.9, pp. 57–58.

5. Gastil, ed., *Freedom* (1982).

6. Banks, ed., *Political Handbook* (1987).

7. Manning Nash, *The Golden Road to Modernity: Village Life in Contemporary Burma* (Chicago: University of Chicago Press, 1965), Ch. 3.

8. See the two reports in the *Washington Post* by William Branigin: "Marcos Trying to Thwart Plans for Election Boycott as Voting Nears," June 14, 1981, and "Marcos Easily Wins a Six-Year Term; Vote Is Marked by Opposition Boycott," June 17, 1981.

9. *The Economist*, May 19, 1984; William Branigin, "Challenges to Marcos: Opposition to Play Key Role in New Assembly," *Washington Post*, August 13, 1984.

10. William Branigin, "1983 Murder Launched Upheaval That Toppled Marcos," *Washington Post*,

February 27, 1986; *The Economist*, February 7, 1987, May 16, 1987; Keith Richburg, "Philippines to Elect National Legislature," *Washington Post*, May 11, 1987; *The Economist*, January 23, 1988.

11. Ivo K. Feierabend et al., eds., *Anger, Violence and Politics: Theories and Research* (Englewood Cliffs, N.J.: Prentice-Hall, 1972). The specific articles from this collection that are discussed are Ivo K. Feierabend and Rosalind L. Feierabend, "Systemic Conditions of Political Aggression: An Application of Frustration–Aggression Theory" (Ch. 9); and Ted Robert Gurr, "A Causal Model of Civil Strife: A Comparative Analysis Using Indices" (Ch. 10).

12. Arthur S. Banks and William Overstreet, eds., *Political Handbook of the World: 1982–1983* (New York: McGraw-Hill, 1983). Banks, ed., *Political Handbook* (1987).

13. Ruth L. Sivard, *World Military and Social Expenditures, 1987–88* (Washington, D.C.: World Priorities, 1987), pp. 29–31. See also Stephen Goose, "Armed Conflicts in 1986, and the Iraq–Iran War," in Stockholm International Peace Research Institute, *SIPRI Yearbook 1987: World Armaments and Disarmaments* (Oxford: Oxford University Press, 1987), pp. 297–320.

14. *The Economist*, March 12, 1988.

15. *The Economist*, January 16, 1988, February 27, 1988, August 15, 1987, and October 10, 1987. Also Goose, "Armed Conflicts."

16. Samuel P. Huntington, *Political Order in Changing Societies* (New Haven, Conn.: Yale University Press, 1968).

17. Manning Nash, "Southeast Asian Society: Dual or Multiple," *Journal of Asian Studies* 23, 3 (May 1964), 417–431.

18. Lucian W. Pye, ed., *Communications and Political Development* (Princeton, N.J.: Princeton University Press, 1963).

19. Robert Redfield, *A Village That Chose Progress: Cham Kom Revisited* (Chicago: University of Chicago Press, 1950), p. 144.

20. Nash, *Golden Road to Modernity*, p. 283.

21. Joseph LaPalombara and Myron Weiner, "The Origin and Development of Political Parties," in LaPalombara and Weiner, eds., *Political Parties and Political Development* (Princeton, N.J.: Princeton University Press, 1966), pp. 3–42.

22. Richard E. Stryker, "A Local Perspective on Developmental Strategy in the Ivory Coast," in Michael F. Lofchie, ed., *The State of the Nations: Constraints on Development in Independent Africa* (Berkeley: University of California Press, 1971), pp. 134–135.

23. Jackson Diehl, "Pragmatic Leader Emerging in Peru," *Washington Post*, December 31, 1984.

24. Henry Bienen, "Political Parties and Political Machines in Africa," in Lofchie, ed., *The State of the Nations*, Ch. 9. See also Banks, ed., *Political Handbook* (1987).

25. *The Economist*, March 5, 1988.

26. Peter C. Lloyd, *Africa in Social Change*, rev. ed. (Baltimore: Penguin, 1975).

27. Bruce H. Millen, *The Political Role of Labor in Developing Countries* (Washington, D.C.: Brookings Institute, 1963); Everett M. Kassalow, "Trade Unionism and the Development Process in the New Nations: A Comparative View," in Solomon Barkin et al., eds., *International Labor* (New York: Harper & Row, 1967), pp. 62–80; Everett M. Kassalow, ed., *National Labor Movements in the Postwar World* (Evanston, Ill.: Northwestern University Press, 1963).

28. Kurian, *Encyclopedia*, 3rd ed., 3 vols.

29. Kurian, ibid.

30. Marlise Simons, "Labor Patriarch Is Key Figure in Evolving Mexico," *Washington Post*, December 28, 1979; William Orme, "Mexico's Labor Patriarch, 83, Faces Unrest," *Washington Post*, March 10, 1984; Jim Brooke, "Union Leader Vexes Brazil's Military Leaders," *Washington Post*, March 4, 1981; Jackson Diehl, "Influence of Peronist Unions Grows in Argentina," *Washington Post*, April 26, 1983; Richard House, "Brazil, Facing Broad Labor Unrest, Settles Major Strike by Mediation," *Washington Post*, May 29, 1985;

"A Survey of Brazil," *The Economist*, April 25, 1987; Jackson Diehl, "Argentine Unions Threaten to Undercut Alfonsin's IMF Challenge," *Washington Post*, June 20, 1984; Jackson Diehl, "Strike Called in Argentina," *Washington Post*, August 30, 1984; Jackson Diehl, "Argentine Unions Strike to Protest Alfonsin's Economic Policies," *Washington Post*, May 24, 1985; Gregg Jones, "Troops Fire on Workers in Philippines Strike," *Washington Post*, August 27, 1987; Keith Richburg, "Labor Strife Damaging to Aquino," *Washington Post*, October 15, 1987; *The Economist*, August 15, 1987.

31. Dale L. Johnson, "The National and Progressive Bourgeoisie in Chile," in James D. Cockcroft et al., eds., *Dependence and Underdevelopment: Latin America's Political Economy* (Garden City, N.Y.: Doubleday, 1972), pp. 201–206.

32. David Lehmann, "Agrarian Reform in Chile, 1965–1972: An Essay in Contradictions," in Lehmann, ed., *Peasants, Landlords and Governments: Agrarian Reform in the Third World* (New York: Holmes & Meier, 1974), p. 109.

33. John D. Powell, "Peasant Society and Clientelistic Politics," *American Political Science Review* 64 (2) (1970), 411–426.

GOVERNMENT INSTITUTIONS IN THE THIRD WORLD

The historical, psychological, social, cultural, and economic features of a society provide the setting within which governments must operate. We have already seen how the setting of politics influences policies designed to increase human dignity. It is now time to examine some of the typical political institutions likely to be found in the Third World. We are looking for links between kinds of formal institutions and levels of human dignity in a given country and across the Third World. Or, to put it another way, are the government structures that are typical of the Third World capable of undertaking policies that vigorously enhance human dignity in their societies? If not, how can we identify and explain major flaws in the political structures of developing countries?

Political Implications of Delayed Industrialization

Most countries in the Third World possess what some scholars have called *regimes of delayed in-* *dustrialization.*[1] This means that these countries typically began their industrialization process considerably after the countries of Western Europe and North America. The reasons for this delay and its consequences are central to an understanding of the prevailing Third World government structures.

Industrialization as a social process is never cheap. In fact, where the process has more or less run its course, the costs have been extremely high. Although the costs of industrialization are always high, regimes handle other important questions of the industrialization process quite differently—for example, which social classes pay the costs, which receive the benefits, and how rapidly the overall process is carried out. The process of industrial growth seems to require a good deal of social coercion, but whether or not it explodes into revolutionary violence or class warfare depends on how a regime answers these questions.

The high costs of industrialization stem directly from the massive shifts in human values, attitudes, resources, and behavior that accompany the change from a preindustrial to an industrial society.[2] Income must be transferred from those who spend unproductively (on luxuries) to those who will spend productively (on capital equipment). Current consumption must be held down in favor of future investment. Unproductive agrarian classes (mostly peasants) must be encouraged or forced to leave their land and move to the cities where they form the large pool of potential laborers.[3] The commercialization of agriculture and the shift of agrarian resources into food production make possible the growing of enough food to maintain the urban working classes in a state of health and vigor adequate to make them productive workers. To cite Barrington Moore, Jr., the policy challenge of industrialization amounts "to using a combination of economic incentives and political compulsion to induce the people on the land to improve productivity and at the same time taking a substantial part of the surplus so generated to construct an industrial society. Behind this problem there stands a political one, whether or not a class of people has arisen in the society with the capacity and ruthlessness to force through the changes."[4]

Countries that began their drive to industrialization relatively late must modernize under much more difficult conditions than such early industrial states as Great Britain or the United States. For the latecomers, internal social structures are not conducive to such far-reaching changes. Language, race, religion, class, and ethnic divisions present seemingly insurmountable obstacles to rapid development. Abroad, the special position enjoyed by the already-industrialized states blocks the developing countries from reaping the benefits of the international trade system. As traditional social structures and attitudes crumble under the strain of modernization, Westernized intellectuals agonize over some new kind of ideology that can guide their people toward a new brand of social cohesion. When industrialization is delayed, the tendency is for the process to take place in an atmosphere of intense feeling, hostility, passion, class, and national prejudices, and there is little inclination to preserve the rights of the individual citizen.

Some late industrializers, including the Soviet Union, China, and Cuba, have chosen to deal with these obstacles by means of the model of development called (by political scientist A. F. K. Organski) the *Stalinist alternative*.[5] Stalinist regimes are characterized by the violent destruction of the premodern rural classes—both landed aristocracy and peasantry—and the accumulation of massive coercive power in the hands of an industrial elite. This elite uses its power to squeeze all possible surplus out of both the urban and the agrarian working classes and fuels the industrialization effort with this surplus. Peasants are driven from the land by collectivization, and the gentry by confiscation. Although the cost in terms of human suffering is high, the results of forced-draft industrialization are impressive.

Most of the other late industrializers, including a majority of the countries of the Third World, have followed still another path to development. *Syncratic politics*, which could be defined literally as "rule by coalition," is the term coined by Organski to describe this model. The chief characteristic of the syncratic model is the way the government attempts to handle the inevitable conflict between the old landlord class and the rising industrialists. In liberal bourgeois democracies, such as Great Britain, the conflict dissolved slowly as the agrarian sector modernized and became commercialized. In Stalinist countries, the industrial elites smashed the antimodern classes, frequently using the peasants as shock troops against the landlords, only to dismantle the peasant class itself once the revolution was consolidated. In the syncratic model, however, agrarian interests are too powerful, or industrial sectors too weak, to permit either of these solutions. The result is a shaky compromise that involves completely different kinds of bargains, payoffs, and protective devices. In sum, syncratic politics refers to the style of governance that emerges in late-industrializing countries when the agrarian class is too strong to be destroyed or converted by the industrial elite and, so, must be brought into some sort of broad coalition to preserve the special premodern conditions of the countryside.

Although they both are members of their nation's economic elite, the landed aristocracy and the industrialists are actually divided from one another by a number of inescapable economic schisms. For one thing, agrarian and industrial elites frequently come from different regions of the country or are members of different ethnic, racial, linguistic, or religious groups. These noneconomic differences may aggravate emerging class distinctions. More important, the economic roles of the two classes are antithetical. Industrialists exist to save, invest, and produce; landlords exist to consume and to withhold resources from production. Urban elites value work and self-sacrifice; agrarian elites regard manual labor as demeaning. Industrialists need a large, mobile, well-educated, disciplined, and motivated workforce and will seek to lure farm workers into the cities to fill this need; landlords want to keep their peasant class docile, traditional, and poorly educated so that its members will not wish to upset the clientelist system. The industrialists intend to squeeze the agricultural sector of its surplus production through taxation and to use the resources to advance the state's industrial base; the landlords quite naturally will try to resist being used in this manner.

In a few instances, the rural and industrial elites have managed to cover over their differences enough to cooperate in governing the country, usually through a semiparliamentary authoritarian regime that, although strong, would still fall short of a military dictatorship. In most cases, however, economic crisis or foreign threat causes internal conditions to deteriorate. As the previously quiet lower classes clamor for change, the coalition loses its nerve and submits either to a syncratic party or to a military dictator who can impose order and establish the conditions necessary for industrialization to continue.

Once in power, a syncratic regime typically undertakes a set of reform measures designed to industrialize the country without disturbing the social structures of the countryside. Traditional territorial divisions, local peculiarities, and internal barriers to trade are suppressed, and strong central government agencies are put in charge of the nation's economic fortunes. The mass of citizens must be brought into the modern social order by means of the expansion of literacy and technical skills. Antimodern loyalties to region, clan, religion, or ethnic kin are overridden. Steps are taken to stimulate latent industrial potential. Government incentives, including protective tariffs, are used to aid native manufacturing. Where the private sector is unwilling or unable to invest in a needed project, the state itself will mobilize the needed capital. Because it appears that these early measures favor the industrial elite, a syncratic regime discovers it must now provide benefits to the other partner in the coalition. Agricultural elites are kept in the partnership through three types of policy. First, they are permitted a great deal of freedom to perpetuate their exploitation of the countryside, and the central government stands ready to suppress rural rebellion where it should occur. Second, by using the threat of revolution, the regime may convince the conservative, traditional elites that they have little choice but to side with the state in the struggle. Finally, industrial workers are kept under control by the enactment of increasingly liberal welfare measures and by the use of corporatist labor organizations that bind the urban proletariat into the structure of the state economic system.

The special compromises struck by the syncratic state mean that the costs of industrial development are allocated much differently than in the liberal bourgeois or Stalinist models. Because the landed upper classes are protected by the syncratic compromise and their hold over the land is left unmolested, the surplus for reinvestment (forced savings) must come from some other source. Occasionally, these resources may be derived through foreign aid from one of the wealthy states in the international system, but this is a weak and insecure support on which to rest the industrialization policy. Eventually, the syncratic state must turn to the only remaining source of capital: the fledgling industrial sector itself. To cite Organski:

> Under a syncratic system, the savings for investment in industry are squeezed primarily out of the industrial sector itself, not gathered from the entire country. To a very large extent, the savings in the industrial sector are created by increases in productivity in the modern portion of the economy and by decreases in the living standard of the industrial proletariat.[6]

Pakistan: A Case Study in Syncratic Rule

The ten-and-a-half-year (1958 to 1969) military regime of General Mohammed Ayub Khan of Pakistan offers a clear example of a syncratic regime in action.[7] The Ayub government took power in Pakistan in October 1958, following a period of prolonged instability, unrest, and violence under the former parliamentary system. The 1958 proclamation of martial law lasted for almost four years, until March 1962. Pakistan lived under martial law for eight years between 1958 and 1971. During the period that Ayub was the chief executive of the country, Pakistanis had little access to open or free government; the executive branch of the government controlled all aspects of the country's political life. The 1962 constitution legitimized one-man rule by placing all political functions—legislative, executive, and judicial—into the hands of Ayub.

From 1958 to 1969, Pakistan's economy experienced a strong growth trend, with gross national product (GNP) rising at the average rate of 6 percent per year during the 1960s. A new business and industrialist class was fostered by government stimulus, but little was done for the urban proletariat or for the landless rural workers. An extremely small number of wealthy families continued to enjoy control of the growing industrial power of the nation, but income inequalities increased during Ayub's regime instead of diminishing.

The rhetorical dimension of Ayub's so-called revolution illustrates the syncratic governance style in action. In the case of land reform, the government responded to a critical problem by creating the Land Reform Commission in 1958. The commission's report, issued in early 1959, contained only the mildest kind of recommendations for Ayub but was still accepted by him with only minor changes. Few large landowners lost land; few, if any, peasants received any land. Apparently, Ayub was unwilling to risk losing support from the wealthy rural sector by imposing forced expropriation of agrarian lands. In other areas, such as equal rights for women or education, far-reaching laws were passed, but little attention was paid to implementation or to the financial burdens of such legislation. The result was a large set of unenforced (probably unenforceable) laws that specified desirable goals, but left unanswered the question of how to reach them.

This gap between rhetoric and reality was not the product of ignorance or incompetence on the part of Ayub Khan and his colleagues; instead, it was a calculated effort on his part to build a governing coalition made up of both elites: the modernizing, urban-based nationalists and the tradition-bound, rural aristocracy. In the cities, Ayub not only sought to stimulate industrial development, but also turned government policy toward strengthening the army, both as a modernizing bureaucracy and as the ultimate arbiter of Pakistan's fate in any armed clashes. In the countryside, as we have seen, Ayub's rule was more notable for what it did not achieve than for what it did. The privileges of the landed elites were maintained and perhaps even strengthened.

Ayub was not without his opponents and, in the end, the disturbances caused by these opposition sectors unseated his government. The major forces against the regime were the disaffected intellectuals of the universities and the professions, religious leaders, the urban middle class, and the urban and rural workers. Toward the end of Ayub's regime in 1968, these groups began to express their displeasure with the fact that they were being asked to carry more than their fair share of the development burden. The result was a series of street clashes between rioting workers and students and the army and police. By 1969, matters had worsened to the point that the army insisted that Ayub step down and allow a successor regime to try to restore order. Faced with these realities, Ayub resigned his office in March 1969 and appointed another general to take his place.

Political unrest and government repression in Pakistan in the 1970s and 1980s illustrate well the continuing agony unleashed by the syncratic approach to politics. In 1977, General Mohammed Zia ul-Haq came to power by a military overthrow of the government of President Zulfikar Ali Bhutto, who was later arrested and executed. When he seized power, Zia promised prompt elections and a return to democracy, but in October 1969, he canceled voting scheduled for that fall. In early 1981, after more than three weeks of student riots, the martial-law government launched an intensive crackdown on dissidents, jailing at least a dozen opposition leaders who had been demanding an end to Zia's rule. Through the first half of the 1980s, Zia attempted to impose on Pakistan a mild form of the Islamic fundamentalist social and political revolution, some aspects of which were borrowed from Iran. The antidemocratic nature of these reforms provoked serious resistance, especially from women, whose very right to vote was threatened. In 1983, police used clubs and tear gas to break up demonstrations by women protesting this new direction in Pakistani politics.[8]

During the last half of the 1980s, however, Pakistan began to take some gradual and halting steps toward the restoration of democracy. In December 1984, General Zia extended his personal rule five more years on the basis of a national referendum on his religious policies. The following February, parliamentary elections were held (the first since Zia came to power) and martial law was lifted. Because no parties were allowed to compete in the elections and all candidates ran as independents, the illegal opposition parties tried to boycott the elections; but voter turnout was slightly more than 50 percent, considered by many to be a victory for Zia. The general's strongest support remained in the rural areas, where landlords and tribal leaders mobilized the voters, and among the military and fundamentalist religious groups. In May 1985, General Zia changed the constitution to strengthen his rule at the same time that he opened the way for a transition from direct military rule to civilian government; and in December, he appointed a civilian prime minister and abandoned direct military control. The following spring, the daughter of the executed President Bhutto, Benazir Bhutto, returned to Pakistan to be received by huge crowds who supported her demand for immediate direct elections. Her major sources of support were the groups that had lost ground in Pakistan's development drive, predominantly the urban poor. In August 1986, Bhutto's new party, the Pakistan People's Party, took to the streets in massive demonstrations intended to force Zia to hold new elections, but the general's military support held fast and the demonstrations subsided. In November 1987, new local elections seemed to offer yet again the promise of a gradual restoration of democracy; and Zia promised to schedule direct parliamentary elections with free competition among all parties for sometime in 1990. Meanwhile, ethnic and communal violence caused the death of more than 500 persons in Karachi alone in 1987, and the country had become Asia's largest producer and trafficker of illicit drugs.

In August 1988, Pakistan was once again plunged into a crisis when General Zia was killed in a still-unexplained airplane crash. Despite speculation that the army would intervene to block any move to replace the general's regime with a democratic system, pro-democracy elements within the army's leadership prevailed. Pakistan's first free elections in more than a decade were held in November. Benazir Bhutto's party won 92 of the 237 parliamentary seats, and she was asked by interim President Ghulam Ishaq Khan to form a government. She was officially sworn into office in December as the world's first female head of state in a Moslem country. Her first year in office was stormy and uncertain, with barely disguised threats emanating not only from the military, which still distrusted her ability to run the country, but also from disaffected ethnic and regional groups. She narrowly survived a parliamentary vote of no-confidence in November 1989, after which she charged that opposition groups had planned to arrest her and more than 100 of her followers if she had lost the vote. Clearly, Pakistan's leaders were finding it especially difficult to overcome the legacy of nearly thirty years of syncratic politics.[9]

Political Institutions: Major and Minor Networks

The syncratic political style is both a cause and a consequence of a social phenomenon we have noted before: the uneven penetration of modernization through various layers of a traditional society. On the one hand, uneven rates of modernization in a traditional society allow the rural elites to retain their stranglehold on the political system despite the progressive modernization of the industrial sector in the cities. At the same time, the syncratic state perpetuates this uneven penetration of modernity simply because it exists by relying on two antithetical social groupings. For these reasons, the syncratic political style is an integral part of Third World social, economic, and political systems today. These systems are separated into dual societies: one modern, rational, secular, urban, and nationalistic; the other traditional, religious (or mystical), rural, and particularistic.

Binding together all these features of Third World politics is a three-tiered institutional arrangement that we now consider in detail. At the top is what we will call (following Robert Gamer[10]) the *major network*. The major network consists of the power elite of the country, the national government ministries, the civil and military bureaucracy, and the industrial-entrepreneurial leaders. These individuals are almost always located in the nation's capital city, cut off from the vast majority of the country. The major network extracts political support, obedience, labor, and agricultural commodities from the general populace with whom it is linked by the second level of institutions (the many *minor networks*). The minor networks consist of the middle-echelon patrons, the leaders of patron–client systems both in the cities and in the countryside. These patrons receive personal rewards for their service that are at least adequate to maintain a satisfactory lifestyle. Below these minor networks lies the vast bulk of the population, usually unorganized and unrepresented in the power structure by any forces other than their patrons. The masses supply the national system with labor and with commodities, and they participate in the system more or less regularly by means of symbolic exercises like voting for similar candidates in fraudulent elections. The patrons maintain their clients in a state of commitment to the system by a variety of means that we will examine shortly.

Minor Networks: Patron–Client Politics

In the small, remote Honduran village of Tocoa in the 1960s there lived a very powerful man named Carlos Bascha. Señor Bascha did not derive his power from any formal elective office, his ownership of large areas of land, or any special religious or ethnic status. Señor Bascha

was, instead, simply the freight agent for the Honduran national airline, which operated (irregularly) a DC-3 flight into Tocoa, the only link between the village and the outside world. Tocoa was at one time situated on a rail line constructed by the United Fruit Company many years ago. With the onset of a blight, the land in the vicinity was rendered useless for growing bananas, so the company took up the line, leaving Tocoa almost completely isolated from the rest of Honduras. All commercial activity, such as the movement of local farm products depended on the air service provided by the government. Because Señor Bascha controlled that service, he rather completely controlled the town. Preferential freight rates tied certain influential villagers to his goodwill, and Bascha's general store (the only one in town) was allowed to dominate the village's local commerce. Señor Bascha was, in our terms, a patron; the people of Tocoa were his clients.[11]

In remote villages of Burma, Manning Nash reports, the patron may not be the elected village headman. In some cases, such as in the village of Nondwin, another man, more powerful than the headman, may be regarded as the local patron. In Nondwin, this local power, U Sein Ko, was not only the richest man in the village, but the person with whom everyone had to consult in case of any dispute or political question. His power derived from the almost mystical aura of *pon*, the Burmese concept of control, which implies one's ability to make others conform to one's wishes. U Sein Ko alone had this ability. Therefore, the village population clustered around him to bask in the warmth of his power and to receive protection from it.[12]

Patron–client systems are important features of urban politics in Third World countries as well. In large cities throughout the Third World, such as Lima or Caracas, the festering slums and impoverished neighborhoods have produced squatters' associations to protect the land rights of the residents. These usually come under the jurisdiction or control of local patrons who defend the interests of their clients and receive deference and respect (as well as more material rewards) from them in return. Several observers of political parties in African cities have likened them to the big-city machines in the United States and other Western countries, especially as they operated before World War II. In Africa, these political machines rarely operate on the basis of ideology or political theory, but more often win their support as patrons win support from clients—by using an intricate mixture of coercion, prestige, material benefits (spoils), bribes, cajolery, and ceremony.[13] Other modern interest groups, such as labor unions, often find themselves infiltrated by tribal-based patron–client systems that use tribal, ethnic, and linguistic cleavages to fragment the unions and render them helpless. The presence of traditional patron–client relationships within their organizations helps explain the weakness of the otherwise powerful copper miners' union in Zambia or the rubber workers' union in Malaysia.[14]

Latin American specialist John Duncan Powell has observed that the patron–client system is marked by three characteristics. First, the tie between patron and client develops between two parties who are unequal in status, wealth, and influence. Second, the formation and maintenance of the relationship depends on the reciprocal exchange of goods or services. Finally, the development and maintenance of the system depends largely on face-to-face contact between patrons and their clients.[15] In his study of Thailand, Clark D. Neher writes,

The ideal superior acts as a patron and is expected to protect, aid, complement, and give generously to those whose status is in-ferior. In return, the subordinate, or client, is expected to act deferentially to the superior, who is his patron. He is expected to perform tasks efficiently and with the least amount of trouble for his superior. The subordinate maintains his inferior position by not challenging the superior or undermining the latter's position.[16]

Patron–client relationships can be classified according to the kinds of values that pass in exchange. Those that are of greatest relevance to the political order involve power, trust, and loyalty. The clients of such a system support their patrons' choices for public office; in return, they receive government services and personal security.

Patron–client systems are crucial to developing countries as links between the national, urban-based modernizing elites, on the one hand, and the mass of urban and rural laborers, on the other hand. Most patron–client systems can be viewed as existing at two levels. At the lowest level, in the rural village or the big-city neighborhood, clientelistic politics involves a relationship between large numbers of low-status persons and a single powerful patron who defends the interests of his or her clients and who receives deference or more material rewards in return. This patron, however, is also a member of another, higher-level patron–client system, but this time as a client to a member of the national, urban elite. The intermediary depends on an elite patron to deliver special treatment to his or her clients, but the intermediary also provides valuable services to the urban elites, particularly by mobilizing the low-status clients for mass manifestations of loyalty to the regime, such as demonstrations and elections. Patron–client systems at the village or neighborhood level are institutions that lean backward toward tradition instead of looking forward toward modernity. At the lowest level of operation, patron–client systems usually do not contribute to the modernization of the nation-state but, instead, detract from this process. In the case of patron–client links that tie intermediaries to national elites, however, the resources and values that are exchanged come closer to characterizing what we think of as modern politics: money, power, and all of the symbolic and tangible manifestations of these (votes, land, and so on).

Because of this dual nature, patron–client political systems can be regarded either favorably or unfavorably for their impact on the overall process of political development. Some observers, such as Robert E. Gamer,[17] are quite critical of clientelistic politics. As they see it, such political processes always work a hardship on the mass of clients at the very bottom of the pyramid. According to this view, patron–client systems owe their origin to the uneven penetration of modernity through the several layers of a traditional social order. The modern nation-state has enough power and organizational ability to reach down into the traditional sectors to manipulate the masses and to mobilize them to perform the symbolic functions of politics, such as voting; but the two-way institutions that are truly indicative of modern politics—political parties and associational interest groups—simply are lacking in most Third World countries. In the absence of parties and interest groups, patrons are brought to the fore to facilitate communication (mostly of a top-down nature) between elites and masses. In the course of this communication process, however, the intermediaries extract their due (and more) from the exchange, and the minor networks end up receiving much less in terms of material well-being than they should. Accordingly, only the creation of truly modern, mass-based institutions, such as political parties, can do away

with the exploitative patron–client systems and extend modernity all the way down to the very lowest level of society.

However, another way of looking at the question (as exemplified by John Duncan Powell[18]) holds that, at the middle level of operation, patron–client systems offer the potential for being transformed into modernizing institutions. Powell cites as an example the various peasant leagues that were created by the Venezuelan reformist political parties, primarily Acción Democrática. These leagues were not, at the outset, what we would regard as modern institutions. They were still operating on the basis of patron–client principles: unequal status, exchange of goods and services, obedience and deference, loyalty and security, a face-to-face communications system, and so forth. Yet, the leaders of Acción Democrática relied on these leagues for the mobilization of the peasants as potential voters, and they used their vigorous land-reform program to attract peasant voters to their party. Thus, Acción Democrática transformed the clientelistic peasant leagues into modernizing institutions capable of linking the peasant (and, subsequently, the middle-class farmer) into the national political system in a way that meets the needs of the low-status members of the network.

The Venezuelan experience, although not unique, is certainly the exception rather than the rule. In the majority of Third World countries, low-status persons, whether in the city or in the country, simply have no other way to communicate with their government other than through their local patron. Transportation and communication gaps cause rigidity in the links between the government and its people; the absence of mass-based, modernizing institutions, such as parties and interest groups, likewise contributes to blocking effective communication. For good or ill, in most developing countries, patron–client systems are almost the only connection between the government and the mass of citizens.

Major Networks: The Separation of Powers

When we in the United States analyze our country's political institutions, we usually begin with the concept *separation of powers*. During the Republic's formative years, the members of the new American colonial elite were so eager to prevent government from abusing the rights of the citizens that they devised a simple formula for keeping the central government weak: Divide power and authority into so many competing institutions that the constant struggle between and among these agencies will occupy their attention and drain their resources so that there will be little of either left over to direct toward the average citizen in private life. John Taylor, a noted liberal writer of the period, expressed the thought this way:

> Power is divided by our policy, that the people may maintain their sovereignty. . . . Our principle of division is used to reduce power to that degree of temperature, which may make it a blessing and not a curse. . . . We do not balance power against power. It is our policy to reduce it by division, in order to preserve the political power of the people.[19]

But it was James Madison, the principal author of the Constitution, who expressed the classic argument in favor of separation of powers:

> But the great security against a gradual concentration of . . . powers in the same department consists in giving to those who administer each department the necessary constitutional means and personal motives to resist encroachments of others. . . . Ambition must be made to counteract ambition. The interest of the man must be connected with the constitutional rights of the place. . . . If men were angels, no government would be necessary. If angels were to govern man, neither external nor internal controls on government would be necessary. In framing a government which is to be administered by men over men, the great difficulty lies in this: you must first enable the government to control the governed; and in the next place oblige it to control itself. A dependence on the people is, no doubt, the primary control on the government; but experience has taught mankind the necessity of auxiliary precautions.[20]

Indeed, much of American political history can be seen as a struggle between and among Madison's auxiliary precautions: the various states against the national government, the legislature against the president, the courts against each of the others, and so on.

Because the principle of separation of powers is so deeply embedded in the American political system, it may seem strange to note that few other countries in the world share our aversion toward centralizing power in the hands of a single institution or person. Among the Third World countries, almost none have political institutions and constitutional structures that try to divide powers among several competing agencies or sources of authority. In Latin America, the Spanish and Portuguese tradition of centralized power in a monarchy was transmitted to the New World in undiluted form and was amalgamated with the indigenous political systems, which were similarly inclined toward centralization of power.[21] In Africa and Asia, the native, precolonial political systems were usually of the centralized and unified type. The introduction of European power did nothing to alter this situation. The practice of direct rule employed by France, Holland, and other continental colonial powers lodged power in the mother country. British indirect rule merely confirmed authority in the local rules (tribal chieftains, village headmen, and so on) who had held centralized power for centuries. Thus, the countries of the Third World came to independence and began their drive to development with little in the way of historical preparation for, or appreciation of, governance by means of separation of powers.

At the same time, Third World leaders confronted problems quite different from those faced by Washington, Madison, Hamilton, and Jefferson. The new country of America came into being determined to free the individual from government interference and, thus, to reduce government power, but the new states of the Third World find that they must *increase* government power to meet the critical problems created by the dual processes of industrialization and modernization. Instead of limiting government's power, what the elites of the Third World want to do is break through the substantial constraints on their power so that they might better cope with their special social and economic difficulties.

Finally, in the industrialized West, we have a tendency to look at government not as a party to a given dispute, but as the reconciler of conflicting interests, the ultimate recourse for the resolution of conflict. This view depends, however, on the prior existence of a rich and accessible network of modern secondary associations that are essentially outside government: political parties, interest groups, and many different kinds of voluntary associations. These institutions are notably lacking in most Third World countries. Voluntary associations are al-

most completely unknown in many developing countries; where they do exist, they are weakened by the traditional mistrust with which such associations are viewed by low-status individuals in poor countries. Parties and interest groups frequently are controlled by the government itself, and they are used not to channel messages upward from the populace, but to channel commands and rhetoric downward from the regime. In this context, government becomes more than a reconciler of interests— it becomes a party to the dispute. Consequently, there is great pressure on the government to adopt a unified position, to employ decision-making techniques that accelerate action and suppress dissent. The result is an inclination to override whatever institutional separation of powers there might have been to begin with.

Major Networks: The Dominant Executive

The notion of separation of powers actually has two different meanings. The first meaning has to do with the separation of powers within the government. Regardless of the form that government may take, there are three more or less distinct functions that must be performed in the course of the policy process: legislation (the adoption of general principles and the statement of general goals); execution (the translation of these principles and goals into politically acceptable actions); and adjudication (the judgment of the fairness of the application of the general principles in specific cases where a party is thought to be damaged). In the United States, we like to think of these three functions as being assigned primarily to the three corresponding institutions: the Congress, the president, and the Supreme Court. (The dividing lines are much fuzzier in practice than they are in theory.) But in the Third World they tend to be performed by the same institution or, in some extreme cases, by the same individual. We call this phenomenon the principle of *executive dominance*. In the struggle among and between competing institutions of government in the developing world, it is the executive power than has won.

Let us consider some concrete manifestations of the executive-dominant system in the Third World. Most observers of politics regard an independent legislature or parliament as the surest check on the power of the executive. A survey of the 102 Third World countries in 1987 reveals that in 22 of them, the legislative branch has been dismissed, dissolved, or suspended indefinitely, or was never even constituted or elected. A number of traditional monarchies, such as Saudi Arabia and Kuwait, have never had an elected legislative assembly; others, like Chile, were under the control of a military regime that suspended the country's legislature when it came to power. In thirty-six other countries, although there is an elected legislature, it consists solely (or largely) of members of the single official party who, in most instances, were elected without opposition. In states with de facto one-party regimes, like Mexico and Egypt, the legislature provides virtually no real check on the executive since the members of the assembly do not represent any independent base of power. In another twenty-four cases, a more or less freely elected legislature is so dominated by a powerful chief executive that it has few real powers and is reduced to ratifying decisions made by the executive. The prime minister of Turkey, Turgot Ozal, enjoyed such power because his party, the Motherland Party, held 292 of the parliament's 450 seats, and the second leading party held only 99. Thus, in only twenty instances can we say that a country's legislative assembly is an effective counterweight to the executive branch.[22]

Another indicator of executive dominance is the degree to which presidents or dictators manipulate or suspend the constitution (completely or in part) or engage in other electoral irregularities to remain in power beyond the end of their legally prescribed term of office. In 1987, at least twenty-nine Third World countries were operating either without any constitution or with their basic law suspended or bypassed by the chief executive. In Kenya in 1986 and 1987, President Daniel arap Moi pushed through constitutional amendments to give him more direct control over the country's judicial system and its public spending control agent, both of which had previously been independent of presidential authority. In Pakistan in late 1985, President (General) Zia ended martial law only after his rubber-stamp legislature had amended the constitution to ensure that his previous martial law decrees would become civilian law, to ratify his continued control over the parliament, and to continue the suspension of numerous human rights guarantees until he decides to restore them. On the other hand, in the late 1980s there were several very important instances of the restoration of constitutional government in the Third World that offered the promise of an eventual return to democracy throughout the southern hemisphere. Some of the more crucial countries where constitutionalism reemerged to regulate executives were the Philippines (where Ferninand Marcos was forced out of office by Corazon Aquino's electoral challenge), Argentina, Brazil, South Korea, and Uruguay. It may well be that as we near the end of the decade, more constitutional regimes will reappear throughout the Third World, and the lengthy period of executive power domination will begin to be offset by new constraints on the power of the executive.[23]

Not all examples of executive dominance are extralegal or unconstitutional. Many Third World executives enjoy extraordinary powers as a consequence of a constitutional grant of authority. The 1962 Republic of Tanganyika Act provided that, "except as may otherwise be provided by law, in the exercise of his functions, the President shall act at his own discretion and shall not be obliged to follow advice tendered by any other person." Following this broad grant of authority, President Julius K. Nyerere acted unilaterally to end discrimination against non-Africans in the civil service; to unite Tanganyika with Zanzibar (creating Tanzania); to introduce a one-party state, making the Tanzania African National Union the sole legal party in the country; to break diplomatic relations with Great Britain in 1965; and to create completely new agencies, such as the Village Resettlement Agency (1963).[24]

Other Third World executives enjoy similar powers. Under the country's 1965 constitution, the president of Brazil could appoint state governors and the mayors of municipalities, and dissolve the Brazilian Congress if it disagreed with his decisions. The prime minister of Singapore imposed one-party rule, jailed political opponents and held them for years without trial, closed down newspapers, and otherwise suppressed public dissent, all within the boundaries of the country's constitution. For seventeen months, from late 1975 through early 1977, India's Prime Minister Indira Gandhi ruled her giant country under the provisions of emergency law, which permitted her to censor the press and jail her opponents for simple acts of dissidence. In all, at least 100,000 dissidents were imprisoned during this period. In parliamentary elections in March 1977, Mrs. Gandhi was defeated. She returned to power and in mid-1980 sought once again to impose emergency police measures in India to suppress un-

rest in rebellious Assam State. Again, as in the other instances just cited, Mrs. Gandhi's acts were all decreed by her as prime minister and were within the bounds imposed by the Indian Constitution.[25]

Executive dominance is also reflected in the relatively high degree of administrative centralization that exists in most Third World countries. Most Third World executives dominate the legislative and judicial branches at the national level, and, because of the concentration of administrative power in the hands of the national government, they also dominate local, provincial, and municipal governments. In the entire Third World, only eleven countries have adopted the federal form of government, which supposes certain political autonomy for provincial or state-level administrative units. Eight of these federal systems are very large countries with land areas of about 1 million square kilometers or more: Argentina, Brazil, India, Mexico, Nigeria, Pakistan, South Africa, and Tanzania. However, even in these few instances, the autonomy of the lower administrative units is more apparent than real. In India, for example, Prime Minister Indira Gandhi acted forcefully in the early 1980s to curtail state powers and even to remove from office state officials who opposed her.

In his analysis of local administration in Thailand, Clark D. Neher has identified three separate but closely interrelated patterns of authority that apply to local populations in that country.[26] The *territorial or provincial administration*, which receives its power and resources from the central government in Bangkok, is the most powerful of the three systems. This administrative system consists of the minister of interior, 71 provincial governors, and 530 district officers. The minister of interior appoints, removes, and transfers both the provincial governors and the district officers; these subordinate officials are, consequently, responsible to the interior minister in all that they do. All major decisions are referred to the minister. The provincial governors are powerful only in a derivative sense; that is, they have no resources themselves but derive power from carrying out central government decrees. District officers' authority seems to be restricted primarily to the supervision of the ministry's local employees and to the filling out and submission of an almost endless number of forms and reports. The second pattern of authority consists of some 50,000 villages that, in turn, are clustered into about 5,000 *communes* for some limited purposes of self-government. Each village elects a headman who, as we saw in the example drawn from Burma earlier, may have considerable social and economic power in addition to his formal political authority. But the actual powers of the village and commune are restricted to making arrests in criminal cases, settling petty disputes and quarrels, submitting reports and information to higher authorities, and deciding how to spend the meager sums distributed to the villages from the central government. The third pattern of authority, called *local self-government units*, is the weakest system of the three. It consists of provincial councils, municipal councils, and sanitation districts. The first two bodies are purely deliberative institutions; all substantive policy decisions remain in the hands of the central government. Sanitation districts are charged with responsibilities in such fields as garbage collection, street paving, street and house lighting, slaughterhouse regulation, water and sewage facilities, and health centers. These units are notoriously inefficient and lack adequate funds for their many operations.

Most local authority in Third World countries effectively lies in the hands of the central governments, primarily in the various ministries of interior and their subordinate units. In in-stances where local units actually have authority, however, a serious lack of resources prevents them from taking advantage of this constitutional delegation of power. Henry Bretton reports that local self-government in many African countries is hampered by a lack of locally obtained and locally expended funds.[27] Local governments either do not have the authority to collect their own taxes or, if they do have such authority, lack the trained personnel to apply the authority efficiently. In addition, where power resides so solidly in the central government, and local governments lack the financial resources to cope with local problems, the obvious strategy for patron–client systems is to bypass the local administrators and go straight to the pertinent ministry in the capital. Such a development further weakens local government and strengthens the central administration's ties over local patrons in a vicious circle of progressive local debilitation. This sort of circumstance seems to be a significant reason why state governors and municipal mayors in Mexico are bypassed by local patrons and interest-group leaders who feel that the only place their problem can be handled is in Mexico City.

Although executive dominance remains the most important characteristic of many Third World governments, in the latter half of the 1980s there were a number of important developments that suggest that we are entering a new era in which the powers of the chief executives increasingly are being curtailed by other resurgent political forces and institutions. For example, in two important countries— Egypt and India—the assassination of powerful, dominant chief executives (Anwar Sadat and Indira Gandhi) was followed by the rise to power of two much more modest leaders (Hosni Mubarak and Rajiv Gandhi) whose more moderate style allowed other forces or institutions to enter actively into national politics. In several instances—the Philippines and South Korea—dictatorships were forced out of office by mass pressures and electoral challenges and were replaced by popularly elected leaders committed to constitutional government (Corazon Aquino and Roh Tae Woo). In a number of instances, although strong-man dictators remained entrenched in office, they were willing to allow other institutions to share power with them, even if gradually and haltingly: in Pakistan, General Zia allowed the parliament to exercise some independent authority; in Indonesia, President (formerly General) Suharto encouraged reforms to make the parliament a much more active force in politics with an independent voice and responsibility; and in Singapore, Prime Minister Lee Kuan Yew even suggested the possibility of a directly elected president who could in time come to rival the prime minister himself. Still, apparently the hardest thing for a Third World executive to do is retire willingly from office and leave power to someone else. Tunisia's legendary president, Habib Bourguiba, held on to power until the age of eighty-four, when it took a coup by one of his young protégés, Prime Minister Zine Abidine Ben Ali, to remove him from office in late 1987. Tanzania's founder and first president, Julius Nyerere, had apparently set a dramatic new precedent in 1985 when he voluntarily stepped down as chief executive and passed power to his successor, Ali Hassan Mwinyi. However, Nyerere held onto his post as chairman of the ruling Revolutionary Party of Tanzania for a term to last no more than two years. As he neared the end of this period, however, Nyerere decided to remain in office, and he had his tenure extended another five years. And in Panama in the first half of 1988, General Manuel Noriega seemed determined to try to resist pressures from the United States to oust him from his position as dictator and commander in chief of the armed forces.

Major Networks: The Military Bureaucracy

As noted earlier, one aspect of separation of powers involves the division of the legislative, executive, and judicial functions of the policy-making process among separate institutions. The second involves separating the institutions that make policy from those that implement it, that is, the civil and military bureaucrats that put the political decisions into effect. It is usually assumed by observers of Western democracy that the individuals who administer or implement policy must be separated from those who make policy because of the need to identify clearly the lines of political responsibility. At least in theory, those who make policy are somehow to be more or less directly responsible to the electorate, who can judge the policies and change them if they desire simply by electing a different group of policymakers. Bureaucrats, on the other hand, are invulnerable to voter pressure; they are not supposed to actually make policy but, instead, should simply apply the decisions of the political officials in specific cases. To the degree that bureaucrats, either civil or military, stray across the line from policy implementation to policy-making, they are acting in an antidemocratic fashion, because they are putting into effect policy decisions over which the sovereign public has no control.[28]

Problems connected with the operations of the civil bureaucracy in the Third World (corruption, lack of training, clientelism) are discussed in Chapter 20. In this section, we concentrate on the intervention of the armed forces into the policy-making process in the developing world.

It is true that, on occasion, supporters of democracy in the Third World have welcomed military intervention in politics to restore order to political life.[29] Yet, in the larger sense, military intervention in civilian politics constitutes a major barrier to Third World political development. Military regimes impose arms expenditures on their countries' fragile economies, diverting resources that could be used for social and economic improvement. The rise to power of military governments is associated with increased numbers of international and internal wars with the resultant widespread killing of civilians. Finally, military regimes tend to use force excessively against their own people, leading to increased human rights violations.[30]

Military intervention in politics has been a major problem of Latin American governments ever since the nineteenth century. During the period from 1930 to 1965, there were 106 illegal and unscheduled changes in the heads of state in the countries of Latin America; all but a tiny portion of these changes were initiated and carried out by the military, although frequently with civilian support and encouragement. There were many observers, however, who believed that the countries of Africa and Asia that became independent after World War II would be spared this dismal history and would demonstrate that civilian constitutional regimes could meet the severe problems of development in a stable and responsive manner without succumbing to military rule. Such hopes have been destroyed by

military coups in most of the countries in Africa, the Middle East, and Asia and by continued military rule in thirty-six of them. Table 19.1 indicates that a coup or attempted coup occurred once every four months in Latin America (from 1945 to 1972), once every seven months in Asia (1947 to 1972), once every three months in the Middle East (1949 to 1972), and once every fifty-five days in Africa (1960 to 1972)!

According to the 1987–88 edition of *World Military and Social Expenditures*, fifty-nine Third World states were under military control, meaning that they met one or more of these criteria; key political leadership by military officers; existence of a state of martial law; extrajudicial authority exercised by security forces; lack of central political control over armed forces rule; and control by foreign military forces. These fifty-nine states had lived under military rule for an average of more than eighteen years, or about two-thirds of the entire period from 1960 to 1987. They had experienced eighty-four successful military interventions, or about one every 100 days throughout the twenty-three-year period from 1960 to 1982. (See Table 19.2.)

The degree of military rule in effect in the Third World today attests to the instability and ineffectiveness of civilian regimes since World War II. Military rule is spread thickly across all four regions of the Third World. (See Tables

Table 19.1 Military Coups in the Third World for Selected Periods, 1945–72

	Successful	*Unsuccessful*	*Total*
Latin America (1945–72)	53	28	81
Asia (1947–72)	21	21	42
Middle East (1949–72)	41	42	83
Africa (1960–72)	32	46	78
Total	147	137	284

(*Source*) Gavin Kennedy, *The Military in the Third World* (New York: Scribner's, 1974), pp. 337–344.

Table 19.2 Third World Countries under Military Control, by Region, 1987

Region	Number of Countries, 1987	Number of Successful Coups, 1960–82	Average Years of Military Rule, 1960–87
Africa	29	35	15.6
Asia	13	15	21.7
Latin America	10	22	19.3
Middle East/North Africa	7	12	25.1
Total Third World	59	84	18.7

(*Source*) Sivard, *World Military and Social Expenditures*, 1987–88, p. 27. Note that this source includes as Third World countries four states classified here as Second World: North Korea, Kampuchea, Laos, and Vietnam.

19.3 and 19.4.) In thirty-eight countries, officers of the armed forces actually occupy key leadership positions, usually without leaving active military service. Africa is the region most susceptible to this sort of institutional decay, but it is not unknown in Latin America, the Middle East, or Asia. In Table 19.4, we see that an additional nineteen countries have military establishments that, although not actually occupying leadership positions, exercise substantial influence in areas besides those traditionally assigned to the armed forces. In many of these countries, civilian rulers must assume that a military coup attempt is being plotted virtually constantly. They must be aware that any deterioration in public order or the financial status of the government could bring the military into control. In some states, the incumbent regime is headed by a former military commander who rose to power at the head of a coup, then resigned his military status to be elected more or less democratically as the chief executive of a newly established constitutional order. These two categories of military rule together account for fifty-seven states in the Third World.

One can learn almost as much about Third World politics by studying countries in which the military is not dominant. For this, we can turn to Table 19.5. We can see that forty-five Third World states have either managed to escape military rule entirely, or, as in the cases of Mexico and Venezuela, have civilian regimes that have defeated military insurgents. Of these forty-five countries, however, twenty-one are quite small (population of less than 5 million in 1985) and consist largely of former British island colonies (Jamaica, Trinidad and Tobago), or traditional monarchies (Bhutan, Swaziland). Of the states that had a population of more than five million in 1985 and that have also escaped military rule, two (Nepal, Saudi Arabia) are autocratic, traditional monarchies, and most of the remainder have one-party civilian regimes that have achieved a poor record in the field of human rights. (See Chapter 21.) Thus, of the entire range of 102 Third World nations, only a comparative handful (Colombia, Costa Rica, India, Kenya, Mexico, Sri Lanka, Tanzania, Tunisia, and Venezuela) have successfully faced the challenges of governing a large, rapidly developing country under a more or less open and constitutional process and, at the same time, have managed to avoid giving the military a reason and an opportunity to intervene.[31]

Table 19.3   Third World States in Which Armed Forces Occupy Key Leadership Positions, 1987 (N = 38)

	Africa	Asia	Latin America	Middle East/North Africa
Military Control Not Yet Ratified by Constitutional Processes	Burkina Faso Central African Republic Chad Ethiopia Ghana Guinea Lesotho Mauritania Niger Nigeria Uganda	Afghanistan	Haiti Panama Suriname	
Military Control Ratified by Constitutional Processes	Benin Burundi Congo Equatorial Guinea Guinea-Bissau Madagascar Mali Rwanda Somalia Sudan Togo Zaire	Bangladesh Burma Indonesia Pakistan	Chile Nicaragua Paraguay	Iraq Libya Syria Yemen A.R.

(*Source*) Banks, ed., *Political Handbook* (1987); George Thomas Kurian, *Encyclopedia of the Third World*, 3rd ed. (New York: Facts on File, 1987), 3 vols.; Sivard, *World Military and Social Expenditures, 1987–88*, p. 27; Raymond D. Gastil, ed. *Freedom in the World: Political Rights and Civil Liberties, 1985–1986* (Westport, Conn.: Greenwood Press, 1987), pp. 74–75.

The massive literature on the role of the military in Third World politics suggests the following arguments to explain the intervention of a country's armed forces into politics.[32]

1. A sharp decline in the prestige of the government or of the ruling political party. This causes the regime to use in-

creasing amounts of physical coercion to maintain order and to stress the imperative of the national unity in the face of crisis, leading consequently to a suppression of dissent.

2. Schisms between or among political leaders, causing military commanders to doubt the continued ability of the

civilian regime to govern effectively.

3. A low probability of external intervention by a major world power or by neighboring states in the event of a coup.

4. Contagion from military coups in neighboring countries.

5. Domestic social unrest, most obviously occurring in countries governed by a minority group (Ibos in Nigeria, Arabs in Zanzibar), and usually marked by high levels of violence.

6. Economic crises, leading to austerity policies that affect the organized, urban sectors of society (labor unions, civil servants).

7. Corruption and inefficiency among government and party officials or a belief that civilian officials are on the verge of selling out the country to some foreign group (Peru, in the case of Fernando Belaunde; Chile, in the case of Salvador Allende).

8. A highly rigid class structure that makes military service the only possible avenue

for a poor boy to move from low to high status.

9. A growing belief among the members of the military that they are the only social class with enough discipline and enough commitment to modernization to move the country out of its traditional ways.

10. Foreign influences. These could include the military representatives of foreign governments, experiences gained in foreign wars (e.g., the Colombian battalion in the Korean War) or in foreign training centers, or foreign aid in the form of equipment and weapons.

11. Defeat of the military in a war with another country, especially when the military leaders are convinced that the civilian government betrayed them by negotiating disadvantageous peace terms or by mismanaging the war effort behind the front lines (Bolivia in the 1940s).

Any one or any combination of these causes could constitute an impressive bill of particulars

Table 19.4 Third World States with High Military Influence and Potential for Military Intervention, 1987 (N = 18)

Africa	Asia	Latin America	Middle East/North Africa
Liberia	Republic of Korea	Argentina	Algeria
Sierra Leone	Philippines	Bolivia	Iran
South Africa	Thailand	Brazil	Lebanon
		El Salvador	Turkey
		Guatemala	Yemen P.D.R.
		Honduras	
		Peru	

(*Source*) See Table 19.3.

Table 19.5 Third World States with Low Military Influence and Low Potential for Intervention, 1987 (N = 45)

	Africa	Asia	Latin America	Middle East/North Africa
Traditional Monarchies	Swaziland	Bhutan Brunei Nepal		Bahrain Jordan Kuwait Oman Qatar Saudia Arabia United Arab Emirates
De facto or Constitutional One-Party States	Angola Cameroon Gabon Ivory Coast Kenya Malawi Mozambique São Tomé and Principe Tanzania Zambia Zimbabwe	Singapore Taiwan	Mexico	Tunisia
Multiparty Democracies	Botswana Gambia Mauritius Senegal	India Malaysia Papua New Guinea Sri Lanka	Belize Colombia Costa Rica Dominican Republic Eduador Guyana Jamaica Trinidad and Tobago Uruguay Venezuela	Morocco

(*Source*) See Table 19.3.

to lay at the doorstep of the ousted civilian government. No doubt some military leaders have intervened in politics primarily (or even solely) out of a desire to advance personal prestige or power. The regimes of Idi Amin in Uganda or of Rafael Trujillo in the Dominican Republic seem to have brought their countries not prosperity and peace, but suppression of human rights in the most brutal fashion and economic stagnation, all for the greater glory of "The Dictator." The evidence seems to indicate, however, that the Amins and the Trujillos

Chilean police patrol the streets of Santiago in September 1983 to suppress popular demonstrations against the military regime of General Augusto Pinochet. These demonstrations were timed to coincide with the tenth anniversary of General Pinochet's rise to power by overthrowing the government of Marxist President Salvador Allende. General Pinochet yielded power to a constitutional government and a popularly elected president, Patricio Aylwin, following election.

are in the minority as far as military governments are concerned. The majority of military regimes in the Third World are in place not primarily because of a desire for personal power, but for the same reason people strive for political power anywhere: to improve the public sector's capacity to solve persistent and annoying (or even critical) problems.

And how well do military regimes perform that function? How effective have military regimes been in their search for economic prosperity and social order? One sort of evidence lies in the life and the death of military governments. On the one hand, most military governments are most reluctant to give power back to civilian authorities, apparently on the assumption that the same circumstances that prompted their original intervention are still present. The civilians simply cannot be trusted with power until the country's stability is assured. On the other hand, most military regimes end the way they began: at the hands of another coup launched by a hostile faction within the military. Gavin Kennedy asserts that of all the precipitating factors that might bring the military into power in the Third World, the most important is simply that the incumbent regime is also a military government that gained power illegally.[33] In other words, the more military coups a country has, the more it is likely to have. The first is the most difficult; they become progressively easier as the military becomes accustomed to holding power. But this observation also suggests that military governments rarely solve the problems they say motivated their entry into politics in the first place.

In recent years, political scientists have begun to assess the economic growth performance of military and civilian regimes in the Third World.[34] In general, their findings suggest that there is really rather little difference between the two kinds of regimes, especially when other such factors as national wealth are held constant. R. D. McKinlay and A. S. Cohan assessed the performance of military and nonmilitary regimes in 101 countries over the period from 1961 to 1970.[35] Their findings revealed that, although there was considerable difference between the two kinds of regimes in political terms (such as the dissolution of legislatures or the banning of opposition political parties), there was relatively little significant difference between the two types in the areas of military policy and economic growth rates. That is, the economies of the countries in question grew rapidly or slowly in response to other factors (their endowment with strategic raw materials, for instance) apart from the kind of regime they possessed.

Our own research in this area suggests that the relationship between level of military control and economic performance is ambiguous. (See Figure 19.1.) It is clear that countries with military regimes that have not yet been ratified by some constitutional process exhibit very low GNP per capita growth rates (less than 1 percent annually for more than twenty years). In contrast, multiparty, civilian, constitutional democracies that have little to fear from military intervention have achieved fairly high economic growth rates (2.1 percent). Countries with military regimes that *have* been ratified by some constitutional process (e.g., Indonesia), as well as those that have civilian regimes but also high levels of military influence (e.g., Argentina, Korea), have also performed poorly on the indicator of GNP per capita growth rates (less then 2.0 percent in both cases). All these data suggest that the relationship between form of government and level of economic performance is extremely complex, and that countries desiring a rapid rate of economic growth will not necessarily accomplish this goal simply by adopting a military form of government.

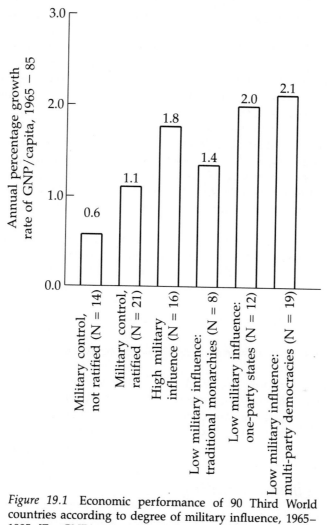

Figure 19.1 Economic performance of 90 Third World countries according to degree of military influence, 1965–1985. [For GNP/capita growth rates: World Bank, *World Development Report: 1987* (New York: Oxford University Press, 1987), Table 1, pp. 202–3. For military influence: Tables 19.3, 19.4, and 19.5.]

Conclusions: Government Institutions and Human Dignity

It seems that many Third World governments suffer from a number of important flaws that block them from making a maximum contribution to the enhancement of human dignity in their countries. Being comparative latecomers in the rush to industrialization, Third World industrial elites have been too weak to absorb or defeat the traditional agrarian elites, so they have been forced to turn to the authoritarian rule of the syncratic regime, which manages to maintain order by refraining from attacking rural landlords and by suppressing mass demands for a better standard of living. Industrialization must proceed at a reduced pace because the rural elites oppose it and because the industrial sector has difficulty financing its own development. Whatever surplus there is must be extracted from the low-income city and village dwellers.

The ability of a syncratic regime to carry out this kind of policy depends largely on three sets of institutions, which we have considered in detail. The first set consists of the network of patron–client systems that link together the urban elites and the low-income citizens in a complex psychological bond that makes it possible for governments to ignore mass demands without provoking mass rebellion. The second set is the country's dominant executive, the president and his or her circle of advisers and experts. Aided by both constitutional grants and extraconstitutional seizures of extraordinary powers, the chief executive can rule without serious challenge from outside interests or groups as long as the patron–client systems remain intact and as long as he or she can control the industrialist–landlord coalition that supports the syncratic regime. Behind many of these regimes, however, stands the third set of institutions—the military—ready to intervene to restore order if the constitutional government should prove unable to govern. The comparative frequency of military interventions in politics in the Third World reflects the continuing inability of civilian, constitutional regimes to break through the barriers of syncratic politics and to master the industrialization process. Levels of human dignity are unlikely to rise greatly in countries where these three institutions remain powerful and unchallenged.

Suggestions for Further Reading

Anderson, James N. E., ed., *Changing Law in Developing Countries* (New York: Praeger, 1963).

Ashford, Douglas E., *National Development and Local Reform: Political Participation in Morocco, Tunisia and Pakistan* (Princeton, N.J.: Princeton University Press, 1967).

Braibanti, Ralph, ed., *Political and Administrative Development* (Durham, N.C.: Duke University Press, 1969).

Burke, Fred G., *Local Government and Politics in Uganda* (Syracuse, N.Y.: Syracuse University Press, 1964).

David, Stephen R., *Third World Coups d'Etat and International Security* (Baltimore: Johns Hopkins University Press, 1986).

Herman, Valentine, *Parliaments of the World* (New York: DeGruyter, 1976).

Horowitz, Irving Louis, *Beyond Empire and Revolution: Militarization and Consolidation in the Third World* (New York: Oxford University Press, 1982).

Janowitz, Morris, *The Military and the Political Development of New Nations* (Chicago: University of Chicago Press, 1964).

Johnson, John J., ed., *The Role of the Military in Underdeveloped Countries* (Princeton, N.J.: Princeton University Press, 1962).

Kaldor, Mary, and **Asbjorn Eide,** eds., *The World Military Order: The Impact of Military Technology on the Third World* (New York: Praeger, 1979).

Kennedy, Gavin, *The Military in the Third World* (New York: Scribner's, 1974).

Kornberg, Allan, and **Lloyd D. Musolf,** eds., *Legislatures in Developmental Perspective* (Durham, N.C.: Duke University Press, 1970).

Lieuwin, Edwin, *Arms and Politics in Latin America* (New York: Praeger, 1960).

_____, *Generals vs. Presidents: Neomilitarism in Latin America* (New York: Praeger, 1964).

Lloyd, P. C., ed., *The New Elites of Tropical Africa* (London: Oxford University Press, 1966).

Park, Richard L., and **Irene Tinker,** eds., *Leadership and Political Institutions in India* (Princeton, N.J.: Princeton University Press, 1959).

Shack, William A., and **Percy S. Cohen,** eds., *Politics in Leadership: A Comparative Perspective* (New York: Oxford University Press, 1979).

Sherwood, Frank P., *Institutionalizing the Grass Roots in Brazil: A Study in Comparative Local Government* (San Francisco: Chandler, 1967).

Simon, Sheldon W., ed., *The Military and Security in the Third World: Domestic and International Impacts* (Boulder, Colo.: Westview Press, 1978).

Smith, Joel, and **Lloyd Musolf,** eds., *Legislatures in Development: Dynamics of Change in New and Old States* (Durham, N.C.: Duke University Press, 1979).

Tinker, Hugh, *Ballot Box and Bayonet: People and Government in Emergent Asian Countries* (New York: Oxford University Press, 1964).

_____, *The Foundations of Local Self-Government in India, Pakistan and Burma* (London: London University Press, 1954).

Uphoff, Norman T., *Local Institutional Development* (West Hartford, Conn.: Kumarian Press, 1987).

Younger, Kenneth, *The Public Service in New States* (London: Oxford University Press, 1969).

Notes

1. Mary Matossian, "Ideologies of Delayed Industrialization: Some Tensions and Ambiguities," *Economic Development and Cultural Change* 6 (3) (1958), 217–228. This important article has been reprinted in several places, including Claude E. Welch, Jr., ed., *Political Modernization* (Belmont, Calif.: Wadsworth, 1967), pp. 332–334.

2. Walt W. Rostow, *The Stages of Economic Growth* (Cambridge: Cambridge University Press, 1960); Rostow, *Politics and the Stages of Growth* (Cam-

bridge: Cambridge University Press, 1971).

3. Barrington Moore, Jr., *Social Origins of Dictatorship and Democracy: Lord and Peasant in the Making of the Modern World* (Boston: Beacon Press, 1966).

4. Ibid., pp. 385–386.

5. A.F.K. Organski, *The Stages of Political Development* (New York: Knopf, 1965).

6. Ibid., p. 139.

7. Robert LaPorte, Jr., "Pakistan and Bangladesh," in Robert N. Kearney, ed., *Politics and Modernization in South and Southeast Asia* (New York: Wiley, 1975), pp. 122–135.

8. Stuart Auerbach, "A Dozen Pakistani Leaders Arrested after Student, Political Unrest," *Washington Post*, February 26, 1981; William Claiborne, "Pakistani Women's Groups Oppose Zia's Drive for Islamic Rules," *Washington Post*, March 28, 1983; *The Economist*, August 4, 1984.

9. William Claiborne, "Pakistan Elects New Legislature," *Washington Post*, February 26, 1985; Richard Weintraub, "Bhutto's Party Splits; New Centrist Group Forms," *Washington Post*, September 1, 1986; Weintraub, "Local Elections to Test Credibility of Pakistan's Two Main Parties," *Washington Post*, November 29, 1987; *The Economist*, March 9, 1985, October 10, 1987, November 21, 1987.

10. Robert E. Gamer, *The Developing Nations: A Comparative Perspective* (Boston: Allyn & Bacon, 1976), Ch. 4.

11. Based on field research in Honduras by Robert Clark.

12. Manning Nash, *The Golden Road to Modernity: Village Life in Contemporary Burma* (Chicago: Chicago University Press, 1965), pp. 73–93.

13. Henry Bienen, "Political Parties and Political Machines in Africa," in Michael F. Lofchie, ed., *The State of the Nations: Constraints on Development in Independent Africa* (Berkeley: University of California Press, 1971), Ch. 8.

14. Henry L. Bretton, *Power and Politics in Africa* (Chicago: Aldine, 1973), p. 258; Gordon P.

Means, "Malaysia," in Kearney, ed., *Politics and Modernization*, p. 202.

15. John D. Powell, "Peasant Society and Clientelistic Politics," *American Political Science Review* 64 (2) (1970), 411–425. See also René Lemarchand, "Political Clientelism and Ethnicity in Tropical Africa: Competing Solidarities in Nation-Building," *American Political Science Review* 64(1) (1972), 68–90.

16. Clark D. Neher, "Thailand," in Kearney, ed., *Politics and Modernization*, p. 228.

17. Gamer, *The Developing Nations*.

18. Powell, "Peasant Society."

19. John Taylor, *Inquiry into the Principles and Policy of the Government of the United States* (New Haven, Conn.: Yale University Press, 1950), pp. 171, 356.

20. Alexander Hamilton, John Jay, and James Madison, *The Federalist*, reprint ed. (New York: Random House, 1937), p. 337.

21. Claudio Veliz, "Centralism and Nationalism in Latin America," *Foreign Affairs* 47(1)(1968), 69–83.

22. Arthur S. Banks, ed., *Political Handbook of the World: 1987* (Binghamton, N.Y.: CSA Publications, 1987); also *The Economist*, March 26, 1988.

23. *The Economist*, October 12, 1985, February 21, 1987; also Banks, ed., *Political Handbook* (1987).

24. R. Cranford Pratt, "The Cabinet and Presidential Leadership in Tanzania: 1960–1966," in Lofchie, ed., *The State of the Nations*, pp. 96, 112, 116.

25. See two *Washington Post* articles by Stuart Auerbach: "Indian Government Increases Powers," September 24, 1980; and "Ghandhi in Crisis as Her Leadership Is Being Openly Questioned," October 16, 1980.

26. Neher, "Thailand," pp. 233–237.

27. Bretton, *Power and Politics*, pp. 141–145.

28. Fred W. Riggs, "Bureaucrats and Political Development: A Paradoxical View," in Joseph LaPalombara, ed., *Bureaucracy and Political De-*

velopment (Princeton, N.J.: Princeton University Press, 1963), Ch. 5.

29. William Attwood, "Guinea's Amazing Coup on Behalf of Democracy," *Washington Post*, September 16, 1984.

30. Ruth L. Sivard, *World Military and Social Expenditures*, 1987–88 (Washington, D.C.: World Priorities, 1988), pp. 26–27.

31. Some readers may disagree with the subjective judgments that place a given country into one category or another. We have tried to give civilian rulers the benefit of the doubt where possible, so, if anything, some countries could be moved from low to high military influence. (Venezuela is one example.)

32. Claude E. Welch, Jr., "Cincinnatus in Africa: The Possibility of Military Withdrawal from Politics," in Lofchie, ed., *The State of the Nations*, Ch. 10. See also Robert P. Clark, *Development and Instability: Political Change in the Non-Western World* (Chicago: Dryden, 1974), pp. 185–186.

33. Gavin Kennedy, *The Military in the Third World* (New York: Scribner's, 1974), pp. 23–30.

34. For a summary of these studies, see Sam C. Sarkesian, "A Political Perspective on Military Power in Developing Areas," in Sheldon W. Simon, ed., *The Military and Security in the Third World: Domestic and International Impacts* (Boulder, Colo.: Westview Press, 1978), Ch. 1.

35. R. D. McKinlay and A. S. Cohan, "Performance and Instability in Military and Nonmilitary Regime Systems," *American Political Science Review* 70(3) (1976), 850–865.

CHAPTER 20

POLICY-MAKING IN THE THIRD WORLD

In preceding chapters, we examined some important social, economic, and psychological dimensions of Third World political life and discussed the major institutions and structures of Third World political systems. The capacity of Third World governments to enhance human dignity in their countries depends largely on how these various ingredients come together to form an effective and creative policy process. The term *policy-making process* refers to the series of steps taken by a government to solve problems, make decisions, allocate resources or values, implement policies, and, in general, to do the things expected of them by their constituents. We cannot appreciate the connections between levels of human dignity and politics until we have analyzed the nature of the policy process in a typical Third World setting.

There is obviously some risk involved in making generalizations about 102 different political systems in an area of social behavior that is so poorly defined. The chapter offers an outline of a policy-making process that we think characterizes most governments in the Third World regardless of their social and economic circumstances or their colonial heritage. The principal components of this process derive largely from the nature of traditional society and personality, from the scarcity and unpredictability of funds needed to carry out government policy, and from a shortage of modernizing institutions to assist governments in making and implementing public policy choices.

Policy-making in the Third World: An Overview

Several years ago, Yale University economist Albert O. Hirschman published the first of a series of books and articles in which he outlined what he understood to be the major reasons that developing countries so frequently fell short of their goals, particularly in the field of economic well-being. Based on his experiences as an economic adviser to the government of Colombia and a number of in-depth studies made in other Latin American countries, Hirschman's analysis eventually focused on what he termed the "failure-prone policy process" in the less developed world.[1]

Hirschman began by considering the fundamental problem of less developed countries—the inability to make decisions that will induce development of the economy. For Hirschman, the inability of development elites to make these decisions could be traced back to certain psychological and social structural inadequacies that prevent the decision makers of the country from bringing to bear the knowledge and commitment needed to make the proper decisions about the allocation of resources. In the face of this recurring inability to meet development problems, struggling groups within the society begin to grow desperate at their failure to penetrate the decision makers' attention screen and attract attention to their problems. As the problems become more and more aggravated, groups are pushed toward acts of violence to attract attention. The consequence is usually an impulsive policy decision taken in the heat of debate or passionate confrontation, without adequate understanding of what is required to solve the problem. The result, not surprisingly, is failure.

The fatal flaw, according to Hirschman, now appears in the decision-making styles of developing countries. Instead of learning from their mistakes, Third World elites typically compound the problem by what Hirschman called *la rage de vouloir conclure*, a phrase taken from Gustave Flaubert that means (approximately) "the mania for wanting to be done with it." At the point of recognizing failure, a great cry arises from the country's intellectuals who call for a comprehensive total attack on the problem. Earlier solutions are decried for being piecemeal, fragmented, less than total, and generally inadequate. Fundamental change must be introduced; anything less will certainly fail. The reformist elites of the country cannot tolerate any further delay in attacking the problem. Very

few countries possess governments with the policymaking apparatus adequate to the task of producing a comprehensive program dealing with a major issue in a span of months; and, certainly, the Third World countries are more poorly equipped in this regard than most other governments. Therefore, calls for comprehensive solutions are met in the only possible way: by introducing policy solutions from abroad. The history of Third World attempts to solve domestic problems is littered with examples of poorly related solutions borrowed from the industrialized states. Successful policy solutions like the Tennessee Valley Authority (TVA) have been copied all over the Third World to solve problems in agrarian reform, flood control, land reclamation, power generation, and pest control, as well as many other issues for which a particular policy tool might actually be inappropriate. Likewise, international agencies like the World Bank and the International Monetary Fund (IMF) are frequently called on to send professional advisers to struggling Third World countries to prescribe an instant remedy for ills that are centuries old.

Not only do the foreign solutions usually fail to resolve the immediate problem, but their very use tends to have an adverse effect on future efforts. For one thing, the nation's intellectual leaders are inhibited from acting on a local problem as long as some foreign miracle is being developed. Anyone who has worked in the field of solving public policy problems knows that before a person can really solve a problem he or she must interact with the problem, become immersed in its very nature, and come to know the problem intimately. There must be, to quote Hirschman, "that long confrontation between man and a situation" before creativity emerges.[2] By introducing foreign solutions on a poorly thought-out crash basis, Third World elites deprive themselves and their

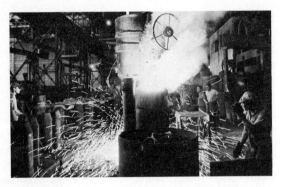

Steel production in this mill in São Paulo, Brazil, is impressive. Yet, production of steel in Brazil almost never reaches predicted levels. Repeated failures of major programs or projects to achieve their goals or targets are depressing to the morale of Third World technicians and political leaders. Government legitimacy must be won through performance, and the failure of many Third World regimes to meet their own stated goals makes them appear incompetent in the eyes of their own citizens.

intellectuals of any chance to master the problem on their own terms. In addition, the continued failure to solve a given problem begins to sap the morale and weaken the resolve of the national political cadres. They begin to believe that they merit the title "failure-prone"; they deprecate the national style; and they either escalate the ideological battle considerably or drop out by resigning themselves to mediocrity or going into self-imposed exile. Each time this sequence is repeated, it erodes the scant supply of problem-solving talent with which Third World political leaders have to work. The long-term consequences of failure-prone politics are to lead the country into a vicious circle of one disaster after another until some authoritarian force, usually the army, steps in to impose discipline on the nation and attempts to reassure the people that they are in control of their destiny once again.

Policy-making in the Third World: Goals, Actions, Outcomes

Setting Goals

The policy-making process begins with the setting of goals. For the average American, the idea of setting national goals is alien, because our system of separation of powers and our cultural predilection against long-range planning obscure the setting of goals in our government. There is, for example, no single document in the U.S. government that could be called "National Goals for 1990." The closest thing we have to that would be the federal government budget for any given fiscal year. Similarly, we do not have any single agency responsible for devising the country's goals for a specific period. The closest agency to this would be the Office of Management and Budget (OMB) located within the Office of the President. The ability of OMB to influence the structure of our national political goals derives almost entirely from its role as the coordinator of the executive branch's budget proposal, which is sent to the Congress for approval each year. It is possible that before the end of the century, even the U.S. government will adopt formal goal-setting procedures for its operations. As of now, however, we still believe that single sets of national goals should not be imposed on our heterogeneous population.

In the Third World, in contrast, there has been great emphasis placed on national goal setting and state-directed economic planning. Ever since 1928, when the Soviet Union launched its first five-year economic plan, leaders of poor countries have seen central state economic planning as an attractive strategy for stimulating the industrialization and modernization of their countries. State intervention has been used in the Third World to catch up with the early-industrializing states since 1933, when the reform government in Turkey of Kemal Ataturk introduced the country's first five-year plan (inspired, and partly financed, by their neighbor, the Soviet Union, but drawn up by American technicians). The definition of *planning* has varied from country to country. In some instances, it simply means state action to support and stimulate private enterprise. In others, planning has been used to get the state into fields that private enterprise is unwilling or unable to exploit. For still others, state intervention means the gradual replacement of private enterprise by collective action and the coordination of all economic activities subject to the criteria of social welfare.[3]

Morocco's first five-year plan (1960 to 1964) listed two chief goals: (1) to lessen the country's dependence on foreign technicians, capital, and markets; and (2) to integrate the traditional sectors into the national economy.[4] These two broad goals led to the establishment of specific programs to increase the number of technicians and other qualified personnel by emphasis on education and training; to stimulate traditional agriculture by giving top priority to agricultural reform and the introduction of modern technology into the rural areas; to establish basic steel and chemical industries by promoting private investment if possible but by state intervention if necessary; and to facilitate the implementation of both plans by reforms in government administration and organization and by the Morocconization of the civil service, that is, gaining control of national agencies for national personnel.

Pakistan's first five-year plan (1953 to 1958) listed these major objectives: (1) to achieve the greatest increase possible in national income and the standard of living; (2) to increase health,

education, housing, and social welfare services justified primarily on grounds other than increasing the national income; (3) to improve the nation's balance of payments by increasing exports and import substitution; (4) to increase opportunities for useful employment; and (5) to increase rapidly the rate of development in East Pakistan and other relatively less developed zones of the country.[5] Although the first four objectives presented problems that were primarily technical in nature, the fifth objective—showing favoritism toward the relatively less developed East Pakistan—was the subject of intense controversy. The controversy was never resolved; East Pakistan seceded from the rest of the country in 1971 to form the new state of Bangladesh.

Where are goals typically formulated in Third World countries? In a few instances, such as in Mexico, countries with very strong official political parties may employ the inner councils of their parties to discuss alternate goals and to formulate a final list for state action. In a small number of traditional monarchies, like Saudi Arabia, the setting of goals amounts to little more than an expression of the personal convictions of the monarch and the monarch's closest advisers. However, in most Third World republics, central economic and social planning agencies have been created and charged with the task of setting goals for public policymakers to follow. In a 1965 study, Albert Waterston listed central-planning institutions in over 100 Third World independent states and (at that time) soon-to-be independent colonies. The World Bank's *World Development Report* for 1983 reports that of some eighty developing countries surveyed, four out of five have multiyear development plans. Over the preceding ten years, more than 200 plan documents had been prepared.[6] Although the degree of sophistication and state control vary considerably from one example to another, the list of those Third World countries that are at least formally committed to some kind of central planning is clear evidence of the strength of the idea of rational government ordering a society's priorities.

Planning in the Third World has usually followed one of three models, depending on the colonial heritage of the country, the type of planning used by the former colonial country, and, most important, the specific economic and social structures in the developing state.[7] At one end of the spectrum are the states that engage in detailed central planning of both the private and the public sectors of the economy. Typical of this style is India, whose civil servants were strongly influenced by the Fabian socialists under whom they studied in Great Britain. India's brand of socialism is rather unconventional, because over 90 percent of the country's business enterprises remain in private hands. This means that the government must set detailed goals and objectives for the businesses in the private sector if the overall goals of the national economic plan are to be realized.

At the other end of the planning spectrum lie the states that are basically committed to reliance on the private sector to achieve the broad goals of the national economy. These countries, such as Malaysia, Pakistan, and the Philippines, typically restrict their planning to the formulation of the broadest goals possible (called *macroplanning*). Thus, a planning document in one of these countries might set as a goal the achievement of an increase of 3 percent in per capita income over the next year without specifying exacty how such a goal is to be accomplished. Then, the plan is augmented through budgetary and other procedures to grant special incentives to the private sector to undertake projects whose overall result will be the fulfillment of the national plan goals. Accordingly, the state does not become involved

in direct industrial activity unless there is clearly no alternative and unless the project in question is badly needed. Another feature of macroplanning is its tendency to encourage and rely on regional planning institutions. As in Malaysia, the national plan is frequently little more than the regional plans collected under one cover.

In the middle of the planning spectrum are the countries that have adopted the French *consultative planning* method, including Chile (before 1970), Morocco, Tanzania, and Tunisia. The French method of planning involves careful consultation between the public sector's planning officials and representatives of the private sector. As a result of this planning style, private industry and commerce leaders leave the consultations knowing (and accepting) what is expected of them in the way of investment and production decisions. The state, for its part, undertakes to provide support for economic activities that conventionally are not financed by private industry: social infrastructure, such as roads and schools, and large projects that cannot pay for their costs of construction, such as huge dams, and so forth.

The choice of an appropriate planning model for any given Third World country depends to a large extent on the role of the government in making economic decisions. Specifically, the key factor in any individual case is the extent to which the government replaces the free market as the instrument for making resource allocation decisions. One way to describe the government's role in economic decision making is to place countries along a spectrum ranging from "socialist," meaning that the government owns most if not all the means of production, to "capitalist," meaning that the government is involved very little, if at all, in production matters. However, in the Third World, this simple descriptive device is complicated greatly by the numerous cases where less than half the country's economy is effectively incorporated into the modern sector. Thus, we have to introduce a second dimension into out analysis. Let us call "inclusive" those economic systems where more than half the economy is included in the modern sector, and "noninclusive" those countries where more than half the economy is located outside the modern realm. This two-dimension framework allows us to classify most Third World countries fairly accurately. (See Table 20.1.)[8]

For example, countries with inclusive capitalist economic systems are states that rely generally on the operation of the market and on the private sector for production and for citizen well-being. Taxes may be high, but they are not confiscatory; and government interference is generally limited to subsidy and regulation. Third World countries with this form would include South Korea, Colombia, and Malaysia. States classified as noninclusive capitalist, such as Ecuador or Honduras, will still have as much as 50 percent of their population living in the traditional, preindustrial sector. In such states, the traditional economy may be individual, communal, or

feudal, but the direction of change is toward capitalism.

The next category, capitalist-statist, includes countries where the bulk of the modern economy remains in private hands, but the government has involved itself in a number of very large productive enterprises, typically in heavy industry or social infrastructure projects. This level of government involvement comes about because of several possible factors, such as a development philosophy that relies only marginally on private enterprise, or a dependence on a key resource, such as oil. Venezuela, Mexico, and Brazil would exemplify the inclusive capitalist-statist model, while Indian and Indonesia typify the noninclusive form.

Mixed capitalist systems, such as Uruguay or Singapore, provide social services on a large scale through governmental agencies, and private control over property is relegated to a lower priority. While capitalism is still regarded in these countries as a legitimate form of enterprise ownership, the private sector is subjected to considerable government control and regulation, and the transition to public ownership through democratic means remains a real possibility.

Table 20.1 Third World Economic Systems, with Government Spending as Percentage of GNP, 1985

	Socialist	Mixed Socialist	Mixed Capitalist	Capitalist-Statist	Capitalist
Inclusive	2 countries Insufficient data	3 countries Insufficient data	10 countries 35.7 percent	19 countries 24.4 percent	12 countries 26.1 percent
Noninclusive	9 countries 24.7 percent	9 countries 25.8 percent		16 countries 24.9 percent	22 countries 25.9 percent

(*Source*) For classification of countries: Raymond D. Gastil, ed., *Freedom in the World: Political Rights and Civil Liberties, 1986–1987* (Westport, Conn.: Greenwood Press, 1987), Table 8, pp. 74–75. For government spending as percentage of GNP: World Bank, *World Development Report: 1987* (New York: Oxford University Press, 1987), Table 23, pp. 246–247.

There are relatively few Third World states in this category, and all of them are of the inclusive variety.

Mixed socialist states, including Libya and Syria, have as their objective (either long-range or near-term) the expansion of the public sector to absorb most of the country's economy; but in actual practice, large portions of the economy remain in private hands. Only a few Third World states are inclusive mixed socialist countries; those that are noninclusive, such as Burma, are slightly more numerous.

Finally, we come to the socialist systems, where the avowed policy goal of the state is to place the entire national economy under direct or indirect governmental control. Where private property is allowed, it is understood that these are exceptions that can be revoked as the government might find necessary. Most Third World socialist countries are of the noninclusive type, such as Angola or Afghanistan, and their relatively primitive economy cannot yet be incorporated into the modern sector to any great degree.

Interestingly, we find very little difference overall between or among forms of economic organization when they are compared on such dimensions as the percentage of GNP accounted for by government spending. Comparative data in this field are difficult to obtain and frequently of doubtful accuracy. Nevertheless, using data drawn from the World Bank's *World Development Report* for 1987, we find that government expenditures as a percentage of GNP varies between 24.4 percent and 35.7 percent for all the categories for which we have sufficient data to make comparisons.

Through the 1970s and into the early 1980s, in many Third World countries socialism was the preferred ideological approach to economic development, and the state was a major shareholder in the economy. As Table 20.2 suggests, in a number of important Third World economic powers, such as Brazil and India, the government held at least three-fourths of the productive facilities in such key sectors as coal, steel, shipbuilding, automobiles, and railway operations. As the decade has worn on, however, the promise of socialism and state ownership of production has dimmed and the trend now is for the state to sell off many of its public corporations to private investors or syndicates. This trend is known as "privatization," and it has been spurred on by similar experiments in advanced industrialized countries, particularly in Britain and Japan. In Turkey, for example, the

Table 20.2   Share of State Ownership of Key Sectors in Selected Third World States in the Early 1980s

State	Sector					
	Oil	Coal	Steel	Railways	Automobiles	Shipbuilding
Brazil	More than ¾	More than ¾	¾	More than ¾	Less than ¼	Less than ¼
India	More than ¾	More than ¾	¾	More than ¾	Less than ¼	More than ¾
Mexico	More than ¾	More than ¾	¾	More than ¾	¼	More than ¾
South Korea	na*	¼	¾	More than ¾	Less than ¼	Less than ¼

*na = Not available.
(*Source*) *The Economist*, December 21, 1985.

government has decided to open up to foreign private consortia the construction of a number of large thermal electric power plants, the first time the government has been willing to turn over such a sensitive economic project to the private sector. In 1985, Tanzanian President Julius Nyerere announced a plan to sell many state-owned farms to private entrepreneurs. Self-proclaimed Marxist states like Mozambique and Zimbabwe have abandoned their ideological stance against private investment and have begun to encourage foreign private ownership of key sectors, particularly involving exploitation of natural resources. In 1983, the Brazilian government listed eighty-nine state-owned firms that it wanted to be rid of, and by 1985 twenty of these had been privatized. By mid-decade, Mexico had identified more than 200 miscellaneous enterprises owned by the state that it wanted to sell back to the private sector. There are major problems with privatization in the Third World, including a lack of available and liquid capital to purchase the businesses. In many instances, the firms or enterprises are money losers, and the private sector wants to have nothing to do with them. In addition, while the state wants to divest itself of these firms, it likely will want to retain some regulatory control over the enterprise and its activities, to ensure that it continues to contribute to the overall economic development effort. Despite these difficulties, it seems increasingly clear that around the Third World as we enter the 1990s the government will have less and less of a role in the economy of its country.[9]

Regardless of the exact model followed by planning agencies in Third World countries, they have often exhibited a tendency to set unrealistic goals, which frequently are followed by failure and a decline in public morale. Hirschman has observed that government decision making can fit into one of two categories:

(1) either capabilities outrun motivation (the technical solution to a problem surfaces before the problem becomes critical), in which case the goals adopted are usually within the reach of government power; or (2) motivation outruns capabilities (as when a problem becomes critical rapidly), in which case the outcome is usually failure. Goal setting in the Third World tends to be of the second type, thus helping to account for the failure-prone political style noted earlier.

Brazilians are accustomed to seeing their government plan grandiose projects. It almost seems as if the enormous size of the country has encouraged its leaders to imagine that they can accomplish miracles. Press reports coming out of Brazil have revealed, however, that several key projects have run seriously behind schedule, contributing even more to disbelief and cynicism in Brazilian and foreign private economic circles.[10] In 1970, for example, Brazil announced that it would increase steel production from 5.4 million ingot tons to 20 million tons by 1980. Shortly thereafter, the goal was raised to 24 million tons and then to 35 million tons by 1985. Actual performance was disappointing. Figures for 1975 showed steel production reaching 8.3 million tons. Most observers admitted that the goal of 35 million tons was totally beyond the country's capacity. Another fantastic project envisioned by Brazilian planners was the Northern Perimetral Highway, a space-age highway intended to link Brazil's northern Amazon region with Venezuela, Colombia, and Peru. Construction was begun in 1973, and completion was promised by 1977. But, by the middle of 1976, only 400 miles of the highway's 2,600-mile length had been completed and construction was proceeding so slowly that the jungle was reclaiming parts of the completed roadway. But, as the Brazilian finance minister was quoted as saying, "It's better to plan for too much than for too little. If your original goals are too high, you can always change your plans. But, if they're too low, progress could become strangled."[11] Perhaps the minister would be correct were it not for the serious blows to national confidence and morale that are suffered each time the government defaults on a promise.

Another example is the huge Helwan steel mill in Egypt. Begun in 1955 by a West German firm, the Helwan iron and steel works was nationalized by the Egyptian government in 1961. As a consequence, Egypt needed continued aid from the Soviet Union to complete Helwan, to expand it, and to keep it running in the face of mounting operation and maintenance problems. Total capital investment in Helwan, one of the largest industrial enterprises in the Middle East, reached $1 billion. Despite Egypt's political break with the Soviet Union, there were in 1976 still 500 Soviet technicians working at Helwan, supplemented by a team of consultants and advisers from U.S. Steel and from the United Nations.

All of these foreign advisers were needed simply because nothing ever seemed to go right at Helwan. Originally designed to be producing 1.5 million tons of steel products by 1976, the plant's output by that time was more like 500,000 tons. Although export sales reached $21 billion in 1975, Egypt spent more than that amount on imports—coal, spare parts, vehicles, and other equipment—needed to keep the plant running. Egyptian iron ore has a very high salt content, which corroded the plant's machinery. Although Helwan had its own plant for converting coal into coke, the coal had to be imported, and was frequently delayed in the country's snarled port facilities. Staffing was a huge problem. There were 20,000 workers, far too many for the plant's needs, but political considerations made layoffs impossible. Low salaries made it difficult to retain middle-level

managers and engineers. Many managers spent more time in their offices than they did supervising operations on the plant floor. Alleged corruption and kickback deals caused plant supplies to lag behind requirements. Improper use of equipment caused much breakage and many maintenance problems. One piece of expensive equipment, designed to last ten years, was broken in four days at Helwan. Finally, the Egyptians depended almost completely on foreign capital and technology to make the plant function properly. In an effort to reduce the cost of importing coal, Egypt tried to convert some of the equipment to run on natural gas, which the country has domestically. Amoco Oil Company ran a pipeline to the plant but could not complete the task because the U.S. law prevented American companies from participating in projects funded by the Soviet Union. The USSR, for its part, refused to connect the pipeline to plant facilities because of its running feud with the late Egyptian President Anwar Sadat. And Helwan stumbled along consuming more wealth than it produced.[12]

Industrial projects are not the only examples of failure to meet unrealistic goals. Massive agricultural developments also have fallen short of high expectations. In the early 1970s, following the increase in world oil prices, the combination of Arab petrodollars, Western technology, and local manpower was supposed to turn the Sudan into the agricultural mainstay of the Arab world. The wide open spaces and favorable climate of the country were thought to be ideal for cattle raising and wheat farming. The region could become the breadbasket of the Arabs, offering them the promise of food self-sufficiency. After less than a decade of effort, the project was bankrupt. With imports running more than $1 billion ahead of exports each year, the Sudan quickly ran up a hugh foreign debt, which by the early 1980s had mounted to more than $2 billion. Arab money sources dried up in the face of the magnitude of the problems. Many of the specific projects were simply too great for the country's overtaxed infrastructure. Western sales representatives delivered outdated and unsound equipment. Government tax, employment, and nationalization policies worked against the very developments they sought to advance. There was no overall planning and little accountability for money borrowed abroad. At the rate the project is moving, it may not be completed until the end of this century.[13]

The Third World inclination to set unrealistic goals has its economic disadvantages in that it distorts the efficient allocation of resources. From our vantage point, the most disturbing consequences of this tendency are political and psychological. Most Third World governments lean on shaky popular support under the best of circumstances. Few governments in the developing world enjoy such popular acclaim that they can maintain their legitimacy in the face of repeated failure. Thus, when failure comes, as it inevitably must if goals are set unrealistically high, one serious effect is to weaken mass confidence in their ruling elites.

Why do Third World political elites set such high goals for themselves and for their political systems? A review of the policy-making literature in developing states suggests at least four reasons. First, political debate in the Third World is carried on with such intensity and fervor that appeals to moderation have little impact. The role of inspirational, charismatic leaders was highly useful during the struggle against the colonial masters when a lethargic populace had to be roused into heroic actions to gain national (and personal) liberation. But, once independence is obtained and the state must settle down into the routine of managing complex economic and social problems, charisma loses it useful-

ness. Legitimacy must be based on real achievement, and regimes based on inspiration and promises do not long survive, as the fate of Sukarno of Indonesia or Kwame Nkrumah of Ghana can attest.

A second source of unrealistic goal setting derives from the general non-Western cultural inclination to deal in the comprehensive and the total. Such cultural predelictions certainly reinforce the already-present institutional tendencies toward global and grandiose projects and goals (what some call grand-design politics).

Third, unrealistic goals are established largely because decision makers lack reliable information on which to base their calculations. The problem of insufficient information is partly derived from inadequate data-gathering services and national statistical agencies. Too often, bureaucrats in developing countries simply cannot obtain complete and reliable data. Even more symptomatic of political underdevelopment, however, is the way in which data are distorted for political purposes. In countries where the population is narrowly balanced between competing and hostile tribal, religious, or ethnic groups, such as Lebanon or Nigeria, even outwardly simple statistical exercises, such as conducting a national census, become the cause of much concern lest the new data reveal that the balance of demographic power has shifted. In Nigeria, this fear became so great that in 1975 the military dictator, Brigadier General Murtala Ramat Muhammad, simply declared the 1973 census to be inoperative and proclaimed that the 1963 census would be used henceforth for planning purposes. A similar example can be seen in Pakistan. The first five-year plan was drafted on the assumptions that (1) the GNP would rise by 20 percent during the period, (2) the population would increase 7.5 percent (a rate of only 1.5 percent annually), and (3) consequently the GNP per capita would grow 12.5

percent. As Waterston reports, according to the deputy chairman of the planning board, it was believed that population was actually growing much faster than 1.5 percent but it was felt that the population growth rate had to be understated in the plan "to keep despair away."[14]

The final cause of incorrect goal setting involves the suppression of dissent in many Third World regimes. In a study of foreign policy decision making in the U.S. government, Irving Janis discovered that policymakers were most prone to make serious errors of judgment whenever the social cohesion of the group imposed a sort of dissent-free atmosphere over the deliberations so that contradictory opinions were suppressed, often by those who held them.[15] Janis labels this phenomenon "groupthink." Any group that is wrestling with a particularly complex problem should take pains to ensure that dissent is protected and encouraged, even institutionalized, to avoid as many errors as possible. In many Third World regimes, however, the opposite is true. Dissent is suppressed and ideological conformity is imposed during all stages of decision making. The consequence of this practice is to lead the government into making numerous errors of judgment and into setting unreasonably high goals.

Taking Actions

Our discussion of unrealistic goals would not be necessary if Third World governments somehow found the ability to carry through their plans and to implement the policy choices they have made. Yet, when we come to this second phase of the policy-making process, we find that many Third World governments must operate under administrative, economic, and political constraints that virtually guarantee

failure at the point where the policy is applied to the society.[16]

It is not easy to generalize about problems of policy implementation in countries as different as those of the Third World. One recent book, edited by political scientist Merilee S. Grindle, highlights a number of factors that affect the ability of Third World governments to implement policies.[17] Some of these factors stem from the policy content (such as who wins and who loses), the type of costs and benefits associated with it, and the extent of change called for by the policy. Other factors have to do with the power, interests, and strategies of the parties involved, or the willingness of the people affected by the policy to comply with its provisions. As they attempt to implement policy, most Third World governments are constrained by three special sets of problems: administrative, economic, and political.

The first kind of constraint on Third World policy actions comes from the *administrative* sphere. Here we note the numerous problems connected with the administration of development plans and specific projects: long delays in execution of the plan (some plans, such as those of Pakistan, were not put into effect until the plan period was more than half over), increased costs over projections because of delays and inflation, inferior construction, low yields on investment, unnecessary dispersal of resources among a number of small and uncoordinated projects, and so forth. The World Bank's *World Development Report* for 1984 reports the findings of a study of about 1,600 large (i.e., worth more than $100 million) projects undertaken in the Third World in the 1970s. Of projects costing between $100 million and $250 million, 21 percent had significant delays or cost overruns averaging 30 percent. Of the projects that cost more than $1 billion, 47 percent had delays or overruns averaging 109 percent. About half the

The failure of many Third World countries to meet debt payments has caused many private and public lenders, like the policymakers for the General Agreement on Tariffs and Trade (G.A.T.T.) pictured here, to restructure or forgive huge amounts of debt.

projects suffered delays of between one and two years; another 25 percent had delays of three to four years.

There are at least three sources of administrative confusion and incompetence. The first is the most obvious—the lack of trained experts to administer the complex programs and projects so vital to economic development. This shortage of expertise brings on poor project preparation, especially in crucial areas, such as economic feasibility (cost–benefit) studies and engineering supervision of the project once under way. A second problem stems from the lack of political support for civil servants and bureaucrats. From Tanzania, for example, we have the report that cabinet officials were so opposed to the basic provisions of that nation's first five-year plan that, even after the plan had been put into effect, they fought for, and secured, major changes in the program. The changes benefited their ministries but eroded the administrators' enthusiasm for the plan. A similar phenomenon was observed in Pakistan, where the planning agency's own analysis for the reasons for plan failure began by accusing the political elites of failing to enforce the plan's provisions. Finally,

623

we must again note the casual way Third World bureaucrats manipulate statistical data to conform to political requirements. This point brings to mind the story told by U.S. political scientist and State Department official Roger Hilsman at the time of America's involvement in the Vietnam War. During the early years of that struggle, Americans were still trying to develop statistical indicators to measure our progress in the war. To which one of the Vietnamese generals replied, "*Ah, les statistiques!* Your Secretary of Defense [Robert S. McNamara] loves statistics. We Vietnamese can give him all he wants. If you want them to go up, they will go up. If you want them to go down, they will go down."[18]

The second kind of constraint on policy implementation is an *economic* one—the lack of funds available to pay for the many projects and programs that all Third World governments would like to establish. Immanuel Wallerstein has shown that in virtually every independent country in Africa, expenditures have exceeded receipts at least in the long run (more than two or three years).[19] Even where some sort of windfall makes new revenues available unexpectedly, as with the negotiation of new arrangements between the Zambian government and the international copper companies, increased needs absorb the new revenues as fast as they become available. Even oil-rich states like Venezuela and Nigeria found themselves in financial straits only a few years after the oil embargo and the rise in oil prices brought them close to the point of luxury for Third World countries.

There are only a limited number of sources from which a development elite can obtain the money needed to pay for its programs. The industrialized states, such as the United States and countries in Western Europe, can provide official government-to-government loans or grants; but these sources attach significant conditions to this money that usually infringe on the power of the developing nation. No Third World country likes to find itself in the situation of India, where 30 percent of the entire income of the third five-year plan had to come from foreign aid. Many Third World countries have sought financial relief by controlling the sale of export commodities, either by administering these sales entirely through some sort of export marketing board (as with cocoa in Ghana) or simply by levying an indirect tax on the exported items. In extreme cases, such as that of oil in Venezuela or copper in Chile, the exporting country's government will actually nationalize or expropriate the commercial, mining, or industrial enterprises so that all foreign exchange from export sales will accrue to the government. Dependence on foreign sales of raw materials is a shaky source of support for government policy because prices are so volatile that it is difficult to predict far in advance exactly how large government revenues are likely to be. Furthermore, many Third World countries are based on monocultural economies, meaning that one single commodity or product dominates the export picture. Fluctuations in the price of that commodity can have disastrous effects on the country's overall economy.

When a development elite turns to its own national resources, the picture is not too bright. Some governments have chosen to avoid the problem of insufficient funds by simply creating money to pay at least their domestic bills. In cases like that of Chile in the 1960s, inflation was used by the government to avoid a clash between economic sectors that were not predisposed to compromise. Inflation was a substitute for taxation and expenditure of real resources. As subsequent events in Chile testify, that kind of policy cannot be maintained for long without tragic results. Only a regime that already maintains a reputation with its people for honesty and legitimacy can afford to run budget deficits and to meet the difference in created money. Governments that do not enjoy legitimacy with their people or with significant disadvantaged sectors do not usually have this option. In addition, inflation caused by creating money at home does not solve the equally severe problem of shortage of foreign exchange, which a government needs to purchase greatly needed imported items for industrial and agricultural modernization.

Thus, development elites are forced to consider the most important of all financial policies—the levy of taxes on private, personal, and corporate income. During the 1950s and early 1960s, the less developed countries typically took between 8 and 15 percent of their GNP to finance government operations. The average for twenty-four developing countries in the 1953–55 period was 11.8 percent. In contrast, the average during that same period for fifteen industrialized countries was 26.2 percent, and several collected more than 30 percent of the GNP in taxes. Since that time, Third World governments have been making great strides in their ability to tax their own countries' wealth. During the period 1972–76, the same twenty-four developing countries averaged 16.3 percent of their GNP in taxes, an increase of 38 percent. From 1972 to 1985, according to the World Bank, total government revenue as a percent of GNP increased slightly in the low-income countries, while taxes on income, profit, and capital gains as a percentage of government revenue declined by 20 percent. (See Table 20.3.) Among lower-middle-income countries, both percentages rose significantly, to the point where they were devoting about one-fifth of GNP to government revenue, and taxes on income, profits, and capital gains represented more than one-third of total government revenue. Upper-middle-in-come countries increased the percentage of GNP going to government by more than one-fourth, but the share of government revenue coming from taxes dropped sharply. After nearly three decades of development, the poor countries were still taking out of their national economies less than half the percentage taxed by industrialized countries, whose figure for the 1972–76 period stood at 36.2 percent. Moreover, since 1975, tax ratios in developing countries have not increased. A 1980 World Bank report found that "the scope for raising taxation is less now than it was 20 years ago."[20]

The typical Third World government's inability to tax income stems from several defects in the political and economic systems: the highly unequal distribution of income combined with the close connection between income distribution and political power; the regressive nature of most Third World tax systems (tax rate goes *up* as income goes *down*); the tendency for the wealthiest sectors of Third World economies to derive their income from inaccessible sources, such as rents and land; and the bureaucratic inadequacies that make levies such as land taxes easy to evade.

This last observation brings us to a consideration of the *political constraints* of policy implementation, which will be subsumed under Gunnar Myrdal's phrase "the soft state."[21] According to Myrdal, all underdeveloped countries are, to one degree or another, soft states. This means that they suffer from social indiscipline, which manifests itself in deficiencies in legislation and, in particular, in law observance and enforcement; a widespread disobedience by public officials of rules and directives handed down to them; and often the collusion of public officials with powerful persons and groups whose conduct they should regulate. Singapore's former minister for foreign affairs and labor, S. Rajaratnam, has called this "govern-

Table 20.3 Government Revenue as Percentage of GNP, Taxes as Percentage of Revenue, 1972 and 1985

	Taxes on Income, Profit, and Capital Gains as Percentage of Revenue		Total Government Revenue as Percentage of GNP	
	1972	*1985*	*1972*	*1985*
Low-income economies	21.0	16.8	13.8	15.6
Lower-middle-income	23.8	34.8	16.5	20.9
Upper-middle-income	27.3	20.3	18.7	23.6
Eight selected Third World countries				
Nigeria	43.0	na*	11.6	na
Tanzania	29.9	na	15.8	na
India	na	16.2	na	14.0
Indonesia	45.5	67.0	13.4	22.5
Mexico	36.4	24.7	10.4	17.6
Brazil	20.0	17.9	19.1	24.7
Egypt	na	15.2	na	39.4
Iran	7.9	9.5	26.2	na

* na = Not available.
(*Source*) World Bank, *World Development Report* (1987), Table 24, pp. 248–249.

ment by kleptocracy." The soft state includes corruption, racketeering, bribes, payoffs, smuggling, kickbacks, black market profits, arbitrary enforcement of the law, lax or nonexistent enforcement of the law, and abuse of power, especially on the local level.

Political and commercial corruption can alter the quality of life in Third World countries in many different ways, ranging from the trivial to the critical. In Lima, Peru, one of the more vexing public policy problems for city officials during the 1980s was what to do about the hordes of street vendors who thronged the city's main avenues selling all manner of consumer products, from clothing to cooking utensils.[22] No one seemed to know just how many such vendors there were. Estimates ranged from 20,000 to 200,000, with the city's official census counting 4,000. One 1987 government report estimated that one-third of the country's urban workforce had entered this underground economy. What everyone knew, however, was that they were operating illegally. In the decade or so that the street vendors had been working the area, however, there had grown up an intricate underground support structure, including license kickbacks and illegal protection rackets. With such a supporting social system, it seemed unlikely that the city government could take the action needed to remove the vendors without a show of armed force.

Halfway around the world, in Nigeria, the issue was much more critical: the price of rice, a staple of the Nigerian diet. Because Nigeria does not produce enough food to feed its own population, the government issues permits to private firms to import 200,000 tons each year. Despite these imports, rice was hard to find during the last half of 1980, and prices continued to rise. The reason, many observers alleged, was that the government had been distributing licenses only to its friends and political allies and that the amount was kept low to keep prices and profits high. Government officials counter-charged that their opponents had been buying up the rice as soon as it got to the country, causing prices to rise and artificial scarcities to develop. As so often is the case, the truth was impossible to ascertain. But, for typical Nigerian citizens, it was imperative that some solution be found to the problem if they were to have enough rice to feed their families.[23]

One aspect of the "soft state" in the Third World that began to have special significance for the United States in the 1980s involved the international narcotics traffic. With only 5 percent of the world's population, the United States consumes between 50 and 60 percent of the world's illegal drugs. Nearly all of these narcotics originate in the Third World; about 80 percent are channeled through one Third World country—Colombia. According to the U.S. Department of State, in 1986 there were about 1,200 to 1,600 metric tons of opium produced in the world, of which between 555 and 885 came from the "Golden Crescent" countries (Afghanistan, Iran, and Pakistan) and 600 to 700 from the "Golden Triangle" countries (Burma, Laos, and Thailand). Production of the coca leaf that is turned into cocaine reached

more than 127,000 metric tons, of which 90,000 came from Peru and 32,000 from Bolivia. Marijuana production was estimated at between 5,000 and 6,000 metric tons, of which 2,500 to 3,000 came from Mexico, and another 500 to 1,200 from Jamaica. While relatively little of the narcotics traffic originates in Colombia, nearly all of the Latin American drugs are funneled through that country's processing laboratories, most of which are buried deep in the country's remote interior. The illegal drug traffic now grosses more than $100 billion annually, a sum equal approximately to the Gross National Product of Sweden, and larger than the GNP of about 150 countries in the world. The United States spends about $40 million each year trying to eradicate cocaine production in Latin America alone, but despite these efforts the war against drugs is steadily slipping back. One major reason for these failures is the "soft state" administration of many Third World countries. The inability of many of these governments to enforce even the most routine laws and regulations has left an enormous vacuum within which narcotics traffickers can operate with impunity.[24]

Before we discuss the specific causes for the soft state, we must discard two erroneous notions. The first is that political corruption in the Third World has something to do with the form of government. Actually, many Third World regimes are soft, lax, and corrupt regardless of whether the chief of state is a military dictator or an elected president, or whether parties and press function freely or are suppressed. The second erroneous idea is that political corruption has something to do with inferior standards of morality. The morality of Third World citizens and public officials is about what it is in most political systems and probably higher than the public morality exhibited by political bosses in some of America's larger cities. If we want to understand the causes of political softness in developing countries, we must learn to look for it in the nature of political power in a less developed political system.

For one thing, we must attempt to put ourselves into the place of the citizens of most Third World countries. Often, low-status and low-income persons from these countries, whether they live in urban or rural areas, have grown up in an environment where the government is feared or hated, and rightly so. In many cases, the precolonial administrations were only slightly benevolent dictatorships; their successors, the colonial regimes, only exceeded their predecessors in the extent to which they could abuse power. Manning Nash's description of politics in a remote Burmese village is significant in this regard.

> Government [to the people of Nondwin village] is one of the five traditional enemies, along with fire, famine, flood, and plague. . . . From the days of arbitrary demands from the royal city to the British colonial administration, through the Japanese occupation and the civil disorders following independence, political power in the shape of government has been something alien, demanding, and usually capricious or enigmatic. Government is identified with the unrestricted use of force. Nondwin villagers seek means to avoid or subvert the force of government, except when there is a local man who also has the kind of power that governments are thought to have.[25]

The effect of this ancient tradition of mistrust of government is to encourage local villagers to look the other way when smuggling or bribery occurs and to engage in passive resistance when the national government enters their village. It seems as if peasants the world over have learned much the same kind of defense against government intruders: Stare at the bureaucrats with a passive, noncommittal look and then wait for them to leave, secure in the knowledge that nothing of consequence will really change, for good or ill.

A second cause of political corruption in the Third World can be traced to the administrative style of many of these countries. Despite a notable lack of real political power and authority, Third World governments have legislated an amazing array of official restrictions and regulations that amount to an open invitation to bribery and payoffs. In Burma, the state attempts to control most retail merchandising by requiring merchants to sell their wares through state-run stores. However, visitors to the official stores find them virtually empty, whereas street vendors a few feet away from the stores display a wide variety of consumer goods—all illegally sold, of course.[26] The customary insistence on a seemingly endless series of forms, permits, licenses, and other devices allows administrative discretion at a very low level, encouraging bureaucrats to take advantage of the helpless business people or consumers. In addition, many Third World countries try to regulate citizen behavior by offering financial subsidies for certain kinds of private decisions—rental of an apartment, for example—which burdens the administrative apparatus and offers further opportunity for abuse. Add to this apparatus the notoriously low salaries earned by civil servants in poor countries and you have a situation open to abuse, corruption, and bribery. Some of the worst offenders appear to be foreign multinational corporations, which regard the bribes they pay to public officials as a normal cost of doing business in developing countries.[27]

A third cause of the soft state lies in the highly unequal distribution of political power in the Third World. We have already seen that Third World governments frequently make use of the syncratic style of governance as they attempt to modernize and industrialize their countries without seriously altering the privileges and special powerful status of the traditional sectors of the country. This effort leads, in turn, to the promulgation of laws, decrees, and proclamations that are more honored in the breach than in the observance. Third World regimes have enacted numerous laws intended to reform the land-tenure patterns of their countries, to curb abuses of power, to grant security of property to peasants, to establish a minimum wage for urban laborers, to provide free health care for the poor, and so on.

What happens to these laws? Most of the provisions of these laws are designed to please either low-status interest group representatives or foreign governments trying to urge local reforms before external assistance is granted. But the really powerful of the country know that the law will contain enough escape provisions (loopholes) that they themselves need never feel the adverse impact of the law. Despite the radical sounds emanating from many national capitals in the Third World, little in the way of radical change ever really takes place because of the elites' ability to block effective enforcement of the law. Thus, we see a growing gap between the symbolic pronouncements of the political leaders and the tangible significance of the regime's actions. There is not a government in the world that does not distribute at least a little symbolism instead of tangible benefits to its people. No government has enough control over real goods (money, food, housing, health care) that it can distribute a satisfactory quantity to each person; so, each government has to concentrate on making its people feel happy instead of enjoying material well-being. Again, as in the case of unrealistic goal setting, the real difficulty arises from a growing class consciousness of low-income persons who are coming to realize

that one cannot live on symbols indefinitely and that, eventually, governments must turn to the real issues of power, wealth, and their unequal concentration.

One final point needs to be made regarding corruption in the soft state. It appears as if the real hidden cause of political softness and public immorality in the Third World lies in the comparatively underdeveloped state of countervailing powers in these societies. Perhaps the chief characteristic of Third World power systems is the relative lack of power anywhere in the system. Coercion, force, and authoritarian rule are all present in abundance, but power is a genuinely scarce commodity. Little power exists outside of the local-level patron–client networks and the international influences, which bear on the national network from both sides. (This theme is examined in greater detail later.) But, at the national level, individuals are not organized into collectivities that can exercise power efficiently. There are few freely operating opposition political parties or independent judiciary systems. Most legislatures are of the rubber stamp variety. Interest groups are primitive and are mostly under the control of the government itself. Press freedom is rare. In other words, there are few checks on the unrestrained and abused power of a dominant executive (civil or military) and its representatives. Laws are made or unmade and enforced or unenforced not according to some master guide, such as a constitution, but according to the whim of the administrator and the special access enjoyed by traditional elites. The founders of the U.S. system did not assume that political leaders were especially moral people. The opposite seems true, because they created the system in such a way as to pit one force against another, each with enough power to defend itself and none with enough power to overwhelm the others. Through the years, that system has been subjected to many threats, but the essential soundness of the principle appears to have been proven. This lack of a system of countervailing powers paradoxically encourages Third World leaders to try to accumulate more and more force and authority. It is paradoxical because even as they violate their own laws and abuse their own supporters to gain more power, in the long run they condemn themselves to further weakness and softness.

Evaluating Outcomes

To complete the picture of the failure-prone policymaking process, we must examine how Third World governments evaluate the outcomes of their policy choices. We find that the defects of the first two stages of decision making (setting goals and taking actions) are compounded by an inability to evaluate policies quickly and accurately, to locate mistakes, and to remedy those errors to avoid serious adverse consequencs.

Several concepts are particularly useful here. We have already encountered the idea of feedback—information about past or present system performance that can be used to improve future system performance. Feedback in the political context means any information about the impact of past and present policy choices to make new decisions about future policy directions. When feedback is lacking, political systems in an environment of rapid change cannot respond to mistakes quickly enough to avoid their adverse consequences. If certain environmental factors, such as population, change by a percentage increment each year instead of by a fixed quantity (e.g., population growth of 2 percent per year instead of 1 million persons per year), we say that these factors are growing exponentially. In contrast to linear growth, when the increments are always of a fixed quantity, exponential growth makes quantities grow surprisingly fast

because the base for growth expands so rapidly. Third World political systems are particularly vulnerable to exponential growth because of their poor facilities for evaluating policy outcomes (feedback), their penchant to make mistakes in the first place, and their limited resources to rectify their errors once detected. When environmental factors change so fast that a mistake cannot be detected until it is too late to avoid its adverse consequence, we say that the system has experienced overshoot. When overshoot is experienced often enough, in enough sectors of the society, and to a strong enough degree, the policymaking mechanism of the system collapses under the burden of repeated failures. This is the situation facing many Third World governments today.

We have discussed some of the characteristics of Third World societies and political systems that contribute to an inability to evaluate policy outcomes. Certainly, the limited communications media available in less developed systems inhibit the free flow of information that is so vital to policymakers in attempting to understand their own societies. Third World governments' policies to constrain a free press also play a key role in undermining their own self-analysis efforts. Political culture, especially in the mass of urban and rural poor, is another important obstacle faced by developing governments. In examples drawn from countries as far apart as Burma and Chile, we have already noted the prevailing peasant response to mistaken policies advanced by bureaucrats from the national government: "They rarely say no; they prefer to nod their heads in agreement, so that the long-winded officials will depart soon, and so that they can continue to pursue their interest in their own way."[28] No government can evaluate its own policies as long as the supposed beneficiaries of these policies remain mute about their defects.

But of all the causes of poor policy evaluation in the Third World, perhaps the most serious is, again, the institutional flaw in developing political systems. There simply are not enough autonomous associations and institutions at work in Third World societies to obtain information about the impact of policies on their members, to assess the costs and benefits of this impact, and to communicate this information to public officials. The policy evaluation tools that have become so familiar to American observers—think tanks, university research facilities and laboratories, investigative journalism—are virtually unknown in the developing countries. And the more conventional feedback mechanisms, such as political parties and interest groups, are either fragmented, not trusted by their constituents, or controlled or ignored by the government. Robert Scott, for example, points out that most Latin American governments have found it exceedingly difficult to respond to the multiple dislocations brought about by rapid social and economic change because of their lack of accurate information about their societies.[29] Most governments in that region have discounted the benefits to be derived from nurturing and encouraging a multiparty system with reform-minded, modernizing political parties. Instead, they have preferred to proceed on the institutional basis of an expanded bureaucracy (civil and military) and the artificial creation of captive interest groups that represent industry, commerce, and agriculture at a minimum. Yet, Scott continues, these awkward and stilted feedback mechanisms simply are not up to the demands of rapid development. Bureaucrats, whether civil or military, tend to see development where there is none—and have the data to prove it. Even in countries where interest groups are nominally independent of government control, as in Chile before 1970, the majority of the business sector has declined

to participate in the activities of their interest group; they fear the group to be ineffective and too subservient to goverment dictates.[30] Finally, where the government sets out to create feedback institutions, as in Pakistan's basic democracies experiment, the regime's opponents quickly learn that dissent within the controlled institutions is permitted only up to the point where it begins to be effective. In other words, the institutionalization of dissent is done more for theatrical purposes than for the purpose of obtaining needed information about the state of affairs in remote areas. (The proof of this flaw lies in Pakistan's inability to sense the depth of grievances in East Pakistan until it was too late and secession was inevitable.) The Tanzanian example seems particularly typical:

[Other than the National Executive Committee of the ruling Tanganyika African National Union (TANU) Party,] there were few other ways for the government to inform itself of popular reactions to its proposals. Parliamentary discussion was none too vigorous and members were very cautious with any criticism they might wish to make of government policies. The newspapers were either controlled by the party or were extremely timid. The trade union movement had been brought increasingly under tighter government control. Within both the civil service and the party bureaucracy the upward flow of information on popular reactions to government policies was sporadic and inadequate.[31]

Myron Weiner writes on one of the key differences between developed and less developed political systems:

A modern political system has no single mechanism, no single procedure, no single institution for the resolution of conflict; indeed, it is precisely the multiplicity of individuals, institutions and procedures for dispute settlement that characterizes the modern political system—both democratic and totalitarian. In contrast, developing societies with an increasing range of internal conflict, typically lack such individuals, institutions and procedures. It is as if mankind's capacity to generate conflict is greater than his capacity to find methods of resolving conflict; the lag is clearly greatest in societies in which fundamental economic and social relationships are rapidly changing.[32]

Conclusions: Policy-making and Human Dignity

As a generalization, let us conclude this analysis by outlining the consequences of the Third World policy-making style: unrealistic goals, ineffectual and underfinanced actions, and poorly evaluated outcomes. Policies designed to enhance human dignity often suffer from the tendency of many Third World states to swing wildly back and forth between two polar extremes, the conservative and the radical approaches, which are drawn here in abstract and general terms. In this analysis, we follow the work of Immanuel Wallerstein on styles of governance in Africa.[33]

The conservative regime, according to Wallerstein, desires above all to maintain a relatively open economy and national society. This has usually meant keeping the country within the zone of some international currency (dollar, pound, franc); maintaining few economic restrictions, such as import quotas, tariffs, or controls, over the transfer of capital; and permitting (and encouraging) foreign private capital investment. At home, agitation from the left is suppressed and human rights do not flourish. As the years pass, the initial difficulties of the conservative regime stem from its growing international problems, with consequent pressure on the government's budget. Declining prices on the world market for the country's raw materials exports cause the nation's foreign-exchange situation to become critical. Much of the national income is spent on imported luxury items, worsening the nation's balance of payments and not contributing to domestic production. Free transfer of capital leads to capital drain or flight, typified by the opening of Swiss bank accounts by the country's elite.[34] Steady expansion of the nation's educational system produces too many overeducated persons for the small number of jobs available in the contracting economy, but the government finds that it cannot do anything to reduce school enrollments. Universities become centers of agitation against the government's hiring policies. Unemployment grows, particularly among the urban lower classes and the young intellectuals, creating an explosive coalition of disaffected masses and restive articulate leaders. Foreign interest in supporting the government declines, either as a result of lessening international tensions (the decline of the Cold War) or because of the decline in the return on foreign investment in domestic enterprises. In the face of growing unemployment, rising prices, and declining government services, the lower classes begin to believe charismatic leaders who offer them simplistic explanations for their plight. In Latin America, these leaders may come from universities or from the trade union movement; in Africa, from tribal leadership positions; and in Asia, from plantation unions or from the elite professions (law, medicine, journalism). Popular pressure on the government provokes considerable suppression of individual rights and reshuffling of the cabinet, but the basic causes of the government's discomfort—economic cramp magnified by international pressure—refuse to go away. As popular rebellion grows, the armed forces are provoked once again to enter the political arena, less for their own benefit (although military budgets *will* increase once they take power) than for a growing realization that the civilian leaders cannot set things right.

Wallerstein's typical radical regime begins with an entirely different set of assumptions. Instead of openness in the economy and polity, the leaders seek to close off the national system from disturbing and imperialistic influences. At the international level, this means breaking ties with the former colonial country's currency zone and establishing strict currency controls. Heavy constraints are placed on imports, currency transactions, and the movement of convertible currencies abroad. Internally, although the growing commercial and industrial bourgeoisie is limited in its development, private foreign investment is not inhibited until it becomes apparent that such investment is working against the best interests of the nation. Then, it is usually confiscated or expropriated by the government, sometimes with compensation (oil companies in Venezuela) and sometimes without adequate compensation. In the international political sphere, the radical regime usually adopts an anti-Western, neutralist position, supporting the national liberation movements in the still-colonized areas of the Third World (southern Africa especially) and the radical opposition parties in conservative states. Internally, the one-party state comes into being, and dissent from the right is suppressed. Human rights are denied, as they were by conservative regimes. Despite the many differences between radical and conservative regimes, their undoing commonly comes from the same place: growing budgetary deficits combined with inflation and economic policies that alienate key political groups. In the case of radical regimes, budget deficits grow because of the desire to spend larger amounts to provide needed social services as well as to create employment. With sufficient jobs, the urban working classes are kept relatively quiet. The problem comes from the taxation side of the equation. To pay for growing government programs, the regime tries to tax the traditional and progressive elites, the cash-crop farmers, the urban middle class, and the urban workers. Government bureaucrats are asked to do more with less in the name of fiscal austerity. Luxury imports are restricted, leading to higher domestic prices for inferior goods and angering the middle class. The leftward shift of the government brings about economic retaliation from the West, manifested by pressures by the World Bank, the IMF, and the U.S. government. Foreign sources of capital begin to dry up. Once again, the dreary picture of instability is displayed. Rising costs, declining incomes, loss of government control over events, and so forth, all lead to growing unrest, disorder, turbulence, the threat of even more radical policies from the far left, and, at last, intervention by the armed forces.

And, so, for nearly three decades, the countries of the Third World have swung back and forth between these two alternative governance styles. Sometimes the period between regimes is marked by military government; sometimes the military takes power permanently and attempts to establish its own style or approach to meeting the nation's problems. The exact sequence of events or the exact labels on all the key participants are not important. What does matter is that each regime lacks the sensory mechanisms necessary to let it know when disaster looms in enough time to pull back from mistaken policies. What we see are a series of experiments in failure as the Third World oscillates from conservative to radical and back again, never finding its own solid path to development and failing to emulate the models from the First and Second Worlds.

Suggestions for Further Reading

Caiden, Naomi, and **Aaron Wildavksy,** *Planning and Budgeting in Poor Countries* (New York: Wiley, 1974).

Dror, Yehezkel, "Public-Policy-Making in Avant-Garde Development States," *Civilisations* 13 (4) (1963), 395–405.

Grindle, Merilee S., ed., *Politics and Policy Implementation in the Third World* (Princeton, N.J.: Princeton University Press, 1980).

Heidenheimer, Arnold J., ed., *Political Corruption* (New York: Holt, Rinehart & Winston, 1970).

Hirschman, Albert O., *Journeys toward Progress: Studies of Economic Policy Making in Latin America* (New York: Twentieth Century Fund, 1963).

———, *The Strategy of Economic Development* (New Haven, Conn.: Yale University Press, 1961).

Honey, John C., *Planning and the Private Sector: The Experience in Developing Countries* (New York: Dunellen, 1970).

Ilchmann, Warren F., and **Norman Thomas Uphoff,** *The Political Economy of Change* (Berkeley: University of California Press, 1969).

Korten, David, and **Felipe Alfonso,** eds., *Bureaucracy and the Poor: Closing the Gap* (West Hartford, Conn.: Kumarian Press, 1985).

LaPalombara, Joseph, ed., *Bureaucracy and Political Development* (Princeton, N.J.: Princeton University Press, 1963).

Marathe, Sharad S., *Regulation and Development: India's Policy Experience of Controls over Industry* (Beverly Hills: Sage, 1987).

Mason, Edward, *Economic Planning in Underdeveloped Areas* (New York: Fordham University Press, 1958).

Montgomery, John D., and **William J. Siffin,** eds., *Approaches to Development: Politics, Administration and Change* (New York: McGraw-Hill, 1966).

Riggs, Fred, *Administration in Developing Countries* (Boston: Houghton Mifflin, 1964).

Scott, James C., *Comparative Political Corruption* (Englewood Cliffs, N.J.: Prentice-Hall, 1972).

Waterston, Albert, *Development Planning: Lessons of Experience* (Baltimore: Johns Hopkins University Press, 1965).

———, *Planning in Morocco* (Baltimore: Johns Hopkins University Press, 1962).

———, *Planning in Pakistan* (Baltimore: Johns Hopkins University Press, 1963).

World Bank, *World Development Report, 1983* (New York: Oxford University Press, 1983), Part II, "Management in Development."

Wraith, Ronald, and **Edgar Simpkins,** *Corruption in Developing Countries* (New York: Norton, 1964).

Yudelman, Sally, *Hopeful Openings: A Study of Five Women's Development Organizations in Latin America and the Caribbean* (West Hartford, Conn.: Kumarian Press, 1987).

Notes

1. Albert O. Hirschman, *Journeys toward Progress: Studies of Economic Policy Making in Latin America* (New York: Twentieth Century Fund, 1963); Hirschman, *The Strategy of Economic Development* (New Haven, Conn.: Yale University Press, 1961).

2. Hirschman, *Journeys toward Progress*, p. 240.

3. Amiya Kumar Bagchi, *The Political Economy of Underdevelopment* (Cambridge: Cambridge University Press, 1982), Ch. 9.

4. Albert Waterston, *Planning in Morocco* (Baltimore: Johns Hopkins University Press, 1962), pp. 28–29.

5. Albert Waterson, *Planning in Pakistan* (Baltimore: Johns Hopkins University Press, 1963), pp. 44, 102.

6. Albert Waterston, *Development Planning: Lessons of Experience* (Baltimore: John Hopkins University Press, 1965), Appendix 3; World Bank, *World Development Report, 1983* (New York: Oxford University Press, 1983), p. 66.

7. John C. Honey, *Planning and the Private Sector: The Experience in Developing Countries* (New York: Dunellen, 1970), Part I.

8. This classification scheme is based on Raymond D. Gastil, ed., *Freedom in the World: Political Rights and Civil Liberties, 1986–1987* (Westport, Conn.: Greenwood Press, 1987), Table 8, pp. 74–75.

9. *The Economist*, December 21, 1985, April 4, 1987; Glenn Frankel, "Socialism Seen Losing Appeal in Africa," *Washington Post*, June 6, 1985; William U. Chandler, "Designing Sustainable Economies," in Lester R. Brown et al., *State of the World: 1987* (New York: Norton, 1987), Ch. 10.

10. Bruce Handler, "Brazil: Big Projects but Big Delays," *Washington Post*, July 20, 1976.

11. Ibid.

12. Thomas W. Lippmann, "Egypt's Large Steel Plant Is Economic Embarrassment," *Washington Post*, October 11, 1976.

13. Jonathan C. Randal, "Debt-Ridden Sudan Mocks Former Promise as Arabs' Breadbasket," *Washington Post*, May 16, 1981.

14. Waterston, *Planning in Pakistan*, p. 46, footnote 29.

15. Irving Janis, *Victims of Groupthink* (Boston: Houghton Mifflin, 1972).

16. On this general subject, see Immanuel Wallerstein, "The Range of Choice: Constraints on the Policies of Governments of Contemporary African Independent States," in Michael F. Lofchie, ed., *The State of the Nations: Constraints on Development in Independent Africa* (Berkeley: University of California Press, 1971), Ch. 2.

17. Merilee S. Grindle, ed., *Politics and Policy Implementation in the Third World* (Princeton, N.J.: Princeton University Press, 1980).

18. Roger Hilsman, *To Move a Nation* (Garden City, N.Y.: Doubleday, 1967), p. 523.

19. Wallerstein, "The Range of Choice."

20. World Bank, *World Development Report* (1980), Table 6.1, p. 73. See also Nicholas Kaldor, "Will Underdeveloped Countries Learn to Tax?" *Foreign Affairs* 41 (2) (1963), 410–419.

21. Gunnar Myrdal, *The Challenge of World Poverty* (New York: Random House, 1970), Ch. 7.

22. Cynthia Gorney, "Lima's Hordes of Street Vendors Enraged by Plan to Relocate Them," *Washington Post*, June 6, 1981; Jackson Diehl, "Lima's Street Vendors Have Economic Clout," *Washington Post*, July 21, 1984; Michael J. Smith, "The 'Underground' Explodes in Peru," *Washington Post*, May 17, 1987.

23. Leon Dash, "Nigeria Rice Prices Fuel Political Feuding," *Washington Post*, December 27, 1980.

24. T. R. Reid, "A New Assault Planned against

Formidable Foe," *Washington Post*, August 10, 1986; Bradley Graham, "With Each Step Forward, the U.S. Loses Ground in Its War on Cocaine," *Washington Post*, June 28, 1987; *The Economist*, April 2, 1988.

25. Manning Nash, *The Golden Road to Modernity: Village Life in Contemporary Burma* (Chicago: University of Chicago Press, 1965), p. 75.

26. William Branigin, "Burmese Rely on Thriving Black Market," *Washington Post*, January 27, 1984.

27. For an example from Nicaragua, see Julia Preston, "Black Marketeers, Sandinistas Battle to Control Distribution of Scarce Food," *Washington Post*, April 16, 1987.

28. David Lehmann, "Agrarian Reform in Chile, 1965–1972: An Essay in Contradictions," in David Lehmann, ed., *Peasants, Landlords and Governments: Agrarian Reform in the Third World* (New York: Holmes & Meier, 1974), p. 109.

29. Robert Scott, "Political Parties and Policy Making in Latin America," in Joseph LaPalombara and Myron Weiner, eds., *Political Parties and Political Development* (Princeton, N.J.: Princeton University Press, 1966), pp. 365–367.

30. Dale L. Johnson, "The National and Progressive Bourgeoisie in Chile," in James D. Cockcroft et al., eds., *Dependence and Underdevelopment: Latin America's Political Economy* (Garden City, N.Y.: Doubleday, 1972), pp. 201–206.

31. R. Cranford Pratt, "The Cabinet and Presidential Leadership in Tanzania: 1960–1966," in Lofchie, ed., *The State of the Nations*, p. 100.

32. Myron Weiner, "Political Integration and Political Development," *The Annals* 358 (1965), 60.

33. Wallerstein, "The Range of Choice," pp. 28–32. See also James D. Cockcroft, "Last Rites for the Reformist Model in Latin America," in Cockcroft et al., eds., *Dependence and Underdevelopment*, pp. 118–119.

34. According to a Swiss Parliament study, there were in 1984 more than $160 billion in numbered Swiss bank accounts held by people living in the Third World, a sum equal to nearly half of the entire foreign debt of Latin America. *El País* (Madrid), November 26, 1984.

POLITICAL PERFORMANCE IN THE THIRD WORLD

Politics is a struggle under the best of circumstances, but the Third World does not enjoy the best of circumstances or even anything approaching the best. Nevertheless, the political life of a community must go forward, for better or worse. The pressure of events is relentless. Our concern as students of comparative politics is to assess the degree of success or failure experienced by Third World regimes in responding to these pressures.

Inquiries such as this are always susceptible to distortions caused by ethnocentrism or the disposition to judge foreign groups by reference to one's own cultural and political customs, institutions, and standards. We have examined Third World governments as they allocate four values: power, well-being, respect, and enlightenment. Although the simple listing of these four values may seem objective enough, the way we interpret each of the four may make a great deal of difference in our findings. Consider, for example, the value of respect. In the industrialized democracies of Western Europe and North America, respect means the guarantee of individual human rights against the pressure of the group or the coercion of the state. In countries inspired by Marxist or Maoist philosophy, respect may mean comradeship or the feeling of being accepted by the ruling group. In many Third World countries (but by no means all), Western norms of individualism are less important. In these countries, respect may mean the domination of one ethnic group by another or the prestige enjoyed by the government in international or regional organizations.

As we apply the four-value framework to political performance in the Third World, we must try to avoid defining values and goals solely by Western norms. Many developing countries have adopted the goal structure of modern, industrialized countries, even if only superficially or partially. Yet, in most instances, the transfer of Western values took place under duress or coercion when the recipient colony could not defend itself and its culture against European influence. Understandably, many Third World leaders are caught uncomfortably between their desire to match the economic and political power and well-being of the industrialized countries, on the one hand, and their need to return to the cultural tradition that characterized their peoples before the arrival of the Europeans. The result has been the emergence of mixed traditional–modern philosophies and ideologies to guide the new states of the developing world. In the 1930s, Victor Raúl Haya de la Torre of Peru began to articulate the doctrine of *aprismo* in an attempt to link together the urban, modernizing elites of his country and the poor Indian villagers of the remote interior. Similarly, Julius K. Nyerere in Tanzania espoused *ujamaa* socialism as the best way to combine traditional village communal values with the benefits of the modern welfare state. Whether any of the mixed ideologies will survive their founders cannot be known this early. At this juncture of history, we can only note the dangers of ethnocentrism, observe the efforts of Third World leaders to define their own goals in terms to which they can relate, and then use these same goals as yardsticks against which to measure their performance.

Goals, Actions, Outcomes: Power

We begin our discussion of political performance in the Third World with the value of power because of the central role of power in any plan to maximize or distribute any of the other values. Possession of power is, by itself, no guarantee that individuals or governments will really try to enhance human dignity in their societies. But, without power, no individual or government can do much to advance this goal.

Power in the Third World can best be visualized as existing in three more or less separate realms: the international, the national-modern, and the local-traditional. Most national governments in Latin America, Asia, Africa, and the Middle East are caught in a squeeze between two largely autonomous power centers, neither of which is much interested in promoting the power of the national regime. One power center lies outside the Third World, that is, the governments of the developed countries (both the industrialized democracies of the West and the communist states); the private, multinational corporations located primarily in Western Europe and North America, many of which are richer and more powerful than entire countries in the Third World; and the international institutions that represent the industrial countries (the United Nations and its subordinate agencies; the International Monetary Fund [IMF]; the World Bank; and the many separate institutions that control the marketing of raw materials). As long as the international economic, military, cultural, and political systems continue to intrude into their national arenas, the Third World's latitude for reform will be defined by what the international system will permit.

The other competing source of power is just as much an obstacle to national development as the international system, but it usually is harder to locate and identify. This second power center consists of the traditional elites of the countryside and the patrons of both the city and the village who manipulate their clients to protect them against an encroaching central government. We have already discussed the agents, moneylenders, plantation owners, slum bosses, local chieftains, village heads, and the many other petty political powers, each guarding his or her province from the national authority and each benefiting from the respect and privilege received from clients.

In view of the fact that both the international and the clientelist power sources are in agreement about the necessity to limit the power of the national government, it is not surprising that we occasionally find them in alliance to undermine a particular reformist elite or to weaken its policies that are designed to strengthen national power. Examples of these alliances are difficult to find in the open literature because they are usually clandestine and are denounced by the government as illegal when they occur. Nevertheless, there are enough cases openly admitted to suggest that such alliances are fairly common in the Third World. Agencies of the U.S. government, for example, have entered into working relationships with local-traditional elites to weaken or unseat reform-minded national regimes on several occasions in Latin America (Chile, Guatemala, Peru). The reasons behind such actions were reviewed in Chapter 16. Here, we simply want to illustrate the informal ties that exist between the international power triad (national governments, multinational corporations, international institutions) and local patrons and other traditional leaders. Together and separately, they render many progressive, reformist regimes in the Third World powerless to carry out their intended transformations of their societies.

Accordingly, the first order of business for reform-minded elites in the Third World must be to concentrate on the accumulation of power at the national level. In the first instance, this means seizing the institutionalized power of the state; in the second, it means securing that power and expanding it to reach into areas of the country and the society previously beyond the control of central authority. Power has been seized in the Third World in many different ways. A few regimes still in existence can trace their legitimacy back through previous rulers, handed down to them by inheritance. These include the traditional monarchies of Jordan and Saudi Arabia. The fate of Ethiopia reveals what happens to this fast-disappearing type of political order if it delays modernization too long. In a second type of regime, also repre-

sented by comparatively few cases, the present rulers were handed power peacefully by the departing colonial regime. A few such regimes are still in power; but as their immediate post-colonial leaders age and either retire or die, even these countries must pass power to new hands. Examples of these changes in the 1980s would include Tanzania (where Julius Nyerere voluntarily retired) and Tunisia (where Habib Bourguiba was deposed by a nonviolent coup). Still another way of achieving power is through violent revolution against a stubborn colonial authority, as in Algeria and Indonesia and (much earlier) in most of the states of Latin America. For most Third World countries, however, the transfer and acquisition of power have now settled down into one of two techniques: either peacefully through democratic procedures, including open elections (Costa Rica, Mexico, Sri Lanka, Venezuela), or violently and extralegally, often through a military coup but also through a civilian seizure of power (as in India prior to the 1977 elections).

Once in power, however, most Third World regimes find that they must devote major resources to the task of remaining there. Of course, simply staying in power is not enough to enable a government to enhance human dignity. The regime must accumulate enough extra power so that some may be diverted to making badly needed changes in the country's society, economy, and culture. Although different strategies are used by different regimes to accumulate power, in essence they all boil down to one significant fact: Virtually all of the country's leaders and most of its mass population must regard the incumbent regime as having the authority to make decisions on behalf of the entire state or the coercive force necessary to require acceptance of these decisions, or both.

Power in this sense can be thought of as a commodity. Power can be exchanged or traded, like money, and it can be taken from one person or group and given to another, like land. In the short run, however, it cannot be increased in absolute terms for an entire society. As a regime increases its power, the power of other groups in society or outside its boundaries must decline by an approximately equivalent amount. If, for example, the government of Peru were to develop the country's industrial base sufficiently to be relatively impervious to the international economy, then the power of the IMF to influence Peruvian politics would decline accordingly. Internally, as the power of the government of India to set a national policy regarding languages increases, the power of various minority linguistic factions must be reduced by the same degree. To the extent that national governments succeed in accumulating and consolidating power, they do so only by influencing competitors to relinquish their power and to transfer their loyalty to the central regime. This is the goal with regard to power.

For regimes that lack control over tangible resources, reliance on the charismatic leader quickly becomes a cornerstone of policies designed to increase power.[1] *Charisma* has been defined as the ability of a person to make others feel more powerful in his or her presence.[2] In politics, charisma involves a complex psychocultural relationship between a leader and the masses who are led to believe themselves more powerful simply by being in the presence of the great ruler. The entire process, then, feeds back into itself. The ruler, by enjoying the enthusiastic support of the mass of followers, does indeed become capable of great things and can lead the country on to high achievements.

Charisma has several functions in a developmental setting. Aided by the apparatus of modern mass communications, the charismatic leader bypasses the traditional bosses, chieftains, and heads of the local areas and reaches out to enter the consciousness of the low-income and low-status citizens who previously were shielded from national politics by their patrons. Thus armed, the charismatic leader can persuade the masses to undergo sacrifices, to unite in national movements to carry out grand schemes, and to feel themselves part of a larger enterprise—the work of a nation. On the foreign scene, a charismatic leader personifies the country in its relations with other states and can, when necessary, direct the sentiment of the people against foreign enemies or to meet external threats.

If the individual leader is not particularly well endowed with charisma, a frequently used substitute is leadership through ideology. Many people in the developing world live in a confusing state of rapid change. One way to secure their support and loyalty is to make rapid change understandable and rational to them. An ideology, in its cohesive and comprehensive picture of the world, makes sense to the populace and enables them to grapple with a world that is more and more threatening. Moreover, the leadership as the custodian of the official ideology is given the authority to carry the ideological prescriptions out to their logical policy conclusions.

Child psychologists tell us that one of the most important early tasks of a mother is to make a child's deprivations and frustrations understandable and rational in a world that the child does not at first grasp. Ideologies and charismatic leaders do much the same sort of thing for illiterate and poor citizens in rapidly changing societies. If the elites perform this function effectively, the masses respond by following them, by obeying their orders, and by quietly enduring the sacrifices imposed on them.

Regimes that rest their power on the personality of a single leader or ideology are in a weak position; individual leaders grow old and die and ideologies lose their significance in the face of rapid change and repeated crisis. Reforming elites who want to endure in power must turn their attention to ways to institutionalize their rule. To institutionalize a particular political phenomenon, such as power, means to depersonalize it, to embed it in a regularized set of interactions and activities that are identified with the name or label of an organization, not with the name of an individual. Any mass of politically aware people must be given a feeling that the enterprise in which they are engaged has a life of its own, that it existed before they joined it, and, most important, that it will persist after they have left so that their contributions will not have been in vain. In the United States, political leaders seek to identify themselves and their followers with the ancient sages and leaders of another era (Thomas Jefferson and Andrew Jackson among the Democrats; Abraham Lincoln among the Republicans) to give members of both parties a sense of the historical ties that bind them not only to earlier generations but also to future ones.

Institution building also has to do with predictability and reliability. Feelings of unpredictability and discontinuity often characterize politics in newly created nations. There is little tradition of the essence of politics: how power is transferred, how ordinary citizens can relate to political leaders, what kind of morality one can expect from elites, and so forth. Political organizations, in performing the same tasks over and over, lend predictability to the political process, and the people soon learn what to expect from elites and from their fellow citizens.

Institutions can also improve communications in a society. Rulers can transmit messages to subordinates and, hence, to mass followings, and they can be reasonably certain that the message that was sent will be the one that arrives. At the same time, the channels of communication are available for the masses to respond, either through acceptance or through protest and dissent. Leaders are well advised to pay attention to the reverse flow of information through institutions because these channels are likely to be the only ones available.

With comparatively few exceptions, political parties, interest groups, and the other institutions of a modern, developed polity have not emerged fully in the Third World. Where they have emerged, as in Sri Lanka, Tunisia, or Venezuela, progressive political leaders have made good use of them to pursue policies that consolidate the power of the ruling elite and that enhance the level of human dignity of the masses of the society. Where they have not emerged, regimes rarely last long enough to embark on fundamental reform or they are so preoccupied with mustering coercive force to suppress dissent that there is little in the way of resources, energy, or time left to devote to bettering the lot of their citizens.

No regime can endure long if it depends solely or even largely on the charismatic charm of a single leader or on the organizational strength and flexibility of a party. At some point, regimes must try to alter certain aspects of the political environment, either inside the country or abroad. At least four kinds of policies have been used by developing regimes in their quest for power: economic development, expansion of political participation, encouragement of ethnonationalism, and foreign relations.

Economic development is one of the most important policies for the maintenance of a regime in power. In societies where many people live at or near subsistence levels, expansion of the overall economic pie is a prerequisite for distribution of income or wealth to the poor. Monuments, sports stadiums, or public works symbolize the presence and the strength of the regime. Communications and transportation media not only facilitate movement of people from the countryside to the cities (thereby throwing off the domination of the local patrons) but also permit extension of central government authority into previously inaccessible regions. National industrial strength enables a developing country to resist international economic pressures, especially as they affect its balance of payments and rate of inflation. Certainly, policies of economic development have their drawbacks, because it is difficult to finance their costs, and benefits appear only after a long waiting period. But few regimes can last for long if they do not have the industrial and agricultural potential for material well-being in their countries.

A second kind of public policy designed to consolidate a regime's power involves the *expansion of political participation*. Several of the more progressive elites in the Third World have come to power supported by sectors of the population that previously had been politically inactive. The new regime reached down into the inert layers of traditional society and awakened groups that had never tried to exert their influence before. The regime must then reinforce the inclination of these new groups to participate by being genuinely responsive to their needs and wishes. Where this has happened, as with the peasants in Venezuela or the rural villagers in Sri Lanka, the political system undergoes a genuine transformation and is never quite the same again.

At times, however, the mobilization of new actors in the political drama takes on an ugly overtone. Regimes may seek to take advantage of smoldering ethnic animosities to secure their power position in society. By pitting one ethnic group against another or by representing themselves as the protectors of formerly oppressed ethnic groups, regimes may purchase some time in the race to develop and modernize

their countries. We have already seen that ideologies are used at times to help define "the enemy" and, quite often, that "the enemy" turns out to have a different skin color, speak a different language, or worship a different god. The cost of such policies can easily be excessive. The hatred and hostility generated by *ethnonationalistic chauvinism* may produce solidarity behind the regime for a time, but it is a weak reed on which to rest an entire national government.

Finally, the *international environment* offers two different kinds of resources that can be directed toward securing domestic power. First, tangible resources, particularly money and military aid, can be of great use to an economic and political development effort, especially if the donors of such aid can be kept at arm's length. Some developing countries have found that they can form regional alliances, free-trade associations, or raw materials cartels, and thereby come to one another's aid in staving off the threat of great power interference in their economies. In addition, the international system offers many important symbolic resources to a struggling young regime. Membership and a speaking platform in the United Nations and related agencies are taken as proof of the state's acceptance as an equal member of the world community. Foreign enemies can also be conjured up to provide justification for solidarity behind the regime. These foreign enemies may be industrial states, like the United States, or they may be regional neighbors that profess differing ideologies (Kenya and Uganda, for example) or that claim the same territory (Bolivia, Chile, and Peru). Although this facet of the international system may turn out to be a disadvantage if hostilities flare into real war (as former Indonesian President Sukarno found out in his confrontation with Malaysia), a sort of psychological mini Cold War may actually help consolidate political power on both sides of the border.

National power is a most elusive concept, one not easily quantifiable. Table 21.1 suggests one way of portraying such a concept, based on the World Power Assessment Project of Ray Cline.[3] According to Cline's formulation, national power is a product of population, territory, economic capability, strategic and conventional military capabilities, strategic purpose, and the will to pursue national objectives. Assessed in this way, the power of the Third World does not appear to be quite as low as one would expect. Of the top ten states on Cline's list of seventy-seven, only one is from the Third World (Brazil, ranked third, after the Soviet Union and the United States); but of the next ten, seven are Third World countries (Indonesia, eleventh; Taiwan, twelfth; South Korea, thirteenth; Egypt, fourteenth; South Africa, fifteenth; Saudi Arabia, seventeenth; and India,

twentieth). (See Table 21.1 for the rankings and scores of eight selected Third World countries.)

Cline has also divided the world into eleven geopolitical zones to assess the way power is distributed regionally. Of these, three zones are roughly what we call the First World: North and Central America (which includes Mexico, Guatemala, Honduras, Costa Rica, Nicaragua, and Panama), which has a score of 388; West Europe, with 458; and Australia/New Zealand, with 106. Thus, the First World is evaluated by Cline as having a cumulative power score of 952, or about 36 percent of the total for eleven zones (2,625). Two of the zones correspond roughly to the Second World: East Europe, with a score of 534; and China, Vietman, and North Korea, with a score of 143. According to this measurement, then, Second World zones account for 677 points, or about 26 percent of the total. The predominantly Third World zones are the Middle East and North Africa, with a

Table 21.1 Ranking of Eight Selected Third World Countries as of 1978 by Ray Cline's World Power Assessment

Country	Ranking*	(C + E + M)†	(S)‡	(W)§	(S + W)	Total‖
Nigeria	27	28	0.4	0.4	0.8	22
Tanzania	54	9	0.5	0.5	1.0	9
India	20	71	0.3	0.2	0.5	36
Indonesia	11	61	0.5	0.4	0.9	55
Mexico	28	32	0.3	0.4	0.7	22
Brazil	3	98	0.6	0.8	1.4	137
Egypt	14	38	0.6	0.6	1.2	46
Iran	40	32	0.2	0.3	0.5	16

* Out of seventy-seven countries ranked. The USSR ranked first with a score of 458; the Unites States, second with a score of 304.

† Critical mass (population + territory) + Economic capability + Military capability.

‡ Strategic purpose.

§ Will to pursue national strategy.

‖ (C + E + M) × (S + W).

(*Source*) Ray S. Cline, *World Power Trends and U.S. Foreign Policy for the 1980s* (Boulder, Colo.: Westview Press, 1980), Table 34.

score of 255 (about 10 percent of the total); South Asia, 69 (about 3 percent); Southeast Asia, 110 (4 percent); East Asia (including Japan), 203 (about 8 percent); South America, 232 (nearly 9 percent); and Africa below the Sahara, 127 (nearly 5 percent). Thus, all Third World zones combined (which includes Japan but excludes Mexico and Central America) account for 996 points, or some 38 percent of the total.

Cline's World Power Assessment Project can tell us something about levels of power in Third World countries as they confront external threats or challenges, but the data say little about the ability of Third World governments to meet and cope with internal threats. Whatever may be a country's standing on the scale of international power, ultimately it is that government's internal power that matters. We have already seen in other chapters the various kinds of threats experienced by Third World regimes in the 1970s and 1980s: military intervention, ethnic separatism, disruptive union work stop-

Units of the Salvadoran army undertake patrol operations against the rural guerrilla army in early 1981. By the late 1980s, the combination of effective counterinsurgent operations and reforms seemed to have strengthened the government's hand against the rebels. Negotiations to end the insurgency began in mid-1990.

In November 1989, six Jesuit priests were assassinated in San Salvador, the capital of El Salvador, apparently by Salvadoran soldiers who were members of the Death Squadron, an armed force of the extreme right. These deaths were among the most dramatic of the thousands that have been inflicted upon both the military and civilian populations since violence began in El Salvador in the early 1980s.

pages, rural guerrilla insurgencies, urban riots and terrorism, and many more. As a very rough measure of the extent of such threats generally across the Third World, if we were to add together the number of countries experiencing serious internal violence with those governed by, or strongly influenced by, military regimes, we would find that probably as many as two-thirds of the states in the Third World were confronted with significant challenges to their internal power. In some cases, the response of the government in power is conciliatory, aimed at relieving the pressure that led to the violence or disorder in the first place. During 1983 and 1984, for example, the president of Colombia, Belisario Betancur, succeeded in negotiating a cease-fire with guerrilla insurgents. Even though many former rebels took part in 1986 elections, violence (much of it related to drug trafficking) continued unabated; and in January 1988 the government decreed new anti-terrorism laws. In El Salvador, newly elected President José Napoleon Duarte in late 1984 began negotiations with rural rebels that offered the promise of bringing to a close that country's civil war after more than seven years of bloodshed. In the Philippines, Corazon Aquino negotiated directly with Communist and Muslim insurgent groups, and succeeded in arranging a two-month cease-fire in December 1986. In February 1987, the violence resumed at before-truce rates. Other governments may have elected to respond to violence with counterviolence, police suppression, martial law, and other repressive tactics. In May 1984, for example, Libyan leader Colonel Muammar el-Qaddaffi reacted to an insurgent attack against his regime with sharp reprisals, arrests, and an increased crackdown on opponents of his government. The government of Burma responded to increased guerrilla insurgency with massive troop deployments into the remote provinces that had been the scene of fighting. The late Indian Prime Minister Indira Gandhi answered a threat from Sikh fundamentalist rebels by sending troops to invade and occupy one of the religious faith's sacred sites, the Golden Temple of Amritsar. Responses may differ, but the general problem remains. Throughout the Third World, governments are having considerable difficulty accumulating and holding enough real power to meet internal threats and to get on with the business of industrializing and modernizing their countries.

With so many state actions available to accumulate and consolidate power at the national level, it is remarkable that in the late 1980s, nearly forty years after the Third World came into being, there is still so little real national power in the region. There remains an abundance of coercive force and personal abuse of power, but the stable, progressive development of power is still a slippery goal that eludes more

Third World regimes than have mastered it. Numerous case studies and articles attest to the continued dominance of the international system in the economies of developing states.[4] There is less firm evidence of the continued power of patrons and antimodern elites, but the fate of radical reformers, such as Chile's Salvador Allende or the leaders of the Palestine Liberation Organization (PLO), reveals that the forces of the status quo retain their stranglehold over development policies throughout most of the Third World. Several countries seem to have broken through these obstacles to develop strong, flexible sources of power that are independent of the international and local spheres: Venezuela, aided by its enormous oil deposits; Sri Lanka, with its relatively high level of education; or Tanzania, with its extraordinarily astute leader. But these are the exceptions.

Goals, Actions, Outcomes: Well-Being

After the seizure, accumulation, and consolidation of power, the next important goal of most developing countries is to enhance the value of well-being. The principal distinguishing feature of the Third World is its grinding and dehumanizing poverty, which is accompanied by a high infant mortality rate, malnutrition, unemployment, lack of housing, social disintegration, and illiteracy. To combat its poverty, almost without exception, nearly every government in the Third World, radical or conservative, must be committed to improving the well-being of its citizens.

Following more than twenty years of general international prosperity during the 1950s and 1960s, the world was shaken by two major recessions in the 1970s and early 1980s. The recession of 1974–75, occasioned by the dis-

Table 21.2   Summary Indicators of Economic Performance, Average Annual Growth Rates (percent)

Country	GNP* per capita, 1965–85	GDP† 1980–85	Agriculture, 1980–85	Industry, 1980–85
Nigeria	2.2	−3.4	1.0	−5.8
Tanzania	(.)	0.8	0.7	−4.5
India	1.7	5.2	2.7	5.4
Indonesia	4.8	3.5	3.1	1.0
Mexico	2.7	0.8	2.3	0.3
Brazil	4.3	1.3	3.0	0.3
Egypt	3.1	5.2	1.9	7.0
Iran	na	na	na	na
37 low-income countries	2.9	7.3	6.0	9.3
36 lower-middle-income countries	2.6	1.6	1.9	0.6
23 upper-middle-income countries	3.3	1.7	2.3	1.4

* GNP = gross national product.
† GDP = gross domestic product.
(.) = less than half a percent.
na = not available.
(*Source*) World Bank, *World Development Report: 1987* (New York: Oxford University Press, 1987), Tables 1, 2, pp. 202–205.

ruption in the world petroleum market after the 1973 Middle East war, was felt most severely in the industrialized countries, where Gross Domestic Product (GDP) grew by only about 3 percent annually through the decade. In the developing countries, the shock effects of the recession were less apparent. During the decade, developing countries saw their economies grow at the rate of about 5 percent per year; and a few countries, such as Brazil, Singapore, and South Korea, achieved growth rates in the 8 to 9 percent range each year.[5] Despite this superficially reassuring growth record in the 1970s, there were some significant flaws in the econ-

omies of many Third World countries that were not to become apparent until after the second recession of 1980–83.

Certainly the chaos that afflicted the world's oil market in the 1970s had a number of negative consequences for the Third World, even for those countries like Brazil and Mexico that seemed to be coping well with the crisis.[6] Many of the problems were related to soaring energy costs and their directly linked problems of inflation, unemployment, an inability of Third World governments to maintain budget surpluses in the midst of worldwide recession, and the resultant heavy borrowing abroad.

In some of the most adversely affected countries, the crisis of the 1970s translated itself into political instability as well. Brazil during the decade accumulated a foreign debt of more than $50 billion, and the country's export earnings were just barely sufficient to service the interest on the debt and pay for imported oil. The annual bill for imported oil in South Korea more than doubled, to $6 billion annually, nearly 10 percent of the country's GNP. In Turkey, payments of interest on foreign loans plus the cost of imported oil equaled the country's entire foreign exchange earnings for the year. Oil import costs consumed about half of the foreign exchange earnings of the Philippines each year. Each of these countries experienced sharp upheavals during the decade, with military intervention and martial law the consequences.

If the world oil crisis of the 1970s shocked many Third World governments, at least they were able to weather the storm because of their ability to continue to borrow abroad, either on the private international capital markets in New York and Europe, or through the International Monetary Fund and the World Bank. The effects of the second worldwide recession were much more severe in the Third World, and they pointed up several soft spots in the economic strategies of many developing countries.[7]

Like the recession of 1974–75, the crisis of 1980–83 was triggered by disruption of the world oil market, this time the result of the Iranian revolution. However, unlike the crisis of the 1970s, the decline of the 1980s was aggravated by a number of counterinflationary policies adopted in the industrialized countries. These policies had a number of adverse consequences for the Third World. For one thing, growing unemployment in the industrialized countries led to pressures for protection against imports, which reduced Third World exports to Europe and the United States and cut into the ability of the developing countries to earn badly needed foreign exchange. The recession prompted cutbacks in investment by American and European firms, which was felt in the Third World directly through declining foreign private investment, and indirectly through falling demand for their exports to the industrial markets. The most severe blow to the Third World, however, involved foreign indebtedness.

As the recession rolled through the industrial countries, their governments initiated a series of counterrecession policies that had as their consequence a sharp increase in budget deficits, especially in the United States. As the government covered these deficits by borrowing in the private capital markets, principally New York, the effect was to drive interest rates up sharply. As interest rates rose, Third World countries found themselves devoting more and more of their foreign exchange earnings just to pay the interest; and the basic debt level began to rise dramatically. From 1970 to 1983, the total debt of the developing countries rose nearly tenfold, from about $68 billion to $595 billion. The ratio of debt to GNP doubled, from 13 percent to 26.7 percent, and the ratio of interest payments to exports rose from 13.5 percent to 20.7 percent. In other words, the Third World was in debt for an amount equal to more than one-fourth of its entire annual production of goods and services, and the amount of money needed just to pay the interest was equal to about one-fifth of its total export earnings.[8] While the international debt crisis affected all Third World countries, it was concentrated in a relatively small group, primarily the larger and more industrialized Latin American countries. In 1984, Brazil's debt had reached about $100 billion; that of Mexico, $94 billion; Argentina, $43.5 billion; Venezuela, $34 billion; and Chile, $21 billion.[9]

The debt crisis reached a turning point in August 1982, when Mexico announced it would be unable to pay the installment due on its interest. The ramifications of this announcement immediately became obvious. If more countries began to default on their interest payments, the private banks would stop loaning money to Third World countries, which in turn would continue to defer payments and in addition reduce their hard-currency purchases from the United States and Europe. The cycle of international crisis loomed large once again. Fortunately, several forces were at work to prevent such a crisis. A number of countries were able to work out a new repayment schedule in 1983 that eased their temporary difficulties. In all, thirty-six countries were able to reschedule the payment of more than $67 billion; and these included some of the principal problem countries—Argentina, Mexico, and Venezuela. The private banking sector and the international lending agencies—especially the IMF—also came to the rescue with emergency loans to enable some countries to make the required installment payments on time. More importantly, however, the general economic recovery in the United States and in some Western European countries allowed Third World exports to grow once again. By late 1984, most observers were pronouncing the Third World foreign debt crisis "resolved." What remained unsolved, however, were the fundamental or structural flaws in the Third World's economies that brought about the crisis in the first place.[10]

Because these structural flaws in the global economic system remained unaffected, by 1988 the foreign debt crisis had returned to plague many of the Third World's leading economies. Early in 1988, the World Bank reported that foreign debt in the Third World had increased from $1.12 trillion in 1986 to an estimated $1.19 trillion in 1987, and was projected to continue to rise to $1.24 trillion in 1988. For the fourth consecutive year, debtor countries in the Third World sent more money to the advanced industrial countries in the form of interest payments on previous loans than they received in new loans. By 1987, Brazil's foreign debt had climbed to $114.5 billion, Mexico's to $105 billion, Argentina's to $49.4 billion, and Venezuela's to $33.9 billion. The debt-to-GNP ratio soared to more than 60 percent; and in a number of countries, including Jamaica, Chile, Morocco, Ivory Coast, Bolivia, and Costa Rica, foreign debt exceeded their annual GNP.[11]

The economic growth potential of any state is a product of both industrial and agricultural strength. Any overall development effort mounted by a Third World government must deal with both of these important elements. To get a clearer picture of economic development in the Third World, then, we must examine both industrial and agricultural policies and accomplishments over the past two decades.

The industrial goal of most developing states is twofold: (1) to increase the amount of inputs available to the industrial sector (capital, energy, raw materials, trained labor, and infrastructural improvements such as roads and telephone service), and (2) to increase the number of outputs received per unit of input (i.e., the productivity of the various production factors). In addition, Third World states would like to channel industrial production away from the extraction of raw materials and toward the manufacture of finished goods, away from industrial systems that were designed with Western societies in mind and toward systems more in keeping with local traditions and resources, away from the manufacture of Western-influenced goods and toward the production of goods that will satisfy real (not manipulated) native demand.

To accomplish these objectives, Third World governments have a wide variety of alternate policy choices available: the regulation of national currency and foreign exchange; the expropriation of private property for public uses; the control of monetary flow and currency levels; propaganda efforts to exhort the citizens to sacrifice for the industrial effort; the power to levy tariffs on imported goods, to tax (or to exempt from taxes) certain industries or firms, or to create money and credit; investment in social and economic infrastructure (roads, electric power, potable water); the granting of credit and technical assistance to productive enterprises; direct investment in productive activity; negotiation of contracts with foreign businesses; and price stabilization of major export commodities.[12]

Governments across the entire ideological spectrum try to stimulate industrial production through many of the same public policies.[13] In India, the nation's industrial sector is divided into three spheres: industries reserved for public ownership (mostly strategic industries, such as iron and steel, and public utilities); industries in which private capital is expected to supplement public investment (machine tools, drugs, aluminum, transport); and industries reserved for the private sector and guaranteed against national expropriation. Even though India professes to be a socialist state, 90 percent of the nation's industrial production remains in private hands. The Indian government, through its central economic planning mechanism, seeks to direct private investment decisions in directions desired by the government. However, the government's paramount position in the country's financial and credit institutions, together with the conventional government monopoly of certain taxing and spending functions, means that much stimulation of industrial growth occurs in the form of traditional incentives, including the licensing of new industrial facilities; in the potential for assuming management of facilities if conditions warrant; and in the control over supply, distribution, and price of a company's production. The Indian government also gives incentives in the form of tax holidays to firms it desires to attract to the country and otherwise provides substantial advisory services for prospective industries. Finally, because of the nation's recurring severe balance-of-payments problems, India has had to apply sharp restrictions on imports, contributing, thereby, to national industrial development through import substitution.

Throughout the 1960s and 1970s and the first third of the 1980s, industry and manufacturing were relatively bright spots in the economic picture of developing countries.[14] In thirty-four low-income countries, industrial production grew at the annual rate of 6.6 percent from 1960 to 1970 and 4.2 percent from 1970 to 1982. In thirty-eight lower-middle-income countries, most of which are in the Third World, industrial production grew annually 6.2 percent from 1960 to 1970 and 5.8 percent from 1970 to 1982. In twenty-two upper-middle-income countries, which include a few non–Third World states like Greece and Israel, industrial output rose a healthy 9.1 percent from 1960 to 1970 and 5.7 percent from 1970 to 1982. Yet, the strength of the Third World industrial and manufacturing base was spread unevenly, with a few countries like Brazil, Nigeria, and South Korea achieving spectacular growth rates, but with many countries (including Chile, Ghana, and Uganda) actually declining during the 1970s.

Between 1980 and 1985, however, industrial and manufacturing growth rates declined sharply throughout the Third World, most noticeably in several important countries that had led the manufacturing surge in the 1970s. Industrial production in the extremely poor low-income countries grew respectably during the period; even without counting the sizable Indian and Chinese manufacturing sectors, growth still exceeded 3.5 percent each year during the first half of the decade. In the lower-middle-income countries, however, growth was virtually stagnant at about 0.6 percent annually; and in the upper-middle-income countries, industry managed only to inch ahead at 1.4 percent each year. Several key countries experienced either stagnation (Brazil and Mexico each recorded growth rates of 0.3 percent annually during the period) or actual decline (Nigeria, minus 5.8 percent; the Philippines, minus 2.8 percent).[15]

While industrial growth slowed in most of the Third World, manufacturing expanded so rapidly in several countries that economists and political scientists began to talk about a new international economic order which they labeled the Global Manufacturing System. In contrast to an earlier period, when the world's economy consisted of industrial states and Third World exporters of raw materials, in the 1980s a number of Third World countries began to export manufactured products in large quantities to the advanced industrial states, where the manufacturing sector had declined and the services and information sectors had expanded. In 1986, for the first time ever, developing countries earned more from exports of manufactures than from agriculture and mining. The leading Third World exporters of manufactured products were Brazil and the so-called Four Tigers of the Pacific rim: Taiwan, South Korea, Hong Kong, and Singapore. Other Third World exporters of manufactured products were Indonesia, Turkey, Mexico, and Malaysia. By 1987, developing countries were accounting for more than 25 percent of the world's refined oil, about 20 percent of its textiles and footwear, about 15 percent of its food products and clothing, and nearly

15 percent in iron and steel, plastics, glass, and industrial chemicals.[16]

The Global Manufacturing System is a complex, highly interconnected set of institutions and economic and technological forces that are rapidly causing manufacturing to be distributed widely around the world instead of being concentrated in the old industrial states of Western Europe, North America, and Japan. One of the leading causes of this trend is the increased mobility of the factors of production. Highly mobile factors of production—such as capital, technology, information, and low-cost labor—are becoming relatively more important to the manufacturing process, while the less mobile factors, like land and raw materials, are becoming less significant. Thus, businesses can relocate more freely around the world in response to the local costs, particularly of labor. These changes have led to the transfer of manufacturing facilities abroad to take advantage of lower labor costs. Many of these transferred facilities do little more than assemble parts manufactured elsewhere. These so-called maquiladora industries, many of which are located near the United States–Mexican border, are in many respects simply the industrial equivalent of the farming and mining enclaves that dominated the colonial economies of an earlier era. These plants and factories are "footloose," in that they can move easily to other countries if the host government fails to provide them with the necessary incentives or if local labor becomes more expensive or restive. Thus, there is a real question as to exactly how much genuine industrial development there has been in the Third World as a result of the Global Manufacturing System.[17]

The dramatic economic growth of a number of Third World countries has not been enough to keep up with, and to absorb, the rapidly growing population, a trend we discussed in

Chapter 16. Thus, another key element in the Global Manufacturing System has been the major shifts in population around the world in the 1980s. Population growth rates have slowed to virtually zero in the advanced industrial countries, leaving Europe and North America with labor shortages in the low-skill, low-pay service sectors like food preparation and building maintenance and construction. Meanwhile, the population of the Third World continues to soar. The resulting imbalance has led to an inevitable outcome: the large-scale immigration of Third World peoples to Europe, Canada, and the United States in search of jobs and a better way of life. In the 1980s, an estimated 30 million Third World natives were living in the First World, about evenly divided between Europe and the United States. In Europe, although many governments have tried to close off the flow of Third World workers, their families continue to immigrate, causing severe problems of housing and job discrimination, social services, education, language differences, and so forth. The principal Third World groups in Europe are from North Africa (primarily Algerians in France), the Middle East (Turks in Germany), and the British Commonwealth (West Indians, Africans, and South Asians in Great Britain). The United States continues to admit about half a million legal immigrants each year, principally from Mexico, Central America, the Philippines, Korea, Vietnam, and other Asian countries. Since the United States is the only First World country with a long, more or less open border with a Third World state, it also receives a large and growing flow of illegal immigrants each year. For the first time since the country's beginning, the United States is starting to question how many more immigrants it can absorb. Third World immigrants, especially those from Latin America, present a challenge to the economic and cultural absorptive capacity of the United States that will surely increase as time goes on.[18]

There are also signs that some of the adverse ecological effects of rapid industrial growth are beginning to be felt in some Third World countries. For some years, Third World leaders have deemphasized the problems of environmental pollution or energy deficiencies as their countries have moved ahead toward industrial status. It would appear that some of the more successful Third World states will now have to consider the adverse impact of their forced-pace industrial programs. Just a few miles outside the industrial city of São Paulo, Brazil, Latin America's largest petrochemical complex has turned the surrounding area into what residents call "the Valley of Death." Air pollution is so bad that the suspended particulate count per cubic meter of air is twice that identified by the World Health Organization as causing excess mortality; monitoring devices installed to measure the contaminants in the air overloaded and broke down. According to the city health director, theoretically, by the level of pollution, "there shouldn't be life there." In Mexico, the issue is nuclear energy, specifically whether or not the government should move ahead with its plans to build a nuclear reactor on the shore of scenic Lake Pátzcuaro, not only one of the most beautiful spots in the country, but also one where many peasants fish to sustain themselves and their families. The coming of the reactor, they fear, will kill the lake's fish population with thermal pollution. In Sri Lanka, the rapid pace of development from 1978 to 1981 produced such an influx of consumer appliances, such as television sets, electric stoves, and air conditioners, that the country's electric grid was overloaded. The government responded with planned power shortages for five and one-half hours each day until the seasonal rains filled the reservoirs of the hydroelectric plants. In 1982, a United Nations report concluded that the rapid economic development in a number of Asian countries was leading to major environmental problems that could threaten their future resources. Some of the problems cited by the report were the destruction of the area's tropical rain forests at an alarming rate, declining productivity of farmland, deterioration of water quality, increasingly serious air pollution, and high concentrations of toxic pesticides such as DDT. In these and many other ways, development elites throughout the Third World are learning what the industrialized world already knew: that development without planning and precautions inevitably brings severe problems and unforeseen costs that eventually must be met if the national quality of life is not to suffer.[19]

The second half of the problem of poverty lies in agriculture. Here, Third World regimes begin with what seems to be a fairly simple overall objective: to increase the food supply available to their people, to avoid famine, to lower rates of malnutrition, and, generally, to raise overall levels of health and physical well-being in their populations. There are, however, two competing strategies for accomplishing this broad objective.

The first strategy, which emphasizes the continued interrelationships between the developing world and the dominant international economy, is based on the maintenance of the agricultural status quo in the Third World. Countries that pursue this dependence strategy will continue to cultivate export crops, such as bananas, coffee, sugar, and cocoa. The foreign exchange gained from these overseas sales will, in turn, be used to purchase food supplies, principally wheat and rice, from the major international sources: Australia, Canada, the United States, and (to a much lesser extent) Argentina. In times of crisis, Third World recipients of food can assume that the world's grain-exporting nations will give them free food or sell it to them at highly subsidized prices, not necessarily out of humanitarian concerns but to guarantee high returns to their own farmers, who constitute a powerful domestic interest that must be treated kindly. The dependence strategy has a few good features. It ensures that food prices will be kept low in the urban areas of the Third World; hopefully, these low prices can be subsequently translated into social peace and support for the incumbent regime. Foreign business enterprises that own plantations are also reassured that they will be treated fairly and profitably.

By all measures, however, the costs of the dependence strategy outweigh the supposed benefits. For one thing, the strategy practically guarantees that the nation's rural areas will remain backward, not only economically but also socially and politically, without the financial incentives that accompany production for the national market. Inflation in the grain-exporting countries means that the purchase price for wheat and rice will continue to rise, draining the Third World of badly needed foreign exchange. Finally, oscillating prices on the world's raw materials markets mean that secure income cannot be predicted and national economic planners in developing countries must be prepared for foreign-exchange shortfalls from year to year. The results of all these factors in recent years have been growing food shortages, starvation, and malnutrition on a planet that theoretically could support 40 billion people at an acceptable level of caloric intake.

Confronted with the defects in the dependence strategy, more and more Third World countries—principally Brazil, India, Mexico, Pakistan, and the Philippines—have now turned their attention to a strategy of self-sufficiency. Most, if not all, Third World countries at one time produced enough food for their own needs. Many would like to return to that status; some actually show promise of being able to do so. The self-sufficiency strategy requires an increase in the productivity of land presently under cultivation as well as bringing new lands under cultivation. For political and technological reasons, the second objective is proving to be more difficult to accomplish than the first. Some presently cultivated land is being used for nonfood export crops, but to bring that land into food production would put the government on a collision course with powerful foreign commercial enterprises, such as United Brands (bananas) and the various international coffee companies. Underutilized haciendas contain much land kept out of production because of either the cautious mentality of the owner or the absence of sufficient price incentive; bringing this land into production would require policies aimed at breaking the power of the landed gentry. There is much land in remote areas of many Third World countries that is essentially untouched; to bring this land under the plow would require enormous investments in infrastructural improvements (especially roads and irrigation) and other agricultural technologies. One authority on the subject has estimated that more than $46 billion would be needed to modernize 50 million hectares of arable but unused land in India. At this same expenditure rate, more than $700 billion spread out over thirty or more years would be required to bring all arable land in developing countries under cultivation.[20]

For these reasons, most developing countries have concentrated their efforts on increasing the agricultural productivity of each unit of land already being used for the cultivation of food. Generally, agricultural development takes place in four relatively well defined stages. Each step represents a definite intermediate goal that must be reached and passed through to make sub-

sequent stages feasible. The first stage, traditional agriculture, was marked by reliance on conventional hand-wielded implements, rudimentary cultivation and ground-breaking practices, and rainfall for water. Land cultivated this way typically yields less than one metric ton of rice per hectare. Most of rural Africa and substantial parts of Latin America (especially in the Andean and Central American mountains) are still farmed in this manner. The second stage is characterized by the introduction of land improvement through irrigation and drainage, the enhancement of soil nutrients through improved incorporation of organic materials, and by better timing of crop production through improved cultivation techniques. Rice yields typically reach two tons per hectare. Nearly all of South and Southeast Asia and much of the remainder of Latin America fall into this category. In the third stage, scientifically developed techniques are introduced, thus raising rice yield to the range of 2.5 to 4 metric tons per hectare. During this stage, improved varieties of seed, fertilizers, pesticides, and improved storage and transportation facilities are introduced. Very few countries in the Third World (Malaysia, Mexico, Taiwan, with Brazil and Venezuela soon to enter) are in this category yet. Finally, during stage 4, institutional and structural reforms are introduced, changing the very nature of agricultural production. Institutions such as research and development laboratories, credit banks, farmers' cooperatives, tractor stations, and farm extension services begin to dot the countryside, making improved food production a regularized and institutionalized matter instead of a question of providence and good weather. Countries fortunate enough to achieve this stage typically produce as much as six tons of rice per hectare, and often more. Relatively few areas of the Third World have reached this stage.[21]

The actions required for a developing country to move its agrarian sector from stage 2 to stage 3 are referred to by the handy but overworked phrase *the Green Revolution*. Ever since 1970, when Norman E. Borlaug won the Nobel Peace Prize for developing a miracle strain of wheat that promised food self-sufficiency to developing countries, the Green Revolution has been looked to for the salvation of hungry millions. The Green Revolution is a summary term for the many scientific and technological advances that were introduced into farming in several developing countries in the 1970s. Foremost among these innovations were the new, high-yield strains of rice and wheat that allowed farmers to irrigate and fertilize their crops to degrees never before possible. But, as many farmers came to understand, the Green Revolution consists of a package of techniques, each of which must be applied efficiently and in conjunction with the others. The absence of any of these other significant factors could erode the gains brought about by the miracle strains of rice and wheat. These additional technologies include improved fertilizers (which, because of their petroleum base, make for increased imports from the oil-exporting countries); wells, pumps, ditches, and embankments for better irrigation; improved harvesting and cultivating machinery; improved facilities to store, transport, and market the additional output; and new pesticides to keep down the rodents and other pests that infest the fields. In addition, certain social factors have to be present as well. The nature of cultivation of the miracle strains requires more labor for a more regular period of time; so, the character of rural employment has to change. Finally, because the investment required to acquire all of these innovations is substantial, progressive farmers have to be guaranteed a satisfactory return on their investment, which, in turn, means the introduction of guaranteed

high prices or subsidies, or both. In any event, major government intervention in both the rural areas and the urban markets seems inevitable with the Green Revolution.[22]

To what extent have these government policies succeeded in actually raising the level of food production in the Third World? Certainly, no one can doubt that some amazing achievements have been recorded by various individual countries. India, for example, one of the leaders of the Green Revolution, raised its rate of increase in farm output from 2.5 percent during the period from 1947 to 1965 to about 3.3 percent during the 1965 to 1971 period. From 1961 to 1976, India's food production grew annually at the rate of 2.6 percent, exceeding slightly the country's population growth rate of 2.4 percent. Between 1974–76 and 1982–84, India's per capita food production increased by more than 10 percent. Even though India's population doubled in the three decades between 1957 and 1987, food production grew 30 percent faster than population. Total production of foodgrains in 1983–84 reached 152 million metric tons, more than three times the level in 1951. Thus, by July 1985 food reserves had reached some 30 million metric tons. When, in 1987, India faced its worst drought in 125 years, there was neither panic nor large food imports of food from abroad; the country had reached the point of self-sufficiency even in trying times. The secrets of India's success include not only planting high-yield seeds on irrigated land with optimal fertilizer, but also an agricultural extension service that ensures that the latest in farming technologies are brought from the laboratory to the individual farmer quickly and efficiently.[23]

Nevertheless, during the 1960s and 1970s, the record of the Third World in food production has been poor. Let us consider gross production indicators from 1963 through 1973. During this eleven-year span, world food production climbed at an average annual rate of 2.8 percent; in the developing countries, the rate was slightly lower, 2.5 percent. In Africa, the worst record was compiled, 1.5 percent annually; Latin America and Asia registered increases of about 2.5 percent; in the Middle East, production climbed about 3 percent. These increases, however, do not take into account population growth. World food production per capita from 1963 through 1973 remained almost stable, with an increase of only 0.6 percent. In the developing world as a whole, per capita food production actually declined by two-tenths of 1 percent as a result of Africa's disastrous record (−1 percent) and relative stability in the other three regions. Of the seventy-one developing countries for which data are available from 1953 to 1971, food production failed to keep pace with population growth in twenty-four; in seventeen more countries, growth in food production fell short of the increased demand for food (a combined result of increased population and rising personal incomes). Thus, in only thirty countries from this sample did food production manage to equal population growth and increased demand. Even in Mexico, where Borlaug developed the miracle strains of wheat, the Green Revolution appears to have run its course, but population growth continues at the rate of 3.5 percent. Mexico was actually exporting wheat, corn, and beans from 1966 to 1969, but, by the early 1970s, the country had to import between 15 and 20 percent of its basic food grains. Despite almost heroic measures in some countries and continued effort in most of the rest, population growth is eroding what little increase in food production there is in the Third World.

Reports based on data from a more recent period are somewhat more promising. The World Bank's *World Development Report* for 1987 reports significant improvement in food production in the low-income and middle-income countries. Using the period 1979–81 as the base equal to 100, the Bank shows that sixty-two of the world's ninety-five poorest countries increased per capita food production by more than 1 percent per year by the 1983–85 period, twenty-one countries more or less held steady with per capita increases of between zero and 1 percent, and only twelve countries actually fell back in per capita food output. The thirty-seven low-income countries increased their index of food production from 100 to 120, although most of that increase was accounted for by China and India. The thirty-six lower-middle-income states increased their index of per capita food output to 111, while the upper-middle-income countries improved their output to 108.[24]

On the other hand, long-range studies done by the United Nations Food and Agriculture Organization (FAO) are much more discouraging. From 1961 to 1976, according to the FAO, food production in ninety-four developing countries grew at a rate of 2.6 percent per year, thus barely staying abreast of population growth. Despite the fact that food production exceeded population growth in twenty-four of these countries, the FAO estimated that more than 23 percent of the people in eighty-six countries with a total population of 1.9 billion were undernourished. The FAO definition of undernourishment means, however, a daily caloric intake per person of only 1,600 calories, a figure regarded by many experts as minimal for maintaining existence but not high enough to permit any kind of strenuous exertion. Studies undertaken of agricultural workmen in the tropics suggest that 3,500 calories per day may be required in these areas. If this threshold of undernourishment is used, then, more than one-fourth of the world's population is undernourished. The results of the FAO estimate are stark enough, however—in the mid-1970s in fifty-two developing countries, the under-

Table 21.3 Indicators of Well-Being in Eight Selected Third World Countries, 1984

Country	Public Expenditures per Capita on Health*	Population per Physician	Infant Mortality Rate†	Life Expectancy‡	Calorie Supply per Capita	Percentage of Population with Safe Water	Physical Quality of Life Index (PQLI)§
Nigeria	5	11,223	129	50	2,061	36	31
Tanzania	5	19,388	111	51	2,314	52	53
India	2	2,550	104	54	2,161	54	44
Indonesia	4	10,332	87	55	2,504	33	55
Mexico	11	1,110	51	66	3,147	74	78
Brazil	23	1,110	68	64	2,629	75	74
Egypt	9	761	94	58	3,262	75	54
Iran	28	2,551	112	58	2,855	71	57

* Per capita public expenditures on health in U.S.$.
† Infant mortality rate in deaths under one year of age per 1,000 live births.
‡ Life expectancy in years.
§PQLI is an index developed by the Overseas Development Council. It is a composite index based on life expectancy, infant mortality, and literacy. All countries are ranked from 1 to 100, with four countries holding the highest rank of 98 and Guinea-Bissau having the lowest score of 15. These data are from 1981.
(*Source*) All data except those for the PQLI are from Ruth Leger Sivard, *World Military and Social Expenditures*, 1987–88 (Washington, D.C.: World Priorities, 1987), Table III, pp. 46–51. PQLI data are from George Thomas Kurian, *The New Book of World Rankings* (New York: Facts on File, 1984), Table 259.

nourished population exceeded 15 percent. Looking to the future, the FAO paints a dismal picture of Third World hunger through the year 2000. By the end of this century, if major increases in agricultural production are not achieved (along with population controls), sixty-four countries—twenty-nine of them in Africa—will not be able to feed their populations, even if every hectare of their cultivable land is farmed.[25] (See Table 21.3 for some additional indicators of well-being in eight Third World countries.)

Goals, Actions, Outcomes: Enlightenment

Third World governments generally accord a higher priority to power and well-being policies and goals than they do to enlightenment and respect. The relative poverty of the Third World in both power and material comfort dictates that any progressive government must attend to these needs first, relegating enlightenment and respect goals to a second level of importance.

Where enlightenment and respect policies do receive great attention, it is usually to serve the goals of power and well-being first. Only secondarily do policies bearing on enlightenment and respect have any intrinsic worth.

In this chapter we examine some data regarding the performance of Third World regimes in the fields of enlightenment and respect. Be aware that we have entered areas of human behavior that defy quantitative analysis. We look at some numerical indicators of performance, but readers should treat all such data with a certain degree of skepticism. At best, the data reflect general orders of magnitude instead of precise levels of performance.

Earlier, we considered what Third World governments attempt to do in the field of enlightenment to increase the values of national power, national unity, integrity, loyalty, and legitimacy. In Chapter 17 we found that the majority of Third World governments exercise some form of control over their nation's news media, especially radio, film, and television. Even in the print media—newspapers and magazines— many Third World regimes exert what amounts to *de facto* censorship in an effort to shape the information given to the mass population.

We are accustomed to seeing press censorship and control of the media as integral parts of authoritarian regimes or dictatorships, whether from left-wing regimes like that of Nicaragua, or from right-wing governments such as that of Chile.[26] As we saw in an earlier chapter (see Figure 17.2), about two-thirds of all Third World governments restrict or limit the freedom of the broadcast media in their countries, while about half restrict the print media in some fashion. In most of these instances, press censorship has been an important element in government policy for many years. What is disturbing is that in the late 1970s and through the 1980s, press censorship began to appear in countries where in the past the media have operated relatively free of official government restraint. India has for decades boasted of having one of the freest newspaper establishments in the Third World. Yet in 1975, Prime Minister Indira Gandhi declared a national state of emergency, censored the press heavily, and arrested a large number of newspaper editors for criticism of the government. Popular reaction against these policies eventually led to Mrs. Gandhi's defeat at the polls in 1977, and press freedom was generally restored in India during the early 1980s. In 1982, however, a court in New Delhi blocked publication of a magazine article about the questionable business dealings of a political ally of Mrs. Gandhi; reporters and editors complained that they were beaten, threatened, and arrested for antigovernment reporting; and several state laws were passed prohibiting the publication, sale, and possession of any printed material that is "scurrilous" in its attacks on public officials. At one point, in September 1982, most of India's 10,000 newspapers closed down in protest over the government's antimedia measures. Throughout 1987, Mrs. Gandhi's son, Rajiv, who had followed his assassinated mother to India's leadership, waged a continuous battle with one of the country's leading newspapers, the *Indian Express*. The *Express* had begun to demand Gandhi's resignation from office because of alleged corruption in his government involving arms purchases in Sweden and secret bank accounts in Switzerland. Gandhi retaliated by sending armed groups to raid the offices of the newspaper, initiating legal proceedings to take over the paper and its building and printing presses, and blocking publication of the paper while its workers were on strike and picketing the press building. At one point in the fall, the paper was shut down for seven weeks; and its editorial staff were attacked with bottles of acid when they attempted to enter the building to resume publication. The government charged that the newspaper had violated Indian law by importing printing press equipment illegally, and that the paper was linked to militant right-wing Hindu activist organizations that seek the downfall of the country's secular regime. Despite India's tradition of a vigorous press, many of the country's newspapers seemed intimidated by these attacks and were reluctant to come to the defense of the *Express*.[27]

Third World governments have demonstrated that they have the power to close down critical newspapers and magazines internally, but they still have not been able to do much about the persistent criticism emanating from the international wire services and other news agencies, such as Reuters or United Press International (UPI). During 1975 and 1976, many developing countries, led by Mexico, began to urge the creation of a Third World news agency to be based in Mexico City. This new agency would foster the publication of news reports favorable to the Third World to counteract the bad impressions left by the critical international news agencies. In October 1976, the issue came to a head at the meeting of the United Nations Educational, Scientific, and Cultural Organization (UNESCO) in Nairobi, Kenya. At the UNESCO meeting, Third World delegates sought to pass a resolution that would go beyond the news-pool idea, and they asserted that governments are responsible for the activities in the international sphere of all mass media under their jurisdiction, a proposition that runs counter to the notion of press freedom.

Since the 1976 meeting in Nairobi, the Third World has acted to establish its own international news service, an information pool operated by a number of nonaligned news agencies that report on events throughout the developing world and send the stories to seven regional centers, the most important of which are Bel-grade, Havana, and New Delhi. From there, the reports are disseminated to media editors and staffs throughout the Third World for subsequent publication. The new service has not prospered for a number of reasons. Many of the developing countries distrust each other almost as much as they do the West, and reports emanating from Third World countries are frequently censored by the affected governments just as if they had been broadcast or written by Western news agencies. The Third World is still largely dependent for the transmission of their stories on the communications technology that is dominated by the Western wire services. In addition, the field of journalism is still a rather new and untested one in many Third World countries; admittedly it is not particularly easy for a journalist to write an engaging and dramatic story about rice production in the Philippines or housing problems in India. Leaders of this news-dissemination effort reply in defense, however, that, since the founding of the pool, the major Western news services—such as Reuters and the Associated Press (AP)—have begun to devote more time to development news, a trend that by itself justifies the creation of the pool.[28]

There were in the 1980s other attempts to break what many Third World leaders regard as a monopoly over global communications held by the Western industrialized democracies. One such effort is the OPEC News Agency (OPECNA), established by the Organization of Petroleum Exporting Countries in Vienna in early 1981. The agency, whose mission is to correct misconceptions about its thirteen member states, issues about 1,000 words a day on economic and other developments within OPEC. And in late 1982, UNESCO itself acted to promote a "new world information order" and to further the development of Third World media through improvement of communications, training of journalists, and lessening of dependence on Western news organizations.[29]

Restrictive policies toward the news media may have promoted national unity and thereby strengthened national governments; but such policies will also concentrate power in fewer and fewer hands. As opposition elites in the media are forced out and replaced by government representatives, power is redistributed toward a single elite beholden to government agencies. The prevailing trend in the Third World is to undertake policies in the field of enlightenment that encourages the growth of power at the national level but that also distributes that power more unequally.

Education policies also have a bearing on enlightenment in the Third World. Third World elites have been greatly influenced by seeing the favorable effects of large expenditures on public education in developed countries. Despite the obvious differences between the economic and cultural environments in developed and less developed countries, Third World leaders are convinced that they can make massive improvements in the economic potential of their countries by investing heavily in the human capital of their society, and that means investing in education.

Through the early 1980s developing countries made major strides forward in public financing of education, and the results have been encouraging. The total public expenditure on education in the developing world rose from about $9 billion (about 2.4 percent of the collective GNP) in 1960 to $38 billion (4.0 percent) in 1976 to more than $100 billion (3.7 percent) in 1984. The number of teachers in the developing countries rose from about 8 million in 1960 to almost 26 million in 1986. (See Table 21.4 for indicators of educational policy effort in selected Third World countries.) As a consequence, by 1980, slightly more than half of all school-age

Table 21.4   Indicators of Educational Policy in Eight Selected Third World Countries, 1984

Country	Percentage of GNP to Education	Public Expenditures per Capita on Education*	Percentage of School-Age Population in School	School-Age Population per Teacher
Nigeria	1.9	15	46	85
Tanzania	3.3	11	44	84
India	3.0	8	46	68
Indonesia	3.3	20	63	37
Mexico	2.6	79	69	42
Brazil	3.9	57	54	42
Egypt	4.3	31	52	60
Iran	7.5	133	53	35

* Per capita public expenditures on education expressed in U.S.$.
(*Source*) Sivard, *World Military and Social Expenditures* (1987–88), Table III, pp. 46–51.

children in the Third World were enrolled in school, although levels of enrollment varied widely according to region (from nearly 60 percent in Latin America and the Far East to about 40 percent in South Asia), sex (enrollment of females typically runs about 20 percentage points behind that of males), income (enrollment of children from the richest households ranges from 20 to 30 percentage points higher than from the poorest households), and area of the country (urban children enroll from 10 to 30 percentage points higher than do rural children).[30]

Beyond the bare statistics of educational expenditures lies a major dispute over whether to stress low-level education to raise literacy rates or high-level education to provide the managers and skilled professionals to run a developing economy. To some degree, the dispute changes focus depending on the relative stage of development of a given country. Countries that are still rather traditional are faced with a major problem in communications. No matter how much they spend on the electronic media (radio and television), there are still many significant kinds of information that can only be communicated by the written or printed word. In an urban setting, well over half of all information is conveyed by written media. A society that enjoys general literacy among its adult population has the potential for a completely different kind of economic and social organization—one that emphasizes bureaucratic rule making and the transmission of formal, written messages as well as one that can be relied on to perform routine tasks efficiently by individuals with a minimum of personal supervision. The drive for adult literacy in developing countries goes far beyond the need for an individual citizen to be able to read a newspaper. It has an impact on the organizational potential of a society. Inasmuch as we have repeatedly stressed the need for Third World countries to enhance their institutional power, both politically and economically, we see that increased literacy is an indispensable component of this approach.

In Table 21.5, we see the results of literacy policies in the eight selected Third World countries. The varying levels of achievement over a twenty-five year period (1960–84) are striking. Countries like Tanzania and Iran, starting from a base of nearly total illiteracy, have made remarkable strides. Others with an already high literacy rate, like Mexico and Brazil, managed an increase at the rate of about 1 percent per year over the period. Still, after two decades of concerted effort to raise the literacy level of

Table 21.5 Changes in Literacy Rates over Time in Eight Selected Third World Countries

Country	Adult Literacy Rates				
	1960	1970	1975	1980	1984
Nigeria	—	—	—	34	42
Tanzania	10	—	66	70	85
India	28	36	36	40	44
Indonesia	39	56	62	67	74
Mexico	65	84	76	83	90
Brazil	61	68	76	76	78
Egypt	26	40	44	50	44
Iran	16	37	50	47	51

(*Source*) World Bank, *World Tables, 1976*, pp. 522–523; World Bank, *World Development Report (1980)*, Table 23, pp. 154–155; Ruth Leger Sivard, *World Military and Social Expenditures, 1983* (Leesburg, Va.: World Priorities, 1983), Table III, pp. 36–41; Sivard, *World Military and Social Expenditures (1987–88)*, Table III, pp. 46–51.

these countries, four of them are still at least 50 percent illiterate, two are in the range of two-thirds to three-fourths literate, and only two are above 80 percent literate.

At the opposite end of the spectrum are those who stress upper-level training to prepare people to staff a complex society and its institutions. According to the International Labor Office, for example, in the United States in 1980 about 10.5 percent of the workforce was classified as "administrative and managerial," while another 14.7 percent worked in "professional and technical" positions. For seven of the eight selected Third World countries (excluding Tanazania, for which data were not available), the corresponding average percentages were 0.98 and 4.97. Overall, the best-endowed country of the eight was Mexico, with 2.6 percent of its workforce in administrative posts and another 6.2 percent devoted to professional and technical jobs.[31]

The gravity of the problem is clear, yet policy solutions are consistently falling short of success for several reasons. For one thing, upper-level training of this sort has been found to be extremely expensive, especially when compared with lower-level, primary-grade education. Although postsecondary education in the United States may cost per pupil about twice what it costs to educate a student in the primary grades, the data indicate that in developing countries the ratio may be 1:40. Pressed by the scarcity of funds, Third World governments may succumb to the apparent bargain they purchase by investing in primary education. A second problem stems from the relatively great prestige of higher education in such fields as the humanities, law, and the social sciences, whereas what developing countries need are students in fields like the physical and natural sciences, engineering, and agronomy. The distortion in university enrollments often means that many students flood the market in law and the hu-

manities and become disgruntled when they fail to find employment. The interaction of an expanding educational system and a stable or contracting economy brings about the third problem in educational policy, the phenomenon of the brain drain—the migration of highly trained professionals from developing countries (where they are needed in theory but where there are often too few real jobs available) to the more highly developed markets of Europe and North America. Finally, we must note the effects of educational policy on equality in the Third World. As Charles Elliott points out, Third World educational programs frequently aggravate the tendency toward differentiation because a certain few individuals are chosen to move up the social, economic, and political ladder by means of a highly selective policy that relegates the vast majority to a continued life of poverty.[32] Educational policies as they are implemented in the Third World usually skew the distribution of income and power even more than would be the case if the government allowed market forces to operate freely. Government loans and scholarships, decisions about where to build schools, teacher assignments, informal ties to certain racial or religious groups that smooth their access to educational resources, and other policies operate to accelerate the rise of a very few individuals at the expense of leaving behind the great bulk of their fellow citizens. We find that educational policies emphasize growth while operating to accentuate inequity.[33]

Goals, Actions, Outcomes: Respect

During his first campaign for the presidency in 1976 and, subsequently, in his administration, Jimmy Carter made clear the concern of the

U.S. government over the plight of political prisoners and over the fate of human rights generally, not only in the Soviet Union but also in many Third World states. The expressions of concern were not limited to rhetoric; foreign military assistance was reduced or eliminated entirely if the recipient was judged to be in violation of human rights and if the aid reduction did not adversely affect America's defense posture. Some of the Third World countries affected were Chile, Ethiopia, and Uruguay. Others, such as Brazil, rejected American aid if it was accompanied by lectures about human rights.

During the 1980 American presidential campaign, one of the major points of disagreement between President Carter and Ronald Reagan involved American policy toward friendly regimes that violated the human rights of their citizens. Once in office, President Reagan made it clear that he would draw a distinction between adversary nations, like the Soviet Union, and those allied with the United States, such as Argentina or Chile, when the violation of human rights was at issue. Further, the president and his secretary of state confirmed their view that it was more effective and proper to work through private diplomatic channels to secure better treatment of prisoners in other countries than to use highly visible and dramatic techniques, such as those favored by Carter. The differences of opinion between these two American leaders illustrate the challenging and divisive nature of the human rights issue in international politics and in the conduct of American foreign policy.

Few policy areas are as difficult to assess as those having to do with human rights violations, and the difficulties are compounded when the region of concern is the Third World. Let us consider first the problem of information. We must recognize the extreme sensitivity of most governments to matters of this sort. Are governments really interested in evaluating policy

outcomes or in measuring political performance in this field? Past experiences and common sense suggest that they are not. Nearly every state in the Third World is a signatory of the United Nations Declaration on Human Rights, yet many of them systematically violate that declaration. Most governments are reluctant to admit any deviation from their professed goals and objectives. Can we expect any less when the issue of concern is so controversial and sensitive? Then, there is the problem of unbiased news reporting in the Third World. Most of the information that we have about human rights violations in the Third World comes from one of a few sources: Amnesty International, Freedom House, and other international human rights reporting agencies; or Western news agencies. Many of these sources have come under fire for biases in their reporting. Critics of Amnesty International complain that it only criticizes right-wing dictatorships, such as Argentina and Chile, and seldom charges left-wing regimes with suppression of human rights. On the other side of the ledger, as we have already seen, many Third World governments have complained of reporting by the Western news agencies (such as UPI and Reuters) and have replaced these services with a Third World news network. In such an emotion-charged area of human relations, can we ever expect to obtain information that would meet scientific standards for objectivity, methodological rigor, and verifiability? The answer seems highly doubtful.

Even if the information problem could be solved, however, we must still deal with the philosophical question of how to interpret news about Third World violations of human rights. Are these events really all that uncommon? We know that many countries that now enjoy a democratic tradition once suppressed dissent and freedom of political thought in the interest of public order and economic progress. Is the

Western tradition entirely applicable here? Perhaps the poverty and illiteracy of many Third World countries work to make freedom of political expression an unacceptable luxury at this early stage of their development. And are there no long-term benefits to be derived from the near-term suppression of human rights? At one time or another, nearly every country on earth, including our own, has denied free expression to certain groups of people in the interest of increasing or preserving the well-being of the remainder.

For their part, many Third World leaders claim that human dignity can be guaranteed and protected without building the intricate structure of institutions and laws that characterize the Western approach to human rights. On the contrary, they argue, many Western traditions actually work to deny individuals their rights in a developing setting. Political parties, for example, only aggravate conflict and institutionalize class strife. Elections polarize opinion and foster disunity when what a country needs is an integrating force. A free press merely serves to enflame passions. Irresponsible demogogues take advantage of free speech to whip up the masses and provoke them to rebellion. Many non-Western societies, such as Indonesia, place greater emphasis on mass, public consensus as a prelude to decision making than they do on dissent and adversary proceedings so important to pluralist democrats in the West. Most important, many Third World leaders assert that public order is required to preserve private rights. Those who would dissent and who would disrupt the public order must be suppressed to protect the rights of those who are loyal to the state.

We may admit the validity of more than one approach to this most complex question, but we may not retreat into ignorance and fuzzy generalizations about human rights. Instead, what we have attempted to do is to survey several sources of information about the status of human rights around the world and categorize the various Third World regimes according to the actions they have taken in this field. The reader must then determine for himself or herself what this information signifies in our overall appraisal of Third World political performance.

We consider here government policies that have to do with political rights, that is, the liberties that a person is thought to enjoy regardless of political opinion, partisan affiliation, or attitude. For a political system to be considered a democracy, three criteria must be satisfied. First, there must be safeguards for each individual to speak and to organize according to his or her political beliefs. Governments that seek to suppress these rights censor or otherwise control the media of mass communications, imprison persons for their beliefs in the political realm, and infringe on the rights of representative assemblies (legislatures, parliaments, congresses) to articulate dissenting opinions. Second, in a democracy, safeguards must exist for the freedom of individuals to remove the existing regime through elections and to replace it with one more to the liking of the people. Furthermore, this freedom must be protected through the creation of appropriate institutions so that exercise of this freedom does not depend on the whim of a single individual. Regimes that intend to suppress these freedoms concentrate their policies on preventing free and open elections, on the prohibition of some or all political parties, and on overriding the constitution by some extralegal procedure. Third, in a democracy, individual citizens must be able to live in peace without fear that the state will terrorize them or allow others to do so for political reasons. Regimes that do not uphold these freedoms practice torture and other human rights violations and encourage vigilante-type groups to engage in illegal but unpunished assassinations of dissenting political leaders.[34]

Figure 21.1 reveals our findings about the extent of human rights violations in the Third World. The rankings used to classify Third World countries in the figure are a composite of two scales issued annually by Freedom House of New York City since 1972. The first measure, dealing with politically rights, ranks countries according to the extent to which the people are able to play an active role in choosing their leaders and in determining the laws under which they live. States ranked either 1 or 2 have a respected electoral procedure, multiple parties, free elections, and political participation by all segments of society. States ranked 3 or 4 have unfair electoral systems that ban opposition parties. States ranked 5 have poor electoral procedures but some opposition. States ranked 6

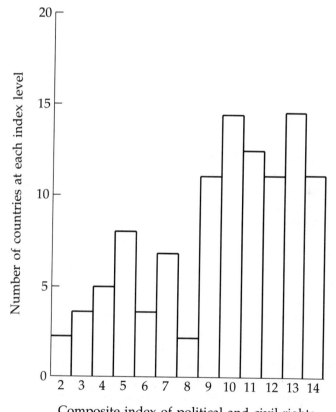

Figure 21.1 Index of political and civil rights for 102 Third World countries, 1986. [Raymond D. Gastil, ed., *Freedom in the World: Political Rights and Civil Liberties*, 1986–1987 (Westport, Conn.: Greenwood Press, 1987), Table 1, pp. 30–34.]

have electoral systems that are manipulated by ruling parties. States ranked 7 do not permit any legal opposition or open elections. The second scale deals with civil rights and also ranks states from 1 to 7, depending on how well they protect four critical rights—freedom from censorship, open public discussion, maintenance of rule of law, and freedom from government terror—and four subsidiary rights—economic independence of the media; freedom of movement; freedom of choice, including religious freedom; and freedom of property. The rankings in Figure 21.1 are achieved by adding together the scores of both scales for each of the 102 countries in the Third World. Thus, countries with a 7 on both the political rights and the civil rights scales have a score of 14. (A score of 1 would not be possible because we are combining two scales, the lowest score on each of which is 1.)

It is obvious that the state of human rights in the Third World leaves much to be desired.[35] Only 29 of the 102 states surveyed fall below the midpoint of the scale, and 17 of these are in Latin America. The scores from 11 to 14 indicate really serious violations of human rights because each country in these groups must have scored near the bottom of the scale on at least one of the two measures of human rights performance. Exactly half the countries surveyed (fifty-one) appear on these upper scales, a sad commentary on the way in which human rights have been abused in developing countries in the 1980s.

Finally, what can we conclude about the economic performance of regimes that are suppressive of civil and political rights? In Figure 21.2, we see the average GNP per capita growth rates from 1965 to 1985 arrayed according to the composite political and civil rights index, as derived from Figure 21.1. It will be clear to the reader that while there is not a direct relationship between economic growth and respect for human rights, there is an unmistakable general tendency for suppressive regimes to register rather low average growth rates, while those with better records on human rights also score better in terms of GNP per capita growth rates. We must be careful not to draw the wrong conclusions here. The data as presented do not indicate whether suppression of human rights causes poor economic performance, or whether authoritarian, antidemocratic regimes come into power spurred by a deteriorating economic picture. Does a policy of abuse of human rights cause economic growth to slow down, or does economic decline cause governments to suppress dissent and opposition? We do not know from examining Figure 21.2, but we can conclude this much: Authoritarian regimes, despite all their claims, perform rather poorly in meeting the challenge of economic distress in developing countries.

Conclusions: Enhancing Human Dignity in the Third World

In the preceding pages, we have assessed the performance of the 102 governments of the Third World as they struggle to improve the level of human dignity in their countries. Not surprisingly, the record is a mixed one. Scattered throughout the developing world are significant cases of impressive success and even of heroic triumph over the obstacles to development. In Colombia, Costa Rica, Sri Lanka, and Venezuela, among others, progressive governments have the development process in hand, and they have achieved this without serious suppression of individual freedoms. In other countries, including some that once offered great promise of success, the results have been decidedly

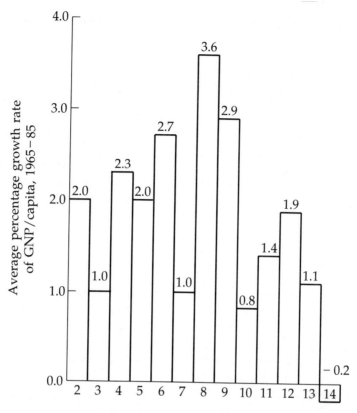

Figure 21.2 Economic performance of 102 Third World countries according to their index of political and civil rights. [For political and civil rights index: See Figure 21.1. For GNP/capita growth rates: World Bank, *World Development Report: 1987* (New York: Oxford University Press, 1987), Table 1, pp. 202–203.]

negative, even bordering on disastrous. Ethiopia, Ghana, and Uganda typify these countries. In general, however, we simply do not know at this stage in their development how most countries will fare in the struggle. Many countries exhibit wide variations in performance from year to year, and most are highly vulnerable to factors beyond their control, such as the condition of the international economy or the weather. With the exception of the older countries of Latin America, most Third World states have not been independent long enough to demonstrate a track record, so it is too early to make any firm judgments about their future.

As most Third World elites know only too well, however, many of the important determinants of human dignity look more like obstacles than opportunities. Power remains divided among three competing forces: local, tradition-bound elites; national governments; and powerful international agencies. Economic development is being advanced somewhat in the industrial sphere, agricultural production has stagnated throughout the area, and exponential population growth threatens to erode progress in both sectors. Enlightenment policies interfere excessively with the free flow of ideas, particularly when they offer criticism of the existing regime, whereas educational expenditures are too little and too late to keep up with population growth. And a growing number of Third World regimes are leaning toward the denial of human rights in an effort (usually futile) to keep order and accelerate economic growth. In sum, the balance sheet of human dignity in the Third World looks mixed but with signs of deterioration over the decade of the 1980s.

The preceding chapters have focused on the separate threads of Third World politics. It is time now to pull these threads together into a coherent picture to explain why many Third World countries find themselves in such difficulty today. Our explanation must deal with three factors: the environment, the individuals who occupy important political roles, and the structural setting within which the political drama is acted. Third World politics is a function of the interaction of these three factors. No single factor can be isolated as being of paramount importance; each interacts with the other two in both cause-and-effect relationships.

First, let us consider the environment. The historical experience of colonialism has left a residue of attitudes and institutions that has proven intractable. The international political and economic systems work against the national interests of poor and developing states, quite apart from whether some evil force so wills it or whether the system is some kind of mammoth practical joke played by impersonal forces on struggling Third World countries. The privileged role enjoyed by traditional elites is also a severe obstacle to more progressive policies at home. The comparative scarcity of natural resources (and of financial ones, too) has aggravated the disadvantage suffered by developing states that are late arrivals on the path to industrialization. At times, it seems that even the weather and other natural forces conspire against the world's poor countries as droughts, monsoons, floods, and earthquakes seem to most affect those nations and peoples who can least protect themselves against their force. In short, the environment within which the Third World must act is mostly unfavorable for the improvement of human dignity.

The human resources of the Third World also offer their share of obstacles to progress. Low levels of health, nutrition, and literacy sap the working class of its strength and productivity and, thereby, make it that much more difficult to launch a flourishing industrial effort with the necessary skilled labor. The prevailing personality structure that characterizes many non-Western societies seems ill suited to the requirements of incremental politics, compromise, joining with others for political gains, or valuing achievement. Many facets of the traditional personality are quite functional in the context of a struggle against colonial powers, for which heroic measures and enormous sacrifice are needed, and compromise is equivalent to betrayal. But, once independence is won and the system settles into the daily routine of meeting economic and social challenges, a new kind of personality is required, and traditional child-rearing and socialization procedures seem badly equipped to shape such a personality. In addition, dimensions of a society, such as the way in which families rear their young, are beyond the reach of most Third World governments. Changes in basic personality may occur, but they will take place more as the result of the gradual impact of economic modernization than as the outcome of intentional public policy. Finally, the heavy reliance of mass populations on charismatic leaders makes it correspondingly more difficult for these same leaders to build the institutions so necessary for a developing country. Again, the charismatic leader is very valuable during the anticolonial struggle, when public commitment must be raised to new heights. Eventually, however, charisma must yield to institutions as the motivating force for political change. Regrettably, many charismatic leaders fail to sense the appropriate time to begin to ease the state to a new foundation, one that will outlast the revolutionary leaders.

These comments bring us to the structural dimension of Third World politics. Readers who have followed our arguments through the book must now realize that the institutionalization of political change must receive top priority from reforming elites. The reasons for this are spelled out in greatest detail in Chapters 18, 19, and 21. The institutional base left behind by colonial economics and politics contains both individuals and regularized relationships that resist and, eventually, undermine efforts to modernize and industrialize. Instead of dealing decisively with these antimodern forces, as has been done in both Western democracies and communist states, most Third World governments have opted for a sort of shaky compromise wherein the traditional elites are left alone and modernization is pursued in only a part of the nation. Not surprisingly, then, the costs of change are borne by those who cannot protect themselves from bearing the burden: the urban and rural poor. The institutions that have come to the aid of these classes in other regions in the past, political parties and interest groups, are ineffectual in most Third World situations, and often they are even captives of the very

regimes whose actions they seek to influence. This is not to say that every country in the Third World must now adopt the two-party system and create a chamber of commerce. The particular institutional network created within each country must be closely related to that country's peculiar social, economic, and historical background. But, without the institutions to mobilize, organize, and shape the collective behavior of the Third World's masses and progress toward distribution of power, well-being, enlightenment, and respect will lag behind the expectations of the bulk of the population.

Why Is There So Little Upheaval in the Third World?

Given the massive discontent that we sense in the developing world, why is there so little actual revolutionary change in these countries? This textbook has tried to make the argument that the average citizen of the Third World must surely note little real improvement in his or her life over the years. Yet, with few exceptions, there seems to be little support for radical change in these countries. Even in those few countries where radicalization has occurred, such as Cuba or Vietnam, the motivation was as least as much one of establishing national independence as it was raising the material standard of living of the mass of the people. Why do the poor of the developing countries accept their fate with so little resistance?

Several explanations have been suggested. Some Western observers point to the apathy, fatalism, and lethargy of the rural masses in traditional countries as factors that rob them of the strength to rebel. Others claim that there is actually a great desire to rebel among the poor but that the cultural obstacles to common causes prevent them from organizing to achieve their goals. Still others assert that there is actually a great deal of violence in politics in the Third World but that the military and the police have so far been able to contain rebellion by sheer coercion and counterterror.

Yet another explanation of mass acceptance of what seems to be a manifestly unjust social system has to do with the difference between symbolic and tangible politics. We begin with a quote by Robert A. Dahl as he discusses ethnic politics in New Haven:

> Politicians who play the game of ethnic politics confer individual benefits like jobs, nominations, bribes, gratuities, and assistance on all sorts of individuals more or less according to ethnic criteria. But ethnic characteristics serve as a kind of comprehensive symbol for class and other criteria. Moreover, benefits conferred on an individual member of an ethnic group are actually shared to some degree by the rest of the group, for every time one member makes a social or economic breakthrough, others are likely to learn of it, to take pride in his accomplishment, and to find it easier themselves to achieve the same sort of advance. The strategies of politicians are designed to confer specific benefits on particular individuals and thus to win the support of the whole group.[36]

What Dahl is describing with regard to ethnic politics in New Haven is a specific example of the more general social institution that Charles Elliott calls the *confidence mechanism*.[37] The confidence mechanism is any social practice or structure that permits real resources to be distributed unequally, but it does so in such a way as to convince those who lose that the system is essentially fair and that they lost because of their own shortcomings. Any confidence mechanism consists of these six characteristics:

there must be competition among the members of a group for individual enrichment; only a few members of the group are chosen to benefit from the enrichment process; the process of selection is biased away from natural abilities or merit and toward some ascriptive criterion, such as race or language; these selective biases are not obvious to those who compete; the system remains sufficiently open (at least to all appearances) to make the process seem legitimate to those who lose; and the overall process of enrichment is controlled by persons who benefit directly or indirectly from it.

Murray Edelman has drawn our attention to the central role of symbols in any political system.[38] In poor countries, symbolic capability may be the key to regime survival. Symbols have their greatest value in politics as media to bestow the psychic benefit of a given policy on those sectors or individuals who do not receive any material benefit from the policy and who did not have the opportunity to participate in its formulation. In other words, political symbols help a government make its people feel good about a policy that does not benefit them materially. In developing countries where there are not many material benefits to distribute, symbolic politics (as administered by confidence mechanisms) takes on heightened importance.

Does this line of analysis suggest that people who benefit from politics only symbolically are being deceived or duped? More radical commentators of Third World politics would certainly answer in the affirmative. To these people, the lower classes are being bought off by essentially worthless symbols, such as racial or ethnic pride, and they must experience an increase in class consciousness to attract more tangible benefits to their lives. On the other hand, argues Dahl, who are we to denigrate another person's values, which may include symbols instead of tangible goods and services? As he says:

> Terms such as benefit and reward are intended to refer to subjective, psychological appraisal by the recipients, rather than appraisals by other observers. An action can be said to confer benefits on an individual . . . if he believes he has benefited, even though, from the point of view of observers, his belief is false or perhaps ethnically wrong.[39]

After all, when people have lost all hope of gaining material rewards commensurate with their efforts, can anyone deny them the right to take refuge in symbols? One of the lasting contributions of Freud to our understanding of human consciousness was to show that our desires are inherently insatiable and that,

therefore, we must engage in psychological exercises to be able to live on a day-to-day basis with frustration and denial our constant companions. Certainly, people who have had their class consciousness raised and who are denied the sanctuary of symbolic gratification are frequently the fuel for the fires of revolution. Nevertheless, traditional identities based on race, religion, tribal affiliation, ethnic characteristics, or language are still powerful in the Third World. They should serve as a constant reminder to potential revolutionaries that the task of mobilization of the poor of their country has so far defied all but the most talented of leaders. Whether this continues to be the case or not is a secret locked in the minds and in the social institutions of the 2½ billion people of the Third World.

Suggestions for Further Reading

Adams, Don, and **Robert M. Bjork,** *Education in Developing Areas* (New York: McKay, 1969).

Aiken, William, and **Hugh La Follette,** eds., *World Hunger and Moral Obligation* (Englewood Cliffs, N.J.: Prentice-Hall, 1977).

Amnesty International Report 1987 (London: Amnesty International, 1987).

Baranson, Jack, *Industrial Technology for Developing Economies* (New York: Praeger, 1969).

Brown, Lester R., et al., *State of the World: 1987* (New York: Norton, 1987).

Carter, Gwendolyn, and **William O. Brown,** *Transition in Africa: Studies in Political Adaptation* (Boston: Boston University Press, 1958).

Cline, Ray S., *World Power Trends and U.S. For-

eign Policy for the 1980s* (Boulder, Colo.: Westview Press, 1980).

Diamond, Larry, Juan Linz, and **Seymour Martin Lipset,** eds., *Democracy in Developing Countries* (Boulder, Colo.: Lynne Reiner Publishers, 1987), 4 vols.

Froelich, Walter, ed., *Land Tenure, Industrialization and Social Stability* (Milwaukee: Marquette University Press, 1961).

Gastil, Raymond D., ed., *Freedom in the World: Political Rights and Civil Liberties, 1986–1987* (Westport, Conn.: Greenwood Press, 1987).

Harrison, Paul, *The Greening of Africa* (New York: Penguin, 1987).

Hermassi, Elbaki, *The Third World Reassessed*

(Berkeley: University of California Press, 1980).

Hill, Kim Q., ed., *Toward a New Strategy for Development* (New York: Pergamon, 1979).

Hoogvelt, Ankie, *The Third World in Global Development* (London: Macmillan, 1982).

Hoselitz, Bert F., and Wilbert E. Moore, eds., *Industrialization and Society* (Paris: UNESCO, 1963).

Kurian, George Thomas, *Encyclopedia of the Third World*, 3rd ed. (New York: Facts on File, 1987), 3 vols.

Livingstone, Arthur, *Social Policy in Developing Countries* (London: Routledge & Kegan Paul, 1969).

Loup, Jacques, *Can the Third World Survive?* (Baltimore: Johns Hopkins University Press, 1983).

Marchal, Jean, and Bernard Ducros, eds., *The Distribution of National Income* (London: Macmillan, 1968).

Newberg, Paula R., ed., *The Politics of Human Rights* (New York: New York University Press, 1980).

Schram, Wilbur, *Mass Media and National Development* (Stanford, Calif.: Stanford University Press, 1964).

Schultz, Thomas W., *Transforming Traditional Agriculture* (New Haven, Conn.: Yale University Press, 1964).

Scientific American, 243 (3) (1980). (Special issue on economic development.)

Sigmund, Paul E., ed., *The Ideologies of the Developing Nations* (New York: Praeger, 1963).

Sivard, Ruth Leger, *World Military and Social Expenditures, 1987–88* (Washington, D.C.: World Priorities, 1987).

Veenhoven, William A., ed., *Case Studies on Human Rights and Fundamental Freedoms: A World Survey*, 2 vols. (The Hague: Martinus Nijhoff, 1975).

Wesson, Robert, ed., *Democracy: World Survey 1987* (Boulder, Colo.: Lynne Reiner Publishers, 1987).

Wriggins, W. Howard, *The Ruler's Imperative: Strategies for Political Survival in Asia and Africa* (New York: Columbia University Press, 1969).

Notes

1. This discussion leans heavily on W. Howard Wriggins, *The Ruler's Imperative: Strategies for Political Survival in Asia and Africa* (New York: Columbia University Press, 1969).

2. David McClelland, "The Two Faces of Power," *Journal of International Affairs* 24 (1) (1970); 29–47.

3. Ray S. Cline, *World Power Trends and U.S. Foreign Policy for the 1980s* (Boulder, Colo.: Westview Press, 1980).

4. James D. Cockcroft et al., eds., *Dependence and Underdevelopment: Latin America's Political Economy* (Garden City, N.Y.: Doubleday, 1972).

5. Hobart Rowen, "World Bank: Next Ten Years May Be Worse," *Washington Post*, September 22, 1980. See also World Bank, *World Development Report: 1984* (New York: Oxford University Press, 1984), Ch. 2.

6. Don Oberdorfer, " 'Me Decade' Looms for Oil Users," *Washington Post*, March 23, 1980.

7. Jonathan Power, "After Decade of Growth, Third World Faces Grim Future," *Washington Post*, June 6, 1989.

8. World Bank, *World Development Report* (1984), Table 2.11, p. 31.

9. James L. Rowe, Jr., "New Debt Repayment Terms Expected," *Washington Post*, August 29, 1984.

10. Hobart Rowen, "World Financiers Gather in Mood of Optimism," *Washington Post*, September 16, 1984.

11. Hobart Rowen, "World Bank Sees 'Bad News' on Third World Debt," *Washington Post*, January 19, 1988; *The Economist*, February 20, 1988.

12. Charles W. Anderson, *Politics and Economic Change in Latin America: The Governing of Restless Nations* (Princeton, N.J.: Van Nostrand, 1967), Table 1, pp. 64–65.

13. This discussion is based on John C. Honey, *Planning and the Private Sector: The Experience in Developing Countries* (New York: Dunellen, 1970), esp. Ch. 6. See also Stanley A. Kochanek, "India," in Robert N. Kearney, ed., *Politics and Modernization in South and Southeast Asia* (New York: Wiley, 1975), pp. 86–89.

14. World Bank, *World Development Report* (1984), Table 2, pp. 220–221.

15. World Bank, *World Development Report* (1987), Table 2, pp. 204–205.

16. *The Economist*, December 6, 1986, October 3, 1987, and March 28, 1987.

17. For a discussion of the elements of the Global Manufacturing System, see Nigel Harris, *The End of the Third World* (New York: Penguin, 1986), and Ankie Hoogvelt, *The Third World in Global Development* (London: Macmillan, 1982).

18. Leon Bouvier and Robert Gardner, *Immigration to the U.S.: The Unfinished Story*, Population Bulletin, vol. 41, no. 4 (Washington, D.C.: Population Reference Bureau, November 1986); Jonathan Power, *Western Europe's Migrant Workers*, Report No. 28 (London: Minority Rights Group, 1978).

19. Michael J. Eden, "Environmental Hazards in the Third World," in Alan B. Mountjoy, ed., *The Third World: Problems and Perspectives* (New York: St. Martin's Press, 1978). Also, from the *Washington Post*: Jim Brooke, "Industrial Pollution Scars Brazil's 'Valley of Death,'" May 10, 1981; Christopher Dickey, "Scenic Mexican Reactor Site Entangles Indians, Unions, Nationalists," May 18, 1981; Stuart Auerbach, "Sri Lanka Discovers Capitalism's Benefits and Pitfalls," May 9, 1981; and William Branigin, "U.N. Study Says Fast-Growing Asia Faces Major Environmental Damage," March 30, 1982.

20. Roger Revelle, "The Resources Available for Agriculture," *Scientific American* 235 (3) (1976); 165–178, esp. p. 172.

21. W. David Hopper, "The Development of Agriculture in Developing Countries," *Scientific American* 235 (3) (1976); 197–205.

22. Zubeida Manzoor Ahmed, "The Social and Economic Implications of the Green Revolution in Asia," *International Labour Review* 105 (1972), 9–34.

23. *The Economist*, July 5, 1986, March 14, 1987, and August 15, 1987.

24. World Bank, *World Development Report* (1987), Table 6, pp. 212–213.

25. Nevin S. Scrimshaw and Lance Taylor, "Food," *Scientific American* 243 (3) (1980); 78–88; Michael Dover and Lee Talbot, "Feeding the Earth: An Agroecological Solution," *Technology Review* (February/March 1988), 27–35.

26. Sanford Ungar, "How Chile Muzzles Its Press," *Washington Post*, January 3, 1988; Julia Preston, "Nicaraguan Radio: Jokes But No News," *Washington Post*, September 27, 1987; "La Prensa Goes to Print," *Washington Post*, October 2, 1987.

27. Stuart Auerbach, "Ban on Article Tests Press Freedom in India," *Washington Post*, March 11, 1982; William Claiborne, "Indian Papers, News Agencies Shut to Protest Tough Press Bill," *Washington Post*, September 4, 1982; Richard Weintraub, "Authorities Raid Offices of Major

Paper in India," *Washington Post*, September 2, 1987; "Gandhi Seeks Takeover of Critical Paper," *Washington Post*, November 18, 1987; Steven Weisman, "Newspaper Is Snared; Did Gandhi Spin the Web?" *New York Times*, December 4, 1987.

28. Michael Dobbs, "Standards for Third World News Agency Still Unsettled," *Washington Post*, December 27, 1979.

29. Tom Heneghan, "OPEC Starts Unit to Distribute News," *Washington Post*, April 6, 1981; "UNESCO Sets Framework for World Press," *Washington Post*, December 4, 1982.

30. World Bank, *World Development Report, 1980* (New York: Oxford University Press, 1980), pp. 46–53. Ruth L. Sivard, *World Military and Social Expenditures* (1987–88), pp. 42–51.

31. Kurian, *The New Book of World Rankings*, Tables 196, 197.

32. Charles Elliott, *Patterns of Poverty in the Third World* (New York: Praeger, 1975), Ch. 9.

33. Many of these issues are discussed in greater detail in Bert F. Hoselitz, "Investment in Education and Its Political Impact," in James S. Coleman, ed., *Education and Political Development* (Princeton, N.J.: Princeton University Press, 1965), Ch. 16.

34. This discussion is based on Rupert Emerson, "The Prospects for Democracy in Africa," in Michael F. Lofchie, ed., *The State of the Nations: Constraints on Development in Independent Africa* (Berkeley: University of California Press, 1971), Ch. 11. See also the important collection of studies in Willem A. Veenhoven, ed., *Case Studies on Human Rights and Fundamental Freedoms: A World Survey*, 2 vols. (The Hague: Martinus Nijhoff, 1975).

35. Data are drawn from Raymond D. Gastil, ed., *Freedom in the World: Political Rights and Civil Liberties, 1986–1987* (Westport, Conn.: Greenwood Press, 1987), Table 1, pp. 30–34.

36. Robert A. Dahl, *Who Governs? Democracy and Power in an American City* (New Haven, Conn.: Yale University Press, 1961), p. 53.

37. Elliott, *Patterns of Poverty*, Ch. 1.

38. Murray Edelman, *The Symbolic Uses of Politics* (Urbana: University of Illinois Press, 1964).

39. Dahl, *Who Governs?* p. 52, footnote 1.

POLITICS AND HUMAN VALUES IN THREE WORLDS

As we conclude this introduction to the study of comparative politics, we want to draw together some of the central themes of the preceding chapters and summarize our findings on the major questions that people around the world face today. It is the nature of politics that few political issues ever are successfully resolved. Some issues gradually disappear from public awareness, some become aggravated and critical, most are simply managed and coped with from year to year, from one generation to another. But some become so urgent that they force governments to attempt, at least, to come to grips with them. Moving from inattention to such issues to feverish efforts to resolve them will not always produce the best results. We urge you to remember that politics is not a neat and tidy process wherein everything nicely comes to a conclusion at an appropriate time and place.

The key questions that remain to be dealt with are these:

1. How do concepts of human dignity vary in the three political worlds?

2. How do levels of political performance compare in the three worlds?

3. Is politics significant in helping us understand the levels of performance in each world? Does politics matter to people trying to improve their lives by achieving their values?

4. What can we say about the state of human values in the future? In what direction are the three worlds apparently headed?

Concepts of Human Dignity in the Three Worlds

On the basis of our findings presented earlier, it seems that one central difference stands out in importance in any discussion of varying perspectives of human dignity. In the *polyarchies* of Western Europe and Japan, making up much of what we have called the First World, there is no single, official, centrally directed and mandated version of human dignity that all citizens must endorse, accept, and obey. Instead,

675

the Western polyarchies encourage multiple concepts of human dignity, the public good, the national interest, and other ambiguous and contentious symbols of the political community. Traditional communist states, on the other hand, did have such an official version of human dignity, and, until recently at any rate, perspectives that challenged this version were not allowed to be disseminated. In the Third World, matters are more complex. Many governments, perhaps even a majority of them, have an official view of human dignity, and they make efforts to have it accepted by the citizenry, either willingly or not. Evidence indicates, however, that many Third World citizens are not willing to accept their governments' official versions of the public good, and challenges to existing regimes have been frequent and sharp. Many Third World states lack either the legitimacy to persuade everyone to agree with the official view of human dignity or the power to force them to accept it. The consequence is and will continue to be a good deal of instability and turbulence in the Third World as its countries go through the difficult process of developing a national identity.

Let us consider some important differences in the ways governments in the three worlds look at the four values we have been discussing throughout this book: *power, well-being, respect,* and *enlightenment.*

When we think about differing versions of power, we must consider three definitions of democracy. In the liberal states of Western Europe and Japan, democracy means polyarchy, a term that suggests competing centers of power, as well as respect for and protection of the right of each citizen to participate in the political process according to the dictates of his or her conscience. Such participation must be significant in that real issues (and not just symbolic ones) are at stake. Elections must be meaningfully contested; the votes must be fairly counted;

and opposition parties must be allowed to assume power if elected. Thus, in the Western view of democracy, politics is basically a form, or structure, intended to guarantee meaningful popular participation. The exact outcomes are not prescribed in the liberal definition of democracy; it is assumed that if the processes are correct, the outcomes also must be.

In traditional Communist Party states, democracy was always a much used term, but the operational definition was changed. Instead of the freewheeling emphasis on mass participation in multiple parties that we see in Western Europe, the communist states emphasized participation by those who shared the official version of the public good (that is, those who did not challenge the right to rule of the Communist Party). Because the state's purported reason for existence was to promote social justice for the workers and because the Communist Party existed for the same purpose, to be loyal to the state was to be loyal to the Communist Party, and vice versa. Until recently, communist leaders saw no need for opposition parties to challenge the regime's policies or right to rule. All debate and dissent were to be carried out within the confines of the Communist Party; anything that could not be done in this way did not deserve to persist because it betrayed the functioning and the purposes of the state—a principle that was forcefully reasserted in May and June of 1989 in China. However, major changes have taken place in East European countries and the Soviet Union. Countries such as Czechoslovakia, Hungary, and Poland have rejected communism and established democratically elected governments. Although the Soviet Union is moving more slowly than its East European counterparts, it is also moving in the direction of greater democracy.

Democracy in the developing countries of the Third World is distinguished by two important exceptions to what we have already considered. First, many governments in these developing countries cannot even consider the question of sharing power until they have created a set of centralized institutions that have power over their societies. Power is a scarce commodity in the Third World. Many national governments find themselves caught in a vise between an inhospitable international system and a set of local chieftains who resist modernization at every turn. The road to democracy in this context means first consolidating power at the national level, perhaps through coercion. Then—and only then—can the issue of sharing power be raised. The second major distinction concerns the democratic nature of public policy. In many cases, political leaders in the Third World think of democracy as what a government does for the people (an output) instead of a set of procedures for organizing and protecting the right of the masses to participate (an input). Social justice and economic progress have higher priority in many of these countries than the guarantee of competing parties, honest elections, and free news media. Nevertheless, democracy reasserts itself from time to time, as it has done in some Latin American and East Asian countries of late. This suggests that democracy remains an aspiration that is high on the priority list of some people in many Third World countries, but it is an aspiration that is very difficult to satisfy. Lasting institutions must be established to translate popular will into public policy.

A comparison of three views of well-being leads us to a discussion of what constitutes the good life in the three worlds. In Western Europe and Japan, most public policy emphasis is on the fine tuning of the economy, that is, how to manipulate the economy to avoid the gross excesses of either depression and unemployment or inflation and financial chaos. The governments of the industrialized West possess the ideology and the skills needed to direct the economy, to maintain growth momentum, and to provide jobs for a slowly growing work force. A variety of problems are still being faced, however: how to adapt industrial sectors to changes in world markets and the major issue of what to do about affluence; how to prevent pollution and the flow of hazardous substances throughout the environment; how to insure a secure source of energy in the years ahead; and how to relieve the tensions and stresses of life in an urban, industrial society.

The communist and post-communist states of the Second World face much more pressing needs as they attempt to secure the good life for their people. Although most of these states are relatively well developed economically, they still face fundamental problems of industrialization, increased food production, housing for an expanding population, and growing public demand for more consumer goods. In many states, such as the Soviet Union, heavy defense expenditures have drained away much needed funds for social welfare projects and for consumer items, such as cars and refrigerators. In Poland, Yugoslavia, and even in the USSR itself, ordinary people are telling their leaders that they expect more. Conditions are more severe in China than in these Eastern European countries. Despite impressive growth at times over the past generation, China is finding social and economic modernization a difficult challenge, with problems not unlike those found in other developing countries.

Developing countries face the greatest challenges in defining the good life for their people; not only must they industrialize and upgrade their agricultural production but they also must experience wrenching psychological changes. Some leaders have suggested that it is possible for the Third World to modernize and industrialize and remain traditional at the same time.

To date, a few countries, such as South Korea and Brazil, have made considerable strides in industrializing, and a few, such as India, have dramatically raised agricultural production. It is still too early to make a judgment, but historical experience does not make us optimistic about the ability of many Third World countries to find a third way to economic well-being and progress.

An examination of the three worlds' perspectives on the human value of respect leads to a consideration of differing views of human rights. In the First World, governments are constitutionally bound to tolerate dissent, although there still are some problems—even in countries famed for their tolerance, such as Great Britain. Most important, Western Europe and Japan have not lost faith in the cornerstone of human rights: the belief that the rights of the individual are paramount and that the rights of the social collective and the state remain secondary, unless an exceptional crisis, such as war or natural disaster, endangers the continued existence of the community.

As the part of the book on the Second World emphasized, traditional communist views of human rights differ sharply from those in the West. Communist systems place emphasis on the rights of the collectivity over those of the individual. Individuals are not allowed to engage in behavior that would have socially adverse repercussions, such as disseminating antistate literature or advocating the right to strike. Instead, national unity and social cohesion are major objectives; the rights of the individual must be submerged. In place of the Western emphasis on the individual, traditional communist states such as China stress the supportive role of the collectivity. Individuals are to find their greatest pleasure and psychological support when they place themselves within the context of a comradely group of fellow workers or citizens. Emphasis is placed not on the immediate gratification of one's personal desires but instead on sharing in a communal context. A problem arises in the case of ethnic minorities and people with strong religious beliefs, because the solidarity of communist society is supposed to supercede these remnants of preindustrial "feudalism," using the Marxist-Leninist jargon. Conflict between such minorities and the larger collectivity must, according to Marxism-Leninism, result in subordination of the former to the latter. Events in Eastern Europe since the late 1980s show that many people have rejected this downgrading of individual and minority rights in favor of the collectivity.

In developing countries, human rights are relegated to a definitely secondary position. The weakness of most Third World governments dictates that power considerations must take first priority, and the shaky nature of most Third World economies means that industrialization and agricultural modernization must receive second place in the goal structure. Thus, few resources are left to shore up the foundations of human rights in developing countries; on the contrary, the leaders in many of these countries insist that too much attention to human rights can block their governments from the actions they need to move their countries forward economically. Opposition parties cannot be allowed to enflame mob passions. The mass media must be harnessed to the needs of the state. Workers cannot be permitted to strike for higher wages when doing so would intensify inflation. In a political sense, human rights suffer (sometimes grievously) in rapidly developing countries. This does not mean, however, that Third World populations have been brutalized to the point of social atomization. There remains at the local, village level considerable concern for the welfare of others and for the maintenance of a warm and nurturant environment. The post-communist governments of Eastern Europe have moved quickly toward the Western conceptions of respect and human rights. The revolutions of 1989 have expanded greatly the people's human rights. However, even more so than in the First and Second Worlds, the lack of respect accorded minority populations in many Third World countries is a serious problem. Government actions or inactions that are harmful to minorities will fan hostilities and resentments into violence, which Third World governments are often too weak to control.

It may be useful to consider the issue of enlightenment in the three worlds by broadly defining and comparing their views of education and knowledge. Because enlightenment in our inquiry is what a person knows about his or her world and the process by which he or she comes to know these things, we must examine how the three worlds deal with these vital variables.

First World governments interpret the issue of enlightenment as involving the nature of public education. The key points are the relative priority of education versus other social expenditures and mass versus elite education. Like all industrialized countries, Western European countries and Japan confront the problem of how to prepare their growing youth for responsible roles in managing a complex economy and society as well as for how to live productive and useful lives. Much contemporary debate surrounds the question of whether quality education geared to a privileged minority should be sacrificed in favor of expanding educational opportunities for the many, the latter being the choice that the United States and a few other First World countries, including Japan, had made earlier.

The traditional Communist Party states were much more ambitious in their approach to knowledge and the process of acquiring it. The traditional governments of China, Cuba, and the Soviet Union wanted to go far beyond the simple requirements of education; they wanted to create a new Soviet (or Cuban, or Chinese) person, one who would welcome the burdens and special demands of life in a Communist Party state, accept the responsibilities imposed by the collectivity, and work productively within the framework established by other forces. A collective spirit was expected to prevail in a communist society, and the educational system was given the task of insuring that such a spirit would emerge. Of course, all other media of expression—the press, the arts, television, and radio—were expected to fit within this same mold. Even the family was expected to do its part in changing the personality type that prevailed in the pre-communist culture. Much of this, of course, is changing in the Soviet Union under glasnost and in the post-communist governments of Eastern Europe. In Czechoslovakia, Hungary, and Poland today, the issue of enlightenment is viewed very much like it is in the First World polyarchies. Censorship has been stripped away and individuals are able to learn much more about their political affairs and the world.

The enlightenment goals of Third World states focus on mass education and on technical/vocational training to manage the nascent industrial base, but there also is an elite educational system that produces liberally trained professionals in far greater numbers than there are jobs available for them. Thus, the educational objectives of developing states must range from the eradication of illiteracy in remote villages to the management of great universities in large urban areas. To complicate matters, developing elites wish to modernize their countries while retaining the beneficial qualities of tradition: respect for the past, the extended family, social cohesion, and stability. The educational system is somehow expected to achieve these multiple objectives, despite their almost inherently contradictory implications. Finally, Third World regimes frequently seek to curb the liberties of the mass media to insure that the press will play a positive role in the overall developmental effort.

Political Performance in Three Worlds

Considered in the very broadest of terms, Japan and the larger industrialized states of Western Europe—Britain, France, West Germany, and Italy—have been quite successful in creating centralized state power and in distributing it widely to citizens who desire access to the political process. Since World War II, these states have not only established effective administrative machinery in Tokyo, London, Paris, and Rome but they have also reaffirmed commitments for widely shared access to those centers of power. Compared with the United States, power is concentrated to a greater degree in these five countries, but because of the rule of law and the self-restraint of bureaucrats at the national level, there is an underlying faith in the ability of government institutions to curb the larger excesses of political leaders. Even in France, where the power of the Chief Executive has gone further than in the rest of these countries, there are fundamental institutional factors that protect the citizenry from being overwhelmed by the exercise of power from the center. Moreover, the ability of the center to ride roughshod over the wishes of the various French regions and localities has been diminished by reforms in the past decade, while during the same period the will of the Executive at the national level has been thwarted from

time to time by the growing countervailing assertiveness of the Constitutional Council. With regard to widespread distribution of power, we must rate the governments of the First World high.

Governments of the traditional communist world approached the problem of power and its distribution in a different way. The goal was to consolidate the power of the Communist Party and to insure that it could not be effectively challenged by opposition groups that might seek to betray the foundations of the state. In the late 1980s, much of this began to change in the Soviet Union and Eastern Europe. Gorbachev's reforms expanded the power of individuals, groups, and even noncommunist parties in the USSR. The revolutionary changes of 1989 in Eastern Europe ushered in a series of democratic experiments in those countries. Only a few of the Second World states, such as China and Cuba, resisted these democratic forces, leaving most observers to wonder how long their resistance can succeed.

Developing countries have concentrated on the creation of power, the consolidation of a particular regime, and the establishment of a set of institutions that can transcend the life of a specific set of elite members. Because of the fragmentation of power in the developing world (i.e., the three-way split among the international system, the national government, and the local power brokers), there usually have been formidable obstacles to the centralization of power in the national government's institutions. Whereas in many Third World countries, very little has been done to move a step beyond this stage and begin to grant some of the government's power to individual citizens, in a few countries, fragile steps have been taken toward democracy. The emphasis should be placed on the word *fragile*, however, because in most of these countries (e.g., Argentina, South Korea, the Philippines, Peru), there has historically been a pendulum swing back and forth between authoritarianism and democracy. In recent times, the authoritarian regimes have logged more years in power than have the democratic ones.

An appraisal of political performance in the domain of well-being involves two questions: (1) How do public policies contribute to the growth of the total economic pie of a country?; and (2) How do public policies affect the way the pie is distributed, especially to the groups and classes that have previously received little from the economic system?

In this regard, the First World countries examined in this text have a mixed record. As a region, Western Europe has reached the post-industrial era, which means it has begun to face many new problems and difficulties. This fact alone is a sign of success, because it indicates the achievement of sustained economic growth since the end of World War II. During the 1950s and 1960s, indicators revealed that Western Europe as a whole achieved surprisingly good economic growth records, with West Germany, France, and Italy scoring better than the United States but not as well as Japan. All of these countries registered less favorable economic indicators in the 1970s and 1980s, but Japan considerably improved its position with respect to the rest during these decades. All five countries are making efforts—but only modest progress—in income redistribution.

On the yardstick of well-being, the communist and post-communist states have achieved less than those of Western Europe and Japan. Economic growth has been stagnant in most Second World countries of late. The picture in the Soviet Union is mixed. On one hand, housing is cheap but scarce, and medical care, health services, and education are of poor quality but free. Until recent years, Soviet citizens seemed relatively content with what they had, perhaps because they could still remember the poverty and sacrifice of the period before and during World War II. More recently, however, the Soviet people have grown increasingly critical of their economic situation. The lack of significant progress and improvements in social well-being will bring great pressure on Soviet officials.

The same is true of the post-communist governments of Eastern Europe. The level of social well-being is far below that of their West European counterparts. Although most do not expect to be on the same level as the Western Europeans, they do expect improvements. The lack of progress will make the Eastern European people restive and could make them critical of their new governments and experimentation with private enterprise and economic reform. In China, an economic slowdown during the past several years has caused ambitious industrial plans to be revised downward. To stimulate economic growth, the Chinese have introduced more wage incentives and material rewards, which in turn are likely to result in greater socioeconomic inequalities. Although economic growth spurted again in the mid-1980s, it has slowed down in recent years, a fact that may have contributed to the Party leaders' fears in the spring of 1989 that student unrest might spread to the society in general.

Economic achievements have been weakest in much of the Third World for reasons that are political and economic. Industrial production in the 1980s managed to creep ahead at a rate of about 2 to 3 percent per capita per year; in many parts of the Third World, where energy supplies are scarce and expensive, industrial growth has been halting. It is in agriculture, however, that the developing world has suffered most. With few exceptions, farm production has not kept up with population growth over the past decade. This situation must change before the Third World's citizens can begin to enjoy the standard of living seen in even the Second World states of Eastern Europe. The standards of living of the First World's industrialized democracies are quite beyond both the short-term and the long-term expectations of Third World countries.

We now move to a comparison of political performance with regard to the value of respect. Here the First World countries have been impressive in their achievements, even if they have fallen short of their own high expectations in several ways. Given their authoritarian and oppressive backgrounds in the 1930s and 1940s, West Germany, Japan, and Italy have gone far toward insuring fair and just treatment of all citizens regardless of their political beliefs. France's record has been equally good. In Great Britain, the special strains introduced by the violence in Northern Ireland have been difficult to withstand, as attested to by the policy employed by the British Army of preventive detention without a trial and by the occasional reports of torture of Irish Republican Army members. It is a reflection of Great Britain's usually high standards in this field, however, that such reports are newsworthy there, whereas in countries with more lax standards, such matters pass unnoticed. We must give high marks to the First World countries for their performance concerning human rights.

The human rights record of the Soviet Union, Eastern Europe, and China at times has raised international public concern. Soviet dissidents have been placed under house arrest, jailed for long periods after trials of doubtful authenticity, or exiled for daring to write or speak their feelings. In 1989, the Chinese communists, going a step further than their Soviet counterparts recently have gone, publicly announced summary trials and executions of people arrested in the aftermath of the confrontation between the regime and the students calling for more

democracy in Tiananmen Square. Such lapses in observing human rights elicited criticism even from fellow Communist Parties (nonruling) in the West, which assert that communism is strong enough to permit dissent and opposition parties and that human rights must be respected in Communist Party states as they are in noncommunist states.

In the late 1980s, the human rights records of the Soviet Union and East European states improved markedly. Gorbachev's reforms accorded Soviet citizens considerably more respect, including a wide range of human rights. Freedom of speech, religion, and assembly, long denied under traditional Soviet communism, began to be provided during the Gorbachev period. The East European communist leaders also began to relax restrictions and allow such rights in the late 1980s. The people began to speak out, demonstrate, and finally called for the overthrow of communist rule. Except for the short period of fighting and bloodshed surrounding the Romanian revolution, the changes showed great respect between the competing groups, including the revolutionaries and the Communist Party elites. Although East European societies continue to suffer from low levels of social well-being, many now enjoy human rights practices that approximate those found in the democracies of Western Europe.

The more than 100 countries of the Third World span the entire range of possibilities in the treatment of human rights. At one end of the spectrum are several scores of countries, such as Costa Rica and Venezuela, that respect human rights to a remarkable degree. At the other end of the scale lie a fairly large number of countries where military rule, press censorship, and political imprisonment are the rule and not the exception. These include Iran, Iraq, and Uganda. In between fall most of the major states of the Third World. In these countries, dissent is limited but not completely stifled. Some opposition parties may be permitted, but they are not expected to get out of line. Elections are held, but votes are not counted honestly. The press functions but not too critically, for it will be shut down or deprived of newsprint if it does. In brief, most Third World countries hover on the brink of serious suppression of human rights, and the merest disturbance or economic crisis may be sufficient to push them over the edge. Certainly, there are few institutionalized barriers to dictatorship when and if the rulers decide to impose it. We should acknowledge, however, that during the 1980s, a number of important Third World states made great strides toward the restoration and strengthening of constitutional regimes that will vigorously protect human rights. In Latin America, Argentina, Uruguay, and Brazil stand out for their progress in this dimension; in Asia, the ability of India to weather the storm of upheaval following Indira Gandhi's assassination in 1984 was a tribute to that country's longstanding commitment to democracy. Next door, in Pakistan, plans to hold free elections had been made before the sudden death in 1988 of autocratic President Zia ul-Haq. The plans were carried out afterward, and the country returned to democratic status. Will the pendulum swing again for these countries?

The fourth value to be considered is enlightenment, or the acquisition of knowledge and information. Our assessment of Western European achievements in this field is that they are reasonably good, although some of the larger countries of Western Europe do not compare favorably with the United States and Japan on all measures of educational effort. The four major European states and Japan spend between 4 and 6 percent of GNP on education, whereas the United States spends about 7 percent and Canada, Sweden, and the Netherlands have

invested more than 7 percent. School enrollment figures confirm these conclusions. Three of the four largest Western European states—Britain, West Germany, and Italy—show between 70 and 80 percent of their secondary school–aged youngsters enrolled in schools. In France, the figure is higher, at 90 percent, but in the United States and Japan, it reaches 95 percent. Even greater differences are observed at the higher levels of education. Western Europe's educational systems begin, at age eleven or twelve, to separate University-bound students from those who will be denied access to higher education because of poor performance. But in terms of upward mobility via the educational system and the quality of scientific and mathematics education, there is reason to believe that the Japanese educational system ranks at the top of the major First World countries, suggesting the more efficient creation of a rich pool of human resources than occurs in the other countries. In other areas of knowledge and information, however, Western European polities rate as high as Japan's. The mass media function freely and prolifically, and media criticism of government is tolerated and legally protected.

Starting from a much lower base both economically and institutionally, the traditional Communist Party states of the Second World recorded significant advancements in their educational systems. From an era when education was reserved for the privileged few, the Soviet Union and China extended mass education down to the most remote village in an effort to make every citizen literate. Similar policies were initiated in most other Communist Party states. In terms of numbers, the Soviet educational system has surely been successful, especially in technological and scientific areas, where it has transformed a backward and traditional country into a well educated society in less than fifty years. The goal of developing a "new communist person" was not nearly as successful. After almost a quarter century of communism in the Soviet Union, communist values seem to be receding rather than growing. This aspect of "communist enlightenment" in Eastern Europe was an even greater failure. The great majority of people rejected communism and now aspire to Western, non-communist conceptions of enlightenment.

What of education, information policies, and enlightenment in the Third World? As earlier discussions indicate, the statistics reflect a major effort by many developing countries to launch crash education programs. Many countries of the Third World spend as great a percentage of their GNP on education as do the Western European countries (3 to 5 percent). Yet, because of institutional rigidities, the scarcity of qualified teachers and learning materials, and high rates of population growth, the majority of the developing countries are just barely managing to hold their own in the battle against illiteracy. Policies toward the mass media span the same range as do those on human rights. Several dozen countries allow the press to operate freely, about a dozen suppress free press operations, and the remainder fit somewhere in between, neither allowing a free press nor suppressing it entirely, using the media to support government policies and to reduce dissent and criticism of government.

Explaining Differences in Performance: Does Politics Matter?

It is good for observers of politics to be modest as they try to construct plausible explanations for complex social phenomena, such as different levels of political performance in three widely varying kinds of political systems. In the explanatory comments that follow, we repeat several of the more important features of our previous analyses, which might lead us to a better understanding of the three worlds. Our discussion here emphasizes the importance of human resources, leadership, environmental factors, and institutions.

The human dimension of politics in the First World has two facets. On one hand, Western European countries and Japan possess an enormous advantage in the relatively well-educated, modernized, well-trained, and motivated labor force available to staff their industrial facilities and farms. Furthermore, the populace actively participates in politics, although exact figures vary widely from country to country and from one kind of activity to another. In recent years, however, some observers have pointed to a growing apathy among the youth of all Western countries that perhaps is warning their political leaders that a new generation is finding politics a useless and deceptive enterprise.

The second facet of the human dimension in First World politics involves leadership styles and patterns. Comparative analysis seems to indicate some correlation between vigorous leadership and determined policies in some countries (West Germany and France much of the time since the 1950s, Great Britain in the 1980s) and between less creative or assertive leadership and political immobilism in others (Italy much of the time since the 1950s, Japan in the late 1980s). This fact should remind us that no matter what environmental advantages a particular country may start out with, little can be done with these assets without creative leadership to mobilize and direct resources toward valued public goals.

This observation leads us to some conclusions about the environment of First World politics, an environment that contains both advantages and disadvantages. The historical residue of World War II, for example, was an advantage for West Germany, Japan, and Italy because they had to struggle to eradicate social, economic, and political characteristics that had made fascism possible. Great Britain seemed to have emerged from the early post-war period with her self-confidence shaken and puzzled about her role in a world then dominated by the two superpowers, the United States and the USSR. On the other hand, Great Britain's long experience with the traditions of representative government have made possible the well-known British tolerance for dissent without excesses of rhetoric or repression. Most of the countries of Western Europe have enjoyed traditional restraints on the arbitrary use of power as well as economic abundance since World War II. However, in many areas, social cleavages and class struggle persist and make the search for social and political consensus more difficult.

In structural terms, the key to political moderation in Western Europe has been the growth of institutionalized restraints on power that do not exist anywhere else in the world. Courts, political parties, the mass media, and traditions of constitutional governance all can be brought to bear to keep a potential dictator under control. Similar institutional restraints have grown up in Japan since World War II. Public opinion as expressed through institutions such as the press and voluntary associations also is a powerful factor in all First World countries. Furthermore, many countries enjoy thoroughly professional bureaucracies that can restrain political leaders who might abuse power and that can provide leadership themselves when the political leaders are indecisive or weak. Finally, polyarchy insures that virtually all citizens will have access to the centers of power and that participation will be significant.

The human dimension of politics in Second World countries also exhibits some interesting interplay between elite-leadership styles and mass participation, although the relationship is far different from that in Western Europe. Without question, the leadership abilities and styles of world figures such as Vladimir Ilyich Lenin, Joseph Stalin, Mao Zedong, Josip Broz Tito, and Ho Chi Minh did much to determine the direction of communist politics, quite removed from any ideological considerations. These men all were of a type: dedicated to the supremacy not only of their ideological system but also of the Party that propelled it into power, unwilling to permit opposition or dissent; and skilled craftsmen in the construction of institutions that outlived the original leadership generation. Each had the ability to sense the real and imagined needs of the people, to articulate these needs on a broader stage, and, therefore, to make politics a real and significant exercise for the many who had previously been excluded from the process. They all were violent men, who will be remembered both for their violent rise to power and for their attempts to radically reconstruct their societies. As communist systems matured, however, they have shown a need for a different type of leader, one who knows how to provide greater scope for individual political and economic initiative while maintaining the capacity of the Communist Party to make coherent collective choices. Mikhail Gorbachev appears to be such a leader, but he faces an extremely difficult task with many potential pitfalls.

For decades, the masses of ordinary citizens in Second World countries adapted to the special demands of communist politics. This resulted, at least partly, from the historical and cultural setting within which they were socialized. Before the communist revolutions in Russia and China, the masses were given virtually no opportunity to participate in politics. Voices of dissent were stilled, and political organizations were suppressed. Thus, the Communist Party states inherited and built on relatively passive political communities. The passivity of communist societies came to an abrupt end in 1989 in Eastern Europe. Once the East European people learned that the Soviet Union would not intervene and crush their desires for democracy, many revolted and got rid of their communist leaders. Whether the same will happen in the Soviet Union, only time will tell.

Many environmental factors conditioned traditional communist politics. As we have mentioned, the historical tradition of autocratic rule facilitated state control of such institutions as schools and mass media. Cultural schisms and strong regional ethnonationalisms (especially in the Soviet Union and Yugoslavia) sensitized many communist leaders to the need for national unity. After World War I, the Soviet Union was buffeted by the turbulence of civil war, foreign intervention, economic crisis, depression, and, finally, the tragedy of World War II. Soviet leaders received a baptism of fire that would have undermined and destroyed weaker regimes. Their survival was due to their ruthlessness in smashing opposition internally; the lessons they learned during this period have been hard to forget. Similar conditions attended the birth of other major Communist Party states, including China, Cuba, and Vietnam, which came into existence in the midst of an international system that regarded them with fear and hostility. Finally, although Karl Marx predicted that communism would first come to the industrialized countries, the reverse was true. Communism became a method for underde-

veloped countries to lift themselves up by mobilizing mass resources. New communist states came into being in backward and poor countries that allowed radical, forceful policies to try to wrench them from the past.

Two structural features influenced the shape of traditional communist politics: one-party rule and state socialism. In every traditional Communist Party country, the key institution, without peer or tolerated opposition, was the Communist Party. The Party controlled access to the centers of power and most public discussion of government policies. It was the device for channeling communications between the elite and the masses and for mobilizing the masses into their participatory roles. The other major institutional factor in communist politics was the central government's direction and management of the economy, including production and pricing decisions and broad investment allocations. Communist governments intervened in almost every economic decision covering both industry and agriculture.

The East European revolutions of 1989 produced new leaders, institutions, politics, and policies. These, in turn, had an impact on the values of power, well-being, respect, and enlightenment. However, the extent and precise nature of the impact remains to be seen. Analyzing these, and the evolution of human dignity in East European societies, will be an exciting challenge to students of comparative politics in the 1990s.

The political performance of the developing countries of the Third World can be accounted for in similar terms. At the level of the masses, individual preparation for modern participatory politics remains poor. The masses of citizens are ill equipped educationally and physically. Many are still illiterate and thereby dependent on the few who control the sources of information, and their physical well-being (health, income, housing, nutrition, clothing, medical care) is usually so precarious that they have little time or energy left over for political activity. In addition, many traditional cultures discourage behavior and attitudes that are important in politics: bargaining, compromise, a positive and instrumental approach to one's environment and one's fellow workers, and a sense of individual efficacy. On the contrary, traditional cultures and psychology encourage fatalism, apathy, and a feeling of inefficacy when dealing with authority figures. Such characteristics must be changed before traditional peoples will be ready for roles in a modern participatory democracy.

Many developing countries are governed by charismatic figures whose major claim to power rests on their ability to sway the masses with their rhetoric. The chief problem with this style of governing lies in the personality of the charismatic leader. Charisma is a valuable leadership trait for countries that are called on for heroic measures, when compromise means defeat. Too frequently, however, charismatic figures cannot settle down to the routine of daily politics after the war is over or the revolution is won. Charisma does not accommodate itself well to the politics of moderation and compromise. Furthermore, charismatic leaders frequently fail to develop the institutional structures that can shape and guide the political process after they are gone. When the leader dies or is deposed, this lack of institutions leaves the state without the sense of predictability and regularity so badly needed in rapidly changing societies.

The environmental problems faced by developing countries are so numerous that we can only list a few of the more important ones. Although colonial regimes did bring some beneficial aspects of European culture to the Third World, the historical legacy of colonialism has been, on the whole, disadvantageous. Nevertheless, the sense left behind by the colonial powers of a native people's inferiority and the disruption of the native economic system have condemned developing states to many years of struggle as they try to catch up with the more developed countries. The international systems—both political and economic—work against the interests of the Third World in many different ways. A combination of scarce resources and late industrialization has meant that developing countries have few resources that they can call on to aid their citizens in achieving their values. Thus, a vicious circle of poverty (low income, low savings, low investment, poverty) affects not only the economies but also the political systems of developing countries.

Many of these environmental and human factors come together in the institutional makeup of the typical Third World country. The syncratic state is one that attempts to industrialize the country without disturbing traditional privilege, a task that requires formidable political skills, large resources, and infinite patience. Most of these requisites are lacking in the Third World, which helps to explain why syncratic regimes (for example, Peron in Argentina, Ayub Khan in Pakistan) fail and are deposed by the country's military. Not only is the syncratic regime attempting the impossible but it also tries to accomplish it without building a suitable institutional base. Institutions are weak in developing countries, and the consequences are well documented—a lack of access to policy-making for the masses, an absence of countervailing powers to prevent an abuse of authority by the political elites, and a lack of a sense of continuity and dependability that is so badly needed in developing states. Finally, because syncratic leaders lack the institutions or the resources to create real power and to distribute tangible benefits, they resort to politics by symbolism, and the people are manipulated with empty slogans, ethnic hatreds, and the rhetoric of class struggle.

It should be evident by now from this comparative overview of the three worlds that politics does indeed matter and that political choices and styles are significant in determining whether or not—and to what extent—people can achieve valued goals in their lives. Certainly, the research of a number of other scholars suggests the importance of political forces, yet we should recognize that domestic factors are not the exclusive determinants of the quality of life or human dignity in countries throughout the world. International events such as wars or economic "super events," such as the Great Depression of the 1930s or the high levels of inflation of the 1970s, can have a powerful impact on what goes on inside countries. The impact of the United States on Western Europe and Japan after World War II and the former and present-day impact of colonialism and neocolonialism on the Third World also have been emphasized in this text. Accordingly, we must recognize that some of what occurs in nation-states is beyond their immediate control. Many contend that this is a growing phenomenon that will continue as countries become more interdependent. The impact of international energy crises on the prospects for improving well-being around the globe is another good example of the power of global forces in the contemporary era.

Although domestic politics is not the sole determinant of human dignity (nor even the primary one in many circumstances), it is still important and worthy of our study and consideration. Political decisions and political institutions do much to shape the world we live in, and they help and hinder us in our efforts to make it better. If each of us lived alone on a desert island or atop a mountain, there would

be no need to coordinate our desires and behaviors with the desires and behaviors of others. Humans do not live alone, however, and somehow the things that people do to reach their goals must be subjected to a certain degree of social and political coordination. Goals must be established for the entire community; resources must be mobilized and deployed, and actions undertaken to reach these goals; outcomes must be evaluated and mistakes corrected; and the costs and benefits of social action must be assessed and allocated. In a simpler time, many human societies used essentially nonpolitical mechanisms for doing these things, for example, the price machinery of the free market, the town meeting, or the voluntary association. Now, however, the public interest requires a more authoritative mechanism for coordinating thousands of private decisions, attitudes, and behaviors. Government is the only agency yet devised that can do many of these things. How these tasks are performed is influenced by some of the human, environmental, and structural factors we have just enumerated. The ways in which these tasks are performed in turn determine the impact of public policies on private human values.

Politics and Human Values: A Look to the Future

Political scientists enjoy no special gifts to see into the future, so our forecasts must, like those of anyone else, be based on the perception of current trends and the projection of those trends into the years ahead. Speaking very broadly, the three political scientists who have written this book in all four editions have discerned two trends that have been particularly noticeable in the half decade since the last edition was published. The first has been a growth in assertiveness of ordinary people in political systems where their previous political voice had been relatively mute. This trend has been accompanied by a corresponding growth in political elites' responsiveness to the popular demand for a growing voice in public affairs. The second trend has been the increasing willingness of government, whether in an essentially capitalist or socialist economy, to reduce its role in economic affairs, leaving greater scope for private initiative. These two trends of democratization and privatization are observable to varying degrees in all three worlds, and they appear also to varying degrees, to have been accelerating for the past half decade. We anticipate that the trend-lines will continue during the 1990s.

Theorists of modernization and political development have argued that these signs of renewed popular participation and market economic behavior in the three worlds vindicate earlier theories that predicted general world development in precisely those directions, including a convergence of capitalist (First World) and socialist (Second World) countries along many of the same lines. Skeptics would point out that developmental theorists were basically elitist in stressing the importance of both intermediary organizations with able leadership that would help to shape and channel popular participation and emerging "civic cultures" that would temper individual political initiative with deference to established elites. They would also point out that convergence theories were less inclined to suggest parallel movements in the First and Second World toward greater private initiative in market-oriented economies than coincident agreement of East and West on some sort of mixed economy, sometimes called social democracy, sometimes market socialism.

The most systematic critics of the developmental theorists of the 1950s and 1960s were the dependency theorists, discussed in Chapter 16 of this text. It was their argument that the most serious developmentalist fallacy lay in the assumption that all three worlds essentially were moving along the same path, although starting at different times and moving at different paces. Developmental theory suggests that the Second and Third Worlds, as their labels might suggest, are being led along the path by the example set earlier by the First World. Dependency theorists stressed that the world has changed drastically since the industrialization of First World countries in the nineteenth and early twentieth centuries, and countries that are late in seeking to industrialize will be unable to follow the same path because of the vicious circle of dependency and underdevelopment imposed on them by the economic order that advanced capitalist countries have successfully perpetuated. But the two general trends previously noted are not what dependency theory predicted.

One fact that we, as well as other political scientists, now recognize is that economic globalization is diminishing the capacity of even the largest and strongest states to regulate their internal affairs. Multinational corporations can evade the control of First World states as they have always been able to do in their dealings with Third World states. This is because, regardless of where their headquarters are located, many of their operations are conducted in a variety of locations around the world and they are able to pick up stakes from one country and move to another, thus posing a disincentive against government controls that are not to their liking. In the Second World, ruling Communist Parties are no longer able to plan for economic growth in isolation from world markets. They have begun to open up their economies in recognition of the fact that to do otherwise would be to relegate their economies to third-class status, and the well-being of their citizenry would slip further behind that of First World peoples and be eclipsed by that of the more rapidly industrializing Third World countries.

As governments discover that the levers of economic guidance they once possessed are no longer effective, they are also finding themselves losing an important justification for continued political inequality between the elites and the masses. People are discovering they no longer need the government to help them regulate their affairs. Their economic links increasingly are with other economies, in that the automobiles, VCRs, and clothes they buy are produced in other countries. If they are themselves producers or sellers of goods and services, they find that their competitors are no longer other firms within their own country but are based all over the world. To compete on their terms, the local firm has to also think in global terms and may have to enter the global market to survive. Thus, the national economy is no longer a coherent unit unless it is artificially insulated by government protectionist measures, which are likely to be detrimental to the fortunes of all parts of the economy that are not protected. To extend the protection throughout the economy, as has been done in Second World and some Third World economies, today seems to be a way of insuring national economic stagnation rather than growth, as it was in earlier times. It also means that government holds on to outmoded powers that are increasingly resented by those who believe they can handle matters more effectively on their own, or who feel they are not being given sufficient voice in national affairs by a small circle of rulers. They no longer accept the rulers' right to give them orders. They ask, "Who needs them?"

Considering the changing role of nation-states and national economies in the larger world, we can point to similar sorts of issues that because they are mobilizing ordinary people in society,

are coming to preoccupy political elites more than they once did. Some of these issues have been around for a long time in one form or another and in one world or another, but they are taking on added significance today. This is especially true in places where they are, in fact, brand new issues. Take the value of power, with which we can identify two kinds of "new-old" issues. The first of these is the issue of *democratic participation*. In all three worlds this is considerably, but not exclusively, an argument between generations, an older generation that is more deferential to elite value definitions and a younger generation that is, on average, better educated, less conformist, perhaps less materialistic, and rebelling against a political leadership that is itself of the older generation and thus representative of that generation's values. This conflict arose in the First World in the 1960s and has perhaps since become institutionalized in the establishment of new political parties and agenda items. However, it is very much at the forefront of political conflict in the Second World today, and in a sense it has been a major feature of Third World political life since their independence. The more striking recent manifestations of intergenerational conflict have been in the major Second World countries. On one hand, Mikhail Gorbachev has identified himself with youths' impatience with the old guard in the Politburo. On the other hand, Deng Xiaoping became too closely identified with a similar old guard and found himself having to use repressive force against students demanding greater democratization in China's political life, that is, a greater role in it for themselves.

The value of power is the focus of another sort of issue that has been an undercurrent in the politics of countries in all three worlds but has of late, surfaced as a major focus of contention in the Second World. The question is whether power is now too centralized in the hands of national governments to meet the challenges of a rapidly changing world. In the First World, steps are being taken to remove powers from the national level to regulate economic and social affairs *upward* from the national to the European regional level. This is not really incompatible with demands for a dispersal of power downward from the central governing units of the nation-state. Because the nation-state is where the greatest concentration of governmental power is found, to shift the locus of that power either upward or downward is to disperse power so as to free members of society to take actions of their own choosing with less fear of restriction. There are in all three worlds advocates of dispersing power from the central to the regional and local levels of government, and their demands are finding increasing response from the general public and even from governments. But they pose a threat to central political elites whose careers have been built on the exercise of central direction, as is the case of Communist Party *apparatchiki* in the Soviet Union. Even Mikhail Gorbachev has found it necessary to rethink his appeals for glasnost, or greater openness, in the face of an overenthusiastic response to his ideas by regions of the Soviet Union where non-Russian minorities are in the majority, as in Armenia and Azerbaijan in the Caucasus, Estonia and Lithuania in the Baltic, and Uzbekistan in Central Asia. Meanwhile, the Yugoslavian communist leaders have been driven apart because of their respective sympathies for the aspirations of the Serbian, Slovenian, Croatian, and Albanian minorities, who are in a country with no ethnic majority. In both Yugoslavia and the USSR, the most disaffected minorities have asserted not just the right for greater autonomy but, in some cases, even the right to secede from the central state.

The issues involving ethnic minorities are also among the most important to include in any discussion of the value of *respect*. They are among the many kinds of issues involving the assertion of the right of some people to be *different* from others and to be respected for their own qualities, rather than those to which someone else, usually someone more powerful, would like them to conform. Women's rights, gay rights, and various other civil libertarian movements in the First World fit into this category of people asserting the right to diversity. Others are demanding respect for alternative goals that they would like the rest of society to accept. These include groups as diverse as the Green movement seeking to preserve the natural environment and to reduce the arsenals of weapons of destruction held by nation-states, the right-to-life movement, movements seeking to restrict the immigration of "guest" workers, and those seeking to establish the rights of these newest minorities to normally live, work, and participate in the First World countries. What is common to these sometimes mutually exclusive movements is the auxiliary demand for respect for their right to advance their views, which are often intensely disliked by governments supported by popular majorities precisely because they are at odds with consensual beliefs. It is always easier for governments to conform to a consensus than it is for them to attempt to lead the majority to an examination of uncomfortable realities. States in all three worlds vary in the degree to which they are willing to open the public agenda to new items, the consequences of which they cannot foresee or control. Strong leadership may increase the likelihood that agendas will be forced open, as Gorbachev has done, or that they will be all the more forcefully closed, as has recurrently been the case of the Nationalist regime in South Africa in the face of demands for changes in the system of *apartheid*.

As far as the value of enlightenment is concerned, in all three worlds there is tension between the widely acknowledged need to train increasing numbers of young people to share in the broader world culture and its technological advances and the need, felt more strongly by some governments than by others, to maintain as many as possible of the beliefs established locally through centuries of tradition or through the imposition of prior regime leaders' ideologies. In the Second World, this takes the form of the Red vs. Expert conflict. This conflict reached its apogee in the USSR in Stalin's purge trials of the 1930s, and was a continuous source of tension in the Stalinist influnced, communist systems of Eastern Europe. In China during Mao Zedong's Cultural Revolution, Red temporarily won over Expert, only to have the verdict reversed after Mao's death a decade later. Today in China, the Red vs. Expert conflict may have reached a new phase, with the unsuccessful assertion by Western-oriented students of their right to sample Western value systems freely and to turn their backs on a dysfunctional enforcement of ideological conformity. Suppression of the democracy movement in China takes the form of a reimposition of tight controls over the system of dissemination of information; the media, the schools, and the daily contact between the Chinese and foreigners. There are other versions of this conflict between local values centered on the way people gain information about the outside world and those more widely recognized. The rise in parts of the Middle East of Islamic fundamentalism involves an explicit attempt to force external influences out of local cultures at the price of national isolation from the worldwide political and economic currents. As another example, one method of control exercised by the white minority in South Africa to keep the black majority relatively quiescent is the screening of news from the outside world in an effort to eliminate information about a world highly critical of the apartheid regime.

As for the value of well-being, new issues—and newly rephrased issues—abound. The trend in all three worlds toward the greater play of market forces has been accompanied by fierce conflict over a series of interrelated issues. Central to these is whether economies should be driven more by *collective or by individual choice mechanisms*. Collective choice mechanisms have ranged from the central planning systems of traditional communism to Keynesian countercyclical macroeconomic policy that prevailed in the First World before the late 1970s. As the nation-state has lost its capacity to control internationally generated economic events, these mechanisms for guiding national economies have yielded to experimentation in state disengagement from the economy, leaving greater scope for private initiative. In the countries of the Second and Third Worlds that are more advanced industrially, steps are being taken to create indigenous private sectors, especially in agriculture and in small-scale marketing of goods. Second and Third World economies have also been opened wider to firms based in the First World that are seeking to sell goods manufactured at home or even to manufacture them in the host country, taking advantage of less expensive labor and relaxation of government restrictions on their activities. In the more centrally controlled economies, these incursions are limited in scope to certain major projects like the participation of the Italian automobile manufacturer Fiat in the production of Soviet cars, in the concessions granted to foreign firms in areas along the China coast, or in special freeports or enterprise zones in a growing number of Third World countries. It remains to be seen whether these developments will produce a distinct and autonomous entrepreneurial class in Second and Third World countries that are moving in this direction. The steps have been taken in the face of strong political opposition that has called attention to possible short-run effects, notably a loss of political and economic independence and a possible worsening of intracountry social and economic inequality.

Some of the motivation of very diverse regimes to at least partially disengage the state from the domestic economy is a desire to make economies more *productive* than they have been under heavy-handed state control and guidance. The enhancement of national productivity is at the heart of governments' preoccupation with economic indicators, especially the catch-all indicator, gross national product. In Second and Third World countries, this preoccupation often cancels out concern for values that might interfere with the largest possible yearly increase in GNP. But these countries are beginning to awaken to the potential adverse side effects of single-minded devotion to production for production's sake. Two general issues involving the conflict between productivity and other concepts of well-being have produced more severe conflicts in the First World for a longer period of time than in the other two worlds.

The first of these issues relates to the fact that if beyond a certain point, greater productivity can only be achieved by allowing market incentives to operate more freely, then the state will have to remove its protection of economic actors who are not in a favorable position to exploit the opportunities that an opening of markets presents. The removal of such protection subjects firms and, indeed, whole sectors of the economy and of the country to competitive forces that they may not be able to withstand. Hence, firms will fold, jobs will be lost, and geographic areas—even whole regions—will become depressed. Economic inequality will grow between different categories of workers and between different parts of the country. Soviet economic reformers are well aware of these

effects, or have been made aware of them by more "conservative" members of the ruling elite, who forcefully argue that to open up the economy (or at least to open it too rapidly) will mean inflicting unacceptable damage on too many people at once. The political backlash, even in a controlled society like the USSR, could be severe. Similar arguments have been posed against "Reaganomics" in the United States and "Thatcherism" in Great Britain, and they find echoes in countries as far removed as India, Turkey, and Mexico.

The other issue that is reverberating from the First World to the other two pits productivity against *environmental well-being*. Over the long term, the two values should not be in conflict. We have seen numerous examples of the environmental consequences of inattention to the side effects of pushing productivity to its limits. Oil spills, nuclear reactor disasters, chemical explosions and spills, acid rain wearing away the faces of buildings and destroying countless acres of beautiful, life-giving, forest—these and many more examples have constantly been in the news for the past half-decade. Despite the growing support for the ecological cause throughout the industrialized part of the world, the incidence of such disasters is higher there than in less-industrialized countries where environmentalism has, at best, a very weak voice in public affairs. But even the least industrialized Third World countries have not escaped environmental fallout. Because they for the most part are located in the tropical zone, they probably will suffer more severely from the depletion of the ozone layer and the consequent rise in world temperatures caused by the emission into the atmosphere of various gasses produced by industry, automobiles, aerosol cans, and other artifacts of "advanced" society. As another example, although the affluence of the West has brought more tourist dollars to Africa, it has assisted in the spread of venereal disease, drugs, needles, and the fatal AIDS virus to parts of the world where the health care facilities are inadequate to reduce the frequency at which the components of this syndrome of related human disasters are contracted and become fatal. In short, productivity as such is a mixed blessing. Its material benefits, so central to the idea of well-being that prevails all over the world, can be enjoyed only in the here and now. Their long-term effects may be catastrophic.

The trends we project here at the conclusion of this text add up to a prediction that is, in one way at least, in stark contrast to the emphasis we placed in the previous section on the importance of politics in determining what shares people will have of the values that make up human dignity. This is true, but only if the term politics is used in the restricted sense, that is, how the nation-state uses power, both domestically and internationally, in pursuit of its policy objectives. From the two main trends discussed at the outset of this section, it appears that central governments of nation-states are losing their capacity to regulate domestic conflict over the values of power, respect, enlightenment, and well-being. It also appears that radical changes in the world economy have hastened this process, so that the important roles played in the past by leadership and by stable governmental institutions may no longer be possible because both leaders and institutions are overwhelmed by changes that are occurring too rapidly for their effects to be centrally controlled.

From another perspective, however, it can be argued that it is precisely in times of rapid change that effective leadership and familiar institutions are especially needed, not only for wise policy decisions to be made and implemented but also to reduce the potential for anxiety and unrest within society. Such was the case in many countries during the turbulent first half of the twentieth century, and the political upheavals that occurred all over the world during that period—the survivals and the disasters—attested to the importance, indeed, the indispensability, of good leadership and well-grounded institutions. Changes are occurring both in people's expectations of the relationship between themselves and the state and in the understanding that governments in all three worlds have of what is and what is not politically feasible. These changing perceptions will generate a great deal of friction for political systems everywhere in the last decade of an eventful century. Countries—if not whole regions or worlds—that are characterized by unimaginative leadership and inflexible institutions will suffer most from the damage inflicted and capitalize least on the opportunities presented by the massive changes that are occurring.

GLOSSARY

Actions—The strategies and tactics implemented by political leaders to achieve their expressed goals.

Administrative elites—High-ranking, university trained civil servants involved in policymaking as well as in overseeing the implementation of policy.

Agenda—The set of goals to which the political leaders of a country assign high priority at a given time.

Aggregate demand—The demand of individuals and groups for goods and services treated as a combined unit in an economy.

Aggregate purchasing power—The purchasing power of all individuals and groups in an economy treated collectively.

Agrarian economy—An economy in which the vast majority of the working population is engaged in agriculture or related pursuits.

Allocation of values—Priority choices made among competing values, that is, policymaking.

Anticlericalism—Opposition to church influence in political matters.

Apparatchiki—Paid Communist Party functionaries who serve in central, regional, and local Party positions.

Aristocracy (German: *Junkers*)—In Europe, a social class located at the top of the social stratification hierarchy whose economic, social, and (formerly) political positions are (were) based on the ownership of land.

Artisans—An occupational type prevalent in preindustrial towns and cities. Those who work with their hands, producing individually made goods primarily for a local market.

Ascriptive—Refers to the belief that society should reward its members for some attribute (usually acquired at birth) other than performance in social roles.

Associational interest groups—Interest groups based on economic functions or other specialized roles played by the members of the group.

Autarky—The pursuit or existence of a self-sufficient national economy, independent of the world market and international trade.

Autonomous behavior—Behavior intended to influence government decisions.

Backbenchers—Rank-and-file members of the majority and opposition parties who are not part of the party leadership and, therefore, are not entitled to sit on the front bench.

Basic Law—The equivalent of a constitution for the Federal Republic of Germany. When drafted in 1949, it was intended to be a temporary instrument until the reunification of East and West Germany.

Basic personality—That personality configuration shared by the bulk of a society's members as a result of the early experiences they have in common.

Betrayal syndrome—Child-rearing practices that teach children to distrust their environment.

Bolsheviks—Lenin's wing of the Russian Social Democratic Labor Party, comprising the more radical Marxist revolutionaries who took power after the October Revolution in 1917. Distinguished from the less revolutionary Mensheviks.

Bourgeoisie (middle class)—The entrepreneurs or property-owning class in modern capitalist systems who control the means of production (according to Marxist theory).

Bundersrat (Federal Council)—The upper house of the German Parliament, made up of delegates from the *land* (state) governments.

Bundestag (Federal Diet)—The lower (directly elected) house of the German Parliament.

Bureaucracy—A multi-level, hierarchical institution comprised of many individuals, bureaus, and departments; overseen by a central administration and responsible for the implementation of public policies within a country.

Cabinet—A body of advisors to the chief executive of a government, or a body that collectively heads the government. Its members usually head government departments and are drawn from the leadership of the political party or parties that form the government.

Capitalism—Economic system characterized by private ownership of property whereby the owners derive profit from the production and sale of goods and services.

Capitalists—Private owners of the means of industrial production in a capitalist economy.

Capitalist-statist economic systems—Economic systems where the bulk of the modern economy remains in private hands, but the government owns a number of very large productive enterprises, typically in heavy industry or social infrastructure.

Central Committee—Large and powerful body in Communist Parties that formally elects members of the Politburo and Secretariat.

Centralism—A distribution of power in which all major decisions are made by individuals or organizations remote from local authorities who lack the real power to govern themselves.

Charisma—The quality of being able to convince others of one's superior powers (bordering on the supernatural)—for example, a charismatic leader.

Christian Democracy—Ideology, found in countries with large Catholic populations, that appeals to devout Catholics who combine political and cultural conservatism with social progressivism.

Civic competence—The belief that one has the capacity, *in actuality*, to influence government decisions.

Civic culture—Term coined by Gabriel Almond and Sidney Verba to denote a political culture in which political participation is highly valued but in which there is sufficient contentment with the political system that most people are not in fact motivated to participate very actively in politics.

Class consciousness—Self-identification as a member of a social class that has interests in common with oneself. These interests are in conflict with those of another class or other classes.

Coalition government—In a parliamentary system, a prime minister and cabinet comprised of, and resting on a parliamentary majority consisting of, more than one political party.

Code law—System of law that prevails in continental European countries, among others, and derives from the Roman law tradition. Laws enacted by parliament are codified into complex bodies of categories and subcategories that contain the legal norms that apply in individual cases.

Codetermination—A system of worker participation in the management of industry whereby workers' representatives sit on the directing boards of private corporations.

Cognition—The mental processes that have to do with the possession of information.

Cognitive dissonance—An individual's awareness of contradictory information, attitudes, or behavior. The contradiction will be dealt with through some psychological mechanism.

Cohabitation—A term specific to French politics, referring to the situation in which a President of the Republic faces a National Assembly majority of the opposition parties. In these circumstances the president may choose as prime minister an opposition leader, thus "cohabiting" power until the next elections, as between 1986 and 1988 in France.

Colonial—A relationship between two groups of people who are culturally alien and geographically distant from one another. The essence of this relationship is its asymmetrical or unequal nature. One group is strong and dominant, the other, weak and dependent. The dominant group receives most of the benefits of the relationship; the dependent group bears most of the costs. The relationship is not amenable to change since the dependent group has little access to the political institutions of the dominant state, and few instruments of power by which to influence its policies.

Command economy—Economic system based on government control of the factors of production and centralized planning; the laws of supply and demand are of little importance in such a system.

Common law—System of law, originating in medieval England, that consists of a body of precedents found in earlier court decisions defining the legal norms that apply in individual cases.

Common Market—The popular term for the European Community (EC)—a customs union of European countries in which customs barriers to trade among the member states have been removed and a common external tariff is enforced vis-à-vis third countries.

Commune—Term for the most basic unit of local government in France, Italy, Yugoslavia and some other countries. Applied to cities, towns, and villages.

Communism—A term meaning many different things, including a theory, movement, or system envisaged in the writings of Karl Marx. Based on the principle, "From each according to his abilities, to each according to his needs." Communism presupposes economic abundance and a classless society.

Communist Information Bureau (Cominform)—A Cold War, Second World international political organization created by Stalin in 1947 to bind the East European socialist states more closely to the USSR. Khrushchev dismantled the Cominform in the late 1950s.

Communist International (Comintern)—A political organization created by Lenin and the Bolsheviks in 1919 to control and monitor the activities of Communist Parties around the world. The Comintern was dissolved in 1943.

Comparison—A mode of analysis that involves a search for similarities and differences among units in a given category (*e.g.*, sovereign states).

Comprehensive schools—British secondary schools promoted by the Labour Party that are designed to break down the three-tiered school system that reinforces social class divisions.

Comradeship—Interpersonal relations based on a universalistic ethic whereby individuals treat others as equal members of a cooperative political community.

Confidence mechanism—Any social practice or structure that permits tangible resources to be distributed unequally but that does so in such a way as to convince those who lose that the system is essentially fair and that they lost because of their own shortcomings.

Conservatism—Ideological defense of the *status quo*,

involving skepticism toward, but not closedminded rejection of, reform proposals.

Constitutional courts—High courts that have the power to determine whether the acts of legislative and executive agencies of government are in accord with a constitution (*e.g.*, the German Federal Constitutional Court).

Constructive vote of nonconfidence—Under the German Basic Law, the Chancellor must resign only if defeated on a motion of nonconfidence in which a successor is named and which passes by a majority of the entire membership of the Bundestag (absolute majority).

Conventional political participation—Acts taken through accepted institutionalized channels (e.g., voting, campaigning, lobbying) by ordinary citizens designed to affect political outcomes. The meaning of the term varies from political system to political system, and, over time, in any given system, depending upon what types of participation are generally accepted as legitimate.

Convergence theory—The theory that societies become more alike culturally as they become industrialized.

Corporatism—A system of government characterized by the formal inclusion of private institutions and parapublic organizations in the processes of state policymaking.

Council for Mutual Economic Assistance (CMEA or COMECON)—A Cold War, Second World international economic institution established, at the insistence of the Soviet Union, to coordinate planning, production, and foreign trade within Eastern Europe.

Cynicism—In a political sense, the belief that all politicians are corrupt and that one is best advised to worry about one's own affairs, thus avoiding the disillusionment inevitably resulting from involvement in politics.

De facto—A condition that exists in reality regardless of whether the law requires or prohibits it.

De facto one-party systems—Political party systems that are dominated by only one party although others are legal.

Deindustrialization—The decline in manufacturing's share of Gross national product (GNP) that occurs in advanced industrial societies. Accompanied by a decline in manufacturing sector employment in absolute numbers as well as percentages, and by a decline in total output of traditional manufacturing sectors, such as steel, shipbuilding, and textiles as markets are lost to newly industrializing countries.

de jure—A condition of formal legitimacy or recognized lawfulness.

Democracy—A system of government in which the majority of the people rule either directly or through the medium of elected representatives.

Democratic centralism—Vladimir Ilyich Lenin's formula whereby members of Communist Parties are encouraged to speak freely until a decision is taken; then, unity is to prevail. In addition, decisions of higher Party bodies are binding on lower ones.

Democratic socialism—Ideology advocating a redistribution of well-being, enlightenment, and respect in favor of groups in society that are relatively deprived of these values, but the ideology is opposed to any fundamental alteration of the structure of power in a polyarchy.

Demographic transition—The change in size and composition of a nation's population brought about by the uneven impacts of hygiene and medicine at first and the changing mores and values later. The effect is a rapidly growing population, owing to declining infant mortality, coupled with continued high birth rates.

Demokratzia—Soviet reform efforts designed to pluralize the decision and policymaking processes within both the Communist Party of the Soviet Union and the Soviet Government.

Département **(French) (Italian counterpart: province)**—French unit of local government encompassing several towns or cities and surrounding territory. Larger than the average U.S. county but much smaller than the average state.

Diffuse support—When most of a nation's population regards political institutions with an allegiance that is sufficiently well-established to withstand adverse political outcomes. Distinct from *specific support*, which rises or falls with the success or failures of current governments. *See* regime.

Disinformation—Government-sponsored campaigns of deception designed to disguise true state policies, intentions, or actions.

Disorganized capitalism—In postindustrial capitalism there is a loss of national economic and political coherence due to the increasing extra-national scale of corporate enterprise and the globalization of markets. The capacity of governments and nationally organized trade unions to influence corporate policies diminishes.

Dissolution—In a parliamentary system, the premature termination of the life of an elected parliamentary body. It is designed to test the respective strengths of the majority and opposition parties.

Division—The mode of voting on important questions in the British House of Commons. The MPs file into separate division lobbies to be counted by tellers as voting aye or no.

Division of labor—The structure of jobs and occupational skills in a society.

Doctrine of harmony of interests—The belief that the interests of the poor are identical with those or the rich in the expansion and growth of the national and international economic systems.

Dual economy—Primarily refers to the division in labor market conditions within a single economy, between larger firms in sectors of the economy with a concentration of production in few firms, and smaller firms in highly competitive sectors where there are many producers. Large firms in concentrated sectors tend to have unionized workforces that are better paid with better working conditions and job security, while workforces in small firms in competitive sectors are less likely to enjoy these advantages.

Early industrialization—Often called the rapid industrialization or take-off stage, it is the period of time when an economy converts from an essentially agrarian base to one in which industry occupies approximately one-half the work force.

Economic enclaves—The system by which foreign economic entities, such as plantations or mines, operate on a country's territory without interacting with that country's economy.

Ego structure—Core mental structures that provide the central regulatory mechanisms for individual personality.

Enlightenment—The process by which individuals learn about themselves and their world by means of formal education, acquisition of information from the mass media, or transmission of informal social mores through family, peer group, or neighborhood. Also, the value attached to this process.

Environment—The social, economic, and cultural setting that surrounds the political process and influences goals, actions and outcomes and, in turn, is influenced by them.

Ethnicity—Social differentiation based on racial or linguistic distinctiveness, often associated with particular regions within countries.

Ethnocentrism—Tendency to judge foreign groups by reference to one's own customs, institutions, and standards.

Ethnonationalism—The belief that people should be governed only by others of their own ethnic group.

Executive dominance—The dominant role played by the political executive in developing countries. This is in contrast to the relatively weak and submissive role played by legislative and judicial branches.

Expansionism—A tendency of nation-states or colonial empires to expand their boundaries and the territory over which they exercise control.

Extractive capabilities—The ability of governing elites to obtain resources from the citizenry, especially the ability to tax income and to conscript to military service.

Extreme (reactionary) right—Political movement exhibiting ideological commitment to nationalism, aversion to big government and big business, and resistance to many of the features accompanying modernization.

Factions—Stable, identifiable subgroups within a political party that usually espouse somewhat different sets of policies from one another or from the official party line; they may also constitute a tight-knit social group in which personal favors play an important role.

Failure-prone policy processes—A term coined by Albert O. Hirschman for a frequently observed tendency in Latin American for the policymaking process to increase rather than decrease the probability of failure.

Fascism—Term applied to extreme right-wing political movements that exhibit strong nationalism and appeal to the authoritarian inclinations of their supporters. Usually headed by a strong leader, as Benito Mussolini, leader of the Italian *fascisti*.

Fatalism—The belief that human beings cannot control their lives or the world around them.

Federalism—A system of vertical power distribution in which there is a constitutionally protected division of power between central and regional units of government.

Feedback—Information about past performance of a political system that is used to correct mistakes or improve future performance.

First World—Countries in North American and Western Europe, plus Australia, Israel, Japan, and New Zealand, that are both industrially advanced and politically pluralistic.

Five-year plans—Government plans for coordinating the economic goals, policies, and programs of traditional Communist and some Third World countries.

Future shock—Individual psychological disorientation caused by rapid change.

Gaullism—A pragmatic blend of strong French nationalism, political conservatism, and economic growth-oriented progressivism, which is characteristic of the followers of General Charles de Gaulle's philosophy.

Glasnost—Soviet reform efforts designed to encourage and foster increased honesty, candor, and open debate within the Communist Party, the Soviet government, and Soviet society at large.

Goals—Objectives advanced by political elites for the allocation of values within their society.

Great Leap Forward—Chinese economic strategy in 1958–1960 that resulted in failure but was intended to make China an economic power—based on loosening restraints, decentralization, and modern and traditional methods of development.

Great Proletarian Cultural Revolution (GPCR)—Attempt to rejuvenate the revolutionary spirit of the Chinese populace in 1966–1969 that resulted in political and economic turmoil.

Green Revolution—Major changes of a scientific and technological nature that were expected to help the Third World solve its food-shortage problems without making changes in the social or institutional structures in the countryside.

Greens—A movement advocating defense of the natural environment through government action to reduce pollution by public and private agencies. As a *political* movement that is particularly strong in Germany and other Western European countries, it has broadened its agenda to include demands for disarmament, women's and minority rights, and aid to Third World countries, among other goals. Specifically, a West German political party, "the Greens" (*die Grune*).

Gross national product (GNP)—The money value of a country's total output of goods and services for a year.

Gross national product (GNP) per capita—The money value of a nation's output of goods and services divided by its population. This permits comparisons of countries that have different population sizes.

Groupthink—A term coined by Irving Janis for a

process in which the government restricts debate on a complex problem; thus, dissent is suppressed in the interest of loyalty to the group and serious error results.

Guerrilla insurgency—A violent political struggle in which the challengers, because of their relative weakness, choose strategies and tactics that minimize their vulnerability and maximize the vulnerability of the opponent.

Head of government—In a traditional communist system, the office responsible for the overall implementation of Party policy by the state bureaucracy, usually the chairman of the council of ministers; in a parliamentary system, the office that leads the majority government and directs the formulation and implementation of state policy, usually the prime minister.

Head of state—In a parliamentary system, the ceremonial, but essentially powerless, representative of the nation. Usually an hereditary monarch or an indirectly elected President of the Republic.

Hectare—A metric measure of area, equal to 2.47 acres.

Horizontal power distribution—Formal distribution of government power among units at the same level (national, regional, or local), for example, the separation of powers between the three branches of the U.S. Government.

Human dignity—A preferred state of being that depends on the ideal mixture of the values of power, well-being, respect, and enlightenment desired by a given society.

Human values—What people want for themselves and, by derivation, what they want from government.

Ideology—Systems of political beliefs adhered to by the more politically alert and active citizens. Serves as the philosophical bases for political party doctrines and platforms and the stated goals of other political movements.

Immigrant workers—Workers originating in less industrially advanced countries who enter the work-forces of more advanced countries. Tend to occupy less well-paid and less desirable jobs; but become the focal point of resentment by native workers as jobs become scarcer.

Imperialism—The expansion of an industrial state's power and authority abroad to many less powerful countries or nations.

Inclusive economic systems (opposite: noninclusive)—Those economic systems where more than half the economy is included in the modern sector.

Incremental policymaking—A mode of policy making that involves *ad hoc*, short-term planning based on incomplete information and resulting in marginal changes in policy.

Indicative planning—System of economic planning that involves targets set by government planners in consultation with economic-sector representatives and state-provided incentives (carrots rather than sticks) to encourage goal fulfillment.

Individualism—A characteristic of Western value systems that is said to be less pronounced in parts of the world other than Western Europe and North America. Especially in Asian value systems (e.g., Japanese and Chinese), *collectivism* is said to prevail. When individuals act on behalf of goals of their own choosing and evaluate the acts and their outcomes in terms of costs and benefits to themselves, and when they expect others to do likewise, they are individualistically oriented. When their standards are determined by or subordinated to the groups to which they belong, they are collectivistically oriented. As a political ideology, individualism means that the state exists for the individual, while collectivism holds the opposite.

Industrialization—The process of changing the ways in which society produces goods and services through the increasing application of technology to allow people to manipulate the natural world.

Industrial maturity—The phase that follows early, rapid industrialization; economic trends, begun in the preceding period, continue and include a growth in the industrial work force (now the majority), a decline in the agricultural work force, and an increase in the size of business firms.

Industrial relations—As an area of public policy, it is the system of conflict and cooperation between employers and employees with the state acting simultaneously as (1) a party to the conflict and (2) an actual or potential intermediary between the conflicting parties.

Industrial Revolution—The transformation from preindustrial to industrial society that took place in Western Europe and North America between the mid-eighteenth and the late nineteenth centuries.

Inflation—An economic condition characterized by increasing prices for consumer goods. This results from increased production costs per unit and an expansion of the money supply at a rate faster than the increased supply of goods and services.

Infrastructure—The underlying network of transportation, communication, and institutions that sustains a society, especially an industrial society.

Interest groups—Groups of people, organized or unorganized, who make claims on other groups and on government for policy outcomes that correspond to the values they seek.

Judicial review—The power of a court to consider whether or not acts of the legislature are in accord with the constitution and to declare them null and void when the finding is negative.

Keynesianism—A blueprint for national economic policymaking stemming from the writings of British economist John Maynard Keynes in the 1920s and 1930s. It prescribes government intervention in the economy in order to smooth business cycles, using fiscal and monetary policy instruments to stimulate the economy when it is in recession and to "cool it off" when there is a danger of inflation.

Komsomol—Soviet youth organization that serves as an agent of political socialization for youth ages 14 to 26.

Laissez faire—The belief that the minimum amount of government intervention in the economy is necessary for economic prosperity.

Land (plural, *länder*)—Regional subdivisions of government in the German system of federalism, similar to the states in the United States.

Land-tenure system—The system by which ownership of land is organized.

Left—The political parties and movements adhering to ideologies descending from 19th century socialism (especially today's Communism and Democratic Socialism) which are distinguished from parties and ideologies of the *center* and *right* by their commitment to a redistribution of well-being, enlightenment, and respect in favor of those in society with lesser amounts of these values.

Lethality—The characteristic of a weapon or weapon system that measures its ability to kill persons or destroy physical structures.

Liberalism—Ideology supporting steady political, social, and economic reform within the framework of capitalism.

Machismo—Latin American cultural characteristic that emphasizes masculinity.

Major networks—The national political elite of a developing country. Includes the national government leaders, the civil and military bureaucracy, and the industrial leadership.

Majority government—In a parliamentary system, the party or coalition of parties which commands a majority of the seats in the parliament and, as a rule, form the cabinet and select the prime minister.

Market socialism—An economic system characterized by both state and private ownership under single party rule. A hybrid system between the pluralist, largely free market systems of the First World and the traditional communist, centrally planned economies of the Second World.

Marxism—Body of political and economic doctrines founded on the writings of Karl Marx. Calls for collective ownership, the abolition of bourgeois morality, and the withering away of the state.

Marxism–Leninism—A body of doctrine based on the writings of Karl Marx and the writings and practical experience of Vladimir Ilyich Lenin. The doctrine establishes the Communist Party as a centralized institution for building socialism and communism.

Mass-line—Pattern of reciprocating communications between Party members and masses in Mao Zedong's China.

Materialism—A personal value system in which priority is given to immediate personal security rather than to the realization of more abstract ideals whose realization appears problematic. Materialists value security from external military threats and from economic uncertainties, while they are relatively indifferent to the demands of others for greater personal freedom, civil rights, or preservation of the natural environment for the benefit of future generations.

Meiji Restoration—The restoration of the authority of the Japanese emperor in 1868, taken as the beginning of modern Japan. A group of provincial leaders, bureaucrats and scholars overthrew the feudalistic Tokugawa Shogunate and reversed its policy of keeping Japan isolated from Western modernizing influences. However, the Meiji rulers were themselves selective in determining which Western ideas and institutions would be borrowed for Japanese culture and society.

Metropolitan country—The dominant and distant state in a colonial relationship.

Minifundia (opposite: latifundia)—Spanish term that means a parcel of agricultural land too small to be worked productively by its owner.

Minority government—A prime minister and cabinet in a parliamentary system who belong to one or more parties that together hold 50 percent or fewer of the seats in parliament but that enjoy the support of a party or parties not included in the cabinet, thus, enabling the government to stay in office.

Minor networks—The middle-echelon political elites of developing countries, typically linked to the major networks by patron-client systems.

Mobilized behavior—Behavior of an actor stimulated by other actors to achieve their goals.

Modernization—The process of individual and societal change that involves the transformation of individual attitudes from fatalistic to activistic and the transformation of society from being relatively unorganized to being relatively highly organized.

Modernization from within—Modernization that occurred in the countries that experienced industrialization earliest (First World countries). It involves little external stimulus in comparison with countries that industrialized in the twentieth century.

Modernization from without—Modernization that accompanied industrialization in the past 100 years; external sources of investment play a major role in fostering industrialization in this kind of modernization.

Modernizing elites—Political elites who seek industrialization, attitudinal modernization, and the development of political system capabilities. Opposed by traditional, anti-industrial groups.

Monetarism—A blueprint for economic policymaking that draws upon classical "liberal" economics and has been successful in the past 15 years in gaining public acceptance as an alternative to the prevailing Keynesianism. Advocates the application of monetary and fiscal policy to keep the increase of money supply at a steady, moderate rate to contain inflation and provide for steady economic growth. Sometimes called "neoliberalism" and "neoclassical economics", which are broader concepts, including the advocacy of a generalized withdrawal of the state from economic involvement.

Mosaic societies—Societies made up of many different culturally distinct pieces (subcultures), each of which adds to the overall society without being absorbed by it.

Motion of confidence—Government-sponsored motion designed to rally majority support behind the policies of the prime minister and cabinet. Defeat on such a motion will force the prime minister to resign or call for new elections. (Censure is an opposition sponsored motion that has the same potential consequences if adopted.)

MPs—Members of Parliament, that is, the elected members of the British House of Commons.

Multinationals—Business firms whose operations and span of ownership and control cross state boundaries and exist in more than one country.

Multiparty system—A political party system that includes more than two parties, each consistently receiving more than 2 percent of the popular vote.

Multiple societies—A divided social order that consists of two separate social systems bound together by a single set of economic, political, and legal bounds.

Nation—An ethnic group whose members share a common identity and desire to create or maintain their own nation-state.

National front—Postwar strategy used by Soviet and East European Communists to unite various groups in antifascist coalitions that were subsequently replaced by Communist regimes.

Nationalism—The belief that one's nation is especially deserving of praise or loyalty; sometimes developed into a political ideology or movement.

Nationalization—State action converting private economic undertakings to state ownership. Opposite: denationalization or *privatization*.

National self-determination—The principle that all nations have the right to choose the system of government under which they live and the people who shall govern them.

Negative corporatism—Cooperation between government and business involving government regulation of industry in return for control over trade union activity designed to restrict wage increases.

Neocolonialism—A condition of economic domination that persists even after formal legal colonialism has been abolished.

Neoliberalism—Renewed assertion of classical economic doctrine that the role of the state should be limited, providing maximum scope for private economic activity.

Neo-Marxism—In postindustrial society, continued perception that the class struggle has not altered and that the proletariat must wage relentless war against capitalism. See also: Radical left.

Neutral civil service—A system of government employment in which strict standards of nonpartisanship prevail in the recruitment and promotion of personnel and in which employees loyally serve the government in power at any given time regardless of its partisan coloration.

New Economic Policy—A set of policies adopted by Soviet Communist Party leaders in the period 1921 to 1928 that permitted private enterprise in an attempt to facilitate economic recovery in the aftermath of the Russian Civil War.

New left—Political parties and movements that have arisen since the late 1960s espousing the ideological goals of *postmaterialism*. Includes the Greens.

Nomenklatura—A list of positions within a traditional Communist Party state, both in the Party and in society at large, that the Party maintains and for which Party approval is necessary before personnel changes, removals, or replacements can be made.

Nominal legislature—Institutions that have no real power but exist for ceremonial, "rubberstamping" purposes; the traditional legislatures in Communist Party states.

North Atlantic Treaty Organization (NATO)—A First World international organization created in 1949 for the purpose of coordinating the defense of Western Europe in the event of an armed communist attack. Historically led by the United States, NATO members have pledged to settle disputes among themselves peacefully, and to defend each other against outside aggressors.

Object loss—An individual's psychological deprivation owing to loss of some valued object or person.

Oligopoly—Control of a particular sector of the economy by a small number of firms.

Organized capitalism—The organization of capitalist production on a hierarchical national basis. Industrial sectors are dominated in a country by one or a few large corporations, which have not yet become *multinational corporations*. Trade unions are consolidated into national peak organizations that can negotiate with peak employers' organizations and with the state. The state gains the capacity to regulate the national economy because the economy is as yet relatively insulated from global economic changes. Organized capitalism prevailed in Western Europe from the late 19th century until the last one-third of the 20th.

Outcomes—The degree of actual success achieved by political leaders as a result of actions taken in pursuit of their goals.

Parliamentary system—A system of government in which executive power is lodged in a prime minister and cabinet responsible to, and removable by, an elected legislative body (parliament).

Particularism—Bestowing one's loyalty on nearby social organizations, such as clan, village, or tribe.

Patron-client systems—A political system consisting of several patrons (or bosses), who control the majority of the country's or region's political resources, and their clients (or followers), who participate only rarely or incompletely in the political process.

Peasants—A generic term for the bulk of the rural population in preindustrial society; excludes large landholders but includes small-farm owners, tenant farmers, sharecroppers, and farm laborers.

Perestroika—Soviet reform efforts designed to restructure the traditional communist economic, political, and social institutions of the Soviet Union into more efficient, effective, and responsive concerns.

Periphery nations—Those raw-materials-producing nations identified in the Prebisch thesis as suffering from the workings of the international system.

Personality structure—The cluster of mental orientations that characterize individuals and guide their behavior.

Petite bourgeoisie (also "middling class")—Owners of small-scale businesses, popularly characterized as conservative and reluctant to take risks.

Pluralism—Refers to a political system. A condition in which many distinct groups with conflicting interests compete for power, thus, ensuring that power will not be concentrated in the hands of an elite few.

Policy—The expressed goals of political elites and the actions taken to implement them.

Policymaking—The process by which goals of political elites are converted into actions and, in turn, into outcomes.

Politburo—The small and most powerful policymaking body in Communist parties.

Political alienation—Absence of the sense that the ruling political elites and the regime on which their rule is based are legitimate, i.e., that they have the right to rule. Based on a lack of trust in the rulers and often a cynical belief that they act on behalf of their own interests and not those of the public.

Political allegiance—The belief that the system of government (regime) is one that works, at least most of the time, and that the people who specialize in the work of government (political elites) are capable of making it work.

Political culture—The pattern of attitudes and beliefs that people in a society hold about their political system.

Political decay—Decreasing ability of political institutions to absorb rising numbers of mass participants in the political process.

Political development—Changes in political structures and attitudes accompanying and supportive of modernization. Includes an accretion of power by political elites and the development of attitudes and institutions that favor popular participation.

Political elites—Those members of a society who are involved in the determining of policy, either directly as occupants of policymaking roles or indirectly as wielders of influence over the policymaking process.

Political immobility (*immobilisme*)—A condition in which government leaders are unable to make coherent policy because of the absence of requisite political support.

Political orientations—The ways in which people think and feel about politics, that is, political attitudes and beliefs.

Political participation—Activity by private citizens to influence government decisions.

Political performance—The extent to which a political system's goals, actions, and outcomes contribute to enhancing human dignity.

Political socialization—The process by which the prevailing political attitudes and beliefs of a society are transmitted to new members and these attitudes and beliefs undergo change.

Political subcultures—Groups within a society that are differentiated on the basis of certain common political orientations as well as more objective characteristics, such as race, religion, or age.

Political system—Distinguished from the narrower concept of government, this concept incorporates all individuals and institutions involved in the political process visualized as interacting systematically.

Polyarchy—The type of political system in which the many rule, at least in the sense that there is meaningful competition among groups contending for power, from among whom the many can choose their rulers.

Positive corporatism—Economic policymaking in which government, business and organized labor cooperate in promoting economic growth with low unemployment while maintaining modest wage increases in order to keep inflation in check.

Postindustrial society—An advanced industrial society in which knowledge has become the most important economic resource. Indicators include a high GNP per capita, a preponderance of service sector employees in the work force, and a rapid increase in the number of employees in professional and technical occupations.

Postmaterialism—A value system in which personal security (see materialism) is subordinate to abstract *wants* beyond the immediate *needs* of the individual. Includes the desire for a more equitable distribution of the values of power and respect within society and globally.

Power—The ability to influence the behavior of others; in a political context, the capacity to change or influence policy outcomes. Also, the value placed on the above.

Prebisch thesis—The theory advanced by Argentine economist Raul Prebisch that the international trade system works automatically and inherently to the disadvantage of the raw-materials-producing countries.

President—In a presidential system of government, an office that is constitutionally independent of the legislature and holds the power of both chief of state and chief political executive; in a parliamentary or traditional communist system of government, an office that holds the powers of chief of state but has minimal political power.

Presidential system—A system of government in which the legislative body and the chief executive (president) are separately elected and exercise constitutionally separated powers.

Prime Minister—The effective head of government in a parliamentary system. Leads the cabinet and is accountable to the majority in parliament. In Germany: the Federal Chancellor (*Bundeskanzler*).

Proletarian dictatorship—Transitional state that follows revolution when the proletariat or those acting

706

in their interests rule. In Marx's words, "in order to establish equality, we must first establish inequality."

Proletarian revolution—Based on the writings of Karl Marx, the idea that the proletariat will develop a political consciousness and overthrow the ruling class (bourgeoisie). In fact, the proletariat did not play a major role in most Marxist–Leninist takeovers.

Proletariat—Propertyless wage earners who sell their labor in exchange for wages to employers.

Proportional representation—A method of distributing seats among political parties on the basis of election results so that each party gets approximately the same proportion of seats as of popular votes.

Radical left—Adherents to the goal of redistributing power, well-being, enlightenment, and respect; heavily criticizing both Western polyarchies and Soviet-style Communist systems for their failure to alter the *status quo*.

Rationalization—The process of social and cultural change by which traditional values are replaced by those based on empirical fact and logic.

Redistributive policies—Policies designed to make a change in the distribution of power, well-being, respect, and/or enlightenment, with greater equality as the intended outcome.

Reform communists—Communist Party members who do not support the maintenance of the Marxist–Leninist–Stalinist status quo in their states. Those who seek alternative political, social, and economic models that abandon both a guaranteed Communist Party monopoloy of political power and a highly centralized, state owned, and centrally planned economy.

Regime—As an object of political orientations (see political culture), it refers both to the way in which power is structured within a political system and to the entire pool of political elites commited to exercising power within these structural limits.

Regional level of government—Government jurisdiction that encompasses an area comprising more

than one city and a significant proportion of a country's population (*e.g.*, U.S. states).

Regional separatism—Political movements seeking to detach particular ethnically distinct regions from a given sovereign state to create a separate nation-state.

Relative deprivation—Perception of a significant gap between individual expectations and capabilities.

Respect—The value placed on enjoyment of secure and supportive relationships with others (including political authorities) in a community, based on honor and prestige, respect for human rights, affection, and loyalty.

Revisionism—Late nineteenth century modification of Marxism, which abandoned revolutionary strategy in favor of the attainment of socialism through obedience to the rules of parliamentary democracy.

Revolution—Violent change in the existing social and political organization of a country, brought about by internal forces.

Right—A catch-all term applying to proponents of the ideologies of Christian Democracy and Conservatism, as well as that of the "extreme right", and to political parties espousing these ideologies. The right resists demands on the left for redistribution of the values of power, well-being, enlightenment, and respect.

Samizdat—Underground, unofficial, and banned publications produced and circulated within the dissident communities of traditional Communist Party states.

Scientific socialism—Theory developed by Karl Marx and Friedrich Engels that claims that a scientific analysis of the evolution of material forces in history leads to the conclusion that socialism is inevitable.

Second World—Communist states wherein the pace of industrialization has historically been forced by modernizing elites guided by Marxist–Leninist ideology and employing a centralized state apparatus.

Secretariat—Organizational arm of the Politburo in Communist Parties. Coordinates the implementation and execution of Party policies through a hierarchy of Party secretaries, the most important being the General Secretary.

Self-managing socialism—Used by the Yugoslavs to identify their more decentralized system of socialism, which asserts that in economic firms and all other organizations (except the military) decisions are to be made by members of those groups.

Separation of powers—A type of government organizational structure that seeks to limit government power by dividing or separating it into autonomous and competing agencies or institutions.

Service sector—Collective term for sectors of the economy that provide services rather than produce goods. Includes transportation, utilities, trade, finance, insurance, real estate, health, education, research, recreation, and government.

Shatter zones—Geopolitical areas characterized by weak governments whose inability to control their internal affairs leads stronger powers to intervene.

Single-member plurality system—An electoral system in which each election district (constituency) returns one member to parliament, the candidate elected in a given constituency being the one who receives more votes than any other single candidate (*i.e.*, a plurality).

Social classes—Categories of members of a society based on occupation and relative economic advantage and arranged hierarchically from upper, through middle, to lower.

Social democracy—A Marxist political tradition which advocates advancement toward socialism in a peaceful, democratic, and evolutionary manner, mindful of national peculiarities and respectful of existing state political institutions. The social democratic tradition contrasts sharply with Marxist–Leninist doctrine that views violence and revolution as being essential in the establishment of a socialist state.

Social faultlines (cleavages)—Those dividing lines or characteristics that separate one social group from another, for example, race, religion, language.

Socialism—System of social and economic organization where the public (or government) controls the means of production and distribution. Also an ideology and political movement advocating such a system.

Socialization—The process by which new members of a society are taught its rules, norms, and mores.

Social mobility—The movement of individuals from one social class to another, as the result of educational, occupational, and other experiences.

Social stratification—The vertical organization of a society based upon social class lines of division.

Soft state—A term coined by Gunnar Myrdal to describe the political system of the typical developing country. The government's ability to achieve goals is undermined by corruption, administrative weakness, and refusal to obey the law.

Stagflation—Simultaneous occurrence of unacceptably high levels of unemployment (re: stagnant economic growth) and unacceptably high levels of inflation.

State—When not used interchangeably with "government," the concept of the state emphasizes the permanent bureaucratic agencies that pursue institutionalized policy objectives that are not always in accord with the dominant political forces of the nation. Viewed as having its own interests, the state is also counterposed against the major economic interests and social classes.

State socialism—Economic and political system in which state ministries and other governmental and political bodies manage the factors of production.

Structural adjustment—That branch of economic policy that brings about changes in the particular sectors of the economy in order to make them more competitive in the light of changes in technology and in world markets.

Subculture—A group of people differentiated from

others in a society on the basis of shared characteristics, such as class or ethnicity, and the holding of common beliefs and opinions.

Syncratic politics—A style of political coalition that attempts to unite both modernizing elites and antimodern elites to govern a modernizing country without disturbing its premodern classes and forces.

Synoptic policymaking—Rational-comprehensive mode of policymaking that involves careful and thorough planning based on systematic analysis of all available information.

Technocrats—Government elites recruited on the basis of their specialized technical expertise who are said to be impatient with the conflicts and compromises endemic to politics.

Technology—Knowledge and tools that are used to manipulate our natural environment.

Terrorism—The application of violence by insurgents with the intent to frighten a particular target group.

Third World—The independent countries of the world located in Latin America, Africa, the Middle East, and Asia that have not yet chosen unequivocally to follow the political models offered by either Western industrialized democracies or traditional Communist authoritarianism.

Totalitarianism—Highly centralized and dictatorial political process in which individuals and groups outside the ruling elite have no influence over decisions affecting their daily lives.

Trade unions (U.S. usage: labor unions)—Organizations of employees formed to promote the economic objectives of their members vis-à-vis employers and vis-à-vis the state.

Traditional (premodern) society—Society that was characterized by relatively low standards of organization and in which people's lives were controlled by custom or by personal standards of the rulers rather than by the rules and standards of bureaucracy.

Two-party system—A political party system in which two (and only two) parties consistently receive more than 2 percent of the popular vote.

Unconventional political participation—Political action by ordinary citizens that is outside the scope of what is generally regarded as normal political activity within a given political culture. In the 1960s this included activities such as demonstrations, unofficial strikes, boycotts and sit-ins, which have since come to be seen as more conventional in advanced industrial societies. Violent activities and activities that are unambiguously illegal, such as terrorist acts, would today still be regarded as unconventional political participation.

Unitary system—A system of vertical power distribution in which a central unit of government determines what powers will be exercised by units of government at lower levels.

Universalism—Giving one's primary loyalty to a social or political entity larger than one's own narrow parochial grouping.

Utopian socialist—Term used by Marxists in criticism of earlier socialist theorists who did not base their theories on a study of material forces, which Marxists regard as the key to history.

Vertical power distribution—Formal distribution of power among different levels of government: national, regional, and local (*e.g.*, federalism).

Warsaw Treaty Organization (Warsaw Pact or WTO)—A military alliance comprised of Second World states in Eastern Europe and the Soviet Union formed in 1955 in response to the inclusion of the Federal Republic of Germany in NATO.

Well-being—The value placed on the enjoyment by groups and individuals of income, goods, services, wealth, safety, and comfort.

Wildcat strikes—Unauthorized strikes initiated locally by trade unionists against the wishes of the union leadership.

Withering away of the state—Largely ignored in states today, this concept from Second World early Marxist–Leninist doctrine holds that once classes are abolished, the "rule over men" will give way to the "administration of things" during the transition to communism and will lead to the end of the state.

PHOTO CREDITS

Photo Credits

INDEX

A

713

Index

Index

Confederation of British Industries (CBI), 183
Confédération Française Démocratique du Travail (CFDT), 186, 203–206
Confédération Générale du Travail (CGT), 186, 203–206
Confidence mechanism, 670
Confindustria, 199
Congress Party, 568, 569
Congress of People's Deputies, 391–392, 393, 394, 395
Conquistadores, 466, 474
Conservatism, ideological aspects, 119
Conservative Party, 39, 125, 127, 131, 136, 138
Constitution of 1958, France, 159, 161
Constitution: of China, 387–388; in communist systems, 381; in executive-dominant system, 596; and separation of powers, 594; of Soviet Union, 368–369, 394–395
Constitutional Council, 226–227
Consumer goods, 294–295, 342
Contras, 564
Convention People's Party, 568
Convergence theory of social change, 523
Cornwallis, Lord, 476
Corporations, multinational, 495–497, 501, 517, 577, 638, 639
Corporatism: characteristics of, 191–192; Great Britain, 193–194; negative corporatism, 192, 194; positive corporatism, 192–193
Corsicans, 81
Costa Rica, 557, 572, 601, 649
Council of the Federation (Soviet Union), 395
Council of Ministers, 244; in communist states, 384, 389
Council for Mutual Economic Assistance (COMECON), 286
County, 172
Craxi, Bettino, 140, 200, 201
Crime, in Soviet Union, 440, 451–452
Croatians, 344
Cuba, 298, 350, 467, 480, 486, 497, 498, 546–547, 563, 586; communist victory in, 271, 273, 274; economy of, 375–376; political socialization in, 317
Cultural inferiority complex, 475–476
Cultural Revolution, 318–319, 327, 336, 337
Culture: definition of, 523; schisms in, 514–517; traditional and modern, 523–524
Czechoslovakia, 48, 277, 350; Communist Party in, 372; communist victory in, 269, 274; economic policy in, 288–289, 428, 430; elections in, 404; government reform in, 372, 402; Prague Spring, 289, 428; wages in, 298

D

Dahl, Robert A., 27, 670–671
Dalton, Russell J., 99, 101
Death rate, 471, 502
Debré, Michel, 159
Decolonization process: in early 1820s, 467; since 1945, 477, 479–480
Defense Council, in communist states, 384
de Gaulle, Charles, 48, 51, 96–97, 158, 159–160, 201–202, 220, 244, 479
Deindustrialization, 195; postindustrial era, 64
Delors, Jacques, 204
Democracy: criteria of, 664–665; definitional difficulties, 93; support for, 92–93
Democratic centralism, 349–365
Democratic Forum (Hungary), 372, 407, 408, 430
Democratic Party of the Ivory Coast (PDCI), 568
Democratic Platform (Soviet Union), 368

Democratic Proletarians, 121
Democratic socialism, ideological aspects, 118, 119
Democratic Socialist Party (DSP), 121, 124, 192
Democratizazia, 361, 414, 416
Demographic factors, political participation, 104–105
Demographic transition, 502
Deng Liqun, 424
Deng Xiaoping, 279, 291, 352, 361, 362, 363, 374, 389, 421–422, 425, 426–427, 455–456
Département, 172
Dependency theory, 500–501
Destourian Socialist Party, 572
Diet, 40, 153, 245, 294, 331, 470, 473, 491
Dimitrov, Georgi, 270
Disease, European: in Third World, 470
Dissent. *See* Subculture
Divine Right, 35
Division of labor, 297
Djibouti, 479
Dobrynin, Anatoly, 361
Domei, 207
Dominican Republic, 467, 476, 498, 557, 605
Dos Santos, Theotonio, 500–501
Drug traffic, political corruption and, 627
Dual economy, 59, 191; characteristics of, 69, 71
Duarte, José Napoleon, 557–558, 646
Duarte, Maria Eva, 494–495
Dubcek, Alexander, 289, 372, 428
Dutch East Indies Company, 467
Duverger, Maurice, 124

E

Eastern Europe: Communist Parties in, 370, 371–374, 399; communist victory in, 267–271, 273, 274; economic policy in, 285–286, 287–289, 291, 427–430, 431; elections in, 371, 372, 373, 403, 404–405, 408; political culture of, 322–323, 330–331, 333, 334, 340; political performance in, 436, 442–444, 448, 449, 450, 454; reform movement in, 325–327, 333, 370–371, 372–374, 397–408, 429–430; and Soviet dominance, 277, 371; standard of living in, 295–296; subcultures in, 344–345
East Germany, 277, 286, 289, 295, 350, 448; Communist Party of, 372; communist victory in, 270, 273, 274; elections in, 404; formation of, 50; reunification, 245–250
East Indies, 466
East Pakistan. *See* Bangladesh
Ecole Nationale d'Administration (ENA), 168
Economic change, characteristics of, 61
Economic Council, 49
Economic environment, postindustrial era, 59
Economic policy: in China, 284–285, 291–292, 421–427, 431, 446–447; in Eastern Europe, 285–286, 287–289, 291, 405, 427–430, 431; Japan's approach to, 241–242; Keynesian economics, 67; macroeconomic policy, 235–236, 241; microeconomic policy, 236, 240; monetarism, 67, 241; political systems and, 235–242; Reaganomics, 241; socialist system and, 286–292; in Soviet Union, 262, 283–284, 287, 289–291, 412–419, 431, 444–446, 448; structural adjustment, 236; supply-side economics, 67–68, 241; Thatcherism, 241
Economic policy-making, 612–634; agriculture, 653–654; corporatism, 191–195; evaluating outcomes, 630–632; failure-prone, 612–614; free market, 417–418, 423–424, 429; goal-setting, 614–622; and human dignity, 632–634; implementation, 622–630; industry, 650; pluralism, 191, 412, 413, 415,

716

Index

Modrow, Hans, 246
Monetarism, 240; view of unemployment, 67
Mongolia, 263, 273, 274, 350, 375
Moore, Barrington, Jr., 586
"Moral Code of the Builder of Communism," 321–322
Morocco, 479, 649; policy goals in, 615, 616
Moro National Liberation Front, 533, 562
Moslems, 516. *See also* Islamic fundamentalism
Mossadegh, Mohammad, 497
Motherland Party, 596
Mozambique, 466, 469, 479, 619
Mubarak, Hosni, 598
Muhammad, Murtala Kamat, 621
Multinational corporations, 495–497, 501, 517, 577, 638, 639
Multiple society, 565–567
Muramatsu, Michio, 163, 171
Mussolini, Benito, 45, 121, 152, 198
Mwinyi, Ali Hassan, 599
Myrdal, Gunnar, 625

N

Nakane, Chie, 207
Namibia, 479–480, 486, 558, 563
Nash, Manning, 558, 565, 567, 591, 628
Nassar, Gamal Abdel, 497
National Action Party (NDP), 571
National Assembly, 158–159, 160, 161, 170
National Confederation of French Employers (CNPF), 183
National Front, 122
National Health Insurance Scheme, 58
National Health Service, 58
Nationalism: ethnonationalism, 304–306, 329, 439, 480–481, 514–515, 642; growth of, 301, 439; intellectuals, 476–477; and Western education, 472–473
Nationalities. *See* Ethnicity
National Party Congress, 354–356
National People's Congress (NPC), 387–388
National Salvation Front (Romania), 373–374
National Union of Mineworkers, 211, 213–214
Nazi Germany, 268, 269, 285
Nazi Party, 45–47, 192, 249; tactics of, 46–47
Negative corporatism, 192, 194
Neher, Clark D., 597
Nelson, Joan M., 552
Nemeth, Miklos, 406, 407
Neocolonialism, 468, 475, 479
Neo-Fascists, 121–122
Nepal, 601
Netherlands: agricultural production in, 509; colonialism, 467, 468, 469, 479, 595
Neves, Tancredo, 558
New Deal, 227
New Economic Mechanism (NEM), 289, 405, 428
New Economic Policy (NEP), 262, 283, 412–413
New Left, 111; Italy, 122; West Germany, 122
New Liberal Club (NLC), 141
Newly industrializing countries (NICs), 65
New People's Army, 562
New Right, 112
News agencies, 544, 546, 659–660, 663
Nicaragua, 375, 497, 498; political violence in, 564
Nicholas II, Tsar of Russia, 261
Nigeria, 473, 478, 480, 498, 509, 514, 528, 562, 624, 650; child-

rearing practices in, 539; economic policy-making in, 621; political corruption in, 627; political parties and labor unions in, 568, 569; press freedom in, 545; tribal conflict in, 516–517, 568; voting turnout in, 555
Nixon, Richard M., 89, 220
Nkrumah, Kwame, 541, 621
Nomenklatura, 365–366
Noriega, Manuel, 558, 599
North Atlantic Treaty Organization (NATO), 49–50
Northern Ireland, 228; conflict with Great Britain, 81–82
North Korea, 267, 273, 274, 350, 486, 643. *See also* Korea; South Korea
North Vietnam, 272
Nyerere, Julius K., 597, 599, 619, 639
Nyers, Rezso, 406

O

Object loss, 530–531
Occupations, postindustrial society, 72
Ochetto, Achille, 120
Official Secrets Act of 1911, 224
Ogionwo, William, 525
Oil embargo, 481, 648
Okinawa, 479
Oksenberg, Michel, 420, 421
Opinion surveys, 314–315
Organization for Economic Cooperation and Development (OECD), 75
Organization of Petroleum Exporting Countries News Agencies (OPECNA), 659–660
Organized labor. *See* Trade unions
Organski, A.F.K., 586, 588
Ortega, Daniel, 375
Ostrovsky, Nikolai, 335
Ottoman Empire, 468
Owen, Dr. David, 138, 139
Ozal, Turgut, 558, 596

P

Pakistan, 473, 477, 481, 627; electoral system in, 590; executive-dominant system, 596, 599; policy evaluation in, 631; policy goals in, 615, 616, 621–622; policy implementation in, 622, 623; syncratic regime in, 588–590; women in, 540
Pakistan People's Party, 590
Palestine, 468, 477
Panama, 599; elections in, 558
Papua New Guinea, 486
Paris Peace Conference of 1919, 264
Parliament, 149, 153
Parliamentary systems, 32, 149–163; compared to American system, 151, 154; characteristics of, 149; coalition cabinet, 151; France, 157–163; Great Britain, 149–155; heads of state in, 152; horizontal power distribution, 149–156; Italy, 149–155; Japan, 40, 149–155; party cabinet and, 154–155; prime minister, 151, 152; single-party cabinet, 151; unclear election return and, 151–152; West Germany, 40, 155–156
Particularism, 527
Party of Democratic Socialism (East Germany), 372
Party systems, 117–118
Pathet Lao, 272
Patron–client politics, 580, 591–594, 638–639
Pay inequality, 71–72
Pearl Harbor, 48

722

Index

Index

Powell, John Duncan, 580, 592, 593
Power, 513–514, 638–646; distribution in United States, 148–149; horizontal distribution of, 148, 149–156; political culture and, 90, 324–328; political performance and, 434–439; political systems and, 219–221; vertical distribution of, 148, 171–172, 174; after World War I, 44
Pozsgay, Imre, 406, 407
Prague Spring, 289, 428
Prebisch, Raul, 498
Prebisch thesis, 498, 499–500
Prefect, 173
Prefecture, 172
Preindustrial Europe: early industrialization, 33–34; economy of, 30–31; political system in, 32–33; social structure of, 31–32
Presidential Council (Soviet Union), 394–395
Presidential power, France, 161–162
Presidium, of communist legislature, 382–383, 394
Press. See Media
Primacy versus recency argument, 108
Prime minister, 151, 152
Private property, dissolution of, 296
Privatization, 618–619
Project 1992, 243
Proletarian dictatorship, 262, 296, 349, 376, 377
Proletarian revolution, 257, 258, 259, 266
Proletariat, 36
Propaganda: Communist Party, 320; in totalitarianism, 46
Proportional representation, 129, 132, 135
Protestantism, and capitalism, 34
Protestant Reformation, 79
Province, 172
Provisional government, 261
Putnam, Robert D., 163

Q

Qadaffi, Muammar el, 646
Qatar, 486
Question of Imperialism, The (Cohen), 497

R

Racial minorities, 228
Radical left, ideological aspects, 120, 122
Radical Party, 122
Rafsanjani, Ali Akbar Hashremi, 536
Rajaratnam, S., 625
Rákos, Mátyás, 270
Rally of the French People, 124
Rationalization, 523
Raw materials, 471, 474, 499, 500, 501
Reactionary right, ideological aspects, 121–122
Reaganomics, 240
Reagan, Ronald, 240, 453, 560, 663
Recession, 42, 646–647, 648; effects of, 64–65
Red Army, 263, 267, 269–270
Redfield, Robert, 567
Red Guards, 285
Redness and expertness, 339–340
Reform Act of 1832, 37
Regimes of delayed industrialization, 585
Reichstag, 38, 46
Reischauer, Edwin O., 45
Relative deprivation, 530–531
Religion: anticlericalism, 79–80; political socialization and, 317;

postindustrial era, 79–80; religious instruction in schools, 106; schisms, 516; and social change, 515. *See also* Islamic fundamentalism
Republican People's Party, 572
Republikaner, 122, 249
Research and development (R & D), 239–240
Resource consumption, population growth and, 505, 507
Respect, 662–666; political culture and, 328–331; political performance and, 439–444
Revolutionary Party of Tanzania, 599
Rhodesia, 498
Right-wing movements: France, 121, 122; ideological aspects, 121–122; Italy, 121–122; West Germany, 122
Rocard, Michel, 144, 160, 227
Rockman, Bert A., 163
Roh Tae Woo, 558, 599
Roman Catholicism, 34, 79, 80
Romania, 349, 350, 448; Communist Party in, 373; communist victory in, 269–270, 273, 274; economic policy in, 430; elections in, 405; National Salvation Front in, 373–374; overthrow of Ceausescu, 373, 401; standard of living in, 295–296
Romanov, Grigori, 360
Roman, Petre, 373
Roosevelt, Franklin, 227
Rose, Richard, 125
"Rule by coalition," 586–587
Rush, Myron, 359
Russia: prerevolutionary, 261–262; totalitarianism, 44, 46; World War I and, 44, 261, 262; World War II and, 48. *See also* Soviet Union
Russians, 301
Russo-Japanese War of 1904–1905, 261
Rwanda, 479
Ryzhkov, Nikolai, 395

S

Sadat, Anwar, 533, 598, 620
Sakharov, Andrei, 393, 440
Salazar, Antonio, 479
Salinas de Gortari, Carlos, 573
Sandinistas, 497, 564
São Tomé, 486
Sarney, José, 558
Sartori, Giovanni, 117
Saudi Arabia, 468, 573, 596, 601, 615, 639, 643; Islamic fundamentalism in, 533
Savry, Alfred, 485
Sawyer, Malcolm, 75
Sayed, Ayatollah, 535
Scargill, Arthur, 213, 214
Schiller, Kurt, 196–197
Schmidt, Helmut, 137, 156, 197, 221, 234
Schuman, Robert, 50
Scottish Nationalist Party, 81, 122
Scottish Presbyterians, 79
Scott, Robert, 631
Secondary picketing, 212
Second World: Communist Parties of, 348–377; economic policymaking in, 411–412; and economic reform, 412–431; economic and social well-being, 292–296; equality in, 296–300; ethnicity in, 300–307; future of, 454–458; government structure in, 380–408; political culture in, 315–345; political performance in, 434–454. *See also* Eastern Europe; specific countries

724

Index

Index